Lecture Notes in Artificial Intelligence     2871
Edited by J. G. Carbonell and J. Siekmann

Subseries of Lecture Notes in Computer Science

T0205310

**Springer**
*Berlin*
*Heidelberg*
*New York*
*Hong Kong*
*London*
*Milan*
*Paris*
*Tokyo*

Ning Zhong   Zbigniew W. Raś
Shusaku Tsumoto   Einoshin Suzuki (Eds.)

# Foundations of Intelligent Systems

14th International Symposium, ISMIS 2003
Maebashi City, Japan, October 28-31, 2003
Proceedings

Springer

Series Editors

Jaime G. Carbonell, Carnegie Mellon University, Pittsburgh, PA, USA
Jörg Siekmann, University of Saarland, Saarbrücken, Germany

Volume Editors

Ning Zhong
Maebashi Institute of Technology
Department of Systems and Information Engineering
460-1 Kamisadori-Cho, Maebashi-City 371-0816, Japan

Zbigniew W. Raś
University of North Carolina
Department of Computer Science
Charlotte, NC 28223, USA

Shusaku Tsumoto
Shimane Medical University
School of Medicine, Department of Medical Informatics
89-1 Enya-cho, Izumo 693-8501, Japan

Einoshin Suzuki
Yokohama National University
Department of Electrical and Computer Engineering
79-5 Tokiwadai, Hodogaya, Yokohama, Kanagawa 240-8501, Japan

Cataloging-in-Publication Data applied for

A catalog record for this book is available from the Library of Congress.

Bibliographic information published by Die Deutsche Bibliothek
Die Deutsche Bibliothek lists this publication in the Deutsche Nationalbibliografie;
detailed bibliographic data is available in the Internet at <http://dnb.ddb.de>.

CR Subject Classification (1998): I.2, H.3, H.2.8, H.4, H.5.2, K.4.4, F.1

ISSN 0302-9743
ISBN 3-540-20256-0 Springer-Verlag Berlin Heidelberg New York

Springer-Verlag Berlin Heidelberg New York
a member of BertelsmannSpringer Science+Business Media GmbH

http://www.springeronline.com

© Springer-Verlag Berlin Heidelberg 2003
Printed in Germany

Typesetting: Camera-ready by author, data conversion by PTP-Berlin GmbH
Printed on acid-free paper    SPIN: 10960912    06/3142    5 4 3 2 1 0

# Preface

This volume contains the papers selected for presentation at the 14th International Symposium on Methodologies for Intelligent Systems, ISMIS 2003, held in Maebashi City, Japan, 28–31 October, 2003. The symposium was organized by the Maebashi Institute of Technology in co-operation with the Japanese Society for Artificial Intelligence. It was sponsored by the Maebashi Institute of Technology, Maebashi Convention Bureau, Maebashi City Government, Gunma Prefecture Government, US AFOSR/AOARD, the Web Intelligence Consortium (Japan), Gunma Information Service Industry Association, and Ryomo Systems Co., Ltd.

ISMIS is a conference series that was started in 1986 in Knoxville, Tennessee. Since then it has been held in Charlotte (North Carolina), Knoxville (Tennessee), Turin (Italy), Trondheim (Norway), Warsaw (Poland), Zakopane (Poland), and Lyon (France).

The program committee selected the following major areas for ISMIS 2003: active media human-computer interaction, autonomic and evolutionary computation, intelligent agent technology, intelligent information retrieval, intelligent information systems, knowledge representation and integration, knowledge discovery and data mining, logic for artificial intelligence, soft computing, and Web intelligence.

The contributed papers were selected from approximately 200 full draft papers by the following program committee members: Kenro Aihara, Troels Andreasen, Nadir Belkhiter, Alan Biermann, Henri Briand, Jacques Calmet, Nick Cercone, John Debenham, Robert Demolombe, Tapio Elomaa, Floriana Esposito, Yutaka Funyu, Koichi Furukawa, Patrick Gallinari, Attilio Giordana, Jerzy Grzymala-Busse, Mohand-Said Hacid, Mirsad Hadzikadic, Howard Hamilton, Dave Hislop, Tu Bao Ho, Guangshu Hu, Kenichi Ida, Mitsuru Ishizuka, Yves Kodratoff, Churn-Jung Liau, Donato Malerba, David Maluf, Stan Matwin, Riichiro Mizoguchi, Hiroshi Motoda, Amihai Motro, Masao Mukaidono, Neil Murray, Hideyuki Nakashima, Maria Orlowska, Lin Padgham, Jeng-Shyang Pan, James Peters, Vijay Raghavan, Gilbert Ritschard, Lorenza Saitta, Nahid Shahmehri, Ayumi Shinohara, Andrzej Skowron, Roman Slowinski, Einoshin Suzuki, Atsuhiro Takasu, Kwok Ching Tsui, Hiroshi Tsukimoto, Shusaku Tsumoto, Haruki Ueno, Akira Utsumi, Lipo Wang, Takashi Washio, Alicja Wieczorkowska, Xindong Wu, Takahira Yamaguchi, Yiyu Yao, Tetsuya Yoshida, and Djamel Zighed.

We wish to express our thanks to Jiming Liu, Hideyuki Nakashima, Raghu Ramakrishnan, and Domenico Talia who presented invited talks at the symposium. We express our appreciation to the sponsors of the symposium and to all who submitted papers for presentation and publication in the proceedings. Our sincere thanks go to the Organizing Committee of ISMIS 2003, in particular to the General Chair, Setsuo Ohsuga, and to the Local Organizing Chair Nobuo Otani. Also, our thanks are due to Alfred Hofmann of Springer-Verlag for his continuous support.

July, 2003                              N. Zhong, Z.W. Ras, S. Tsumoto, E. Suzuki

# Table of Contents

## Invited Papers

New Challenges in the World Wide Wisdom Web (W4) Research ....... 1
    *Jiming Liu*

Grounding to the Real World – Architecture for
Ubiquitous Computing – .......................................... 7
    *Hideyuki Nakashima*

Data Mining: Fast Algorithms vs. Fast Results....................... 12
    *Raghu Ramakrishnan*

Knowledge Discovery Services and Tools on Grids ..................... 14
    *Domenico Talia*

## Regular Papers

### 1A Knowledge Discovery and Data Mining (1)

Space Decomposition in Data Mining: A Clustering Approach .......... 24
    *Lior Rokach, Oded Maimon, Inbal Lavi*

Time Series Rule Discovery: Tough, Not Meaningless .................. 32
    *Zbigniew R. Struzik*

Mining Diagnostic Rules with Taxonomy from Medical Databases ....... 40
    *Shusaku Tsumoto*

Comparing Simplification Methods for Model Trees with Regression
and Splitting Nodes .............................................. 49
    *Michelangelo Ceci, Annalisa Appice, Donato Malerba*

Goodness-of-Fit Measures for Induction Trees ....................... 57
    *Gilbert Ritschard, Djamel A. Zighed*

### 1B Knowledge Representation and Integration

PDL with Maximum Consistency Monitors........................... 65
    *Elisa Bertino, Alessandra Mileo, Alessandro Provetti*

Comparing and Merging Ontologies: A Concept Type
Hierarchy Approach .............................................. 75
    *Dan Corbett*

Integrating Information under Lattice Structure ...................... 83
    V. Phan-Luong, T.T. Pham, R. Jeansoulin

Functional Ontology for Intelligent Instruments ...................... 88
    Richard Dapoigny, Eric Benoit, Laurent Foulloy

Constructing an Ontology Based on Hub Words ...................... 93
    Sang Ok Koo, Soo Yeon Lim, Sang Jo Lee

## 2A Intelligent Information Systems (1)

Integration of Heterogeneous, Imprecise and Incomplete Data:
An Application to the Microbiological Risk Assessment ................ 98
    Patrice Buche, Ollivier Haemmerlé, Rallou Thomopoulos

Intelligent Protein 3D Structure Retrieval System .................... 108
    Yiqiang Chen, Wen Gao, Lijuan Duan, Xiang Chen, Charles X. Ling

Cognitive Vision Systems in Medical Applications .................... 116
    Marek R. Ogiela, Ryszard Tadeusiewicz

An Automated School Timetabling System Using Hybrid
Intelligent Techniques ............................................ 124
    Alvin C.M. Kwan, Ken C.K. Chung, Kammy K.K. Yip, Vincent Tam

Representing Audio Data by FS-Trees and Adaptable TV-Trees ......... 135
    Alicja A. Wieczorkowska, Zbigniew W. Raś, Li-Shiang Tsay

## 2B Rough Sets

A Framework of Rough Sets Based Rule Generation in
Non-deterministic Information Systems ............................. 143
    Hiroshi Sakai

Granular Computing Based on Rough Sets, Quotient Space Theory,
and Belief Functions.............................................. 152
    Yiyu Yao, Churn-Jung Liau, Ning Zhong

Searching for the Complex Decision Reducts: The Case Study of the
Survival Analysis ................................................ 160
    Jan Bazan, Andrzej Skowron, Dominik Ślęzak, Jakub Wróblewski

Clustering Supermarket Customers Using Rough Set Based
Kohonen Networks ............................................... 169
    Pawan Lingras, Mofreh Hogo, Miroslav Snorek, Bill Leonard

Multi-rough Sets and Generalizations of Contexts in
Multi-contexts Information System ................................. 174
    Rolly Intan, Masao Mukaidono

## 3A Intelligent Agent Technology (1)

MetaNews: An Information Agent for Gathering News Articles on
the Web .......................................................... 179
   *Dae-Ki Kang, Joongmin Choi*

Enacting an Agent-Based Digital Self in a 24×7 Web
Services World..................................................... 187
   *Steve Goschnick*

Light-Weight Agents for E-learning Environments .................... 197
   *Kevin Chan, Leon Sterling*

Towards a Pragmatic Methodology for Open Multi-agent Systems....... 206
   *Philippe Mathieu, Jean-Christophe Routier, Yann Secq*

Using Similarity to Implement Distributed Ubiquitous
Software Services ................................................. 211
   *Abdelkader Gouaich*

MIC*: Algebraic Agent Environment ................................ 216
   *Abdelkader Gouaich, Yves Guiraud*

Using the SPACE Intermediate Model to Help to Implement Agents .... 221
   *Dominique Fournier, Bruno Mermet, Gaële Simon, Marianne Flouret*

Belief Revision and Text Mining for Adaptive Recommender Agents..... 226
   *Raymond Y.K. Lau, Peter van den Brand*

## 3B Intelligent Information Systems (2)

NETMARK: A Schema-Less Extension for Relational Databases for
Managing Semi-structured Data Dynamically......................... 231
   *David A. Maluf, Peter B. Tran*

Program Generation for Application Domain Users by Selecting
Model Candidates.................................................. 242
   *Takumi Aida, Setsuo Ohsuga*

Traffic Sign Recognition in Disturbing Environments ................ 252
   *Hsiu-Ming Yang, Chao-Lin Liu, Kun-Hao Liu, Shang-Ming Huang*

Design Patterns in Intelligent Systems ............................. 262
   *James F. Peters*

Temporal Feature Extraction from Temporal Information Systems ...... 270
   *Piotr Synak*

Parallel Ant Colony Systems ....................................... 279
   *Shu-Chuan Chu, John F. Roddick, Jeng-Shyang Pan, Che-Jen Su*

Some Case-Refinement Strategies for Case-Based Criminal
Summary Judgments .............................................. 285
    *Chao-Lin Liu, Tseng-Chung Chang*

G-STRIPS – A Generalized STRIPS System for Handling State
Change over Dynamic Domains .................................. 292
    *Yan Zhang, Yun Bai*

**4A Text Mining**

Classifying Document Titles Based on Information Inference ........... 297
    *Dawei Song, Peter Bruza, Zi Huang, Raymond Lau*

Building Topic Maps Using a Text Mining Approach .................. 307
    *Hsin-Chang Yang, Chung-Hong Lee*

Improving the Performance of Text Classifiers by Using
Association Features ............................................. 315
    *Yang Zhang, Lijun Zhang, Zhanhuai Li, Jianfeng Yan*

Korean Document Summarization Using Topic Phrases Extraction and
Locality-Based Similarity ......................................... 320
    *Je Ryu, Kwang-Rok Han, Kee-Wook Rim*

Improving Naïve Bayes Text Classifier with Modified EM Algorithm ..... 326
    *Han-joon Kim, Jae-young Chang*

Mining Environmental Texts of Images in Web Pages for
Image Retrieval ................................................. 334
    *Hsin-Chang Yang, Chung-Hong Lee*

Towards a Contextual Content of Ontologies ........................ 339
    *Djamal Benslimane, Catherine Roussey, Christelle Vangenot,
    Ahmed Arara*

An Email Classifier Based on Resemblance ......................... 344
    *Chung Keung Poon, Matthew Chang*

**4B Logic for AI and Logic Programming**

The Characterization on the Uniqueness of Answer Set for
Prioritized Logic Programs ....................................... 349
    *Yan Zhang, Yun Bai*

A New Approach to Constraint Inductive Logic Programming .......... 357
    *Lei Zheng, Chunnian Liu, Dong Jia, Ning Zhong*

Extending the CLP Engine for Reasoning under Uncertainty ........... 365
    *Nicos Angelopoulos*

Logic for Multi-path Message Forwarding Networks for Mobile Agents ... 374
  *Masahito Kurihara, Masanobu Numazawa*

θ-Subsumption and Resolution: A New Algorithm ..................... 384
  *S. Ferilli, N. Di Mauro, T.M.A. Basile, F. Esposito*

Supporting E-consent on Health Data by Logic ...................... 392
  *Chun Ruan, Vijay Varadharajan*

Towards the Theory of Relaxed Unification ......................... 397
  *Tony Abou-Assaleh, Nick Cercone, Vlado Kešelj*

Probability Logic Modeling of Knowledge Discovery in Databases ....... 402
  *Jitender Deogun, Liying Jiang, Ying Xie, Vijay Raghavan*

## 5A  Soft Computing

Constructing Extensions of Bayesian Classifiers with Use of
Normalizing Neural Networks ...................................... 408
  *Dominik Ślęzak, Jakub Wróblewski, Marcin Szczuka*

Fuzzy Multiset Model for Information Retrieval and Clustering
Using a Kernel Function .......................................... 417
  *Kiyotaka Mizutani, Sadaaki Miyamoto*

Validation of Fuzzy Partitions Obtained through Fuzzy C-Means
Clustering ....................................................... 422
  *Dae-Won Kim, Kwang H. Lee*

Generating Fuzzy Thesaurus by Degree of Similarity in Fuzzy Covering .. 427
  *Rolly Intan, Masao Mukaidono*

Design of Iconic Language Interface for Semantic Based Korean
Language Generation .............................................. 433
  *Kyonam Choo, Hyunjae Park, Hongki Min, Yoseop Woo,
  Seokhoon Kang*

Incremental Feature Extraction Based on Empirical Kernel Map ........ 440
  *Byung Joo Kim, Joo Yong Shim, Chang Ha Hwang, Il Kon Kim,
  Joon Hyun Song*

## 5B  Knowledge Discovery and Data Mining

On Lookahead Heuristics in Decision Tree Learning ................... 445
  *Tapio Elomaa, Tuomo Malinen*

Empirical Evaluation of Dissimilarity Measures for Time-Series
Multiscale Matching .............................................. 454
  *Shoji Hirano, Shusaku Tsumoto*

First-Order Rules Mining Guided by Information Gain ................ 463
   *Xinwu Yang, Chunnian Liu, Ning Zhong*

Simultaneous Row and Column Partitioning: Evaluation of a Heuristic... 468
   *Gilbert Ritschard, Djamel A. Zighed*

Partial Prefix Sum Method for Large Data Warehouses ................ 473
   *Seok-Ju Chun*

Spatio-Temporal Association Mining for Un-sampled Sites ............. 478
   *Dan Li, Jitender Deogun*

**6A Intelligent Information Retrieval**

Development of Generic Search Method Based on
Transformation Invariance ........................................ 486
   *Fuminori Adachi, Takashi Washio, Hiroshi Motoda, Atsushi Fujimoto,
   Hidemitsu Hanafusa*

Hierarchical Ordering for Approximate Similarity Ranking ............. 496
   *Joselíto J. Chua, Peter E. Tischer*

Space Transformation Based Approach for Effective Content-Based
Image Retrieval ................................................... 501
   *Biren Shah, Vijay Raghavan*

Collaborative Filtering – Safe and Sound? .......................... 506
   *Michael P. O'Mahony, Neil J. Hurley, Guénolé C.M. Silvestre*

**6B Autonomic and Evolutionary Computation**

RNA Structure as Permutation: A GA Approach Comparing Different
Genetic Sequencing Operators ...................................... 511
   *Kay C. Wiese, Edward Glen*

Evolutionary Computation for Optimal Ensemble Classifier in
Lymphoma Cancer Classification .................................... 521
   *Chanho Park, Sung-Bae Cho*

Floorplan Design Using Improved Genetic Algorithm ................. 531
   *Kenichi Ida, Yosuke Kimura*

Some Enhancements in Genetic Learning: A Case Study on
Initial Population ................................................. 539
   *Ivan Bruha*

## 7A Intelligent Information Systems

Comparing Hierarchical Markov Networks and Multiply Sectioned
Bayesian Networks ...................................................... 544
  *C.J. Butz, H. Geng*

Constraint Propagation to Semantic Web Services Discovery ........... 554
  *Salima Benbernou, Etienne Canaud, Mohand-Said Hacid,
  Farouk Toumani*

Reasoning in Data Integration Systems: Why LAV and GAV
Are Siblings ........................................................... 562
  *Andrea Calì*

Design of an Adaptive Web Merchandising System Using Data Mining ... 572
  *Sung Ho Ha*

## 7B Multi-media Data Processing

Minutiae Extraction from Fingerprint Images Using Run-Length Code ... 577
  *Jung-Hwan Shin, Hui-Yeoun Hwang, Sung-Il Chien*

Endpoint Detection of Isolated Korean Utterances for Bimodal
Speech Recognition in Acoustic Noisy Environments................... 585
  *Hyun-Hwa Oh, Hong-Seok Kwon, Jong-Mok Son, Keun-Sung Bae,
  Sung-Il Chien*

Enhanced Active Shape Models with Global Texture Constraints for
Image Analysis ....................................................... 593
  *Shiguang Shan, Wen Gao, Wei Wang, Debin Zhao, Baocai Yin*

Discovering Structures in Video Databases .......................... 598
  *Hicham Hajji, Mohand-Said Hacid, Farouk Toumani*

## 8A Intelligent Agent Technology

Theoretical Evaluation of Ring-Based Architectural Model for
Middle Agents in Agent-Based System ............................... 603
  *Chunsheng Li, Chengqi Zhang, Longbing Cao*

Multi-attributes-Based Negotiation Agent and E-marketplace in
Customer-to-Customer Electronic Commerce ......................... 608
  *Wooju Kim, June S. Hong, Yong U. Song*

A Feature Analysis Framework for Evaluating Multi-agent System
Development Methodologies ........................................ 613
  *Quynh-Nhu Numi Tran, Graham Low, Mary-Anne Williams*

Decentralized Control (Obligations and Permissions in Virtual
Communities of Agents) ............................................. 618
  *Guido Boella, Leendert van der Torre*

An Intelligent Agent for Automatic Course Adaptation ................ 623
  *Mohammed Abdel Razek, Claude Frasson, Marc Kaltenbach*

An Exploration of Bugs and Debugging in Multi-agent Systems ........ 628
  *David Poutakidis, Lin Padgham, Michael Winikoff*

## 8B Intelligent Information Systems

A Framework for Building Competency-Based Systems Dedicated to
Human Resource Management ...................................... 633
  *Francky Trichet, Michel Leclère*

Extracting the Most Discriminant Subset from a Pool of Candidates
to Optimize Discriminant Classifier Training ........................ 640
  *Carlos E. Vivaracho, Javier Ortega-Garcia, Luis Alonso,
  Q. Isaac Moro*

Knowledge Engineering of Intelligent Sales-Recruitment System
Using Multi-layered Agent Methodology ............................ 646
  *R. Khosla, T. Goonesekera, Y. Mitsukura*

The KAMET II Methodology: A Modern Approach for Building
Diagnosis-Specialized Knowledge-Based Systems ..................... 652
  *Osvaldo Cairó, Julio César Alvarez*

A Formal Approach to Describing Action Concepts in Taxonomical
Knowledge Bases ................................................. 657
  *Christel Kemke*

An Efficient Algorithm for Computing Core Attributes in
Database Systems ................................................ 663
  *Jianchao Han, Xiaohua Hu, T.Y. Lin*

## 8C Soft Computing

Similarity Graphs ................................................. 668
  *Rasmus Knappe, Henrik Bulskov, Troels Andreasen*

Image-Based Flame Control of a Premixed Gas Burner Using
Fuzzy Logics .................................................... 673
  *Apichart Tuntrakoon, Suwat Kuntanapreeda*

Intelligent Pattern Recognition by Feature Selection through
Combined Model of DWT and ANN.................................. 678
  *Cheol-Ki Kim, Eui-Young Cha, Tae-Soo Chon*

Applying Neural Networks to Study the Mesoscale Variability of
Oceanic Boundary Currents ..................................... 684
    *Silvia S.C. Botelho, Mauricio M. Mata, Rodrigo de Bem,*
    *Igor Almeida*

Dialog Planning and Domain Knowledge Modeled in Terms of Tasks
and Methods: A Flexible Framework for Dialog Managing.............. 689
    *Fabien Delorme, Jérôme Lehuen*

**Author Index** ............................................... 695

# New Challenges in the World Wide Wisdom Web (W4) Research

Jiming Liu

Web Intelligence Consortium (WIC) &
Computer Science Department, Hong Kong Baptist University
Kowloon Tong, Hong Kong
jiming@comp.hkbu.edu.hk
http://robotics.comp.hkbu.edu.hk/~jiming

**Abstract.** This talk addresses the research and development needs for creating the new paradigm shift in Internet computing. In particular, it presents a promising answer to such needs, called the **World Wide Wisdom Web** (W4), and identifies several research challenges and enabling technologies in developing the W4.

## 1 The Emergence of Web Intelligence (WI)

Web Intelligence (WI) was first introduced by Zhong, Liu, Yao, and Ohsuga [7], as a joint research effort in developing the next generation Web-based intelligent systems, through combining their expertise in Data-Mining, Agents, Information Retrieval, and Logic.

Broadly speaking, WI encompasses the scientific research and development that explores the fundamental roles as well as practical impacts of Artificial Intelligence (AI), such as autonomous agents and multi-agent systems, machine learning, data mining, and soft-computing, as well as advanced Information Technology (IT), such as wireless networks, grid computing, ubiquitous agents, and social networks, on the next generation of Web-empowered products, systems, services, and activities. WI is the key and the most urgent research field of IT today.

As more detailed blueprints and issues of Web Intelligence (WI) are being evolved and specified [4,6,8,9], numerous WI related research studies and business enterprises have been established around the world. WI companies and research centres or labs have been launched in North America, Europe, and Asia. Each of them focuses on certain specific WI issues, products, and/or services.

In the meantime, international forums, such as IEEE/WIC International Conference on Web Intelligence (WI'01, WI'03) and Atlantic Web Intelligence Conference (AWIC'03), were also organized with overwhelming interests and positive responses. Successful experiences in the development of WI technologies have been reported in the special issues of some leading journals and magazines, and documented in details in the first text on Web Intelligence published by Springer [10].

N. Zhong et al. (Eds.): ISMIS 2003, LNAI 2871, pp. 1–6, 2003.

The challenges of Internet computing research and development in the next decade will be Web Intelligence (WI) centric, focusing on how we can intelligently make the best use of the widely available Web connectivity. The new WI technologies being developed will be precisely determined by *human needs in a post-industrial era*; namely:

1. **information** empowerment;
2. **knowledge** sharing;
3. virtual **social** communities;
4. **service** enrichment;
5. practical **wisdom** development.

This talk advocates that one of the most promising paradigm shifts in WI will be driven by the notion of *wisdom*. *Wisdom*, according to the Webster Dictionary (Page: 1658) [5], implies the following meanings:

1. The quality of being wise; knowledge, and the capacity to make due use of it; **knowledge of the best ends and the best means**; discernment and judgment; discretion; sagacity; skill; dexterity.
2. The results of wise judgments; scientific or practical truth; acquired knowledge; erudition.

## 2   Wisdom Oriented Computing

**Wisdom oriented computing** is a new computing paradigm aimed at providing not only a medium for seamless information exchange and knowledge sharing [2] but also a type of *man-made resources for sustainable knowledge creation, and scientific and social evolution*. The **World Wide Wisdom Web** (W4), *i.e.*, the Web that empowers wisdom oriented computing, will reply on *grid-like service agencies* that self-organize, learn, and evolve their courses of actions in order to perform service tasks as well as their identities and interrelationships in Web communities. They will cooperate and compete among themselves in order to optimize their as well as others resources and utilities.

Self-organizing, learning agents are computational entities that are capable of self-improving their performance in dynamically changing and unpredictable task environments. In [3], Liu has provided a comprehensive overview of several studies in the field of **autonomy oriented computing**, with in-depth discussions on self-organizing and adaptive techniques for developing various embodiments of agent based systems, such as autonomous robots, collective vision and motion, autonomous animation, and search and segmentation agents. The core of those techniques is the notion of synthetic or emergent autonomy based on behavioral self-organization.

Developing the **World Wide Wisdom Web** (W4) will become a tangible goal for WI researchers and practitioners. The W4 will enable us to *optimally* utilize the global connectivity, as offered by the Web infrastructure, and most importantly, to gain the practical wisdoms of living, working, and playing, in addition to information search and knowledge queries.

In order to effectively develop the new generation WI systems, we need to define *benchmark* applications, *i.e.*, a new *Turing Test*, that will capture and demonstrate the W4 capabilities.

Take the wisdom oriented computing benchmark as an example. We can use a service task of compiling and generating a market report on an existing product or *a potential market report on a new product*. In order to get such service jobs done, an information agent on the W4 will mine and integrate available Web information, which will in turn be passed onto a market analysis agent. Market analysis will involve the quantitative simulations of customer behavior in a marketplace, instantaneously handled by other service agencies, involving a large number of semantic or computational grid agents (*e.g.*, [1]). Since the number of variables concerned may be in the order of hundreds or thousands, it can easily cost a single system years to generate one predication.

## 3   The Laws of the W4

An important challenge in the W4 research is to discover the law of pattern-oriented adaptation in W4 services, that is, to identify the interrelationships among different W4 services. By understanding such interrelationships, we aim to develop adaptive W4 brokering tools that facilitate and personalize W4 operations.

Another interesting endeavor in the W4 research is to identify and understand the law of self-organizing W4 communities. In addressing this challenge, it is necessary to analyze and characterize user behavior and W4 service regularities. Researchers have recently discovered several interesting, self-organized regularities on the World Wide Web, ranging from the structure and growth of the Web to the access patterns in Web surfing.

This talk will present our initial efforts on the characterization of strong Web regularities with an information foraging agent-based model. The results of this work can readily provide us with insights into the potential regularities in W4 communities.

Specifically, we will demonstrate and formulate:

1. A white-box model that incorporates the behavioral characteristics (*i.e.*, motivation aggregation) of Web users with measurable and adjustable factors, and exhibits the regularities as found in empirical Web data. The foraging operations in the model correspond to the surfing operations in the real-world Web server.

2. Different user strategies that lead to different emergent regularities. In the cases of rational and recurrent agents, the *power law* in link-click-frequency distribution becomes ubiquitous. The distinction among the different categories of agents in the information foraging model lies in their abilities to predict which of linked next-level sites may contain more relevant contents.

By way of experimenting with the agent-based decision model, we will be able to explain how services and user behavioral factors interact with each other. Our work offers a means for studying strong Web regularities with respect to user Interest Profiles, Web Content Distribution and coupling, and user navigation strategies. It enables us to predict the effects on emergent usage regularities if certain aspects of Web servers or user foraging behaviors are changed.

## 4   From Semantic Web to "Knowledge of the Best Ends and the Best Means"

The notion of Semantic Web originated in response to the demands for knowledge management, reuse, and sharing over the Internet [2]. The underlying technology utilizes a machine-understandable language to define the ontology of a certain domain, upon which content information on the Web can be semantically described and accessed by software agents. In the core of the semantic Web technology lies in the eXtensible Markup Language (XML) that allows users to define their own Web document tags, which in turn may constitute the standard ontology of a knowledge domain [13]. Resource Description Framework (RDF), at the same time, provides a model for encoding Web information using the user-defined XML tags. RDF Schema (RDFS), a lightweight schema language, further defines the structures of the encoded Web information in terms of their classes and properties. Also built on top of RDF models with XML tags, DARPA Agent Markup Language (DAML) presents yet another ontology markup option that offers more sophisticated class definitions than RDFS [11].

The above mentioned semantic Web languages enable users to query Web information according to the semantic meanings of information rather than the occurrence of keywords, and at the same time, support software agents to access Web resources or services and understand the contents based on their ontology-based descriptions.

This talk will show that the scope of the semantic Web technology can be extended from ontology-based knowledge search to wisdom search, *i.e.*, discovering "knowledge of the best ends and the best means" − one of the essential meanings of *wisdom*. In particular, it will demonstrate a new ontology-based planning capability with an implemented, semantic Web supported planner, called OntoPlan.

Generally speaking, planning represents one of the most important human activities in daily life, work, or play. It involves not only the understanding of domain knowledge, whether declarative or procedural, but also the manipulation of such knowledge into a plan of actions that allow one to achieve a certain goal. This talk will describe how OntoPlan defines, represents, and hence interprets the state of the world in predicate logic as well as a planning domain. In OntoPlan, planning knowledge is specified in the above mentioned semantic Web documents. The meanings and relationships of the embedded classes and their properties are specified using the standard DAML. There are limited tools for the manipulation of DAML documents. Jena API for Java [12], as developed by Hewlett Packard Semantic Web Research Laboratory, provides an API for processing RDF and DAML documents. OntoPlan utilizes this API to read DAML ontology and instance files for the purpose of planning. By retrieving user-defined semantic planning documents, `OntoPlan` can readily generate a plan. In so doing, it performs Partial-Order Planning (POP) by searching a space of partial plans.

This talk will provide details on how to represent the basic constructs in planning, including the representations of a logic-based language to describe the states and goal of a planning problem.

## 5   WIC: A Consortium for the W4 Research and Development

In order to best exchange and coordinate the W4 research and development efforts, and effectively promote and share the WI technologies, Ning Zhong (Maebashi Institute of Technology, Japan) and Jiming Liu (Hong Kong Baptist University), together with Edward A. Feigenbaum (Stanford University, USA), Setsuo Ohsuga (Waseda University, Japan), Benjamin Wah (University of Illinois at Urbana-Champaign, USA), Philip Yu (IBM T. J. Watson Research Center, USA), and L.A. Zadeh (UC Berkeley, USA), formally established the Web Intelligence Consortium (WIC) in 2002.

The WIC is an international non-profit organization dedicated to the promotion of world-wide scientific research and industrial development in the era of Web and agent intelligence, through collaborations among world-wide WI research centres and organizational members, technology showcases at WI conferences and workshops, WIC official book and journal publications, WIC newsletters, and WIC official releases of new industrial solutions and standards.

## References

1. Berman, F.: From TeraGrid to knowledge grid. Communications of the ACM, 44:27–28, 2001.
2. Berners-Lee, T., Hendler, J., Lassila, O.: The semantic Web. Scientific American, 284:34–43, 2001.
3. Liu, J.: Autonomous Agents and Multiagent Systems, World Scientific Publishing, 2001.
4. Liu, J., Zhong, N., Yao, Y. Y., Ras, Z. W.: The Wisdom Web: New challenges for Web Intelligence (WI). Journal of Intelligent Information Systems, Kluwer Academic Publishers, 20(1):5–9, 2003.
5. Porter, N. (ed.): Webster's Revised Unabridged Dictionary, G&C. Merriam Co., 1913.
6. Yao, Y. Y., Zhong, N., Liu, J., Ohsuga, S.: Web Intelligence (WI): Research challenges and trends in the new information age. N. Zhong, Y. Y. Yao, J. Liu, and S. Ohsuga (eds.), Web Intelligence: Research and Development, LNAI 2198, pages 1–17, Springer, 2001.
7. Zhong, N., Liu, J., Yao, Y. Y., Ohsuga, S.: Web Intelligence (WI). In Proceedings of the 24th IEEE Computer Society International Computer Software and Applications Conference (COMPSAC 2000), pages 469–470, IEEE Computer Society Press, Taipei, Taiwan, October 25–28, 2000.

8. Zhong, N., Yao, Y. Y., Liu, J., Ohsuga, S. (eds.): Web Intelligence: Research and Development, LNAI 2198, Springer, 2001.
9. Zhong, N., Liu, J., Yao, Y. Y.: In search of the Wisdom Web. IEEE Computer, 35(11):27–31, November 2002.
10. Zhong, N., Liu, J., Yao, Y. Y. (eds.): Web Intelligence, Springer, 2003.
11. The DARPA Agent Markup Language Homepage, http://www.daml.org
12. Jena Semantic Web Toolkit, http://www.hpl.hp.com/semweb/jena.htm
13. Resource Description Framework (RDF), W3C, http://www.w3.org/RDF/

# Grounding to the Real World – Architecture for Ubiquitous Computing –

Hideyuki Nakashima

Cyber Assist Research Center, AIST
2-41-6 Aomi, Koto-Ku, Tokyo 135-0064 Japan
h.nakashima@aist.go.jp

## 1  Introduction

As requirements from the information oriented society, it is desired that anyone can utilize information processing technology anywhere in the world. The Goal of the Cyber Assist Project is realization of a ubiquitous information society in which all can benefit from assistance of information processing technology (IT hereafter) in all situations of daily life.

Traditional IT is accessible only through computers sitting on a desktop, or worse, in a computer room. Its accessibility is broadening recently with the spread of mobile devices including PDA and mobile phones with *i*-mode. Nevertheless, such technology is appreciated only by a small portion of people in rather limited scenarios of their everyday lives. IT should be able to support human in every aspect of everyday life with information processing units embedded in the environment which communicate with portable or wearable personal devices. Keywords are "here, now and me". IT will be able to help human daily life by automatically booking a seat in a train according to an individual schedule, by guiding a user through a shopping mall while providing necessary information about goods, or automatically calling a taxi or requesting bus service when needed. Through this technology, we believe that IT can boost the quality of life in economy, politics, culture, and education.

To widen up the range of opportunity for receiving assistance from IT, computers should be able to share the semantics of tasks with humans. We must pull computers out of their digital world into our physical world by providing various sensors and visual and acoustic recognition technologies. For instance, if a mobile phone can understand that its holder has a visitor and is discussing an important issue, it may be able to automatically forward incoming calls to the user's secretary.

We need new network architecture to support the technology. It must be capable of dynamic reconfiguration and connection with very low latency, creating "responsive" network technology.

As the access becomes ubiquitous, other problems will become evident. One of them is information overload. We need some supporting technology to help us access only relevant information to our needs. A major cause of information overload and the "digital divide" is the semantic gap between humans and computers; humans are

N. Zhong et al. (Eds.): ISMIS 2003, LNAI 2871, pp. 7–11, 2003.

adapted to dealing with deep meaning, while machines excel at processing explicit syntax. The only feasible way to fill this gap systematically is to make the semantic structure of information content explicit so that machines can manage them too [Hasida 2000]. Worldwide document processing with tagging, ontology, and semantic search is proposed in the Semantic Web project. We cooperate with that movement and will develop "intelligent content" technologies.

Another problem is protection of personal information from its abuse. In the society where everyone is connected to the network all the time, personal data is easy to be accessed and hard to protect. Moreover, on-line data are easy to copy and distribute. There are laws against abuse of on-line personal data. But technological support for this problem is very limited. Encryption does not protect data from abuse of the server itself that manipulates the data.

Our goal is to develop human-centered information processing assistance systems (intelligence booster) usable without special knowledge or training, while addressing the problems of information overload and privacy. We are aiming at the construction of a system to provide situated information that I-want-here-now through "natural interface." In other words, we are strengthening a variety of technologies that link digital realm represented by Internet to us people who live in the real world.

## 2  Cyber Assist Approach

We develop new communication methodology based on location, which is the integration/amalgamation of information processing technology and the real physical world through situated communication. One of the key issues is the reorganization of information according to its semantics (often called "grounding" in AI community). It is achieved through sensors, actuators and information processing over them. Therefore, our use of "cyber" differs from those in mass media, where the word is synonymous to "digital." In fact, we define "cyber" as follows: cyber = digital + real, meaning that cyber world implies grounding of digital, or logical, information to the real, or physical, world.

The main (positive) target of our project is situated information support. If a server knows the user's situation, it can provide more fine-tuned information support without querying the user's selections. There may be many keys to this; we regard location as a most prominent physical property.

One form of location-based service is to provide information only to a certain area of 3D space. For example, in a museum, detailed information of an entry is broadcast to the area in front of an exhibition, but only to those facing it.

As a communication device to receive such information, we developed a very simple compact battery-less information terminal called CoBIT [Nishimura 2002]. In our design, devices embedded in the environment play many important roles. CoBIT is equipped with a reflective sheet whose location can be identified easily from cameras mounted in the environment. Then an infrared beam is projected toward the direction from a LED scanner that is capable of tracking CoBIT movement. Note that there is no need for any ID to establish communication. Physical location of the terminal is an essential and unique key of the device. The infrared signal is modulated using a sound wave; CoBIT replays it as auditory information. The infrared beam itself is the power source of CoBIT; thus, there is no need to have any internal power supply. Cameras in the environment will see the reflection from the reflective sheet of CoBIT to know its location, direction and movement (gesture). Therefore, CoBIT functions as a two way communication terminal even without its own internal power source.

There exist two global communication networks: the telephone network and the Internet. Telephone systems use a phone number as a global ID to reach each telephone in the world. Communication over the Internet is based on IP-addresses, which are also a global ID for each processing unit connected to the network. When communication is overheard, it is easy to connect content to recipients using those global ID's. In a ubiquitous computing environment, the majority of communication is computer to computer: frequency is much larger in magnitude. If ubiquitous computing follows this tradition, it may endanger privacy protection. For instance, if someone discovers the IP address of a TV set, all programs a user watches may be monitored. It is therefore recommended to use locally- resolved ID's wherever possible. It is even better to use no ID's at all.

# 3  Multiagent Architecture

In ubiquitous computing, many devices in the vicinity of the user are used. How does one know which devices are near to the user, and free to use? The location of user may be given by the name of the building, or longitude and latitude of GPS positioning. Those must be converted from one to another. Multiagent architecture plays important roles for access control of those devices. We are developing location identification (including conversion between coordinates and names) and access control architecture called CONSORTS [Kurumatani 2003].

The main claim of this paper is that multiagent architecture with physically grounded agents is the essential element of ubiquitous computing.

First of all, why do we need agents? An agent is pieces of programs that has its own goals and judgments. The goals originate from the user's specification of the task given to the agent. In other words, an agent in our context is a delegate of the user. We need software agents in ubiquitous computing environment (1) to cope with many devices and filter only important information to human, and (2) to act as interpreter of different languages and ontologies used in different devices and human, and (3) to maintain security and privacy of the user.

Secondly, why do we need multiagent architecture? Multiagent system deals with (4) integration of partial information distributed among agents, and (5) distributed resources and their management.

We will elaborate on each point in the following.
1. Intelligent information filter. Low-level sensor data are not of interest to human. They must be filtered or integrated into higher-level information before delivered to the user.

2. (1) Interpreter to human. Raw data are not necessarily interpretable to human. The user prefers higher-level symbol description, and the same data correspond to different classification in different situations. When a user requests information of a certain location, the reciprocal processing is necessary. (2) Inter-device interpreter. Different sensor may use different metrics. Or they use relative values. Those data must be translated between each other or some bias must be added to convert them into absolute values.

3. Security and privacy control. As the user move through the environment, there will be many connections to the devices in the environment and personal information may be requested. Some of the requests are passed up to the user for permission but the agent handles many portions automatically. Security of connection must be maintained. Passwords, which by definition must be in the head of the user rather than written in a file, cannot be used for each automatic connection to embodied devices. New method is required here. Private information may or may not be given out depending on the need of the user or trustworthiness of the server. For example, one does not want to broadcast its location to all over the world. Location information must be maintained by a personal agent and given to only those authorized to access it. The agent should do most of the decision without bothering the user.

4. Information integration. This item must be obvious without further explanation. Multimodal data from many different sensors must be integrated to model the user and the situation.

5. Resource management. There are many users and many devices. If every user tries to get access to each of the surrounding devices, someone must arbitrate the access. Otherwise there will be many conflicting traffic. If there are $n$ users and $m$ devices and they communicate each other directly, $n \times m$ access connections must be maintained. If we add a middle layer of access manager, it can be reduced to $n + m$. Moreover, resource management and negotiation in case of the conflict are long studied in multiagent.

# 4  Summary

We are conducting Cyber Assist project to install ubiquitous computing technology to support ordinary people in their ordinary life.

One of the aspect not acknowledged by majority of research communities is that the necessity of multiagent architecture for ubiquitous computing. It is essential for device control, human cognition aid, and grounding.

## References to Our Further Work

[Hasida 2000] Koiti Hasida: GDA: Annotated Document as Intelligent Content. Invited talk at *COLING 2000 Workshop on Semantic Annotation and Intelligent Content*, Luxembourg. 2000.

[Kurumatani 2003] Koichi Kurumatani: Social Coordination with Architecture for Ubiquitous Agents: CONSORTS, *Proc. of International Conference on Intelligent Agents, Web Technologies and Internet Commerce* IAWTIC'2003 (Vienna), 2003.

[Nakashima 2002] Hideyuki Nakashima: Cyber Assist Project for Situated Human Support. Keynote Speech, *Proc. The Eights International Conference on Distributed Multimedia Systems*, Knowledge Systems Institute, ISBN 1-891706-11-X, pp. 3–7, 2002

[Nakashima 2003] Hideyuki Nakashima: Cyber Assist Project and Its Security Requirements. *Proc. The First International Conference on Security in Pervasive Computing*, Springer, 2003

[Nakashima 2003] Hideyuki Nakashima, Masatomo Hashimoto and Akira Mori: UBKit for Cyber Assist. *Active Media Technology*. World Scientific, 2003.

[Nishimura 2002] Takuichi Nishimura, Hideo Itoh, Yoshinov Yamamoto and Hideyuki Nakashima: A Compact Battery-less Information Terminal (CoBIT) for Location-based Support Systems. *In Proc. of International Symposium on Optical Science and Technology (SPIE)*, 4863B-12. 2002.

# Data Mining: Fast Algorithms vs. Fast Results

Raghu Ramakrishnan

Computer Sciences Department
University of Wisconsin, Madison, USA

**Abstract.** Exploratory data analysis is typically an iterative, multi-step process in which data is cleaned, scaled, integrated, and various algorithms are applied to arrive at interesting insights. Most algorithmic research has concentrated on algorithms for a *single step* in this process, e.g., algorithms for constructing a predictive model from training data. However, the speed of an individual algorithm is rarely the bottleneck in a data mining project. The limiting factor is usually the difficulty of understanding the data, exploring numerous alternatives, and managing the analysis process and intermediate results. The alternatives include the choice of mining techniques, how they are applied, and to what subsets of data they are applied, leading to a rapid explosion in the number of potential analysis steps.

An important direction for research is how to provide better support for multi-step analyses. I will discuss this problem, and describe a novel framework called *subset mining* that we are developing and evaluating in the application domain of atmospheric aerosol analysis. As the name suggests, the goal is to identify subsets of data that are "interesting", or have interesting relationships between them. The use of the approach for multi-step mining is based on the idea that each step in an analysis is focused on some subset of the data, and that multi-step analyses can be understood and composed in terms of the underlying data subsets and their properties. We hope to achieve two kinds of benefits with respect to multi-step analyses: (1) Focus the computation across multiple steps by exploiting their relationship. (2) Facilitate rapid exploration of many analysis alternatives by using semi-automatic generation and testing of potentially interesting data subsets and hypotheses using analyst-provided domain knowledge.

We illustrate the subset mining paradigm through an example taken from the application domain that we are currently investigating, analysis of atmospheric aerosols. Consider a table of hourly wavelength-dependent light absorption coefficients, with one row for each reading, and another table of ion-concentration readings, also measured hourly. Consider the following query, which is of great interest in atmospheric studies: *Are certain ranges of light absorption levels strongly correlated to unusually high concentrations of particulate metal ions?* This is an example of a subset mining query, and the complexity arises from the lack of restriction on the ranges of light absorption coefficients and ion concentrations to be considered. We must consider all possible light absorption coefficient ranges, and for each, carry out (at a minimum) a SQL query that calculates corresponding ion concentrations. In addition, like typical "data mining" questions, this query involves inherently fuzzy criteria ("strong correlation", "unusually high") whose precise formulation gives us some latitude. As another example, if we have identified *clusters* based on the location of each reading, we can

N. Zhong et al. (Eds.): ISMIS 2003, LNAI 2871, pp. 12–13, 2003.
© Springer-Verlag Berlin Heidelberg 2003

readily refine the previous query to ask whether there are such correlations (for some ranges of reactive mercury levels) at certain locations.

To summarize, there are three main parts to a subset mining query: (1) A criterion that generates several subsets of a table, (2) A correspondence—e.g., a relational expression—that generates a subset of a second table for each of these subsets, and (3) A measure of interestingness for the second subset (that indirectly serves as a similar measure for the original subset).

To see why subset mining queries are especially useful for integrated analysis of multiple datasets, using a combination of mining techniques, observe that Steps (1) and (3) could both be based on the results of (essentially any) mining techniques, rather than just simple SQL-style selections and aggregation. Further, we can analyze a single table by simply omitting Step (2); intuitively, this allows us to compare an arbitrary number of "groups" in the data to see if they are correlated to, or deviate from, other groups in terms of high-level properties. Examples include the dominant sources of certain elements in observed particles or the correlation between temperatures and light-absorption of atmospheric aerosols. Thus, subset mining offers a promising approach to the broader challenge of describing and optimizing multi-step mining tasks.

A significant technical challenge is to optimize subset mining, at least for several particular instances (i.e., query classes). This will require research into *cost estimation* for the data mining techniques used as components of the subset mining instance, as well as ways to "push" abstract constraints derived from the subset-generation component into the interestingness-measure component (and vice-versa). While there are parallels in database query optimization and evaluation for relational algebra operations, we expect that these issues will have to be tackled on a case-by-case basis for different data mining techniques when they are used to instantiate the subset mining framework.

# Knowledge Discovery Services and Tools on Grids

Domenico Talia

DEIS
University of Calabria,
87036 Rende (CS), Italy
talia@deis.unical.it

**Abstract.** The Grid is today mainly used for supporting high-performance computing intensive applications. However, it could be effectively exploited for deploying data-driven and knowledge discovery applications. To support this class of applications, tools and services for knowledge discovery are vital. The Knowledge Grid is an high-level system for providing Grid-based knowledge discovery services. These services allow professionals and scientists to create and manage complex knowledge discovery applications composed as workflows that integrate data sets and mining tools provided as distributed services on a Grid. They also allow users to store, share, and execute these knowledge discovery workflows as well as publish them as new components and services. The Knowledge Grid provides a higher level of abstraction of the Grid resources for knowledge discovery activities, thus allowing end users to concentrate on the knowledge discovery process without worrying about Grid infrastructure details.

## 1 Introduction

As Grid technology becomes more and more mature and both Grid tools and applications increase in number, variety, and complexity, the user community use Grids for implementing a larger set of applications [1]. New projects are started in different areas, such as data archives (e.g., a Grid for the Library of Congress), medicine (e.g., Access Grid for battling SARS), drug design, and financial modeling.

The Grid is today mainly used for supporting high-performance computing intensive applications in science and engineering. However, it could be effectively exploited for implementing data-driven and knowledge discovery applications. To support this class of applications, tools and services for data mining and knowledge discovery on Grids are vital. The Knowledge Grid is a high-level system for providing Grid-based knowledge discovery services [2]. These services allow professionals and scientists to create and manage complex knowledge discovery applications composed as workflows that integrate data sets, mining tools, and computing and storage resources provided as distributed services on a Grid. Knowledge Grid facilities allow users to compose, store, share, and execute these knowledge discovery workflows as well as publish them as new components and services on the Grid.

N. Zhong et al. (Eds.): ISMIS 2003, LNAI 2871, pp. 14–23, 2003.

The knowledge building process in a distributed setting involves collection/generation and distribution of data and information, followed by collective interpretation of processed information into "knowledge." Knowledge building depends not only on data analysis and information processing but also on interpretation of produced models and management of knowledge models. The knowledge discovery process includes mechanisms for evaluating the correctness and accuracy and usefulness of processed data sets, developing a shared understanding of the information, and filtering knowledge to be kept in accessible organizational memory. The Knowledge Grid provides a higher level of abstraction and a set of services based on the use of Grid resources to support all those phases of the knowledge discovery process. Therefore, it allows end users to concentrate on the knowledge discovery process they must develop without worrying about Grid infrastructure and fabric details.

This paper discusses knowledge discovery services and features of the Knowledge Grid system. The next sections discuss knowledge discovery services and describe the system architecture and how its components can be used to design and implement knowledge discovery applications for science, industry, and commerce. We also discuss relationship between knowledge discovery services and emerging models such as OGSA, ontologies for Grids, and peer-to-peer computing protocols and mechanisms for Grids.

## 2 Knowledge Discovery Services

Nowadays several public organizations, industries, and scientific labs produce and manage large amounts of complex data and information. This information patrimony can be effectively exploited if it is used as a source to produce knowledge necessary to support decision making. This process is both computationally intensive and collaborative and distributed in nature. Unfortunately, high-level tools to support the knowledge discovery and management in distributed environments are lacking. This is particularly true in Grid-based knowledge discovery [3].

The Knowledge Grid [2] provides a middleware for knowledge discovery services for a wide range of high performance distributed applications. The data sets, and data mining and data analysis tools used in such applications are increasingly becoming available as stand-alone packages and as remote services on the Internet. Examples include gene and DNA databases, network access and intrusion data, drug features and effects data repositories, astronomy data files, and data about web usage, content, and structure.

Knowledge discovery procedures in all these applications typically require the creation and management of complex, dynamic, multi-step workflows. At each step, data from various sources can be moved, filtered, and integrated and fed into a data mining tool. Based on the output results, the analyst chooses which other data sets and mining components can be integrated in the workflow or how to iterate the process to get a knowledge model. Workflows are mapped on a Grid assigning its nodes to the Grid hosts and using interconnections for communication among the workflow components (nodes).

The Knowledge Grid supports such activities by providing mechanisms and higher level services for searching resources and representing, creating, and managing knowledge discovery processes and for composing existing data services and data mining services in a structured manner, allowing designers to plan, store, document, verify, share and re-execute their workflows as well as their output results.

The Knowledge Grid architecture is composed of a set of services divided in two layers: the *Core K-Grid layer* that interfaces the basic and generic Grid middleware services and the *High-level K-Grid* layer that interfaces the user by offering a set of services for the design and execution of knowledge discovery applications. Both layers make use of repositories that provide information about resource metadata, execution plans, and knowledge obtained as result of knowledge discovery applications.

In the Knowledge Grid environment, discovery processes are represented as workflows that a user may compose using both concrete and abstract Grid resources. Knowledge discovery workflows are defined using visual interface that shows resources (data, tools, and hosts) to the user and offers mechanisms for integrating them in a workflow. Single resources and workflows are stored using an XML-based notation that represents a workflow as a data flow graph of nodes, each representing either a data mining service or a data transfer service. The XML representation allows the workflows for discovery processes to be easily validated, shared, translated in executable scripts, and stored for future executions. Figure 1 shows the main steps of composition and execution process of a knowledge discovery application on the Knowledge Grid.

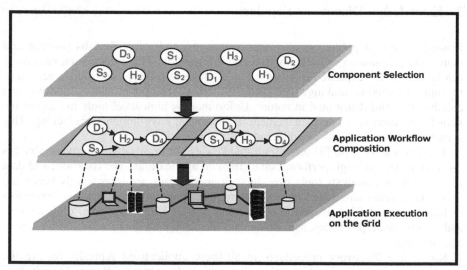

**Fig. 1.** Main steps of application composition and execution in the Knowledge Grid.

## 3 Knowledge Grid Components and Tools

Figure 2 shows the general structure of the Knowledge Grid system and its main components and interaction patterns. The High-level K-Grid layer includes services used to compose, validate, and execute a parallel and distributed knowledge discovery computation. Moreover, the layer offers services to store and analyze the discovered knowledge. Main services of the High-level K-Grid are:

- The *Data Access Service (DAS)* it does search, selection, transfer, transformation, and delivery of data to be mined.

- The *Tools and Algorithms Access Service (TAAS)* is responsible for searching, selecting and downloading data mining tools and algorithms.

- The *Execution Plan Management Service (EPMS)*. An execution plan is represented by a graph describing interactions and data flows between data sources, extraction tools, data mining tools, and visualization tools. The Execution Plan Management Service allows for defining the structure of an application by building the corresponding graph and adding a set of constraints about resources. Generated execution plans are stored, through the RAEMS, in the Knowledge Execution Plan Repository (KEPR).

- The *Results Presentation Service (RPS)* offers facilities for presenting and visualizing the knowledge models extracted (e.g., association rules, clustering models, classifications). The resulting metadata are stored in the KMR to be managed by the KDS (see below).

The Core K-Grid layer includes two main services:

- The *Knowledge Directory Service (KDS)* that manages metadata describing Knowledge Grid resources. Such resources comprise hosts, repositories of data to be mined, tools and algorithms used to extract, analyze, and manipulate data, distributed knowledge discovery execution plans and knowledge obtained as result of the mining process. The metadata information is represented by XML documents stored in a Knowledge Metadata Repository (KMR).

- The *Resource Allocation and Execution Management Service (RAEMS)* is used to find a suitable mapping between an "abstract" execution plan (formalized in XML) and available resources, with the goal of satisfying the constraints (computing power, storage, memory, database, network performance) imposed by the execution plan. After the execution plan activation, this service manages and coordinates the application execution and the storing of knowledge results in the *Knowledge Base Repository (KBR)*.

A software prototype that implements the main components of the Knowledge Grid environment, comprising services and functionalities ranging from information and discovery services to visual design and execution facilities is VEGA (Visual Environment for Grid Applications) [4]. It is useful to offer the users a simple way to design and execute complex Grid applications by exploiting advantages coming from a Grid environment in the development of distributed knowledge discovery applications.

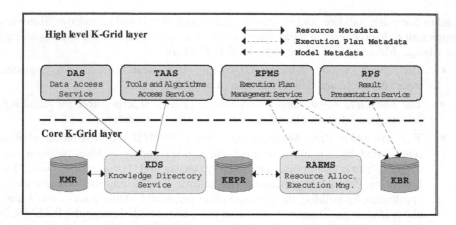

**Fig. 2.** The Knowledge Grid general structure and components.

The main goal of VEGA is to offer a set of visual functionalities that give the users the possibility to design applications starting from a view of the present Grid status (i.e., available nodes and resources), and composing the different steps inside a structured environment, without having to write submission scripts or resource description files.

The high-level features offered by VEGA are intended to provide the user with easy access to Grid facilities with a high level of abstraction, in order to leave her/him free to concentrate on the application design process. To fulfill this aim VEGA builds a visual environment based on the component framework concept, by using and enhancing basic services offered by the Knowledge Grid and the Globus Toolkit.

VEGA overcomes the typical difficulties of Grid application programmers offering a high-level graphical interface and by interacting with the Knowledge Grid Knowledge Directory Service (*KDS*), to know available nodes in a Grid and retrieve additional information (metadata) about their published resources. Published resources are those made available for utilization by a Grid node owner by means of the insertion of specific entries in the Globus Toolkit monitoring and discovery service (MDS). So, when a Grid user starts to design its application, she/he needs to obtain first of all metadata about available nodes and resources. After this step, she/he can select and use all found resources during the application design process. This first feature aims at making available useful information about Grid resources and to show the user their basic characteristics, permitting her/him to design an application.

The application design facility allows the user to build typical Grid applications in an easy, guided, and controlled way, having always a global view of the Grid status and the overall building application. To support structured applications, composed of multiple sequential stages, VEGA makes available the *workspace* concept, and the *virtual resource* abstraction. Thanks to these entities it is possible to compose applications working on data processed in previous phases even if the execution has not been performed yet.

Once the application design has been completed, resulting job requests are to be submitted to the proper Globus Resource Allocation Manager (*GRAM*). VEGA includes in its environment the execution service, which gives the designers the possibility to execute an application and to view its output.

## 4  Knowledge Grid and OGSA

Grid technologies are evolving towards an open Grid architecture, called *the Open Grid Services Architecture (OGSA)*, in which a Grid provides an extensible set of services that virtual organizations can aggregate in various ways [5].

OGSA defines a uniform exposed-service semantics, the so-called Grid service, based on concepts and technologies from both the Grid computing and Web services communities. Web services define a technique for describing software components to be accessed, methods for accessing these components, and discovery methods that enable the identification of relevant service providers. Web services are in principle independent from programming languages and system software; standards are being defined within the World Wide Web Consortium (W3C) and other standards bodies. The OGSA model adopts three Web services standards: the Simple Object Access Protocol (SOAP) [32], the Web Services Description Language (WSDL), and the Web Services Inspection Language (WS-Inspection). Web services and OGSA aim at interoperability between loosely coupled services independent of implementation, location or platform. OGSA defines standard mechanisms for creating, naming and discovering persistent and transient Grid service instances, provides location transparency and multiple protocol bindings for service instances, and supports integration with underlying native platform facilities. The OGSA effort aims to define a common resource model that is an abstract representation of both real resources, such as processors, processes, disks, file systems, and logical resources. It provides some common operations and supports multiple underlying resource models representing resources as service instances.

In OGSA all services adhere to specified *Grid service* interfaces and behaviors defined in terms of WSDL interfaces and conventions and mechanisms required for creating and composing sophisticated distributed systems. Service bindings can support reliable invocation, authentication, authorization, and delegation. To this end, OGSA defines a Grid service as a Web service that provides a set of well-defined WSDL interfaces and that follows specific conventions on the use for Grid computing.

The Knowledge Grid, is an abstract service-based Grid architecture that does not limit the user in developing and using service-based knowledge discovery applications. We are devising an implementation of the Knowledge Grid in terms of the OGSA model. In this implementation, each of the Knowledge Grid services is exposed as a persistent service, using the OGSA conventions and mechanisms. For instance, the EPMS service implements several interfaces, among which the notification interface that allows the asynchronous delivery to the EPMS of notification messages coming from services invoked as stated in execution plans. At the same time, basic knowledge discovery services can be designed and deployed by using the KDS services for discovering Grid resources that could be used in composing knowledge discovery applications.

## 5  Knowledge Grid, Ontologies, and Peer-to-Peer

The Semantic Web is an emerging initiative of World Wide Web Consortium (W3C) aiming at augmenting with semantic the information available over Internet, through document annotation and classification by using ontologies, so providing a set of tools able to navigate between concepts, rather than hyperlinks, and offering semantic search engines, rather than key-based ones. In the Grid computing community there is a parallel effort to define a so called *Semantic Grid* (www.semanticgrid.org).

The Semantic Grid vision is to incorporate the Semantic Web approach based on the systematic description of resources through metadata and ontologies, and provision for basic services about reasoning and knowledge extraction, into the Grid. Actually, the use of ontologies in Grid applications could make the difference because it augments the XML-based metadata information system associating semantic specification to each Grid resource. According to this approach we may have a set of basic services for reasoning and querying over metadata and ontologies, semantic search engines, etc. These services could represent a significant evolution with respect to current Grid basic services, such as the Globus MDS pattern-matching based search.

An effort is on the way to provide ontology-based services in the Knowledge Grid [6]. It is based on extending the architecture of the Knowledge Grid with ontology components that integrate the KDS, the KMR and the KEPR. An ontology of data mining tasks, techniques, and tools has been defined and is going to be implemented to provide users semantic-based services in searching and composing knowledge discovery applications.

Another interesting model that could provide improvements to the current Grid systems and applications is the peer-to-peer computing model. P2P is a class of self-organizing systems or applications that takes advantage of distributed resources — storage, processing, information, and human presence — available at the Internet's edges. The P2P model could thus help to ensure Grid scalability: designers could use the P2P philosophy and techniques to implement nonhierarchical decentralized Grid systems.

In spite of current practices and thoughts, the Grid and P2P models share several features and have more in common than we perhaps generally recognize. broader recognition of key commonalities could accelerate progress in both models. A synergy between the two research communities, and the two computing models, could start with identifying the similarities and differences between them [7]. The Grid was born to support the creation of integrated computing environments in which distributed organizations could share data, programs, and computing nodes to implement decentralized services. Although originally intended for advanced scientific applications, Grid computing has emerged as a paradigm for coordinated resource sharing and problem solving in dynamic, multi-institutional, virtual organizations in industry and business. Grid computing can be seen as an answer to drawbacks such as overloading, failure, and low QoS, which are inherent to centralized service provisioning in client–server systems. Such problems can occur in the context of high-performance computing, for example, when a large set of remote users accesses a supercomputer.

Resource discovery in Grid environments is based mainly on centralized or hierarchical models. In the Globus Toolkit, for instance, users can directly gain information about a given node's resources by querying a server application running on it or running on a node that retrieves and publishes information about a given organization's node set. Because such systems are built to address the requirements of organizational-based Grids, they do not deal with more dynamic, large-scale distributed environments, in which useful information servers are not known a priori.

The number of queries in such environments quickly makes a client–server approach ineffective. Resource discovery includes, in part, the issue of presence management — discovery of the nodes that are currently available in a Grid — because global mechanisms are not yet defined for it. On the other hand, the presence-management protocol is a key element in P2P systems: each node periodically notifies the network of its presence, discovering its neighbors at the same time.

Future Grid systems should implement a P2P-style decentralized resource discovery model that can support Grids as open resource communities. We are designing some of the components and services of the Knowledge Grid in a P2P manner. For example, the KDS could be effectively redesigned using a P2P approach. If we view current Grids as federations of smaller Grids managed by diverse organizations, we can envision the KDS for a large-scale Grid by adopting the super-peer network model. In this approach, each super peer operates as a server for a set of clients and as an equal among other super peers. This topology provides a useful balance between the efficiency of centralized search and the autonomy, load balancing, and robustness of distributed search. In a Knowledge Grid KDS service based on the super-peer model, each participating organization would configure one or more of its nodes to operate as super peers and provide knowledge resources. Nodes within each organization would exchange monitoring and discovery messages with a reference super peer, and super peers from different organizations would exchange messages in a P2P fashion.

## 6 Final Remarks

The Grid is today mainly used for supporting high-performance computing-intensive applications [8]. However, it could be effectively exploited for deploying data-driven and knowledge discovery applications. To support this class of applications, tools and services for knowledge discovery are vital. The Knowledge Grid is an high-level system for providing Grid-based knowledge discovery services. These services allow professionals and scientists to create and manage complex knowledge discovery applications composed as workflows that integrate data sets and mining tools provided as distributed services on a Grid. They also allow users to store, share, and execute these knowledge discovery workflows as well as publish them as new components and services. The Knowledge Grid provides a higher level of abstraction of the Grid resources for knowledge discovery activities, thus allowing the end-users to concentrate on the knowledge discovery process without worrying about Grid infrastructure details.

In the next years the Grid will be used as a platform for implementing and deploying geographically distributed knowledge discovery [9] and knowledge management platforms and applications. Some ongoing efforts in this direction have been recently started. Example of systems such as the Discovery Net [10], the AdAM system [11], and the Knowledge Grid discussed here show the feasibility of the approach and can represent the first generation of knowledge-based pervasive Grids.

The wish list of Grid features is still too long. Here are some main properties of future Grids that today are not available:

- Easy to program,
- Adaptive,

- Human-centric,
- Secure,
- Reliable,
- Scalable,
- Pervasive, and
- Knowledge-based.

The future use of the Grid is mainly related to its ability embody many of those properties and to manage world-wide complex distributed applications. Among those, knowledge-based applications are a major goal. To reach this goal, the Grid needs to evolve towards an open decentralized infrastructure based on interoperable high-level services that make use of knowledge both in providing resources and in giving results to end users. Software technologies as knowledge Grids, OGSA, ontologies, and P2P we discussed in this paper will provide important elements to build up high-level applications on a World Wide Grid. These models, techniques, and tools can provide the basic components for developing Grid-based complex systems such as distributed knowledge management systems providing pervasive access, adaptivity, and high performance for virtual organizations.

**Acknowledgements.** This research has been partially funded by the Italian MIUR project GRID.IT.

# References

[1]    I. Foster, C. Kesselman, J. M. Nick, and S. Tuecke. The Physiology of the Grid: An Open Grid Services Architecture for Distributed Systems Integration. Technical report, http://www.globus.org/research/papers/ogsa.pdf, 2002.

[2]    M. Cannataro, D. Talia, The Knowledge Grid, *Communications of the ACM*, 46(1), 89–93, 2003.

[3]    F. Berman. From TeraGrid to Knowledge Grid. *Communications of the ACM*, 44(11), pp. 27–28, 2001.

[4]    M. Cannataro, A. Congiusta, D. Talia, P. Trunfio, "A Data Mining Toolset for Distributed High-Performance Platforms", *Proc. 3rd Int. Conference Data Mining 2002*, WIT Press, Bologna, Italy, pp. 41–50, September 2002.

[5]    D. Talia, "The Open Grid Services Architecture: Where the Grid Meets the Web", *IEEE Internet Computing*, Vol. 6, No. 6, pp. 67–71, 2002.

[6]    M. Cannataro, C. Comito, "A Data Mining Ontology for Grid Programming", *Proc. 1st Int. Workshop on Semantics in Peer-to-Peer and Grid Computing*, in conjunction with WWW2003, Budapest, 20–24 May 2003.

[7]    D. Talia, P. Trunfio, "Toward a Sinergy Between P2P and Grids", *IEEE Internet Computing*, Vol. 7, No. 4, pp. 96–99, 2003.

[8]    F. Berman, G. Fox, A. Hey, (eds.), *Grid computing: Making the Global Infrastructure a Reality*, Wiley, 2003.

[9]    H. Kargupta, P. Chan, (eds.), *Advances in Distributed and Parallel Knowledge Discovery*, AAAI Press 1999.

[10] M. Ghanem, Y. Guo, A. Rowe, P. Wendel, "Grid-based Knowledge Discovery Services for High Throughput Informatics", *Proc. 11th IEEE International Symposium on High Performance Distributed Computing,* p. 416, IEEE CS Press, 2002.

[11] T. Hinke, J. Novotny, "Data Mining on NASA's Information Power Grid," *Proc. Ninth IEEE International Symposium on High Performance Distributed Computing*, pp. 292–293, IEEE CS Press, 2000.

# Space Decomposition in Data Mining: A Clustering Approach

Lior Rokach, Oded Maimon, and Inbal Lavi

Tel-Aviv University, Department of industrial engineering
Ramat Aviv, Tel Aviv 69978, Israel
{liorr, maimon}@eng.tau.ac.il

**Abstract.** Data mining algorithms aim at searching interesting patterns in large amount of data in manageable complexity and good accuracy. Decomposition methods are used to improve both criteria. As opposed to most decomposition methods, that partition the dataset via sampling, this paper presents an accuracy-oriented method that partitions the instance space into mutually exclusive subsets using K-means clustering algorithm. After employing the basic divide-and-induce method on several datasets with different classifiers, its error rate is compared to that of the basic learning algorithm. An analysis of the results shows that the proposed method is well suited for datasets of numeric input attributes and that its performance is influenced by the dataset size and its homogeneity. Finally, a homogeneity threshold is developed, that can be used for deciding whether to decompose the data set or not.

## 1 Introduction

Clustering and classification are both basic tools in the data-mining task. In essence, the difference between clustering and classification lies in the manner knowledge is extracted from data: whereas classification is a supervised learning method, clustering is an unsupervised one. Clustering, however, finds its own classes without any guidance from the user.

Fayyad *et al* [3] claim that the explicit challenges for the KDD research community is to develop methods that facilitate the use of data mining algorithms for real-world databases. One of the characteristics of such databases is high volume.

A possible way of tackling very large databases is the decomposition approach, according to which one or more subsets of the data are selected, based on some selection procedure. Learning algorithms are run on each of the subsets, and the concept descriptions (or classifiers in the case of classification problems) produced are combined by some combining procedure into a final model [9].

Decomposition may divide the database horizontally (subsets of rows or tuples) or vertically (subsets of attributes – see, for instance [8]). This paper deals with the former, namely tuple decomposition.

N. Zhong et al. (Eds.): ISMIS 2003, LNAI 2871, pp. 24–31, 2003.

Many methods have been developed for partitioning the tuples into subsets. Some of them are aimed at minimizing space and time needed for the classification of a dataset; whereas others attempt to improve accuracy. These methods may be roughly divided according to the manner in which tuples are divided into subsets:

Sample-based tuple decomposition – tuples are divided into subsets via sampling. This category includes sampling, as well as multiple model methods. The latter may be sequential, trying to take advantage of knowledge gained in one iteration, and use it in the successive one. Combining the classifiers simply means selecting the last classifier produced. Such methods include algorithms as windowing, trying to improve the sample they produce from one iteration to another, and also the boosting algorithm, increasing the probability of selecting instances that are misclassified by the current classifier for constructing the next one, in order to improve accuracy [1].

Many multiple model methods were showed to improve accuracy. This accuracy gain may stem from the variation in classifiers, built by the same algorithm, or from the advantages of the sequential process. Despite their advantages, using multiple models is characterized with low understandability. The classification of an instance employs many classifiers, the distinction between which is not clear. In addition, such methods require determining several characteristics of the process, including the number of subsets, the distribution according to which instances are sampled and the combination method to be used. Each of these characteristics may influence performance, yet their optimal values are not necessarily known in advance, or initially set by the algorithm.

Space-based decomposition - tuples are divided into subsets according to their belonging to some part of space. Kusiak [7] describes feature value decomposition – objects are partitioned into subsets according to the value of selected input attributes, and decision value decomposition – objects are partitioned according to the value of the decision (or more generally, the target attribute).

Kusiak does not describe a way for determining which attribute/s is preferable to partition by, or which values should belong to each subset. He only deals with rules in the decision-making process, and does not offer some automated version of space-based decomposition.

This paper presents a space-decomposition algorithm, exploiting the K-means clustering algorithm. It is aimed at decreasing error rate compared to the simple classifier embedded in it, while being rather understandable.


# 2  Problem Formulation

The problem of decomposing the data space, presented in this paper, is accuracy related. Our aim is to achieve a decomposition of the data space, such that if a learning algorithm is built on each data subset, it will achieve a lower generalization error compared to a classifier built on the entire data set using the same algorithm. Formally the problem may be defined as follows:

Given an inducer $I$, a training set $S$ with input attribute set $A=\{a_1,...,a_n\}$ and target attribute $y$ from a distribution $D$ over the labeled instance space, the goal is to find an optimal decomposition $W_{opt}$ of the instance space $X$ into $\Psi$ mutually exclusive and collectively exhaustive subspaces, such that the generalization error of the induced classifiers will be minimized over the distribution $D$.

The generalization error in this case is defined as follows:

$$\varepsilon(W,I) = \sum_{x \in X} \sum_{v_{y,j} \in V_y} \sum_{B_k \in W} L(x, v_{y,j}, B_k, I) \cdot P_D(x, v_{y,j}) \tag{1}$$

Where the loss function is as:

$$L(x, v_{y,j}, B, I) = \begin{cases} 1 & if\ v_{y,j} \neq \arg\max_{v_{y,j}^* \in V_y} \hat{P}_{I(S \cap B)}(y = v_{y,j} | x)\ and\ x \in B \\ 0 & otherwise \end{cases} \tag{2}$$

It should be noted that the optimal is not necessarily unique.

## 3  Algorithmic Framework

One of the main issues arising when trying to address the problem formulated in section 2 concerns the question of what sort of instance space division should be taken in order to achieve as high accuracy as possible. One may come up with quite a few ways for dividing the instance space, varying from using one attribute at a time (similarly to decision tree construction) to the use of different combinations of attribute values for the same goal.

The search of the required division approach is guided by another important question: Should there be a recommended division in any given domain? After all, it is not clear that in all cases, dividing the instance space would yield any significant result.

In order to understand whether the instance space of a certain data set should be divided, we define the following:

Let $X$ be an instance space of the input data (the unlabeled instance space), from which instances are produced according to some distribution $R$. The resulting data set is an *heterogeneous data set* if exits a partition $W=\{B_1, B_2,...B_j\}$ of $X$, such that instances belonging to each of the partition products comprise a separate population.

Let $A=\{a_1,a_2,...,a_n\}$ be an input attribute set, of the domain $X=V_1*V_2*...*V_n$. Instances belonging to a sub space $B_K$ of $X$ are a *population* if, according to some training set $S$, unlabeled instances within $B_K$ are similar among their selves and different from data instances belonging to $X-B_K$.

The above definitions guide us in determining whether the instance space should be divided at all, and if so – in what manner. The main assumption is that data sets for which space decomposition may yield an accuracy gain are heterogeneous, namely consist of different populations of unlabeled data. Since these populations are different in some way, not yet defined, they might be assigned to different classes according to different models. They may even have target domains that consist of different subsets of the original one. When constructing a single classifier on the entire data set, such specific behavior will probably be lost, since the algorithm will "average" on all instances.

The above definition of population leads us towards using some clustering method as a possible tool for detecting populations. That is since "clustering is the grouping of similar objects" [4], whereas different objects belong to different clusters. We choose to define the similarity of unlabeled data via the distance metric. In particular, the metric used will be the Euclidean metric for continuous attributes, involving simple matching for nominal ones (very similar to the similarity measure used by [5] in the K-prototypes algorithm, except for the fact that there is no special cluster-dependent weight for the categorical attributes). The reason for this particular metric chosen lies in the clustering method we prefer for this work, namely the K-means algorithm.

### 3.1 The K-Means Algorithm as a Decomposition Tool

The K-means algorithm is one of the simplest and most commonly used clustering algorithms. This algorithm heuristically attempts to minimize the sum of squared errors:

$$SSE = \sum_{k=1}^{K} \sum_{i=1}^{N_k} \left\| x_i - \mu_k \right\|^2 \tag{3}$$

where $N_k$ is the number of instances belonging to cluster $k$ and $\mu_k$ is the mean of cluster no. $k$, calculated as the mean of all the instances belonging to that cluster:

$$\mu_{k,i} = \frac{1}{N_k} \sum_{q=1}^{N_k} x_{q,i} \, \forall i \tag{4}$$

The algorithm starts with an initial set of cluster centers, chosen at random or according to some heuristic. In each iteration, each instance is assigned to its nearest cluster center according to the Euclidean distance between the two. Then the cluster centers are re-calculated.

A number of convergence conditions are possible, including no reduction in error as a result of the relocation of centers, no (or minimal) reassignment of instances to new cluster centers, or exceeding a pre-defined number of iterations.

The K-means algorithm is very popular among researchers mainly due the following properties: low computational complexity, ease of interpretation, simplicity of implementation, speed of convergence and adaptability to sparse data [2].

Having intended to use a clustering algorithm as a means for partitioning large data sets, we choose to integrate this specific clustering method in the proposed met.

## 3.2  Determining the Number of Subsets

In order to proceed with the decomposition of unlabeled data, a significant parameter should be at hand – the number of subsets, or in our case, clusters, existing in the data.

The K-means algorithm requires this parameter as input, and is affected by its value. Various heuristics attempt to find an optimal number of clusters when no prior knowledge is available. A few of them concentrate on the intra-cluster performance measure, trying to minimize it for achieving compact clusters. Such methods are the within cluster decay (see for instance [11] and [12]) and SSE decay, which are graphical methods, assuming the intra cluster distance first declines rapidly and then flattens, as it reaches the optimal number of clusters. These methods also include Hartigan's *F* statistic [4] and the PRE (proportional reduction in error) method, which suggests the number of clusters should be increased from K to K+1 only if the reduction rate in SSE is sufficiently large.

The above methods all suffer from drawbacks: graphical methods are quite subjective, especially since the intra-cluster curves do not always fit the expected behavior pattern; the PRE and Hartigan's method require a threshold that is not trivial to determine; and the latter is also based on a number of incorrect assumptions. In addition to these individual drawbacks, all intra-cluster based methods are characterized with a weakness that is difficult to overlook. Trying to minimize intra-cluster distance in each cluster, such methods tend to over-partition the data, namely split some rather distinct cluster, compared to other clusters, in order to achieve an additional decline in the intra-cluster distances in each cluster.

To avoid such over-partitioning, some methods use not only an intra-cluster measure, but an inter-cluster measure as well. Thus, a cluster that is relatively far from other clusters will not be further partitioned even if it may decrease the intra-cluster measure some more. Heuristics belonging to this category include, for example, the measure described in [10]. Minimizing this measure that equals the ratio of intra-cluster scatter and inter-cluster scatter is equivalent to both minimizing the intra-cluster scatter and maximizing the inter-cluster scatter. This research uses a similar method known as the validity index, offered by Kim *et al* [6].

## 3.3  Algorithm Overview

The basic K-classifier algorithm employs the K-means algorithm for the purpose of space decomposition and uses the validity index described in [6] for determining the number of clusters. The algorithm follows the following stages:

1.  Apply the K-means algorithm to the training set $S$ using $K=2,3,...K_{max}$.
2.  Compute the validity index for $K=2,...,K_{max}$ and choose the optimal number of clusters $K^*$.
3.  Produce $K$ classifiers of the induction algorithm $I$, each produced on the training data belonging to a subset $k$ of the instance space.

New instances are classified by the K-classifier as follows:

1. The instance is assigned to the most nearest cluster (using Euclidean distance).
2. The classifier induced using $B_k$ is employed for assigning a class to the instance.

# 4 Experimental Study

We analyze the extent to which the conditions surrounding the basic K-classifier may lead to its success or failure. This is done using three representative classification algorithms: C4.5 Decision Tree, Back-Propagation Neural Network and Naive Bayes. These algorithms, are employed on 8 databases from the UCI repository, once in their basic form and once combined with the K-classifier. The classification error rate, resulting from the decomposition, is measured and compared to that achieved by the basic algorithm. The maximum number of clusters is set to a sufficiently large number (25).

These experiments are executed 5 times for each database and each classifying algorithm, so as to reduce the variability resulting from the random choice of training set. Table 1 summarizes the results obtained by the above experiments. For each database the average error rate of each inducer with clustering and without clustering is detailed. A superscript of "+" or "-" indicates whether the improvement or deterioration of the k-classifier framework is significant according to McNemar's test [13]. The last column indicates the number of clusters obtained for each database.

**Table 1.** Partial results of the K-classifier compared to three learning algorithms

| Database Name | Decision Tree | | Neural Networks | | Naive Bayes | | # of Clusters |
|---|---|---|---|---|---|---|---|
| | K-classifier | Regular | K-classifier | Regular | K-classifier | Regular | |
| Adult | $0.1656^-$ | 0.1564 | $0.1994^-$ | 0.1806 | $0.19025^-$ | 0.17425 | 10.72 |
| Japanese vowels | $0.1234^+$ | 0.139 | $0.0902^+$ | 0.1712 | $0.08625^+$ | 0.16675 | 11.95 |
| Indonesia Prevalence Survey | 0.5042 | 0.485 | 0.5102 | 0.5196 | 0.51075 | 0.53225 | 8.4 |
| LED 17 | $0.6602^-$ | 0.4382 | $0.6904^-$ | 0.4546 | $0.5084^+$ | 0.40775 | 14.4 |
| MONSK1 | 0.3756 | 0.2878 | 0.3026 | 0.1024 | 0.29275 | 0.2625 | 13.57 |
| Nurse | $0.0556^-$ | 0.0342 | $0.0464^-$ | 0.0286 | 0.09 | 0.0975 | 11.8 |
| OP-digits | $0.0752^+$ | 0.1032 | 0.0558 | 0.0396 | $0.06175^+$ | 0.088 | 8.83 |
| PEN-digits | $0.0346^+$ | 0.0444 | $0.0364^+$ | 0.0806 | $0.053^+$ | 0.14025 | 8.33 |

In order to analyze the causes for the K-classifier's success or failure, a matrix of 5*120 is constructed. The matrix contains a row for each experiment on each database with each classifying algorithm. Its columns correspond to the characteristics of the experiment:

- The number of records divided by the number of attributes –expresses the size of the database, namely are there enough records in the database compared to its dimensionality?
- Initial PRE – the reduction in the SSE, resulting from partitioning the data set from one cluster (the non partitioned form) to two. This characteristic was chosen since we suspect it indicates whether the data set should be partitioned at all.
- Classification method – the classification algorithm employed on the database.
- Result Class – Indicates whether employing the K-classifier has obtained significant improvement, significant deterioration, or insignificant result.

Using the above matrix, a meta-classifier is constructed. The classifying method employed for this purpose is the C4.5 decision tree. The input attributes for the classifier are the record-attribute ratio, the initial PRE and the classification method. As may be learned from the obtained tree, the two attributes that determine whether or not the K-classifier would achieve a significant decrease in error rate are the record-attribute ratio and the initial PRE. A significant decrease in error rate may occur when the former characteristic exceeds 20.67 and the latter exceeds 0.2.

Another conclusion that may be drawn from this stage is that the K-classifier algorithm works better on integer or continuous-valued attributes. Though the algorithm did not significantly decrease error on all databases of such values, the ones on which error decreased significantly all contained integer attributes, continuous-valued attributes or some combination of these two kinds.

## 5   Conclusions

This paper presents a space decomposition approach to data mining and implements it using the K-means clustering algorithm. An important conclusion derived from our experiments regards the heterogeneity of the data set: If it exist, it is very likely that space-based decomposition would improve accuracy. Specifically, we derived a PRE threshold for determining heterogeneity and combined it in our algorithm.

Other parameters that affect the effectiveness of the decomposition are also related to the degree to which the instance space and dataset are likely to be separable: record-attribute ratio as well as input data type.

Our heterogeneity detecting decomposition algorithm decreased error rate on what appeared to be heterogeneous datasets and did not increase it on almost all of the others. That was done in the expense of some additional complexity. In contrary to popular sample-based decomposition methods, such as bagging, this method is also relatively understandable: it may be translated into a decision-tree like scheme, describing the model to be used in case an instance is close to any of the cluster means (which are also easy to understand).

# References

1.  Bauer, E. and Kohavi, R. An empirical comparison of voting classification algorithms: bagging, boosting and variants. Machine learning, 36, 105–142, 1999.
2.  Dhillon, I. S. and Modha, D. S. A data clustering algorithm on distributed memory machines. In M. Zaki and C.-T. Ho, editors, Lecture Notes in Artificial Intelligence, 1759: pp 245–260, 2000.
3.  Fayyad, U., Piatesky-Shapiro, G., and Smyth P., From Data Mining to Knowledge Discovery: An Overview, in U.Fayyad, G. Piatetsky-Shapiro, P. Smyth, and R. Uthurusamy, editors, Advances in Knowledge Discovery and Data Mining, pp 1–30, MIT Press, 1996.
4.  Hartigan, J. A. Clustering algorithms. John Wiley & Sons., 1975.
5.  Huang, Z. Clustering large data sets with mixed numeric and categorical values. In proceedings of the first Pacific-Asia conference on knowledge discovery and data mining, Singapore, 1997.
6.  Kim, D.J., Park, Y.W. and Park,. A novel validity index for determination of the optimal number of clusters. IEICE Trans. Inf., Vol. E84-D, no.2 (2001), 281–285.
7.  Kusiak, A. Decomposition in data mining: An industrial case study, IEEE Trans. Electron. Packag. Manufact., vol. 23, pp. 345–353, Oct. 2000.
8.  Maimon, O. and Rokach L. Theory and Applications of Attribute Decomposition. In IEEE International Conference on Data Mining, 473–480, 2001.
9.  Provost, F.J. and Kolluri, V. A Survey of Methods for Scaling Up Inductive Learning Algorithms. Proc. 3rd International Conference on Knowledge Discovery and Data Mining, 1997.
10. Ray, S., and Turi, R.H. Determination of Number of Clusters in K-Means Clustering and Application in Color Image Segmentation. Monash university, 1999.
11. Tibshirani, R., Walther, G. and Hastie, T. (2000). Estimating the number of clusters in a dataset via the gap statistic. Tech. Rep. 208, Dept. of Statistics, Stanford University.
12. Wang, X. and Yu, Q. Estimate the number of clusters in web documents via gap statistic. May 2001.
13. Dietterich, T. G. (1998). Approximate statistical tests for comparing supervised classification learning algorithms. Neural Computation, 10 (7).

# Time Series Rule Discovery: Tough, Not Meaningless

Zbigniew R. Struzik

Centrum voor Wiskunde en Informatica (CWI)
Postbus 94079, NL-1090 GB, Amsterdam, The Netherlands
Zbigniew.Struzik@cwi.nl

**Abstract.** 'Model free' rule discovery from data has recently been subject to considerable criticism, which has cast a shadow over the emerging discipline of time series data mining. However, other than in data mining, rule discovery has long been the subject of research in statistical physics of complex phenomena. Drawing from the expertise acquired therein, we suggest explanations for the two mechanisms of the apparent 'meaninglessness' of rule recovery in the reference data mining approach.

One reflects the universal property of self-affinity of signals from real life complex phenomena. It further expands on the issue of scaling invariance and fractal geometry, explaining that for ideal scale invariant (fractal) signals, rule discovery requires more than just comparing two parts of the signal. Authentic rule discovery is likely to look for the possible 'structure' pertinent to the failure mechanism of the (position and/or resolution-wise) invariance of the time series analysed.

The other reflects the redundancy of the 'trivial' matches, which effectively smoothes out the rule which potentially could be discovered. Orthogonal scale space representations and appropriate redundancy suppression measures over autocorrelation operations performed during the matches are suggested as the methods of choice for rule discovery.

## 1 Introduction

Recently, there has been considerable criticism of the mainstream rule discovery algorithm in data mining [1]. By performing scrutiny testing [1] suggests that the discussed algorithm [2] based rule discovery does not produce meaningful rules. In particular, the confidence of the rules recovered is not to be distinguished from the rules obtained from random noise. The overwhelming conclusions of the article would be disastrous for the domain of research in question if they lacked full explanation and understanding. In addition to the explanation provided in [1], the purpose of our paper is to propose a different look at the possible and plausible causes for the result reported in [1].

The primary investigated example in [1], coinciding with the example used by the primarily criticised paper by Das et al [2], is that of the S&P500 financial index. Indeed, the authors of [1] suggest that there is no more confidence in the particular rule advocated in [2] than in any other deterministic rule. Thus any

N. Zhong et al. (Eds.): ISMIS 2003, LNAI 2871, pp. 32–39, 2003.

rule might do, which in actual fact means that such a rule is useless and irrelevant, holding at random, statistically meaningless instances. The mechanism of proving this conclusion has been devised by comparing the rule discovery algorithm from [2] on both the test time series (S&P500) and the surrogate time series (random walk). However, as the authors of [1] rightly indicate, the evidence for the lack of correlations in a financial time series like the S&P 500 index is so overwhelming that the 'meaninglessness' of any deterministic rule discovered may not seem surprising [3,4,5,6,7,8].

The article [1] suggests, however, that the same degree of meaninglessness is obtained no matter what input time series is used. The primary cause attributed to this failure is not in the clustering algorithm, which is the only rule extraction mechanism investigated, but in the pre-processing of the time series. In particular, the 'moving window' overlapping selection of candidate time series intervals leads to so-called spurious matches, destroying the resolution of the clustering algorithm.

The purpose of this writing is to look closer at the likely cause for the inability of the algorithms discussed blindly to extract rules from real life time series. In particular, the issue of scale invariance will be addressed, which characterises not only an overwhelming range of real-life and artificial time series but can also be attributed to isolated singularities - often the building blocks of the real-life and artificial time series.

Additionally, scaling invariance will be linked to the rate of auto-correlation decay, which determines the impact of 'redundant' spurious matches on the blind clustering algorithms. While auto-correlation decay is considered an important diagnostic tool in the study of long range dependence, for the purpose of blind clustering only the extrema (maxima or minima) of the autocorrelation (or the local match) may need to be considered to provide rule extraction with sufficient resolution and sensitivity.

## 2   Redundant Information → Spurious Matches

The primary cause of the meaninglessness of the rule discovery has been attributed by the authors of the critical work [1] to the shortcoming of the time series pre-processing algorithm and in particular to the redundancy of the matching operation through the so-called 'trivial' matches. Indeed, matching two time-series intervals shifted with respect to one another by a time lag will indeed in many cases show a slow rate of decorrelation – which is referred to as partial, trivial matches in [1].

Apart from the entire plethora of possible distance measures, the standard way of calculating the inner product of two time series is used for evaluating their 'correlation' level. For the time lag $t$ shifted versions, the definition of the autocorrelation product/function $C(t)$ of a function $f(t)$ reads:

$$C(t) = \int_{-\infty}^{\infty} \bar{f}(\tau) \, f(t + \tau) \, d\tau \qquad (1)$$

where $\bar{f}(\tau)$ is the complex conjugate of $f(t)$. Amazingly, the autocorrelation is simply given by the Fourier transform $\mathcal{F}$ of the absolute square of $f(t)$:

$$C(t) = \mathcal{F}(|f(t)|^2) , \tag{2}$$

and, of course, the Fourier transform of the second moment of the function is nothing else than its power spectrum $P(\omega) = \mathcal{F}(|f(t)|^2)$. This relationship is known by the name of the Wiener Khinchin theorem.

Thus, interestingly, the Fourier power spectrum is also related to the likely cause of the inability of the rule discovery to be selective enough in its pre-processing phase (feeding the rule extraction algorithms.) The importance of this in the context of our discussion lies in the fact that it links the scaling properties of the Fourier power spectrum with the decay rate of the auto-correlation function. Thus any property of the scaling invariance as discussed above will reveal itself in the invariance of the auto-correlation function. In particular, it will also determine the rate of decay of the auto-correlation function and will be inherited by the cross-correlation products of the time series with its sub-parts.

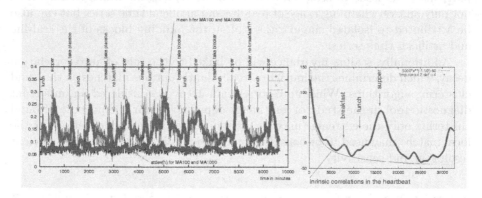

**Fig. 1.** Left: the plot of the variability of human heartbeat from a seven day long experiment where the test persons were given placebo or beta-blocker. For the variability estimate, local roughness (local correlation) exponent $h$ is used, smoothed with a moving average (MA) filter with 100 and 1000 long window. An interesting pattern of response to food is evident [9]. Right: autocorrelation function confirms the presence of an invariant, intra-day periodic structure. The autocorrelation plot is in fact the autocorrelation of the local correlation exponent (as described with the Hölder $h$ exponent.)

The sub-part matching operation is the key operation used in the rule discovery algorithms [2,1] and it clearly inherits the self-similarity properties of the time series. The explanation of the 'trivial match' redundancy which contributes to the inability of the algorithm to select sound rules thus comes from the spectral properties of the time series. The same spectral properties which, as we will show in the following, describe self-similarity properties of the time series.

It is worth noting that the autocorrelation decay is an important diagnostic tool widely used in investigating long range dependence (correlations), see e.g. [4] in the context of S&P500 analysis. However, due to the (Wiener Khinchin) equivalence referred to above, power spectrum decay has been extensively investigated in the same context. A modern method which allows local multiscale or multi-resolution decomposition of non-stationary signals as opposed to the global Fourier approach (useful for stationary processes), is the recently introduced wavelet transform. It allows local location-wise (temporal) and scale-wise (frequency) extraction of required information, including moments of the decomposition measure and regularity (scaling) exponents.

## 3   Estimating Regularity Properties of Rough Time Series

The advent of multi-scale techniques (like WT), capable of locally assessing the singular behaviour, greatly contributed to the advance of analysis of 'strange' signals, including (multi)fractal functions and distributions. The wavelet transform [10,11,12,13] is a decomposition of the input time series into the discrete or continuous basis of localised (often compactly supported) functions - the wavelets. This decomposition is defined through an inner product of the time series with the appropriately rescaled and translated wavelet of a fixed shape. Wavelet decomposition schemes exist which allow decomposition optimisation through the choice from various wavelet bases [14,15] or adaptive decomposition (notably the lifting scheme [16]).

In the continuous formulation, the wavelet transform can be seen as a convolution product of the signal with the scaled and translated kernel, the wavelet $\psi(x)$:

$$(Wf)(s,b) = \frac{1}{s} \int dx\ f(x)\ \psi(\frac{x-b}{s})  \qquad (3)$$

where $s, b \in \mathbf{R}$ and $s > 0$ for the continuous version.

For analysis purposes, one is not so much concerned with numerical or transmission efficiency or representation compactness, but rather with accuracy and adaptive properties of the analysing tool. Therefore, in analysis tasks, continuous wavelet decomposition is mostly used. The space of scale $s$ and position $b$ is then sampled semi-continuously, using the finest data resolution available. The numerical cost of evaluating the continuous wavelet decomposition is not as high as it may seem. Algorithms have been proposed which (per scale) have a complexity of the order $n$, the number of input samples, at a relatively low constant cost factor [17]. Additionally, computationally cheap, discretised, semi-continuous versions of the decomposition are possible [18,19].

In figure 2, we plot the input time series which is a part of the S&P index containing the crash of '87. In the same figure, we plot corresponding maxima derived from the WT decomposition with the Mexican hat wavelet. The maxima converging to the strongest singularity - the '97 crash have been highlighted in the top view.

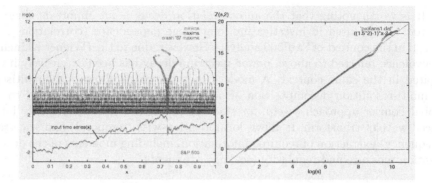

**Fig. 2.** Left: the L1 normalised S&P500 index time series with the derived WT maxima tree above it in the same figure. The strongest maxima correspond to the crash of '87. Right: the second moment of the partition function over the entire CWT (thus not only the maxima lines) see Eq. 4, shows consistent scaling invariance with the exponent $H + 1 = 1.5$. This corresponds with the Brownian walk scaling invariance exponent at $H = 0.5$.

There is an ultimate link between the global scaling exponent: the Hurst exponent $H$ (compare figure 3), and the Fourier power spectral exponent. The power spectrum of the input signal and the corresponding scaling exponent $\gamma$ can be directly evaluated from the second moment of the partition function $Z(s, q = 2)$:

$$\mathcal{Z}(s, q) = \sum_{\Omega(s)} (W f \omega_i(s))^q , \qquad (4)$$

where $\Omega(s) = \{\omega_i(s)\}$ is the set of maxima $\omega_i(s)$ at the scale $s$ of the continuous wavelet transform $W f(s, t)$ of the function $f(t)$.

Indeed the wavelet transform decomposes the signal into scale (and thus frequency) [1] dependent components (scale and position localised wavelets), comparably to frequency localised sines and cosines based Fourier decomposition, but with added position localisation. Scaling of the second moment of the decomposition coefficients provides $\gamma$, the power spectrum scaling, through $\gamma = 2H + 1$, the relation which links the spectral exponent $\gamma$ with the Hurst exponent $H$.

## 4    Rules within Rules, or the Principle of Self-Similarity

Contrary to the long and widely accepted (Euclidean) view, real world time series/ signals are not smooth, but they are often non-differentiable and densely packed with singularities. Rough and wildly changing records are ever-present in nature [24,25,26,27,28]. The frequently adopted view that these signals consist of some smooth information carrying a component with superimposed noise is

---

[1] The working scale of the wavelet $s$ is inversely proportional to the (Fourier) frequency $f \sim 1/s$ and the continuous wavelet used is the second derivative of the Gaussian curve (*Mexican hat*).

also very often inaccurate. Real life records are not necessarily contaminated by 'noise'. Instead, in the case of the lack of a better model, they often intrinsically consist exclusively of noise - indeed, they are 'noise' themselves.

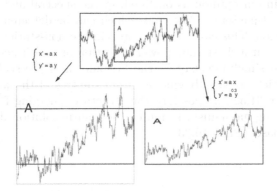

**Fig. 3.** The principle of self-affinity; *similar* rescaling in the bottom left figure versus *affine* rescaling, bottom right, of the fractional Brownian motion of $H = 0.3$. The rescaling factor used for the affine rescaling of the $(x, y)$ axis is $(a, a^{0.3})$, while for a similar case both axes were rescaled using the $a$ factor.

Their 'noisy' components are often distributed at various resolution and length scales - in other words each sub-part of the record is equally noisy and statistically similar (after affine rescaling of $x,y$ coordinates with some factors $\beta_x, \beta_y$) to the entire record (or any other subpart). This kind of similarity can often be characterised by one single exponent $h = \log(\beta_y)/\log(\beta_x)$ for a range of $\beta$ rescaling factors. This is the concept of local scaling which has been explored with the wavelet transform local scaling estimates in section 3. Additionally, the local scaling is often isotropic and the same one unique exponent can characterise both global and local ratio of the similarity rescaling. E.g. this is the case for 1-dim Brownian walk - the integral of white noise for which $h = 0.5$, and equals global $H = 0.5$, the so-called Hurst exponent. Such global scaling rules have been addressed through the partition function multifractal formalism [21].

Indeed the very essence of scaling, i.e. scale invariance, has the consequence that statistically similar patterns may occur at any resolution or scale length. This property characterising many real life signals may be behind the limited ability to extract meaningful deterministic 'rules' from such records [1], although it does permit statistical rule discovery [4,22]. Such can be used for distance evaluation for detecting rule violation for whole time series or streaming diagnosis etc., or streaming time series novelty assessment through departure from the model 'rule'.

In conclusion, the kind of redundancy inherent to a variety of signals analysed in [1] (for the discussion of the algorithm of [2]), as revealed in the 'trivial or spurious matches' has been the subject of research into scaling, (multi-)fractal and long-range correlation properties in real-life phenomena and technology.

Recently this has also been done using the advanced multiscale technique of wavelet transform permitting advanced 'inverse problem' type rule recovery.

The pressing question of course remains, what then is the meaningful methodology/strategy for dealing with signals inherently tough for rule discovery. The answer resides, in our opinion as outlined, in the spectral and auto-correlation properties of the time series. The rules which can be detected are instances of invariance violation, This can be manifested in the non-stationarity of spectral characteristics, be it a short-time power spectrum or multifractal spectrum. Or alternatively and simultaneously, in the breakdown of the scaling invariance - the structure which potentially emerges from the tree of the wavelet transform maxima [23,29,30,31,32], or possibly the structure emerging from the conduct of the self-adapting mechanism in multiscale/multiresolution decomposition or approximation bases [14,15,16,33].

# References

1. J. Lin, E. Keogh, W. Truppel, When is Time Series Clustering Meaningful?, *preprint* Workshop on Clustering High Dimensional Data and its Applications, SDM 2003. will appear on the workshop site:
   www.cs.utexas.edu/users/inderjit/sdm03.html
2. G. Das, K. Lin, H. Mannila, G. Renganathan, P. Smyth, Rule Discovery from Time Series, in proceedings of the ..th Intl. Conference on Knowledge Discovery and Data Mining, New York, NY, Aug 27-31, 1998, pp 16–22, (1998).
3. R.N. Mantegna and H.E. Stanley, *An Introduction to Econophysics: Correlations and Complexity in Finance* Cambridge, England: Cambridge University Press, (2000).
4. A. Arneodo, J.F. Muzy, D. Sornette, Eur. Phys J. B, **2**, 277 (1998).
   http://xxx.lanl.gov/ps/cond-mat/9708012
5. A. Johansen, D. Sornette, Stock Market Crashes are Outliers, Eur.Phys.J. B 1, pp. 141–143 (1998).
   A. Johansen, D. Sornette, Large Stock Market Price Drawdowns Are Outliers arXiv:cond-mat/0010050, 3 Oct 2000, rev. 25 Jul 2001.
6. B. Podobnik, P.Ch. Ivanov, Y. Lee, and H.E. Stanley. "Scale-invariant Truncated Lévy Process". Europhysics Letters, **52** pp 491–497, (2000).
7. Z. R. Struzik. Wavelet Methods in (Financial) Time-series Processing. Physica A: Statistical Mechanics and its Applications, 296(1-2):307–319, June 2001.
8. D. Sornette, Y. Malevergne, J.F. Muzy, Volatility Fingerprints of Large Shocks: Endogeneous Versus Exogeneous, arXiv:cond-mat/0204626, (2002).
9. Z. R. Struzik. Revealing Local Variablity Properties of Human Heartbeat Intervals with the Local Effective Hölder Exponent. Fractals **9**, No 1, 77–93 (2001).
10. S. Jaffard, Multifractal Formalism for Functions: I. Results Valid for all Functions, II. Self-Similar Functions, *SIAM J. Math. Anal.*, 28(4): 944–998, (1997).
11. I. Daubechies, *Ten Lectures on Wavelets*, (S.I.A.M., 1992).
12. M. Holschneider, *Wavelets – An Analysis Tool*, (Oxford Science Publications, 1995).
13. S.G. Mallat and W.L. Hwang, Singularity Detection and Processing with Wavelets. *IEEE Trans. on Information Theory* **38**, 617 (1992).
    S.G. Mallat and S. Zhong Complete Signal Representation with Multiscale Edges. *IEEE Trans. PAMI* **14**, 710 (1992).

14. S. Mallat, Z. Zhang, Matching Pursuit in a Time-frequency Dictionary, *IEEE Transactions on Signal Processing*, **41** pp. 3397–3415, (1993).
15. R.R. Coifmann M.V. Wickerhauser, Entropy-based Algorithm for Best-basis Selection. *IEEE Transactions on Information Theory*, **38**, pp. 713–718, (1992).
16. W. Sweldens, The Lifting Scheme: Construction of Second Generation Wavelets, *SIAM J. Math. Anal.* **29**, (2), pp 511–546, (1997).
17. A. Muñoz Barrutia, R. Ertlé, M. Unser, Continuous Wavelet Transform with Arbitrary Scales and O(N) Complexity, Signal Processing, vol 82, no. 5, pp. 749–757, May 2002
18. M. Unser, A. Aldroubi, S.J. Schiff, Fast Implementation of the Continuous Wavelet Transform with Integer Scales, IEEE Transactions on Signal Processing, vol. 42, no. 12, pp. 3519–3523, December 1994.
19. Z. R. Struzik, Oversampling the Haar Wavelet Transform. Technical Report INS-R0102, CWI, Amsterdam, The Netherlands, March 2001.
20. A. Arneodo, E. Bacry, J.F. Muzy, Oscillating Singularities in Locally Self-Similar Functions, *PRL*, **74**, No 24, 4823–4820, (1995).
21. A. Arneodo, E. Bacry and J.F. Muzy, The Thermodynamics of Fractals Revisited with Wavelets. *Physica A*, **213**, 232 (1995).
   J.F. Muzy, E. Bacry and A. Arneodo, The Multifractal Formalism Revisited with Wavelets. *Int. J. of Bifurcation and Chaos* **4**, No 2, 245 (1994).
22. A.C.-C.Yang, S.-S. Hseu, H.-W. Yien, A.L. Goldberger, C.-K. Peng, Linguistic Analysis of the Human Heartbeat using Frequency and Rank Order Statistics, *PRL*, in press, (2003).
23. Z.R. Struzik, Taming Surprises, in proceedings of the *New Trends in Intelligent Information Processing and Web Mining* conference, Zakopane June 2–5, (2003).
24. K. Falconer, Fractal Geometry: Mathematical Foundations and Applications, John Wiley, 1990; paperback 1997.
25. A. Arneodo, E. Bacry, J.F. Muzy, Wavelets and Multifractal Formalism for Singular Signals: Application to Turbulence Data, *PRL*, **67**, No 25, 3515–3518, (1991).
26. H.E. Stanley, P. Meakin, Multifractal Phenomena in Physics and Chemistry, Nature, vol 335, 405–409, (1988)
27. P.Ch. Ivanov, M.G. Rosenblum, L.A. Nunes Amaral, Z.R. Struzik, S. Havlin, A.L. Goldberger and H.E. Stanley, Multifractality in Human Heartbeat Dynamics, *Nature* **399**, 461–465, (1999).
28. A. Bunde, J. Kropp, H.J. Schellnhuber, (Eds), The Science of Disasters, Climate Disruptions, Heart Attacks, and Market Crashes, Springer, (2002).
29. A. Arneodo, E. Bacry and J.F. Muzy, Solving the Inverse Fractal Problem from Wavelet Analysis, *Europhysics Letters*, **25**, No 7, 479–484, (1994).
30. A. Arneodo, A. Argoul, J.F. Muzy, M. Tabard and E. Bacry, Beyond Classical Multifractal Analysis using Wavelets: Uncovering a Multiplicative Process Hidden in the Geometrical Complexity of Diffusion Limited Aggregates. *Fractals* **1**, 629 (1995).
31. Z.R. Struzik The Wavelet Transform in the Solution to the Inverse Fractal Problem. *Fractals* **3** No.2, 329 (1995).
32. Z. R. Struzik, A. P. J. M. Siebes. Wavelet Transform in Similarity Paradigm. In Proceedings of the Pacific-Asia Conference on Knowledge Discovery and Data Mining, Volume 1394 of Lecture Notes in Artificial Intelligence, pp 295–309, Melbourne, Australia, April 1998.
33. A. Smola, B. Schölkopf, A Tutorial on Support Vector Regression, NeuroCOLT2 technical report NC-TR-1998-030, (1998).

# Mining Diagnostic Rules with Taxonomy from Medical Databases

Shusaku Tsumoto

Department of Medical Informatics,
Shimane Medical University, School of Medicine,
89-1 Enya-cho Izumo City, Shimane 693-8501 Japan
tsumoto@computer.org

**Abstract.** Experts' reasoning in which selects the final diagnosis from many candidates consists of hierarchical differential diagnosis. In other words, candidates gives a sophisticated hiearchical taxonomy, usally described as a tree. In this paper, the characteristics of experts' rules are closely examined from the viewpoint of hiearchical decision steps and and a new approach to rule mining with extraction of diagnostic taxonomy from medical datasets is introduced. The key elements of this approach are calculation of the characterization set of each decision attribute (a given class) and the similarities between characterization sets. From the relations between similarities, tree-based taxonomy is obtained, which includes enough information for diagnostic rules.

## 1 Introduction

Rule mining has been applied to many domains. However, empirical results show that interpretation of extracted rules deep understanding for applied domains. One of its reasons is that conventional rule induction methods such as C4.5[4] cannot reflect the type of experts' reasoning. For example, rule induction methods such as PRIMEROSE[7] induce the following common rule for muscle contraction headache from databases on differential diagnosis of headache:

$$[location = whole] \land [\text{Jolt Headache} = no] \land [\text{Tenderness of M1} = yes]$$
$$\rightarrow \text{muscle contraction headache.}$$

This rule is shorter than the following rule given by medical experts.

$[\text{Jolt Headache} = no]$
$\land ([\text{Tenderness of M0} = yes] \lor [\text{Tenderness of M1} = yes] \lor [\text{Tenderness of M2} = yes])$
$\land [\text{Tenderness of B1} = no] \land [\text{Tenderness of B2} = no] \land [\text{Tenderness of B3} = no]$
$\land [\text{Tenderness of C1} = no] \land [\text{Tenderness of C2} = no] \land [\text{Tenderness of C3} = no]$
$\land [\text{Tenderness of C4} = no]$
$\rightarrow \text{muscle contraction headache}$

where $[\text{Tenderness of B1} = no]$ and $[\text{Tenderness of C1} = no]$ are added.

One of the main reasons why rules are short is that these patterns are generated only by a simple criteria, such as high accuracy or high information gain.

N. Zhong et al. (Eds.): ISMIS 2003, LNAI 2871, pp. 40–48, 2003.

The comparative studies[7,9] suggest that experts should acquire rules not only by a single criteria but by the usage of several measures. For example, the classification rule for muscle contraction headache given in Section 1 is very similar to the following classification rule for disease of cervical spine:

[Jolt Headache = $no$]
$\wedge$([Tenderness of M0 = $yes$] $\vee$[Tenderness of M1 = $yes$] $\vee$[Tenderness of M2 = $yes$])
$\wedge$([Tenderness of B1 = $yes$] $\vee$[Tenderness of B2 = $yes$] $\vee$[Tenderness of B3 = $yes$]
$\quad$ $\vee$[Tenderness of C1 = $yes$] $\vee$[Tenderness of C2 = $yes$] $\vee$[Tenderness of C3 = $yes$]
$\quad$ $\vee$[Tenderness of C4 = $yes$])
$\quad$ $\rightarrow$ disease of cervical spine

The differences between these two rules are attribute-value pairs, from tenderness of B1 to C4. Thus, these two rules are composed of the following three blocks:

$$A_1 \wedge A_2 \wedge \neg A_3 \rightarrow muscle\ contraction\ headache$$
$$A_1 \wedge A_2 \wedge A_3 \rightarrow disease\ of\ cervical\ spine,$$

where $A_1$, $A_2$ and $A_3$ are given as the following formulae:
$A_1$ = [Jolt Headache = $no$], $A_2$ = [Tenderness of M0 = $yes$] $\vee$ [Tenderness of $M1$ = $yes$] $\vee$ [Tenderness of M2 = $yes$], and $A_3$ = [Tenderness of C1 = $no$] $\wedge$ [Tenderness of C2 = $no$] $\wedge$ [Tenderness of C3 = $no$] $\wedge$ [Tenderness of C4 = $no$]. The first two blocks ( $A_1$ and $A_2$ ) and the third one ( $A_3$ ) represent the different types of differential diagnosis. The first one $A_1$ shows the discrimination between muscular type and vascular type of headache. Then, the second part shows that between headache caused by neck and head muscles. Finally, the third formula $A_3$ is used to make a differential diagnosis between muscle contraction headache and disease of cervical spine. Thus, medical experts first select several diagnostic candidates, which are very similar to each other, from many diseases and then make a final diagnosis from those candidates.

In this paper, the characteristics of experts' rules are closely examined from the viewpoint of hierarchical decision steps. Then, extraction of diagnostic taxonomoy from medical datasets is introduced, which consists of the following three procedures. First, the characterization set of each decision attribute (a given class) is extracted from databases. Then, similarities between characterization sets are calculated. Finally, the concept hierarchy for given classes is calculated from the similarity values.

## 2   Rough Set Theory: Preliminaries

In the following sections, we use the following notations introduced by Grzymala-Busse and Skowron[6], which are based on rough set theory[3].

Let $U$ denote a nonempty, finite set called the universe and A denote a nonempty, finite set of attributes, i.e., $a : U \rightarrow V_a$ for $a \in A$, where $V_a$ is called the domain of $a$, respectively.Then, a decision table is defined as an information system, $A = (U, A \cup \{d\})$.

The atomic formulae over $B \subseteq A \cup \{d\}$ and $V$ are expressions of the form $[a = v]$, called descriptors over B, where $a \in B$ and $v \in V_a$. The set $F(B, V)$ of formulas over B is the least set containing all atomic formulas over $B$ and closed with respect to disjunction, conjunction and negation. For example, $[location = occular]$ is a descriptor of $B$. For each $f \in F(B, V)$, $f_A$ denote the meaning of $f$ in $A$, i.e., the set of all objects in U with property $f$, defined inductively as follows: (1) If $f$ is of the form $[a = v]$ then, $f_A = \{s \in U | a(s) = v\}$ (2) $(f \wedge g)_A = f_A \cap g_A$; $(f \vee g)_A = f_A \vee g_A$; $(\neg f)_A = U - f_a$

By the use of the framework above, classification accuracy and coverage, or true positive rate is defined as follows.

**Definition 1.**
*Let R and D denote a formula in $F(B, V)$ and a set of objects which belong to a decision d. Classification accuracy and coverage(true positive rate) for $R \to d$ is defined as:*

$$\alpha_R(D) = \frac{|R_A \cap D|}{|R_A|}(= P(D|R)), \ and \ \kappa_R(D) = \frac{|R_A \cap D|}{|D|}(= P(R|D)),$$

*where $|S|$, $\alpha_R(D)$, $\kappa_R(D)$ and P(S) denote the cardinality of a set S, a classification accuracy of R as to classification of D and coverage (a true positive rate of R to D), and probability of S, respectively.*

It is notable that $\alpha_R(D)$ measures the degree of the sufficiency of a proposition, $R \to D$, and that $\kappa_R(D)$ measures the degree of its necessity.

Also, we define partial order of equivalence as follows:

**Definition 2.** *Let $R_i$ and $R_j$ be the formulae in $F(B, V)$ and let $A(R_i)$ denote a set whose elements are the attribute-value pairs of the form $[a, v]$ included in $R_i$. If $A(R_i) \subseteq A(R_j)$, then we represent this relation as: $R_i \preceq R_j$.*

Finally, according to the above definitions, probabilistic rules with high accuracy and coverage are defined as:

$$R \xrightarrow{\alpha, \kappa} d \ s.t. \ R = \vee_i R_i = \vee \wedge_j [a_j = v_k], \ \alpha_{R_i}(D) \geq \delta_\alpha \ and \ \kappa_{R_i}(D) \geq \delta_\kappa,$$

where $\delta_\alpha$ and $\delta_\kappa$ denote given thresholds for accuracy and coverage, respectively.

## 3    Characterization Sets

### 3.1    Characterization Sets

In order to model medical reasoning, a statistical measure, coverage plays an important role in modeling. Let us define a characterization set of $D$, denoted by $L(D)$ as a set, each element of which is an elementary attribute-value pair R with coverage being larger than a given threshold, $\delta_\kappa$. That is,

**Definition 3.** *Let R denote a formula in $F(B, V)$. Characterization sets of a target concept (D) is defined as: $L_{\delta_\kappa}(D) = \{R | \kappa_R(D) \geq \delta_\kappa\}$*

Then, three types of relations between characterization sets can be defined as follows: (1) Independent type: $L_{\delta_\kappa}(D_i) \cap L_{\delta_\kappa}(D_j) = \phi$, (2) Overlapped type: $L_{\delta_\kappa}(D_i) \cap L_{\delta_\kappa}(D_j) \neq \phi$, and (3) Subcategory type: $L_{\delta_\kappa}(D_i) \subseteq L_{\delta_\kappa}(D_j)$. All three definitions correspond to the negative region, boundary region, and positive region, respectively, if a set of the whole elementary attribute-value pairs will be taken as the universe of discourse.

Tsumoto focuses on the subcategory type in [8] because $D_i$ and $D_j$ cannot be differentiated by using the characterization set of $D_j$, which suggests that $D_i$ is a generalized disease of $D_j$. Then, Tsumoto generalizes the above rule induction method into the overlapped type, considering rough inclusion[9]. However, both studies assumes two-level diagnostic steps: focusing mechanism and differential diagnosis, where the former selects diagnostic candidates from the whole classes and the latter makes a differential diagnosis between the focused classes.

The proposed method below extends these methods into multi-level steps. In this paper, we consider the special case of characterization sets in which the thresholds of coverage is equal to 1.0: $L_{1.0}(D) = \{R_i | \kappa_{R_i}(D) = 1.0\}$ It is notable that this set has several interesting characteristics.

**Theorem 1.** *Let $R_i$ and $R_j$ two formulae in $L_{1.0}(D)$ such that $R_i \preceq R_j$. Then, $\alpha_{R_i} \leq \alpha_{R_j}$.*

**Theorem 2.** *Let $R$ be a formula in $L_{1.0}(D)$ such that $R = \vee_j[a_i = v_j]$. Then, $R$ and $\neg R$ gives the coarsest partition for $a_i$, whose $R$ includes $D$.*

**Theorem 3.** *Let $A$ consist of $\{a_1, a_2, \cdots, a_n\}$ and $R_i$ be a formula in $L_{1.0}(D)$ such that $R_i = \vee_j[a_i = v_j]$. Then, a sequence of a conjunctive formula $F(k) = \wedge_{i=1}^{k} R_i$ gives a sequence which increases the accuracy.*

## 4  Rule Induction with Diagnostic Taxonomy

### 4.1  Intuitive Ideas

As discussed in Section 2, When the coverage of $R$ for a target concept $D$ is equal to 1.0, $R$ is a necessity condition of $D$. That is, a proposition $D \rightarrow R$ holds and its contrapositive $\neg R \rightarrow \neg D$ holds. Thus, if $R$ is not observed, $D$ cannot be a candidate of a target concept. Thus, if two target concepts have a common formula $R$ whose coverage is equal to 1.0, then $\neg R$ supports the negation of two concepts, which means these two concepts belong to the same group. Furthermore, if two target concepts have similar formulae $R_i, R_j \in L_{1.0}(D)$, they are very close to each other with respect to the negation of two concepts. In this case, the attribute-value pairs in the intersection of $L_{1.0}(D_i)$ and $L_{1.0}(D_j)$ give a characterization set of the concept that unifies $D_i$ and $D_j$, $D_k$. Then, compared with $D_k$ and other target concepts, classification rules for $D_k$ can be obtained. When we have a sequence of grouping, classification rules for a given target concepts are defined as a sequence of subrules. From these ideas, a rule induction algorithm with grouping target concepts can be described as a combination of grouping (Figure 1) and rule induction(Figure 2).

**procedure** *Grouping* ;
  **var inputs**
    $L_c$ : *List*;
    /* A list of Characterization Sets */
    $L_{id}$ : *List*;
    /* A list of Intersection */
    $L_s$ : *List*;
    /* A list of Similarity */
  **var outputs**
    $L_{gr}$ : *List*;
    /* A list of Grouping */
  **var**
    $k$ : *integer*;     $L_g, L_{gr}$ : *List*;
  **begin**
    $L_g := \{\}$ ;
    $k := n$
    /* n: A number of Target Concepts*/
    Sort $L_s$ with respect to similarities;
      Take a set of $(D_i, D_j)$, $L_{max}$
        with maximum similarity values;
      k:= k+1;
      **forall** $(D_i, D_j) \in L_{max}$ **do**
      **begin**
        Group $D_i$ and $D_j$ into $D_k$;
        $L_c := L_c - \{(D_i, L_{1.0}(D_i)\}$;
        $L_c := L_c - \{(D_j, L_{1.0}(D_j)\}$;
        $L_c := L_c + \{(D_k, L_{1.0}(D_k)\}$;
        Update $L_{id}$ for $DD_k$;
        Update $L_s$;
        $L_{gr} := ($
          *Grouping* for $L_c$, $L_{id}$, and $L_s$) ;
        $L_g := L_g + \{\{(D_k, D_i, D_j), L_g\}\}$;
      **end**
    **return** $L_g$;
  **end** {*Grouping*}

**procedure** *RuleInduction* ;
  **var inputs**
    $L_c$ : *List*;
    /* A list of Characterization Sets */
    $L_{id}$ : *List*; /* A list of Intersection */
    $L_g$ : *List*; /* A list of grouping*/
    /* $\{\{(D_{n+1}, D_i, D_j), \{(DD_{n+2}, .)...\}\}\}$ */
    /* n: A number of Target Concepts */
  **var**
    $Q, L_r$ : *List*;
  **begin**
    $Q := L_g$; $L_r := \{\}$;
    **if** $(Q \neq \emptyset)$ **then do**
      **begin**
        $Q := Q - first(Q)$;
        $L_r := Rule\ Induction\ (L_c, L_{id}, Q)$;
      **end**
    $(DD_k, D_i, D_j) := first(Q)$;
    **if** $(D_i \in L_c$ and $D_j \in L_c)$ **then do**
      **begin**
        Induce a Rule $r$ which discriminate
        between $D_i$ and $D_j$;
        $r = \{R_i \to D_i, R_j \to D_j\}$;
      **end**
    **else do**
      **begin**
        Search for $L_{1.0}(D_i)$ from $L_c$;
        Search for $L_{1.0}(D_j)$ from $L_c$;
        **if** $(i < j)$ **then do**
          **begin**
            $r(D_i) := \vee_{R_l \in L_{1.0}(D_j)} \neg R_l \to \neg D_j$;
            $r(D_j) := \wedge_{R_l \in L_{1.0}(D_j)} R_l \to D_j$;
          **end**
        $r := \{r(D_i), r(D_j)\}$;
      **end**
    **return** $L_r := \{r, L_r\}$ ;
  **end** {*Rule Induction*}

**Fig. 1.**   An   Algorithm   for
Grouping

**Fig. 2.** An Algorithm for Rule Induction

## 4.2   Similarity

To measure the similarity between two characterization sets, we can apply several indices of two-way contigency tables. Table 1 gives a contingency table for two rules, $L_{1.0}(D_i)$ and $L_{1.0}(D_j)$. The first cell $a$ (the intersection of the first row and column) shows the number of matched attribute-value pairs. From this table, several kinds of similarity measures can be defined[1,2].

In this paper, we focus on the two similarity measures: one is Simpson's measure: $\frac{a}{min\{(a+b),(a+c)\}}$ and the other is Braun's measure: $\frac{a}{max\{(a+b),(a+c)\}}$.

As discussed in Section 4, a single-valued similarity becomes low when $L_{1.0}(D_i) \subset L_{1.0}(D_j)$ and $|L_{1.0}(D_i)| << |L_{1.0}(D_j)|$. For example, let us consider when $|L_{1.0}(D_i)| = 1$. Then, match number is equal to 1.0, which is the lowest value of this similarity. In the case of Jaccard's coefficient, the value is $1/1 + b$ or $1/1 + c$: the similarity is very small when $1 << b$ or $1 << c$. Thus, these similarities do not reflect the subcategory type. Thus, we should check the difference between $a + b$ and $a + c$ to consider the subcategory type. One solution

**Table 1.** Contingency Table for Similarity

| | | $L_{1.0}(D_j)$ | | |
| | | Observed | Not Observed | Total |
|---|---|---|---|---|
| $L_{1.0}(D_i)$ | Observed | $a$ | $b$ | $a + b$ |
| | Not observed | $c$ | $d$ | $c + d$ |
| | Total | $a + c$ | $b + d$ | $a + b + c + d$ |

is to take an interval of maximum and minimum as a similarity, which we call an interval-valued similarity.

For this purpose, we combine Simpson and Braun similarities and define an interval-valued similarity: $\left[ \frac{a}{max\{(a+b),(a+c)\}}, \frac{a}{min\{(a+b),(a+c)\}} \right]$ If the difference between two values is large, it would be better not to consider this similarity for grouping in the lower generalization level. For example, when $a + c = 1 (a = 1, c = 0)$, the above value will be: $\left[ \frac{1}{1+b}, 1 \right]$ If $b >> 1$, then this similarity should be kept as the final candidate for the grouping.

The disadvantage is that it is difficult to compare these inverval values. In this paper, the maximum value of a given interval is taken as the representative of this similarity when the difference between min and max are not so large. If the maximum values are equal to the other, then the minimum value will be compared. If the minimum value is larger than the other, the large one is selected.

# 5   Example

Let us consider the case of Table 2 as an example for rule induction. For a similarity function, we use a matching number[2] which is defined as the cardinality of the intersection of two the sets. Also, since Table 2 has five classes, $k$ is set to 6. For extraction of taxonomy, the interval-valued similarity is applied.

## 5.1   Grouping

From this table, the characterization set for each concept is obtained as shown in Fig 3. Then, the intersection between two target concepts are calculated. In the first level, the similarity matrix is generated as shown in Fig. 4.

Since *common* and *classic* have the maximum matching number, these two classes are grouped into one category, $D_6$. Then, teh characterization of $D_6$ is obtained as : $D_6 = \{[loc = lateral], [nat = thr], [jolt = 1], [nau = 1],$ $[M1 = 0], [M2 = 0]$. In the second iteration, the intersection of $D_6$ and others is considered and the similarity matrix is obatined: as shown in Fig 5. From this matrix, we have to compare three candidates: $[2/8,2/4]$, $[3/7,3/6]$ and $[2/7,2/4]$.

**Table 2.** A small example of a database

| No. | loc | nat | his | prod | jolt | nau | M1 | M2 | class |
|---|---|---|---|---|---|---|---|---|---|
| 1 | occular | per | per | 0 | 0 | 0 | 1 | 1 | m.c.h. |
| 2 | whole | per | per | 0 | 0 | 0 | 1 | 1 | m.c.h. |
| 3 | lateral | thr | par | 0 | 1 | 1 | 0 | 0 | common. |
| 4 | lateral | thr | par | 1 | 1 | 1 | 0 | 0 | classic. |
| 5 | occular | per | per | 0 | 0 | 0 | 1 | 1 | psycho. |
| 6 | occular | per | subacute | 0 | 1 | 1 | 0 | 0 | i.m.l. |
| 7 | occular | per | acute | 0 | 1 | 1 | 0 | 0 | psycho. |
| 8 | whole | per | chronic | 0 | 0 | 0 | 0 | 0 | i.m.l. |
| 9 | lateral | thr | per | 0 | 1 | 1 | 0 | 0 | common. |
| 10 | whole | per | per | 0 | 0 | 0 | 1 | 1 | m.c.h. |

Definition. loc: location, nat: nature, his:history,
Definition. prod: prodrome, nau: nausea, jolt: Jolt headache,
M1, M2: tenderness of M1 and M2, 1: Yes, 0: No, per: persistent,
thr: throbbing, par: paroxysmal, m.c.h.: muscle contraction headache,
psycho.: psychogenic pain, i.m.l.: intracranial mass lesion, common.:
common migraine, and classic.: classical migraine.

$$L_{1.0}(m.c.h.) = \{([loc = occular] \lor [loc = whole]), [nat = per], [his = per],$$
$$[prod = 0], [jolt = 0], [nau = 0], [M1 = 1], [M2 = 1]\}$$
$$L_{1.0}(common) = \{[loc = lateral], [nat = thr], ([his = per] \lor [his = par]), [prod = 0],$$
$$[jolt = 1], [nau = 1], [M1 = 0], [M2 = 0]\}$$
$$L_{1.0}(classic) = \{[loc = lateral], [nat = thr], [his = par], [prod = 1],$$
$$[jolt = 1], [nau = 1], [M1 = 0], [M2 = 0]\}$$
$$L_{1.0}(i.m.l.) = \{([loc = occular] \lor [loc = whole]), [nat = per],$$
$$([his = subacute] \lor [his = chronic]), [prod = 0],$$
$$[jolt = 1], [M1 = 0], [M2 = 0]\}$$
$$L_{1.0}(psycho) = \{[loc = occular], [nat = per], ([his = per] \lor [his = acute]),$$
$$[prod = 0]\}$$

**Fig. 3.** Characterization Sets for Table 2

|  | m.c.h. | common | classic | i.m.l. | psycho |
|---|---|---|---|---|---|
| m.c.h. | − | [1/8,1/8] | [0,0] | [3/8,3/7] | [2/8,2/4] |
| common | − | − | [6/8,6/8] | [4/8, 4/7] | [1/7,1/4] |
| classic | − | − | − | [3/8, 3/7] | 0 |
| i.m.l. | − | − | − | − | [2/7, 2/4] |

**Fig. 4.** Interval-valued Similarity of Two Characterization Sets (Step 2)

From the minimum values, the middle one: $D_6$ and $i.m.l.$ is selected as the second
grouping. Thus, $D_7 = \{[jolt = 1], [M1 = 0], [M2 = 0]\}$. In the third iteration,
the intersection matrix is calculated as Fig 6 and $m.c.h.$ and $psycho$ are grouped
into $D_8$: $D_8 = \{$ [nat=per], [prod=0] $\}$.

| | m.c.h. | $D_6$ | i.m.l. | psycho |
|---|---|---|---|---|
| m.c.h. | – | 0 | [3/8, 3/7] | [2/8,2/4] |
| $D_6$ | – | – | [3/7,3/6] | 0 |
| i.m.l. | – | – | – | [2/7,2/4] |

**Fig. 5.** Interval-valued Similarity of Two Characterization Sets after the first Grouping (Step 3)

| | m.c.h. | $D_7$ | psycho |
|---|---|---|---|
| m.c.h. | – | [0, 0] | [2/8,2/4] |
| $D_7$ | – | [0, 0] | [0,0] |

**Fig. 6.** Interval-valued Similarity of Two Characterization Sets after the second Grouping (Step 4)

### 5.2 Rule Induction

The grouping obtained shows the candidate of the differential diagnosis for matching number and interval-valued similarity. For differential diagnosis, First, this model discriminate between $D_7$(*common*, *classic* and *i.m.l.*) and $D_8$ (*m.c.h.* and *psycho*). Then, $D_6$ and *i.m.l.* within $D_7$ are differentiated. Finally, *common* and *classic* within $D_7$ are checked. Thus, a classification rule for *common* is composed of two subrules: (discrimination between $D_7$ and $D_8$), (discrimination between $D_6$ and *i.m.l.*), and (discrimination within $D_6$).

The first part can be obtained by the intersection for Figure 6. That is,

$$D_8 \to [nat = per] \wedge [prod = 0]$$

$$\neg[nat = per] \vee \neg[prod = 0] \to \neg D_8.$$

Then, the second part can be obtained by the intersection for Figure 5. That is,

$$\begin{aligned}&\neg([loc = occular] \vee [loc = whole]) \vee \neg[nat = per]\\ &\qquad \vee \neg([his = subacute] \vee [his = chronic])\\ &\qquad\qquad \vee \neg[prod = 0] \to \neg i.m.l.\end{aligned}$$

Finally, the third part can be obtained by the difference set between $L_{1.0}(common)$ and $L_{1.0}(classic) = \{[prod = 1]\}$.

$$[prod = 0] \to common.$$

Combining these three parts, the classification rule for *common* is

$$\begin{aligned}&(\neg[nat = per] \vee \neg[prod = 0])\\ &\qquad \wedge (\neg([loc = occular] \vee [loc = whole]) \vee \neg[nat = per]\\ &\qquad \vee \neg([his = subacute] \vee [his = chronic]) \vee \neg[prod = 0])\\ &\qquad\qquad \wedge [prod = 0] \to common.\end{aligned}$$

After its simplification, the rule is transformed into:

$$\begin{aligned}&[nat = thr] \wedge ([loc = lateral] \vee \neg([his = subacute] \vee [his = chronic]))\\ &\qquad\qquad \wedge [prod = 0] \to common.\end{aligned}$$

whose accuracy is equal to 2/3.

It is notable that the second part ($[jolt = 1] \wedge [M1 = 0] \wedge [M2 = 0]$) is redundant in this case, compared with the first model. However, from the viewpoint of characterization of a target concept, it is very important part.

## 6  Conclusion

In this paper, the characteristics of experts' rules are closely examined, whose empirical results suggest that grouping of diseases is very important to realize automated acquisition of medical knowledge from clinical databases. Thus, we focus on the role of coverage in focusing mechanisms and propose an algorithm for grouping of diseases by using this measure. The above example shows that rule induction with this grouping generates rules, which are similar to medical experts' rules and they suggest that our proposed method should capture medical experts' reasoning. This research is a preliminary study on a rule induction method with grouping and it will be a basis for a future work to compare the proposed method with other rule induction methods by using real-world datasets.

**Acknowledgments.** This work was supported by the Grant-in-Aid for Scientific Research (13131208) on Priority Areas (No.759) "Implementation of Active Mining in the Era of Information Flood" by the Ministry of Education, Science, Culture, Sports, Science and Technology of Japan.

## References

1. Cox, T. F. and Cox, M. A. A. *Multidimensional Scaling (Second Edition)*, Chapman & Hall/CRC, Boca Raton, 2000.
2. Everitt, B. S., *Cluster Analysis*, 3rd Edition, John Wiley & Son, London, 1996.
3. Pawlak, Z., *Rough Sets*. Kluwer Academic Publishers, Dordrecht, 1991.
4. Quinlan, J.R., *C4.5 – Programs for Machine Learning*, Morgan Kaufmann, Palo Alto, 1993.
5. *Readings in Machine Learning*, (Shavlik, J. W. and Dietterich, T.G., eds.) Morgan Kaufmann, Palo Alto, 1990.
6. Skowron, A. and Grzymala-Busse, J. From rough set theory to evidence theory. In: Yager, R., Fedrizzi, M. and Kacprzyk, J.(eds.) *Advances in the Dempster-Shafer Theory of Evidence*, pp. 193–236, John Wiley & Sons, New York, 1994.
7. Tsumoto, S., Automated Induction of Medical Expert System Rules from Clinical Databases based on Rough Set Theory. *Information Sciences* **112**, 67–84, 1998.
8. Tsumoto, S., Extraction of Experts' Decision Rules from Clinical Databases using Rough Set Model *Intelligent Data Analysis*, 2(3), 1998.
9. Tsumoto,S. Extraction of Hierarchical Decision Rules from Clinical Databases using Rough Sets. *Information Sciences*, 2003 (in print)

# Comparing Simplification Methods for Model Trees with Regression and Splitting Nodes

Michelangelo Ceci, Annalisa Appice, and Donato Malerba

Dipartimento di Informatica, Università degli Studi
via Orabona, 4 - 70126 Bari - Italy
{ceci, appice, malerba}@di.uniba.it

**Abstract.** In this paper we tackle the problem of simplifying tree-based regression models, called model trees, which are characterized by two types of internal nodes, namely regression nodes and splitting nodes. We propose two methods which are based on two distinct simplification operators, namely pruning and grafting. Theoretical properties of the methods are reported and the effect of the simplification on several data sets is empirically investigated. Results are in favor of simplified trees in most cases.

## 1    Introduction

Model trees are tree-structured regression models that associate leaves with multiple linear regression functions. Internal nodes are typically splitting tests that partition the space spanned by $m$ independent (or predictor) random variables $x_i$ (both numerical and categorical). Regression models at the leaves capture the linear dependence between one or more independent variables and the continuous dependent (or response) variable $y$, locally to a partition of the sample space. Several methods have been proposed for the construction of the tree and for the estimation of the linear dependence at the leaves on the basis of a training sample. They have been implemented in some well-known model tree induction systems such as M5 [10], RETIS [5], M5' [14], HTL [12], TSIR [6] and SMOTI [7]. All these systems perform a *top-down* induction of model trees (TDIMT). However, the last two systems are characterized by two types of internal nodes: *regression nodes*, which perform only straight-line regressions, and *splitting nodes*, which partition the sample space. The regression model at a leaf is obtained by combining the straight-line regression functions associated to the regression nodes along the path from the root to the leaf. In SMOTI, the composition of straight-line regressions can be statistically interpreted as a multiple linear model built *stepwise*.

When building model trees, it is common practice to discard parts of the tree that describe spurious effects in the training sample rather than true features of the underlying phenomenon. The application of model tree simplification (pruning) methods follows the generation (growing) of the tree itself and tries avoid the overfitting problem under control. Several simplification methods have been reported in the literature, most of which are derived from those developed for decision trees [4]. For instance, RETIS bases its pruning algorithm on Niblett and Bratko's method

N. Zhong et al. (Eds.): ISMIS 2003, LNAI 2871, pp. 49–56, 2003.

[8], extended later by Cestnik & Bratko [2]. M5 uses a pessimistic-error-pruning-like strategy since it compares the error estimates obtained by pruning a node or not. The error estimates are based on the training cases and corrected in order to take into account the complexity of the model in the node. Similarly, in M5' the pruning procedure makes use of an estimate, at each node, of the expected error for the test data. The estimate is the resubstitution error compensated by a factor that takes into account the number of training examples and the number of parameters in the linear model associated to the node [14]. A method à la error-based-pruning is adopted in HTL, where the upper level of a confidence interval of the resubstitution error estimate is taken as the most pessimistic estimate of the error node [12]. A different solution has been proposed by Robnik-Sikonja and Kononenko [11] who applied the MDL principle. This principle is based on the coding of the possible solutions to the problem and the selection of the instance with the shortest code as the result.

A common characteristic of all these methods is that they have been defined for model trees whose internal nodes are only splitting tests. Since SMOTI has a different tree structure, it is necessary to develop new methods that correctly operates on the two types of internal nodes. It is noteworthy that no simplification method was proposed in TSIR, the only other system that induces trees with two types of nodes. In this paper, two methods are proposed: they are based on two distinct simplification operators, namely pruning and grafting. They are described in Section 3, after a brief introduction of SMOTI (next section). Experimental results are reported and discussed in Section 4.


## 2   Stepwise Induction of Model Trees

In this section we briefly recall some characteristics of SMOTI. A more detailed explanation of SMOTI and a comparison with other TDIMT methods are reported in [7]. In SMOTI the top-down induction of models trees is performed by considering *regression steps* and *splitting tests* at the same level. The former compute straight-line regression, while the latter partition the feature space. They pass down observations to their children in two different ways. For a splitting node $t$, only a subgroup of the $N(t)$ observations in $t$ is passed to each child (left or right). No change is made on training cases. For a regression node $t$, all the observations are passed down to its only child, but the values of both the dependent and independent numeric variables not included in the multiple linear model associated to $t$ are transformed in order to remove the linear effect of those variables already included. Thus, descendants of a regression node will operate on a modified training set. This is done in accordance to the statistical theory of linear regression, where the incremental construction of a multiple linear model is made by removing the linear effect of introduced variables each time a new independent variable is added to the model. In this way, a *multiple linear model* can be associated to each leaf. It involves all the numerical variables in the regression nodes along the path from the root to the leaf. Variables involved in regression nodes at top levels of the tree capture global effects, while those involved in regression nodes close to the leaves capture local effects.

During the tree growing phase, nodes are selected on the basis of an evaluation function. For a splitting node $t$ it is defined as:

$$\sigma(t) = \frac{N(t_L)}{N(t)}R(t_L) + \frac{N(t_R)}{N(t)}R(t_R) \, ,$$

where $N(t)$ is the number of cases reaching the current splitting node $t$, $N(t_L)$ ($N(t_R)$) is the number of cases passed down to the left (right) child of $t$, and $R(t_L)$ ( $R(t_R)$ ) is the resubstitution error of the left (right) child, computed as follows:

$$R(t_L) = \sqrt{\frac{1}{N(t_L)} \sum_{j=1}^{N(t_L)} (y_j - \hat{y}_j)^2} \quad \left( R(t_R) = \sqrt{\frac{1}{N(t_R)} \sum_{j=1}^{N(t_R)} (y_j - \hat{y}_j)^2} \right).$$

The estimate $\hat{y}_j = a_0 + \sum_{s=1}^{m} a_s x_s$ is computed by combining all univariate regression lines associated to regression nodes along the path from the root to $t_L$ ($t_R$).

The evaluation of a regression step at node $t$ cannot be naïvely based on the resubstitution error $R(t)$. Indeed, the splitting node "looks-ahead" to the best multiple linear regressions after the split is performed, while the regression step does not. A fairer comparison would be growing the model tree at a further level in order to base the computation of $\rho(t)$ on the best splitting node $t'$ after the current regression node $t$ is performed. Therefore, $\rho(t)$ is defined as follows:

$$\rho(t) = min \ \{R(t), \sigma(t')\}.$$

Both $\sigma(t)$ and $\rho(t)$ are compared to choose between three different possibilities: i) growing the model tree by adding a regression node $t$; ii) growing the model tree by adding a splitting node $t$; iii) stopping the tree's growth at node $t$.

Five different stopping criteria are used in SMOTI. The first performs the partial F-test to evaluate the contribution of a new independent variable to the model [3]. The second requires the number of cases in each node to be greater than a minimum value. The third operates when all continuous variables along the path from the root to the current node are used in regression steps and there are no discrete variables in the training set. The fourth creates a leaf if the error in the current node is below a fraction of the error in the root node [13, p. 60]. The fifth stops the growth when the *coefficient of determination* is greater than a minimum value [15, pp. 18-19].

# 3    Simplification Methods for Model Trees

The two proposed methods are both based on the use of an independent pruning set, but they adopt two distinct simplification operators (see Fig. 1), namely:

- the *pruning operator*, $\pi_T$, which associates each internal node $t$ with the tree $\pi_T(t)$ having all the nodes of T except the descendants of $t$, and
- the *grafting operator*, $\gamma_T$, which associates each couple of internal nodes $<t,t'>$ directly connected by an edge with the tree $\gamma_T$ ($<t,t'>$) having all nodes of T except those in the branch between $t$ and $t'$.

The two methods are detailed in the next two subsections.

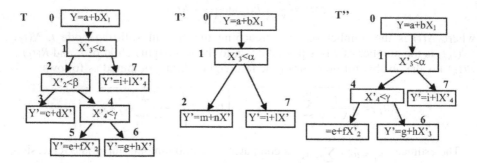

**Fig. 1.** The model tree T' is obtained by pruning T in node 2, while T" is obtained by grafting the subtree rooted in node 4 onto the place of node 2.

### 3.1    Reduced Error Pruning (REP)

This method is based on the Reduced Error Pruning (REP) proposed by Quinlan for decision trees [9]. It uses a pruning set to evaluate the goodness of the subtrees of a model tree T. The pruning set is independent of the set of observations used to build the tree T, therefore, the training set must be partitioned into a *growing* set used to build the tree and a *pruning* set used to simplify T.

The algorithm analyzes the complete tree T and, for each internal node $t$, it compares the mean square error (MSE) computed on the pruning set when the subtree $T_t$ is kept, with the MSE computed on the same set when $T_t$ is pruned and the best regression function is associated to the leaf $t$. The MSE is defined as follows:

$$MSE(T) = \frac{1}{N} \sum_{t \in \tilde{T}} \sqrt{\sum_{x_i \in t} (y_i - \hat{y}_i)^2} \,,$$

where $N$ is the number of examples $(\mathbf{x}_i, y_i)$ in the pruning set, $\tilde{T}$ is the set of leaves of the tree T, and $\hat{y}_i$ is the estimate of the response variable computed according to the multiple linear model associated to a leaf.

If the simplified tree has a better performance than the original one, it is advisable to prune $T_t$. The pruning is repeated on the simplified tree until further pruning increases the MSE. The nodes to be pruned are examined according to a bottom-up traversal strategy. When the node $t$ is turned into a leaf the model associated to $t$ is entirely determined on the basis of the growing set.

The following optimality theorem can be proven [1]:

**Theorem.** Given a model tree T constructed on a set of observations $O$ and a pruning set $O'$, the REP version that determines the regression model on $O$ returns the smallest pruned subtree of T with the lowest error with respect to $O'$.

The specification "the REP version that determines the regression model on $O$" refers to the fact that once a node $t$ has been pruned, the model associated to $t$ is determined on the basis of the same growing set $O$. Alternatively, it could be determined on the basis of either the pruning set or the whole training set.

Finally, the computational complexity of REP is linear in the number of internal nodes, since each node is visited only once to evaluate the opportunity of pruning it.

## 3.2    Reduced Error Grafting

The Reduced Error Grafting (REG) is conceptually similar to REP and uses a pruning set to evaluate the goodness of T', a subtree of T. The algorithm operates recursively. It analyzes the complete tree T and, for each splitting node $t$, it compares the MSE made on the pruning set when the subtree $T_t$ is kept, with the MSE made on the pruning set when $T_t$ is turned into REG($T_{t_1}$) or REG($T_{t_2}$), where $t_1$ and $t_2$ are children of $t$. Sometimes, the simplified tree has a better performance than the original one. In this case, it appears convenient to replace $t$ with its best simplified subtree (left of right). This grafting operation is repeated on the simplified tree until the MSE increases. The nodes to be pruned are examined according to a bottom-up traversal strategy.

This method is theoretically advantaged with respect to REP, since it allows the replacement of a subtree by one of its branches. Indeed, if $t$ is a node that should be pruned according to some criterion, while $t'$ is a child of $t$ that should not be pruned according the same criterion, such simplification strategy either prunes and loses the accurate branch $T_{t'}$ or does not prune at all and keeps the inaccurate branch $T_t$. On the contrary, REG acts by grafting $T_{t'}$ onto the place of $t$, so saving the good sub-branch and deleting the useless node $t$.

Similarly to REP, a theorem on the optimality of the pruned tree can be proven [1]. **Theorem**. Given a model tree T constructed on a set of observations $O$ and a pruning set $O'$, the REG version that determines the regression model on $O$ returns the smallest grafted subtree of T with the lowest error with respect to $O'$.

The complexity of REG is $O(|N_T| \log_2 |N_T|)$, where $N_T$ is the set of nodes in T.

## 4    Comments on Experimental Results

The experiment aims at investigating the effect of simplification methods on the predictive accuracy of the model trees. REP and REG were implemented as a module of KDB2000 (http://www.di.uniba.it/~malerba/software/kdb2000/) and have been empirically evaluated on ten datasets listed in table 1.

**Table 1.** Datasets used in the empirical evaluation of SMOTI.

| Dataset | No. Cases | No. Attributes | Continuous | Discrete |
|---|---|---|---|---|
| Abalone | 4177 | 10 | 9 | 1 |
| Auto-Mpg | 392 | 8 | 5 | 3 |
| Auto-Price | 159 | 27 | 17 | 10 |
| Bank8FM | 4499 | 9 | 9 | 0 |
| Cleveland | 297 | 14 | 7 | 7 |
| Housing | 506 | 14 | 14 | 0 |
| Machine CPU | 209 | 10 | 8 | 2 |
| Pyrimidines | 74 | 28 | 28 | 0 |
| Triazines | 74 | 61 | 61 | 0 |
| Wisconsin Cancer | 186 | 33 | 33 | 0 |

Each dataset is analyzed by means of a 10-fold cross-validation. For every trial, the training set is partitioned into growing (70%) and pruning set (30%). SMOTI is trained on the growing set, pruned on the pruning set and tested on the hold-out block (testing set). Comparison is based on the average mean square error (*Avg.MSE*) made on the testing sets and on the average number of leaves. The stopping criteria used in the experimentation are fixed as follows: the significance level $\alpha$ used in the F-test is set to 0.075, the minimum number of cases falling in each internal node must be greater than the square root of the number of cases in the entire training set, the error in each internal node must be greater than the 0.01% of the error in the root node, the coefficient of determination in each internal node must be below 0.90 for model trees induced on the entire training set and 0.99 for model trees induced on the growing set and after simplified by means of REP or REG method.

Experimental results are listed in Table 2, which reports the average MSE of (unpruned/pruned) SMOTI trees built on training/growing set. For comparison purposes, results obtained by M5' are reported as well. They show that pruning is generally beneficial since REP and REG decrease the average MSE of SMOTI trees built on the growing set. The two methods also drastically reduce the size of the induced trees, often of an order of magnitude, although REG tends to be more conservative than REP. The pruning method implemented in M5' outperforms both REP and REG in most data sets. However, the worst performance of REP and REG can be justified if we consider that M5' pruned a model tree which was originally more accurate than that pruned by REP and REG because of the full use of the cases in the training set.

This result is similar to that reported in [4] for decision trees. Even in that case, it was observed that methods requiring an independent pruning set are at a disadvantage. This is due to the fact that the set of pre-classified cases is limited and, if part of the set is put aside for pruning, it cannot be used to grow a more accurate tree. A clear example is represented by the Auto-Price dataset, where the average number of leaves of REG and M5' is the same (1.6) while the accuracy is different.

**Table 2.** Experimental results of pruning methods for SMOTI and M5'.

| | SMOTI un-pruned trees | | | | SMOTI pruned trees | | | | M5' | | | |
| | Tree built on training set | | Tree built on growing set | | REP | | REG | | Tree built on training set | | Pruning | |
| | Avg MSE | Avg Leaves | Avg MSE | Avg Leaves | Avg MSE | Avg Leaves | Avg MSE | Avg Leaves | Avg MSE | Avg No Leaves | Avg MSE | Avg Leaves |
|---|---|---|---|---|---|---|---|---|---|---|---|---|
| Abalone | 2.5364 | 143 | 6.724 | 95.6 | 2.185 | 5.4 | 2.179 | 25.4 | 2.7724 | 281.4 | 2.126 | 11 |
| AutoMpg | 3.1493 | 13.7 | 4.4866 | 19.2 | 3.5633 | 3.1 | 3.7436 | 8.5 | 3.2010 | 22.6 | 2.835 | 4.6 |
| Auto Price | 2246.0 | 4.3 | 2481.7 | 8 | 2746.3 | 1.6 | 2890.4 | 4.1 | 2358.8 | 12.4 | 2390.1 | 1.6 |
| Bank8FM | 0.0383 | 2.2 | 0.0427 | 68.8 | 0.035 | 5.6 | 0.034 | 30.2 | 0.0409 | 417.7 | 0.0319 | 27 |
| Cleveland | 1.3160 | 21.7 | 1.521 | 17.3 | 0.914 | 2.3 | 0.934 | 5.2 | 1.2496 | 28.1 | 0.9028 | 1.6 |
| Housing | 3.58 | 8.8 | 5.717 | 19.6 | 4.080 | 3.1 | 3.912 | 7.6 | 4.2792 | 50.7 | 3.815 | 14.5 |
| MachineCPU | 55.314 | 4.0 | 71.699 | 6 | 70.953 | 2.7 | 69.145 | 2.4 | 57.352 | 12 | 58.341 | 3.8 |
| Pyrimidines | 0.1056 | 3.8 | 0.1872 | 6.4 | 0.1034 | 1.8 | 0.1352 | 1.8 | 0.0927 | 3.4 | 0.0864 | 3 |
| Triazines | 0.2017 | 16.6 | 0.1820 | 13.3 | 0.155 | 1.2 | 0.229 | 3.8 | 0.1550 | 9.1 | 0.131 | 3.5 |
| Wisconsin | 51.413 | 18.4 | 72.376 | 11.5 | 33.464 | 1.2 | 37.455 | 1.9 | 45.406 | 32.1 | 34.397 | 2.7 |

**Table 3.** Average percentage of the MSE for pruned trees w.r.t. the MSE of un-pruned trees. MSE is computed on the testing set. Best values are in bold.

| Data Set | REP/unpruned SMOTI | REG/unpruned SMOTI | Pruned M5'/unpruned M5' |
|---|---|---|---|
| Abalone | 32.49% | **32.40%** | 76.68% |
| AutoMpg | **79.42%** | 83.4% | 88.56% |
| Auto Price | 110.66% | 116.46% | **101.32%** |
| Bank8FM | 81.96% | 79.62% | **77.99%** |
| Cleveland | **60.09%** | 61.40% | 72.24% |
| Housing | 71.36% | **68.42%** | 89.15% |
| Machine CPU | 98.96% | **96.44%** | 101.72% |
| Pyrimidines | **55.23%** | 72.23% | 93.20% |
| Triazines | 85.71% | 125.86% | **84.51%** |
| Wisconsin Cancer | **46.23%** | 51.75% | 75.75% |

A different view of results is offered in Table 3, which reports a percentage of the Avg. MSE made by pruned trees on the testing sets with respect to the average mean square error made by un-pruned trees on the same testing sets. The table emphasizes the gain of the use of pruning. In particular, pruning is beneficial when the value is less than 100%, while it is not when the value is grather than 100%. Results reported confirm that pruning is beneficial for nine out of ten datasets. Moreover, the absolute difference of Avg. MSE for REP and REG is below 5% in seven datasets. Finally, it is worthwhile to notice that the gain of REP and REG is better than the corresponding gain of M5' pruning method in six datasets. This induces to hypothesize that the better absolute performances of M5' are mainly due to the fact that the tree to be pruned is more accurate because of the full use of training cases.

# 5    Conclusions

SMOTI is a TDIMT method which integrates the partitioning phase and the labeling phase. Similar to many decision tree induction algorithms, SMOTI may generate model trees that overfit training data. In this paper, the *a posteriori* simplification (or pruning) of model trees has been investigated in order to solve this problem. Two methods, named REP and REG, have been defined. They are both based on the use on an independent pruning set, but adopt different simplification operators. Some experimental results have been reported on the pruning methods and show that pruning is generally beneficial. Moreover, the comparison with another well-known TDIMT method, namely M5', which uses the training data both for growing and for pruning the tree, has shown that putting aside some data for pruning can lead to worse results. As future work, we plan to extend this comparison to other TDIMT systems (e.g. HTL and RETIS). Moreover, we intend to implement a new simplification method based on both pruning and grafting operators and to eventually extend MDL-based pruning strategies developed for regression [11] trees to the case of SMOTI trees. This extension should overcome problems we observed for small datasets since the new pruning algorithm will not require an independent pruning set.

**Acknowledgments.** The work presented in this paper is partial fulfillment of the research objective set by the MIUR COFIN-2001 project on "Method for the extraction, validation and representation of statistical information in decision context".

# References

1.  Ceci, M., Appice, A. & Malerba D.: Simplification Methods for Model Trees with Regression and Splitting Nodes. In P. Perner, & A. Rosenfeld (Eds.), *Machine Learning and Data Mining in Pattern Recognition,* Lectures Notes in Artificial Intelligence, 2734, Springer, Berlin (2003), in press.
2.  Cestnik B. and Bratko I.: On estimating probabilities in tree pruning, *Proc. of the Fifth European Working Session on Learning*, Springer, (1991), 151–163.
3.  Draper N.R. and Smith H.: *Applied regression analysis*, John Wiley & Sons, (1982).
4.  Esposito F., Malerba D., Semeraro G.: A comparative analysis of methods for pruning decision trees. *IEEE Trans. PAMI*, Vol. 19, Num. 5, (1997), 476–491.
5.  Karalic A.: Linear regression in regression tree leaves, in *Proceedings of ISSEK '92 (International School for Synthesis of Expert Knowledge)*, Bled, Slovenia, (1992).
6.  Lubinsky D.: Tree Structured Interpretable Regression, in Learning from Data, Fisher D. & Lenz H.J. (Eds.), Lecture Notes in Statistics, 112, Springer, (1996), 387–398.
7.  Malerba D., Appice A., Ceci M., Monopoli M. : Trading-off Local versus Global Effects of Regression Nodes in Model Trees. In H.-S. Hacid, Z.W. Ras, D.A. Zighed, Y. Kodratoff (Eds), *Proceedings of the 13th International Symposium, ISMIS'2002*, Lecture Notes in Artificial Intelligence, 2366, Springer, Berlino, Germania, (2002), 393–402.
8.  Niblett, T. & Bratko I.: Learning decision rules in noisy domains. In Bramer, M. A., *Research and Development in Expert Systems III*, Cambridge University Press, Cambridge, (1986), 25–34.
9.  Quinlan J.R.: Simplifying decision trees. *International Journal of Man-Machine Studies;* 27, (1987), 221–234.
10. Quinlan J.R.: Learning with continuous classes, in *Proceedings AI'92*, Adams & Sterling (Eds.), World Scientific, (1992), 343–348.
11. Robnik-Šikonja M., Kononenko I.: Pruning Regression Trees with MDL. In H. Prade (Ed.), Proceedings of the 13th European Conference on Artificial Intelligence, John Wiley & Sons, Chichester, England, (1998), 455–459.
12. Torgo L.: Functional Models for Regression Tree Leaves, in *Proceedings of the Fourteenth International Conference (ICML '97)*, D. Fisher (Ed.), Nashville, Tennessee, (1997).
13. Torgo L.: *Inductive Learning of Tree-based Regression Models*, Ph.D. Thesis, Department of Computer Science, Faculty of Sciences, University of Porto. (1999).
14. Wang Y. & Witten I.H.: Inducing Model Trees for Continuous Classes, in *Poster Papers of the 9th European Conference on Machine Learning (ECML 97)*, M. van Someren, & G. Widmer (Eds.), Prague, Czech Republic, (1997), 128–137.
15. Weisberg S.: *Applied regression analysis*, 2nd edn. New York: Wiley, (1985).

# Goodness-of-Fit Measures for Induction Trees

Gilbert Ritschard[1] and Djamel A. Zighed[2]

[1] Dept of Econometrics, University of Geneva, CH-1211 Geneva 4, Switzerland
`ritschard@themes.unige.ch`
[2] Laboratoire ERIC, University of Lyon 2, C.P.11 F-69676 Bron Cedex, France
`zighed@univ-lyon2.fr`

**Abstract.** This paper is concerned with the goodness-of-fit of induced decision trees. Namely, we explore the possibility to measure the goodness-of-fit as it is classically done in statistical modeling. We show how Chi-square statistics and especially the Log-likelihood Ratio statistic that is abundantly used in the modeling of cross tables, can be adapted for induction trees. The Log-likelihood Ratio is well suited for testing the significance of the difference between two nested trees. In addition, we derive from it pseudo $R^2$'s. We propose also adapted forms of the Akaike (AIC) and Bayesian (BIC) information criteria that prove useful in selecting the best compromise model between fit and complexity.

## 1 Introduction

Decision tree induction has become since Breiman et al. [4] one of the most popular supervised learning tool. It consists in seeking, through successive splits of the learning data set, some optimal partition of the predictor space for predicting the value of the response variable. Once the membership to a class of the partition is established, the prediction is given by the majority rule that assigns the most frequently observed value of the response variable in that class. Though the primary use of decision trees is classification, they provide a useful description of how the distribution of the response variable is conditioned by the values of the predictors. A tree may exhibit for instance how attributes like age, gender, education level and profession influence the probability of solvency of customers. In this respect, induced trees model the effect of the predictors upon the response variable in the same way as linear or logistic regression. In this paper, we focus on this descriptive modeling feature of induction trees. We introduce and discuss criteria for measuring the reliability of the description provided by a tree.

It is worth mentioning that the criteria we are interested in are not intended to measure the classification performance of the tree. The error rate that focuses on the fit of individual values is well suited for this purpose and has already been largely studied. For the reliability of the description, individual predictions do not matter. Rather, we focus on the posterior distribution of the response variable, i.e. on the distribution conditioned by the values of the predictors. Our concern is thus to measure how well a tree may predict these conditional

N. Zhong et al. (Eds.): ISMIS 2003, LNAI 2871, pp. 57–64, 2003.

distributions. This is a goodness-of-fit issue very similar to that encountered in the statistical modeling of multiway cross tables. According to our knowledge, however, it has not been addressed so far for induced trees.

In statistical modeling, e.g. linear regression, logistic regression or more generally generalized linear models (GLM), the goodness-of-fit is usually assessed by two kinds of measures. On the one hand, indicators like the coefficient of determination $R^2$ or pseudo $R^2$'s tell us how better the model does than some naive baseline model. On the other hand we measure, usually with divergence Chi-square statistics, how well the model reproduces some target or, in other words, how far we are from the target.

Our contribution is a trick that permits to use this statistical machinery with induced trees. The trick allows us to propose, among others, an adapted form of the Likelihood Ratio deviance statistic with which we can test statistically the significance of any expansion of a tree. Other criteria discussed are $R^2$ like measures and the powerful model selection AIC and BIC criteria.

The paper is organized as follows. Section 2 enlightens different kinds of fit that make sense in supervised learning. In Section 3 we formalize our fit issue in terms of table comparison and describe the trick for induced trees. Section 4 proposes and discusses goodness-of-fit measures. Finally, the concluding Section 5 shortly discusses possible further developments.

## 2  Descriptive Ability versus Classification Performance

The goodness-of-fit of a statistical model refers to its capacity to reproduce the data. In a predictive framework, it is measured by a decreasing function of the prediction error, i.e. of the discrepancy between the observed values $y_\alpha$ and the predicted states $\hat{y}_\alpha = f(\mathbf{x}_\alpha)$ of the response variable, with $\alpha = 1, \ldots, n$, $n$ being the number of cases. In classification, the response variable $y$ is categorical with say $r$ values and we have to distinguish between two kinds of predictions. For given values $\mathbf{x} = (x_1, \ldots, x_p)$ of the predictors, we may be interested in predicting the class or in predicting the probability to be in a given class. This suggests to distinguish between the *descriptive probability model* $\hat{\mathbf{p}}(\mathbf{x})$ and the *classifier* itself $f(\mathbf{x}) = g(\hat{\mathbf{p}}(\mathbf{x}))$, with $\hat{\mathbf{p}}(\mathbf{x}) = (\hat{p}_1(\mathbf{x}), \ldots, \hat{p}_r(\mathbf{x}))$ being the prediction of the probability distribution $\mathbf{p}(\mathbf{x}) = (p(Y = y_1|\mathbf{x}), \ldots, p(Y = y_r|\mathbf{x}))$ of the response variable $y$ given $\mathbf{x}$, and $g(\cdot)$ denoting the majority vote rule $g(\hat{\mathbf{p}}(\mathbf{x})) = \arg\max_i \hat{p}_i(\mathbf{x})$.

Many supervised classification tools, among which logistic regression, but also the induction trees, follow a two steps process: First predict the class probabilities by fitting a descriptive model $\mathbf{p}(\mathbf{x})$, then classify according to the majority rule $g(\hat{\mathbf{p}}(\mathbf{x}))$. It makes then sense to assess the fit of both the descriptive and the classification models.

If the final goal is to predict the class, the classification error rate based on the discrepancy between the $y_\alpha$'s and $\hat{y}_\alpha$'s provides undoubtedly the relevant information on how well the classifier fits the data. Nevertheless, users may be interested in the description provided by the descriptive model rather than

**Table 1.** Example of a response × predictors contingency table **T**

| married | male | | | female | | | total |
|---|---|---|---|---|---|---|---|
| | primary | secondary | tertiary | primary | secondary | tertiary | |
| no | 11 | 14 | 15 | 0 | 5 | 5 | 50 |
| yes | 8 | 8 | 9 | 10 | 7 | 8 | 50 |
| total | 19 | 22 | 24 | 10 | 12 | 13 | 100 |

in classification itself. Indeed, logistic regressions as well as induction trees or graphs typically provide useful insights on how predictors jointly affect the probabilities to be in given classes. It is then this representation that goodness-of-fit measures should assess. Hence, the measures should report how well the model $\hat{\mathbf{p}}(\mathbf{x})$ predicts the conditional distributions $\mathbf{p}(\mathbf{x})$ of the response variable, rather than the classification performance of the resulting classifier.

With $n$ cases, the classifier $f(\mathbf{x})$ has to fit $n$ values of $y$. The target of the descriptive model $\hat{\mathbf{p}}(\mathbf{x})$ is quite different. It has to fit a probability distribution $\mathbf{p}(\mathbf{x}) \in \mathbb{R}^r$ for each of the $c$ different[1] observed profiles $\mathbf{x}$. Hence it has to predict $rc$ probabilities (indeed only the non zero probabilities.) Notice that $c \leq n$ is often much smaller than $n$, especially when all predictors are categorical and $n$ is large. The target of the descriptive model is thus a $r \times c$ cross table that synthesizes the relevant information contained in the data. Goodness-of-fit should here assess how well the model reproduces this synthetic representation.

## 3   Target Table and Predicted Table

When all variables are discrete, the empirical counterpart of the conditional distributions $\mathbf{p}(\mathbf{x})$ can be derived from the $r \times c$ contingency table **T** that cross classifies the $r$ values of $Y$ with the $c$ profiles. Table 1, for example, synthesizes 100 data used for predicting the *marital status* (yes, no) with the two predictors *gender* (M = male, F = female) and *activity sector* (P = primary, S = secondary, T = tertiary). Letting $n_{ij}$ denote an element of table **T** and $n_{.j}$ the total of column $j$, the maximum likelihood estimation of $\mathbf{p}_{|j} = \mathbf{p}(\mathbf{x}_j)$ is indeed the vector of the observed frequencies $n_{ij}/n_{.j}, i = 1, \ldots, r$. Each column of the table **T** corresponds to the terminal node of a so called *saturated tree*, i.e. the tree that exhausts all splits and generates the finest partition for the retained predictors (see Figure 1, left.)

As will be shown, an induced tree provides a prediction $\hat{\mathbf{T}}$ of **T**. Measuring the (descriptive) goodness-of-fit of the tree consists then in measuring how well $\hat{\mathbf{T}}$ fits **T**. To explain how we get $\hat{\mathbf{T}}$ from an induced tree, we consider the following rebuilding model where $\hat{\mathbf{T}}_j$ stands for the $j$-th column of $\hat{\mathbf{T}}$

$$\hat{\mathbf{T}}_j = n\, a_j \hat{\mathbf{p}}_{|j}, \quad j = 1, \ldots, c \tag{1}$$

---

[1] If each predictor $x_s$, $s = 1, \ldots, p$ has $c_s$ different values, the number $c$ of possible different profiles, and hence conditional distributions, is at most $\prod_{s=1}^{p} c_s$.

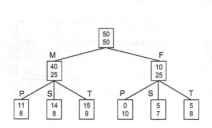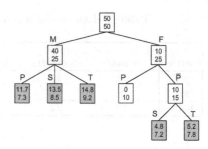

**Fig. 1.** (left) saturated tree and (right) an induced tree (white nodes) together with its maximal extension (white + grey nodes). The predictors are the gender (M, F) and the sector of activity (P=primary, S=secondary, T=tertiary) and the response variable is the marital status (yes, no). Observe that the distribution in the grayed nodes is the same as in their parental white node.

The parameters are the total number of cases $n$, the proportions $a_j$ of cases in column (terminal node) $j = 1, \ldots, c$ and the $c$ column distribution vectors $\mathbf{p}_{|j}$. The $a_j$'s are naturally estimated by $n._j/n$. The only trick required concerns the estimation of the $\mathbf{p}_{|j}$'s. Indeed, the induced tree has generally $q < c$ terminal nodes which generate a $r \times q$ table $\mathbf{T}^a$ not conformable with $\mathbf{T}$. To render table $\mathbf{T}^a$ conformable, we have to extend it or equivalently extend the induced tree.

**Definition 1.** *The* maximal extension *of an induced tree is obtained by maximally further splitting each terminal node $k = 1, \ldots, q$ of the tree and by distributing the cases in each new node according to the distribution $\mathbf{p}^a_{|k}$ of its parent terminal node of the induced tree. (See Figure 1, right.)*

Formally, letting $\mathcal{X}_k$ denote the subset of profiles that belong to the group defined by the terminal node $k$, the maximally extended tree leads to the following estimations of $\mathbf{p}_{|j}$

$$\hat{\mathbf{p}}_{|j} = \mathbf{p}^a_{|k} \quad \text{for all } \mathbf{x}_j \in \mathcal{X}_k \ \ k = 1, \ldots, q \tag{2}$$

For example, if the induced tree is the tree with the white nodes in the right part of Figure 1, its maximal extension is obtained by completing the tree with the grayed nodes. The distributions in the six terminal nodes of the extension follow from those of the three (white) leaves of the induced tree: $\hat{\mathbf{p}}_{|MP} = \hat{\mathbf{p}}_{|MS} = \hat{\mathbf{p}}_{|MT} = \mathbf{p}^a_{|M} = (40/65, 25/65)$, $\hat{\mathbf{p}}_{|FP} = \mathbf{p}^a_{|FP} = (0/10, 10/10)$, $\hat{\mathbf{p}}_{|FS} = \hat{\mathbf{p}}_{|FT} = \mathbf{p}^a_{|F\bar{P}} = (10/25, 15/25)$. From the leaves of the extension we derive the predicted table $\hat{\mathbf{T}}$ depicted in Table 2.

## 4    Goodness-of-Fit Measures for Induction Trees

Having defined the target table $\mathbf{T}$ and the one $\hat{\mathbf{T}}$ predicted by the induced tree, we can now apply the statistical tests and goodness indicators used in

**Table 2.** The predicted table $\hat{\mathbf{T}}$

| married | male | | | female | | | total |
|---|---|---|---|---|---|---|---|
| | primary | secondary | tertiary | primary | secondary | tertiary | |
| no | 11.7 | 13.5 | 14.8 | 0 | 4.8 | 5.2 | 50 |
| yes | 7.3 | 8.5 | 9.2 | 10 | 7.2 | 7.8 | 50 |
| total | 19 | 22 | 24 | 10 | 12 | 13 | 100 |

the statistical modeling of cross tables (see for instance [1].) We first discuss statistics that measure the divergence between the predicted and target tables or, equivalently, between the induced and saturated trees. We then address the issue of trees comparison and propose some $R^2$ like indicators that measure the improvement over a baseline model. We complete the Section with AIC and BIC information criteria for induced trees.

## 4.1   Chi-Square Statistics

The most popular divergence Chi-square statistics are the Pearson $X^2$ and the deviance $G^2$ statistics. Under some regularity conditions (see for instance [3] chap. 14) these statistics have, when the induced tree is correct, an asymptotical Chi-square distribution. In our case, the deviance $G^2$ reads

$$G^2 = 2 \sum_{j=1}^{c} \sum_{i=1}^{r} n_{ij} \ln \left( \frac{n_{ij}}{\hat{n}_{ij}} \right).$$

For practical use of these statistics, we have to determine the associated degrees $d$ of freedom. These are given by the number of independent constraints (2) on the posterior probability vectors $\mathbf{p}_{|j}$'s. Each vector $\mathbf{p}_{|j}$ has $r-1$ independent terms and there are only $q \leq c$ different distributions among the $c$ vectors. Hence the degrees of freedom are: $d = (r-1)(c-q)$. The independence model $I$ between the predictors and the response corresponds to the tree with the sole root node. In this case, we have $q = 1$ and get the well known number $d_I = (r-1)(c-1)$ of degrees of freedom for the independence test. Likewise, for the saturated model $S$, we have $q = c$, which gives $d_S = 0$. For the white induced tree $M$ in the right panel of Figure 1, we get $G^2(M) \simeq 0.18$. Since $r = 2$, $c = 6$ and $q = 3$, we have $d_M = 3$ degrees of freedom. The value of the $G^2$ is in this example very small. Its $p$-value is about 98%, which indicates an excellent fit.

Thanks to an additive property, $G^2$ permits to test the difference between nested models. Let $M_2$ be a restricted form of model $M_1$. Then, the deviance between the two models is (see [1] p. 211) $G^2(M_2|M_1) = G^2(M_2) - G^2(M_1)$ which, if $M_2$ is correct, has an asymptotic Chi-square distribution with $d_2 - d_1$ degrees of freedom.

For induction trees, the deviance between nested trees, i.e. between a tree and the same tree after the pruning of a subtree of interest, provides a natural way to test the statistical relevance of the subtree. In the example of Figure 1, we can for instance test if the activity sector has a significant role, by comparing the induced tree $M_1 = M$ with the tree $M_2$ that includes only the split by gender. For the latter, we get $G^2(M_2) = 8.41$ with $d_2 = 4$ degrees of freedom. The divergence between the two trees is thus $G^2(M_2|M_1) = 8.41 - 0.18 = 8.23$ with $d_2 - d_1 = 4 - 3 = 1$. Its $p$-value is 0.4%. This is clearly less than the usual 5% threshold from which we conclude that the split is statistically significant.

## 4.2   Comparison with a Baseline Model

This Section is devoted to $R^2$-type indicators that measure the relative quality improvement over a baseline tree. For trees, a natural choice for the naive baseline model is the tree with the sole root node, i.e. the independence case.

*Proportion of reduction in the error rate.* Though we are not interested in the prediction of individual values, it is worth mentioning that $R^2$-type measures make also sense for the error rate. The proportion of reduction of the learning error rate corresponds indeed to the Goodman and Kruskal [5] first association measure $\lambda_{y|\text{partition}}$. The literature [6,9] gives formulas of its asymptotic variance that can be used to test its statistical significance.

*Information Gain.* The gain in information is typically measured by the reduction in the entropy of the response variable. Since we are interested in quality measures of the whole tree, we consider the global reduction achieved by the induced tree when compared with the root node. This should not be confused with the local entropy reduction that some tree growing algorithms maximize at each node. The relative gain of information with respect to the root node can for instance be measured with $\hat{\tau}_{M|I} = \left( n \sum_i \sum_j \frac{\hat{n}_{ij}^2}{n_{\cdot j}} - \sum_i n_{i\cdot}^2 \right) / \left( n^2 - \sum_i n_{i\cdot}^2 \right)$ or with $\hat{u}_{M|I} = \left( \sum_i \frac{n_{i\cdot}}{n} \log_2 \frac{n_{i\cdot}}{n} - \sum_j \frac{n_{\cdot j}}{n} \sum_i \frac{\hat{n}_{ij}}{n_{\cdot j}} \log_2 \frac{\hat{n}_{ij}}{n_{\cdot j}} \right) / \left( \sum_i \frac{n_{i\cdot}}{n} \log_2 \frac{n_{i\cdot}}{n} \right)$. The $\hat{\tau}_{M|I}$ is the second nominal association measure of Goodman and Kruskal [5]. It measures the proportion of reduction in the quadratic entropy $H_Q(\mathbf{p}) = \sum_i p_i(1-p_i)$ also known as the Gini variation index. The $\hat{u}_{M|I}$ is known in statistics as the Theil uncertainty coefficient [11]. It measures the proportion of reduction in Shannon's entropy $H_S(\mathbf{p}) = -\sum_i p_i \log_2 p_i$. For our induced tree $M$ in Figure 1, we have for example $\hat{\tau}_{M|I} = 0.145$ and $\hat{u}_{M|I} = 0.132$. These values indicate a relative gain of information of about 14%. This should in turn be compared with the gains achieved by the saturated tree that are respectively $\hat{\tau}_{S|I} = 0.146$ and $\hat{u}_{S|I} = 0.134$, from which it appears that the induced tree captures almost the whole potential gain we can get from the predictors.

For testing the statistical significance of the information gain, i.e. the hypotheses $H_0 : \tau_{M|I} = 0$ and $H_0 : u_{M|I} = 0$, there are two possibilities. We can use available asymptotic variances [9] and a Gaussian approximation. It is most powerful, however, to use the following transformations of the indexes: $C(I|M) = (n-1)(r-1)\hat{\tau}_{M|I}$ and $G^2(I|M) = \left( -2 \sum_i n_{i\cdot} \log(n_{i\cdot}/n) \right) \hat{u}_{M|I}$. The first has been suggested by Light and Margolin [8]. In a setting corresponding to the case where the tree is the saturated tree $M = S$, these authors show that under the independence hypothesis ($\tau_{S|I} = 0$), the quantity $C(I|S)$ follows asymptotically a $\chi^2$ with $d_I$ degrees of freedom. Replacing $S$ with a restraint model $M$ just requires adjusting the degrees of freedom. Hence, for the general case, $C(I|M)$ has a $\chi^2$ distribution with $d_I - d_M$ degrees of freedom. The transformation of $\hat{u}_{M|I}$ shows that testing the significance of $u_{M|I}$ is equivalent to testing the difference in fit between $I$ and $M$ with $G^2(I|M) = G^2(I) - G^2(M)$. Both transformations have thus, under $H_0$, the same asymptotic $\chi^2$ distribution with $d_I - d_M$ degrees of freedom. For our illustrative induced tree, we get $C(I|M) = 14.32$ and $G^2(I|M) = 18.36$. These are large values for the degrees of freedom $d_I - d_M = 5 - 3 = 2$. They confirm the statistical significance of the global information gain.

*Pseudo $R^2$.* The goal is here to measure the proportion of the divergence between the baseline and saturated trees that can be catched by the induced tree. If we measure the divergence with the $G^2$ statistic, we can use for example the pseudo $R^2 = 1 - G^2(M)/G^2(I)$ or its form adjusted for the degrees of freedom $R^2_{\text{ajust}} = 1 - [G^2(M)d_I]/[G^2(I)/d_M]$. For our example, we have $G^2(I) = 18.55$, $d_I = 5$, $G^2(M) = .18$ et $d_M = 3$ from which we get $R^2 = .99$ and $R^2_{\text{ajust}} = .984$. Again, these values confirm that the induced tree catches almost the entire lack of fit of the independence tree.

## 4.3   Goodness-of-Fit and Complexity

Clearly, the more we grow a tree the better is the fit. For description purposes the tree should on the contrary be as simple as possible. Parsimony is not only an interpretability requirement. It is also essential to ensure the stability of the description. Thus when selecting a descriptive tree we have to trade off between fit and complexity. This is precisely what the Akaike (AIC) [2] and Bayesian (BIC) [10,7] information criteria are intended for. Their principle is simply to penalize the fit for the complexity. In their definition the AIC and BIC measure the complexity in terms of the number of independent parameters of the model. For trees, we have to count the independent parameters of the rebuilding formula (1). This gives $qr - q + c$ and the AIC and BIC read thus $\text{AIC}(M) = G^2(M) + 2(qr - q + c)$ and $\text{BIC}(M) = G^2(M) + (qr - q + c)\log(n)$. The BIC penalizes complexity increasingly with $n$ and more strongly than does AIC. These information criteria are specially useful for model selection. Among several trees, the one that minimizes the criteria provides the best compromise between fit and adjustment. To illustrate, let us compare our induced tree $M$ with the variant $M^*$ where the node "female" is split into the three sectors $P, S, I$ instead of the binary split into primary $P$ and not primary $\bar{P}$. For both trees we have $n = 100$, $c = 6$ and $r = 2$. For $M$, we have $q = 3$ and hence $(qr - q + c) = 9$, and for $M^*$, $q = 4$ and $(qr - q + c) = 10$. Since $G^2(M) = 0.18$ and $G^2(M^*) = .16$, we get $\text{AIC}(M) = 18.18$ and $\text{AIC}(M^*) = 20.16$. Likewise, we get $\text{BIC}(M) = 41.63$ and $\text{BIC}(M^*) = 46.21$. Both criteria indicate the the simpler tree $M$ should be preferred to $M^*$. The fit improvement of $M^*$ over $M$ is not sufficient to justify the increase in complexity. Note that the induced tree outperforms both the independence model $(\text{AIC}(I) = 32.55,\ \text{BIC}(I) = 50.78)$ and the saturated tree $(\text{AIC}(S) = 24,\ \text{BIC}(S) = 55.26)$.

## 5  Conclusion

We have addressed the issue of evaluating the descriptive quality of an induced tree. The central point in the approach presented is the trick of the extended tree that allows comparison with the target saturated tree. The approach is quite simple and its implementation as an a posteriori quality measure in tree building softwares should be straightforward. Its main limitation is the number of profiles involved by the predictors that should not be too huge.

Criteria like the AIC and BIC are powerful model selection tools. We plan therefore to use them at the tree building stage. Two aspects merit here special attention. First, we should establish some local criteria that when optimized (at each node) provides a solution equivalent to the global minimization of the AIC or BIC. Second, there is the issue of continuous attributes. Induction tree methods usually discretize them dynamically, i.e. optimally during the tree building process. We have then to solve the question of the a priori target table to use for the computation of the divergence Chi-squares.

## References

1. Agresti, A.: *Categorical Data Analysis.* Wiley, New York (1990)
2. Akaike, H.: Information theory and an extension of the maximum likelihood principle. In Petrox, B.N., Caski, F., eds.: *Second International Symposium on Information Theory.* Akademiai Kiado, Budapest (1973) 267
3. Bishop, Y.M.M., Fienberg, S.E., Holland, P.W.: *Discrete Multivariate Analysis.* MIT Press, Cambridge MA (1975)
4. Breiman, L., Friedman, J.H., Olshen, R.A., Stone, C.J.: *Classification And Regression Trees.* Chapman and Hall, New York (1984)
5. Goodman, L.A., Kruskal, W.H.: Measures of association for cross classifications. *Journal of the American Statistical Association* **49** (1954) 732–764
6. Goodman, L.A., Kruskal, W.H.: Measures of association for cross classifications IV: simplification of asymptotic variances. *Journal of the American Statistical Association* **67** (1972) 415–421
7. Kass, R.E., Raftery, A.E.: Bayes factors. *Journal of the American Statistical Association* **90** (1995) 773–795
8. Light, R.J., Margolin, B.H.: An analysis of variance for categorical data. *Journal of the American Statistical Association* **66** (1971) 534–544
9. Olszak, M., Ritschard, G.: The behaviour of nominal and ordinal partial association measures. *The Statistician* **44** (1995) 195–212
10. Schwarz, G.: Estimating the dimension of a model. *The Annals of Statistics* **6** (1978) 461–464
11. Theil, H.: On the estimation of relationships involving qualitative variables. *American Journal of Sociology* **76** (1970) 103–154

# PDL with Maximum Consistency Monitors*

Elisa Bertino[1], Alessandra Mileo[1], and Alessandro Provetti[2]

[1] Dipartimento d'Informatica e Comunicazione
Università degli studi di Milano. Milan, I-20135 Italy
{bertino, mileo}@dico.unimi.it.
[2] Dipartimento di Fisica
Università degli studi di Messina. Messina, I-98166 Italy
ale@unime.it

**Abstract.** In the context of Network management, Chomicki, Lobo and Naqvi have defined the specification language PDL (Policy Description Language) and later extended it by introducing monitors: constraints on the actions that the network manager cannot execute simultaneously. We argue that PDL with monitors is an appealing language that can be applied to specification and implementation of intelligent systems beyond network management. To do so, we discuss two extensions of it. In the first extension monitors are defined as computing a *maximum* set of actions compatible with the constraints, rather than a *maximal* one. The inevitably higher computational complexity of this extension is assessed. In the second extension, negative events, a device already introduced by Chomicki et al., are treated as equivalent to regular events, thus allowing more intuitive results from monitor application.

## 1 Introduction

Policies are widely used and play a relevant role in several different contexts, such as network management, access control, trust management and telecommunication systems. Many of those environments are, however, characterized by complex policies, taking into account a large variety of events, conditions and actions to be executed. Developing and analyzing a given base of policies can be thus quite a complex task, in particular if one wants to ensure *policy consistency*, that is, for example, that no two different policies result in conflicting actions to be executed. In order to address such a requirement, declarative approaches to policy specification languages, appear to be a promising solution.

We believe that policy specification and enforcement are a key enabling technology for intelligent systems. In fact, policy languages such as PDL can be seen as bringing together advances from the Database field, where the emphasis is on scalability and practical deployment, and Logic Programming, where the emphasis is on ease of representation and declarative semantics.

* This work was partially funded by the Information Society Technologies programme of the European Commission, Future and Emerging Technologies under the IST-2001-33058 PANDA and IST-2001-37004 WASP projects.

N. Zhong et al. (Eds.): ISMIS 2003, LNAI 2871, pp. 65–74, 2003.

Chomicki, Lobo and others have been among the first to address issues related to policy specification and in the context of network services management by defining a high-level specification language, called Policy Description Language (PDL). In that context, a policy is a description of how events received over a network (e.g., queries to data, connection requests etc.) are served by some given network terminal, often identified as *data server*. PDL allows network/system managers to specify policies independently from the details of the particular device executing it. For each device, a PDL *wrapper* is provided that maps PDL actions into actual commands understood by the device. [Virmani et al., 2000] describes one of the PDL wrappers now used in industry. PDL's abstraction from device seems to a great advantage in heterogeneous networks, and very promising for application elsewhere. We refer the reader to [Lobo et al., 1999], [Chomicki et al., 2000], [Virmani et al., 2000] and [Chomicki et al., 2003] for a complete introduction and motivation for PDL.

In their recent work, Chomicki et al. have extended the syntax and semantics of PDL to allow specifying *monitors*: descriptions of sets of actions that cannot be executed simultaneously. This type of constraint primitives has been added to PDL to allow specifying illegal, hazardous or physically impossible situations and to prevent policy application from generating them. However, in our opinion some issues need further consideration, if we want to make PDL with monitors an appealing specification language also outside heterogeneous network management. In this article we investigate monitors that, unlike the approach by Chomicki et al., yield maximum sets of actions as a result. We argue that such monitors capture more closely the intended meaning of a monitor, but their application may become computationally intractable. Next, we consider *negative actions* of PDL syntax and show how to handle them in the complex scenario of Event-cancellation monitors.

This article is organized as follows. In Section 2 we introduce the syntax of PDL and its translation into Answer Set Programming, used to define its semantics. Then, in Section 3 we argue for extending PDL. Subsequent sections describe formally the proposed extensions.

## 2    Introduction to PDL

PDL can be described as an evolution of the typical Event-Condition-Action (ECA) schema of active databases. A PDL policy is defined as a set of rules of the form

$$e_1, \ldots e_m \textbf{ causes } a \textbf{ if } C$$

where $C$ is a Boolean condition and $e_1, \ldots e_m$ are events, which can be seen as input requests. For the sake of simplicity, in this article we consider only constant (propositional) events. For each primitive event $e$, Chomicki et al. introduce a *dual* event $!e$ representing the fact that $e$ *has not occurred*. Finally, $a$ is an action, which is understood to be a configuration command that can be executed by the network manager.

PDL assumes that events and actions are syntactically disjoint and that rules are evaluated and applied in parallel. One may notice the lack of any explicit reference to time. In fact, PDL rules are interpreted in a discrete-time framework as follows. If at a given time $t$ the condition is evaluated true and all the events are received from the network, then at time $t + 1$ action $a$ is executed. As a result, we can see PDL policies as describing a transducer. [Chomicki et al., 2000] give a precise formal semantics of PDL policies by showing a translation into function-free [disjunctive] logic programs, which have Gelfond-Lifschitz Answer Set semantics [Gelfond and Lifschitz, 1991]. So, the semantics of a policy written in PDL (and its extensions) is given in terms of the Answer Sets of the translated policy. This article adopts the same methodology and discusses semantics always in terms of Answer Sets.

## 2.1 Introduction to Consistency Monitors

In [Chomicki et al., 2003] PDL has been extended to allow describing constraints on sets of actions executing together. This is the syntax of the new rules:

$$\textbf{never } a_1 \dots a_n \textbf{ if } C$$

where $C$ is a Boolean condition and $a_1 \dots a_n$ are actions; it prohibits the simultaneous execution of $a_1 \dots a_n$. A set of such rules is called a *consistency monitor*. Consistency monitors can be used to specify hazardous, insecure or physically impossible situations that should be forbidden. At this point, clearly, the question becomes what to do when applying the policy yields a set of actions that actually violates one of the rules in the monitor. Applying a monitor means filtering actions that follow from a policy application, *canceling* some of them.

In conflict resolution, cancellation can be understood and performed in different ways. [Chomicki et al., 2003] proposes two alternative semantics for cancellation; the first semantics, called Action-cancellation monitor, consists of dropping some of the actions to be executed so that to *respect* the monitor.

The second semantics, called Event-cancellation monitor, consists of dropping some of the events from the input, and then re-applying the original policy, which, having lesser conditions satisfied, this time will yield a set of to-be-executed actions that does not violate any of the constraints in the monitor.

Unlike Action-cancellation, Event-cancellation has the property of *unobtrusiveness:* in case of a violation, the original policy is applied (in some sense, re-applied) *as is,* to a possibly smaller set of input events. Chomicki et al. argue that this is a very appealing property of EC-monitors over AC monitors since the latter may dictate a set of actions where certain *causal connections* among actions are lost.

## 2.2 Formal Definitions

Let us describe the formal setting used in the rest of the article. First of all, following Chomicki et al., we slightly simplify the notation by restricting to policies and monitors with empty condition $C$. Second, we recall that the event $(\mathcal{E})$ and action $(\mathcal{A})$ alphabets are assumed to be disjoint. Also, $\mathcal{E}$ is implicitly extended by introducing for each event $e$ its opposite $!e$. As described earlier, the intended meaning of $!e$, $e$ did not happen, is captured by the next definition.

**Definition 1.** *A set $E$ of events observed on the network, sometimes called epoch, is completed by $E^c = E \cup \{!e_i \ : \ e_i \notin E\}$.*

Next definitions concern the encoding of PDL policies as Answer Set Programs. The set of observed events, $E$, is represented by a set $occ(E)$ of *occurs* facts. Policies are encoded as follows.

**Definition 2.** *Let $\mathcal{E}$ and $\mathcal{A}$ be event and action alphabets, respectively and let $\mathcal{E} \cap \mathcal{A} = \emptyset$. A policy $P$ over $\mathcal{E}$ and $\mathcal{A}$ is a set of rules of the form ($e_i \in \mathcal{E}$, $a \in \mathcal{A}$):*

$$exec(a) \ :- \ occ(e_1), \ldots occ(e_l), \\ not \ occ(e_{l+1}), \ldots not \ occ(e_m). \tag{1}$$

Clearly, a set of *occurs* facts together with rules describing *exec* makes up a simple (stratified) ASP program, for which there is a unique answer set.

**Definition 3.** *Let $occ(E)$ be a set of occurs facts and $P$ a policy. The consequence set of $E$ w.r.t. a policy $P$, denoted $P(E)$, is the (unique) set of all actions implied by program $occ(E) \cup P^1$: $a \in P(E) \leftrightarrow occ(E) \cup P \models_{asp} exec(a)$.*

Let us now introduce consistency monitors as ASP programs. By lack of space, we will only show the most complex one, Event-Cancellation, in the Chomicki et al. encoding.

## 2.3   Encoding Consistency Monitors in ASP

Chomicki et al. define Event-Cancellation monitors, in ASP as a set of rules of two types. In the first type we have, for each constraint of the form "**never** $a_1, \ldots, a_n$" the rule

$$block(a_1) \ \vee \ \ldots \ \vee \ block(a_n) \ :- \ exec(a_1), \ldots, \ exec(a_n). \tag{2}$$

The second type of rule is instead relative to the policy. Each rule "$e_1, \ldots, e_n$ **causes** a" in $P$, is translated into two rules, a *blocking* rule:

$$ignore(e_1) \ \vee \ldots \vee \ ignore(e_n) \ :- \ occ(e_1), \ldots, occ(e_n), \\ block(a). \tag{3}$$

and an *accepting* rule:

---
[1] The ASP declarative semantics, with the definition of $\models_{asp}$, is found in [Gelfond and Lifschitz, 1991]

$$accept(a) \; :- \; occ(e_1), \ldots, \; occ(e_n),$$
$$not \; ignore(e_1), \ldots, \; not \; ignore(e_n). \tag{4}$$

respectively[2]. Given a PDL policy $P$ and a set of input events $E$, we define the ASP program $\pi_P(E)$ as containing i) $occ(E)$, ii) the definition of exec, as in 2) and the definition of *ignore* and *accept* as above. Unlike program $P \cup occ(E)$ of Definition 3, $\pi_P(E)$ may have several answer sets. In each of them we find a collection of *accept* facts that describe actions satisfying the monitor under Event-cancellation semantics. Indeed, from the point of view of consistency monitoring, since all answer sets describe a *maximal* monitor, they are equivalent, so one can just pick the first. Finally, we remind the reader that answer sets of $\pi_P(E)$ can be computed in practice by feeding it to and ASP solver such as DLV [Systems].

## 3   Review of PDL with Monitoring

The concept of monitor, in our opinion, captures crucial aspects of policy specification and application in realistic contexts. Indeed, it gives a formal, abstract language by which system/network/database administrators can specify the policy with which a certain service handles incoming requests.

Chomicki et al. work on theory and implementation of PDL gives a careful assessment of tractability (polynomial time complexity) of computing the output of monitors. *However, we believe that in their work tractability is guaranteed at the price of reducing, to a significant extent, the properties of the monitors being dealt by.* There are two areas where intuition and a clean semantics are compromised. Let us discuss them here.

First, in the introduction to their work, Chomicki et al. argue convincingly that monitors, while prohibiting the simultaneous execution of some set of actions

> [...] should cancel as few actions as possible. ([Chomicki et al., 2003])

We understand this requirement as saying that the output of a monitor, under any of the proposed semantics, should contain the *maximum,* in the sense of set cardinality, set of actions that are sanctioned by the policy and compatible with the constraints defined in the monitor. Contrary to our intuition, Chomicki et al. semantics for monitors dictates that output of a monitor is a *maximal,* in the sense of set containment, set of actions. We believe that their definition can be a good starting point in the formal treatment of monitors but that it does not capture the requirement that *as many requests as possible* are satisfied. We will show that going from Chomicki et al.'s maximality requirement to a more realistic maximum-cardinality requirement makes monitoring intractable for large inputs.

The second issue that needs attention is the treatment of negative actions. Recall that a *negative* event $!e$ is considered as part of the input whenever

---

[2] Remind that rules defining *exec* (2) are still part of the encoding.

no event of type $e$ is recorded in the input. Negative events are a very convenient syntactic device as they allow describing a desired behavior of the system when some expected event actually does not happen, thus pointing to some failure/disconnection in the system.

In Sec. 3.5 of [Chomicki et al., 2003], to avoid nonmonotonic effects (i.e., canceling an event triggers some new actions) Chomicki et al. limit event-cancellation to policies without negative events only. In the last section we discuss event-cancellation in general, and we show an implementation in Logic Programming and hint at the foreseeable complexity of PDL with monitors under that interpretation.

## 4    Maximum Consistency Monitors

In this section we define maximal monitors and maximum consistency monitors, and discuss their computational complexity. The following definition is intended to capture the maximality requirement of [Chomicki et al., 2003].

**Definition 4.** *(rephrases Definition 10 of [Chomicki et al., 2003])*
*An epoch $E$ is $P$-consistent w.r.t. a monitor $M$ if the output of $P$ does not violate the constraints in $M$. An epoch $E'$ is a $(P,AC)$-consistent reduction of an epoch $E$ if $E' \subseteq E$ and $E'$ is $P$-consistent w.r.t. monitor $M$. The reduction is maximal if there is no $(P,AC)$-consistent reduction $E''$ of $E$ such that $E' \subseteq E''$ and $E' \neq E''$.*

We can now give a stronger conditions on the output of a policy+monitor.

**Definition 5.** *MAXAC-MONITOR*
*For an arbitrary policy $P$, monitor $M$ and epoch $E$ (defined over the same language), $MAXACM(P, M, E)$ is a set of actions $A$ s.t. i) $A' \subseteq P(E)$, ii) $A$ is consistent w.r.t $M$ and iii) for any other set of actions $A'' \subseteq P(E)$ consistent w.r.t. $M$, $|A''| \leq |A'|$.*

**Definition 6.** *MAXEC-MONITOR*
*For an arbitrary policy $P$, monitor $M$ and epoch $E$ (defined over the same language), $MAXECM(P, M, E)$ is a sub-epoch $E' \subseteq E$ such that i) $E'$ is a $(P,AC)$-consistent reduction of $E$ and ii) for any other $E''$ which is a $(P,AC)$-consistent reduction of $E$ , $|E''| \leq |E'|$.*

### 4.1    A Lower Bound for Complexity of Maximum Monitors

We shall show that the problem of finding the Maximum AC- EC- Monitor is NP-hard by reducing the well-known 3SAT problem [Papadimitriou, 1994] (in its decision version). Some notation is needed. Consider a finite set of Boolean variables $x_1 \ldots x_n$. Let a literal $l$ be either a proposition, $x_i$, or its negation $\neg x_i$. A propositional formula is a 3-clause if it has the form: $l_1 \vee l_2 \vee l_3$. A formula $\phi$ built using variables from $x_1 \ldots x_n$ and standard structural induction is said to be in 3-CNF normal form if it corresponds to a conjunction of 3-clauses. From now on, by a formula $\phi$ we intend a formula in 3-CNF normal form.

**Definition 7.** *3SAT*

**instance:** *a formula $\phi$ in 3-CNF normal form*
**question:** *does $\phi$ admit a model, i.e. $\exists i : \{x_1, \ldots, x_n\} \rightarrow \{t, f\}$ s.t. $[[\phi]]^i = t$?*

Let us establish a polynomial reduction from the 3SAT problem to maximum-consistency monitors, thus giving a lower bound to EC-monitor complexity. We will present the reductions in reverted order, since the reduction to MAX EC-MONITOR may be easier to grasp.

**Reduction from 3SAT to MAXEC-MONITOR.** Consider an arbitrary 3CNF formula $\phi$ containing $m$ 3-clauses over $n$ variables; each clause $c_k$ will be denoted $(l_1^k \vee l_2^k \vee l_3^k)$, $k = 1..m$. Now, we start describing a PDL policy+monitor by defining events. $\mathcal{E} = \{t(x_i), f(x_i) : i = 1..n\}$ Intuitively, event $t(x_i)$ (resp. $f(x_i)$) means that we take $x_i$ true (resp. false). As for action, $\mathcal{A} = \{x_i, n\_x_i : i = 1..n\} \cup \{unsat(c_k) : k = 1..m\}$. Now, policy $P_{3SAT-EACM}(\phi)$ is defined as follows: $P_{3SAT-ECM}(\phi) = \{$

$\tilde{\forall} \, i = 1..n :$
$t(x_i)$ **causes** $x_i$,
$f(x_i)$ **causes** $n\_x_i$,

$\tilde{\forall} \, k = 1..m :$
$\overline{l_1^k}, \overline{l_2^k}, \overline{l_3^k}$, **causes** $unsat(c_k)$. {where $\overline{l} = f(x_i)$ if $l = x_i$ and $\overline{l} = t(x_i)$ if $l = \neg x_i$}
$\}$
The corresponding monitor $M_{3SAT-ECM}$ is defined as follows:
$M_{3SAT-ECM}(\phi) = \{$

$\tilde{\forall} \, i = 1..n :$
**never** $x_i, n\_x_i$.

$\tilde{\forall} \, k = 1..m :$
**never** $unsat(c_k)$.
$\}$

Now, consider the input $E = \{t(x_i), f(x_i) : i = 1..n\}$. We can prove the correctness of the reduction.

**Theorem 1.** *(3SAT $\leq_p$ MAXECM)*
*A 3CNF formula $\phi$ is satisfiable if and only if the result of MAX-EC Monitor over $P_{3SAT-ECM}(\phi)$ has cardinality exactly $n$.*

To prove the statement it suffices to notice that, even though $E$ contains $2n$ events, the first $n$ constraints in $P_{3SAT-ECM}(\phi)$ imply blocking one action each. If the maximum monitor has cardinality $n$ then no further event has been blocked in order to respect the remaining $m$ constraints (which impose satisfaction of each clause).

**Corollary 1.** *MAX EC-monitor is NP-hard.*

*Proof.* It follows from the fact that the 3SAT problem is in NP [Papadimitriou, 1994] and Theorem 1 above.

**Reduction from 3sat to MAXACM.** In a similar way we can establish a polynomial reduction from 3SAT problem to AC-monitor only by slightly modifying our policy and monitor as follows.
$P_{3SAT-ACM}(\phi) = \{$

$\tilde{\forall}\, i = 1..n :$
$t(x_i)$ **causes** $x_i$,
$f(x_i)$ **causes** $n\_x_i$,
$\}$

The corresponding monitor $M_{3SAT-ACM}$ is defined as follows:
$M_{3SAT-ACM}(\phi) = \{$

$\tilde{\forall}\, i = 1..n :$
**never** $x_i,\ n\_x_i$.

$\tilde{\forall}\, k = 1..m\ :$
**never** $\overline{l_1^k},\ \overline{l_2^k},\ \overline{l_3^k}$. {where $\overline{l} = n\_x_i$ if $l = x_i$ and $\overline{l} = x_i$ if $l = \neg x_i$)}
$\}$
Consider the same input as above: $E = \{t(x_i),\ f(x_i)\ :\ i = 1..n\}$. We can prove the correctness of the reduction.

**Theorem 2.** *(3SAT $\leq_p$ MAXACM)*
*A 3CNF formula $\phi$ is satisfiable if and only if the result of MAX-AC Monitor over $P_{3SAT-ACM}(\phi)$ has cardinality exactly n.*

As for MAXECM, to prove the statement it suffices to notice that, even though $E$ contains $2n$ events, the first $n$ constraints in $P_{3SAT-ACM}(\phi)$ imply blocking one action each.

## 5   Extending Monitors to Treat Negative Events Properly

We would like to allow negative (!e) events to be used in policy rules *even under event-cancellation monitor*. This can be useful in many cases, when an action should be triggered by an event *not occurred* (a signal not received, an update not done and so on). Allowing negated literals in policies leads to a different concept of *unobtrusiveness* than that described by [Chomicki et al., 2003]. We illustrate the concept by means of an example where negative events are used in the policy specification.

*Example 1.* (Starving from resources) Consider the following policy.
$P_{starve} = \{\, \tilde{\forall}\, x :$
$\qquad\qquad e_x$ **causes** $eat\_banana_x$,
$\qquad\qquad !e_x$ **causes** $eat\_mango_x.\}$
and the monitor

$M_{starve} = \{ \tilde{\forall} \, x, \, y, \, x \neq y :$
    **never** $eat\_banana_x, \, eat\_banana_y.$
    $\tilde{\forall} \, x :$
    **never** $eat\_banana_x, \, eat\_mango_x.\}$

where $x$ and $y$ represent users needing a resource, *mango* is supposed to be an unlimited resource while *banana* is limited to one for iteration. The second constraint is added to make sure that each user eats at most one fruit per iteration.

Now, suppose that the input $E = \{e_{u1}, e_{u2}\}$ is received *repeatedly*. At each policy application a conflict arises and we have to block one action among those indicated in the first *block* rule. Suppose $block(eat\_banana_{u2})$ is non-deterministically chosen; from the second *ignore* rule, the event triggering the blocked action is ignored, so we remain with the reduced (and, incidentally, maximum) epoch $E' = \{occ(e_{u1})\}$. A re-application of the original policy to $E'$ returns $exec(eat\_banana_{u1})$ (with no conflict), while we are expected to obtain also $exec(eat\_mango_{u2})$. Since the choice of the event to block is non-deterministic at each execution, we may well end up blocking user $u_2$ from getting any resource over and over again, even though there is an unlimited supply of mangos!

Example 1 shows how, if we allow negated events to appear in a policy, we cannot grant our Event-Cancellation monitor to be *unobtrusive*, because ignoring a negated event $!e_i$ which triggers some new action, we fail to derive consequences from *lack of* $e_i$ and the behavior produced by the policy using a reduced epoch as actual input may be incorrect. This problem may be overcome by adding, for each event $e_i$, an *unobtrusiveness rule* as follows:

$$occ(!e_i) \; :\!\!- \; ignore(e_i). \tag{5}$$

We believe that this proposed extension to the monitor semantics is needed to allow reasoning with missing events. However, it does come to a price. First of all, the correspondence between the answer sets of the resulting program and monitors needs to be reproved. Second, we believe that the new formulation of Event-cancellation monitor may increase the computational complexity of finding monitors even further. We propose the following conjecture.

*Conjecture 1.* Computing the maximum monitor under Event-cancellation semantics is asymptotically more complex than computing the maximum monitor under Action-cancellation semantics.

## 6   Discussion and Future Work

The intractability of maximum consistency monitors proved in this article should not be taken as an argument against neither their further study nor their implementation and testing. Simply, it gives a roadmap to what type of computational logic support, and what type of optimization techniques should be tried out in this context. Theorem 2 justifies the choice of [Chomicki et al., 2003] of disjunctive logic programming, a formalism for which satisfiability is above NP, as the implementation tool for consistency monitors.

The results presented in this paper can be extended in various directions. In particular, we are interested in investigating whether the maximality requirement is a *strong* requirement in many common applications, or it can be -at least partially- released. We believe that flexible policy languages, with underlying formal semantics, are required by which applications can specify whether to enforce or not the maximality requirement.

# References

[Chomicki et al., 2000] Chomicki J., Lobo J. and Naqvi S., 2000. *A logic programming approach to conflict resolution in policy management.* Proc. of KR2000, 7th Int'l Conference on Principles of Knowledge Representation and Reasoning, Morgan Kaufmann, pp 121–132.

[Chomicki et al., 2001] J. Chomicki, J. Lobo, 2001. *Monitors for History-Based Policies.* Proc. of Int'l Workshop on Policies for Distributed Systems and Networks. Springer-Verlag, LNCS 1995, pp. 57–72.

[Chomicki et al., 2003] Chomicki J., Lobo J. and Naqvi S., 2003. *Conflict Resolution using Logic Programming.* To appear on IEEE Transactions on Knowledge and Data Engineering (TKDE) 15(1): 244-249. Available from *http://www.cs.buffalo.edu/~chomicki/*

[Gelfond and Lifschitz, 1991] Gelfond, M. and Lifschitz, V., 1991. Classical negation in logic programs and disjunctive databases. New Generation Computing: 365–387.

[Liberatore, 1999] Liberatore, P., 1999. Algorithms and Experiments on Finding Minimal Models. Tech. Report 09–99, DIS, University of Rome "La Sapienza."

[Lobo et al., 1999] Lobo J., Bhatia R. and Naqvi S., 1999. A Policy Description Language, in *AAAI/IAAI, 1999*, pp. 291–298.

[Papadimitriou, 1994] Papadimitriou, C., 1994. *Computational Complexity,* Addison Wesley.

[Schlipf, 1995] Schlipf, J., 1995. *The expressive powers of the logic programming semantics,* Journal of Computer and Systems Sciences 51, pp. 64–86.

[Systems] Web location of the most known ASP solvers:
aspps: *http://www.cs.uky.edu/ai/aspps/*
CCalc: *http://www.cs.utexas.edu/users/tag/cc/*
Cmodels: *http://www.cs.utexas.edu/users/tag/cmodels.html*
DLV: *http://www.dbai.tuwien.ac.at/proj/dlv/*
NoMoRe: *http://www.cs.uni-potsdam.de/ linke/nomore/*
SMODELS: *http://www.tcs.hut.fi/Software/smodels/*

[Virmani et al., 2000] Virmani, J., Lobo, L. and Kohli, M., 2000. *NETMON: Network Management for the SARAS Softswitch* Proc. of IEEE/IFIP Network Operations and Management Symp.

# Comparing and Merging Ontologies: A Concept Type Hierarchy Approach

Dan Corbett

Advanced Computing Research Centre
School of Computer and Information Science
University of South Australia
Adelaide, South Australia 5095

**Abstract.** In this paper we explore the issue of using some aspects of the Conceptual Graph Theory formalism to define functions on ontologies. We exploit the formal definitions of type hierarchy and projection to define operations on an ontology. We discuss the definition of an ontology, and demonstrate that projection as defined in Conceptual Graph Theory can then be used for comparing and merging ontologies. We then explore how these formal definitions can be used to implement merging and comparison of ontologies.

## 1   Introduction

An ontology, in the Knowledge Engineering and Artificial Intelligence sense, is a framework for the domain knowledge of an intelligent system. An ontology structures the knowledge, and acts as a container for the knowledge. While there has been much discussion in the literature regarding the structure and logical foundations of ontologies, few researchers are looking at the issues of sharing knowledge between intelligent systems, or reusing knowledge gathered in ontologies by agents.

There are many papers reporting attempts and some successes on the use of ontologies *within* applications [Jasper and Uschold 1999]. However, there are few reports on the *reuse* of *existing ontologies,* apart from some top-level linguistic ontologies. One of the important steps within a methodology for the "use of ontologies within an application" that Pinto and Gomez-Pérez [Pinto and Gomez-Pérez 1999] have identified, is to compare several ontologies to discover whether they are compatible among themselves. This step applies to the reuse of more than one existing ontology, and to the reuse of an existing ontology with a new ontology.

We define *Knowledge Conjunction* as one or more agents using multiple ontologies to perform tasks and understand the domain. Once a common ontology is agreed upon, the agents then have a common background in which to share knowledge. No current method exists that allows intelligent agents to agree on a common framework for sharing knowledge, although there has been some work in comparing semantic meanings within an ontology [Yang and Kifer 2002]. This means that agents are unable to use the knowledge of another agent, as the knowledge is meaningless if it isn't presented in a proper context or a common "language."

There has also been discussion in recent Conceptual Graph (CG) literature about using CGs as the representation scheme for knowledge bases, knowledge frameworks and ontologies (see, for example, [Tepfenhart 1998; Mineau 2002; Ribière and Dieng-

N. Zhong et al. (Eds.): ISMIS 2003, LNAI 2871, pp. 75–82, 2003.
© Springer-Verlag Berlin Heidelberg 2003

Kuntz 2002]). Much of this work has concentrated on the use of graphs as the representation scheme for the ontology, or as the knowledge base structure.

In this paper, we take a different point-of-view for the representation of ontologies. Rather than constructing a CG to represent the ontology, we assert that the CG formalism is better exploited by using a concept type hierarchy to act as the framework for the knowledge base. An unpopulated ontology (which is simply a framework for the knowledge) is represented by the type hierarchy without specific individuals, while the populated ontology (the framework, as well as the knowledge of the domain) is represented by a hierarchy and the specific conceptual graphs which instantiate individuals, constraints, situations or concepts. Our definition for ontology is a functional one. We can define what an ontology *does* more easily than we can define what it *is*.

## 2    Projection as an Ontology Operator

We base our formal definition of ontology on the CG Theory definition of canon, as defined in [Mugnier and Chein 1996; Corbett 2003] and others. A canon in the sense discussed here is the set of all CGs which are well-formed, and meaningful in their domain. Canonical formation rules specify how ontologies can be legally built and guarantee that the resulting graphs satisfy "sensibility constraints," called the Canonical Basis. The canonical basis is a set of rules in the domain which specifies how the relations can be legally used, for example that the concept *eats* must have a theme which is *food*.

A type hierarchy can then be established for both the concepts and the relations within a canon. A type hierarchy is based on the intuition that some types subsume other types, for example, every instance of *cat* would also have all the properties of *mammal*. This hierarchy is expressed by a subsumption or generalization order on types. We formalize these ideas below.

**Definition 1. Ontology.** An ontology is a tuple $(T, I, \leq, ::, B)$ where

$T$ is the set of types. We will further assume that $T$ contains two disjunctive subsets $C$ and $R$ containing types for concepts and relations. Relations are functions with arguments, where each $arg_i : R \rightarrow C$ is a partial function where $arg_i(r)$ indicates the i-th argument of the relation $r$.

$I$ is the set of individuals, sometimes called referents.

$\leq \subseteq T \times T$ is the subtype relation. It is assumed to be a lattice (so there are types top ($\top$) and bottom ($\bot$) and lattice operations join ($\vee$) and meet ($\wedge$)).

$:: \subseteq I \times T$ is the conformity relation. The conformity relation relates type labels to individual markers. This is essentially the relation which ensures that the typing of the concepts makes sense in the domain.

$B$ (also called $\sigma$ by some authors) is the Canonical Basis, a function which associates each relation type with the concept types that may be used with that relation. This helps to guarantee well-formed graphs.

The set T of types is arranged into a type hierarchy, ordered according to the specificity of each type. Separate type hierarchies are established for the concepts and the relations within a canon, expressed by a generalization order on the types. A type t is said to be more specific than a type s if t specializes some of the concepts from s.

Projection is the function which determines the specialization/generalization relation between two concepts. The standard definition of projection used in recent Conceptual Graph literature [Mugnier and Chein 1996; Corbett 2001a] is:

**Definition 2. Projection.**

$G = (C, R, type, referent, arg_1, \ldots, arg_m)$ is said to have a projection into (subsume) $G' = (C', R', type', referent', arg'_1, \ldots, arg'_m)$, $G \geq G'$, if and only if there is a pair of morphisms $h_C: C \to C'$ and $h_R: R \to R'$, such that:

$\forall c \in C$ and $\forall c' \in C'$, $h_C(c) = c'$ only if $type(c) \geq type'(c')$, and $referent(c) = *$ or $referent(c) = referent(c')$

$\forall r \in R$ and $\forall r' \in R'$, $h_R(r) = r'$ only if $type(r) \geq type'(r')$

$\forall r \in R$, $arg'_i(h_R(r)) = h_C(arg_i(r))$,

$\forall c \in C$ there is a concept $c' \in C'$, such that $h_C(c) = c'$

This definition of projection then gives us a formal definition for subtype and supertype and for subsumption on the partial order of the types in the hierarchy. All of these operations are now simply applications of the projection operator. Finding types which are compatible is now a matter of finding a common subtype (join) of the two types. If the only common subtype is $\perp$ then there can be no unification.

## 3 Knowledge Conjunction

As an operator for ontology comparison, the use of the projection operator becomes obvious. When comparing two ontologies, one need only determine whether the two concepts under consideration (one from each ontology) are in a subtype-supertype relation. This means that there needs to be a way for specifying which two types to compare. As discussed for CG unification in [Corbett and Woodbury 1999], the user will need to specify a starting node, or in this case a starting type in each ontology. This may simply be T, but can be any node that the user wants to specify.

Many terms (or types in our case) are not in any subsumption relation, for example *cat* and *dog*, or *wood* and *mammal*. Inheritance hierarchies can be seen as lattices that admit unification and generalization [Knight 1989]. So, in our case, combining two ontologies is the process of finding the common points in the two ontologies (represented as lattices) and merging the rest of the structures together.

An example for such an approach is H. Aït-Kaci's Login [Aït-Kaci and Nasr 1986], where first-order terms are replaced by feature terms. In the ψ-terms of Aït-Kaci [Aït-Kaci and Nasr 1986] subterms are labeled symbolically, rather than by argument position, and there is no fixed arity. The novel contribution of ψ-terms is in the use of type inheritance information. Aït-Kaci's view of unification was as a filter for matching partial structures, using functions and variables as the "filters." Then, his unification technique uses information from a taxonomic hierarchy to achieve a more gradual filtering.

An example of Aït-Kaci's ideas from Knight [Knight 1989] illustrates this gradual filtering technique. Assume that we have the following inheritance information, as illustrated in Figure 1: Birds and fish are animals; a fish-eater is an animal; a trout is a fish; and a pelican is both a bird and a fish-eater. Then unifying the following ψ-terms:

> *fish-eater (likes → trout)*
> *bird (color → brown; likes → fish)*

will yield the new ψ-term:

> *pelican (color → brown; likes → trout)*

Unification does not fail on comparing *fish-eater* to *bird*, or *trout* to *fish*. Instead, the conflict is resolved by finding the greatest lower bound on each of the two pairs of items in the taxonomic hierarchy, in this case *pelican* and *trout*, respectively. In this manner, Aït-Kaci's system naturally extends the information-merging (or *knowledge conjunction*) nature of unification.

The merging of two ontologies is somewhat more complicated, and also more interesting and useful than merely an extension of the projection operation. A unification of two graphs contains neither more nor less information than the two graphs being unified. This is the idea behind knowledge conjunction. The merging of two ontologies is a matter of finding a common starting point on the two hierarchies (usually with the assistance of the user) and then continuing outward from that point in a depth-first manner to find other matching points.

The main thrust of previous research has been the unification of Conceptual Graphs in terms of conjoining the knowledge contained in two different graphs [Corbett and Woodbury 1999; Corbett 2001b]. In our case, these pieces of partial information are represented by Conceptual Graphs. However, our current work involves combining the knowledge of two entire domains. We want to be able to combine the expert knowledge of two systems, or even combine knowledge from different sources, not merely gather additional information.

When an ontology is represented by a type hierarchy constructed in this way, subsumption can be used to combine, refine and reuse the knowledge contained in the graphs. This further allows us to perform reasoning over the knowledge in the graphs as concepts. Reasoning is not limited to objects, classes or libraries, but can also be applied to generic concepts in the knowledge.

## 4   Conjunction of Ontologies

The knowledge conjunction of ontologies can take two forms: merging the ontologies into one new ontology, or placing links between the ontologies to indicate semantic identities while maintaining two separate ontologies. Creating a new, merged ontology has the advantage of maintainability. Keeping the ontologies separate has the advantage that an owner of an ontology can

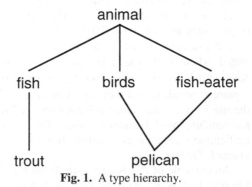

**Fig. 1.** A type hierarchy.

"borrow" concepts from another ontology without the need of reorganizing one's own ontology.

Let us first examine the issue of linking two separately-maintained ontologies. As our example ontologies, let us use the simple taxonomies from Aït-Kaci's work expressed in Figures 1 and 2. As with the unification of two CGs, the user starts by specifying a start node for the comparison. This would normally just be the top concept, but provision is made for the user to specify any concept in the lattice. Comparison then continues from the specified node to the nodes that are subsumed by that node. The algorithm proceeds by comparing the name of each type to check for an exact match. If there is an exact match, then a link is created from one ontology to the other. In this way, the two ontologies are linked, but not merged. Issues of distributed knowledge bases and dynamically changing ontologies are not addressed in this method.

The second method involves creating a completely new ontology by merging the two ontologies. The algorithm starts in a similar manner, with the user selecting the start node for the merge. The algorithm again proceeds by comparing the name of each type to check for an exact match. If there is an exact match, then that type and everything subsumed by that type in both ontologies is copied into a new lattice.

We can now employ standard graph spanning and unification algorithms which recursively move down through the subsumption relations from the start node. Informally, our algorithm starts by comparing the start nodes, q and q´ for compatibility, that is, that they are the same type or that the type of one subsumes the type of the other. Given compatible start nodes, the algorithm selects a subsumption relation s from all of the subsumption relations that lead from the head node q, and seeks its projection s´ in the second lattice from the subsumption relations that lead from q´. If none is found, then the subsumed type s becomes part of the unified graph trivially. If the projection is present in the second graph, then the unification algorithm is called recursively on the types subsumed by type s. If all these types s prove to be compatible, then the two sublattices are joined, and attached to the unified top, q´´. The algorithm proceeds depth-first through the lattice. When all types subsumed by the start concept in both graphs have been successfully

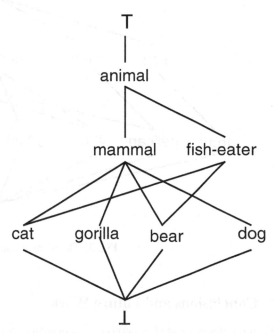

**Fig. 2.** Another ontology from the same domain.

processed in this way, the algorithm terminates successfully. Figure 3 shows the result of applying the Merge algorithm to the lattices in Figs. 1 and 2.

The algorithm presented below shows the procedure formally. $L = (T, q, S)$ represents the lattice in question, T is the set of types, $q \in T$ is the chosen start node in lattice L, and S is the set of subsumption relations. Each $r \in S$ is a relation which maps a supertype to a subsumed subtype, $r(p) = s$ when s is a subsumed subtype of p. Subsumption of types is determined by projection. This is basically just a depth-first search of the two lattices.

**Algorithm 1. Merge** $(L, L')$.

• **If** $q \neq q'$ **then** terminate with failure.

• Construct the set $M_S$ of all $s \in S$ and $s' \in S'$, where $r(q) = s$

• While there is an $s \in M_S$:

    • **If** there is an $s' = r(q)$ **then** Merge$((T, r(q), S), (T', r'(q), S'))$

        **else** set $s'' = r(q)$

• Return $L'' = (T'', q'', S'')$ .

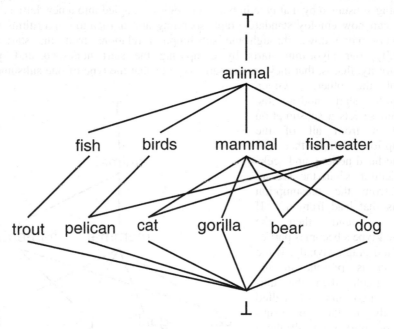

**Fig. 3.** The merged ontology

## 5 Conclusions and Future Work

We have demonstrated a method for automated comparison of ontologies represented as concept type hierarchies. Type hierarchies and the canonical formation rules efficiently specialize ontologies into concrete instances by instantiating canonical CGs from the hierarchies. A simple merge operation, using join and type subsumption, is used to perform knowledge conjunction of the concepts represented in the ontologies. The significance of our work is that the previously static knowledge representation of ontology is now a dynamic, functional reasoning system. This extension of ontologies using Conceptual Graph Theory helps to strengthen the use of ontologies as a knowledge representation and reasoning system.

The method described above works well when the user can guarantee that a given type name has the same meaning in all ontologies. However, problems arise when a given label has different meanings in two ontologies, or when the semantics of the types vary. This is the classic problem presented by many ontology authors [van Zyl and Corbett 2000; Buccafurri et al. 2002]. Overcoming the problems of synonymy and heterogeneity requires the examination of the semantic links of each type.

Comparing the semantic links of each type requires that the software understands the "neighborhood" of each type, and has a basic understanding of how to compare the neighboring nodes for semantic similarity. Again, while some authors have attempted to define solutions for this problem, the issue of applying those techniques to conceptual type hierarchies is future work.

There are still two main issues which need to be resolved before knowledge conjunction with ontologies can be a useful tool: how does the user decide which concept to start with, and can the process be automated so that two ontologies can be merged without user intervention. Both of these questions are still being investigated.

The question of automating the process may subsume the first question, especially if a successful method is found. Right now, our thinking runs to examining the semantic neighborhood of each type to see if two concept types have a common semantic context. There are also many investigations into how to make this sort of semantic comparison [Buccafurri et al. 2002]. The goal would be to automatically examine two ontologies to find the starting point in both (which may be domain dependant). But this almost begs the question, in that it seems to require an ontology which describes the knowledge contained in the two ontologies in question.

Another issue which arises is that there is no real difference between a (unpopulated) reference ontology and (populated) local ontology. An ontology is just a framework for the knowledge, but also expresses the basic format and rules of the domain. A reference ontology then would just be a concept type hierarchy. The local ontology would be the concept type hierarchy which specializes right down to all the individuals I in the domain. There is a sense then that the canonical formation rules also form part of the ontology, in the sense that they are used to determine when a graph can be specialized. If a CG can be specialized, refined or unified with another CG under the canonical formation rules, then it is a valid expression under the ontology as well.

# References

Aït-Kaci, H. and R. Nasr (1986). "LOGIN: A Logic Programming Language with Built-in Inheritance." *Journal of Logic Programming* **3**.

Buccafurri, F., G. Lax, D. Rosaci and D. Ursino (2002). "A User Behavior-Based Agent for Improving Web Usage". In *Proc. International Conference on Ontologies, Databases and Applications of Semantics*, Irvine, California, USA, Springer-Verlag, October, 2002.

Corbett, D.R. (2001a). "Conceptual Graphs with Constrained Reasoning". *Revue d'Intelligence Artificielle* **15**(1): 87–116.

Corbett, D.R. (2001b). "Reasoning with Conceptual Graphs". In *Proc. Fourteenth Australian Joint Conference on Artificial Intelligence*, Adelaide, South Australia, Springer, December, 2001.

Corbett, D.R. (2003). *Reasoning and Unification over Conceptual Graphs*. New York, Kluwer Academic Publishers.

Corbett, D.R. and R.F. Woodbury (1999). "Unification over Constraints in Conceptual Graphs". In *Proc. Seventh International Conference on Conceptual Structures*, Blacksburg, Virginia, USA, Springer-Verlag, July, 1999.

Jasper, R. and M. Uschold (1999). "A Framework for Understanding and Classifying Ontology Applications". In *Proc. Twelfth Workshop on Knowledge Acquisition, Modeling and Management*, Banff, Alberta, Canada, 1999.

Knight, K. (1989). "Unification: A Multidisciplinary Survey". *ACM Computing Surveys* **21**(1): 93–124.

Mineau, G. (2002). "A First Step Toward the Knowledge Web: Interoperability Issues Among Conceptual Graph Based Software Agents, Part I". In *Proc. International Conference on Conceptual Structures*, Borovets, Bulgaria, Springer-Verlag, July, 2002.

Mugnier, M.-L. and M. Chein (1996). "Représenter des Connaissances et Raisonner avec des Graphes". *Revue d'Intelligence Artificielle* **10**(6): 7–56.

Pinto, H.S. and A. Gomez-Pérez (1999). "Some Issues on Ontology Integration". In *Proc. International Joint Conference on Artificial Intelligence Workshop on Ontologies and Problem-Solving Methods*, Stockholm, Sweden, August, 1999.

Ribière, M. and R. Dieng-Kuntz (2002). "A Viewpoint Model for Cooperative Building of an Ontology". In *Proc. Tenth International Conference on Conceptual Structures*, Borovets, Bulgaria, Springer-Verlag, July, 2002.

Tepfenhart, W.M. (1998). "Ontologies and Conceptual Structures". In *Proc. Sixth International Conference on Conceptual Structures*, Montpellier, France, Springer-Verlag, August, 1998.

van Zyl, J.D. and D.R. Corbett (2000). "A Framework for Comparing Methods for Using or Reusing Multiple Ontologies in an Application". In *Proc. Eighth International Conference on Conceptual Structures*, Darmstadt, Germany, Shaker Verlag, August, 2000.

Yang, G. and M. Kifer (2002). "Well-Founded Optimism: Inheritance in Frame-Based Knowledge Bases". In *Proc. International Conference on Ontologies, Databases and Applications of Semantics*, Irvine, California, USA, Springer-Verlag, October, 2002.

# Integrating Information under Lattice Structure

V. Phan-Luong[1], T.T. Pham[2], and R. Jeansoulin[2]

[1] L.I.F. Laboratoire d'Informatique Fondamentale de Marseille,
[2] L.S.I.S. Laboratoire des Sciences de l'Information et des Systèmes,
C.M.I. de l'Université de Provence
39, rue F. Joliot Curie, 13453 Cedex 13, France
{phan,pham,jeansoulin}@gyptis.univ-mrs.fr

**Abstract.** Different observations on a domain framework can result in different information sources, which can be complementary or in conflict with each other. In this paper, we propose a framework to deal with this problem, assuming the information space has a lattice structure. When inconsistencies exist in information sources, our approach can allow consensus solutions for integration. Our approach can apply for integrating geographic information, in particular, the spatio-thematic information.

## 1 Introduction

With the widespread development of distributed applications, people can easily access to voluminous information from several sources (searching information on the world-wide web, querying distributed databases, querying distributed geographic information systems, etc). Information from several sources can be redundant, complementary, or contradictory with each other. Determining which pieces of information are essential, complete and consistent is one of the important tasks in research in data integration [1,2,3,4]. Most approaches to the problem deal with the semantic heterogeneity and uncertainty of data in different information sources. They are usually based on logic and probability theory, which represent information in propositional or first-order logic languages. However, information from different sources can be different in sense of precision or taxonomy. For instances, in land cover, an observation on an area that results in "land of vegetation" is less precise than one that results in "land of agriculture". In general, information has naturally a partial order on its elements, which can play an important role in the result of data integration.

In this work we study the possibility of integration where information with the partial order forms a lattice structure. Instances of this problem occur in merging ontologies [5,6], merging information in knowlegde bases [1], integrating geographic information [7], etc.

## 2 Preliminaries

An ordered set is a pair $(P, \preceq)$, where $P$ is a set, and $\preceq$ is a partial order on $P$. We denote $x \prec y$, if $x \preceq y$ and $x \neq y$. Let $X \subseteq P$ such that $X \neq \emptyset$. An element

N. Zhong et al. (Eds.): ISMIS 2003, LNAI 2871, pp. 83–87, 2003.
© Springer-Verlag Berlin Heidelberg 2003

$a \in X$ is called a *minimal* (resp. *maximal*) of $X$, if there exists no $x \in X$ such that $x \prec a$ (resp. $a \prec x$). The set of all minimal (resp. maximal) elements of $X$ is denoted by $min(X)$ (resp. $max(X)$). If $a$ is the unique minimal (resp. maximal) element of $X$, then $a$ is called the *least* (resp. *greatest*) element of $X$. An element $a \in P$ is an *upper bound* (resp. *lower bound*) of $X$ if for all $x \in X, x \preceq a$ (resp. $a \preceq x$). The least upper bound of $X$, if exists, is denoted by $\vee X$, and called the *join* of $X$. The greatest lower bound of $X$, if exists, is denoted by $\wedge X$, and called the *meet* of $X$. In particular, $\vee\{x, y\}$ is denoted by $x \vee y$, and $\wedge\{x, y\}$ is denoted by $x \wedge y$. The least upper bound and the greatest lower bound of $P$, if exist, are denoted by $\top$ and $\bot$, respectively. An ordered set $(P, \preceq)$ is a $\vee$-semi lattice ($\wedge$-semi lattice) if for any $x, y \in P$, $x \vee y$ (resp. $x \wedge y$) always exists. $(P, \preceq)$ is a lattice if it is a $\vee$-semi lattice and also a $\wedge$-semi lattice.

## 3   Information Spaces

**Definition 1.** *An* information space *is a lattice* $(\mathcal{I}, \preceq)$ *which contains* $\bot$ *and* $\top$. $\bot$ *represents the information* null, *and* $\top$ *represents the information* all.

Let $x, y \in \mathcal{I}$. If $x \prec y$ then $y$ is called *more complete or more specific* than $x$. The elements $\bot$ and $\top$ represent unknown and inconsistent, respectively. If $x \vee y \neq \top$, then $x$ and $y$ are called *complementary* to one another. If $x \vee y = \top$ then $x$ and $y$ are called in *conflict* with each other. The conflict between $x$ and $y$ is total if $x \wedge y = \bot$, as $x$ and $y$ do not share any common information. Otherwise it is partial, and $x \wedge y$ is called a *consensus* of $x$ and $y$. In what follows, we consider an information space $(\mathcal{I}, \preceq)$.

**Definition 2.** *Let $I$ and $J$ be subsets of $\mathcal{I}$. We define $I \sqsubseteq J$ if $I = \emptyset$, or for each $x \in I$, there exists $y \in J$ such that $x \preceq y$.*

Intuitively, $I \sqsubseteq J$ means that $J$ contains as much information as $I$. Notice that if $I \subseteq J$ then $I \sqsubseteq J$. But the inverse is not true.

**Definition 3.** *Let $I, J$ be subsets of $\mathcal{I}$. Define $I \simeq J$ iff $I \sqsubseteq J$ and $J \sqsubseteq I$.*

Clearly, $\simeq$ is an equivalence relation. For any $I, J \subseteq \mathcal{I}$, we have $I \simeq max(I)$, and $I \simeq J$ if and only if $max(I) = max(J)$.

**Definition 4.** *Let $(\mathcal{I}, \preceq)$ be an information space. Let $I$ and $J$ be subsets of $\mathcal{I}$. If $I$ and $J$ are non-empty, then define*

$$I \otimes J = max(\{x \wedge y \mid x \in I, y \in J\}) \, ,$$

$$I \oplus J = max(\{x \vee y \mid x \in I, y \in J\}) \, .$$

*If $I = \emptyset$ (or $J = \emptyset$), then define $I \otimes J = \emptyset$, and $I \oplus J = max(J)$ (resp. $max(I)$).*

Intuitively, $I \otimes J$ computes the common information that $I$ and $J$ carry, and $I \oplus J$ computes the information we can get using $I$ and $J$ as complementary to one another.

**Proposition 1.** *Let $I_1$ and $I_2$ be subsets of $\mathcal{I}$. If $I_1 \simeq I_2$ then for any $J \subseteq \mathcal{I}$, we have $I_1 \otimes J \simeq I_2 \otimes J$, and $I_1 \oplus J \simeq I_2 \oplus J$.*

**Proposition 2.** *Let $I$ and $J$ be subsets of $\mathcal{I}$. We have:*
*(a) $I \otimes J \sqsubseteq I$, $I \otimes J \sqsubseteq J$, and $I \cap J \sqsubseteq I \otimes J$.*
*(b) If $I \sqsubseteq J$ then $I \sqsubseteq I \otimes J$.*

**Proposition 3.** *$I \sqsubseteq I \oplus J$ and $J \sqsubseteq I \oplus J$, and $I \cup J \sqsubseteq I \oplus J$.*

**Proposition 4.** *$I \otimes J \sqsubseteq I \cup J \sqsubseteq I \oplus J$.*

## 4 Information Sources

We call a (finite) *collection* of $X$ a set $\{X_1, ..., X_k\}$ such that $X_i \subseteq X, 1 \le i \le k$, and a *covering* of $X$ is a collection $\{X_1, ..., X_k\}$ of $X$ such that $\cup_{i=1,k} X_i = X$.

**Definition 5. Information Source.** *Let $\mathcal{I}$ be an information space, and $\mathcal{S}$ be a non-empty set of objects, called objects space. An information source is a triple $\mathcal{D} = (P(\mathcal{S}), C(\mathcal{I}), R)$, where $P(\mathcal{S})$ is a covering of $\mathcal{S}$, $C(\mathcal{I})$ is a collection of $\mathcal{I}$, and $R$ is a binary relation on $P(\mathcal{S})$ and $C(\mathcal{I})$.*

We call the *source mapping* of $\mathcal{D}$ the function $f$ defined as follows: for each $x \in \mathcal{S}$, $f(x) = \{i \in \mathcal{I} \mid \exists (X, I) \in R, x \in X, i \in I\}$. $\mathcal{S}$ is then *partitionned* by the equivalence $\sim$: for any $x, y \in \mathcal{S}$, $x \sim y$ iff $f(x) = f(y)$, and $\mathcal{D}$ can be represented by the set of pairs $(X_i, I_i)$, where $1 \le i \le k$, and $I_i = f(p)$, for every $p \in X_i$.

**Definition 6. Source Equivalence** *Let $\mathcal{D}_1 = (P_1(\mathcal{S}), C_1(\mathcal{I}), R_1)$ and $\mathcal{D}_2 = (P_2(\mathcal{S}), C_2(\mathcal{I}), R_2)$ be information sources on a same objects space $\mathcal{S}$ and a same information space $\mathcal{I}$. Let $f_1$ and $f_2$ be the source mappings of $\mathcal{D}_1$ and $\mathcal{D}_2$, respectively. $\mathcal{D}_1$ is $\simeq$-equivalent to $\mathcal{D}_2$, denoted by $\mathcal{D}_1 \simeq \mathcal{D}_2$, if for each $p \in \mathcal{S}, f_1(p) \simeq f_2(p)$.*

Information sources can contain redundancies in sense of $\simeq$-equivalence. Consider pairs $(X_1, I_1)$ and $(X_2, I_2)$ of a source $\mathcal{D} = (P(\mathcal{S}), C(\mathcal{I}), R)$.

**Information Redundancy.** If $max(I)$ is strictly included in $I$, then the pair $(X, I)$ has *information redundancy*.

**Object Redundancy.** If $I_1 \sqsubseteq I_2$ and $X_1 \cap X_2 \neq \emptyset$, then the pair $(X_1, I_1)$ contains object redundancy, as the information associated with $X_1 \cap X_2$ by $(X_1, I_1)$ can be deduced from $(X_2, I_2)$. Hence, $(X_1, I_1)$ is replaced by $(X_1 \backslash X_2, I_1)$. In particular, if $I_1 \sqsubseteq I_2$ and $X_1 \subseteq X_2$, then $(X_1, I_1)$ is removed from $R$.

## 5 Integration of Information Sources

**Definition 7.** *Let $\mathcal{D}_1 = (P_1(\mathcal{S}), C_1(\mathcal{I}), R_1)$ and $\mathcal{D}_2 = (P_2(\mathcal{S}), C_2(\mathcal{I}), R_2)$ be two information sources on a same objects space $\mathcal{S}$ and a same information space $\mathcal{I}$, with the source mappings $f_1$ and $f_2$, respectively. An integration of $\mathcal{D}_1$ and $\mathcal{D}_2$ is a source $\mathcal{D} = (P(\mathcal{S}), C(\mathcal{I}), R)$ with the source mapping $f$ satisfying: for each $p \in \mathcal{S}, f_1(p) \otimes f_2(p) \sqsubseteq f(p) \sqsubseteq f_1(p) \oplus f_2(p)$. Let us denote $f = f_1 \theta f_2$, and call $\mathcal{D}$ the $\theta$-integration of $\mathcal{D}_1$ and $\mathcal{D}_2$.*

**ALGORITHM D-Reduce**
*Input:* an information source $\mathcal{D} = (P(\mathcal{S}), C(\mathcal{I}), R)$.
*Output:* $\mathcal{D}' = (P'(\mathcal{S}), C'(\mathcal{I}), R')$ information and object reduced, and $\mathcal{D}' \simeq \mathcal{D}$.
*Method:*
1. Computing the source mapping $f$ of $\mathcal{D}$.
2. Let $R_\sim$ be the set of pairs $(X_i, I_i)$, where $X_i$ is in the partition of $\mathcal{S}$ by $f$, and $I_i = f(p)$ for every $p \in X_i$.
3. Replace each pair $(X, I)$ in $R_\sim$ by $(X, max(I))$.
4. Regrouping: In the result of step 3, replace all pairs $(X_1, I_1), ..., (X_k, I_k)$ such that
   $I_1 = ... = I_k = I$ by the pair $(X_1 \cup ... \cup X_k, I)$.
5. Return the final result of step 4.

**Fig. 1.** Algorithm for reducing information sources

After Proposition 2, $f_1(p) \cap f_2(p) \sqsubseteq f_1(p)\theta f_2(p)$, for every $\theta$-integration. This corresponds to the natural intuition on integration. However, under lattice structure with the order $\preceq$, $x \wedge y \preceq x$ and $x \wedge y \preceq y$, the condition $f_1(p) \otimes f_2(p) \sqsubseteq f_1(p)\theta f_2(p)$ is justified. On the other hand, after Proposition 4, we could accept $f_1(p) \cup f_2(p)$ in the result of integration. Furthermore, in sense of the complement relation, we could accept $f_1(p) \oplus f_2(p)$ as the result of integration at $p$, because $\mathcal{D}_1$ and $\mathcal{D}_2$ can complement to one another.

The integration is *pessimistic* (resp. *optimistic*) if for all $p \in \mathcal{S}$, $f_1(p)\theta f_2(p) = f_1(p) \otimes f_2(p)$ (resp. $f_1(p)\theta f_2(p) = f_1(p) \oplus f_2(p)$).

**ALGORITHM $\theta$-Integrate**
*Input:* $\mathcal{D}_1 = (P_1(\mathcal{S}), C_1(\mathcal{I}), R_1)$ and $\mathcal{D}_2 = (P_2(\mathcal{S}), C_2(\mathcal{I}), R_2)$.
*Output:* $\mathcal{D} = (P(\mathcal{S}), C(\mathcal{I}), f)$ an integration of $\mathcal{D}_1$ and $\mathcal{D}_2$.
*Method:*
1. Let $\mathcal{D}'_1 = $ D-Reduce$(\mathcal{D}_1)$ and $\mathcal{D}'_2 = $ D-Reduce$(\mathcal{D}_2)$.
2. Let $\mathcal{D} = (P(\mathcal{S}), C(\mathcal{I}), R)$, where $P(\mathcal{S}) = \emptyset$, $C(\mathcal{I}) = \emptyset$, and $R = \emptyset$.
3. For each pair $(X_1, I_1)$ in $\mathcal{D}'_1$ do
        For each pair $(X_2, I_2)$ in $\mathcal{D}'_2$ do begin
            Produce $(X_1 \cap X_2, I_1\theta I_2)$;
            If $X_1 \cap X_2 \neq \emptyset$, then insert $X_1 \cap X_2$ into $P(\mathcal{S})$,
                $I_1\theta I_2$ into $C(\mathcal{I})$, and $(X_1 \cap X_2, I_1\theta I_2)$ into $R$;
        end;
4. Return D-Reduce$(\mathcal{D})$.

**Fig. 2.** Algorithm for $\theta$-integrating

*Example 1.* Let $\mathcal{S} = \{1, 2, 3, 4\}$, $\mathcal{I} = \{a, b, c, d, e, f, g, \bot, \top\}$ with the partial order $\preceq$ defined by $\{\bot \prec d, \bot \prec e, d \prec a, d \prec b, e \prec b, e \prec c, a \prec f, b \prec f, b \prec g, c \prec g, f \prec \top, g \prec \top\}$.

Let $\mathcal{D}_1$ be an information source with $R_1$: $\{(\{1\}, \{a, d, e, f\}), (\{2\}, \{a, b, e\}), (\{3\}, \{b, d, e\}), (\{1, 4\}, \{a, f\}), (\{1, 2\}, \{a, e\}), (\{2, 3\}, \{b, e\})\}$.

The result of D-Reduce: $\{(\{1, 4\}, \{f\}), (\{2\}, \{a, b\}), (\{3\}, \{b\})\}$.

Let $\mathcal{D}_2$ with $R_2$:

$\{(\{1\}, \{b, c\}), (\{2\}, \{a, e\}), (\{3\}, \{a, b\}), (\{1, 3\}, \{b\}), (\{3, 4\}, \{d, e\})\}.$
The result of D-Reduce: $\{(\{1\}, \{b, c\}), (\{2\}, \{a, e\}), (\{3\}, \{a, b\}), (\{4\}, \{d, e\})\}.$
The $\theta$-integration of $\mathcal{D}_1$ and $\mathcal{D}_2$ is:
$(\{1\}, \{b, c\}\theta\{f\}), (\{2\}, \{a, b\}\theta\{a, e\}), (\{3\}, \{b\}\theta\{a, b\}, (\{4\}, \{f\}\theta\{d, e\})).$
The pessimistic integration consists of: $(\{1, 3\}, \{b\}), (\{2\}, \{a, e\}), (\{4\}, \{d, e\}).$
The optimistic integration consists of: $(\{1\}, \{\top\}), (\{2, 3, 4\}, \{f\}).$

An intermediate integration, defined by $f_1\theta f_2(I) = f_1(I) \cup f_2(I)$, consists of:
$(\{1\}, \{b, c, f\}), (\{2\}, \{a, b, e\}), (\{3\}, \{a, b, \}), (\{4\}, \{d, e, f\}).$ Applying D-Reduce
on this result, we obtain: $(\{1\}, \{c, f\}), (\{2, 3\}, \{a, b\}), (\{4\}, \{f\}).$

# 6    Related Work and Conclusions

The lattice structure required for the information space is not a strong constraint,
as it can apply to all cases studied in [7], for integrating spatio-thematic information, in particular under the hierarchical structure with single inheritance.
The lattice structure is more general than the hierarchical structure with single
inheritance. Our approach uses the operations that are more general than the
set intersection or product, which are exclusively used in the approach of [7]. In
the important aims of data integration: identification and refinement of information collected from several sources, with the notion $\theta$-integration, we can search
for the compromises between consistency and completeness. For further work,
uncertainty and imprecision can be considered in the notion of $\theta$-integration.

**Acknowledgement.** This work is supported by the REVIGIS FET (Future &
Emerging Technologies) IST-1999-14189 project of the European Community.

# References

1. S. Benferhat, D. Dubois, J. Lang, H. Prade, A. Saffiotti, and P. Smets: A general approach for inconsistency handling and merging information in prioritized knowledge
   bases. In Proc of KR'98, Trento, 1998.
2. L. Cholvy: Applying theory of evidence in multisensor data fusion: a logical interpretation. In Proc. of FUSION, Paris, 2000.
3. F. Fonseca, M. Egenhofer, P. Agouris, and G. Camara: Using ontologies for integrated geographic information systems. Trans. in Geo. Inform. Systems, 6(3), 2002.
4. V. Kashyap and A. Sheth: Semantic heterogeneity in global information systems:
   the role of metadata, context and ontologies. In M.P. Papazoglou and G. Schlageter,
   editors, *Cooperative Information Systems*, Academic Press, San Diego, 1998.
5. D. L. McGuinness, R. Fikes, J. Rice, and S. Wilder: An environment for merging
   and testing large Ontologies. In Proc. KR '00, Colorado, USA, 2000.
6. G. Stumme and A. Maedche: FCA-Merge: Bottom-Up Merging of Ontologies. In
   Proc. 17th Intl. Joint Conf. on Artificial Intelligence, JCAI'01, San Francisco, 2001.
7. M. Worboys and M. Duckham: Integrating spatio-thematic information. In Proc.
   the Intl. Conf. GIScience, Colorado, USA, 2002.

# Functional Ontology for Intelligent Instruments

Richard Dapoigny, Eric Benoit, and Laurent Foulloy

Laboratoire d'Informatique des Systèmes, du Traitement de l'Information et de Commande, University of Savoie, BP 806, 74016 ANNECY Cedex
{richard.dapoigny,eric.benoit,laurent.foulloy}@univsavoiefr
http://avaunivsavoiefr

**Abstract.** As a general and challenging task of decisional process in distributed environments, the individual nodes of the network need to exchange specific knowledge in order to achieve their goal. This is the case in distributed instrumentation where a network of intelligent components interact each other to realize some task. A conceptualization of functional knowledge is proposed and we argue that this conceptualization will be represented by ontologies based on mereology and topology. A synthesis of many works in knowledge engineering leads us to propose a knowledge representation with a dual objective. First, it provides instruments designers with a structural and logical framework that allows for easy reuse and secondly, it enable a distributed behavior based on causal representation and on dependencies between functional and behavioral knowledge on each node.

## 1 Introduction

Technological advances in the areas of industrial networks and microcontroller capabilities encourage the design of systems composed of smart components[1] which are either sensing their environment or acting upon it. Their fundamental property is the inclusion of an active processing element (a microcontroller) which encapsulates a number of functionalities, known as external services, and that are accessible through a network interface via perceptual channels [1]. A basic model has been proposed that is based on the notions of operating modes, services and internal services. In a first step, the dedicated tool called CAPTOOL [2] enters a design engineering phase in which requirement specifications of an instrument at the functional level is translated into a set of services, internal services, events ... The problem is that implicit knowledge cannot be shared due to its implicitness and no reuse is possible within an application involving several intruments. The second step, focusses on the control or the monitoring of an application involving many instruments interacting together. Most often, instruments need some external information (external variables values, external services capabilities in relation with their own goal, ...). The other problem concerns the unability of instruments to require appropriate external resources during the runtime process avoiding automatic diagnosis decisions based on the environment behavior (CAPTOOL doesn't take distrib-

---

1. Also called *Intelligent Instruments*

N. Zhong et al. (Eds.): ISMIS 2003, LNAI 2871, pp. 88–92, 2003.

uted knowledge into consideration nor access to dynamic knowledge). Taking in account these problems and the capabilities of new embedded microcontrollers, a conceptual framework centered on functional and behavioral modeling will be investigated. This paper provides a description of a functional model dedicated to intelligent instruments, with a a potential use in measurement systems. As the application deals with approximations of physical processes by mathematical relations, the study can be limited to discrete processes in which the concepts of state and event are the main basis.

## 2  The Intelligent Instruments Basic Modeling

For the conception of large applications, an external model of an intelligent instrument was proposed, based on services and operating modes [3]. Services are organized into subsets called "USer Operating Modes" (USOM). In this model, a given service can be required, only if the current active USOM includes this service. This prevents requiring services when they can not be available. Intelligent instruments are considered as entities that offer some more or less complex services. These services represent the instrument functionalities from the user's point of view. At a lower level, each instrument service is defined as a set of internal services. In each service, the internal services are linked through an ordered graph which behave like a plan in the AI framework. Existing instruments are modelised from the external point of view, but despite of its internal intelligent behavior, that external model is inadequate to build a global behavioral model for an application involving many instruments. The previous approach must be extended to a more global view in which a functional formalization of services is closely related to the concepts of function and behavior.

## 3  Function Conceptualization

We assume the teleological nature of intelligence, where purposes are assigned to functions and mechanisms are described by function implementation. A function describes what a system or an agent is supposed to do and is closely related to the notion of goal. In the industrial engineering area, the concept of function consists of the task a given device may achieve. Function is being explicitly represented and used in applications as diverse as Diagnosis [4][7] or Device Design [5]. For some, the function is indissociable from the behavior [6]  while for others, a function appears as a desired effect on the environment [8] or "How the system achieves its behavior"[9]. An important feature of function is that it may be used to address the scaling problem, in the sense of the discrimination among results during diagnosis.

In the context of intelligent instruments, functions represent the functional role that supports a given physical process, and the function concept is achieved by the *iservice*. The *iservices* are either extracted from functional patterns dedicated to specific instruments or defined by the end user. As previously shown, functions and goals are strongly coupled [7], and we take this result as a basic assumption of the instrument model. A first classification of elementary functions based on state changes has been proposed with  generic elementary acts whose the result are elementary state changes. With regard to this classification, the actions can only be achieved, provided some pre-conditions are fulfilled. Therefore, in the functional model, any functional concept will be described by a (sub-)goal definition which is related to the intensional aspect of function and some predicates expressing the required pre-conditions in order to fulfill the intended (sub-)goal. Representation of functions as "to do X" has been used by several researchers and we adopt that textual definition of the function goal. The functional model must define the terms that correspond to actions and the terms that are objects of the actions. Thus, functional specifications must include a variety of qualifying information that can help to narrow the search, such as the concerned physical object and its physical role. An atomic (sub-)goal represents the mapping $A \times R \times \Phi \rightarrow G$ as the tuple $<a, r, \varphi>$ ;$a \in A$;$r \in R$;$\varphi \in \Phi$ where A , R, $\Phi$ and G are the sets associated with the respective sorts of elementary actions, the sort of physical roles (physical quantities or control/monitoring roles), the sort of physical entities of the physical system related to the instrument, and the sort of elementary sub-goals. In such a way, a functional model of the physical system is built by associating the teleological part of functions with the physical components of the system. Examples of atomic sub-goals for *iservices* are:

$g_1$=<To_acquire, x_spectral_sensitivity, sample>
$g_2$=<To_act_upon, position, Valve>
$g_3$=<To_act_upon, angle, axis>

Taking into consideration the constraints attached to intelligent instruments, a limited set of appropriate elementary goals can be proposed. With a few number of generic verbs, one can create elementary sub-goals and associate them to form more complex goals at the service level or the mode level. In addition, we introduce two special goals related to message exchanges between instruments (i.e., send and receive actions). Table 1 summarizes the basic elementary goals available in different instrument types.

**Table 1.**

| Action | Actuator | Sensor | Sensor and actuator | calculator |
|---|---|---|---|---|
| to_acquire | – | yes | yes | – |
| to_act_upon | yes | – | yes | – |
| to_compute | yes | yes | yes | yes |
| to_control | yes | yes | yes | yes |
| to_send | yes | yes | yes | yes |
| to_receive | yes | yes | yes | yes |

Examples of goals defined for services:

$G_1$=<To_control, flow, water>
$G_2$=<To_measure, x_spectral_sensitivity, y_spectral_sensitivity, z_spectral_sensitivity , Sample>

where $G_1$ is composed of the following sub-goals:

<to_acquire, pressure, position1>,
<to_acquire, pressure, position2>,
<to_acquire, pressure, position1>,
<to_compute, speed, water_s1, level, water_s1>,

<to_control, speed, water_s1>,
<to_act_upon, position, Valve>.

and $G_2$ with the sub-goals:

<to_acquire, spectrum, Sample>,
<to_compute, x_spectral_sensitivity, Sample, y_spectral_sensitivity, Sample, z_spectral_sensitivity, Sample>,
<to_send, x_spectral_sensitivity, Sample, y_spectral _sensitivity, Sample, z_spectral_sensitivity, Sample>.

In the previous examples, several pairs $<r, \varphi>$ can be distributed over a given action. This is an effect of aggregation illustrating the principle of mereological fusion. As suggested in related works concerned with the functional modeling of physical and industrial environments [12], the verb plays a central role in the functional formalization. In addition, a semantic link is established with physical information via the introduction of pairs <physical role, physicial entity>. The combination of logic within a mereology provides a language that can express relationships about the entities in the domain of interest. The functional modeling is addressed in terms of mereological and topological primitives. Therefore, functional elements are separate entities than can be connected to form a higher functional structure with a higher level of abstraction, the functional knowledge being expressed with i) mereological relationships where the functional elements of the instrument are described by a part-of decomposition into subelements, ii) topological relationships where the functional elements are connected with events and iii) system ontology where the boundaries and atoms for the objects in relation with functional elements are defined.

The multi-level reasoning has been widely explored in representation of physical systems, mainly for its ability to integrate several points of view. From the basic instrument modeling, we can identify four abstraction levels (see figure 1).

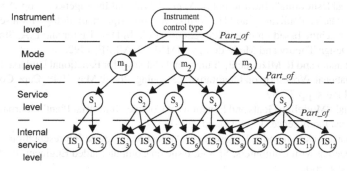

**Fig. 1.** The functional partonomic abstraction hierarchy

The highest one is the instrument level seen as a set of instrument functioning modes expressed as global goals. The mode level represents the set of available services in a given mode, where each service is described as a goal (*To_control_speed*, *To_Measure_xyz*, ...). The *service* level captures the internal way of achievement of its intended goal with a unique sequence of alternate states and actions, in which each action can be either an event occurrence or a *iservice* execution. Finally, the *iservice* level reduces to describe the sub-goal expressing the intended action attached to each *iservice*. As a consequence, related functional concepts are organized into an abstraction hierarchy which captures the connections between terms for describing functions at different levels of detail.

## 4    Conclusion

The functional mereology extended with the behavioral one provides many advantages such as modularity, easy dependency analysis between instruments and easy reuse between applications. Implementations with Java platforms are in progress in addition with a graphical tool. The modeling is applied both in a design step, in order to check its consistency, and in the run-time process where dynamic dependences between entities can be achieved. As the control system has the possibility to modify the knowledge during run-time, works in progress focusses on the temporal aspects. As a consequence, temporal constraints between events and actions must be represented explicitly.

## References

[1]    A. Bouras, M. Staroswiecki, "How can Intelligent Instruments Interoperate in an Application Framework ? A Mechanism for Taking into Account Operating Constraints", Proc. of Int. Conf. SICICA'97 (9–11 juin 1997) Annecy, France.

[2]    Tailland J., Foulloy L., Benoit E., "Automatic Generation of Intelligent Instruments from Internal Model", Proc. of 4th IFAC Int.Symp. SICICA'2000, Buenos Aires, Argentina, Sept. 2000, pp 337–342.

[3]    J.M. Riviere, M. Bayart, J.M. Thiriet, A. Bouras, M. Robert, "Intelligent instruments: some modelling approaches", Measurement and Control, Vol.29, pp.179–186, 1996.

[4]    R. Hawkins, J. K. McDowell, J. Sticklen, T. Hill, and R. Boyer, "Function-based modeling and troubleshooting", Int. Journal of Applied Artificial Intelligence, 8, pp 285–302, 1994.

[5]    Y. Umeda, T. Tomiyama, and H. Yoshikawa, "A design methodology for a self-maintenance machine based on functional redundancy", In D.L. Taylor and L.A. Stauffer, editors, Design Theory and Methodology - DTM '92. ASME, 1992.

[6]    Y. Kitamura and R. Mizoguchi, "Functional Ontology for Functional Understanding", 12th International Workshop on Qualitative Reasoning, 26–29 May 1998, Cape Cod, USA, AAAI Press, pp 77–87

[7]    M. Lind, "Modeling Goals and Functions of Complex Industrial Plant", Journal of Applied Artificial Intelligence, 1994, (8), pp 259–283

[8]    B. Chandrasekaran and J. R. Josephson, "Function in device Representation", Journal of Engineering with Computers, Special Issue on Computer aided Engineering, 16, pp 162–177, Sept. 2000

[9]    F.A. Salustri, "Function Modeling for an Integrated Framework: A progress Report", Procs. of FLAIRS'98, D. Cook, Eds., 1998, AAAI, pp 339–343

[10]    Y. Umeda et al.," Supporting conceptual design based on the function-behavior-state modeler", Artificial Intelligence for Engineering Design, Analysis and Manufacturing, 1996, 10(4), pp. 275–288

[11]    L. Qian, and J.S. Gero, "Function-behavior-structure paths and their role in analogy-based design", Artificial Intelligence for Engineering Design, Analysis and Manufacturing, 1996, 10(4), pp. 289–12.

[12]    Y. Kitamura, T. Sano, K. Namba and R. Mizogushi, "A Functional Concept Ontology and its Application to Automatic Identification of Functional Structures", Advanced Engineering Informatics, 16(2), pp. 145–163, 2002.

# Constructing an Ontology Based on Hub Words

Sang Ok Koo, Soo Yeon Lim, and Sang Jo Lee

Department of Computer Engineering, Kyungpook National University,
Daegu, 702-701, Korea
tomatofall@msn.com, nadalsy@hotmail.com, sjlee@knu.ac.kr

**Abstract.** This paper suggests a semi-automatic ontology construction method based on hub words. To do this, we define the words that are related to many other words as *hub words*. We determine the hub words by the statistical analysis of documents. Additionally, we discuss the base ontology construction process based on hub words and automatic ontology extension method. The proposed ontology can be used like an index file for traditional document retrieval and can offer more semantic information than simple index files.

## 1 Introduction

In recent years ontologies have become a topic of interest in computer science. In its most prevalent use in computer science, an ontology refers to an engineering artifact constituted by a specific vocabulary used to describe a certain reality, and a set of explicit assumptions regarding the intended meaning of the vocabulary[6].

So far, famous ontologies like MikroKosmos, HowNet, SENSUS, CYC, and WordNet are have been constructed by human labor and applied to the general domain. However, ontologies that contain more domain-specific knowledge are needed for real application systems, because the concepts of words are somewhat different in each domain such as economic, electronic, medical, and so on. In recent researches, there have been many attempts to construct an ontology automatically or semi-automatically[5]. We propose a method to build a domain specific ontology. Guarino [4] has suggested the development of different kinds of ontologies by specializing the concepts introduced in the top-level ontology. In this paper, we do not use the any top-level ontology. This paper suggests a simple method that is able to construct a light-weight ontology in an economic domain semi-automatically by analyzing many texts in a document collection.

## 2 Proposed Ontology Construction Process Based on Hub Words

Our process of constructing an ontology is as follows: First, we find the words with high-term frequency in a text collection because we assume that the words with high-term frequency are closely related to many other words in the documents. Then, we manually construct the base ontology using these words. At last, we extend the ontology automatically by adding the words related with the selected hub words. For this, we analyze the Wall Street Journal documents in TREC text collection volume 2.

N. Zhong et al. (Eds.): ISMIS 2003, LNAI 2871, pp. 93–97, 2003.

## 2.1   Extracting Hub Words

We regard ontology as a kind of network comprised of many lexical items. Networks such as the Internet have a small subset of nodes with a great number of links. A few hubs with many links play an important role in the entire network. The link distribution of a web page accords to *Power Law*. We assume that the distribution of word frequency accords to *Power Law*.

In this paper, we define *hub words* as words that are related to many other words in the document collection and we construct the base ontology using these hub words. To determine the hub words, we first extracted all nouns except the stop words in the document collection. We assumed that the nouns with high frequency have many relations with other nouns in the documents and then we computed the *tf(term frequency)* and *idf(inverted document frequency)* values of each noun.

As a result of selecting in nouns with very high *tf* values, we determined a few *hub words*, which consist of 505 nouns and 65 proper nouns. 505 nouns, 0.78% of the total nouns number, occupy more than 54% of total noun frequency. Because proper nouns such as person, country or city names are important in the economic domain, we treat proper nouns as general nouns.

Hub words selected in the economic domain are different from those of other domains like medical science. For example, 'company" has many links to other words such as 'share", 'interests", 'stock", 'tra    de', 'loan", 'officer", and 'lawyer" in economics domain, but in the medical science domain 'company" has few links. Hub words tend to be domain-dependent and we extract the hub words of the economic domain using Wall Street Journal documents.

## 2.2   Constructing the Base Ontology

In this section, we describe how to manually construct a base ontology using selected hub words and how to automatically extend a base ontology. First, we connect a hub word with other hub words in relation to that word in context. Based on the assumption that the co-occurring words are interconnected, we extract 4 words around a hub word in the document collection and compute their frequencies. Table 1 shows that the examples of the hub words, and their co-occurring noun lists. As referring to Table 1, we create the network that has hub words as nodes and co-occurring words as links. Fig. 1(a) shows the co-occurrence network comprised of words in Table 1.

To define relations, we extract all verbs of the documents as well as nouns. We select verbs with high frequency and define 50 main relations as classifying these verbs and including syntactic relations like the possessive. Then we make a noun list that occurs around the main relations in the documents. The task of constructing the base ontology is finished with adding relations to the network. Fig. 1(b) shows results of adding the semantic relations between hub words by manual editing. In this network, nouns represent concepts and verbs represent the relation between the concepts.

**Table 1.** The words around hub words

| company | million, mr, year, share, **stock**, company, quarter, earnings, market, sales, business, insurance, oil, spokesman, bank, billion, years, debt, companies, products, corp, officials, group, time, plan, analysts, plans, management, operations, executive, loss, profit, investment, president, price, board, services, assets, sale, parent, employees, interest, **chairman**, revenue, growth, state, investors, securities, results, shareholders, unit, capital, **trading**, ..., **staff**, ... |
|---|---|
| trade | market, **stock**, mr, board, futures, deficit, prices, japan, group, year, agreement, stocks, investors, **trade**, exchange, billion, trading, dollar, industry, chicago, shares, world, securities, bond, yen, commission, talks, government, bonds, index, oil, million, york, surplus, **company**, day, **traders**, issues, currency, association, analysts, program, interest, week, bank, ... |
| stock | exchange, market, york, **trading**, **company**, shares, price, prices, million, stock, cents, mr, investors, year, tokyo, futures, fund, dividend, issues, volume, cash, times, earnings, options, record, bond, world, friday, analysts, billion, time, growth, plan, decline, **traders**, corp, investment, brokers, purchase, money, bank, june, quarter, morgan, split, loans, securities, collateral, crash, points, trends, london, counter, arbitrage, exchanges, news, holders, class, shareholders, ownership, ... |
| staff | mr, house, members, **company**, john, chief, member, year, president, committee, employees, million, reporter, people, time, cuts, commission, wall, plans, reductions, support, work, office, sec, bank, headquarters, sales, years, department, security, companies, part, ms, number, chiefs, senate, agency, chairman, jobs, business, **staff**, finance, attorney, months, operations, force, securities, magazineoffices, management, executive, spokesman, executives, firms, darman, problems, lawyers, ... |
| chairman | **executive**, chief, mr, officer, company, committee, president, john, board, corp, robert, vice, william, year, years, alan, greenspan, richard, bank, house, james, group, jr, post, director, budget, exchange, michael, david, reserve, smith, banking, **chairman**, charles, senate, million, lee, subcommittee, seidman, thomas, council, stephen, breeden, services, founder, paul, business, time, commission, york, securities, shares, allen, panetta, panel, martin, finance, george, ..., **staff** ... |

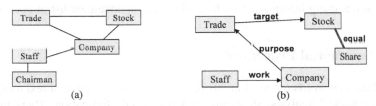

(a)                                                    (b)

**Fig. 1.** Example of co-occurence network(a) and base ontology added relations(b)

## 2.3 Extending the Ontology

After constructing of the base ontology, we attempt to extend the base ontology automatically. The process of adding relation to the network is similar with the process of building the base ontology. After sentence analysis, we extract the relations according to the Relation Extraction Rules made manually. We aimed at automatically inserting relations between a hub word and other hub words and also inserting relations between a hub word and non-hub words.

Our method of adding relations to the ontology has the following two steps. First, nouns around hub words are extracted from the documents. In this process, sentence extraction and sentence analysis techniques are needed. Second, the relations are established between hub words and other words by relation extraction rules. For example, if a verb like 'belong" or 'include" is between two nouns, we can add a 'belongTo" relation to the ontology. Mostly, nouns become instances of ontology concepts and verbs become relations between concepts. Fig. 2 shows the result of establishing concepts and relations around hub word 'Company."

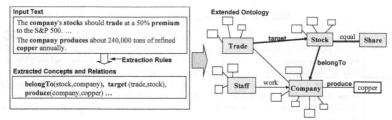

**Fig. 2.** Sketch of establishing concepts and relations around hub word

# 3 Application of Ontology for Document Retrieval

Most traditional Information Retrieval systems use noun lists extracted from documents[2]. However, a simple noun vector cannot represent semantic information between nouns. To represent semantic information, ontologies that have the relations of words describing certain knowledge topics are used in many areas.

In our research, we process queries with reference to the ontology after converting the input query to RDF(Resource Description Framework) format[3]. In our ontology, each node represents a word, that has a related document list. We can retrieve the document using information such as relations and document list of our ontology.

# 4 Experimental Procedures

To find the hub words reported in this paper, we performed general text analysis such as morphological analysis, stemming, and stop word elimination. Then, in the first place, we extracted nouns from 627,649 documents of the Wall Street Journal in TREC collection volume 2.

Table 2 shows the distribution of the frequency for nouns, proper nouns, and verbs. The words with frequency more than 1000 are over 54% of total word frequency. Therefore, we built our ontology based on 505 hub words selected in words that appeared more than 1000 times in the document collection.

Fig. 3 shows the distribution of word frequency. Fig. 3(a) is the distribution for 64,040 nouns in the document collection and Fig. 3(b) shows the distribution of hub words that occurred more than 1000 in the document collection.

**Table 2.** The Distribution of the frequency for each Part of Speech.

| POS | The Number of Words (N) | Total Frequency (TF) | Frequency > 100 | | Frequency > 1000 | |
|---|---|---|---|---|---|---|
| | | | N | TF | N | TF |
| Noun | 64,040 | 2,779,889 | 3,236 (5.05%) | 2,342,944 (84.2%) | 505 (0.79%) | 1,506,003 (54.18%) |
| Proper Noun | 28,567 | 399,854 | 598 (2.09%) | 277,003 (69.3%) | 65 (0.23%) | 138,234 (34.6 %) |
| Verb | 7,281 | 684,607 | 1,257 (17.3%) | 571,099 (83.4%) | 124 (1.7 %) | 243,446 (35.6 %) |

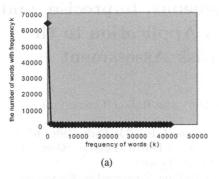
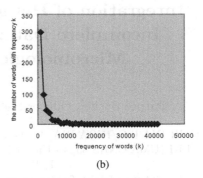

(a)                                    (b)

**Fig. 3.** Distribution of the word frequency(a) and Distribution of the frequency of hub words(b)

As a general rule, the words with very high term frequency have very low inverted document frequency. Therefore, a hub word reported in this paper is not important as an index term in document retrieval. Hub words play a role as mediators of index terms.

The ontology which was constructed by the method proposed in this paper has 5,200 nodes and 50 relations. The average relation number of hub words is 127 and a few hub words have relations with more than 1000.

## 5   Conclusions

In this paper, we discussed how documents in a specific domain are dominated by a small number of hub words. We suggest a method to create an ontology based on hub words. Our method does not use existing resources and is based entirely on text analysis. In our experiments, we identified hub words in documents of the Wall Street Journal in TREC collection and semi-automatically constructed an ontology based on hub words and contextual information. We plan to extend the ontology for sophisticated query processing and analyze the structure or properties of the ontology based on hub words.

## References

1.   Albert-László Barabási, LINKED: Th    e New Science of Networks. (2002)
2.   Baeza-Yates, R., Robeiro-Neto, B.: Modern Information Retrieval. ACM Press (1999)
3.   Brickley, D. and Guha, R.V.: Resource Description Framework (RDF) Schema Specification 1.0. http://www.w3.org/TR/2000/CR-rdf-schema-20000327/ (2000)
4.   Guarino, N.: Formal ontology and information systems. IOS press (1998)
5.   Kang, S. J. and Lee, J. H.: Semi-Automatic Practical Ontology Construction by Using a Thesaurus, Computational Dictionaries, and Large Corpora. ACL 2001 Workshop on Human Language Technology and Knowledge Management, Toulouse, France (2001)
6.   Maedche, A.: Ontology learning for the semantic web. Kluwer (2002)

# Integration of Heterogeneous, Imprecise, and Incomplete Data: An Application to the Microbiological Risk Assessment

Patrice Buche[1], Ollivier Haemmerlé[1,2], and Rallou Thomopoulos[1]

[1]UMR INA P-G/INRA BIA, 16 rue Claude Bernard, F-75231 Paris Cedex 05, France
[2]LRI (UMR CNRS 8623 - Université Paris-Sud) / INRA (Futurs), Bâtiment 490,
F-91405 Orsay Cedex, France
{Patrice.Buche,Ollivier.Haemmerle,Rallou.Thomopoulos}@inapg.fr

**Abstract.** This paper presents an information system developed to help the assessment of the microbiological risk in food products. UQS (Unified Querying System) is composed of two distinct bases (a relational database and a conceptual graph knowledge base) which are integrated by means of a uniform querying language. The specificity of the system is that both bases include fuzzy data. Moreover, UQS allows the expression of preferences into the queries, by means of the fuzzy set theory.

## 1   Introduction

Following several food safety problems, the Marrakech Agreement was signed in 1994 during the creation of the World Trade Organization. Included in this agreement, the SPS Agreement (Sanitary and Phytosanitary measures) concerns the international trade of food, and targets the safety and protection of human health. One important principle of the SPS Agreement is the study of risk analysis. Our research project is part of a French programme that aims at building a tool for microbiological risk analysis in food products. This tool is based on a relational database containing data extracted from scientific publications in microbiology. As changing the schema of the database is quite an expensive operation, we decided to use an additional base in order to store information that was not expected when the schema of the database was designed, but is useful nevertheless. We chose to use the conceptual graph model [1] for many reasons: (i) its graph structure which appeared as a flexible way of representing complementary information; (ii) its readability for a non-specialist; (iii) its interpretation in first order logic (FOL) which provides a robust theoretical framework; (iv) the availability of a development platform providing efficient algorithms; (v) the distinction between the terminological part and the assertional part of the knowledge (as in Description Logics, for example).

In UQS (Unified Querying System), both bases are queried simultaneously by a unified querying mechanism. Both have to deal with the following two specificities. Firstly, some of the data are imprecise, like data whose precision is limited by the measuring techniques. For instance by using a method allowing

N. Zhong et al. (Eds.): ISMIS 2003, LNAI 2871, pp. 98–107, 2003.
© Springer-Verlag Berlin Heidelberg 2003

one to detect bacteria beyond a given concentration threshold (e.g. $10^2$ cells per gramme), not detecting any bacterium means that their concentration is below this threshold, which is an imprecise value noted "$< 10^2$ cells/g". Secondly, the bases are incomplete, as they will never contain information about all possible food products and all possible pathogenic germs. Those two characteristics led us to propose, firstly the handling of imprecise values, and secondly the expression of different levels of preferences in the user's selection criteria so as to allow flexible querying. In the bibliography concerning databases, the fuzzy set framework has been shown to be a sound scientific way of modelling both flexible queries [2] and imprecise values by means of possibility distributions [3].

In this paper, we remind briefly the Conceptual Graph model and the fuzzy set theory in section 2. In section 3, we present our query language which allows the expression of preferences. Then both relational database system and Conceptual Graph knowledge base system are presented in section 4 and 5.

## 2    Preliminary Notions

### 2.1    The Conceptual Graph Model

The Conceptual Graph model (or CG) [1] is a knowledge representation model based on labelled graphs. We use the formalization presented in [4]. In the following, we present the *support* which contains the terminological knowledge, the *conceptual graphs* which contain the assertional knowledge, and the *specialization relation* on CGs.

**The support.** The support provides the ground vocabulary used to build the knowledge base: the types of concepts used, the instances of these types, and the types of relations linking the concepts.

The *set of concept types* is partially ordered by a *kind of* relation. *Universal* and *Absurd* are respectively its greatest and lowest elements. Fig. 1 presents a part of the set of concept types used in the application.

The concepts can be linked by means of relations. The support contains the *set of relation types*. Each relation type has a given arity. An example of relation is *agent* which is a binary relation allowing one to link an *Action* with a *Germ* (which are both concept types).

The third set of the support is the *set of individual markers*, which represent the instances of the concepts. For example, *Celsius degree* can be an instance of *Degree*. The generic marker (noted $*$) is a particular marker referring to an unspecified instance of a concept.

**The conceptual graphs.** The CGs, built upon the support, express the factual knowledge. A CG is composed of: (i) a set of *concept vertices* (noted in rectangles) which represent the entities, attributes, states, events; (ii) a set of *relation vertices* (noted in ovals) which express the nature of the relationship between concepts; (iii) a set of edges linking relation vertices to concept vertices; (iv) a

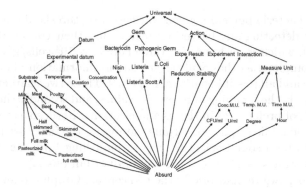

**Fig. 1.** A part of the concept type set for the microbial application

*label* for each vertex or edge: the label of a concept vertex is a pair composed of a concept type and a marker (individual or generic) of this type, the label of a relation vertex is its relation type, the label of an edge is its rank in the total order on the neighbours of a given relation vertex.

For example, the CG given in Fig. 2 is a representation of the following information: "the experiment E1 carries out an interaction I1 between Nisin and Listeria Scott A in skimmed milk and the result is reduction".

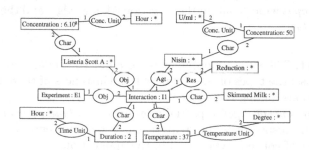

**Fig. 2.** An example of a Conceptual Graph

**Specialization relation, projection operation.** The set of CGs is partially pre-ordered by the *specialization relation* (noted ≤), which can be computed by the *projection operation* (a graph morphism allowing a restriction of the vertex labels): $G' \leq G$ if and only if there is a projection of $G$ into $G'$.

**Definition 1.** *A* **projection** $\Pi$ *from a CG G into a CG G' is a pair $(f, g)$ of mappings, f (resp. g) from the set of relation vertices (resp. concept vertices) of G to the set of relation vertices (resp. concept vertices) of G' such that: (i) the edges and their labels are preserved; (ii) the vertex labels may be restricted.*

An example is given in Fig. 3. The projection is a ground operation in the CG model since it allows the search for answers, which can be viewed as specializations of a query.

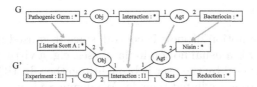

**Fig. 3.** There is a projection from $G$ into $G'$, $G' \leq G$ ($G'$ is a specialization of $G$)

## 2.2   The Fuzzy Set Theory

In this paper, we use the representation of fuzzy sets proposed in [5, 6].

**Definition 2.** *A fuzzy set $A$ on a domain $X$ is defined by a membership function $\mu_A$ from $X$ to [0, 1] that associates the degree to which $x$ belongs to $A$ with each element $x$ of $X$.*

A fuzzy set can be defined on a continuous or on a discrete domain, as illustrated in Fig. 4.

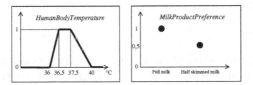

**Fig. 4.** Two fuzzy sets defined respectively on a continuous and on a discrete domain

The fuzzy set formalism can be used in two different ways:

— in the queries, in order to express preferences on the domain of a selection criterion. For example the fuzzy set *HumanBodyTemperature* in Fig. 4 may be interpreted as a preference on the required value of the criterion *Temperature*: a value between 36.5 and 37.5 degrees is fully satisfactory; values outside this interval may also be acceptable with smaller preference degrees;
— in the data, in order to represent imprecise data expressed in terms of possibility distributions. For example the fuzzy set *MilkProductPreference* in Fig. 4 may be interpreted as an imprecise datum if the kind of milk that was used in the experiment is not clearly known: it is very likely to be full milk, but half-skimmed milk is not excluded.

## 3   The Query Language

This section presents the query language used in both the Relational Database (RDB) and the Conceptual Graph Knowledge Base (CGKB). In the following, we present the notions we use in terms of domain relational calculus [7].

## 3.1    The Views

In our system, the notion of view is central, since it is used in the RDB and in the CGKB. A view is a usual notion in databases, e.g. a virtual table in which all the information needed by the user is brought together. In UQS, the set of views can be compared to a mediated schema. We define a view by a set of attribute names which are consultable (they can be used as projection attributes or as selection attributes), and by a logical predicate which defines the way the view is computed. The nature of such a predicate will be precised in sections 4 and 5.

**Definition 3.** *A* **view** *$V$ on $n(n > 0)$ attributes $a_1, \ldots, a_n$ is defined by $V = \{a_1, \ldots, a_n | \exists b_1, \ldots, b_m P_V(a_1, \ldots, a_n, b_1, \ldots, b_m)\}$ where $P_V$ is a predicate which characterizes the construction of the view, $b_1, \ldots, b_m$ being the attributes belonging to the definition of the view without being consultable[1].*

**Example 1** BacteriocinInteraction    =    {*PathogenicGerm,    Bacteriocin, ExpeResult,    Substrate,    Duration,    Temperature    | $P_{BacteriocinInteraction}(PathogenicGerm, Bacteriocin, ExpeResult, Substrate, Duration, Temperature)$}. That view concerns the interaction of bacteriocins (which are kinds of bacteria) on pathogenic germs.*

## 3.2    The Queries

A query in UQS is always asked on a given view, by precising a set of projection attributes and a set of selection criteria using the form <attribute/value>.

**Definition 4.** *A* **query** *$Q$ asked on a view $V$ defined on $n$ attributes $\{a_1, \ldots, a_n\}$ is defined by $Q = \{a_1, \ldots, a_l | \exists a_{l+1}, \ldots, a_n (P_V(a_1, \ldots, a_n) \wedge (a_{l+1} = v_{l+1}) \wedge \ldots \wedge (a_m = v_m))\}$ $1 \leq l \leq m \leq n$, where $P_V$ is the predicate which characterizes the construction of the view $V$, $a_1, \ldots, a_l$ are the projection attributes, $a_{l+1}, \ldots, a_m$ are the selection attributes with their respective values $v_{l+1}, \ldots, v_m$ (the attributes $a_{m+1}, \ldots, a_n$ are not used in that query). The values $v_i$ are given as selection values by the user. They can be precise values as well as a fuzzy sets. In the case of a fuzzy set, such a value is interpreted as an expression of preferences.*

A query is a partial instanciation of a given view by specifying the projection attributes and by giving selection values to some other attributes.

**Example 2** *$Q = \{PathogenicGerm, ExpeResult | \exists Substrate, Duration (P_{BacteriocinInteraction}(PathogenicGerm, Bacteriocin, ExpeResult, Substrate, Duration, Temperature) \wedge (Temperature = HumanBodyTemperature) \wedge (Bacteriocin =' Nisin'))\}$*
*The query $Q$ expresses that we want to obtain the PathogenicGerm and the ExpeResult from the view BacteriocinInteraction when the Temperature is a HumanBodyTemperature (see Fig. 4) and the Bacteriocin is Nisin.*

---

[1] For readability reasons, we do not mention the attributes $b_1, \ldots, b_m$ in the following definitions and examples

**Definition 5.** *An* **answer** *A to a query Q in UQS is a set of tuples, each of the form $\{v_1, \ldots, v_l, \delta\}$, $v_1, \ldots, v_l$ corresponding to the values (which can be fuzzy values) associated with each projection attribute $a_1, \ldots, a_l$ of Q, $\delta$ being the degree of adequation of the answer to the query, presented in [8].*

The query processing in UQS is the following: when a query is asked, the system searches for the considered view both in the RDB and in the CGKB. Then the RDB engine and/or the CGKB engine are run in parallel, each subsystem building partial answers to the query. The global answer results from the merging of the partial answers. Note that all the views of the system need not exist in both RDB and CGKB parts of the system.

In the two following sections we present the RDB subsystem very briefly, then the CGKB subsystem in more details. We will explain the link between a query in UQS and its translation, by means of "wrappers", into a query designed for the RDB and/or into a query designed for the CGKB.

## 4    The RDB Subsystem

### 4.1    Presentation of the Subsystem

The first subsystem is composed of an RDB implemented in Oracle. It is composed of about 90 tables, which contain data extracted from about 500 scientific publications in microbiology. A preliminary version of this subsystem has been presented in [9]. An extended version of this work is under submission.

### 4.2    The RDB Wrapper

The access to the RDB is done by means of views, which consist in pre-written SQL queries.

**Definition 6.** $\mathcal{V}_{db} = \{Vr_1, \ldots, Vr_n\}$ *is the set of views on the relational database, with $P_{Vr_1}, \ldots, P_{Vr_n}$ the predicates characterizing each view.*

**Remark 1** *The predicate $P_{Vr_i}$ corresponding to a view $Vr_i$ is the translation in terms of relational calculus of the SQL query which defines the view.*

Thus the querying mechanism consists in specifying the values of the selection attributes, then in asking that complemented SQL query on the RDB.

## 5    The CG Subsystem

### 5.1    Extension of the CG Model to the Representation of Fuzzy Values

The second subsystem is composed of a knowledge base expressed in terms of CGs. In order to allow the storage of data with the same expressivity as the data stored in the RDB, we chose to extend the CG model to the representation of numerical and fuzzy values in concept vertices. This work is presented in details in [8]. We only recap it through examples.

A fuzzy set can appear in two ways in a concept vertex (Fig. 5): (i) as a marker: this fuzzy set can be continuous or discrete; (ii) as a fuzzy type defined on a subset of the set of concept types. In the extension of the model to the representation of fuzzy sets, we have extended the projection operation in order to take into account the concept vertices with a fuzzy type or a fuzzy marker. Intuitively, the notion of specialization for fuzzy sets is based on the inclusion relation: if $A$ and $B$ are fuzzy sets, $A$ is a specialization of $B$ if and only if $A$ is included in $B$.

Fig. 5 presents an example of a projection involving fuzzy markers. There is a projection because, in addition to the usual projection criteria, the fuzzy marker in the second CG is more specific than the fuzzy marker in the first CG (its characteristic function is lower on the whole definition domain).

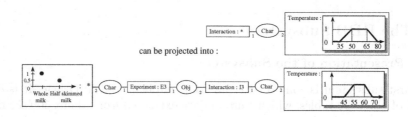

**Fig. 5.** An example of a projection involving fuzzy concepts

## 5.2   Presentation of the Subsystem

**Definition 7.** *In UQS, the CGKB, which contains the weakly structured knowledge of our system, is a set of connected, possibly cyclic CGs.*

At the moment, the CGKB contains about 100 CGs corresponding to scientific publications which do not fit the RDB schema. These CGs have been built manually by analyzing the pertinent sentences of these publications. The CG presented in Fig. 2 belongs to the CGKB.

## 5.3   The CG Wrapper

The CG subsystem relies on a set of *schema graphs* which allows us to define views on the CGKB.

**Definition 8.** *A* **schema graph** *$S$ associated with a view $V$ on $n$ attributes $\{a_1, \ldots, a_n\}$ is a pair $\{g, C\}$ where $g$ is an acyclic CG and $C = \{c_1, \ldots, c_n\}$ is a set of distinct concept vertices of $g$. Each $c_i$ has $a_i$ as a concept type.*

A schema graph is thus a CG with a set of distinguished concept vertices, which correspond to the attributes of the view. The graph presented in Fig. 6 is a schema graph for the view *BacteriocinInteraction*, the concepts of $C$ are framed in bold.

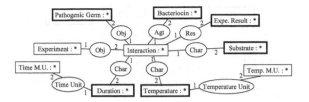

**Fig. 6.** An example of a schema graph for the view BacteriocinInteraction

**Definition 9.** $\mathcal{V}_{cg} = \{Vg_1, \dots, Vg_m\}$ *is the set of views on the CGKB, with* $P_{Vg_1}, \dots, P_{Vg_m}$ *the predicates characterizing each view.*

A CG can be interpreted in terms of FOL by means of the $\Phi$ operator [1]. The FOL which can be represented by CGs is limited to conjunctive formulae with only existential quantifiers, without negation.

**Definition 10.** *The predicate* $P_{Vg_i}$ *associated with a view* $Vg_i$ *corresponds to the logical interpretation* $\Phi(g_i)$ *of the schema graph* $g_i$ *which defines the view.*

**Example 3** *If a view* $V_{g_1}$ *is defined by the following CG, and if the only attributes which can be used in a query are PathogenicGerm and Bacteriocin*

$$[PathogenicGerm:*] \xrightarrow{\;2\;} (obj) \xrightarrow{\;1\;} [Interaction:*] \xrightarrow{\;1\;} (agt) \xrightarrow{\;2\;} [Bacteriocin:*]$$

*then the view* $V_{g_1}$ *is* $\{x, y | \exists z P_{Vg_1}(x, y, z)\}$ *with* $P_{Vg_1} = (PathogenicGerm(x) \wedge Interaction(z) \wedge Bacteriocin(y) \wedge obj(z, x) \wedge agt(z, y)).$

## 5.4   Query Processing

When a query is asked on the CGKB, the schema graph corresponding to the considered view is specialized by the instantiation of concept vertices in order to take into account the selection attributes, giving a *query graph.*

**Example 4** *The query graph presented in Fig. 7, which is a specialization of the schema graph presented in Fig. 6, corresponds to the query Q presented in Example 2. Note that the "instantiation" of the selection attributes is done in two different ways: the selection attribute* $<$ *Temperature : HumanBodyTemp.* $>$ *is instantiated by defining a marker (which is a fuzzy one in that example), while the selection attribute* $<$ *Bacteriocin, Nisin* $>$ *is instantiated by restricting the concept type "Bacteriocin" to its subtype "Nisin". This results from our choice to let the designer of a knowledge base the possibility to define instances of a concept type by means of individual markers or by means of subtyping [10].*

The following step of the query processing consists in projecting the query graph into all the CGs of the CGKB. In other words, we search for assertions in our KB which contain information more precise than that of the query graph.

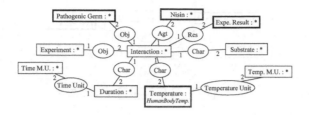

**Fig. 7.** An example of a query graph

**Remark 2** *Given two CGs G and H, it is proven[2] that $G \leq H$ iff $\Phi(G) \to \Phi(H)$ [1, 11]. The logical formula associated with a query graph, which is a specialization of the associated schema graph, implies then the logical formula associated with the schema graph itself. We are currently working on the extension of that property when the considered CGs involve fuzzy sets [12]. When the query graph $Q_G$ can be projected into a fact graph $F_G$, then $F_G$ is a specialization of $Q_G$: $\Phi(F_G)$ implies $\Phi(Q_G)$.*

For each projection of the query graph, we extract the values of the projection attributes, in order to build the result of the query. For example, if we ask the query of Fig. 7 on a CGKB containing the CG of Fig. 2, the resulting tuple would be: $<'$ *Listeria'*,*' Reduction'* $>$. Note that the question of the existence of a projection of a graph into another graph is NP-complete. However there are polynomial cases, for instance the question of the existence of a projection of an acyclic graph into a graph. In UQS, we use the polynomial algorithm of [13].

## 6   Conclusion and Perspectives

In this paper, we have presented a work which is part of a food risk control application using two different knowledge sources: a relational database and a CG knowledge base. These two knowledge sources allow the user: (i) to insert data involving fuzzy values represented in terms of fuzzy sets as well as (ii) to query the base with the expression of preferences, also represented by means of fuzzy sets. The integration of these two subsystems is done by means of a uniform querying language plugged into two wrappers which realize the translation of the query into queries fitting one subsystem or the other.

Our system is composed of a common interface developed in Java. That interface queries both subsystems and merges their partial answers into a global answer. The CG subsystem consists in a 5.000 lines supplement of C++, implemented on the CoGITaNT platform [14]. It includes all the mechanisms presented in this paper. It has been successfully presented to our microbiologist partners and is now operational.

Among the multiple perspectives induced by this work, two are to be studied very soon. The first one is the study of enlargement querying mechanisms,

---

[2] $G$ and $H$ must be normalized, i.e. each individual marker appears at most once

extending those yet implemented in the RDB [9] and in the CGKB [10]. The second one is the integration of our system into a more ambitious project, called "e.dot", which involves three computer science laboratories and a firm[3]. The goal is to build a data warehouse composed of our bases, completed by data extracted from the Web.

# References

1. J.F. Sowa. *Conceptual structures - Information processing in Mind and Machine.* Addison-Welsey, 1984.
2. P. Bosc, L. Lietard, and O. Pivert. Soft querying, a new feature for database management system. In *Proceedings DEXA'94 (Database and EXpert system Application), Lecture Notes in Computer Science*, volume 856, pages 631–640. Springer-Verlag, 1994.
3. H. Prade. Lipski's approach to incomplete information data bases restated and generalized in the setting of zadeh's possibility theory. *Information Systems*, 9(1):27–42, 1984.
4. M.L. Mugnier and M. Chein. Représenter des connaissances et raisonner avec des graphes. *Revue d'Intelligence Artificielle*, 10(1):7–56, 1996.
5. L.A. Zadeh. Fuzzy sets. *Information and Control*, 8:338–353, 1965.
6. L.A. Zadeh. Fuzzy sets as a basis for a theory of possibility. *Fuzzy Sets and Systems*, 1:3–28, 1978.
7. J.D. Ullman. *Principles of database and knowledge-base systems.* Computer Science Press, 1988.
8. R. Thomopoulos, P. Buche, and O. Haemmerlé. Representation of weakly structured imprecise data for fuzzy querying. *to appear in Fuzzy Sets and Systems*, 2003.
9. P. Buche and S. Loiseau. Using contextual fuzzy views to query imprecise data. In *Proceedings DEXA'99 (Database and EXpert system Application), Lecture Notes in Computer Science #1677*, pages 460–472, Florence, Italy, August 1999. Springer.
10. P. Buche and O. Haemmerlé. Towards a unified querying system of both structured and semi-structured imprecise data using fuzzy views. In *Proceedings of the 8th International Conference on Conceptual Structures, Lecture Notes in Artificial Intelligence #1867*, pages 207–220, Darmstadt, Germany, August 2000. Springer.
11. M. Chein and M.L. Mugnier. Conceptual graphs, fundamental notions. *Revue d'Intelligence Artificielle*, 6(4):365–406, 1992.
12. R. Thomopoulos, P. Bosc, P. Buche, and O. Haemmerlé. Logical interpretation of fuzzy conceptual graphs. In *Proceedings of the NAFIPS'2003 Conference (to appear)*, Chicago, USA, July 2003.
13. M.L. Mugnier and M. Chein. Polynomial algorithms for projection and matching. In *Proceedings of the 7th annual Workshop on Conceptual Graphs, Lecture Notes in Artificial Intelligence #754*, pages 239–251, Las Cruces, NM, USA, July 1992. Springer-Verlag.
14. D. Genest and E. Salvat. A platform allowing typed nested graphs: How cogito became cogitant. In *Proceedings of the 6th International Conference on Conceptual Structures (ICCS'1998), Lecture Notes in Artificial Intelligence #1453*, pages 154–161, Montpellier, France, August 1998. Springer.

---

[3] LRI/IASI, Paris XI University, INRIA/Verso, Xyleme and INA P-G, www.inria.fr/edot

# Intelligent Protein 3D Structure Retrieval System

Yiqiang Chen[1], Wen Gao[1,2], Lijuan Duan[1], Xiang Chen[1], and Charles X. Ling[3]

[1](Institute of Computing Technology, Chinese Academy of Sciences, 100080)
[2](Department of Computer Science, Harbin Institute of Technology, 150001)
[3](Department of Computer Science, University of West Ontario, CA )
(yqchen@ict.ac.cn;86-10-82649008;86-10-82649298)

**Abstract.** Since the 3D structure of a protein determines its function, the protein structural identification and comparison system is very important to biologists. In this paper, an intelligent protein 3D structure retrieval system is described. The system is intelligent since it integrates the moment feature extraction technology and the relevant feedback method in Artificial Intelligence (AI). As there is no universal agreement on the similarity of proteins structures, the major advantage of our system compared to other previous systems is that we use the relevance feedback technology to aid the biologists to find the similar protein structures more effectively. The similarity metric formula is improved dynamically by biologists' interaction through relevance feedback. The experimental results show that the proposed approach can capture the biologists' intentions in real-time and obtain good performance in the protein 3D structure retrieval. The ratio of total improvement is about 15.5% on average, which is quite significant compared to the improvements obtained in some previous work.

## 1 Introduction

Most biological actions of proteins, such as catalysis or regulation of the genetic messages, depend on certain particular components of their three-dimension (3D) structures. Proteins with similar 3D structures often show similar biological properties, or have the same functions [1]. It is therefore highly desirable to measure the similarities between protein 3D structures. One of the primary goals of protein structural alignment programs is to quantitatively measure the level of structural similarity between pairs of known protein structures.

There have been several previous methods that compare protein structures and measure the degree of structural similarity between them. For instance, 3dSEARCH [2] is based on geometric hashing, an object recognition algorithm developed in the field of computer vision. Dali Server [3] presents a general approach to aligning a pair of proteins represented by two-dimension distance matrixes. Another well-known algorithm called Combinatorial Extension (CE) defines aligned fragment pairs (AFPs) to confer structure similarities of proteins [4]. In recent years, the method of moments and mesh representation for 3D model retrieval, which succeeds in computer vision [5], is adapted and extended to perform retrieval of 3D protein structures [6].

Since there is no universal agreement on the similarity of proteins, it is not easy to assess the results of similarity retrieval systems to tell which one is the best [7]. The

N. Zhong et al. (Eds.): ISMIS 2003, LNAI 2871, pp. 108–115, 2003.
© Springer-Verlag Berlin Heidelberg 2003

biologists intend to use their own similarity measure to formulate their queries. In the systems mentioned above, the parameters and methods of feature extraction and similarity measurement are pre-determined, and they cannot be adjusted intelligently according to the experimental conditions. Thus the biologists' subjective perceptions could not effectively be modeled by the features and their associated weights used in assessing protein similarities. To resolve this problem, relevance feedback is adapted in our system. Relevance feedback is a powerful tool, and it has been successfully used in text or image retrieval [8,9,10,11]. Retrieval system based on the relevance feedback allows users to provide coarse queries initially. The system provides an interface to allow the users to decide which answers are correct or incorrect, and then the system learns from the positive (correct) and negative (incorrect) examples submitted by the users, and submit a more accurate set of answers to the users. The process may iterate several times until users are satisfied with the answer. As it is often difficult for users to express their intention, the approach of relevance feedback will be very effective in retrieving proteins that users have desired.

A new intelligent protein 3D structure retrieval system, integrating moment feature extracting technology and relevance feedback method, is proposed in this paper. Figure 1 shows the framework of our intelligent protein 3D structure retrieval system. It not only obtains 3D features but also refines the queries and the similarity metric in the retrieval process. The similarity metric formula can be improved dynamically according to users' interaction with the system. Experiments show that this system can satisfy users' queries.

Two key technologies used in our system can be further explained here. One is the feature extraction technology (see Section 2). From the PDB [13], we can extract two kinds of features: protein 3D structural features (such as the geometric shape feature or the moment [6]) and protein description features (such as the number of atoms, the weight of each atoms, and the name of each atoms). The features can be normalized for similarity measurement.

The other key technology is relevance feedback (see Section 3), which, as far as we know, has not been applied in protein retrieval systems previously. Relevance feedback allows users to iteratively retrieve similar protein structures from any large protein 3D structure database, such as PDB. A user can browse the protein database and investigate the detailed structure for each protein. Once he/she finds a protein structure of interests, that protein structure is submitted as a query. The system computes the similarity between proteins in the database and the query protein, and ranks them according to the similarity scores. If the user wants to improve the retrieval results, he can submit some positive or negative examples to the system. The system computes the similarity scores according to our relevance feedback method [12], and ranks proteins again. The above process is repeated until user is satisfied with the results.

Figure 2 illustrates a concrete query process with relevance feedback. In Figure 2, the query protein is displayed at the upper left corner, and the best 20 retrieved proteins are displayed in the right window (but only 9 of them are shown here due to picture size). Users can put a check mark or cross mark on each protein retrieved, and then the proteins with the check marks on them are submitted as positive examples, while the proteins with the cross marks are submitted as negative examples. The system takes in the users' feedback, adjusts the feature weights and the similarity metric formula (see Section 3), and re-computes the similarity score and produces a new ranked list that will contain more proteins with the similar features as the user has chosen. This process may repeat several times until the user is satisfied.

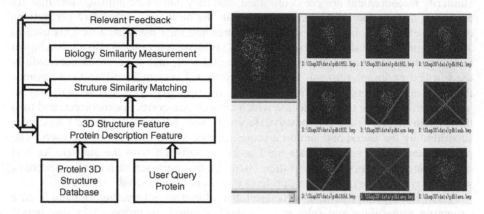

Fig. 1. System Overview          Fig. 2. User Interaction

The paper is organized as follows. Section 2 describes feature extraction and matching technology. Section 3 gives our relevance feedback method. Experimental results and conclusion are given in section 4 and section 5 respectively.

## 2  Feature Extraction

First of all, we must find the best alignment of two proteins before we extract the features for matching. All the chemical atoms of the protein are treated as equally weighted points in our algorithm. The center of mass of each protein therefore is easily computed and then the protein can be centered at the origin. This method is commonly used to find center of the mass before alignment [6]. After that, in order to align the 3D protein structures which can rotate freely, a 3x3 matrix C is constructed by the covariance of the three dimensional model:

Assume $A=[x, y, z]^T$ and Ai is the (x,y,z) coordinates of each atom. The following formula calculates the covariance matrix C.

$$\mu = \frac{1}{M}\sum_{i=1}^{M} A_i \qquad\qquad C = \frac{1}{M}\sum_{i=1}^{M} [A_i - \mu][A_i - \mu]^T \qquad (1)$$

The principle axis is then obtained by computing the eigenvectors of matrix C, which is also known as the principle component analysis (PCA). The eigenvector corresponding to the largest eigenvalue is the first principal axis. The next eigenvector corresponding to the secondary eigenvalue is the second principal axis, and so on. The two proteins will then be rotated the atom sets to their own principal axes for best alignment. PCA-based protein 3D alignment can make the two proteins to be rotated to their maximal various directions. Then we need not consider the effect of different direction rotation of each protein in the following feature extraction.

After alignment, we extract geometry-based features of a set of points combined with protein description features before performing matching and retrieval. In classical mechanics and statistical theory, the concept of moments is used extensively [6]. We can extract nine features of each protein: the number of atoms, the weight of atoms, the render scale, two aspect ratios defined by height and depth divided by width, and four 2nd and 3rd order moments including $M_{200}, M_{210}, M_{102}, M_{201}$. Those nine features have been regarded as the most crucial features in protein structural description [6]. Then we can assign each feature a weight. The next section will give the method how to adjust the weight to make the protein retrieval standard more consistent with biologist judgment.

## 3  Relevance Feedback

For most previous retrieval systems (such as [8,9,10]), the retrieval processing follows steps below: Firstly, each object is represented by a set of selected features. Secondly, during the retrieval process, the user provides a query example or a set of feature values representing the query object and specifics a weight for each feature to assess the similarity between the query object and objects in the database. Finally, based on the selected features and specified weights, the retrieval system tries to find object similar to the user's query. The weights are fixed during the retrieval process.

Definition 1 (distance between two object)

Each object $O$ is represented by a feature vector $f = [f_1, ..., f_n]$ ($n$ is the dimension of the feature). The distance between two objects is defined as

$$ dist\ (f_j, f_k, w) = \left[ \sum_{i=1}^{n} w_i \left| f_{ji} - f_{ki} \right|^2 \right]^{\frac{1}{2}} \tag{2} $$

We assume that the weights are normalized. As we have seen, for most retrieval systems, the weights are fixed. The query model could not adapted to user's intention, which is often difficult to specify for users. To better capture the right weights reflecting users intention, relevance feedback is introduced in our system. The system provides an interface to gather user's evaluating information and learn from the positive and negative examples submitted by the user. Then the system computes the weights. The technique is called re-weighting. Rui [8] proposed a global re-weighting technique. We find that if positive examples are not consistent in some features, the efficiency of Rui's re-weighting method is very low. We propose a relevance feedback approach based on subspace to improve the retrieval efficiency.

### 3.1  Subspace Based Relevance Feedback Retrieval

The detail of the processing is shown as following steps.

1. At the initial retrieval time, the system computes the distance from query example to each object according to definition 1 and ranks the objects according to the distance value. The most similar object is ranked at the first and the minor is at the second.

2. If user is not satisfied with the retrieval results, he can give some positive examples and negative example.

3. The system clusters these positive examples into several subspaces, and creates some exceptions according to the negative examples.

4. The system computes the distances according to the new retrieval models and display retrieval results.

5. Repeat step 2 to 4, until user is satisfied the retrieval result.

## 3.2  Subspace Definition

Subspaces are obtained by clustered the training example sets. The training example sets are composed of query examples and positive examples supposed in relevance feedback retrieval. We partition these features of training examples into several subspaces.

A subspace represents a set of features that are similar in feature space. Each subspace $S =< m, C, R, W, P >$ consists of a set of weights $W = \{ w_1, ..., w_n \}$, a set of training examples $P = \{ p_1, ..., p_m \}$ that are clustered into the subspace, a centroid $C$ that is the center of $P$ and a radius that repents the mean distance from training examples of the subspace to centroid $C$. $m$ is the number of training examples clustered into the subspace.

After each feedback, the system should compute distances of examples from subspaces. If the distance is less than or approximately equal to the radius the subspace, the new example is added to the subspace. . When a new example is added, it is either merged into an existing subspace or starts off a new subspace. If the number of subspace exceed $N_{sub\_max}$, certain two subspaces are merged into one subspace. The nearest two subspaces are merged according to following distance.

$$dist (S_j, S_k) = \frac{n_j}{n_j + n_k} * dist (C_j, C_k, W_j) + \frac{n_k}{n_k + n_j} * dist (C_k, C_j, W_k) \qquad (3)$$

Either adding new examples to subspace or merging two subspaces, the related parameters are set again. We use the re-weight method proposed by Rui [14]. After re-weighting and computing new centroid, the radius is changed according to the mean distance from every example to centroid.

## 3.3  Exception Definition

It is obviously that using reasonable negative information can improve the performance of system. But superabundant negative information will destroy the query model and degrade the efficiency of retrieval [15]. For most systems, the abilities to process negative information are finite.

In general, negative examples' are similar to query object in term of feature. Lacking of effective negative information processing ability will not only lose a part of feedback information, but also affect the retrieval efficiency.

Negative examples are regarded as exception. In other word, they are not selected as train examples to create subspace. On the contrary, we create many small negative example clusters that called exceptions.

Each exception $E =< m, C, R, W, N >$ consists of a set of weights $W = \{ w_1, ..., w_n \}$, a set of negative examples $N = \{ n_1, ..., n_m \}$ that clustered into the exception, a centroid $C$ that is the center of $N$ and a radius that repents the mean distance from negative examples of the exception to centroid $C$. $m$ is the number of negative examples clustered into the exception.

After each feedback, the exceptions are updated according to the new negative examples provided by the user. The distances from negative example to each exception are computed. If the distance is larger than the radius of the exception, a new exception is created.

## 3.4  Similarity Definition

Through above-mentioned process, the positive examples are clustered into several clusters. These clusters represent the distribution of query objects. The retrieval process converts to compute from each object to these subspaces.

The radii of each subspace are different, which will affect the similarity judgment of the system. There are need a normalization schema. We define a sort of normalization method, which uses subspace radius to adjust the distance as following.

$$
Dist_k(O) = \begin{cases} 1 - \dfrac{1 - Dist_k(f, C_k, W_k)}{1 - R_k}, & if \quad Dist_k(o) >= R_k \\ 0, & if \quad Dist_k(o) < R_k \end{cases} \tag{4}
$$

$Dist_k(f, C_k, W_k)$ is the distance from object $O$ to subspace $S_k$. $R_k, C_k$ and $W_k$ are parameters related to subspace $S_k$. If an object is similar to the centroid of certain subspace, the object is a good result. The similarity from object $O$ to query is defined as following.

$$
Sim(O, Q) = \max(1 - Dist'_k(O)), \quad k = 1, ..., N_{sub} \tag{5}
$$

Sometimes the centroid of exception is very near to the centroid of certain subspace. If the distance from object to certain exception is smaller than the radii of the exception, it is considered that $Sim(O, Q) = 0$.

## 4  Experiment

The experiments are conducted on the public database PDB (Protein Data Bank) [13], which includes 18691 protein files (As September 10, 2002) and FSSP database [16], in which the fold classification is based on structure-structure alignment of proteins, and which includes all protein chains (>30 residues) from the PDB. FSSP database is based on search results of Dali engine (mainly based on the Z-score) and divides proteins in PDB into families. Each protein family has a representative protein. At the same time some of the results in FSSP have been revised by biologists. The FSSP database we used has 2860 protein families, which represent 27181 protein structures.

Since there is no universal agreement on the similarity of proteins and FSSP database is relatively objective and maintained by biologists, we use the FSSP classification results as the ground truth to make assessment of our retrieval system. The results are showed in Table 1. In the table, Representative Protein ID means the ID (entry) of the representative protein from each protein family in FSSP database. The Retrieval Accuracy is computed as follows: choose N (in our experiments, N=20) proteins whose similarity scores are ranked top in all proteins in PDB. Find M proteins that also belong to the same family as the representative protein in FSSP. Then the retrieval accuracy is simply M/N. As we can see, the first and second rounds of relevant feedback always improve the retrieval accuracy, and the ratio of total improvement is about 15.5% on average. This improvement is quite significant compared to the improvements obtained in some previous work [6].

**Table 1.** Retrieval Accuracy of different representative sets

| Representative Protein ID | Initial Matching (Retrieval Accuracy) | First Relevant Feedback (Retrieval Accuracy) | Second Relevant Feedback (Retrieval Accuracy) |
|---|---|---|---|
| 1cxq | 80% | 90% | 100% |
| 1a6m | 80% | 90% | 95% |
| 1abw | 90% | 100% | |
| 1ba1 | 85% | 100% | |
| 1b8j | 70% | 75% | 75% |
| 1ctq | 45% | 65% | 75% |
| 1djx | 40% | 45% | 55% |
| 1fnc | 35% | 40% | 40% |
| 1crb | 20% | 25% | 30% |
| 1ckq | 30% | 35% | 40% |

# 5 Conclusion

In this paper, an intelligent protein 3D structure retrieval system is proposed. It is a novel matching method, which not only obtains 3D features with the moment technology, but also refines the query and the similarity metric in the retrieval process with relevant feedback. Since there is no universal agreement on the similarity of proteins, the major advantage of our system compared to other previous systems is that the relevance feedback technology is adapted to improve the similarity metric formula dynamically with biologist's interaction. The experimental results show that the proposed approach can capture the biologist's intention and obtain significant improvement in the protein 3D structure retrieval.

**Acknowledgments.** This research is supported by National Key Basic Research & Development Program. (No. 2002CB713807)

# References

[1]   Singh, A. P. and Brutlag, D. L. (2001). Protein Structure Alignment: A comparison of methods. Nature Structural Biology, Submitted.

[2]   http://gene.stanford.edu/3dSearch

[3]   Holm L, Sander C (1993). Protein structure comparison by alignment of distance matrices. J Mol Biol 233, 123–138.

[4]   Tsigelny1 I., Shindyalov I. N., Bourne P. E., Südhof T. and Taylor P.( 2000) Common EF-hand Motifs in Cholinesterases and Neuroligins Suggest a Role for CA2+ Binding in Cell Surface Associations. Protein Science 9(1) 180–185.

[5]   C. Zhang and T. Chen, "Efficient Feature Extraction for 2D/3D Objects in Mesh Representation", ICIP, 2001.

[6]   Shann-Ching Chen and Tsuhan Chen, Retrival of 3D protein structures", ICIP, 2002.

[7]   Ingvar Eidhammer, Inge Jonassen, William R. Taylor, Structure Comparison and Structure Patterns, Reports in Informatics No. 174, Department of Informatics, University of Bergen, Norway, July 1999.

[8]   Yong Rui, Thomas S. Huang, Sharad Mehrotra, and Michael Ortega. Relevance Feedback: a power tool for interactive content-based object retrieval. IEEE trans. Circuits and systems for video technology, vol. 8, no. 5, pp. 644–655, Sep. 1998.

[9]   Yoshiharu Ishikawa, Ravishankar Subramanya, and Christos Faloutsos Mindreaner: Query Databases Through Multiple Examples. In Proc. of the 24th VLDB Conference, (New York), 1998.

[10]  Catherine. Lee, Wei-Ying Ma, Hongjiang Zhang. Information Embedding Based on User's Relevance Feedback for Object Retrieval. Technical report HP Labs, 1998.

[11]  Nuno Vasconcelos and Andrew Lippman. Bayesian Representations and Learning Mechanisms for Content Based Object Retrieval. SPIE Storage and Retrieval for Media Databases 2000, San Jose, California, 2000.

[12]  Lijuan Duan Wen Gao Jiyong Ma. Rich Get Richer Strategy for Content-Based Image Retrieval, Robert Laurini (Ed.): Advances in Visual Information Systems, 4th International Conference, VISUAL 2000, Lyon, France, November 2–4, 2000, Proceedings. Lecture Notes in Computer Science 1929 Springer 2000, pp 290–299.

[13]  H.M. Berman, J. Westbrook, Z. Feng, G. Gilliland, T.N. Bhat, H. Weissig, I.N. Shindyalov, P.E. Bourne: The Protein Data Bank. Nucleic Acids Research, 28 pp. 235–242 ,2000

[14]  Y. Rui, T. S. Huang, A novel relevance feedback technique in image retrieval, ACM Mulitmedia 1999.

[15]  J. J. Rocchio, Relevance feedback in information retrieval, In The SMART Retrieval System, Experiments in Automatic Document Processing, Pages 313–323. Prentice Hall, Engle-wood Cliffs, New Jersey, USA, 1971.

[16]  L. Holm and C. Sander , Mapping the protein universe. Science 273:595–602, 1996.

# Cognitive Vision Systems in Medical Applications

Marek R. Ogiela and Ryszard Tadeusiewicz

AGH University of Science and Technology, Institute of Automatics
Al. Mickiewicza 30, PL-30-059 Kraków, Poland
{mogiela, rtad}@agh.edu.pl

**Abstract.** This paper presents new opportunities for applying linguistic description of the picture merit content and artificial intelligence methods to undertake tasks of the automatic understanding of images semantics in intelligent medical information systems. A successful obtaining of the crucial semantic content of the medical image, thanks to the application of the methods presented in this paper, may contribute considerably to the creation of new intelligent multimedial cognitive medical systems. Similar systems are now constructed in many labs for textual database, especially for web crawling using selected ontology, nevertheless methodology described in this paper gives possibilities perform that function also on the basis of multimedia data. Thanks to the new idea of cognitive resonance between stream of the data extracted from the image using linguistic methods and expectations taken from the representation of the medical knowledge we can understand the merit content of the image even if the form of the image is very different from any known pattern. In the future the technique of automatic understanding of images may become one of the effective tools for semantic interpreting, and intelligent storing of the visual data in scattered multimedia databases and knowledge based systems. This article proves that structural techniques of artificial intelligence may be applied in the case of tasks related to automatic classification and machine perception based on semantic pattern content in order to determine the semantic meaning of the patterns. In the paper we describe some examples presenting ways of applying such techniques in the creation of cognitive vision systems for selected classes of medical images. On the base of scientific research described in the paper we try to build some new systems for collecting, storing retrieving and intelligent interpreting selected medical images. The proposed approach will be described in selected examples of medical images obtained in radiological and MRI diagnosis, however the methodology under consideration can be used also for general applications.

## 1 Introduction

Traditional approach to automated analysis of medical data is mostly based on databases, statistical analysis, signal processing, features extraction and pattern recognition – recently powered by Internet and other networks in terms so called telemedicine. By means of all such methods and techniques we can obtain many valuable items, e.g. computer based tracking of patients moving and control of medical treatment, remote consulting in case of complex diseases, computer powered physiologi-

N. Zhong et al. (Eds.): ISMIS 2003, LNAI 2871, pp. 116–123, 2003.
© Springer-Verlag Berlin Heidelberg 2003

cal, pathological and epidemiological investigations, computer aided diagnosis making and cure performing (including telesurgery), and many others.

Although results of traditional applications of computers and informatics in medicine are so impressive, still there are many problems not solvable by means of computers and reserved for human medical staff only. Such problems are mainly connected with medical information interpretation. When the goal can not be reached by the simple processing of the data and it needs understanding of the semantic content of the electronically collected information – we must engage human intelligence instead of computer performance. This is very important limitation of most popular medical information systems. When the medical data under consideration are represented in the form of the text data, for example description of the actual state of patient, results of medical investigation, anamnesis etc. we can use new methods of the semantic analysis of the data developed recently for intelligent searching of the selected alphanumerical data by means of semantic networks using syntactic analysis and advanced ontology. Unfortunately all new methods designed for intelligent searching of texts in databases (or in web) totally failed when we have multimedial data including many kind of medical images and also other signals (e.g. bioelectric records like RCG, EEG, MCG, or sound signal like pathological speech records) instead of simple numerical data and texts.

This limitation can be broken by means of the new ideas and the problem of automatic understanding of medical data can be solved by development of scientific research, it needs only the time for new methods formation and new ideas development. This paper try to give answer for at least one important question from this area. The question is: Do machine can understand multimedial medical data?

The answer is "yes", but only if we can use new methods of semantic analysis of the merit content of the multimedial medical data (especially images) instead of simple data processing, signal analysis and pattern classification. For this purpose we need new methods and new philosophy, described in this paper. Until now computer can only perform data processing tasks, but understanding, what the data means – was reserved for human specialists. Nevertheless sometimes we do need automatic understanding of medical data e.g. for intelligent helping of diagnosis process or for semantic based searching in big multimedia medical databases. Such tasks may be done using cognitive analysis in the intelligent visual data processing systems, which allow to make a semantic perception of analyzed visualization. Generally the perception of an image requires a deeper analysis aimed at the determination of significant semantic features. Such features enable a further semantic image interpretation or a semantically oriented indexation when in images objects are retrieved that come from various diagnostic examinations or determine different disease entities. Due to the fact that the number of combinations of features that characterize images is not limited, it can be assumed that perception may refer the image to potentially unlimited number of classes. This indicates that when understanding an image one should refer to a tool that can currently generate its semantic descriptions and not just select a suitable item from a prepared list. Therefore for cognitive analysis, specified languages of image description must be used, and the whole field must be based on mathematical linguistics.

## 2 Cognitive Analysis in Intelligent Systems

In this paper we try to show, how we do solve the problem of automatic understanding of some classes of medical images. By means of proper application of cognitive-based approach we can automatically describe important, from diagnostic point of view, features of analyzed images using special kind picture description languages. Linguistic description of picture contents, obtained by means of special goal-oriented preprocessing of the medical image can be next analyzed by means of finite automate called parser. During parsing process we can solve problem of generalization of features of selected image up to obtaining semantic description of the contents of image. Parsing process is based on special kind graph-grammar (prepared especially for this goal) and on knowledge based analysis. Most important part of this analysis depends on the process named "cognitive resonance", when features of real image are compared with demands taken from the knowledge base, applying both knowledge elements of pathological morphology and medical practice.

More precisely in cognitive analysis the image understanding process is characterised by a two-way flow of information. The stream of empirical data, registered by cognitive vision system, interferes with the stream of expectations originate from knowledge database. The expectations can have features with some postulates specifying the important features of the analysed image with the assumption that the content of the image corresponds to one possible variant of its semantic interpretation. It is assumed that the system understating images has a set of generators for the previously mentioned expectations and its disposal; the generators are connected with various hypothetical methods of the meritorious interpretation of the image content [2]. Such a structure of the image understanding system generally corresponds to one of the psychological models of visual perception which is based on the concept of the use of knowledge about objects perceived.

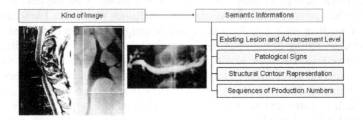

**Fig. 1.** Analysed images of the spinal cord (left) urinary tracts (middle) and pancreatic duct (right) and semantic information necessary to understand the medical meaning of the pathologies visible in them.

Constructing those systems is extremely efficient in the case of the structural analysis of complex shapes of chest or abdominal cavity organs which are characterised by an occurrence of morphological lesions typical of developing disease processes. A possibility to conduct such a cognitive analysis will be presented on the examples of analysis of patterns received during the diagnostic examinations of renal pelvis, pancreatic ducts and the spinal cord (Fig. 1).

For the cognitive analysis of the mentioned structures a graph grammar of type EDT [1, 2] and an attributed context-free grammars of type LALR (1) have been proposed.

Before coming to the interpretation of the changes it is necessary to preserve the sequence of operations, which are included in the image pre-processing [3, 6]. The goal of this analysis is to obtain new representation in the form of width graphs, which show the pathological changes occurring in these structures.

During the initial analysis of visualisations, the following operations are executed: segmentation, skeletonization, and the application of a straightening transformation to transform the contour of the analysed structure into two-dimensional graph, which shows a profile of a straightened organ [1]. The graphs obtained in such way are the starting point in the classification of morphological features by using context-free grammars.

In order to define primary components on the obtained width graphs as terminal symbols describing these components, an algorithm of line approximation was used [3]. As a result, sequence of terminal symbols for every graph was received, which constitute an input to syntax analysers and semantic classifiers. An example of application of such operations is presented on Fig. 2.

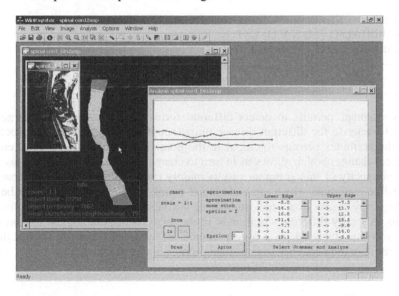

**Fig. 2.** An example of the application of preliminary processing stages, and the way of creating syntactic descriptions for the outer boundaries.

## 3  Spinal Cord Cognitive Analysis

The application of cognitive analysis to extract important semantic information from images will be shown in the example of syntactic analysis of spinal cord images.

In the case of the spine and spinal cord MRI image analyses, the aim of the diagnosis is to find changes that may be evidence of several disease entities such as encephalomeningocele, different inflammatory states, ischaemia of the meninges or the spinal cord, and the most serious cases of intraspinal and extraspinal tumours. An unambiguous identification of all entities with the application of the diagnostic program is extremely difficult due to rather subtle differences that are decisive in a correct classification. However, it turns out that a structural analysis may be very useful when determining the degree of the progression of an illness entity by means of defining the level of changes in the spinal cord morphology and determining the degree of the spinal cord and spinal compression [5].

For an analysis of this structure a context-free grammar was prepared which allows us to identify symptoms, and to draw diagnostic conclusions concerning the essence of visible pathology. In the case of the analysis of the spinal cord image, the grammar was defined in the following way:

$V_N$ = {LESION, NARROWING, ENLARGEMENT, N, U, D}- set of non-terminal symbols
$V_T$ = {n, u, d} for n∈[-10°, 10°], u∈(10°, 180°), d∈(-10°, -180°) - set of terminal symbols
STS = LESION - starting symbol of grammar
SP: set of production

1.  LESION → NARROWING | ENLARGEMENT
2.  NARROWING → D N U | D U | D N
3.  ENLARGEMENT → U N D | U D | U N
4.  N → n | n N          $w_{sym}:=w_{sym}+w_n$; $h_{sym}:=h_{sym}+h_n$
5.  U → u | u U          ...
6.  D → d | d D          ...

This grammar permits to detect different forms of narrowing and enlargements which characterise the different disease units (neoplasm or inflammation processes). Using the attributes permits to calculate the numerical parameters of detected morphological changes which allows us in turn to characterize the degree of lesions.

The simplicity of this grammar results mainly from the big generation capacity of context-free grammars which are understood mainly as possibilities to describe complex shapes by means of a small number of introductory rules that are grammar productions. A totally different situation is in the analysis of pathological lesions in the main pancreatic ducts where a bigger number of symptoms and the variety of their shapes result in the necessity to introduce more complex grammar [1].

## 4   Graph Grammar Perception in Case of Renal Pelvis Analysis

An example of understanding the gist of morphological lesions of the shape with the use the graph grammars will be presented on an actual task in which an analysis of the correctness of the renal pelvis and renal calyxes.

Although these structures are characterized by unusual shape variations [3], it is possible to distinguish certain common features which characterize all proper structures using a number of smaller and bigger calyxes revealed in the renal sinus [5]. To describe the shapes of these structures we have suggested an expansive EDT graph grammar [2] defined with the aim of analyzing the skeleton morphology of investigated renal pelvises and renal calyxes.

To characterize the original components which are used in graph grammar, an approximation algorithm for the skeleton branches in the pelvis and the renal calyxes can be applied. Then each branch can be identified with a single section whose ends are determined by the ends of the approximated branch. Next, to each determined segment are assigned edge terminal labels, depending on the angle of its inclination [3].

To diagnose morphological changes in renal pelvises the following graph grammar was used: $G_{EDT}=(\Sigma, \Gamma, r, P, Z)$, where $\Sigma = \Sigma_N \cup \Sigma_T$ is a set of terminal and non-terminal vertex labels defined in the following way:

$\Sigma_T$ = {pelvis_renalis, calix_major, calix_minor, papilla_renalis}

$\Sigma_N$ = {PELVIS_RENALIS, CALIX_MAJOR,CALIX_MINOR}

r - is a function which assigns to the graph vertex the number of its consequents

$\Gamma = \{x, y, z\}$ - is a set of edge labels for $y \in (-30°, 30°)$, $x \in (30°, 180°)$, $z \in (-30°, -180°)$

Z={PELVIS_RENALIS} - is a finite set of starting graphs

P- is a set of production:

1.  PELVIS_RENALIS → pelvis_renalis($x$CALIX_MAJOR $y$CALIX_MAJOR $z$CALIX_MAJOR)
    → pelvis_renalis($x$CALIX_MAJOR $y$CALIX_MAJOR)
    → pelvis_renalis($x$CALIX_MAJOR $z$CALIX_MAJOR)
    → pelvis_renalis($y$CALIX_MAJOR $z$CALIX_MAJOR)
2.  CALIX_MAJOR → calix_major($x$CALIX_MINOR $y$CALIX_MINOR $z$CALIX_MINOR)
    → calix_major($x$CALIX_MINOR $y$CALIX_MINOR)
    → calix_major($x$CALIX_MINOR $z$CALIX_MINOR)
    → calix_major($y$CALIX_MINOR $z$CALIX_MINOR)
3.  CALIX_MINOR → calix_minor($x$papilla_renalis) | calix_minor($y$papilla_renalis)
    → calix_minor($z$papilla_renalis) | calix_minor($x$papilla_renalis $y$papilla_renalis)
4.  CALIX_MINOR → calix_minor($x$papilla_renalis $z$papilla_renalis)
    → calix_minor($y$papilla_renalis $z$papilla_renalis)

The first group of productions defines the different kinds of normal renal pelvises i.e. having two or three smaller calyxes. The succeeding productions define the form of bigger calyxes formed from two or more smaller calyxes. The last group defines the proper form of renal papillae which obtains a fork form during the skeletonisation, which means that it finishes with short branches which arise only when it is concave to the interior of a smaller calyx. Convex forms during skeletonisation are thinned to the line without end branches, which results from the properties of skeletonisation algorithms.


# 5  Selected Results

As a result of cognitive analysis it is possible to understand pathogenesis of the deformations viewed on x-ray images of the organs under consideration, what means the possibility of recognize some kind of diseases even on images absolutely not similar one to other. This cognitive approach is slightly different form typical analysis and recognition of medical images, because during recognition process it try to find, to which template can be pursuit the image, and during automatic understanding process intelligent system try to find, what does it means, that the image includes objects having particular shapes. Presented approach is applicable even if no templates of healthy and pathological organs at all or if number of recognized classes goes to infinity. In particularly applications of the presented grammars deliver almost complete information concerning the visual morphological irregularities of investigated organs. An analysis of the morphological changes was carried out on the basis of a set containing over one hundred images (urograms, pancreatic, and spinal cord images). The efficiency of gaining recognition of information with semantic character, in all cases exceeded the threshold of 90%. In the pancreatic duct image analysis, owing to the additional use of procedures based on languages of description of shape features, the efficiency reached 95%. The grammar for the analysis of pancreas images was presented in [1, 2].

In Fig. 3 are presented examples which show the description of the changes in question for pancreatic duct and spinal cord images. The recognition process is based on production numbers generated as an output string by syntax analyzers.

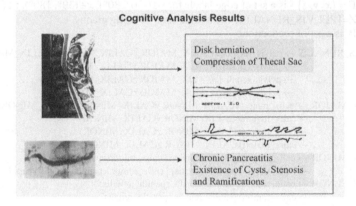

**Fig. 3.** Results of disease symptom recognition and understanding using syntactical methods of pattern recognition. Width diagrams show the place in which the looked-for lesion was diagnosed. Its structural description with the use of terminal symbols and the proper production sequences constitutes theirs unambiguous descriptions.

# 6   Conclusion

The development of the Internet and techniques of visual data storing (including medical data) made access to practically any database, with the information coming from diagnostic research, extremely easy. However, the automatic analysis and intelligent interpretation of the data by the information system is still a significant problem. In order to solve this problem advanced techniques of artificial intelligence must be applied that will enable the creation of systems that can both recognize and understand (to some degree, of course) processed data in the form of images.

Thus the aim of the presented algorithms was to show an innovative concept of the application of structural algorithms of artificial intelligence in the creation of cognitive vision systems aimed at understanding and determining the semantic meaning of medical images of certain classes. It is worth mentioning that machine perception using such methods may lead to an automatic interpretation of medical images in the way it is done by a specialist. It may enable the determination of not only crucial changes but also the consequences of existing irregularities and finally the optimal directions and methods of conducting a suitable therapy. Automatic understanding of the image content can have numerous further applications for example such information can be used to monitor therapeutic processes or to forecast disease development as well as the patient's future state of health.

Cognitive approach developed for understanding of presenting medical images can be easy extended for solving problems of cognitive analysis of many other medical data. In fact pathological process always gives many kind of deformation observed in medical data, but interpretation of such deformations in complex cases can not be done using only simple recognition methods – it needs sometimes understanding, what does it means that analyzed data have exactly such values. For example the authors tried to apply this methodology to understanding of pathological speech deformations and they also obtained very good results.

**Acknowledgement.** This work was supported by the AGH University of Science and Technology under Grant No. 10.10.120.39.

# References

1. Ogiela, M.R., Tadeusiewicz, R.: Syntactic pattern recognition for X-ray diagnosis of pancreatic cancer. IEEE Engineering In Medicine and Biology Magazine, 19 (2000) 94–105
2. Ogiela, M.R., Tadeusiewicz, R.: Syntactic reasoning and pattern recognition for analysis of coronary artery images, Artificial Intelligence in Medicine, 26 (2002) 145–159
3. Ogiela, M.R., Tadeusiewicz, R.: Visual Signal processing and image understanding in Biomedical systems, Proceedings of the 2003 IEEE International Symposium on Circuits and Systems - ISCAS 2003, Bangkok, Thailand (2003), Vol5 17–20
4. Sonka, M., Fitzpatrick, J.M. (eds.): Handbook of Medical Imaging: Vol. 2 – Medical image processing and analysis. SPIE PRESS, Bellingham WA (2000)
5. Burgener, F.A., Meyers, S.P., Tan, R.: Differential diagnosis in Magnetic Resonance Imaging. Thieme, Stuttgart (2001)
6. Javidi, B. (ed.): Image Recognition and Classification. Marcel Dekker, Inc., New York (2002)

# An Automated School Timetabling System Using Hybrid Intelligent Techniques

Alvin C.M. Kwan[1], Ken C.K. Chung[2], Kammy K.K. Yip[2], and Vincent Tam[3]

[1] CITE, University of Hong Kong, Pokfulam Road, Hong Kong SAR, China
alvin@cite.hku.hk

[2] Real Logic Technology, Suite A & B, 23/F Seabright Plaza, 9-23 Shell Street,
North Point, Hong Kong, China
{kenchung, kammyyip}@reallogictech.com

[3] Dept. of Electrical & Electronic Engineering, University of Hong Kong, Pokfulam Road,
Hong Kong SAR, China, vtam@eee.hku.hk

**Abstract.** School timetabling is typically hard to resolve and the problem gets harder when teaching resources are scarce. The need for supporting stringent teaching requirements such as co-teaching and split-class teaching complicates the problem even more. In this paper, we describe an automated school timetabling system called @PT that reasons about sophisticated timetabling requirements. @PT makes use of a number of intelligent techniques including constraint technology, heuristics, local search operators, and tabu-list like data structure. It also changes its search behavior dynamically at run-time. Experimental results show that @PT is robust and manages to solve real problem instances effectively within minutes.

## 1 Introduction

School timetabling has been studied for decades [3, 15, 1] and is still regarded as one of the most difficult scheduling problems nowadays. A number of techniques including graph coloring, tabu search, simulated annealing, evolutionary algorithms and constraint based approach, *etc.*, for tackling the problem have been studied [14]. In this paper, we describe an automated school timetabling system called @PT (standing for *academic planning and timetabling*) that employs hybrid techniques in its problem solving. Special design issues have been considered so as to make @PT suitable for tackling school timetabling in Hong Kong.

@PT adopts a range of intelligent techniques that include constraint technology, customized lesson selection and timeslot selection heuristics, sophisticated local search operators and tabu-list like data structure. It is adaptive in the sense that it changes its search behavior based on dynamic information collected during problem solving such as the amount of time remained for its execution. @PT provides important facilities like resources capacity analysis and post-generation decision support tuning facilities to help its end-users compile school timetables throughout the timetabling process. It also allows end-users to switch between auto-generation and manual tuning modes during timetable construction. Furthermore, end-users may set

N. Zhong et al. (Eds.): ISMIS 2003, LNAI 2871, pp. 124–134, 2003.

up an ordered list of preferred but relaxable timetabling requirements in case some of those requirements are to be relaxed in order to generate a feasible timetable.[1]

This paper aims at describing the scheduling algorithm of @PT. Essence of the key heuristics adopted by the algorithm is described. So far, @PT has been tested on real data sets collected from a number of Hong Kong schools. In the next section, background information about school timetabling in Hong Kong is introduced. A description of the scheduling algorithm is detailed afterwards. Experimental results of applying @PT to tackle three real instances of school timetabling problem (STP) are then presented and discussed. Conclusions are given in the last section.

## 2     School Timetabling in Hong Kong

In Hong Kong, school timetable is structured as a sequence of periods within a given number of days. Each student is assigned to a class in every academic year. Unless a school does not have enough classrooms (which is very common for secondary schools in Hong Kong), a standard classroom is allocated to each class such that most of lessons for the class will take place in that "home" room of the class. A lesson is referred to as a session during which a course be scheduled to be taught to a group of students by one or more teachers. Classes without a "home" room are known as "floating" classes as they need to attend lessons in various rooms including special rooms (e.g., art room) and "home" rooms of other classes (while those classes are taking their own lessons in special rooms such as computer laboratory). Usually students of the same class are required to take the same courses at the same time together. Subject to curriculum requirements, one or more classes may need to be split, and sometimes spit-and-combined, into groups to take different lessons at the same time occasionally.

Timetable scheduling in Hong Kong is usually hard to deal with due to its high room utilization. Two other factors that make the STP hard to resolve are: (1) virtually no students have free periods in their timetables; and (2) the complicated timetabling requirements involved (with some of those listed below.)

- For a given class, lessons of some subjects must not be held in the same day. Those subjects form a *mutually exclusive subject group*. For example, lessons for English dictation and Chinese dictation should not be held in the same day for any class.
- Subjects may need to be taught in alternate weeks/cycles. Moreover, a lesson may need to be held at two different teaching venues in alternate week/cycles.
- Some lessons demand split-class and split-subject requirements, e.g., two classes may be split into three groups, with each group taking the same or a different subject, taught by various teachers at three different venues.
- For the sake of a balanced timetable, a class should take no more than one lesson (of arbitrary length) of any given subject in any single day.
- For a given class, lessons of some subjects may need to be scheduled to non-successive days. A scenario that requires the enforcement of the requirement is to

---

[1] More description about @PT is available at http://www.reallogictech.com/.

allow pupils to have enough time to wash and dry their sports uniform between sports lessons.

*   All multi-period lessons must not be scheduled across a *hard break*, e.g., lunch break, although user-specified multi-period lessons are allowed, but preferably not, to be scheduled across a *soft break*, e.g., recess.

A more detailed description of some common timetabling requirements in Hong Kong schools can be found in [7]. Note that similar timetabling requirements can also be found in schools of other countries such as Singapore and Australia.

# 3     Scheduling Algorithm

The scheduling algorithm consists of an initialization phase and an improvement phase. The initialization procedure attempts to schedule all concerned lessons onto the master timetables. Should there be any unscheduled lessons remained at the end of the initialization phase, the scheduling algorithm enters into the improvement phase for further processing.

## 3.1     Initialization Phase

As shown in Figure 1, the initialization algorithm has three key components which are lesson selection, timeslot selection and repair heuristics. It assigns a selected lesson to a feasible timeslot in accordance with the lesson selection and timeslot selection heuristics. Should no feasible timeslot be identified for a selected lesson, the repair heuristics will be applied to try to fix the problem by rescheduling some already scheduled lessons to other feasible timeslots. If the repair heuristics cannot fix the problem, the concerned lesson will be left to be handle by the improvement phase. The process repeats until all lessons are handled.

```
// V = set of all lessons
// S = set of scheduled lessons
// F = set of fail-to-schedule lessons
// Note that V = S ∪ F and S ∩ F = ∅ after the initialization phase.
// v ∈ V, i.e., v is a lesson
// D(v) = domain of variable v, i.e., feasible timeslots that lesson v
//    can be scheduled to.
1    procedure initializationPhase(V, S, F)
2      Y := V
3      while (v := chooseVariable(Y)) != NIL
4        Y := Y - {v} // remove v from set of yet-to-schedule lesson
5        d := chooseValue(D(v)) // get a feasible timeslot for lesson v
6        if d != NIL  // feasible timeslot found
7          bind(v, d) // place lesson v to timeslot d and re-compute
                      // feasible timeslots for all affected lessons
8          S := S + {v}
9        else if repair(v, V, Y, F)
10         S := S + {v} // repair succeeded
11       else // repair failed
12         F := F + {v} // put v in failed list
```

```
13           increaseFailedCount(v)
14      end-while
15      return (S, F)
16   end-procedure
```

**Fig. 1.** Initialization phase of @PT's scheduling algorithm.

**Lesson Selection Heuristic.** The heuristic used for lesson selection is an enhanced version of the K-value heuristic [8], a variant of the fail-first heuristic [4] for timetabling applications. The enhanced K-value heuristic computes the constrainedness of a lesson as the number of ways that the selected lesson can be inserted in the timetable divided by the number of lessons of the same subject to be taught to the concerned class. This simple modification enables the heuristic to take even distribution of lessons across a class timetable into account.

**Timeslot Selection Heuristic.** The heuristic adopted is called COTS [6] which is inspired by the ORR heuristic designed for constraint-directed job-shop scheduling [12]. COTS aims to assign a value (in our case, a timeslot) to a variable (in our case, a lesson) that imposes least restriction to the unlabeled variables. The degree of restriction is measured according to how intensive those yet-to-assign lessons contend for a timeslot. Note that COTS is rather generic and can be applied to any CSP that involves disequality constraints.

**Repair Heuristic.** If there is no feasible timeslot for accommodating a selected lesson, the initialization procedure will use two local search operators, namely the billiard and double-billiard movements [5], to try to escape from the dead-end situation. The essence of billiard movement is based on the observation that although there may be no feasible timeslot for accommodating a yet-to-schedule lesson (say X), it may be able to be assigned the lesson to some timeslot that is currently occupied by another lesson (say Y). The billiard movement moves Y to another feasible timeslot and assigns X to the timeslot that was originally occupied by Y. The double-billiard movement extends the idea further by allowing the displacement of Y to trigger the execution of another billiard movement if Y cannot be scheduled to any timeslot after being displaced by X. An example that shows how the double-billiard movement works is given below.

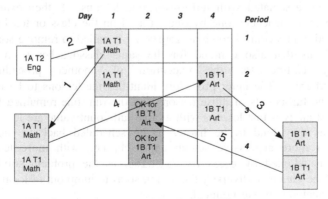

**Fig. 2.** An example use of the double-billiard movement.

In Figure 2, the numbers that label the arrows stand for the sequence of actions. Here we would like to schedule a single-period English lesson taught to class 1A by teacher T2. Suppose no feasible timeslot can be found for the lesson but it can be scheduled to the first period in Day 1 if class 1A's double-period Mathematics lesson (taught by T1) can be moved to a new timeslot. Apparently there is no other feasible timeslot for the Mathematics lesson to move to. However, should class 1B's Art double-period lesson (taught by T1 too) be moved to Day 2, the Mathematics lesson may then put to the timeslot formerly occupied by the Art lesson. With the series of movements, all the lessons concerned can be scheduled.

The computational effort for the double-billiard movement can be high. According to Kaneko *et. al.* [5], when combining with the double-billiard movement the computational time taken by a really-full-lookahead greedy search [16] augmented by the min-conflict hill-climbing algorithm [10] is twenty or more times longer than the time required by a similar algorithm that uses the billiard movement instead. Kaneko *et. al.* are dismissive of the usefulness of the double-billiard movement as in their experiments the improvement in solution quality is minimal. We however notice in our experiments that a successive application of billiard and double-billiard movements does improve the solution quality without spending too much time if the double-billiard movement is carefully implemented. Due to space limitation, those implementation details are omitted in this paper.

**Fail-count.** Whenever a lesson is selected for scheduling but fails to be assigned with any timeslot even after the application of local search operators, its fail-count will be incremented. The value serves as a measure reflecting the degree of difficulty of scheduling the corresponding lesson. Those fail-counts give hints as to which lessons be unscheduled if the scheduling process is trapped in local optima. Lessons associated with a larger fail-count value are less likely to be unscheduled when performing some aggressive lesson unscheduling operations (in the improvement phase only).

## 3.2    Improvement Phase

In the improvement phase, the scheduling algorithm first identifies classes and teachers that are associated with fail-to-schedule lessons. It then examines those classes, followed by teachers, one by one. Based on the class or teacher currently being examined, a procedure known as improve is called to remove some already-scheduled lessons that also contend for the same class/teacher from the master timetable by calling for the execution of another procedure named extractVictims. The latter procedure identifies the lessons to be unscheduled according to the fail-counts of those lessons and the run-time remained for problem solving. The strategy is that lessons with a large fail-count value are less likely to be unscheduled as they tend to be harder to be scheduled back to the timetable. Furthermore, a more aggressive search approach, i.e., with more lessons being unscheduled, is adopted by extractVictims as the problem solving time is running out. The idea is to diversify the search so as to jump out of local optima that are otherwise unable to be surmounted.

After the selected lessons are unscheduled, the improve procedure calls a procedure called solve to try to resolve the timetabling problem. The implementation of the solve procedure is similar to that of the initialization algorithm except that it makes use of additional local search operators which supports sideway (instead of hill-climbing only) movement across the search space when a dead-end is met. Furthermore, it allows a case-specific relaxation of preferred timetabling requirement should the local search be unable to resolve a dead-end. Note that all these do not guarantee that the solve procedure be able to return a solution better than the recorded best solution due to the heuristic nature of the scheduling algorithm. The process of unschedule-and-schedule-lessons will be repeated a number of times. If there exist any unscheduled lessons, preferred timetabling requirements will be relaxed one-by-one in accordance with the user-defined relaxation order. If the generated (partial) solution is no better than the best solution recorded, the best solution will be copied as the current solution for the next iteration of the improvement phase. Note that due to the changes in the fail-counts of lessons caused by the recently applied local search operators, a different sequence of actions is likely to be chosen to work on the current solution in the new iteration.

# 4    Experiments

## 4.1    Experimental Setup

The problem instances for experimentation were obtained from two primary schools and one secondary school. The percentage of timetable completion, i.e., the total number of timeslots occupied by scheduled lessons divided by total number of timeslots in the timetable to be filled up, and the solution time required are used to evaluate the effectiveness of scheduling algorithm. @PT was run on each of the three problem instances five times and the best, worst and mean results were collected for analysis. In all the experiments, @PT was enforced to terminate after running on a 700MHz Pentium® III processor with 256 megabytes of memory for eight minutes. Currently @PT is implemented in Java 2.

## 4.2    Problem Instances

Table 1 gives some basic data reflecting the structures and sizes of the three problem instances. For ease of reference, the instances are named LCS, HPS and WWM respectively. HPS and WWM were obtained from two primary schools whereas LCS was obtained from a secondary school.

The lessons mentioned in Table 1 include single-period and multi-period lessons. Some of them are special lessons. A *special lesson* is a lesson that has to be scheduled with at least one other special lesson to the same timeslot. Examples of special lesson are lessons co-taught by multiple teachers (at the same venue), and split-class or split-subject lessons (of the same or different subjects) that require multiple teachers to teach at different venues.

**Table 1.** Structures and sizes of the problem instances

|  | LCS | HPS | WWM |
|---|---|---|---|
| Timetable structure | 7 days 8-9 periods/day | 6 days 7 periods/day | 5 days 5 periods/day |
| No. of classes | 28 | 30 | 24 |
| No. of teachers | 51 | 47 | 35 |
| No. of rooms | 41 | 36 | 30 |
| No. of lessons | 1,324 | 1,070 | 600 |
| No. of types of constraints that @PT is allowed to relax in auto-generation | 3 | 3 | 0 |

Although there exist dozens of timetabling requirements in the problem instances, only three of them are allowed to be relaxed in LCS and HPS. For both problems, during requirement relaxation stage, soft break relaxation is enabled (i.e., a multi-period lesson for selected subjects may be scheduled across a recess) and classes are allowed to have two single-period lessons of any subject in any single day (i.e., upon relaxation, a class may take either one multi-period lesson or up to two single-period lessons of the same subject in a day). The relaxation also allows split of any double-period lessons into two single-period lessons for LSC, and the "removal" of the mutually exclusive subject group for HPS. For WWM, no requirement relaxation is allowed. Although some other timetabling requirements may be relaxable too, timetablers typically do not allow automatic relaxation on certain relaxable timetabling requirements in practice as they want to have a tighter control on those requirements relaxation via manual tuning. To respect the schools' requests, no timetabling requirements other than those mentioned above were relaxed in our first set of experiments.

Table 2 displays the mean utilization rates of classes, teachers and rooms for each problem. The *utilization rate* of a resource is defined as the number of timeslots occupied by those lessons that require the resource divided by the number of available timeslots for that resource. As we understand, those utilization rates given in Table 2 are higher than the corresponding rates in many other countries. The table reflects some typical features of the STPs in Hong Kong schools. First, the class utilization is typically 100%, i.e., classes have no free period. Second, both teacher and room utilization are high and these make timetabling difficult.

**Table 2.** Resource utilization of the problem instances

| Utilization (mean) | LCS | HPS | WWM |
|---|---|---|---|
| Class | 100% | 100% | 100% |
| Teacher | 87% | 86% | 87% |
| Room | 77% | 77% | 78% |

In general, high schools tend to have more special classrooms such as laboratories which are not suitable for general teaching. Thus, the effective room utilization in schools that include a substantial number of technical subjects in their curriculum (like LCS) is in fact much higher than the apparent figures. Furthermore, some school timetabling requirements may reduce the number of feasible timeslots for a teaching venue. For example, some schools allow no physical education lesson be held on playground when a music lesson is held in the hall if the hall is next to the playground. When those factors are considered, the effective room utilization rate of Hong Kong schools often exceeds 90%.

## 4.3    Results Analysis

The mean, best and worst performance of @PT for solving each problem instance in terms of percentage of timetable completion and solution time over the five test runs are shown in Table 3. From the table, we can see that @PT is robust as its performance differences between the best and worst cases are small.

**Table 3.** The performance of @PT on the test instances (over 5 test runs)

|       | Percentage of timetable completion | | | Run time (rounded to the nearest second) | | |
|-------|-------|-------|-------|-------|-------|-------|
|       | LCS   | HPS   | WWM   | LCS   | HPS   | WWM   |
| Mean  | 99.90 | 99.96 | 99.83 | 417   | 264   | 321   |
| Best  | 100   | 100   | 100   | 275   | 188   | 78    |
| Worst | 99.75 | 99.82 | 99.67 | 480   | 480   | 480   |

On average, no more than two periods of lessons were left unscheduled in the test runs. The average numbers of occasions that a requirement was relaxed for LSC and HPS are 20 and 30 respectively. Note that @PT is equipped with interactive tuning module that provides decision support facilities to help users schedule any lessons remained unscheduled after auto-generation.

**Table 4.** Number of times that @PT successfully solved the test instances within 8 minutes (over 5 test runs)

| No. of times that a problem was totally solved | | |
|-------|-------|-------|
| LCS   | HPS   | WWM   |
| 3     | 4     | 2     |

Table 4 displays the number of cases out of the five test runs that @PT successfully scheduled all lessons for each problem instance within eight minutes. Although @PT was only able to generate complete timetables in 9 out of 15 runs, the success rate is expected to go up if more computational time is given. Currently the end-users opt to have a tight control over most of the timetabling requirement relaxation and prefer to deal with any remaining lessons using @PT's interactive tuning facility. Another experiment was conducted by relaxing a few more timetabling requirements in the auto-generation phase. Every test instance was solved in each of the five test runs in the experiment. The mean run times for tackling LCS, HPS and WWM are 57.8, 105 and 10.4 respectively as shown in Table 5.

**Table 5.** The performance of @PT on the test instances with additional timetabling requirements relaxed (over 5 test runs)

| | Percentage of timetable completion | | | Run time (rounded to the nearest second) | | |
| | LCS | HPS | WWM | LCS | HPS | WWM |
| --- | --- | --- | --- | --- | --- | --- |
| Mean | 100 | 100 | 100 | 58 | 105 | 10 |
| Best | 100 | 100 | 100 | 53 | 87 | 4 |
| Worst | 100 | 100 | 100 | 63 | 125 | 14 |

The numbers of occasions that a timetabling requirement was relaxed for the "relaxed" version of LCS, HPS and WWM are only 8, 15 and 10 respectively on average. The numbers for LCS and HPS are even smaller than the corresponding numbers in the original version. It is due to the fact that some requirements such as teacher's daily load limit, which were only allowed to be relaxed in the "relaxed" problem version in auto-generation mode, have a much higher impact to timetable completion than those relaxable requirements specified in the original version.

According to the end-users, a timetabling group consisting of two to three teachers typically takes five or more days to construct a timetable for each test instance. When the group tackles the instances with a decision support timetabling software called TESS [11], it needs two to three days to achieve a solution of similar quality for each test instance. TESS adopts a heuristic approach to put lessons to a timetable automatically in the *conflict free* stage until no unscheduled lessons can be placed to the partial filled timetable without displacing any already scheduled lessons. It tries to finish the timetabling task by interleaving between the *conflict avoidance* stage and *conflict resolution* stage during which decision tools and heuristic procedures are provided to help a timetabler to resolve conflicts.

# 5    Conclusion

Despite the progress in school timetabling research over the last few decades, most schools in Hong Kong still construct their timetables manually because they found existing timetabling software packages incapable of representing their timetabling requirements or generating any feasible solutions. For example, TESS does not support the timetabling requirement that demands lessons to be scheduled to non-successive days. @PT is designed to tackle those problems. By incorporating a range of sophisticated techniques in its implementation, @PT has successively improves both efficiency and effectiveness of the timetabling process. In fact there is a growing interest in using hybrid techniques for tackling timetabling problems in recent years [13, 2, 9].

In addition to the uses of hybrid intelligent techniques in its implementation, a number of novel techniques are adopted in this research. These include the enhanced K-value heuristic, COTS heuristic and double-billiard movement, *etc.* Despite the techniques were derived for STP, they can be easily adapted for tackling other timetabling problems. In fact, we have been successfully applied those heuristics to tackle the course timetabling problem of a community college in Hong Kong recently.

With the aid of @PT, the time required for timetable scheduling has been significantly reduced from days, if not weeks, to minutes. Its impressive performance has attracted the Education and Manpower Bureau of the Hong Kong to adopt the scheduling engine of @PT in the timetabling module of WebSAMS which is a web based school administration and management system. At the time of preparing this manuscript, the system development of WebSAMS is in the stage of user-acceptance testing. According to the project schedule, the system will be delivered to more than 1,100 schools, virtually all government funded schools in Hong Kong by August 2004.

# References

1.  Burke, E. & Erben, W. (Eds.) 2001. *Practice and Theory of Automated Timetabling III.* Lecture Notes in Computer Science 2079, Springer.
2.  David, P. 1997. A constraint-based approach for examination timetabling using local repair techniques. In: Burke, E., Ross, P. (Eds.), *Practice and Theory of Automated Timetabling II*, Lecture Notes in Computer Science, vol. 1408. Springer, 169–186.
3.  Gotlieb, C.C. 1963. The construction of class-teacher time-tables. In Popplewell C.M. (ed.): *Proceedings of IFIP Congress 62*, Amsterdam, North-Holland, 73–77.
4.  Haralick, R.M. & Elliott, G.L. 1980. Increasing tree search efficiency for constraint satisfaction problems. *Artificial Intelligence*, **14**: 263–313.
5.  Kaneko, K., Yoshikawa, M. & Nakakuki, Y. 1999. Improving a heuristic repair method for large-scale school timetabling problems. In Joxan Jaffar (Ed.): *Proceedings of the 5th International Conference Principles and Practice of Constraint Programming*. Lecture Notes in Computer Science 1713, Springer, 275–288.
6.  Kwan, A.C.M. & Chung, K.C.K. 2002. A contention-oriented timeslot selection heuristic for school timetabling. In Bramer, M., Preece, A. & Coenen, F. (Eds.): *Proceedings of the 22nd SGAI International Conference on Knowledge Based Systems and Applied Artificial Intelligence*, Springer, 381–394.
7.  Kwan, A.C.M., Chung, K.C.K. & Yip K. K. K. 2002. Data Modeling for School Timetabling - A Case Study. In Torrellas, G.A.S. & Uskov, V. (Eds.): *Proceedings of the 5th IASTED International Multi-Conference on Computers and Advanced Technology in Education*, ACTA Press, 211–215.
8.  Kwan, A.C.M. & Chan, H.L. 1999. Efficient lesson selection heuristic for high school timetabling. In Hamza, M.H. (Ed.): *Proceedings of the IASTED International Conference Artificial Intelligence and Soft Computing*, ACTA Press, 323–327.
9.  Merlot, L., Boland, N., Hughes, B. & Stuckey P.J. 2003. A hybrid algorithm for the examination timetabling problem. In: *Proceedings of PATAT2002*, LNCS, page to appear. Springer.
10. Minton, S., Johnston, M.D., Philips, A.B. & Laird, P. 1992. Minimizing conflicts: a heuristic repair method for constraint satisfaction and scheduling problems. *Artificial Intelligence*, **58**: 161–205.

11. Ng, W-Y. 1997. TESS: an interactive support system for school timetabling. In Fung, A.C.W. (Ed.): *Information Technology in Education Management for the Schools of the Future*, Chapman and Hall, 131–137.
12. Sadeh, N. 1991. *Lookahead techniques for micro-opportunistic job-shop scheduling*. PhD thesis, Carnegie-Mellon University. CMU-CS-91-102.
13. Schaerf, A. 1997. Combining local search and look-ahead for scheduling and constraint satisfaction problems. In: *Proceedings of the International Joint Conference on Artificial Intelligence*, 1254–1259.
14. Schaerf, A. 1999. A survey of automated timetabling. *Artificial Intelligence Review*, 13 (2): 87–127.
15. Schmidt, G. & Strohlein, T. 1979. Timetabling construction – an annotated bibliography. *The Computer Journal*, 23(4): 307–316.
16. Yoshikawa, M., Kaneko, K., Nomura, Y. & Watanabe, M. 1994. A constraint-based approach to high-school timetabling problems: a case study. In: *Proceedings of the 12th National Conference on Artificial Intelligence*, 1111–1116.

# Representing Audio Data by FS-Trees and Adaptable TV-Trees

Alicja A. Wieczorkowska[1], Zbigniew W. Raś[2,3], and Li-Shiang Tsay[2]

[1] Polish-Japanese Institute of Information Technology, Koszykowa 86,
02-008 Warsaw, Poland
[2] University of North Carolina, Department of Computer Science,
Charlotte, N.C. 28223, USA
[3] Polish Academy of Sciences, Institute of Computer Science,
Ordona 21, 01-237 Warsaw, Poland
{awieczor,ras,ltsay}@uncc.edu

**Abstract.** An automatic content extraction from multimedia files based both on manual and automatic indexing is extensively explored. However, in the domain of musical data, an automatic content description of musical sounds has not been broadly investigated yet and still needs an intensive research. In this paper, spectro-temporal sound representation is used for the purpose of automatic musical instrument recognition. Assuming that musical instruments can be learned in terms of a group of features and also based on them either automatic or manual indexing of an audio file is done, Frame Segment Trees (FS-trees) can be used to identify segments of an audio marked by the same indexes. Telescopic vector trees (TV-trees) are known from their applications in text processing and recently in data clustering algorithms. In this paper, we use them jointly with FS-trees to construct a new Query Answering System (QAS) for audio data. Audio segments are returned by QAS as answers to user queries. Heuristic strategy to build adaptable TV-trees is proposed.

## 1  Introduction

Indexing and searching multimedia data is a non-trivial task, which requires signal analysis and processing. Standardization of content labeling of multimedia data is addressed by Moving Picture Experts Group in MPEG-7 standard, named Multimedia Content Description Interface [11]. This standard provides numerous descriptors for labeling audio and visual data. However, algorithms for searching through the labeled data are behind the scope of MPEG-7, since their standardization is not required, thus leaving space for further development. Therefore, research on efficient searching through audio data represented by descriptors is still desirable. Additionally, the use of new descriptors may be necessary for more efficient searching or more detailed labeling of multimedia data. This is why we decided to explore a new data structure based on TV-trees jointly with FS-trees for representation of multi-dimensional audio data, in order to allow efficient searching of specific audio segments (fulfilling not only index

N. Zhong et al. (Eds.): ISMIS 2003, LNAI 2871, pp. 135–142, 2003.

type properties, but also some similarity criteria). We focus our attention on musical instrument sounds.

## 2   Descriptors of Musical Audio Data

In the research published so far, various methods for musical data parameterization have been used. The parameters (descriptors) can be based on time domain features, spectrum, or/and other analyses. Time-domain parameters of musical instrument sounds may describe the duration of particular phases of the sound (the attack, quasi-steady state and ending transient) or properties of sound wave, like number of zero-crossings in time unit etc. [14]. Also, features of sound envelope can be used as descriptors [21].

Descriptive features of sound can also be extracted from spectral analysis. These features may describe contents of the selected groups of harmonics in spectrum, like even/odd harmonics, or lower/middle/higher harmonics [14], [19]. Also fundamental frequency and its variance (vibrato) are used as descriptors [16], [24]. Other parameters describe statistical properties of spectrum, like average amplitude and frequency deviations, average spectrum, standard deviation, auto- and cross-correlation functions [1], [5]. Such properties of spectrum as higher order moments, such as skewness and kurtosis, as well as brightness and spectral irregularity, are also used for musical sound parameterization [8], [23].

Sound descriptors can be also derived from other analyzes. Results published so far are based on constant-Q coefficients [4], [12], auditory model [16], cepstral and mel-cepstrum coefficients and derivatives [2], [4], [7], multidimensional scaling analysis trajectories [12], wavelets [13], [23], Bark scale bands [7] and other [9], [25]. A set of descriptors for audio content description is also provided in MPEG-7 standard [11]; these descriptors are aimed to aid musical instrument timbre description, audio signature, sound description etc. Apart from higher-level descriptors, the audio framework in MPEG-7 includes 17 temporal and spectral low-level descriptors, divided into the following groups [15]:

- basic: instantaneous waveform and power values,
- basic spectral: log-frequency power spectrum envelopes, spectral centroid, spectrum spread, and spectrum flatness,
- signal parameters: fundamental frequency and harmonicity of signal,
- timbral temporal: log attack time and temporal centroid,
- timbral spectral: spectral centroid, harmonic spectral centroid, and harmonic spectral deviation, harmonic spectral spread, harmonic spectral variation,
- spectral basis representations: spectrum basis and spectrum projection.

These features can be used to describe a segment with a summary value or with a series of sampled values that apply to the entire segment, with exception of the timbral temporal group, applied to segments as a whole only.

Sound description schemes presented above focus on digital and compact sound representation for classification purposes. Assuming feature vector is given, our aim is to propose a new searching method through audio data based on tree-like structures.

In our research, we are dealing with recordings containing singular sounds of musical instruments. We apply descriptors which have been already used in experiments and which gave good results, i.e. up to 70% of correct classification, which is comparable with results of similar worldwide research [9], [21]. These descriptors characterize temporal and spectral features of short sound frames and sound as a whole. Temporal group includes the following descriptors [21]:

- *Length*: Signal length,
- *Attack*, *Steady* and *Decay*: Relative length of the attack, i.e. the onset portion of sound (till reaching 75% of maximal amplitude), quasi-steady state (after the end of attack, till the final fall under 75% of maximal amplitude) and decay time (the rest of the signal), respectively,
- *Maximum*: Moment of reaching maximal amplitude,
- *Env1*, ..., *Env7*: Envelope parameters: average values of envelope of sound amplitude in consequent 7 intervals of equal width,
- *EnvFill*: Area of envelope,
- *Cluster*: Number of cluster (obtained through clusterization of envelope vectors for the whole data set into 6 clusters) closest to the analyzed sound, with respect to Euclidean metric.

Spectral descriptors include [23]:

- *Frequency*: Fundamental frequency,
- *Br* and *Ir*: Brightness *Br* and irregularity *Ir* of spectrum, defined as

$$Br = \frac{\sum_{n=1}^{N} n A_n}{\sum_{n=1}^{N} A_n} \quad Ir = \log\left(20 \sum_{k=2}^{N-1} \left| \log \frac{A_k}{\sqrt[3]{A_{k-1} A_k A_{k+1}}} \right| \right) \tag{1}$$

where $A_n$ - amplitude of $n^{th}$ harmonic, $N$ - number of available harmonics,
- *Ev* and *Odd*: Contents of even *Ev* and odd *Od* harmonics in spectrum:

$$Ev = \sqrt{\frac{\sum_{k=1}^{M} A_{2k}^2}{\sum_{n=1}^{N} A_n^2}} \quad Od = \sqrt{\frac{\sum_{k=2}^{L} A_{2k-1}^2}{\sum_{n=1}^{N} A_n^2}} \tag{2}$$

where $M = \lfloor N/2 \rfloor$ and $L = \lfloor N/2 + 1 \rfloor$,
- *Tristimulus*1, 2, 3: Tristimulus [19] parameters given by:

$$Tr_1 = \frac{A_1^2}{\sum_{n=1}^{N} A_n^2} \quad Tr_2 = \frac{\sum_{n=2,3,4} A_n^2}{\sum_{n=1}^{N} A_n^2} \quad Tr_3 = \frac{\sum_{n=5}^{N} A_n^2}{\sum_{n=1}^{N} A_n^2} \tag{3}$$

All these parameters were calculated for the whole sounds of musical instruments of definite pitch. Additionally, spectral parameters and maximal amplitude were calculated for consequent short frames, covering this sound. The length of analyzing frame was equal four times the sound period. Most common length of analyzing frame is about 20–30 ms [2], [4], [5], [7], whereas in our case it is 2–125 ms. Shorter frames allow observation of fast changes, especially for pizzicato sounds and during transients; longer frames are taken in case of the lowest sounds. Calculation of sound descriptors using sliding window allows observation of changes of parameters values in time. The obtained attribute values produce time series, which are next analyzed to discover patterns characterizing sound evolution in time, specific for some groups of sounds [21]. This way, new descriptors of musical sounds are generated.

Observations of parameters using sliding window is also a step towards experiments with ordinary, unstructured recordings, which require segmentation through discovering changes in sound characteristics.

## 3   Classification of Data

The descriptors presented in the previous section were applied to recordings of consequent singular sounds of musical instruments of definite pitch, taken from MUMS stereo recordings [18]. These CD's are widely used in musical instrument sound research [7], [8], [12], [16], [24], so they can be considered as a standard. The parameterized 667 sounds represent 11 instruments, played using various articulation techniques. The data objects are grouped into the following 19 classes, with respect to both instrument and articulation [24]: violin vibrato, violin pizzicato, viola vibrato, viola pizzicato, cello vibrato, cello pizzicato, double bass vibrato, double bass vibrato, double bass pizzicato, flute, oboe, b-flat clarinet, trumpet, trumpet muted, trombone, trombone muted, French horn, French horn muted, and tuba. These objects are stored in a decision table. Formally, the decision table is defined as $\mathbf{A} = (U, A \cup \{d\})$, where each attribute $a \in A \cup \{d\}$ is identified with a function $a : U \rightarrow V_a$ from the universe of objects $U$ into the set $V_a$ of all possible values of $a$. Values $v_d \in V_d$ correspond to mutually disjoint decision classes of objects. In our case, each element $u \in U$ corresponds to a sound sample, elements $a \in A$ are numeric features corresponding to sound descriptors and the decision attribute $d \notin A$ labels particular object (sound) with integer code representing the instrument.

The data placed in decision table can be used for generalization, i.e. prediction of decision class based on information provided by some attributes of new objects. This is achieved through construction of classifiers, such as decision trees, rule-based classifiers, $k$-nearest neighbor classifiers, neural nets, etc. The issue of musical instrument sound recognition has been brought up in several research studies, applying various methods [10], [21]. The most common one is $k$-nearest neighbor algorithm, applied in [7], [8], [12], [16]. Brown in her research [4] applied clustering and Bayes decision rules, using $k$-means algorithm to calculate clusters, and forming Gaussian probability density functions from the mean and variance of each of the clusters. Martin and Kim (1998) used maximum a posteriori classifiers, based on Gaussian models obtained through Fisher multiple-discriminant analysis. Gaussian classifier was also used by Eronen and Klapuri (2000). Other applied methods include binary trees, used in [23], hidden Markov models, reported in [2], and rough set approach [24].

## 4    Audio Content Representation Using FS-Trees and Adaptable TV-Trees

Rules describing different sounds in terms of features from $A$ can be extracted from the table $\mathbf{A} = (U, A \cup \{d\})$. When applied to a new audio signal they can be considered as a tool for its automatic indexing. For audio files containing only sounds of singular instruments this tool has been already successful [23] due to the high confidence of rules describing singular sounds. Now, assuming that indexing of audio files both automatic and manual is done, FS-trees [22] can be used for a compact content description representation of audio data and also for efficient processing of audio queries based on this indexing. But, users may want to submit additional queries which are audio signals represented as frames. Query Answering System (QAS), based not only on FS-trees but also on trees similar to binary Telescopic Vector trees (TV-trees) [22], [25] is used by us to search for frames similar to a frame representing user's query.

Now, we outline the strategy for construction our TV-trees. Each audio signal is divided into frames of length four times the fundamental period of the sound. Each frame is represented as a vector consisting of $K$ acoustic descriptors. So, any collection of audio signals can be seen as a set of $K$-dimensional vectors. We represent this set as $(K \times N)$-matrix where $N$ is the number of frames in all audio signals in the database. If needed, we reduce $K$ to a smaller number using Singular Value Decomposition method [22]. The notion of a distance between two vectors, used by us, is a standard one. These vectors are seen as points in $K$-dimensional space. They are partitioned into disjoint clusters in a such way that points similar with respect to maximal number of coordinates are kept in each cluster. These coordinates are called active dimensions. To define $a$ as an active dimension in a cluster, we require that the span of values of $a$ in that cluster has to be below some threshold value. For example, if $\{1, \ldots, 100\}$ is the domain of an attribute and its corresponding threshold value is $1/20$, then this attribute is active in a cluster of $N$ vectors if the distance between values of this attribute for any 2 vectors in that cluster is not greater than 5. Assume now that our goal is to represent the set of $N$ points as a TV-tree of order 2, which means that only 2 clusters per node can be constructed. So, we divide the set of $N$ points into 2 clusters maximizing the total number of active dimensions in both clusters. For each cluster we repeat the same procedure, again maximizing the total number of active dimensions in the corresponding sub-clusters. For instance, if $\{[5, 3, 20, 1, 5], [0, 0, 18, 41, 4], [0, 0, 19, 39, 5], [11, 10, 2, 0, 5]\}$ is the initial cluster, then the following 2 sub-clusters are generated: $\{[0, 0, 18, 41, 4], [0, 0, 19, 39, 5]\}$, $\{[5, 3, 20, 1, 5], [11, 10, 2, 0, 5]\}$. The initial cluster has only the last dimension active. After split, the first sub-cluster has 5 dimensions active and second one has the last 2 dimensions active. We continue this procedure till all sub-clusters are relatively dense (all points are close to each other with respect to all dimensions). For instance, in the example above, the first sub-cluster is dense. The underlying structure for this method is a binary tree with nodes storing information about the center (c) of a corresponding cluster, the smallest radius (r) of a sphere containing this cluster, and its list of active dimensions [25].

Our heuristic procedure to construct a binary TV-tree (part of QAS) for a collection of audio signals is similar to the one used in Rosetta or See5 system for discretizing numerical attributes [20], [17]. For $m$-element domain of an attribute, $m - 1$ splitting points are considered (alternatively, the splitting points can be placed between consecutive dense groups of values of an attribute). Saying more precisely, if $v_1$, $v_2$ are neighboring values of the attribute $a$, then an audio signal with value of $a$ less than or equal to $[v_1 + v_2]/2$ is placed in the left subtree and all other audio signals are placed in the right subtree. When this is done, the total number of active dimensions in both left and right subtree is checked. We repeat this step for each attribute and for its all splitting points mentioned above. A split which gives the maximal number of active dimensions, for both left and right sub-tree, is the winning split and it is used to build two children of the current node. The above procedure is recursively repeated at two children nodes just created.

Now, let us assume that QAS is based both on a TV-tree and an FS-tree and user submitting an audio query to QAS is looking for audio files satisfying certain properties corresponding to indexes used in FS-trees. User's audio query contains also a sub-query represented in QAS as a vector similar to vectors stored in a TV-tree. For this type of queries, FS-tree is searched first for audio files satisfying desired properties (index-based search). Next, the TV-tree is searched to identify which files retrieved from FS-tree also satisfy the additional sub-query. Our initial results with respect to precision and recall from testing QAS are very encouraging.

## 5   Construction of Adaptable TV-Trees

Let us assume that audio data are stored in a relational table, where attributes are either features computed from the raw data given by users or indexes provided by experts. By an adaptable TV-tree, we mean a TV-tree built from a relational table, where each splitting attribute is chosen not only on the basis of how to maximize the total number of active features in children nodes it generates, but also on the basis which attributes are used most frequently in user queries. Such attributes are called *popular*. The idea here is to make popular attributes active as soon as we can so they are used by QAS in searching its TV-tree at the very beginning of a query answering process.

Assume that $a_1$, $a_2$, $a_3$,...,$a_K$ is an ordered set (with respect popularity) of all acoustic descriptors in the relational table (the most popular descriptors are listed first). Let $k_i$ is a frequency of occurrence of a descriptor $a_i$ in vectors representing audio queries submitted to QAS. In order to build an adaptable TV-tree we consider a function from $\{a_1, a_2, a_3, ..., a_K\}$ into $\{1, 2, 3, ..., K\}$, defined as $f(a_i) = (K - i + 1)$. To evaluate a relational table from the point of view of a descriptor $a_i$, we multiply $1/f(a_i)$ by the number of cuts needed in $Dom(a_i)$ to make $a_i$ active. Let's denote the resulting number by $h(a_i)$. Descriptor with a cut making $h(a_i)$ the smallest is chosen as the new node of adaptable TV-tree. This tree is called adaptable since the construction of its nodes is driven by a function $h(a_i)$, which may change in time as new queries are submitted to QAS. For simplicity reason only one of the easiest versions of the function $f(a_i)$ was presented here, but more complex definitions of $f(a_i)$ have been tested as well.

## 6   Conclusion

Automatic indexing of multimedia databases is of great importance, and ISO/IEC decided to provide MPEG-7 standard for multimedia content description. However, this standard does not comprise the extraction of descriptors (nor search algorithms). Therefore, there is a need to elaborate extraction of sound descriptors that would be attached to sound files.

This paper reviews some audio descriptors based on various kinds of sound analysis. We use them, for instance, to learn definitions of musical instruments (to construct a new audio descriptor). This new audio descriptor is only an example of a descriptor useful for an automatic indexing of musical files. Finally, we use all our audio descriptors to construct QAS based on FS-tree and adaptable TV-tree to allow efficient access to audio data. The initial results related to precision and recall of our QAS are good.

The main goal of this paper is to find a new data representation suitable for handling audio queries based not only on indexes, but also containing semantic type of information, which cannot be expressed in index-type languages.

**Acknowledgements.** This research was sponsored by the Research Center of PJIIT, supported by the Polish National Committee for Scientific Research (KBN).

## References

1. Ando, S., Yamaguchi, K.:  Statistical Study of Spectral Parameters in Musical Instrument Tones. *J. Acoust. Soc. of America* 94(1) (1993) 37–45
2. Batlle, E., Cano, P.: Automatic Segmentation for Music Classification using Competitive Hidden Markov Models. *Int. Sym. Mus. Inf. Retr.* Plymouth, MA (2000)
3. Beauchamp, J. W., Maher, R., Brown, R.    Detection of Musical Pitch from Recorded Solo Performances. 94th AES Convention, preprint 3541, Berlin (1993)
4. Brown, J.: Computer identification of musical instruments using pattern recognition with cepstral coefficients as features. *J.Acoust.Soc.Am.* 105 (1999) 1933–1941

5. Brown, J., Houix, O., McAdams, S.: Feature dependence in the automatic identification of musical woodwind instruments. *J. Acoust. Soc. Am.* 109 (2001) 1064–1072
6. Cook, P. R., Morrill, D., Smith, J. O.: An Automatic Pitch Detection and MIDI Control System for Brass Instruments. Invited for special session on Automatic Pitch Detection, Acoustical Society of America, New Orleans (1992)
7. Eronen, A., Klapuri, A.: Musical Instrument Recognition Using Cepstral Coefficients and Temporal Features. *Proc. IEEE International Conference on Acoustics, Speech and Signal Processing ICASSP 2000* Plymouth, MA. (2000) 753–756
8. Fujinaga, I., McMillan, K.: Realtime recognition of orchestral instruments. *Proceedings of the International Computer Music Conference* (2000) 141–143
9. Herrera, P., Amatriain, X., Batlle, E., Serra X.: Towards instrument segmentation for music content description: a critical review of instrument classification techniques. In *Proc.Int.Sym.Music Inf.Retr. (ISMIR 2000)*, Plymouth, MA (2000)
10. Herrera, P., Peeters, G., Dubnov, S.: Automatic Classification of Musical Instrument Sounds *Journal of New Music Research* 32(1) (2003)
11. ISO/IEC JTC1/SC29/WG11: MPEG-7 Overview (2002)
12. Kaminskyj, I.: Multi-feature Musical Instrument Classifier. *MikroPolyphonie* 6 (2000) (online journal at http://farben.latrobe.edu.au/)
13. Kostek, B. and Czyzewski, A.: Representing Musical Instrument Sounds for Their Automatic Classification. *J. Audio Eng. Soc.* 49(9) (2001) 768–785
14. Kostek, B., Wieczorkowska, A.: Parametric Representation of Musical Sounds. *Arch. Acoustics* 22(1), Inst. Fund. Tech. Research, Warsaw, Poland (1997) 3–26
15. Lindsay, A. T., Herre, J.: MPEG-7 and MPEG-7 Audio – An Overview. *J. Audio Eng. Soc.* 49(7/8) (2001) 589–594
16. Martin, K., Kim, Y.: 2pMU9. Musical instrument identification: A pattern-recognition approach. 136-th meeting Acoustical Soc. America, Norfolk, VA (1998)
17. Øhrn, A., Komorowski, J., Skowron, A., Synak, P. The design and implementation of a knowledge discovery toolkit based on rough sets: The ROSETTA system. In: Polkowski, L., Skowron, A. (Eds.), *Rough Sets in Knowledge Discovery 1: Methodology and Applications*, number 18 in Studies in Fuzziness and Soft Computing, chapter 19, Physica-Verlag, Heidelberg, Germany (1998) 376 399
18. Opolko, F., Wapnick, J.: MUMS – McGill University Master Samples. CD's (1987)
19. Pollard, H. F., Jansson, E. V.: A Tristimulus Method for the Specification of Musical Timbre. *Acustica* 51 (1982) 162–171
20. Quinlan, J. R.: *C4.5: Programs for Machine Learning*, Morgan Kaufmann, San Mateo, California (1993)
21. Ślęzak, D., Synak, P., Wieczorkowska, A., Wróblewski, J.: KDD-based approach to musical instrument sound recognition. In: Hacid, M.-S., Ras, Z., Zighed, D., Kodratoff, Y. (Eds.), *Found. Intel. Syst.* LNCS/LNAI 2366, Springer (2002) 29–37
22. Subrahmanian, V. S.: *Multimedia Database Systems*. Morgan Kaufmann Publishers, San Francisco, CA (1998)
23. Wieczorkowska, A. A.: The recognition efficiency of musical instrument sounds depending on parameterization and type of a classifier. PhD thesis (in Polish), Technical University of Gdansk, Poland (1999)
24. Wieczorkowska, A.: Rough Sets as a Tool for Audio Signal Classification. In: Ras, Z. W., Skowron, A. (Eds.), *Foundations of Intelligent Systems* (pp. 367–375). LNCS/LNAI 1609, Springer (1999)
25. Wieczorkowska, A. A., Raś, Z. W. Audio Content Description in Sound Databases. In: Zhong, N., Yao, Y., Liu, J., Ohsuga, S. (Eds.), *Web Intelligence: Research and Development* LNCS/LNAI 2198, Springer (2001) 175–183

# A Framework of Rough Sets Based Rule Generation in Non-deterministic Information Systems

Hiroshi Sakai

Department of Computer Engineering,
Kyushu Institute of Technology,
Tobata, Kitakyushu 804, Japan
sakai@comp.kyutech.ac.jp

**Abstract.** Rule generation in non-deterministic information systems, which follows rough sets based rule generation in deterministic information systems, is studied. For possible implications in non-deterministic information systems, six kinds of classes are newly introduced, and certain rules are defined by possible implications belonging to a class. Similarly, possible rules are defined by possible implications belonging to other three kinds of classes. Furthermore, the lower and upper approximations of criteria, i.e., *support*, *accuracy* and *coverage* of rules, are introduced. Finally a tool, which extracts minimal certain and minimal possible rules based on a total order over attributes, has been implemented.

## 1 Introduction

Rough set theory is seen as a mathematical foundation of soft computing. This theory usually handles tables with deterministic information, which we call *Deterministic Information Systems* (*DISs*). Many applications of this theory to rule generation, machine learning and knowledge discovery have been presented [1,2,3,4].

*Non-deterministic Information Systems* (*NISs*) and *Incomplete Information Systems* have been proposed for handling information incompleteness in *DISs*, like null values, unknown values, missing values and etc. In this extension, the concept of modality is introduced into *NISs*, and an axiomatization of logic in *NISs* has been studied [5,6,7,8]. Most of work related to *NISs* is research of logic with modal operators [ ] and <>, and focuses on valid formulas.

Very few work deals with algorithms for handling *NISs* on computers. In [7,8], Lipski showed a question-answering system besides an axiomatization of logic. In [9,10], Grzymala-Busse surveyed the unknown attribute values, and studied the learning from examples with unknown attribute values. In [11,12], Kryszkiewicz discussed rules in incomplete information systems. These are the most important work for handling incomplete information on computers.

N. Zhong et al. (Eds.): ISMIS 2003, LNAI 2871, pp. 143–151, 2003.

We follow such previous work, and have already proposed rule generation by using *possible equivalence relations* [13,14]. Possible equivalence relations solve most of the problems in rule generation. In this paper, we also propose rule generation without using possible equivalence relations. This new method is more efficient than the method by using possible equivalence relations, because manipulations of possible equivalence relations are not necessary. However in this case, we can not apply lots of effective algorithms, like an algorithm for checking data dependency in $NISs$ [15], based on possible equivalence relations.

In the subsequent sections, definitions related to $DISs$ are surveyed. Then, *possible implications* are introduced into $NISs$. Possible implications are divided into six kinds of classes, and *certain rules* are defined by possible implications belonging to a class. Similarly, *possible rules* are defined by possible implications belonging to other three kinds of classes. For certain and possible rules, we assign the lower and upper approximations of *support*, *accuracy* and *coverage*. These values are important criteria for characterizing rules. Because, it is possible to know the worst case and the best case of three values. Finally, we propose the problem of rule generation in $NISs$, and show a real execution by implemented programs.

## 2    Definitions in DISs

A *Deterministic Information System* $(DIS)$ is a quadruplet $(OB, AT, \{VAL_A|$ $A \in AT\}, f)$, where $OB$ is a finite set whose elements are called *objects*, $AT$ is a finite set whose elements are called *attributes*, $VAL_A$ is a finite set whose elements are called *attribute values* and $f$ is such a mapping that $f : OB \times AT \rightarrow$ $\cup_{A \in AT} VAL_A$ which is called a *classification function*. If $f(x, A)=f(y, A)$ for every $A \in ATR \subset AT$, we see there is a relation between $x$ and $y$ for $ATR$. This relation is an equivalence relation over $OB$. Let $[x]_{ATR}$ denote an equivalence class $\{y \in OB|f(y, A)=f(x, A)$ for every $A \in ATR\}$.

Let us consider two sets $CON \subset AT$ which we call *condition attributes* and $DEC \subset AT$ which we call *decision attributes*. An object $x \in OB$ is *consistent* (with any distinct object $y \in OB$ between $CON$ and $DEC$), if $f(x, A)=f(y, A)$ for every $A \in CON$ implies $f(x, A)=f(y, A)$ for every $A \in DEC$. For any $x \in OB$, let $imp(x, CON, DEC)$ denote a formula called *implication*: $\wedge_{A \in CON}[A, f(x, A)] \Rightarrow \wedge_{A \in DEC}[A, f(x, A)]$, where a formula $[A, f(x, A)]$ implies that $f(x, A)$ is the value of the attribute $A$. This is called a *descriptor* in [7,12].

## 3    Possible Implications in NISs

A *Non-deterministic Information System* $(NIS)$ is also a quadruplet $(OB, AT, \{VAL_A|A \in AT\}, g)$, where $g : OB \times AT \rightarrow P(\cup_{A \in AT} VAL_A)$ (a power set of $\cup_{A \in AT} VAL_A$). Every set $g(x, A)$ is interpreted as that there is an actual value in this set but this value is not known. Especially if the actual value is not known at all, $g(x, A)$ is equal to $VAL_A$. This is called *null value* interpretation.

**Definition 1.** Let us consider a $NIS=(OB, AT, \{VAL_A|A \in AT\}, g)$, a set $ATR \subset AT$ and a mapping $h : OB \times ATR \to \cup_{A \in ATR} VAL_A$ such that $h(x, A) \in g(x, A)$. We call a $DIS=(OB, ATR, \{VAL_A|A \in ATR\}, h)$ a *derived DIS* (*for ATR*) *from NIS*.

**Definition 2.** Let us consider a $NIS$ and a set $ATR=\{A_1, \cdots, A_n\} \subset AT$. For any $x \in OB$, let $PT(x, ATR)$ denote the Cartesian product $g(x, A_1) \times \cdots \times g(x, A_n)$. We call every element a *possible tuple* (*for ATR*) *of* $x$. For a possible tuple $\zeta=(\zeta_1, \cdots, \zeta_n) \in PT(x, ATR)$, let $[ATR, \zeta]$ denote a formula $\bigwedge_{1 \le i \le n}[A_i, \zeta_i]$.

**Definition 3.** For any $NIS$, let $CON$ be condition attributes and let $DEC$ be decision attributes. For any $x \in OB$, let $PI(x, CON, DEC)$ denote a set $\{[CON, \zeta] \Rightarrow [DEC, \eta]|\zeta \in PT(x, CON), \eta \in PT(x, DEC)\}$. We call an element of $PI(x, CON, DEC)$ a *possible implication* (*for CON and DEC*) *of* $x$.

**Example 1.** Let us consider $NIS_1$ in Table 1. There are about $10^{14}$ derived $DISs$ for all attributes. As for $CON=\{A, B\}$ and $DEC=\{C\}$, there are 1492992 ($=2^{11} \times 3^6$) derived $DISs$. Here, $PT(1, \{A, B\})=\{(3, 1), (3, 2), (3, 4)\}$, $PT(1, \{C\}) =\{(3)\}$ and $PI(1, \{A, B\}, \{C\})$ consists of three possible implications $[A, 3] \wedge [B, 1] \Rightarrow [C, 3]$, $[A, 3] \wedge [B, 2] \Rightarrow [C, 3]$ and $[A, 3] \wedge [B, 4] \Rightarrow [C, 3]$. Each possible implication appears in 497664($= 1492992/3$) derived $DISs$ for $\{A, B, C\}$.

**Definition 4.** Let us consider a $NIS$, condition attributes $CON$ and decision attributes $DEC$. For any $\tau \in PI(x, CON, DEC)$, let $DD(\tau, x, CON, DEC)$ denote a set $\{\varphi| \varphi$ is such a derived $DIS$ for $CON \cup DEC$ that an implication $imp(x, CON, DEC)$ in $\varphi$ is equal to $\tau\}$.

**Definition 5.** Let us consider a $NIS$, condition attributes $CON$ and decision attributes $DEC$. If $PI(x, CON, DEC)$ is a singleton set $\{\tau\}$, we say $\tau$ (from $x$) is *definite*. Otherwise we say $\tau$ (from $x$) is *indefinite*. If a set $\{\varphi \in DD(\tau, x, CON, DEC)| x$ is consistent in $\varphi\}$ is equal to $DD(\tau, x, CON, DEC)$, we say $\tau$ is *globally consistent* (*GC*). If this set is equal to $\emptyset$, we say $\tau$ is *globally inconsistent* (*GI*). Otherwise we say $\tau$ is *marginal* (*MA*). By combining two

**Table 1.** A Table of $NIS_1$

| OB | A | B | C | D | E | F |
|---|---|---|---|---|---|---|
| 1 | $\{3\}$ | $\{1, 2, 4\}$ | $\{3\}$ | $\{1, 2\}$ | $\{1, 2, 3\}$ | $\{1, 2\}$ |
| 2 | $\{1, 4\}$ | $\{1, 2, 3\}$ | $\{2\}$ | $\{2, 4\}$ | $\{2\}$ | $\{1, 2, 4\}$ |
| 3 | $\{2, 4\}$ | $\{1, 3\}$ | $\{1, 3\}$ | $\{2\}$ | $\{2\}$ | $\{1, 3, 4\}$ |
| 4 | $\{1\}$ | $\{1\}$ | $\{1, 2\}$ | $\{1, 2, 3\}$ | $\{1, 3\}$ | $\{1, 2, 4\}$ |
| 5 | $\{1\}$ | $\{1, 2\}$ | $\{3\}$ | $\{4\}$ | $\{1, 3, 4\}$ | $\{4\}$ |
| 6 | $\{2, 3\}$ | $\{1, 4\}$ | $\{1, 2\}$ | $\{1, 3, 4\}$ | $\{1, 2, 4\}$ | $\{2, 3\}$ |
| 7 | $\{2, 3, 4\}$ | $\{1, 2\}$ | $\{1, 2, 4\}$ | $\{1, 2, 3\}$ | $\{2, 4\}$ | $\{4\}$ |
| 8 | $\{1\}$ | $\{1, 2\}$ | $\{4\}$ | $\{2\}$ | $\{4\}$ | $\{1, 2, 4\}$ |
| 9 | $\{2, 3, 4\}$ | $\{3\}$ | $\{3\}$ | $\{3\}$ | $\{1, 3, 4\}$ | $\{1, 2\}$ |
| 10 | $\{2, 3, 4\}$ | $\{1\}$ | $\{3\}$ | $\{1, 2, 3\}$ | $\{4\}$ | $\{4\}$ |

cases, i.e., 'D(efinite) or I(ndefinite)' and '$GC$ or $MA$ or $GI$', we define six classes, $D\text{-}GC$, $D\text{-}MA$, $D\text{-}GI$, $I\text{-}GC$, $I\text{-}MA$, $I\text{-}GI$, for possible implications.

A possible implication $\tau_1$ belonging to $D\text{-}GC$ class is consistent in all derived $DISs$, and this $\tau_1$ is not influenced by the information incompleteness, therefore we especially say $\tau_1$ is a *certain rule*. A possible implication $\tau_2$ (from object $x$) belonging to $I\text{-}GC$ class is consistent in every $\varphi \in DD(\tau_2, x, CON, DEC)$, too. However, one of $PI(x, CON, DEC)$ is the real implication with unknown truth attributes values, therefore we say $\tau_2$ is a *possible rule*. A possible implication $\tau_3$ belonging to $MA$ class is consistent in some derived $DISs$. Because there may be a derived $DIS$ with unknown truth attributes values, we also say $\tau_3$ is a *possible rule*.

The definition of classes $GC$ and $MA$ is semantically the same as the definition in [12]. For handling the information incompleteness in $NISs$, we introduced possible implications. In [12], Kryszkiewicz proposed *generalized decision* $\partial_{AT}(x)$ for handling null values in $DISs$. In definite class, our definition and Kryszkiewicz's definition specify the same implications. However, there exists a difference. Example 2 shows it.

**Example 2.** Let us consider Table 1. A possible implication $\tau{:}[A, 1] \wedge [C, 3] \Rightarrow [F, 4] \in PI(5, \{A, C\}, \{F\})$ is definite, and $DD(\tau, 5, \{A, C\}, \{F\})$ consists of $3359232(= 2^9 \times 3^8)$ derived $DISs$. Since $[A, 1] \wedge [C, 3]$ occurs in only object 5, $\tau$ is a certain rule in our framework. Now, let us consider null value interpretation for object 9, namely we suppose $g(9, A){=}VAL_A$ instead of $g(9, A){=}\{2, 3, 4\}$. Then, $\tau' : [A, 1] \wedge [C, 3] \Rightarrow [F, 1] \in PI(9, \{A, C\}, \{F\})$ holds, and objects 5 and 9 are inconsistent in some derived $DISs$. Each null value '$*$' is replaced with every value in $VAL$, so $\tau$ is not a certain rule in [12].

# 4    Necessary and Sufficient Conditions for Possible Implications

This section presents necessary and sufficient conditions for characterizing $GC$, $MA$ and $GI$ classes.

**Definition 6.** Let us consider a $NIS$ and a set $ATR \subset AT$. For any $\zeta \in PT(x, ATR)$, we fix the tuple of $x$ to $\zeta$, and define (1) and (2) below.
(1) $inf(x, \zeta, ATR){=}\{x\} \cup \{y \in OB | PT(y, ATR){=}\{\zeta\}\}$,
(2) $sup(x, \zeta, ATR){=}\{y \in OB | \zeta \in PT(y, ATR)\}$.

In Definition 6, $inf(x, \zeta, ATR)$ implies a set of objects whose tuples are $\zeta$ and definite. $sup(x, \zeta, ATR)$ implies a set of objects whose tuples may be $\zeta$. Clearly $\{x\} \subset inf(x, \zeta, ATR) \subset sup(x, \zeta, ATR)$ holds.

**Theorem 1.** For any $NIS$, let $CON$ be condition attributes, let $DEC$ be decision attributes and let us consider a possible implication $\tau{:}[CON, \zeta] \Rightarrow [DEC, \eta] \in PI(x, CON, DEC)$. Then, the following holds.
(1) $\tau$ belongs to $GC$ class iff $sup(x, \zeta, CON) \subset inf(x, \eta, DEC)$.
(2) $\tau$ belongs to $MA$ class iff $inf(x, \zeta, CON) \subset sup(x, \eta, DEC)$.
(3) $\tau$ belongs to $GI$ class iff $inf(x, \zeta, CON) \not\subset sup(x, \eta, DEC)$.

**Example 3.** Let us continue the discussion on Example 1. For $\tau$:$[A,3] \wedge [B,1] \Rightarrow [C,3] \in PI(1,\{A,B\},\{C\})$, $sup(1,(3,1),\{A,B\})=\{1,6,7,10\}$ and $inf(1,(3), \{C\})=\{1,5,9,10\}$ hold. Therefore, $sup(1,(3,1),\{A,B\}) \not\subset inf(1,(3),\{C\})$ holds, and condition (1) in Theorem 1 does not hold. Similarly, $inf(1,(3,1),\{A,B\})= \{1\}$ and $sup(1,(3),\{C\})=\{1,3,5,9,10\}$ hold, so $inf(1,(3,1),\{A,B\}) \subset sup(1, (3),\{C\})$ is derived. In this way, it is possible to conclude that $\tau$ belongs to $I$-$MA$ class.

Here, we show a useful property for calculating $inf$ and $sup$. This property is effective for examining conditions in Theorem 1.

**Proposition 2.** For any $NIS$, let $ATR \subset AT$ be $\{A_1, \cdots, A_n\}$, and let a possible tuple $\zeta \in PT(x, ATR)$ be $(\zeta_1, \cdots, \zeta_n)$. Then, the following holds.
(1) $inf(x,\zeta,ATR)=\cap_i inf(x,(\zeta_i),\{A_i\})$.
(2) $sup(x,\zeta,ATR)=\cap_i sup(x,(\zeta_i),\{A_i\})$.

By using Theorem 1 and Proposition 2, it is possible to decide a class of each possible implication. Namely, we first prepare $inf(x,(\zeta_{i,j}),\{A_i\})$ and $sup(x,(\zeta_{i,j}),\{A_i\})$ for any $x \in OB$, any $A_i \in AT$ and any $(\zeta_{i,j}) \in PT(x,\{A_i\})$. Then, we produce $inf(x,\zeta,CON)$, $sup(x,\zeta,CON)$, $inf(x,\eta,DEC)$ and $sup(x, \eta,DEC)$ by using Proposition 2. Finally, we apply Theorem 1 to them.

## 5    The Lower and Upper Approximations of Support, Accuracy, and Coverage

In [4], rules in $DISs$ are defined by implications $\tau : imp(x,CON,DEC)$, which satisfy conditions by the next three criteria, $support(\tau)=|[x]_{CON} \cap [x]_{DEC}|/|OB|$, $accuracy(\tau) =|[x]_{CON} \cap [x]_{DEC}|/|[x]_{CON}|$ and $coverage(\tau)=|[x]_{CON} \cap [x]_{DEC}|/ |[x]_{DEC}|$. Therefore, three criteria are very important for rule generation in $DISs$. In this section, three criteria are extended to the lower and upper approximations of them in $NISs$.

**Definition 7.** For a $NIS$, let us consider a possible implication $\tau$:$[CON,\zeta] \Rightarrow [DEC,\eta] \in PI(x,CON,DEC)$ and $DD(\tau,x,CON,DEC)$. Then, let $minsup(\tau)$ denote $min_{\varphi \in DD(\tau,x,CON,DEC)}\{support(\tau) \text{ in } \varphi\}$, and let $maxsup(\tau)$ denote $max_{\varphi \in DD(\tau,x,CON,DEC)}\{support(\tau) \text{ in } \varphi\}$. As for $accuracy$ and $coverage$, we also define $minacc(\tau)$, $maxacc(\tau)$, $mincov(\tau)$ and $maxcov(\tau)$.

**Proposition 3.** For a $NIS$, let us consider a possible implication $\tau$:$[CON,\zeta] \Rightarrow [DEC,\eta] \in PI(x,CON,DEC)$. The following holds.
(1) $minsup(\tau)=|inf(x,\zeta,CON) \cap inf(x,\eta,DEC)|/|OB|$,
(2) $maxsup(\tau)=|sup(x,\zeta,CON) \cap sup(x,\eta,DEC)|/|OB|$.

**Proposition 4.** For a $NIS$, let us consider a possible implication $\tau$:$[CON,\zeta] \Rightarrow [DEC,\eta] \in PI(x,CON,DEC)$. Let $INACC$ denote a set $[sup(x,\zeta,CON) - inf(x,\zeta,CON)] \cap sup(x,\eta,DEC)$, and let $OUTACC$ denote a set $[sup(x,\zeta, CON) - inf(x,\zeta, CON)] - inf(x,\eta,DEC)$. Then, the following holds.
(1) $minacc(\tau)=\frac{|inf(x,\zeta,CON) \cap inf(x,\eta,DEC)|}{|inf(x,\zeta,CON)|+|OUTACC|}$.
(2) $maxacc(\tau)=\frac{|inf(x,\zeta,CON) \cap sup(x,\eta,DEC)|+|INACC|}{|inf(x,\zeta,CON)|+|INACC|}$.

**Proposition 5.** For a $NIS$, let us consider a possible implication $\tau$:$[CON,\zeta] \Rightarrow [DEC,\eta] \in PI(x,CON,DEC)$. Let $INCOV$ denote a set $[sup(x,\eta,DEC) - $

$inf(x, \eta, DEC)] \cap sup(x, \zeta, CON)$, and let $OUTCOV$ denote a set $[sup(x, \eta,$ $DEC) - inf(x, \eta, DEC)] - inf(x, \zeta, CON)$. Then, the following holds.

(1) $mincov(\tau) = \frac{|inf(x,\zeta,CON) \cap inf(x,\eta,DEC)|}{|inf(x,\eta,DEC)| + |OUTCOV|}$.

(2) $maxcov(\tau) = \frac{|sup(x,\zeta,CON) \cap inf(x,\eta,DEC)| + |INCOV|}{|inf(x,\eta,DEC)| + |INCOV|}$.

**Example 4.** Let us continue the discussion on Example 3. For $\tau : [A, 3] \wedge [B, 1] \Rightarrow [C, 3] \in PI(1, \{A, B\}, \{C\})$, $inf(1, (3, 1), \{A, B\}) = \{1\}$, $sup(1, (3, 1), \{A, B\}) = \{1, \quad 6, 7, 10\}$, $inf(1, (3), \{C\}) = \{1, 5, 9, 10\}$ and $sup(1, (3), \{C\}) = \{1, 3, 5, 9, 10\}$ hold. By Proposition 3, $minsup(\tau) = |\{1\} \cap \{1, 5, 9, 10\}|/10 = 0.1$ and $maxsup(\tau) = |\{1, 6, \quad 7, 10\} \cap \{1, 3, 5, 9, 10\}|/10 = 0.2$ hold. By Proposition 4, $INACC = [\{1, 6, 7, 10\} - \{1\}] \cap \{1, 3, 5, 9, 10\} = \{10\}$ and $OUTACC = [\{1, 6, 7, 10\} - \{1\}] - \{1, 5, 9, 10\} = \{6, 7\}$. Since $\tau \in PI(y, \{A, B\}, \{C\})$ holds for any $y \in INACC$, every $y \in INACC$ increases the value of *accuracy*. On the other hand, $(3, 1) \in PT(z, \{A, B\})$ and $\tau \notin PI(z, \{A, B\}, \{C\})$ hold for any $z \in OUTACC$, namely every $z \in OUTACC$ decreases the value of *accuracy*. $minacc(\tau) = |\{1\} \cap \{1, 5, 9, 10\}|/(|\{1\}| + |\{6, 7\}|) = 0.33$ holds, and $maxacc(\tau) = |\{1\} \cap \{1, 5, 9, 10\}| + |\{10\}|/(|\{1\}| + |\{10\}|) = 1.0$ holds.

## 6   Minimal Possible Implications and Rules in NISs

This section focuses on reduction of condition attributes in possible implications.
**Definition 8.** For any $NIS$, let $CON$ be condition attributes, let $DEC$ be decision attributes and let us consider a possible implication $\tau : [CON, \zeta] \Rightarrow [DEC, \eta]$. Let us suppose $\tau$ belongs to a class. If there is no proper subset $CON^* \subset CON$ such that $[CON^*, \zeta^*] \Rightarrow [DEC, \eta]$ belongs to this class, we say $\tau$ is *minimal* (in this class).

Now, it is possible to define the problem of rule generation in $NISs$.
**Problem 1.** For any $NIS$, let $DEC$ be decision attributes and let $\eta$ be a tuple of decision attributes values for $DEC$. Then, find all minimal certain or minimal possible rules in the form of $[CON, \zeta] \Rightarrow [DEC, \eta]$. For additional information, calculate the lower and upper approximations of *support*, *accuracy* and *coverage* of rules, too.

Several work deals with reduction for finding minimal reducts. For solving this problem, a *discernibility function* is proposed in [2], and this function is extended to a discernibility function in incomplete information systems [11]. In [10], an algorithm for finding a minimal complex is presented. However, finding a minimal reduct in a $DIS$ is proved to be NP-hard [2]. This means that to compute reducts is a non-trivial task. Therefore in $NISs$, some assumptions may be necessary for finding all minimal rules.

In such a situation, we introduce a total order, which is defined by the significance of attributes, over $(AT-DEC)$, and we think about rules based on this order. For example, let us suppose $\{A, B, C, D, E\}$ be an ordered set, and let $[A, \zeta_A] \wedge [B, \zeta_B] \wedge [C, \zeta_C] \wedge [D, \zeta_D] \Rightarrow [F, \eta_F]$ and $[B, \zeta_B'] \wedge [E, \zeta_E'] \Rightarrow [F, \eta_F]$ be certain rules. The latter seems simple, but we choose the former rule according to the order of significance. In this case, each attribute $A_i \in (AT-DEC)$ is sequentially picked up based on this order, and the necessity of the descriptor $[A_i, \zeta_{i,j}]$ is checked. Then, Proposition 2 and Theorem 1 are applied. Under this assumption, we have realized a tool for solving Problem 1. We show a real execution in the appendix. Of course, the introduction of total order over attributes is too strong simplification of the problem. Therefore, it is necessary to solve the problem of reduction in $NISs$ without using any total order.

## 7 Concluding Remarks

A new framework of rules in $NISs$ is proposed, and an overview of algorithms is presented. This work followed the research by Lipski, Grzymala-Busse and Kryszkiewicz, and produced a tool for $NISs$. From now on, it is necessary to cope with the following issues in $NISs$.
(1) An issue of finding all minimal reducts without any order over attributes,
(2) An issue of examining computational complexities of algorithms,
(3) An issue of applying this framework to real rule generation.

**Acknowledgment.** The author would be grateful to anonymous referees for their useful comments.

## References

1. Pawlak,Z.: Rough Sets. Kluwer Academic Publisher (1991)
2. Komorowski,J., Pawlak,Z., Polkowski,L., Skowron,A.: Rough Sets: a tutorial. Rough Fuzzy Hybridization. Springer (1999) 3–98
3. Nakamura,A., Tsumoto,S., Tanaka,H., Kobayashi,S.: Rough Set Theory and Its Applications. J.JSAI 11(2) (1996) 209–215
4. Tsumoto,S.: Knowledge Discovery in Clinical Databases and Evaluation of Discovered Knowledge in Outpatient Clinic. Information Sciences 124 (2000) 125–137
5. Orłowska,E., Pawlak,Z.: Representation of Nondeterministic Information. Theoretical Computer Science 29 (1984) 27–39
6. Orłowska,E. (ed.): Incomplete Information: Rough Set Analysis. Physica-Verlag (1998)
7. Lipski,W.: On Semantic Issues Connected with Incomplete Information Data Base. ACM Trans. DBS 4 (1979) 269–296
8. Lipski,W.: On Databases with Incomplete Information. Journal of the ACM 28 (1981) 41–70
9. Grzymala-Busse,J.: On the unknown attribute values in learning from examples. Proc. ISMIS'91, Lecture Notes in AI, Vol.542. Springer-Verlag (1991) 368—377
10. Grzymala-Busse,J., Werbrouck,P.: On the Best Search Method in the LEM1 and LEM2 Algorithms. Incomplete Information: Rough Set Analysis. Physica-Verlag (1998) 75-91
11. Kryszkiewicz,M.: Rough Set Approach to Incomplete Information Systems. Information Sciences 112 (1998) 39–49
12. Kryszkiewicz,M.: Rules in Incomplete Information Systems. Information Sciences 113 (1999) 271–292

13. Sakai,H.: Effective Procedures for Handling Possible Equivalence Relations in Non-deterministic Information Systems. Fundamenta Informaticae 48 (2001) 343–362
14. Sakai,H.: On a Method to Extract Rules from a Table with Non-deterministic Information: A Rough Sets based Approach. Bulletin of Informatics and Cybernetics 34(1) (2002) 13–28
15. Sakai,H.: Some Effective Procedures for Data Dependencies in Information Systems. Rough Set Theory and Granular Computing, Studies in Fuzziness and Soft Computing, Vol.125. Springer-Verlag (2003) 167–176

# Appendix: Real Execution

We show a real execution related to $NIS_1$ in Table 1. Programs *translate, rule, certain-rule*, etc. are implemented on a workstation with 450MHz UltraSparc CPU. A file 'data.pl' stores contents of $NIS_1$. For example, data(1,[3,[1,2,4],3,[1,2],[1,2,3],[1,2]]) is the real data expression for object 1. Here, we set $DEC=\{F\}$ and $\eta=(4)$, namely we think about rules like $[CON,\zeta] \Rightarrow [F,4]$. The order over attributes is sequentially $A,B,C,D$ and $E$. These definitions are stored in a file named 'attrib.pl'. Program *translate* produces internal expressions, i.e., $inf$ and $sup$, from data.pl and attrib.pl.

```
?-translate.
File Name for Read Open:'data.pl'.
Decision Definition File:'attrib.pl'.
File Name for Write Open:'data.rs'.
EXEC_TIME=0.096(sec)
yes
?-rule.
Rs File:'data.rs'.
DECLIST:<[F,4],definite=[5,7,10],indefinite=[2,3,4,5,7,8,10]>
<<Rules from object 2>>
=== One Attribute ===
[A,4]⇒[F,4]  [23328/139968,I-MA]  [(0.1,0.4),(0.33,1.0),(0.14,0.8)]
[B,2]⇒[F,4]  [20736/186624,I-MA]  [(0.1,0.4),(0.33,1.0),(0.14,0.8)]
[C,2]⇒[F,4]  [5184/15552,I-MA]  [(0.1,0.3),(0.33,1.0),(0.14,0.6)]
[D,4]⇒[F,4]  [34992/209952,I-MA]  [(0.2,0.2),(0.66,1.0),(0.28,0.5)]
=== Combined Attributes ===
[A,1]&[B,2]&[C,2]⇒[F,4]  [53747712/967458816,I-GC]  [(0.1,0.1),(1.0,1.0),(0.14,0.25)]
[A,1]&[B,3]⇒[F,4]  [2239488/40310784,I-GC]  [(0.1,0.1),(1.0,1.0),(0.14,0.25)]
         :      :      :
<<Rules from object 10>>
=== One Attribute ===
[A,2]⇒[F,4]  [46656/139968,I-MA]  [(0.1,0.3),(0.25,1.0),(0.14,0.75)]
[A,4]⇒[F,4]  [46656/139968,I-MA]  [(0.1,0.4),(0.25,1.0),(0.14,0.8)]
         :      :      :
[A,4]&[B,1]&[C,3]&[D,3]⇒[F,4]  [34828517376/313456656384,I-GC]  [(0.1,0.1),···,(0.14,0.33)]
EXEC_TIME=0.501(sec)
yes
?-certain-rule.
DECLIST:<[F,4],definite=[5,7,10],indefinite=[2,3,4,5,7,8,10]>
<<A certain rule from object 5>>
[A,1]&[C,3]⇒[F,4]  [3359232/3359232,D-GC]  [(0.1,0.1),(1.0,1.0),(0.14,0.33)]
<<A certain rule from object 7>>
<<A certain rule from object 10>>
[B,1]&[C,3]&[E,4]⇒[F,4]  [1451188224/1451188224,D-GC]  [(0.1,0.2),(1.0,1.0),(0.14,0.66)]
EXEC_TIME=0.129(sec)
yes
```

Program *rule* finds minimal possible implications (based on a total order over attributes) belonging to $GC$ or $MA$ classes. The descriptor [F,4] appears in

**Table 2.** Definitions of $NISs$ and each execution time(sec)

| $NIS$ | $|OB|$ | $|AT|$ | $Derived\_DISs$ | $translate$ | $rule$ | $certain\_rule$ |
|---|---|---|---|---|---|---|
| $NIS_1$ | 10 | 6 | $1.0 \times 10^{14} (= 2^{18} \times 3^{18})$ | 0.096 | 0.501 | 0.129 |
| $NIS_2$ | 50 | 5 | $120932352 (= 2^{11} \times 3^{10})$ | 0.173 | 0.086 | 0.039 |
| $NIS_3$ | 100 | 5 | $1451188224 (= 2^{13} \times 3^{11})$ | 0.612 | 0.599 | 0.391 |
| $NIS_4$ | 300 | 5 | $2.4 \times 10^{16} (= 2^{18} \times 3^{23})$ | 11.252 | 12.987 | 7.629 |

seven objects 2,3,4,5,7,8,10, so a procedure is sequentially applied to these seven objects. For each object, $\tau{:}[CON, \zeta] \Rightarrow [F, 4]$ ($CON \in \{A, B, C, D, E\}$) are examined at first. If there is no rules in $GC$ class, $CON$ is extended to a subset of $\{A, B, C, D, E\}$ for obtaining rules in $GC$ class. The notation $P/Q$ beside every rule implies that $P$ is $|\{\varphi \in DD(\tau, x, CON, DEC)|x$ is consistent in $\varphi\}|$ and $Q$ is $|DD(\tau, x, CON, DEC)|$. Furthermore, the lower and upper approximations $[(minsup,maxsup),(minacc,maxacc), (mincov,maxcov)]$ are displayed. Program $certain$-$rule$ extracts only certain rules. In this execution, the descriptor $[F,4]$ is definite for object 5,7,10, so a procedure is sequentially applied to these three objects.

For examining the overview of the execution time, we show each execution time of $translate$, $rule$ and $certain$-$rule$ for four kinds of $NISs$.

# Granular Computing Based on Rough Sets, Quotient Space Theory, and Belief Functions

Yiyu (Y.Y.) Yao[1], Churn-Jung Liau[2], and Ning Zhong[3]

[1] Department of Computer Science, University of Regina
Regina, Saskatchewan, Canada S4S 0A2. yyao@cs.uregina.ca
[2] Institute of Information Science, Academia Sinica
Taipei, Taiwan, liaucj@iis.sinica.edu.tw
[3] Department of Information Engineering, Maebashi Institute of Technology
Maebashi 371, Japan, zhong@maebashi-it.ac.jp

**Abstract.** A model of granular computing (GrC) is proposed by reformulating, re-interpreting, and combining results from rough sets, quotient space theory, and belief functions. Two operations, called zooming-in and zooming-out operations, are used to study connections between the elements of a universe and the elements of a granulated universe, as well as connections between computations in the two universes. The operations are studied with respect to multi-level granulation structures.

## 1 Introduction

Granular computing (GrC) is a label of theories, methodologies, techniques, and tools that make use of granules, i.e., groups, classes, or clusters of a universe, in the process of problem solving [15,20]. There is a fast growing and renewed interest in the study of granular computing [4,8].

There are many fundamental issues in granular computing, such as granulation of the universe, description of granules, relationships between granules, and computing with granules [15]. Many models of granular computing have been proposed and studied [16,20]. However, each model only captures certain aspects of granular computing. There is still a need for formal and concrete models for systematic studies of fundamental issues of granular computing.

The main objective of this paper is to propose a concrete model of granular computing based on a simple granulation structure, namely, a partition of a universe. Results from rough sets [9], quotient space theory [21,22], belief functions [12], and power algebra [1] are reformulated, re-interpreted, and combined for granular computing. With respect a two-level granulation structure, namely, a universe and the quotient universe induced by an equivalence relation, we introduce two basic operations called zooming-in and zooming-out operations. Zooming-in allows us to expand an element of the quotient universe into a subset of the universe, and hence reveals more detailed information. Zooming-out allows us to move to the quotient universe by ignoring some details. Computations in both universes can be connected through zooming operations. The study of two-level structures is generalized to multi-level granulation structures.

N. Zhong et al. (Eds.): ISMIS 2003, LNAI 2871, pp. 152–159, 2003.

# 2   Granulation and Approximations

This section studies a simple granulation of a universe, i.e., a partition induced by an equivalence relation. The discussion is basically a reformulation, re-interpretation, and combination of results from Shafer's work on belief functions [12], Pawlak's work on rough sets [9], and Zhang and Zhang's work on quotient space theory for problem solving [21,22].

## 2.1   Granulation by an Equivalence Relation

Suppose $U$ is a finite and nonempty set called the universe. Let $E \subseteq U \times U$ be an equivalence relation on $U$. The pair $apr = (U, E)$ is called an approximation space [9,10]. The relation $E$ can be conveniently represented by a mapping from $U$ to $2^U$, where $2^U$ is the power set of $U$. The mapping $[\cdot]_E : U \longrightarrow 2^U$ is given by: $[x]_E = \{y \in U \mid xEy\}$. The subset $[x]_E$ is the equivalence class containing $x$. The family of all equivalence classes is commonly known as the quotient set and is denoted by $U/E = \{[x]_E \mid x \in U\}$. It defines a partition of the universe, namely, a family of pairwise disjoint subsets whose union is the universe.

Under the equivalence relation, we only have a coarsened view of the universe. Each equivalence class is considered as a whole granule instead of many individuals [16]. They are considered as the basic or elementary definable, observable, or measurable subsets of the universe [10,14]. The equivalence class $[x]_E$ containing $x$ plays dual roles. It is a subset of $U$ if considered in relation to the universe, and an element of $U/E$ if considered in relation to the quotient set. In clustering, one typically associates a name with a cluster such that elements of the cluster are instances of the named category or concept [5]. Lin [7], following Dubois and Prade [3], explicitly used $[x]_E$ for representing a subset of $U$ and $Name([x]_E)$ for representing an element of $U/E$.

With a partition, we have two views of the same universe, a coarse-grained view $U/E$ and a detailed view $U$. A concept, represented as a subset of a universe, is thus described differently under different views. As we move from one view to the other, we change our perceptions and representations of the same concept.

## 2.2   Zooming-in: Refinement

Each element in the coarse-grained universe $U/E$ is a name associated with a subset of the universe $U$. For an element $X_i \in U/E$, a detailed view can be obtained at the level of $U$ from the subset of $U$ corresponding to $X_i$. This can be easily extended to any subset $X \subseteq U/E$. The expansion of an element of $U/E$ into a subset of $U$ is referred to as a zooming-in operation. With zooming-in, we are able to see more details.

Formally, zooming-in can be defined by an operator $\omega : 2^{U/E} \longrightarrow 2^U$. Shafer [12] referred to the zooming-in operation as refining. For a singleton subset $\{X_i\} \in 2^{U/E}$, we define [3]:

$$\omega(\{X_i\}) = [x]_E, \quad X_i \text{ is the name of the equivalence class } [x]_E. \tag{1}$$

For an arbitrary subset $X \subseteq U/E$, we have:

$$\omega(X) = \bigcup_{X_i \in X} \omega(\{X_i\}). \tag{2}$$

By zooming-in on a subset $X \subseteq U/E$, we obtain a unique subset $\omega(X) \subseteq U$. The set $\omega(X) \subseteq U$ is called the refinement of $X$.

The zooming-in operation has the following properties [12]:

(zi1)    $\omega(\emptyset) = \emptyset$,

(zi2)    $\omega(U/E) = U$,

(zi3)    $\omega(X^c) = (\omega(X))^c$,

(zi4)    $\omega(X \cap Y) = \omega(X) \cap \omega(Y)$,

(zi5)    $\omega(X \cup Y) = \omega(X) \cup \omega(Y)$,

(zi6)    $X \subseteq Y \Longleftrightarrow \omega(X) \subseteq \omega(Y)$,

where $^c$ denotes the set complement operator, the set-theoretic operators on the left hand side apply to the elements of $2^{U/E}$, and the same operators on the right hand side apply to the elements of $2^U$. From these properties, it can be seen that any relationships of subsets observed under coarse-grained view would hold under the detailed view, and vice versa. For example, in addition to (zi6), we have $X \cap Y = \emptyset$ if and only if $\omega(X) \cap \omega(Y) = \emptyset$, and $X \cup Y = U/E$ if and only if $\omega(X) \cup \omega(Y) = U$. Therefore, conclusions drawn based on the coarse-grained elements in $U/E$ can be carried over to the universe $U$.

## 2.3    Zooming-out: Approximations

The change of views from $U$ to $U/E$ is called a zooming-out operation. By zooming-out, a subset of the universe is considered as a whole rather than many individuals. This leads to a loss of information. Zooming-out on a subset $A \subseteq U$ may induce an inexact representation in the coarse-grained universe $U/E$.

The theory of rough sets focuses on the zooming-out operation. For a subset $A \subseteq U$, we have a pair of lower and upper approximations in the coarse-grained universe [2,3,13]:

$$\underline{apr}(A) = \{[x]_E \mid [x]_E \in U/E, [x]_E \subseteq A\},$$
$$\overline{apr}(A) = \{[x]_E \mid [x]_E \in U/E, [x]_E \cap A \neq \emptyset\}. \tag{3}$$

The expression of lower and upper approximations as subsets of $U/E$, rather than subsets of $U$, has only been considered by a few researchers in rough set community [2,3,13,19]. On the other hand, such notions have been considered in other contexts. Shafer [12] introduced those notions in the study of belief functions and called them the inner and outer reductions of $A \subseteq U$ in $U/E$. The connections between notions introduced by Pawlak in rough set theory and these introduced by Shafer in belief function theory have been pointed out by Dubois and Prade [3].

The expression of approximations in terms of elements of $U/E$ clearly shows that representation of $A$ in the coarse-grained universe $U/E$. By zooming-out, we only obtain an approximate representation. The lower and upper approximations satisfy the following properties [12,19]:

(zo1)  $\underline{apr}(\emptyset) = \overline{apr}(\emptyset) = \emptyset$,

(zo2)  $\underline{apr}(U) = \overline{apr}(U) = U/E$,

(zo3)  $\underline{apr}(A) = (\overline{apr}(A^c))^c$,     $\overline{apr}(A) = (\underline{apr}(A^c))^c$;

(zo4)  $\underline{apr}(A \cap B) = \underline{apr}(A) \cap \underline{apr}(B)$,     $\overline{apr}(A \cap B) \subseteq \overline{apr}(A) \cap \overline{apr}(B)$,

(zo5)  $\underline{apr}(A) \cup \underline{apr}(B) \subseteq \underline{apr}(A \cup B)$,     $\overline{apr}(A \cup B) = \overline{apr}(A) \cup \overline{apr}(B)$,

(zo6)  $A \subseteq B \Longrightarrow [\underline{apr}(A) \subseteq \underline{apr}(B), \overline{apr}(A) \subseteq \overline{apr}(B)]$,

(zo7)  $\underline{apr}(A) \subseteq \overline{apr}(A)$.

According to properties (zo4)-(zo6), relationships between subsets of $U$ may not be carried over to $U/E$ through the zooming-out operation. It may happen that $A \cap B \neq \emptyset$, but $\underline{apr}(A \cap B) = \emptyset$, or $A \cap B = \emptyset$, but $\overline{apr}(A \cap B) \neq \emptyset$. Similarly, we may have $A \neq B$, but $\underline{apr}(A) = \underline{apr}(B)$ and $\overline{apr}(A) = \overline{apr}(B)$. Nevertheless, we can draw the following inferences:

(i1)    $\underline{apr}(A) \cap \underline{apr}(B) \neq \emptyset \Longrightarrow A \cap B \neq \emptyset$,

(i2)    $\overline{apr}(A) \cap \overline{apr}(B) = \emptyset \Longrightarrow A \cap B = \emptyset$,

(i3)    $\underline{apr}(A) \cup \underline{apr}(B) = U/E \Longrightarrow A \cup B = U$,

(i4)    $\overline{apr}(A) \cup \overline{apr}(B) \neq U/E \Longrightarrow A \cup B \neq U$.

If $\underline{apr}(A) \cap \underline{apr}(B) \neq \emptyset$, by property (zo4) we know that $\overline{apr}(A) \cap \overline{apr}(B) \neq \emptyset$. We say that $A$ and $B$ have a non-empty overlap, and hence are related, in $U/E$. By (i1), $A$ and $B$ must have a non-empty overlap, and hence are related, in $U$. Similar explanations can be associated with other inference rules.

## 2.4   Zooming-out and Zooming-in: Classical Rough Set Approximations

Given a subset $A \subseteq U$, we perform the zooming-out operation and obtain a pair of subsets $\underline{apr}(A) \subseteq \overline{apr}(A) \subseteq U/E$. By zooming-in on the two subsets, we derive the classical rough set approximations [9,10,13]:

$$\omega(\underline{apr}(A)) = \bigcup_{X_i \in \underline{apr}(A)} \omega(\{X_i\}) = \bigcup\{[x]_E \mid [x]_E \in U/E, [x]_E \subseteq A\},$$

$$\omega(\overline{apr}(A)) = \bigcup_{X_i \in \overline{apr}(A)} \omega(\{X_i\}) = \bigcup\{[x]_E \mid [x]_E \in U/E, [x]_E \cap A \neq \emptyset\}. \quad (4)$$

For a subset $X \subseteq U/E$ we can zoom-in and obtain a subset $\omega(X) \subseteq U$, and then zoom-out to obtain a pair of subsets $\underline{apr}(\omega(X))$ and $\overline{apr}(\omega(X))$. The compositions of zooming-in and zooming-out operations have the properties [12]: for $X \subseteq U/E$ and $A \subseteq U$,

$$(\text{zio1}) \quad \omega(\underline{apr}(A)) \subseteq A \subseteq \omega(\overline{apr}(A)),$$
$$(\text{zio2}) \quad \underline{apr}(\omega(X)) = \overline{apr}(\omega(X)) = X.$$

The composition of zooming-out and zooming-in cannot recover the original set $A \subseteq U$. The composition zooming-in and zooming-out produces the original set $X \subseteq U/E$. A connection between the zooming-in and zooming-out operations can be established. For a pair of subsets $X \subseteq U/E$ and $A \subseteq U$, we have [12]:

$$(1) \quad w(X) \subseteq A \Longleftrightarrow X \subseteq \underline{apr}(A),$$
$$(2) \quad A \subseteq \omega(X) \Longleftrightarrow \overline{apr}(A) \subseteq X.$$

Property (1) can be understood as follows. Any subset $X \subseteq U/E$, whose refinement is a subset of $A$, is a subset of the lower approximation of $A$. Only a subset of the lower approximation of $A$ has a refinement that is a subset of $A$. It follows that $\underline{apr}(A)$ is the largest subset of $U/E$ whose refinement is contained in $A$, and $\overline{apr}(A)$ is the smallest subset of $U/E$ whose refinement containing $A$.

The rough set approximations can be related to the notion of dilation and erosion operations in mathematical morphology [11]. They have been considered by Zhang and Zhang in the quotient space theory for problem solving [21,22].

## 3   Granulation and Computations

The zooming-in and zooming-out operations provide a linkage between subsets of universe and subsets of granulated universe. Based on such connections, we can study the relationships between computations in two different universes.

### 3.1   Zooming-in: Set-Based Computations

Suppose $f : U \longrightarrow \Re$ is a real-valued function on $U$. One can lift the function $f$ to $U/E$ by performing set-based computations [17]. The lifted function $f^+$ is a set-valued function that maps an element of $U/E$ to a subset of real numbers. More specifically, for an element $X_i \in U/E$, the value of function is given by:

$$f^+(X_i) = \{f(x) \mid x \in \omega(\{X_i\})\}. \tag{5}$$

The function $f^+$ can be changed into a single-valued function $f_0^+$ in a number of ways. For example, Zhang and Zhang [21] suggested the following methods:

$$f_0^+(X_i) = \min f^+(X_i) = \min\{f(x) \mid x \in \omega(\{X_i\})\},$$
$$f_0^+(X_i) = \max f^+(X_i) = \max\{f(x) \mid x \in \omega(\{X_i\})\},$$
$$f_0^+(X_i) = \text{average} f^+(X_i) = \text{average}\{f(x) \mid x \in \omega(\{X_i\})\}. \tag{6}$$

The minimum, maximum, and average definitions may be regarded as the most permissive, the most optimistic, and the balanced view in moving functions from $U$ to $U/E$. More methods can be found in the book by Zhang and Zhang [21].

For a binary operation $\circ$ on $U$, a binary operation $\circ^+$ on $U/E$ is defined by [1,17]:

$$X_i \circ^+ X_j = \{x_i \circ x_j \mid x_i \in \omega(\{X_i\}), x_j \in \omega(\{X_j\})\}, \tag{7}$$

In general, one may lift any operation $p$ on $U$ to an operation $p^+$ on $U/E$, called the power operation of $p$. Suppose $p : U^n \longrightarrow U$ $(n \geq 1)$ is an $n$-ary operation on $U$. Its power operation $p^+ : (U/E)^n \longrightarrow 2^U$ is defined by [1]:

$$p^+(X_0, \ldots, X_{n-1}) = \{p(x_0, \ldots, x_{n-1}) \mid x_i \in \omega(\{X_i\}) \text{ for } i = 0, \ldots, n-1\}, \tag{8}$$

for any $X_0, \ldots, X_{n-1} \in U/E$. This provides a universal-algebraic construction approach. For any algebra $(U, p_1, \ldots, p_k)$ with base set $U$ and operations $p_1, \ldots, p_k$, its quotient algebra is given by $(U/E, p_1^+, \ldots, p_k^+)$.

The power operation $p^+$ may carry some properties of $p$. For example, for a binary operation $p : U^2 \longrightarrow U$, if $p$ is commutative and associative, $p^+$ is commutative and associative, respectively. If $e$ is an identity for some operation $p$, the set $\{e\}$ is an identity for $p^+$. Many properties of $p$ are not carried over by $p^+$. For instance, if a binary operation $p$ is idempotent, i.e., $p(x, x) = x$, $p^+$ may not be idempotent. If a binary operation $g$ is distributive over $p$, $g^+$ may not be distributive over $p^+$.

## 3.2   Zooming-out: Inner and Outer Fuzzy Measures

Suppose $\mu : 2^{U/E} \longrightarrow [0, 1]$ is a set function on $U/E$. If $\mu$ satisfies the conditions, (i). $\mu(\emptyset) = 0$, (ii). $\mu(U/E) = 1$, and (iii). $X \subseteq Y \implies \mu(X) \leq \mu(Y)$, $\mu$ is called a fuzzy measure [6]. Examples of fuzzy measures are probability functions, possibility and necessity functions, and belief and plausibility functions.

Information about subsets in $U$ can be obtained from $\mu$ on $U/E$ and the zooming-out operation. For a subset $A \subseteq U$, we can define a pair of inner and outer fuzzy measures [18]:

$$\underline{\mu}(A) = \mu(\underline{apr}(A)), \qquad \overline{\mu}(A) = \mu(\overline{apr}(A)). \tag{9}$$

They are fuzzy measures. If $\mu$ is a probability function, $\underline{\mu}$ and $\overline{\mu}$ are a pair of belief and plausibility functions [12,18]. If $\mu$ is a belief function, $\underline{\mu}$ is a belief function, and if $\mu$ is a plausibility function, $\overline{\mu}$ is a plausibility [18].

# 4   Multi-level Granulations and Approximations

The simple granulation structure can be used to construct a multi-level granulation or a hierarchy [16,21]. The zooming-in and zooming-out operations can be defined on any two adjacent levels.

The ground level, $l_0$, is the universe $U_0 = U$. The next level, $l_1$, constructed through an equivalence relation $E_0$ or the corresponding partition, is $U_1 = U/E_0$. The elements of $U_1$ are names assigned to subsets of $U_0$. From the universe $U_i$ at level $i \geq 0$, the next level of universe is given by $U_{i+1} = U_i/E_i$, where $E_i$ is an equivalence relation on $U_i$. The elements of $U_{i+1}$ are names associated with subsets of $U_i$. Thus, we have a multi-level representation of the universe $U$ with different grain sizes [21].

The connection between different granulated views can be easily established by the zooming-in and zooming-out operations. Let $\omega_i$ and $(\underline{apr}_i, \overline{apr}_i)$, $i \geq 0$, denote the zooming-in and zooming-out operations defined between $U_{i+1}$ and $U_i$. For a ground level subset $A$, its approximations at level $k > 0$ is given by:

$$\underline{apr}_{k-1}(\ldots \underline{apr}_0(A)), \qquad \overline{apr}_{k-1}(\ldots \overline{apr}_0(A)). \tag{10}$$

They are obtained by the composition of $k$ zooming-out operations, namely, $\underline{apr}_{k-1} \circ \ldots \circ \underline{apr}_0$, and $\overline{apr}_{k-1} \circ \ldots \circ \overline{apr}_0$. For a subset $X \subseteq U_k$, its ground level refinement is given by:

$$\omega_0(\ldots \omega_{k-1}(X)). \tag{11}$$

It is obtained by the composition of $k$ zooming-in operations, namely, $\omega_0 \circ \ldots \circ \omega_{k-1}$. We can establish a connection between subsets in any two levels in the multi-level granulation by treating the lowest level as the ground level.

By zooming-in, we can move downwards in the multi-level granulation, which enables us to examine more details. By zooming-out, we can move upwards in the multi-level granulation, which enables us to ignore details and obtain a more abstract level description. Zhang and Zhang [21] applied this simple principle to solve many problems in artificial intelligence and developed a granular computing theory for problem solving.

Although we illustrate the idea of granulations, as well as the zooming-in and zooming-out operations, by using a simple and concrete framework based on the notion of partitions, the argument can be easily applied to other granulation structures. For example, one may use partial orders to model granulation structures [21]. A crucial step is the introduction of operations that allow us to navigate (change views) in the granulation structures. The operations, such as zooming-in and zooming-out, also allow us to establish connections between elements of different granulated views of the universe. It may be desirable that the granulated universe keep some properties of the original universe [21]. Computations under multi-level granulation structures can be done by extending the computational methods presented in Section 3 under the two-level structure.

## 5    Conclusion

We review, compare, reformulate and re-interpret results from rough sets, quotient space theory, belief functions, and power algebras. The results enable us to build a concrete model for granular computing. The granular computing model offers a unified view to examine many notions studied in several related fields. More insights may be obtained in one particular field from studies in other fields. The combination of results from different fields under the umbrella term of granular computing may eventually lead to new theories and methodologies for problem solving.

# References

1. Brink, C. Power structures, *Algebra Universalis*, **30**, 177–216, 1993.
2. Bryniarski, E. A calculus of rough sets of the first order, *Bulletin of the Polish Academy of Sciences, Mathematics*, **37**, 71–77, 1989.
3. Dubois, D. and Prade, H. Rough fuzzy sets and fuzzy rough sets. *International Journal of General Systems*, **17**, 191–209, 1990.
4. Inuiguchi, M., Hirano, S. and Tsumoto, S. (Eds.), *Rough Set Theory and Granular Computing*, Springer, Berlin, 2003.
5. Jardine, N. and Sibson, R. *Mathematical Taxonomy*, Wiley, New York, 1971.
6. Klir, G.J. and Folger, T.A. *Fuzzy Sets, Uncertainty, and Information*, Prentice Hall, Englewood Cliffs, 1988.
7. Lin, T.Y. Topological and fuzzy rough sets, in: *Intelligent Decision Support: Handbook of Applications and Advances of the Rough Sets Theory*, Slowinski, R. (ed.), Kluwer Academic Publishers, Boston, 287–304, 1992.
8. Lin. T.Y., Yao, Y.Y. and Zadeh, L.A. (Eds.) *Rough Sets, Granular Computing and Data Mining*, Physica-Verlag, Heidelberg, 2001.
9. Pawlak, Z. Rough sets, *International Journal of Computer and Information Sciences*, **11**, 341–356, 1982.
10. Pawlak, Z. *Rough Sets: Theoretical Aspects of Reasoning about Data*, Kluwer Academic Publishers, Boston, 1991.
11. Serra, J. *Imagine Analysis and Mathematical Morphology*, Academic Press, London, 1982.
12. Shafer, G. *A Mathematical Theory of Evidence*. Princeton University Press, Princeton, 1976.
13. Yao, Y.Y. Two views of the theory of rough sets in finite universes, *International Journal of Approximation Reasoning*, **15**, 291–317, 1996.
14. Yao, Y.Y. On generalizing Pawlak approximation operators, *Proceedings of the First International Conference, RSCTC'98*, LNAI 1424, 298–307, 1998.
15. Yao, Y.Y. Granular computing: basic issues and possible solutions, *Proceedings of the 5th Joint Conference on Information Sciences*, 186–189, 2000.
16. Yao, Y.Y. Information granulation and rough set approximation, *International Journal of Intelligent Systems*, **16**, 87–104, 2001.
17. Yao, Y.Y. and Noroozi, N. A unified framework for set-based computations, *Proceedings of the 3rd International Workshop on Rough Sets and Soft Computing*, The Society for Computer Simulation, 252–255, 1995.
18. Yao, Y.Y. and Wong, S.K.M. Representation, propagation and combination of uncertain information, *International Journal of General Systems*, **23**, 59–83, 1994.
19. Yao, Y.Y., Wong, S.K.M. and Lin, T.Y. A review of rough set models, in: *Rough Sets and Data Mining: Analysis for Imprecise Data*, Lin, T.Y. and Cercone, N. (Eds.), Kluwer Academic Publishers, Boston, 47–75, 1997.
20. Zadeh, L.A. Towards a theory of fuzzy information granulation and its centrality in human reasoning and fuzzy logic, *Fuzzy Sets and Systems*, **19**, 111–127, 1997.
21. Zhang, B. and Zhang, L. *Theory and Applications of Problem Solving*, North-Holland, Amsterdam, 1992.
22. Zhang, L. and Zhang, B. The quotient space theory of problem solving, *Proceedings of International Conference on Rough Sets, Fuzzy Set, Data Mining and Granular Computing*, LNCS 2639, 11–15, 2003.

# Searching for the Complex Decision Reducts: The Case Study of the Survival Analysis

Jan Bazan[1], Andrzej Skowron[2], Dominik Ślęzak[3,4], and Jakub Wróblewski[4]

[1] Institute of Mathematics, University of Rzeszów
Rejtana 16A, 35-959 Rzeszów, Poland
[2] Institute of Mathematics, University of Warsaw
Banacha 2, 02-097 Warsaw, Poland
[3] Department of Computer Science, University of Regina
Regina, SK, S4S 0A2 Canada
[4] Polish-Japanese Institute of Information Technology
Koszykowa 86, 02-008 Warsaw, Poland

**Abstract.** Generalization of the fundamental rough set discernibility tools aiming at searching for relevant patterns for complex decisions is discussed. As an example of application, there is considered the post-surgery survival analysis problem for the head and neck cancer cases. The goal is to express dissimilarity between different survival tendencies by means of clinical information. It requires handling decision values in form of plots representing the Kaplan-Meier product estimates for the groups of patients.

## 1 Introduction

In many rough set approaches to data analysis, especially these dedicated to (strongly) inconsistent data tables, where the decision class approximations cannot be determined to a satisfactory degree, decisions can take more complex forms, e.g., the collections or probabilistic distributions of the original decision values (cf. [6,10]). In the same way, one could consider, e.g., statistical estimates, plots, etc., definable using the original attributes, in a way appropriate for a particular decision problem. Then, one should search for relevant patterns for approximation of such decision structures. We study how complex decision semantics can influence the algorithmic framework and results of its performance. We show that quite unusual structures can be still handled using just slightly modified rough set algorithms based on discernibility and Boolean reasoning [9].

Complex attribute values occur often in the medical domain, while analyzing heterogeneous data gathering series of measurements, images, texts, etc. [2]. We illustrate our approach using data representing medical treatment of patients with the head and neck cancer cases. The data table, collected for years by Medical Center of Postgraduate Education in Warsaw, Poland, consists of 557 patient records described by 29 attributes. The most important attributes are

N. Zhong et al. (Eds.): ISMIS 2003, LNAI 2871, pp. 160–168, 2003.

well-defined qualitative features. The decision problem, however, requires approximation of especially designed complex decision attribute, corresponding to the needs of the survival analysis [3].

One may conclude that the proposed methodology is applicable not only to the presented case study but also to other medical, as well as, e.g., multimedia or robotics problems. The results can also be treated as a step towards hybridization of case-based reasoning with the rough set approach [4,7].

## 2   Illustrative Example

In rough set theory the sample of data takes the form of an information system $\mathbb{A} = (U, A)$, where each attribute $a \in A$ is a function $a : U \to V_a$ from the universe $U$ into the set $V_a$ of all possible values of $a$. Figure 1 illustrates the meaning of the attribute values for the information system $\mathbb{A} = (U, A)$, where $A = \{\#, ttr, st_l, st_{cr}, loc, gap, rec\}$. $U$ gathers 557 patients labelled with their values for the elements of $A$. For instance, the object with the vector of values $(1, after, T2, cN3, throat, 3.5, 1)$ corresponds to a patient, who was treated with one-sided operation, after unsuccessful radiotherapy, with the local stage of cancer classified as $T2$, the regional stage clinically (before the operation) classified as $cN3$, with the cancer recognized in the throat, the last notification done after 3.5 years, during which the cancer recurrence was observed.

| Column with description | Values with description |
|---|---|
| # – No. of Sides Operated | 1 – operation needed at one side; 2 – at both sides |
| *ttr* – Type of Treatment | *only* – only operation applied; *radio* – together with radiotherapy; *after* – after unsuccessful radiotherapy |
| *st$_l$* – Local Stage | *T1, T2, T3, T4* |
| *st$_{cr}$* – Clinical Regional Stage | *cN0, cN1, cN2, cN3* |
| *loc* – Localization | *larynx, throat, other* |
| *gap* – Time Interval Gap | the gap between operation and the last notification |
| *rec* – Recurrence Notification | 1 – recurrence observed; 0 – otherwise |

**Fig. 1.** The selected attributes of medical data

Object $u \in U$ *supports descriptor* $a = v_a$ iff $a(u) = v_a$. Descriptors, treated as *boolean unary predicates*, are atomic logical formulas. Descriptors for quantitative attributes can be built using also, e.g., inequalities. According to the experts, a person who survives more than 5 years after surgery is regarded as the *success* case, even if the same type of cancer repeats after. A person who dies within 5 years can be the *defeat* or *unknown* case due to the reason of death. We obtain the following *decision classes* of patients, described by means of conjunctions of descriptors built over qualitative *rec* and quantitative *gap*:

1. **defeat**: the set of objects, which support conjunction $rec = 1 \land gap < 5$
2. **unknown**: the set of objects, which support conjunction $rec = 0 \land gap < 5$
3. **success**: the set of objects, which support descriptor $gap \geq 5$

One of the aims of rough set theory is to approximate decision classes by means of *conditional attributes* [5]. We want to approximate *defeat, unknown,* and *success* using clinical information. We consider *decision table* $\mathbb{A} = (U, C \cup \{d\})$ with conditional attributes $C = \{\#, ttr, st_l, st_{cr}, loc\}$ and distinguished *decision attribute* $d \notin C$, which indicates decision classes defined above.

Decision approximation is usually stated by means of *"if .. then .."* *rules*, such that (*almost*) all objects that support the conditional part of the rule, drop into the specified decision class. *Inconsistency* of $\mathbb{A} = (U, C \cup \{d\})$ can be expressed by, e.g., *boundary regions* of decision classes [5], *generalized decision sets* [8,9], or *rough memberships* [6,10], which label each $u \in U$ with distribution of its *indiscernibility class* $[u]_C = \{u' \in U : \forall_{a \in C}(a(u) = a(u'))\}$ among decisions:

$$\vec{\mu}_{d/C}(u) = \left\langle \frac{|[u]_C \cap defeat|}{|[u]_C|}, \frac{|[u]_C \cap unknown|}{|[u]_C|}, \frac{|[u]_C \cap success|}{|[u]_C|} \right\rangle \quad (1)$$

Inconsistency of $\mathbb{A}$ corresponds to distributions, which do not specify a unique decision class for some $u \in U$. Figure 2 illustrates such distributions for a couple of elements of $U$. In this case one can expect difficulties in constructing reasonable decision rules. We discuss a solution of this problem in the next section.

| $u$ | $\#$ | $ttr$ | $st_l$ | $st_{cr}$ | $loc$ | $\|[u]_C\|$ | $\|[u]_C \cap def\|$ | $\|[u]_C \cap unk\|$ | $\|[u]_C \cap suc\|$ |
|---|---|---|---|---|---|---|---|---|---|
| 0 | 1 | *only* | $T3$ | $cN1$ | *larynx* | 25 | 15 | 4 | 6 |
| 4 | 1 | *after* | $T3$ | $cN1$ | *larynx* | 38 | 8 | 18 | 12 |
| 24 | 1 | *radio* | $T3$ | $cN1$ | *larynx* | 23 | 6 | 7 | 10 |
| 28 | 1 | *after* | $T3$ | $cN0$ | *throat* | 18 | 4 | 8 | 6 |
| 57 | 1 | *after* | $T4$ | $cN1$ | *larynx* | 32 | 12 | 14 | 6 |
| 91 | 1 | *after* | $T3$ | $cN1$ | *throat* | 35 | 5 | 16 | 14 |
| 152 | 1 | *only* | $T3$ | $cN0$ | *larynx* | 27 | 9 | 14 | 4 |
| 255 | 1 | *after* | $T3$ | $cN0$ | *larynx* | 15 | 2 | 6 | 7 |
| 493 | 1 | *after* | $T3$ | $cN1$ | *other* | 19 | 6 | 7 | 6 |
| 552 | 2 | *after* | $T4$ | $cN2$ | *larynx* | 14 | 6 | 3 | 5 |

**Fig. 2.** Statistics for randomly selected objects. The first column contains the object's ordinal number. The next five columns contain the attribute values. The last four columns contain cardinalities enabling calculation of the rough membership coefficients.

# 3   Discernibility-Based Reduction

Approximation of decision classes corresponds to the construction of an *approximation space* [8], where objects with similar decisions are well described by conditional formulas. Given $\mathbb{A} = (U, C \cup \{d\})$, we search for indiscernibility classes $[u]_C$, such that if $u' \in [u]_C$, then $d(u')$ is *close to* $d(u)$. We also try to generalize such classes by reducing the number of needed attributes (cf. [8,9]). Let us consider *discernibility matrix* $\mathbb{M}_{\mathbb{A}}$ (cf. [9]), where:

1. columns correspond to attributes $a \in C$
2. rows correspond to the pairs of objects $(u, u')$ such that $d(u) \neq d(u')$
3. for row $(u, u')$ and column $a \in C$ we put 1, if $a(u) \neq a(u')$ and 0 otherwise

Any *irreducible covering* $B \subseteq C$ of $\mathbb{M}_\mathbb{A}$ [1] corresponds to a *decision reduct* – an irreducible subset of attributes providing consistent subtable $\mathbb{B} = (U, B \cup \{d\})$.

For inconsistent $\mathbb{A} = (U, C \cup \{d\})$ there is impossible to cover $\mathbb{M}_\mathbb{A}$ at all. Still, one can search for reducts as the *approximate* coverings of $\mathbb{M}_\mathbb{A}$ or as the coverings of *modified* matrices (cf. [8,9,10]). For instance, the rows of a discernibility matrix can correspond to the pairs of objects with different rough membership distributions. Any irreducible covering of such a matrix corresponds to a decision reduct for consistent decision table $\mathbb{A} = (U, C \cup \{\vec{\mu}_{d/C}\})$. Then, however, we cannot group the objects with *very similar* distributions. A solution ([10]) is to consider only the pairs $(u, u')$ with *enough distant* distributions, i.e. such that

$$\varrho\left(\vec{\mu}_{d/C}(u), \vec{\mu}_{d/C}(u')\right) \geq \alpha \tag{2}$$

for a specified function $\varrho$ and threshold $\alpha > 0$. Irreducible coverings of such obtained matrix, further denoted by $\mathbb{M}_\mathbb{A}^\alpha$, provide $\alpha$-*approximate decision reducts* $B \subseteq C$, which *approximately* preserve information induced by $C$ about $d$. Condition (2) can be applied with *any other* function $\varrho$, which measures distances between *any other* complex decision values calculated for classes $[u]_C$, $u \in U$.

| $u$ | $u'$ | $\#$ | $ttr$ | $st_l$ | $st_{cr}$ | $loc$ |
|---|---|---|---|---|---|---|
| 0 | 255 | 0 | 1 | 0 | 1 | 0 |
| 0 | 91 | 0 | 1 | 0 | 0 | 1 |
| 0 | 4 | 0 | 1 | 0 | 0 | 0 |
| 0 | 28 | 0 | 1 | 0 | 1 | 1 |
| 0 | 152 | 0 | 0 | 0 | 1 | 0 |
| 0 | 24 | 0 | 1 | 0 | 0 | 0 |

| $u$ | $u'$ | $\#$ | $ttr$ | $st_l$ | $st_{cr}$ | $loc$ |
|---|---|---|---|---|---|---|
| 152 | 255 | 0 | 1 | 0 | 0 | 0 |
| 152 | 552 | 1 | 1 | 1 | 1 | 0 |
| 91 | 552 | 1 | 0 | 1 | 1 | 1 |
| 57 | 255 | 0 | 0 | 1 | 1 | 0 |
| 255 | 552 | 1 | 0 | 1 | 1 | 0 |
| 24 | 152 | 0 | 1 | 0 | 1 | 0 |

**Fig. 3.** $\mathbb{M}_\mathbb{A}^\alpha$ for $U = \{0, 4, 24, 28, 57, 91, 152, 255, 493, 552\}$. The rows correspond to the pairs, for which Euclidean distance between distributions is not lower than $\alpha = 0.365$. One can see that the only irreducible covering takes the form of the set $B = \{ttr, st_{cr}\}$. This is the only $\alpha$-approximate decision reduct in this case.

The main theoretical contribution of this paper is the reduction methodology based on conditions similar to (2), but at the level of *local decision reducts* [9]. An $\alpha$-*approximate* local reduct is built by discerning a given $u \in U$ from all $u' \in U$ such that inequality (2) holds. It corresponds to operations on matrix $M_\mathbb{A}^\alpha(u)$, which is $M_\mathbb{A}^\alpha$ restricted to the rows related to $u$. A covering $B \subseteq C$ of $M_\mathbb{A}^\alpha(u)$ generates the rule described by the $u$'s values on $B$: if $u' \in U$ supports descriptors $a = a(u)$ for all $a \in B$, then the decision of $u'$ is *close to* that of $u$.

---

[1] The covering of binary $\mathbb{M}_\mathbb{A}$ takes the form of any subset of columns $B \subseteq C$ such that for any row we have at least one $a \in B$ with value 1 on this row.

Just like at the level of decision reducts, we can consider arbitrary criteria for measuring the decision distances. A general problem is that sometimes there can be objects $u', u'' \in U$, which do not need to be discerned from $u$ but their decision characteristics are too distant to each other to put both of them to the same class.[2] Therefore, we should add to $M_{\mathbb{A}}^{\alpha}(u)$ also the rows encoding the need of keeping at least one of objects $u', u''$ outside the support of any local reduct derived at the basis of $u$. It is illustrated in Figure 4 for criterion (2). This is a novel approach, which can be extended to other types of complex decisions, assuming a distance measure between the decision values is given.

| $u$ | $u'$ | $\#$ | $ttr$ | $st_l$ | $st_{cr}$ | $loc$ |
|---|---|---|---|---|---|---|
| 0 | 91 | 0 | 1 | 0 | 0 | 1 |
| 152 | 255 | 0 | 1 | 0 | 1 | 1 |
| 91 | 552 | 1 | 0 | 1 | 1 | 1 |
| 57 | 255 | 0 | 0 | 1 | 1 | 1 |
| 24 | 152 | 0 | 1 | 0 | 1 | 1 |

**Fig. 4.** Matrix $M_{\mathbb{A}}^{\alpha}(u)$ for $u = 91$ and $\alpha = 0.365$. Its coverings correspond to $\alpha$-*approximate local reducts* $B1 = \{ttr, st_l\}$, $B2 = \{st_l, st_{cr}\}$, and $B3 = \{loc\}$. Their supports are equal $[u]_{B1} = \{4, 28, 91, 255, 493\}$, $[u]_{B2} = \{4, 57, 91, 493\}$, and $[u]_{B3} = \{28, 91\}$. They correspond to patterns $ttr = after \wedge st_l = T3$, $ttr = after \wedge st_{cr} = cN1$, and $loc = throat$.

Another problem corresponds to the task of case-based reasoning, aiming at deriving new decisions from the clusters of objects with similar decision characteristics (cf. [4,7]). As an example, let us consider the case of handling rough membership distributions. We can label a given cluster $[u]_B$, obtained as the support of $\alpha$-approximate local reduct $B \subseteq C$ obtained at the basis of $u \in U$, with distribution $\vec{\pi}_{d/B}(u)$ calculated as (1), for $[u]_B$ instead of $[u]_C$. One can rewrite $\vec{\pi}_{d/B}(u)$ as the average of distributions $\vec{\pi}_{d/C}(u')$, $u' \in U$.

It is shown in [10] that if Euclidean distances between distributions $\vec{\pi}_{d/C}$ of all elements of $[u]_B$ are lower than $\alpha$, what is the case for $\alpha$-approximate local reducts, then the same can be said about distances between $\vec{\pi}_{d/C}(u')$ and $\vec{\pi}_{d/B}(u)$, for any $u' \in [u]_B$. Therefore, we can talk about a *complex decision rule* saying that if a given object supports descriptors $a = a(u)$, for any $a \in B$, then its decision distribution is *close to* $\vec{\pi}_{d/B}(u)$.

The above kind of case-based reasoning analysis should be reconsidered for any other applied decision and distance semantics. For instance, in the following sections we discuss the local reduct patterns grouping *similar* plots representing the Kaplan-Meier product estimates (cf. [3]). Although we can search for the groups of such plots using the same discernibility procedure as above, further research is needed to examine to what extent the estimate calculated for some class $[u]_B$, $u \in U$, $B \subseteq C$, can be regarded as a *representative* for the collection of mutually similar estimates calculated locally for classes $[u']_C$, $u' \in [u]_B$.

---

[2] This problem does not occur in the classical case, where objects $u', u'' \in U$ need not to be discerned from $u$, iff $d(u) = d(u')$ and $d(u) = d(u'')$, what implies $d(u') = d(u'')$.

## 4   Discernibility Approach to the Survival Analysis

In the survival analysis, one distinguishes *complete* and *censored* objects. In case of the considered medical data, the set of complete objects coincides with the *defeat* decision class. The Kaplan-Meier product-limit estimate (cf. [3]) provides the means for construction of *survival function* $S(t)$, which returns cumulative proportion of cases surviving up to the time $t$ after operation. We define it as

$$S(t) = \prod_{u \in defeat:gap(u) \leq t} \frac{|U| - \|\|gap \leq gap(u)\|_{\mathbb{A}}|}{|U| - \|\|gap \leq gap(u)\|_{\mathbb{A}}| + 1} \qquad (3)$$

where $\|gap \leq gap(u)\|_{\mathbb{A}} = \{u' \in U : gap(u') \leq gap(u)\}$. $S(t)$ can be recalculated for any subset of $U$ as illustrated in Figure 5. Since all the cases $u \in U$, such that inequality $gap(u) > 5$ is satisfied, are censored (because they are *successes*), we restrict ourselves to the survival plots within the range of $[0, 5]$ years.

One used to assume that a given attribute provided more information, if it split data onto subtables with less similar survival plots. For instance, Figure 5 illustrates the meaning of *ttr*. The patients not treated with radiotherapy seem to have more chances for survival, because the corresponding plot has the highest level of chances after 5 years. It does not mean, however, that radiotherapy should not be applied. The type of treatment *ttr = only* is applied to relatively less severe cases, which makes the corresponding survival characteristics more optimistic "by definition". This is an example why the decision behaviors corresponding to the values of single attributes should be analyzed in the context of other attributes. It was a motivation for applying to this data the proposed generalization of the rough set approach to searching for approximate reducts.

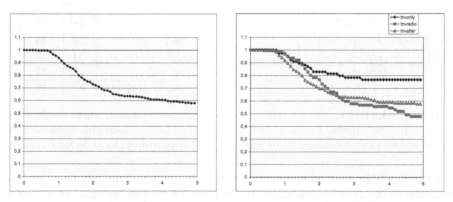

**Fig. 5.** The plots of function $S(t)$. The left plot corresponds to the whole $U$. The right plots correspond to subtables filtered with respect to foregoing values of attribute *ttr*.

Let us label each $u \in U$ with the survival function $S_u^C(t)$ obtained for the indiscernibility class $[u]_C$. Since functions $S_u^C(t)$ seem to contain more adequate information than $\overrightarrow{\mu}_{d/C}(u)$, we repeat the discernibility reduction process described in the previous section for the survival plot decisions. To do this, we can follow the same procedures of creating and analyzing $\alpha$-approximate discernibility matrices $M_\mathbb{A}^\alpha$ and $M_\mathbb{A}^\alpha(u)$, but for the decision distances calculated between the survival plots instead of Euclidean distances between distributions.

We considered two examples of distances enabling to compare pairs of objects $u, u' \in U$. The first one, $\varrho_{area}(u, u')$, equals the area between the plots of $S_u^C(t)$ and $S_{u'}^C(t)$. The second one, $\varrho_{merged}(u, u')$, refers more to particular cases than to the plots. It averages the differences between the survival estimates for the *defeat* objects in $[u]_C \cup [u']_C$ before and after merging $[u]_C$ and $[u']_C$ within a more general cluster. A broader family of distances should be analyzed in future.

Given functions $\varrho_{area}$ or $\varrho_{merged}$, we can search for clusters of objects with $\alpha$-approximately similar Kaplan-Meier characteristics. Procedure based on discernibility matrices $M_\mathbb{A}^\alpha(u)$ assures that any local reduct $B \subseteq C$ obtained for a given $u \in U$ forms the cluster $[u]_B$ of $\alpha$-approximately similar objects. A question is whether the plots $S_u^B(t)$ corresponding to such clusters can be regarded as their *representatives* in the same way as discussed for distributions $\vec{\mu}_{d/B}(u)$. As mentioned before, it must be analyzed, whether mutual closeness of estimates $S_{u'}^C(t)$ for all $u' \in [u]_B$ assures the same kind of closeness to $S_u^B(t)$. Although the experiments confirm this tendency, further theoretical studies are needed.

## 5   Selected Experimental Results

We performed experiments for the data table described by conditional attributes $C = \{\#, ttr, st_l, st_{cr}, loc\}$. Just like in Section 3, we were generating $\mathbb{M}_\mathbb{A}^\alpha$ and $\mathbb{M}_\mathbb{A}^\alpha(u)$ basing on criterion (2), now applied for distances $\varrho_{area}$ and $\varrho_{merged}$.

| $\alpha$ | $\varrho_{area}$ | $\varrho_{merged}$ | $\varrho_{area}$ | $\varrho_{merged}$ |
|---|---|---|---|---|
| 0.3 | $\{\#, ttr, st_l, st_{cr}, loc\}$ | $\{ttr, st_l, st_{cr}, loc\}$ | 57 | 37 |
| 0.4 | $\{ttr, st_l, st_{cr}, loc\}$ | $\{ttr, st_l, loc\}$ | 39 | 43 |
| 0.5 | $\{ttr, st_l, st_{cr}, loc\}$ | $\{st_l, st_{cr}, loc\}, \{\#, st_l, st_{cr}\}, \{ttr, st_l\}$ | 34 | 43 |
| 0.6 | $\{st_l, st_{cr}\}$ | $\{st_l, st_{cr}\}, \{ttr, st_l\}$ | 25 | 27 |
| 0.7 | $\{st_l, st_{cr}\}, \{ttr, st_l, loc\}$ | $\{st_{cr}, loc\}, \{st_l, st_{cr}\}, \{ttr\}$ | 13 | 18 |

**Fig. 6.** The reduction results for various approximation thresholds, where the first column contains the threshold value $\alpha$, two next columns contain $\alpha$-approximate decision reducts, and two last columns contain numbers of $\alpha$-approximate local decision reducts.

Because of the lack of space, we focus just on two observations. The first one concerns the type of treatment $ttr$. In Figure 6 we can see that $ttr$ occurs in majority of reducts, for various approximation thresholds. In case of $\varrho_{merged}$ and $\alpha = 0.7$ it even begins to be an approximate reduct itself. On the other hand, the occurrence of $ttr$ together with other attributes for lower thresholds suggests that it should not be considered totally independently, as noticed in Section 4.

The most frequent attribute occurring in Figures 6, 7 is the local cancer stage $st_l$. This is very surprising because the initial hypothesis formulated by medical experts was that $st_l$ can be reduced given the rest of considered clinical features.

| $\|[u]_B\|$ | $B$ | $\#$ | $ttr$ | $st_l$ | $st_{cr}$ | $loc$ |
|---|---|---|---|---|---|---|
| 79 | $\{ttr\}$ | * | $only$ | * | * | * |
| 132 | $\{ttr\}$ | * | $radio$ | * | * | * |
| 346 | $\{ttr\}$ | * | $after$ | * | * | * |
| 82 | $\{st_l\}$ | * | * | $T2$ | * | * |
| 361 | $\{st_l\}$ | * | * | $T3$ | * | * |
| 276 | $\{st_{cr}\}$ | * | * | * | $cN1$ | * |
| 174 | $\{loc\}$ | * | * | * | * | $throat$ |
| 46 | $\{\#,loc\}$ | 1 | * | * | * | $other$ |
| 62 | $\{\#,loc\}$ | 2 | * | * | * | $larynx$ |

| $\|[u]_B\|$ | $B$ | $\#$ | $ttr$ | $st_l$ | $st_{cr}$ | $loc$ |
|---|---|---|---|---|---|---|
| 25 | $\{st_l,st_{cr}\}$ | * | * | $T4$ | $cN0$ | * |
| 27 | $\{st_l,st_{cr}\}$ | * | * | $T4$ | $cN2$ | * |
| 6 | $\{st_l,st_{cr}\}$ | * | * | $T4$ | $cN3$ | * |
| 102 | $\{st_{cr},loc\}$ | * | * | * | $cN0$ | $larynx$ |
| 49 | $\{st_{cr},loc\}$ | * | * | * | $cN2$ | $larynx$ |
| 14 | $\{st_{cr},loc\}$ | * | * | * | $cN3$ | $larynx$ |
| 11 | $\{st_{cr},loc\}$ | * | * | * | $cN0$ | $other$ |
| 6 | $\{st_{cr},loc\}$ | * | * | * | $cN2$ | $other$ |
| 5 | $\{st_{cr},loc\}$ | * | * | * | $cN3$ | $other$ |

**Fig. 7.** $\alpha$-approximate local reducts obtained for $\alpha = 0.7$ and $\varrho_{merged}$. The first column contains the number of supporting objects. The second column contains attributes defining the reduct. The last five columns describe the reduct patterns. For instance, $*, *, T4, cN3, *$ corresponds to pattern $st_l = T4 \wedge st_{cr} = cN3$, supported by 6 objects.

Actually, $st_l$ does seem to provide less amount of information than the other attributes while comparing the Kaplan-Meier estimates for their particular values. However, as often happens in the rough set reduction processes, potentially least valuable attributes turn out to be crucial for discerning important cases.

## 6   Conclusions

We discussed a rough set approach to extraction of relevant patterns for compound decisions. We considered decision values modeled by rough membership distributions (cf. [6,10]) and the Kaplan-Meier's product-limit survival estimates (cf. [3]). We focused on searching for possibly minimal subsets of attributes approximately preserving the decision information, as well as the clusters of objects with approximately similar decision characteristics, described by possibly general patterns. The solutions were presented as approximate reducts derived using appropriately modified rough set discernibility procedures (cf. [9]).

In future we plan to develop a general approach to visualization of the chains of patterns characterized by various thresholds for decision distances, as initiated in [1]. We are going to strengthen the correspondence between the issue of the unified representation of the classes of objects with similar decision characteristics and the case-based reasoning challenges (cf. [7]). We also plan to continue the experiments concerning the considered medical data, in purpose of extending the results of this paper, as well as our previous experiences in this area.

**Acknowledgements.** Supported by Polish State Committee for Scientific Research (KBN) grant No. 8T11C02519. The fourth author also supported by the Research Center of PJIIT. Special thanks to Dr. Antoni Osmólski from the Medical Center of Postgraduate Education in Warsaw, Poland.

# References

1. Bazan J., Osmólski A., Skowron A., Ślęzak D., Szczuka M., Wróblewski J.: Rough set approach to the survival analysis. In Proc. of RSCTC'02 (2002).
2. Cios K.J., Kacprzyk J. (eds): Medical Data Mining and Knowledge Discovery. Studies in Fuzziness and Soft Computing 60, Physica Verlag, Heidelberg (2001).
3. Hosmer D.W. Jr., Lemeshow S.: Applied Survival Analysis: Regression Modeling of Time to Event Data. John Wiley & Sons, Chichester (1999).
4. Lenz M., Bartsch-Spoerl B., Burkhard H.-D., Wess S. (eds): Case-Based Reasoning Technology – From Foundations to Applications. LNAI 1400, Springer (1998).
5. Pawlak Z.: Rough sets – Theoretical aspects of reasoning about data. Kluwer Academic Publishers (1991).
6. Pawlak Z., Skowron A.: Rough membership functions. In: R.R. Yaeger, M. Fedrizzi, J. Kacprzyk (eds), Advances in the Dempster Shafer Theory of Evidence. Wiley (1994) pp. 251–271.
7. Polkowski L., Skowron A., Komorowski J.: Approximate case-based reasoning: A rough mereological approach. In: Proc. of the 4-th German Workshop on Case-Based Reasoning, System Developments and Evaluation (1996) pp. 144–151.
8. Skowron A., Pawlak Z., Komorowski J., Polkowski L.: A rough set perspective on data and knowledge. In: W. Kloesgen, J. Żytkow (eds), Handbook of KDD. Oxford University Press (2002) pp. 134–149.
9. Skowron A., Rauszer C.: The discernibility matrices and functions in information systems. In: R. Słowiński (ed.), Intelligent Decision Support. Handbook of Applications and Advances of the Rough Set Theory, Kluwer Academic Publishers, Dordrecht (1992) pp. 311–362.
10. Ślęzak D.: Various approaches to reasoning with frequency-based decision reducts: a survey. In: L. Polkowski, S. Tsumoto, T.Y. Lin (eds.), Rough Sets in Soft Computing and Knowledge Discovery: New Developments. Physica Verlag (2000).

# Clustering Supermarket Customers Using Rough Set Based Kohonen Networks

Pawan Lingras[1], Mofreh Hogo[2], Miroslav Snorek[2], and Bill Leonard[1]

[1] Department of Mathematics and Computing Science
Saint Mary's University, Halifax, Nova Scotia, B3H 3C3, Canada.
Pawan.Lingras@StMarys.CA
[2] Department of Computer Science and Engineering
Faculty of Electrical Engineering, Czech Technical University
Karlovo Nam. 13, 121 35 Prague 2, Czech Republic.

**Abstract.** This paper describes the creation of intervals of clusters of supermarket customers based on the modified Kohonen self-organizing maps. The supermarket customers from three different markets serviced by a Canadian national supermarket chain were clustered based on their spending and visit patterns. The resulting rough set based clustering captured the similarities and differences between the characteristics of the three regions.

## 1   Introduction

Any classification scheme can be represented as a partition of a given set of objects. Objects in each equivalence class of the partition are assumed to be identical or similar. In data mining, it is not possible to provide an exact representation of each class in the partition. Rough sets [4] enable us to represent such classes using upper and lower bounds. Researchers in rough set theory are showing increasing interest in clustering. Lingras [1,3] described how rough set theory can be used to modify some of the popular clustering methods such as Genetic Algorithms, K-means, and Kohonen self-organizing maps. The proposed rough set based clustering methods were successfully used to create interval clusters of web users on a number of educational web sites. This paper applies the modified Kohonen self-organizing maps for clustering supermarket customers. The data is obtained from three regions served by a national supermarket chain in Canada. The first region is a rural area, which is serviced by a single store. The second region is also a rural area serviced by five stores. The third region is an urban area serviced by six stores. The analysis of results seems to suggest that the intervals of clusters were able to distinguish the characteristics of these regions.

## 2   Rough Set Based Kohonen Self-Organizing Maps

Incorporating rough sets into the Kohonen algorithm requires an addition of the concept of lower and upper bounds in the equations, which are used for updating

N. Zhong et al. (Eds.): ISMIS 2003, LNAI 2871, pp. 169–173, 2003.

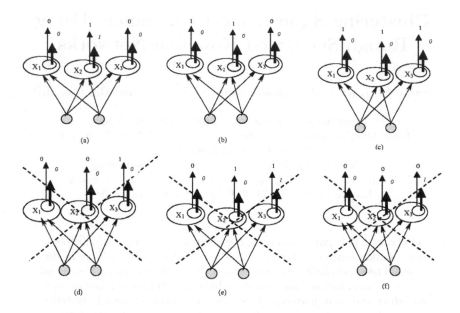

**Fig. 1.** Valid and invalid outputs from Kohonen rough set layer

the weights of the winners. The Kohonen rough set architecture is similar to the conventional Kohonen architecture. It consists of two layers, an input layer and the Kohonen rough set layer (rough set output layer). These two layers are fully connected. Each input layer neuron has a feed forward connection to each output layer neuron. Fig.1 illustrates the Kohonen rough set neural network architecture for one-dimensional case. A neuron in the Kohonen layer consists of two parts, a lower neuron and an upper neuron. The lower neuron has an output of 1, if an object belongs to the lower bound of the cluster. Similarly, a membership in the upper bound of the cluster will result in an output of 1 from the upper neuron. Since an object belonging to the lower bound of a cluster also belongs to its upper bound, when lower neuron has an output of 1, the upper neuron also has an output of 1. However, membership in the upper bound of a cluster does not necessarily imply the membership in its lower bound. Therefore, the upper neuron contains the lower neuron. Fig. 1 provides some cases to explain outputs from the Kohonen rough set neural network. Fig. 1(a-c) shows some of the possible outputs, while Fig. 1(d-f) shows some of the invalid outputs from the network. The interval clustering provides good results, if initial weights are obtained by running the conventional Kohonen learning. The next step in the modification of the Kohonen algorithm for obtaining rough sets is to design criteria to determine whether an object belongs to the upper or lower bounds of a cluster. For each object vector, $\mathbf{v}$, let $d(\mathbf{v}, \mathbf{x_i})$ be the distance between itself and the weight vector $\mathbf{x}_i$ of cluster $X_i$. The ratios $\frac{d(\mathbf{v}, \mathbf{x_i})}{d(\mathbf{v}, \mathbf{x_j})}$, were used to determine the membership of $\mathbf{v}$ as follows: Let $d(\mathbf{v}, \mathbf{x_i}) = \min_{1 \le j \le k} d(\mathbf{v}, \mathbf{x_j})$ and $T = \{j : d(\mathbf{v}, \mathbf{x_i}) - d(\mathbf{v}, \mathbf{x_j}) \le threshold$ and $i \ne j\}$.

1. If $T \neq \emptyset$, $\mathbf{v} \in \overline{A}(\mathbf{x}_i)$ and $\mathbf{v} \in \overline{A}(\mathbf{x}_j), \forall j \in T$. Furthermore, $\mathbf{v}$ is not part of any lower bound. The weight vectors $\mathbf{x_i}$ and $\mathbf{x_j}$ are modified as:
   $\mathbf{x_i}^{new} = \mathbf{x_i}^{old} + \alpha_{upper}(t) \times (\mathbf{v} - \mathbf{x_i}^{old})$, and
   $\mathbf{x_j}^{new} = \mathbf{x_j}^{old} + \alpha_{upper}(t) \times (\mathbf{v} - \mathbf{x_j}^{old})$.
2. Otherwise, if $T = \emptyset$, $\mathbf{v} \in \underline{A}(\mathbf{x}_i)$. In addition, $\mathbf{v} \in \overline{A}(\mathbf{x}_i)$. The weight vectors $\mathbf{x_i}$ is modified as:
   $\mathbf{x_i}^{new} = \mathbf{x_i}^{old} + \alpha_{lower}(t) \times (\mathbf{v} - \mathbf{x_i}^{old})$, and

Usually, $\alpha_{lower} > \alpha_{upper}$. The above algorithm preserves some of the important properties of rough sets [3]. It should be emphasized that the approximation space $A$ is not defined based on any predefined relation on the set of objects. The upper and lower bounds are constructed based on the criteria described above. Lingras, *et al.* [3] conducted experiments with web logs on three web sites, which suggests that the modification of the Kohonen neural networks provide reasonable interval set representations of clusters. The next section describes interval clustering of supermarket customers from three different regions.

## 3    Results and Discussions

The data used in the study was supplied by a national Canadian supermarket chain. Data consisted of transactional records from three regions. The first region, S1, consisted of one store in a rural setting. The second rural region (S2) was served by five stores, while the third region was an urban area with six stores. The data was collected over a twenty-six weeks period: October 22, 2000 – April 21, 2001. Lingras and Adams [2] used data on the spending and visits of supermarket customers for clustering those customers. The use of average values of these variables may hide some of the important information present in the temporal patterns. Therefore, Lingras and Adams [2] used the weekly time series values. It is possible that customers with similar profiles may spend different amounts in a given week. However, if the values were sorted, the differences between these customers may vanish. For example, three weeks spending of customer A may be $10, $30, and $20. Customer B may spend $20, $10, and $30 in those three weeks. If the two time-series were compared with each other, the two customers may seem to have completely different profiles. However, if the time-series values were sorted, the two customers will have identical patterns. Therefore, the values of these variables for 26 weeks were sorted, resulting in a total of 52 variables. A variety of values of K (number of clusters) were used in the initial experiments. After experimenting with a range of values, the threshold was set at 0.7, $\alpha_{lower}$ was chosen to be 0.01, 0.005 was used as the value of $\alpha_{upper}$, and 1000 iterations were used for the training phase of each data set.

Fig. 2 shows the average spending and visit patterns for the lower bounds of the five clusters. The patterns enable us to distinguish between the five types of customers as: loyal big spenders (G1), loyal moderate spenders (G2), semi-loyal potentially big spenders (G3), potentially moderate to big spenders with limited loyalty (G4), and infrequent customers (G5).

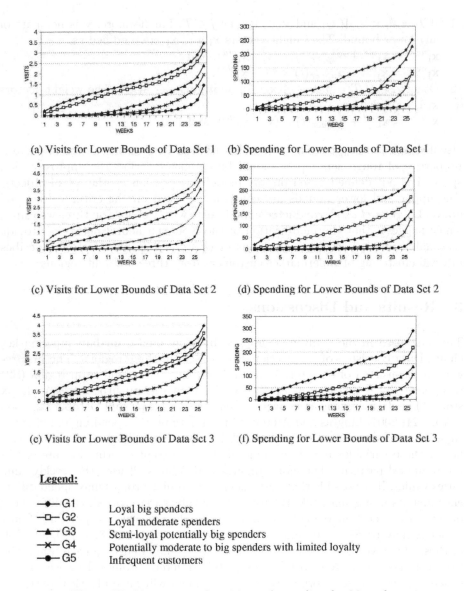

(a) Visits for Lower Bounds of Data Set 1    (b) Spending for Lower Bounds of Data Set 1

(c) Visits for Lower Bounds of Data Set 2    (d) Spending for Lower Bounds of Data Set 2

(e) Visits for Lower Bounds of Data Set 3    (f) Spending for Lower Bounds of Data Set 3

**Legend:**

| | | |
|---|---|---|
| ◆ G1 | | Loyal big spenders |
| □ G2 | | Loyal moderate spenders |
| ▲ G3 | | Semi-loyal potentially big spenders |
| ✕ G4 | | Potentially moderate to big spenders with limited loyalty |
| ● G5 | | Infrequent customers |

**Fig. 2.** Weekly patterns for visits and spending for 26 weeks

The patterns of these classes for the three regions were mostly similar. However, there was an interesting difference in S1 region. Even though for most weeks *loyal moderate spenders* (G2) had higher spending than *semi-loyal potentially big spenders* (G3), the highest spending of G3 was higher than G2. The region has only one store and hence it is likely that *semi-loyal potentially big spenders* do not find it convenient to shop at the supermarket on a regular basis.

# 4    Summary and Conclusions

This paper describes creation of interval clusters of supermarket customers using a modification of Kohonen self-organizing maps. The modification is based on rough set theoretic properties. The modified Kohonen algorithm was used to create interval clusters of customers from the three regions serviced by a Canadian supermarket chain. The resulting clusters seem to identify the differences between the regional characteristics. The percentages of loyal customers tended to be higher in an urban area with six stores than the rural regions. A well serviced rural region (with five stores) tended to attract higher customer loyalty than a rural region with only a single store. A detailed study of the characteristics of rough set based clusters will be helpful for the marketing analysts.

# References

1. P. Lingras: Unsupervised Rough Set Classification using GAs. Journal Of Intelligent Information Systems, Vol. 16:3 (2001) 215–228
2. P. Lingras and G. Adams: Selection of Time-Series for Clustering Supermarket Customers. Technical Report 2002_006, Department of Mathematics and Computing Science, Saint Mary's University, Halifax, N.S., Canada. http://cs.stmarys.ca/tech_reports/ (2002).
3. P. Lingras, M. Hogo and M. Snorek: Interval Set Clustering of Web Users using Modified Kohonen Self-Organization Maps based on the Properties of Rough Sets. submitted to Web Intelligent and Agent Systems: an International Journal, (2003).
4. Z. Pawlak: Rough Sets: Theoretical Aspects of Reasoning about Data. Kluwer Academic Publishers (1992).
5. L. Polkowski and A. Skowron: Rough Mereology: A New Paradigm for Approximate Reasoning. International Journal of Approximate Reasoning, Vol. 15(4) (1996) 333–365.
6. A. Skowron and J. Stepaniuk: Information granules in distributed environment. In Zhong, N. Skowron, A. Ohsuga, S. (eds.): New Directions in Rough Sets, Data Mining, and Granular-Soft Computing, Lecture notes in Artificial Intelligence, Vol. 1711. Springer-Verlag, Tokyo (1999) 357–365
7. Y.Y. Yao, X. Li, T.Y. Lin, and Q. Liu: Representation and Classification of Rough Set Models. Proceeding of Third International Workshop on Rough Sets and Soft Computing, San Jose, California (1994) 630–637.

# Multi-rough Sets and Generalizations of Contexts in Multi-contexts Information System

Rolly Intan[1,2] and Masao Mukaidono[1]

[1] Meiji University, Kawasaki-shi, Kanagawa-ken, Japan
[2] Petra Christian University, Surabaya, Indonesia 60236

**Abstract.** In previous paper, we introduced a concept of multi-rough sets based on a multi-contexts information system (MCIS). The MCIS was defined by a pair $\mathbf{I} = (U, \mathbf{A})$, where $U$ is a universal set of objects and $\mathbf{A}$ is a set of contexts of attributes. For every $A_i \in \mathbf{A}$ is a set of attributes regarded as a context or background, consequently, if there are $n$ contexts in $\mathbf{A}$, where $\mathbf{A} = \{A_1, \ldots, A_n\}$, it provides $n$ partitions. A given set of object, $X \subseteq U$, may then be represented into $n$ pairs of lower and upper approximations defined as *multi-rough sets* of $X$. In this paper, our primary concern is to discuss three kinds of general contexts, namely AND-general context, OR-general context and OR$^+$-general context.

## 1 Introduction

In [3], we introduced a concept of multi-rough sets based on a multi-contexts information system (MCIS). The MCIS was defined by a pair $\mathbf{I} = (U, \mathbf{A})$, where $U$ is a universal set of objects and $\mathbf{A}$ is a set of contexts of attributes. A context can be viewed as a background or situation in which somehow we need to group some attributes as a subset of attributes and consider the subset as a context. For every $A_i \in \mathbf{A}$ is a set of attributes regarded as a context or background, consequently, if there are $n$ contexts in $\mathbf{A}$, where $\mathbf{A} = \{A_1, \ldots, A_n\}$, it provides $n$ partitions. A given set of object, $X \subseteq U$, may then be represented into $n$ pairs of lower and upper approximations defined as *multi-rough sets* of $X$. Our primary concern in this paper is to generalize contexts in the presence of MCIS. Three kinds of general contexts, namely AND-general context, OR-general context and OR$^+$ general context, are proposed. We show that AND-general context and OR$^+$-general context provide (disjoint) partitions but OR-general context provides covering of the universe. Then, rough sets of a given crisp set are derived from partitions as well as covering of the general contexts. Their relations to summary multi-rough sets are examined.

## 2 Multi-rough Sets

A concept of *multi-rough sets* is proposed based on multi-contexts, where every context is considered as a subset of attributes. Partitions in corresponding to

N. Zhong et al. (Eds.): ISMIS 2003, LNAI 2871, pp. 174–178, 2003.

multi-contexts are generated from a *multi-contexts information system* (MCIS). Formally, the MCIS is defined by a pair $\mathbf{I} = (U, \mathbf{A})$, where $U$ is a universal set of objects and $\mathbf{A}$ is a non-empty set of contexts such as $\mathbf{A} = \{A_1, \ldots, A_n\}$. $A_i \in \mathbf{A}$ is a set of attributes and denoted as a context. Every attribute, $a \in A_i$, is associated with a set of $V_a$ as its values called domain of $a$. It is NOT necessary for $i \neq j \Rightarrow A_i \cap A_j = \emptyset$. Therefore, for $x \in U$, $a(x)^i \in V_a$ is denoted as the value of attribute $a$ for objects $x$ in the context $a \in A_i$. An indiscernibility relation (equivalence relation) is then defined in terms of context $A_i$ such as for $x, y \in U$: $R_{A_i}(x, y) \Leftrightarrow a(x)^i = a(y)^i$, $a(x)^i, a(y)^i \in V_a$, $\forall a \in A_i$. Equivalence class of $x \in U$ in the context $A_i$ is given by $[x]_{A_i} = \{y \in U | R_{A_i}(x, y)\}$. From the set of contexts $\mathbf{A}$, a set of partitions of universal objects are derived and given by $\{U/A_1, \ldots, U/A_n\}$, where $U/A_i$ as a partition of the universe based on context $A_i$ contains all equivalence classes of $[x]_{A_i}$, $x \in U$. More properties and discussion about MCIS can be found in [3].

Based on the MCIS, a multi-rough sets can be defined as follow: Let U be a non-empty universal set of objects. $R_{A_i}$ and $U/R_{A_i}$ are equivalence relation and partition with respect to a set of attributes in the context of $A_i$. For $X \subseteq U$, corresponding to a set of contexts, $\mathbf{A} = \{A_1, A_2, \ldots, A_n\}$, $\mathbf{X}$ is defined as multi-rough sets of $X$ and given by:

$$\mathbf{X} = \{(\underline{apr}_1(X), \overline{apr}_1(X)), (\underline{apr}_2(X), \overline{apr}_2(X)), \ldots, (\underline{apr}_n(X), \overline{apr}_n(X))\},$$

where $\underline{apr}_i(X) = \{u \in U \mid [u]_{A_i} \subseteq X\} = \bigcup\{[u]_{A_i} \in U/A_i \mid [u]_{A_i} \subseteq X\}$ and $\overline{apr}_i(X) = \{u \in U \mid [u]_{A_i} \cap X \neq \emptyset\} = \bigcup\{[u]_{A_i} \in U/A_i \mid [u]_{A_i} \cap X \neq \emptyset\}$. Some basic relations and operations have been proposed in [3].

Similar to *bags* (multiset) as proposed in [1,6], a multi-rough sets, $\mathbf{X}$, is characterized by a counting function $\Sigma_{\mathbf{X}}$ such that: $\Sigma_{\mathbf{X}} : \mathcal{P}(U)^2 \to \mathbb{N}$, where $\mathbb{N}$ is a set of non-negative integers and $\mathcal{P}(U)$ is power set of $U$. Clearly, for any pair of lower and upper approximations $(M, N) \in \mathcal{P}(U)^2$, $\Sigma_{\mathbf{X}}((M, N))$ counts number of occurrences the pair $(M, N)$ in the multi-rough sets $\mathbf{X}$, where it should be clarified that $(M, N) \notin \mathbf{X} \Rightarrow \Sigma_{\mathbf{X}}((M, N)) = 0$. Also, a support set of $\mathbf{X}$ denoted by $\mathbf{X}^*$ is defined by satisfying : $(M, N) \in \mathbf{X}^* \Leftrightarrow \Sigma_{\mathbf{X}}((M, N)) > 0$, where $\forall (M, N) \in \mathbf{X}^*$, $\Sigma_{\mathbf{X}^*}((M, N)) = 1$. It can be proved that if $\mathbf{X} = \mathbf{X}^*$ then set of contexts $\mathbf{A}$ is free from redundancy (see [3]), not vice versa. Related to the occurrence of elements and despite the order of elements in multi-rough sets, we may consider the following basic operations and relations.

(m1) Containment: $\mathbf{X} \sqsubset \mathbf{Y} \Leftrightarrow \Sigma_{\mathbf{X}}((M, N)) \leq \Sigma_{\mathbf{Y}}((M, N))$, $\forall (M, N)$;
(m2) Equality: $\mathbf{X} \equiv \mathbf{Y} \Leftrightarrow \Sigma_{\mathbf{X}}((M, N)) = \Sigma_{\mathbf{Y}}((M, N))$, $\forall (M, N)$;
(m3) Union: $\Sigma_{\mathbf{X} \oplus \mathbf{Y}}((M, N)) = \max[\Sigma_{\mathbf{X}}((M, N)), \Sigma_{\mathbf{Y}}((M, N))]$, $\forall (M, N)$;
(m4) Intersection: $\Sigma_{\mathbf{X} \otimes \mathbf{Y}}((M, N)) = \min[\Sigma_{\mathbf{X}}((M, N)), \Sigma_{\mathbf{Y}}((M, N))]$, $\forall (M, N)$;
(m5) Insertion: $\Sigma_{\mathbf{X} + \mathbf{Y}}((M, N)) = \Sigma_{\mathbf{X}}((M, N)) + \Sigma_{\mathbf{Y}}((M, N))$;
(m6) Minus: $\Sigma_{\mathbf{X} - \mathbf{Y}}((M, N)) = \max[\Sigma_{\mathbf{X}}((M, N)) - \Sigma_{\mathbf{Y}}((M, N)), 0]$;

When union and intersection are applied for all pair elements of multi-rough sets $\mathbf{X}$, we have:

$$\Gamma(X) = \bigcup^i \overline{apr}_i(X), \quad \Upsilon(X) = \bigcap^i \overline{apr}_i(X),$$
$$\Phi(X) = \bigcup^i \underline{apr}_i(X), \quad \Psi(X) = \bigcap^i \underline{apr}_i(X), \quad \forall i \in \mathbb{N}_n,$$

where $\overline{apr}(\mathbf{X}) = \{(\Gamma(X), \Upsilon(X))\}$ and $\underline{apr}(\mathbf{X}) = \{(\Phi(X), \Psi(X))\}$ are defined as a summary multi-rough sets in which they have only one pair element. It can be easily verified their relationship by: $\Psi(X) \subseteq \Phi(X) \subseteq X \subseteq \Upsilon(X) \subseteq \Gamma(X)$, where we may consider pair of $(\Phi(X), \Upsilon(X))$ as a finer approximation and pair of $(\Gamma(X), \Psi(X))$ as a worse approximation of $X \subseteq U$. From the definition of summary multi-rough sets, it satisfies some properties such as:

(1) $X \subseteq Y \Leftrightarrow [\Psi(X) \subseteq \Psi(Y), \Phi(X) \subseteq \Phi(Y), \Upsilon(X) \subseteq \Upsilon(Y), \Gamma(X) \subseteq \Gamma(Y)]$,
(2) $\Psi(X) = \neg\Gamma(\neg X)$, $\Phi(X) = \neg\Upsilon(\neg X)$, $\Upsilon(X) = \neg\Phi(\neg X)$, $\Gamma(X) = \neg\Psi(\neg X)$,
(3) $\Psi(U) = \Phi(U) = \Upsilon(U) = \Gamma(U) = U$, $\Psi(\emptyset) = \Phi(\emptyset) = \Upsilon(\emptyset) = \Gamma(\emptyset) = \emptyset$,
(4) $\Psi(X \cap Y) = \Psi(X) \cap \Psi(Y)$, $\Phi(X \cap Y) = \Phi(X) \cap \Phi(Y)$,
 $\Upsilon(X \cap Y) \leq \Upsilon(X) \cap \Upsilon(Y)$, $\Gamma(X \cap Y) \leq \Gamma(X) \cap \Gamma(Y)$,
(5) $\Psi(X \cup Y) \geq \Psi(X) + \Psi(Y) - \Psi(X \cap Y)$, $\Phi(X \cup Y) \geq \Phi(X) + \Phi(Y) - \Phi(X \cap Y)$,
 $\Upsilon(X \cup Y) \leq \Upsilon(X) + \Upsilon(Y) - \Upsilon(X \cap Y)$, $\Gamma(X \cup Y) \leq \Gamma(X) + \Gamma(Y) - \Gamma(X \cap Y)$,

## 3 Generalization of Contexts

Generalization of contexts means that all contexts of attributes are combined for the purpose of providing the one general context. Here, we propose three kinds of general context, namely AND-general context, OR-general context and OR$^+$-general context, .

First, general context provided by AND logic operator to all attributes of all contexts, called AND-*general context*, is simply constructed by collecting all elements of attributes of all contexts to the general context as defined by the following definition.

**Definition 1.** *Let* $\mathbf{A} = \{A_1, A_2, \ldots, A_n\}$ *be a set of contexts.* $A_\wedge$ *is defined as AND-general context by* $A_\wedge = A_1 \wedge A_2 \wedge \cdots \wedge A_n$, *where* $A_\wedge$ *is a result of summation of all conditions as given by all attributes in* $A_i, \forall i \in \mathbb{N}_n$ *or simply,* $A_\wedge = A_1 + A_2 + \cdots + A_n$.

In Definition 1, nevertheless, it was defined before in Section 2 that $i \neq j \nRightarrow A_i \cap A_j = \emptyset$, every attribute is regarded uniquely and independently in providing value of the attribute corresponding to a given object in terms of a certain context. It can be proved that $A_\wedge$ satisfies $|A_\wedge| = \sum_{i=1}^n |A_i|$. Also, $\forall [u]_{A_\wedge}, \forall i \in \mathbb{N}_n, \exists [u]_{A_i}$ such that $[u]_{A_\wedge} \subseteq [u]_{A_i}$. For a given $X \subseteq U$, $\underline{apr}_\wedge(X)$ and $\overline{apr}_\wedge(X)$ are defined as lower and upper approximations of $X$ provided by the set of attributes, $A_\wedge$. Approximation space performed by AND-general context is regarded as the finest disjoined partition by combining all partition of contexts and considering every possible area of intersection among equivalence classes as an equivalence class of AND-general context. Therefore, it provides the finest approximation of rough set.

Second, if relations among contexts are operated by OR logic operator, the independency of every context persists in the process of generalization. Clearly, it provides a covering of the universal objects instead of a disjoint partition. Since the general context provides covering [2], it may also be called *Cover-general context* (*C-general context*, for short) and defined as follows.

**Definition 2.** *Let* $\mathbf{A} = \{A_1, A_2, \ldots, A_n\}$ *be a set of contexts.* $A_\vee$ *is defined as C-general context by:* $A_\vee = A_1 \vee A_2 \vee \cdots \vee A_n$, *such that* $U/A_\vee = \bigcup_{i=1}^{n} U/A_i$, *where* $U/A_\vee$ *is a covering of the universe as union of all equivalence classes in* $U/A_i$, $i \in \mathbb{N}_n$.

Consequently, $|U/A_\vee| \leq \sum_{i=1}^{n} |U/A_i|$ and $\forall C \in U/A_\vee$, $\forall i \in \mathbb{N}_n$, $\exists [u]_{A_i}$ such that $C = [u]_{A_i}$, where $C$ is *a similarity class* in covering and $[u]_{A_i}$ is an equivalence class in the partition of $U/A_i$. We call $C$ as a similarity class as a means to distinguish between equivalence class provided by equivalence relation as usually used in partition and one used in covering. Every similarity class might take overlap one to each other. A given object $u \in U$ possibly belongs to more than one similarity classes. It can be verified that for $X \in U$, $\overline{apr}_\vee(X)$ and $\underline{apr}_\vee(X)$, as a pair of upper and lower approximations of $X$ in terms of $A_\vee$, can be defined by, $\overline{apr}_\vee(X) = \bigcup_{i=1}^{n} \overline{apr}_i(X)$, $\underline{apr}_\vee(X) = \bigcup_{i=1}^{n} \underline{apr}_i(X)$, where $\overline{apr}_i(X)$ and $\underline{apr}_i(X)$ are upper and lower approximations of $X$ based on the context $A_i$. It can be proved that iterative operation is applied in the upper approximation operator, for $\overline{apr}_\vee(X) \subseteq \overline{apr}_\vee(\overline{apr}_\vee(X))$. We may then consider $M(\overline{apr}_\vee(X))$ as a maximum upper approximation given by $\overline{apr}_\vee(X) \subset \overline{apr}(\overline{apr}_\vee(X)) \subset \cdots \subset M(\overline{apr}_\vee(X))$, where the iterative operation is no longer applied in the maximum upper approximation or $M(\overline{apr}_\vee(X)) = \overline{apr}_\vee(M(\overline{apr}_\vee(X)))$. Related to the covering of the universal objects, some properties are given in [2]. Moreover, related to summary multi-rough sets as defined in the previous section, we found that $\overline{apr}_\vee(X) = \Gamma(X)$ and $\underline{apr}_\vee(X) = \Phi(X)$.

The third general context is called $OR^+$-*general context* in which transitive closure operation is applied to the covering as result of OR-general context or C-general context. In other words, equivalence classes of $OR^+$-general context are provided by union of all equivalence classes of all partitions (of all contexts) that overlap one to each other. Similarity classes of $OR^+$-*general context* are defined as the following definition.

**Definition 3.** *Let* $\mathbf{A} = \{A_1, A_2, \ldots, A_n\}$ *be a set of contexts.* $A_\vee^+$ *is defined as* $OR^+$-*general context by:* $A_\vee^+ = A_1 \circ A_2 \circ \cdots \circ A_n$, *such that* $y \in [x]_{A_\vee^+}$ *iff* $(\exists C_i \in U/A_\vee, \; x, y \in C_i)$ OR $(\exists C_{i1}, C_{i2}, \ldots, C_{im} \in U/A_\vee,$ $x \in C_{i1}, \; C_{ik} \cap C_{ik+1} \neq \emptyset, \; k = 1, \ldots, m-1, \; y \in C_{im})$, *where* $m \leq n$ *and* $[x]_{A_\vee^+}$ *is an equivalence class containing* $x$ *in terms of* $A_\vee^+$.

For $U/A_\vee$ be a set of similarity classes provided by all contexts, equivalence classes generated by $A_\vee^+$ are able to be constructed by the following algorithm: $S_i \in U/A_\vee^+$, $i \in \mathbb{N}$: Equivalence classes of $OR^+$-general context.

```
p = 0; SC = U/A_∨;
while SC ≠ ∅ do {
p = p + 1; Sₚ = ∅;
SC = SC − {M};  M is an element (similarity class) in SC.
Sₚ = M;
SS = SC;
while SS ≠ ∅ do {
SS = SS − {M};  M is an element (similarity class) in SS.
```

$if\ S_p \cap M \neq \emptyset\ then\ \{$
$S_p = S_p \cup M;$
$\mathbf{SC} = \mathbf{SC} - \{M\};$
$\}$
$\}$
$\}$

Finally, by the above algorithm, there will be $p$ equivalence classes. Possibly, $p$ might be equal to 1 in case all elements in $U/A_\vee$ transitively join each other. It can be proved that all equivalence classes in $U/A_\vee^+$ are disjoint. Also, $\forall S \in U/A_\vee^+$ such that $\forall i \in \mathbb{N}_n$, $\exists M \in U/A_i$, $M \subseteq S$. For a given $X \subseteq U$, $\underline{apr}_\vee^+(X)$ and $\overline{apr}_\vee^+(X)$ are defined as lower and upper approximation of $X$ provided by set of attributes, $A_\vee^+$. Approximation space performed by OR$^+$-general context is regarded as the worst disjoined partition. Therefore, it provides the worst approximation of rough set. Related to the maximum upper approximation based on C-general context, it can be verified that $\overline{apr}_\vee^+(X) = M(\overline{apr}_\vee(X))$. Compare to summary multi-rough sets and approximation based on AND-general context, we have

$$\underline{apr}_\vee^+(X) \subseteq \Psi(X) \subseteq \Phi(X) \subseteq \underline{apr}_\wedge(X) \subseteq X \subseteq \overline{apr}_\wedge(X) \subseteq \Upsilon(X) \subseteq \Gamma(X) \subseteq \overline{apr}_\vee^+(X).$$

## 4    Conclusion

This paper proposed multi-rough sets based on a MCIS. Related to the MCIS, we proposed three types of general contexts, namely AND-general context, C-general context and OR$^+$-general context. This paper also discussed briefly relation among approximations provided by the general contexts. In the future work, we need to apply and implement the concept of multi-rough sets in the real-world application.

## References

1. Cerf, V., Fernandez, E., Gostelow, K., Volansky, S., 'Formal Control Flow Properties Flow Properties of a Model of Computation', *Report ENG-7178*, Computer Science Department, UCLA, (December 1971).
2. Intan, R., Mukaidono, M., 'Generalized Fuzzy Rough Sets By Conditional Probability Relations', *International Journal of Pattern Recognition and Artificial Intelligence 16(7)*, World Scientific, (2002), pp. 865–881.
3. Intan, R., Mukaidono, M., 'Multi-Rough Sets Based on Multi-Contexts of Attributes', *Proceeding of RSFDGrC 2003, LNAI 2639, Springer-Verlag*, (2003), pp. 279–282.
4. Komorowski, J., Pawlak, Z., Polkowski, L., Skowron, A., 'Rough Sets: A Tutorial', In S.K Pal and A. Skowron (Eds.), *Rough Fuzzy Hybridization*, (1999), pp. 3–98.
5. Pawlak, Z., Rough sets, *International Journal Computation & Information Science*, *11*, (1982), pp. 341–356.
6. Yager, R. R., 'On The Theory of Bags', *Int. J. General Systems*, *13*, (1986), pp. 23–37.

# MetaNews: An Information Agent for Gathering News Articles on the Web

Dae-Ki Kang[1] and Joongmin Choi[2]

[1] Department of Computer Science
Iowa State University
Ames, IA 50011, USA
dkkang@cs.iastate.edu
[2] Department of Computer Science and Engineering
Hanyang University
Ansan, Kyunggi-Do 426-791, Korea
jmchoi@cse.hanyang.ac.kr

**Abstract.** This paper presents *MetaNews*, an information gathering agent for news articles on the Web. MetaNews reads IITML documents from online news sites and extracts article information from them. In order to recognize and extract articles from an HTML document, MetaNews removes redundant HTML tags, builds *a reference string* which is a sequence of semantic components of a noise-removed document, and performs pattern matching between the reference string and each of pre-defined *information patterns* for articles. With a few training inputs from the operator with intermediate-level skills, MetaNews is capable of adding new sites easily and extracting articles in real time. By reducing the complexity of designing and creating wrapper interfaces, the proposed techniques in MetaNews are useful for many information-mediator applications such as meta-search engines, information-push solutions, and comparison-shopping agents.

## 1 Introduction

The World Wide Web has been growing rapidly, and as a result, it is becoming more difficult to find the right information that users really need. The main issue that is raised commonly from many applications such as online shopping and meta-search systems is how to integrate semi-structured and heterogeneous Web information sources and provide a uniform way of accessing them. *Wrapper* has been suggested for this kind of integration[7,8].

Most wrapper interfaces have been implemented in an ad-hoc way that the knowledge about information sources is obtained manually and hard-coded into the program. In this approach, however, whenever the information structure of a site is changed, the corresponding wrapper should be rewritten accordingly. The modification of a handwritten wrapper is not trivial, since it may include the rewriting of program codes that requires at least a moderate level of programming skills. Furthermore, handwritten wrappers are not scalable. That is, since

N. Zhong et al. (Eds.): ISMIS 2003, LNAI 2871, pp. 179–186, 2003.

a handwritten wrapper corresponds only to a single Web information source, adding a new Web site requires building a new wrapper by creating a program code for the site. For these reasons, automated methods for wrapper generation have been suggested[3,5,7]. However, most previous studies related to the automatic wrapper generation have some drawbacks in actual applications. First, a small change in the corresponding Web site such as changing text colors or font sizes might affect the wrapper significantly. Second, pattern-matching process based on regular expression is complex. Only a few experts who are knowledgeable on both domain features and regular grammars can build patterns in a regular-expression form for new application domains.

In this paper, we present an efficient method for relaxing the overheads in generating wrapper interfaces and promoting the scalability of adding and changing semi-structured Web information sources. *Effective noise removal* and *fast pattern matching of strings* are the two key features in this method. With these features, information-mediator applications can retrieve the needy information more efficiently in real time, and are immune to small format changes in retrieved documents. To show the effectiveness of our approach, we developed *MetaNews*, an information agent for gathering online news articles that can manipulate over 100 international news sites. By categorizing various news sites in a systematic way, MetaNews provides the knowledge about each site and up-to-date articles. In addition, MetaNews has an interesting feature for ubiquitous Web browsing that transmits collected articles to a PDA so that users can read them even when they are away from their desktops.

The characteristics of MetaNews can be described in four ways. First, the back-end analyzer of MetaNews can focus only on meaningful information through preprocessing that removes noisy HTML tags and annotations. Second, even with a small amount of knowledge, users can find the right information they need. Third, the wrapper interface is not affected by trivial changes in the corresponding Web site. Fourth, it is quite easy to add a new site to the system with only a small amount of additional information. The method is effective not only for the MetaNews agent but also for other information-mediator applications such as meta-search engines, push solutions, and comparison-shopping agents[3].

This paper is organized as follows. In Section 2, we describe the system architecture and the features of MetaNews, focusing on noise removal and pattern matching. In Section 3, we present some empirical results to show the practical merits of MetaNews. Finally, in Section 4, we conclude with a summary and future direction.

## 2    MetaNews

MetaNews is an information agent for gathering news articles on the Web. The goal of MetaNews is to extract news articles from periodically updated online newspapers and magazines. More specifically, MetaNews collects HTML documents from online newspaper sites, extracts articles by using the techniques of

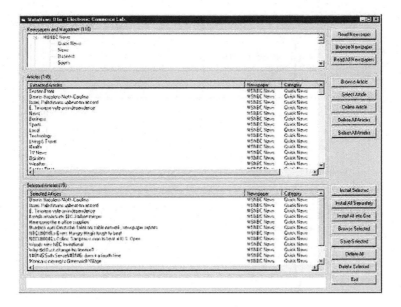

**Fig. 1.** Main interface of MetaNews

noise removal and pattern matching, and provides the user with the titles of extracted articles and the hyperlinks to their contents.

Figure 1 shows the main interface of MetaNews which has three display windows. The upper window provides a hierarchical view in a way that each top-level node corresponds to a news site and its subnodes denote topic categories. In the figure, the "MSNBC News" site is displayed with its categories including "QuickNews", "News", "Business", and "Sports". The center window lists the extracted news articles. The user can see the titles not the contents, and select interesting articles from several news sites. The selected articles are displayed at the bottom window, where the user can save them to files or install them in a PDA. At any window, the user can see the content of an article by double-clicking its title that invokes an ActiveX-controlled Web browser.

Figure 2 shows the architectural diagram of MetaNews. The control flow of MetaNews can be explained in three different stages. At the *initial configuration stage*, MetaNews is given with the URLs of a site's homepage and its subcategory pages and also with the information patterns for article extraction. This information is used for the addition of new sites. At the *article retrieval stage*, the user selects specific news in the control panel, and then MetaNews gets HTML documents from the selected Web sites in real time. After that, noise removal and substring pattern matching are performed on the documents, and the informative records of articles in the matched documents are extracted. MetaNews has an embedded Web browser with ActiveX control for convenient article display. At the *article saving stage*, the user can select interesting articles and save

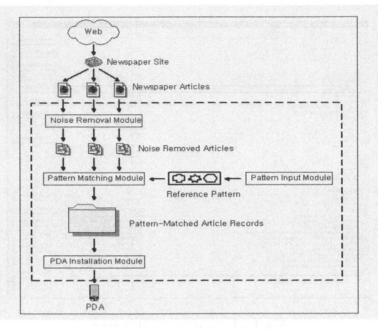

**Fig. 2.** Architecture of the MetaNews agent

them to files or install them in a PDA. With a minimal editing work, a new site can be easily added to MetaNews.

We now discuss in more detail about the key techniques in our method: noise removal and pattern matching.

## 2.1   Noise Removal

MetaNews extracts the articles' titles and relevant URLs from the category pages of a news site. Since HTML is mainly used for displays and hyperlinks, most HTML tags are irrelevant to the information content. Although some of these tags may be useful for emphasizing or giving weights to terms, we are certain from the empirical results that removing these tags is not harmful in analyzing the document for the extraction. Furthermore, for the applications like MetaNews in which the priorities of information in the document is not so important and most pieces of information are equally useful and needed, removing tags is always advantageous. This process is called *noise removal*.

A category page of a news site contains the list of news article records, and each article record contains a hyperlink surrounded by some anchor tags. These anchor tags are treated as useful HTML tags, and the URL in each anchor tag of a hyperlink is converted into a simplified canonical form by the anchor tag conversion module. Also, some of table-related tags including `<table>`, `<tr>`, and `<td>` are also considered as useful tags. Other redundant tags are simply removed by the tag removal module.

The noise remover in MetaNews is implemented in Fast LEX (FLEX), a clone of LEX which has more expressive power and generates an efficient binary executable. Each regular expression in the FLEX code can be regarded as a rule/action pair for noise removal purpose. Fig. 3 shows an example of noise-removed part of a document.

```
<TABLE>
<TR>
<TD>
</TD>
<TD>
<A>
HREF=303767.asp
With a heavy heart, crew leaves Mir
</A>
</TD>
</TR>
<TR>
<TD>
</TD>
<TD>
Amid sadness and ceremony, a Russian-French crew left the
13-year-old Mir space station unoccupied and returned
to earth.
</TD>
</TR>
</TABLE>
```

**Fig. 3.** Noise removed document

Note that the noise removal module makes it possible to use the same wrapper interface for different news sites. This advantage also applies to the situation when the external layout of a news site is changed.

## 2.2   Pattern Matching

In MetaNews, *pattern matching* is performed to recognize and extract articles from the noise-removed document. Pattern matching is composed of three sub-processes. First, the noise-removed document is converted into a *reference string* which is a sequence of semantic components. Next, the string matching is performed between the reference string and each of the *information pattern* strings. An information pattern (also called a reference pattern) is also a sequence of semantic components that comprises an article. Information patterns for articles are predefined by the operator. Finally, the substrings in the reference string that are matched with any information pattern are extracted and displayed.

To help understand the operation of this module, we revisit the example in Fig. 3 which represents a single record. This record can be converted into a reference string "**TRDdDAUXadrRDdDXdrt**", by applying a simple conversion rule described in Fig. 4 to each line .

In contrast with the reference string that is generated automatically by the conversion rules, the information pattern for an article is built manually. For

| | | |
|---|---|---|
| &lt;TABLE&gt; | → | **T** |
| &lt;/TABLE&gt; | → | **t** |
| &lt;TR&gt; | → | **R** |
| &lt;/TR&gt; | → | **r** |
| &lt;TD&gt; | → | **D** |
| &lt;/TD&gt; | → | **d** |
| &lt;A&gt; | → | **A** |
| &lt;/A&gt; | → | **a** |
| *hyperlink* (HREF=. . .) | → | **U** |
| *other* (*general text*) | → | **X** |

**Fig. 4.** Rules for reference string generation

example, the title of a news article is normally surrounded by hyperlink tags, so we might induce that the information pattern for an article can be "**AUXa**". In this pattern, '**A**' indicates the beginning of an anchor tag (&lt;a&gt;), '**U**' is the URL of an article (href=http://...), '**X**' is the title text of an article, and '**a**' is the ending anchor tag (&lt;/a&gt;). With some intuitive heuristics, this simple pattern can be used effectively for locating the title of a news article with the corresponding hyperlink. Since this information pattern is a substring of the reference string for the record in Fig. 3, MetaNews can recognize it as an article. Figure 1 shown in the previous section is the result of applying pattern matching algorithm to the QuickNews section of the MSNBC News.

Note that, in the online shopping domain, each record corresponds to a product description with the product name and the price. In this case, the information pattern for a record can be "**DXd**", which consists of table tags and the text for product description. The information pattern denotes how the desired information is encoded in a noise-removed HTML page, so it may be changed in different domains.

Our pattern matching scheme has advantages in terms of simplicity and scalability. Especially, at the stage of pattern matching, extracting information can be done by just one string matching which is supported by most programming languages. Also, since these information patterns are encoded in a data file instead of being hard-coded into the program, a trained operator can add new sites easily by just inserting less than fifty lines of data including the URLs and the information patterns.

## 3   Evaluation

The MetaNews agent can extract articles and their hyperlinks from 116 news sites. MetaNews is scalable in a sense that a new site can be added by inserting a few lines of pattern data, even for a large news site. For our actual experiments of reading news, only three information patterns were needed for all cases: "**AUXa**", "**XAUa**", and "**AUaX**".

Since MetaNews does not depend on a morphological analyzer or a stemming program, it does not have the language limit. Therefore, without changing any program code, MetaNews can be used for sites with various languages such as English, Korean, or Japanese.

In order to evaluate the performance of MetaNews, *precision* and *recall* values are estimated by using positive false and negative false data.

*Positive false* refers to the data that are not news articles but extracted by MetaNews since they contain fragments matched with the information patterns. Examples of positive false are quick links for other sections, cool links, advertisement links, etc. We have tested MetaNews for 116 sites, and Fig. 5 shows the comparison between the number of total data and the number of positive false data gathered by MetaNews for each site. Note, in the graph, that the first 90 sites are the news sites which have the 3-level information structure consisting of the main page, the category pages, and the actual article pages, and the last 26 are the magazine sites which have the 2-level information structure with the main and article pages, without category pages. MetaNews extracts more articles from 3-level sites since the category page plays an important role in pattern matching. Positive false affects the precision value of the system, and MetaNews shows the average precision value of 88% for the news sites, and about 82% for the magazine sites.

On the other hand, *negative false* occurs when MetaNews fails to recognize and extract news articles, and this phenomenon affects the recall value of the system. With just three information patterns, however, MetaNews does not produce any negative false data for all 116 sites, so the recall can be said as 100% in our experiments.

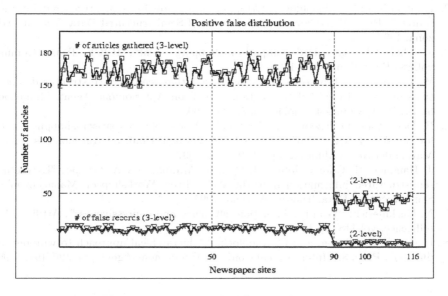

**Fig. 5.** Positive false distribution on test sites

# 4   Conclusions

We have presented MetaNews, an information gathering agent for news articles on the Web. With a few training inputs from the operator with intermediate-level skills, MetaNews is able to add a new site easily and extract articles in real time. Our method is simple but powerful enough to reduce the complexity in designing and creating wrapper interfaces, and is useful for many information-mediator applications such as meta-search engines, information-push solutions, and comparison-shopping agents.

Several problems exist for MetaNews that will be handled in the future. First, we need to work out for the removal of false record with post-processing after pattern matching. If the information pattern is not too long or too general, false links can be regarded as news articles. The three information patterns used in this paper can be generalized but it is difficult to set more constraints to our pattern matching approach. A keyword filter can be helpful for reducing the ratio of false records. For example, if the user sets a keyword filter as *Clinton*, only the articles with the title containing *Clinton* will be gathered. Also, a deny list could be maintained in post-processing. Second, we need to search for the *back issues* to extract past articles. MetaNews should be able to deal with the CGI scripts of news sites to achieve this. Finally, porting MetaNews to the conduit mechanism for mobile communication will be an interesting topic.

# References

1. D. Angluin, "Interface of reversible languages", Journal of ACM, vol.29, no.3, pp.741–765, 1982.
2. N. Ashish and C. Knoblock, "Wrapper generation for semi-structured Internet sources", Proc. Workshop on Management of Semistructured Data, Tucson, Arizona, 1997.
3. J. Choi, "A customized comparison-shopping agent", IEICE Trans. Comm., vol.E84-B, no.6, pp.1694–1696, 2001.
4. W. Cohen, "A web-based information system that reasons with structured collections of text", Proc. 2nd International Conf. on Autonomous Agent, Minneapolis/St. Paul, Minnesota, pp.400–407, May 1998.
5. R. Doorenbos, O. Etzioni, and D. Weld, "A scalable comparison-shopping agent for the World Wide Web", Proc. 1st International Conf. on Autonomous Agent, Marina del Rey, California, pp.39–48, Feb. 1997.
6. J. Hammer, H. Garcia-Molina, J. Cho, R. Aranha, and A. Crespo, "Extracting semistructured information from the Web", Proc. Workshop on Management of Semistructured Data. Tucson, Arizona, 1997.
7. N. Kushmerick, "Wrapper induction: efficiency and expressiveness", Artificial Intelligence, vol.118, pp.15–68, 2000.
8. I. Muslea, S. Minton, and C. Knoblock, "A hierarchical approach to wrapper induction", Proc. 3rd International Conf. on Autonomous Agents, pp.190–197, 1999.

# Enacting an Agent-Based Digital Self in a 24x7 Web Services World

Steve Goschnick

Intelligent Agent Lab
Department of Information Systems
University of Melbourne, 3010, Australia
`gosh@staff.dis.unimelb.edu.au`

**Abstract.** As broadband access to the Internet becomes pervasive, the need for a 24 hours a day, seven days a week (24x7) interface within the client devices, requires a level of sophistication that implies agent technology. From this situation we identified the need for a user-proxy++, something we have termed the *Digital Self* that acts for the user gathering appropriate information and knowledge, representing and acting for them when they are off-line. With these notions in mind we set about defining an agent architecture, sufficiently complex to deal with the myriad aspects of the life of a busy time-poor modern user, and we arrived at the Shadowboard architecture. For the theory, for the model of mind, we drew upon the *Psychology of Subselves*, a modern strain of Analytical Psychology. For the computation engine we drew upon Constraint Logic Programming. For the hundreds of sources of sub-agency and external intelligence needed to enact a Digital Self within the 24x7 Internet environment, we drew upon the Web Services paradigm. This paper presents the theory, the architecture and the implementation of a prototype of the Shadowboard agent system.

## 1 Introduction

There were two driving motivations for the research and development outlined in this paper. Firstly, our continual connection to the Internet 24x7, usually as a by-product of broadband, leaves us connected to a world of disparate services and external computational intelligence, largely under-utilized while we are either: asleep, away from our desktops, or otherwise occupied. Secondly, the time-poor lives that many of us live, in our busy modern modes of existence, where we each have numerous and increasing roles, each with associated obligations, needs and desires, often operating concurrently – eg. one may be a *parent*, a *teacher*, a *domain expert*, an *artist*, a *traveler*, an *investor* – sometimes all at once. We have set out to harness the untapped potential of the first, to improve the quality of life observed in the second.

By creating and then using a sufficiently complex agent architecture on the client device, we are able to harness external services and growing intelligence out on the web, in a systematic and synergetic way, providing a serious bid to buy back some

N. Zhong et al. (Eds.): ISMIS 2003, LNAI 2871, pp. 187–196, 2003.

quality time for the well connected user. We term this fully configured system for a given individual user, their *Digital Self*.

In Section 2 we outline the theory by introducing the *Psychology of Subselves* as the complex model of mind from which we inferred the Shadowboard agent architecture. In Section 3 we introduce the *Shadowboard architecture*, looking at its different components. In Section 4 we briefly look at the *methodology* still being evolved, that is designed to get the best match for an individual user, of a combination of sub-agents that will in concert, represent their Digital Self. In Section 5 we outline the development of a prototype. It includes: *ShadowFaces* an agent-metaphor interface which is more appropriate for a Digital Self operating 24x7 than the document-centric desktop metaphor; the use of CoLoG a constraint logic language as the computational engine; and the wrapping of hundreds of SOAP web services into the sub-agents that make the Digital Self viable and useful in the near term.

# 2    Theory

The BDI agent architecture [14] is one of a number of architectures that enact deliberative agents. BDI calls upon the mentalistic notions of *Beliefs*, *Desires* and *Intentions* from *Folk Psychology*, as abstractions to encapsulate the hidden complexity of the inner functioning of an *individual* agent. Folk psychology is the name given to everyday talk about the mind, the vocabulary we use to explain ourselves such as: *beliefs, desires, intentions, fears, wishes, hopes*. As people, the use of such language gives us an efficient method for understanding and predicting behaviour, although the model of mind it presents is very course-grained and therefore not suitable for a complex Digital Self. However BDI sets a precedent in its use of a psychology other than cognitive psychology, as fertile ground for computational agent models.

| Main exponent: | Sigmund Freud | Carl Jung | Roberto Assagioli | Hal Stone & Sidra Winkelman (Psychoanalysis & Psychosynthesis) |
|---|---|---|---|---|
| *Technique* | Psychoanalysis | | Psychosynthesis | Voice Dialogue |
| *Model divisions of the human psyche* | Ego | Persona | Centre | Aware Ego |
| | | Self, self | Self | |
| | Super Ego | Higher Self | | Protector/Controller Inner Critic |
| | Id *repression* | The Shadow | | Several *Disowned Selves* |
| | | Anima/ Animus | Many sub-selves | Pusher, Pleaser, Parental and many other subselves |
| | | Archetypes | Evolved Subselves | |

**Fig. 1.** Lineage of sub-personality exponents and some of their divisions of the psyche

Western psychology has many rich branches from which one could draw models of agency including: *analytical psychology, humanistic psychology, developmental psychology*. Shadowboard, the agent architecture we have developed, draws upon *analytical psychology*, in particular a contemporary stream encompassing refinements of Freudian [15], Jungian [9] and Assagiolian [1] concepts. The approach is known as the

*Psychology of Subselves,* an attempt to understand the whole personality of an individual - in order to model consciousness, deliberation and action [15; 17].

Figure 1 above represents a scant overview of the divisions of the psyche that different influential analytical psychologists identified and named. Beginning with Freud about 100 years ago, followed by Carl Jung these psychologists identified substrata within the psyche of an individual. As we move across the columns in Figure 1 from left to right, we move forward to contemporary theory on sub-selves within the psyche. The most easily identified sub-selves of a person often align with the *roles* in their lives – *teacher, parent, domain expert, artist, sibling, traveler,* etc. A comparative description of the different psychologies we considered and the subsequent development of the Shadowboard *architecture*, is detailed extensively elsewhere [4].

## 3   Architecture

Figure 2 below is a graphic overview of the Shadowboard architecture, collectively representing an individual *whole agent* made up of numerous sub-components – the structural implications are inferred from the Psychology of Subselves. In the centre of the agent is the *Aware Ego Agent* – the dominant sub-agent in the whole cluster of sub-agents. In the figure, the Aware Ego Agent is surrounded by eight first-level sub-agents, diagrammatically drawn as circles the same size as the Aware Ego Agent. Five of these example sub-agents are not nested any deeper (i.e. sub-agents can be clustered recursively), while the other three have clusters of circles within them, representing a second-level of sub-agents, grouped into numerous Envelope-of-Capability (EoC).

Each *EoC*, of which there are arbitrarily eight in the figure, represent different areas of expertise that a particular whole agent embodies. As such the whole agent could perform a number of consecutive and diverse tasks, depending on what goals via what roles it has taken on in the outer world.

Each EoC contains a number of sub-agents with similar capabilities, but each different from it neighbors in some specialized way. At the two far ends of an EoC are two diametrically skilled agents - in Figure 2 the two are adjacent, one is white the other is black, separated by a dotted radial line.

One is the *basic reactive sub-agent* a purely reactive agent [2] with a hard-wired rule-action mechanism and no deliberative capability. It is usually called upon within a particular EoC when time or other resources are severely constrained.

At the other end of the scale is an *archetypal sub-agent*, one that has maximum deliberative ability used when time and other resources are plentiful.

The *aware ego agent,* as well as each of the other sub-agents (*delegation sub-agents*) that are shaded as spheres, have *knowledge of the capabilities* of sub-agents in their EoC. They use this knowledge to select the appropriate sub-agent to achieve the particular goal that has been sent their way from higher up in the recursive hierarchy.

When a sub-agent has been found lacking in capability to achieve a specific intention, or when an external (and available) agent matches the particular specialty better than any internal sub-agents, an external agent can be called upon as if it were an internal sub-agent. This process is termed *disowning a sub-agent*.

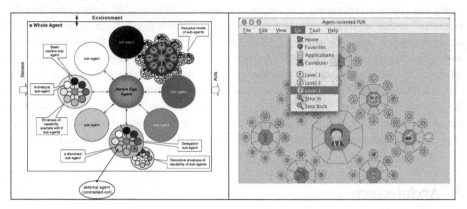

**Fig. 2.** The Shadowboard Architecture and the Implemented Prototype

## 3.1 Sub-agents as Subselves

The mentalistic notion of a *subself* at work within the psyche of an individual, is a metaphor for the *sub-agent* of a Shadowboard agent. To broadly place this work in context of research upon multi-agent systems (MAS) - most MAS can be described as *inter*-agent systems. In contrast, the Shadowboard theory and architecture is an *intra*-agent system, one enabling the incorporation of many components that together represent one *whole* agent, albeit a very sophisticated one. Such a *whole agent* built upon the Shadowboard architecture – the *Digital Self* – seen from without, should be seen as a fully *autonomous* individual agent, one compatible with contemporary definitions of agency, such as that of Wooldridge [19].

Unlike the autonomous whole agent, the inner sub-agents are semi-autonomous or even totally subservient to the *Aware Ego Agent* - the executive controller within a Shadowboard agent. Sub-agents may themselves be sophisticated agents capable of their own semi-autonomous work, or they may be conventional application programs, expert systems, or even wrapped Web Services as we shall see further down. This is a significant relaxation on the need in most MAS systems (at least in theory) for each individual agent to be a fully functioning autonomous agent. This flexibility in capability provided within a Shadowboard agent, is attained by making all sub-agents ultimately subordinate to the *Aware Ego Agent*.

## 4  Methodology

Building a Digital Self involves building a comprehensive *user-proxy++* - something much more wide ranging than a user surrogate. In order to do so for the vast diversity of individuals, we are developing a methodology. It begins with the definition of a generic range of sub-agent *types* that are likely to encapsulate the sorts of EoC any given user may want to choose from to build into their Digital Self. This list of Shadowboard sub-agent types include: *DecisionMaker, Manager, Protector, PersonalAssistant, Advisor, Critic, Initiator, Adventurer, KnowledgeSeeker, Logician, Player, Teacher, Mentor, Engineer, Artist, Intuitive, Intrapersonal, ContextSituator*. Most often these sub-agent types represent an *envelope-of-capability (EoC)*, which in turn have a range of like-functioned sub-agents within it, but covering a range of capabilities and/or degrees of agencies from highly deliberative to reactive. An example of sub-agents (their generic names) within one of the EoCs above (ie. Manager) include: *Benevolent* (archetypal), *Conciliatory, Planner, Scheduler, Coordinator, Recycler, Decisive* (reactive). Similarly, there are lists of further sub-agents for each of the other EoCs above. These are fully detailed in [4], which together cover many of the roles and activities an individual may be involved in.

Other EoCs outside this starting range, may draw upon agent ontologies compiled by other people, and can occupy any level within the recursive hierarchy of Shadowboard. For example Hristozova [7] specified a range of *Middle Agents: Matchmaker Agent, Recommender Agent, Mediator Agent, Facilitator agent, Broker agent* – which establish, maintain and complete communications with end agents, in a graduated range of capability. In other words, the methodology for building a Digital Self, is very much about utilizing third party agents and ranges of agents, as sub-agents within the Shadowboard architecture framework.

# 5 Implementation

Enacting the Shadowboard architecture has been hastened by the use of several existing technologies at our disposal, which we have modified, enhanced and integrated. There are several levels of technology. At the base is a system called ShadowSpaces [6], which is a dynamic model of the hierarchy of sub-agents which are later intertwined with logic programming. There is an interface system called ShadowFaces, which the user uses as both an editor to create and modify their Digital Self, and as an interface to their running Digital Self system. Notifications, filtered information and those decisions that the Digital Self defers back to the user, all percolate up through the interface. There is our underlying constraint logic language parser called CoLoG, which uses constraint logic programming [13], to bind together the various sub-agents into a powerful and dynamic computational system.

## 5.1 ShadowSpaces – a Dynamic Object System

ShadowSpaces is not unlike the W3C DOM (Document Object Model), and with some effort could be made to be DOM compliant [18]. In our case, it is used to dynamically maintain a hierarchy of objects, which are independent of the way the objects are instantiated and stored in the language the system is created in. ie. Java. As with the

W3C DOM, the ShadowSpace tree is *mutable* - able to deal with events that modify the structure of the tree.

## 5.2 The ShadowFaces Interface

The ShadowFaces interface we have built adopts an *agent-metaphor* [11] (in addition to it being an agent technology), rather than the *desktop metaphor* of most systems today – which we consider to be a severely challenged metaphor in the 24x7 space.

ShadowFaces displays three levels of the hierarchy of sub-agents at a time, and can be thought of as a *lens* that the user can use to navigate through the recursive structure of the Shadowboard architecture. See right-hand-side of Figure 2 above. The advantages of this interface are numerous:

- It has an agent-metaphor rather than the document-centric interface of the desktop metaphor, making it applicable non-desktop systems.
- Up to 589 individual items in the hierarchy can be displayed and are selectable at the one time, versus the use of a tree manager approach (eg. Windows Explorer).
- The shape echoes the graphic depiction of the Shadowboard architecture, reinforcing the *system image* in the user's mind – useful when introducing a new software interface [16].
- The interface can be expanded to full-screen or reduced down to the size of a handheld screen (as low as 160x160 pixels), making it an ideal interface for a number of different consumer devices – PDAs and newer mobile phones.
- It has an eight-way navigational action making it equally suitable to: the mouse, the keypad, function-key pads, and game console joystick interfaces – again making it ideal for 24x7 operation via suitability to different types of consumer devices, each applicable to different locales.
- The same interface can be used to: zoom, navigate, filter and get details-on-demand (see Figure 3 below, editing an Envelope-of-capability).

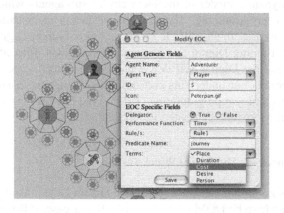

**Fig. 3.** Editing the current Envelope-of-Capability (EoC)

## 5.3   The CoLoG Computation Engine

To understand the computation engine and how it inter-operates with both individual *sub-agents* and the *EoCs* in which they are clustered, we examine a small *Constraint Logic Program*, and observe how it is carved up within the Shadowboard system. Figure 4 below is the constraint logic program called *Journey*. It has single *Rule* at the top, consisting of the *conjunction* (represented by commas) of numerous *Predicates*, together with two *constraints*, both of which use the >= operator.

Following the Rule is a series of *ground terms* which conform to the predicates *destination(...)*, *money(...)* and *available_time(...)*, such that: *destination(...)* represents all holiday locations for which a traveler may choose, the second argument is the amount of money it costs, and the third argument is the number of days the travel/holiday package deal includes; *money(...)* represents a number of individuals and the amount of money each has available; *available_time(...)* represents the amount of days each individual has available to travel.

Here are a series of Queries/Goals that the program Journey is capable of answering, expressed in both English and in predicate logic:

- *Which people could go to Brisbane?*   journey(**brisbane**, Duration, Cost, Desire, Person)?

- *What places could Jill travel to?*   journey(Place, Duration, Cost, Desire, **jill**)?

- *What does it cost to go to Canberra?*   destination(**canberra**, Cost, Duration)?

- *How much time does John have to travel?*   available_time(**john**, Time)?

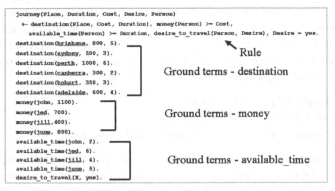

**Fig. 4.** Constraint Logic Program - *Journey*

The range of queries/goals that this program can answer, is typical of the flexibility of most logic languages.

A Shadowboard EoC holds *rules, constraints* and *performance functions,* with links to appropriate sub-agents next step down in the recursive hierarchy. The Journey example has only one rule, however the EoC may hold several alternative rules, the order of choice guided by the *performance-function*.

Looking at the detail in Figure 3 you will see that the *'Modify EOC'* dialog box, represents the EoC that has program *journey* as its *Predicate Name*. Predicate *journey* has five terms: *Place, Duration, Cost, Desire* and *Person*. It has a rule called *Rule1*.

In this computational system, sub-agents that are not EoCs have a single *predicate* for which they may *get, generate* and *manage* ground terms. In our example we have a sub-agent called the *Travel Sub-agent*, which manages just those ground terms for the predicate *destination(Place, Cost, Duration)*.

The standalone example constraint logic program *Journey* represented in Figure 4 is capable of *goal driven processing* only. Shadowboard exhibits both *goal driven* and *data driven reasoning*. Ie. The sub-agents are able to source new/updated ground terms, which in turn trigger the appropriate EoCs to recalculate – which in turn pass their derived terms up the hierarchy to their parent EoC. Although the computation engine within Shadowboard uses constraint logic programming, it is more like a generalized constraint solver in its operation [13].

### 5.4 Wrapping Web Services as Sub-agents

The ground terms managed by a particular sub-agent are not a static set. A sub-agent may generate them itself. A whole ShadowBoard Agent in the form of a Digital Self can accommodate multiple: Personal Assistant agents, notification, filtering [12] and other agent types, application programs and other less complex processes – given the definition of sub-agency in Shadowboard. However, there is a need for hundreds of third-party sub-agents to make a user's Digital Self, genuinely useful in the near term.

*Web Services*, particularly in the form of SOAP Web Services, are of interest to us as the primary source of much external intelligence. Several recent papers document other efforts to utilize web services within the agent paradigm of programming [3; 10]. There are hundreds of single/limited purpose web services already available across the Internet and that number is accelerating. Web Services offer a programmatic interface to services, many of which were only available previously as browser-oriented services. Three consolidating standards are of interest to us:

- SOAP - *Simple Object Access Protocol*
- WSDL - *Web Services Description Language*
- UDDI - *Universal Description Discovery and Integration*

In short, these represent the *wiring, description* and *discovery* stacks respectively, of web services. UDDI in particular, is still under-developed. However, numerous manually built and managed directories detail a growing number of services from which a user can choose, to wrap a Shadowboard sub-agent around. For example see the directories at: www.xmethods.com and www.salcentral.com.

To give the reader a flavour of what is available, the following is a short, terse description of a small sample of the web services listed there: *eBay Price Watcher; FedEx Package Tracker; BabelFish language translation; Stock Quote; Traffic Conditions; Barnes and Noble Price Quote; Amazon; Currency Exchange Rate; Whois by IP addresses, domain; Location by IP (longitude, latitude); Top Music Charts; etc).*

The format of data that are retrievable from these by SOAP RPC for example, are lists of values which match a fixed set of attributes - very much like the ground term tuples that a sub-agent stores in the Shadowboard computational system. So far we have built into the ShadowFaces interface the ability to define a wrapper around a known SOAP RPC Web Service. We intend to extend the wrapping to other protocols including WSDL described services in the near future.

By wrapping web services individually within sub-agents we are able to orchestrate numerous independent web services into synergies of capability via the CoLoG constraint logic programming enacted at the EoC level of Shadowboard.

## 6  Conclusions

In recent times, since we proposed the Shadowboard architecture as a blueprint for the resulting technology [4], several agent architectures and methodologies have come forward with hierarchies of agent roles as a feature [8]. Several people have since questioned our use and continued emphasis of the Psychology of Subselves as the theory behind the Shadowboard hierarchy of sub-agents. To paraphrase the question: *'Why highlight the psychology when the ends is simply a hierarchical role structure?'*

The answer is: *the journey is easily as important as the destination* – particularly when insights are still being gained. Numerous insights have been derived from the psychology:

- *Computational implications* from the Psychology of Subselves include:
  - Notions of decomposition, of sub-agents without full-autonomy, with an overriding executive controller with full self-knowledge of the system – the *Aware Ego* agent.
  - Notions of diversity in both the sub-agents and in their capabilities – allowing lesser applications, such as web services to be wrapped as sub-agents, without diluting the theory.
  - Internalizing external services and capabilities, for pragmatic purposes.
  - Learning from external agencies as archetypes and mentors.
- *Structural implications* from the Psychology of Subselves include:
  - Hierarchy of sub-agency equating to a hierarchy of roles.
  - Application of numerous ontologies at sub-levels of a model.
  - Storage of ground terms at the sub-agent level, is akin to the memory storage/retrieval of war-stories associated with a sub-self/role in a personal history.

The psychology continues to guide the developing *Shadowboard methodology* outlined in Section 4 above. Now that the development is well advanced and the working prototype is being enhanced, new questions are coming to the fore with respect to fertile ground for future research. We would like to address the following research questions in the near future:

- Will the use of the software validate theories of the Analytical Psychology?
- What are the consequences of externalizing aspects of Self?
- How will people be influenced and what can they learn about the real *Self*, from this model of Self with augmented functionality?

It is now obvious to us that the cross-fertilization between the fields of Computer Science and Psychology are only at the beginning.

# References

[1]   Assagioli, Roberto: *Psychosynthesis*. New York. Viking, (1965)

[2]   Brooks, R. A.: Intelligence Without Representation, Workshop in Foundations of Artificial Intelligence, Endicott House, Dedham, MA, (1987)

[3]   Buhler, P.A. and Vidal, J.M.: Toward the synthesis of web services and agent behaviors. Proceedings of the International Workshop on Challenges in Open Agent Systems, (2002)

[4]   Goschnick, S.B.: Shadowboard: an Agent Architecture for enabling a sophisticated Digital Self, Thesis, 180 pages, Dept. of Computer Science, University of Melbourne, Sep. (2001)

[5]   Goschnick S.B.: Shadowboard: A Whole-Agent Architecture that draws Abstractions from Analytical Psychology, Proceedings of PRIMA 2000, Melbourne (2000)

[6]   Goschnick, S.B. & Sterling, L.: Enacting and Interacting with an Agent-based Digital Self in a 24x7 Web Services World. To appear in the Workshop on Humans and Multi-Agent Systems, at the AAMAS-2003 conference, (2003)

[7]   Hristozova, M.: Middle Agents. Presentation, Agent Lab, Department of Computer Science, University of Melbourne (2002)

[8]   Juan,T., Pearce,A.R. and Sterling, L.: ROADMAP: extending the gaia methodology for complex open systems. AAMAS (2002) 3–10

[9]   Jung C.G.: *Man and his Symbols*. Aldus Books, (1964)

[10]  Kuno, H. and Sahai, A.: My agent wants to talk to your service: personalizing web services through agents. In Proceedings of the First International Workshop on Challenges in Open Agent Systems, (2002)

[11]  Lewis M.: Designing for Human-Agent Interaction. AI Magazine, Summer (1998) 67–78

[12]  Maes P. and Kozierok R.: Learning Interface Agents. In *Proceedings of AAAI Conference*, (1993)

[13]  Marriott, K. and Stuckey, P.J.: Programming with Constraints: an Introduction, MIT Press, (1998)

[14]  Rao A.S. and Georgeff M.P.: An Abstract Architecture for Rational Agents. Proceedings of the Third International Conference on Principles of Knowledge Representation and Reasoning, (1992) 439–449

[15]  Sliker, G.: Multiple Mind - Healing the Split in Psyche and World. Shambhala Publications Inc. (1992)

[16]  Shneiderman, B.: Designing the User Interface, Strategies for Effective Human-Computer Interaction, third edition, Addison-Wesley, (1997)

[17]  Stone, H. and Winkelman, S.: Embracing Ourselves – the Voice Dialogue Manual. New World Library. (1989)

[18]  World Wide Web Consortium Document Object Model (DOM). Documentation available at <http://www.w3.org/DOM/> (2003)

[19]  Wooldridge, M. and Jennings, N.: Intelligent Agents: Theory and Practice. Knowledge Engineering Review, 10(2), (1995) 115–152

# Light-Weight Agents for E-learning Environments*

Kevin Chan and Leon Sterling

Department of Computer Science and Software Engineering,
University of Melbourne,
Victoria 3010, Australia

**Abstract.** Web-based delivery of educational courses is becoming increasingly common. There is great scope for light-weight AI methods in enhancing web-based education. We describe the design, prototype implementation and use of QuizHelper, a system of light-weight agents that provides feedback to students taking online quizzes. We discuss AgentSquare, the framework used to build QuizHelper. AgentSquare supports adding agent intelligence to websites.

## 1 Introduction

Educational courses delivered via the World Wide Web are becoming more numerous and common [3]. The courses range in style from static HTML pages, to interactive, real-time courses taught in chat-room-style environments. A goal for all of these courses is to provide students with a positive learning environment. One way to enhance the learning experience is through the addition of AI elements into the course delivery system.

A large amount of work has been done in applying stronger AI techniques to enhancing computer-based education. Most of the work has been in the area of Intelligent Tutoring Systems (ITS). ITS are usually built on expert systems, requiring a detailed model of the domain being taught [10]. However, some topics cannot be modelled in an ITS. For example, in subjects such as English Literature, there is often no single correct answer to a question, and there are no pre-defined steps that a student must follow in answering a question. These topics are not suitable for use with an ITS. Additionally, the creation of an expert system is a major development task that requires technical expertise [2], making the development of ITS very costly.

There is scope for simpler systems. In this paper, we investigate the suitability of light-weight AI techniques for enhancing online education. These techniques do not use detailed models of the material being taught, enabling flexible systems that can be used with a wide range of course topics.

In particular, we examine how light-weight AI techniques were applied in the design of QuizHelper, light-weight agents that provide feedback to students taking online quizzes. QuizHelper was implemented using AgentSquare, a simple framework that enables agent intelligence to be added to a variety of web applications.

---

* This project was funded by ARC Spirt Grant C001066966, "Agent based Knowledge Assimilation and Maintenance for online learning", supported by Hearne Scientific Software.

N. Zhong et al. (Eds.): ISMIS 2003, LNAI 2871, pp. 197–205, 2003.

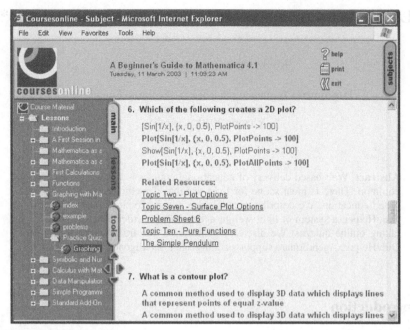

**Fig. 1.** Quiz results from CoursesOnline. Question 6 was answered incorrectly, so QuizHelper provides links to the course materials to help the student correct their answer.

## 2  Overview of QuizHelper

QuizHelper is an agent-based system that operates in conjunction with CoursesOnline (http://www.coursesonline.com.au), an online education website developed by Hearne Scientific Software (http://www.hearne.com.au). QuizHelper provides feedback to students after they complete quizzes. For any question that a student answers incorrectly, QuizHelper provides the student with hypertext links to course materials that the student can use to learn from their mistakes. QuizHelper automatically analyses the quiz questions and selects relevant course materials for each question. The author does not need to specify the relevant resources manually, nor provide addition information about the quiz questions and course materials. This enables QuizHelper to work with existing courses, and means that course authors do not need to do any extra work to use QuizHelper with their courses.

At first glance, the task required of QuizHelper seems similar to writing an agent that can find the answer to any quiz question. That is an extremely difficult problem. However, there are three differences that make QuizHelper's task more achievable. Firstly, QuizHelper has access to the answer for each question. These are stored in the CoursesOnline database. Secondly, the system does not need to generate answers for the questions; it only needs to locate information that can help students to understand the answers. Thirdly, the system does not need to find the exact line, phrase, words that the student needs to read in order to answer the question. It is sufficient to simply point the student to the correct page or correct section. It is beneficial for the student to reread the section that he or she misunderstood.

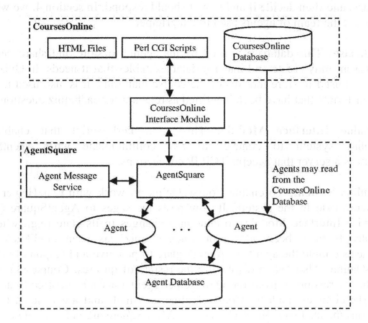

**Fig. 2.** AgentSquare Architecture.

# 3  The AgentSquare Framework

CoursesOnline was already completed and in operation when we began work on QuizHelper. Because of this, one of our design goals was to ensure that QuizHelper could be easily added to CoursesOnline. To accomplish this, we designed AgentSquare, a simple framework which can be used to add agent intelligence to web applications. The following sections briefly describe the components of AgentSquare.

**AgentSquare:** AgentSquare is a Java application that acts as an agent server. It functions as a container for the agents to execute in, and allows other programs to connect to it and give it commands (e.g. posting messages to the agents inside AgentSquare, asking AgentSquare to start up or shut down agents, etc).

**Agent Message Service:** This component is part of the AgentSquare application. This facility enables agents to send messages to each other. Programs connected to AgentSquare can also use this facility to send messages to the agents. Messages can be sent to all agents, to a specific agent instance, or to all agents who are able to perform a particular role.

**Agents:** Each agent executes in its own Java thread. Agents send, receive and respond to messages via the Agent Message Service. It is the agent's responsibility to examine each message, and then decide if and how it should respond. In section 4, we will look more closely at the team of agents used in QuizHelper.

**Agent Database:** This database is used by the agents to store and share persistent data. Each agent may create and manage database tables that it needs. In QuizHelper the database is used to store indexes of the course materials. It is also used to record the course materials that have been identified as relevant for each quiz question.

**CoursesOnline Interface Module:** This is a Perl script that enables the CoursesOnline system to connect to and communicate with AgentSquare. AgentSquare is a server that accepts TCP/IP connections.

**CoursesOnline System:** To enable CoursesOnline to work with QuizHelper, a few changes were made to the system. It now posts messages to AgentSquare (via the CoursesOnline Interface Module) to announce changes in its state (e.g., when new course materials have been added, or when a quiz has been modified). These announcements enable the agents in AgentSquare to perceive and respond to changes in CoursesOnline. Also, when displaying the results of quizzes, CoursesOnline now obtains a list of resources from the QuizHelper agent for each incorrectly answered question. The changes made to CoursesOnline are small and are isolated to a few locations. This means that CoursesOnline and AgentSquare are only loosely coupled.

## 4 The Agents of QuizHelper

In this section, we provide an overview of the agents used in QuizHelper. We will look more closely at the details of these agents in sections 5, 6 and 7.

We decided on the techniques that are used in the QuizHelper agents by examining the quizzes and course materials in a typical web-based course. We looked at the content of the course, and considered how a human might decide which course materials were relevant to each quiz question. We then examined how these techniques could be generalised and implemented in the QuizHelper agents.

The course that we used in the analysis is "A Beginner's Guide to Mathematica 4.1" [8]. The course contains a significant amount of technical information, enabling us to investigate the effectiveness of light-weight AI methods on technical material.

The resulting design for QuizHelper consisted of five agents:
- QuizHelper Agent: This agent is responsible for interacting with the CoursesOnline system. When a student answers a quiz questions incorrectly, CoursesOnline will send requests to this agent to get course materials that are relevant to incorrectly answered questions. The agent determines what resources to return by examining the indices created by the GeneralQuizSearch and MathQuizSearch agents.
- Index Agent: This agent is responsible for indexing the course materials and updating the index on notification that the course materials have changed.

- GeneralQuizSearch Agent: This agent is responsible for determining which course materials are relevant to each quiz question. It updates the resources for each question when the course materials are reindexed or when the quiz questions are changed.
- MathIndex and MathQuizSearch Agents: These two agents are similar to the Index and GeneralQuizSearch agents, respectively. However, they use techniques that are specific for the Mathematica course.

## 5   Design of Index Agent

The Index Agent creates indexes that are used by the GeneralQuizSearch and MathQuizSearch agents. The Index Agent uses standard indexing methods [12] to record the occurrences of words in the course materials. Additionally, the Index agent also records context information about the indexed material. There are three main pieces of context information that the Index agent records.

**Section Headers:** When keywords appear in a section header or title, that section is usually a useful resource to return. As a result, the search agents give preference to resources in which the keywords appear in section headers or titles. To enable this, the Index Agent records which words appeared in section headers or titles.

**Formatted Text:** In the Mathematica course, when a term or concept is defined, the item being defined is shown bolded. It is a general convention that text is bolded to indicate its importance. The search agents will give preference to resources that contain the keywords bolded over resources that just contain the keywords. To support this, the Index Agent marks as "highlighted text" any words that are bolded, underlined or italicised.

**Content Pages:** In the Mathematica course, there is a contents page at the start of each lesson. These pages list the topics covered in each lesson, and are often selected by the search agents. However, contents pages are not useful for students. To enable the search agents to identify and ignore these pages, the Index Agent marks materials from the contents page as "contents". To detect contents pages, the Index Agent uses a "number of links to number of words" ratio as a heuristic for deciding which pages are content pages. Currently, we count any page that has more than 1 link per 10 words as a contents page.

## 6   Design of GeneralQuizSearch Agent

The GeneralQuizSearch agent is responsible for analysing the quiz questions, and finding resources to help students understand questions that they have answered incorrectly. This agent extracts keywords from quiz questions/answers, searches for the keywords in the Index agent's index, and determines what course materials are the most relevant to each quiz question. It then records these results in the Agent Database, where it can be read by the QuizHelper agent.

Extracting useful keywords from quiz questions/answers is one of the GeneralQuizSearch agent's primary tasks. The GeneralQuizSearch agent extracts these words automatically as we want the QuizHelper system to be able to handle existing courses that have not been specially "annotated" for QuizHelper. (In the future, we may also allow course authors to optionally specify keywords for each quiz question. Specifying these manually may help improve the search results.)

## 6.1  Handling Common Words and Estimating Word Significance

GeneralQuizSearch agent extracts keywords from the question/answer texts and searches for them from the Index Agent's index. The GeneralQuizSearch agent needs to determine which words in the question/answer text are relevant and should be searched for, and which should be ignored.

As part of this, we dynamically determine which words are common, and ignore those. For each word that appears in a question and its answer, the GeneralQuizSearch agent queries the database on the word's frequency of occurrence. The agent places a higher importance on words that appear less frequently. If the number of occurrences is higher than a set threshold (twenty in the current implementation), the word is ignored and treated as a common word.

Additionally, this heuristic is also applied by the GeneralQuizSearch agent to rank the remaining non-common words in the question/answer. This heuristic assumes that words which appear less frequently have a higher significance than words which appear more frequently. The GeneralQuizSearch Agent searches for course materials containing the less common question words.

A word which appears frequently throughout a course is treated as a common word and not considered important. However, when a word that is uncommon (in the context of the entire course) appears multiple times within a single question/answer, the GeneralQuizSearch Agent considers the word likely to be significant for that question, and gives preference to the resources found using that word.

## 6.2  Extracting Keywords from the Question and Answer Text

In sections 6.1, we discussed some generic techniques used by the GeneralQuizSearch Agent to prioritise the words, from the question/answer text. In this section, we look at the three question types supported by CoursesOnline, and examine how we extract keywords from them.

**Multiple Choice Questions:** The question text and correct answer provides useful information that is searched for by the GeneralQuizSearch agent. However, examiners often write incorrect multiple choice answers that appear similar to the correct answer, reducing the opportunity for students to guess. The GeneralQuizSearch agent takes advantage of this by looking for words that appear simultaneously in correct and incorrect answers, and giving those words a higher significance.

**Numeric Answer Questions:** Questions that require numeric answers usually ask the student to perform calculations. Searching on the answer text for calculation questions does not usually find relevant resources. For example, if the answer for a calculation is 32, occurrences of "32" in the course materials do not indicate useful resources. The GeneralQuizSearch agent extracts keywords from the question text of numeric questions, ignoring the answer text.

**Short/Long Text Answers:** The question and answer text for short and long answer questions usually contain materials from the course, and searching for the words from these answers usually provides useful results.

## 6.3  Granularity of Resource Returned

At what level of granularity should the GeneralQuizSearch agent return resources to the student? It could point to a particular file, a particular page, a particular section, or even to a particular paragraph. The smaller the section pointed to, the more accurate the returned results must be. Identifying the exact paragraph to return is difficult, requiring a deep understanding of the question and the course material. However, if the student is directed to a page containing multiple paragraphs related to the question, it is likely that there will be material related to the answer on that page. So, from a technical perspective, it is easier to present the student with a wider region of course material.

Additionally, as we want the student to learn from their mistakes, we might not want to pin-point the exact paragraph where the answer is. By pointing the student to a wider section, it encourages the student to read through that section again to discover the answer. So, from an educational perspective, it may also be **∗ ∗ ∗ ∗** a slightly wider region of course material to the student. As the Mathematica course is presented using short HTML pages, returning HTML files to the student is usually the ideal level of detail from an educational perspective.

## 7  Design of MathIndex and MathQuizSearch Agents

The MathIndex and MathQuizSearch agents perform similar functions to the Index and GeneralQuizSearch agents, respectively. However, these two agents take advantage of Mathematica-specific techniques to improve the search results. Functions are an important part of the Mathematica course. Lessons are often focused on a set of related functions and how they can be used. There are many quiz questions that ask the student to specify what a given function does or returns.

The MathIndex and MathQuizSearch agents have the ability to recognise functions. They distinguish between normal words and function names (e.g. Plot and Plot[...]). For example, the word "plot" appears in more places than the function "Plot[]". So, for a question that involves the "Plot[]" function, searching specifically for the function "Plot[]" will return more accurate results than searching for the word "plot". The MathIndex agent indexes the occurrences of function names. The

MathQuizSearch agent identifies Mathematica functions in the quiz questions and searches for them in the index created by the MathIndex agent.

Section 6.1 discussed how the GeneralQuizSearch agent can identify common words. The MathQuizSearch agent uses a similar technique to identify and ignore frequently occurring functions, such as Cos[], when searching for relevant resources.

# 8   QuizHelper in Operation

The following are the results from an initial trial of the prototype. For each question, we manually selected a resource that we thought would be the most useful to a student answering the question. Next, we used the prototype QuizHelper to locate resources for the quiz questions. Finally, we compared the resources returned by QuizHelper with the resources we selected manually. The "first correct" results are the numbers of questions in the quiz for which QuizHelper returned the manually selected link as the first link. The "in first three" results are the numbers of questions in the quiz for which QuizHelper returned the manually selected link as one of its top 3 links.

**Table 1.** Initial trial results

| Lesson | First Correct | In First Three |
|---|---|---|
| *Lesson 1: A First Session in Mathematica* | 3 out of 5 | 4 out of 5 |
| *Lesson 3: Mathematica as a Publishing Tool* | 2 out of 5 | 5 out of 5 |
| *Lesson 4 First Calculations with Mathematica* | 4 out of 12 | 4 out of 12 |
| *Lesson 6: Graphing with Mathematica* | 8 out of 12 | 8 out of 12 |
| *Lesson 8: Calculus with Mathematica* | 6 out of 12 | 7 out of 12 |
| *Lesson 11: Standard Add-on Packages* | 3 out of 5 | 5 out of 5 |

We found that QuizHelper is generally able to find relevant resources for text and descriptive questions. However, the cases where QuizHelper performed badly tended to be questions that contain mainly Mathematica expressions. We believe that the results will continue to improve as we improve the implementations of the MathIndex and MathQuizSearch agents to handle more Mathematica specific constructs.

# 9   Summary and Further Work

In this paper, we described the design and prototype implementation of QuizHelper, an application that operates in conjunction with CoursesOnline. QuizHelper extends the online quiz functionality of CoursesOnline, providing feedback to students taking online quizzes. While implementing QuizHelper, we also developed the AgentSquare framework. The framework enables agent-based applications to be easily added to new and existing websites.

The design of QuizHelper was based on an analysis of the web-based course "A Beginner's Guide to Mathematica 4.1". Through the analysis, we developed light-weight AI methods that have been applied in the design. We believe that light-weight methods would be useful for constructing other agents for use in online education.

There are several areas that we are continuing to investigate:

- Adding functionality to search the World Wide Web (in addition to the course materials) for relevant resources.
- Using a student's performance in previous quizzes to determine the student's education needs, and re-prioritising the resources shown to the student.
- Investigate how well the agents in QuizHelper generalise to other domains (e.g. History).
- Further develop and refine the AgentSquare framework by using it for other agent-based applications.
- Are some course structures /styles are more suited for use with QuizHelper? Investigate this and develop some guidelines for creating suitable courses.

# References

1.  Baker M.: The roles of models in Artificial Intelligence and Education research: a prospective view. International Journal of Artificial Intelligence in Education, 11:122–143 (2000)
2.  Baldoni, M., Baroglio, C., Patti, V., Torasso, L.: Using a rational agent in an adaptive, web-based tutoring system. Workshop on Adaptive Systems for Web-based Education, 2nd International Conference on Adaptive Hypermedia and Adaptive Web Based Systems. Malaga, Spain (2002)
3.  Brusilovsky, P.: Adaptive and intelligent technologies for web-based education. Special Issue on Intelligent Systems and Teleteaching, (Kunstliche Intelligenz), 4:19–25 (1999)
4.  El-Khouly, M., Far, B., Koono, Z.: A Multi-Agent Internet Based Tutoring System (I-ATCL) for Teaching Computer Programming Languages, Advanced Research in Computers and Communications in Education, G. Cummings et al. (Eds.), IOS Press (1999)
5.  Fenton-Kerr, T., Clark, S., Cheney, G., Koppi, T., Chaloupka, M.: Multi-Agent Design in Flexible Learning Environments, ASCILITE (1998)
6.  Giraffa, L., Viccari, R.: The use of Agents techniques on Intelligent Tutoring Systems, IV Congresso RIBIE, Basilia (1998)
7.  Hara, N., Kling, R.: Students' Frustrations with a Web-Based Distance Education Course. First Monday, 12(4), December (1999) http://www.firstmonday.org/issues/issue4_12/hara/index.html
8.  Hearne Scientific Software: A Beginners Guide for Mathematica 4.1, CoursesOnline, www.coursesonline.com.au. (2001)
9.  Juan, T., Pearce, A. and Sterling, L.: ROADMAP: Extending the Gaia Methodology for Complex Open Systems. AAMAS 2002, Bologna, Italy (2002).
10. McArthur, D., Lewis M. and Bishay, M.: The Roles of Artificial Intelligence in Education: Current Progress and Future Prospects. Published on www: http://www.rand.org/education/mcarthur/Papers/role.html
11. Whitson, G.: An Application of Artificial Intelligence to Distance Education, 29th ASEE/IEEE Frontiers in Education Conference, San Juan, Puerto Rico (1999)
12. Witten, I., Moffat A. and Bell, C.: Managing Gigabytes: Compressing and Indexing Documents and Image. Morgan Kaufmann Publishers (1999)
13. Wooldridge, M., Jennings, N. and Kinny, D.: The Gaia Methodology for Agent-Oriented Analysis and Design. J.Autonomous Agents and Multi-Agent Systems 3 (3). 2000, 285–312.

# Towards a Pragmatic Methodology for Open Multi-agent Systems

Philippe Mathieu, Jean-Christophe Routier, and Yann Secq

Laboratoire d'Informatique Fondamentale de Lille – CNRS UMR 8022
Université des Sciences et Technologies de Lille
59650 Villeneuve d'Ascq Cedex
{mathieu,routier,secq}@lifl.fr

**Abstract.** This paper introduces the RIO methodology, which relies on the notions of Role, Interaction and Organization. We define a model of *runnable* specification of interaction protocols that represents interactions between agents globally, and that can be processed in orsder to generate Colored Petri Nets that handle agent conversations. Moreover, these specifications are not tied to a particular agent model and could therefore be used to enable multi-agent systems interoperability.

The RIO methodology aimes at the design of open multi-agent systems, and is based on an engineering of these *runnable* interaction protocols. They are described in term of conversation between *micro-roles* characterized by their skills, then *micro-roles* are gathered in *composite roles*. These *composite roles* are used to build *abstract agents*. Lastly, these latter can be distributed among the agents of a running multi-agent system.

## 1 Introduction

The idea of an agent based software engineering has appeared roughly ten years ago, with the paper from Shoham entitled *Agent Oriented Programming*[6]. Since these days, several methodologies have been proposed to help developers in their analysis and design[3,1]. These methodologies are interesting but they generally do not propose pragmatic concepts or principles facilitating the realization of such systems. Moreover, they do not tackle the problem of multi-agent systems interoperability that should be a primary concern as more and more agent models and agent platforms are becoming available.

The FIPA association has published some standard specifications that provide a first step towards interoperability. Sadly, we believe that without a strong commitment to interaction specification and standardized ontologies, interoperability will not be reached. Thus, our proposal is a pragmatic methodology to ease the design of open multi-agent systems. To achieve this goal, we rely on a model of *runnable* specification of interaction protocols, which describes a global sight of the conversations between the agents of the system. Unlike AGENTUML [5], our model of interaction is more than a description or a notation: we use it to generate code to handle agent conversations.

N. Zhong et al. (Eds.): ISMIS 2003, LNAI 2871, pp. 206–210, 2003.

The following definition given by Singh[7] of the interaction oriented approach, characterizes our approach:

*We introduce interaction-oriented programming (IOP) as an approach to orchestrate the interactions among agents. IOP is more tractable and practical than general agent programming, especially in settings such as open information environments, where the internal details of autonomously developed agents are not available.*

It is the point of view that we adopt by proposing a formalism for the *runnable* specifications of interaction protocols.

## 2 RIO: Roles, Interactions and Organizations

The RIO methodology that we are developing relies on the concept of *runnable* specification of interaction protocols. This methodology falls under the line of GAIA[8], and thus aims the same applicability. However, GAIA remains too general to ease the transition from the system design stage to its realization. The purpose of our proposal is to facilitate this transition. The RIO methodology relies on four stages (figure 1), the two first represent reusable specifications, while the two last are specific to the targeted application. Moreover, we will not speak about building an *application*, but about designing an agent society. Indeed, the RIO methodology proposes an incremental and interactive construction of multi-agent systems.

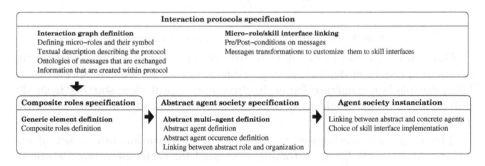

**Fig. 1.** The stages of the RIO methodology

*Interaction protocols specification.* The first stage consists in identifying the involved interactions and roles. The purpose of these runnable interaction protocol specifications, is the checking and the deployment of interaction protocols within multi-agent systems. On all these stages, the designer has to define the specification, the other stages being automated. For that, we define a formalism representing the global view of an interaction protocol, and a projection mechanism which transforms this global view into a set of local views dedicated to each role. The creation *ex-nihilo* of the specification of an interaction protocol consists in specifying the interaction protocol by detailing its cartouche (figure 2). The specialization makes it possible to annotate an existing cartouche. Finally, the composition consists in assembling existing protocols by specifying

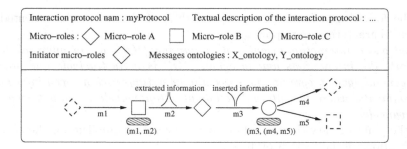

**Fig. 2.** Cartouche that specifies interaction protocols

associations of *micro-roles* and information transfers. The figure 3 illustrates a specification of the FIPA Contract Net Protocol.

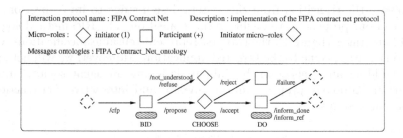

**Fig. 3.** The FIPA Contract Net interaction protocol

Once an interaction protocol, that gives to the designer a global view of the interaction, has been defined, it is possible to obtain a *runnable* specification. The principle is to generate for each *micro-role* a local view starting from the global view. This one could then be distributed dynamically to the agents of the system.

The projection mechanism transforms the specification into a set of automata. More precisely, an automata is created for each *micro-role* (figure 4). This automata manages the course of the protocol: coherence of the protocol (messages scheduling), messages types, side effects (skill invocation). The implementation of this mechanism is carried out by the generation of Colored Petri Nets[2] (CPN) for each *micro-role*, and we transform this CPN description to a JAVA class. This class is then integrated within a skill, which is used by the conversation manager skill. The interest of this approach is that the designer graphically specifies the global view of the interaction, the projection mechanism generates the skill needed to the management of this interaction. Moreover, thanks to the dynamic skill acquisition, it is possible to add new interaction protocols to running agents of the system [4]. At the end of this stage, the designer has defined a set of interaction protocols. He can then go to the next stage: the description of *composite roles*, which will allow the aggregation of *micro-roles* that are involved in complementary interactions.

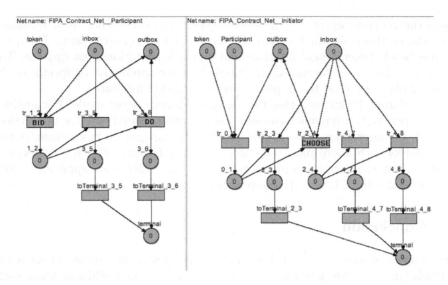

**Fig. 4.** Generated Colored Petri Nets for FIPA Contract Net protocol.

***Composite roles specification.*** This second stage specifies role models. These models are abstract reusable descriptions, which correspond to a logical gathering of *micro-roles*. These patterns define *abstract* roles, which gather a set of consistent interaction protocols. Indeed, a role is generally composed of a set of tasks which can be, or which must be carried out by the agent playing this role. Each one of these tasks can be broken up and be designed as a set of interactions with other roles. The concept of *composite role* is thus used to give a logical coherence between the *micro-role* representing the many facets of a role.

***Agent societies specification.*** This third stage can be regarded as a specification of an abstract agent society, i.e. a description of *abstract agents* and their occurrence, as well as the link between *composite roles* and organizations. Once the set of *composite roles* is created, it is possible to define the *abstract agents*, which are defined by a set of *composite roles*. *Abstract agents* can be seen as agent patterns, or agent templates: they define a type of agent relying on interactions that the agent can be involved in. For the designer, these *abstract agents* describe applicative agent models. Because these models introduce strong dependencies between composite roles, they are specific to the targeted applications and can therefore hardly be reused. The second part of this stage consists in specifying for each *abstract agent*, and even for the *composite roles* of these agents, which organization should be used to find their acquaintances at runtime.

***Instantiating an agent society in a multi-agent system.*** This last stage specifies deployment rules of the *abstract agents* on the running agents of a system. We have a complete specification of the agent society, that can be mapped onto the concrete agents of the multi-agent system. For that, it is necessary to indicate the assignments from *abstract agents* to concrete ones. Then, the connection between a skill interface and its implementation is carried out. The designer indeed must, according to criteria that are applicative or specific to the hosting platform, bind the implementation with skill interfaces.

It is during deployment that the use of our generic agent model[4] is justified as a support to the dynamic acquisition of new skills related with the interaction. Indeed, the interaction, once transformed by the projection mechanism, is represented for each *micro-role* by a Colored Petri Net (figure 4) and its associated skills. All these information are sent to the agent, which adds applicative skills and delegates the CPN to the conversation manager.

## 3   Conclusion

Multi-agent systems are now becoming a new design paradigm. Many agent models have been proposed, as well as many multi-agent toolkits or framework. This diversity poses the problem of multi-agent systems interoperability. In this paper, we have presented the RIO methodology, which is based on the notions of role, interaction and organization. We use these notions to propose an engineering of interaction protocols and to enable interoperability for open multi-agent systems.

We are working on an agent platform and its associated tools to support the RIO methodology.

## References

1. F. M. T. Brazier, B. M. Dunin-Keplicz, N. R. Jennings, and J. Treur. DESIRE: Modelling multi-agent systems in a compositional formal framework. *Int Journal of Cooperative Information Systems*, 6(1):67–94, 1997.
2. Kurt Jensen. Coloured petri nets – basic concepts, analysis methods and practical use, vol. 1: Basic concepts. In *EATCS Monographs on Theoretical Computer Science*, pages 1–234. Springer-Verlag: Berlin, Germany, 1992.
3. E. A. Kendall, M. T. Malkoun, and C. H. Jiang. A methodology for developing agent based systems. In Chengqi Zhang and Dickson Lukose, editors, *First Australian Workshop on Distributed Artificial Intelligence*, Canberra, Australia, 1995.
4. P. Mathieu, J.C. Routier, and Y. Secq. Dynamic skill learning: A support to agent evolution. In *Proceedings of the AISB'01 Symposium on Adaptive Agents and Multi-Agent Systems*, pages 25–32, 2001.
5. J. Odell, H. Parunak, and B. Bauer. Extending uml for agents, 2000.
6. Y. Shoham. Agent-oriented programming. *Artificial Intelligence*, 60:51–92, 1993.
7. Munindar P. Singh. Towards interaction-oriented programming. Technical Report TR-96-15, 16, 1996.
8. M. Wooldridge, NR. Jennings, and D. Kinny. The GAIA methodology for agent-oriented analysis and design. *Journal of Autonomous Agents and Multi-Agent Systems*, 2000.

# Using Similarity to Implement Distributed Ubiquitous Software Services

Abdelkader Gouaich[1,2]

[1] LIRMM, Montpellier, France,
gouaich@lirmm.fr
[2] Centre de Recherche Motorola, Paris, France,
gouaich@crm.mot.com

**Abstract.** This paper presents both theoretical and experimental results enabling the distributed implementation of ubiquitous software services.

## 1 Introduction

Advances in network technologies, small equipments manufacturing and distributed software engineering allow nowadays the design and deployment of high-level software services defined everywhere and available at anytime, namely *ubiquitous software services*. Ubiquity of a software service is defined as its ability to provide its functionalities to other components (clients) coherently and continuously everywhere within a defined space. To achieve this, most current approaches adopt a centralised vision by assuming that the distributed software system composed by the ubiquitous service and its clients are able to interact everywhere. This paper presents a different approach enabling a globally coherent ubiquitous service implemented by several distributed and disconnected entities (*service instances*) using only local peer-to-peer interactions.

### 1.1 MIC* Deployment Environment Model

In order to understand the environment surrounding a multi-agents system an algebraic model, {Movement, Interaction, Computation}*, has been introduced in [3]. It defines an abstract structure where autonomous, mobile and interacting entities may be deployed. Within this framework, agents interact by exchanging *interaction objects*, found in a set represented as $\mathcal{O}$, through *interaction spaces*. The mobility of the agents is described as the mobility of interaction objects over interaction spaces. MIC* describes the dynamics of the environmental structure as a composition of three elementary evolutions: the movement, the interaction and the computation.

## 2 Theoretical Foundations

This section presents the theoretical foundations required to enable distributed implementation of ubiquitous services. A dialogue represents a sequence of interactions. Within the MIC* framework, a dialogue can be represented by a *sequence* of interaction

N. Zhong et al. (Eds.): ISMIS 2003, LNAI 2871, pp. 211–215, 2003.

objects generated by the free monoid $\mathcal{O}^*$ that is built using, . (dot), a non-commutative law on interaction objects. The sequence structure is used as an interaction object to encode the *memory* of the conversation. The ubiquity property is defined as an ability to be present everywhere within a defined space [1]. Formally, this definition is expressed as follows:

**Definition 1.** *A computational entity $p \in \mathcal{A}$ is said to be ubiquitous within a defined topology $\delta \subset \Delta$ iff:*

$$\forall x \in \delta, \pi(p, x) = 1$$

$$\forall o \in \mathcal{O}^*, \forall x, y \in \delta, \gamma(p_x, o) = \gamma(p_y, o)$$

Where $\Delta$ represents a space. $\pi : \mathcal{A} \times \Delta \rightarrow \{0, 1\}$ is a characteristic function that equals 1 when a process $p \in \mathcal{A}$ is located in $x \in \Delta$ and 0 otherwise. $\gamma : \mathcal{A} \times \mathcal{O}^* \rightarrow \mathcal{O}^*$ is the calculus function presented in MIC*, that maps the perceptions of an agents to its observable emitted interaction objects. The notation $p_x$ is used to identify the process $p$ located at coordinate $x$ of the space. The first assertion of definition 1 expresses the fact that the entity has to be located everywhere in $\delta$. The second assessment expresses that from an external point of view, the entity behaves as a single process.

The mapping relation defines where the software processes are actually located in the space. This is defined formally as follows:

**Definition 2.** *A mapping, $m$, is a relation defined on $\mathcal{A} \times \Delta$ that links processes to space coordinates.*

An agent process $p \in \mathcal{A}$ is said to be similar to another agent process $q \in \mathcal{A}$ when both are observed similarly by an external observer. This definition is formalised as follows:

**Definition 3.** *Similarity $\sigma : \mathcal{A} \times \mathcal{A}$ relation is defined as follows: $\sigma(p, q) \Leftrightarrow \forall o \in \mathcal{O}^*, \gamma(p, o) = \gamma(q, o)$*

Obviously, $\sigma$ is an equivalence relation on $\mathcal{A} \times \mathcal{A}$. Thus, $\sigma$ defines an equivalence class of an element $p$ as follows $\hat{p} = \{q \in \mathcal{A} : \sigma(p, q)\}$. The notation, $\hat{p}$, represents then the set of processes that are similar to $p$.

**Definition 4.** *The covered topology $\delta_{\hat{p},m}$ of an equivalence class $\hat{p}$ according to the mapping $m$ is defined as follows: $\delta_{\hat{p},m} = \bigcup_{p \in \hat{p}} \{x \in \Delta | (p, x) \in m\}$*

$\delta_{\hat{p},m}$ represents the space covered by all the similar processes according to a particular mapping $m$.

**Proposition 1.** *Let $\Delta$ be a space, $\mathcal{A}$ an agent set, $m$ a $(\mathcal{A} \times \Delta)$-mapping. If $\hat{p}$ is $\sigma$-equivalence class, then $\hat{p}$ is a ubiquitous entity on $\delta_{\hat{p},m}$.*

The first assessment of definition 1 is verified since all processes belonging to $\hat{p}$ belong to $\delta_{\hat{p},m}$ according to definition 4. Concerning the second part of the ubiquity definition, if $\hat{p}$ is not a ubiquitous entity, this means that:

$$\neg ubiquity(\hat{p}, \delta_{\hat{p},m}) \Rightarrow \exists o \in \mathcal{O}^*, \exists x, y \in \delta_{\hat{p},m} : \gamma(\hat{p}_x, o) \neq \gamma(\hat{p}_y, o)$$

$$\Rightarrow \exists p, q \in \hat{p} \wedge (p, x), (q, y) \in m : \gamma(p, o) \neq \gamma(q, o)$$

$$\Rightarrow \neg \sigma(p, q), \text{ which contradicts } p, q \in \hat{p} \qquad \square$$

Proposition 1, theoretically proves that similarity between independent and autonomous processes naturally builds a ubiquitous entity spread over the space occupied by all its processes. The next section shows how to implement the similarity relation between autonomous and disconnected processes.

## 3   Achieving Similarity in Distributed and Disconnected Environment

In order to behave coherently, each instance of the ubiquitous service $\hat{p}$ should be able to continue coherently any interaction that was initiated with another $\sigma$-equivalent process. To achieve this, ubiquitous service instances have to know about history of ongoing interactions. This interaction memory can be shared among the instances following different mechanisms. For instance, a common accessible storage space can be used to share information. However, implementing this mechanism is difficult in a disconnected and asynchronous environment. Encapsulating the interaction memory in the interaction itself seems to be an interesting alternative. Hence, any instance of the service is able to rebuild locally the memory of the ongoing dialogue when needed. Having this memory of the dialogue, the service instance is then expected to react similarly to other instances. According to proposition 1, this defines a virtual ubiquitous service. Using the dialogue as an interaction object raises also some problems that are summarised as follows:

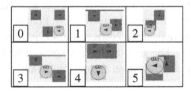

**Fig. 1.** Elementary situations between a user agent (ua), light grey box, and several ubiquitous service instances (s): dark grey boxes

- 'Remember' a dialogue-level communicative act: The problem appears when the client agent interacts with the ubiquitous service (situation 1 in figure 1) and is suddenly disconnected while expecting a response (situation 0 in figure 1). When reconnected to another instance of the ubiquitous service (situation 1 in figure 1), the newly met service instance has no knowledge about the ongoing dialogue and the client agent is waiting for an answer. This creates a dialogue deadlock. This deadlock is resolved by introducing a neutral communicative act about the conversation. Hence, the client agent asks the service agent to *remember* what was the last interaction stream.
- Ubiquitous service instances synchronisation : Although ubiquitous service instances are distributed and autonomous, some critical actions implying side effects have to be synchronised. For instance, the payment action for a particular service should be performed once by a service instance and the user should not be charged

again by other instances. This is an important feature to be guaranteed in order to meet ubiquitous service definition. In fact, if the service's client observes any inconsistency then the ubiquity property presented in definition 1 is lost. Consequently, service instances have to coordinate their side-effects actions.

## 4 Experiments

In order to correctly simulate ubiquitous environment a three layers architecture has been used:

1. Movement simulator: The movement simulator represents the low-level geometric communication range of the entities and handles their movement in a two dimensional space.
2. MIC* environment: a MIC* term represents the deployment environment of agents. Thus, agents' processes are deployed on MIC* terms that are linked when their geometric representations overlap.
3. Agents: agents' processes react to perceived interaction objects by emitting other interaction objects. Since agents interact only when they are in the same deployment environment, the geometric overlapping becomes a sine qua non condition to agents' interactions.

The experiment scenario simulates a virtual city where both user agents and service agents move and may interact. For this demonstration a single ticket buying service has been implemented in the virtual city. The user agent goal is to buy a ticket from a ticket selling service while moving in the city. Notice that service agents also move which raises the dynamics of the system. The user agent is expected to perceive a single coherent ubiquitous service implemented by several distributed and disconnected entities.

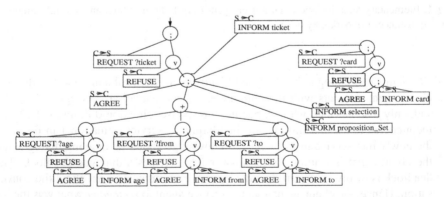

**Fig. 2.** Ticket buying interaction protocol between the user agent (C) and the service (S)

**Ticket buying interaction protocol:** In order to validate the presented approach, a simple interaction protocol has been defined in order to buy a ticket from the ticket selling service. The notations that are used to describe this interaction protocol are the following: $(a); (b)$ expresses a sequence between two interactions $a$ and $b$. This interaction is valid if and only if $a$ happens first followed by $b$. $(a) \vee (b)$ expresses an exclusive choice between $a$ and $b$. This interaction is valid if and only if $a$ or $b$ hold. $(a) + (b)$ expresses parallel interactions that hold in an unordered manner. Hence, this interaction is valid if and only if $a$ and $b$ happen no matter which first. Having these notations the 'ticket-buying' interaction protocol is described in figure 2. The user agent (C) initiates this protocol by sending a request to the service (S). After this, the service agent may agree to respond to the request or not. When agreeing, the service agent asks the user agent some information about the starting point; the destination of his travel and the traveller's age. After gathering these data, the service agent delivers some propositions to the user agent. When the user agent selects an offer, he informs the service agent about it. After the payment procedure, the offer is acknowledged and the dialogue is closed. The interaction protocol is specified from the viewpoint of an external observer. Having this specification a MIC*-deployment environment is generated. This process is discussed more on details in [2]. All autonomous agents are executed as concurrent processes that interact with the deployment environment with explicit interaction objects sent via low-level TCP/IP sockets. Despite disconnections due to the mobility of the entities, the user agent succeeds each time in buying a travel ticket. The debug traces show also that several service instances have been involved in the interaction with the user agent. The user agent perceives a single coherent ubiquitous service spread in the surface occupied by its instances. The experimental work presented in this section validates the theoretical results presented in section 2.

## 5   Conclusion

This paper has defined the ubiquity of a software entity as its presence, as a coherent whole, in a certain spatial topology. The theoretical result has proved that achieving similarity among software processes defines a virtually distributed ubiquitous entity. Using the composition property of the MIC* formal model and defining dialogue structure, the similarity property has been successfully implemented in a highly distributed and disconnected context. The implementation of this property has also raised some problems such as the need of a neutral communicative, 'Remember', act to restart a frozen dialogue. Consistency of the memory of the dialogue is also an important issue that has not been specifically addressed in this paper and should be handled by future works.

## References

1. *Le Petit Larousse Illustré*. Larousse, 2001.
2. Abdelkader Gouaich. Implementing interaction norms is open, distributed and disconnected multi-agent software systems. Submitted to AOSE 2003. Url: http://www.lirmm.fr/~gouaich/research.html, 2003.
3. Abdelkader Gouaich, Yves Guiraud, and Fabien Michel. Mic*: An agent formal environment. To appear in the 7th World Multiconference on Systemics, Cybernetics and Informatics (SCI 2003), 7 2003. Orlando, USA.

# MIC*: Algebraic Agent Environment

Abdelkader Gouaich[1,2] and Yves Guiraud[1,3]

[1] LIRMM, Montpellier, France,
{gouaich,guiraud}@lirmm.fr
[2] Centre de Recherche Motorola, Paris, France,
gouaich@crm.mot.com
[3] Laboratoire Géométrie, Topologie, Algèbre – Université Montpellier 2 – France
guiraud@math.univ-montp2.fr

**Abstract.** This paper presents the MIC* algebraic structure modelling an environment where autonomous, interacting and mobile entities evolve.

## 1 Introduction

Understanding and representing explicitly the *deployment environment* where software processes or *agents* are deployed is a crucial issue especially for dynamical and open software environment such as ubiquitous software systems. In fact, as mentioned by [2] ignoring properties of the deployment environment may lead to dysfunctions that cannot be explained when the software system is isolated from its deployment environment. This paper presents an algebraic model, named MIC*, of such deployment environment where autonomous, interacting and mobile agents evolve. Multi-agents system (MAS) considers a computational system as a coherent aggregation of autonomous entities, named *agents*. The deployment environment has already been pointed out as a fundamental concept for the design and implementation of MAS-based applications [8, 4]. However, few works have actually addressed the problem of studying the general properties of this entity. By contrast to MAS, mobile computing [7] and coordination communities have represented explicitly the deployment environment that joins respectively mobile entities and coordinables in order to establish their interactions [5,1]. We suggest generalising their concepts in order to define a deployment environment that rules interactions among entities; their movement laws and how to react to their actions. On the other hand, formal models of mobile and distributed calculus such as $\pi$-calculus [6], Ambient [2] and Join calculus [3] present a formal programming language capturing modern computing concepts such as mobility and distribution. MIC* adopts a different view by clearly separating the calculus from its environment. Consequently, mobility, interaction and observations of the entities' computation are defined and studied at the environmental level.

## 2 Informal Example: Ubiquitous Electronic Chat Scenario

In order to introduce the MIC* formal structure, this section extracts main concepts starting from a simple ubiquitous application scenario. The ubiquitous electronic chat

N. Zhong et al. (Eds.): ISMIS 2003, LNAI 2871, pp. 216–220, 2003.

application emulates verbal conversations between several humans about some specific topics. Users are no longer connected permanently to a central network but own a small device equipped with some ad hoc networking capabilities. Thus, when several users are spatially joined they can converse together. The general description of the application can be summarised as following: *(i)* each user *participates* in one or several *discussions*; *(ii)* the interaction between the users are conducted by explicitly sending *messages*. The first reflection concerns the interactions among agents. These interactions are materialised by concrete objects that we identify as *interaction objects*. Interaction objects are structured objects. For instance, they can be composed in simultaneous interactions. Moreover, a special empty interaction object (the zero 0) can be abstractly identified to express 'no interaction'. In the presented scenario, messages represent the interaction objects and receiving simultaneous messages is viewed as receiving a *sum* $(\sum o)$ of interaction objects. *Interaction spaces* are abstract locations where several entities interact by exchanging explicitly interaction objects. An interaction space rules interactions among agents and may alter the exchanged interaction objects. In the ubiquitous chat scenario, each topic is represented by an interaction space, where several *human agents* can exchange messages. Concerning the mobility over the interaction spaces, it is easy to encode the agents' desires to participate in certain topics as a logical movement inside these interaction spaces. *Agents* perceive and react to external interaction objects by a local computation and the emission of other interaction objects in interaction spaces. These reactions are considered as *attempts* to influence the universe (others) that are committed only when they are coherent with the deployment environment rules.

## 3 {Movement, Interaction, Computation}* (MIC*)

Due to space constraints this section presents semi-formally and briefly some aspect of the {Movement, Interaction, Computation}* structure. The algebraic theoretical definitions are omitted. Thus, a more intuitive view of the manipulated algebraic objects is designed using matrices. In fact, matrix representations are familiar to computer scientists and give spatial representation better than complex linear formulas. To present the matrix view, the reader should assume the following minimal definitions:

- $(\mathcal{O}, +)$ represents the commutative group of interaction objects. This means that interaction objects can be composed commutatively by the $+$ law, and that the empty interaction object exists ($0 \in \mathcal{O}$). Furthermore, each interaction object $x$ has an opposite $(-x)$ and $x + (-x) = 0$;
- $\mathcal{A}$ and $\mathcal{S}$ represent respectively the sets of agents and interaction spaces. $\mathcal{S}$ contains a special element: $1 \in \mathcal{S}$ representing the universe as a global interaction space. Moreover, this special element has the following features: *(i)* no interaction between the entities is possible; *(ii)* all the interaction objects can move inside or outside this interaction spaces without restriction.

Each MIC* term is represented by the following matrices:

Outboxes Matrix: Rows of this matrix represent agents $A_i \in \mathcal{A}$ and the columns represent the interaction spaces $S_j \in \mathcal{S}$. Each element of the matrix $o_{(i,j)} \in \mathcal{O}$ is the representation of the agent $A_i$ in the interaction space $S_j$.

Inboxes Matrix: Rows of this matrix represent agents $A_i \in \mathcal{A}$ and the columns represent the interaction spaces $S_j \in \mathcal{S}$. Each element of the matrix $o_{(i,j)} \in \mathcal{O}$ defines how the agent $A_i$ perceives the universe in the interaction space $S_j$.

Memories Vector: Agents $A_i \in \mathcal{A}$ represent the rows of the vector. Each element $m_i$ is an abstraction of the internal memory of the agent $A_i$. Except the existence of such element that can be proved using the Turing machine model, no further assumptions are made in MIC* about this element.

MIC* terms model naturally ubiquitous environments. In fact, the union or split of computational environments are simply represented as an addition $+$ and a subtraction $-$ defined between the sub matrices representing sub environments.

### 3.1 MIC* *Dynamics*

This section characterises three main transformations of environmental terms : the movement, the interaction and the computation.

- Movement $\mu$: A movement is a transformation $\mu$, of the environment where both inboxes and memories matrices are unchanged, and where outboxes matrix interaction objects are changed but globally invariant. This means that interaction objects of an agent can change their positions in outboxes matrix and no interaction object is created or lost.
- Interaction $\phi$: Interaction is characterised by a transformation $\phi$ that leaves both outboxes and memories matrices unchanged and transform a row of the inboxes matrix. Thus, interaction is defined as modifying the perceptions of the entities in a particular interaction space.
- Computation $\gamma$: An observable computation of an entity transforms its representations in outboxes matrix and the memories vector. For practical reasons, the inboxes of the calculating entity are reset to 0 after the computation.

Finally, the structure of MIC* is fully defined for a particular system by giving the interaction objects group; the sets of processes and interaction spaces; the sets of transformations defining its dynamics.

## 4 Ubiquitous Chat

### 4.1 Situation A

Each topic is represented by an interaction space. For instance, "sport" and "computing" topics are represented by two interaction spaces (figure 1). When the user selects a chat topic $x$, this is expressed as sending an interaction object $go^x$. This interaction object is absorbed by the *correct* interaction space. In fact, the interaction space controls its local movement policy allowing certain interaction objects to enter and refusing access to others. Here the movement policy of an interaction space $x$ is to absorb $go^x$ and to move outside $-go^x$. Situation expressed in figure 1 is be described formally as follows:

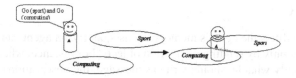

**Fig. 1.** Agent 'A' moving inside two interaction spaces

$$e_0^{outbox} = \frac{\quad}{A\left|go^{sport}+go^{computing}\right.} \begin{array}{|c|c|} \hline 1 & \\ \hline sport & computing \\ \hline 0 & 0 \\ \hline \end{array} \text{ that evolves to :}$$

$$\mu(\mu((e_0^{outbox})) = e_1^{outbox} = \begin{array}{c|c|c|c} & 1 & sport & computing \\ \hline A & 0 & go^{sport} & go^{computing} \end{array}$$

After these two movements, agent $A$ exists in both interaction spaces: *sport* and *computation*.

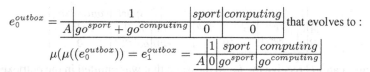

**Fig. 2.** Union and disjunction of environments

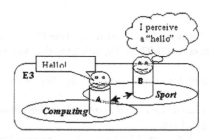

**Fig. 3.** Interaction among agents

## 4.2  Situation B

As illustrated in figure 2, when two environments $E_1$ and $E_2$ are joined a new environment $E_3$ is defined. This environment, the interaction schema among the entities is modified. On the other side, when the physical network link is disconnected, the environment $E_3$ is split into $E_1$ and $E_2$. This situation is formally described as follows:

$$\begin{array}{c|c|c|c} & 1 & sport & computing \\ \hline A & 0 & go^{sport} & go^{computing} \end{array} + \begin{array}{c|c|c|c} & 1 & sport & computing \\ \hline B & 0 & go^{sport} & 0 \end{array} \rightarrow \begin{array}{c|c|c|c} & 1 & sport & computing \\ \hline A & 0 & go^{sport} & go^{computing} \\ \hline B & 0 & go^{sport} & 0 \end{array}$$

## 4.3   Situation C

Computation modifies the agent's memory. Consequently, an agent can modify the surrounding entities only by sending interaction objects. For instance, when a human agent computes internally what he should write as message, the observation of this process is the written message (interaction object). The surrounding entities receive this message through the interaction space (see figure 3). For instance, when agent $A$ writes a *hello* message, the outboxes matrix is changed as follows:

$$\begin{array}{c|c|c|c} & |1| & sport & computing \\ \hline A & |0| & go^{sport} & go^{computing} \\ \hline B & |0| & go^{sport} & 0 \end{array} \rightarrow \begin{array}{c|c|c|c} & |1| & sport & computing \\ \hline A & |0| & hello & hello \\ \hline B & |0| & go^{sport} & 0 \end{array}$$

Both agents $A$ and $B$ receive the *hello* message that was emitted in the outboxes matrix.

## 5   Conclusion

This paper has presented, semi-formally, the MIC* algebraic structure modelling combinable environments where mobile, autonomous and interacting entities evolves. Evolutions of this environment are described as composition of three atomic evolutions: movement, interaction and computation. The next step of our works is to generate specific environments and interaction spaces starting form the engineering specification of a system. Following the MIC* approach, it would be possible to guarantee these specifications in an unpredictable and dynamic environments such as ubiquitous systems.

## References

1. Giacomo Cabri, Letizia Leonardi, and Franco Zambonelli. Coordination in mobile agent applications. Technical Report DSI-97-24, Dipartimento di Scienze dell Ingegneria Universitá di Modena, 1997.
2. Luca Cardelli. Abstractions for mobile computation. *Secure Internet Programming*, pages 51–94, 1999.
3. Cedric Fournet. *Le Join-Calcul: Un Calcul Pour la Programmation Repartie et Mobile*. PhD thesis, Ecole Polytechnique, 1998.
4. James J. Odell, H. Van Dyke Parunak, Mitch Fleischer, and Sven Brueckner. Modeling agents and their environment. In *AOSE 2002, AAMAS 2002*, Bologna, 2002.
5. George A. Papadopoulos. Models and technologies for the coordination of Internet agents: A survey. In Andrea Omicini, Franco Zambonelli, Matthias Klusch, and Robert Tolksdorf, editors, *Coordination of Internet Agents: Models, Technologies, and Applications*, chapter 2, pages 25–56. Springer-Verlag, March 2001.
6. Milner Robin, Parrow Joachim, and Walker David. A calculus for mobile processes, parts 1 and 2. *Information and Computation*, 100(1), 1992.
7. G.-C. Roman, G. P. Picco, and A. L. Murphy. Software engineering for mobility: A roadmap. *The Future of Software Engineerin,*, pages 241–258, 2000.
8. Stuart Russell and Peter Norvig. *Artificial Intelligence: A Modern Approach*. Prentice Hall, 1995.

# Using the SPACE Intermediate Model to Help to Implement Agents

Dominique Fournier, Bruno Mermet, Gaële Simon, Marianne Flouret
Laboratoire d'informatique du Havre – BP 540
76058 Le Havre Cedex
FRANCE

**Abstract.** In this article, an intermediate model for specifying agents is described. This model makes easier the transition between a conceptual model (like the BDI one) and a multiagent environment. The SPACE model is specified. An example of application to BDI agents is also presented.

**Keywords:** Multiagent systems, model, software engineering, validation

## 1 Introduction

For the last decade, in order to answer to the growing interest for multi–agent systems (MAS) development, several models and tools have been proposed ([3, 6, 8]). Among them, there are some methods ([2, 8]), agents models ([1, 5]), MAS models and MAS development environments. Our research focuses on the design of a MAS development method allowing, at the same time, validation, verification or even system proof. Few already proposed methods provide enough elements necessary to achieve these tasks. In [7], we have described a first development of our method dedicated to optimization problems. The main goal of this paper is to propose an agent model allowing to completely and precisely specify agents produced by our method. This model must also provide an easy way to operationalize these agents.

This model, called SPACE (Structure, Perception, Action, Comportment and Environment) can be seen as an interface between agents models, like BDI, Aalaadin, Vowel, ... ([1, 5]) used to characterize agents behaviour, and their corresponding implementation in a MAS development environment.

A SPACE specification of an agent gives the most declarative operational view as possible of this agent. This property gives the basis to potentially future validations of the agent implementation.

The first part of this paper deals with a SPACE model description. The second part describes the operational semantics of the model. Finally, the third one focuses on a case study that deals with BDI model and gives its expression with SPACE.

## 2 The Agent Model: SPACE

In this part, we present the different elements of the SPACE agent model. As explained before, this model is designed in order to be a good compromise between a purely executable agent specification about which it is not possible to reason and a more formal specification not really implementable. We try to obtain an almost runnable agent specification while keeping the most declarative description as possible. As a consequence, the resulting specification can be considered as an

N. Zhong et al. (Eds.): ISMIS 2003, LNAI 2871, pp. 221–225, 2003.

operational one: we provide not only models but also an operational semantics describing the effective operation of the agent from these models.

In SPACE, an agent is represented by three complementary models and a structure: the perceptions model, the actions model, the behaviour model, the inner structure. These different elements are described in the following paragraphs. They are of course not independent from each other. That is why they must satisfy a set of consistency rules we yet defined [4] but that are not presented in this paper.

## 2.1 Perceptions Model

This model describes the set of perceptions of the agent, that is to say, whatever is likely to modify the actions the agent may do. There are two kinds of perceptions: Messages perceptions and Variables Perceptions.

### 2.1.1 Variables Perceptions (EVP/IVP)

These perceptions are connected to inner and environment variables. The environment in which the agent is living is considered as a set of variables. The environment evolution implies changes on the values of the variables. *A priori*, an agent has only a partial and biased view of the environment. This view is also biased because it depends on the agent interpretation. By this way, it is easy to take into account the point of view of the agent in its behaviour. Thus, some elements of the environment may be considered differently according to the goal of the agent.

An Environment Variable Perception associates a particular value to a subset of values of significant environment variables for the agent. It allows to design the agent point of view on the environment. For example, let us consider weather variables like wind, hygrometry and temperature. The perception "weather" could have four values : nice, very nice, bad and very bad. Thus, when the wind speed is lower than 15 mph, the hygrometry fewer than 60% and the temperature between 20°c and 25°c, the weather perception shall be nice.

Inner variables perceptions rely on the same principles, but they are not based on the same kind of variables. It is assumed that an agent maintains some variables during its life. Generally, these variables are connected to the problems and goals the agent has to achieve. They are designed to manage some aspects of the agent behaviour.

Formally, variables perceptions are defined by a 5–tuple (N, C, V, T, F) with:

| name | type | role |
|------|------|------|
| N | String | Name of the perception |
| C | {EVP,IVP} | Kind of the perception |
| V | {variables} | Set of significant variables |
| T | {values} | Set of potential values |
| F | Function | Function from V to T describing the value of the perception according to the value of the concerned variables |

### 2.1.2 Messages Perceptions (IMP/RMP)

A first class of messages perceptions is *Information Messages Perceptions* (IMP). These perceptions are based on information messages. An information message is considered as a set of variables. Receiving these variables may modify a subset of receiver's inner variables. Yet, every values are not necessarily useful to the receiver. An IMP allows to define which elements of the message are relevant. The IMP also provides the way to read and use the information the message contains.

These perceptions are defined by a 5–tuple (N, C, S, V, F) with:

| name | type | role |
|------|------|------|
| N | String | Name of the perception |
| C | IMP | Kind of the perception |
| S | Class | Message structure (name and type of each variable) |
| V | {inner variables} | List of inner variables the perception may modify |
| F | Function | Casting function from S to V |

We defined also another class of messages perceptions : the *Request Messages Perceptions* (RMP), that are described in [4].

## 2.2  The Actions Model

The actions model allows to describe the entire set of actions the agent is able to do. It also allows to conditions in which they can be performed (precondition), and also properties (on inner or environment variables) always having to be checked after their execution (postcondition). We can notice that sending messages is considered as specific actions. The associated precondition describes, in this case, when the agent can send the message.

An action is then defined by a 3–tuple (Pre, M, Post) with:

| name | type | role |
|------|------|------|
| PRE | Event | Precondition. Preconditions are specified by events (see below) |
| M | Method | Describes what the action does |
| POST | {properties} | Postcondition, expressed as a set of properties. A property is a constraint over one or more inner or environment variables |

An event is a couple (name, function). The function is defined on values of one or more perceptions or events, and its result is in B = {True, False}. This notion allows to specify a significant special context for the agent behaviour, i.e. in which the agent can implement specific actions.

For example, if an agent wants to play tennis, several conditions have to be checked. To express them, an event "tennis condition" will be defined. This event takes into account values of perceptions as "weather" (see paragraph 2.1.1) and "free partner". Thus, this event will be "true" if the "weather" perception value is "nice" or "very nice", and if the "free partner" perception value is "true".

## 2.3  The Behaviour Model

A part of the agent behaviour is formalised by specific automata which are transducers [7]. Within the framework of our model, the agent  automaton is in fact the representation of a decomposition of its goals. We give below the state and transition patterns with more details.

A state $p$ is defined by a 7–tuple (N, L, M, Ve, Vs, V, $\pi$) such that N is a string labelling the state, L={(E, A)} is an ordered list of couples (event, action) –an action A can be realized only if the associated event E is true –, M is a method, possibly neutral, which sorts actions of L if a specific order is needed, Ve is the set of input variables, i.e. variables the agent can read when it tries to reach the goal $p$, Vs is the set of output variables, i.e. the ones it can modify during its stay in state $p$, V is the variant of the goal $p$, and $\pi$ is the choice policy of transitions (priority order,...) starting from state $p$ when several events are realized.

A transition between two states Ed and Ea is defined by a 4–tuple (Ed, Ea, E, A). Such a transition shall be fired when the current state is Ed and when event E is true. The action A will then be run and the current state becomes Ea.

## 2.4  Inner Structure of the Agent

The inner structure of the agent contains the set of inner variables which represent, in real time, the evaluation the agent can do of its own situation. It contains also a list of waiting resquests.

The inner structure of the agent is also made up of its relationships, in fact the list of other agents it knows. This list shall be linked with a qualitative judgment about the kind of relationship (friends, enemies,...). Last but not least, the inner structure includes the behaviour automaton, and a reference to the current state in which the agent is.

# 3  Application to BDI Agents

BDI agents ([5]) rely on 3 essential characteristics : their beliefs, their desires and their intentions. Beliefs correspond to how the agents percieve their environment and their inner state. In our model, beliefs of BDI agents can be easily translated into perceptions.

Desires correspond to the set of goals an agent may have. In SPACE, the behaviour of an agent being described by an automaton whose states are associated to goals, the set of desires of a BDI agent will correspond to the set of states of the automaton.

Finally, intentions correspond to the current goal and eventually to an intention about next goals or actions. The current goal is represented, in SPACE, by the current state. The intentions about the next goals or actions can be modelised by inner variables. The latter must be taken into account by the events associated to transitions.

The typical algorithm describing how a BDI agent works is the following :

| | |
|---|---|
| *initial−state();* | *execute();* |
| *repeat* | *get−new−external−events();* |
|   *options := option−generator(event−queue);* | *drop−successful−attitudes();* |
|   *selected−option := deliberate(options);* | *drop−impossible−attitudes();* |
|   *update−intention(selected−options);* | *end repeat* |

This algorithm can also be translated easily into SPACE. The option generation corresponds to the calculus of the perceptions associated to the transitions starting from the current state. The choice of the option and the updating of the intentions of the agent corresponds to the choice of the transition if several are fireable.  The executed statement is similar to the standard behaviour of the SPACE agents when they are in a given state. Let us notice it is not necessary to translate  the *get−new−external−events()* function because require events are automatically evaluated before executing actions. As well, the deletion of successful goals is a consequence of the automaton structure. Indeed, solving a goal implies the evaluation of the transitions coming from the state associated to this goal. By this way, the current state and as a consequence the current goal of the agent change. Finally, the deletion of impossible attitudes can be taken into account by adding an inner variable indicating when a goal is impossible. Then, transitions ending in the state associated to this goal must evaluate this variable.

# 4  Conclusion

The aim we had when we developed the SPACE model was to enlight as many properties as possible that could be necessary to validate the produced Multi–Agent System. Previous works were realized with the same goal. This is for instance the case of Metatem[2] and Gaïa[8]. A comparison of them with SPACE can be found in [4].

SPACE is designed to be a bridge between higher–level (in terms of abstraction) models like BDI, Eco–Agent, ... and their corresponding implementation in a MAS development platform. The main goal is to provide a runnable description of an agent, while keeping a description level which allows to reason about it, especially for verification and validation purpose. It is the main interest and contribution of the SPACE model.

Our work will focus on the design of a MAS development method integrating the SPACE model. More precisely, the goal is to extend the method we have already proposed in a previous paper [7], in order to produce an agent model expressed with SPACE. This method must also provide tools allowing to use the different components of the SPACE model in order to verify and validate the produced agents and then the entire MAS.

# References

1. Jacques Ferber and Olivier Gutknecht, *A meta–model for  the analysis of Multi–agent Organisations in multi–agent systems*. In Third International Conference on Multi–Agent Systems (ICMAS 98) proceedings. IEEE Computer Society, p128–135, 1998.
2. M. Fisher. *A Survey of Concurrent MetateM – the Language and its Applications*. In D.M. Gabbay and H.J. Ohlbach, editors, Temporal Logic – Proceedings of the First International Conference, number 827 in LNAI, pages 480–505. Springer Verlag, 1994.
3. Carlos Iglesias, Mercedes Garrijo, and José Gonzalez. *A survey of agent–oriented methodologies*. In Jörg Müller, Munindar P. Singh, and Anand S. Rao, editors, Proceedings of the 5th International Workshop on Intelligent Agents: Agent Theories, Architectures, and Languages (ATAL–98), volume 1555, pages 317–330. Springer–Verlag: Heidelberg, Germany, 1999.
4. Bruno Mermet, Gaële Simon, Dominique Fournier, Marianne Flouret, *From the problem to its implementation, a methodology and the SPACE model to design Multi–Agents Systems*, ProMAS 2003, Melbourne (Australia), 2003 *to appear*.
5. A. Rao, M. Georgeff, *BDI Agents from Theory to Practice*, Technical Note 56, AAII, April 1995.
6. Arsène Sabas, Sylvain Delisle, and Mourad Badri. *A comparative analysis of multiagent system development methodologies : Towards a unified approach*. In Robert Trappl, editor, Cybernetics and Systems, pages 599–604. Austrian Society for Cybernetics Studies, 2002.
7. Gaële Simon, Marianne Flouret, Bruno Mermet, A methodology to solve optimisation problems with MAS ; application to the graph colouring problem, AIMSA 2002, Varna 2002.
8. Michael Wooldridge, Nicholas R. Jennings, and D. Kinny, *The Gaia Methodology for Agent Oriented Analysis and Design*, Journal of Autonomous Agents and Multi–Agent Systems, 3(3), p 285–312, 2000.

# Belief Revision and Text Mining for Adaptive Recommender Agents

Raymond Y.K. Lau and Peter van den Brand

Centre for Information Technology Innovation
Faculty of Information Technology
Queensland University of Technology
GPO Box 2434, Brisbane, Qld 4001, Australia
{r.lau, p.vandenbrand}@qut.edu.au

**Abstract.** With the rapid growth of the number of electronic transactions conducted over the Internet, *recommender systems* have been
proposed to provide consumers with personalized product recommendations. This paper illustrates how belief revision and text mining can be
used to improve recommender agents' *prediction effectiveness*, *learning
autonomy*, *adaptiveness*, and *explanatory capabilities*. To our best
knowledge, this is the first study of integrating text mining techniques
and belief revision logic into a single framework for the development of
adaptive recommender agents.

**Keywords:** Belief Revision, Text Mining, Recommender Agents.

## 1 Introduction

Applying a symbolic framework to develop recommender agents [5,6] is intuitively attractive because a consumer's product preferences can be formally represented as *beliefs* in a recommender agent's knowledge base. Then, the consumer's implicit needs can be deduced by the agent based on formal reasoning.
In particular, a symbolic framework offers sufficient expressive power to capture
a *recommendation context* (e.g., the associations between products, correlation
between consumers, background of specific consumers, etc.). Hence, *proactive*
recommendation is possible. For instance, the agent may recommend "Ford Falcon" to its user given the facts that the user is interested in "Family Car", and
"Ford Falcon" is a "Family Car". In fact, the above reasoning is based on the
sound inference rule called Modus Ponens. Since a consumer's needs can only
be partially represented in a recommender agent, the above reasoning process
involves uncertainty. The belief revision logic is just able to support this kind
of reasoning e.g., the prediction that a consumer is interested in "Ford Falcon" is true to a certain degree. As less direct feedback is required to train the
recommender agents, the *learning autonomy* of these agents is enhanced. It is
believed that *autonomy*, *proactiveness*, and *adaptiveness* are among the essential properties of intelligent agents [9]. Since a consumer's preferences will change
over time, recommender agents must be *adaptive* in the sense that the agents

N. Zhong et al. (Eds.): ISMIS 2003, LNAI 2871, pp. 226–230, 2003.

can make sensible recommendations based on the consumer's latest preferences. This is another reason why a belief revision logic is required to develop adaptive recommender agents. Classical logic is *monotonic* and so it is ineffective to model changing recommendation contexts. The AGM belief revision framework provides a rigorous formal foundation to model belief changes in rational agents under the guiding principle of *minimal* and *consistent* belief revision [3]. The inductive power brought by the text mining method is just able to complement the nonmonotonic reasoning capability offered by a belief revision system. Last but not least, a symbolic framework can improve recommender agents' explanatory power as the agents can explain their decisions based on appropriate recommendation contexts (e.g., the association rules). Enhanced explanatory power help improve users' trust on using the recommender agents.

## 2  The AGM Belief Revision Framework

The AGM belief revision framework is one of the most influential works in the theory of belief revision [3]. The framework formalises *consistent* and *minimal* belief changes by sets of postulates and belief functions e.g., *expansion* $(K_\alpha^+)$, *contraction* $(K_\alpha^-)$, and *revision* $(K_\alpha^*)$ via *epistemic entrenchment* $(\leqslant)$ [3]. For a computer-based implementation of the AGM framework, the *finite partial entrenchment ranking* **B** which ranks a finite subset of beliefs with the minimum possible degree of entrenchment $(\leqslant_\mathbf{B})$ was proposed by Williams [7]. In addition, several transmutation methods were developed to implement iterated belief revision based on finite partial entrenchment rankings. One of them is the Maxiadjustment transmutation method [8]. Belief revision is not just taken as adding or removing a belief from a knowledge base but the *transmutation* of the underlying epistemic entrenchment ranking. The explicit beliefs of an agent is denoted $exp(\mathbf{B}) = \{\alpha \in dom(\mathbf{B}) : \mathbf{B}(\alpha) > 0\}$. The set of implicit beliefs $Cn(exp(\mathbf{B}))$ is denoted $content(\mathbf{B})$, where $Cn$ is the classical consequence operator. In the proposed recommender agent model, a recommendation context (i.e., a consumer's product preferences and the background information about the consumers and the products) is represented by a set of beliefs **B**. When a user's needs change, the entrenchment degrees of the corresponding beliefs are raised or lowered in the agent's knowledge base. Raising or lowering the entrenchment degree of a belief is conducted via a transmutation operation $\mathbf{B}^\star(\alpha, i)$ where $\alpha$ is a belief and $i$ is the new entrenchment degree. In particular, the Rapid Maxi-adjustment (RAM) method which was developed based on the Maxi-adjustment transmutation strategy [8] is applied to develop the learning and reasoning components of adaptive recommender agents.

## 3  Knowledge Representation and Reasoning

### 3.1  Representing a Consumer's Preferences

Each product description $D$ (e.g., a Web page) is pre-processed according to traditional IR techniques so that a set of *tokens* (e.g., stems, n-grams, or phrases) is extracted as its representation. At the symbolic level, each token $k$ is mapped to a proposition $q$ of the classical propositional Horn language $\mathcal{L}_{Horn}$. On the other hand, a user's product preferences is induced based on a set of rated product descriptions. In particular, $D^+$ represents a consumer's positive interests (i.e., positive training examples) and $D^-$ is the set of items that the consumer does not like (i.e., negative training examples). Essentially, there are three types of tokens that can be induced from $D^+$ and $D^-$. *Positive tokens* represent specific items that the consumer likes; *negative tokens* indicate what the consumer dislikes; *neutral tokens* are not good indicators of the a consumer's preferences. The following formula is used to distinguish positive, negative or neutral tokens, and their *preference values* which are used to derive the *epistemic entrenchment* of corresponding beliefs.

$$pre(k) = \xi \times (pos \times \tfrac{df^+(k)}{|D^+|} - neg \times \tfrac{df^-(k)}{|D^-|}) \tag{1}$$

where $pre(k)$ is the induced preference value of a token $k$, and $\xi$ is a scaling factor. Since all beliefs induced in this way are contractable, their degrees of entrenchment must be less than the maximal degree 1. *pos* and *neg* are the weight factors for positive and negative training examples respectively. $df^+(k)$ or $df^-(k)$ is the term frequency of $k$ appearing in the set of positive $D^+$ or negative $D^-$ items. $|D^+|$ and $|D^-|$ are the cardinalities of the respective training sets. A positive $pre(k)$ indicates that the underlying token $k$ is a positive token, whereas a negative preference value implies that $k$ is a negative token. If the preference value of a token is below a threshold $\lambda$, the token is considered neutral. A positive token is mapped to a literal such as $p$ of $\mathcal{L}_{Horn}$, whereas a negative token is mapped to a negated literal such as $\neg p$. The entrenchment degree of a belief corresponding to a token $k$ (i.e., $\mathbf{B}(\alpha_k)$) is computed according to the following formula:

$$\mathbf{B}(\alpha_k) = \begin{cases} \frac{(|pre(k)|-\lambda)}{1-\lambda} & \text{if } |pre(k)| > \lambda \\ 0 & \text{otherwise} \end{cases} \tag{2}$$

where $\lambda$ is a parameter used to filter insignificant beliefs.

## 3.2   Mining Contextual Knowledge

The *unsupervised* text mining method employed in the recommender agent system is based on the Apriori algorithm [1]. A database (i.e., a document collection for text mining) contains a set of transactions (i.e., documents) with each transaction $t$ containing a subset of *items* (i.e., tokens) from a finite set of items $\mathcal{I} = \{k_1, k_2, \ldots, k_n\}$. The Apriori algorithm successively finds *large item sets* $L_k$ which satisfy the minimal *support*. Then, association rules are constructed based on each element $Z \in L_k$ which satisfies the minimal *confidence*. An association rule is an implication of the form $X \to Y$, where $X \subset Z$, $Y \subset Z$, and $X \cap Y = \emptyset$. Rule support is the priori probability $Pr(Z) = \dfrac{\text{No. trans. containing } z}{\text{Total no. of trans.}}$, and rule confidence is the conditional probability $Pr(Z|X) = \dfrac{\text{No. trans. containing } z}{\text{No. of trans. containing } x}$.

Since our prototype agent system employs propositional Horn logic $\mathcal{L}_{Horn}$ as its representation language, the consequent $Y$ must be a single item. To convert the term association rules to beliefs in an agent's knowledge base, the entrenchment degree $\mathbf{B}(\alpha)$ is derived by multiplying the rule support $s$ and rule confidence $c$ by an adjustment factor $\epsilon$, where $\alpha$ is an association rule.

Apart from term association rules, a recommender agent can make use of other semantic relationships such as *information preclusion* [2] to characterise a recommendation context so as to enhance *precision* of its recommendations. An information preclusion relation such as $\alpha \perp \beta$ indicates that a token $\alpha$ precludes another token $\beta$. For example, $car \perp boat$ may hold if a consumer is only interested in "car" rather than "boat". Therefore, information preclusion relations are driven by a consumer's specific interests, and so they should be induced dynamically. The down side of the information preclusion relations is that they can only be discovered via supervised text mining. Formally, an information preclusion relation between two tokens $\alpha \perp \beta$ can be represented by a rule $\alpha \rightarrow \neg \beta$. In the current prototype system, only strict preclusion rules are induced. For any token $k$ from $D^+$ and $D^-$, if $df^+(k) > \gamma$ and $df^-(k) = 0$, $k$ is added to a set $L$. Similarly, for a token $k$ satisfying $df^-(k) > \gamma$ and $df^+(k) = 0$, it is added to a set $R$. Then, for each token $k_i \in L$, generate a rule $k_i \rightarrow \neg k_j$ for each $k_j \in R$. The entrenchment degree of such a rule is derived by: $Pr(k_i) \times Pr(k_j) \times \delta$.

### 3.3    Computing Recommendations

An entrenchment-based similarity measure $Sim(\mathbf{B}, d)$ Eq.(3) is developed to approximate the *semantic correspondence* $Sim(Ctx, D)$ between a recommendation context $Ctx$ and a product description $D$.

$$Sim(Ctx, D) \approx Sim(\mathbf{B}, d)$$
$$= \frac{\sum_{l \in d}[degree(\mathbf{B}, l) - degree(\mathbf{B}, \neg l)]}{|S|} \tag{3}$$

Eq.(3) combines the advantages of quantitative ranking and symbolic reasoning in a single formulation. The basic idea is that a product description $D$ is represented by a set of positive literals $d = \{l_1, l_2, \dots, l_n\}$. If an agent's knowledge base $K$ logically entails an atom $l_i$, a positive contribution is made to the overall similarity score because of the partial semantic correspondence between $Ctx$ and $D$. This kind of logical entailment is non-classical. Conceptually, information matching is underpinned by $q \underset{E}{\hspace{0.5pt}\mid\hspace{-3pt}\sim} d$, where $\underset{E}{\hspace{0.5pt}\mid\hspace{-3pt}\sim}$ is a nonmonotonic inference relation [4]. On the other hand, if $K$ implies the negation of a literal $l_i \in d$, it shows the *semantic distance* between $Ctx$ and $D$. Therefore, the similarity value $Sim(\mathbf{B}, d)$ is reduced by a certain degree. The set $S$ is defined by $S = \{l \in d : degree(\mathbf{B}, l) > 0 \vee degree(\mathbf{B}, \neg l) > 0\}$.

## 4    Discussion and Future Work

The AGM belief revision framework provides a rigorous formal foundation to model non-monotonicity of changing recommendation contexts. The induction power brought by text mining is complementary to the nonmonotonic reasoning capability of a belief revision system. Our preliminary evaluation was based on the set of book descriptions found on the Prentice-Hall academic catalogue (http://vig.prenhall.com/). Essentially, each category of books (e.g., computer science, Agriculture, Biology, etc.) represents a consumer's initial interest. Our recommender agent was loaded with an initial interest (e.g., book category description) together with the contextual association rules mined from the book dataset to predict if a book was relevant with respect to the recommendation context captured in its knowledge base. The same procedure was applied to a recommender agent developed based on the vector space IR model (i.e., no contextual rules available). Our experiment showed that the integrated belief revision and text mining approach improved the recommender agents' prediction accuracy over four different book categories. More effective text mining methods will be examined to improve the agents' prediction effectiveness in future research. Large IR bench-mark collections will also be used to evaluate the effectiveness and efficiency of the belief-based recommender agents.

# References

1. R. Agrawal and R. Srikant. Fast algorithms for mining association rules in large databases. In Jorge B. Bocca, Matthias Jarke, and Carlo Zaniolo, editors, *VLDB'94, Proceedings of 20th International Conference on Very Large Data Bases*, pages 487–499, Santiago de Chile, Chile, September 12–15 1994. Morgan Kaufmann Publishers.
2. P.D. Bruza and T.W.C. Huibers. Investigating Aboutness Axioms Using Information Fields. In W.B. Croft and C.J. van Rijsbergen, editors, *Proceedings of the 17th Annual International ACM SIGIR Conference on Research and Development in Information Retrieval*, pages 112–121, Dublin, Ireland, July 1994. ACM Press.
3. P. Gärdenfors. *Knowledge in flux: modeling the dynamics of epistemic states.* The MIT Press, Cambridge, Massachusetts, 1988.
4. P. Gärdenfors and D. Makinson. Nonmonotonic inference based on expectations. *Artificial Intelligence*, 65(2):197–245, 1994.
5. N. Good, J. Schafer, J. Konstan, A. Borchers, B. Sarwar, J. Herlocker, and J. Riedl. Combining collaborative filtering with personal agents for better recommendations. In *Proceedings of the 6th National Conference on Artificial Intelligence (AAAI-99)*, pages 439–446, Menlo Park, California, July 18–22 1999. MIT Press.
6. P. Resnick and H. Varian. Recommender systems. *Communications of the ACM*, 40(3):56–58, March 1997.
7. M.-A. Williams. Iterated theory base change: A computational model. In Chris S. Mellish, editor, *Proceedings of the Fourteenth International Joint Conference on Artificial Intelligence*, pages 1541–1547, Montréal, Canada, August 20–25, 1995. Morgan Kaufmann Publishers.
8. M.-A. Williams. Anytime belief revision. In Martha E. Pollack, editor, *Proceedings of the Fifteenth International Joint Conference on Artificial Intelligence*, pages 74–79, Nagoya, Japan, August 23–29, 1997. Morgan Kaufmann Publishers.
9. M. Wooldridge and N. Jennings. Intelligent Agents: Theory and Practice. *Knowledge Engineering Review*, 10(2):115–152, 1995.

# NETMARK: A Schema-Less Extension for Relational Databases for Managing Semi-structured Data Dynamically

David A. Maluf and Peter B. Tran

NASA Ames Research Center, Mail Stop 269-4
Moffett Field, California, USA
maluf@ptolemy.arc.nasa.gov
pbtran@mail.arc.nasa.gov

**Abstract.** Object-Relational database management system is an integrated hybrid cooperative approach to combine the best practices of both the relational model utilizing SQL queries and the object-oriented, semantic paradigm for supporting complex data creation. In this paper, a highly scalable, information on demand database framework, called NETMARK, is introduced. NETMARK takes advantages of the Oracle 8i object-relational database using physical addresses data types for very efficient keyword search of records spanning across both context and content. NETMARK was originally developed in early 2000 as a research and development prototype to solve the vast amounts of unstructured and semi-structured documents existing within NASA enterprises. Today, NETMARK is a flexible, high-throughput open database framework for managing, storing, and searching unstructured or semi-structured arbitrary hierarchal models, such as XML and HTML.

## 1 Introduction

During the early years of database technology, there were two opposing research and development directions, namely the relational model originally formalized by Codd [1] in 1970 and the object-oriented, semantic database model [2][3]. The traditional relational model revolutionized the field by separating logical data representation from physical implementation. The relational model has been developed into a mature and proven database technology holding a majority stake of the commercial database market along with the official standardization of the Structured Query Language (SQL)[1] by ISO and ANSI committees for a user-friendly data definition language (DDL) and data manipulation language (DML).

The semantic model leveraged off from the object-oriented paradigm of programming languages, such as the availability of convenient data abstraction mechanisms, and the realization of the *impedance mismatch* [4] dilemma faced

---

[1] The Structured Query Language (SQL) is the relational standard defined by ANSI (the American National Standard Institute) in 1986 as SQL1 or SQL-86 and revised and enhanced in 1992 as SQL2 or SQL-92.

N. Zhong et al. (Eds.): ISMIS 2003, LNAI 2871, pp. 231–241, 2003.

between the popular object-oriented programming languages and the underlining relational database management systems (RDBMS). Impedance mismatch here refers to the problem faced by both database programmers and application developers, in which the way the developers structure data is not the same as the way the database structures it. Therefore, the developers are required to write large and complex amounts of object-to-relational mapping code to convert data, which is being inserted into a tabular format the database can understand. Likewise, the developers must convert the relational information returned from the database into the object format developers require for their programs. Today, in order to solve the impedance mismatch problem and take advantage of these two popular database models, commercial enterprise database management systems (DBMS), such as Oracle, IBM, Microsoft, and Sybase, have an integrated hybrid cooperative approach of an *object-relational model* [5].

In order to take advantage of the object-relational (OR) model defined within an *object-relational database management system* (ORDBMS) [5][6], a standard for common data representation and exchange is needed. Today, the emerging standard is the *eXtensible Markup Language* (XML) [7][8] known as the next generation of HTML for placing structure within documents. Within any large organizations and enterprises, there are vast amounts of heterogeneous documents existing in HTML web pages, word processing, presentation, and spreadsheet formats. The traditional document management system does not provide an easy and efficient mechanism to store, manage, and query the relevant information from these heterogeneous and complex data types.

To solve the vast quantities of heterogeneous and complex documents existing within NASA enterprises, NASA at Ames Research Center initially designed and developed an innovative schema-less, object-relational database integration technique and framework referred to hereby as *NETMARK*. Developed in early 2000 as a rapid, proof-of-concept prototype, NETMARK, today, is a highly scalable, open enterprise database framework (architecture) for dynamically transforming and generating arbitrary schema representations from unstructured and/or semi-structured data sources. NETMARK provides automatic data management, storage, retrieval, and *discovery* [17] in transforming large quantities of highly complex and constantly changing heterogeneous data formats into a well-structured, common standard.

This paper describes the NETMARK schema-less database integration technique and architecture for managing, storing, and searching unstructured and/or semi-structured documents from standardized and interchangeable formats, such as XML in relational database systems. The unique features of NETMARK take advantages from the object-relational model and the XML standard described above, along with an open, extensible database framework in order to dynamically generate arbitrary schema stored within relational databases, object-relational database management system.

# 2    Background

## 2.1    Object-Relational DBMS

The object-relational model takes the best practices of both relational and object-oriented, semantic views to decouple the complexity of handling massively rich data representations and their complex interrelationships. ORDBMS employs a data model that attempts to incorporate object-oriented features into traditional relational database systems. All database information is still stored within relations (tables), but some of the tabular attributes may have richer data structures. It was developed to solve some of the inadequacies associated with storing large and complex multimedia objects, such as audio, video, and image files, within traditional RDBMS. As an intermediate hybrid cooperative model, the ORDBMS combined the flexibility, scalability, and security of using existing relational systems along with extensible object-oriented features, such as data abstraction, encapsulation, inheritance, and polymorphism.

In order to understand the benefits of ORDBMS, a comparison of the other models need to be taken into consideration. The 3x3 database application classification matrix [6] shown in Table 1 displays the four categories of general DBMS applications—simple data without queries (file systems), simple data with queries (RDBMS), complex data without queries (OODBMS), and complex data with queries (ORDBMS). For the upper left-handed corner of the matrix, traditional business data processing, such as storing and managing employee information, with simple normalized attributes, such as numbers (integers or floats) and character strings, usually needs to utilize SQL queries to retrieve relevant information. Thus, RDBMS is well suited for traditional business processing; but this model cannot store complex data, such as word processing documents or geographical information. The lower right-handed corner describes the use of persistent object-oriented languages to store complex data objects and their relationships. The lower right-handed corner represents OODBMS, which either have very little SQL-like queries support or none at all. The upper right-handed corner with the dark gray colored cell is well suited for complex and flexible database applications that need complex data creation, such as large objects to store word processing documents, and SQL queries to retrieve relevant information from within these documents. Therefore, the obvious choice for NETMARK is the upper right-handed corner with the dark gray colored cell as indicated in Table 1.

The main advantages of ORDBMS, are scalability, performance, and widely supported by vendors. ORDBMS have been proven to handle very large and complex applications, such as the NASDAQ stock exchange, which contains hundreds of gigabytes of richly complex data for analyst and traders to query stock data trends. In terms of performance, ORDBMS supports query optimization, which are comparable to RDBMS and out performs most OODBMS. Therefore, there is a very large market and future for ORDBMS. This was another determining factor for using ORDBMS for the NETMARK project. Most ORDBMS supports the SQL3 [9] specifications or its extended form. The two basic characteristics of SQL3 are crudely separated into its "relational features" and its "object-oriented features". The relational features for SQL3 consist of new data types, such as large objects or LOB and its variants. The object-oriented features of SQL3 include structured user-defined types called *abstract data types* (ADT) [10][11] which can be hierarchical defined (inheritance feature), invocation routines called methods, and REF types that provides reference values for unique row objects defined by *object identifier* (OID) [11] which is a focus of this paper.

**Table 1.** Database Application Classification Matrix

| Query | **RDBMS** (Traditional Business Data Processing) | **ORDBMS** (NETMARK) |
|---|---|---|
| **No Query** | **File Systems** (Simple Text Editors) | **OODBMS** (Persistent OO Languages) |
| | **Simple Data** | **Complex Data** |

Adapted from M. Stonebraker, "Object-Relational DBMS - The Next Wave",
Informix Software (now part of the IBM Corp. family), Menlo Park, CA

## 2.2 Large Objects

ORDBMS was developed to solve some inadequacies associated with storing large and complex data. The storage solution within ORDBMS is the large object data types called LOBs [9][11]. There are several LOB variants, namely binary data (BLOB), single-byte character data set (CLOB), multi-byte character data (NCLOB), and binary files (BFILE). BLOBs, CLOBs, and NCLOBs are usually termed *internal LOBs* [11], because they are stored internally within the database to provide efficient, random, and piece-wise access to the data. Therefore, the data integrity and concurrency of external BFILEs are usually not guaranteed by the underlining ORDBMS. Each LOB contains both the data value and a pointer to the data called the *LOB locator* [9]. The LOB locator points to the data location that the database creates to hold the LOB data. NETMARK uses LOBs to store large documents, such as word processing, presentation, and spreadsheet files, for later retrieval of the document and its contents for rendering and viewing.

## 2.3 Structuring Documents with XML

XML is known as the next generation of HTML and a simplified subset of the Standard Generalized Markup Language (SGML)[2]. XML is both a semantic and structured markup language [7]. The basic principle behind XML is simple. A set of meaningful, user-defined tags surrounding the data elements describes a document's structure as well as its meaning without describing how the document should be

---

[2] The Standard Generalized Markup Language (SGML) is the official International Standard (ISO 8879) adopted by the world's largest producers of documents, but is very complex. Both XML and HTML are subsets of SGML.

formatted [12]. This enables XML to be a well-suitable meta-markup language for handling loosely structured or *semi-structured data*, because the standard does not place any restrictions on the tags or the nesting relationships. Loosely structured or semi-structured data here refers to data that may be irregular or incomplete, and its structure is rapidly changing and unpredictable [12]. Good examples of semi-structured data are web pages and constantly changing word processing documents being modified on a weekly or monthly basis.

XML encoding, although more verbose, provides the information in a more convenient and usable format from a data management perspective. In addition, the XML data can be transformed and rendered using simple *eXtensible Stylesheet Language* (XSL) specifications [8]. It can be validated against a set of grammar rules and logical definitions defined within the *Document Type Definitions* (DTDs) or *XML Schema* [14] much the same functionality as a traditional database schema.

## 2.4  Oracle ROWIDs

ROWID is an Oracle data type that stores either physical or logical addresses (row identifiers) to every row within the Oracle database. Physical ROWIDs store the addresses of ordinary table records (excluding indexed-organized tables), clustered tables, indexes, table partitions and sub-partitions, index partitions and sub-partitions, while logical ROWIDs store the row addresses within indexed-organized tables for building secondary indexes. Each Oracle table has an implicit pseudo-column called ROWID, which can be retrieved by a simple SELECT query on the particular table. Physical ROWIDs provide the fastest access to any record within an Oracle table with a single read block access, while logical ROWIDs provide fast access for highly volatile tables. A ROWID is guaranteed to not change unless the rows it references is deleted from the database.

The physical ROWIDs have two different formats, namely the legacy *restricted* and the new *extended* ROWID formats. The restricted ROWID format is for backward compatibility to legacy Oracle databases, such as Oracle 7 and/or earlier releases. The extended format is for Oracle 8 and later object-relational releases. This paper will only concentrate on extended ROWID format, since NETMARK was developed using Oracle 8i (release 8.1.6). For example, the following displays a subset of the extended ROWIDs from a NETMARK generated schema. It is a generalized 18-character format with 64 possibilities each:

### AAAAAA | BBB | CCCCC | DDD

The extended ROWIDs could be used to show how an Oracle table is organized and structured; but more importantly, extended ROWIDs make very efficient and stable unique keys for information retrievals, which will be addressed in the following subsequent section below (3.3).

## 3    The NETMARK Approach

Since XML is a document and not a data model per se, the ability to map XML-encoded information into a true data model is needed. The NETMARK approach allows this to occur by employing a customizable data type definition structure defined by the NETMARK SGML parser to model the hierarchical structure of XML data regardless of any particular XML document schema representation. The customizable NETMARK data types simulate the Document Object Model (DOM) Level 1 specifications [15] on parsing and decomposition of element nodes. The SGML parser is more efficient on decomposition than most commercial DOM parsers, since it is much more simpler as defined by node types contained within configuration files. The node data type format is based on a simplified variant of the *Object Exchange Model* (OEM) [13] researched at Stanford University, which is very similar to XML tags. The node data type contains an object identifier (node identifier) and the corresponding data type. Traditional object-relational mapping from XML to relational database schema models the data within the XML documents as a tree of objects that are specific to the data in the document [14]. In this model, element type with attributes, content, or complex element types are generally modeled as classes. Element types with parsed character data (PCDATA) and attributes are modeled as scalar types. This model is then mapped to the relational database using traditional object-relational mapping techniques or via SQL3 object views. Therefore, classes are mapped to tables, scalar types are mapped to columns, and object-valued properties are mapped to key pairs (both primary and foreign). This traditional mapping model is limited since the object tree structure is different for each set of XML documents. On the other hand, the NETMARK SGML parser models the document itself (similar to the DOM), and its object tree structure is the same for all XML documents. Thus, NETMARK is designed to be independent of any particular XML document schemas and is termed to be schema-less.

NETMARK is even flexible to handle more than just XML. It is also a SGML-enabled, open enterprise database framework. The term SGML-enabled means NETMARK supports both HTML and XML sets of tags through a set of customizable configuration files utilized by the NETMARK SGML parser for dynamically generating arbitrary database schema as shown in section (3.2) and in Figure 2. The NETMARK SGML parser decomposes either the HTML or XML document into its constituent nodes and inserted the nodes as individual records within Oracle tables. This dynamic schema representation and generation without requiring to write tedious and cumbersome SQL scripts or having to depend on experienced database administrators (DBAs) saves both time and valuable resources. Thus, this makes the storage model of NETMARK a general-purpose HTML or XML storage system.

### 3.1  Architecture

The NETMARK architecture comprises of the distributed, *information on demand* model, which refers to the "plug and play" capabilities to meet high-throughput and constantly changing information management environment. Each NETMARK modules are extensible and adaptable to different data sources. NETMARK consists of (1) a set of interfaces to support various communication protocols (such as HTTP,

FTP, RMI-IIOP and their secure variants), (2) an information bus to communicate between the client interfaces and the NETMARK core components, (3) the daemon process for automatic processing of inputs, (4) the NETMARK keyword search on both document context and content, (5) a set of extensible application programming interfaces (APIs), (6) and the Oracle backend ORDBMS.

The three core components of NETMARK consist of the high-throughput information bus, the asynchronous daemon process, and the set of customizable and extensible APIs built on Java enterprise technology (J2EE) and Oracle PL/SQL stored procedures and packages [11]. The NETMARK information bus allows virtually three major communication protocols heavily used today—namely HTTP web-based protocol and its secure variant, the File Transfer Protocol (FTP) and its secure variant, and the new Remote Method Invocation (RMI) over Internet Inter-Orb Protocol from the Object Management Group (OMG) Java-CORBA standards—to meet the information on demand model. The NETMARK daemon is a unidirectional asynchronous process to increase performance and scalability compared to traditional synchronous models, such as Remote Procedure Call (RPC) or Java RMI mechanisms. The NETMARK set of extensible Java and PL/SQL APIs are used to enhance database access and data manipulation, such as a robust Singleton database connection pool for managing check-ins and checkouts of pre-allocated connection objects.

## 3.2  Universal Process Flow

The NETMARK closed-loop universal process flow is shown in Figure 1. The information bus comprises of an Apache HTTP web server integrated with Tomcat Java-based JSP/Servlet container engine. It waits for incoming requests from the various clients, such as an uploaded word processing document from a web browser. The bus performs a series of conversion and transformation routines from one specific format to another using customized scripts. For instance, the NETMARK information bus will automatically convert a semi-structured Microsoft Word document into an inter-lingual HTML or XML format. A copy of the original word document, the converted HTML or XML file, and a series of dynamically generated configuration files will be handed to the NETMARK daemon process.

The daemon process checks for configuration files, the original processed files, and notifies the NETMARK SGML parser for decomposition of document nodes and data insertion. The daemon has an automatic logger that outputs both successful and event errors by date and time stamps with periodical archival and cleanup of log files. The daemon accepts three types of configuration files—(1) the request file, (2) the HTML/XML configuration file, and (3) the metadata configuration file. The request file is required by the daemon to proceed to process the correct information, whereas the HTML/XML configuration file and the metadata file are optional. If there is no HTML/XML configuration file provided to the daemon, a default configuration file located on the server is used. If there is no request file, the daemon issues an appropriate error message, logs the message to the log files for future reference, performs cleanup of configuration files, and waits for the next incoming request.

If the daemon can read the request file from the incoming request directory, it locks the file and extracts the name-value pairs from the request file for further processing. After extraction of the relevant attribute values, the request file is unlocked and a child process is spawned to process the incoming files. The child process locks the request file again to prevent the parent process from reprocessing the same request file and calling the SGML parser twice to decompose and insert the same document. The child process then calls the NETMARK SGML parser with the appropriate flag options to decompose the HTML or XML document into its constituent nodes and insert the nodes into the specified database schema. After the parsing and insertion completes, the source, result, and metadata files along with its corresponding configuration files will be cleanup and deleted by the daemon.

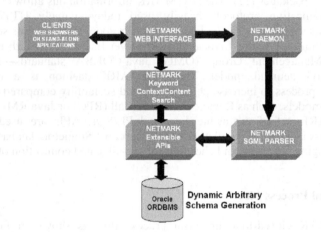

**Fig. 1.** NETMARK Universal Process Flow

The NETMARK SGML parser decomposes the HTML or XML documents into its constituent nodes and dynamically inserts them into two primary database tables—namely, XML and DOC—within a NETMARK generated schema. The descriptions of the XML and DOC tables along with their respective relationships are listed in Figure 2. The SGML parser is governed by five different node data types, which are specified in the HTML or XML configuration files passed by the daemon. The five NETMARK node data types and their corresponding node type identifier as designated in the NODETYPE column of the XML table are as follows: (1) ELEMENT, (2) TEXT, (3) CONTEXT, (4) INTENSE, and (5) SIMULATION.
The node type identifier is a single character data type inserted by the SGML parser to the XML table for each decomposed XML or HTML nodes. The node type identifiers will be used in the keyword-based context and content search.

The XML table contains the node tree structure as specified by the rules governed by the HTML or XML configuration files being used by the SGML parser to decompose the original HTML or XML documents into its constituent nodes. The DOC table holds the source document metadata, such as FILE_NAME, FILE_TYPE, FILE_DATE, and FILE_SIZE. Each NETMARK generated schema contains these two primary tables for efficient information retrievals as explained in the subsequent section (3.3). In order to store, manipulate, and later on retrieve unstructured or semi-structured documents, such as word processing files, presentations, flat text files, and spreadsheets, NETMARK utilizes the LOB data types as described in section (2.2) to

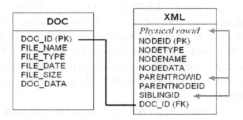

**Fig. 2.** NETMARK Generated Schema

store a copy of each processed document. In Figure 2 both the XML and the DOC table utilize CLOB and BLOB data types, respectively within the NODEDATA attribute for the XML table and the DOC_DATA column for the DOC table.

### 3.3 NETMARK Keyword Search

There are two ways that the Oracle database performs queries—either by a costly full table scan (with or without indexes) or by ROWIDs. Since a ROWID gives the exact physical location of the record to be retrieved by a single read block access, this is much more efficient as the database table size increases. As implied in the earlier section (2.4), ROWIDs can be utilized to very efficiently retrieve records by using them as unique keys. The NETMARK keyword search takes advantage of the unique extended ROWIDs for optimizing record retrievals based on both context and content. The keyword-based search here refers to finding all objects (elements or attributes) whose tag, name, or value contains the specified search string.

The NETMARK keyword search is built on top of Oracle 8i *interMedia Text* index [11][17] for retrieving the search key, and it is based on the Object Exchange Model [13] researched at Stanford University as mentioned earlier in section (3). Oracle interMedia is also known as Oracle Text in later releases of Oracle 9i and formerly known as the ConText [16] data cartridge. Oracle interMedia text index creates a series of index tables within the NETMARK generated schema to support the keyword text queries. The interMedia text index is created on the NODEDATA column of the XML table as shown in Figure 2. The NODEDATA column is a CLOB data type (character data). As described in Figure 2, the NETMARK XML table is consisted of eight attributes (columns) plus one physical ROWID pseudo-column. Each row in the XML table describes a complete XML or HTML node. The main attributes being utilizing by the search are DOC_ID, NODENAME, NODETYPE, NODEDATA, PARENTROWID, and SIBLINGID from the XML table. The DOC_ID column is used to refer back to the original document file. As the name implies, NODENAME contains the name of the node; whereas NODETYPE, as described earlier in section (3.2), identifies the type of node it is and informs NETMARK how to process this particular node. Reiterating the five specialized node data types: (1) ELEMENT, (2) TEXT, (3) CONTEXT, (4) INTENSE, and (5) SIMULATION. TEXT is a node whose data are free text or blocks of text describing a specific content. An ELEMENT, similar to a HTML or XML element, can contain multiple TEXT nodes and/or other nested ELEMENT nodes. Within NETMARK search, CONTEXT is a parent ELEMENT whose children elements contain data describing the contents of the following sibling nodes. INTENSE is another CONTEXT, which itself contains meaningful data. SIMULATION is a node data type reserved for special purposes and future implementation. NODEDATA is an Oracle CLOB data type used to store TEXT data. PARENTROWID and SIBLINGID are used as references for identifying the parent node and sibling node, respectively, and are of data type ROWID.

The NETMARK keyword-based context and content search is performed by first querying text index for the search key. Each node returned from the index search is then processed based on its designated unique ROWID. The processing of the node involves traversing up the tree structure via its parent or sibling node until the first context is found. The context is identified via its corresponding NODETYPE. The context refers to here as a heading for a subsection within a HTML or XML document, similar to the <H1> and <H2> header tags commonly found within HTML pages. Thus, the context and content search returns a subsection of the document where the keyword being searched for occurs. Once a particular CONTEXT is found, traversing back down the tree structure via the sibling node retrieves the corresponding content text. The search result is then rendered and displayed appropriately.

# 4   Conclusion

NETMARK provides an extensible, schema-less, information on demand framework for managing, storing, and retrieving unstructured and/or semi-structured data. NETMARK was initially designed and developed as a rapid, proof-of-concept prototype using a proven and mature Oracle backend object-relational database to solve the vast amounts of heterogeneous documents existing within NASA enterprises. NETMARK is currently a scalable, high-throughput open database framework for transforming unstructured or semi-structured documents into well-structured and standardized XML and/or HTML formats.

**Acknowledgement.** The authors of this paper would like to acknowledge NASA Information Technology-Based program and NASA Computing, Information, and Communication Technologies Program.

# References

1.  Codd, E. F.: A Relational Model of Data for Large Shared Data Banks, Communications of the ACM, 13(6), (1970) 377–387
2.  Hull, R. and King, R.: "Semantic Database Modeling: Survey, Applications, and Research Issues", ACM Computing Surveys, 19(3), (1987) 201–260
3.  Cardenas, A. F., and McLeod, D. (eds), Research Foundations in Object-Oriented and Semantic Database Systems, New York: Prentice-Hall, (1990) 32–35

4.  Chen, J. and Huang, Q.: Eliminating the Impedance Mismatch Between Relational Systems and Object-Oriented Programming Languages, Australia: Monash University (1995)
5.  Devarakonda, R. S.: Object-Relational Database Systems – The Road Ahead, ACM Crossroads Student Magazine, (February 2001)
6.  Stonebraker M.: Object-Relational DBMS: The Next Wave, Informix Software (now part of the IBM Corp. family), Menlo Park, CA
7.  Harold, E. R.: XML: Extensible Markup Language, New York: IDG Books Worldwide, (1998) 23–55
8.  Extensible Markup Language (XML) World Wide Web Consortium (W3C) Recommendation, (October 2000)
9.  Eisenberg, A., and Melton, J.:  SQL:1999, formerly known as SQL3, (1999)
10. ISO/IEC 9075:1999, "Information Technology – Database Language – SQL – Part 1: Framework (SQL/Framework)", (1999)
11. Loney, K. and Koch, G.: Oracle 8i: The Complete Reference, 10th edition, Berkeley, CA: Oracle Press Osborne/McGraw-Hill, (2000) 69–85; 574–580; 616–644; 646–663
12. Widom, J.: Data Management for XML Research Directions, Stanford University, (June 1999) http://www-db.stanford.edu/lore/pubs/index.html
13. Lore XML DBMS project, Stanford University (1998) http://www-db.stanford.edu/lore/research/
14. Bourret, R.: Mapping DTD to Databases, New York: O'Reilly & Associates, (2000)
15. Wood, L. et al.: "Document Object Model (DOM) Level 1 Specification", W3C Recommendation, (October 1998)
16. Oracle8 ConText Cartridge Application Developer's Guide (Release 2.4), Princeton University Oracle Reference (1998)
17  Maluf, D. A. and Tran, P. B.: "Articulation Management for Intelligent Integration of Information", IEEE Transactions on Systems, Man, and Cybernetics Part C: Applications and Reviews, 31(4) (2001) 485–496

# Program Generation for Application Domain Users by Selecting Model Candidates

Takumi Aida[1] and Setsuo Ohsuga[2]

[1] Department of Computer Science, Waseda University,
3-4-1 Okubo, Shinjuku, Tokyo 169-8555, Japan
takumi@aoni.waseda.jp
http://www.aoni.waseda.jp/takumi/
[2] Emeritus Professor, the University of Tokyo, JAPAN
ohsuga@fd.catv.ne.jp

**Abstract.** This study has proposed a method for software development in application domains such as control engineering. A new method is requested: (1) to reduce or remove communication between application domain and software engineering domain, (2) to provide a simple modeling scheme, and (3) to decrease *knowledge-capturing* cost. The process of the method is: capturing the knowledge in the target domain, defining the target program denotatively, generating model candidates automatically, selecting the model satisfied requirements, transforming the model into source code in a target language automatically, and evaluating the source code. This cooperation between computers and domain experts achieves both automatic model construction and identifying the solution.

## 1 Introduction

In software development, requirements engineering is considered to be the most important task. As computer application area expands, software requirements vary in expressions or criteria. This variety causes communication gaps between application engineers and software engineers. Furthermore, even among engineers with the same background, difference of viewpoints can cause inconsistency [1, 2]. Some investigation reveals us that two thirds of software failures occur at the upstream of programming; the half of them came from their incorrectness of making requirements and the rest came from their misunderstanding by programmers.

There have been a number of studies on requirements engineering: eliciting requirements, requirements modeling and analysis, requirements validating[3], rapid prototyping, executable specification, and transformational implementation[4]. However, little has discussed both capturing-cost reduction and automatic model generation. This paper therefore focuses on: (1) human-computer collaboration in building program models, (2) automatic generation of program model candidates. Transformation of a program model into a source code is automated as well.

N. Zhong et al. (Eds.): ISMIS 2003, LNAI 2871, pp. 242–251, 2003.

Section 2 describes characteristics and problems of software development in application domains, and then Section 3 shows the proposed method. Section 4 introduces an experiments in car engine control system development. Finally Section 5 summarizes the study.

## 2  Software Development in Application Domains

In principle requirements in application domain should be provided by application engineers. In most cases, however, they can not make their requirements model themselves because of two major reasons: to build requirements models needs to consider transformation of the models into program code, and typical modeling schemes in application domains are unsuitable for program modeling.

A requirements model must involve a program model in the sense that the latter is deduced from the former. However, it is not expected in many cases that application engineers have enough programming knowledge. They consequently require software engineers to help building the models. The need for this cooperation can cause the *communication-gap* errors. In order to reduce or remove communication gap problem, knowledge-based methods are being studied, but these are not yet applied in a practical use because of *knowledge capturing problem*. Murphy et al. propose *reflection model* that summarizes source level models from viewpoint of design level model[5], and Kitamura et al. propose a method for understanding correspondence between behavioral model and functional model with ontology[6]; these methods can assist redesign.

Almost all application domains have their own modeling scheme. But not every modeling scheme is suited for representing program models. Technical fields such as control engineering often use mathematical modeling. Even mathematical modeling scheme is not necessarily suited for the purpose. For example, in control engineering, models are represented as differential and/or integral equations, and represented in the form of block diagram. In order to deal with this model in computer, first the variables are quantized and the model is transformed into a discrete-time system, i.e. a sampling system. The time interval must be small enough for keeping the faithful correspondence between original (continuous time) system and its sampled-time system. On the other hand, in order to meet the real-time condition every necessary operation must be achieved in this small sample time period. It depends on CPU power and also programs that are generated from this model. It needs high-level programming technique. It means that the model must be made taking the program as the product from it into account. In many cases it is difficult to estimate program behavior directly from the model and this is a big hazard involved in this approach. Usually mathematical model is used in control engineering only for the performance evaluation of the system but completely different model is used for program development. There is no formal method to make correspondence between them and suitableness of the program model must be assured depending on the programmer's skill and experience. It causes often to result in incorrect program as mentioned communication gap before. A new method is necessary.

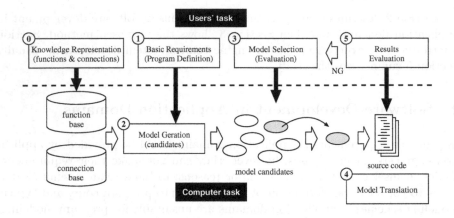

**Fig. 1.** The process of proposed method

## 3  The Method

A new method should: (1) reduce or remove communication gap problem between different fields, (2) provide a simple modeling scheme, and (3) decrease *knowledge-capturing* cost. In order to satisfy these requirements, an approach is proposed. It is based on program modeling as functional model generation.

### 3.1  Overview

The process of the proposed method is: (0) to capture the knowledge in the target domain, (1) to define the target program denotatively, (2) to generate model candidates, (3) to select the most appropriate model, (4) to transform the model into source code in a target language, and (5) to evaluate the source code (Fig.1.)

As illustrated in Fig.1, (0),(1),(3), and (5) are assigned to application domain experts, (2), and (4) to computers.

### 3.2  Prepared Knowledge

Explicit knowledge needed in the method is only functional information. Fig.2 shows sample data formats of *functions* and *connection*.

**Functions.** A *function* is a unit of an operation or an action in an application domain. Functions are defined and stored in the function base of the domain in advance. They can be used at every design time. Some functions have their program code as a component program and some are macro functions composed of the other functions.

Implementations of functions are stored in the implementation base of the domain. Implementations are needed to generate source code. How to implement

*Function Data*

```
<function id="Base Ignition Timing">
  <in>
    <port id="Engine Rev."
      type="rpm"
      domain="[0,10000]"
      domaintype="range" />
    <port id="Intake Press."
      type="mmHg"
      domain="[0,1000]"
      domaintype="range" />
    <port id="Throttle Pos."
      type="percent"
      domain="[0,100]"
      domaintype="range" />
  </in>
  <out>
    <port id="Igt. Time"
      type="CA"
      domain="[-10,100]"
      domaintype="range" />
  </out>
  <description></description>
</function>
```

*Connection Data*

```
<connection id="conn04">
  <sendFunction>
    <functionInfo
      id="Base Ignition Timing"
      portId="Igt. Time">
  </sendFunction>
  <recvFunction>
    <functionInfo
      id="Ignition Compensation"
      portId="Igt. Time">
  </recvFunction>
</connection>
```

**Fig. 2.** Sample data formats of *function* and *connection*

functions is an important issue, but there is no place to go into detail in this paper.

**Connections.** A *connection* is information to direct the way of using *functions* in an application domain. It shows that an output of a function, called sender, can be used as an input of another function, called receiver. Connections are defined by application domain experts, and stored in the connection base.

A connection which a range of the output of the sender is larger than domain of the input of the receiver, is called *OR connection*. It is called so because in order for an output being accepted the sender requires more-that-one receivers connected in disjunctive way. OR connections can be a conditional branch. Correspondingly the other is called *AND connection*.

### 3.3   Definition of Programs

In order to automatically generate an internal structure of the target program, application engineers provide the program definition. Generally, a program is a function that takes some values, and calculates them, and then gives the results. A initial definition of programs therefore is given as a combination of inputs and outputs.

### 3.4   Model Candidates Generation

Program model candidates are automatically generated with functions and connections data. This phase consists of two tasks; one makes parts for program structures, another builds up them into a program structure.

**Forward search for data flows.** This task means shrinking sets of functions and connections, and building parts for program structures.

The prepared sets of function and connection may be partially required to compose a program structure. As programs must use only given inputs in order to produce outputs, tracking data flows forwards, from the inputs to the outputs, can leave footprints of use on a necessary and sufficient set of functions. Furthermore, combinations of data flows for branching and recombining as program structures must be generated from the necessary and sufficient set. So data flows should be arranged as consistent short paths for this purpose. The algorithm of this task is shown below.

1. Focus on one of the initial input functions defined as the initial requirements.
2. Search such connections as related to the outputs of the currently handled function from the connection base.
3. Try to obtain functions connected by the connection(s) from the function base.
   a) If no function is found, the current path will be terminated.
   b) If only one function is found, and
      i. if the function has *not* been introduced before in this search process, the function will be directly connected to the current function. This forms a *data flow path*. The function will be registered in the *introduced function list*.
      ii. if the function has been appeared before i.e. it's already been in the introduced function list, the current path will be terminated, and a *directed link* from the current function to the path including the function is made[1].
   c) Otherwise — if more than one functions are found, the current path will be terminated, and each function will be dealt with separately:
      i. Newly introduced function: a new path beginning with the function found is created. Then a *directed link* from the current function to the new path is established. The function will be registered in the introduced function list.
      ii. A function appeared before: a directed link from the current function to the path including the function is made[1].
4. if the new function appeared either in 2-(b)-i or 2-(c)-i above is the output of the target program, then the path to which the function belongs is terminated.
5. When all the paths has been terminated, this task ends[2]. If not, each function at the end of paths that have not been terminated is processed by 1 above.

A *path* can be regarded as one closed cluster of functions. In addition a program structure is represented as *graph* composed of paths. Therefore a path is called a *node* hereafter.

---

[1] "Including" means that there is the function in the path. This type of link may wedge into the path and break its consistency. In this case the path must be divided there into two parts so that both of them can keep their consistencies.

[2] This repetitive process will come to an end because the number of functions and connections is finite.

**Backward search for program structures.** The next task is to build the candidates of program model. These model candidates must be free from inconsistency and ambiguity.

Such program models are generated by tracking the selected functions backwards from outputs to inputs. In order for program models to promise to produce outputs, a function that calculates the outputs must surely get its inputs. Recurrently, in order for the function to obtain its inputs, a function that produce a value of the inputs must surely get inputs for itself. This can determine the necessary functions of program models.

The algorithm of the task, which is shown below, is based on *constraint solver*. In this case constraints are represented as *"can the input port get any value?"*

1. Focus on one of the output functions defined as the initial requirements.
2. Create *constraints* for the input ports of the currently handled *node*.
3. Try to propagate the constraints to node(s) linked from the input ports through *directed link* backwards.
    a) If the current node has only one input port, directly transfer the constraint to the next node.
    b) Otherwise — if the current node furnishes more than one input ports, the constraint is decomposed into separate constraints for those input ports. If and only if all of these constraints are satisfied, the constraint for the node is satisfied.
4. If the constraint was propagated through an *OR-connection* link, the connection will be *also* propagated *forwards* to the other OR-connection links.
    a) If the constraint reaches the (input) port of the node which supplied the constraint, the constraint will be satisfied. whichever one of OR-connection links is chosen can provide the result for the node, which is the origin of the constraint.
    b) If the node which received the constraint from its input port has other input ports, create a new constraint for the input ports, then propagate them.
5. If the checking process reaches the node including one of the input functions defined as the initial requirements, it ends in success.
6. If the constraint is not satisfied, abandon the checking path.
7. If the checking has finished, gather the nodes whose constraints have been satisfied, then promote this node set to a program model candidate.
8. When all combinations of propagation have been checked, this task ends.

## 3.5    Model Selection

A program model is chosen from the candidates by users. Syntactically, each candidate is correct, and can be transformed into source code in a target programming language. The users therefore should only pay attention to its semantic correctness and requirements fulfillment.

**Table 1.** Transformation rules for coding (with example *function* name)

| Node type | | Code |
|---|---|---|
| Normal | | $e=E(x);$ |
| Conditional Branch | | $b = B(\ x\ );$<br>**if(** $cond_1(b)$ **){}**<br>**else if(** $cond_2(b)$ **){}**<br>...<br>**else if(** $cond_n(b)$ **){}** |
| Loop Begin | | **while(** true **){**<br>    $a=A(x)$<br>**}**<br>ESCAPE_LOOP_A:<br>**switch(** $flag$ **){**<br>    **default:**<br>        **break;**<br>**}** |
| Loop Escape | | – in a conditional branch<br>$flag$=toH; $hi = b$;<br>**goto** ESCAPE_LOOP_A;<br><br>– in **switch** after the goto label<br>**case** toH;<br>    $h=H(hi);$ |
| Loop End | | /* *storing variable i1*<br>    *for the start node* */<br>$i1=F(x);$<br>**continue;** |

The user's criteria for evaluating a program model are often not made explicit. It is inexpressive or informal, which are known as non-functional requirements, or know-how. Useful information has been gained from experience.

The proposed method doesn't force users to represent such knowledge explicitly, but let them evaluate candidates as a selection of the best one in the set of candidates using the implicit knowledge in their mind. Well-thought-out actions of experts correspond to the expertise. The proposed method regards the selection as the task to be achieved depending on expertise.

Effective evaluation methods such as simulation should be provided for users, but given the space available it can't be discussed in this paper.

## 3.6   Transformation of Program Model to Source Code

In the task of model generation, each node in the program model is assigned the role as the element of program structure such as branch or loop. The nodes which are arranged in the way of extended topological sort are transformed into source code with rules. Table 1 illustrates the transformation rules, and Figure 3 demonstrates the transformation.

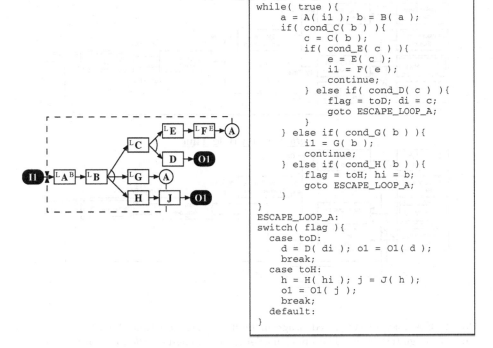

```
while( true ){
    a = A( i1 ); b = B( a );
    if( cond_C( b ) ){
        c = C( b );
        if( cond_E( c ) ){
            e = E( c );
            i1 = F( e );
            continue;
        } else if( cond_D( c ) ){
            flag = toD; di = c;
            goto ESCAPE_LOOP_A;
        }
    } else if( cond_G( b ) ){
        i1 = G( b );
        continue;
    } else if( cond_H( b ) ){
        flag = toH; hi = b;
        goto ESCAPE_LOOP_A;
    }
}
ESCAPE_LOOP_A:
switch( flag ){
    case toD:
        d = D( di ); o1 = O1( d );
        break;
    case toH:
        h = H( hi ); j = J( h );
        o1 = O1( j );
        break;
    default:
}
```

**Fig. 3.** A sample program structure with loops

## 4   Experiment

The experiment illustrated here is a case of development of car engine control systems, especially ignition timing controller.

Ignition timing controller decides timing of the firing of the spark plug. The spark plug must be fired at a proper point in the combustion cycle in order to obtain good performance; car engines must meets strict requirements such as emission and fuel economy. The engine controllers generally use a multi-mode control scheme. For example, one mode can be suited for idling, and another for warming-up. The larger number of sensors and modes makes control systems more complex [7].

At first, functions and connections for engine controls were prepared, then four inputs and one output were defined as follows: coolant temperature sensor, engine revolution sensor, intake pressure sensor, throttle position sensor, and actuators of igniters included in the engine model. the engine model here is not for controlling function, but a model of a controlled object is needed in embedded software development. Next, model candidates were automatically generated. In the candidates, two models were initially selected as proper ignition controllers (Fig. 4); one is for an engine with an internal igniter driver, another is for one without the driver. At this design, the target engine had an internal igniter

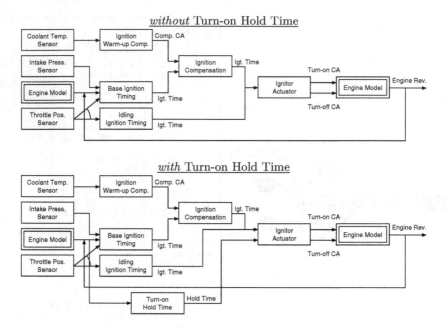

**Fig. 4.** Examples of generated program models. "Turn-on Hold Time" function is a part of an igniter driver. The upper model is for an engine *with* an igniter driver, the lower one for an engine *without* an igniter driver.

*without* Turn-on Hold Time

```
1: while( true ){
2:    a = coolant_temp_sensor();
3:    b = intake_press_sensor();
4:    d = throttle_pos_sensor();
5:    if( cond_BIT( d ) ){
6:       e = igt_warmup_comp( a );
7:       f = base_igt_timing( b, c, d );
8:       g = igt_comp( e, f );
9:    } else if( cond_IIT( d ) ){
10:      g = idling_igt_timing( d );
11:   }
12:   (h1, h2) = igt_actuator( g );
13:   c = engine_model( h1, h2 );
14:   continue;
15: }
16: ESCAPE_LOOP_ENGIN_MODEL:
17: switch( flag ){
18:   default:
19:      break;
20: }
```

*with* Turn-on Hold Time

```
1: while( true ){
2:    a = coolant_temp_sensor();
3:    b = intake_press_sensor();
4:    d = throttle_pos_sensor();
5:    e = turnon_hold_time( c );
6:    if( cond_BIT( d ) ){
7:       f = igt_warmup_comp( a );
8:       g = base_igt_timing( b, c, d );
9:       h = igt_comp( f, g );
10:   } else if( cond_IIT( d ) ){
11:      h = idling_igt_timing( d );
12:   }
13:   (k1, k2) = igt_actuator( h, e );
14:   c = engine_model( k1, k2 );
15:   continue;
16: }
17: ESCAPE_LOOP_ENGIN_MODEL:
18: switch( flag ){
19:   default:
20:      break;
21: }
```

**Fig. 5.** Examples of source code (partial) translated from Fig. 4.

driver, so the former model was finally chosen. Figure 5 partially shows a pair of sample source code from both two models.

# 5 Summary

This study has proposed a method for software development in application domains. It seems to be still difficult to sufficiently collect software requirements or knowledge from the experts. The method requires only two types of very formal but simple knowledge; *functions and their connections*. Making use of these information can "haphazardly" construct program models, but can not identify the best one. We regard selection by experts as the most important task because well-thought-out actions of experts corresponds to expertise. Both of constructing automatically and selecting wisely can be achieved in the method.

**Acknowledgment.** This study was performed through Special Coordination Funds for Promoting Science and Technology from the Ministry of Education, Culture, Sports, Science and Technology of the Japanese Government.

# References

1. Finkelstein, A.C.W., Gabbay, D., Hunter, A., Kramer, J., Nuseibeh, B.: Inconsistency handling in multiperspective specifications. IEEE Transactions on Software Engineering **20** (1994) 569–578
2. Sommerville, I., Sawyer, P., Viller, S.: Managing process inconsistency using viewpoints. IEEE Transactions on Software Engineering **25** (1999) 784–799
3. Nuseibeh, B., Easterbrook, S.: Requirements engineering: A roadmap. In Finkelstein, A., ed.: The Future of Software Engineering, ACM (2000) 37–46
4. Tsai, J.J.P., Liu, A., Juan, E., Sahay, A.: Knowledge-based software architectures: Acquisition, specification, and verification. IEEE Transactions on Knowledge and Data Engineering **11** (1999) 187–201
5. Murphy, G.C., Notkin, D., Sullivan, K.J.: Software reflexion models: Bridging the gap between design and implementation. IEEE Transactions on Software Engineering **27** (2001) 364–380
6. Kitamura, Y., Sano, T., Namba, K., Mizoguchi, R.: A functional concept ontology and its application to automatic identification of functional structures. Advanced Engineering Informatics **16** (2002) 145–163
7. Wolf, W.: Computers as Components — Principles of Embedded Computing System Design. Morgan Kaufmann Publishers (2001)

# Traffic Sign Recognition in Disturbing Environments

Hsiu-Ming Yang, Chao-Lin Liu, Kun-Hao Liu, and Shang-Ming Huang

Department of Computer Science, National Chengchi University
Taipei 11605, Taiwan
chaolin@cs.nccu.edu.tw

**Abstract.** Traffic sign recognition is a difficult task if we aim at detecting and recognizing signs in images captured from unfavorable environments. Complex background, weather, shadow, and other lighting-related problems may make it difficult to detect and recognize signs in the rural as well as the urban areas. We employ discrete cosine transform and singular value decomposition for extracting features that defy external disturbances, and compare different designs of detection and classification systems for the task. Experimental results show that our pilot systems offer satisfactory performance when tested with very challenging data.

## 1 Introduction

Computer vision has been applied to a wide variety of applications for intelligent transportations systems. For instance, researchers have developed vision-based techniques for traffic monitoring, traffic-related parameter estimation, driver monitoring, and intelligent vehicles, etc. [1]. Traffic sign recognition (TSR) is an important basic function of intelligent vehicles [7], and TSR problems have attracted attention of many research groups since more than ten years ago [16]. In this paper, we report experiences in detection and recognition of traffic signs when images of the traffic signs are severely disturbed by external factors.

Detection and recognition are two major steps for determining types of traffic signs [6]. Detection refers to the task of locating the traffic signs in given images. It is common to call the region in a given image that potentially contains the image of a traffic sign the region of interests (ROI). Taking advantages of the special characteristics of traffic signs, TSR systems typically rely on the color and geometric information in the images to detect the ROIs. Hence, color segmentation is common to most TSR systems, so are edge detection [9,14] and corner detection techniques [4].

After identifying the ROIs, we extract features of the ROIs, and classify the ROIs using the extracted feature values. Researchers have explored several techniques for classifying the ideographs, including artificial neural networks (ANNs) [4], template matching [14], chain code [15], and matching pursuit methods [9].

Detection and recognition of traffic signs become very challenging in a noisy environment [14]. Traffic signs may be physically rotated or damaged for different reasons. View angles from the car-mounted cameras to the traffic signs may lead to artificially rotated and distorted images. External objects, such as tree leaves, may occlude the traffic signs, and background conditions may make it difficult to detect traffic signs. Bad weather conditions may have a detrimental effect on the quality of the images.

N. Zhong et al. (Eds.): ISMIS 2003, LNAI 2871, pp. 252–261, 2003.
© Springer-Verlag Berlin Heidelberg 2003

To confront these challenges, researchers have designed techniques for raising the quality of the recognition results. Sandoval et al. develop methods for generating convolution masks that are then used for position-dependent edge detection of circular signs [17]. Kehtarnavaz and Ahmad apply Fourier and log-polar-exponential grid transformations for extracting invariant feature values of the traffic signs [11]. Piccioli et al. focus more on detection of traffic signs in cluttered background. Assuming constant orientation of images of the detected signs, they apply template-matching methods to pick candidate signs, and claim 98% of correct classification [14].

We consider that occluded and poor-quality images of traffic signs are not uncommon in reality. Images in Fig. 1 and the Appendix illustrate some of these challenging scenarios. As a result, we believe that templates alone will not always work perfectly for traffic sign recognition. Even if images of the traffic signs are partially occluded by objects or interfered by shadow, human may guess

**Fig. 1.** Selected "hard" traffic signs. The left sign did not face the camera directly, and had a red background. The middle picture was taken in the dusk. The signs in the rightmost image were in the shadow.

what the signs are using the limited available information, so we charge ourselves with the task of detection and recognition of 45 triangular signs in challenging scenes. Besides some selected raw image data, we employ discrete cosine transform [5] and singular value decomposition methods [2] to acquire some invariant features of the traffic signs as features, and apply these features in different ways. Similar to many other researchers, we use the extracted feature values as input to ANNs for classifying the captured images. We also test the integration of ANNs and Naïve Bayes models, and examine the applicability of $k$ nearest neighbor methods. As we will explain, different setups of our systems recognize around 70% of the test signs.

Section 2 provides details of our approaches to traffic sign detection and recognition. Section 3 presents empirical results of our recognition systems. It turned out that our systems detected and recognized signs in the leftmost and the rightmost images in Fig. 1. We wrap up this paper with discussions in Section 4.

## 2  Traffic Sign Detection and Recognition

### 2.1  ROI Detection

Transportation engineers design traffic signs such that people can recognize them easily by using distinct colors and shapes for the signs. Similar to many other countries, Taiwan uses triangles and circles for signs that carry warning and forbidding messages, respectively. These signs have thick and red borders for visibility from apart. Hence, we may use color and shape information for detecting traffic signs.

### Color Segmentation

Identifying what pixels of the images are red is a special instance of the *color segmentation* problems. This task is not easy because images captured by cameras are affected by a variety of factors, and the "red" pixels as perceived by human may not be encoded by the same pixel values all the time.

Assuming no directly blocking objects, lighting conditions affect the quality of the color information the most. Weather conditions certainly are the most influential factor. Nearby buildings or objects, such as trees, may also affect quality of the color information because of their shadows. It is easy to obtain very dark images, e.g., the middle image in Fig. 1, when we are driving in the direction of the sun.

As a consequence, "red" pixels can be embodied in a range of values. Hence, we attempt to define the range for the red color. We convert the original image to a new image using a pre-selected formula. Let $R_i$, $G_i$, and $B_i$ be the red, green, and blue component of a given pixel in the original image. We encode the pixels of the new image by $R_o$, $G_o$, and $B_o$. Based on results of a few experiments, we found that the following conversion most effective: $R_o = \max(0, (R_i - G_i) + (R_i - B_i))$, $G_o = 0$, and $B_o = 0$. After the color segmentation step, only pixels whose original red components dominate the other two components can have a nonzero red component in the new image most of the time.

**Region of Interests**

We then group the red pixels into separate objects, apply the *Laplacian of Gaussian* (LoG) edge detector [8] to this new image, and use the 8-connected neighborhood principle for determining what pixels constitute a connected object. We consider any red pixels that are among the 8 immediate neighbors of another red pixel *connected*.

After grouping the red pixels, we screen the object based on four features to determine what objects may contain traffic signs. These features are areas, height to width ratios, positions, and detected corners of the objects.

According to the government's decrees for traffic sign designs, all traffic signs must have standard sizes. Using our camera, which is set at a selected resolution, to take pictures of warning signs from 100 meter apart, the captured image will occupy 5x4 pixels. Due to this observation, we ignore objects that contain less than 40 red pixels. We choose to use this threshold because it provided a good balance between recall and precision, defined in (3) in Section 3.2, when we applied the *Detection* procedure to the training data. Two other reasons support our ignoring these small objects. Even if the discarded objects were traffic signs, it would be very difficult to recognize them correctly. Moreover, if they are really traffic signs that are important to our journey, they would get closer and become bigger, and will be detected shortly.

The decrees also allow us to use shapes of the bounding boxes of the objects to filter the objects. Traffic signs have specific shapes, so heights and widths of their bounding boxes must also have special ratios. The ratios may be distorted due to such reasons as damaged signs and viewing angles. Nevertheless, we can still use an interval of ratios for determining whether objects contain traffic signs.

Positions of the objects in the captured images play a similar role as the decrees. Except driving on rolling hills, we normally see traffic signs above a certain horizon. Due to this physical constraint and the fact that there are no rolling hills in Taiwan, we assume that images of traffic signs must appear in a certain area in the captured image, and use this constraint for filtering objects in images.

Since we focus on triangular signs in our experiments, we can rely on features specific to triangles for determining

**Fig. 2.** Using corners for identifying triangular borders

whether the objects are likely to contain triangular signs. We divide the bounding boxes of the objects into nine equal regions, and check whether we can detect corners in selected regions. The leftmost image in Figure 2 illustrates one of these patterns by the blue checks. More patterns are specified in the following *Detection* procedure. If none of the patterns is satisfied, chances are very low that the object could contain a triangular sign. Using this principle, we were able to detect the rightmost four signs in Fig. 2.

**Procedure** *Detection* (Input: an image of 640x480 pixels; Output: an ROI object list)
**Steps**:
1    Color segmentation
2    Detect edges with the LoG edge detector.
3    Remove objects with less than 40 red pixels.
4    Mark the bounding boxes of the objects.
5    Remove objects whose highest red pixel locates below row 310 of the original images, setting the origin (0,0) of the coordinate system to the upper-left corner.
6    Remove objects with height/width ratios not in the range [0.7, 1.3].
7    Check existence of the corners of each object.
　　7.1　Find the red pixel with the smallest row number. When there are many such pixels, choose the pixel with the smallest column number.
　　7.2　Find the red pixels with the smallest and the largest column numbers. If there are multiple choices, choose those with the largest row numbers.
　　7.3　Mark locations of these three pixels in the imaginary nine equal regions, setting their corresponding containing regions by 1.
　　7.4　Remove the object if these pixels do not form any of the patterns listed aside.
8    For each surviving bounding box, extract the corresponding rectangular area from the original image and save it into the ROI list.

| | | | | |
|---|---|---|---|---|
| 010 | 010 | 010 | 100 | 001 |
| 100 | 001 | 000 | 000 | 000 |
| 001 | 100 | 101 | 101 | 101 |

Fig. 3 illustrates how we detect a triangular sign with the *Detection* procedure. Notice that the sing in (f) is not exactly upright. The tree trunks and red sign behind the sign made our algorithm unable to extract the complete red border. All objects detected by *Detection* are very likely to contain a triangular traffic sign. They will be used as input to the recognition component after the preprocessing step.

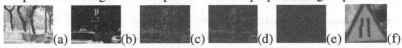

(a)　　　　(b)　　　　(c)　　　　(d)　　　　(e)　　　　(f)

**Fig. 3.** An illustration of detection steps: (a) the original image; (b) result of color segmentation; (c) result of edge detection; (d) result of removing small objects; (e) results of filtering objects by step 7; (f) the enlarged image of the detected sign

## 2.2 Preprocessing

**Procedure** *Preprocessing* (Input: an ROI object list; Output: an object list)
**Steps**:
For each object in the ROI list, do the following:

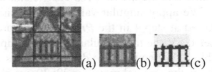

(a)　　　(b)　　　(c)

**Fig. 4.** An illustration of preprocessing steps

1     Normalize the object to the standard size 80x70.
2     Extract the rectangle of 32x30 pixels from (25,30).
3     Remove remaining red pixels.
4     Convert the object to a gray-level image.

As the first step of the preprocessing, we normalize all objects to the 80x70 standard size. After a simple analysis of the 45 standard triangular signs, we found that the ideographs appear in a specific region in the normalized images. As shown in Fig. 4(a), we can extract the ideographs from a particular rectangular area in the image. We extract the ideograph from a pre-selected area of 32x30 pixels from the normalized image. The coordinates of the upper left corner of the extracted rectangle is (25, 30). Notice that, although we have attempted to choose the rectangular area such that it may accommodate distorted and rotated signs, the extracted image may not include all the original ideographs all the time. Fig. 4(b) shows that the bottom of the ideograph was truncated. Similarly, the extracted area may contain noisy information.

After extracting the rectangular area that might contain the ideograph, we remove red pixels in the extract. We use a more stringent standard for defining "red." Let $R$, $G$, and $B$ be the red, green, and blue component of a pixel. A pixel is red if $R>20$, $(R-B)>20$, and $(R-G)>20$.

After removing the red pixels, we convert the result into a gray-level image. We adjust pixel values based on the average luminance to increase contrast of the image. We compute the YIQ values [18] of each pixel from its RGB values, set their gray levels to their luminance values, and compute the average gray levels of all pixels. Let the average be $\alpha$. We invert the colors of the pixels by deducting the amount of $(\alpha-100)$ from the gray levels of all pixels.

Then, pixels whose remaining gray levels are smaller than 70 are set to 0, and others are set to 255. However, if using 70 as the threshold gives us less than 10 pixels with value 255 or 10 pixels with value 0, we apply another slightly more complex method. We calculate the average gray level of the pixel values, and use this average, $\lambda$, as the cutting point for assigning pixel values in the gray-level image. Pixels whose gray levels are less than $\lambda$ are set to 0, and others are set to 255. Fig. 4(c) shows such a gray-level image.

## 2.3   Traffic Sign Recognition

After the preprocessing procedure, each object becomes a rectangle of 32x30 pixels. We can use these raw data as features for recognition. In addition, we employ the discrete cosine transform (DCT) and the singular value decomposition (SVD) procedures for extracting the invariant features of the ideographs.

DCT is one of the popular methods for decomposing a signal to a sequence of components and for coding images [5]. We concatenate rows of a given object, generated at step 5 in *Preprocessing*, into a chain, and apply the one-dimension DCT over the chain, and use the first 105 coefficients as the feature values.

We apply singular value decomposition to the matrices of the objects that are obtained at step 4 in the *Preprocessing* procedure for extracting features of the objects. Let $U\Sigma V^T$ be the singular value decomposition [2] of the matrix that encodes a given object. We employ the diagonal values in $\Sigma$ as the feature values of the given object. Since the original matrix is 32x30, we obtain 30 feature values from $\Sigma$.

We investigate the effectiveness of artificial neural networks, $k$-nearest-neighbor ($k$NN) models, and naïve Bayes models for the recognition task. All these three alternatives are commonly used for pattern recognition tasks [3]. We use the collected features as input to different combinations of these techniques, test the integrated systems with test data, and report their performance in the next section.

# 3 Empirical Results

## 3.1 Data Source

We trained our clssifiers with feature values of perfect signs, real-world signs, and artificially created signs. We created more than 10000 imperfect signs

**Fig. 5.** Sample training patterns

using perfect images of the 45 triangular signs. We gradually rotated the signs both clockwise and counterclockwise by the amount of one degree. The first row of Fig. 5 shows ten rotated signs. We added Gaussian noise of varying means and variances to the perfect signs. We created signs in the middle row by adding Gaussian noise of increasing means, and the leftmost five signs in the last row by adding Gaussian noise of increasing variances. We also created training patterns by shifting the perfect signs to their north, east, south, and west. The rightmost five signs in the bottom illustrate such operations.

We used the *Preprocessing* procedure to process our training data. As described in Section 2.3, for each pattern, we obtained the values of the 32x30 pixels, the 105 DCT coefficients, and the SVD vector of 30 components. (For easy reference, we refer to the vectors formed by the diagonal of the $\Sigma$ matrix by *SVD vectors* henceforth.)

## 3.2 Experiments and Results

We tested our systems with 210 signs in pictures that were not used in the training phase, and all of these pictures are shown in the Appendix. The pictures were taken at the 640x480 resolution with Nikon Coolpix 775 digital camera. We report results of five sets of experiments. For each experiment, we measured the performance by standard definitions of *precision* ($P$), *recall* ($R$), and $F$ [12]. Precision is the portion of total number of correctly classified signs in the total number of classified objects. Recall is the portion of total number of correctly classified signs in the total number of real signs in the testing images. $F$ measure is a function of $P$ and $R$, and $F(\beta) = ((\beta^2 + 1)PR)/(\beta^2 P + R)$. We set $\beta$ to 1 because we considered precision and recall are equally important for TSR.

**Basic Methods**

In the first experiment, we used the pixel values and their DCT coefficients as input to an ANN for recognition. The ANN had 1065 input units, each for the 32x30 pixel values and the 105 DCT coefficients. There were 400 hidden units and 45 output units.

The values of the output units indicated the likelihood of the detected object being the sign represented by the unit.

In the second experiment, we rely on the SVD vectors of the objects for classification. We computed the Euclidean distances of SVD vector of the object to those of the training patterns, and applied the $k$NN principle for classification. The closest 100 neighbors voted for the class of the test object.

**Integrated Methods**

We combine the original pixel values, DCT coefficients, and SVD vectors for recognition in three ways. Here, we reused the ANN in the first experiment, but used SVD vectors in a slightly different way. We normalized each SVD vector by dividing its components by the largest component before we computed distances. This was partially due to the fact the outputs of our ANN were normally below 2, while values of components of original SVD vectors fell in a much wider range. We normalized the values in SVD vectors to balance the influences of the ANN and SVD vectors.

The first integration of ANN and SVD assigned equal weights to the scores given by ANN and SVD. We separately normalized ANN scores and the SVD distances to the range [0,1]. Let $Score_A(sign)$ be the likelihood of the object being the *sign* determined by output units of the ANN, and $Score_S(sign)$ be the distances between the SVD vector of the test object and the SVD vector of the perfect image of *sign*. The possibility of the test object being a particular sign is determined by the following score function. The subtraction was due to the fact that we computed distances with SVD vectors, and large values suggest different signs.

$$Score(sign) = Score_A(sign) - Score_S(sign)$$

We may also assign different weights to the scores given by ANN and SVD. We determined the weights based on the classification performances of setups used in the first and the second experiments over the training data.

We used the ANN for the first experiment and the SVD vectors for the second experiment to classify the training data, and collected their $F$ measures for individual sign classes. These $F$ measures reflected how well the ANN-based and SVD-based classifiers performed on the training data, so we used this information to weight their predictions for the test data. Let $F_A$ and $F_S$ be the $F$ measures so collected for the ANN and SVD, respectively. In this experiment, we computed the scores of a sign class, $s_j$, using the following formula to choose the best candidate solutions.

$$Score(s_j) = F_A(s_j) \cdot Score_A(s_j) + F_S(s_j) \cdot (2 - Score_S(s_j))$$

The last experiment employed the components of the SVD vectors as features in a Naïve Bayes model. We assumed that the distributions of the feature values are mutually independent and normally distributed given the signs. Let $v_i$ be the $i^{th}$ component in the SVD vector. As shown below, we used the training data to estimate the means, $u_{ij}$, and variances, $\sigma_{ij}^2$, of the distributions of $v_i$ given sign $s_j$.

$$f_{ij}(v_i | s_j) = \frac{1}{\sqrt{2\pi\sigma_{ij}^2}} \exp\left(-(v_i - \mu_{ij})^2 / (2\sigma_{ij}^2)\right)$$

Because each SVD vector contained 30 components, and we had 45 triangular signs, we would have to estimate 2700 parameters for 1350 distributions. Since we had only slightly more than 10000 training data, which did not appear to be sufficient for estimating 2700 parameters, we chose to use only the largest 10 components in the

SVD vectors for this experiment, so we had to estimate only 900 parameters for 450 normal distributions.

To apply the naïve Bayes model, we needed to know the prior distribution over the 45 signs. Normally, this information would be trained with the frequencies of the signs in the training data. This standard method could not work for us. We could not guarantee that the frequencies of signs that were collected in our training set reflected the relative likelihood of coming across the signs. As an alternative, we employed the output of the ANN component as the surrogate for the prior distribution. As just mentioned, the ANN component gave a score for each of the different targeted signs. We mapped the ANN scores to the interval [0,1], and used the results as $\Pr(s_j)$.

Let $v_k$ be the $k^{th}$ largest component in the SVD vector of the object being recognized. At the recognition phase, we computed the following score, and assigned object the sign $s_j$ that maximized the following score.

$$Score(s_j) = \Pr(s_j)\prod_{k=1}^{10} f_{kj}(v_k \mid s_j) \tag{1}$$

In all of these experiments, we used the absolute values of the ANN scores and SVD distances as extra filters to determine what objects were very unlikely to contain a triangular sign. The current object would not be considered as a traffic sign if any of the following conditions satisfied.

1. if the SVD distance between the current object to all perfect signs is greater than 5
2. if the highest ANN score of the current object is less than 0.3
3. if all the following conditions hold: the highest ANN score is less than 1.5 times the second highest ANN score; the second highest ANN score is less than 2 times the third highest ANN score; the third highest ANN score is less than 3 times the fourth highest ANN score

**Results**
Using the output of the *Detection* procedure as the gauging point for computing the precision and recall of our detection component, we achieved 93% in recall, and 78% in precision. We deliberatively allowed higher recall and lower precision at the detection phase because it offered better prospect of higher recognition rate of the overall system.

**Table 1.** Experimental results of classifying objects into 45 triangular signs

| Classifiers | Single Candidate | | | Single Candidate | | |
|---|---|---|---|---|---|---|
| | Precision | Recall | F | Precision | Recall | F |
| EXP1: ANN | 63% | 71% | 67% | 68% | 78% | 73% |
| EXP2: kNN | 28% | 40% | 34% | 36% | 50% | 43% |
| EXP3: ANN+SVD | 66% | 76% | 71% | 72% | 83% | 78% |
| EXP4: ANN+SVD+F | 62% | 73% | 68% | 72% | 83% | 78% |
| EXP5: ANN+SVD+NB | 45% | 54% | 50% | 56% | 65% | 61% |

Table 1 shows the recognition rates of our experiments over the test data that are publicized in the Appendix. The **Single Candidate** column shows the performance measures when our recognizer returned only the most possible traffic sign as the answer. The **Three Candidates** column shows the performance measures when we allowed our recognizer to return the three most possible signs.

Although SVD distances alone did not perform very well, according to results of the second experiment, they worked quite well with the ANN scores. The direct integration of ANN scores and SVD distances turned out to be the best classifier, followed by their integration using the $F$ measures as the weights. Integrating ANN scores and SVD distances via the naïve Bayes model did not perform as well as we expected. After analyzing the errors, we found that using the product formula in (1) allowed SVD-based features to dominate the classification decisions, which is not a very good design as already suggested by results of the second experiment. In contrast, the third and the fourth experiments gave more balanced weights to ANN scores and SVD distances, and achieved better performances.

In Exp4, which provides the best performance, the average time spent on detection was 4.05 seconds for each input image. The standard deviation was 0.501 seconds. The average time spent on recognition for each ROI was 0.168 seconds, and the standard deviation was 0.0146 seconds. The timing statistics were collected when we ran our system on a 1 GHz Pentium III CPU with 256 Mbyte SDRAM, using interpreted Matlab programs.

## 4   Discussions

Although we have discussed designs of our experiments using the RGB color system, we did have tried the HSI system [18]. The HSI system may be more resilient to the disturbance caused by lighting problems, but did not improve performances of our systems significantly.

The problems we are tackling are more difficult than we thought. Consider the following signs. Telling signs (a) through (d) apart in a noisy environment can be a difficult job even for human eyes. Signs (e) through (g) form another confusing group. We found that, in many cases, drivers could guess types of the signs by contextual information while driving.

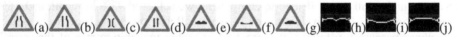

It has been tempting to us to apply low-level information, such as morphological information [10], for recognition. One may compute the skeleton of the ideographs for sign recognition. Although we did not report results of our effort on this front, our experiences indicated that skeletons alone might not be very fruitful. For instance, skeletons of ideographs in (e) through (g), shown in (h) through (j), may look very similar when we take their images in noisy environments.

Nevertheless, the extremely similar signs in these sample images strongly suggest the necessity of low-level information for high quality of recognition. A robust template-based matching can be very useful if integrated with an active vision system [13]. If we use one camera to search for ROIs that may contain traffic signs in the viewing area, and use another camera to zoom in the ROIs for clearer images of the candidate areas, we may apply template-based matching for high performance systems. However, we are not sure if it is feasible to install two cameras on passenger cars while maintaining the affordability.

The applicability of our current system is quite limited by the facts that it employs several human selected parameters and rules. Many of these settings are not well supported by any theories, but were set to their current values based on limited experiments over the training data. Improving the recognition rate and the generalizability of our methods requires a lot of more future work.

**Acknowledgments.** We thank anonymous reviewers for the invaluable comments on the original manuscript. Although we cannot follow all the comments partially due to page limits, we will do so in an expanded version of this paper. We also thank Mr. Chang-Ming Hsieh of the Taichung Bureau of Transportation for his providing perfect images of the traffic signs. This project was supported in part by Grant NSC-91-2213-E-004-013 from the National Science Council of Taiwan.

# References

We use ITS and IV for *Intelligent Transportation Systems* and *Intelligent Vehicles*, respectively.

1. *Proc. of the IEEE 5$^{th}$ Int'l Conf. on ITS*, 2002.
2. Ž. Devčić and S. Lončarić, SVD block processing for non-linear image noise filtering, *J. of Computing and Information Technology*, **7**(3), 255–259, 1999.
3. R. O. Duda, P. E. Hart, and D. G. Stork, *Pattern Classification*, John-Wiley & Sons, 2001.
4. A. de la Escalera, L. E. Moreno, M. A. Salichs, and J. M. Armingol, Road traffic sign detection and classification, *IEEE Trans. on Industrial Electronics*, **44**(6), 848–859, 1997.
5. O. Egger, P. Fleury, T. Ebrahimi, and M. Kunt, High-performance compression of visual information: A tutorial review, Part I: still pictures, *Proc. of the IEEE*, **87**(6), 976–1011, 1999.
6. D. M. Gavrila. Traffic sign recognition revisited, *Proc. of the 21$^{st}$ DAGM Symp. für Mustererkennung*, 86–93, 1999.
7. D. M. Gavrila, U. Franke, C. Wöhler, and S. Görzig, Real-time vision for intelligent vehicles, *IEEE Instrumentation & Measurement Magazine*, **4**(2), 22–27, 2001.
8. R. Haralick and L. Shapiro, *Computer and Robot Vision*, Vol. 1, 346–351, Addison-Wesley, 1992.
9. S.-H. Hsu and C.-L. Huang, Road sign detection and recognition using matching pursuit method, *Image and Vision Computing*, **19**(3), 119–129, 2001.
10. G. Y. Jiang, T. Y. Choi, and Y. Zheng, Morphological traffic sign recognitions, *Proc. of the 3$^{rd}$ Int'l Conf. on Signal Processing*, 531-534, 1996.
11. N. Kehtarnavaz and A. Ahmad, Traffic sign recognition in noisy outdoor scenes, *Proc. of the IEEE IV 1995 Symp.*, 460–465, 1995.
12. C. D. Manning and H. Schutze. *Foundations of Statistical Natural Language Processing*. The MIT Press, 1999.
13. J. Miura, T. Kanda, and Y. Shirai, An active vision system for real-time traffic sign recognition, *Proc. of the IEEE 3$^{rd}$ Int'l Conf. on ITS*, 52–57, 2000.
14. G. Piccioli, E. De Micheli, P. Parodi, and M. Campani, A robust method for road sign detection and recognition, *Image and Vision Computing*, **14**(3), 209–223, 1996.
15. L. Priese, R. Lakmann, and V. Rehrmann, Ideograph identification in a realtime traffic sign recognition system, *Proc. of the IEEE IV 1995 Symp.*, 310–314, 1995.
16. W. Ritter, Traffic sign recognition in color image sequences, *Proc. of the IEEE IV 1992 Symp.*, 12–17, 1992.
17. H. Sandoval, T. Hattori, S. Kitagawa, and Y. Chigusa, Angle-dependent edge detection for traffic signs recognition, *Proc. of the IEEE IV 2000 Symp.*, 308–313, 2000.
18. M. Sonka, V. Hlavac, and R. Boyle, *Image Processing, Analysis, and Machine Vision*, PWS Publishing, 1999.

# Appendix

**http://www.cs.nccu.edu.tw/~chaolin/papers/ismis03/testdata.html** (Please contact the author should the link became inaccessible in the future.)

# Design Patterns in Intelligent Systems

James F. Peters

Department of Electrical and Computer Engineering, University of Manitoba
Winnipeg, Manitoba R3T 5V6 Canada
jfpeters@ee.umanitoba.ca

**Abstract.** This article introduces design patterns useful in intelligent systems engineering. The basic approach in this research has been influenced by recent work on design patterns in systems engineering, pattern recognition for humans and machines and on the identification of components of an approximation space approach to understanding and crafting intelligent systems. In general, an IS pattern is seen an entity that is vaguely defined relative to structural and functional features of a component of an intelligent system. A complete IS pattern map is given in this paper. The application of IS patterns is illustrated in the reverse engineering of a life form that has pattern recognition capabilities (e.g., identifying the location of cached food by Nucifraga columbiana (Clark's nutcracker)). The contribution of this paper is to introduce an approach to forward engineering robotic devices that embody IS patterns and to reverse engineering existing robotic or living systems using IS patterns either singularly or in networks as classifiers where a feature set embodied in an IS pattern matches *to a degree* features of a subsystem of an existing system.

**Keywords**: Classification, design pattern, intelligent systems engineering, pattern recognition, reverse engineering.

## 1 Introduction

This article introduces a pattern-based approach to designing intelligent systems based. The basic approach in this research has been influenced by recent work on architectural patterns [1], modeling design patterns in systems engineering [2], pattern recognition [3]-[5], the ideas concerning knowledge, classification and machine learning in rough set theory [6] and work on an approximation space approach to intelligent systems [7], [9], [15]. Patterns commonly found in intelligent systems are represented using class, collaboration, interaction, and state diagrams from the Unified Modeling Language (UML) [17]. In general, an IS pattern is seen an entity that is vaguely defined relative to structural and functional features of a component of an intelligent system.

The notation ≪Pattern≫ denotes a stereotype for a particular pattern named inside guillemets ≪≫. A stereotype is a new class of metamodel element that represents an extension of elements of UML introduced for some special purpose. For example, the pattern ≪Neuron≫ specifies a collaboration

N. Zhong et al. (Eds.): ISMIS 2003, LNAI 2871, pp. 262–269, 2003.

between a number of objects such as Actuator, Approximation, Reason, and Sensor. When it is clear from the context, pattern names are given without the surrounding guillemets ≪≫. A number of IS patterns have been identified, namely, Actuator, Aggregation, Approximation, Category, Change, Classifier, Computation, DataMining, Detection, Design, Emotion, Granule, Harmony, Isomorphism, Judgment, KnowledgeBase, Learning, Map, Measure, Measurement, Model, Navigation, Neuron, Order, Pattern, Selector, Sensor, and Set pattern.

In this work, we adopt a paradigm-oriented approach to discerning the structural and functional features found in components of an intelligent system. A paradigm of intelligence (typical example, model, pattern) characterizes a class of objects found in intelligent systems. Such a class is collection where each object in the collection has *to some degree* the same form. The contribution of this paper is the introduction to a unified approach to the design of intelligent systems viewed as a weaving together of design patterns associated with intelligence.

This paper has the following organization. A partial catalogue and map of IS patterns is given in Section 2. In addition, a suggested use of collaborations in the realization of IS patterns is also presented in Section 2. An introduction to the notion of an IS classification scheme is presented in Section 3. A very brief illustration of how one might apply IS patterns in reverse engineering a living intelligent system is given in Section 3.

## 2 Intelligent Systems Patterns

It has been suggested that the basic object of design is form [18]. A basic tenet in intelligent systems engineering is that it is possible to achieve some degree of match between a pattern (well-understood form of the function and structure of an IS component) and its context (particular application requiring some form of sapient-like behavior). In general, a pattern provides a paradigm or typical example that is a model for a collection of individual objects. In this work, every IS pattern is a collection of classifiers that can be considered either structurally (diagram of the pattern) and functionally (actions defined by methods belonging to each class in the pattern). In some sense, an IS pattern provides a means of satisfying a requirement for the design of a component in a sapient-like machine.

The context for an IS system defines an IS design problem to be solved. It can be seen that IS patterns have a hierarchical organization, where a pattern such as Set and Granule are super-patterns relative to the Aggregation ($\sum$, $\int$), Approximation and Change ($\Delta$, d, $\partial$) patterns. A partial IS pattern catalogue and corresponding map is given in Fig. 1. The map in Fig. 1 is organized relative to how each pattern (represented by a named box) relates to other patterns in an IS system. The sensors in an intelligent system provide a basis for a Sensor pattern (this includes Filter and Noise subclasses) that is a super-pattern of (has a link to) what are known as Approximation, Measurement, Selector, and Map patterns. The Set pattern is a basic pattern in the design of intelligent systems. This pattern has a Methods interface which can be implemented in different ways (e.g., Zermelo-Fraenkel axiomatic set theory, fuzzy sets [13], rough sets[6]) depending on the interpretation of the inclusion operation. In this paper, the Set and Granule patterns are modeled with respect to rough sets in the context of a calculus of granules and measures useful in approximate reasoning [7-12]. The Approximation design pattern is fundamental in providing a basis for reasoning and decision-making by an intelligent system.

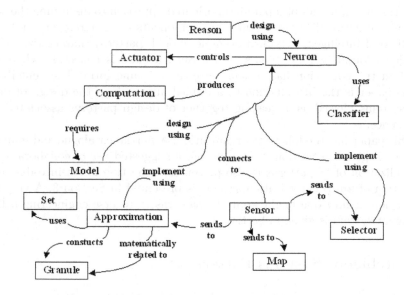

**Fig. 1.** Partial IS Pattern Map

The ≪Neuron≫ pattern is a basic pattern in the design of intelligent systems (see Fig. 2). This pattern is modeled as a collection of classifiers, each with its own role in a collaboration that makes a particular form of pattern recognition possible. The ≪Approximation≫ classifier in Fig. 2 has an ≪ApproxMethods≫ interface which can be implemented in different ways (e.g., rough sets[7], [11]) depending on the interpretation of the inclusion operation. In this paper, the Set and Granule patterns are modeled with respect to rough sets in the context of a calculus of granules and measures useful in approximate reasoning [9]. Notice that a model of the ≪Approximation≫ pattern (modeled statically as a class diagram) is also included in Fig. 2 This pattern provides a basis for approximate reasoning and decision-making (see, e.g., [7]).

## 3   Design Patterns: Basic Approach

The basic approach in this research is to design and build robotic devices that embody IS patterns and to reverse engineer existing robotic or living systems

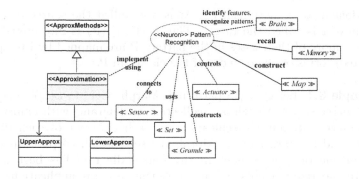

**Fig. 2.** ≪Neuron≫ pattern

using IS patterns either singularly or in networks as classifiers (i.e., where a feature set embodied in an IS pattern matches *to a degree* features of a subsystem of an existing system such as a Cephalopod (e.g., octopus)). Template matching [4] and 3D objection recognition [3] are used to describe, model and recognize IS patterns. Other approaches to modeling and recognizing IS patterns (e.g., statistical pattern recognition [4]) are possible but are outside the scope of this paper. In addition, the basic idea of an IS architectural pattern based mainly on physical features of a system is briefly described. In identifying an IS pattern, we use knowledge both about the structure (interfaces, superclasses, hierarchies, stereotypes, associations, classifiers) and the function (i.e., what one class does in relation to other classes (stereotypes), interactions and the exchange of information between objects (informorphisms)) represented by a design pattern. The principle of comprehension is used in establishing the type of a pattern [14]. The application of IS patterns is illustrated in the reverse engineering of a life form that has pattern recognition capabilities (e.g., identifying the location of cached food by Nucifraga columbiana (Clark's nutcracker)). The availability of IS patterns provides an approach to forward engineering robotic devices that have some measure of intelligence and to reverse engineering existing robotic or living systems using IS patterns either singularly or in networks.

The IS design process can be viewed as a form of IS classification similar to the classification scheme defined in [15] and in [16]. In what follows, an IS pattern is viewed as a set of classifiers with specified relationships to each other.

**Definition 3.1.** IS Classification. Let $P$, $\wp(P)$, $M$, $\aleph$, $\delta$ be a set of patterns, family of sets of patterns, set of morphisms (set functions from $\wp(P)$ to $\wp(P)$), set of requirements for an intelligent system, and $\delta$: $\wp(P) \rightarrow [0,1]$, respectively. Let $A \subseteq \wp(P)$. Further, let $\models_\Im \in M \times \wp(P)$ denote a satisfaction relation where $A \models_{\Im,\delta} f$ asserts that $f(A)$ satisfies a requirement $\delta \in \aleph$ for an IS classification $\Im$ provided $\delta(f(A)) = 1$. Then an IS classification is defined in (1).

$$\Im = (\wp(P), M, \aleph, \models_{\Im,\delta}) \tag{1}$$

The domain of a morphism f ∈ M is also called the source of f, and the co-domain of f is called the target. The function f(P) is interpreted to mean that one or more of the classes in the pattern P are mapped by f to specialized (interpreted) forms of one or more of the classes in P.

**Example 3.1.** Let Q = {IS patterns}, Morph = {f | f : ℘(Q) → ℘(Q)} such that the source of f ∈ Morph is a collection of diagrams with empty methods and generalized attribute specifications in each classifier of each diagram of the source and the target of f ∈ Morph is a set specialized patterns (i.e., each method in one or more classes in the source diagram has been specialized relative to the requirements for an intelligent systems application, and each attribute in one or more source classes has been tailored to the needs of an application). Let A ⊆ ℘(Q). Then A ⊨$_{\Im,\delta}$ f is interpreted to mean that the target f(A) satisfies requirement δ in ℵ, i.e., δ(f(A)) = 1. Then the tuple (℘(Q), Morph, ℵ, ⊨$_{\Im,\delta}$) is a form of IS classification.

**Example 3.2.** Let Q = {IS patterns}, Morph = {f | f : ℘(Q) → ℘(Q), M ⊆ Morph such that M is set of patterns for sensors. Each pattern in M is of the form shown in Fig. 3. The target of the morphism f is a new pattern where the measureStimulus method in the Stimulus interface has been specialized.

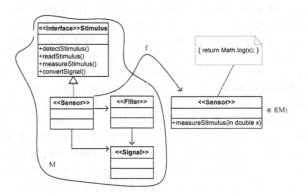

**Fig. 3.** Sample IS Pattern Morphism Target

Refinements made to classifiers in an IS pattern can be viewed as composite mappings.

**Definition 3.2.** Composite IS Pattern. Let ℑ = (℘(P), M, ℵ, ⊨$_{\Im,\delta}$) be an IS classification where A, B, C are subsets of ℘(P). Given that f: ℘(P) → ℘(P) and g: ℘(P) → ℘(P) so that f(A) = B and g(B) = C, then the composite g∘f is defined by the rule g∘f(A) = g(f(A)) as shown in Fig. 4.

**Proposition 3.1.** The target of a composite IS pattern g∘f is an IS pattern.

That the target of a composition IS pattern g∘f is also an IS pattern follows immediately from the definition of IS composites.

**Proposition 3.2.** Let $\Im = (\wp(P), M, \aleph, \models_{\Im,\delta})$ and that f: $\wp(P) \rightarrow \wp(P)$ and g: $\wp(P) \rightarrow \wp(P)$ for A,B,C $\subseteq \wp(P)$, f(A) = B and g(B) = C. A $\models_{\Im,\delta}$ f and B $\models_{\Im,\delta}$ g if, and only if A $\models_{\Im,\delta}$ g∘f.

# 4  Reverse Engineering an Intelligent System

Birds such as Clark's Nutcracker that cache food use distinctive rocks, logs, and other habitat features as clues to the locations of buried food [19-20]. The beginning of a reverse engineered bird starts with collaborations that realize use cases associated with an avian model. For example, consider the forage use case shown in Fig. 4. The behavior associated with the ≪Neuron≫ pattern in the context of the forage use case is represented by the collaboration of the Brain, Memory, Map and Search stereotypes shown in Fig. 4.

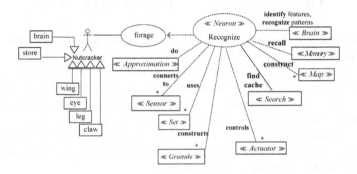

**Fig. 4.** Avian Pattern Recognition Model

In Fig. 4, the boxes labeled brain, store, wing, eye, leg, claw represent actors that provide generalizations of the actor named Nutcracker, which is associated with the forage use case. The roles of the objects named ≪Brain≫, ≪Memory≫, ≪Sensor≫, and ≪Actuator≫ in the Recognize collaboration (instance of the ≪Neuron≫ pattern) provide a realization of the behavior of the physical, avian subsystems represented by the forage use case. The ≪Approximation≫, ≪Map≫ and ≪Search≫ patterns are allied with approximate reasoning by an avian intelligence. Finally, the ≪Set≫ and ≪Granule≫ patterns are allied with the byproducts of approximate reasoning, where the feature sets and aggregates of feature values provide an idealized basis for avian reasoning (matching physical features of a landscape with recalled feature values) and memorizing (storing object configurations in locations where food has been cached). The ≪Approximation≫ pattern seems to be an appropriate basis for reasoning by a caching bird because current stored feature values used to identify the location of cached food will probably not match exactly the future configurations of objects that have changed because of the influences of such as things as weather, biodeterioration, movements of objects by foraging animals.

The ≪Brain≫ pattern provides a basis for modeling the brain of Clark's Nutcracker. Its role is to identify features of the landscape and to classify patterns that make it possible for the Nutcracker to find cached food. One possible interaction between a partial representation of the objects in a foraging behavior is shown in the sequence diagram in Fig. 5.

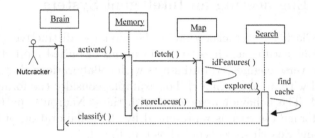

**Fig. 5.** Partial Sequence Diagram for Forage Use Case

The construction of the partial sequence diagram in Fig. 5 has been guided by the roles of the objects exhibited in the collaboration representing the ≪Neuron≫ pattern (see Fig. 4). The reverse engineering of the Nutcracker continues at the level of patterns such as ≪Sensor≫ and ≪Actuator≫, ≪Approximation≫, ≪Actuator≫, and ≪Granule≫ to arrive at the basis for a simulation of a caching bird such as Clark's Nutcracker. The quality of mappings of IS patterns to component designs also needs to be measured relative to requirements (known features) for a model of avian mapping and pattern recognition. This is considered outside the scope of this paper.

## 5   Conclusion

An approach to designing intelligent systems based on selections from a catalogue of patterns has been introduced in this article. An IS pattern represents a well-understood paradigm useful in constructing components of a system that has some measure of intelligence. The quality of IS designs can be measured in the context of an IS classification, where each mapping of classes in a pattern to a target design can be measured relative to system requirements. Elaboration of IS patterns, augmentation of the IS pattern catalogue, refinement and extension of pattern maps, and consideration of properties of classification schemes are part of the future work in this research.

**Acknowledgements.** This research has been supported by the Natural Sciences and Engineering Research Council of Canada (NSERC) grant 185986. Many thanks to Maciej Borkowski for preparing the LATEXversion of this paper.

# References

1. C. Alexander, S. Ishikawa, M. Silverstein, M. Jacobson, I. Fiksdahl-King, S. Angel, A Pattern Language. Oxford University Press, UK, 1977.
2. E. Gamma, R. Helm, R. Johnson, J. Vlissides, Design Patterns: Elements of Reusable Object-Oriented Software. Addison-Wesley, Toronto, 1995. ISBN 0-201-633612.
3. L. Stark, K. Bowyer, Achieving generalized object recognition through reasoning about association of function to structure, IEEE Trans. on Pattern Analysis and Machine Intelligence 13(10), 1991, 1097–1104.
4. A.K. Jain, R.P.W. Duin, J. Mao, Statistical pattern recognition, IEEE Trans. on pattern analysis and machine intelligence, vol. 22, no. 1, Jan. 2000, 4-37.
5. S. Watanabe, Pattern Recognition: Human and Mechanical. Wiley, London, 1985.
6. Z. Pawlak, Rough Sets: Theoretical Aspects of Reasoning About Data, Boston, MA, Kluwer Academic Publishers, 1991.
7. J.F. Peters, A. Skowron, J. Stepaniuk, S. Ramanna, Towards an ontology of approximate reason, Fundamenta Informaticae, Vol. 51, Nos. 1, 2, June 2002, 157–173.
8. J.F. Peters, W. Pedrycz, Computational Intelligence. In: J.G. Webster (Ed.), Encyclopedia of Electrical and Electronic Engineering. 22 vols.NY, John Wiley & Sons, Inc., 1999.
9. A. Skowron, Toward intelligent systems: Calculi of information granules. In: S. Hirano, M. Inuiguchi, S. Tsumoto (Eds.), Bulletin of the International Rough Set Society, vol. 5, no. 1 / 2, 2001, 9–30.
10. A. Skowron, J. Stepaniuk, J.F. Peters, Extracting patterns using information granules. In: S. Hirano, M. Inuiguchi, S. Tsumoto (Eds.), Bulletin of the International Rough Set Society, vol. 5, no. 1/2, 2001, 135–142.
11. A. Skowron, J. Stepaniuk, Information granules and approximation spaces. In: Proc. of the $7^{th}$ Int. Conf. on Information Processing and Management of Uncertainty in Knowledge-based Systems (IPMU'98), Paris, France, 6–10 July 1998, 1354–1361.
12. A. Skowron, J. Stepaniuk, J.F. Peters, Hierarchy of information granules. In: H.D. Burkhard, L. Czaja, H.S. Nguyen, P. Starke (Eds.), Proc. of the Workshop on Concurrency, Specification and Programming, Oct. 2001, Warsaw, Poland , 254–268.
13. L.A. Zadeh, Fuzzy sets, Information Control 8, 1965, 338–353.
14. R. Goldblatt, Topoi: The Categorical Analysis of Logic, North-Holland Publishing Co., Amsterdam, 1979.
15. A. Skowron, J. Stepaniuk, J.F. Peters, Rough sets and informorphisms, Fundamenta Informaticae XXI, 2003, 1001–1015.
16. J.F. Peters, A. Skowron, J. Stepaniuk, Types, classification and information systems: A rough set approach. In: Proc. of Workshop on Rough Sets and Knowledge Discovery, Warsaw, Poland, April 2003 [to appear].
17. OMG Unified Modeling Language Specification, Object Management Group, http://www.omg.org.
18. C. Alexander, Notes on the Synthesis of Form. Cambridge, MA, Harvard University Press, 1964.
19. C. Elphick, J.B. Dunning, D.A. Sibley (Eds.), The Sibley Guide to Bird Life & Behavior. NY, Alfred A. Knopf, 2001.
20. D.A. Sibley, The Sibley Guide to Birds. NY, Alfred A. Knopf, 2001.

# Temporal Feature Extraction from Temporal Information Systems*

Piotr Synak

Polish-Japanese Institute of Information Technology
Koszykowa 86, 02-008 Warsaw, Poland

**Abstract.** We present a framework for new feature extraction from temporal information systems. Such systems provide information about behaviour of object(s) in time and state of an object is described by some attributes. We propose a modification of Apriori algorithm for frequent episode detection across many series. The episodes are built from events being temporal patterns found in temporal information system.

## 1 Introduction

Temporal data analysis is a topic of high interest in many real world applications like weather forecasting or web log processing. There are several kinds of temporal data, from classical time series, through temporal sequences to temporal information systems. Each type of data, as well as field of application, arises new problems, which in many cases are very hard to solve. Therefore, there is no any universal method that could be applied to temporal data of any kind.

In the paper we focus on temporal information systems, which describe objects changing in time, in terms of attributes. The attributes can be both of numerical or symbolic type. In our approach we search for temporal patterns in series related to investigated objects. Some specific configurations of discovered patterns may appear to be characteristic to, e.g., particular groups or classes of objects. Thus, we search across many objects for kind of episodes described in a language of temporal patterns. We propose an algorithm for such episodes detection, which is a modification of Apriori algorithm. Episodes specific to groups or classes of objects can leverage the clustering or classification algorithms.

We present a complete framework describing all the basic stages of analysis, from temporal information system processing to new feature extraction. The framework is highly parameterised, so tuning parameters is an important step of the presented method. We present some results of experiments related to musical instrument sound analysis. They seem to be very satisfactory.

---

* Supported by Polish National Committee for Scientific Research (KBN) grant No. $8T11C02519$ and PJIIT grant No.$PJ/AI/03/2002$.

| A | User_id | Page | Duration |
|---|---------|------|----------|
| $t_1$ | 1 | a.htm | 5 |
| $t_2$ | 3 | b.htm | 4 |
| $t_3$ | 1 | b.htm | 4 |
| $t_4$ | 2 | a.htm | 6 |
| $t_5$ | 3 | a.htm | 1 |
| $t_6$ | 1 | c.htm | 1 |
| $t_7$ | 1 | d.htm | 2 |
| $t_8$ | 2 | d.htm | 5 |
| $t_9$ | 3 | c.htm | 3 |
| $t_{10}$ | 3 | d.htm | 5 |

**Fig. 1.** A temporal multiple information system – each $User\_id$ represents one series.

## 2  Temporal Data

There are many kinds of temporal data being investigated in real applications. The most commonly known are *time series* data, which are results of some observations usually ordered in time, i.e. $X = \{x_t : t = 1, \ldots, n\}$, where $x_t$ is a numerical value observed in time $t$. There are several examples of time series: data describing seismic activity, stock market indicator's changes or EEG signals. The following are examples of problems related to time series analysis: forecasting – for a given sequence predict the future values, or predict occurrence of some special events (e.g. earthquakes); clustering – for given sequences group them into clusters of similar series; classification – for a given sequence classify it to the right class. Time series are widely studied in the literature [7,5,10].

*Temporal sequences* are another class of temporal data. There is given an alphabet $E$ of event types. An event is a pair $(e, t)$, where $e \in E$ and $t$ is time index. Events can be of numerical or symbolic type and time is discrete. Temporal sequence is then sequence of events. There are several examples of temporal sequences, e.g. logs of telecommunication network monitors or web logs. In the first case event types are different notification types in the network, in the second – different pages of given web site. There can be several problems formulated for this kind of data including searching for frequent episodes, i.e. collections of events occurring frequently in data [11,12].

In several cases temporal data are described by many features of both numerical and symbolic types. *Temporal information system* is a system, which describes behaviour of one object in time. It is a pair $A = (\{x_1, x_2, \ldots, x_n\}, A)$ of universe ordered in time and set of attributes $A$. An example is a system describing behaviour of stock market in time. There can be several economic and market indicators used to describe the situation on a market. One row of such system describes situation at given time index. In this case we can formulate e.g. classification problem: given values of indicators classify the the situation described by them [20].

Temporal information system is a special case of *temporal multiple information system* that describes behaviour in time of many objects. We can consider e.g. several users visiting a web site. Each request can be described by several

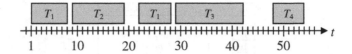

**Fig. 2.** An example of temporal templates found for one series.

attributes including referrer, elapsed time, etc. In this case the system describes several series (user sessions) in terms of attributes. The problems considered in this case include clustering – find sessions with similar behaviour and prediction – find characteristic patterns that precede given action taken by the user.

## 3    Temporal Templates

In this section we present the notion of temporal templates, i.e. temporal patterns that can be generated from temporal information systems. Temporal templates can be of numerical or symbolic type. They are built by using expressions $(a \in V)$, where $a$ is an attribute and $V$ is a set of values.

Let $\mathbb{A} = (\{x_1, x_2, \ldots, x_n\}, A)$ be a temporal information system. By *descriptor* over $\mathbb{A}$ we understand any expression of form $(a \in V)$, where $a \in A$ and $V$ is a subset of $V_a$ – domain of attribute $a$. *Temporal template* is then a set of expressions involving any subset $B \subseteq A$: $\mathbf{T} = (T, t_s, t_e)$, where $T = \{(a \in V) : a \in B, V \subseteq V_a\}$ and $1 \le t_s \le t_e \le n$. The set of descriptors $T$ we call a *template* (or *generalised template*). Temporal templates are intensively studied in the literature ([1], [15], [20]). To outline the intuition which is in behind, let us understand temporal template as strong regularity occurring in time.

There can be defined several properties of temporal templates. By *width* of $\mathbf{T} = (T, t_s, t_e)$ we mean $t_e - t_s + 1$. *Support* of $\mathbf{T}$ is the number of objects from interval $[t_s, t_e]$ that match all of the descriptors from $T$. The *precision* of template $T$ in $\mathbb{A}$ we define by

$$S_{\mathbb{A}}(T) = \sum_{(a \in V) \in T} s_{\mathbb{A}}^{T}((a \in V)), \tag{1}$$

where $s_{\mathbb{A}}^{T}((a \in V))$ is a measure of how much a descriptor $(a \in V)$ is specific (the exact definition can be found in [20]). If template $T$ consists of many descriptors that describe the whole domain of attributes, it is a general template (not precise). If $T$ consists of one-value descriptors only, it is very specific (precise) and then $S_{\mathbb{A}}(T)$ gives the number of descriptors of $T$ (length of $T$). Upon to the investigated problem we can also define *quality* of temporal template as some function of width, support, number of descriptors and precision.

Let us outline an algorithm for temporal templates generation [20]. It uses time window of given size, which is moved across information system. In each window there is generated an optimal template, which is compared to that from previous time window. In this way we can compute time of validity $[t_s, t_e]$ of found template. The algorithm results with a sequence of temporal templates found for the whole temporal information system. However, there can be a time interval without any satisfactory (in terms of quality function) template at all, i.e. without any strong regularity.

# 4    Temporal Feature Extraction

In this section we present a step-by-step schema of temporal feature extraction process from temporal multiple information systems. This schema consists of many parameters that are about to be tuned up while applying to the real problem. There are five main steps. In the first step the input information system is pre-processed. Then for each sequence there are computed temporal patterns (templates). Next, found patterns need to be processed in order to, e.g., decrease the total amount of different patterns, so the extracted information is more general. In the fourth step we search for collections of patterns (episodes) appearing in sequences frequently. Finally, we generate new attributes from found frequent episodes.

## 4.1    Data Pre-processing

Information stored in data can be of numerical and/or symbolic type. In case when there are too many different values no strong regularity may occur at all. Thus, the pre-processing step is needed to discretise (numerical case) or group (symbolic case) stored information. In the simplest case real-value attributes can be discretised by using a uniform scale quantisation (the number of intervals is a parameter). More sophisticated methods can be found, e.g., in [14].

## 4.2    Temporal Patterns Extraction

We propose to search for temporal patterns in series – their collections may be specific to some groups of investigated objects, what can be very helpful in solving clustering or classification problems. Because temporal multiple information systems consists of many series, i.e. objects changing in time, we propose to search for temporal templates in each series separately. The mentioned algorithm for temporal templates generation results with a sequence of templates for each series, i.e. with a set of sequences of temporal templates. Let us observe that this set may consist of relatively large number of different (in terms of descriptors only) templates. In the pessimistic case there can be no repeating templates at all, and then it makes no sense to search for combinations of templates occurring across sequences frequently. Therefore, we propose to search for template representatives and use them only for encoding of sequences of templates. Such template representatives are computed from the set of all templates by taking optimal ones with respect to some quality measures. In the simplest case we can compute frequencies of templates, i.e., number of different sequences containing given template. We can use the information about decision class where given

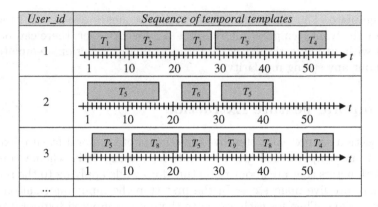

**Fig. 3.** A sequence of temporal templates found for each series (*User_id*).

sequence belongs to, i.e. we can generate most frequent templates for each class separately. The following measures are examples based on theories of machine and statistical learning, as well as rough sets. Let $\mathbf{T} = (T, t_s, t_e)$ be a temporal template. Measure

$$BayesDist(T) = \sum_{v_d \in V_d} |P(T/v_d) - P(T)| \qquad (2)$$

describes the impact of decision classes onto probability of $T$. By $P(T)$ we mean simply the prior probability that elements of the universe satisfy $T$, estimated directly from data. By $P(T/v_d)$ we mean the same probability, but derived from the decision class corresponding to $v_d \in V_d$. If we regard $T$ as the left side of an inexact decision rule $T \Rightarrow d = v_d$, then $P(T/v_d)$ describes its sensitivity [13]. Quantities $|P(T/v_d) - P(T)|$ express a kind of degree of information we gain about $T$ given knowledge about membership of the analysed objects to particular decision classes. According to the Bayesian reasoning principles [6], $BayesDist(T)$ provides the degree of information we gain about decision probabilistic distribution, given additional knowledge about satisfaction of $T$. The second exemplary measure

$$RoughDisc(T) = P(T)(1 - P(T)) - \sum_{v_d \in V_d} P(T, v_d)(P(v_d) - P(T, v_d)) \qquad (3)$$

is an adaptation of one of the rough set measures used, e.g., in [14] and [21] to express the number of pairs of objects belonging to different decision classes, being discerned by a specified condition. Normalisation, understood as division by the number of all possible pairs, results with (3), where $P(T)$ is understood as before, $P(v_d)$ denotes the normalised cardinality of the decision class corresponding to $v_d \in V_d$ and $P(T, v_d)$ is the joint probability of satisfying conditions $T$ and $d = v_d$.

## 4.3    Temporal Patterns Processing

We use template representatives to replace all the templates in found sequences of templates. Any template is substituted with the closest representative. In this way the total number of different templates is limited to the number of representatives, which is a parameter. There can be defined several measures of closeness between templates. In general the closeness can be defined as follows:

$$cl(T_1, T_2) = \sum_{a \in A} cl_a(T_1(a), T_2(a)) \tag{4}$$

where $T_i(a)$, $i = 1, 2$, is the descriptor of template $T_i$ corresponding to attribute $a$ (or empty set if there is no such descriptor), and $cl_a$ is closeness function between descriptors related to $a$. Let us note that attributes can be of both numerical or symbolic type and closeness can be defined in different ways for different attributes. For example, if $a$ is a real attribute and descriptors of temporal templates are described by intervals, we can have the following definition:

$$cl_a((a \in v_1), (a \in v_2)) = \frac{|v_1 \cap v_2|}{|v_1 \cup v_2|} \tag{5}$$

where $|.|$ is the length of interval. In case when $a$ is numerical, but templates are built from one-value descriptors we can define closeness by

$$cl_a((a = v_1), (a = v_2)) = 1 - \frac{|v_1 - v_2|}{|V_a|} \tag{6}$$

where $|V_a|$ is the length of domain of attribute $a$. For symbolic attributes we can define the closeness by

$$cl_a((a \in v_1), (a \in v_2)) = \frac{card(v_1 \cap v_2)}{card(v_1 \cup v_2)}. \tag{7}$$

## 4.4    Frequent Episode Generation

Till now, for each series we have generated a sequence of temporal templates, each of them being replaced by the closest representative. We can expect that some combinations of representative templates may be specific to particular decision classes (one or more). Let us reformulate this problem in terms of events. We can treat each template representative as an *event*. Then any sequence of templates is a sequence of events and any collection of templates is an *episode*. Thus, from sequences of templates we can discover frequent episodes – collections of templates occurring together [12,20]. We say that an episode *occurs* in a sequence of templates if each element (template) of the episode exists in the sequence and the order of occurrence is preserved. For example, an episode $AAC$ occurs in a sequence $B\underline{A}\underline{C}AB B\underline{C}$. Definition of episode occurrence depends on the particular application. We can modify the above definition by not preserving order of occurrence of events in episodes. In this way we obtain parallel episodes while in the former case we have serial episodes.

We propose an algorithm, based on Apriori method [2,12], which discovers frequently occurring episodes with respect to some occurrence measure $Occ$. The main difference, comparing, e.g., to Winepi algorithm [12], is that here we are looking for episodes across many series of events. The input to the algorithm is a set of template sequences and the frequency threshold $\tau$.

---

Detection of episodes occurring frequently

1. $\mathcal{F}_1 = \{1\text{-sequences occurring frequently}\}$
2. for $(l = 2;\ \mathcal{F}_{l-1} \neq \emptyset;\ l{+}{+})$ {
3.     $\mathcal{C}_l = GenCandidates(\mathcal{F}_1, \mathcal{F}_{l-1}, l)$
4.     $\mathcal{F}_l = \{c \in \mathcal{C}_l : Occ(c) \geq \tau\}$ }
5. return $\bigcup_l \mathcal{F}_l$

---

At first, we check which templates occur frequently enough in all sequences. That forms the set $\mathcal{F}_1$ of frequent episodes of length one. We can use several measures of occurrence. The fundamental one is the number of occurrences, however, by being "frequent" we can also understand frequent occurrence in one class and rare occurrence in another classes. Thus, we can adapt measures (2), (3) to the definition of function $Occ$. Next, we recursively create a set of candidates $\mathcal{C}_l$ by combining frequent templates ($\mathcal{F}_1$) with frequently occurring episodes of size $l - 1$ ($\mathcal{F}_{l-1}$). The last step is to verify the set of candidates $\mathcal{C}_l$ and eliminate infrequent episodes. The algorithm stops if there are no more candidates.

## 4.5    New Attributes Generation

Frequent episodes can be used for new feature generation. They carry information about combinations of temporal patterns specific to particular classes. Such a new feature can be used as additional attribute in an information system describing investigated series. New attributes may support process of series clustering or, in decision case, series classification.

We propose two definitions of new attributes based on occurrence of frequent episodes. Let us assume that in the training step we have computed frequent episodes for all series in the training sample. There can be several episodes out of them that occur in a testing object (series). The value of such a new attribute is simply the most frequent episode (in terms of function $Occ$). In the second case we take the longest episode occurring in a testing object. If there are several such episodes we choose the most frequent one (up to $Occ$).

Let us note that in both cases the attributes are of symbolic type. One can consider also numerical attributes generated from several properties of episodes.

## 5    Results of Experiments

The presented method requires evaluation of many parameters. The most important ones are: window size (when generating temporal templates), number of representative templates, quality and frequency measure, and frequency threshold. We have tested the method on musical instrument sound data [16]. The investigated problem is to classify samples of sound to one out of 18 classes (11 instruments + different articulations). There are 667 different samples in the database and for each sample we generated 16 spectral attributes (see [22] for details). In the experiments we built a classifier, based on decision rules generation by using rough set theory. For evaluation we used standard CV-5 method.

After tuning the parameters we have obtained an attribute with average prediction quality higher than 40%. The result seems to be significant – in [22] several spectral attributes give about 15%. It is also comparable to temporal attributes presented in [22], however here the result is for one single attribute.

## 6   Conclusions

We have presented a framework for supporting analysis of, so called, temporal multiple information systems, i.e., information systems describing temporal behaviour of objects. We have shown how notion of temporal templates can be used to temporal patterns extraction from sequences. We have also proposed modification of Apriori algorithm for frequent episodes detection in many series. The presented approach can be used for new temporal features extraction and supporting clustering or classification problems.

Further research is needed to establish a broader family of valuable episode based descriptors. Mainly, investigation of numerical features based on frequent episodes seems to be of high importance.

## References

1. R. Agrawal, H. Mannila, R. Srikant, H. Toivonen, and A. I. Verkamo. Fast discovery of association rules. In *Advances in Knowledge Discovery and Data Mining*, pp. 307–328, 1996. AAAI Press.
2. R. Agrawal and R. Srikant. Mining sequential patterns. In P. S. Yu and A. S. P. Chen (eds.), *XIX Int. Conf. on Data Engineering*, pp. 3–14, 1995. IEEE Press.
3. J. Bazan, H. S. Nguyen, S. H. Nguyen, P. Synak, and J. Wróblewski. Rough set algorithms in classification problems. L. Polkowski, T. Y. Lin, S. Tsumoto (eds.), *Studies in Fuzziness and Soft Computing*, vol. 56, pp. 49–88. Springer, 2000.
4. J. Bazan, A. Skowron, and P. Synak. Market data analysis: A rough set approach. ICS Research Reports 6, Warsaw Univeristy of Technology, Warsaw, Poland, 1994.
5. B. Bollobas, G. Das, D. Gunopulos, and H. Mannila. Time-series similarity problems and well-separated geometric sets. In *Symposium on Computational Geometry*, pp. 454–456, 1997.
6. Box, G., and Tiao, G. C. Bayesian Inference in Statistical Analysis. Wiley, 1992.
7. P.J. Brockwell and R. Davis. *Introduction to Time-Series and Forecasting*. Springer-Verlag, Berlin, Germany, 1996.
8. G. Das, D. Gunopulos, and H. Mannila. Finding similar time series. In *Principles of Data Mining and Knowledge Discovery*, pp. 88–100, 1997.
9. V. Guralnik and J. Srivastava. Event detection from time series data. In *Fifth ACM SIGKDD Int. Conf. on KDD*, pp. 33–42, 1999. ACM Press.

10. E. Keogh and M. Pazzani. An enhanced representation of time series which allows fast and accurate classification, clustering and relevance feedback. In R. Agrawal, P. Stolorz, and G. Piatetsky-Shapiro (eds.), *IV Int. Conf. on KDD*, pp. 239–241, 1998. ACM Press.
11. H. Mannila, H. Toivonen, and A. I. Verkamo. Discovering frequent episodes in sequences. *First Int. Conf. on KDD*, pp. 210–215, 1995. AAAI Press.
12. H. Mannila, H. Toivonen, and A. I. Verkamo. Discovery of frequent episodes in event sequences. *Data Mining and Knowledge Discovery*, 1(3):259–289, 1997.
13. Mitchell, T. Machine Learning. Mc Graw Hill, 1998.
14. H. S. Nguyen. *Discretization of Real Value Attributes, Boolean Reasoning Approach*. PhD thesis, Warsaw University, Poland, 1997.
15. S. H. Nguyen. *Regularity Analysis And Its Applications In Data Mining*. PhD thesis, Warsaw University, Poland, 2000.
16. Opolko, F., Wapnick, J.: MUMS – McGill University Master Samples. CD's (1987).
17. Z. Pawlak. *Rough Sets: Theoretical Aspects of Reasoning about Data, Series D: System Theory, Knowledge Engineering and Problem Solving*, vol. 9. Kluwer, 1991.
18. L. Polkowski and A. Skowron (eds.), *Rough Sets in Knowledge Discovery 1: Methodology and Applications, Studies in Fuzziness and Soft Computing*, vol. 18. Physica-Verlag, 1998.
19. Richard J. Povinelli. Identifying temporal patterns for characterization and prediction of financial time series events. In J. F. Roddick and K. Hornsby (eds.), LNCS 2007, pp. 46–61, 2000. Springer-Verlag.
20. P. Synak. Temporal templates and analysis of time related data. In W. Ziarko and Y. Yao (eds.), LNAI 2005, pp. 420–427, 2000. Springer-Verlag.
21. D. Ślęzak. Approximate decision reducts. Ph.D. thesis, Institute of Mathematics, Warsaw University, 2001.
22. A. Wieczorkowska, J. Wróblewski, P. Synak, and D. Ślęzak. Application of temporal descriptors to musical instrument sound recognition. *Journal of Intelligent Information Systems*, 21(1), 2003.

# Parallel Ant Colony Systems

Shu-Chuan Chu[1], John F. Roddick[1], Jeng-Shyang Pan[2,3], and Che-Jen Su[2]

[1] School of Informatics and Engineering,
Flinders University of South Australia,
GPO Box 2100, Adelaide 5001, South Australia.
{shuchuan.chu, roddick}@infoeng.flinders.edu.au
[2] Department of Electronic Engineering,
Kaohsiung University of Applied Sciences
Kaohsiung, Taiwan
jspan@cc.kuas.edu.tw
[3] Department of Automatic Test and Control,
Harbine Institute of Technology
Harbine, China

**Abstract.** In this paper a Parallel Ant Colony System ($PACS$) is developed. Three communication methods for updating the pheromone level between groups in $PACS$ are proposed and work on the traveling salesman problem using our system is presented. Experimental results based on three well-known traveling salesman data sets demonstrate the proposed $PACS$ is superior to the existing Ant Colony System ($ACS$) and Ant System ($AS$) with similar or better running times.

## 1 Introduction

Swarm intelligence research originates from work into the simulation of the emergence of collective intelligent behavior of real ants. Ants are able to find good solutions to the shortest path between the nest and a food source by laying down, on their way back from the food source, a trail of an attracting substance – a *pheromone*. Communication is based on the pheromone level – the shortest path being considered that with the greatest density of pheromone and with ants tending to follow the path with more pheromone. Dorigo *et al.* were the first to apply this idea to the traveling salesman problem [1,2]. The initial algorithm was referred to as the *Ant System* ($AS$) algorithm and a later enhanced method was also developed and referred to as the *Ant Colony System* ($ACS$) algorithm [3]. The Ant System and Ant Colony System algorithms have been applied successfully in many applications such as the quadratic assignment problem [4], data mining [5] and space-planning [6].

Parallelization strategies for $AS$ [7] and $ACS$ [8] have been investigated, however, these studies are based on simply applying $AS$ or $ACS$ on the multiprocessor, ie. the parallelization strategies simply share the computation load over several processors. No experiments demonstrate the sum of the computation time for all processors can be reduced compared with the single processor works on the $AS$ or $ACS$.

N. Zhong et al. (Eds.): ISMIS 2003, LNAI 2871, pp. 279–284, 2003.

In this paper, we apply the concept of parallel processing to the Ant Colony System $(ACS)$ and a *Parallel Ant Colony System* $(PACS)$ is proposed. The purpose of the $PACS$ is not just to reduce the computation time. Rather a parallel formulation is developed which gives not only reduces the elapsed and the computation time but also obtains a better solution. The artificial ants are firstly generated and separated into several groups. The Ant Colony System is then applied to each group and communication between groups is applied according to some fixed cycles. The basic idea of the communication is to update the pheromone level for each route according to the best route found by neighbouring groups or, in some cases, all groups. Three communication methods are proposed for $PACS$. Experimental results based on the traveling salesman problem confirm the efficiency and effectiveness of the proposed $PACS$.

## 2   Parallel Ant Colony System

A parallel computer consists of a large number of processing elements which can be dedicated to solving a single problem at a time. Pipeline processing and data parallelism are two popular parallel processing methods. Data parallelism has been applied to genetic algorithms by dividing the population into several groups and running the same algorithm over each group using different processor [9]. The resulting parallel genetic algorithm has been successfully applied to noise reduction of vector quantization based communication [10]. In this paper, we apply the idea of data parallelism to Ant Colony Systems $(ACS)$ in order to reduce running time and obtain a better solution. The Parallel Ant Colony System $(PACS)$ is described as follows:

**Step 1: Initialization** – Generate $N_j$ artificial ants for the $j$th group, $j = 0, 1 \ldots G - 1$. $N_j$ and $G$ are the number of artificial ants for the $j$th group and the number of groups, respectively. Randomly select an initial *city* for each ant. The initial pheromone level between any two cities is set to be a small positive constant $\tau_0$. Set the cycle counter to be 0.

**Step 2: Movement** – Calculate the next visited city $s$ for the $i$th ant in the $j$th group according to

$$s = \begin{cases} arg\ max_{u \in J_{i,j}(r)}[\tau_j(r,u)] \cdot [\eta(r,u)]^\beta & , \ if\ q \leq q_0\ (exploitation) \\ P_{i,j}(r,s) & , \ otherwise\ (biased\ exploration) \end{cases}$$

$$P_{i,j}(r,s) = \begin{cases} \dfrac{[\tau_j(r,s)] \cdot [\eta(r,s)]^\beta}{\sum_{u \in J_k(r)}[\tau_j(r,u)] \cdot [\eta(r,u)]^\beta} & , \ if\ s \in J_{i,j}(r) \\ 0 & , \ otherwise \end{cases}$$

where $P_{i,j}(r,s)$ is the transition probability from city $r$ to city $s$ for the $i$th ant in the $j$th group. $\tau_j(r,s)$ is the pheromone level between city $r$ to city $s$ in the $j$th group. $\eta(r,s) = \frac{1}{\delta(r,s)}$ the inverse of the distance $\delta(r,s)$

between city $r$ and city $s$. $J_{i,j}(r)$ is the set of cities that remain to be visited by the $i$th ant in the $j$th group and $\beta$ is a parameter which determines the relative importance of pheromone level versus distance. $q$ is a random number between 0 and 1 and $q_0$ is a constant between 0 and 1.

**Step 3: Local Pheromone Level Updating Rule** – Update the pheromone level between cities for each group as

$$\tau_j(r, s) \longleftarrow (1 - \rho) \cdot \tau_j(r, s) + \rho \cdot \Delta\tau(r, s)$$

$$\Delta\tau(r, s) = \tau_0 = (n * L_{nn})^{-1}$$

where $\tau_j(r, s)$ is the pheromone level between cities $r$ and $s$ for the ants in the $j$th group, $L_{nn}$ is an approximate distance of the route between all cities using the *Nearest Neighbour Heuristic*, $n$ is the number of cities and $0 < \rho < 1$ is a pheromone decay parameter. Continue Steps 2 and 3 until each ant in each group completes the route.

**Step 4: Evaluation** – Calculate the total length of the route for each ant in each group.

**Step 5: Global Pheromone Level Updating Rule** – Update the pheromone level between cities for each group as

$$\tau_j(r, s) \longleftarrow (1 - \alpha) \cdot \tau_j(r, s) + \alpha \cdot \Delta\tau_j(r, s)$$

$$\Delta\tau_j(r, s) = \begin{cases} (L_j)^{-1} & , \quad if\ (r, s) \in best\ route\ of\ jth\ group \\ 0 & , \quad otherwise \end{cases}$$

where $L_j$ is the shortest length for the ants in the $j$th group and $\alpha$ is a pheromone decay parameter.

**Step 6: Updating from Communication** – Three communication methods are proposed as follows:

- **Method 1:** Update the pheromone level between cities for each group for every $R_1$ cycles as

$$\tau_j(r, s) \longleftarrow \tau_j(r, s) + \lambda \cdot \Delta\tau_{best}(r, s)$$

$$\Delta\tau_{best}(r, s) = \begin{cases} (L_{gb})^{-1} & , \quad if\ (r, s) \in best\ route\ of\ all\ groups \\ 0 & , \quad otherwise \end{cases}$$

where $\lambda$ is a pheromone decay parameter and $L_{gb}$ is the length of the best route of all groups, i.e., $L_{gb} < L_j$, $j = 0, 1 \ldots G - 1$.

- **Method 2:** Update the pheromone level between cities for each group for every $R_2$ cycles as

$$\tau_j(r, s) \longleftarrow \tau_j(r, s) + \lambda \cdot \Delta\tau_{ng}(r, s)$$

$$\Delta\tau_{ng}(r, s) = \begin{cases} (L_{ng})^{-1} & , \quad if \ (r, s) \in best \ route \ of \ neighbour \ group \\ 0 & , \quad otherwise \end{cases}$$

where neighbour is defined as being the group whose binary representation of the group number $j$ differs by the least significant bit. $\lambda$ is a pheromone decay parameter and $L_{ng}$ is the length of the shortest route in the neighbour group.

- **Method 3:** Update the pheromone level between cities for each group using both Method 1 and Method 2.

**Step 7: Termination** – Increment the cycle counter. Move the ants to the originally selected cities and continue Steps 2 to 6 until the stagnation or a present maximum number of cycles has reached, where a stagnation indicated by all ants taking the same route.

## 3   Experimental Results

Experiments were carried out to test the performance of the Ant System ($AS$), Ant Colony System ($ACS$) and Parallel Ant Colony System ($PACS$) for the traveling salesman problem. Three generally available and typical data sets, EIL101, ST70 and TSP225 were used as the test material[1]. EIL101, ST70 and TSP225 are data sets with 101, 70 and 225 cities, respectively. The number of ants for $AS$, $ACS$ and $PACS$ was set to be 80, with the ants divided into 4 groups of 20 for $PACS$. All results shown are averaged over 5 runs. The parameters were set to the following values: $\beta = 2$, $q_0 = 0.9$, $\alpha = \rho = \lambda = 0.1$. The number of cycles between updates of the pheromone level from communication for methods 1 and 2 in $PACS$ were set to 80 and 30, respectively.

The data sets for the first and second experiment were EIL101 and ST70. We recorded the shortest length of the route for a fixed running time of 300 secs. The TSP225 data set was used for the third experiment and the shortest length of the route for an execution time of 600 secs was recorded. $PACS$ with method 1, method 2 and method 3 for communication are referred to as $PACS1$, $PACS2$ and $PACS3$, respectively. The experimental results of the data sets EIL101 for one seed are shown in Figure 1. The experimental results shown in Table 1 are the average shortest length over 5 runs for all data sets.

---

[1] available from *http://www.iwr.uniheidelberg.de/groups/comopt/software/*

The average improvement on three data sets for the proposed $PACS1$, $PACS2$ and $PACS3$ compared with $ACS$ was 4.17%, 4.11% and 4.35%, respectively. Compared with $AS$, the $PACS1$, $PACS2$ and $PACS3$ shows improvements of 9.32%, 9.27% and 9.49%, respectively.

**Table 1.** Performance Comparison of the shortest length for Three Datasets

| Data sets | $AS$ | $ACS$ | $PACS1$ | $PACS2$ | $PACS3$ |
|---|---|---|---|---|---|
| EIL101 | 718.5917 | 670.8689 | 646.4660 | 648.6656 | 645.9640 |
| TSP225 | 4536.8308 | 4199.8483 | 3939.4237 | 3934.4802 | 3916.0839 |
| ST70 | 711.4132 | 696.1061 | 677.4363 | 677.1765 | 678.5531 |

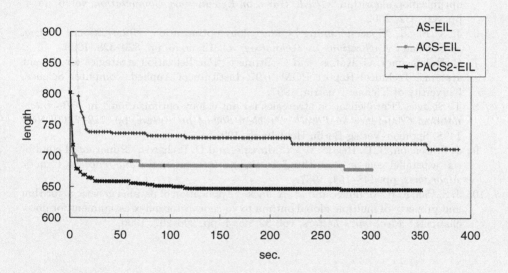

**Fig. 1.** Performance Comparison of $AS$, $ACS$, $PACS2$ for EIL101.tsp data sets

## 4 Conclusions

The main contribution of this paper is to propose a parallel formulation for the Ant Colony System ($ACS$). Three communication methods between groups which can be used to update the pheromone levels are presented. From our experiments, the proposed Parallel Ant Colony System ($PACS$) outperforms both $ACS$ and AS based on three available traveling salesman data sets. We will continue to work on new communication strategy for updating the pheromone level in $PACS$ and we are interested in applying the $PACS$ to data clustering in future.

# References

1. A. Colorni, M. Dorigo, and V. Maniezzo, "Distributed optimization by ant colonies," in *First Europ. Conference Artificial Life* (F. Varela and P. Bourgine, eds.), pp. 134–142, 1991.
2. M. Dorigo, V. Maniezzo, and A. Colorni, "Ant system: optimization by a colony of cooperating agents," *IEEE Trans. on Systems, Man, and Cybernetics-Part B: Cybernetics*, vol. 26, no. 1, pp. 29–41, 1996.
3. J. M. Dorigo and L. M. Gambardella, "Ant colony system: a cooperative learning approach to the traveling salesman problem," *IEEE Trans. on Evolutionary Computation*, vol. 1, no. 1, pp. 53–66, 1997.
4. V. Maniezzo and A. Colorni, "The ant system applied to the quadratic assignment problem," *IEEE Trans. on Knowledge and Data Engineering*, vol. 11, no. 5, pp. 769–778, 1999.
5. R. S. Parpinelli, H. S. Lopes, and A. A. Freitas, "Data mining with an ant colony optimization algorithm," *IEEE Trans. on Evolutionary Computation*, vol. 6, no. 4, pp. 321–332, 2002.
6. J. A. Bland, "Space-planning by ant colony optimization," *International Journal of Computer Applications in Technology*, vol. 12, no. 6, pp. 320–328, 1999.
7. B. Bullnheimer, G. Kotsis, and C. Strauss, "Parallelization strategies for the ant system," Technical Report POM 9/97, Institute of Applied Computer Science, University of Vienna, Austria, 1997.
8. T. Stutzle, "Parallelization strategies for ant colony optimization," in *Fifth International Conference on Parallel Problem Soving for Nature*, pp. 722–731, LNCS 1498, Springer-Verlag Berlin Heidelberg, 1998.
9. J. P. Cohoon, S. U. Hegde, W. N. Martine, and D. Richards, "Punctuated equilibria: a parallel genetic algorithm," in *Second International Conference on Genetic Algorithms*, pp. 148–154, 1987.
10. J. S. Pan, F. R. McInnes, and M. A. Jack, "Application of parallel genetic algorithm and property of multiple global optima to vq codevector index assignment for noisy channels," *Electronics Letters*, vol. 32, no. 4, pp. 296–297, 1996.

# Some Case-Refinement Strategies for Case-Based Criminal Summary Judgments

Chao-Lin Liu and Tseng-Chung Chang

Department of Computer Science, National Chengchi University
Taipei 11605, Taiwan
chaolin@nccu.edu.tw

**Abstract.** We report means for simplifying case instances in a case-based reasoning system for criminal summary judgments in Taiwan. We merge similar case instances, remove irrelevant terms, and weight important terms. The best method combination reduces the size of the case database by more than 60% of the most complete case database while maintaining the classification quality at about 80%.

## 1 Introduction

Case-based reasoning (CBR) has been applied to intelligent systems for legal informatics since more than ten years ago [3], and real systems have been put into work, e.g., CATO applies CBR for helping students to practice argument formulation [2]. Unfortunately, except the existence of some databases that offer legal information in Chinese [1], there has not been any reported attempt to actively apply these on-line information sources for applications such as computer-assisted sentencing [7] and drafting [4]. This paper reports some experiences in creating more compact and more representative case databases based on our previous experience in applying CBR to criminal summary judgments in which one defendant commits only one crime [5].

Section 2 outlines background information for computer-assisted criminal summary judgments using Chinese documents. Section 3 presents how we obtain and apply cases from documents for previously closed lawsuits. Section 4 elaborates strategies for making the case database in our CBR system more compact yet maintaining system's quality of classification. Section 5 presents and discusses experimental results of applying our CBR methods to the lawsuit classification problem.

## 2 Background

Criminal summary judgment (CSJ) is a special section in criminal judgment. Lawsuits that are judged in the CSJ courts are relatively simple than those judged in full scaled criminal courts. Public prosecutors institute a lawsuit against the defendant by issuing a prosecution document, and judges publicize whether the defendants should be sentenced by issuing a judgment document.

N. Zhong et al. (Eds.): ISMIS 2003, LNAI 2871, pp. 285–291, 2003.

The prosecution documents contain a section that describes the defendants' criminal activities found by the prosecutors. The following Chinese excerpt extracted from a prosecution document describes a drunk driver who caused a traffic accident. For privacy consideration, we replaced names with "〇", and improvised plate numbers.

吳〇〇於民國九十年十月二十七日上午十時十分許，在某ＫＴＶ店內服用酒類，致
其反應能力降低，已不能安全駕駛動力交通工具後，仍駕駛車號ＨＹ－１２３４號
自用小客車沿板橋市文化路往台北方向行駛，在行經臺北縣板橋市文化路與站前路
路口時，撞及自對向車道駛來，欲左轉站前路，由林〇〇所駕駛之Ｚ３－５６７８
號自用小客車，嗣經警方處理，對吳〇〇施以酒精測試，其測定值為０．八五ＭＧ
／Ｌ，始循線查知上情。

The judgment documents also contain a section that describes the defendants' related activities found by the judges and their assistants. For convenience, we call the section that describes the defendants' activities, whether found by the prosecutors or the judges, by the section of the alleged criminal action (SACA). In addition to SACA, the judgment documents include the judges' decisions over the lawsuits.

Our system attempts to determine the prosecution reason, assuming the truth of the information in the SACA of the prosecution document. The system categorizes test lawsuits into 13 classes of CSJs, including the "unknown" class. Putting a test lawsuit into the "unknown" class is to show that the classifier knows its limitation. We achieve this by building a CBR system using documents for closed lawsuits, and use the cases in the CBR for classifying future lawsuits [5].

# 3   Case Construction and Applications

## 3.1   Case Generation

Due to the page limits, we could not provide sufficient details about the generation process. In short, we convert the SACA of each training lawsuit into a sequence of keywords, use each such a sequence as a case instance, and assign the prosecution reason or the training lawsuit to this case instance. The ordering of the keywords is an important aspect in applying the cases. Given the Chinese text that appeared in Section 2.1, we create the following keyword sequence. For more details, please refer to our previous work [5].

內服 反應 能力 降低 不能 安全駕駛 動力 交通工具 車道 左轉 駕駛 自用
客車 警方 處理 施以 酒精 測試 測定

## 3.2   Case Applications

Given a set of instances generated by methods discussed in Section 3.1, we can apply the $k$-Nearest-Neighbor principle for classification. To this end, we must define a measure for "similarity" so that we can establish the notion of nearest neighbors of the current lawsuit [5].

Hence, we convert the SACA of the current lawsuit into an ordered list using the same method for generating instances. This ordered list, $X$, is then compared with each prior case, $Y$. Taking the order of keywords into consideration, the comparison will find the number of common keywords that appear in the same order in both $X$ and $Y$. Let $OCW$ be a function that will return the number of ordered, common words in its input word lists, and $Counts$ be a function that will return the number of words in its input word list. The similarity between the current lawsuit and a prior case of the second type is defined as follows.

$$s(X,Y)=\frac{1}{2}\left(\frac{OCW(X,Y)}{Counts(X)}+\frac{OCW(X,Y)}{Counts(Y)}\right) \tag{1}$$

## 4  Case Refinement

We report three different methods for refining the case database, and compare the resulting performances experimentally in Section 5.

### 4.1  Merging Similar Cases

The first alternative is to identify similar case instances, and somehow merge them into one case. Clearly not all our machine-generated cases are required, and, if we can identify and keep those that are more representative than others, we may achieve the same accuracy of classification at reduced computational costs.

To this end, we must define a measure for "similarity" for merging instances. Since our original instances are already tagged with the classes, i.e., the prosecution reasons, we can merge case instances with the same classes. Let $X$ and $Y$ be two such machine-generated instances. We define the overlapping portion, $Com(X,Y)$, of $X$ and $Y$ to be the ordered common keywords in $X$ and $Y$. $Merge2Instances$ determines how to merge (or not to merge) two given instances, where $p$ is a percentage threshold selected by the instance database manager. Let IDB be the instance database that contains the instances being considered to merge, I[j] be the j[th] instance in the IDB, and S be current number of instance in the IDB. We use $MergeAllInstances$ to merge all instances in the IDB [5]. Notice that S may decrease as we remove instances from the IDB when we call $Merge2Instances$.

```
Procedure MergeAllInstances(IDB)
S = current size of the IDB
do { for j = 1 to S-1
        for k = j+1 to S
            Merge2Instances(I[j], I[k]);
    } while (new cases were added to the IDB);
Procedure Merge2Instances(X, Y)
if (OCW(X, Y)≥p*Counts(X)) and (OCW(X, Y)≥p*Counts(Y))) {
  Remove X and Y from the instance database;
  Add COM(X, Y) into the instance database; }
else if ((OCW(X, Y)<p*Counts(X)) and (OCW(X, Y)≥p*Counts(Y)))
```

```
    Remove Y from the instance database;
else if (OCW(X,Y)≥p*Counts(X)) and OCW(X,Y)<p*Counts(Y))
    Remove X from the instance database;
```

## 4.2   Removing Irrelevant Terms

The second alternative is to remove irrelevant keywords in cases. We define relevancy in a way similar to the term-frequency-inverse-document-frequency used in the information retrieval community [6]. Assume that there are $n(c)$ instances tagged with the $c^{th}$ prosecution reason, that each distinct keyword is assigned an ID number, and that $k(m,c)$ be the total number of times the $m^{th}$ distinct keyword appears in instances in the $c^{th}$ prosecution reason. We define the average occurrence frequency (AOF) of the $m^{th}$ keyword appearing in lawsuits under the $c^{th}$ prosecution reason by $AOF(m,c) = k(m,c)/n(c)$. We remove the $g^{th}$ keyword from case instances with the $c^{th}$ prosecution reason, if the keyword meets the following two conditions: (1) $AOF(g,c) \leq r$, and (2) the $g^{th}$ keyword also appears in case instances with a different prosecution reason. In other words, we remove keywords that are both relatively infrequent and may suggest more than one prosecution reasons. We will set $r$ to some possible values in our experiments. After we remove the irrelevant keywords from the case instances, we apply them with the method described in Section 3.2.

## 4.3   Weighting Important Terms

Instead of removing irrelevant words, we can weight keywords differently in (1) so that more important words have stronger influences on the lawsuit classification. Keywords are weighted using the following assignment steps. In (1), each keyword has the same weight, i.e. 1. We add extra weights to the keywords using the following procedure.

```
    1.  Compute AOF(m,c) for all mᵗʰ keywords and all cᵗʰ prosecution
        reasons.
    2.  Compute the average AOF, denoted  AAOF(c), of all keywords
        that appear in case instances with the cᵗʰ prosecution rea-
        son for all c.
    3.  If ( AOF(m,c)≤0.3 ) Set EW(m,c) to 0
        else if (the keyword does not appear in instances with
                other prosecution reasons) Set EW(m,c) to  AOF(m,c)
        else if ( AOF(m,c)≤0.75×AAOF(c) ) Set EW(m,c) to  AOF(m,c)
        else Set EW(m,c) to 0
```

At step 3, we add no extra weights to infrequent keywords, which has small AOFs. We add no extra weights to a keyword, if it has an above-the-average AOF and it is related to multiple prosecution reasons. If the keyword is related to multiple prosecution reasons, but has only median AOF, we use its AOF as its extra weight. Currently, the parameters of the procedure, i.e., 0.3 and 0.75, are set arbitrarily at seemingly reasonable levels.

When we compute the similarity, in (1), between a future lawsuit and a case instance with the $c^{th}$ prosecution reason, we use $1 + EW(m,c)$ as the weight for the $m^{th}$ keyword that appear in $X$ and $Y$.

## 5  Experimental Results

We compared classification quality for the three methods for refining case database. In addition to applications of the three basic methods, we refined the case database with their combination. Our system classified test lawsuits into twelve groups ($C_1$-$C_{12}$) and possibly the unknown group ($C_{13}$). We obtained two seasons of documents for CSJs. We used the documents for lawsuits occurred in the first season as the training data, and tested the resulting system with the lawsuits that occurred in the second season. Table 1 shows the amount of cases.

**Table 1.** Statistics of case quantities

|          | $C_1$ | $C_2$ | $C_3$ | $C_4$ | $C_5$ | $C_6$ | $C_7$ | $C_8$ | $C_9$ | $C_{10}$ | $C_{11}$ | $C_{12}$ | $C_{13}$ |
|----------|-----|-----|-----|-----|-----|-----|-----|-----|-----|------|------|------|------|
| Season 1 | 158 | 26 | 30 | 14 | 99 | 15 | 9 | 15 | 19 | 16 | 19 | 9 | 74 |
| Season 2 | 142 | 19 | 39 | 15 | 139 | 24 | 11 | 21 | 23 | 7 | 25 | 11 | 27 |

We applied the k-Nearest-Neighbor method for determining the prosecution reasons of the test lawsuits. Rather than selecting a particular $k$, we set a threshold for determining which prior cases could vote for the test lawsuit. For experiments that did not use extra weights for keywords, the threshold was 0.3; otherwise, it was 0.4. Only prior cases whose similarity scores exceeded the threshold could cast the votes. The prosecution reason that received the most number of votes became the prosecution reason of the test lawsuit. If there were multiple winning prosecution reasons, we compared the exact total similarity scores for these winning prosecution reasons, and the one that had the highest score won.

We evaluated the performance with the F measure with $\beta=0.5$ because we considered precision to be more important than recall in the task [6]. A misclassified lawsuit may demand more human power to correct the error than an unclassified lawsuit would require. For each prosecution reason, we computed the precision and recall, and then obtained the F measure, $f_i$. Let $c_i$ be the case amount of prosecution reason $C_i$, the performance measure WF was calculated by $\sum_{i=1}^{13} c_i f_i / \sum_{i=1}^{13} c_i$ [5].

Table 2 shows the WF values of two sets of experiments. The "Merging" row shows the results of applying only the merging procedure discussed in Section 4.1 to the case database that was created from the documents for lawsuits occurred in the first season. When $p=1$, there is no merging operation at all. One can observe that the number of remaining case instances continued to drop as we increased $p$. The results in Table 2 indicate that we may maintain classification quality above 85% as long as we merge case instances modestly ($p \geq 0.5$). For comparison purpose, we have a set of 24 human-constructed cases for assigning prosecution reasons, and the performance of this set of cases was 88%. Cases provided by human experts are clearly more effective. Adding extra weights, as described in Section 4.3, did not seem to help or hurt the performance as suggested by the last row of Table 2.

**Table 2.** Merging reduces number of case instances at no extra costs

| $p$ | 1 | 0.7 | 0.6 | 0.5 | 0.4 | 0.3 | 0.2 |
|---|---|---|---|---|---|---|---|
| Number of cases | 429 | 283 | 215 | 136 | 92 | 47 | 18 |
| Merging | 88% | 88% | 88% | 87% | 83% | 71% | 62% |
| Merging+Weighting | 87% | 88% | 87% | 86% | 85% | 73% | 62% |

We conducted a test for checking the effects of the keyword removing procedure, as described in Section 4.2. We varied the parameter from r=0.5 to r=3. The resulting performance did not change significantly, and hanged between 85% and 88%.

The charts in Fig. 1 show the results of a particular combination of the merging, weighting, and removing operations. We removed irrelevant keywords before we merged case instances. We use r=0 to indicate the situation when we did not remove keywords at all.

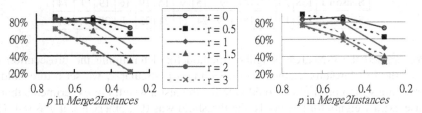

**Fig. 1.** The vertical axes show the WF of each experiment. The left chart shows the results of weighting all keywords equally, and the right chart the results of assigning extra weights to selected keywords. Curves for r=2 and r=3 almost overlap in both charts

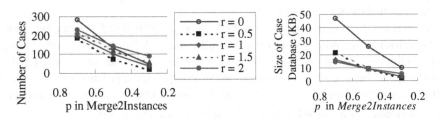

**Fig. 2.** Removing common keywords refined the case database

Not surprisingly, the performance degraded as we removed keywords and merged case instances more and more aggressively. Curves for r=0 and r=0.5 suggest that removing keywords conservatively will not hurt the performance of the classifier significantly, while we do not merge case instances aggressively at the same time. This offers a great chance for us to simplify the case instances and reducing number of case instances while maintaining the classification performance. Curves for r=2 and

$r$=3 suggest that the weighting procedure helped to slow the degradation in performance when we aggressively removed keywords from the case instances.

Maintaining the performance while simplifying the case instances means that we can save both time for computation and space for storing case instances. Charts in Fig. 2 show how much storage we had saved by removing common keywords from case instances. Because the case instances became increasingly different as we removed common keywords, the number of resulting case instances increased as we increased $r$. Nevertheless, the sizes of the resulting databases did not grow. Fig. 1 shows that, for the combination r=0.5 and p=0.7, our system achieved almost the same performance as it did when it used the case database directly trained from the lawsuits. Fig. 2 shows that, using this combination, the case database occupied 21 Kbytes, just a bit below one third the size of the original case database.

## 6  Conclusion

We have reported methods for refining the case instances while maintaining the classification quality at a satisfactory level. The techniques can be applied to computer-supported case-instance generation for legal informatics.

**Acknowledgements.** We thank the anonymous reviewers for their invaluable comments, but we could not follow all the comments partially due to page limits. We also thank Judge Jim-How Ho for being our consultant on legal knowledge. This research was support in part by Grant NSC-91-2213-E-004-013 from the National Science Council of Taiwan.

## References

1.   The Judicial Yuan (wjirs.judicial.gov.tw/jirs/); The Legislative Yuan (www.ly.gov.tw); The Ministry of Justice (www.moj.gov.tw); Lawbank Information Inc. (www.lawbank.com.tw); www.ordos.nm.cn/haoxia/navigation/zhengfa.htm
2.   Aleven, V. *Teaching Case-Based Argumentation Through a Model and Examples*, Ph.D. Dissertation, University of Pittsburgh, Pittsburgh, Ohio, USA  (1997).
3.   Ashley, K. D. *Modeling Legal Argument: Reasoning with Cases and Hypotheticals*, MIT Press, 1990.
4.   Branting, L. K, Lester, J., and Callaway, C. Automating judicial document drafting: A discourse-based approach. *AI & Law*, 6(2-4), 111–149, 1998.
5.   Liu, C.-L., Chang, C.-T., and Ho, J.-H., Classification and clustering for case-based criminal summary judgments, *Proc. of the 9$^{th}$ Int'l Conf. on AI and Law* (2003), to appear.
6.   Manning, C. D. and Schutze, H. *Foundations of Statistical Natural Language Processing*, The MIT Press, 1999.
7.   Schild, U. J. Intelligent computer systems for criminal sentencing, *Proc. of the 5$^{th}$ Int'l Conf. on AI and Law*, (1995), 229–238.

# G-STRIPS – A Generalized STRIPS System for Handling State Change over Dynamic Domains

Yan Zhang and Yun Bai

School of Computing and Information Technology
University of Western Sydney
Penrith South DC, NSW 1797, Australia
{yan,ybai}@cit.uws.edu.au

**Abstract.** State change is an essential issue in robotic dynamics modeling. In this paper, we investigate this issue over *dynamic domains* in the sense that an object in the domain may be created or destroyed by executing some plan of the system. It is observed that current logic based dynamic systems, e.g. the STRIPS-like systems, are semantically problematic to deal with dynamic domains in state change. It turns out that representing nonexisting objects in a logic system becomes a key point to handle this problem. Based on this observation, we define $N$-structures for an arbitrary first order language where syntactic terms are allowed to denote nonexisting objects with respect to the domain of quantification. Using $N$-structures to model dynamic domains, we then generalize classical STRIPS to G-STRIPS which can represent and reason about state change involving creation or destruction of objects. We also specify a provably correct semantics for a class of G-STRIPS systems based on $N$-structures.

**Keywords:** Reasoning about change, commonsense reasoning, knowledge representation, logic of AI

## 1 Introduction

Given a dynamic system, state change occurs over the domain of the system if some plan of the system is executed. Conventionally, the domain of a system may be viewed as a collection of objects dealt with in the system activities. For example, in a dynamic system of modeling a blocks world, the domain of the system could include objects of a number of blocks and a table, and effects of the system operators may change positions or colors of these blocks. By examing current logic based dynamic systems, e.g. [8,5], it is clear that these systems only deal with *static domains* in state change where objects in the domain of a system are usually fixed from the beginning and system operators may just change objects' properties (e.g. paint block $A$ to red color) or relationships among different objects (e.g. move block $A$ onto block $B$). However, in many situations, the domain of a system may change from time to time. For instance, a tower may be built from three individual blocks. But before the proper plan of building a tower is performed, there was no such object named *tower* in the domain. Also,

N. Zhong et al. (Eds.): ISMIS 2003, LNAI 2871, pp. 292–296, 2003.

after burning a letter, the object named *letter* does not exist in the domain any more.

In this paper, we investigate state change over *dynamic domains* in the sense that an object in the domain may be created (e.g. building a tower from individual blocks) or destroyed (e.g. burning a letter) by executing some plan of the system. It is observed that current logic based dynamic systems, e.g. the STRIPS-like systems, are semantically problematic to deal with dynamic domains in state change. It turns out that representing nonexisting objects in a logic system becomes a key issue to handle this problem. Our idea is to propose non-classical structures, named $N$-structures, for an arbitrary first order language where syntactic terms are allowed to denote nonexisting objects with respect to domains of quantification of the structures. Using $N$-structures to model dynamic domains, we show how the classical STRIPS can be generalized to G-STRIPS which can represent and reason about state change involving creation or destruction of objects.

## 2    State Change, Domains, and Nonexisting Objects

In this section, throughout a particular example, we examine the semantic problem caused by state change over dynamic domains within the classical STRIPS formalism.

We start with an arbitrary first order language $\mathcal{L}$. Following Lifschitz's specification on STRIPS [4], a *world description* is a finite set of sentences of $\mathcal{L}$. A *state* of a world description is a structure of $\mathcal{L}$ in which each sentence of the world description is true. An *operator description* is a triple $(P, D, A)$, where $P$ is a sentence of $\mathcal{L}$ (i.e. the *precondition*), and $D$ and $A$ are finite sets of sentences of $\mathcal{L}$ (i.e. the *delete-list* and *add-list*).

A *STRIPS system* is then defined as $\Sigma = (W_0, \{(P_\alpha, D_\alpha, A_\alpha)\}_{\alpha \in OP})$, where $W_0$ is the *initial world description*, $OP$ is a set of operators and each $\alpha$ in $OP$ is associated with its precondition $P_\alpha$, delete-list $D_\alpha$ and add-list $A_\alpha$. We also assume that the initial world description $W_0$ may contain some *constraints* that should *not* be included in any operator's delete-list.

Given a STRIPS system $\Sigma$, a *plan* is defined to be any finite sequence of its operators. Each plan $\overline{\alpha} = <\alpha_1, \cdots, \alpha_k>$ defines a sequence of world descriptions $W_0, W_1, \cdots, W_k$, where $W_0$ is the initial world description and $W_i = (W_{i-1} - D_{\alpha_i}) \cup A_{\alpha_i}$, $(i = 1, \cdots, k)$. A plan $\overline{\alpha} = <\alpha_1, \cdots, \alpha_k>$ is *acceptable* by $\Sigma$ if $W_{i-1} \models P_{\alpha_i}$ $(i = 1, \cdots, k)$. A sentence (*goal*) $G$ is *achieved* by a plan $\overline{\alpha} = <\alpha_1, \cdots, \alpha_k>$ of $\Sigma$ if $\overline{\alpha}$ is acceptable by $\Sigma$ and $W_k \models G$. The *domain* of $\Sigma$ at world description $W$ is usually viewed as a collection of all possible objects that are dealt with in $W$. Sometimes, if the world description is not specifically interested in our context, we also say the domain of $\Sigma$ without indicating the specific world description.

Now we define $N$-structures for an arbitrary first order language $\mathcal{L}$ where syntactic terms are allowed to denote nonexisting objects with respect to the domain of quantification.

**Definition 1.** *A $N$-structure $M$ of $\mathcal{L}$ is any ordered pair $(D, \mathcal{F})$, where $D$ is a set of objects (to be called the* domain*) and $\mathcal{F}$ is a unary function such that:*

*(i)  $\mathcal{F}$ is total to assign every n-placed predicate symbol $P$ a set of ordered n-placed tuples of elements of $D$;*

*(ii)  $\mathcal{F}$ is partial to assign every defined ground term an element of $D$;*

**Definition 2.** *Given a N-structure $M = (D, \mathcal{F})$, a primary assignment $\alpha_M$ in $M$ is a partial unary function from the set of sentences of $\mathcal{L}$ to $\{\mathrm{T},\ \mathrm{F}\}$ such that*

*(i)  if $\varphi$ is of the form $P(a_1, \cdots, a_n)$ and $\mathcal{F}(a_i)$ is defined for every $i$ ($1 \leq i \leq n$), then $\alpha_M(\varphi) = \mathrm{T}$ if $(\mathcal{F}(a_1), \cdots, \mathcal{F}(a_n)) \in \mathcal{F}(P)$, and otherwise $\alpha_M(\varphi) = \mathrm{F}$;*

*(ii)  (a) if $\varphi$ is of the form $a = b$ and both $\mathcal{F}(a)$ and $\mathcal{F}(b)$ are defined, then $\alpha_M(\varphi) = \mathrm{T}$ if $\mathcal{F}(a) = \mathcal{F}(b)$, and otherwise $\alpha_M(\varphi) = \mathrm{F}$; (b) if $\varphi$ is of the form $a = b$ and exactly one of $\mathcal{F}(a)$ and $\mathcal{F}(b)$ is defined, then $\alpha_M(\varphi) = \mathrm{F}$;*

*(iii)  for any other $\varphi$, $\alpha_M(\varphi)$ is not defined.*

**Definition 3.** *Given a N-structure $M = (D, \mathcal{F})$, a completion of $M$ is a N-structure $M' = (D', \mathcal{F}')$ such that*

*(i)  $D \subseteq D'$;*

*(ii)  for any predicate symbol $P$, $\mathcal{F}(P) \subseteq \mathcal{F}'(P)$;*

*(iii)  for every individual ground term $a$, $\mathcal{F}'(a)$ is defined and $\mathcal{F}'(a) = \mathcal{F}(a)$ if $\mathcal{F}(a)$ is also defined.*

Intuitively, a completion $M'$ of $M$ is a classical structure in which every ground term is defined, and for a term that is defined in $M$, its interpretation in $M'$ is consistent to that in $M$. For a given $N$-structure $M$, $M$ may have many different completions. We denote the set of all completions of $M$ as $Comp(M)$.

**Definition 4.** *Let $M = (D, \mathcal{F})$ be a N-structure, $M' = (D', \mathcal{F}')$ a completion of $M$. A supplementary assignment $\alpha_{M,M'}$ in $M$ with respect to completion $M'$ is a total unary function from the set of sentences of $\mathcal{L}$ to $\{\mathrm{T}, \mathrm{F}\}$ such that*

*(i)  if $\varphi$ is atomic and $\alpha_M(\varphi)$ is defined, then $\alpha_{M,M'}(\varphi) = \alpha_M(\varphi)$;*

*(ii)  if $\varphi$ is atomic and $\alpha_M(\varphi)$ is not defined, then $\alpha_{M,M'}(\varphi) = \alpha_{M'}(\varphi)$;*

*(iii)  if $\varphi$ is of the form $\neg\psi$, then $\alpha_{M,M'}(\varphi) = \mathrm{T}$ iff $\alpha_{M,M'}(\psi) = \mathrm{F}$, and otherwise $\alpha_{M,M'}(\varphi) = \mathrm{F}$;*

*(iv)  if $\varphi$ is of the form $\psi \wedge v$, then $\alpha_{M,M'}(\varphi) = \mathrm{T}$ iff $\alpha_{M,M'}(\psi) = \alpha_{M,M'}(v) = \mathrm{T}$, and otherwise $\alpha_{M,M'}(\varphi) = \mathrm{F}$;*

*(v)  if $\varphi$ is of the form $\forall x\psi$ then $\alpha_{M,M'}(\varphi) = \mathrm{T}$ iff $\alpha_{M,M'}(\psi_x[a]) = \mathrm{T}$ for every individual ground term $a$ such that $\mathcal{F}(a)$ is defined, and otherwise $\alpha_{M,M'}(\varphi) = \mathrm{F}$.*

**Definition 5.** *Let $M = (D, \mathcal{F})$ be a N-structure, and $Comp(M)$ the set of all completions of $M$. The assignment $\alpha_M^*$ in $M$ is a partial unary function from the set of sentences of $\mathcal{L}$ to $\{\mathrm{T}, \mathrm{F}\}$ such that*

*(i)  $\alpha_M^*(\varphi) = \mathrm{T}$ iff $\alpha_{M,M'}(\varphi) = \mathrm{T}$ for every completion $M'$ of $M$ in $Comp(M)$;*

*(ii)  $\alpha_M^*(\varphi) = \mathrm{F}$ iff $\alpha_{M,M'}(\varphi) = \mathrm{F}$ for every completion $M'$ of $M$ in $Comp(M)$;*

*(iii)  $\alpha_M^*(\varphi)$ is not defined in all other cases.*

**Definition 6.** *A sentence $\varphi$ is $N$-satisfiable iff there exists some $N$-structure $M$ such that $\alpha_M^*(\varphi) =$ T. $\varphi$ is $N$-invalid iff there exists some $N$-structure $M$, either $\alpha_M^*(\varphi) =$ F or $\alpha_M^*(\varphi)$ is not defined. $\varphi$ is $N$-valid, denoted as $\models_N \varphi$, iff $\varphi$ is not $N$-invalid.*

As mentioned earlier, a specific $N$-structure is usually associated with a set of ground terms in which only terms in the set are defined. Sometimes, as will be seen in next section, it is important to decide the $N$-satisfaction of a set of sentences in a $N$-structure with a fixed set of defined terms. We define a $N$-*theory* to be a pair $<T, C>$, where $T$ is a set of sentences and $C$ is a nonempty set of ground terms of $\mathcal{L}$.

**Definition 7.** *Given a $N$-theory $<T, C>$. $M$ is a $N$-model of $<T, C>$ if*

(i)   *every ground term in $C$ is defined in $M$ and all other ground terms of $\mathcal{L}$ are not defined in $M$;*

(ii)  *every sentence of $T$ is $N$-satisfied in $M$.*

$<T, C>$ is *finite* if both $T$ and $C$ are finite sets. A sentence $\varphi$ is $N$-*entailed by* $<T, C>$, denoted as $<T, C> \models_N \varphi$, if $\varphi$ is $N$-satisfied in every $N$-model of $<T, C>$.

# 3   A Generalized STRIPS System

In this section, we extend the classical STRIPS to a Generalized STRIPS, denoted as G-STRIPS, which overcomes the difficulty of STRIPS over dynamic domains.

We still start with an arbitrary first order language $\mathcal{L}$. We extend a *world description* to be a finite $N$-theory $<W, C_W>$. A *state* $S_W$ of $<W, C_W>$ is a $N$-model of $<W, C_W>$. An *operator description* is a tuple $(P, D, A, C_D, C_A)$, where $P$, $D$ and $A$ are defined as previously, and $C_D$ and $C_A$, which are called *destroyed-object-list* and *created-object-list* respectively, are finite sets of ground terms of $\mathcal{L}$ associated with delete-list $D$ and add-list $A$ respectively. Each element of $C_D$ denotes an object that is destroyed by the operator specified as $(P, D, A, C_D, C_A)$, while each element of $C_A$ denotes an object that is created by this operator. Now a *G-STRIPS system* $\Sigma^g$ is then defined as

$$\Sigma^g = (< W_0, C_{W_0} >, \{(P_\alpha, D_\alpha, A_\alpha, C_{D\alpha}, C_{A\alpha})\}_{\alpha \in OP}),$$

where $<W_0, C_{W_0}>$ is the initial world description, $OP$ is a set of operators and each $\alpha$ in $OP$ is associated with its precondition $P_\alpha$, delete-list $D_\alpha$, add-list $A_\alpha$, destroyed-object-list $C_{D\alpha}$, and created-object-list $C_{A\alpha}$. A *plan* $\overline{\alpha} = <\alpha_1, \cdots, \alpha_k>$ defines a sequence of world descriptions $<W_0, C_{W_0}>$, $\cdots$, $<W_k, C_{W_k}>$, where $<W_0, C_{W_0}>$ is the initial world description and $W_i = (W_{i-1} - D_{\alpha_i}) \cup A_{\alpha_i}$, $C_{W_i} = (C_{W_{i-1}} - C_{D\alpha_i}) \cup C_{A\alpha_i}$, $(i = 1, \cdots, k)$. A plan $\overline{\alpha} = <\alpha_1, \cdots, \alpha_k>$ is *acceptable* by $\Sigma^g$ if $<W_{i-1}, C_{W_{i-1}}> \models_N P_{\alpha_i}$ $(i = 1, \cdots, k)$. A sentence (*goal*) $G$ is *achieved* by a plan $\overline{\alpha} = <\alpha_1, \cdots, \alpha_k>$ of $\Sigma^g$ if $\overline{\alpha}$ is acceptable by $\Sigma^g$ and $<W_k, C_{W_k}> \models_N G$. Finally, the *domain* of $\Sigma^g$ associated with world description $<W, C_W>$ is a collection of all objects denoted by elements of $C_W$.

# 4    Concluding Remarks

We have observed that current logic based dynamic systems cannot deal with state change over dynamic domains properly due to the fact that classical first order structures are inappropriate to model dynamic domains. From our observation, we argued that representing nonexisting objects in a logic system is a key issue to handle dynamic domains in state change. Our approach then was to propose non-classical $N$-structures for an arbitrary first order language where syntactic terms of the language are allowed to denote some nonexisting objects with respect to the domain of such structures. Based on $N$-structures, we extended classical STRIPS to G-STRIPS whcih can represent and reason about state change involving creation or destruction of objects.

We should mention that *Free logic* has been studied in philosophical logics [1] in which terms can denote somethings that are not in the universe. Nevertheless, to the best of our knowledge, there is no detailed study on how free logic can be applied in reasoning about state change, it is not clear to us yet whether we can directly use free logic to achieve our purpose addressed in this paper. In this sense, it appears that our work here presents an original contribution to handle dynamic domains in reasoning about action and change.

# References

1. E. Bencivenga, Free logic. *Handbook of Philosophical Logic*, Vol. III, pp 373–426, 1986.
2. R.E. Fikes and N.J. Nilsson, STRIPS: A new approach to the application of theorem proving to problem solving. *Artificial Intelligence* **2**:189–208, 1971.
3. N.Y. Foo, A. Nayak, M. Pagucco, P. Peppas and Y. Zhang, Action localness, genericity and invariants in STRIPS. In *Proceedings of the 15th International Joint Conference on Artificial Intelligence (IJCAI'97)*, pp 549–554. Morgan Kaufmann Publishers Inc., 1997.
4. V. Lifschitz, On the semantics of STRIPS. In *Proceedings of 1986 Workshop on Reasoning about Actions and Plans*, pp 1–9. Morgan Kaufmann Publishers Inc., 1987.
5. F. Lin and R. Reiter. How to progress a database. *Artificial Intelligence*, **92**:131–167, 1997.
6. E.P. Pednault. ADL: exploring the middle ground between STRIPS and the situation calculus. In *Proceedings of KR-89*, pages 324–332, 1989.
7. R. Reiter, On closed world data bases. In *Logic and Database*, pp 55–6. Ed., H. Gallaire and J. Minker. Plenum Press, 1978.
8. M. Winslett, Reasoning about action using a possible models approach. In *Proceedings of the Seventh National Conference on Artificial Intelligence (AAAI'88)*, pp 89–93. Morgan Kaufmann Publishers, Inc., 1988.

# Classifying Document Titles Based on Information Inference

Dawei Song[1], Peter Bruza[1], Zi Huang[2], and Raymond Lau[3]

[1] Distributed Systems Technology Centre
The University of Queensland, QLD 4072 Australia
{dsong, bruza}@dstc.edu.au
[2] School of Information Technologies and Electrical Engineering
The University of Queensland, QLD 4072 Australia
huang@itee.uq.edu.au
[3] Centre for Information Technology Innovation
Faculty of Information Technology
Queensland University of Technology
GPO Box 2434, Brisbane, Q4001, Australia
r.lau@qut.edu.au

**Abstract.** We propose an intelligent document title classification agent based on a theory of information inference. The information is represented as vectorial spaces computed by a cognitively motivated model, namely Hyperspace Analogue to Language (HAL). A combination heuristic is used to combine a group of concepts into one single combination vector. Information inference can be performed on the HAL spaces via computing information flow between vectors or combination vectors. Based on this theory, a document title is treated as a combination vector by applying the combination heuristic to all the non-stop terms in the title. Two methodologies for learning and assigning categories to document titles are addressed. Experimental results on Reuters-21578 corpus show that our framework is promising and its performance achieves 71% of the upper bound (which is approximated by using whole documents).

## 1 Introduction

There has been ever expanding vast amount of electronic information available to us to process. In situations involving large amounts of incoming electronic information (e.g., defense intelligence), judgments about content (whether by automatic or manual means) are sometimes performed based simply on a *title* description or brief caption because it is too time consuming, or too computationally expensive to peruse whole documents. Many of us also do this daily while scanning the subject descriptions of emails, or the title captions in the result set from a search engine.

A human can quickly make the judgment that a web page title "Welcome to Penguin Books, U.K" refers to Penguin, the publisher. In regard to the following text "Linux Online: Why Linus chose a Penguin?", some agents can infer readily that "Li-

N. Zhong et al. (Eds.): ISMIS 2003, LNAI 2871, pp. 297–306, 2003.
© Springer-Verlag Berlin Heidelberg 2003

nus" refers to Linus Torvalds, the inventor of Linux system, and the penguin mentioned here has to do with the Linux logo. In this way, the user can classify the incoming documents into different categories, e.g., "publisher", "birds", "logo", etc., by scanning their titles, instead of spending much time browsing and reading the whole articles. Suppose a user is only interested in Linux logo penguin. He can then simply filter out the documents about penguin publisher.

At the first glance, it shows similarity to the Text Categorization (TC), whose task is to assign a number of pre-defined category labels to a document by learning a classification scheme from a set of labeled training data. The result of the learning is a classifier associated with each category C, which can decide whether an arbitrary document should be classified with C. A number of statistical learning algorithms have been investigated, such as K-nearest neighbour (KNN) [2, Naïve Bayes (NB) [7], Support Vector Machines (SVM) [11], and Neural Network (NN) [7], etc. These are supervised approaches- they make use of the manually pre-assigned categories associated with the training documents. For example, given a test document, the KNN algorithm gets the K nearest (i.e. most similar) neighbours of the test document from the training set. The categories of the K neighbours are ranked according to the degree of similarity between each neighbour and the test document as well as a score to each category in each neighbour.

As mentioned previously, many practical situations do not conform to the above format of text categorization. For example, labeled training may not be available. As a consequence, unsupervised techniques are required in order to produce a classifier. In data intensive domains for example, defense intelligence, incoming documents may need to be classified on the basis of titles alone. Note that the categories like "publisher", "birds" and "logo" may not explicitly appear in the document titles. In other words, they are inferred.

In short, agents can generally make robust judgments about what information fragments are, or are not about, even when the fragments are brief or incomplete. The process of making such "aboutness" judgements has been referred to as *informational inference* in our recent work [3, 9]. We have developed an information flow inference model to automatically discover the implicit information flows from the terse text fragments. This model is a reflection of how strongly *Y* is *informationally contained* within *X*. The goal of this paper is to propose an intelligent agent to drive the use of information flow model for category learning and information classification from document titles.

# 2   Information Inference via Information Flow

## 2.1   Vector Representation of Information via HAL

A human encountering a new concept draws its meaning via an accumulation of experience of the contexts in which the concept appears. This opens the door to "learn" the meaning of a concept through how a concept appears within the context of other concepts. Following this idea, Burgess and Lund  [6] developed a model called *Hy-*

*perspace Analogue to Language* (HAL), which automatically constructs a high dimensional semantic space from a corpus of text.

Given an *n*-word vocabulary, the HAL space is a $n \times n$ matrix constructed by moving a window of length *L* over the corpus by one word increment ignoring punctuation, sentence and paragraph boundaries. All words within the window are considered as co-occurring with each other with strengths inversely proportional to the distance between them. After traversing the corpus, an accumulated co-occurrence matrix for all the words in a target vocabulary is produced. HAL is direction sensitive: the co-occurrence information for words preceding every word and co-occurrence information for words following it are recorded separately by its row and column vectors.

In our work, the row and column vectors in the HAL matrix corresponding to a word are added to produce a single vector representation for that word. It is sometimes useful to identify the so called *quality properties* of a HAL-vector. Quality properties are identified as those dimensions in the HAL vector for *c* which are above a certain threshold (e.g., above the average weight within that vector). HAL vectors are normalized to unit length before information flow computation. For example, the following is part of the cosine-normalized HAL vector for *"Iran"* computed derived from applying the HAL method to the Reuters-21578 collection with stop words removed, which consists of Reuters new articles in the mid-late eighties.

This example demonstrates how a word is represented as a weighted vector whose dimensions comprise other words. The weights represent the strengths of association between "iran" and other words seen in the context of the sliding window: the higher the weight of a word, the more it has lexically co-occurred with "iran" in the same context(s). The dimensions reflect aspects which were relevant to the respective concepts during the mid to late eighties. For example, Iran was involved in a war with Iraq, and president Reagan was involved in an arms scandal involving Iran.

The quality of HAL vectors is influenced by the window size; the longer the window, the higher the chance of representing spurious associations between terms. A window size of eight or ten has been used in various studies [3, 6, 9, 10].

**Table 1.** HAL vector.

| Iran | |
|---|---|
| Dimension | Value |
| arms | 0.64 |
| iraq | 0.28 |
| scandal | 0.22 |
| gulf | 0.18 |
| war | 0.18 |
| sales | 0.18 |
| attack | 0.17 |
| oil | 0.16 |
| offensive | 0.12 |
| missiles | 0.10 |
| reagan | 0.09 |
| ... | ... |

More formally, a concept *c* is a vector representation: $c = < w_{cp_1}, w_{cp_2}, ...., w_{cp_n} >$ where $p_1, p_2, ... p_n$ are called dimensions of *c*, *n* is the dimensionality of the HAL space, and $w_{cp_i}$ denotes the weight of $p_i$ in the vector representation of *c*. A dimension is termed a property if its weight is greater than zero. A property $p_i$ of a concept *c* is a termed a *quality property* iff $w_{cp_i} > \partial$, where $\partial$ is a non-zero threshold value. Let $QP_\partial(c)$ denote the set of quality properties of concept *c*. $QP_\mu(c)$ will be used to denote the set of quality properties above mean value, and $QP(c)$ is short for $QP_0(c)$.

## 2.2 Computing Information Flow in HAL Spaces

Barwise and Seligman [1] have proposed an account of information flow that provides a theoretical basis for establishing informational inferences between concepts. For example, *penguin, books* |- *publisher* denotes that the concept "publisher" is carried informationally by the combination of the concepts "penguin" and "books". Said otherwise, "publisher" *flows* informationally from "penguin" and "books". Such information flows are determined by an underlying information state space. A HAL vector can be considered to represent the information "state" of a particular concept (or combination of concepts) with respect to a given corpus of text. The degree of information flow is directly related to the degree of inclusion between the respective information states represented by HAL vectors. Total inclusion leads to maximum information flow. Inclusion is a relation $\lhd$ over HAL vectors.

**Definition 1 ( HAL-Based Information Flow)**

$$i_1, \ldots, i_k |- j \text{ iff } \text{degree}(\oplus c_i \lhd c_j) > \lambda$$

where $c_i$ denotes the conceptual representation of token $i$, and $\lambda$ is a threshold value. ($\oplus c_i$ refers to the combination of the HAL vectors $c_1, \ldots, c_k$ into a single vector representation representing the combined concept. Details of a concept combination heuristic can be found be in [10].

Note that information flow shows truly inferential character, i.e., concept $j$ is not necessarily a dimension of the $\oplus c_i$. The degree of inclusion is computed in terms of the ratio of intersecting quality properties of $c_i$ and $c_j$ to the number of quality properties in the source $c_i$:

$$\text{degree}(c_i \lhd c_j) = \frac{\sum\limits_{p_l \in (QP_\mu(c_i) \wedge QP(c_j))} w_{c_i p_l}}{\sum\limits_{p_k \in QP_\mu(c_i)} w_{c_i p_k}}$$

**Table 2.** Information flows from "Gatt talks".

| Information Flows | Degree |
|---|---|
| gatt | 1.00 |
| trade | 0.96 |
| agreement | 0.96 |
| world | 0.86 |
| negotiations | 0.85 |
| talks | 0.84 |
| set | 0.82 |
| states | 0.82 |
| EC | 0.81 |
| japan | 0.78 |
| ... | ... |

The underlying idea of this definition is to make sure that a majority of the most important quality properties of $c_i$ appear in $c_j$. Note that information flow produces truly inferential character, i.e., concept $j$ need not be a property dimension of $c_i$. Table 2 shows an example of information flow computation where the weights represent the degree of information flows derived from the combination of "GATT" (General Agreement on Tariffs & Trade, which is a forum for global trade talks) and "talks".

# 3   Classifying Document Titles via Information Flow Inference

The architecture of information flow based information classification agent is depicted in the following figure:

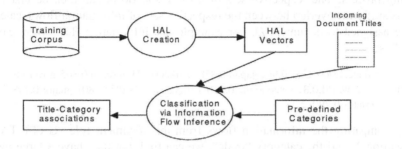

**Fig. 1.** Architecture of the intelligent classification agent

## 3.1   HAL Construction

A weighted vector represented HAL space will be produced from a large scale training collection. Once the HAL space has been created, it is ready for use by the information inference module. The training corpus may be dynamic — it could be expanded when new information comes in. The changes of HAL vectors from the new data can then be updated accordingly. This module can be pre-processed and kept updated in the background.

## 3.2   Classification via Information Flow Inference

The HAL space will then feature a module of informational inference, which is sensitive to the context of local collection, which refers to incoming document titles. The information flow theory introduced in Section 2 allows information classification to be considered in terms of information inference.

### 3.2.1   Methodology-1

Suppose the user has a list of pre-defined categories. Consider the terms $i_1, \ldots, i_n$ being drawn from the title of an incoming document $D$ to be classified. The concept combination heuristic can be used to obtain a combination vector $i_1 \oplus i_2 \oplus \ldots \oplus i_n$. The degree of information flow from $i_1 \oplus i_2 \oplus \ldots \oplus i_n$ to a category $j$ can be calculated. If it is sufficiently high, category $j$ can be assigned to $D$.

For example, "trade" is inferred from "GATT TALKS" with a high degree 0.96. The document titled ""GATT TALKS" can then be classified with category "trade".

### 3.2.2 Methodology-2

A variation of Methodology-1 can also be applied. A set of information flows can be computed from the document title terms $i_{1}, \ldots, i_{n}$. Similarly, a set of information flows can be computed on the basis of the category $j$. This is indeed a category learning process. The respective sets of information flows can then be matched. If there is sufficient overlap between the respective sets of information flows, category $j$ can be assigned to document $D$. For example, the information flows from category "trade" is:

**trade** |-  < trade:1.000 U.S.:0.967 japan:0.878 market:0.871 foreign:0.865 government:0.843 countries:0.837 world:0.816 economic:0.810 officials:0.810 dlrs:0.801 major:0.798 international:0.790 states:0.790 ... >

By comparing the information flows from the document title "GATT TALKS" (see section 2) and the category "trade", we can find that they have a large overlap, for example, "trade", "japan", "world", "states", etc. Such overlap provides the basis of assigning the category "trade" to the document in question, even though "trade" does not explicitly appears in the document title.

## 4 Experiments

The effectiveness of this module is evaluated empirically on the Reuters-21578 corpus, which has been a commonly used benchmark for text classification. This corpus consists of 21578 Reuters news articles, among which 14688 are training documents and the rest are test documents. The human indexers have pre-defined 120 topics (categories) and labeled the documents using the corresponding topics assigned to them.

In our experiments, seventeen categories (topics) were selected from the total of 120 topics. The 14,688 training documents were extracted, and pre-labeled topics were removed, i.e., there won't be any explicit topic information in the training set. This training set is then used to construct a HAL space from which information flows can be computed. After removing stop words, the total size of vocabulary for the training set is 35,860 terms.

In addition, a collection of 1,394 test documents, each of which con-

**Table 3.** Test topics.

| Topics | Number of relevant documents |
|---|---|
| acq (acquisition) | 719 |
| coconut | 2 |
| coffee | 28 |
| crude | 189 |
| grain | 149 |
| interest | 133 |
| nickel | 1 |
| oat | 6 |
| peseta | 0 |
| plywood | 0 |
| rice | 24 |
| rupiah | 0 |
| rye | 1 |
| ship | 89 |
| sugar | 36 |
| tea | 4 |
| trade | 118 |

tains at least one of the 17 selected topics, is formed. Similarly, the topic labels are removed. With respect the test set, only 14 topics have relevance information (i.e., assigned to at least one test document). Among the 14 topics, five have above 100 relevant documents and four have below 10 relevant documents. The average number of relevant documents over the 14 topics is 107. We chose this set of topics because they vary from the most frequently used topics in Reuters collection like "acquisition" to some rarely used ones such as "rye". Note that we use the real English word "acquisition" instead of the original topic "acq" for information flow computation. Table 3 lists the selected topics and their relevance information.

### Experiment 1 – Effectiveness of Methodology 1

The aim is this experiment is to test the effectiveness of deriving categories directly from document titles information flow model. We use only titles of test documents. The average title length is 5.38 words. The concept combination is applied to each title to build title vector. The top 80 Information flows with associated degrees are derived from each title vector. If a topic appears in the list of information flows of a title, it is then considered to be relevant to this title. Our previous experiments in query expansion via information flow shows that keeping top 80 information flows produces the best results [3]. This parameter setting will be used throughout this paper. Figure 3 illustrates this experiment.

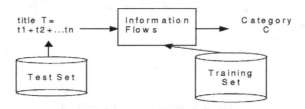

**Fig. 2.** Methodology of Experiment 1

### Experiment 2 – Effectiveness of Methodology 2

The aim of this experiment is to use information flow model to expand document titles and categories, instead of deriving categories from titles directly as in experiment 1. Similarly only titles of test documents are used. The top 80 Information flows are derived from each title vector, and then used to match top 80 information flows of each topic using dot product function. Figure 4 summaries experiment 2.

### Experiment 3 – Upper Bound

The upper bound of document title classification module can be roughly measured by using the whole document to match the categories. In our case, this involves computing the information flows on the basis of a category $j$, and using the resultant informa-

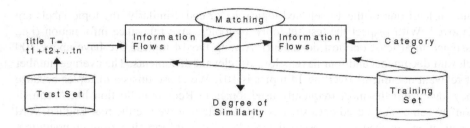

**Fig. 3.** Methodology of Experiment 2

tion flows as expansion terms. These can then be matched with the document $D$. If the match is deemed sufficient, $D$ can be classified with $j$.

The test documents are indexed using the document term frequency and inverse collection frequency components of the Okapi BM-25 (Robertson et al. 1995) formula. The average document length in the test set is 77.7 words. They are matched against the top 80 information flows of each topic using dot product. The methodology of experiment 3 is visualized as below:

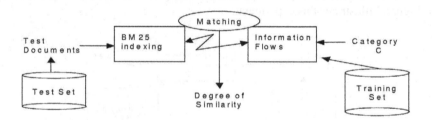

**Fig. 4.** Methodology of Experiment 3

**Experimental Results**

The performance measures used in the paper include interpolated 11-point Average Precision[1], Initial precision (i.e. interpolated precision at 0% recall) and R-precision (i.e. precision after R (= number of documents which actually belong to a category) documents have been retrieved). We choose them because we think people care more about the precision of the top ranked documents with respect to a category. In our experiments, the documents are ranked by their similarity to the topics. The experiment results are shown in Table 4 and Figure 5.

---

[1] Precision is the proportion of documents classified with a category that really belong to that category. Recall is the proportion of the documents belonging to a category that are actually assigned that category. The average precision is computed across at 11 evenly spaced recall points (0, 0.1, 0.2, ...1.0), and averaged over all the queries (categories). It is corresponding to the micro averaged precision in the text categorization context.

**Table 4.** Comparison of performance between three experiments.

|                | Avg Precision | Initial Precision | *R-Precision* |
| -------------- | ------------- | ----------------- | ------------- |
| **Experiment-1** | 0.461         | 0.786             | 0.454         |
| **Experiment-2** | 0.404         | 0.819             | 0.406         |
| **Experiment-3** | 0.721         | 0.911             | 0.640         |

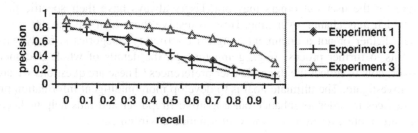

**Fig. 5.** Precision Recall curves of three experiments

**Discussions**

Experiment 3 serves as a baseline and sets a somehow upper bound for the other two experiments. Compared to the baseline, Experiment 1 and 2 both performs reasonably well. In particular, the precision values at low recall points 0.0, 0.1 and 0.3 are pretty high. Their R-precisions achieved separately 71% and 64% of the upper bound. This indicates the information flow model seems promising for reasoning about terse text fragments.

Experiment 1, which applies information flow model to derive categories from titles directly, performs better than experiment 2, which is based on the similarity between expanded titles and categories. This indicates that the document title classification could be considered more like an inference process rather than similarity.

## 5 Conclusions and Future Work

We have proposed an intelligent agent for classifying incoming document titles, based on a theory of information inference. The information is represented as vectorial spaces computed by a cognitively motivated model namely Hyperspace Analogue to Language (HAL). A combination heuristic is used to combine a group of concepts into one single combination vector. Information inference can be performed on the HAL spaces via computing information flow between vectors or combination vectors. Based on this theory, a document title is treated as a combination vector by applying the combination heuristic to all the non-stop terms in the title. A number of predefined categories, which also among the set of top-ranked information flows inferred from this combination vector, can be assigned to this title. Alternatively, the categories can also be represented as HAL vectors. Information flows inferred from category vectors are used to match against the information flows inferred from document title vectors. The categories with sufficiently high similarity scores are assigned to the corresponding document titles. Experimental results on Reuters-21578 corpus show that our framework is promising and its performance achieves 71% of the upper bound (which is approximated by using whole documents).

The story would not end yet. The classification agent assigns a number of categories to a document title. However, there may exist conflicts – some categories may be desirable for the user but others may not. Users always have their specific preferences, which may change over time. How to resolve these conflicts, i.e., how to determine whether or not a document assigned conflicting categories is really what a user wants to further process (e.g., going through the details of whole document)? Moreover, how to reflect the dynamic user preferences? These are questions we are to further investigate. The ultimate goal is to develop more intelligent information processing devices in order to enhance our cognitive firepower and thus help us become more aware in our ever more complex information environment.

**Acknowledgements.** The work reported in this paper has been funded in part by the Cooperative Research Centres Program through the Department of the Prime Minister and Cabinet of Australia.

# References

1. Barwise, J. and Seligman, J. (1997) *Information Flow: The Logic of Distributed Systems.* Cambridge Tracts in Theoretical Computer Science, 44.
2. Dasarathy, B.V. (1991) *Nearest Neighbor (NN) Norms: NN Pattern Classification Techniques.* IEEE Computer Society Press.
3. Bruza, P.D. and Song, D. (2002) Inferring Query Models by Computing Information Flow. *Proceedings of the 12$^{th}$ International Conference on Information and knowledge Management (CIKM2002),* pp. 260–269.
4. Burgess, C., Livesay, K. and Lund K. (1998) Explorations in Context Space: Words, Sentences, Discourse. *Discourse Processes, 25(2&3),* 211–-257.
5. Gärdenfors, P. (2000) *Conceptual Spaces: The Geometry of Thought.* MIT Press.
6. Lund, K. and Burgess C. (1996) Producing High-dimensional Semantic Spaces from Lexical Co-occurrence. *Behavior Research Methods, Instruments, & Computers, 28(2),* 203–208.
7. Mitchell, T. (1996) *Machine Learning.* McGraw Hill.
8. Robertson, S.E., Walker, S., Spark-Jones, K., Hancock-Beaulieu, M.M., and Gatford, M. (1995) OKAPI at TREC-3. In *Proceedings of the 3$^{rd}$ Text Retrieval Conference (TREC-3).*
9. Song, D. and Bruza, P.D. (2001) Discovering Information Flow Using a High Dimensional Conceptual Space. In Proceedings of the *24th Annual International Conference on Research and Development in Information Retrieval (SIGIR'01),* pp. 327–333.
10. Song, D. and Bruza, P.D. (2003) Towards A Theory of Context Sensitive Informational Inference. *Journal of American Society for Information Science and Technology, 54(4).* pp. 326–339.
11. Vapnic, V. (1995) The Nature of Statistical Learning Theory. Springer.

# Building Topic Maps Using a Text Mining Approach

Hsin-Chang Yang[1] and Chung-Hong Lee[2]

[1] Department of Information Management, Chang Jung University,
Tainan, 711, Taiwan
[2] Department of Electric Engineering, National Kaohsiung University of Applied
Sciences, Kaohsiung, Taiwan

**Abstract.** Topic maps standard (ISO-13250) has been gradually recognized as an emerging standard for information exploration and knowledge organization in the web era. One advantage of topic maps is that they enable a user to navigate and access the documents he wants in an organized manner, rather than browsing through hyperlinks that are generally unstructured and often misleading. Nowadays, the topic maps are generally manually constructed by domain experts or users since the functionality and feasibility of automatically generated topic maps still remain unclear. In this work we propose a semi-automatic scheme to construct topic maps. We first apply a text mining process on a corpus of information resources to identify the topics and discover the relations among these topics. Necessary components of topic maps such as topics, topic types, topic occurrences, and topic associations may be automatically revealed by our method.

## 1 Introduction

Topic maps provide a general, powerful, and user-oriented way to navigating the information resources under consideration in any specific domain. A topic map provides a uniform framework that not only identifies important subjects from an entity of information resources and specifies the information resources that are semantically related to a subject, but also explores the relations among these subjects. When a user needs to find some specific information on a pool of information resources, he only needs to examine the topic maps of this pool, selects the topic he thought interesting, and the topic maps will show him the information resources that are related to this topic as well as its related topics. He will also recognize the relationships among these topics and the roles the topics play in such relationships. With the help of the topic maps, we no longer have to browse through a set of hyperlinked documents and hope they may eventually reach the information we need in a finite amount of time even when we know nothing about where we should start. We also don't have to gather some words and hope that they may perfectly symbolize the idea we interest and are conceived well by a search engine to obtain reasonable result. Topic

N. Zhong et al. (Eds.): ISMIS 2003, LNAI 2871, pp. 307–314, 2003.

maps provide us a way to navigate and organize information, as well as to create and maintain knowledge in an infoglut.

To construct a topic map for a set of information resources, human intervention is unavoidable in present time. We need human effort in tasks such as selecting topics, identifying their occurrences, and revealing their associations. Such need is acceptable only when the topic maps are used merely for navigation purpose and the volume of the information resource is considerably small. However, a topic map should not only be a 'topic navigation map'. Besides, the volume of information resource under consideration is generally large enough to prevent manual construction of topic maps. To expand the applicability of topic maps, some kind of automatic process should involve during the construction of topic maps. The degree of automation in such construction process may differ for different users with different needs. One may only need a friendly interface to automate the topic map authoring process, and another one may try to automatically identify every components of a topic map for a set of information resources from the ground up. In this work, we recognize the importance of topic maps not only as a navigation tool but also an desirable scheme for knowledge acquisition and representation. According to such recognition, we try to develop a scheme based on a proposed text mining approach to automatically construct topic maps for a set of information resources. Our approach is opposite to the navigation task performed by a topic map to obtain information. We extract knowledge from a corpus of documents to construct a topic map. Although the proposed approach cannot fully construct the topic maps automatically in present time, our approach still seems promising in developing a fully automatic scheme for topic map construction.

## 2   Related Work

Topic map standard is an emerging standard so there are few works about it. Most of the early works about topic maps focus on providing introductory materials [5,1]. Few of them are devoted to automatic construction of topic maps. Two works that addressed this issue were reported in [6] and [4]. Rath [6] discussed a framework for automatic generation of topic maps according to a so-called 'topic map template' and a set of generation rules. The structural information of topics is maintained in the template. They used a generator to interpret the generation rules and extract necessary information that fulfills the template to create the topic map. However, both the rules and the template are to be constructed explicitly and probably manually. Moore [4] discussed topic map authoring and how software may support it. He argued that the automatic generation of topic maps is a useful first step in the construction of a production topic map. However, the real value of a topic map comes through the involvement of people in the process. This argument is true if the knowledge that contained in the topic maps can only be obtained by human efforts. Fully automatic generation process is possible only when such knowledge may be discovered from the underlying set of information resources through an automated process, which is generally known as knowledge discovery from texts or *text mining*.

# 3   The Text Mining Process

Before we can create topic maps, we should first perform a text mining process on the set of information resources to reveal the relationships among the information resources. Here we only consider those information resources that can be represented in regular texts. Examples of such resources are web pages, ordinary books, technical specifications, manuals, etc. The set of information resources is collectively known as *the corpus* and individual resource is referred as a document in the following text. To reveal the relationships between documents, the popular self-organizing map (SOM) [3] algorithm is applied to the corpus to cluster documents. We adopt the vector space model [7] to transform each document in the corpus into a binary vector. These document vectors are used as input to train the map. We then apply two kinds of labeling process to the trained map and obtained two feature maps, namely the document cluster map (DCM) and the word cluster map (WCM). In the document cluster map each neuron represents a document cluster that contains several similar documents with high word co-occurrence. In the word cluster map each neuron represents a cluster of words that reveal the general concept of the corresponding document cluster associated with the same neuron in the document cluster map.

The text mining process described above provides us a way to reveal the relationships between the topics of the documents. We introduce here a method to identify topics and the relationships between topics. The method also arranges these topics in a hierarchical manner according to their relationships. As we mentioned before, a neuron in the DCM represents a cluster of documents that contain words that often co-occurred in these documents. Besides, documents that associate with neighboring neurons contain similar set of words. Thus we may construct a super-cluster by combining neighboring neurons. To form a super-cluster, we first define the distance between two clusters:

$$D(i, j) = H(||\mathbf{G}_i - \mathbf{G}_j||), \tag{1}$$

where $i$ and $j$ are the neuron indices of the two clusters and $\mathbf{G}_i$ is the two-dimensional grid location of neuron $i$. $||\mathbf{G}_i - \mathbf{G}_j||$ measures the Euclidean distance between the two coordinates $\mathbf{G}_i$ and $\mathbf{G}_j$. $H(x)$ is a bell-shaped function that has maximum value when $x = 0$. We also define the dissimilarity between two clusters:

$$\mathcal{D}(i, j) = ||\mathbf{w}_i - \mathbf{w}_j||, \tag{2}$$

where $\mathbf{w}_i$ denotes the synaptic weight vector of neuron $i$. We may then compute the *supporting cluster similarity* $\mathcal{S}_i$ for a neuron $i$ from its neighboring neurons by

$$S(i, j) = \frac{\text{doc}(i)\text{doc}(j)}{F(D(i, j)\mathcal{D}(i, j))}$$

$$\mathcal{S}_i = \sum_{j \in B_i} S(i,j), \qquad (3)$$

where $\text{doc}(i)$ is the number of documents associated with neuron $i$ in the document cluster map and $B_i$ is the set of neuron indices in the neighborhood of neuron $i$. The function $F : \mathbf{R}^+ \to \mathbf{R}^+$ is a monotonically increasing function. A *dominating neuron* is the neuron which has locally maximal supporting cluster similarity. We may select dominating neurons by the following algorithm:

**Step 1.** Find the neuron with the largest supporting cluster similarity. Selecting this neuron as dominating neuron.
**Step 2.** Eliminate its neighbor neurons so that they will not be considered as dominating neurons.
**Step 3.** If there is no neuron left or the number of dominating neurons exceeds a predetermined value, stop. Otherwise go to Step 1.

A dominating neuron may be considered as the centroid of a super-cluster, which contains several clusters. We assign every cluster to some super-clusters by the following method. The $i$th cluster (neuron) is assigned to the $k$th super-cluster if

$$\mathcal{D}(i,k) = \min_l \mathcal{D}(i,l), \qquad l \text{ is a super}-\text{cluster.} \qquad (4)$$

A super-cluster may be thought as a category that contains several sub-categories. Let $C_k$ denote the set of neurons that belong to the $k$th super-cluster, or category. The category topics are selected from those words that associate with these neurons in the WCM. For all neurons $j \in C_k$, we select the $n^*$th word as the category topic if

$$\sum_{j \in C_k} w_{j_{n^*}} = \max_{1 \le n \le N} \sum_{j \in C_k} w_{j_n}. \qquad (5)$$

Eq. 5 selects the word that is the most important to a super-cluster since the components of the synaptic weight vector of a neuron reflect the willingness that the neuron wants to learn the corresponding input data, i.e. words.

The topics that are selected by Eq. 5 form the top layer of the category hierarchy. To find the descendants of these topics in the hierarchy, we may apply the above process to each super-cluster and obtain a set of sub-categories. These sub-categories form the new super-clusters that are on the second layer of the hierarchy. The category structure can then be revealed by recursively applying the same category generation process to each new-found super-cluster. We decrease the size of neighborhood in selecting dominating neurons when we try to find the sub-categories.

## 4   Automatic Topic Maps Construction

The text mining process described in Sec. 3 reveals the relationships between documents and words. Furthermore, it may identify the topics in a set of documents, reveals the relationships among the topics, and arrange the topics in a hierarchical manner. The result of such text mining process can be used to construct topic maps. We will discuss the steps in topic maps construction in the following subsections.

## 4.1  Identifying Topics and Topic Types

The topics in the constructed topic map can be selected as the topics identified by Eq. 5. All identified topics in every layer of the hierarchy can be used as topics. Since topics in different layers of the hierarchy represent different levels of significance, we may constrain the significance of topics in the topic map by limiting the depth of hierarchy that we select topics from. If we only used topics in higher layers, the number of topics is small but the topics represent more important topics. The significance level can be set explicitly in the beginning of the construction process or determined dynamically during the construction process. A way to determine the number of topics is by the size of the self-organizing map.

The topic types can also be determined by the constructed hierarchy. As we mentioned before, a topic on higher layers of the hierarchy represents a more important concept than those on lower layers. For a parent-child relationship between two concepts on two adjacent layers, the parent topic should represent a important concept of its child topic. Therefore, we may use the parent topic as the type of its child topics. Such usage also fulfills the requirement of the topic map standard that a topic type is also a topic.

## 4.2  Identifying Topic Occurrences

The occurrences of a identified topic are easy to obtain after the text mining process. Since a topic is a word labeled to a neuron in the WCM, its occurrences can be assigned as the documents labeled to the same neuron in the DCM. That is, let a topic $\tau$ be labeled to neuron $A$ in the WCM, the occurrences of $\tau$ should be those documents labeled to the same neuron $A$ in the DCM. For example, if the topic 'text mining' was labeled to the 20th neuron in the WCM, all documents labeled to the 20th neuron in the DCM should be the occurrences of this topic. Furthermore, we may create more occurrences of this topic by allowing documents labeled to lower levels of the hierarchy being also included. For example, if neuron 20 in the above example located on the second level of a topic hierarchy, we may also allow the clusters of documents associated with topics below this level being also occurrences of this topic. Another approach is to use the DCM directly such that we also include the documents associated with the neighboring neurons of the neuron associated with a topic as its occurrences.

## 4.3  Identifying Topic Associations

The associations among topics can be identified by two ways in our method. The first is to use the developed hierarchy structure among topics. A topic is associated with the other if there existed a path between them. We should limit the lengths of such paths to avoid establishing associations between pairs of unrelated topics. For example, if we limited the length to 1, only topics that are direct parents and children are associated with the topic under consideration. The type of such associations is essentially an instance-class association. The second way to identify topic associations simply examines the WCM and finds the associations. To establish associations to a topic $\tau$, we first find the neuron $A$ that $\tau$ is labeled to. We then establish associations between $\tau$ and every topic associated with some neighboring neuron of $A$. The neighboring neurons are selected from a neighborhood of $A$ that are arbitrarily set by the creator. Obviously, a large neighborhood will create many associations. We should at least create associations between $\tau$ and other topics associated with the same neuron $A$ since they are considered as very related topics in the text mining process. The association types are not easy to reveal by the method since we do not fully reveal the semantic relations among neurons after text mining process. An alternative method to determine the association type between two topics is to use the semantic relation defined in a well-developed ontology such as WordNet [2].

## 5    Experimental Result

We performed the experiments on a set of news articles that were collected from a Chinese newswire site [1]. Two corpora were constructed in our experiments. The first corpus (CORPUS-1) contains 100 news articles posted during Aug. 1-3, 1996. The second corpus (CORPUS-2) contains 3268 documents posted during Oct. 1-9, 1996. A word extraction process was applied to the corpora to extract Chinese words. Total 1475 and 10937 words were extracted from CORPUS-1 and CORPUS-2, respectively. To reduce the dimensionality of the feature vectors we discarded those words that occur only once in a document. We also discarded the words that appear in a manually constructed stoplist and reduced the number of words to 563 and 1976 for CORPUS-1 and CORPUS-2, respectively. A reduction rate of 62% and 82% is achieved for the two corpora, respectively.

To train CORPUS-1, we constructed a self-organizing map that contains 64 neurons in 8×8 grid format. The number of neurons is determined experimentally such that a better clustering can be achieved. Each neuron in the map contains 563 synapses. The initial training gain is set to 0.4 and the maximal training time is set to 100. These settings are also determined experimentally. We tried different gain values ranged from 0.1 to 1.0 and various training time setting ranged from 50 to 200. We simply adopted the setting which achieves the most satisfying result. After training we labeled the map by documents and words respectively and obtained the DCM and the WCM for CORPUS-1. The above process was also applied to CORPUS-2 with a $20 \times 20$ neuron map and obtained the DCM and the WCM for CORPUS-2.

---

[1] http://www.cna.com.tw

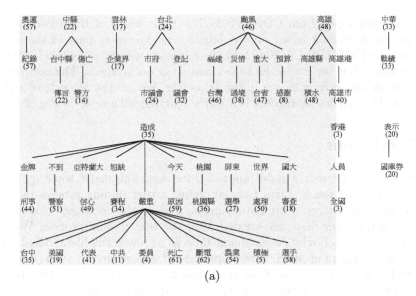

Fig. 1. The category hierarchies of CORPUS-1

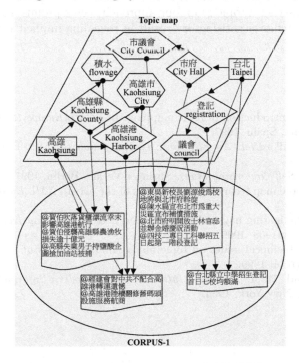

Fig. 2. Part of the topic map of CORPUS-1

We applied the hierarchy generation process after the clustering process to the DCM to obtain the category hierarchies. In Figure 1 we show the overall hierarchies developed from CORPUS-1. The topic maps of these two corpora can then be generated based on the hierarchies. We show part of the overall topic map for CORPUS-1 in Fig. 2. In the figure we use the same two-layer view of topic maps that separates the topics and their occurrences. The occurrences of a topic are collectively shown in the same box. We use the subjects of articles to refer to the articles. A subject is a string starting with a '@' in Fig. 2.

## 6    Conclusions

In this work we present a novel approach for semi-automatic topic map construction. The approach starts from applying a text mining process on a set of information resources. Two feature maps, namely the document cluster map and the word cluster map, are created after the text mining process. We then apply a category hierarchy development process to reveal the hierarchical structure of the document clusters. Some topics are also identified by such process to indicate the general subjects of those clusters located in the hierarchy. We may then create topic maps according to the two maps and the developed hierarchy automatically. Although our method may not identify all kinds of components that should construct a topic map, our approach seems promising since the text mining process achieves satisfactory result in revealing implicit topics and their relationships.

## References

1. M. Biezunski. Introduction to topic mapping. In *SGML Europe 1997 GCA Conference*, Barcelona, Spain, 1997.
2. C. Fellbaum. *WordNet: An Electronic Lexical Database*. MIT Press, Cambridge, MA, 1998.
3. T. Kohonen. *Self-Organizing Maps*. Springer-Verlag, Berlin, 1997.
4. G. Moore. Topic map technology – the state of the art. In *XML Europe 2000*, Paris, Frace, 2000.
5. S. Pepper. Navigating haystacks, discovering needles. *Markup Languages: Theory and Practice*, 1:41–68, 1999.
6. H. H. Rath. Technical issues on topic maps. In *Proceedings of Metastructures 99 Conference, GCA*, 1999.
7. G. Salton and M. J. McGill. *Introduction to Modern Information Retrieval*. McGraw-Hill, New York, 1983.

# Improving the Performance of Text Classifiers by Using Association Features

Yang Zhang, Lijun Zhang, Zhanhuai Li, and Jianfeng Yan

Dept. Computer Science & Engineering, Northwestern Polytechnical University, China
{zhangy, zlj, lzh}@co-think.com, yanjf@mail.nwpu.edu.cn

**Abstract.** The co-occurrence of words can make contribution to text classification. However, current text classification technology failed to take full advantage of this information. In this paper, we use association features to describe this information and present the algorithm for creating association feature set to make the association features we selected be good discriminators. The experiment results show that the performance of Naïve Bayes text classifier and decision tree text classifier could be improved by using association features.

## 1 Introduction

For text classification, the co-occurrence of primitive features can make contribution to classifiers. For example, the primitive feature *mining* is helpless when it is used to distinguish document class *Data Mining* from *Coal Mining*, while the co-occurrence information of *mining* and *classification* can strongly imply that the document class is *Data Mining*. In other words, the association feature *{mining, classification}* can make contribution to automatic text classification. However, current text classification technology failed to take full advantage of this co-occurrence information.

In order to take advantage of this co-occurrence information, we introduce the entity *association feature* into text mining to represent the co-occurrence of primitive features, and enhance the performance of text classifiers by using association features.

In [1][2], researchers studied improving the performance of classifiers by using itemsets, which suggests us to improve the performance of text classifiers by using association features. The difference between our work and [1][2] is that for text categorization, there are always thousands of primitive features, and it is a challenge to create association feature set form such a big primitive feature set. In [3][4], researchers use *n*-grams, which are sequences of *n* words, to improve the performance of text classifiers. The association features could be recognized as an expansion to *n*-grams.

## 2 Association Features

Let W be the set of primitive features on a set of text documents, we say that each arbitrary non-empty proper subset of W ($\forall f$ ($f \subset W \wedge f \neq \varnothing$)) is an association feature.

N. Zhong et al. (Eds.): ISMIS 2003, LNAI 2871, pp. 315–319, 2003.
© Springer-Verlag Berlin Heidelberg 2003

The Naïve Bayes classifier estimate the document class for a text document by the *Naïve Bayes assumption*, which assumes that the occurrence of a feature in a document class is independent of the occurrence of other features. Obviously, this assumption is not true for text categorization, and it is generally recognized that the relaxation of *Naïve Bayes assumption* could lead to a better performance of Naïve Bayes classifier. Association features could be used to describe the dependence information, which is helpful to text categorization, among primitive features. For example, the association feature *{mining, classification}* can represent the dependence between *mining* and *classification*. By using association features, the *Naïve Bayes assumption* is relaxed. Therefore, the performance of Naïve Bayes classifier could be improved.

A well-known fundamental limitation of primitive feature based decision tree algorithms is that when primitive features are not adequate for describing theories to be learned, their performance in terms of prediction accuracy and theory complexity is usually poor. The replication problem of decision trees, which makes decision trees deep and difficult to understand, is a manifestation of this fundamental limitation. In replication a portion of a subtree is constructed multiple times. Association features can help to solve this problem. For example, suppose a subtree, which comprises node *mining* and node *classification*, emerges multiple times in a decision tree. This subtree could be replaced by the node *{mining, classification}*, so as to simplify the tree.

## 3   Creating Association Feature Set

Let $F_{nItemSet}$ represent frequent association feature set and $F_{1ItemSet}$ represent primitive feature set, then the association feature set $F = F_{nItemSet} \cup F_{1ItemSet}$.

There is a lot of noise and redundant information in the association feature set defined above. Eliminating these noise and redundant information could help to improve the performance and efficiency of text classifiers, and this process takes two steps. 1, Carrying out redundancy pruning on frequent association feature set $F_{nItemSet}$. 2, Carrying out feature selection on association feature set F.

### 3.1   Redundancy Pruning

In our experiment, we used an Apriori-like algorithm to mine association features whose occurring frequency is higher than the predefined parameter, *minSupport*.

In real life application, the size of sample data for each document class may not be the same. For this reason, in our algorithm we partition the training document set into groups by the class label of text documents. Then, we mine frequent association features in each group, and combine all these features into frequent association feature set $F_{nItemSet}$.

For document class $C_1$, its positive document set includes all of the training documents that are labeled as $C_1$, and its negative document set includes all of the training documents that are not labeled as $C_1$. Let $\text{Conf}(f_j, C_1) = P(f_j | C_1)$ be the confidence for association feature $f_j$ to occur in positive document set of class $C_1$, and

$Conf(f_j, \overline{C_l}) = P(f_j | \overline{C_l})$ be the confidence for $f_j$ to occur in negative document set of class $C_l$. The following formula is used to estimate the discriminative ability of $f_j$:

$$maxConf(f_j) = max(Conf(f_j, C_l), Conf(f_j, \overline{C_l})) \cdot$$

**Definition 1.** The size of association feature $f_j$, $size(f_j)$, is defined as the count of primitive features in $f_j$.

**Definition 2.** Containing Relationship $\subset$ for Association Features: For association feature $f_i$ and $f_j$, $f_i \neq f_j$, if $\forall w$   $w \in f_i$, we have $w \in f_j$, then we say $f_i \subset f_j$.

**Definition 3.** Redundant Feature: For association feature $f_i$ and $f_j$, if $f_i \subset f_j$ and $maxConf(f_i) > maxConf(f_j)$, then we say $f_j$ is a redundant feature with respect to $f_i$.

The redundancy pruning on frequent association feature set $F_{nItemSet}$ takes two steps: 1, According to definition 1, all association features are sorted into a queue in size ascending order. 2, According to definition 3, all redundant features are eliminated from this queue.

## 3.2 Feature Selection

We chose to use IG (Information Gain) for feature selection because IG works well and has been often used for text categorization [5]. The IG value for feature $f_j$ with respect to document class $C_l$ is defined as:

$$IG(f_j) = \sum_{c \in \{C_l, \overline{C_l}\}} \sum_{f \in \{f_j, \overline{f_j}\}} P(c, f) \lg \frac{P(c, f)}{P(c)P(f)} \cdot$$

Let $F_{1ItemSet}$ be the primitive feature set; $F_{nItemSet}'$ be the frequent association feature set after redundancy pruning; $M, N, K$ be three integer parameters. The feature selection on association feature set takes four steps: 1, All features in $F_{1ItemSet}$ are sorted in IG descending order, $F_{1ItemSet}'$ is created by the top $M$ features in this order. 2, Variable $IGatN$ is set to the IG value of the $N^{th}$ feature in this order. 3, $F_{nItemSet}'' = \{f_i | f_i \in F_{nItemSet}' \wedge IG(f_i) \geq IGatN \cdot K\}$. 4, $F' = F_{nItemSet}'' \cup F_{1ItemSet}'$, is the association feature set after feature selection.

## 4 Experiment Result

Here we report our experiment result on Reuters21578, a benchmark dataset for automatic text classification. We experiment with a multi-variate Bernoulli model Naïve Bayes classifier and C4.5, a decision tree classifier.

We simply set parameter $N=100$ and $K=1$ for feature selection. Fig. 1, Fig. 2 gives the experiment results for Naïve Bayes classifier and C4.5 classifier in macro-average $F_1$ respectively, which is widely used for measuring the classification performance of text classifiers [5]. (Please refer to [5] for details about macro-average $F_1$.) Here, *pre* represents the experiment result when only primitive features are used; *supp=0.1* represents the experiment result of *minSupport=0.1* when association features are used. Others are similar. The horizontal axis *F1itemset*, represents the size of primitive feature set.

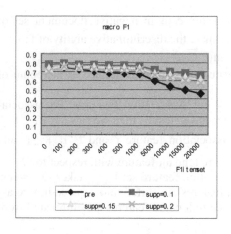

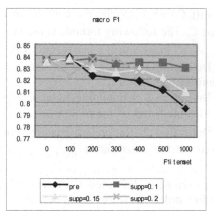

**Fig. 1.** Macro $F_1$ for Naïve Bayes Classifier      **Fig. 2.** Macro $F_1$ for C4.5 classifier

From these figures, it is obvious that the performance of Naïve Bayes classifier and C4.5 classifier could be improved by taking full advantage of the selected set of association features. When association features are used for representing text document, considering the different sizes of primitive feature sets, the performance of text classifiers varies less than when primitive features are used.

In our experiment, the processing of creating association feature set took about 87 seconds on a computer with single 1.80 GHz Pentium 4 CPU and 256 MB memory.

## 5   Conclusions and Future Work

In this paper, we propose an approach to enhance the performance of Naïve Bayes text classifier and decision tree text classifier by using association features. We present the algorithm for creating association feature set, which means that the association features which we selected are more likely to be good discriminators and less likely to be noisy. The experiment results show that the performance of Naïve Bayes text classifier and decision tree text classifier could be improved by a selected set of association features.

In the future, we plan to find a better algorithm for creating association feature set.

## References

1. Mukund Deshpande, George Karypis.: Using Conjunction of Attribute Values for Classification. In Proc. of 11th ACM Int. Conf. Information and Knowledge Management (CIKM'02), 2002.
2. Neal Lesh, Mohammed J. Zaki, Mitsunori Ogihara.: Mining features for Sequence Classification. In Proc. of 5th ACM SIGKDD Int. Conf. on Knowledge Discovery and Data Mining (KDD'99), 1999.

3. D. Mladenic, M. Grobelnik.: Word Sequences as Features in Text-learning. In Proc. of the 17th Electrotechnical and Computer Science Conference, Ljubljana, Slovenia, 1998.
4. Chade-Meng Tan, Yuan-Fang Wang, Chan-Do Lee.: The Use of Bigrams to Enhance Text Categorization. Information Processing and Management, 1(38), 2002.
5. Fabrizio Sebastiani.: Machine learning in automated text categorization. ACM Computing Surveys, 34(1): 1–47, 2002.

# Korean Document Summarization Using Topic Phrases Extraction and Locality-Based Similarity

Je Ryu[1], Kwang-Rok Han[1], and Kee-Wook Rim[2]

[1] Graduate School of Venture, Hoseo University
A-San, Chungnam, Korea
ryuje@shinbiro.com,krhan@office.hoseo.ac.kr
[2] Dept. of Knowledge information Industrial Engineering, Sunmmon University
A-San, Chungnam, Korea
rim@omega.sunmoon.ac.kr

**Abstract.** We describe a hybrid approach to summarize the document content using the topic phrases extraction and the query-based summary. The topic phrases are extracted using machine learning algorithm. We use these topic phrases as the query terms with locality-based similarity calculation in order to extract highly ranked sentences or paragraph. We experiment with three machine learning methods, Naive Bayesian, decision tree and supported vector machine, for extracting the topic phrases effectively and discuss the results. The overall summaries have been evaluated for the extraction accuracy compared with the human-selected summaries.

## 1 Introduction

The text summarization is regarded as an abstraction of source document or a simplification process like the summarization of the scientific paper.

In the case of web document summarization, because there are massive volumes of data to process for summarizing, it needs to implement a system that satisfies the correctness and effectiveness based on document condensing[2,11,12,13].

In this paper we describe a hybrid approach to use the topic phrase extraction and the query-based summary for summarizing the content of document. At first the topic phrases, which pay an important role in a document and can be a word or a phrase, are extracted using machine learning algorithm. We use these topic phrases as the query terms for locality-based similarity heuristics[1]. Once all query term locations have been processed using locality-based similarity, a partial sort is used to extract the required number of ranked answers. For each answer that is to be presented to the user the corresponding file is opened at the relevant byte location, and a small window of text extracted and formatted for display. We experiment with three machine learning methods, Naïve Bayesian, decision tree and supported vector machine for extracting the topic phrases effectively and discuss the results[5]. The overall summaries have been evaluated for extraction accuracy and by human subjects for informativeness of extracts.

N. Zhong et al. (Eds.): ISMIS 2003, LNAI 2871, pp. 320–325, 2003.

## 2 Summary System

In section 2.1 we outline the overall architecture of our system, in section 2.2 we describe in more detail the topic phrase extractor and summary extractor

### 2.1 System Architecture

Our experimental system is composed of three units:

**Model Builder :** The learning models are built from learning documents in order to extract topic phrases. We use three different learning algorithms, Naïve Bayesian, Decision Tree and Supported Vector Machine.

**Topic Phrase Extractor :** The topic phrase extractor extracts the topic phrases automatically from new document based on the model.

**Summary Extractor :** The summary extractor outputs the summary of the document using query-based summary which considers the extracted topic phrases as queries and calculates the locality-based similarity of each topic phrase.

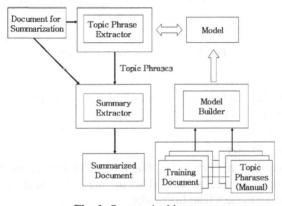

**Fig. 1.** System Architecture

### 2.2 Topic Phrase Extractor

Topic phrase extraction does not use a controlled vocabulary, but instead chooses topic phrases from text itself. We employ lexical and information retrieval techniques to extract from the document that is likely to characterize it[3,4,8,12]. In this approach, the training data is used to tune the parameters of extraction algorithm. Figure 2 shows the process to extract the topic phrases from document.

#### 2.2.1 Preprocess for Candidate Phrases

*A. Content words are selected by Korean morphological analyzer.*

Morphological analyzer allows us to identify the content words and remove all of the functional words[6, 10, 13]. A preprocess of Korean text for this system is shown in Figure 3.

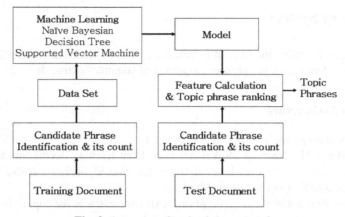

**Fig. 2.** A process of topic phrase extraction

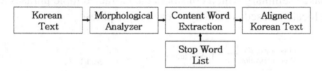

**Fig. 3.** A preprocess of Korean text

*B. Punctuation marks, brackets and numbers are replaced by phrase boundaries.*
*C. Apostrophes are removed.*

### 2.2.2  Building the Model
There are many learning methods in building the model, but we build the model using Naive Bayesian, decision tree, supported vector machine and discuss the final summary result according to each learning model.

### 2.2.3  Topic Phrases Extraction
The model determines the overall probability that each candidate is a topic phrase, and then a post-processing operation selects best topic phrases [7,9].

When the Naïve Bayesian model is used on a candidate phrase with feature value *tif*(for *TFxIDF*) and *dis*(for *distance of first occurrence*), two quantities are computed:

$$P[yes] = \frac{Y}{Y+N} P_{TFxIDF}[tif \mid yes] P_{dis\,tance}[dis \mid yes] \tag{1}$$

$$P[no] = \frac{N}{Y+N} P_{TFxIDF}[tif \mid no] P_{dis\,tance}[dis \mid no] \tag{2}$$

where Y is the number of positive instances in training files and N is the number of negative instances. The overall probability that the candidate phrase is a topic phrase can be calculated:

$$p = P[yes] / (P[yes] + P[no]) \tag{3}$$

Candidate phrases are ranked according to this value and the higher-ranking phrases are extracted as the topic phases from the candidate phrases.

### 2.3 Summary Extractor

We calculate the feature value of the document text and build a model using the learning method described previous chapter. Topic phrases for new documents are extracted using the model.

In this section we describe a hybrid approach to searching that offers the ranked queries and similarity matching of a genuine information retrieval system, but does so without any need for an index to be precomputed. We use these topic phrases as the query terms for locality-based similarity heuristics.

One of the principal advantages of locality-based querying compared with more conventional document-based querying is that the system becomes far less reliant upon formal document boundaries being established and takes a set of query terms and a set of files and determines words locations within the files that are of interest with respect to the query using a locality-based similarity heuristics.

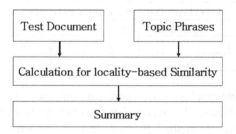

**Fig. 4.** A process of summarization using topic phrases.

Figure 4 shows the process of summarization using topic phrases which extracted from previous section. The system extracts summary automatically by calculating locality-based similarity of each topic phrases, which are extracted from previous section 3, as a query.

## 3 Evaluation and Discussion

We designed an experiment to evaluate the summaries obtained by topic phrase and locality based similarity with a summary constructed by human. We also compared the summaries with those obtained by the Microsoft Summarizer available inWord97. Fifty articles were selected for comparison. For each article, two extracts were constructed manually. Each summary constructed 20% length of a document. For convenience, percent of length was computed in terms of number of sentences.

For each automatic summarization system, four quantities were computed.

**Optimistic:** since the two manual extracts for an article are different, the amount of overlap between an automatic and a manual extract depends on which manual extract is selected for comparison. The optimistic evaluation for an algorithm is done by selecting the manual extract with which the automatic extract has a higher overlap, and measuring this overlap.

**Pessimistic:** Analogously, a pessimistic evaluation is done by selecting the manual extract with which the automatic extract has a lower overlap.

**Intersection:** for each article, an intersection of the two manually generated summaries is computed. The fact that the sentences in this intersection were deemed important by both the readers suggests that they may, in fact, be the most important sentences in the article. We compute the percentage of these sentences that is included in the automatic extract.

**Union:** we also calculate the percentage of automatically selected sentences that is selected by at least one of two users. This is, some sense, a precision measure, since it provides us with a sense of how often an automatically selected paragraph is potentially important.

**Table 1.** Evaluation result for automatic extraction methods

(%)

| Overlap between manual extracts : 47% | | | | |
|---|---|---|---|---|
| Method | Optimistic | Pessimistic | Intersection | Union |
| Suggested Method | 47 | 30 | 50 | 55 |
| MS Word 97 | 43 | 26 | 38 | 52 |

The most unexpected result of our experiment was the low level of agreement between two human subjects. The overlap between two manual extracts is only 47% on an average. However, our method showed better performance than method of MS-Word. As a result of the experiment, we find that the summarization performance is the best at topic phrase extraction when the number of topic phrase is 3-4 when Decision Tree is used internally.

# 4  Conclusion

For the automatic text summarization, we use a hybrid approach to extract topic phrases using machine learning and to select a summary using locality-based similarity. The topic phrases are considered as the queries while computing the similarity. The learning models are built from learning documents in order to extract topic phrases. We use Naive Bayesian, Decision Tree and Supported Vector Machine as the machine learning algorithm. The system extracts topic phrases automatically from new document based on these models and outputs the summary of the document using query-based summary which considers the extracted topic phrases as queries and calculates the locality-based similarity of each topic phrase. We examine how topic phrase affects the summarization and how many phrases are proper to extract the summary, evaluate and compare each machine learning result.

In this research, we have empirically proved that our hybrid method can be well applied to document summarization.

# References

[1] Owen de Kretser and Alistair Moffat, "Needles and Haystacks: A Search Engine for Personal Information Collections", de Kretser, Moffat. Proc. 23rd Australasian Computer Science Conference, Canberra, January 2000, pp 58–65.

[2] Timm Euler, *Tailoring Text Using Topic Words: Selection and Compression.* Proceedings of the 13th International Workshop on Database and Expert Systems Applications (DEXA), IEEE Computer Society Press, 2002.

[3] Frank, E., Paynter, G.W., Witten, I.H., Gutwin, C. and Nevill-Manning, C.G. (1999) Domain-specific keyphrase extraction.Proc Int Joint Conf on Artificial Intelligence, pp. 668–673, Stockholm, Sweden

[4] Witten I. H., Paynter G. W., Frank E., Gutwin C., Nevill-Manning C. G.: *KEA: Practical Automatic Keyphrase Extraction*, ACM DL, 254–255, 1999

[5] Michael Pazzani, Larry Nguyen & Stefanus Mantik, "Learning from hotlists and coldlists: Towards a WWW information filtering and seeking agent", *http://www.ics .uci.edu/ ~pazzani/Coldlist.html*

[6] Jérôme Mathieu, "Adaptation of a Keyphrase Extractor for Japanese Text", *http://extractor.iit.nrc.ca/ reports/CAIS99.ps.Z*

[7] Witten I. H., Paynter G W., Frank E., Gutwin C., Nevill-Manning C. G.: "KEA : Practical Automatic Keyphrase Extracting", ACM DL, 254–255, 1999.

[8] Owen de Kretser, Alistair Moffat "Needles and Haystacks: A Search Engine for Personal Information Collections", de Kretser, Moffat. Proc. 23rd Australasian Computer Science Conference, Canberra, January 2000, pp.58–65, 2000.

[9] Frank, E., Paynter, G.W., Witten, I.H., Gutwin, C. and Nevill-Manning, C.G. (1999) "Domain-Specific Keyphrase Extraction", Proc. Sixteenth International Joint Conference on Artificial Intelligence, Morgan Kaufmann Publishers, San Francisco, CA, pp.668–673, 1999.

[10] Min-Yen Kan, Kathleen R. McKeown and Judith L. Klavans "Domain-specific informative and indicative summarization for information retrieval." In Proceedings of the Document Understanding Workshop (DUC 2001), New Orleans, USA: September, 2001.

[11] Francine R. Chen, Dan S. Bloomberg, "Extraction of Inductive Summary Sentences from Imaged Documents", ICDAR97, pp. 227–232, Aug., 1997.

[12] Min-Yen Kan, Kathleen R. McKeown, Judith L. Klavans "Applying Natural Language Generation to Indicative Summarization" In Proceedings of 8th European Workshop on Natural Language Generation, Toulouse, France, pp.92–100, July, 2001.

[13] Je Ryu, Kwang-Rok Han, *etal,,* "Automatic Extraction of Core Sentences from Document", ICEIC 2000, 2000. 08.

# Improving Naïve Bayes Text Classifier with Modified EM Algorithm*

Han-joon Kim[1] and Jae-young Chang[2]

[1] Department of Electrical and Computer Engineering, University of Seoul, Korea
khj@uos.ac.kr
[2] School of Computer Engineering, Hansung University, Korea
jychang@hansung.ac.kr

**Abstract.** This paper presents the method of significantly improving conventional Bayesian statistical text classifier by incorporating accelerated EM (Expectation Maximization) algorithm. EM algorithm experiences a slow convergence and performance degrade in its iterative process, especially when real textual documents do not follow EM's assumptions. We propose a new accelerated EM algorithm that is simple yet has a fast convergence speed and allow to estimate a more accurate classification model on Bayesian text classifier.

**Keywords:** Text classification, Naïve Bayes, EM algorithm, selective sampling, classification uncertainty

## 1 Introduction

One of most important difficulties in machine-learning based classification algorithms is that they require sufficiently large number of labelled training examples to build an accurate classification model. Assigning class labels to unlabelled documents should be performed by human labeller, which is a highly time-consuming and expensive task. To resolve such a problem, active learning approach was proposed in which the learner can actively choose the training documents from a pool of unlabelled documents [1]. As another solution, EM (Expectation Maximization) algorithm has been evaluated to be a practical and excellent solution to the problem of lack of training examples in text classification systems [6]. EM algorithm is an iterative method for finding maximum likelihood in problems with incomplete (or unlabelled) data. EM algorithm allows to learn more accurate text classifiers from only a few labelled examples by augmenting the labelled documents with a large pool of unlabelled documents.

However, the basic EM algorithm has the following several limitations. First, when the number of labelled documents is already large enough to obtain reasonably good classification model parameters, unlabelled data do not contribute to achieve better performance any longer and even often spoil well developed classification model. Secondly, the convergence of the EM algorithm can be quite

---

* This research was financially supported by Hansung University in the year of 2003.

N. Zhong et al. (Eds.): ISMIS 2003, LNAI 2871, pp. 326–333, 2003.

slow when the proportion of unlabelled data is high. Lastly, EM is sensitive to initial starting condition and its model parameters converge to one of numerous local optimum.

In order to overcome the above drawbacks, this paper presents a modified EM technique with automatically augmenting training documents in the framework of Bayesian text classifier. The rationale behind the technique is that class labels of particular unlabelled documents can be reliably determined only if the documents can be recognized not to be uncertain of their classification.

## 2  Preliminaries

### 2.1  Statistical Formal Framework for Text Classification

For our classifier, we adopted Naïve Bayes (NB) learning method because this learning method is a simple yet surprisingly accurate technique and it has been used in many text classification projects [2]. Learning a Naïve Bayes text classifier consists of estimating the parameters of generative model by using a set of labelled training data. The estimated classification model is composed of two parameter: the word probability estimates $\hat{\theta}_{w|c}$, and the class prior probabilities $\hat{\theta}_c$ ; that is, classification model $\hat{\theta}_{NB} = \{\hat{\theta}_{w|c}, \hat{\theta}_c\}$. Each parameter can be estimated according to maximum a posteriori (MAP) hypothesis.

For classifying a given document, Naïve Bayes learning method estimates the posterior probability of a class via Bayes' rule; that is, $P(c_j|\mathbf{d}_i) = \frac{P(c_j) \cdot P(\mathbf{d}_i|c_j)}{P(\mathbf{d}_i)}$, where $P(c_j)$ is the class prior probability that any random document from the document collection belongs to the class $c_j$, $P(\mathbf{d}_i|c_j)$ is the probability that a randomly chosen document from documents in the class $c_j$ is the document $\mathbf{d}_i$, and $P(\mathbf{d}_i)$ is the probability that a randomly chosen document from the whole collection is the document $\mathbf{d}_i$. The document $\mathbf{d}_i$ is then assigned to a class $argmax_{c_j \in C} P(c_j|\mathbf{d}_i)$ with the most posterior. Here, the document $\mathbf{d}_i$ is represented by a bag of words $(w_{i1}, w_{i2}, \cdots, w_{i|\mathbf{d}_i|})$ where multiple occurrences of words are preserved. the Naïve Bayes classifier is based on the simplifying assumption that the terms in a document are mutually independent and the probability of term occurrence is independent of position within the document. This assumption results in the classification function $f_{\theta_{NB}}(\mathbf{d}_i) = argmax_{c_j \in C} P(c_j|\mathbf{d}_i) = argmax_{c_j \in C} P(c_j) \cdot \prod_{k=1}^{|\mathbf{d}_i|} P(w_{ik}|c_j)$. To generate this classification function, $P(c_j)$ can be simply estimated by counting the frequency with which each class value $c_j$ occurs in a set of the training documents $D^{tl}$, where $P(c_j|\mathbf{d}_i) \in \{0, 1\}$, given by the class label. That is, $\hat{\theta}_{c_j} = P(c_j) = \frac{\sum_{i=1}^{|D^{tl}|} P(c_j|\mathbf{d}_i)}{|D^{tl}|}$. As for $P(w_{ik}|c_j)$, its maximum likelihood estimate using Laplace's law of succession [5] is $\hat{\theta}_{w_{ik}|c_j} = P(w_{ik}|c_j) = \frac{tf_{c_j}(w_{ik}) + 1}{\sum_{w \in V} tf_{c_j}(w) + |V|}$, where $tf_{c_j}(w)$ is the number of occurrences of the word $w$ in the class $c_j$ and $V$ denotes the set of significant words extracted from the training documents.

Most machine learning methods including Naïve Bayes assumes the existence of good quality documents for training. However, this assumption is not effective

**Table 1.** Basic EM algorithm

---

Input: Training documents $D^t = D^{tl} \cup D^{tu}$
Output: Classification model $\hat{\theta}_{NB} = \{\hat{\theta}_{w|c}, \hat{\theta}_c\}$

---

$l_{NB}(D^{tl}) \equiv argmax_{\hat{\theta}_{NB}} P(D^{tl}|\hat{\theta}_{NB}) \cdot P(\hat{\theta}_{NB})$ /* MAP estimation */
$\hat{\theta}_{NB} = l_{NB}(D^{tl})$; $D^{temp} = D^{tl}$ /* Initial estimation */
**while** (Currently estimated model $\hat{\theta}_{NB}$ improves)
    (E-step) $D^{temp} = D^{temp} \cup \{\langle \mathbf{d}_i, f_{\hat{\theta}_{NB}}(\mathbf{d}_i) \rangle\}$ **for each** $\mathbf{d}_i \in D^{tu}$
    (M-step) $\hat{\theta}_{NB} = l_{NB}(D^{temp})$; $D^{temp} = D^{tl}$

---

in real world operational environments. Thus, how to obtain training examples has become an important issue in practically developing a text classifier. In this regard, EM algorithm is a very successful solution to the problem of difficulty of obtaining training documents. In particular, Naïve Bayes in combination with EM algorithm dramatically improved overall accuracy of text classification with only a few labelled training examples [6].

## 2.2   Basic EM Algorithm

EM algorithm is the semi-supervised learning in which classifiers can be more precisely learned by augmenting a few labelled training data with many un-labelled data. This can be seen as a form of clustering algorithm that clusters the unlabelled data around the labelled data, even though probabilistic membership is used. Table 1 shows the basic procedure of EM algorithm. As mentioned before, learning Naïve Bayes classifier corresponds to calculating a maximum a posteriori estimate of $\theta$ given a set of training examples $D^{tl}$; that is, $l_{NB}(D^{tl}) \equiv argmax_{\hat{\theta}_{NB}} P(D^{tl}|\hat{\theta}_{NB}) \cdot P(\hat{\theta}_{NB})$. Initially, the model parameters $\hat{\theta}_{w|c}, \hat{\theta}_c$ are estimated from only the labelled training documents $D^{tl}$. Then in E-step, *learner* module assigns probabilistic class label, $P(c_j|\mathbf{d}_i)$, to each of unlabelled documents $\mathbf{d}_i \in D^{tu}$ with the current estimated parameters $\hat{\theta}$. In M-step, a new MAP estimate for the parameters $\hat{\theta}$, using the current estimates for $P(c_j|\mathbf{d}_i)$. The algorithm iterates over the E-step and M-step until it converges to a stationary point where $\hat{\theta}$ does not change from one iteration to the next. As shown in [4], at each iteration, EM process is guaranteed to find model parameters that have equal or higher likelihood than at the previous iteration.

This algorithm contributes to dramatically improve the accuracy of text classifier even though there are a small number of labelled training examples. In [6], to obtain 70% accuracy of text classifier, the Naïve Bayes requires 2,000 training examples whereas the Naïve Bayes combined with EM only requires about 600 training examples. However, when the number of labelled documents is already large enough to obtain reasonably good classification model parameters, unlabelled data do not contribute to achieve better performance any longer and even

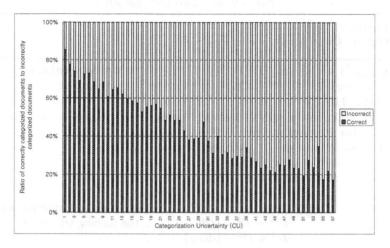

**Fig. 1.** Changes in classification correctness with classification uncertainty (CU)

often spoil well developed classification model parameters. Also, the convergence of the EM algorithm can be quite slow when the proportion of unlabelled data is relatively high. Furthermore, EM is sensitive to initial starting condition and thus its model parameters converge to one of numerous local optimum.

# 3   The Proposed Method

## 3.1   Basic Idea

In the context of EM algorithm, the only significant effect of the labelled data is to initialize the classification parameters that determines EM's starting point for hill-climbing [4]. In general, the expected model estimation error $|\theta - \hat{\theta}|$ converges to zero at a rate proportional to $\frac{1}{\sqrt{|D^{tl}|}}$ [3], where $\theta$ is a true model, $\hat{\theta}$ is an estimated model, and $|D^{tl}|$ is the number of training documents. In basic EM algorithm, the set of unlabelled documents does not change even though the algorithm estimates probabilistic class label of unlabelled documents. However, over EM iteration, if we provide additional labelled documents in E-step, then we can expect that the rate of convergence of the estimation error is accelerated. The problem is how to isolate the best candidate training examples from the unlabelled data. Since labelling requires human effort, we consider the method of sampling candidates for training examples among the unlabelled documents. In this paper, the sampling process is performed based on classification uncertainty, which is the degree of uncertainty in the classification of the example with respect to the current model derived from given training examples. Whenever the model parameters remain unchanged after sufficient number of EM iterations, we carefully incorporate some best classified documents from the unlabelled documents into the set of labelled documents.

**Table 2.** Modified EM algorithm

---

Input: Training documents $D^t = D^{tl} \cup D^{tu}$
Output: Classification model $\hat{\theta}_{NB} = \{\hat{\theta}_{w|c}, \hat{\theta}_c\}$

---

(1) $l_{NB}(D^{tl}) \equiv argmax_{\theta_{NB}} P(D^{tl}|\theta_{NB}) \cdot P(\theta_{NB})$ /* MAP estimation */
(2) $\hat{\theta}_{NB} = l_{NB}(D^{tl})$; $D^{temp} = D^{tl}$
(3) while (TRUE)
(4)     if (Currently estimated model $\hat{\theta}_{NB}$ improves) $Augment$ = FALSE
(5)     else $Augment$ = TRUE
(6) (E-step) $D^{tc} = \{\langle \mathbf{d}_i, f_{\hat{\theta}_{NB}}(\mathbf{d}_i)\rangle\}$ for each $\mathbf{d}_i \in D^{tu}$
(7)         $D^{temp} = D^{temp} \cup D^{tc}$
(8)     if ($Augment$ is TRUE)
(9)         $\mathbf{d}_{best} = argmin_{\mathbf{d}_j \in D^{tc}} CU_{NB}(\mathbf{d}_j)$
(10)         if ($CU_{NB}(\mathbf{d}_{best}) > \mu$)      /* $\mu$ is a threshold value for augmenting
(11)             $D^{tu} = D^{tu} - \{\mathbf{d}_{best}\}$          the training set $D^{tl}$.*/
(12)             $D^{tl} = D^{tl} \cup \{\mathbf{d}_{best}\}$
(13)         else EXIT
(14) (M-step) $\hat{\theta}_{NB} = l_{NB}(D^{temp})$
(15)         $D^{temp} = D^{tl}$

---

## 3.2   Selective Sampling of Candidate Training Documents

As we have already seen, Naïve Bayes learning method develops the probability distribution over words $W$ for each given class $c$ (i.e., $P(W|c)$) that accounts for the concept of that class. In this regard, if a document's classification is *uncertain* under the current model, we can say that the word distribution for its correct class is still not well developed for classification. In such case, the probability distribution over words occurring in the input document for its correct class is similar (or near) to those of other classes. From this, we find that the classification uncertainty can be determined by measuring the distances between the word distributions learned. Now, we propose an uncertainty measure based on the Kullback-Leibler (KL) divergence, which is a standard information-theoretic measure of distance between two probability mass functions. For a document $d$, its KL divergence between the word distributions induced by the two classes $c_i$ and $c_j$, $KLdist_d(P(W|c_i), P(W|c_j))$ is defined as $\sum_{w_k \in d} P(w_k|c_i) \cdot \log\frac{P(w_k|c_i)}{P(w_k|c_j)}$. Its classification uncertainty $CU(d)$ is defined as follows:

$$CU(d) = 1 - \frac{\sum_{c_i, c_j \in C} KLdist_d(P(W|c_i), P(W|c_j))}{|C| \cdot (|C| - 1)} \qquad (1)$$

where $|C|$ denotes the total number of the existing classes. Note that the value of $KLdist_d(\cdot)$ is measured, not over all words but over only those words belonging to a categorized document $d$.

Figure 1 shows that the documents with high uncertainty of classification are likely to be incorrectly categorized. In this figure, the horizontal axis has ticks for the values of $CU(\cdot)$ in ascending order and the bars denote the ratio of correctly categorized documents to incorrectly categorized documents. As the value of $CU(\cdot)$ becomes larger, incorrectly categorized documents become more common than correctly categorized documents. This empirical result implies that class labels of particular unlabelled documents can be reliably determined only if the documents can be recognized not to be uncertain of their classification.

### 3.3 Building Naïve Bayes Classifier with Modified EM Algorithm

Based on the above discussion, we firt apply one EM step with the given trained data sets, and then it draws candidate training data from a large pool of un-labelled data with currently estimated model. Table 2 shows a modification of the basic EM algorithm. When the model parameters remain unchanged after sufficient number of EM iterations, we begin augmenting the labelled documents through selective sampling. Thus, before starting EM steps, the algorithm checks whether the current classification model improves than the previous iteration. If the model does not improve, then the switch variable named *Augment* is assigned to TRUE, else it is assigned to FALSE (See lines (4)-(5)). When the augmentation is allowed, the best probable documents are picked up from the set of documents $D^{tc}$ that probabilistic class labels are allocated to $D^{tu}$ (See line (9)). The selected document is then checked whether its classification uncertainty is larger than a given threshold value (See line (10)). After the training documents arc sufficiently augmented, the uncertainty value of the best candidate document is lower than the threshold value. Then, EM process stops and generates a final classification model. To determine whether current estimated model improves or not, we use the following formula that was given in [6].

$$l(\theta_{NB}|D^{tl}) = \log P(\theta_{NB}) + \log P(D^{tl}|\theta_{NB}) \tag{2}$$

$$= \sum_{j=1}^{|C|} \log P(c_j|\theta_{NB}) \cdot \prod_{t=1}^{|V|} P\left(w_t|c_i;\theta_{NB}\right) + \sum_{d_i \in D^{tl}} \sum_{j=1}^{|C|} z_{ij} \cdot \log P(c_j|\theta_{NB}) \cdot P(d_i|c_j;\theta_{NB})$$

where $z_{ij}$ is an entry member of binary indicator variable $Z_i =< z_{i1}, \cdots, z_{i|C|} >$, and $z_{ij} = 1$ iff the class label of $d_i$ is $c_j$ else $z_{ij} = 0$.

## 4   Experimental Results

To evaluate the proposed method, we used the Reuters-21578 collection [7]. As a feature selection method, we used a document frequency (DF)-based method. According to DF-based feature selection, the lowest frequency of occurrence in a corpus is not helpful to document clustering (or classification) [8]. Thus, after removing the stopwords, we chose the 3,000 top-ranked most frequent words to favor words with a higher DF value. In our experiment, the simulation results are discussed with respect to the categorization accuracy, which is the proportion of categorizations that are correct.

Figure 2 shows the changes in F1-measure from varying the size of the labelled documents $|D^{tl}|$ for the basic EM and the proposed EM algorithm. As shown in

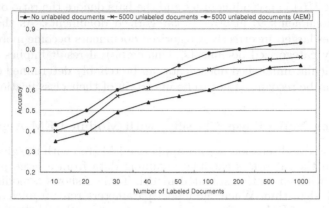

**Fig. 2.** Changes in F1-measure from varying the size of $|D^{tl}|$

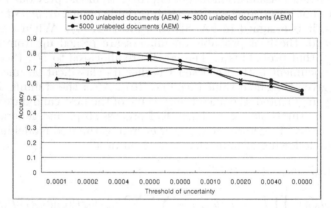

**Fig. 3.** Changes in F1-measure from varying the value of threshold for selecting candidate training examples

[6], the basic EM algorithm improves Naïve Bayes classifier compared to when not providing the unlabelled documents. However, when sufficient number of labelled documents are already given, the unlabelled documents do not help to enhance classification model, as shown in Figure 2. When the size of $D^{tl}$ approaches to 500, unlabelled documents do not contribute to obtain good model parameters no longer. In contrast, the proposed algorithm allows the classifier to more precisely classify the given unknown documents although sufficient number of labelled documents are already given. In addition, regardless of the number of labelled training examples, the proposed algorithm outperforms the basic EM algorithm. This experimental result proves that candidate training examples selected from unlabelled documents are given their corresponding true class label.

As stated before, one of the most important things that determine the performance of classifiers is the threshold value of classification uncertainty by which the candidate training examples are selected. Figure 3 presents changes in F1-

measure from varying the value of threshold for selecting candidate training examples. In this figure, we have observed that an appropriate value of threshold should be selected for effective model estimation, For example, in case of *3000 unlabelled documents (AEM)*, the method shows the best performance when the value of threshold is 0.0006. Too smaller value cannot obtain additional candidate training examples well enough to recognize best (or near best) classification model. In contrast, if too many unlabelled documents are selected as labelled documents, wrongly classified documents with relatively large uncertainty value can weaken classification model estimated with other truly classified document.

## 5    Summary

We propose a new accelerated EM algorithm on Naïve Bayes text classifier to resolve the problem of difficulty of obtaining training documents. The Naïve Bayes categorizer with EM process is further enhanced by selecting optimal training examples, based on the proposed KL distance based uncertainty measure fit for the Naïve Bayes learning method. The key point is to select best training documents from a given pool of unlabelled documents. The proposed EM technique with selective sampling of training documents can be used as a practical solution for operational text classification systems that requires continuous update of classification models.

## References

1. S. A.-Engelson, and I. Dagan, "Committee-Based Sample Selection for Probabilistic Classifiers," *Journal of Artificial Intelligence Research*, Vol. 11, pp. 335–360, 1999.
2. R. Aggrawal, R.J. Bayardo, and R. Srikant, "Athena: Mining-based Interactive Management of Text Databases," *Proceedings of the $7^{th}$ International Conference on Extending Database Technology (EDBT 2000)*, pp. 365–379, 2000.
3. V. Castelli, and T.M. Cover, "On the Exponential Value of Labeled Samples," *Pattern Recognition Letters*, Vol. 16, No. 1, pp. 105–111, 1995.
4. A.P. Dempster, N. Laird, and D.B. Rubin, "Maximum Likelihood from Incomplete Data via the EM Algorithm," *Journal of the Royal Statistical Society*, Vol. B39, pp. 1–38, 1977.
5. T.M. Mitchell, "Bayesian Learning," *Machine Learning*, McGraw-Hill, New York, pp. 154–200, 1997.
6. K. Nigam, A. McCallum, S. Thrun, and T.M. Mitchell, "Learning to Classify Text from Labeled and Unlabeled Documents," *Proceedings of the $15^{th}$ National Conference on Artificial Intelligence and the $10^{th}$ Conference on Innovative Applications of Artificial Intelligence*, pp. 792–799, 1998.
7. D.D. Lewis, "Reuters-21578 text categorization test collection," 1997. http://www.daviddlewis.com/resources/testcollections/reuters21578/
8. Y. Yang, and J.O. Pedersen, "A Comparative Study on Feature Selection in Text Categorization," *Proceedings of the 14th International Conference of Machine Learning (ICML '97)*, pp. 412–420, 1997.

# Mining Environmental Texts of Images in Web Pages for Image Retrieval

Hsin-Chang Yang[1] and Chung-Hong Lee[2]

[1] Department of Information Management, Chang Jung University, Tainan, Taiwan
hcyang@mail.cju.edu.tw
[2] Department of Electric Engineering, National Kaohsiung University of Applied
Sciences, Kaohsiung, Taiwan
leechung@mail.ee.kuas.edu.tw

**Abstract.** In this paper we propose a novel method to discover the semantics of an image within a web page and bridge the semantic gap
between the image features and a user's query. Since an image is always
accompanied with some text segments which are closely related to the
image, we propose that the semantics of the image may be discovered
from such text segments through a data mining process on these texts.
Based on such recognition, we applied a text mining process on the ac-
company texts of an image to discover the themes of this image, which
constitute the semantics of this image. The self-organizing map algorithm
is first applied to cluster a set of preprocessed web pages. Based on the
clustering result, we design a theme identification process to identify a
set of words which constitute the semantics of an image. We performed
experiments on a small set of images and obtained promising results.

## 1 Introduction

Unlike CBIR systems which use 'contents' to retrieve images, semantic image
retrieval (or semantic-based image retrieval, SBIR) systems try to discover the
real semantic meaning of an image and use it to retrieve similar images. However, understanding and discovering the semantics of a piece of information are
high-level cognitive tasks and thus hard to automate. Several attempts have
been made to tackle this problem. Most of the methods inherit from the CBIR
techniques such that primitive features were used to derive higher order image
semantics. However, CBIR systems use no explicit knowledge about the image
and limit their applications to fields such as fingerprint identification and trade
mark retrieval, etc. To levitate the users' satisfaction about the query result,
we must incorporate more semantics into the retrieval process. However, there
are three major difficulties in such incorporation. The first is that we must have
some kind of high-level description scheme for describing the semantics. The second, a semantics extraction scheme is necessary for mapping visual features to
high-level semantics. Finally, we must develop a query processing and matching
method for the retrieval process. Many works have been devised to remedy these
difficulties, as we will discuss later. In this work we propose a novel approach to

N. Zhong et al. (Eds.): ISMIS 2003, LNAI 2871, pp. 334–338, 2003.

solve these difficulties using a simple framework. First we incorporate explicit knowledge into the framework by representing the images with their surrounding texts in the web pages. Such representation also solve the difficulty of semantics representation. The semantics extraction process is achieved in our framework by using a text mining process on these texts. We also design a semantic similarity measure for matching the user's query and images in the corpus. This solves the third difficulty. Our idea comes of the recognition that it is too hard to directly extract semantics from images. Thus we avoid direct access of the image contents which is generally time-consuming and imprecise. Instead, we try to obtain image semantics by their environmental texts which are generally contextually relevant to the images.

## 2    Discovering Image Semantics

### 2.1    Document Preprocessing

A document in our corpus is a typical web page which contains both texts and images. In this article we interest in image retrieval so we should first extract images from the documents. We then extract environmental texts from the web pages corresponding to the extracted images.

**Extracting Images from Web Pages.** In HTML we use the `<img>` tag to add images to the web pages. Thus we can extract images from the web pages by examining the `<img>` tags.

**Extracting Environmental Texts.** The remaining part of the web page is further processed to extract necessary texts. These texts are called the environmental texts (ETs) of these images. There are several types of environmental texts which are related to an image. In this article, two types of ETs are extracted. The first type (denoted by ET-Normal) is the ordinary texts which locate outside any HTML tags. The second type (denoted by ET-Caption) includes alternate texts, captions, and filenames that are extracted from the `<img>` tag.

ET-Normal includes the nearby texts of an image. The nearby texts include texts that satisfy the following criteria:

1. texts in the same row or column of the image if the image occurs in a table environment
2. texts in the same paragraph of the image
3. texts with a small distance to the `<img>` tag

A word extractor is used to segment the ETs associated with each image into a list of terms.

**Encoding Images.** We adopt the vector space model to encode the images. All the ETs associated with an image are collectively transformed to a binary vector such that each component corresponds to an EK associated with this image. A component of the vector with value 1 and 0 indicate the presence and absence of an EK in its associated document respectively.

## 2.2   Discovering Image Semantics by Text Mining

In this subsection we will describe how to organized images and EKs into clusters by their co-occurrence similarities. The images in the corpus are first encoded into a set of vectors as described in Sec. 2.1. We intend to organize these images into a set of clusters such that similar images will fall into the same cluster. Moreover, similar clusters should be 'close' in some manner. That is, we should be able to organize the clusters such that clusters that contain similar images should be close in some measurement space. The unsupervised learning algorithm of SOM networks [1] fulfills our needs. The SOM algorithm organizes a set of high-dimensional vectors into a two-dimensional map of neurons according to the similarities among the vectors. Similar vectors, i.e. vectors with small distance, will map to the same or nearby neurons after the training (or learning) process. That is, the similarity between vectors in the original space is preserved in the mapped space. Applying the SOM algorithm to the image vectors, we actually perform a clustering process about the corpus. A neuron in the map can be considered as a cluster. Similar images will fall into the same or neighboring neurons (clusters). Besides, the similarity of two clusters can be measured by the geometrical distance between their corresponding neurons. To decide the cluster to which an image or an EK belongs, we apply a labeling process to the images and the EKs, respectively. After the labeling process, each image associates with a neuron in the map. We record such associations and form the image cluster map (ICM). In the same manner, we label each EK to the map and form the keyword cluster map (KCM). We then use these two maps for image semantics discovery. Detailed text mining technique can be found in [2].

## 2.3   Image Retrieval by Semantics

After obtaining the image clusters and keyword clusters, we may use them for semantic image retrieval. Two types of query methods are allowed in our scheme, namely the keyword-based queries and query by example. We will discuss them in the following subsections.

**Semantic Image Retrieval by Keywords.** When a user specifies some keywords as a query, the images that are semantically relevant to this query can be retrieved by using the KCM. Basically, the query is transformed to a query vector in the same way as the image vector. Let $\mathbf{q} = \{q_i \in \{0,1\} | 1 \leq i \leq N\}$ denote the query vector, where $N$ is the number of EKs. We also transform each keyword cluster in KCM to a vector. Let $\mathbf{k}_j = \{k_{j_i} \in \{0,1\} | 1 \leq i \leq N\}$ be the encoded vector for the keyword cluster associated with neuron $j$. The similarity between the query vector and an image vector is calculated with an extension of the cosine measurement in the vector space model:

$$S_{\mathbf{q},\mathbf{x}} = A \frac{|\mathbf{q} \cdot \mathbf{k}_j|}{|\mathbf{q}||\mathbf{k}_j|} + \frac{|\mathbf{q} \cdot \mathbf{x}|}{|\mathbf{q}||\mathbf{x}|}. \qquad (1)$$

We let $\mathbf{x}$ be the encoded vector of an image associated with neuron $j$. The first term of the right hand side of Eq. 1 measures the similarity between the query vector and the cluster vector. The second term measures the similarity between the query vector and an image vector associated with neuron $j$. $A$ is a scaling parameter that is big enough to differentiate the contributions from cluster and individual image. That is, $A$ must be big enough so that the order of the second term will not exceed the order of the first term and change the rank of a cluster. We let $A$ be big enough since the degree of match between keywords should be the major part of the similarity. The similarity between the query and each individual image is used only to differentiate the images in the same cluster. For example, let the query be "semantic retrieval" and let neuron 20 be labeled by keywords "semantic", "image", and "retrieval". We also let this neuron be labeled by images 1, 7, 20, and 34. The first term in Eq. 1 may find that neuron 20 is the closest to the query. However, the rank of the four images labeled to this neuron is determined by the second term in Eq. 1. A typical value of $A$ should be the maximum number of images associated with a cluster.

## 3    Experimental Result

We test the method with a set of manually collected web pages. The web pages were collected according to the Yahoo! web site directory. The reason for using Yahoo! directory hierarchy is that it has been a standard test bed for categorization and semantics development of web pages. Thus many works have used Yahoo! hierarchy in their experiments. One advantage of Yahoo! hierarchy is that it was constructed by human linguistic and domain experts, thus makes it "semantically correct". That is, web pages that have been assigned to the same category should be semantically relevant in general. Moreover, the relationships among directories are also carefully revealed and assigned so that directories in the same hierarchy obey their inherent semantic structures. All categories are arranged in a hierarchical manner. There are 14 top-level category in the Yahoo! directory. We adopt the "Art & Humanity" category as our source of web pages. The Art category contains 26 sub-categories. We denote these sub-categories level-1 categories. Each level-1 category also contains several sub-categories. We denote them level-2 categories. A level-1 or level-2 category contains two parts of hyperlinks. The first part is denoted by 'Categories' and contains hyperlinks which link to lower level categories, i.e. level-$(n+1)$ category where $n$ is the current level. The second part is the 'Site Listings' and includes the instantiation hyperlinks which link to corresponding web pages. In this work we collect web pages which are linked by all instantiation hyperlinks in all level-1 and level-2 categories. The statistics of those selected web sites are listed in Table 1. There are total 7736 web pages in the corpus. All pages were preprocessed so that images are extracted and their ETs are also identified. The ETs used in the experiments consist of ET-Normal and ET-Caption as described in Sec. 2.1. We then transformed each image to a image vector as in Sec. 2.1. We extracted 44782 images from the 7736 pages and discarded 8932 unqualified images as described in Sec. 2.1. Since the `alt` strings are often used to describe the semantics of the image and thus images without `alt` strings may be considered less important, we may further reduce the number of images to 27567 by discarding those images without `alt` strings. We adopted this approach and used these 27567 images as the training vectors.

**Table 1.** The statistics of web pages in the corpus

| | |
|---|---|
| Number of level-1 categories | 27 |
| Number of level-1 web pages | 1785 |
| Number of level-2 categories | 436 |
| Number of level-2 web pages | 5951 |

To train the image vectors we constructed a self-organizing map which consists of 400 neurons in $20 \times 20$ grid format. The number of neurons is determined by a simple rule of thumb that the dimension of the map should be close the average number of items associated with a neuron. The initial gain is set to 0.4 and the maximum training time is set to 500 in the training process. Both parameters are determined experimentally to obtain a better result. After the training, we label each image to a neuron as described in Sec. 2.2.

## 4    Conclusions

In this work we propose a novel approach for semantic-based image retrieval. The method applies a proposed text mining approach to discover the semantically related images. Unlike other semantic-based image retrieval approach, we avoid direct analysis of images and rely on their environmental texts to discover their semantics. The approach was applied on a set of web pages and obtained promising result. Our method can only apply on documents with both images and texts.

## References

1. T. Kohonen. *Self-Organizing Maps.* Springer-Verlag, Berlin, 1997.
2. H. C. Yang and C. H. Lee. Mining text documents for thematic hierarchies using self-organizing maps. In J. Wang, editor, *Data Mining: Opportunities and Challenges,* pages 199–219. Idea Group Publishing, Hershey, PA., 2003.

# Towards a Contextual Content of Ontologies

Djamal Benslimane[1], Catherine Roussey[1], Christelle Vangenot[2], and
Ahmed Arara[1]

[1] LIRIS, Université Lyon 1, IUT A 69622 Villeurbanne, France
{djamal.benslimane, catherine.roussey, ahmed.arara}@iuta.univ-lyon1.fr
[2] Swiss Federal Institute of Technology,
Database Laboratory, Lausanne, Switzerland
christelle.vangenot@epfl.ch

**Abstract.** In this paper, we propose an ontology representation language that should provide contextual representation and contextual querying. Our proposal relies on the description logics formalism and the stamping mechanism proposed in database field. Our approach consists of defining contextual concepts by adding stamps to constructors of complex concepts. Such stamped constructors are interpreted according to the contexts they hold in their definition. Thus, contextual concepts denote different sets of individuals with varying attributes.

## 1 Introduction

The objective of this paper is to specify contextual ontologies. Contextual ontologies provide descriptions of concepts that are context-dependent, and that may be used by several user communities. Contextual ontologies do not contradict with the usual assumption that an ontology provides a shared conceptualization of some subset of the real world. Many different conceptualizations may exist for the same real world phenomenon, depending on many factors. The objective of contextual ontologies is to gather into a single organized description several alternative conceptualizations that fully or partly address the same domain. The proposed solution has several advantages: First, it allows to maintain consistency among the different local representations of data. So, update propagation from one context to another is possible. Moreover, it enables navigating among contexts (i.e. going from one representation to another).

Beyond the multiple description aspect, the introduction of context into ontologies has many other important benefits. Indeed, querying global shared ontologies is not a straightforward process as users can be overburdened with lots of information. In fact, a great deal of information are not always relevant to the interest of particular users. For instance when querying information about land parcels, city administrators may get all information about parcels even if they are just interested only in their land use. Ontologies should provide each user with only the specific information that he or she needs and not provide every user with all information. The introduction of the notion of context in ontologies will also provide an adapted and selective access to information. Thus

N. Zhong et al. (Eds.): ISMIS 2003, LNAI 2871, pp. 339–343, 2003.
© Springer-Verlag Berlin Heidelberg 2003

contextual ontologies provide contextual representation and contextual querying of data. They extend classical ontologies and thus allow to represent the same concept according to some contexts (for instance traffic control, transportation, land use management, etc): the concept may be described using different terms or with different structures according to the different contexts. When contextual querying is done according to context, part of information may be hidden as needed: context-dependent semantics are returned.The underlying key idea of our work is to adapt the stamping mechanism proposed in [3] for the needs of multi-representation of spatial databases to meet our needs. Thus, We propose an extension of a sub-language of Description Logics (DLs) with the stamping mechanism. Section 2 presents our contextual extension of the sub-language of DL. Section 3 is devoted to the presentation of the syntax and semantic of our contextual language. Finally, section 4 concludes the paper.

## 2    Presentation of the Contextual Ontology Language

Description logics are a family of logics designed to represent taxonomic and conceptual knowledge of a particular application domain in an abstract and logical level [1]. Basically, $DL^1$ provides the definition of concepts (unary predicates) and roles (binary predicates or binary relationships between two concepts). Complex concepts and roles are derived from their atomic ones by applying constructors. A classical example is the complex concept Mother defined from the two atomic concepts Woman and Person and the atomic role hasChild by the expression: $Woman \sqcap \forall hasChild.Person$.
In order to specify contextual ontologies, we propose the notion of contextual concepts (i.e. concepts whose definition is dependant on one or more contexts). Contextual concepts are derived from atomic concepts by using a set of contextual constructors and/or a set of non-contextual ones. Contextual concepts may be partially or completely available according to context: they are interpreted according to the contexts associated with their definition. The examples used to illustrate the contextual constructors below come from a conference ontology that may be used for various conferences (e.g. ISMIS, CAISE, ... ). Indeed each conference description is similar but it also has its own particularities, like for instance a different number of reviews for the selection of papers, ...etc. In this particular example, each conference may be seen as a different context. Our examples rely on only two contexts, two different conferences using the same ontology, that are designated by $s_1$ and $s_2$ below. An extract of the conference ontology is presented in table 1 (shown in the last page of this paper). Our proposal is based on the following contextual constructors:

**The contextual value restriction constructor** $(\forall_{s_1,\cdots,s_m} R.C)$: It defines a new concept all of whose instances are related via the role $R$ only to the individuals of class $C$ and in the contexts $s_1$ to $s_m$. For example, in two contexts

---
[1] Due to space limitation, non-contextual aspects of description logics are not presented in this paper. For more details readers are referred to [2]

$s_1$ and $s_2$, the concept SubmittedPaper is defined as individuals with either an attribute title in context $s_1$ or an attribute paperId in context $s_2$. The concept is expressed as follows:

$$SubmittedPaper = \forall_{s_1} title.string \sqcup \forall_{s_2} paperId.integer$$

Outside of the two contexts $s_1$ and $s_2$, the concept *SubmittedPaper* corresponds to an empty set.

**The contextual existential quantification constructor** $(\exists_{s_1,\cdots,s_m} R.C)$: It will construct a new concept all of whose instances are related via the role R to at least one individual of type C and only in contexts $s_1$ to $s_m$. For instance, the following expression describes that student is an individual that has at least one graduation diploma in context $s_1$ and in the same time participates in at least one course in context $s_2$:

$$Student = \exists_{s_1} Diploma.Graduate \sqcap \exists_{s_2} Register.Course$$

The interpretation of Student is :

- in the context $s_1$ or $s_2$ separately it gives an empty concept,
- in both contexts ($s_1$ and $s_2$) it corresponds to individuals satisfying the two conditions of the expression.

**The contextual number (at most, at least) restriction constructors** $(\leq_{s_1,\cdots,s_m} nR, \geq_{s_1,\cdots,s_m} nR)$: They specify the number of role-fillers. The $\leq_{s_1,\cdots,s_m} nR$ is used to indicate the maximum cardinality whereas, the expression $\geq_{s_1,\cdots,s_m} nR$ indicates the minimum cardinality in the given contexts $s_1$ to $s_m$. The following example illustrates the use of different cardinalities according to contexts: context $s_1$ where a paper is considered as an accepted paper if it has two positive reviews and context $s_2$ where a paper is considered as an accepted paper if it has four positive reviews.

$$AcceptedPaper = SubmittedPaper \sqcap (\forall_{s_1,s_2} hasReview.PositiveReview) \sqcap$$
$$(\leq_{s_1} 2hasReview \sqcup \leq_{s_2} 4hasReview)$$

The interpretation of the expression AcceptedPaper is:

- in the context $s_1$ (respectively $s_2$), AcceptedPaper consists of submitted paper (always interpreted as it holds no stamps) that has at least two (respectively four) positive reviews.
- outside $s_1$ and $s_2$, the interpretation gives the empty set.

**The contextual conjunction** $(C \sqcap_{s_1,\cdots,s_m} D:)$ It will define either a concept resulting of the conjunction of the two concepts $C$ and $D$ in the defined contexts $s_1$ to $s_m$, or a concept equivalent to concept $C$ outside of all the given contexts ($s_1$ to $s_m$). For instance, the following expression describes a Poster as being in all contexts a SubmittedPaper that is not an AcceptedPaper except in context $s_1$ where it must also have at least one positive review.

$$Poster = (SubmittedPaper \sqcap \neg AcceptedPaper) \sqcap_{s_1}$$
$$(\exists_{s_1} hasReview.PositiveReview)$$

# 3  Syntactical and Semantical Aspects of Contextual Ontologies

**Definition 1. (Syntax of contextual concept terms)** *Let* $s_1, \cdots, s_m$ *be a set of context names. Contextual concept terms* $C$ *and* $D$ *can be formed by means of the following syntax:*

$C, D \longrightarrow$

$\quad\quad\quad \exists_{s_1, \cdots, s_m} R.C \mid$ (contextual existential quantification)

$\quad\quad\quad \forall_{s_1, \cdots, s_m} R.C \mid$ (contextual value restriction)

$\quad\quad\quad (\leq_{s_1, \cdots, s_m} nR) \mid$ (contextual at most number restriction)

$\quad\quad\quad (\geq_{s_1, \cdots, s_m} nR) \mid$ (contextual at least number restriction)

$\quad\quad\quad C \sqcap_{s_1, \cdots, s_m} D$ (contextual conjunction)

To define the semantics of the contextual constructors, we assume having a set of context names $S = \{s_1, s_2, ..., s_t\}$.

**Definition 2. (Semantics of contextual concept terms)** *The semantics of the contextual part of the language is given by a contextual interpretation defined in a context* $j$ *over* $\mathcal{S}$. *A context* $j$ *is either a simple context name belonging to* $\mathcal{S}$ *or a composed context defined as a conjunction of simple contexts*[2]. *A contextual interpretation* $\mathcal{CI} = (\mathcal{I}_0, \mathcal{I}_1, \cdots, \mathcal{I}_j, \cdots, \mathcal{I}_t)$ *is obtained by associating to each context* $j$ *a non-contextual interpretation* $\mathcal{I}_j = (\Delta^{\mathcal{I}}, \cdot^{\mathcal{I}j})$, *which consists of an interpretation domain* $\Delta^{\mathcal{I}}$, *and an interpretation function* $\cdot^{\mathcal{I}j}$. *The interpretation function* $\cdot^{\mathcal{I}j}$ *maps each atomic concept* $A \in \mathcal{C}$ *to a subset* $A^{\mathcal{I}}j \subseteq \Delta^{\mathcal{I}}$ *and each role name* $R \in \mathcal{R}$ *to a subset* $R^{\mathcal{I}}j \subseteq \Delta^{\mathcal{I}} \times \Delta^{\mathcal{I}}$. *Let* $Co(j)$ *be a function which returns a set of all context names appearing in a simple/composed argument context* $j$[3]. *The extension of* $\cdot^{\mathcal{I}j}$ *to arbitrary concepts is inductively defined as follows:*

$(\exists_{s_1, \cdots, s_m} R.C)^{\mathcal{I}}j = \{x \in \Delta^{\mathcal{I}} \mid \exists y : (x, y) \in R^{\mathcal{I}}j \wedge y \in C^{\mathcal{I}}j \wedge Co(j) \cap \{s_1, \cdots, s_m\} \neq \emptyset\}$

$(\forall_{s_1, \cdots, s_m} R.C)^{\mathcal{I}}j = \{x \in \Delta^{\mathcal{I}} \mid \forall y : (x, y) \in R^{\mathcal{I}}j \to y \in C^{\mathcal{I}}j \wedge Co(j) \cap \{s_1, \cdots, s_m\} \neq \emptyset\}$

$(\leq_{s_1, \cdots, s_m} nR)^{\mathcal{I}}j = \{x \in \Delta^{\mathcal{I}} \mid Co(j) \cap \{s_1, \cdots, s_m\} \neq \emptyset \quad \|\{y \mid (x, y) \in R^{\mathcal{I}}j\}\| \leq n\}$

$(\geq_{s_1, \cdots, s_m} nR)^{\mathcal{I}}j = \{x \in \Delta^{\mathcal{I}} \mid Co(j) \cap \{s_1, \cdots, s_m\} \neq \emptyset \quad \|\{y \mid (x, y) \in R^{\mathcal{I}}j\}\| \geq n\}$

$(C \sqcap_{s_1, \cdots, s_m} D)^{\mathcal{I}}j = \{x \in \Delta^{\mathcal{I}} \mid x \in C^{\mathcal{I}}j\} if Co(j) \cap \{s_1, \cdots, s_m\} = \emptyset,$

$= \{x \in \Delta^{\mathcal{I}} \mid x \in C^{\mathcal{I}}j \cap D^{\mathcal{I}}j\} if Co(j) \cap \{s_1, \cdots, s_m\} \neq \emptyset$

A terminological axiom $A = D$ is satisfied by a contextual interpretation $\mathcal{CI}$ if $A^{\mathcal{I}}j = D^{\mathcal{I}}j$ for every context $j$. A contextual interpretation $\mathcal{CI}$ is a model for a $TBox$ $\mathcal{T}$ if and only if $\mathcal{CI}$ satisfies all the assertions in $\mathcal{T}$. Finally, a concept $D$ subsumes a concept $C$ iff $C \sqsubseteq D$ is satisfied in every contextual interpretation $\mathcal{CI}$. The contextual constructors proposed in this paper can be viewed as an adaptive constructors that specialize the non-contextual ones. With respect to the decidability problem the reducing of our language to the decidable modal description logics language [4] is under consideration.

---

[2] $j = s_1$ and $j = s_1 \wedge s_2$ are two examples of simple context and composed context respectively.

[3] $Co(s_1 \wedge s_2) = \{s_1, s_2\}$ and $Co(s_1) = \{s_1\}$ are two examples of the function $Co$.

**Table 1.** Contextual Ontology Example of Conferences

---

Concepts defintion

---

**SubmittedPaper** $= ((\geq_{s_1,s_2} 1HasAuthor) \sqcap (\forall_{s_1,s_2} HasAuthor.Author) \sqcap$
$( \leq_{s_1,s_2} 1Title) \sqcap (\geq_{s_1,s_2} 1Title) \sqcap (\forall_{s_1,s_2} Title.String)) \sqcup$
$(\leq_{s_1} 1Id) \sqcap (\geq_{s_1} 1Id) \sqcap (\forall_{s_1} Id.Integer))$

**AcceptedPaper** $= SubmittedPaper \sqcap (\forall_{s_1,s_2} HasReview.PositiveReview) \sqcap$
$(\geq_{s_1} 2HasReview) \sqcap (\geq_{s_2} 4HasReview)$

**Poster** $= SubmittedPaper \sqcap \neg AcceptedPaper$
$\sqcap_{s_1} (\exists_{s_1} hasReview.PositiveReview)$

**PublishedPaper** $= AcceptedPaper \sqcap_{s_1} Poster$

**FreeParticipant** $= Student \sqcup InvitedSpeaker$

**Student** $= \exists_{s_1} Diploma.Graduate \sqcap \exists_{s_2} Register.Course$

---

# 4   Conclusion

In this paper, we proposed an ontology representation language that should provide contextual representation and contextual querying of data. Our proposal
relies on the description logics formalism and the stamping mechanism proposed
in database field. In our approach contextual concepts are classical concepts
holding stamps. They are interpreted according to the contexts in which they
are defined : the same concept denotes a different set of individuals in different contexts. We are actually working on the assertional part on the language.
Our contextual language for ontologies is still under construction. Moreover, we
intend to define a class-based logic query language to deal with the need of
browsing and searching concepts in large contextual ontologies.

# References

1. Franz Baader, Ian Horrocks, and Ulrike Sattler. Description logics as ontology
   languages for the semantic web. In *In Dieter Hutter and Werner Stephan, editors,
   Festschrift in honor of Jörg Siekmann, Lecture Notes in AI. Springer,* 2003.
2. M. Buchheit, F.M. Donini, and A. Scharaef. Decidable reasoning in terminological
   knowledge representation systems. *Journal of AI Research,* 1:109–138, 1993.
3. C. Vangenot, C. Parent, and S. Spaccapietra. Supporting decision-making with
   alternative data representations. *Journal of Geographic Information and Decision
   Analysis,* 5/2, 2001. Available : http://www.geodec.org/.
4. F. Wolter and M. Zakharyaschev. Satisfiability problem in description logics with
   modal operators. In *In Proceedings of the 6th Int. Conf. on Knowledge Representation and Reasonning, KR'98, Trento, Italy, June 1998.,* pages 512–523, 2001.

# An Email Classifier Based on Resemblance

Chung Keung Poon and Matthew Chang

Dept. of Computer Science, City U. of Hong Kong, China
ckpoon@cs.cityu.edu.hk

**Abstract.** In this paper, we study the email classification problem. We apply the notion of shingling to capture the concept of phrases. For each email, we form a sketch which is compact in size and the sketch of two emails allows for computation of their resemblance. We then apply a $k$-nearest neighbour algorithm to classify the emails. Experimental evaluation shows that a high degree of accuracy can be obtained.

## 1 Introduction

Nowadays, most common email clients provide users with handy facilities to detect spam mails. However, the process of email filing is still by-and-large done manually. Thus the problem of automatic email classification has attracted a lot of attentions. classification.

Rule-based approach is one of the most popular approaches applied in email classification. Earlier systems, such as ISHMAIL ([4]), made use of handcrafted rules. Newer systems studied in [3,7,5] aim at automatically generating rules. While they generate human-readable rules, they are not very adaptable to changes in classification requirement.

A number of different approaches fall into the general framework of TF-IDF. First, each email is mapped to a vector of keyword weightings based on the concept of term frequency and inverse document frequency. The *term frequency* (TF) of a keyword in a document is the number of times it appears in that document. However, if the keyword appears in many documents as well, it will not be as discriminating as a keyword that appears only in a certain class of documents. The *inverse document frequency* (IDF) captures the idea by having a decreasing value as the number of documents containing the keyword increases. In the extreme case, if the keyword appears in all the documents (e.g., words like "a", "the"), the keyword is useless. These are called *stopwords* and are often removed from consideration. For the relevant keywords, we can multiply the TF and IDF to form their keyword weightings. Other methods of combining the TF and IDF are possible, depending on specific methods.

After mapping the emails to vectors, classification can be done in a number of ways, including the $k$-means algorithm (e.g., [6,10]), the $k$-nearest neighbour algorithm (e.g., [7]), Support Vector Machines (SVM) (e.g. [2]) and even the naive Bayesian classifier (e.g., [9]).

While the TF-IDF framework is based on individual keywords, our approach works with phrases. Specifically, we applied a sketching technique due to Broder

N. Zhong et al. (Eds.): ISMIS 2003, LNAI 2871, pp. 344–348, 2003.

[1] to compute a sketch for each email body. The sketches, though compact in size, allow for the computation of a similarity measure called *resemblance* between two emails. We believe that this measure better captures the concept of phrases in a document. Also, no stopword removal and stemming are needed in our method.

After mapping the emails to sketches, we apply a variant of $k$-nearest neighbour algorithms to classify each new email. This simple idea allows us to adapt to changes in classification requirement easily.

Furthermore, notice that an email differs from a document in the traditional document clustering problem in that it has, besides the message content, other components such as sender, subject, date, etc. It is expected that the relationship between a sender and a receiver is rather stable. Hence the sender field can give some clue to the classification. However, the reply-address and the subject may be misleading sometimes. Thus we will only use these information in a careful way so as not to introduce error as far as possible. Details will be given in the full paper.

Our experimental results show that our system achieves a high degree of accuracy. Moreover, the execution time is reasonably fast.

In Section 2, we will introduce the concept of shingles and resemblance. In Section 3, we discuss the classification based on message content and the email headers. Section 4 presents some experimental results.

## 2    Resemblance of Emails

Here, we assume a document is a sequence of words separated by blanks. We define a $w$-shingle of a document as a contiguous sequence of $w$ words in the document. The $w$-shingling of a document $A$, denoted $S_w(A)$, is defined as the multi-set of all $w$-shingles in $A$. The *resemblance* of documents, $A$ and $B$, is defined as $r_w(A, B) = \frac{|S_w(A) \cap S_w(B)|}{|S_w(A) \cup S_w(B)|}$.

It is possible that $r_w(A, B) = 1$ but $B$ is quite different from $A$. For example, consider $w = 1$ and $B$ is any permutation of $A$. In general, the larger value of $w$, the more stringent requirement we impose on $A$ and $B$ in order to classify them as similar. In our application here, we aim at capturing phrases of length 2 to 4. Hence we will choose $w = 2$ to 4.

Note that the size, $|S_w(A)|$, of the $w$-shingling of $A$ is equal to $n - w + 1$ when $A$ is a document with $n$ words. That means, storing $S_w(A)$ requires storing $w(n - w + 1)$ (English) words, which is larger than the original document by a factor of $w$. To reduce the storage cost and computation time, for each email, we take a sample of a fixed number, $s$, of shingles and store them using Rabin's fingerprint [8]. In short, Rabin's fingerprinting technique involves picking a random hash function $f$ to map each shingle to an $l$-bit number (the fingerprint) for some suitable parameter $l$. In practice, choosing $l = 64$ and taking a sample of $s = 100$ shingles achieve a satisfactory accuracy as well as a fast execution time and reasonable storage requirement. For more detail explanation on the mathematical foundation, see [1].

## 3    Message Content Classification

First of all, a preprocessing step is done to remove any formatting information such as HTML tags from the message content. Then we compute the $w$-shingling of the email content and store a sample of $s$ shingles using their fingerprints. In practice, the sampling is done by first computing the fingerprint of each shingle and then taking the smallest $s$ fingerprints. This is done for each classified email in the system.

To classify a new email $A$, we employ a variant of the $k$-nearest neighbour algorithm detailed as follows. We calculate the resemblance of $A$ with all the existing classified emails in the system. We take the top 10 emails according to the resemblance and take note of their folders. We sum the total resemblance of each folder among these 10 emails and choose the folder with the highest total resemblance as the candidate. (Weighting by resemblance is necessary because one almost identical email in a folder is a better match than 3 somewhat similar emails in another folder.)

If the score is above a threshold (currently chosen as 0.1), we classify the new email $A$ as belonging to the top folder. Otherwise, we consider the new email as belonging to a new folder.

## 4    Experimental Results

We tested our system with a mail store consisting of 649 emails distributed in 14 folders. There is one dense folder which accounts for almost half of the emails. There are also 6 sparse folders each containing 11 emails or less. The other folders are medium-sized. The folder sizes are shown in Figure 1 (a) below. Note that this represents a typical scenario in which the folder sizes are highly uneven.

In each test, we give the system emails one by one. For each new email, the system chooses the best folder. Otherwise, it opens a new folder. Then the system is informed of the correct classification before taking the next email. At the end, we record the precision and recall of each folder. We also keep track of the overall accuracy as the system goes through the emails. Notice that the first email of each folder does not contribute to the statistics.

The precisions and recalls shown in Figure 1 (a) are obtained when we set $w = 2$, $s = 100$ and we have made use of the sender information.

Figure 1 (b) shows the learning rate as well as the effect of the sender field in the accuracy. The upper (resp. lower) curve is the overall accuracy with (resp. without) sender information. It shows a significant improvement in accuracy when the sender information is used.

### 4.1    Effect of $w$ and $s$

The table on the left hand side in Figure 2 shows the overall accuracy when using different values of $w$. The sample size $s$ is fixed at 100 and the sender information is not used.

| Folder ID | No. of emails | Precision | Recall |
|---|---|---|---|
| 11 | 338 | 96.19% | 97.33% |
| 8 | 77 | 98.70% | 100.00% |
| 23 | 47 | 97.44% | 82.61% |
| 10 | 38 | 84.21% | 86.49% |
| 5 | 37 | 100.00% | 83.33% |
| 21 | 28 | 100.00% | 92.59% |
| 20 | 26 | 100.00% | 80.00% |
| 18 | 18 | 100.00% | 94.12% |
| 25 | 11 | 100.00% | 80.00% |
| 16 | 10 | 100.00% | 100.00% |
| 17 | 8 | 100.00% | 100.00% |
| 14 | 4 | 100.00% | 100.00% |
| 27 | 4 | 66.67% | 66.67% |
| 22 | 3 | 100.00% | 100.00% |

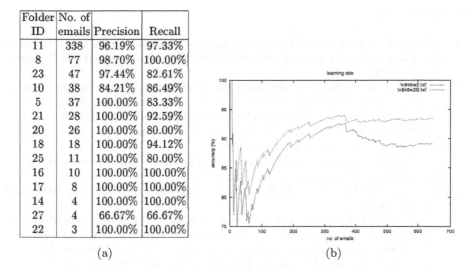

(a)                                    (b)

**Fig. 1.** (a) The size, precision and recall of each folder, (b) the learning curve

| $w$ | overall accuracy |
|---|---|
| 1 | 81.36% |
| 2 | 89.21% |
| 3 | 85.82% |
| 4 | 86.28% |

| $s$ | overall accuracy |
|---|---|
| 25 | 92.46% |
| 50 | 93.69% |
| 75 | 93.38% |
| 100 | 93.53% |

**Fig. 2.** Effect of $w$ (left) and effect of $s$ (right)

It shows that for $w = 2, 3, 4$, the accuracy is significantly better than $w = 1$, i.e., when individual keywords are considered. (A similar pattern is exhibited with the sender information is used and we omitted it in this paper.) We believe that it is because the 1-shingling contains a lot of stopwords and hence create a lot of matchings. Thus we tested our method again by removing the stopwords before computing the 1-shingles. We found that accuracy is improved dramatically from 81.36% to 87.06%. Interestingly, we found that for $w = 2$, the accuracy slightly decreases after stopword removal. This agrees with previous research work suggesting that stopwords are not redundant in a phrase.

The table on the right hand side in Figure 2 shows the overall accuracy when using different number of samples of shingles. The value of $w$ is fixed at 2 and the sender information is used. It seems that there is not much degradation in the accuracy when we decrease the sample size $s$.

# References

1. A.Z. Broder. On the resemblance and containment of documents. In *Compression and Complexity of Sequences (SEQUENCES'97)*, pages 21–29. IEEE Computer Society, 1997.
2. C. Brutlag and J. Meek. Challenges of the email domain for text classification. In *17th International Conference on Machine Learning*, pages 103–110, July 2000.
3. W.W. Cohen. Learning rules that classify e-mail. pages 18–25, 1996.
4. J. Helfman and C. Isbell. Ishmail: immediate identification of important information. Technical report, AT&T Labs, 1995.
5. J. Itskevitch. Automatic hierarchical e-mail classification using association rules. Master's thesis, Simon Fraser University, 2001.
6. G. Manco, E. Masciari, M. Ruffolo, and A. Tagarelli. Towards an adaptive mail classifier, 2002.
7. T. Payne and P. Edwards. Interface agents that learn: an investigation of learning issues in a mail agent interface. *Applied Artificial Intelligence*, 11:1–32, 1997.
8. M.O. Rabin. Fingerprint by random polynomials. Technical Report TR-15-81, Center for Research in Computing Technology, Harvard University, 1981.
9. Jason Rennie. ifile: an application of machine learning to e-mail filtering. In *Proceedings of the KDD-2000 Workshop on Text Mining*, 1995.
10. B.R. Segal and J.O. Kephart. Mailcat: an intelligent assistant for organizing email. In *Proc. of the 3rd International Conference on Autonomous Agents*, pages 276–282, 1999.

# The Characterization on the Uniqueness of Answer Set for Prioritized Logic Programs

Yan Zhang and Yun Bai

School of Computing and Information Technology
University of Western Sydney
Penrith South DC, NSW 1797, Australia
{yan,ybai}@cit.uws.edu.au

**Abstract.** Prioritized logic programming has illustrated its rich expressiveness and flexibility in knowledge representation and reasoning. However, some important aspects of prioritized logic programs have yet to be thoroughly explored. In this paper, we investigate basic properties of prioritized logic programs in the context of answer set semantics. Specifically, we propose a characterization on the uniqueness of answer set for prioritized logic programs, which has a weaker form than the traditional local stratification for general logic programs.

**Keywords:** Foundation of logic programming, knowledge representation, semantics

## 1 Introduction

Prioritized logic programming has illustrated its rich expressiveness and flexibility in knowledge representation, reasoning about action and logic program based updates [2,5,7,8]. However, some important aspects of prioritized logic programs have yet to be thoroughly explored. In this paper, we investigate several properties of prioritized logic programs in the context of answer set semantics. Specifically, we propose a characterization on the uniqueness of answer set for prioritized logic programs. We show that our characteristic condition is weaker than the traditional local stratification for general logic programs [1]. The paper is organized as follows. Section 2 briefly reviews the syntax and semantics of prioritized logic programs. Section 3 proves a unique answer set theorem for prioritized logic programs. Finally, section 4 concludes the paper with some remarks.

## 2 Prioritized Logic Programs

To begin with, we first briefly review prioritized logic programs (PLPs) proposed by the author recently [7]. To specify PLPs, we first introduce the extended logic program and its answer set semantics developed by Gelfond and Lifschitz [4]. A language $\mathcal{L}$ of extended logic programs is determined by its object constants, function constants and predicates constants. *Terms* are built as in the

N. Zhong et al. (Eds.): ISMIS 2003, LNAI 2871, pp. 349–356, 2003.

corresponding first order language; *atoms* have the form $P(t_1, \cdots, t_n)$, where $t_i$ $(1 \le i \le n)$ is a term and $P$ is a predicate constant of arity $n$; a *literal* is either an atom $P(t_1, \cdots, t_n)$ or a negative atom $\neg P(t_1, \cdots, t_n)$. A *rule* is an expression of the form:

$$L_0 \leftarrow L_1, \cdots, L_m, not L_{m+1}, \cdots, not L_n, \tag{1}$$

where each $L_i$ $(0 \le i \le n)$ is a literal. $L_0$ is called the *head* of the rule, while $L_1, \cdots, L_m, not\ L_{m+1}, \cdots, not\ L_n$ is called the *body* of the rule. Obviously, the body of a rule could be empty. A term, atom, literal, or rule is *ground* if no variable occurs in it. An *extended logic program* $\Pi$ is a collection of rules.

To evaluate an extended logic program, Gelfond and Lifschitz proposed answer set semantics for extended logic programs. Let $\Pi$ be an extended logic program not containing *not* and *Lit* the set of all ground literals in the language of $\Pi$. The *answer set* of $\Pi$, denoted as $Ans(\Pi)$, is the smallest subset $S$ of *Lit* such that (i) for any rule $L_0 \leftarrow L_1, \cdots, L_m$ from $\Pi$, if $L_1, \cdots, L_m \in S$, then $L_0 \in S$; and (ii) if $S$ contains a pair of complementary literals, then $S = Lit$. Now let $\Pi$ be an arbitrary extended logic program. For any subset $S$ of *Lit*, let $\Pi^S$ be the logic program obtained from $\Pi$ by deleting (i) each rule that has a formula *not L* in its body with $L \in S$, and (ii) all formulas of the form *not L* in the bodies of the remaining rules[1]. We define that $S$ is an *answer set* of $\Pi$, denoted by $Ans(\Pi)$, iff $S$ is an answer set of $\Pi^S$, i.e. $S = Ans(\Pi^S)$.

It is easy to see that an extended logic program may have one, more than one, or no answer set at all. The language $\mathcal{L}^P$ of PLPs is a language $\mathcal{L}$ of extended logic programs [4] with the following augments:
- *Names:* $N, N_1, N_2, \cdots$.
- A strict partial ordering $<$ on names.
- A naming function $\mathcal{N}$, which maps a rule to a name.
A *prioritized logic program* (PLP) $\mathcal{P}$ is a triple $(\Pi, \mathcal{N}, <)$, where $\Pi$ is an extended logic program, $\mathcal{N}$ is a naming function mapping each rule in $\Pi$ to a name, and $<$ is a strict partial ordering on names. The partial ordering $<$ in $\mathcal{P}$ plays an essential role in the evaluation of $\mathcal{P}$. We also use $\mathcal{P}(<)$ to denote the set of $<$-relations of $\mathcal{P}$. Intuitively $<$ represents a preference of applying rules during the evaluation of the program. In particular, if $\mathcal{N}(r) < \mathcal{N}(r')$ holds in $\mathcal{P}$, rule $r$ would be preferred to apply over rule $r'$ during the evaluation of $\mathcal{P}$ (i.e. rule $r$ is more preferred than rule $r'$). Consider the following classical example represented in our formalism:

$\mathcal{P}_1$:
$N_1 : Fly(x) \leftarrow Bird(x),\ not\ \neg Fly(x)$,
$N_2 : \neg Fly(x) \leftarrow Penguin(x),\ not\ Fly(x)$,
$N_3 : Bird(Tweety) \leftarrow$,
$N_4 : Penguin(Tweety) \leftarrow$,
$N_2 < N_1$.

Obviously, rules $N_1$ and $N_2$ conflict with each other as their heads are complementary literals, and applying $N_1$ will defeat $N_2$ and *vice versa*. However, as

---

[1] We also call $\Pi^S$ is the Gelfond-Lifschitz transformation of $\Pi$ in terms of $S$.

$N_2 < N_1$, we would expect that rule $N_2$ is preferred to apply first and then defeat rule $N_1$ after applying $N_2$ so that the desired solution $\neg Fly(Tweety)$ can be derived.

In a PLP or an extended logic program, we usually view a rule including variables to be the set of all ground instances of this rule formed from the set of ground literals in the language.

**Definition 1.** *Let $\Pi$ be a ground extended logic program and $r$ a rule with the form $L_0 \leftarrow L_1, \cdots, L_m, \text{ not } L_{m+1}, \cdots, \text{ not } L_n$ ($r$ does not necessarily belong to $\Pi$). Rule $r$ is defeated by $\Pi$ iff $\Pi$ has an answer set and for any answer set $Ans(\Pi)$ of $\Pi$, there exists some $L_i \in Ans(\Pi)$, where $m + 1 \le i \le n$.*

The evaluation of a PLP will be based on its ground form. That is, for any PLP $\mathcal{P} = (\Pi, \mathcal{N}, <)$, we consider its *ground instantiation* $\mathcal{P}' = (\Pi', \mathcal{N}', <')$, where $\Pi'$, $\mathcal{N}'$ and $<'$ are ground instantiations of $\Pi$, $\mathcal{N}$ and $<$ respectively[2]. However, this requires some restriction on a PLP since not every PLP's ground instantiation presents a consistent information with respect to the original PLP.

Given a PLP $\mathcal{P} = (\Pi, \mathcal{N}, <)$. We say $\mathcal{P}$ is *well formed* if there does not exist a rule $r'$ that is an instance of two different rules $r_1$ and $r_2$ in $\Pi$ and $\mathcal{N}(r_1) < \mathcal{N}(r_2) \in \mathcal{P}(<)$. In the rest of this paper, we will only consider well formed PLPs in our discussions, and consequently, the evaluation for an arbitrary program $\mathcal{P} = (\Pi, \mathcal{N}, <)$ will be based on its ground instantiation $\mathcal{P}' = (\Pi', \mathcal{N}', <')$. Therefore, in our context a ground prioritized (or extended) logic program may contain infinite number of rules. In this case, we will assume that this ground program is the ground instantiation of some program that only contains finite number of rules.

Let us consider program $\mathcal{P}_1$ once again. Since $N_2 < N_1$ and $N_1$ is defeated by $\mathcal{P}_1 - \{N_1\}$ (i.e. the unique answer set of $\mathcal{P}_1 - \{N_1\}$ is $\{Bird(Tweety), Penguin(Tweety), \neg Fly(Tweety)\}$), rule $N_1$ should be ignored during the evaluation of $\mathcal{P}_1$.

**Definition 2.** *Let $\mathcal{P} = (\Pi, \mathcal{N}, <)$ be a prioritized extended logic program. $\mathcal{P}^<$ is a reduct of $\mathcal{P}$ with respect to $<$ if and only if there exists a sequence of sets $\Pi_i$ ($i = 0, 1, \cdots$) such that:*

1. $\Pi_0 = \Pi$;
2. $\Pi_i = \Pi_{i-1} - \{r_1, r_2, \cdots \mid$ *(a) there exists $r \in \Pi_{i-1}$ such that for every $j$ ($j = 1, 2, \cdots$), $\mathcal{N}(r) < \mathcal{N}(r_j) \in \mathcal{P}(<)$ and $r_1, \cdots$, are defeated by $\Pi_{i-1} - \{r_1, r_2, \cdots\}$, and (b) there does not exist a rule $r' \in \Pi_{i-1}$ such that $N(r_j) < N(r')$ for some $j$ ($j = 1, 2, \cdots$) and $r'$ is defeated by $\Pi_{i-1} - \{r'\}\}$*;
3. $\mathcal{P}^< = \bigcap_{i=0}^{\infty} \Pi_i$.

In Definition 2, $\mathcal{P}^<$ is a ground extended logic program obtained from $\Pi$ by eliminating some rules from $\Pi$. In particular, if $\mathcal{N}(r) < \mathcal{N}(r_1)$, $\mathcal{N}(r) <$

---

[2] Note that if $\mathcal{P}'$ is a ground instantiation of $\mathcal{P}$, then $\mathcal{N}(r_1) < \mathcal{N}(r_2) \in \mathcal{P}(<)$ implies $\mathcal{N}'(r_1') <' \mathcal{N}'(r_2') \in \mathcal{P}'(<')$, where $r_1'$ and $r_2'$ are ground instances of $r_1$ and $r_2$ respectively.

$\mathcal{N}(r_2)$, $\cdots$, and $\Pi_{i-1} - \{r_1, r_2, \cdots\}$ defeats $\{r_1, r_2, \cdots\}$, then rules $r_1, r_2, \cdots$ will be eliminated from $\Pi_{i-1}$ if no *less preferred rule* can be eliminated (i.e. conditions (a) and (b)). This procedure is continued until a fixed point is reached. It is worth to note that the generation of a reduct of a PLP is based on the ground form of its extended logic program part. Furthermore, if $\mathcal{N}(r_1) < \mathcal{N}(r_2)$ holds in a PLP where $r_1$ or $r_2$ includes variables, then $\mathcal{N}(r_1) < \mathcal{N}(r_2)$ is actually viewed as the set of $<$-relations $\mathcal{N}(r_1') < \mathcal{N}(r_2')$, where $r_1'$ and $r_2'$ are ground instances of $r_1$ and $r_2$ respectively.

**Definition 3.** *Let $\mathcal{P} = (\Pi, \mathcal{N}, <)$ be a PLP and Lit the set of all ground literals in the language of $\mathcal{P}$. For any subset $S$ of Lit, $S$ is an answer set of $\mathcal{P}$, denoted as $Ans^P(\mathcal{P})$, iff $S = Ans(\mathcal{P}^<)$ for some reduct $\mathcal{P}^<$ of $\mathcal{P}$. Given a PLP $\mathcal{P}$, a ground literal $L$ is entailed from $\mathcal{P}$, denoted as $\mathcal{P} \models L$, if $L$ belongs to every answer set of $\mathcal{P}$.*

Using Definitions 2 and 3, it is easy to conclude that $\mathcal{P}_1$ has a unique reduct as follows:

$$\mathcal{P}_1^< = \{\neg Fly(x) \leftarrow Penguin(x), \ not\ Fly(x),$$
$$Bird(Tweety) \leftarrow, Penguin(Tweety) \leftarrow\},$$

from which we obtain the following answer set of $\mathcal{P}_1$:

$$Ans^P(\mathcal{P}_1) = \{Bird(Tweety), \ Penguin(Tweety), \neg Fly(Tweety)\}.$$

Now we consider another program $\mathcal{P}_2$:

$$N_1 : A \leftarrow,$$
$$N_2 : B \leftarrow not\ C,$$
$$N_3 : D \leftarrow,$$
$$N_4 : C \leftarrow not\ B,$$
$$N_1 < N_2, N_3 < N_4.$$

According to Definition 2, it is easy to see that $\mathcal{P}_2$ has two reducts:

$$\{A \leftarrow, \quad D \leftarrow, \quad C \leftarrow not\ B\}, \text{ and}$$
$$\{A \leftarrow, \quad B \leftarrow not\ C, \quad D \leftarrow\}.$$

From Definition 3, it follows that $\mathcal{P}_2$ has two answer sets: $\{A, C, D\}$ and $\{A, B, D\}$.

## 3   A Unique Answer Set Theorem

Now we try to provide a unique characterization of the answer set for a prioritized logic program. To investigate this issue, we first extend the concept of local stratification for general logic programs [1] to extended logic programs.

**Definition 4.** *Let $\Pi$ be an extended logic program and Lit be the set of all ground literals of $\Pi$.*

1. A local stratification *for $\Pi$ is a function* stratum *from Lit to the countable ordinals.*
2. *Given a local stratification* stratum, *we extend it to ground literals with negation as failure by setting* stratum$(not\ L) = $ stratum$(L) + 1$, *where $L$ is a ground literal.*
3. *A rule* $L_0 \leftarrow L_1, \cdots, L_m,\ not\ L_{m+1}, \cdots,\ not\ L_n$ *in $\Pi$ is locally stratified with respect to* stratum *if*
   stratum$(L_0) \geq$ stratum$(L_i)$, *where* $1 \leq i \leq m$, *and*
   stratum$(L_0) >$ stratum$(not L_j)$, *where* $m + 1 \leq j \leq n$.
4. $\Pi$ *is called* locally stratified *with respect to* stratum *if all of its rules are locally stratified. $\Pi$ is called* locally stratified *if it is locally stratified with respect to some local stratification.*

Let $\Pi$ be a ground extended logic program and $r$ be a rule in $\Pi$ of the form:

$$L_0 \leftarrow L_1, \cdots, L_m,\ not\ L_{m+1}, \cdots,\ not\ L_n.$$

We use $pos(r)$ to denote the set of literals in the body of $r$ without negation as failure $\{L_1, \cdots, L_m\}$, and $neg(r)$ the set of literals in the body of $r$ with negation as failure $\{L_{m+1}, \cdots, L_n\}$. We specify $body(r)$ to be $pos(r) \cup neg(r)$. We also use $head(r)$ to denote the head of $r$: $\{L_0\}$. Then we use $lit(r)$ to denote $head(r) \cup body(r)$. By extending these notations, we use $pos(\Pi)$, $neg(\Pi)$, $body(\Pi)$, $head(\Pi)$, and $lit(\Pi)$ to denote the unions of corresponding components of all rules in $\Pi$, e.g. $body(\Pi) = \bigcup_{r \in \Pi} body(r)$. If $\Pi$ is a non-ground program, then notions $pos(\Pi)$, $neg(\Pi)$, $body(\Pi)$, $head(\Pi)$, and $lit(\Pi)$ are defined based on the ground instantiation of $\Pi$.

**Definition 5.** *Let $\Pi$ be an extended logic program and $r_p$ and $r_q$ be two rules in $\Pi$. We define a set $\mathcal{D}(r_p)$ of literals with respect to $r_p$ as follows:*

$\mathcal{D}_0 = \{head(r_p)\};$
$\mathcal{D}_i = \mathcal{D}_{i-1} \cup \{head(r) \mid head(r') \in pos(r)$ *where* $r \in \Pi$ *and* $r'$ *are those rules such that* $head(r') \in \mathcal{D}_{i-1}\};$
$\mathcal{D}(r_p) = \bigcup_{i=1}^{\infty} \mathcal{D}_i.$

*We say that $r_q$ is* defeasible through $r_p$ *in $\Pi$ if and only if $neg(r_q) \cap \mathcal{D}(r_p) \neq \emptyset$. $r_p$ and $r_q$ are called* mutually defeasible *in $\Pi$ if $r_q$ is defeasible through $r_p$ and $r_p$ is defeasible through $r_q$ in $\Pi$.*

Intuitively, if $r_q$ is defeasible through $r_p$ in $\Pi$, then there exists a sequence of rules $r_1, r_2, \cdots, r_l, \cdots$ such that $head(r_p)$ occurs in $pos(r_1)$, $head(r_i)$ occurs in $pos(r_{i+1})$ for all $i = 1, \cdots$, and for some $k$, $head(r_k)$ occurs in $neg(r_q)$. Under this condition, it is clear that by triggering rule $r_p$ in $\Pi$, it is possible to defeat rule $r_q$ if rules $r_1, \cdots, r_k$ are triggered as well. As a special case that $\mathcal{D}(r_p) = \emptyset$, $r_q$ is defeasible through $r_p$ iff $head(r_p) \in neg(r_q)$. The following proposition simply describes the relationship between local stratification and mutual defeasibility.

**Proposition 1.** *Given a ground extended logic program $\Pi$. If $\Pi$ is locally stratified, then there are no mutually defeasible pairs of rules in $\Pi$.*

It is easy to observe that the converse of Proposition 3 does not hold. Consider an extended logic program consisting of three rules

$A \leftarrow,$
$B \leftarrow notC, notA,$
$C \leftarrow B, notA.$

There does not exist two rules in this program that are mutually defeasible. But this program is not locally stratified.

**Proposition 2.** *Let $\Pi$ be a ground extended logic program. If $\Pi$ is locally stratified, then $\Pi$ has a unique answer set*[3].

The above result is easy to prove from the corresponding result for general logic programs showed in [3] based on Gelfond and Lifschitz's translation from an extended logic program to a general logic program [4]. It is observed that for a PLP $\mathcal{P} = (\Pi, \mathcal{N}, <)$, if $\Pi$ is locally stratified, then $\mathcal{P}$ will also have a unique answer set. In other words, $\Pi$'s local stratification implies that $\mathcal{P}$ has a unique answer set. However, this condition seems too strong because many prioritized logic programs will still have unique answer sets although their corresponding extended logic programs are not locally stratified. For instance, program $\mathcal{P}_1$ presented in section 2 has a unique answer set but its corresponding extended logic program is not locally stratified. But one fact is clear: the uniqueness of reduct for a PLP is necessary to guarantee this PLP to have a unique answer set.

The above observation suggests that we should first investigate the condition under which a prioritized logic program has a unique reduct. Then by applying Proposition 3 to the unique reduct of the PLP, we obtain the unique answer set condition for this PLP.

**Definition 6.** *Let $\mathcal{P} = (\Pi, \mathcal{N} <)$ be an arbitrary PLP. A $<$-partition of $\Pi$ in $\mathcal{P}$ is a finite collection $\{\Pi_1, \cdots, \Pi_k\}$, where $\Pi = \Pi_1 \cup \cdots \cup \Pi_k$ and $\Pi_i$ and $\Pi_j$ are disjoint for any $i \neq j$, such that*

1. $\mathcal{N}(r) < \mathcal{N}(r') \in \mathcal{P}(<)$ *implies that there exist some $i$ and $j$ ($1 \leq i < j$) such that $r' \in \Pi_j$ and $r \in \Pi_i$;*
2. *for each rule $r' \in \Pi_j$ ($j > 1$), there exists some rule $r \in \Pi_i$ ($1 \leq i < j$) such that*
$\mathcal{N}(r) < \mathcal{N}(r') \in \mathcal{P}(<).$

*Example 1.* Consider a PLP $\mathcal{P}_4 = (\Pi, \mathcal{N}, <)$:

$\mathcal{P}_4$:
$\quad N_1 : A \leftarrow not\ B, not\ C,$
$\quad N_2 : B \leftarrow not\ \neg C,$
$\quad N_3 : C \leftarrow not\ A, not\ \neg C,$
$\quad N_4 : \neg C \leftarrow not\ C,$
$\quad N_1 < N_2, N_2 < N_4, N_3 < N_4.$

It is easy to verify that a $<$-partition of $\Pi$ in $\mathcal{P}_4$ is $\{\Pi_1, \Pi_2, \Pi_3\}$, where

---
[3] Recall that if $\Pi$ has an inconsistent answer set, we will denote it as *Lit*.

$\Pi_1$:

$\qquad N_1 : A \leftarrow not\ B,\ not\ C,$
$\qquad N_3 : C \leftarrow not\ A,\ not\ \neg C,$

$\Pi_2$:

$\qquad N_2 : B \leftarrow not\ \neg C,$

$\Pi_3$:

$\qquad N_4 : \neg C \leftarrow not\ C.$

In fact, this program has unique answer set $\{B, C\}$.

**Theorem 1.** *Every prioritized logic program has a $<$-partition.*

**Theorem 2.** *(Unique Answer Set Theorem) Let $\mathcal{P} = (\Pi, \mathcal{N}\ <)$ be a ground PLP and $\{\Pi_1, \cdots, \Pi_k\}$ be a $<$-partition of $\Pi$ in $\mathcal{P}$. $\mathcal{P}$ has a unique reduct if there does not exist two rules $r_p$ and $r_q$ in $\Pi_i$ and $\Pi_j$ $(i, j > 1)$ respectively such that $r_p$ and $r_q$ are mutually defeasible in $\Pi$. $\mathcal{P}$ has a unique answer set if $\mathcal{P}$ has a unique locally stratified reduct.*

*Proof.* According to Proposition 3, it is sufficient to only prove the first part of this theorem: $\mathcal{P}$ has a unique reduct if there does not exist two rules $r_p$ and $r_q$ in $\Pi_i$ and $\Pi_j$ $(1 < i, j)$ respectively such that $r_p$ and $r_q$ are mutually defeasible in $\Pi$.

We assume that $\mathcal{P}$ has two different reducts, say $\mathcal{P}^{<(1)}$ and $\mathcal{P}^{<(2)}$. This follows that there exist at least two different rules $r_p$ and $r_q$ such that (1) $r_p \in \Pi_i$ and $r_q \in \Pi_j$, where $1 < i, j$; (2) $r_q \in \mathcal{P}^{<(1)}$, $r_q \notin \mathcal{P}^{<(2)}$, and $r_p \notin \mathcal{P}^{<(1)}$; and (3) $r_p \in \mathcal{P}^{<(2)}$, $r_p \notin \mathcal{P}^{<(1)}$, and $r_q \notin \mathcal{P}^{<(2)}$. According to Definition 2, $\mathcal{P}^{<(1)}$ and $\mathcal{P}^{<(2)}$ are generated from two reduct chains $\{\Pi_0^{(1)}, \Pi_1^{(1)}, \cdots\}$ and $\{\Pi_0^{(2)}, \Pi_1^{(2)}, \cdots\}$ respectively.

Without loss of generality, suppose that for all $0 \leq i < k$, $\Pi_i^{(1)} = \Pi_i^{(2)}$, and

$$\Pi_k^{(1)} = \Pi_{k-1}^{(1)} - \{r_1, \cdots, r_l, r_p, \cdots\},$$
$$\Pi_k^{(2)} = \Pi_{k-1}^{(2)} - \{r_1, \cdots, r_l, r_q, \cdots\},$$

where we set $\Pi_{k-1} = \Pi_{k-1}^{(1)} = \Pi_{k-1}^{(2)}$ and the only difference between $\Pi_k^{(1)}$ and $\Pi_k^{(2)}$ is due to rules $r_p$ and $r_q$. Let $r_p$ and $r_q$ have the following forms:

$$r_p : L_p \leftarrow \cdots, not\ L'_p, \cdots,$$
$$r_q : L_q \leftarrow \cdots, not\ L'_q, \cdots.$$

Comparing $\Pi_k^{(1)}$ and $\Pi_k^{(2)}$, it is clear that the only difference between these two programs is about rules $r_p$ and $r_q$. Since Since $\Pi_k^{(1)}$ defeats $r_p$ and $\Pi_k^{(2)}$ defeats $r_q$, it follows that $L'_q \in S_k^{(1)}$ and $L'_p \in S_k^{(2)}$, where $S_k^{(1)}$ and $S_k^{(2)}$ are answer sets of $\Pi_k^{(1)}$ and $\Pi_k^{(2)}$ respectively. Then there must exist some rule in $\Pi_k^{(1)}$ of the form:

$$r^{(1)} : L'_p \leftarrow \cdots,$$

and some rule in $\Pi_k^{(2)}$ of the form:

$$r^{(2)} : L'_q \leftarrow \cdots.$$

Furthermore, since $\Pi_k^{(1)} - \{r_p, r_q\}$ does not defeat rule $r_p$ and $\Pi_k^{(2)} - \{r_p, r_q\}$ does not defeat rule $r_q$ (otherwise $\Pi_k^{(1)} = \Pi_k^{(2)}$), it is observed that rule $r_q$ triggers rule $r^{(1)}$ in $\Pi_k^{(1)}$ that defeats $r_p$, and rule $r_p$ triggers rule $r^{(2)}$ in $\Pi_k^{(2)}$ that defeats $r_q$. This follows that $r_p$ and $r_q$ are mutually defeasible in $\Pi$. ∎

## 4   Concluding Remarks

In this paper we investigated basic properties of PLPs under answer set semantics and provided a unique characterization for the answer set of PLPs. It should be noted that although the uniqueness of answer set for general and extended logic programs has been studied previously, this paper presents the first investigation on this issue for prioritized logic programs. The detailed comparison between our prioritized logic programs and other related proposals is beyond the scope of this paper. Here we only illustrate the most important feature of our approach in preferred defeasible reasoning. The major difference between our approach and other approaches is that by viewing the preference to be defeasible, our approach guarantees that every prioritized logic program has an answer set iff the underlying extended logic program has one – this principle is essential for dealing with logic program update in many situations as we have shown in [8]. So in general our approach provides a flexible framework for prioritized defeasible reasoning.

## References

1. K.R. Apt and R.N. Bol, Logic programming and negation: A survey. *Journal of Logic Programming*, **19,20** (1994) 9–71.
2. G. Brewka and T. Eiter, Preferred answer sets for extended logic programs. *Artificial Intelligence*, **109** (1999) 297–356.
3. M. Gelfond and V. Lifschitz, The stable model semantics for logic programming. In *Proceedings of the Fifth Joint International Conference and Symposium*, pp 1070–1080. MIT Press, 1988.
4. M. Gelfond and V. Lifschitz, Classical negation in logic programs and disjunctive databases. *New Generation Computing*, **9** (1991) 365–386.
5. B.N. Grosof, Prioritized conflict handling for logic programs. In *Proceedings of the 1997 International Logic Program Symposium (ILPS'97)*, pp 197–212. MIT Press, 1997.
6. V. Lifschitz and H. Turner, Splitting a logic program. In *Proceedings of Eleventh International Conference on Logic Programming*, pp 23–37. MIT Press, 1994.
7. Zhang and N.Y. Foo, Answer sets for prioritized logic programs. In *Proceedings of the 1997 International Logic Programming Symposium (ILPS'97)*, pp 69–83. MIT Press, 1997
8. Y. Zhang, Logic program based updates. Manuscript, 2003.

# A New Approach to Constraint Inductive Logic Programming*

Lei Zheng[1], Chunnian Liu[1], Dong Jia[1], and Ning Zhong[2]

[1] School of Computer Science, Beijing Polytechnic University Beijing Municipal Key
Laboratory of Multimedia and Intelligent Software Technology
100022 Beijing, China ai@bjpu.edu.cn
[2] Department of Information Engineering, Maebashi Institute of Technology
371-0816 Maebashi-City, Japan
zhong@maebashi-it.ac.jp

**Abstract.** A continuing problem with Inductive Logic Programming
(ILP) [1] has been the poor handling of numbers. Constraint Inductive Logic Programming (CILP) aims to solve this problem. We propose
a new approach to CILP, and implement a prototype of CILP system
called BPU-CILP. In our approach, methods from pattern recognition,
such as Fisher's linear discriminant [2] and prototype-based partitional
clustering [3], are introduced into CILP. BPU-CILP can generate various forms of polynomial constraints in multiple dimensions, without
additional background knowledge. As results, a CLP program covering
all positive examples and consistent with all negative examples can be
automatically derived.

## 1 Introduction

Inductive Logic Programming(ILP) aims at a formal framework as well as practical algorithms for inductive learning of relational descriptions in the form of
logic programs. Despite the success of ILP, number handling problem is to be
solved. Constraint Inductive Logic Programming (CILP) is the research area
that aims to solve the problem of number handling in ILP.

Several other researchers have addressed the problem of handling numbers in
ILP. Within the representation language of conventional logic programs, Muggleton and Page [4] examined the use of higher-order predicates. In their work, the
authors restrict themselves to only four forms of equations, and no relationship
in more than two dimensions can be find. Srinivasan [5] has built-into Progol a
form of lazy evaluation allowing constants in literals to be left unevaluated until
refinement. The apparent shortcoming of this approach is that if the positive
training examples distribute on two lines, the completeness requirement of this
approach necessitates fitting a line though all the positive examples, producing
a very poor fit. Sebag and Rouveirol [6] have also examined the possibility of

---

* The work is supported by the Natural Science Foundation of China (60173014) and
Beijing Municipal Natural Science Foundation (4022003).

N. Zhong et al. (Eds.): ISMIS 2003, LNAI 2871, pp. 357–364, 2003.

using CLP to improve number handling in ILP. They reformulate the search of the refinement space as a Constraint Satisfaction Problem (CSP), and restrict a numerical literal to be a simple equation or inequation of the form:$X < c$ or $X - Y < c$ (for some constant c). Within a top-down (or refinement-based) setting, Anthony and Frisch [7] present an algorithm called NUM. NUM generates numerical literals during the refinement of a top-down ILP system. The authors assume the existence of a constraint solver capable of solving conjunctions of linear equations, or simplifying conjunctions of linear inequations and dis-equations, and restrict the form of numerical literals to which can be handled by the constraint solver.

This paper proposes a new approach to CILP. Using the approach we have implemented a prototype of top-down CILP system called BPU-CILP, which can generate literals built over not only usual non-numerical predicates but also numerical predicates. When literals are to be built over numerical predicates, we apply methods from pattern recognition, such as Fisher's linear discriminant and prototype-based partitional clustering, to generate various forms of polynomial constraints in multiple dimensions, without additional background knowledge and any constraint solver.

The remainder of this paper is organized as follows. Section 2 describes the framework of BPU-CILP. In section 3, we detail the approach to generating numerical candidate literals with methods from pattern recognition. In section 4, BPU-CILP shows the ability to handle numbers with two examples. We conclude in section 5, and discuss the further extension of this approach.

## 2    The Framework of BPU-CILP

BPU-CILP is a top-down system, which uses separate-and-conquer method. During refinement, BPU-CILP considers the following three forms of numerical literals:

- Inequations of the form $p > 0$ or $p < 0$, where $p$ is a polynomial
- Inexact equations of the form $p \approx 0$, where $p$ is a polynomial consisting of 3 terms (including a constant term). $p \approx 0$ is interpreted, for some specified error term $\varepsilon > 0$, as $p \approx 0 \Leftrightarrow (p - \varepsilon < 0) \bigwedge (p + \varepsilon > 0)$,and
- Inexact dis-equations of the form $p \neq 0$, where $p$ is a polynomial consisting of 3 terms (including a constant term). $p \neq 0$ is interpreted, for some specified error term $\varepsilon > 0$, as $p \neq 0 \Leftrightarrow (p - \varepsilon > 0) \bigvee (p + \varepsilon < 0)$.

The search strategy of BPU-CILP is beam search, and the search heuristic of adding a literal $L$ to clause $C$ is the weighted information gain [8] penalized by the complexity of $L$. The search heuristic is defined as:

$$H(L,C) = t \times \left( \log_2 \frac{p_1}{p_1 + n_1} - \log_2 \frac{p_0}{p_0 + n_0} \right) - \alpha \times CP(L) \qquad (1)$$

where $p_0$ and $n_0$ are respectively the number of positive and negative bindings of clause $C$. Let $C'$ be the clause created by adding literal $L$ to $C$, $p_1$ and $n_1$

are respectively the number of positive and negative bindings of $C'$, and $t$ is the number of positive bindings that still cover by $C'$. $\alpha$ is the coefficient of the penalty and in this paper is 0.2. $CP(L)$ evaluates the complexity of $L$ and its definition is as follows:

$$CP(L) = \begin{cases} the\ arity\ of\ L, & if\ L\ is\ a\ normal\ literal \\ the\ sum\ of\ degrees\ of\ terms\ of\ L, & if\ L\ is\ a\ constraint \end{cases} \quad (2)$$

In one step specialization, BPU-CILP generates normal candidate literals as usual. To generate numerical candidate literals, BPU-CILP projects the bindings of the clause to be specialized to points in $R^n$, where n is the number of numerical attributes of each binding. Then, observing all projection points labelled as positive or negative, BPU-CILP introduces methods from pattern recognition to generate candidate numerical literals heuristically. Given a clause $C$ to be specialized, heuristic values of all candidate literals, including normal literals and numerical literals, are evaluated by formula 1 and some optimal literals are selected to refine $C$ in the beam search frame.

## 3    Generating Numerical Candidate Literals

Given labelled points in $R^n$, formula 1 can be reformulated as:

$$H(L, p_0, n_0, p_1, n_1) = p_1 \times \left( \log_2 \frac{p_1}{p_1 + n_1} - \log_2 \frac{p_0}{p_0 + n_0} \right) - \alpha \times CP(L) \quad (3)$$

where $L$ is a numerical candidate literal. Let $E$ be the labelled points set, $p_0$ and $n_0$ are respectively the number of positive and negative points of $E$, $p_1$ and $n_1$ are respectively the number of positive and negative points of $E$ covered by $L$. $\alpha$ and CP(L) are identical with which appeared in formula 1.

For the sake of perspicuity, we will illustrate methods to generate linear constraints, and then generalize these methods to generate polynomial constraints.

### 3.1    Finding Linear Inequations

The linear inequations we discussed in this paper have the form:

$$w_1 x_1 + w_2 x_2 + \cdots + w_n x_n + w_0 > 0 \quad (4)$$

or

$$w_1 x_1 + w_2 x_2 + \cdots + w_n x_n + w_0 < 0 \quad (5)$$

where $w_1, w_2, ..., w_n$ and $w_0$ are constants and $x_1, x_2, ..., x_n$ are variables that appear in the body of the clause to be specialized.

Given two classes of points in $R^n$, the task of generating a candidate linear inequation is to determine the values of constants of formula 4 or 5, such as the linear inequation is optimal $w.r.t.$ Formula 3. Accordingly, methods in pattern recognition to design linear classifier can be used for reference.

Fisher's linear discriminant [3] is a classification method that projects high-dimensional data onto a line and performs classification in this one-dimensional space. The projection maximizes the distance between the means of the two classes while minimizing the variance within each class. This defines the Fisher criterion, which is maximized over all linear projections, $W$:

$$J(W) = \frac{|m_1 - m_2|^2}{s_1^2 + s_2^2} \tag{6}$$

where $m$ represents a mean, $s^2$ represents a variance, and the subscripts denote the two classes. Maximizing this criterion yields a closed form solution that involves the inverse of a covariance-like matrix. In pattern recognition, the threshold is determined by optimizing a cost function on the training set.

In BPU-CILP, we use Fisher criterion to find candidate linear inequations heuristically. We define the algorithm named GCLI for generating candidate linear inequations as follows:

```
procedure GCLI (Examples, k)
    InequationStore=NULL
    p0=number of positive points of Examples
    n0=number of negative points of Examples
    W=the projection vector for Examples calculated by Fisher's
        linear discriminant
    ProjectionStore=one dimension labelled points generated
                    by projecting Examples to one dimension with W
    IntervalSet=intervals generated by ProjectionStore
    for each interval in IntervalSet
        w0= -1*(midpoint of the interval)
        pl=number of elements in ProjectionStore,
            who are less than w0 and whose labels are positive
        nl=number of elements in ProjectionStore,
            who are less than w0 and whose labels are negative
        literal_l=the inequation constructed by W, w0,
            and the constraint symbol'<'
        HeuristicValueL=H(literal_l, pl, nl, p0, n0)
        InequationStore=InequationStore+{(literal_l, HeuristicValueL)}
        pr= number of elements in ProjectionStore,
            who are greater than w0 and whose labels are positive
        nr= number of elements in ProjectionStore,
            who are greater than w0 and whose labels are negative
        literal_r=the inequation constructed by W,
            w0, and the constraint symbol '>'
        HeuristicValueR=H(literal_r, pr, nr, p0, n0)
        InequationStore=InequationStore+{(literal_r, HeuristicValueR)}
    end for
    InequationStore={x|x is one of the k best elements of
                    InequationStore according to its heuristic value}
    Return InequationStore
```

We shall use a worked example to illustrate the operation of the algorithm GCLI. Consider the following problem of generating candidate inequations, given the labelled points in cartesian space as:

Positive points: (8, 6), (11, 8), (8, 7), (4, 6), (10, 6), (5, 5), (7, 5), (12, 9)
Negative points: (10, 8), (7, 6), (9, 6)

In the experiment, the limit to the number of candidate $k$ is 2. According to Fisher criterion, the normalized projection vector $W$ is evaluated as: $W = (-0.8425, 0.5387)$. The two candidate inequations generated by GCLI are: $-0.8425X + 0.5387Y + 4.7098 < 0$, whose heuristic value is 1.1783 and $-0.8425X + 0.5387Y + 3.8604 > 0$, whose heuristic value is 0.7820. Figure 1 shows the labelled points and the candidate linear inequations.

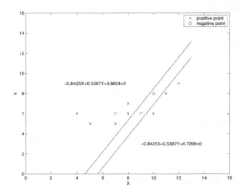

**Fig. 1.** The labelled points and the candidate linear inequations

## 3.2   Finding Linear Inexact Equations and Inexact Dis-equations

For handling the imprecise data, we consider generating candidate linear inexact equations and inexact dis-equations. Also, we restrict our attention to the 2-dimension space (the plane) and then a normalized linear inexact equation is of the form:

$$w_1 x_1 + w_2 x_2 + w_0 \approx 0 \tag{7}$$

and represents a region which consists of all points $(x_1, x_2)$, such that, for a specified error term $\varepsilon$, the Euclidean distance between $(x_1, x_2)$ and the line $w_1 x_1 + w_2 x_2 + w_0 = 0$ is less than $\varepsilon$.

In the methods of cluster analysis, the prototype-based partitional clustering [4] is the principal method to detect linear shape sub-clusters in examples. In prototype-based partitional clustering, the line prototype $L_i$ of a linear shape sub-cluster $S_i$ is defined as $L_i = (u_n, v_n)$, where $u_n$ is a direction and $v_n$ is a point. With line prototypes, a prototype-based partitional clustering method can detect linear shape sub-clusters in examples. The proximity measure between a point and a line prototype is defined as the squared distance from the point to the line specified by the line prototype. The clustering criterion is error square sum and the clustering procedure is similar to that of the well-known k-means clustering. Thus, the outline algorithm for generating candidate linear inexact equations is as follows:

- Points= all positive points of examples $(x_1(i), ..., x_n(i))$, $i = 1, ..., k$
- for all possible (j1,j2), $1 \leq j1 < j2 \leq n$
  - SubPoints= $(x_{j1}(i), x_{j2}(i))$ ,$i = 1, ..., k$
  - for i=1 to a specified limit k1
    Clusters[i]= the result of detecting i linear shape sub-cluster(s) in Sub-Points
    end for
  - determine the most sensible Clusters[j] according to the clustering criterion
  - construct inexact equtions according to Clusters[j] and save them in Buffer
  end for
- CandidateEquations= k optimal elements of Buffer according to formula 3

The method to generate candidate linear inexact dis-equations is similar to the method we presented above, except to detect sub-clusters in negative points.

## 3.3   Generating Polynomial Constraints

We turn to generalize methods above for generating polynomial candidate literals. For simplicity, we suppose the dimension of labelled points is 2 and the degree of the polynomial is 2. Given labelled points $(u(i), v(i))$, $i = 1, ..., n$. Let $x_1 = u$, $x_2 = v$, $x_3 = uv$, $x_4 = u^2$ and $x_5 = v^2$, then labelled points can be transformed into $(x_1(i), x_2(i), x_3(i), x_4(i), x_5(i))$, $i = 1, ..., n$. Thus, the problem of generating polynomial constraints from labelled points is transformed into the problem of generating linear constraints from transformed labelled points, which have been solved. In this way, theoretically, we can generate polynomial constraints of any degree.

## 4   Two Examples

With the following two worked examples, BPU-CILP shows its ability in number handling. In our system, the width of the beam is 5. In these experiments, we use a computer with Pentium processor running at $1.7GHz$ and 128M RAM. Experiment 1: Given training examples and background knowledge as follows:

Positive   examples:   t(a,b,2,2,2),   t(c,d,3,3,2),   t(d,k,3,4,3),   t(b,o,3,4,4), t(e,f,4,3,5), t(g,m,4,4,3), t(e,l,4,4,4), t(h,k,4,3,4), t(g,h,5,2,3), t(f,c,5,5,3)

Negative examples: t(j,c,3,3,3), t(i,k,3,3,4), t(m,f,3,4,3), t(a,c,4,3,5), t(b,m,4,4,4), t(d,l,4,4,3), t(a,i,5,5,7), t(h,n,4,6,7), t(g,h,7,5,5), t(c,d,7,7,7), t(b,o,7,7,8), t(g,m,7,8,7), t(h,k,7,8,8), t(d,k,7,7,9)

Background knowledge: p(a), p(b), p(c), p(d), p(e), p(f), p(g), p(h), q(a,b), q(a,i), q(j,b), q(j,c), q(c,d), q(d,k), q(i,k), q(b,o), q(e,f), q(e,l), q(m,f), q(g,m), q(g,h), q(h,k), q(h,n), q(f,c)

To find the definition of the target predicate $t(A, B, C, D, E)$.

BPU-CILP gave out the CLP program consisting of a single clause: $t(A, B, C, D, E) : --0.3041D - 0.9529E + 5.9833 > 0, p(A), q(A, B)$. The clause covers all positive examples and is consistent with all negative examples (see figure 2 for the snapshot of BPU-CILP interface for this example). The running time of this example is 0.712 second.

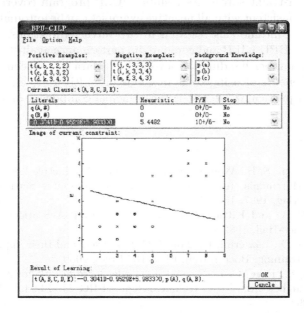

**Fig. 2.** The snapshot of BPU-CILP interface for Experiment 1

**Experiment 2:** In this experiment, we applied BPU-CILP on the data set named balance-scale [5]. Balance-scale consists of 625 examples, and each of them describes a lever with four attributes: Left-Weight, Left-Distance, Right-Weight and Right-Distance. These attributes have the same domain: {1,2,3,4,5}. All examples have been classified into three groups: Left-down group (288 examples), Right-down group (288 examples) and the Balance-state group (49 examples).

In this experiment, positive examples are those in Balance-state group, and negative examples are the rest. Without any back ground knowledge, BPU-CILP successfully found the rule of lever balance state:$B(LW, LD, RW, RD) :$ $--0.7071 * LW * LD + 0.7071 * RW * RD + 0 \approx 0$. The running time of this example is 15.844 seconds. Further more, we set the error term of inexact equation as $\varepsilon = 0.1$, and purposely added a random noise term $\delta$, $-0.01 \leq \delta \leq 0.01$, to each attribute of all examples, BPU-CILP still found the same rule, owning to the clustering method introduced into BPU-CILP.

## 5   Conclusions

CILP aims to solve the problem of number handling in ILP. We propose a new approach to CILP, and implement a prototype of CILP system called BPU-CILP. In our approach, methods from pattern recognition are introduced into CILP, and then BPU-CILP can generate various forms of polynomial constraints in multiple dimensions, without any additional background knowledge, and no need of any constraint solver. As results, a CLP program covering all positive examples and consistent with all negative examples can be automatically derived.

We plan to continue this research in two further directions. The first is to further improve BPU-CILP and compare its performance against other proposed approaches to number handling on several large data sets. Secondly, we hope to consider the benefits of using some methods in multivariate statistical analysis in learning. Of particular interest is the principal component analysis [10].

## References

1. Nienhuys-Chen, S.-H., Wolf, R. de. Foundations of Inductive Logic Programming. In: Goos, Hartmanis, (eds). Lecture Notes in Computer Science 1228, Berlin: Springer-Verlag, 1997. 163–177.
2. Devijver, P. A. and Kittler, J. Pattern Recognition: A Statical Approach, New York: Prentice-Hall, 1982.
3. Dumitrescu, D., Lazzerini, B., Jain, L.C. Fuzzy sets and their application to clustering and training, Boca Raton, FL: CRC Press, 2000.
4. Muggleton, S., Page, C. D. Beyond first-order learning: inductive logic programming with higher-order logic. Technical Report PRG-TR-13-94, Oxford University, Oxford, 1994.
5. Srinivasan, A., Camacho, R. Experiments in numeric reasoning with inductive logic programming. Technical Report PRG-TR-22-96, Oxford University, Oxford, 1996.
6. Sebag, M., Rouveirol, C. Constraint Inductive Logic Programming. In: de Raedt, ed. Advances in ILP. IOS Press, 1996. 277–294.
7. Anthony, S., Frisch, A. Generating numerical literals during refinement. In: Dzeroski, Lavrac, eds. Proceedings of the 7th International Workshop on Inductive Logic Programming. Lecture Notes in Computer Science 1297, Berlin: Springer-Verlag, 1997. 61–76.
8. Quinlan, J.R. Learning logical definitions from relations. Machine Learning, 1990. 5:239–266.
9. http://axon.cs.byu.edu/~martinez/classes/470/MLDB/balance-scale/
10. Everitt B.S., Dunn G., Applied Multivariate Data Analysis. London: Arnold, 2001.

# Extending the CLP Engine for Reasoning under Uncertainty

Nicos Angelopoulos

Department of Computer Science, York University, York
nicos@cs.york.ac.uk

**Abstract.** We show how the amalgamation of Logic Programming with probabilistic reasoning enhances its capabilities for intelligent reasoning. Unlike current approaches we use concepts from Constraint Logic Programming in order to achieve this. In particular, we use the constraint store for storing probabilistic information and inference, and finite domains as sets of basic elements over which distributions can be defined. We describe a new language, Probabilistic finite domains and show how it can be used to code code two examples. First the Monty Hall problem is coded and the extensional means of simulating intelligence within our system are described. Second, we illustrate the benefits of the probabilistic information over the crisp finite domains in solving a simple encoding scheme. Aspects of a prototype implementation, a Prolog meta-interpreter, are discussed.

## 1 Introduction

Logical and probabilistic reasoning are integral parts of intelligent behaviour. In a systemic context, Logic Programming (LP) has been successful as a platform for implementing Logic based intelligent systems. Although there have been a number of proposals for enhancing LP with probabilistic reasoning capabilities, there has not emerged a platform for providing these capabilities in a general problem solving setting.

Current probabilistic extensions to Logic Programming can be thought of as either Bayesian [9,8] or Markovian [4,6]. These attach the probabilities either to the clause definition, or to clauses of restricted form. The Bayesian approaches have difficulties with interpreting the probability of predicates that include variables and in general the form of the clause is altered substantially. In effect, the logical (crisp) reasoning is subordinate to the probabilistic inference. On the other hand, Markovian approaches subordinate the latter to the former; as a result they are more successful for parameter estimation and machine learning tasks rather than as a tool for modelling intelligent behaviour.

Our approach, Probabilistic finite domains (*Pfd*) is in effect a Bayesian approach, however, probabilistic information is not presented in the form of clauses but as constraints. By using Constraint Logic Programming (CLP) ideas on how to extend the reasoning capabilities of the Logic Programming engine, *Pfd* alleviates some of the Bayesian limitations. First we use the store to hold probabilistic

N. Zhong et al. (Eds.): ISMIS 2003, LNAI 2871, pp. 365–373, 2003.

information, thus extricating the deduction process from probabilistic inference tasks. Second, probability distributions are ascribed over finite domains. Third, probabilistic events are mapped to goals containing probabilistic variables.

We assume some familiarity with LP and grasp of the basic intuitions in Constraint Logic Programming. The rest of the paper is structured as follows. The following section briefly introduces the *Pfd* language and an implementation of the language. Section 3 details a *Pfd* program for the Monty Hall problem. Section 4 illustrates how probabilistic information can enhance crisp computation in a Caesar encoding scenario. Final conclusions are in Section 5.

## 2    The Language

**Probabilistic Variables.** A finite domain variable is a logical variable with a restricted set of possible values (its finite domain). Here we will we use lists of distinct objects (e.g. $[a, b, c, \ldots]$) for finite domains. Based on this, a probabilistic variable has two parts; (a) a *finite domain*, which at each stage holds the collection of possible values that can be assigned to the variable, and (b) a *probability assigning function* (or simply function) which is used to assign probabilities to the elements of the domain. The probability function declares the basic statistical behaviour of the variable. In *Pfd*, the two constituents of a probabilistic variable are kept separate. There are two benefits in such an approach. Firstly, the variable is still capable of participating in finite domain constraints. Secondly, probabilistic functions capture the probabilistic behaviour in a manner which is, to a large extent, independent of specific domain values.

**Construct 1.** Let $Fd$ be a list of distinct objects representing a finite domain, $\phi_v$ be a probability function defined over all sublists of $Fd$ and *Arguments* a list of arguments that customise $\phi_v$. Probabilistic variable $V$ is introduced to the store with    $V \in_{\mathbf{p}} \phi_v(Fd, Arguments)$

Two examples of how the introduced variable definition can be applied in practice are:    $Die \in_{\mathbf{p}} \texttt{uniform}([i, ii, iii, iv, v, vi])$

and $Coin \in_{\mathbf{p}} \texttt{finite\_geometric}([head, tail], 2)$.

Function **uniform** takes no other arguments. The behaviour it describes is that the remaining elements of its domain (a sublist of $[i, ii, iii, iv, v, vi]$ in this case) are, in the absence of other evidence, equiprobable. Function **finite_geometric** defines a geometric probability distribution over the domain elements. In this instance, the deterioration factor of the progression is 2. Table 1, presents some variations of how the two examples, can be used. Rows three and four show the formulae for these two functions, while the lower rows give concrete examples with associated distributions.

**Events.** In Probability Theory events collate subsets of random variables' values into semantic units. Predicates containing probabilistic variables can be viewed as such events over the Cartesian space of these probabilistic variables. The main intuition is that the probability assigned to an event is proportional to the space covered by combinations leading to successful derivations. Let $pvars(E)$ be the

**Table 1.** Examples of probabilistic variable definitions

| $\phi_V$ | $Fd$ | $Arguments$ | $Distribution$ |
|---|---|---|---|
| Descriptions | | | |
| uniform | $[El_1, \ldots, El_n]$ | | $[1/n, \cdots, 1/n]$ |
| finite_geometric | $[El_1, \ldots, El_n]$ | $F$ | $[_{j=1}^{n} F^{n-j} / \sum_{i=0}^{n-1} F^i]$ |
| Examples | | | |
| uniform | $[i, ii, iii, iv, v, vi]]$ | | $[1/6, 1/6, 1/6, 1/6, 1/6, 1/6]$ |
| uniform | $[i, ii, iv, v, vi]$ | | $[1/5, 1/5, 1/5, 1/5, 1/5]$ |
| finite_geometric | $[head, tail]$ | 2 | $[2/3, 1/3]$ |
| finite_geometric | $[low, med, high]$ | 2 | $[4/7, 2/7, 1/7]$ |

**Table 2.** Left: Definition for lucky/2. Right: Probability of event example query.

lucky( iv, head ).

lucky( v, head ).

lucky( vi, head ).

?- $Die \in_p$ uniform($[i, ii, iii, iv, v, vi]$),

$LCoin \in_p$ finite_geometric($[head, tail], 2$),

$PLucky$ is $\mathbf{p}(\texttt{lucky(Die, LCoin)})$.

PLucky = 1/3

probabilistic variables in $E$, $e$ be a vector collecting one element from the finite domain of each variable in $pvars(E)$, $p(e)$ be the corresponding vector of probability values, $\mathcal{P}$ be the program defining $E$, and $\mathcal{S}$ be a particular constraint store (a set of constraints). $E/e$ denotes predicate $E$ with its probabilistic variables replaced by their respective elements in $e$. Also, in what follows we use $\mathcal{S} \vdash$, store-derives, to mean $\mathcal{S} \cup \mathcal{P} \vdash$, store-and-program-derive. The probability of predicate $E$ with respect to store $\mathcal{S}$ is

$$P_{\mathcal{S}}(E) = \sum_{\substack{\forall e \\ S \vdash E/e}} P_{\mathcal{S}}(e) = \sum_{\substack{\forall e \\ S \vdash E/e}} \prod_i p(e_i)$$

**Construct 2.** The probability of predicate $E$ with respect to current store $\mathcal{S}$ is assigned to unbound logical variable $Probability$ by : $Probability$ is $\mathbf{p}(\mathrm{E})$

An example of how to query the probability of a predicate is shown in Table 2.

**Conditional Constraint.** The store may contain different kinds of probabilistic information involving probabilistic variables. Here we use a restricted form of the conditional constraints presented in [1].

**Construct 3.** For probabilistic variables $Dependent$ and $Qualifier$, and probability $\pi, 0 \leq \pi \leq 1$, the conditional states: $Dependent$ ⫤ $Qualifier$

If no $\pi$ is given, it is assumed to be equal to one. The conditional should be read as $Dependent \neq X : \pi \oplus Dependent = X : (1 - \pi) \mid Qualifier = X$. For a free variable $X$, this reads as the value of $Dependent$ being different from that of $Qualifier$ with probability $\pi$ and equal to it with probability $1 - \pi$. We say that $Dependent$ depends on $Qualifier$.

For the probability of *Dependent* in an arbitrary store we need to consider the following: (a) each variable, upon which it depends must be assigned a value from its finite domain (b) the weight of each such assignment is equal to the product of the probability for the assigned elements (c) all possible assignments must be considered (d) $\neq$ and $=$ parts, across multiple constraints conditioning the variable, are considered in a multiplicative way ($\otimes$).

Finite domain solvers provide labelling predicates. These, instantiate a variable to one element of each domain at a time, backtracking into the predicate in order to instantiate the variable to all possible values. Similarly, *Pfd* provides for the labelling of variables the **label**(*Vars, Select, Probs, Total*) predicate. *Vars* are labelled by the method described by *Select*. Associated probabilities are in *Probs*. *Total* holds the sum of products of all *Probs* seen so far. *Select* directs the way in which the probability associated with the finite domain elements influences labelling.

**A meta-interpreter.** We have built a prototype system implementing *Pfd*. This has the form of a Prolog meta-interpreter. The full featured system runs on SICStus 3.8.5 or later, while restricted versions run on the Yap 2.3.19 and Swi 5.0.1 Prolog systems. The main restriction, for the two latter systems, is the lack of FD interaction since they do not provide a clp(fd) library. In what follows, we refer to the system behaviour under the SICStus engine. Features of the meta-interpreter include:

1. Rational numbers are represented as quotients of integers, with the underlying prolog engine providing fast, arbitrarily long integer arithmetic.
2. An approximate algorithm, labelling many variables at once. This is selected with `mua` labelling method.
3. Graph algorithms maintain the consistency of variable dependencies.

The labelling method used here, `mua` (maximum unique alternative), implements an approximate search on the tree of all possible valuations. Unlike other approaches this approximation does not compromise the semantics of the reasoning. What is approximated is the order in which the different combinations of values for the labelled variables appear. Some form of approximation is in general needed in this setting, since finding the most promising combination in most cases collapses to a breadth first search. Our algorithm traverses the space of possible valuations according to an approximating heuristic. Each branch upon introduction to the tree, is assigned a value which approximates the branch's final probability. At each stage the children of the most promising branch are added to the tree (in the case of a leaf, its total probability is returned to the top level). Thus, at a random time the tree is expected to have branches at various depths. Children of the selected branch are found by instantiating one of the still free variables to a number of its possible values (starting from the most probable ones). The metric used in `mua` is $M = ParentM + f(MarginalP - MaxAlternativePrb)$ where $M$ and $ParentM$ are the obvious variables, $MarginalP$ is the probability of the instantiated

curtains( gamma, Swt, Prb ) :-
$\qquad$ $Gift \in_{\mathbf{p}} \mathtt{uniform}([a, b, c])$, $\qquad$ $First \in_{\mathbf{p}} \mathtt{uniform}([a, b, c])$,
$\qquad$ $Reveal \in_{\mathbf{p}} \mathtt{uniform}([a, b, c])$, $\qquad$ $Second \in_{\mathbf{p}} \mathtt{uniform}([a, b, c])$,
$\qquad$ $Reveal$ **|≠** $Gift$, $\qquad\qquad\qquad$ $Reveal$ **|≠** $First$,
$\qquad$ $Second$ **|≠** $Reveal$ , $\qquad\qquad$ $Second$ **|≠**$_{Swt}$ $First$ ,
$\qquad$ $Prb$ $is$ $\mathbf{p}(Second{=}Gift)$.

**Fig. 1.** *Pfd* clause for probability of win under strategy $\gamma$.

*Variable* to assume the particular value (which differentiates this child from its siblings) and *MaxAlternativePrb* is the maximum probability assigned to this value in any of the non selected Variables. Function $f$ ensures that the resulting number is an integer value within certain limits. These limits are evaluated when setting-up the labelling procedure and depend on the number of variables and the number of alternative values for each one of them.

# 3   Monty Hall

We first examine a problem which is often used to demonstrates that reasoning with probability is hard and often leads to wrong answers. In the Monty hall tv show, [5, p.137] there are three curtains. Behind these, a car and two goats are concealed. A contestant chooses an initial curtain. One of the remaining curtains is then drawn revealing one of the goats. The contestant is hence asked to make a final choice. Whatever is behind this final curtain is the contestant's gift. We will say the contestant won if his final choice is the curtain concealing the car.

Can the contestant develop a strategy that will increase their winning chances? By far, most people believe that this is not possible, and that both options at the second choice (stay-with-same, against switch-to-other curtain) have the same probability (1/3). However, a closer look reveals that the latter choice is twice as likely to lead to a win. (For a justification see [5].) Furthermore, both choices can be seen as part of a single strategy; that of switching with probability $Swt$. The first, stay-with-same is equivalent to $Swt = 0$ and switch-to-other to $Swt = 1$. Lets call this unifying strategy $\gamma$ . Then probability of win is $P(\gamma) = \frac{1+Swt}{3}$.

An intelligent system would ideally be able to construct the analytical formula from a basic description of the problem. However, this is a very ambitious target. Instead, we require that the system, given a description, should perform computations that provide the same answers to those computed by the formula. In *Pfd* the program modelling the game, is used to extensionally compute the answers given by the analytical formula, from the constituents parts of the problem. The *Pfd* clause for strategy $\gamma$ is shown in Fig. 2. The reading for the clause is that *Prb* is the probability of a win given that the player switched with probability *Swt*. Probabilistic variables *First*, *Gift*, *Reveal* and *Second* have no prior information that distinguishes the three values in their domains. Constraint **|≠** is used to declare pairs of variables that must be different (for example the revealed curtain cannot be the player's first choice *Reveal* **|≠** *First*). Variable

**Table 3.** Example encoding. Letters not in dictionary words, are not encoded.

| dictionary words | amicable | cohered | euphoria | mutant | shame | verb |
|---|---|---|---|---|---|---|
| Caesar encoding | twcbtspo | bfhoyoa | onrhfyct | wnvtdv | mhtwo | loys |

| dict. letter | a b c d e h i l m o p r s  t u v |
|---|---|
| encoded by | t s b a o h c p w f r y m v n l |

*Second* is defined to be different than *First* with probability *Swt* and to be the same as *First* with probability $1 - Swt$. $P(\gamma)$ is assigned to *Prb* with the call to `is/2`. Querying this program with `curtains(gamma, 1/2, Prb)` provides the answer $Prb = 1/2$. The meta-interpreter, when trying to prove `is/2` starts giving values to *Gift*, *First* and *Reveal*. This is because variables in *Second* = *Gift*, the goal for which we wish to find the probability, depend on them. The distribution of *Second* can then be established for each set of values from the final conditional. Note that each such set has an associated probability. The total probability of *Second* is equal to the sum of all sub-probabilities.

## 4    Caesar Encoding

Caesar's scheme is one of the earliest encoding schemes [7], where each letter of the alphabet is encoded by another (unique) letter. Also, each letter in the encoding correspond to a single decoded letter (see Table 3 for an example of a valid encoding). We consider codings of words formed from lower case letters drawn from a dictionary (the Unix[1] words dictionary was used in our experiments). We let each input, encoded, letter correspond to a unique variable. The domain of this variable is all the possible decodings of the encoded letter it stands for (i.e. all letters in the alphabet). For ease of reference we will use $X_i$ for the variable corresponding to the $i$th lower case letter. For example, the encoded word 'bfhoyoa', will be represented by $< X_2, X_6, X_8, X_{15}, X_{25}, X_{15}, X_1 >$ with $X_i \in \{a, \dots, z\}$. Furthermore the desired solution for this example is : $< X_2 = c, X_6 = o, X_8 = h, X_{15} = e, X_{25} = r, X_1 = d >$. So, in order to get the original words (decode) we replace in encoded words c's for b's, o's for h's , etc.

The model, so far, is applicable to both finite domain variables and to probabilistic ones. The full size of the search tree for a word with four free variables, which is our starting point, is $26!/22! = 358800$. The classical approach in solving the Caesar encodings, is to order the combinations in accordance to some likelihood measure. Normally this is done with specialised algorithms in imperative languages and the order is dictated by the proximity of two frequencies. The first frequency is the relative number of occurrences of a single letter in the dictionary and the second is the letter occurrences in the encoded words. The intuition behind this approach is that letters will appear equally often in both, the dictionary and in the encoded words.

---

[1] In our system this contains 25143 words

**Table 4.** Top: dictionary frequencies in units of 260 occurances. Bottom: Proximity based probabilities.

| $D_i$ | a | b | c | d | e | f | g | h | i | j | k | l | m | n | o | p | q | r | s | t | u | v | w | x | y | z |
|---|---|---|---|---|---|---|---|---|---|---|---|---|---|---|---|---|---|---|---|---|---|---|---|---|---|---|
| freq($D_i$) | 24 | 8 | 14 | 12 | 31 | 5 | 8 | 6 | 23 | 0 | 1 | 14 | 6 | 20 | 16 | 4 | 0 | 18 | 18 | 16 | 7 | 2 | 1 | 1 | 4 | 1 |

| $X_i$ | $E_i$ | $f(E_i)$ | $px(X_i, a)$ | $px(X_i, b)$ | $px(X_i, c)$ | $px(X_i, d)$ | out of | ... |
|---|---|---|---|---|---|---|---|---|
| $X_1$ | a | 5/38 | 5883 | 5731 | 5788 | 5769 | /149500 | ... |
| $X_2$ | b | 2/38 | 1898 | 1942 | 1993 | 1980 | /49900 | ... |
| ... | ... | ... | | | | | | ... |

```
probabilistic_method( proximity(Fd,Marker,Frqs,Prbs) ) :-
    rationals_subtract_list_from( Frqs, Marker, Subtr ),
    maplist( rationals_abs, Subtr, Abstr ),
    rationals_add_list( Abstr, Sum ),
    rationals_subtract_list_from( Abstr, Sum, Diffs ),
    rationals_to_probabilities( Diffs, Prbs ).
```

**Fig. 2.** Clause for Proximity Method Definition

For example the frequency of encoded letters can be used as a marker. Then, the probabilistic distribution for the corresponding variable is a function of the differences the dictionary frequencies have to this marker. In Table 4 we give an example of some calculated values for our **proximity** function ($px(X, D)$), which calculates the proximity probability between encoded and dictionary letters). These calculations are based on the frequencies of encoded letters $X_i$ and dictionary letters $D_i$, $freq(X_i)$ and $freq(D_i)$ respectively. In full we have:

$$px(X_i, D_j) = \frac{\mid freq(X_i) - freq(D_j) \mid}{\sum_k \mid freq(X_i) - freq(D_k) \mid} \tag{1}$$

**Programs.** We have programmed two solutions to the Caesar encoding. One based on clp(fd) [2] and a *Pfd* one, based on the proximity probabilities given above. Both run on the SICStus prolog engine. However, clp(fd) is a system library, while the *Pfd* solution runs over an extra meta-interpretation layer. We have tried to make the two programs as similar as possible, while taking care not to compromise the efficiency of either. The two programs (fd.pl and pfd.pl) can be downloaded from http://www.doc.ic.ac.uk/~nicos/sware/pbs/caesar/. The *Pfd* program differs to the clp(fd) one, in two aspects: (a) in the variable definitions and (b) in labelling. Probabilistic variables are introduced with $X_i \in_{\mathbf{p}}$ proximity($Alphabet, [Marker, Freqs]$) with $X_i$, the variable declared as probabilistic. *Alphabet* and *Freqs* are invariants that refer to the dictionary alphabet ('a'-'z' here) and frequencies. *Marker* is the frequency of the encoded letter that corresponds to the variable $X_i$. The probability construction method proximity, an implementation of Eq. 1, is shown in Figure 2. Predicates with names prefixed by *rationals*, refer to a library implementing rational arithmetics.

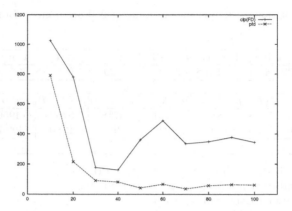

**Fig. 3.** *Pfd* versus clp(fd) timings comparison.

The decoding of words proceeds by selecting the word which currently has the least degrees of freedom (equal to the number of distinct variables times the elements in each variable's domain). All variables in the word are then labelled and their instantiated form checked against the decoded words. The predicate succeeds on backtracking, until a word is found in the dictionary. For word variables, *WordVs*, the call **label**(*WordVs*, mua, *Probs*, *AccProb*) was used for labelling in the *Pfd* program (Section 2).

**Results.** For each $N$ in $\{10, 20, \ldots, 100\}$ we encoded 10 sets of $N$ random words from our dictionary. Only words of four distinct letters or more were considered. The comparative mean execution times for the *Pfd* and clp(fd) programs, in solving these sets of encodings are shown in Fig. 3. In Caesar encoding problems the hardest word to decode is very often by far the first one. For the solution presented here, as well as most of the solutions in the literature, the easiness with which the solution is found, is determined by the closeness of the two letter frequencies (dictionary versus encoded). This in turn is dependent on the number of words to decode. Intuitively, the more words to decode, the more likely it is to have a frequency similar to the dictionary one. Thus fewer combinations will have to be considered before finding the correct decoding. (Note there is no such concept as a hard or easy encoding for a given set of words.)

Our experiments found a boundary in the region of thirty words. Thirty or more random words, as can been seen in Fig. 3 provide enough probabilistic information that help *Pfd* solve the problem in time significantly reduced in comparison to the clp(fd) program. Because clp(fd) is implemented natively whereas *Pfd* relies on an extra layer of meta-interpretation, it is likely that the improvement in performance effected by *Pfd* is greater than Fig. 3 suggests. The increase in time required by clp(fd) occurring after the thirty word mark is mainly due to the amount of wrong decodings the program has to try before it finds the correct one.

Another encouraging factor, in the analysis of performance, is that approximately half the of the execution time, is consumed in garbage collection. The main data-structure that attributes to this is the `mua` labelling procedure. This will be substantially reduced in an Object Oriented or imperative implementation of *Pfd* or even in Prolog systems that implement *Pfd* labelling natively.

# 5 Conclusions

We presented a language integrating logical and probabilistic reasoning seamlessly. This integration is crucial in intelligent systems platforms. Our approach is based on constraints ideas on how to extend the LP paradigm. The integration is facilitated by the use of (a) the store for probabilistic knowledge representation and reasoning (b) finite domains as units over which probabilistic distributions are defined and (c) reading of goals as events in the probability space.

A prototype implementing *Pfd* has been built to provide initial feedback. This can be downloaded and tested on-line at

http://www.doc.ic.ac.uk/~nicos/sware/pfds/ .

The prototype system has been used to demonstrate both the soundness of probabilistic inference from intuitive first principles and the exploitation of probabilistic information for improvements in performance within a declarative framework. However, the meta-interpreter presented here is a research tool, using very simple techniques. Past trends in Constraint Programming have shown that constraint networks are best implemented using Object Oriented or imperative languages. For example, [3] describes such an approach within CLP. We feel that similar techniques will also lead to substantial performance improvements for *Pfd* constraints.

**Acknowledgements.** Thanks to Tarhata Orlanes for corrections in the prose, to James Cussens for forcing me to think more about the maths and to the anonymous referees for their corrections and suggestions.

# References

1. N. Angelopoulos. *Probabilistic Finite Domains*. PhD thesis, City U., London, 2001.
2. M. Carlsson, G. Ottosson, and B. Carlson. An open-ended finite domain constraint solver. In *Progr. Languages: Implem., Logics, and Programs*, 1997.
3. Philippe Codognet and Daniel Diaz. Compiling constraints in clp(FD). *Journal of Logic Programming*, 27(3):185–226, 1996.
4. James Cussens. Stochastic logic programs: Sampling, inference and applications. In *16th Conference on Uncertainty in AI (UAI-2000)*, pages 115–122, 2000.
5. C. M. Grinstead and J. L. Snell. *Introduction to Probability*. AMS, 1997.
6. Yoshitaka Kameya and Taisuke Sato. Efficient learning with tabulation for parameterized logic programs. In *1st Int. Conf. on Comput. Logic*, pages 269–294, 2000.
7. Alan G. Konheim. *Cryptography, a primer*. John Willey & Sons, 1981.
8. Thomas Lukasiewicz. Probabilistic logic programming. In *13th biennial European Conference on Artificial Intelligence*, pages 388–392, Brighton, UK, August 1999.
9. R. Ng and V. Subrahmanian. Probabilistic logic programming. *Information and Computation*, 101:150–201, 1992.

# Logic for Multi-path Message Forwarding Networks for Mobile Agents

Masahito Kurihara[1] and Masanobu Numazawa[2]

[1] Hokkaido University, Sapporo, 060-8628, JAPAN
kurihara@main.eng.hokudai.ac.jp
[2] Otaru University of Commerce, Otaru, 047-8501, JAPAN
numazawa@res.otaru-uc.ac.jp

**Abstract.** We discuss how mobile agents, moving in the Internet from node to node, can communicate with each other by forwarding messages in a robust way. As a solution, we present the general idea of a class of communication networks called the *multi-path message forwarding networks* (MMFNs), which can transmit the messages to mobile agents at the current location in a robust way based on multiple paths between the nodes and the target. The networks are formally defined in terms of graph theory, and the dynamic nature of the networks (i.e., how they evolve) is represented by a logical system, named $\mathcal{L}_n$, consisting of six inference rules. It is shown that the system is sound in the sense that it generates only MMFNs. A computational interpretation of $\mathcal{L}_n$ is also discussed.

## 1 Introduction

The notion of agents can be described in terms of various attributes such as intelligence, autonomy, mobility, communication ability, etc. In this paper we focus on mobility and discuss how mobile agents [1,2,3,4], moving in the Internet from node to node, can communicate with each other in a robust way. In particular, we are interested in *location transparent* mobile agent systems, in which the agents need not be aware of the actual locations of peer agents, the agents with which they wish to communicate.

Three basic models for implementing location transparency have been identified [5, 6]: *searching*, *registering*, and *forwarding*. In this paper our focus is on the forwarding (also called *logging*), in which the (target) agents store in the current node the pointer to the next destination before they move there. The future messages are forwarded to the target agents along the path defined by the chain of those pointers. However, the weakness of the forwarding is its lack of robustness, because the messages will never reach the target if a single node on the chain is broken.

In this paper, we solve this problem by proposing a class of networks called *multi-path message forwarding networks (MMFNs)*, which can transmit the messages to the targets in a robust way based on multiple paths between the nodes and the target. More precisely, each MMFN is associated with an integer $n$ called its *degree* and ensures the existence of a path from every node to the target if the number of broken nodes is at most $n$.

The remaining of this paper is organized as follows. Section 2 presents a formal definition of MMFNs in terms of graph theory, and proves their robustness. In Section

N. Zhong et al. (Eds.): ISMIS 2003, LNAI 2871, pp. 374–383, 2003.
© Springer-Verlag Berlin Heidelberg 2003

3, the dynamic nature of the networks (i.e., how they evolve) is represented by a logical system, named $\mathcal{L}_n$, consisting of six inference rules. It is shown that $\mathcal{L}_n$ is sound in the sense that it generates only MMFNs. A computational interpretation of $\mathcal{L}_n$ and related work are also discussed. The final section provides our brief conclusion.

# 2 Multi-path Message Forwarding Networks

## 2.1 Preliminary

Before describing our main idea, we present a brief review of graph theory.

A (directed) *graph* $G = (V, E)$ consists of a set $V$ of *nodes* (or vertices) and a set $E$ of *links* (or directed edges). If $V$ and $E$ are finite sets, then $G$ is *finite*.

A link is conventionally denoted by an ordered pair $(v, w)$ of nodes but in this paper we denote it by $v \to w$, where $v$ is called the *start node* of the link and $w$ the *end node*. In this case, we say that $v \to w$ is *outgoing* from $v$. The *outdegree*, $od(v)$, of a node $v$ is the number of the links outgoing from $v$. Links with the same start node and the same end node are *parallel*. Graphs with no parallel links are *simple*.

A (directed) *path* is a sequence $v_0 \to v_1 \to \ldots \to v_p$ of links $v_i \to v_{i+1}, 0 \le i < p$, *from $v_0$ to $v_p$ passing through* $v_1, \ldots, v_{p-1}$. If $v_0 = v_p$, it is a (directed) *circuit*. Graphs with no circuits are *acyclic*.

In this paper, we deal with only finite, simple, acyclic graphs.

## 2.2 Definition of MMFN

We present the graph-theoretical, formal definition of MMFNs.

**Definition 1.** A *multi-path message forwarding network (MMFN) of degree* $n$ (where $n$ is a nonnegative integer) is a finite, simple, acyclic graph $G = (V, E)$ such that

- for all node $v \in V$, $od(v) \le n + 1$, and
- for each $i, 0 \le i \le n$, there exists the unique node $v \in V$ with $od(v) = i$.

The unique node $s_i$ with $od(s_i) = i, 0 \le i \le n$, is called the *special node* of degree $i$. In particular, the special node $s_0$ of degree 0 is called the *target* and often written as $t$.

The rest of the nodes $r$, satisfying $od(r) = n + 1$, are called the *residual nodes*.

Based on this classification, we often split $V$ into two disjoint sets $S = \{s_n, s_{n-1}, \ldots, s_0\}$ and $R = V \backslash S$, and write $G = (R, S; E; n)$ for a MMFN $G = (R + S, E)$ of degree $n$, where, in general, the union of two *disjoint* sets $X$ and $Y$ is denoted by $X + Y$ and their difference by $X \backslash Y = X \cap \overline{Y}$ in this paper.

Instances of MMFNs of degrees 0, 1, and 2 are depicted in Fig. 1.

From the definition, we can derive the following fact.

**Proposition 1.** *If $G = (R, S; E; n)$ is a MMFN, then for every special node $s_i \in S$, it holds that $s_i \to s_j \in E$ for all $j, 0 \le j < i$.*

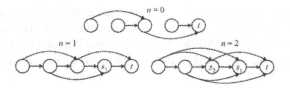

**Fig. 1.** Instances of MMFNs of degree $n$

*Proof.* Since $G$ is acyclic, we can *topologically sort* the nodes $V$ and associate each node $v$ with an integer label $lab(v)$ by a *one-to-one* mapping $lab$ from $V$ to $\{0, 1, \dots, |V|-1\}$ such that if $v \to w \in E$ then $lab(v) > lab(w)$.

To prove the proposition, we need to verify the following claim.

CLAIM. For each $i \in \{0, 1, \dots, n\}$, there exists the unique special node $v \in S$ such that $lab(v) = od(v) = i$. (Indeed, $v = s_i$.)

The claim is proved by induction on $i$, but the complete proof is omitted because of the space limitation.

It is clear that the main proposition follows from this claim. Indeed, the special node $s_i$ has the label $i$ and as many as $i$ outgoing links connecting to nodes $\{v \mid 0 \le lab(v) < i\}$.

$\square$

## 2.3   Robustness of MMFN

Suppose that a message received by a node $v$ should be forwarded to the target $t$ along a path from $v$ to $t$ of the MMFN of degree $n$. We show that if at most $n$ nodes are abnormal, messages can be forwarded to the target. We say that MMFNs are *robust* in this sense. The idea is graph-theoretically formalized as the following theorem.

**Theorem 1.** *Let $G = (V, E)$ be a MMFN of degree $n$ and let $t$ be its target. Then for every node $v \in V$ and every set $A \subseteq V - \{v, t\}$ with $|A| \le n$, there exists a path from $v$ to $t$ without passing through any nodes of $A$.*

*Proof.* We reuse the labeling function $lab(v) : V \mapsto \{0, 1, \dots, |V| - 1\}$ introduced in the proof of Proposition 1 and prove the theorem by induction on $lab(v)$.

The base case $lab(v) = 0$ is trivial, because by Proposition 1 we see $v = t$, thus there exists a required path of length 0.

Consider the case $lab(v) = k > 0$, assuming, as the induction hypothesis, that the theorem holds for $lab(v) < k$. We can identify two cases.

If $v$ is a special node, then by Proposition 1 there exists a link $v \to t \in E$ directly connecting to the target, thus a required path.

Otherwise, $v$ is a residual node. Let $W = \{w \mid v \to w \in E\}$ be the set of end nodes of the links outgoing from $v$. Since $od(v) = n + 1$ and $G$ is simple, those end nodes are mutually distinct, i.e. $|W| = n + 1$. This is compared with $|A| \le n$ to deduce that there exists a node $w \in W$ such that $w \notin A$. Since $lab(w) < lab(v) = k$, we can use the induction hypothesis to show that there exists a path from $w$ to $t$ without passing through any nodes of $A$. Concatenation of the edge $v \to w$ and this path yields a required path.    □

# 3   Evolution of MMFN

In this section we discuss the dynamic nature (evolution) of MMFNs. We present our design as a form of a logical system consisting of six inference rules, and then prove its soundness.

## 3.1   Logical System $\mathcal{L}_n$

We have introduced the notation $(R, S; E; n)$ for representing a MMFN in the previous section. In this section we call it a *configuration* and interpret it as a logical expression that means that the graph $G = (R + S, E)$ is a MMFN of degree $n$ with the special nodes $S$ and the residual nodes $R$.

Since $S$ contains exactly one special node $s_i$ of degree $i$ for each $i \in \{0, 1, \ldots, n\}$, we regard it as an ordered set, arranging the elements in the descending order of $i$, and write it as a sequence $s_n.s_{n-1}.\cdots.s_0$ delimiting the elements by the concatenation operator *dot(.)*. In addition, we use lower case letters for denoting a node and upper case letters for a sequence; thus, for example, $s.S$ denotes the sequence consisting of the first (leftmost) element $s$ followed by the sequence $S$. The empty set or sequence is denoted by $\emptyset$.

Every time the mobile agent moves from node to node, the configuration should be changed so that the resultant network preserves the properties required for MMFNs. Let us formally represent such a dynamic mechanism of the network by the following logical system consisting of six inference rules, where the letters $s$, $S$, etc. are variables denoting arbitrary elements or sequences except that $n$ is fixed to a constant.

**Definition 2.** Let $n$ be a nonnegative integer. Then the logical system $\mathcal{L}_n$ is defined by the following six inference rules.

START $a$

$$\overline{(\emptyset, a; \emptyset; 0)}$$

EXTEND BY $u$

$$\frac{(\emptyset, S; E; k) \quad u \notin S \quad k < n}{(\emptyset, S.u; E \cup \{v \to u \mid v \in S\}; k+1)}$$

MOVE TO NEW $u$

$$\frac{(R, s.S; E; n) \quad u \notin R + s.S}{(R + \{s\}, S.u; E + \{v \to u \mid v \in s.S\}; n)}$$

MOVE TO SPECIAL $s$

$$\frac{(R, S.s.S'; E + \{s \to v \mid v \in S'\}; k) \quad S' \neq \emptyset}{(R, S.S'.s; E + \{v \to s \mid v \in S'\}; k)}$$

MOVE TO RESIDUAL $r$

$$\frac{(R + \{r\}, s.S; E; n)}{(R + \{s\}, S.r; E \backslash E_1 + E_2; n)}$$

where

$$E_1 = \{r \to v \in E\}$$

$$E_2 = \{v \to r \mid v \in s.S\}$$

BYPASS $v$

$$\frac{(R, S; E + \{u \to v, v \to w\}; n) \quad u \to w \notin E}{(R, S; E + \{u \to w, v \to w\}; n)}$$

Each inference rule $\mathcal{I}$ of the form

$$\frac{G \; C_1 \cdots C_m}{G'}$$

proclaims that the configuration $G'$ is *inferred* from the configuration $G$ if all the conditions $C_1 \cdots C_m$ are true (under the ordinary arithmetic and the set calculus). In this case, we write $G[\mathcal{I}]G'$. (For the first rule, START, we simply write $[Start \; a]G'$.)

If $G_i[\mathcal{I}_i]G_{i+1}$ for all $i$, $0 \le i < d$, $d \ge 0$, we write

$$G_0[\mathcal{I}_0]G_1[\mathcal{I}_1]G_2 \ldots [\mathcal{I}_{d-1}]G_d$$

and say that the configuration $G_d$ is *derived* from the configuration $G_0$. In this case, we may also write

$$G_0[\mathcal{I}_0; \mathcal{I}_1; \ldots ; \mathcal{I}_{d-1}]G_d$$

by leaving out the intermediate configurations. Note that this looks like a pseudo program code with the pre- and post-conditions $G_0$ and $G_d$. If we are not interested in the inference rules in the derivation, we write $G_0 \vdash G_d$. In particular, if $\mathcal{I}_0$ is the START rule, we leave out $G_0$ and write $\vdash G_d$. The intended meaning of the inference rules will be described in illustrations in the following example and in words in the proof of Theorem 2.

*Example 1.* Let $n = 1$. We can verify that the following sequence is a valid derivation in $\mathcal{L}_1$. See Fig. 2.

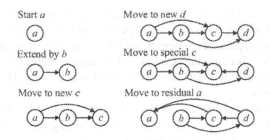

**Fig. 2.** An example of derivation

[START $a$]
$(\emptyset, a; \emptyset; 0)$
[EXTEND BY $b$]
$(\emptyset, a.b; \{a \to b\}; 1)$
[MOVE TO NEW $c$]
$(\{a\}, b.c; \{a \to b, a \to c, b \to c\}; 1)$
[MOVE TO NEW $d$]
$(\{a, b\}, c.d; \{a \to b, a \to c, b \to c, b \to d, c \to d\}; 1)$
[MOVE TO SPECIAL $c$]
$(\{a, b\}, d.c; \{a \to b, a \to c, b \to c, b \to d, d \to c\}; 1)$
[MOVE TO RESIDUAL $a$]
$(\{b, d\}, c.a; \{b \to c, b \to d, d \to c, c \to a, d \to a\}; 1)$

### 3.2 Soundness

In the previous section we introduced a notation $\vdash G$ to mean that the configuration $G$ is derived (or *generated*) by our logical system $\mathcal{L}_n$. Let us introduce a similar notation $\models G$ to mean that the logical expression $G$ is *true* under the interpretation given in the previous section, i.e., $G$ is a MMFN satisfying all the conditions of Definition 1. The following theorem shows the *soundness* of $\mathcal{L}_n$ in the sense that all the expressions it generates are true.

**Theorem 2.** *If $\vdash G$, then $\models G$.*

*Proof.* First of all, it is clear that the network $G = (\emptyset, a; \emptyset; 0)$, consisting of the single node $a$ and no links, generated by the inference rule START is a MMFN of degree 0. Therefore, it is sufficient to show that for each of the remaining rules $\mathcal{I}$, if $G = (R, S; E; k)$ is a MMFN of degree $k$ and $G[\mathcal{I}]G'$, then $G' = (R', S'; E'; k')$ is a MMFN of degree $k'$. This involves verifying that $G'$ is a finite, simple, acyclic graph such that $od(v) \leq k' + 1$ for all node $v$ and for each $i \leq k'$, there exists the unique node $v$ with $od(v) = i$. Since the finiteness is clear, we only show the other properties for each inference rule, one by one. Because of the space limitation, we only present the arguments for EXTEND BY and MOVE TO NEW, skipping the remaining three cases.

EXTEND BY $u$: This inference rule generates $G'$ by introducing a fresh node $u$ and adding the links which connect each of the special nodes $S$ to $u$. Clearly, $G'$ is a simple graph, because $G$ is simple and contains no edges added by the inference rule. Also clear is the acyclicity of $G'$, because the acyclicity of $G$ ensures that if $G'$ contained a circuit, the circuit would involve at least one newly added link $v \to u$. However, there is no links outgoing from $u$.

Consider the outdegrees of the nodes of $G'$. Since $G$ is a MMFN of degree $k$, we can write $S = s_k.s_{k-1}.\cdots.s_0$, with $od(s_i) = i$. By adding the links, the outdegrees of the nodes $S$ are increased by one, and thus we can write $S.u = s_k.s_{k-1}.\cdots.s_0.u$, with $od(s_i) = i + 1$ and $od(u) = 0$. Therefore, $G'$ is a MMFN with degree $k + 1$.

MOVE TO NEW $u$: This rule is similar to the previous one in that it introduces a fresh node $u$. The difference is that it may be used only when the network has the full degree $n$ (thus the degree is not increased any more) and the leftmost special node $s$, with $od(s) = n$, of $G$ now becomes a residual node, with $od(s) = n + 1$, in $G'$. The arguments for the previous inference rule can be reused here to verify that $G'$ is a MMFN of degree $n$.

$\square$

## 3.3   Computational Interpretation

It is clear that the inference rules of $\mathcal{L}_n$ can be interpreted computationally. More precisely, each graphical node may be interpreted as a computational node which has computational resources such as processors, memory, and communication ports. Each link $v \to w$ can be interpreted as a pointer (or reference) to the node $w$, stored in the node $v$. The entire set of such pointers define a communication network in a natural way so that the current location of the mobile agent is at the target $t$ and messages received by a node $v$ are forwarded to $t$ along a path from $v$ to $t$. (Instead of messages, we may think of queries for locating the mobile agent.) Theorem 1 ensures that even if there are $n$ abnormal nodes other than $v$ and $t$, there exists a path from $v$ to $t$ without passing through those abnormal nodes.

For each inference rule, we can think of a remote operation (or a procedure or a command) that modifies the pointers of appropriate nodes to update the configuration of the networks. We start with the initial, trivial network consisting of a single node, defined by the START operation. When the agent has moved to a fresh node, we can use either the EXTEND operation (if the degree of the network, $k$, is smaller than $n$) or the MOVE TO NEW operation (if $k = n$). When it has moved to a special node, the MOVE TO SPECIAL operation is used. Similarly, move to a residual node is implemented by the MOVE TO RESIDUAL operation, but this can be used only when $k = n$. The BYPASS operation can be used to reduce the number of hops (from $u$ to $w$ via $v$) by one and gain efficiency of message delivery by shortening paths that involve those hops.

A possible implementation involves having the mobile agents carry with themselves the locations of the special nodes including where they reside now. This only requires the additional memory space proportional to $n + 1$ for each agent. Let us denote this location information by $S.t$, as suggested by the notation of the inference rules. For example, after the MOVE TO NEW $u$ operation has completed, the agent can send to each agent at $S$ the remote command that request the addition of the pointer to $u$. Then it can update its own $S$ information by removing the leftmost element and adding $u$ as the rightmost element, as specified by the inference rule.

Let us discuss the computational complexity of the system. We measure the time complexity of $\mathcal{L}_n$ by the number of links added or removed for each operation. The space complexity is defined by the total number of links (or pointers) of the network for each agent. Let $V = R + S$ be the set of nodes of the network $(R, S; E; n)$. It is easy to verify the following theorem, which states that, given fixed $n$, the time complexity is constant (independent of $|V|$) and the space complexity is linear in $|V|$.

**Theorem 3.** *The time complexity of $\mathcal{L}_n$ is bounded by $2(n + 1)$. The space complexity of $\mathcal{L}_n$ is bounded by $(n + 1)|V|$.*

*Proof.* For the time complexity, the worst case is the MOVE TO RESIDUAL operation, which requires removal of $n+1$ links and addition of $n+1$ links. For the space complexity, each node of $V$ contains at most $n + 1$ pointers.                                         □

Note that the agents can have mutually different degrees ($n$'s) and network sizes ($|V|$'s). The space requirement for the overall system can be obtained by summing up the spaces required for each agent.

### 3.4   Related Work

Our work is concerned with the *location transparency* of mobile agent systems. In location transparent systems, every agent can communicate with other (peer) agents without knowing where they actually reside. For attaining this property, two general problems must be solved. First, the peer agent must be located by some mechanism that maps an agent's unique name onto its current location. Second, messages must be sent to the peer. (This can be difficult because mobile agents might "run away" from messages, making the location information outdated.)

Based on [5,6], we identify three basic models for location transparency: *searching*, *registering*, and *forwarding*.

In the searching model, the agents should have a priori knowledge of the locations where their peers possibly reside, and before sending messages to a mobile peer, they find its current location by broadcasting search queries to all of those locations [7]. When the number of those locations is huge, it causes a serious inefficiency, but if we have knowledge on the probability distribution of the current location of the peer, we can improve the performance by sending the query messages in an appropriate way [8].

The registering is a classic server-based model. The agents need to update their location in a predefined directory server, which can be either a central node or the agent's home host [9]. The single directory server may become the bottleneck of the system performance and the reliability. One approach to overcome this problem is a distributed directory to share the load [10]. The model developed in [11] is scalable to the Internet and accounts for security issues.

The MMFN model developed in this paper is basically classified as the forwarding model, where locating a peer and delivering a message are both done in a single phase. Every time the agents move to a node, they put in the previous node the pointer to the new node as the trace information so that future messages can be forwarded along the extended path. A closely-related model is a *locate-and-transfer*, where the target is located in the first phase, and in the second phase the messages are transferred to it directly. The theory of MMFNs in this paper is relevant to both models, because it discusses only the network configuration.

In [12,13], the network is assumed to be a tree, so there is exactly one path from every node to the root node where the target agent resides. This causes the lack of robustness, because a single broken node makes the target agent unreachable. Our previous work in [14] defines a network where at most one broken node is allowed. It can be seen as a MMFN of degree $n = 1$. This paper extends this theoretical framework to $n = 0$ and $n \geq 2$. Note that MMFNs of degree $n = 0$ are trees, which are common to existing forwarding models. To the best of our knowledge, no models equivalent to MMFNs of degree $n \geq 2$ have been proposed in the literature.

Another disadvantage of the forwarding model is the degrading of the system performance when messages are large in size and take multi-hops before they reach the target. A well-known solution to this problem is dynamically shortening the paths contained in the network as, for example, in [15]. The inference rule BYPASS in this paper incorporates this technique in a basic way.

There exist combinations of basic models. A combination of registering and forwarding is proposed in [16], where the central directory server is asked to deliver the message only when the forwarding fails. Another hybrid model combining registering and forwarding is proposed in [17], where the mailbox-based algorithm decentralizes the role of the directory server and forwards each message at most once.

The choice of models depends on the application domains and the environments. Our work is not intended to replace any of the existing sophisticated models, but can be incorporated into some models to improve the robustness to arbitrary degree.

# 4   Conclusion

We have proposed the multi-path message forwarding networks for location transparent communications between mobile agents. We believe that we have provided the foundations for studying this kind of networks and their possible extensions by introducing rigorous formalisms based on graph theory and the logical system $\mathcal{L}_n$ as well as the mathematical results of the robustness, the soundness, and the computational complexity.

A natural theoretical question is whether or not the system $\mathcal{L}_n$ is *complete*. By completeness, we mean the converse of the soundness: if $\models G, then \vdash G$. If the system is complete, it provides a universal mechanism for creating all MMFNs. This is currently an open question, but we have a conjecture that the answer is affirmative, because we have recently obtained an informal proof of the completeness for the case of degree $n = 1$.

For practical side, an interesting engineering problem is how to determine the degree $n$. This will depend on the nature and goals of the environments and applications, but a basic guideline should be sought.

There are a lot of notable ideas for location transparency proposed in the literature. It would be our pleasure if our work would be combined with some of them to improve the state-of-the-art architectures of mobile agent systems.

# References

1. S. Appleby and S. Steward: Mobile software agents for control in telecommunication networks. in A.L.G. Hayzelden, et al. (ed.), Software Agents for Future Communication Systems, Springer-Verlag (1999) 270–286
2. W.R. Cockayne and M. Zyda: *Mobile Agents*. Manning Publications (1998)
3. D. Kotz, el al.: Mobile agents for mobile Internet computing. IEEE Internet Computing, 1, 4 (1997) 58–67.
4. A. Pham and A. Karmouch,: Mobile software agents: an overview. IEEE Communications magazine, 36, 7 (1998) 26–37
5. Y. Aridor and M. Oshima: Infrastructure for mobile agents: requirements and design. Proc. 2nd Intern. Workshop on Mobile Agents, Stuttgart, Germany, Lecture Notes in Comp. Sci. 1477, Springer-Verlag (1998) 38–49
6. D. Milojicic, W. LaForge, and D. Chauhan: Mobile objects and agents. Proc. 4th USENIX Conf. on Object-Oriented Technologies and Systems (1998)
7. A.L. Murphy and G.P. Picco: Reliable communication for highly mobile agents. Proc. 1st Intern. Symposium on Agent Systems and Applications, and 3rd Intern. Symposium on Mobile Agents, IEEE Computer Society Press (1999) 141–150
8. W.-S.E. Chen and C.-W. R. Leng: A novel mobile agent search algorithm. Proc. 1st Intern. Workshop on Mobile Agents, Berlin, Germany, Lecture Notes in Comp. Sci. 1219, Springer-Verlag (1997) 162–173
9. T. Xianping, J. Lu, et al.: Communication mechanism in Mogent system. Journal of Software 2000, 11, 8 (2000) 1060–1065
10. M. van Steen, F.J. Hauck, P. Homburg, and A.S. Tanenbaum: Locating objects in wide-area systems. IEEE Communications Magazine, 36, 7 (1998) 104–109
11. V. Roth and J. Peters: A scalable and secure global tracking service for mobile agents. Proc. 5th Intern. Conf. on Mobile Agents, Atlanta, USA, Lecture Notes in Comp. Sci. 2240, Springer-Verlag (2001) 169–181
12. S. Lazar, I. Weerakoon, and D. Sidhu: A scalable location tracking and message delivery scheme for mobile agents. Proc. 7th IEEE Intern. Workshop on Enabling Technologies: Infrastructure for Collaborative Enterprises, IEEE Computer Society Press (1998) 243–248
13. W. van Belle, K. Verelst, and T. D'Hondt: Location transparent routing in mobile agent systems merging name lookups with routing. Proc. 7th IEEE Workshop on Future Trends of Distributed Computing Systems (1999) 207–212
14. M. Kurihara and M. Numazawa: Evolution and maintenance of proxy networks for location transparent mobile agents and formal representation by graph transformation rules. Proc. Pacific Asian Conf. on Intelligent Systems (2001) 151–155
15. L. Moreau: Distributed directory service and message routing for mobile agents. Technical Report ECSTR M99/3, Department of Electronics and Computer Science, Univ. Southampton (1999)
16. P. Wojciechowski and P. Sewell: Nomadic Pict: Language and infrastructure design for mobile agents. Proc. 1st Intern. Symposium on Agent Systems and Applications, and 3rd Intern. Symposium on Mobile Agents, IEEE Computer Society Press (1999) 821–826
17. X. Feng, J. Cao, J. Lü, and H. Chan: An efficient mailbox-based algorithm for message delivery in mobile agent systems. Proc. 5th Intern. Conf. on Mobile Agents, Atlanta, USA, Lecture Notes in Comp. Sci. 2240, Springer-Verlag (2001) 135–151

# θ-Subsumption and Resolution: A New Algorithm

S. Ferilli, N. Di Mauro, T.M.A. Basile, and F. Esposito

Dipartimento di Informatica
Università di Bari
via E. Orabona, 4 – 70125 Bari – Italia
{ferilli,nicodimauro,basile,esposito}@di.uniba.it

**Abstract.** Efficiency of the first-order logic proof procedure is a major issue when deduction systems are to be used in real environments, both on their own and as a component of larger systems (e.g., learning systems). This paper proposes a new θ-subsumption algorithm that is able to return the set of all substitutions by which such a relation holds between two clauses without performing backtracking. Differently from others proposed in the literature, it can be extended to perform resolution, also in theories containing recursive clauses.

## 1 Introduction

Logic Programming [6] is a computer programming approach based on the representation of programs as first-order logic theories made up of Horn clauses, whose execution is reduced to proving statements in the given theory. Since the classical provability relation, logic implication, is undecidable [10], the weaker but decidable generality relation of θ-subsumption is often used in practice. Given $C$ and $D$ clauses, $C$ θ-subsumes $D$ (often written $C \leq D$) iff there is a substitution $θ$ such that $Cθ \subseteq D$. A substitution is a mapping from variables to terms, often denoted by $θ = \{X_1 \rightarrow t_1, \ldots, X_n \rightarrow t_n\}$, whose application to a clause $C$, denoted by $Cθ$, rewrites all the occurrences of variables $X_i$ ($i = 1 \ldots n$) in $C$ by the corresponding term $t_i$.

Since in this framework program execution corresponds to proving a theorem, efficiency of the generality relation used is a key issue that deserves great attention, whichever application Logic Programming is used for. In Theorem Provers, explosion of the possible interactions between clauses is often limited by deleting all clauses that are discovered to be already subsumed by other clauses in the theory. In Inductive Logic Programming (ILP), a large amount of tests is needed to check completeness and consistency of new hypotheses against all given examples. Another exploitation of θ-subsumption tests is to compute the reduction of clauses, i.e. a clause that is equivalent to a given one but from which all redundant (superfluous) literals have been deleted.

In the following, we will assume that $C$ and $D$ are Horn clauses having the same predicate in their head, and that the aim is checking whether $C$ θ-subsumes $D$. Note that $D$ can always be considered ground (i.e., variable-free) without loss

N. Zhong et al. (Eds.): ISMIS 2003, LNAI 2871, pp. 384–391, 2003.
© Springer-Verlag Berlin Heidelberg 2003

of generality. Indeed, in case it is not, each of its variables can be replaced by a new constant not appearing in $C$ nor in $D$, obtaining a new clause $D'$, and it can be proven that $C$ $\theta$-subsumes $D$ iff $C$ $\theta$-subsumes $D'$. Since the test if $C$ $\theta$-subsumes $D'$ can be cast as a refutation of $\{C\} \cup \neg D'$, a basic algorithm can be obtained in Prolog by asserting $C$ plus all the literals in the body of $D'$, and finally querying the head of $D'$. The outcome is computed by Prolog through SLD resolution [8], which can be very inefficient under some conditions.

*Example 1.* Given the following two clauses:

$$h(X) \;\texttt{:-}\; p(X, X_1), p(X, X_2), \ldots, p(X, X_n), q(X_n).$$
$$h(c) \;\texttt{:-}\; p(c, c_1), p(c, c_2), \ldots, p(c, c_m).$$

SLD-resolution will have to try all $m^n$ possible mappings (backtrackings) before realizing that the former does not subsume the latter because of the lack of property $q$. Thus, the greater $n$ and $m$, the sooner it will not be able to compute subsumption between them two clauses within acceptable time.

The next section presents related work in this field; then, Section 3 introduces the new subsumption algorithm, while Section 4 shows how it can be used to perform resolution. Lastly, Section 5 concludes the paper.

## 2 Related Work

The great importance of finding efficient $\theta$-subsumption algorithms is reflected by the amount of work carried out so far in this direction in the literature. Two classical algorithms are based on resolution: The former, by Chang and Lee [1], carries out a complete resolution of each literal in $C$ with all possible literals in the negation of $D$, whereas the latter, by Stillman [11], chooses one at each step and then exploits backtracking in case of wrong choice. The latter uses backtracking to avoid the computation of further, useless unifications once a solution is found. Based on such considerations, Gottlob and Leitsch [4] defined a new backtracking algorithm that attacks the problem complexity by first partitioning the clause into independent subsets, and then applying resolution separately to each of them, additionally exploiting a heuristic that resolves each time the literal with the highest number of variables that occur also in other literals.

A more formal approach was then taken by Kiets and Lübbe [5]. They first identify the subset of $C$ that deterministically $\theta$-subsumes $D$, and then separate the rest of $C$ into independent parts that can be handled separately by $\theta$-subsumption algorithms. Scheffer, Herbrich and Wysotzki [9] transposed the problem into a graph framework, in which additional techniques can be exploited. They take into account not just single literals, but also their 'context' (i.e., the literals to which they are connected via common variables). Indeed, by requiring that two literals have the same context in order to be matched, the number of literals in $C$ that have a unique matching candidate in $D$ potentially grows. The remaining (non-determinate) part of $C$ is then handled by mapping the subsumption problem onto a search for the maximum clique in a graph, for which known efficient algorithms are known, and can be properly tailored.

All the techniques presented so far rely on backtracking, and try to limit its effect by properly choosing the candidates in each tentative step. Hence, all of them return only the first subsuming substitution found, even if many exist.

Finally, Maloberti and Sebag [7] face the problem of $\theta$-subsumption by means of a Constraint Satisfaction Problem (CSP) approach by transforming each literal involved in the hypothesis into a CSP variable with proper constraints encoding the $\theta$-subsumption structure. Given such a representation, different versions of a correct and complete $\theta$-subsumption algorithm, named *Django*, were built, each implementing different (combinations of) CSP heuristics. Experiments in various domains prove a difference in performance of several orders of magnitude in favor of Django compared to the algorithms described above, thus comparison of new algorithms to just this system should be enough to evaluate their efficiency. Note that Django only gives a binary (*yes* or *no*) answer to the subsumption test, without providing any matching substitution in case of positive outcome.

## 3   A New Matching Algorithm

Ideas presented in Section 2 aim at identifying subparts of the given clauses for which the $\theta$-subsumption test can be computed with reduced complexity, and base their efficiency on the retrieval of just one solution (substitution). Then, only classical algorithms can be applied to the remaining parts. In those cases, the CSP approach proves very efficient, but at the cost of not returning any substitution by which the matching holds. This suggests that they would not be able to support resolution, in particular when recursive clauses are involved. The proposed algorithm, on the contrary, returns *all* possible matching substitutions, without performing any backtracking in their computation. Such a feature is important, since the found substitutions can be made available to further matching problems, thus allowing to perform resolution.

Before discussing the new procedure proposed in this paper, it is necessary to give some definitions on which the algorithm is based. In the following we will assume $C$ and $D$ to be clauses, such that $C$ is constant-free and $D$ is ground.

**Definition 1 (Matching substitution).** *A* matching substitution *from a literal $l_1$ to a literal $l_2$ is a substitution $\mu$, such that $l_1\mu = l_2$.*

The set of all matching substitutions from a literal $l \in C$ to some literal in $D$ is denoted by [2]:
$$uni(C, l, D) = \{\mu \mid l \in C, l\mu \in D\}.$$

Let us start by defining a structure to compactly represent sets of substitutions.

**Definition 2 (Multisubstitutions).** *A* multibind *is denoted by $X \to T$, where $X$ is a variable and $T \neq \emptyset$ is a set of constants. A* multisubstitution *is a set of multibinds $\Theta = \{X_1 \to T_1, \dots, X_n \to T_n\} \neq \emptyset$, where $\forall i \neq j : X_i \neq X_j$.*

Informally, a *multibind* identifies a set of constants that can be associated to a variable, while a *multisubstitution* represents in a compact way a set of possible substitutions for a tuple of variables. In particular, a single substitution is represented by a multisubstitution in which each constants set is a singleton.

*Example 2.* $\Theta = \{X \to \{1,3,4\}, Y \to \{7\}, Z \to \{2,9\}\}$ is a multisubstitution. It contains 3 multibinds, namely: $X \to \{1,3,4\}$, $Y \to \{7\}$ and $Z \to \{2,9\}$.

Given a multisubstitution, the set of all substitutions it represents can be obtained by choosing in all possible ways one constant for each variable among those in the corresponding multibind.

*Example 3.* The set of all substitutions represented by the multisubstitution $\Theta = \{X \to \{1,3,4\}, Y \to \{7\}, Z \to \{2,9\}\}$ is the following:
$\{\{X \to 1, Y \to 7, Z \to 2\}, \{X \to 1, Y \to 7, Z \to 9\}, \{X \to 3, Y \to 7, Z \to 2\},$
$\{X \to 3, Y \to 7, Z \to 9\}, \{X \to 4, Y \to 7, Z \to 2\}, \{X \to 4, Y \to 7, Z \to 9\}\}.$

**Definition 3 (Union of multisubstitutions).** *The union of two multisubstitutions* $\Theta' = \{\overline{X} \to T', X_1 \to T_1, \dots, X_n \to T_n\}$ *and* $\Theta'' = \{\overline{X} \to T'', X_1 \to T_1, \dots, X_n \to T_n\}$ *is the multisubstitution defined as*

$$\Theta' \sqcup \Theta'' = \{\overline{X} \to T' \cup T''\} \cup \{X_i \to T_i\}_{1 \leq i \leq n}$$

Note that the two input multisubstitutions must be defined on the same set of variables and must differ in at most one multibind.

*Example 4.* The union of two multisubstitutions $\Sigma = \{X \to \{1,3\}, Y \to \{7\}, Z \to \{2,9\}\}$ and $\Theta = \{X \to \{1,4\}, Y \to \{7\}, Z \to \{2,9\}\}$, is: $\Sigma \sqcup \Theta = \{X \to \{1,3,4\}, Y \to \{7\}, Z \to \{2,9\}\}$ (the only different multibinds being those referring to variable $X$).

**Definition 4 (merge).** *Given a set* $\mathcal{S}$ *of substitutions on the same variables,* merge($\mathcal{S}$) *is the set of multisubstitutions obtained according to Algorithm 1.*
*Example 5.* merge($\{\{X \to 1, Y \to 2, Z \to 3\}, \{X \to 1, Y \to 2, Z \to 4\}, (X \to 1, Y \to 2, Z \to 5\}\}$) = merge($\{\{X \to \{1\}, Y \to \{2\}, Z \to \{3,4\}\}, \{X \to \{1\}, Y \to \{2\}, Z \to \{5\}\}\}$) = $\{\{X \to \{1\}, Y \to \{2\}, Z \to \{3,4,5\}\}\}$.
This way we can represent 3 substitutions with only one multisubstitution.

**Definition 5 (Intersection of multisubstitutions).** *The intersection of two multisubstitutions* $\Sigma = \{X_1 \to S_1, \dots, X_n \to S_n, Y_1 \to S_{n+1}, \dots, Y_m \to S_{n+m}\}$ *and* $\Theta = \{X_1 \to T_1, \dots, X_n \to T_n, Z_1 \to T_{n+1}, \dots, Z_l \to T_{n+l}\}$, *where* $n, m, l \geq 0$ *and* $\forall j, k : Y_j \neq Z_k$, *is the multisubstitution defined as:*
$$\Sigma \sqcap \Theta = \{X_i \to S_i \cap T_i\}_{i=1 \dots n} \cup \{Y_j \to S_{n+j}\}_{j=1 \dots m} \cup \{Z_k \to T_{n+k}\}_{k=1 \dots l}$$
*iff* $\forall i = 1 \dots n : S_i \cap T_i \neq \emptyset$; *otherwise it is undefined.*

---

**Algorithm 1 merge($\mathcal{S}$)**

---

**Require:** $\mathcal{S}$: set of substitutions (each represented as a multisubstitution)
    **while** $\exists u, v \in \mathcal{S}$ such that $u \neq v$ and $u \sqcup v = t$ **do**
      $\mathcal{S} := (\mathcal{S} \setminus \{u, v\}) \cup \{t\}$
    **return** $\mathcal{S}$

---

*Example 6.* The intersection of $\Sigma = \{X \to \{1,3,4\}, Z \to \{2,8,9\}\}$ and $\Theta = \{Y \to \{7\}, Z \to \{1,2,9\}\}$ is: $\Sigma \sqcap \Theta = \{X \to \{1,3,4\}, Y \to \{7\}, Z \to \{2,9\}\}$. The intersection of $\Sigma = \{X \to \{1,3,4\}, Z \to \{8,9\}\}$ and $\Theta = \{Y \to \{7\}, Z \to \{1,2\}\}$ is undefined.

The above $\sqcap$ operator is able to check if two multisubstitutions are compatible (i.e., if they share at least one of the substitutions they represent). Indeed, given two multisubstitutions $\Sigma$ and $\Theta$, if $\Sigma \sqcap \Theta$ is undefined, then there must be at least one variable $X$, common to $\Sigma$ and $\Theta$, to which the corresponding multibinds associate disjoint sets of constants, which means that it does not exist a constant to be associated to $X$ by both $\Sigma$ and $\Theta$, and hence a common substitution cannot exist as well. The $\sqcap$ operator can be extended to the case of sets of multisubstitutions. Specifically, given two sets of multisubstitutions $\mathcal{S}$ and $\mathcal{T}$, their intersection is defined as the set of multisubstitutions obtained as follows:

$$\mathcal{S} \sqcap \mathcal{T} = \{\Sigma \sqcap \Theta \mid \Sigma \in \mathcal{S}, \Theta \in \mathcal{T}\}$$

Note that, whereas a multisubstitution (and hence an intersection of multisubstitutions) is or is not defined, but cannot be empty, a set of multisubstitutions can be empty. Hence, an intersection of sets of multisubstitutions can be empty (which happens when all of its composing intersections are undefined).

**Proposition 1.** *Let* $C = \{l_1, \dots, l_n\}$ *and* $\forall i = 1 \dots n : T_i = merge(uni(C, l_i, D))$; *let* $\mathcal{S}_1 = \mathcal{T}_1$ *and* $\forall i = 2 \dots n : \mathcal{S}_i = \mathcal{S}_{i-1} \sqcap \mathcal{T}_i$. $C$ $\theta$-subsumes $D$ iff $\mathcal{S}_n \neq \emptyset$.

This result, whose proof we omit, leads to the $\theta$-subsumption procedure reported in Algorithm 2. Note that the set of multisubstitutions resulting from the merging phase could be not unique. In fact, it may depend on the order in which the two multisubstitutions to be merged are chosen at each step. The presented algorithm does not specify any particular principle according to which performing such a choice, but this issue is undoubtedly a very interesting one, and deserves a specific study (that is outside the scope of this paper) in order to understand if the quality of the result is affected by the ordering and, in such a case, if there are heuristics that can suggest in what order the multisubstitutions to be merged have to be taken in order to get an optimal result.

*Example 7.* Given the following substitutions: $\theta = \{X \leftarrow 1, Y \leftarrow 2, Z \leftarrow 3\}$, $\delta = \{X \leftarrow 1, Y \leftarrow 2, Z \leftarrow 4\}$, $\sigma = \{X \leftarrow 1, Y \leftarrow 2, Z \leftarrow 5\}$, $\tau = \{X \leftarrow 1, Y \leftarrow$

---

**Algorithm 2 matching($C, D$)**

---

**Require:** $C : c_0 \leftarrow c_1, c_2, \dots, c_n$, $D : d_0 \leftarrow d_1, d_2, \dots, d_m$: clauses
   **if** $\exists \theta_0$ substitution such that $c_0 \theta_0 = d_0$ **then**
      $S_0 := \{\theta_0\}$;
      **for** $i := 1$ to $n$ **do**
         $S_i := S_{i-1} \sqcap merge(uni(C, c_i, D))$
   **return** $(S_n \neq \emptyset)$

---

$5, Z \leftarrow 3\}$ one possible merging sequence is $(\theta \sqcup \delta) \sqcup \sigma$, that prevents further merging $\tau$ and yields the following set of multisubstitutions:
$$\{\{X \leftarrow \{1\}, Y \leftarrow \{2\}, Z \leftarrow \{3,4,5\}\}, \{X \leftarrow \{1\}, Y \leftarrow \{5\}, Z \leftarrow \{3\}\}\}$$
Another possibility is first merging $\theta \sqcup \tau$ and then $\delta \sqcup \sigma$, that cannot be further merged and hence yield:
$$\{\{X \leftarrow \{1\}, Y \leftarrow \{2,5\}, Z \leftarrow \{3\}\}, \{X \leftarrow \{1\}, Y \leftarrow \{2\}, Z \leftarrow \{4,5\}\}\}$$

Considering that the proposed algorithm yields all the possible substitutions by which $\theta$-subsumption holds, its time performance, even on hard problems, turns out to be in most cases comparable, and in any case at least acceptable, with respect to Django. The experimental results confirming such a claim are not reported in this paper due to lack of space.

## 4   Resolution

The effectiveness of the new algorithm can be appreciated by considering that it allows to perform resolution between Horn Clauses, avoiding backtracking. This is possible thanks to its feature of returning all the substitutions for a matching problem. Algorithm 3 shows how the matching procedure has to be modified in order to perform resolution. First, the head of the example must be separated from its body (the "observation"): the former will represent the top level goal of the resolution process and will be used only once (at the beginning); the atoms in the latter must be available at each resolution step. Note that the goal of resolution must not be necessarily ground, which allows to use the given procedure also to get computed answer substitutions [6] for unbound variables.

The algorithm has two basic behaviours. The former regards the proof of *basic literals*, i.e. literals that don't have a definition in the theory, but that can be proved using only literals in the example. In this case, all the possible substitutions between the literal to be proven and those in the observation are collected and represented by a single multisubstitution. The latter behaviour concerns the literals built on predicates that have a definiton in the theory. Whenever a literal of this kind is encountered, we are interested in all the possible substitutions coming from any rule that defines the corresponding predicate. Hence, for each such rule, a new child matching process is started on each of its literals and the corresponding results are intersected. The outer loop collects all possible substitutions that make true $g$ with respect to $O$. Recursive clauses in the theory would lead to non-termination. This can be avoided by handling recursive definitions in a slightly different way, i.e. considering only one clause at a time and performing backtracking just like Prolog does.

*Example 8.* Given the following theory $T$:

```
h(X) :- p(X,Y), q(Y,Z), t(X,Z).   % 1
p(X,Y) :- g(X,Y), s(Y).           % 2
t(X,Y) :- f(X,Y).                 % 3
t(X,Y) :- d(X,Z), t(Y,Z).         % 4 (recursive clause)
```

and the following example $E$:

```
h(1) :- g(1,2), g(1,3), g(1,4), s(2), s(3), f(4,5),
        q(2,3), q(3,4), q(3,5), d(1,2), d(1,5), d(1,4).
```

The algorithm chooses from $T$ a clause $C$ whose head is unifiable with the head of $E$ (if any, otherwise it fails). Hence, it chooses clause (1) (with the multisubstitution $\{\{X\rightarrow\{1\}\}\}$) and begins to prove it by selecting $p(X,Y)$. To solve $p(X,Y)$ clause (2) is choosen, that is verified by the multisubstitution $\{\{X\rightarrow\{1\},Y\rightarrow\{2,3\}\}\}$. Indeed, literal $g(X,Y)$ yields the multisubstitution $\{\{X\rightarrow\{1\}, Y\rightarrow\{2,3,4\}\}\}$, that intersected with the multisubstitution associated to literal $s(Y)$, $\{\{Y\rightarrow\{2,3\}\}\}$, gives the final multisubstitution for clause (2) (note that the multisubstitutions for the literals $g(X,Y)$ and $s(Y)$ are obtained using literals in $E$ because there are no clauses for these predicates in $T$). Now, the algorithm must prove literal $q(Y,Z)$, that is true for $\{\{Y\rightarrow\{2\}, Z\rightarrow\{3\}\}, \{Y\rightarrow\{3\}, Z\rightarrow\{4,5\}\}\}$ by exploiting literals in $E$. The partial multisubstitution $\{\{X\rightarrow\{1\}, Y\rightarrow\{2\}, Z\rightarrow\{3\}\}, \{X\rightarrow\{1\}, Y\rightarrow\{3\}, Z\rightarrow\{4,5\}\}\}$ for clause (1) is obtained. Finally, to prove $h(1)$ it is necessary to prove literal $t(X,Z)$ in clause (1). Predicate $t$ is recursively defined in the theory (clauses (3) and (4)), thus the algorithm selects first clause (3), that is true for $\{\{X\rightarrow\{4\}, Y\rightarrow\{5\}\}\}$ but incompatible with the partial multisubstitution obtained so far. Then, it selects clause (4), it solves literal $d(X,Z)$ with $\{\{X\rightarrow\{1\}, Z\rightarrow\{2,4,5\}\}\}$ and then calls recursively $t(Y,Z)$, that returns (using this time clause (3)) the multisubstitution $\{\{Y\rightarrow\{4\}, Z\rightarrow\{5\}\}\}$. Finally, the algorithm returns for literal $t(X,Z)$ in clause (1) the multisubstitution $\{\{X\rightarrow\{1\}, Z\rightarrow\{4\}\}\}$ that is compatible with the partial one yielding the final multisubstitution $\{\{X\rightarrow\{1\}, Y\rightarrow\{3\}, Z\rightarrow\{4\}\}\}$. This process proves that $h(1)$ is true in $T$ via resolution.

## 5   Conclusions and Future Work

This paper proposed a new algorithm for computing $\theta$-subsumption, that is able to carry out its task with high efficiency and can be extended in order to

---

**Algorithm 3** Resolution

---

**Resolution(g,T,O):S**
**Given** a goal g, a theory $T$ and an observation $O$
**if** $g$ is unifiable with some literal in $O$ **then**
    $S \leftarrow merge(uni(C,g,O))$
**else**
    $S \leftarrow \emptyset$
    **for** all clauses $C \in T$ such that head($C$) and $g$ are unifiable **do**
        $C \leftarrow C\theta$, s.t. $head(C)\theta = g$
        $S' \leftarrow merge(\theta)$ {applies only to constants in $\theta$}
        **for** each literal $l \in body(C)$ **do**
            $S' \leftarrow S' \sqcap$ Resolution($l,T,O$)
        $S \leftarrow S \sqcup S'$
**return**($S$)

---

perform resolution. A Prolog version of the extended algorithm is currently used in the ILP system *INTHELEX* [3]. Future work will concern an analysis of the complexity of the presented algorithm, and the definition of heuristics that can further improve its efficiency.

**Acknowledgements.** This work was partially funded by the EU project IST-1999-20882 COLLATE. The authors are grateful to M. Sebag and J. Maloberti for making available their system Django, and for the kind suggestions on its use and features.

# References

[1] C.L. Chang and R.C.T. Lee. *Symbolic Logic and Mechanical Theorem Proving.* Academic Press, New York, 1973.

[2] N. Eisinger. Subsumption and connection graphs. In J. H. Siekmann, editor, *GWAI-81, German Workshop on Artificial Intelligence, Bad Honnef, January 1981*, pages 188–198. Springer, Berlin, Heidelberg, 1981.

[3] F. Esposito, G. Semeraro, N. Fanizzi, and S. Ferilli. Multistrategy Theory Revision: Induction and abduction in INTHELEX. *Machine Learning Journal*, 38(1/2):133–156, 2000.

[4] G. Gottlob and A. Leitsch. On the efficiency of subsumption algorithms. *Journal of the Association for Computing Machinery*, 32(2):280–295, 1985.

[5] J.-U. Kietz and M. Lübbe. An efficient subsumption algorithm for inductive logic programming. In W. Cohen and H. Hirsh, editors, *Proc. Eleventh International Conference on Machine Learning (ML-94)*, pages 130–138, 1994.

[6] J. W. Lloyd. *Foundations of Logic Programming.* Springer-Verlag, Berlin, second edition, 1987.

[7] J. Maloberti and M. Sebag. θ-subsumption in a constraint satisfaction perspective. In Céline Rouveirol and Michèle Sebag, editors, *Inductive Logic Programming, 11th International Conference, ILP 2001, Strasbourg, France*, volume 2157, pages 164–178. Springer, September 2001.

[8] J. A. Robinson. A machine-oriented logic based on the resolution principle. *Journal of the ACM*, 12(1):23–49, January 1965.

[9] T. Scheffer, R. Herbrich, and F. Wysotzki. Efficient θ-subsumption based on graph algorithms. In Stephen Muggleton, editor, *Proceedings of the 6th International Workshop on Inductive Logic Programming (ILP-96)*, volume 1314 of *LNAI*, pages 212–228, Berlin, August 26–28 1997. Springer.

[10] M. Schmidt-Schauss. Implication of clauses is undecidable. *Theoretical Computer Science*, 59:287–296, 1988.

[11] R.B. Stillman. The concept of weak substitution in theorem-proving. *Journal of ACM*, 20(4):648–667, October 1973.

# Supporting E-consent on Health Data by Logic

Chun Ruan[1] and Vijay Varadharajan[1,2]

[1] School of Computing and Information Technology
University of Western Sydney, Penrith South DC, NSW 1797 Australia
{chun,vijay}@cit.uws.edu.au
[2] Department of Computing
Macquarie University, North Ryde, NSW 2109 Australia
vijay@ics.mq.edu.au

**Abstract.** In our previous work, we have developed a Delegatable Authorization Program (DAP) to support delegatable authorizations, where negation as failure, classical negation and rules inheritance are all allowable. In particular, a conflict resolution policy has been proposed which can support the controlled delegation and exception. This paper discusses an application of DAP in health care: electronic consent (e-consent). It examines a range of types of e-consent and shows how our proposed authorization models can well support these e-consent models. We will use DAP to develop a means of representing and evaluating patient consent to the disclosure of their data, with particular emphasis on security.

## 1   Introduction

More and more coordination of health care relies on the electronic transmission of confidential information about patients between different health and community care services. This health care system brings new uses and disclosures of patient data. However, since the patient data is confidential, the need for electronic forms of patient consent, referred to as e-consent [1] has to be considered. Patients should be able to give or withhold e-consent to those who wish to access their electronic health information.

At present, individuals working in the health system are responsible for obtaining consent from a patient, or determining whether consent exists for using or passing on a patient's information. In an electronic environment, the existence of patient consent is determined by automatic processes. For example, a set of computer rules can be defined to determine whether clinical staff working in a hospital might have their right to access electronic patient records. This is actually the so-called access control in computer information security. In the area of health care, a patient's privacy is not just the personal data. However, this paper is concerned with e-consent in relation to health data disclosure. While much is known about the access control technology, very little work exists to determine how a patient's consent to view private information is expressed and evaluated in an on-line electronic environment.

In our previous work [2], we proposed a logic program based formulation that supports delegatable authorizations, negation as failure and classical negation,

N. Zhong et al. (Eds.): ISMIS 2003, LNAI 2871, pp. 392–396, 2003.
© Springer-Verlag Berlin Heidelberg 2003

and rules inheritance. A conflict resolution policy has been developed in our approach that can be used to support the controlled delegation and exception. In our framework, authorization rules are specified in a Delegatable Authorization Program (DAP) which is an extended logic program associated with different types of partial orderings on the domain, and these orderings specify various inheritance relationships among subjects, objects and access rights in the domain.

In this paper, we will use DAP to develop a means of representing and evaluating patient consent to the disclosure of their data, with particular emphasis on security. We show how DAP with the proposed conflict resolution policy can suit the different needs of various e-consent models. We will first examine a range of types of e-consent and then show how our proposed authorization models can well support various e-consent models.

## 2   Basic Types of E-consent

[1] has presented four basic types of e-consent in health care context. We extend it to six here.

(1) Consent/delegation by default. Consent/delegate to exposure of patient information is assumed for any person, any data and any access except explicit denial exists.
(2) General consent/delegation. This is a general consent given by a patient for an individual or a particular party to access/delegate some or all of his/her health information without exception.
(3) General consent/delegation with specific denial. In this case, a patient provides a general consent/delegate to a broadly-defined class but with exceptions to some of its subclasses, such as denying consent/delegate to the disclosure of particular information.
(4) General denial with specific consent/delegation. In this case, a patient generally denies access to their health data but with exceptions, such as consent/delegate to the disclosure of particular information.
(5) General denial. In this case, a patient generally denies all or part of the information to be used by a particular party or anyone without exception. Contexts in which consumers would be likely to use this are treatments for STD, drug rehabilitation and psychiatric treatment.
(6) Denial by default. Denial is assumed for any person, any data and any purpose except explicitly expressed consent exist.
It should be noted that, from (1) to (6), the degree to support accessibility of health carer decreased but the privacy degree increased. The above basic consent models could be combined to form more complex consent models where different hierarchies of qualifications are allowed.

## 3   Using the Logic Model to Support E-consent

In this section, we show how to use the Delegatable Authorization Program (DAP) developed in [2] to support E-consent model. Recall that our language

$\mathcal{L}$ is a many-sorted first order language, with four disjoint *sorts* $S, O, A, T$ for subject, object, access right and authorization type respectively. Three partial orders are defined on subject, object and access right respectively to represent the inheritance hierarchies. Variables are denoted by a string preceded by an underscore. A Delegatable Authorization Program, DAP, consists of a finite set of rules which are statements of the form:

$$b_0 \leftarrow b_1, ..., b_k, not\, b_{k+1}, ..., not\, b_m, m >= 0$$

where $b_0, b_1, ..., b_m$ are literals, and not is the negation as failure symbol. We first use the authorization predicate *grant* to define consent and denial in the context of health care.

**Definition 1.** *A subject (individual/role) s consents/denies/delegate another subject s' to exercise access right a on patient data o, which is defined by* $grant(s', o, +, a, p, s)$ /$grant(s', o, -, a, p, s)$/$grant(s', o, *, a, p, s)$.

For example, $grant(Bob, health\text{-}data, +/-/*, read, Alice)$ means that Alice consents/denies/delegate Bob to read his health-data. Next we show how different types of consent can be supported by DAP.

1. Consent/Delegation by Default

The following rule expresses that a patient Alice wants to use "consent by default model" for her health data. That is, a subject can access her data if the explicit denial does not exist.

$$grant(\_s, all\text{-}data, +, \_a, Alice) \leftarrow not\, grant(\_s, all\text{-}data, -, \_a, Alice)$$

Intuitively, the rule says, $grant(\_s, all\text{-}data, +, \_a, Alice)$ is true if no information indicates that $grant(\_s, all\text{-}data, -, \_a, Alice)$ is true. Similarly, the following rule expresses that a patient Bob wishes to use "delegation by default model" for his health data. That is, a subject can disclose Bob's data to others if the explicit opposites do not exist.

$$grant(\_s, all\text{-}data, *, \_a, Bob) \leftarrow not\, grant(\_s, all\text{-}data, -, \_a, Bob),$$
$$not\, grant(\_s, all\text{-}data, +, \_a, Bob)$$

Intuitively, the rule says, $grant(\_s, all\text{-}data, *, \_a, Bob)$ is true if no information indicates that $grant(\_s, all\text{-}data, -, \_a, Bob)$ or $grant(\_s, all\text{-}data, +, \_a, Bob)$ is true. Please note that $grant(\_s, all\text{-}data, +, \_a, Bob)$ means a subject can exercise $\_a$ on all-data, but not further grant $\_a$ to other subject.

2. General Consent/Delegation

Suppose a patient Alice wants to give a general consent(delegation) to all the health carers for all the access rights on her health data, which can be represented by the following rule.

$grant(all\text{-}health\text{-}carer, all\text{-}data, +(*), \_a, Alice) \leftarrow$

Another patient Bob may only wish to disclose his health details to all health carers for reading. The following rule can express this.

$grant(all\text{-}health\text{-}carer, health\text{-}detail, +, read, Bob) \leftarrow$

### 3. General Consent/Delegation with Specific Denial

Suppose a patient Alice provides a general delegation to a health care professional, but expressly precludes the disclosure of information about sensitive medical history, such as an STD condition or gynaecological procedure, to her family GP. The following rules express this situation.

$grant(all\text{-}health\text{-}carer, all\text{-}data, *, \_u, Alice) \leftarrow$
$grant(familyGP, sensitive\text{-}history, -, \_a, Alice) \leftarrow$

Let us have a closer look at how this works. Suppose $all\text{-}health\text{-}carer <$ $familyGP$, and $all\text{-}data < sensitive\text{-}history$. The first rule is a general rule which will propagate downward the subject and object hierarchies defined by the above relations, since consent inheritance is supported. Hence the family GP will be able to access sensitive-history. However the second rule says the opposite. Since Alice is the grantor of both rules, and the second rule is more specific than the first one, the second one will override the first one on sensitive-history according to our conflict resolution policy. On the other hand, since Alice has delegated the grant right to all-health-carer, the health professionals can grant consent on her health data thereafter. Suppose a doctor Bob has given her familyGP a consent on sensitive-history, as shown in the following rule:

$grant(familyGP, sensitive\text{-}history, +, \_a, Bob) \leftarrow$

This rule is conflicting with the second rule granted by Alice. In this situation, as Bob was given his privilege to grant consent by Alice, his positive grant to the familyGP will be overridden by the negative grant from Alice, according to our conflict resolution policy (Priority decreases along the delegation relation). In fact, except for the administrator, Alice's grant on her own data will not be overridden by any other person's grant.

### 4. General Denial with Specific Consent/Delegation

For example, a patient Alice provides a general denial to a health care professional, but consent the disclosure to her family GP. This could be expressed by the following two rules.

$grant(all\text{-}health\text{-}carer, all\text{-}data, -, \_a, Alice) \leftarrow$
$grant(familyGP, all\text{-}data, +, \_a, Alice) \leftarrow$

The second "more-specific" rule will override the first one on familyGP. The reason for this is similar to 3.

### 5. General Denial

The following rule expresses that a patient Alice give a general denial to all the health carers for all the access rights on her data.

$$grant(all\text{-}health\text{-}carer, all\text{-}data, -, \_a, Alice) \leftarrow$$

The following rule expresses that a patient Alice give a general denial to a doctor Bob for all the access rights on her data.

$$grant(Bob, all\text{-}data, -, \_a, Alice) \leftarrow$$

### 6. Denial by Default

The following rule expresses a patient Alice wants to use "denial by default" model for her health data. That is, a subject can not access her data if the explicit consent or delegation does not exist.

$$grant(\_s, all\text{-}data, -, \_a, Alice) \leftarrow not\ grant(\_s, all\text{-}data, +, \_a, Alice),$$
$$not\ grant(\_s, all\text{-}data, *, \_a, Alice)$$

## 4   Conclusion

In this paper, we apply our logic authorization model proposed in [2] to a real world application, e-consent on health data. We show how Delegatable Authorization Program (DAP) can be used to specify and evaluate different types of e-consent. It is shown that DAP provides users a good framework to express different e-consent models and the conflict control policy can support well controlled consent delegation.

## References

1. Enrico Coiera, Consumer consent in electronic health data exchange. *Report*, the University of New South Wales, 2001.
2. C. Ruan,V. Varadharajan and Y.Zhang, Logic-based reasoning on delegatable authorizations. In *Proc. of the 13th International Symposium on Methodologies for Intelligent Systems*, pp 185–193, 2002.
3. V. Varadharajan and Claudio Calvelli, An access control model and its use in representing mental health application access policy. *IEEE Transaction on Knowledge and Data Engineering*, 8(1):81–95, 1996.

# Towards the Theory of Relaxed Unification

Tony Abou-Assaleh, Nick Cercone, and Vlado Kešelj

Faculty of Computer Science, Dalhousie University,
Halifax, Ontario, B3H 1W5, Canada,
{taa,nick,vlado}@cs.dal.ca

**Abstract.** Classical unification requires a perfect agreement between the terms being unified. In practice, data is seldom error-free and can contain inconsistent information. Classical unification fails when the data is imperfect. We propose the *Theory of Relaxed Unification* as a new theory that relaxes the constraints of classical unification without requiring special pre-processing of data. Relaxed unification tolerates possible errors and inconsistencies in the data and facilitate reasoning under uncertainty. The Theory of Relaxed Unification is more general and has higher efficacy than the classical Theory of Unification. We present the fundamental concepts and an algorithm for relaxed unification.

## 1 Introduction

The classical unification function takes two terms as input and produces a boolean value indicating whether the unification can be performed successfully. In case of a result of true, the function also returns a substitution that unifies these two terms. The unification fails if the same feature is assigned different values in the objects being unified. This process places rigid constraints on the data requiring it to be correct and consistent. Since real-world data is seldom perfect, classical unification fails when it encounters the slightest error. Erroneous data often contains enough information that one can exploit to overcome the errors. In other cases, it is possible to draw approximate or uncertain conclusions.

Probabilistic logic encapsulates the probability theory with first-order logic. It provides a mechanism for specifying different degrees of belief and evidence to propositions. Although this area has been investigated for several decades, it is still under development. Inconsistencies in the data set are problematic.

Relaxed unification provides a method for extracting information from imperfect data. To achieve this functionality, we relax the strict true/false result of classical unification and replace it by a real number in the range $(0, 1]$ that indicates the correctness of the unification. A correctness value of 1 would represent a success under the classical unification; any other value would represent a failure. Relaxed unification does not includes a notion of failure; the unification always succeeds and returns a substitution.

N. Zhong et al. (Eds.): ISMIS 2003, LNAI 2871, pp. 397–401, 2003.

## 2    Related Work

The Theory of Unification is a well formalized and understood. Robinson [9] was the first to introduce unification in 1965. Knight [7] provided an extensive survey of representations, algorithms, and applications of unification. More recently, Kešelj [6] introduced an efficient general-purpose graph unification algorithm and discussed the low-level details of its implementation.

Several attempts have been made to facilitate reasoning under uncertainty by defining probabilities over first-order languages. These attempts lacked a unified representation model and were limited in their expressive power. Bacchus [4] separated probabilities into statistical and propositional probabilities, which allowed him to represent and perform probabilistic inference in a natural and unified formalism.

Multi-valued attributes have had a limited success in unification [8,5], however, their use was specialized and was not developed into a complete general theory. Relaxed unification [1,2] was the first attempt to formalize the concept of unifying sets of values. Further work has led to proposing the Theory of Relaxed Unification [3], which is the first coherent and complete formalization of the theory along with an implementation of a relaxed unification system.

## 3    Representation

Symbolically, shared structures are represented by suffixing a boxed index to the elements being shared. Graphically, a relaxed term is represented as a directed rooted graph. The nodes in the graph represent sets and functions. Edges directed from set nodes to function nodes are labelled with the function symbols of the elements of the set. Edges directed from function nodes to set nodes are labelled with the positional index of the arguments, starting from 1. Variables are represented in the graph by empty sets with the variable symbol attached to the label of the set node. Sets cannot contain sets or variables as elements.

*Example 1.* Relaxed Terms

  (a)    Empty Set. $t = \{\}$.
  (b)    Set Elements. $t = \{a, b\}$.
  (c)    Function Arguments. $t = \{f(\{a\}, \{b\})\}$.
  (d)    Shared Functions. $t = \{h(\{a\})\,\boxed{1}\,, f(\{h\,\boxed{1}\,\})\}$.
  (e)    Shared Sets. $t = \{f(\{a, b\}\,\boxed{1}\,), h(\{\}\,\boxed{1}\,)\}$.
  (f)    Recursive Structure. $t = \{f(\{\}\,\boxed{1}\,)\}\,\boxed{1}\,$.
  (g)    Combination With Variables. $t = \{a\,\boxed{1}\,, f(x, \{h(\{a\,\boxed{1}\,\}, x), a\})\}$.

## 4    Definitions

**Definition 1 (Relaxed Function).** *A function is an element from a countably infinite set of functions F. Each function has zero or more arguments. Each argument is a relaxed term. A function symbol is an element from the set $\Sigma_F = \{f, g, h, \ldots\}$.*

**Definition 2 (Relaxed Constant).** *A constant is an element from a countably infinite set of nullary functions (functions that do not have arguments) A, i.e, $A \subset F$. A constant symbol is an element from the set $\Sigma_A = \{a, b, c, \ldots\}$.*

**Definition 3 (Relaxed Variable).** *A variable is an element from the infinite set of variables $V$. A variable can be substituted by any relaxed term. A variable symbol is an element from the set $\Sigma_V = \{x, y, z, \ldots\}$.*

**Definition 4 (Relaxed Term).** *We construct a term algebra $T(S_F, V)$ where $S_F$ is a set of all of the subsets of the set of functions $F$ and $V$ is the set of variables. A term can be an empty set $\emptyset = \{\}$, a set of constants and functions, or a variable. A term symbol is an element from the set $\Sigma_T = \{t, u, v, \ldots\}$. Structure sharing is allowed and is represented symbolically by suffixing a boxed index to the shared elements. The graphical representation is a directed rooted graph where each set and function is represented by a node. Since each node is the root of a subterm, we use the terms node and subterm interchangeably.*

**Definition 5 (Perfect Term).** *A perfect term is a relaxed term in which all sets are either empty or singleton. Each classical term has a corresponding perfect term that is formed by encapsulating each function in a set.*

**Definition 6 (Path).** *A path to a node $u$ in a term $t$, denoted as $\pi(u)$, is a sequence of edges that connects the root of the graph of $t$ to $u$. The set of all paths from the root to $u$ is denoted as $\Pi(u)$.*

**Definition 7 (Relaxed Substitution).** *A substitution is a mapping from variables to sets of functions and from sets of functions to sets of functions. A substitution symbol is one of $\{\sigma, \tau, \theta, \ldots\}$. The application of a substitution $\sigma$ to a term $t$, denoted as $t\sigma$, is defined as*

$$
t\sigma = \begin{cases} u & \text{if } t = x \text{ and } x \mapsto u \in \sigma \\ u & \text{if } \Pi(v) \cap \Pi(t) \neq \emptyset \text{ and } v \mapsto u \in \sigma \\ f(t_1\sigma, \ldots, t_n\sigma) & \text{if } t = f(t_1, \ldots, t_n) \\ \{t_1\sigma, \ldots, t_n\sigma\} & \text{if } t = \{t_1, \ldots, t_n\} \\ t & \text{otherwise} \end{cases}.
$$

*Basically, the mapping rule is applied if it matches the node. Otherwise we recursively descend through function arguments and set elements.*

*Substitutions can be combined by applying one substitution to another. The application of a substitution $\tau$ to $\sigma$, denoted $\sigma\tau$, is achieved by applying $\tau$ to the term of each mapping rule in $\sigma$ and merging the mapping rules in $\tau$ with the mapping rules in $\sigma$. The merging is done by adding a mapping rule from $\tau$ to $\sigma$ if $\sigma$ does not contain a mapping rule with the same right-hand-side. If $\sigma$ does contain such a mapping rule then the left-hand-sides of the two mapping rules are relax unified. Substitution combination is associative, i.e., $(\sigma\tau)\theta = \sigma(\tau\theta)$ but generally is not commutative, i.e., $\sigma\tau \neq \tau\sigma$.*

**Definition 8 (Relaxed Unification).** *Two terms, $t$ and $u$, are always unifiable with a unifying substitution $\sigma$ such that $t\sigma = u\sigma$. The term resulting from the unification is denoted $t \sqcup_R u$, i.e., $t \sqcup_R u \iff \exists \sigma : t\sigma = u\sigma$. The unifying substitution $\sigma$ is called a* relaxed unifier *for the terms $t$ and $u$ and must meet the following restriction. For each mapping $v \mapsto w \in \sigma$, if $v$ is a set node then $w = v_t \cup v_u$ where $v_t$ is the corresponding set of $v$ in $t$ and $v_u$ is the corresponding set of $v$ in $u$. This restriction is necessary to prevent substitutions such as $\sigma = \{[rootset] \mapsto \emptyset\}$ from unifying terms by changing their structure to a predefined term independent of the terms being unified and consequently losing all the information associated with them.*

**Definition 9 (Most General Relaxed Unifier).** *A unifier $\sigma$ of terms $t$ and $u$ is the most general unifier if for any other unifier $\theta$ there exists a substitution $\tau$ such that $\sigma\tau = \theta$.*

**Definition 10 (Evaluation Function).** *An evaluation function maps relaxed terms to a real number. An evaluation function symbol is an element from the set $\Delta = \{\alpha, \beta, \delta, \ldots\}$.*

**Definition 11 (Correctness Function).** *A correctness function $\delta$ is an evaluation function that satisfies 1) the range of $\delta$ is $(0, 1]$; 2) for any two relaxed terms $t$ and $u$, $\delta(t) > \delta(u) \iff t$ is more accurate than $u$ according to some user-defined measure of correctness; and 3) for any relaxed term $t$, $\delta(t) = 1 \iff t$ is a perfect term.*

## 5    Algorithm

A high-level algorithm for relaxed unification is provided below as the function RelaxUnify (Algorithm 1). It takes the roots of the terms to be unified as arguments $u$ and $v$ and returns the root of the unified graph $t$ and a unifier $\sigma$. The more-detailed algorithm with illustrative examples can be found in [3]

**Algorithm 1** *Relaxed Unification by Recursive Descent Algorithm*

**global** $\sigma$ : Substitution := $\emptyset$
**function** RelaxUnify($u$ : Node, $v$ : Node) $\Rightarrow$ ($t$ : Node, $\sigma$ : Substitution)
**begin**
   $u := u\sigma$
   $v := v\sigma$
   **if** $u = \{u_1, u_2, \ldots, u_n\}$ **and** $v = \{v_1, v_2, \ldots, v_m\}$ for $n, m \geq 0$ **then**
      $t$ := merge $u$ and $v$ unifying edges with identical labels
      **if** $t \neq u$ **then** $\sigma := \sigma\{u \mapsto t\}$
      **if** $t \neq v$ **then** $\sigma := \sigma\{v \mapsto t\}$
   **else** $u = f(u_1, u_2, \ldots, u_n)$, $v = f(v_1, v_2, \ldots, v_n)$ for $n \geq 0$
      $t := f(t_1, t_2, \ldots, t_n)$ where $t_i := $ RelaxUnify($u_i, v_i$)
   **end if**
   **return** $(t, \sigma)$
**end**

A user-defined correctness function is used to determine the correctness value of the resulting term. The choice of a correctness function depends on the semantics of the relaxed term in a particular application.

# 6   Conclusion

Throughout this work, we propose a new unification theory that we call the *Theory of Relaxed Unification*. The purpose of this novel theory is to enable reasoning under uncertainty. Relaxed unification emerged from the limitation of classical unification that requires a perfect match between the unified terms. Relaxed unification succeeds where classical unification fails. In fact, relaxed unification always succeeds, which allows for reasoning in contradicting, erroneous, and uncertain data sets, as well as in consistent data sets.

This work is the first step towards developing the Theory of Relaxed Unification into a complete coherent theory. To uncover the full potential of relaxed unification, probabilities can be assigned to nodes. Stochastic relaxed unification is our main goal of future work.

Some of the specific theoretical aspects that we will address are: proving the correctness and effectiveness of the relaxed unification algorithm; deriving the runtime and space complexities of the relaxed unification algorithm; developing probabilistic models for assigning weights and probabilities to attributes and values and providing meaningful interpretations for these models; and deriving a scheme for computing the stochastic correctness of the unified objects.

# References

1. Abou-Asslaeh, T. and Cercone, N.: Relaxed Unification – Proposal. In: R. Cohen and B. Spenser (Eds.), Lect. Notes Artif. Int.: 15th Conference of the Canadian Society for Computational Studies of Intelligence, AI 2002. Springer (2002) 364–365
2. Abou-Assaleh, T. and Cercone, N.: Relaxed Unification – Proposal. Appl. Math. Lett. Elsevier Science (to appear)
3. Abou-Assaleh, T.: Theory of Relaxed Unification – Proposal. Master Thesis. School of Computer Science, Univeristy of Waterloo, Waterloo, Ontario, Canada (2002)
4. Bacchus, F.: Representing and Reasoning with Probabilistic Knowledge. The MIT Press (1990)
5. Carpenter, B.: The Logic of Typed Feature Structures. Cambridge Tracts in Theoretical Computer Science **32**, Cambridge University Press (1992)
6. Keselj, V. and Cercone, N.: A Graph Unification Machine for NL Parsing. Comput. Math. Appl. (to appear)
7. Knight, K.: Unification: A Multidisciplinary Survey. ACM Comput. Surv. **21** (1) (1989) 93–124
8. Pollard, C.J. and Moshier, M.A: Unifying partial descriptions of sets. In: P.P. Hanson (Ed.), Information, Language, and Cognition, University of British Columbia Press, Vancouver (1990) 285–322
9. Robinson, J.A.: A Machine-Oriented Logic Based on the Resolution Principle. J. ACM **12** (1) (1965) 23–41

# Probability Logic Modeling of Knowledge Discovery in Databases

Jitender Deogun[1], Liying Jiang[1], Ying Xie[2], and Vijay Raghavan[2]

[1] Department of Computer Science and Engineering, University of Nebraska-Lincoln, Lincoln, NE 68588-0115, U.S.A.
[2] The Center for Advanced Computer studies, University of Louisiana at Lafayette, Lafayette, LA 70504-4330, U.S.A

**Abstract.** A Knowledge discovery in databases (KDD) system with probability deduction capability is expected to provide more information for decision making. Based on Bacchus probability logic and formal concept analysis, we propose a logic model for KDD with probability deduction. We use formal concept analysis within the semantics of probability logic to import the notion of concept into modeling of KDD. One of the most important features of a KDD system is its ability to discover previously unknown and potentially useful patterns. We formalize the definitions of previously unknown and potentially useful patterns.

## 1 Introduction

Knowledge Discovery in Databases (KDD) provides automatic or semi-automatic means for exploring and analyzing data to discover new knowledge. For example, it is of interest to a supermarket manager to know that 80% of the customers who buy bagels also buy cream cheese. Suppose we know that a customer is buying bagels, then we conclude that with 80% probability this customer will also buy cream cheese. This deduction is natural in logic and the assertion with probability is logically sound. Identifying such new assertions with statistical or propositional probabilities inherent in the data helps a domain expert to learn from past data and make informed decisions for the future. An interesting problem then is whether the propositional probability can be directly inferred from the statistical knowledge obtained through the KDD process. To investigate this, we need a theoretical framework for KDD with probability deduction capability.

It is generally accepted that the unique and most important feature of a KDD system lies in its ability to discover *previously unknown* and *potentially useful* patterns. If a new pattern can be easily derived from previous patterns, we do not regard it as a previously unknown pattern, that is, previous unknown depends on deductive complexity. Potentially useful patterns are widely believed to be user-dependent and hence hard to formalize with simple logic alone. Thus to formalize KDD, we must build a logic model that has the capability to express complex concepts like previously unknown and potentially useful.

In this paper, we propose a probability logic model for KDD that presents a logic foundation for KDD process. Our logic model is based on Bacchus probability logic [1] and formal concept analysis [6]. Formal concept analysis facilitates

N. Zhong et al. (Eds.): ISMIS 2003, LNAI 2871, pp. 402–407, 2003.

importation of the notion of *concept* into modeling of KDD. Bacchus probability logic represents and reasons with both statistical probability and propositional probability, which make it suitable for modeling knowledge discovery process with probability inference. Its powerful expression capability makes it possible and suitable for defining complicated concepts, like *previously unknown* and *potentially useful*. In modeling KDD, we investigate logic representation of knowledge in databases and formalize KDD as a process to find *previously unknown* and *potentially useful patterns*, logic definitions theirof are also formalized.

## 2    Probability Logic

### 2.1    Bacchus Probability Logic

Bacchus probability logic [1] is based on first-order logic and extends it with probability expression capability. Probability logic defines a logic language on *statistical probability* and *propositional probability* which represents degree of individual belief.

Probability logic includes a set of *object variables*, a set of *n-ary predicate symbols* that represent propositional functions, propositional probability operator *prob* and statistical probability operator [*]. If $P$ is an n-ary object predicate symbol and $t_1, ..., t_n$ are object variables, then $P(t_1, ..., t_n)$ is a *formula*; If $\alpha$, $\beta$ are formulas, so are $\neg \alpha$, $\alpha \wedge \beta$. If $\alpha$ is a formula, then $prob(\alpha)$ denotes the propositional probability of the formula in possible worlds. If $\alpha$ is a formula and $\overrightarrow{x}$ is a vector of $n$ object variables $\langle x_1, ..., x_n \rangle$, then $[\alpha]_{\overrightarrow{x}}$ denotes statistical probability of the formula in real world.

In terms of formalizing KDD with probability logic, the way is to make propositions to describe the relations among objects by their features. Statistical probability of propositions is used to statistically measure knowledge derived directly from the databases, while proposition probability offer the capability of predicting knowledge in KDD.

Logic semantic structure $M = \langle O, S, \vartheta, \mu_O, \mu_S \rangle$ is defined to interpret symbols and formulas in probability logic. $O$ is a set of objects in the domain of interest. $S$ is a set of possible worlds. $\vartheta$ is a function that associates an interpretation of the language with each world. $\mu_O$ is discrete probability function over $O$, for $A \subseteq O$, $\mu_O(A) = \sum_{a \in A} \mu_O(a)$ and $\mu_O(O) = 1$. $\mu_S$ is discrete probability function over $S$.

### 2.2    Logic Representation of Knowledge in Databases

Developing probability logic model for representing knowledge in databases actually is to build logic semantics structure $M$ from a database context. If we consider representing knowledge in databases alone, the real world is the only world considered logically, it follows that the logic semantic structure $M = \langle O, S, \vartheta, \mu_O, \mu_S \rangle$ reduces to a triple $\langle O, \vartheta, \mu = \mu_O \rangle$. We express the logic semantic structure of a database as: $M = \langle O, \vartheta, \mu \rangle$, where $O$ is the object set of database, $\mu$ is the discrete probability function, $\mu(o) = \frac{1}{|O|}$ for any object $o \in O$, and $\vartheta: V \to O$ where $V$ is the set of object predicate symbols. In KDD object predicate symbols are interpreted as propositions on conjunction of features. To understand $\vartheta$, for each object predicate symbol $\vartheta$ assigns to it a set of objects possessing the features represented by the predicate symbol.

# 3   Formal Concepts in Probability Logic

## 3.1   Formal Concept Analysis

Formal concept analysis (FCA) helps to bridge the gap between probability logic and database system. The basic notions of formal concept analysis are those of a formal context and formal concepts. A *formal context* is a triple $(\mathcal{G}, \mathcal{M}, \mathcal{I})$ where $\mathcal{G}$ is a set of objects, $\mathcal{M}$ is a set of features or attributes, and $I$ is a binary relation from $\mathcal{G}$ to $\mathcal{M}$. $gIm$ means that the object $g$ possesses the feature $m$ [4, 6]. For a set of objects $A \subseteq \mathcal{G}$, $\beta(A)$ is defined as the maximum set of features shared by all the objects in $A$. Similarly, for $B \subseteq \mathcal{M}$, $\alpha(B)$ is defined as the maximum set of objects that posses all the features in $B$.

**Definition 1.** *A formal concept in the context* $(\mathcal{G}, \mathcal{M}, \mathcal{I})$ *is a pair* $(A, B)$ *such that* $\beta(A) = B$ *and* $\alpha(B) = A$, *where* $A \subseteq \mathcal{G}$ *and* $B \subseteq \mathcal{M}$. *The set $A$ is called* the extent *of the concept and $B$ is called the* intent *of the concept.*

From the point of view of logic, the intent of a formal concept can be seen as a conjunct of features that each object of the extent must possess. Let $\mathcal{C}(\mathcal{G}, \mathcal{M}, \mathcal{I})$ denote the set of all formal concepts of the context. An order relation on $\mathcal{C}(\mathcal{G}, \mathcal{M}, \mathcal{I})$ is defined as follows: $(A_1, B_1) \leq (A_2, B_2)$ iff $A_1 \subseteq A_2$ (or equivalently $B_1 \supseteq B_2$). The concept $(A_1, B_1)$ is called a subconcept of the concept $(A_2, B_2)$ and $(A_2, B_2)$ is called a superconcept of $(A_1, B_1)$ [4]. The fundamental theorem of Wille on concept lattices, establishes that $(\mathcal{C}(\mathcal{G}, \mathcal{M}, \mathcal{I}), \leq)$ is a complete lattice called the *concept lattice* of the context $(\mathcal{G}, \mathcal{M}, \mathcal{I})$ [5,6].

## 3.2   Defining Formal Concepts in Probability Logic

A formal context in probability logic modeling of KDD is a triple $(O, V, \vartheta)$, where $O$ is object set of the database, $V$ is set of predicate symbols defined over set of features, and $\vartheta: V \to O$. We represent the elements of databases with the notations of probability logic in the following way. A predicate symbol is interpreted as a proposition on a conjunction of features, and represents possible *intent* of a concept. Object variables stands for objects in the databases, and represents possible *extent* of a concept. Thus a formula $P(t_1, ..., t_n)$, where $P$ is an object predicate symbol and $t_1, ..., t_n$ are object variables, represents a *concept*. Now, we are ready to define the notion of *concept* in probability logic.

**Definition 2.** *Elementary concept is defined as a formula* $P(t_1, ..., t_n)$ *where $P$ is an n-ary object predicate symbol and* $t_1, ..., t_n$ *are object variables, we simply denote it as concept $P$. Derived concepts are defined as follows: if* $P_1, P_2, ..., P_j$

*are elementary or derived concepts, then* $Q = P_1 \wedge P_2 ... \wedge P_j$ *is a derived concept. A derived concept is called a* concept.

There are two special concepts: i) $\phi$, a concept whose intent is null, that is, predicate symbol of which is defined on the conjunction of no features; and ii) $\mathcal{A}$, a concept whose extent is null, that is, predicate symbol of which is defined on the conjunction of all features. It is noted that $\phi \wedge P = \phi$ and $\mathcal{A} \wedge P = P$, where $P$ is any concept; $\phi \wedge \mathcal{A}$ is undefined.

If Q is a derived concept of $P_1, P_2,...,P_j$, then Q is called a *superconcept* of $P_i$ and $P_i$ is called a *subconcept* of Q, $1 \leq i \leq j$. Following the discussion on FCA, it is easy to see that the subconcept–superconcept relation defines a partial order on the set of all concepts in a given context.

# 4  Logic Modeling of Knowledge Discovery in Databases

## 4.1  Previously Unknown Patterns

The main task of KDD is to find new knowledge, or new patterns. To formalize KDD, we need to formalize the notion of *pattern*. In terms of statistical knowledge, patterns can be viewed as the quantitative description of concepts and the relationships between concepts. Therefore, a logic definition of pattern is based on the logic definition of *concept*. We formalized the notion of *concept* in probability logic in section 3.2, now we are ready to give a formal definition of *pattern*.

**Definition 3.** Pattern. *If P is a concept, and* $r \in \Re$, *the set of reals, then* $[P]_{\overrightarrow{x}} = r$ *and is a pattern; and if P, Q are concepts and* $Q \neq \phi$, *then* $[P|Q]_{\overrightarrow{x}} = r$ *is a pattern.*

In KDD, a given database always provides some background knowledge that can be expressed as known patterns whose statistical probabilities can be derived from the database. Let $K$ denoted the known knowledge base which is represented as a conjunction of all known patterns.

To motivate formal definition of previously unknown patterns, we consider the following scenario. Assume we only have the following two pieces of previously known knowledge: 1) Less than 80% of the students get A in the test; 2) Every graduate student in the class got A. Now suppose we obtained a new pattern through some discovery process: Less than 80% of the students are graduate students. The question is, does it belong to previously unknown pattern? We may agree that it does not, because this pattern can be easily deduced from the former two patterns. Therefore, logically defining previously unknown pattern depends on the complexity of deducting unknown patterns from the known patterns. Only those unknown patterns with sufficient high deductive complexity can be defined as previously unknown pattern. Now, we formalize our logic definition of *previously unknown patterns*.

**Definition 4.** Previously unknown patterns. *Assume there exists an efficient deductive algorithm Alg based on Bacchus probability logic. A pattern* $[P]_{\overrightarrow{x}} = r$

*(or $[P|Q]_{\overrightarrow{x}} = r$) is called previously unknown pattern if no pattern like $[P]_{\overrightarrow{x}} = r_1$(or $[P|Q]_{\overrightarrow{x}} = r_1$) $\wedge$ $(r - e < r_1 < r + e)$ where $r_1 \in \Re$, can be deduced by algorithm Alg in at most c steps. We denote the deductive process as $K \models_{Alg(c)}$ $[P]_{\overrightarrow{x}} = r$(or $[P|Q]_{\overrightarrow{x}} = r$). Parameter c is called complexity controller, which is used to control the complexity of deduction and induction processes. Parameter e is called error controller, which is used for error tolerance.*

## 4.2  Potentially Useful Patterns

As datamining process tends to find a lot of trivial patterns along with useful patterns, identifying and eliminating uninteresting patterns discovered are important problem. We therefore define the notion of *potentially useful pattern* — those patterns that are previously unknown and are potentially interested to the user. Usually, the usefulness of a pattern is deemed as user-dependent, which make it difficult to give a formal logic definition. We adopt the *direct reference mechanism* which gives a possible logic solution for *potentially useful patterns*.

Direct inference adopts the reference class principle that says the probability of an individual having a property should be equal to the relative frequency of that property among the proper reference class which that individual belongs to [1]. Intuitively, the mechanism for choosing proper reference class used by probability logic can be described as follows. If we have the knowledge that the probability over a narrower reference class is significantly different from the wider reference class, the narrower reference class should be chosen as the proper class. For example, there are three concepts A, B and $B \wedge C$, which respectively represent a disease, population of an area, sub-population of this area. Suppose we deduct two patterns: $[A|B]_{\overrightarrow{x}}$=40% and $[A|B \wedge C]_{\overrightarrow{x}}$=45%. Now we will say the pattern $[A|B \wedge C]_{\overrightarrow{x}}$=45% is potentially useful since it reflects the important information that the sub-population of the area have the disease at a rate higher than average, and we notice $(B \wedge C)$ is a narrower class than $B$.

We consummate our idea of "potential usefulness" as follows: if a narrower reference class provides more knowledge than any of the wider reference class about a property, the statistical information of this narrower reference class (among the classes the individual belongs to) will be potentially useful in deciding the probability of any individual having that property.

**Definition 5.** Potential useful pattern. *Let $C$, $Q$ be any concept except $\phi$, and $P_1, P_2, ... P_l$ be all subconcepts of Q. A pattern T: $[C|Q]_x = r$ is a (i) positive pattern if $r - max([C|P_i]_{\overrightarrow{x}}) > s$; or (ii) negative pattern if $min([C|P_i]_{\overrightarrow{x}}) - r > s$, where $1 \le i \le l$ and $s > 0$.*

*Parameter s is called significance controller. Both positive patterns and negative patterns are potential useful patterns.*

## 5  Conclusion

In this paper, we propose a logic foundation for knowledge discovery in databases based on probability logic and formal concept analysis. This foundation provides a solution of representing knowledge and reasoning with probability in knowledge discovery system. Moreover, we introduce the formal logic definition of two important concepts in KDD: previously unknown patterns and potentially useful patterns. For future study, we will develop efficient reasoning algorithm to find potentially useful patterns.

# References

1. F. Bacchus, 1990, Representing and Reasoning With Probabilistic Knowledge, MIT Press, Cambridge, Massachusetts, London, England.
2. C. H. Papadimitriou, 1993, computational complexity, MIT, 87–91.
3. H. Reichenbach, 1949, Theory of Probability, University of California Press, Berkely.
4. J. Deogun and J. Saquer, preprint 2003, Monotone Concepts for Formal Concept Analysis.
5. R. Wille, 1982, Restructuring Lattice Theory: an Approach Based on Hierarchies of Concepts, in: Ivan Rival, ed., Ordered sets, Reidel, Dordecht-Boston, 445–470.
6. B. Ganter and R. Wille, 1999, Formal Concept Analsis: Mathematical Foundations, Berlin.

# Constructing Extensions of Bayesian Classifiers with Use of Normalizing Neural Networks

Dominik Ślęzak[1,2], Jakub Wróblewski[2], and Marcin Szczuka[3]

[1] Department of Computer Science, University of Regina
Regina, SK, S4S 0A2, Canada
[2] Polish-Japanese Institute of Information Technology
Koszykowa 86, 02-008 Warsaw, Poland
{slezak,jakubw}@pjwstk.edu.pl
[3] Institute of Mathematics, Warsaw University
Banacha 2, 02-097 Warsaw, Poland, szczuka@mimuw.edu.pl

**Abstract.** We introduce a new neural network model that generalizes the principles of the Naïve Bayes classification method. It is trained with use of backpropagation-like algorithm, in purpose of obtaining optimal combination of several classifiers. Experimental results are presented.

## 1  Introduction

In the classification tasks we search for a method that assigns class/decision value to each given example. In doing so we try to incorporate various kinds of information in the this process. We can look at, e.g., the most probable decisions or the entire vectors of probabilistic decision distributions, for some data-derived patterns. One of the best known classification models, in which the decision probabilities pop up quite naturally, is the Naïve Bayes classifier. It uses vectors of the attribute value probabilities subject to particular decision classes.

In this paper we construct a neural network based model that combines, compares and optimizes probabilistic components of the Naïve Bayes classifier. We propose the network architecture, which processes the whole vectors of the decision probabilities. We introduce a concept of normalizing neural network (NNN), where the neuron transition functions accept and return the vectors of real values instead of single values [9]. We provide the foundations, implement, and verify experimentally the NNN (backpropagation-like) learning algorithm.

## 2  The Starting Point – the Naïve Bayes Classifier

We are dealing with the task of classification [5]. In the beginning we are given a set of examples (training sample) $T$ drawn from some universe $X$. We assume that every example $u \in X$ is represented by a vector of attribute (feature, measurement) values $a_1(u), ..., a_n(u)$, where $a_i : X \to A_i$, $i = 1, ..., n$. The set $A_i$ is referred to as the *attribute value space*. The examples are also labeled with

N. Zhong et al. (Eds.): ISMIS 2003, LNAI 2871, pp. 408–416, 2003.
© Springer-Verlag Berlin Heidelberg 2003

the value of decision $d$, treated as an additional attribute. We denote by $C_k \subset X$ the $k$-th decision class, i.e., the subset of examples labeled with decision value $k \in \{1, ..., r\}$.

Our goal in the classification problem is to find with some algorithm a hypothesis $h : X \rightarrow \{1, ..., r\}$, i.e. a mapping from $X$ onto the set of decision values. Mapping $h$ is often assumed to be highly consistent with the training sample $T$. In other words, one expects that $d(u)$ should be similar to $h(u)$ for $u \in T$. Mapping $h$ should be also – what is far more important – inductively correct, which means that it should be properly applicable for new, not labeled examples. Consistency with the training data hardly provides the inductive correctness. It is often better to base on less accurate, but less complex models (cf. [6]).

An example of the model, which is approximately consistent with the training cases, is the Naïve Bayes classifier. Although it ignores the attribute dependencies derivable from the data, it is proven to behave in a way very close to optimal in many classification problems [2]. It establishes $h$ on the basis of probabilities $Pr(\cdot)$ estimated from sample $T$. The estimates are very simple, based on counting the occurrence of the attribute-value patterns in data (cf. [5,6]). We use them as follows:

$$h(u) = \arg\max_{k \in \{1,...,r\}} \Pr(d = k) \prod_{i=1}^{n} \Pr(a_i = a_i(u)|d = k) \qquad (1)$$

In the next sections, we are also going to refer to an extended version of Naïve Bayes classifier, which is more flexible and less dependent on the "Naive" assumptions about data independence. Let us present it using (natural) logarithms of probabilities:

$$h(u) = \arg\max_k v_0 \log \Pr(d = k) + \sum_{i=1}^{n} v_i \log(\Pr(a_i = a_i(u)|d = k)) \qquad (2)$$

Weights $v_i$ determine the importance of attributes $a_i$ in classification process. One of contributions in this paper is a method for learning these weights using the backpropagation-like technique for the generalized neural network model.

## 3   Normalizing Neural Networks

Normalizing neural networks (NNNs) were introduced in [9]. It is an attempt to devise a mechanism for establishing compound decision distributions with use of an analogon of artificial neural network. Given the list of the classifier components (like e.g. single attributes in the Naïve Bayes method), we put to the input layer neurons responsible for processing their classification preferences. We assume that each component provides the vector of $r$ real values expressing how it is likely to classify each given example to particular decision classes. The difference with respect to the standard artificial network is that now we are going to combine the vectors instead of single real values. The input to the neuron is a collection of vectors and the output is going to be a vector of $r$ real values too. Abbreviation NNN comes from the fact that the weighted sums of vectors undergo normalization by means of the neuron transition functions $\phi : \mathbb{R}^r \rightarrow \triangle_{r-1}$ into the $(r-1)$-dimensional simplex of probabilistic distributions.

The structure of NNN with one hidden layer is presented in Figure 1. Vectors $x_i \in \mathbb{R}^r$ correspond to the classifier components for $i = 0, ..., n$. [1] Each $j$-th neuron in the hidden layer, for $j = 1, ..., m$, takes as input the vector $s_j \in \mathbb{R}^r$ and provides as output the vector $y_j = \phi(s_j)$, where $y_j \in \triangle_{r-1}$ and $\phi : \mathbb{R}^r \to \triangle_{r-1}$. The input to the output neuron is denoted by $t \in \mathbb{R}^r$ and its output takes the form of $h = \phi(t)$, which is the result of the NNN calculations. Vectors $s_1, ..., s_m, t \in \mathbb{R}^r$ are the weighted sums of the outcomes of previous layers, i.e.:

$$t = \sum_{j=1}^{m} w_j y_j \quad \text{and} \quad s_j = \sum_{i=0}^{n} v_{ij} x_i \quad \text{for } j = 1, ..., m \tag{3}$$

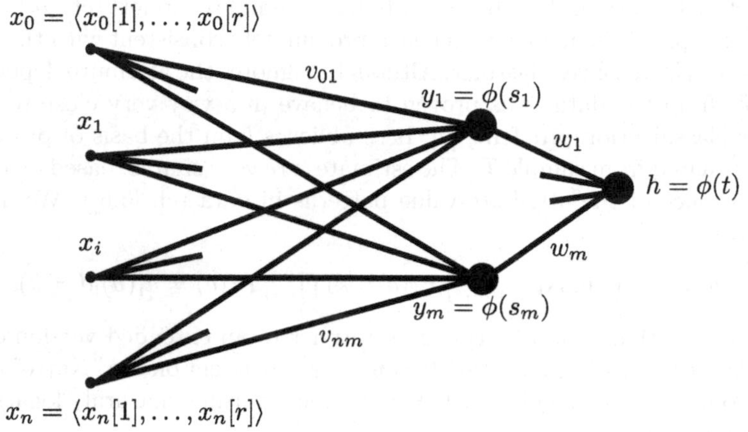

**Fig. 1.** The architecture of NNN with one hidden layer.

## 3.1  The NNN Transition Functions

Transition functions in NNN should be defined in a way that assures both the proper behaviour of calculation procedures and direct interpretation in extended neural network model. They should comply to some conditions, which generalize those formulated for classical transition functions (cf. [3,4,5]). In NN we use (mostly sigmoidal) monotone functions. In case of NNN, one can say that transition function $\phi : \mathbb{R}^r \to \triangle_{r-1}$ is monotone, if it satisfies the following:

1. Inequality $s[k] > s[l]$ between the input vector coordinates results in inequality $\phi(s)[k] > \phi(s)[l]$ between the output vector coordinates, for $k, l = 1, ..., r$.
2. The increase in the input vector coordinate $s[k]$ results in increase of the corresponding output vector coordinate $\phi(s)[k]$, as well as decrease of the other coordinates $\phi(s)[l]$, for $l \neq k$.

We will use the following monotone function $\phi_\alpha : \mathbb{R}^r \to \triangle_{r-1}$, where parameter $\alpha > 0$ determines the steepness of transition:

---

[1] Iteration $i = 0, ..., n$ is consistent with the application described in the next sections.

$$\phi_\alpha(s) = \left\langle \frac{e^{\alpha s[1]}}{\sum_{l=1}^r e^{\alpha s[l]}}, \ldots, \frac{e^{\alpha s[k]}}{\sum_{l=1}^r e^{\alpha s[l]}}, \ldots, \frac{e^{\alpha s[r]}}{\sum_{l=1}^r e^{\alpha s[l]}} \right\rangle \qquad (4)$$

Behavior of $\phi_\alpha$ is illustrated in Figure 2, for two decision classes, i.e. $r = 2$.

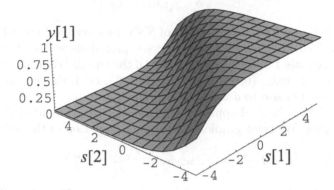

**Fig. 2.** Coordinate $y[1]$ of function $y = \phi_\alpha(s)$ for $\alpha = 1$ and $s \in \mathbb{R}^2$.

In the next section we generalize the backpropagation algorithm [3,4,6] in purpose of tuning the NNN weights. The advantage of using sigmoidal functions in this method is the way of calculating their derivatives. Figure 3 shows that $\phi_\alpha$ generalizes the behavior of classical sigmoidal functions also at this level.

$$\alpha \cdot \begin{bmatrix} \phi_\alpha(s)[1](1 - \phi_\alpha(s)[1]) \cdots & -\phi_\alpha(s)[1]\phi_\alpha(s)[k] & \cdots & -\phi_\alpha(s)[1]\phi_\alpha(s)[r] \\ \vdots & \ddots & \vdots & \ddots & \vdots \\ -\phi_\alpha(s)[k]\phi_\alpha(s)[1] & \cdots \phi_\alpha(s)[k](1 - \phi_\alpha(s)[k]) \cdots & -\phi_\alpha(s)[k]\phi_\alpha(s)[r] \\ \vdots & \ddots & \vdots & \ddots & \vdots \\ -\phi_\alpha(s)[r]\phi_\alpha(s)[1] & \cdots & -\phi_\alpha(s)[r]\phi_\alpha(s)[k] & \cdots \phi_\alpha(s)[r](1 - \phi_\alpha(s)[r]) \end{bmatrix}$$

**Fig. 3.** Derivative matrix $D\phi_\alpha(s)$ for the function $\phi_\alpha : \mathbb{R}^r \to \triangle_{r-1}$ defined by (4).

## 3.2   Backpropagation in NNN

The key issue is to equip the NNNs with an analogon of backpropagation procedure (cf. [3,4]). In a nutshell, in the classical neural network model there exists effective method for calculating the error (gradient) ratios used in the weight updates. The error values for the output layer can be easily derived from the differences between the network outcomes and true answers for the training cases. For the hidden layers, the errors are calculated on the basis of linear combination of the error components propagated from the next layer.

The above method can also be applied in case of NNNs. Let us denote by $d = \langle d[1], \ldots, d[r] \rangle$ the distribution, which we would like to obtain for a given training example. Let us consider the error function

$$E = \frac{1}{2} \sum_{k=1}^{r} (h[k] - d[k])^2 \tag{5}$$

where $h = \langle h[1], \ldots, h[r] \rangle$ is the output of NNN, as shown in Figure 1. Formula 5 is the normalized Euclidean distance between probabilistic distributions [8]. Its upper bound equals 1 and it is reached only if the two distributions have ones at different positions (e.g., $\langle 0, 0, 1, 0, 0 \rangle$, $\langle 0, 1, 0, 0, 0 \rangle$), i.e. if the output $h$ is totally incorrect in comparison to $d$ for a given training example.

Just like in the classical approach, we use negative gradient of $E$ to tune the network weights. We treat gradient of (5) as the function of the weight vectors:

$$\frac{\partial E}{\partial w_j} = \left\langle h - d \,\middle|\, \frac{\partial h}{\partial w_j} \right\rangle \qquad \text{where} \qquad \frac{\partial h}{\partial w_j} = \left\langle \frac{\partial h[1]}{\partial w_j}, \ldots, \frac{\partial h[r]}{\partial w_j} \right\rangle \tag{6}$$

Let us recall that $h = \phi(t)$ for $\phi : \mathbb{R}^r \to \triangle_{r-1}$ and $t = \sum_{j=1}^{m} w_j y_j$. We obtain

$$\left[ \frac{\partial h}{\partial w_j} \right]^T = D\phi(t) \, [y_j]^T \tag{7}$$

where $D\phi$ denotes the derivative matrix of $\phi$. Further, let us consider

$$\frac{\partial E}{\partial v_{ij}} = \left\langle h - d \,\middle|\, \frac{\partial h}{\partial v_{ij}} \right\rangle \tag{8}$$

Let us recall that $y_j = \phi(s_j)$ for $s_j = \sum_{i=0}^{n} v_{ij} x_i$, $j = 1, \ldots, m$. We obtain

$$\left[ \frac{\partial h}{\partial v_{ij}} \right]^T = D\phi(t) w_j D\phi(s_j) \, [x_i]^T \tag{9}$$

Formula (9) provides an interpretation similar to that concerning backpropagation, described at the beginning of this subsection. For the consecutive layers, the error vectors are calculated on the basis of the error components propagated from the next layer. The way of calculations of $D\phi(t)$ and $D\phi(s_j)$ depends on the choice of $\phi$. In our research we apply function $\phi_\alpha$ introduced in Section 3.1.

## 3.3   NNNs for Bayesian Classification

Now we show how to implement the concept of NNN in connection with the Naïve Bayes scheme. We consider the NNN architecture described in Figure 1. Given an example $u \in X$ to be classified, for each $i = 1, \ldots, n$, we put

$$x_i = \langle \log \Pr(a_i = a_i(u) | d = 1), \ldots, \log \Pr(a_i = a_i(u) | d = r) \rangle \tag{10}$$

We also add a special input that corresponds to the bias connection in a classical multilayer, feedforward neural network:

$$x_0 = \langle \log \Pr(d = 1), \ldots, \log \Pr(d = k), \ldots, \log \Pr(d = r) \rangle \tag{11}$$

For each $j = 1, ..., m$, we get the following formula for the coordinates of the input $s_j \in \mathbb{R}^r$ to the $j$-th neuron in the hidden layer:

$$s_j[k] = v_{0j} \log \Pr(d = k) + \sum_{i=1}^{n} v_{ij} \log \Pr(a_i = a_i(u)|d = k) \qquad (12)$$

It corresponds to the extended Naïve Bayes classifier (2). Since the NNN transition function $\phi$ is assumed to be monotone also in the sense of the properties presented in Subsection 3.1, we obtain that $\arg\max_k s_j[k] = \arg\max_k y_j[k]$. Hence, if we classify cases using a single neuron with output $y_j$ calculated from inputs (10,11), then the most probable decision class coincides with that given by (2).

Construction of the hidden layer with $m$ neurons enables to learn automatically, using the generalized backpropagation introduced in Section 3.2, the coefficients of the ensemble of the weighted Naïve Bayes classifiers (2) and then – to synthesize them at the level of the output neuron $h = \phi(t)$. Such an approach closely follows the idea of classifier ensemble as introduced in [1].

In the next section we show the experiments with the application of function $\phi_\alpha$. Used in the structure from Figure 1, $\phi_\alpha$ results with the vector coordinates

$$y_j[k] = \frac{\Pr(d = k)^{\alpha v_{0j}} \prod_{i=1}^{n} \Pr(a_i = a_i(u)|d = k)^{\alpha v_{ij}}}{\sum_{l=1}^{r} \Pr(d = l)^{\alpha v_{0j}} \prod_{i=1}^{n} \Pr(a_i = a_i(u)|d = l)^{\alpha v_{ij}}} \qquad (13)$$

at the level of the hidden layer, and with the final output coordinates

$$h[k] = \frac{\prod_{j=1}^{m} e^{\alpha w_j y_j[k]}}{\sum_{l=1}^{r} \prod_{j=1}^{m} e^{\alpha w_j y_j[l]}} \qquad (14)$$

Vectors $y_j$ can take the form of arbitrary elements of $\triangle_{r-1}$ except its vertices. $h$ can approach a vertex of $\triangle_{r-1}$ only up to the vector of the form $\langle \frac{1}{e^\alpha + r - 1}, ..., \frac{e^\alpha}{e^\alpha + r - 1}, ..., \frac{1}{e^\alpha + r - 1} \rangle$. This is why we decided to learn the NNNs using the reference vectors taking the following form for the training case $u \in T$:

$$d[k] = \begin{cases} \frac{e^\alpha}{e^\alpha + r - 1} & \text{iff } d(u) = k \\ \frac{1}{e^\alpha + r - 1} & \text{iff } d(u) \neq k \end{cases} \qquad (15)$$

Using (15) decreases the risk of overfitting, what was confirmed by experiments.

## 4    Experiments

We implemented the generalized backpropagation algorithm described in Section 3.2 and applied it to learning the NNN model described in Section 3.3. Several data sets of different size and layout have been selected for this purpose (see Table 1). In most cases the split into training and test samples is inherited with the data set. The main observed value in all experiments is the ratio (percentage) of correctly classified objects in the training and testing sets. The presented results are averaged over several algorithm runs (usually 20 or more). They are

414     D. Ślęzak, J. Wróblewski, and M. Szczuka

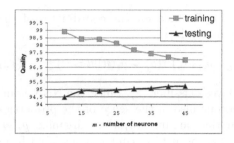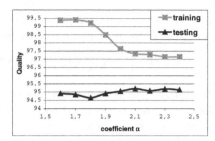

**Fig. 4.** Classification quality on DNA_small data with changing $m$ and $\alpha$.

compared with the results obtained with use of classical Naïve Bayes classifier. Experiments were also repeated with different choice of the NNN parameters.

The used data sets are taken from [10]. These are standard, well described benchmark data tables for which it is possible to find good reference results (see e.g. [6]). DNA_small is derived from the original table by taking only 20 attributes (out of 60), which are known to provide the largest amount of information (cf. [10]); DNA_large is the binary version of original data. Soybean and primary_tumor contain missing values.

The experiments were performed using the NNN network with one hidden layer composed 30-50 neurons in the hidden layer and the neuron transition function $\phi_\alpha$ for $\alpha = 2$. In case of all data sets it was possible to obtain good classification results on training samples after reasonably small number of iterations of backpropagation algorithm (running about 2000 iterations by default). It confirms the idea of backpropagation presented in Section 3.2.

The results are summarized in Table 1 together with these obtained using the Naïve Bayes (NB) classifier. They are generally close to the best known results obtained for the data sets in discourse (cf. [6,10]) and are significantly higher than some other classifier synthesis methods [9,11]. In all cases the NNNs are noticeably better than NB classifiers on the training sets. In three out of four train/test cases (except DNA_small) the same may be told about the testing set.

Relatively high classification rate (comparing to the best results known so far) on the primary_tumor data is encouraging. It was obtained as an average of several 10-fold cross-validation runs.

**Table 1.** Description of data sets (number of objects, attributes and decision classes) and summary of experimental results ($\alpha = 2, m = 30$).

| Name | train/test obj. | attr./dec. | NNN–test | NB–test |
|---|---|---|---|---|
| DNA_small | 2000/1187 | 20/3 | 95.34% | 95.62% |
| DNA_large | 2000/1187 | 180/3 | 95.85% | 93.34% |
| Soybean | 307/376 | 35/19 | 91.14% | 88.56% |
| SAT | 4435/2000 | 36/6 | 82.96% | 82.35% |
| primary_tumor | 339/CV-10 | 17/21 | 45.55% | 45.86% |

The results of the NNN model are parameterized by the number $m$ of neurons in the hidden layer and the value of parameter $\alpha$. Figure 4 illustrates how the choice of these two parameters influences learning process and classification results. In case of the DNA_small data set, there is noticeable tendency suggesting that the larger number of neurons in the hidden layer contributes to the reduction of overfitting effect. These proves to be especially true for data sets with large number of decision values (small representation for each decision class) like primary_tumor and Soybean, for which the increase (from 30 to 40 and more) in the number of hidden neurons resulted in classification quality improvement. Optimal $\alpha$ value seems to be close to $\alpha = 2$, which can be deduced from Figure 4 and results (not presented) of the wider experiment, comparing the $\alpha$ values between 1.5 and 5.0. More massive experiments are obviously needed in purpose of finding optimal configurations of the NNN parameters.

## 5  Conclusions

We introduced a concept of normalizing neural network (NNN), where the probabilistic vectors appear both on inputs and output of every neuron. Description of the NNN architecture and the foundations of its learning algorithm (backpropagation) was presented as well. It effectively extends classical Bayesian approach to classification problems. Presented experimental results demonstrate the ability of NNN to both learn and generalize information. In several cases, Bayesian NNN classifier outperforms classical Naïve Bayes method.

**Acknowledgements.** Partially supported by the Polish State Committee for Scientific Research (KBN) grant No. 8T11C02519. The first author partially supported by the Research Center of PJIIT.

## References

1. Dietterich, T.: Machine learning research: four current directions. *AI Magazine* **18/4** (1997) pp. 97–136.
2. Domingos, P., Pazzani, M.: On the Optimality of the Simple Bayesian Classifier under Zero-One Loss. Machine Learning **29** (1997) pp. 103–130.
3. Hecht-Nielsen, R.: Neurocomputing, Addison-Wesley, New York (1990).
4. le Cun, Y.: A theoretical framework for backpropagation. In: Neural Networks – concepts and theory, IEEE Computer Society Press, Los Alamitos (1992).
5. Mitchell T.M., Machine Learning, McGraw Hill, Boston (1997)
6. Michie D., Spiegelhalter D.J., Taylor C.C.(eds), Machine Learning, Neural and Statistical Classification, Ellis Horwood, London (1994)
   http://www.amsta.leeds.ac.uk/~charles/statlog/
7. Ślęzak, D.: Normalized decision functions and measures for inconsistent decision tables analysis. *Fundamenta Informaticae* **44/3** (2000), pp. 291–319.
8. Ślęzak, D.: Various approaches to reasoning with frequency-based decision reducts: a survey. In: Polkowski, L., Tsumoto, S., Lin, T.Y. (eds): Rough Set Methods and Applications: New Developments in Knowledge Discovery in Information Systems. Physica Verlag, Heidelberg (2000) pp. 235–285.

9. Ślęzak D., Wróblewski J., Szczuka M., Neural Network Architecture for Synthesis of the Probabilistic Rule Based Classifiers, *ENTCS* **82.4**, Elsevier, (2003) http://www.elsevier.nl/locate/entcs/volume82.html

10. UCI Repository of ML databases, University of California, Irvine, (1998) http://www.ics.uci.edu/~mlearn/MLRepository.html.

11. Wróblewski J.: Ensembles of classifiers based on approximate reducts. Fundamenta Informaticae **47** (3,4), IOS Press (2001) 351–360.

# Fuzzy Multiset Model for Information Retrieval and Clustering Using a Kernel Function

Kiyotaka Mizutani[1] and Sadaaki Miyamoto[2]

[1] Graduate School of Systems and Infomation Engineering
University of Tsukuba, Ibaraki 305-8573, Japan
kiyotaka@odin.esys.tsukuba.ac.jp
[2] Institute of Engineering Mechanics and Systems
University of Tsukuba, Ibaraki 305-8573, Japan
miyamoto@esys.tsukuba.ac.jp

**Abstract.** A method of fuzzy clustering based on a fuzzy multiset model is proposed. Data clustering has frequently been discussed in relation to information retrieval models and on the other hand fuzzy multisets provide an appropriate model of information retrieval on the WWW. A dissimilarity measure on fuzzy multisets is proposed. A method of fuzzy $c$-means using this measure is studied and fuzzy $c$-means clustering using a kernel function employed in nonlinear transformation into a high dimensional feature space in Support Vector Machine is discussed.

## 1 Introduction

Search engines on the WWW produce retrieved documents with degrees of relevance, whereby those documents are presented according to the decreasing order of the degrees. Several engines admit multiple occurrences of the same objects with different degrees.

A mathematical framework that captures these two features of multiple occurrences of a subject item with degree of relevance is the theory of fuzzy multisets. Multisets [2,5] and fuzzy multisets [6,9] have been studied in relation to a variety of information systems including relational databases [3]. It is thus necessary to apply this theory to establishing a model of information retrieval on the WWW.

Data clustering has frequently been studied in relation to information retrieval models [7], clustering of data is useful for reducing information amount. By establishing a representative for a group of data, a multiset of information items can be allocated to the nearest representative.

In this paper we thus consider clustering of documents based on a fuzzy multiset model. Among various methods of clustering, fuzzy $c$-means, best-known and widely investigated, are studied herein.

First, we briefly review fuzzy multisets, and a dissimilarity measure on fuzzy multisets is proposed. Second, a method of fuzzy $c$-means using this measure is studied. Moreover, a kernel function employed in nonlinear transformation into a high dimensional feature space in Support Vector Machine(SVM) [10] is considered for clustering.

N. Zhong et al. (Eds.): ISMIS 2003, LNAI 2871, pp. 417–421, 2003.

## 2    Fuzzy Multisets

Let us assume for simplicity that the universal set $X = \{x_1, \ldots, x_n\}$ on which fuzzy multisets are defined is finite. Let us first review crisp multisets.

A crisp multiset $M$ is a collection of multiple occurrences of objects, e.g., $M = \{x_i, \ldots, x_i, x_j \ldots, x_j\}$: it is characterized by the *Count* function (*Count*: $X \rightarrow \{0, 1, 2, \ldots\}$). This function represents multiplicity of an object, if $Count(x_1) = 3$ then there are 3 occurrences of $x_1$ in $M$. Details of multisets are omitted here (see [2,4]).

As Yager [9] has defined, a fuzzy multiset $A$ of $X$ is characterized by the *Count* function that takes the value of a crisp multiset of the unit interval $I = [0, 1]$. Namely,

$$Count_A(x) = \{\nu, \nu', \ldots, \nu''\}, \quad \nu, \nu', \ldots, \nu'' \in I.$$

For simplicity we assume the multisets of $I = [0, 1]$ are finite. The collection of all fuzzy multisets of $X$ is denoted by $\mathcal{FM}(X)$.

Basic operations of fuzzy multisets require the *membership sequence*, that is, the decreasingly ordered sequence of $Count_A(x)$ denoted by

$$Count_A(x) = (\mu_A^1(x), \mu_A^2(x), \ldots),$$

where $\mu_A^1(x) \geq \mu_A^2(x) \geq \cdots$.

### 2.1    Norm of Fuzzy Multisets

Let us define the length of a membership sequence:

$$L(x; A) = \max\{j : \mu_A^j(x) > 0\}.$$

We define a norm of a fuzzy multiset:

$$\|A\|_2 = \sqrt{\sum_{x \in X} \sum_{j=1}^{L(x;A)} \{\mu_A^j(x)\}^2}.$$

### 2.2    Dissimilarity Measure

We consider the cosine correlation as a dissimilarity measure between fuzzy multisets.

For $A, B \in \mathcal{FM}(X)$, we define

$$d(A, B) = 1 - \frac{\sum_{x \in X} \sum_{j=1}^{L(x;A) \wedge L(x;B)} \mu_A^j(x) \mu_B^j(x)}{\|A\|_2 \|B\|_2}. \tag{1}$$

This measure is frequently used for similarity retrieval and clustering of documents.

## 3    Fuzzy $c$-Means Clustering

Assume fuzzy multisets $A_1, \ldots, A_n$ are given. We consider fuzzy clustering of these multisets using the above dissimilarity measure.

The method of fuzzy $c$-means is alternative minimization of a criterion [1]. We consider the following entropy-based objective function with variable for cluster sizes [11].

$$
J_e(U, V, \alpha) = \sum_{k=1}^{n} \sum_{i=1}^{c} \left\{ u_{ik} d(A_k, v_i) + \lambda^{-1} u_{ik} \log \frac{u_{ik}}{\alpha_i} \right\}, \tag{2}
$$

where $\lambda$ is a positive constant.

$U = (u_{ik})$ is the membership matrix: $u_{ik}$ is the degree by which $x_k$ belongs to cluster $i$; the matrix $U$ should be subject to the constraint

$$
M = \left\{ (u_{ik}) : \sum_i u_{ik} = 1, \ \forall k ; \ u_{jk} \geq 0, \ \forall j, k \right\}.
$$

$V = (v_1, \ldots, v_c)$; $v_i$ is the center of cluster $i$, $1 \leq i \leq c$. Notice that $v_i$ is a fuzzy multiset: $v_i \in \mathcal{FM}(X)$. $\alpha = (\alpha_1, \ldots, \alpha_c)$; $\alpha_i$ is the regulation variable for cluster sizes; $\alpha$ should be subject to the constraint

$$
\mathcal{A} = \left\{ \alpha : \sum_i \alpha_i = 1 ; \ \alpha_i \geq 0, \ i = 1, \cdots, c \right\}.
$$

Since we consider alternative minimization of the above function [11], the iterative solutions are

$$
u_{ik} = \frac{\alpha_i \exp(-\lambda d(A_k, v_i))}{\sum_{j=1}^{c} \alpha_j \exp(-\lambda d(A_k, v_j))}, \tag{3}
$$

$$
v_i = \frac{\sum_{k=1}^{n} u_{ik} A_k}{\| \sum_{k=1}^{n} u_{ik} A_k \|}, \tag{4}
$$

$$
\alpha_i = \frac{1}{n} \sum_{k=1}^{n} u_{ik}. \tag{5}
$$

## 4    High Dimensional Space and Kernel Function

A high dimensional space used in SVM [10] is denoted by $H$ here which is called the feature space, whereas the original space $\mathbf{R}^p$ is called the data space. $H$ is in general an infinite dimensional inner product space. Its inner product is denoted by $\langle \cdot, \cdot \rangle$; the norm of $H$ is denoted by $\| \cdot \|_H$.

Notice that in SVM, a mapping $\Phi \colon \mathbf{R}^p \to H$ is employed and $x_k$ is transformed into $\Phi(x_k)$. An explicit representation of $\Phi(x_k)$ is not usable in general but the inner product $\langle \Phi(x_k), \Phi(x_\ell) \rangle$ is expressed by a kernel:

$$
K(x_k, x_\ell) = \langle \Phi(x_k), \Phi(x_\ell) \rangle.
$$

## 4.1    Fuzzy $c$-Means Using a Kernel Function

Assume fuzzy multisets $A_1, \ldots, A_n$ are given. Instead of (1), we use a dissimilarity measure in a high dimensional feature space;

$$d_H(\varPhi(A_k), w_i) = 1 - \frac{\langle \varPhi(A_k), w_i \rangle}{\|\varPhi(A_k)\|_H \|w_i\|_H}, \tag{6}$$

where $\langle \cdot, \cdot \rangle$ is the inner product of $H$ and $\| \cdot \|_H$ is the norm of $H$.

We consider the following objective function.

$$J_e(U, W, \alpha) = \sum_{k=1}^{n} \sum_{i=1}^{c} \left\{ u_{ik} d_H(\varPhi(A_k), w_i) + \lambda^{-1} u_{ik} \log \frac{u_{ik}}{\alpha_i} \right\}, \tag{7}$$

where $\lambda$ is a positive constant. Fuzzy multiset $A_k (k = 1, \ldots, n)$ is regarded as a vector and mapped into $\varPhi(A_k)$. $W = (w_1, \ldots, w_c)$ is the cluster centers in the high dimensional feature space.

It is easily seen that the optimal solution of **FCMA1** is

$$u_{ik} = \frac{\alpha_i \exp(-\lambda d(\varPhi(A_k), w_i))}{\sum_{j=1}^{c} \alpha_j \exp(-\lambda d(\varPhi(A_k), w_j))}. \tag{8}$$

Let $K(x, y) = \langle \varPhi(x), \varPhi(y) \rangle$ be a kernel function and put $K_{\ell h} = \langle \varPhi(A_\ell), \varPhi(A_h) \rangle$. Various kernel functions have been proposed from which the Radial Basis Function(RBF) kernel

$$K_{\ell h} = \exp \left( -cnst \sum_{x \in X} \sum_{j=1}^{L(x; A_\ell) \vee L(x; A_h)} | \mu_{A_\ell}^j(x) - \mu_{A_h}^j(x) |^2 \right), \quad (cnst > 0)$$

is used here, we have

$$d_H(\varPhi(A_k), w_i) = \sum_{g=1}^{n} \frac{u_{ig} K_{gk}}{\sqrt{\sum_{\ell=1}^{n} \sum_{h=1}^{n} u_{i\ell} u_{ih} K_{\ell h}}}. \tag{9}$$

The following algorithm **K-FCMA** is fuzzy $c$-means clustering algorithm in which the kernel function is used.

**Algorithm K-FCMA.**

**K-FCMA0.** Set an initial value of $d_H$ and $\alpha$.

**K-FCMA1.** Calculate $U = (u_{ik})$ by Eq.(8).

**K-FCMA2.** The dissimilarity measure $d_H$ is updated by Eq.(9).

**K-FCMA3.** The parameter $\alpha_i$ is updated by Eq.(5).

**K-FCMA4.** If the solution $U = (u_{ik})$ is convergent, stop; else go to **K-FCMA1**.

**End K-FCMA.**

Notice that in **K-FCMA**, $w_i$ is not explicitly calculated but calculation of (8),(9) and (5) are repeated until convergence. Hence the convergence in **K-FCMA4** should be based on $U$, and not $W$.

We omit a numerical example in this paper due to page limitation, but readers may refer to

http://odin.esys.tsukuba.ac.jp/paper/ISMIS2003mizutani.pdf.

## 5   Conclusion

In this paper, we have proposed the cosine correlation as a type of dissimilarity measures between fuzzy multisets for an application to the information retrieval model of fuzzy multisets, and clustering algorithm by the fuzzy c-means has been examined. Moreover a kernel function has been introduced to extend the fuzzy c-means by using a mapping into a high dimensional feature space. Application to information retrieval is done by using a multiset-valued term-document matrix.

Crisp multisets have been studied with applications to relational databases as well as new computing paradigms. Hence future studies of fuzzy multisets concerning such applications seem promising.

Multisets should moreover be remarked in relation to rough sets [8]. Information system models using rough sets and fuzzy multisets need further considerations.

This research has partially been supported by the Grant-in-Aid for Scientific Research (C), Japan Society for the Promotion of Science, No.13680475.

## References

1. J. C. Bezdek, *Pattern Recognition with Fuzzy Objective Function Algorithms*, Plenum, New York, 1981.
2. W. Blizard, Real-valued multisets and fuzzy sets, *Fuzzy Sets and Systems*, Vol. 33, pp. 77–97, 1989.
3. J. Celko, *Joe Celko's SQL for Smarties: Advanced SQL Programming*, Morgan Kaufmann, 1995.
4. Z. Manna, R. Waldinger, *The Logical Basis for Computer Programming, Vol. 1: Deductive Reasoning*, Addison-Wesley, Reading, Massachusetts, 1985.
5. S. Miyamoto, *Fuzzy Sets in Information Retrieval and Cluster Analysis*, Kluwer Academic Publishers, Dordrecht, 1990.
6. S. Miyamoto, Fuzzy multisets with infinite collections of memberships, *Proc. of the 7th International Fuzzy Systems Association World Congress (IFSA'97)*, June 25–30, 1997, Prague, Czech, Vol.1, pp. 61–66, 1997.
7. G. Salton, M. J. McGill, *Introduction to Modern Information Retrieval*, McGraw-Hill, 1983.
8. Z. Pawlak, *Rough Sets*, Kluwer, Dordrecht, 1991.
9. R. R. Yager, On the theory of bags, *Int. J. General Systems*, Vol. 13, pp. 23–37, 1986.
10. V. Vapnik, *Statistical Learning Theory*, Wiley, New York, 1998.
11. S.Miyamoto, K.Umayahara, Fuzzy c-means with variable for cluster sizes, *Proc. of the 16th Fuzzy System Symposium*, Sept. 6-8, 2000, Akita, pp. 537–538, 2000 (in Japanese).

# Validation of Fuzzy Partitions Obtained through Fuzzy C-Means Clustering

Dae-Won Kim[1] and Kwang H. Lee[1,2]

[1] Department of Electrical Engineering and Computer Science, KAIST
305-701, Yusung-gu, Daejon, Korea
[2] Department of BioSystems, KAIST, 305-701, Yusung-gu, Daejon, Korea
{dwkim,khlee}@if.kaist.ac.kr

**Abstract.** A new cluster validity index is proposed to determine the optimal number of clusters for fuzzy partitions obtained from the fuzzy $c$-means algorithm. The proposed validity index exploits an overlap measure and a separation measure between clusters. A good fuzzy partition is expected to have a low degree of overlap and a larger separation distance. Testing of the proposed index on well-known data sets showed its superior effectiveness and reliability in comparison to other indexes.

## 1 Introduction

The objective of a fuzzy clustering algorithm is to partition a data set $X$ into $c$ homogeneous fuzzy clusters. The most widely used fuzzy clustering algorithm is the fuzzy $c$-means (FCM) algorithm proposed by Bezdek [1]. This algorithm generates a fuzzy partition that provides a degree of membership $\mu_{F_i}(x_j)$ of each data $x_j$ to a given cluster $F_i$ ($i = 1, ..., c$) for unlabeled data set $X = \{x_1, ..., x_n\}$ and the number of clusters "$c$" [2]. However, the FCM clustering requires the user to pre-define the number of clusters; it is not always possible to know the number of clusters in advance. Different fuzzy partitions are obtained at different values of $c$. Thus, an evaluation methodology is required to validate each of the fuzzy c-partitions to obtain the optimal number of clusters, $c$.

Many validation criteria have been proposed for validating fuzzy partitions [1]-[12]. Bezdek proposed partition coefficient ($v_{PC}$) and partition entropy ($v_{PE}$) [3][4]. The optimal partition (or the optimal value of $c$) is obtained by maximizing $v_{PC}$ (or minimizing $v_{PE}$) for $c = 2, 3, ..., c_{max}$. Xie and Beni proposed a validity index that focused on compactness and separation [6]. The most desirable partition is obtained by minimizing $v_{XB}$ for $c = 2, 3, ..., c_{max}$. Fukuyama and Sugeno also tried to model the cluster validation ($v_{FS}$) by exploiting the compactness and separation [7]. Kwon ($v_k$) extended the index of Xie and Beni to eliminate its tendency to monotonically decrease by introducing a punishing function to $v_{XB}$ [8]. Rezaee combined a scattering function for $c$ clusters with a distance functional ($v_{CWB}$) [9]. Boudraa also suggested taking a variance-based dynamic estimation approach to the design of the validity index ($v_{B_{crit}}$) [10]. In this approach, the optimal number of clusters $c$ is obtained by minimizing $v_{B_{crit}}$ for $c = 2, 3, ..., c_{max}$.

N. Zhong et al. (Eds.): ISMIS 2003, LNAI 2871, pp. 422–426, 2003.

Most of validation indexes have largely depended on cluster centroids. However, the classical indexes have some drawbacks. As Pal [5] and Kwon [8] pointed out, these indexes show a monotonic decreasing tendency when "$c$" approaches to "$n$". The indexes are limited to validate partitions for large values of $c$. Furthermore, traditional validity indexes also suffer from their approach to separation. Most separation measures between clusters are obtained by computing the distance between cluster centroids. However, the separation distance based only on the cluster centroid is unable to tell the difference between two partitions that have both different shape of clusters and the same distances between centroids.

## 2   Validation Based on Overlap and Separation Measures

To manage the abovementioned problems, the proposed index considers each fuzzy cluster $F_i$ as a fuzzy set and utilizes the overall geometric structure between clusters. The proposed index consists of two properties: (1) an overlap measure representing the degree of overlap between fuzzy clusters and (2) a separation measure representing the distance between fuzzy clusters; thus, a good fuzzy partition is expected to have a low degree of overlap and a large separation distance.

### 2.1   Overlap and Separation Measures

**Overlap measure.** The degree of overlap between clusters can be quantified by computing an inter-cluster overlap. For each fuzzy cluster $F_i$, we obtain the overlap value between two fuzzy clusters at each point of membership degree ($\mu$) before computing the total inter-cluster overlap. The overlap function $f(\mu)$ at the specific $\mu$ between two fuzzy clusters $F_p$ and $F_q$ is defined as:

$$f(\mu : F_p, F_q) = \begin{cases} \sum_{j=1}^{n} \omega(x_j) & \text{if } \mu \leq \mu_{F_p}(x_j) \text{ and } \mu \leq \mu_{F_q}(x_j) \\ 0.0 & \text{otherwise} \end{cases} \quad (1)$$

$f$-function returns a overlap value of $\omega(x_j)$ when the membership degrees of the two clusters are both greater than $\mu$; otherwise, it returns 0.0. $\omega(x_j)$ assigns a weight for vague data. The weight value of $\omega(x_j) \in [0.0, 1.0]$ is determined by the degree of overlap of data point $x_j$ between clusters. Vague data are given greater weight than clearly classified data.

Having established the overlap degree at the specific $\mu$ between two clusters, we define the overlap measure for fuzzy partition. Let $F_p$ and $F_q$ be two fuzzy clusters belonging to a pattern matrix $U$. Let $f(\mu : F_p, F_q)$ be an overlap function at a given membership degree $\mu$ between $F_p$ and $F_q$. And let the number of clusters and the computation number for the overlap between the fuzzy clusters be denoted by $c$ and $_cC_2$, respectively. Then, the overlap measure $Overlap(U : X)$ is defined as

$$Overlap(U : X) = \frac{1}{_cC_2} \sum_{p=1}^{c} \sum_{q=p+1}^{c} \sum_{\mu} f(\mu : F_p, F_q) \quad (2)$$

where $\sum_\mu f(\mu : F_p, F_q)$ indicates a total inter-cluster overlap between $F_p$ and $F_q$, which is obtained by summing $f(\mu)$ over the whole range of membership degrees. $Overlap(\cdot)$ gives the average degree of overlap for all clusters in a fuzzy $c$-partition. A small value of $Overlap(\cdot)$ indicates a well-classified fuzzy $c$-partition.

**Separation measure.** The proposed separation distance is obtained by using the distance measure in the fuzzy sets. To obtain the distance between fuzzy sets, we utilize the similarity measure suggested by Lee et al. [13]. The similarity $S(F_p, F_q)$ between two fuzzy sets $F_p$ and $F_q$ is defined as

$$S(F_p, F_q) = \underbrace{max}_{x \in X} min(\mu_{F_p}(x), \mu_{F_q}(x)) \tag{3}$$

The similarity measure provides answers what degree can two clusters be co-related? and, what is the guaranteed minimum level of co-relation between two clusters? [13]. Based on this observation, we derive the following definition of the separation measure of a given fuzzy partition. Let $F_p$ and $F_q$ be two fuzzy clusters belonging to a pattern matrix $U$. Let $S(F_p, F_q)$ be the similarity between $F_p$ and $F_q$. And let the number of clusters be denoted by $c$. Then, the separation measure $Sep(U : X)$ is defined as

$$Sep(U : X) = 1 - \underbrace{min}_{p \neq q} S(F_p, F_q) \tag{4}$$

The separation measure $Sep(\cdot)$ uses the minimum dissimilarity (or distance) for all pairs of fuzzy clusters. A large value of $Sep(\cdot)$ indicates a well-separated fuzzy $c$-partition.

## 2.2    The Proposed Validity Index

With the abovementioned overlap and separation measures, we now define the proposed fuzzy cluster validity index. Let $U$ and $c$ be the partition matrix and the number of clusters, respectively. Let $Overlap(U : X)$ be the degree of overlap measure for a fuzzy partition with a particular $U$ and $c$. Let $Sep(U : X)$ be the separation measure for a fuzzy partition with a particular $U$ and $c$. Then, the proposed fuzzy cluster validity index $v_{OS}(U : X)$ is defined as

$$v_{OS}(U : X) = \frac{Overlap(U : X)}{Sep(U : X)} \tag{5}$$

$v_{OS}(U : X)$ is defined as the ratio of the overlap degree to the separation. A small value of $v_{OS}(U : X)$ indicates a partition in which the clusters are overlapped to a lesser degree and are more separated from each other. Therefore, the optimal fuzzy $c$-partition or the optimum value of $c$ is obtained by minimizing $v_{OS}(c, U)$ over $c = 2, 3, ..., c_{max}$.

# 3   Experimental Results

To demonstrate the effectiveness of the proposed index, we conducted extensive comparisons with other indexes on a number of widely used data sets. The proposed index $v_{OS}$ was compared with seven fuzzy cluster validity indexes. Five data sets were used to evaluate the performance reliability of each index. For each data set, we run the FCM for $c = 2, ..., c_{max} = \sqrt{n}$ [5][6].

**Table 1.** Validity values for the BENSAID data set for $c = 2, .., c_{max} = \sqrt{n} \approx 7$

| $c$ | $v_{PC}$ | $v_{PE}$ | $v_{XB}$ | $v_{FS}$ | $v_K$ | $v_{CWB}$ | $v_{B_{crit}}$ | $v_{OS}$ |
|---|---|---|---|---|---|---|---|---|
| $c = 2$ | 0.72 | **0.19** | 0.24 | 3671.01 | 11.89 | 0.84 | 8.00 | 214.55 |
| $c = 3$ | **0.75** | 0.20 | **0.07** | -15676.31 | **4.12** | 0.62 | **4.46** | **60.01** |
| $c = 4$ | 0.61 | 0.32 | 0.27 | -15035.68 | 15.87 | 0.58 | 8.19 | 110.68 |
| $c = 5$ | 0.66 | 0.29 | 0.12 | -27285.22 | 8.71 | 0.46 | 7.69 | 94.90 |
| $c = 6$ | 0.63 | 0.33 | 0.10 | -28692.18 | 8.14 | **0.43** | 8.15 | 87.00 |
| $c = 7$ | 0.61 | 0.36 | 0.10 | **-29292.01** | 9.20 | 0.44 | 9.09 | 92.87 |

**Table 2.** Values of $c$ preferred by each cluster validity index for five data sets

| Data set | $c_{optimal}$ | $v_{PC}$ | $v_{PE}$ | $v_{XB}$ | $v_{FS}$ | $v_K$ | $v_{CWB}$ | $v_{B_{crit}}$ | $v_{OS}$ |
|---|---|---|---|---|---|---|---|---|---|
| BENSAID | 3 | **3** | 2 | **3** | 7 | **3** | 6 | **3** | **3** |
| X30 | 3 | **3** | **3** | **3** | 4 | 2 | **3** | **3** | **3** |
| STARFIELD | 8 | 2 | 2 | 6 | 7 | 6 | **8** | 5 | **8** |
| IRIS | 2 | **2** | **2** | **2** | 3 | **2** | 3 | 3 | **2** |
| BUTTERFLY | 2 | **2** | **2** | **2** | 3 | **2** | **2** | **2** | **2** |

The first data set present here is the BENSAID data set [11]. The data set comprises 49 data points in two dimensional measurement space, and consists of three clusters. Table 1 shows the results obtained using the various validity indexes. The optimal number of clusters in the BENSAID ($c = 3$) was correctly recognized by five cluster validity indexes including the proposed index $v_{OS}$. Among the unsuccessful algorithms, $v_{PE}$ indicates the presence of two clusters, and $v_{FS}$ and $v_{CWB}$ indicate optimal values of $c = 7$ and $c = 6$, respectively.

Table 2 summarizes the results obtained when the eight different validity indexes were applied to five well-known data sets. X30 contains $n = 30$ points, which has $c = 3$ compact, well-separated clusters with 10 points per cluster [12]. STARFIELD data set contains 66 data points where eight or nine clusters are a reasonably optimal partition [6]. IRIS has $n = 150$ data points in a four-dimensional measurement space that represent three physical clusters. We take $c = 2$ as the optimal choice in view of the geometric structure of IRIS as mentioned by Pal and Bezdek [5]. The BUTTERFLY data set comprises $n = 15$ data points and contains $c = 2$ clusters [8]. The column $c_{optimal}$ gives the optimal number of clusters for each data sets, and the other columns show the optimal cluster numbers obtained using each index. The proposed index, $v_{OS}$, is the only index that correctly recognizes the number of clusters for all data sets; hence $v_{OS}$ is the most reliable of the indexes considered. $v_{XB}$ correctly identifies the optimal $c$ in all data sets except STARFIELD. On the other hand, $v_{PC}$ and $v_{PE}$ incorrectly identify the optimum as $c = 2$ for the STARFIELD data set, $v_{PE}$ additionally fails to identify $c_{optimal}$ in the BENSAID set. The index $v_K$ fails to recognize $c_{optimal}$ in the X30 and STARFIELD sets, while $v_{CWB}$ correctly identifies the optimal cluster number only in the X30, STARFIELD, and BUTTERFLY sets. The index $v_{B_{crit}}$ incorrectly recognizes the optimal cluster numbers in the STARFIELD and IRIS sets. $v_{FS}$ proved the most unreliable of the indexes considered.

## 4   Conclusions

A new cluster validity index for the fuzzy $c$-means algorithm has been proposed. The proposed index introduced two measures: the overlap and separation measures. A low degree of overlap between clusters indicates that each data point is likely to be clearly classified to each cluster and not to be vague. A larger distance represents a larger separation. The proposed index $v_{OS}$ was defined as the ratio of the overlapping degree to the separation. Thus, the optimal fuzzy $c$-partition is obtained by minimizing $v_{OS}$ with respect to $c$. Tests of the performance of the proposed index on various data sets demonstrated its effectiveness.

## References

1. Bezdek, J.C.: Pattern Recognition with Fuzzy Objective Function Algorithms. Plenum, New York (1981).
2. Bezdek, J.C. et al: Fuzzy Models and Algorithms for Pattern Recognition and Image Processing, Boston: Kluwer Academy Publishers (1999).
3. Bezdek, J.C.: Numerical taxonomy with fuzzy sets. J. Math. Biology 1 (1974) 57–71.
4. Bezdek, J.C.: Cluster validity with fuzzy stes. J. Cybernit. 3 (1974) 58–72.
5. Pal, N.R., Bezdek, J.C: On cluster validity for the fuzzy c-means model. IEEE Trans. on Fuzzy Systems 3 (1995) 370–379.
6. Xie, X.L., Beni, G.: A validity measure for fuzzy clustering. IEEE Trans. on Pattern Analysis and Machine Intelligence 13 (1991) 841–847.
7. Fukuyama, Y., Sugeno, M.: A new method of choosing the number of clusters for the fuzzy c-means method. Proceedings of 5th Fuzzy Systems Symposium (1989) 247–250.
8. Kwon, S.H.: Cluster validity index for fuzzy clustering. Electronics Letters 34 (1998) 2176–2177.
9. Rezaee, M.R., Lelieveldt, B.P.F., Reiber, J.H.C.: A new cluster validity index for the fuzzy c-mean. Pattern Recognition Letters 19 (1998) 237–246.
10. Boudraa, A.O.: Dynamic estimation of number of clusters in data sets. Electronics Letters 35 (1999) 1606–1607.
11. Bensaid, A.M. et al: Validity-guided (re)clustering with applications to image segmentation. IEEE Trans. on Fuzzy Systems 4 (1996) 112–123.
12. Bezdek, J.C., Pal, N.R.: Some new indexes of cluster validity. IEEE Trans. on Systems, Man, and Cybernetics-Part B: Cybernetics 28 (1998) 301–315.
13. H. Lee-Kwang, Y.S. Song, K.M. Lee: Similarity measure between fuzzy sets and between elements. Fuzzy Sets and Systems 62 (1994) 291–293.

# Generating Fuzzy Thesaurus by Degree of Similarity in Fuzzy Covering

Rolly Intan[1,2] and Masao Mukaidono[1]

[1] Meiji University, Kawasaki-shi, Kanagawa-ken, Japan
{rolly,masao}@cs.meiji.ac.jp
[2] Petra Christian University, Surabaya, Indonesia 60236

**Abstract.** A notion of *fuzzy covering* over a set of terms was proposed as a generalization of a well known fuzzy partition. Degree of similarity relationship between fuzzy classes (subsets) on the set of terms (subjects) as results of the fuzzy covering is approximately calculated using a *fuzzy conditional probability relation* by which degree of similarity relationship between two terms can be determined. An associated function was defined to calculate degree of association between two terms. Special attention will be given to generate a concept of fuzzy thesaurus using the associated function. Its some properties are discussed and examined. A simple example is given to demonstrate the concept.

## 1 Introduction

In [3], a notion of fuzzy covering was introduced as a generalization of a well known fuzzy partition (see [1,5]). In the fuzzy covering, an element of data may totally (with the degree of 1) belong to more than one fuzzy class. Formally, let $D = \{d_1, ..., d_n\}$ be a given domain of data. A fuzzy covering on $D$ is a family of fuzzy subsets or fuzzy classes in P, denoted by $P = \{p_1, p_2, ..., p_c\}$, which satisfies

$$\sum_{i=1}^{c} \mu_{p_i}(d_k) \geq 1, \ \forall \, k \in \mathbb{N}_n, \quad \text{and} \quad 0 < \sum_{k=1}^{n} \mu_{p_i}(d_k) < n, \ \forall \, i \in \mathbb{N}_c, \qquad (1)$$

where $c$ is a positive integer and $\mu_{p_i}(d_k) \in [0, 1]$. Degree of similarity between two fuzzy classes is approximately calculated by *a fuzzy conditional probability relation*. Characteristics of this relation are neither necessarily symmetric nor necessarily transitive as discussed in [2]. Let $\mu_{p_i}$ and $\mu_{p_j}$ be two membership functions over a given domain $D$ for two fuzzy classes $p_i$ and $p_j$, respectively. A fuzzy conditional probability relation is a mapping, $R : P \times P \to [0, 1]$ by:

$$R(p_i, p_j) = \mathrm{P}(p_i \mid p_j) = \frac{|p_i \cap p_j|}{|p_j|} = \frac{\sum_{d \in D} \min\{\mu_{p_i}(d), \mu_{p_j}(d)\}}{\sum_{d \in D} \mu_{p_j}(d)}, \qquad (2)$$

where $R(p_i, p_j)$ means the degree $p_j$ supports $p_i$ or the degree $p_j$ is similar to $p_i$ and $|p_j| = \sum_{d \in D} \mu_{p_j}(d)$ is regarded as cardinality of $p_j$.

N. Zhong et al. (Eds.): ISMIS 2003, LNAI 2871, pp. 427–432, 2003.

On the other hand, every element of data in $D$ can also be represented as a fuzzy subset in terms of the fuzzy classes in $P$ by

$$\mu_{d_i}(p_j) = \frac{\mu_{p_j}(d_i)}{\sum_{d \in D} \mu_{p_j}(d)}. \tag{3}$$

Again, a degree of similarity between two elements of data, $d_i, d_j \in D$ can be determined using a fuzzy conditional probability relation as follows.

$$R(d_i, d_j) = \frac{\sum_{p \in P} \min\{\mu_{d_i}(p), \mu_{d_j}(p)\}}{\sum_{p \in P} \mu_{d_j}(p)}. \tag{4}$$

Moreover, as discussed in [4], in the presence of crisp granularity, for $\alpha \in [0, 1]$, two asymmetric similarity classes of $d_i \in D$ can be defined by:

$$\mathcal{S}_\alpha(d_i) = \{d \in D | R(d_i, d) \geq \alpha\}, \quad (5) \qquad \mathcal{P}_\alpha(d_i) = \{d \in D | R(d, d_i) \geq \alpha\}. \quad (6)$$

Clearly, by omitting $\alpha$-cut, in the presence of fuzzy granularity, two asymmetric similarity classes of $d_i$ are represented as two fuzzy classes and given by $\mu_{\mathcal{S}(d_i)}(d) = R(d_i, d)$ and $\mu_{\mathcal{P}(d_i)}(d) = R(d, d_i), \forall d \in D$.

In the next section, we will discuss and define an associated function in order to calculate degree of association between two elements of data in $D$ by using their similarity classes. Then, a concept of fuzzy thesaurus can be generated by using the degree of association as introduced in [4]. Our primary concern in this paper is to discuss and examine more extended properties of the fuzzy thesaurus. Finally, a simple example is given to demonstrate the concept.

## 2   Fuzzy Thesaurus

Thesaurus serves to associated entry terms (subjects) with related terms in order to provide associative information in *information retrieval* [6]. Generally, related terms are divided into three categories: Broader Terms (BT), Narrower Terms (NT) and Related Terms (RT). Terms categorized under BT have broader meanings than the entry term. Contrary to BT, terms categorized under NT have narrower meanings than the entry term. Terms categorized under RT have similar meanings that are related to the entry term. Some methods have been developed and studied for generating thesaurus such as done by Salton (1971) [7].

Related to the fuzzy covering (see (1)), in [4], we have introduced an alternative concept in generating a fuzzy thesaurus based on a crisp and fuzzy granularity as proposed in (5). The concept showed that naturally a term has an association to the other terms when they are together included, for example, in the same documents as keywords or subjects. They will have stronger relationship if they are included in more the same documents. In this section, the method was recalled and discussed to provide more extended properties.

Still related to the previous section, let $P = \{p_1, ..., p_n\}$ denote a finite and non-empty set of documents (i.e., papers, articles, etc) and $D = \{d_1, ..., d_m\}$ be a set of terms (i.e., subjects or keywords). $p_i \in P$ regarded as a fuzzy class on $D$ is defined as a mapping from $D$ to the closed interval $[0,1]$ characterized by a membership function $\mu_{p_i} : D \to [0,1]$, where $P$ may represent a fuzzy covering over $D$ as discussed in the previous section. On the other hand, by (3), $d_j \in D$ could be defined as a fuzzy class on $P$ characterized by a membership function $\mu_{d_j} : P \to [0,1]$, where $D$, on the contrary, represents a fuzzy covering over $P$. Degree of similarity between two terms can be calculated by using the fuzzy conditional probability relation in (4). We then defined two kinds of asymmetric similarity classes of a given term $d_i$ in the presence of crisp granularity as given in (5) and (6). $\mathcal{S}_\alpha(d_i)$ can be interpreted as a set of terms that is similar to $d_i$. On the other hand, $\mathcal{P}_\alpha(d_i)$ can be considered as a set of terms to which $d_i$ is similar. Then, an associated function, denoted by $\delta(d_i, d_j)$, is defined to calculate degree of association between two terms, $d_i$ and $d_j$ in the presence of crisp and fuzzy granularities, as follows:

$$\delta(d_i, d_j) = \frac{|\mathcal{S}_\alpha(d_i) \cap \mathcal{S}_\alpha(d_j)|}{|\mathcal{S}_\alpha(d_j)|} = \frac{\sum_d \min(\mu_{S(d_i)}(d), \mu_{S(d_j)}(d))}{\sum_d \mu_{S(d_j)}(d)}, \qquad (7)$$

where $|.|$ denotes the cardinality of set. Intuitively, $\mathcal{S}_\alpha(d_i)$ or $\mathcal{S}(d_i)$ is used in (7) rather than $\mathcal{P}_\alpha(d_i)$ or $\mathcal{P}(d_i)$, for $d_i$ is regarded as a core of the set given other terms. Degree of association is used to define a fuzzy thesaurus; $\forall d \in D$,

$$\mu_{BT(d_i)}(d) = \begin{cases} \delta(d, d_i), & \delta(d, d_i) \geq \delta(d_i, d) \\ 0, & \text{otherwise}, \end{cases} \qquad (8)$$

$$\mu_{NT(d_i)}(d) = \begin{cases} \delta(d_i, d), & \delta(d, d_i) \leq \delta(d_i, d) \\ 0, & \text{otherwise}, \end{cases} \qquad (9)$$

$$\mu_{RT(d_i)}(d) = \frac{|\mathcal{S}_\alpha(d_i) \cap \mathcal{S}_\alpha(d)|}{|\mathcal{S}_\alpha(d_i) \cup \mathcal{S}_\alpha(d)|} = \frac{\sum_d \min(\mu_{S(d_i)}(d), \mu_{S(d_j)}(d))}{\sum_d \max(\mu_{S(d_i)}(d), \mu_{S(d_j)}(d))}, \qquad (10)$$

where $BT(d_i)$, $NT(d_i)$ and $RT(d_i)$ are broader, narrower and related terms of $d_i$. By definitions we can obtain some properties such as: If $\mu_{BT(d_i)}(d_j) = \mu_{NT(d_i)}(d_j)$ and $\mu_{BT(d_i)}(d_j) > 0$ then $d_i$ and $d_j$ have the same range of meaning. If $d_i$ and $d_j$ are not semantically related, then $\delta(d_i, d_j) = \delta(d_j, d_i) = 0$. Hence, there are no relation between $d_i$ and $d_j$ in $BT$, $NT$ and $RT$. $RT$ satisfies symmetric property such as: $\mu_{RT(d_i)}(d_j) = \mu_{RT(d_j)}(d_i)$, $\forall d_i, d_j \in D$. If $\mu_{RT(d_i)}(d_j) = 1$, then $d_i$ and $d_j$ are regarded as synonymous. Similarly, if $\mu_{BT(d_i)}(d_j) = \mu_{NT(d_i)}(d_j) = 1$ then $\mu_{RT(d_j)}(d_i) = 1$. If $\mu_{RT(d_i)}(d_j) > \mu_{RT(d_i)}(d_k)$, then $d_i$ is more similar to $d_j$ than to $d_k$. If $\mu_{BT(d_i)}(d_j) = 1$, then the concept of $d_i$ is completely included in the concept of $d_j$. On the other hand, if $\mu_{NT(d_i)}(d_j) = 1$, then the concept of $d_j$ is completely included in the concept of $d_i$. If $\mu_{BT(d_i)}(d_j) > \mu_{BT(d_i)}(d_k)$, then degree of inclusion of the concept of $d_i$ in the concept of $d_j$ is greater than degree of inclusion of the concept of $d_i$ in the concept of $d_k$.

## 3   An Illustrative Example

Let $P = \{p_1, p_2, \ldots, p_6\}$ be a set of documents (papers or articles) and $D = \{d_1, d_2, \ldots, d_8\}$ be a set of terms (keywords or subjects). Also, $P$ is regarded as a set of fuzzy classes performing a fuzzy covering on $D$ as restricted by (1), such as arbitrarily given by:

$$p_1 = \{0.3/d_2, 0.7/d_5, 1/d_7, 1/d_8\}, \qquad p_4 = \{1/d_1, 0.5/d_3, 0.8/d_4, 0.8/d_6\},$$
$$p_2 = \{1/d_2, 0.8/d_5, 0.8/d_7, 1/d_8\}, \qquad p_5 = \{0.1/d_2, 0.7/d_5, 1/d_4, 1/d_8\},$$
$$p_3 = \{0.9/d_1, 0.9/d_3, 1/d_4, 0.8/d_6\}, \qquad p_6 = \{0.9/d_2, 1/d_5, 0.8/d_4, 1/d_8\},$$

where i.e., $\mu_{p_1}(d_2) = 0.3$. Degrees of similarity relationship between fuzzy classes in $P$ are calculated using fuzzy conditional probability relation in (2) as represented by Table 1.

**Table 1.** Degree of Similarity, $R(x, y)$, for $x, y \in P$

| $x \backslash y$ | $p_1$ | $p_2$ | $p_3$ | $p_4$ | $p_5$ | $p_6$ |
|---|---|---|---|---|---|---|
| $p_1$ | 1.00 | 0.78 | 0 | 0 | 0.64 | 0.54 |
| $p_2$ | 0.93 | 1.00 | 0 | 0 | 0.64 | 0.73 |
| $p_3$ | 0 | 0 | 1.00 | 0.97 | 0.36 | 0.22 |
| $p_4$ | 0 | 0 | 0.83 | 1.00 | 0.29 | 0.22 |
| $p_5$ | 0.60 | 0.50 | 0.28 | 0.26 | 1.00 | 0.70 |
| $p_6$ | 0.67 | 0.75 | 0.22 | 0.26 | 0.93 | 1.00 |

Table 1 shows an asymmetric property, for $R(p_1, p_2) = 0.78$, but $R(p_2, p_1) = 0.93$. Also, $R(p_1, p_2) < R(p_2, p_1)$ means that $p_2$ takes a wider meaning in $D$ than $p_1$. On the other hand, by using (3), every term in $D$ can be represented as a fuzzy class on $P$ as follows.

$$d_1 = \{0.25/p_3, 0.32/p_4\}, \qquad d_5 = \{0.23/p_1, 0.22/p_2, 0.25/p_5, 0.27/p_6\},$$
$$d_2 = \{0.1/p_1, 0.28/p_2, 0.06/p_5, 0.24/p_6\}, \quad d_6 = \{0.22/p_3, 0.26/p_4\},$$
$$d_3 = \{0.25/p_3, 0.16/p_4\}, \qquad d_7 = \{0.33/p_1, 0.22/p_2\},$$
$$d_4 = \{0.28/p_3, 0.26/p_4, 0.36/p_5, 0.27/p_6\}, \quad d_8 = \{0.33/p_1, 0.28/p_2, 0.36/p_5, 0.27/p_6\}.$$

It can be proved that the above results also satisfy (1) performing a fuzzy covering on $P$. Similarly, degrees of similarity relationship between terms in $D$ can be calculated by (4) as given in Table 2.

**Table 2.** Degree of Similarity, $R(x, y)$, for $x, y \in D$

| $x \backslash y$ | $d_1$ | $d_2$ | $d_3$ | $d_4$ | $d_5$ | $d_6$ | $d_7$ | $d_8$ |
|---|---|---|---|---|---|---|---|---|
| $d_1$ | 1.00 | 0 | 1.00 | 0.44 | 0 | 1.00 | 0 | 0 |
| $d_2$ | 0 | 1.00 | 0 | 0.26 | 0.64 | 0 | 0.58 | 0.53 |
| $d_3$ | 0.72 | 0 | 1.00 | 0.35 | 0 | 0.79 | 0 | 0 |
| $d_4$ | 0.89 | 0.44 | 1.00 | 1.00 | 0.54 | 1.00 | 0 | 0.51 |
| $d_5$ | 0 | 0.91 | 0 | 0.44 | 1.00 | 0 | 0.82 | 0.86 |
| $d_6$ | 0.84 | 0 | 0.93 | 0.41 | 0 | 1.00 | 0 | 0 |
| $d_7$ | 0 | 0.47 | 0 | 0 | 0.46 | 0 | 1.00 | 0.49 |
| $d_8$ | 0 | 1.00 | 0 | 0.54 | 1.00 | 0 | 1.00 | 1.00 |

From Table 2, we can construct two asymmetric similarity classes for every term in the presence of crisp granularity with $\alpha = 0.5$, by using (5) and (6):

$$
\begin{aligned}
S_{0.5}(d_1) &= \{d_1, d_3, d_6\}, & \mathcal{P}_{0.5}(d_1) &= \{d_1, d_3, d_4, d_6\}, \\
S_{0.5}(d_2) &= \{d_2, d_5, d_7, d_8\}, & \mathcal{P}_{0.5}(d_2) &= \{d_2, d_5, d_8\}, \\
S_{0.5}(d_3) &= \{d_1, d_3, d_6\}, & \mathcal{P}_{0.5}(d_3) &= \{d_1, d_3, d_4, d_6\}, \\
S_{0.5}(d_4) &= \{d_1, d_3, d_4, d_5, d_6, d_8\}, & \mathcal{P}_{0.5}(d_4) &= \{d_4, d_8\}, \\
S_{0.5}(d_5) &= \{d_2, d_5, d_7, d_8\}, & \mathcal{P}_{0.5}(d_5) &= \{d_2, d_4, d_5, d_8\}, \\
S_{0.5}(d_6) &= \{d_1, d_3, d_6\}, & \mathcal{P}_{0.5}(d_6) &= \{d_1, d_3, d_4, d_6\}, \\
S_{0.5}(d_7) &= \{d_7\}, & \mathcal{P}_{0.5}(d_7) &= \{d_2, d_5, d_7, d_8\}, \\
S_{0.5}(d_8) &= \{d_2, d_4, d_5, d_7, d_8\}, & \mathcal{P}_{0.5}(d_8) &= \{d_2, d_4, d_5, d_8\}.
\end{aligned}
$$

The associated function in (7) is used to calculate degree of association between two terms as shown in Table 3.

**Table 3.** Degree of Association, $\delta(x, y)$, for $x, y \in D$

| $x \backslash y$ | $d_1$ | $d_2$ | $d_3$ | $d_4$ | $d_5$ | $d_6$ | $d_7$ | $d_8$ |
|---|---|---|---|---|---|---|---|---|
| $d_1$ | 1.00 | 0 | 1.00 | 0.50 | 0 | 1.00 | 0 | 0 |
| $d_2$ | 0 | 1.00 | 0 | 0.33 | 1.00 | 0 | 1.00 | 0.80 |
| $d_3$ | 1.00 | 0 | 1.00 | 0.50 | 0 | 1.00 | 0 | 0 |
| $d_4$ | 1.00 | 0.50 | 1.00 | 1.00 | 0.50 | 1.00 | 0 | 0.60 |
| $d_5$ | 0 | 1.00 | 0 | 0.33 | 1.00 | 0 | 1.00 | 0.80 |
| $d_6$ | 1.00 | 0 | 1.00 | 0.50 | 0 | 1.00 | 0 | 0 |
| $d_7$ | 0 | 0.25 | 0 | 0 | 0.25 | 0 | 1.00 | 0.20 |
| $d_8$ | 0 | 1.00 | 0 | 0.50 | 1.00 | 0 | 1.00 | 1.00 |

Finally, from Table 3, BT and NT can be generated by using (8) and (9):

$$
\begin{aligned}
BT(d_1) &= \{1/d_1, 1/d_3, 1/d_4, 1/d_6\}, & NT(d_1) &= \{1/d_1, 1/d_3, 1/d_6\}, \\
BT(d_2) &= \{1/d_2, 0.5/d_4, 1/d_5, 1/d_8\}, & NT(d_2) &= \{1/d_2, 1/d_5, 1/d_7\}, \\
BT(d_3) &= \{1/d_1, 1/d_3, 1/d_4, 1/d_6\}, & NT(d_3) &= \{1/d_1, 1/d_3, 1/d_6\},
\end{aligned}
$$

$$\vdots \qquad\qquad , \qquad\qquad \vdots \qquad\qquad ,$$

We leave further calculation of BT, NT and RT for other $d \in D$ to the reader.

# 4    Conclusion

Fuzzy covering was introduced in [3] as a generalization of fuzzy partition which is mostly used in quantization and clustering. Every element, object, or whatever will have a relation (similarity) to the others because of their association in the same groups (classes). In this case, their degree of similarities can be approximately calculated corresponding to their association in the same groups (classes) by using a fuzzy conditional probability relation. Finally, we applied the concept of similarity classes in fuzzy covering for generating a concept of fuzzy thesaurus.

# References

1. Bezdek, J. C., *Pattern Recognition with Fuzzy Objective Function Algorithms*, (Plenum Press, New York, 1981).
2. Intan, R., Mukaidono, M., 'Conditional Probability Relations in Fuzzy Relational Database ', *Proc. of RSCTC'00*, LNAI 2005, Springer-Verlag, (2000), pp. 251–260.
3. Intan, R., Mukaidono, M., 'Degree of Similarity in Fuzzy Partition', *Proceedings of AFSS'02*, LNAI 2275, Springer-Verlag, (2002), pp. 20–26.
4. Intan, R., Mukaidono, M., 'A Proposal of Fuzzy Thesaurus Generated by Fuzzy Covering', *Proceedings of NAFIPS 2003*, IEEE Press., (2003), in press.
5. Klir, G.J., Yuan, B., *Fuzzy Sets and Fuzzy Logic: Theory and Applications*, (Prentice Hall, New Jersey, 1995).
6. Sadaaki Miyamoto, *Fuzzy Sets in Information Retrieval and Cluster Analysis*, (Kluwer Academic Publishers 1990).
7. Salton G. ed., *The SMART Retrieval System: Experiments in Automatic Document Processing*, (Prentice Hall, Englewood Cliffs, New Jersey 1971).

# Design of Iconic Language Interface for Semantic Based Korean Language Generation

Kyonam Choo, Hyunjae Park, Hongki Min, Yoseop Woo, and Seokhoon Kang

Dept. of Information and Telecommunication Engineering, University of Incheon
402-749, 177 Dowha-Dong, Nam-Gu, Incheon, Korea
{g971163, now92, hkmin, yswooo}@incheon.ac.kr
Division of Internet Engineering, Dongseo University
617-716, San 69-1, Churye-Dong, Sasang-Gu, Pusan, Korea
hana@tecace.com

**Abstract.** The iconic language interface is designed to provide more convenient communication environments to the system compared with the existing keyboard input system. The iconic language interface consisting of pictures, which indicate meanings that are easily recognizable to users, is the supplemental language interface for creating the Korean language and the commands to control system through configuration of various situation information such as word, grammar, and meaning from the various iconic stream the user select. Based on this, the algorithm to generate the Korean language from the iconic interface is suggested.

## 1 Introduction

Various technological environments have been established, which allow people to acquire information of knowledge base on the Internet by using common languages without any special training. By this reason, studies on natural language processing for communications between people using different languages or between computer and human draw special attentions. However, these valuable and effective Internet services have considerable limitation to be world-widely used due to the difficulties of natural language processing caused by native linguistic characteristics of each country. Because most system environments depend on the simple input of letters through a keyboard, it is difficult to have precise and composite communications with the system. And, it gives problems of information alienation to the disabled people who can hardly operate keyboards. Therefore, the development of general-purpose interface is required.

In this paper, the concept based iconic language interface is suggested which can provide convenient system control to users as well as reflect the characteristics of natural language. The iconic interface environment is a method to transmit a situation

N. Zhong et al. (Eds.): ISMIS 2003, LNAI 2871, pp. 433–439, 2003.
© Springer-Verlag Berlin Heidelberg 2003

to the system that needs to be delivered by selecting numbers of icons consisting of pictures that can be easily identified by users. The system provides the environment to recognize and analyze the selected iconic stream into the property of natural language after reconfiguration.

The existing studies use similar interfaces [1,2] for the linguistically disabled in the supplemental communication system. However, they have a lot of limitations to process features of natural language, for example matching one picture to simple word or sentence and so on. Since the iconic language interface used in this study is designed applying the concept of natural language system to the icon, it could be used either as the system interface of an independent semantic based language system or as the intermediate language of multi-lingual translation system. In this study, the linguistic word system of icons is defined, and the system, which can generate the Korean language in certain domain, is designed.

## 2  Definition and Characteristics of Iconic Language Interface

The iconic language interface consists of meaningful pictures that can be identified by users, and it is the supplemental language interface to create the Korean language and commands to control the system through configuring various situational information such as word, grammar and meaning from the various iconic streams a user select.

The iconic language system that generates meaning for users through symbol or picture has the following characteristics:
1. The iconic language is applicable to various system environments as an interface, and it is the general-purpose language for ordinary people and for the disabled who have the restriction in expressing their opinions as well.
2. Because icons contain situation-focused meanings, the user can deliver meaning by composing appropriate situations through connection of each icon without the precise linguistic expression.
3. Each icon externally provides consistent interface to users, and internally allows convenient addition of linguistic features like meaning and parts of speeches for the various expressions of natural languages.
4. It could play the role of a meta-language in expressing common elements of meaning to languages. Because icons express each situation in the instinctive picture, it is possible to express common meaning structures in each language and could play the role of an intermediate language in machine translation among different languages.

## 3  Definition of Grammatical Structure of the Iconic Language

In order to configure a situation to transmit through making a combination of icons by users, linguistic characteristics that each icon expresses must be defined such as parts of speech, syntactic relation, meanings and so forth.

## 3.1  Parts-of-Speech Set of the Iconic Language

The iconic language is a kind of artificial language made for the use in the domains whose objectives are clear. In the iconic language, the parts-of-speech set is defined and designed in consideration of the following items:

1. The iconic language consists of head words indicating meaning like a substantive and an inflected word, modifier like a pre-noun and adverb, and sentence information, not like Korean which is the agglutinative and additive language that needs dependent forms such as suffix and affix or a particle.
2. Each icon could have more than one part of speech according to properties of displayed pictures.
3. Upon generation of the Korean language, each part of speech of iconic language is designed to correspond to those of the Korean language.

**Table 1.** Relation between Parts of Speech of the Iconic Language and Korean One

| Part of speech of iconic language | Korean part of speech | Descriptions |
|---|---|---|
| Noun (N) | NG | Noun group except the numerals |
|  | NA | Noun transformed into adverb |
| Numerals (NU) | NU | Numerals |
| Predicate (V) | VG | Common Predicate (verb, adjective) |
|  | DV | Transformed into the pre-noun |
|  | AV | Transformed into the adverb |
| Pre-noun (DT) | DT | Pure pre-noun |
| Adverb (AD) | AD | Pure adverb |
| Negative (F) | NF | Antonym of noun |
|  | VF | Antonym of vocabulary |

And upon generating the Korean language from the configuration of iconic languages, ending sentence, tense and pattern must be also considered for more precise communication.

# 4  Constructing the Part of Speech Corpus of Iconic and Korean Languages

To assign appropriate scope of utilization to the iconic language and meanings to each icon and to express those in instinctive pictures for user's easy understanding, the domain to apply should be selected and sentence samples should be collected. The scope of application in this paper is defined as the situations for traffic and shopping for the disabled who have clear objectives, and possible conversation samples in each situation are established as the raw ignition corpus of frequently occurred sentences in common considering worker's insight and the frequency of vocabulary and expression.

The raw ignition corpus, collected differently from the establishment of morphological analysis corpus of Korean language, considered as the sentences to exemplify situations, is established as the corpus of iconic parts of speech that workers assign parts of speech and head words such as appropriate substantive and vocabulary. In the process of assigning parts of speech of iconic language, the analysis method for sentences of sign language that is similar to the linguistic system of this study is applied to the raw ignition corpus and referred for part of speech information to the vocabulary information that could be occurred by the icons. Upon assigning the iconic part of speech and extracting the meaning, it is conducted based on the items:

1. Various vocabulary forms and corresponding parts of speech are assigned by extracting the representative core vocabulary, which can play the role of effective reduced vocabulary that commonly occurs in the raw ignition sentence, and by considering ambiguity of parts of speech and meaning occurred in the process of expressing as icons.
2. When comprising vocabulary of ignition sentence is dividable into representative single words, the part of speech is assigned to the divided each word.
     Ex. 관광객(traveler) = i관광(travel)/N + i사람(man)/N (* i : icon)
        고속버스(express-bus) = i빠른(fast)/V + i버스(bus)/N
3. For the words consisting of numerals and unit noun, since the vocabulary that can be expressed as icons is limited, they are expressed only in single numerals.
     Ex. 한 장(a sheet), 한 개(an unit) = i하나(one)/NU
4. When tagging, it is allowed for the given situation example to display sentence information.
5. For the cases that affixes are added to noun and the words are changed to predicative form, parts of speech are given by the declinable words.
6. When sub-vocabulary is connected to the vocabulary in the ignition sentence, the generation of Korean language assigns the part of speech of vocabulary with the core vocabulary for using as the reference data.
     Ex. 놀러 가다(go to play) = i놀다(play)/V + i가다(go)/V
7. The declarative and time-now sentences, which are commonly occurred upon tagging sentence information, are set to the basic tag, and the interrogative such as "Where" is allowed to omit it's question tag upon assigning the tag.
8. In order to express emphasis by the vocabulary that can be transformed to noun or adverb, the same iconic vocabulary is allowed to repeat twice in sequence.
     Ex. 최고급(high-end) = i좋다(good)/V + i좋다(good)/V

Table 2 shows examples of part-of-speech iconic corpus.

**Table 2.** Example of Iconic Corpus where Part of Speech is tagged

| Raw Sentence | Part of speech conferred iconic row |
|---|---|
| 첫 기차는 몇시에 있습니까?<br>**What time does the first**<br>**train leave?** | i시작(start)/N i기차(train)/N i시간(time)/N i언제(when)/N /SQ |
|  | i처음(first)/N i기차(train)/N i시간(time)/N /SQ |

# 5 Semantic Dictionary for Korean Language Generation

In this study, in order to generate the semantic-based Korean language, semantic relation for each iconic vocabulary is examined and the relation of semantic independence of headwords is analyzed and processed. Accordingly, the hierarchic thesaurus[3] consisting of iconic vocabulary and the sub-categorization dictionary[4] focused on the iconic vocabulary of declinable words are established.

**Table 3.** Example of the Sub-categorization Dictionary

| Head<br>Predicate | Information of essential complement element |
|---|---|
| 가다<br>(Go) | [Pattern] 1 가(is)[AGT] + 2 를(to)[RNG]<br>[Concept] 1. 인간(Human)  2. 장소(Place) |
|  | [Pattern] 1 가(is)[AGT] + 2 에서(from)[SRC]<br>+ 3 로(to)[PTH] + 4 에게(to)[GOL]<br>[Concept] 1. 인간(Human), 인간이외의동물(Animal besides human),<br>탈것(things to ride)<br>4. Place, human, direction, building |

Each user might use different way of communication by using icons. As stated on the previous example, if the noun [Express Bus] is not expressed in icons, it could be expressed by pressing [Fast] and [Bus]. It is possible due to that the iconic interface allows the reflected content to be expressed as combination of icons in the domain whose objectives are clear. Various relational information among the icons needs to be collected as a dictionary form and managed in order to be used in generating the Korean language.

# 6 Korean Language Generation of the Iconic Language Interface

An algorithm to generate the Korean language from the iconic interface is designed using the iconic Korean vocabularies extracted from the parts-of-speech corpus based on the iconic linguistic system previously discussed and numbers of dictionaries.

To the parts of speech of the icons and vocabulary that users enter, the semantic relation is analyzed and the Korean language is generated as the following order:

1. Apply the selectional restriction[5] to the inputted iconic stream based on the semantic dictionary (thesaurus of icons and sub-categorization dictionary).
2. For the icons that are not dependent to the selectional restriction, analyze the bigram with neighboring icons.

The sub-categorization dictionary of iconic predicate contains the functional morphology such as case particle of Korean language, so that the basic Korean sentence can be generated according to the grammatical role of each vocabulary. And, the ending sentence selected by the user is designed to express tenses and patterns using the vocabulary dictionary of predicate.

And also, numbers of agglutinative languages such as time and place are considered to make the natural expression by connecting the basic functional morphology. Figure 1 and Figure 2 show the process of generating the Korean language from the iconic interface.

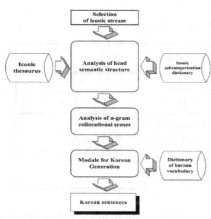

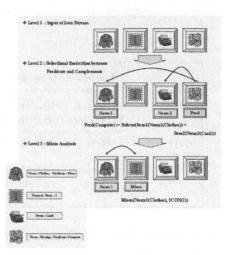

**Fig. 1.** Process of Generating the Korean Language of Iconic Language Interface

**Fig. 2.** Example of Selectional Restriction and Dependency Relation of Icon Stream

## 7   Conclusion

For the Internet users' smooth communication, we design the iconic language interface consisting of pictures that are convenient to use and more instinctive than natural language interface which receives and controls the letters from keyboards. As the iconic language interface consists of pictures that express the application meaning, it has the excellence to be used for language disorders and general-purpose system interface as well.

For the iconic language interface, the grammatical system of iconic language is defined in this paper. Also, conversation examples of domain to be applied are collected, and the iconic corpus are established after applying the grammar of iconic language to the collected examples. In addition, for generating the Korean language based on semantic, various dictionaries are established such as the sub-categorization dictionary, the dictionary of generating vocabulary, and the iconic thesaurus, and based on those, the Korean generation system on semantic is designed.

A problem to be solved in the future is to define pictures for vocabulary of each icon that can be easily identified by users. Even though the vocabulary information is established through the analysis of conversation samples to be applied, a lot of discussions between the worker and the users are needed to express each vocabulary in the appropriate picture to be instinctively recognized. It is obvious that icons express certain meaning; On the other hand, it may also express plenty of ambiguities as well. Therefore, more conversation corpus to be applied needs to be analyzed and established in order to build the secure grammatical system of iconic language.

**Acknowledgements.** This study was supported by research fund from University of Incheon and Multimedia Research Center of the Korea Science and Engineering Foundation(KOSEF)

# References

1. Kathleen F. McCoy and Patrick Demasco, "Some Applications of Natural Language Processing to the Field of Augmentative and Alternative Communication" In Proceedings of the IJCAI-95 Workshop on Developing AI Applications for People with Disabilities, Montreal, Canada, August, 1995.
2. Injeong Hwang, "Design of supplemental communication devices by the semantic symbol", paper of master's degree in Incheon University, 1998. 12
3. Younghun Seo, "Development of Korean analyzer based on the token-establishment of Korean semantic analysis dictionary and sub-categorization dictionary", Report of Korea Electronic Telecommunication Research Institute, 1998
4. Seunghyun Yang and Yoseop Woo, "Constructing a Korean Subcategorization Dictionary with Semantic Roles using Thesaurus and Predicate Patterns", Paper of Information and Science Association, 2000. 6
5. Kyonam Choo, "Korean Lexical Sense Analysis for the Concept-Based Information Retrieval", Paper of master's degree in Incheon University, 1998. 12

# Incremental Feature Extraction Based on Empirical Kernel Map

Byung Joo Kim[1], Joo Yong Shim[2], Chang Ha Hwang[2], Il Kon Kim[3], and
Joon Hyun Song[3]

[1] Youngsan University. School of Computer and Information Engineering, Korea,
bjkim@ysu.ac.kr,
[2] Catholic University of Daegu Dept. of Statistical Information, South Korea,
{jyshim,chhwang}@cu.ac.kr,
[3] Kyungpook National University Dept. of Computer Science, South Korea,
ikkim@knu.ac.kr,jhsong00@hitel.net

**Abstract.** A new incremental kernel principal component analysis is
proposed for the nonlinear feature extraction from the data. The problem
of batch kernel principal component analysis is that the computation
becomes prohibitive when the data set is large . Another problem is
that, in order to update the eigenvectors with another data, the whole
decomposition from scratch should be recomputed. The proposed method
overcomes these problems by incrementally update eigenspace and using
empirical kernel map as kernel function. The proposed method is more
efficient in memory requirement than a batch kernel principal component
and can be easily improved by re-learning the data. In our experiments
we show that proposed method is comparable in performance to a batch
kernel principal component for the classification problem on nonlinear
data set.

## 1 Introduction

Principal Component Analysis(PCA) is a powerful technique for extracting
structure from possibly high-dimensional data sets. It is easily performed by
solving eigenvalue problem. In this paper, we are not focus on principal components in input space, but rather in principal components of variables, or features,
which are nonlinearly related to the input variables. An approach for nonlinear
feature extraction has been taken by Tipping and Bishop[1]. Various global nonlinear approaches have also been developed such as auto-associative multi-layer
perceptrons minimizing the reconstruction error and principal curves[2,3]. The
disadvantage of earlier research is that they require nonlinear optimization techniques. Recently, the kernel trick has also been applied to PCA in terms of the
dot product matrix instead of the covariance matrix[4]. This makes it possible to
extract non-linear features using kernel functions by solving an eigenvalue problem like PCA. Though kernel PCA(KPCA) is capable of extracting nonlinear
features, KPCA has several disadvantages. Firstly standard methods for solving
eigenvalue problems need to store the entire kernel matrix which can become

N. Zhong et al. (Eds.): ISMIS 2003, LNAI 2871, pp. 440–444, 2003.

infeasible for a large number of data N. Secondly standard PCA is usually performed in a batch mode, more specifically, requires all the training data. Thirdly in order to update the subspace of eigenvectors with another training data, we have to recompute the whole decomposition from scratch. In this paper, we propose a incremental approach of making PCA nonlinear using empirical kernel map [5], describing how an incremental KPCA(IKPCA) alleviates the need for storing the kernel matrix and makes KPCA more tractable on large data sets. The empirical kernel map is briefly described in Section 2. The incremental PCA outlined in Section 3. The IKPCA which involves an adaption of the standard formulation of KPCA is described in Section 4. In Section 5 we present the results of the experiments which show the feasibility of our approach. We give the conclusion and the remark in Section 6.

## 2   Empirical Kernel Map

To explain empirical kernel map we denote $\{X_N\}$ be a data set with $N$ examples of dimension $d$ which is mapped into feature space $\{\Phi(x_N)\}$ and suppose the mapped data to be centered $\sum_{i=1}^{N} \Phi(x_i) = 0$. The matrix $X = [\Phi(x_1), \ldots, \Phi(x_N)]$ represent the data in a compact way. In KPCA the data set $\{\Phi(x_N)\}$ is high dimensional and can most of the time not even be calculated explicitly. A way around this problem is the idea of an empirical kernel map [5] $\Psi_N \cdot \mathbf{R}^d \to \mathbf{R}^N$

$$
\Psi_N(x) = [\Phi(x_1) \cdot \Phi(x), \cdots, \Phi(x_N) \cdot \Phi(x)]^T
$$
$$
= [K(x_1, x), \cdots, K(x_N, x)]^T
$$

(1)

The empirical map does not map the data into feature space but into a space of size $N$. The covariance matrix of the empirically mapped data is:

$$
C_\Psi = \frac{1}{N}\Psi\Psi^T = NKK^T = NK^2
$$

(2)

In case of empirical kernel map, we diagonalize $NK^2$ instead of $K$ as in KPCA. Mika shows that the two matrices have the same eigenvectors $\{u_k\}$[6]. The eigenvalues $\{\lambda_k\}$ of $K$ are related to the eigenvalues $\{k_k\}$ of $NK^2$ by

$$
\lambda_k = \sqrt{\frac{k_k}{N}}
$$

(3)

and as before we can normalize the eigenvectors $\{v_k\}$ for the covariance matrix $C$ of the data by dividing each $\{u_k\}$ by $\sqrt{\lambda_k N}$. Instead of actually diagonalize the covariance matrix $C_\Psi$, the IKPCA is applied directly on the mapped data $\Psi = NK$. This makes it easy for us to adapt the incremental eigenspace update method to KPCA such that it is also correctly takes into account the centering of the mapped data in an incremental way. By this result, we only need to apply the empirical map to one data point at a time and do not need to store the $N \times N$ kernel matrix.

## 3   Incremental Eigenspace Update

To explain incremental PCA, we assume we have already built a set of eigenvectors $U = [u_j], j = 1, \cdots, k$ after having trained the input data $\mathbf{x}_i, i = 1, \cdots, N$. The corresponding eigenvalues are $\lambda$ and $\bar{\mathbf{x}}$ is the mean of input vector. Incremental building of eigenspace requires to update these eigenspace to take into account of a new input data . Here we give a brief summarization of the method which is described in [7]. First, we update the mean:

$$\bar{x}' = \frac{1}{N+1}(N\bar{x} + x_{N+1}) \tag{4}$$

We then update the set of eigenvectors to reflect the new input vector and to apply a rotational transformation to $U$. For doing this, it is necessary to compute the orthogonal residual vector $\hat{h} = (Ua_{N+1} + \bar{x}) - x_{N+1}$ and normalize it to obtain $h_{N+1} = \frac{h_{N+1}}{|h_{N+1}|_2}$ for $|h_{N+1}|_2 > 0$ and $h_{N+1} = 0$ otherwise. We obtain the new matrix of eigenvectors $U'$ by appending $h_{N+1}$ to the eigenvectors $U$ and rotating them :

$$U' = [U, h_{N+1}]R \tag{5}$$

where $R \in \mathbf{R}^{(k+1) \times (k+1)}$ is a rotation matrix. $R$ is the solution of the eigenproblem of the following form:

$$DR = R\Lambda' \tag{6}$$

where $\Lambda'$ is a diagonal matrix of new eigenvalues. We compose $D \in \mathbf{R}^{(k+1) \times (k+1)}$ as:

$$D = \frac{N}{N+1}\begin{bmatrix} \Lambda & 0 \\ 0^T & 0 \end{bmatrix} + \frac{N}{(N+1)^2}\begin{bmatrix} aa^T & \gamma a \\ \gamma a^T & \gamma^2 \end{bmatrix} \tag{7}$$

where $\gamma = h_{N+1}^T(x_{N+1} - \bar{x})$ and $a = U^T(x_{N+1} - \bar{x})$. Though there are other ways to construct matrix $D$[8,9], the only method ,however, described in [4] allows for the updating of mean.

## 4   Incremental Kernel PCA

Although incremental PCA builds the subspace of eigenvectors incrementally, it is restricted to apply the linear data. For the case of nonlinear data set, applying feature mapping function method to incremental PCA may be one of the solutions. This is performed by so-called *kernel-trick*, which means an implicit embedding to an infinite dimensional Hilbert space[5](i.e. feature space) $F$.

$$K(x, y) = \Phi(x) \cdot \Phi(y) \tag{8}$$

Where $K$ is a given kernel function in an input space. When $K$ is semi positive definite, the existence of $\Phi$ is proven[10]. Most of the case, however, the mapping $\Phi$ cannot be obtained explicitly. The vector in the feature space is not observable and only the inner product between vectors can be observed via a kernel function. However, for a given data set, it is possible to approximate $\Phi$ by empirical kernel map described in Section 2.

# 5   Experiment

In our experiment, we will evaluate the usefulness of the nonlinear feature extraction by IKPCA, as a preprocessing step for classification. For this purpose, extracted features by IKPCA will be used for training a simple linear classifier. Among many linear classifier, we take linear least squares support vector machine(LS-SVM) proposed by Suykens[11]. The reason why we use LS-SVM in this paper is that LS-SVM method is computationally attractive and easier to extend than standard support vector machine(SVM). In order to evaluate the IKPCA feature extraction capability, we take data sets from UCI machine learning repository which is a famous bench marking data in machine learning community. In all experiments we set eigenspace updating threshold value as 0.8.

## 5.1   Heart Disease Data

To test the performance of IKPCA for real world data, we use the Cleveland heart disease data obtained from the UCI Machine Learning Repository. This data set has 303 patterns and each pattern has 13 attributes. The two classes are highly overlapped. The goal is to distinguish between presence and absence of heart disease in a patient. Like two-spiral data classification problem, the same procedure is applied. A RBF kernel has been taken with $\sigma^2 = 0.1$. The correct classification ratio of a linear LS-SVM is 100%. For this particular data experiment, we can see that IKPCA extracts nonlinear features well on real world data.

## 5.2   Wine Data

The earlier experiments were carried to classify a two class problem. Here we extend our experiment to multiclass classification problem. Training data is the wine data obtained from the UCI Machine Learning Repository. Detailed attributes are available from http://www.ics.uci.edu/~mlearn/MLSummary.html. The Number of instances per class are 59 for class 1, 71 for class 2, and 48 for class 3 respectively. In this case we use a classifier as a multiclass LS-SVM proposed by Suykens[12]. The three classes have been encoded by taking $m = 2$. A RBF kernel has been taken with $\sigma_1^2 = \sigma_2^2 = 0.1$ and $\gamma = 1$. Correct classification ratio of linear multiclass LS-SVM is 100%.

# 6   Conclusion and Remarks

This paper is devoted to the exposition of a new technique on extracting nonlinear features from the incremental data. To develop this technique, we apply an incremental eigenspace update method to KPCA with an empirical kernel map approach. Proposed IKPCA has following advantages. Firstly, IKPCA has similar feature extracting performance for incremental and nonlinear data comparable to batch KPCA. Secondly, IKPCA is more efficient in memory requirement than batch KPCA. In batch KPCA the $N \times N$ kernel matrix has to be stored, while for IKPCA requirements are $O((k+1)^2)$. Here $k(1 \leq k \leq N)$ is the number of eigenvectors stored in each eigenspace updating step, which usually takes a number much smaller than $N$. Thirdly, IKPCA allows for complete incremental learning using the eigenspace approach, whereas batch KPCA recomputes whole decomposition for updating the subspace of eigenvectors with another data. Fourthly, IKPCA can easily be improved by re-learning the data. Fifthly IKPCA do not require nonlinear optimization techniques. Finally, experimental results show that extracted features from IKPCA lead to good performance when used as a pre-preprocess data for a linear classifier. Future work is combining IKPCA with excellent classifier so make the system do well in classification task.

# References

1. Tipping, M.E. and Bishop, C.M. :Mixtures of probabilistic principal component analysers. Neural Computation 11(2), (1998) 443–482
2. Kramer, M.A.:Nonlinear principal component analysis using autoassociative neural networks. AICHE Journal 37(2),(1991) 233–243
3. Diamantaras, K.I. and Kung, S.Y.:Principal Component Neural Networks: Theory and Applications. New York John Wiley & Sons, Inc.(1996)
4. Scholkopf, B. Smola, A. and Muller, K.R.:Nonlinear component analysis as a kernel eigenvalue problem. Neural Computation 10(5), (1998) 1299–1319
5. Scholkopf, B. Mika, S. Burges, C. Knirsch, P. Muller, K.R. Ratsch, G. and Smola, A.J.:Input Space versus Feature Space in Kernel-based Methods. IEEE Transactions on Neural Networks, vol. 10, September (1999) 1000–1017
6. Mika, S.: Kernel algorithms for nonlinear signal processing in feature spaces. Master's thesis, Technical University of Berlin, November (1998)
7. Hall, P. Marshall, D. and Martin, R.: Incremental eigenalysis for classification. In British Machine Vision Conference, volume 1, September (1998)286–295
8. Winkeler, J. Manjunath, B.S. and Chandrasekaran, S.: Subset selection for active object recognition. In CVPR, volume 2, IEEE Computer Society Press, June (1999) 511–516
9. Murakami, H. Kumar, B.V.K.V.: Efficient calculation of primary images from a set of images. IEEE PAMI, 4(5), (1982) 511–515
10. Vapnik, V. N.: Statistical learning theory. John Wiley & Sons, New York (1998)
11. Suykens, J.A.K. and Vandewalle, J.: Least squares support vector machine classifiers. Neural Processing Letters, vol.9, (1999) 293–300
12. Suykens, J.A.K. and Vandewalle, J.: Multiclass Least Squares Support Vector Machines, In: Proc. International Joint Conference on Neural Networks (IJCNN'99), Washington DC (1999)

# On Lookahead Heuristics in Decision Tree Learning

Tapio Elomaa and Tuomo Malinen

Department of Computer Science, University of Helsinki, Finland
{elomaa,tamaline}@cs.helsinki.fi

**Abstract.** In decision tree learning attribute selection is usually based on greedy local splitting criterion. More extensive search quickly leads to intolerable time consumption. Moreover, it has been observed that lookahead cannot benefit prediction accuracy as much as one would hope. It has even been claimed that lookahead would be mostly harmful in decision tree learning.

We present a computationally efficient splitting algorithm for numerical domains, which, in many cases, leads to more accurate trees. The scheme is based on information gain and an efficient variant of lookahead. We consider the performance of the algorithm, on one hand, in view of the greediness of typical splitting criteria and, on the other hand, the possible pathology caused by oversearching in the hypothesis space. In empirical tests, our algorithm performs in a promising manner.

## 1   Introduction

Decision tree learning is a recursive partitioning strategy for constructing, based on a given training sample, a classifier to predict the class label of other similar cases. In it one expands a leaf node unless the given *stopping criterion* is satisfied. All calculations are based on the training examples that reach the leaf under consideration. If one decides to expand a leaf, subtrees will be recursively grown for it. A *splitting criterion* is invoked to decide a suitable test for the leaf in question; the test also determines the number of subtrees and the examples that each of them receives.

Most typically a test concerning the value of a single attribute is assigned to the node that will become the root of the evolving subtree. Greedy attribute selection is based on probabilistic calculations of the information gained on the class value by dividing the data as determined by the splitting criterion. The greediness manifests itself in the fact that only local changes to, e.g., entropy are considered in deciding the attribute to be assigned to node.

Intuitively it would seem that reducing the degree of greediness by calculating the effects of the choice of the attribute deeper down the tree should benefit the process. However, this intuition has turned out false in game tree evaluation [13, 14]. The usefulness of lookahead has also been refuted in decision tree learning [17,12]. Of course, lookahead is costly in computation and has, thus, been used in decision tree learning only seldom [20,18,4]. In this paper we, nevertheless,

N. Zhong et al. (Eds.): ISMIS 2003, LNAI 2871, pp. 445–453, 2003.
© Springer-Verlag Berlin Heidelberg 2003

seek to chart whether lookahead could be performed without prohibitive cost and in a useful manner.

Bounded lookahead, on the other hand, can be implemented efficiently and has been observed beneficial in connection of tree searching [8,9,19,3]. In this paper, we apply such ideas to decision tree learning, but instead of trying to find the split that produces the optimal tree, we use a greedy measure to find the locally optimal binary split and then look at the subtree that is grown after this split. If the subtree produces heuristic evidence of the global unoptimality of the split, we choose another attribute in its stead. Thus, we are tuning the splitting criterion to be less greedy. We present empirical evidence, which shows the algorithm to be useful in many cases.

The remainder of this paper is organized as follows. Sect. 2 describes the top-down induction of decision tree learning setting in more detail. In Sect. 3 we present the lookahead and voting method and give an example where it seems useful. We also discuss related work and give some theoretical motivation for the algorithm. Then in Sect. 4 we give the results of our empirical comparisons. Sect. 5 discusses the work, draws the conclusions, and considers further work.

## 2    Decision Tree Learning

We employ the usual framework for supervised learning from examples: Let $\mathcal{X}$ be the instance space. Each instance $x \in \mathcal{X}$ is described by the values of a set of attributes $\mathcal{A} = \{ a_1, \ldots, a_k \}$. We suppose that the domain of each attribute $a_i \in \mathcal{A}$ is numerical, i.e., $\mathrm{dom}(a_i) = \mathbb{R}$ for all $i$. Let $\mathcal{Y} = \{ y_1, \ldots, y_m \}$ be the set of class labels. A labeled example is then a pair $(x, y) \in \mathcal{X} \times \mathcal{Y}$, where $y$ is the correct class of instance $x$. Suppose we are given a training set $S$ of $n$ labeled examples $\{ s_1, \ldots, s_n \}$.

The basic algorithm for top-down learning of decision trees is informally described as follows. First, all the examples $S$ are assigned to a single leaf with no children, the root node. Then, if $S$ contains examples with different class labels, the set $S$ is partitioned into two and the resulting subsets are assigned to two new children of the root node. This process is then iterated on these new leaves.

We will only consider numerical attributes in this paper. For such an attribute a split divides the real axis in a number of intervals. The examples are thus passed on down the tree with respect to their value and the attribute chosen for the split. There exist a number of approaches for choosing the intervals. The simplest is called *binarization*, where the real axis is split in half, e.g., in the midpoint of the attribute values in the leaf. This is efficient, but may not yield as small tree as possible. *Multi-splitting*, on the other hand, means dividing the real axis in many intervals. In this approach one has to decide the number of intervals and the places of interval borders. Multi-splitting in general is computationally expensive, since the number of possible splits is exponential, but can be carried out efficiently for some common evaluation functions [7,5].

Within each leaf node to be split, we need a suitable partition for the examples that reach it. A common criterion for finding these partitions is information gain, i.e., the decrease in entropy of class labels that follows from a split of the set of examples. In case of an attribute with a numerical domain, one has to choose values by which the examples are divided. As discussed above, finding optimal split points is not trivial. We employ the scheme of choosing the midpoint of the values of the examples assigned to the leaf in presenting our algorithm, although other choices, including multi-split, could be used as well within the scheme. Note also that a multi-way split can be achieved using many binary splits.

Now suppose we want to split a set $S$. The information gain (see e.g. [15]) for this binary split, using attribute $a_i$ with the interval border at $b$ is defined as the difference in entropy between the unpartitioned data and the data partitioned by the chosen split $H(S) - (H(S_{a_i \leq b}) + H(S_{a_i > b}))$, where

$$H(S) = \sum_{j \in \{1,\dots,m\}} \mathbf{Pr}\,(y = y_j) \cdot \log_2 \left( \frac{1}{\mathbf{Pr}\,(y = y_j)} \right)$$

and

$$H(S_{a_i \leq b}) = \sum_{j \in \{1,\dots,m\}} \mathbf{Pr}\,(a_i \leq b, y = y_j) \cdot \log_2 \left( \frac{1}{\mathbf{Pr}\,(y = y_j \mid a_i \leq b)} \right).$$

Also $H(S_{a_i > b})$ is defined similarly. Note that the actual border point $b$ is not interesting, we may place the examples having value $b$ in either leaf. The probabilities are approximated by *data priors*, i.e., they are computed from the given training data. For example, in order to approximate the conditional probability $\mathbf{Pr}\,(y = y_j \mid a_i \leq b)$, we first count the number of those examples in $S$ that fulfill the condition $a_i \leq b$, and then compute the fraction of those that have $y = y_j$ within the resulting set. This is used as the estimate of the probability.

In top-down induction the tree growing usually continues until the data has been partitioned into subsets that are as class-uniform as possible. This will, however, mean that the induced decision tree will be over-fitted to the training set characteristics. Because the sample does not necessarily reflect the true characteristics of the underlying instance space—the elements of which we are supposed to classify in the future—we need somehow to reduce the decision tree's dependency on the peculiarities of the training set. Thus, the tree growing phase is usually followed by a tree *pruning* phase in which the decision tree is restructured somehow to be less particularly a classifier for the training data. We will not, however, apply tree pruning in this study. For surveys and empirical evaluations of decision tree pruning see, e.g., [10,6].

## 3  Reducing Greediness with Lookahead

Now we examine how to reduce the greediness of split selection through lookahead without using too much computational effort. We apply lookahead of limited depth and combine this process with a voting algorithm to decide the test of a node on the basis of results from this lookahead.

## 3.1   The Feature Selection Voting Algorithm

Suppose that we have grown a decision tree $\mathcal{T}$, which includes a leaf $\ell$ that does not fulfill the stopping criterion. Thus, we want to find an attribute by which to split the leaf $\ell$. Let $S_\ell$ be the set of training examples assigned to the leaf $\ell$ and $I(S_\ell)$ the attribute chosen to $\ell$ greedily using information gain.

The idea of the following algorithm can loosely be described as follows: We first split $\ell$ with $I(S_\ell)$ and then recursively build the subtree rooted at $\ell$ until the stopping criterion is fulfilled for all leaves or the subtree reaches a given maximum depth $d$. Each node in the subtree then takes part in a voting procedure to decide the final attribute to split $\ell$ by. Thus, the final decision of splitting $\ell$ is deferred until information concerning the initial greedy choice has been gathered.

In order to implement the voting, we associate with each decision tree node $\ell$ a real-valued weight $w(\ell)$ and a $k$-array $V^\ell$ of real numbers. Each item of $V^\ell$ corresponds to an attribute and is used in the voting procedure. For a leaf $\ell$ to be split, we calculate the information gain score for each attribute. Let $i_1^\ell, \ldots, i_k^\ell$ denote these values. The algorithm also inputs the maximum lookahead depth $d$.

Let $\ell_0$ now be a leaf to be expanded. We proceed, in the first place, just as in basic top-down induction algorithm. However, the depth of the tree is limited to $d$. Thus, whenever a leaf either fulfills the stopping condition or is at depth $d$ from $\ell_0$, we call it a leaf.

After the subtree for $\ell_0$ has been built, we invoke the voting procedure. In it the idea is that each node $v$ in the subtree of $\ell_0$ votes all attributes $a_j, 0 \le j \le k$, by adding its weighted information score to the attribute's total count: $V_j^{\ell_0} \leftarrow V_j^{\ell_0} + i_j^v \cdot w(v)$. The vote is uneven if nodes get different weights. The underlying idea is that we wish to give nodes farther away from $\ell_0$ less consideration in the vote, as they are not likely to tell us as much about situation in $\ell_0$ as nodes above. We give two ways to define $w(v)$. The more straightforward option is to define it as the number of examples in the node $\ell_i$, which clearly reduces when moving downwards in the tree. The more complicated one is formulated recursively: Root node $\ell_0$ has weight 1. Its children $\ell_i$ have weight $w(\ell) \cdot \max_k i_k^{\ell_i}$, i.e., the maximum information gain score for node $\ell_i$ multiplied by weight of father. This is carried on down the tree. This is likely to go to zero even faster than weights according to the first definition.

Denote the final attribute chosen to split $\ell$ by $N(\ell)$. Now $N(\ell)$ is defined as

$$N(\ell) = \arg\max_i V_i^\ell,$$

i.e., the attribute that gathers most "vote mass".

We employed binary splitting above, but the scheme naturally suggests a multi-interval split. Suppose we have decided to split by $N(\ell)$. This is due to a number of, one or several, splits in the subtree that takes part in the voting. We may, instead of choosing the binary split, split at each of these intervals, or a subset of these.

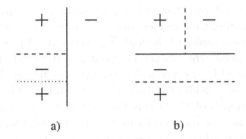

**Fig. 1.** A tree by IG, on the left, and nvIG, on the right

The algorithm suggests a number of modifications. First of all, the weights issued to the nodes of the lookahead tree can be tuned in various ways. For example, we can, instead of using the number of examples in a node, use their number squared, which leads to a more conservative splitting criterion. In the empirical tests, this turned out to be in many cases more stable with respect to lookahead depth and, in some cases, also produce more accurate trees.

Then, to save in running time, one way to define the depth of the lookahead is to terminate building the tree when the weight defined by information gain products reaches some threshold value; in the vote, leaves with low values are likely to have little effect.

A surprisingly simple, and efficient, approach is to build just one branch of the tree, to some depth $d$, and let the nodes along this path vote. For many datasets, the trees turned actually more accurate than with the voting scenario described above. Also, clearly this is quite efficient, as the extra factor due to lookahead is then linear in $d$. Notably, with data set `glass`, this approach was clearly useful, with the best accuracy being 70.95 with lookahead depth 2 compared to 65.71 with information gain splitting.

In terms of computational complexity, the voting algorithm is relatively inexpensive. Growing the lookahead trees of depth $d$ for each leaf adds a factor that grows exponentially in $d$. This factor, however, stays rather small for practical values of $d$. Also, not all of the lookahead trees of depth, say 10, are likely to be complete. Some examples of running times are given with the empirical results in Sect. 4.

### 3.2   Greediness, Oversearching, and Pathology

To make the algorithm described above more intuitive, we give an example of a scenario where the chosen attribute is different from what we would have chosen by information gain, and the algorithm seems useful.

In Fig. 1, we see a simple training set consisting of four examples on a plane, each belonging to one of two classes marked with $+$ and $-$. Two decision trees are represented by the lines dividing the plane. The solid lines mean the split employed in the root node, the dashed lines mean the splits in the children of the root node and the dotted lines means the splits on the third level. The left tree is induced by the standard information gain measure, as given in the previous section. In this example, we consider only the binary split, where the interval is in the middle of the examples of the leaf. The vertical split clearly provides some separation of the classes, whereas the horizontal split would yield no information at all; we choose greedily the vertical attribute to split by. The right side now contains only one example and can be pronounced a leaf. The left side needs two further splits. The depth of the tree is thus 3 and it is rather unbalanced.

On the right is the tree induced by nvIG using the first way to define weights. In the example, splitting first in vertical direction leads to two further horizontal splits on the left side as seen in the tree on the left in Fig. 1. These votes turn the situation in the root in favor of the horizontal split, as the information gained by the vertical split in the root node is quite low. Now, both the up and down side can be completely separated with single splits. We end up with a balanced tree of height 2, which seems to be the simpler of the two hypotheses.

Intuition suggest that doing more search to determine the splitting criterion would help to find a better decision than a simple greedy heuristic such as information gain. The goodness of a decision tree might be measured, e.g., by its prediction accuracy or its size. However, it has often been observed that lookahead can rather hurt than help the process [17,12]. What is the reason for this? One possible explanation is given by Quinlan and Cameron-Jones [17]: In performing more extensive search (lookahead) we increase the probability of finding a "fluke" hypothesis (decision tree) that fits the data (too) well. In carrying out greedy search, so few hypotheses are examined that the probability of stumbling into a fluke hypothesis remains low.

On the other hand, greedy splitting may lead to splitting the instance space too often on some attribute. Then we could, as well, split with that attribute right away. That is what the above-described lookahead-voting scheme attempts to do. In balancing between oversearching and greediness it is a conservative approach. The idea of different weights is to adjust the conservativity of the algorithm: Information gain products are more conservative and go to zero rather fast. The number of examples in the node, on the other hand, approaches zero slowly, which means that lookahead will have an important role in the algorithm.

The empirical evidence concerning lookahead seems to back up the existence of pathology in decision tree learning; the positive results have been few. The idea of the algorithms presented in this paper is not to perform actual lookahead, but to reduce the greediness of information gain split. They are parametrized as are most algorithms of lookahead, i.e., the depth of the lookahead can be varied. But as we are not performing look ahead *per se*, we can assume that pathology does not show up as quickly as in case of actual lookahead.

## 4    Empirical Evaluation

The proposed algorithm was tried out on many all-numerical datasets from the UCI Repository of Machine Learning Databases [1] using 10-fold cross validation. The comparison was against the basic top-down-algorithm with splitting

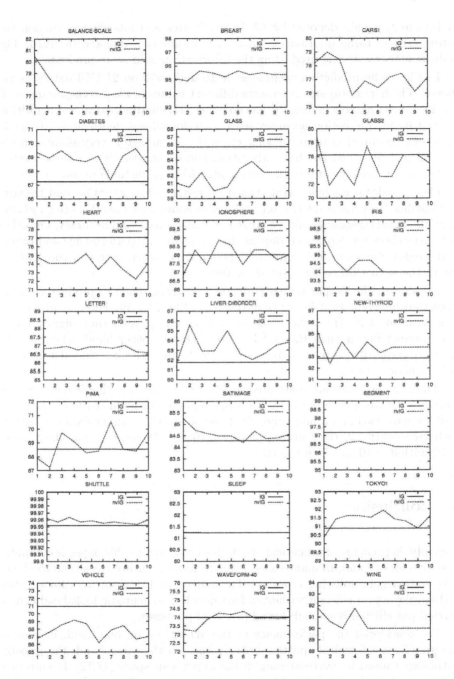

**Fig. 2.** The empirical results: $x$-axis represents depth of lookahead and $y$-axis classification accuracy obtained

by information gain denoted by IG. In the figures and following discussion the voting scheme using information gain score products is denoted by nvIG. The node weights were computed using the information gain score products.

In Fig. 2 the prediction accuracies of IG and nvIG on 21 UCI data sets are shown. The horizontal axis represents different values of the depth parameter $d$. For IG this parameter, naturally, has no effect. The limited lookahead algorithm showed better prediction accuracy with some lookahead depth in 14 of the 21 data sets examined in total (in some cases the advantage is very slight). In the remaining 7 datasets, the basic algorithm turned constantly out to be better. However, the performance of the voting algorithm is unstable in some cases.

On some data sets (e.g., diabetes, liver-disorder, shuttle, and letter) all lookahead depths lead to better performance and on some others (e.g., glass, breast, heart, segment, and vehicle) to worse prediction accuracy. On other data sets there are lookahead depths that improve the performance and others that weaken the result. It is hard to find common characteristics for the domains where the algorithm either succeeds or fails.

In general, the deeper search performed by nvIG tends to produce decision trees that are somewhat larger than those produced by IG. These results somewhat coincide with [11], who found in their empirical tests that slightly larger trees predict better than the smallest ones. On the other hand, whenever the voting scheme turned out to give better results than the baseline algorithm, it built shallower trees.

The running times are quite predictable. On a relatively simple data set, like tokyo1 with tree depth of ca. 14, the learning phase of nvIG (with $d = 10$) took 2.48 seconds, two and a half times the time of IG. On a larger data set letter with tree depth 22, the learning phase of IG was 18 seconds and the time of nvIG with $d = 10$ was 75 seconds.


## 5   Conclusion

The splitting scheme of numerical attributes presented in this paper is computationally efficient and, in many cases, leads to more accurate trees than the basic information gain splitting criterion. The scheme is based on information gain and employing an efficient variant of lookahead. The heuristic lookahead can be carried out efficiently enough for all practical purposes.

We considered the performance of the algorithm, on one hand, in view of the greediness of typical splitting criteria and, on the other hand, the possible pathology caused by oversearching in the hypothesis space [17,12]. In empirical tests, our algorithm performed in a promising manner. The results suggest that a very moderate search in the hypothesis space could prove beneficial. In this paper, instead of looking for the globally best split, we just wanted to see if the locally best split leads to a pathological situation. There might also be other ways to conduct moderate search in the hypothesis space.

# References

1. Blake, C.L., Merz, C.J.: UCI repository of machine learning databases, University of California, Department of Information and Computer Science, Irvine, CA (1998)
2. Breiman, L., Friedman, J.H., Olshen, R.A., Stone, C. J.: Classification and Regression Trees. Wadsworth, Pacific Grove, CA (1984)
3. Devroye, L.: Branching processes and their applications in the analysis of tree structures and tree algorithms. In: Habib, M., McDiarmid, C., Ramirez-Alfonsin, J., Reed, B. (eds.): Probabilistic Methods for Algorithmic Discrete Mathematics. Algorithms and Combinatorics, Vol. 16. Springer, New York (1998) 249–314
4. Dong, M., Kothari, R.: Look-ahead based fuzzy decision tree induction. IEEE Trans. Fuzzy Syst. **9** (2001) 461–468
5. Elomaa, T., Rousu, J.: Generalizing boundary points. In: Proc. Seventeenth National Conference on Artificial Intelligence. AAAI Press, Menlo Park, CA (2000) 570–576
6. Esposito, F., Malerba, D., Semeraro, G.: A comparative analysis of methods for pruning decision trees. IEEE Trans. Pattern Anal. Mach. Intell. **19** (1997) 476-491
7. Fulton, T., Kasif, S., Salzberg, S.: Efficient algorithms for finding multi-way splits for decision trees. In: Prieditis, A., Russell, S. (eds.): Proc. Twelfth International Conference on Machine Learning. Morgan Kaufmann, San Francisco, CA (1995) 244–251
8. Karp, R.M., Pearl, J.: Searching for an optimal path in a tree with random costs. Artif. Intell. **21** (1983) 99–117
9. McDiarmid, C., Provan, G.M.A.: An expected-cost analysis of backtracking and non-backtracking algorithms. In: Proc. Twelfth International Joint Conference on Artificial Intelligence. Morgan Kaufmann, San Mateo, CA (1991) 172–177
10. Mingers, J.: An empirical comparison of pruning methods for decision tree induction. Mach. Learn. **4** (1989) 227-243
11. Murphy, P., Pazzani, M.: Exploring the decision forest: An empirical investigation of Occam's Razor in decision tree induction. J. Artif. Intell. Res. **1** (1994) 257–275
12. Murthy, S., Salzberg, S.: Lookahead and pathology in decision tree induction. In: Proc. Fourteenth International Joint Conference on Artificial Intelligence. Morgan Kaufmann, San Francisco, CA (1995) 1025–1031
13. Nau, D.S.: Decision quality as a function of search depth on game trees. J. ACM **30** (1983) 687-708
14. Pearl, J.: Game tree pathology. Artif. Intell. **20** (1983) 427–453
15. Quinlan, J.R.: Induction of decision trees. Mach. Learn. **1** (1986) 81–106
16. Quinlan, J.R.: C4.5: Programs for Machine Learning. Morgan Kaufmann, San Mateo, CA (1993)
17. Quinlan, J.R., Cameron-Jones, M.: Oversearching and layered search in empirical learning. In: Proc. Fourteenth International Joint Conference on Artificial Intelligence. Morgan Kaufmann, San Francisco, CA (1995) 1019–1024
18. Ragavan, H., Rendell, L.: Lookahead feature construction for learning hard concepts. In: Proc. Tenth International Conference on Machine Learning. Morgan Kaufmann, San Francisco, CA (1993) 252–259
19. Sarkar, U.K., Chakrabarti, P.P., Ghose, S., DeSarkar, S.C.: Improving greedy algorithms by lookahead-search. J. Alg. **16** (1994) 1–23
20. Shepherd, B., Piper, J., Rutovitz, D.: Comparison of ACLS and classical linear methods in a biological application, In: Hayes, J.E., Michie, D., Richards, J. (eds.): Machine Intelligence, Vol. 11: Logic and the Acquisition of Knowledge. Oxford University Press, Oxford, UK (1988) 423–434

# Empirical Evaluation of Dissimilarity Measures for Time-Series Multiscale Matching

Shoji Hirano and Shusaku Tsumoto

Department of Medical Informatics, Shimane Medical University, School of Medicine
89-1 Enya-cho, Izumo, Shimane 693-8501, Japan
hirano@ieee.org, tsumoto@computer.org

**Abstract.** This paper reports the results of empirical evaluation of the dissimilarity measure for time-series multiscale matching. In order to investigate fundamental characteristics of the dissimilarity measure, we performed quantitative analysis of the induced dissimilarities using simple sine wave and its variants, and compared them with dissimilarities obtained by dynamic time warping. The results showed that differences on the amplitude, phase and trends were respectively captured by the terms on rotation angle, phase and gradient, although they also showed weakness on the linearity.

## 1 Introduction

Temporal data mining has attracted much interests in the areas such as marketing and medicine since it provides tools for discovering unknown temporal structure hidden in the data. One of the remarkable characteristics of temporal data is that events in the data have temporal contiguity. Therefore, finding a subsequence that takes interesting course and frequently appears in the data is a key process of temporal data mining. For example, a remarkable temporal pattern may be observed in the electroencephalography of a patient while he/she is in convulsion, and from the pattern medical doctors may obtain sufficient information for making diagnosis. Clustering of subsequences is a promising approach for efficient discovery of the patterns and a lot of methods have been proposed [1].

An important issue in subsequence clustering is selection of the length of the subsequences. Because the length directly affects the types of events to be captured, its selection should be performed carefully. Especially, if one has no prior knowledge about the events expected to be observed in the data, it should not be fixed in advance. In many cases of practical data mining, such unknown lengths of events are covered by preparing some sets of subsequences obtained using different widths and performing clustering on each of them. However, this approach involves two problems:

1. A subsequence may not correctly represent an event
   A subsequence is usually obtained by copying a part of the original sequence that overlaps with a given masking window of the fixed length. This means

N. Zhong et al. (Eds.): ISMIS 2003, LNAI 2871, pp. 454–462, 2003.

that no feature points of the original sequences, i.e., inflection points and local maxima/minima, are taken into account for determining the shape of the subsequences. Therefore, one cannot guarantee that the subsequence correctly covers the event, namely, whether the head and tail of the subsequence precisely match the start and end of the event respectively.

2. Concatenated events of different lengths may not be correctly captured
   Connectivity of subsequences is not guaranteed when they are obtained using different types of masking windows. In other words, there is no guarantee that a set of concatenated subsequences exactly match to a contiguous subpart of the original sequence. This is because no structural information of the original sequence is taken into account in generating the subsequences. Therefore, it is hard to obtain a cluster containing the similar types of concatenated events, i.e., one-week increase followed first by the two-week decrease and then by the one-week increase.

In order to overcome these problems, we have proposed a grouping method [2] for temporal sequences based on multiscale matching [3]. Multiscale matching is a method for comparing two planar curves by partially changing observation scales. We have also proposed a dissimilarity measure that compares subsequences according to the following aspects: rotation angle, length, phase and gradient. However, it empirically became apparent that it was difficult to understand from the results that which aspects were really contributed to the resultant dissimilarity of the sequences, because the pairs should be determined in a complex way. In order to investigate fundamental characteristics of the dissimilarity measure, we performed quantitative analysis of the induced dissimilarity using simple sine wave and its variants.

## 2   Dissimilarity Measure in Multiscale Matching

Multiscale matching, proposed by Mokhtarian [3], is originally developed as a method for comparing two planar curves by partly changing observation scales. It divides a contour of the object into partial contours based on the place of inflection points. After generating partial contours at various scales for each of the two curves to be compared, it finds the best pairs of partial contours that minimize the total dissimilarity while preserving completeness of the concatenated contours. This method can preserve connectivity of partial contours by tracing hierarchical structure of inflection points on the scale space. Since each ends of a partial contour exactly corresponds to an inflection point and the correspondence between inflection points at different scales are recognized, the connectivity of the partial contours are guaranteed.

Now let us introduce the basics of multiscale matching for one-dimensional temporal sequence. First, we represent time-series $A$ using multiscale description. Let $x(t)$ represent an original temporal sequence of $A$ where $t$ denotes a time of data acquisition. The sequence at scale $\sigma$, $X(t, \sigma)$, can be represented as a convolution of $x(t)$ and a Gauss function with scale factor $\sigma$, $g(t, \sigma)$, as follows:

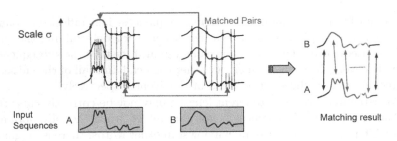

**Fig. 1.** Multiscale matching.

$$X(t,\sigma) = x(t) \otimes g(t,\sigma) = \int_{-\infty}^{+\infty} x(u) \frac{1}{\sigma\sqrt{2\pi}} e^{-(t-u)^2/2\sigma^2} du. \qquad (1)$$

Figure 1 shows an example of sequences in various scales. From Figure 1 and the function above, it is obvious that the sequence will be smoothed at higher scale and the number of inflection points is also reduced at higher scale.

The next step is to find inflection points according to change of the sign of the curvature and to construct segments. A segment is a subsequence whose ends respectively correspond to the adjacent inflection points. Let $\mathbf{A}^{(k)}$ be a set of $N$ segments that represents the sequence at scale $\sigma^{(k)}$. $\mathbf{A}^{(k)}$ can be represented as

$$\mathbf{A}^{(k)} = \left\{ a_i^{(k)} \mid i = 1, 2, \cdots, N^{(k)} \right\}. \qquad (2)$$

In the same way, for another temporal sequence $B$, we can obtain a set of segments $\mathbf{B}^{(h)}$ at scale $\sigma^{(h)}$ as

$$\mathbf{B}^{(h)} = \left\{ b_j^{(h)} \mid j = 1, 2, \cdots, M^{(h)} \right\}, \qquad (3)$$

where $M$ denotes the number of segments of $B$ at scale $\sigma^{(h)}$.

The main procedure of multiscale structure matching is to find the best set of segment pairs that minimizes the total difference. Figure 1 illustrates the process. For example, five contiguous segments at the lowest scale of Sequence $A$ are integrated into one segment at the highest scale, and the integrated segments well match to one segment in Sequence $B$ at the lowest scale. Thus the set of the five segments in Sequence $A$ and the one segment in Sequence $B$ will be considered as a candidate for corresponding subsequences. While, another pair of segments will be matched at the lowest scale. In this way, matching is performed throughout all scales. The matching process can be fasten by implementing dynamic programming scheme [4].

Obviously, the definition of the dissimilarity measure between segments is critical in finding the best set of subsequences that matches the human perception. For planar curves, Ueda et al. defined a dissimilarity measure $d(a_i^{(k)}, b_j^{(h)})$ between segments $a_i^{(k)}$ and $b_i^{(h)}$, which employs difference on their rotation angles and lengths as follows.

$$d(a_i^{(k)}, b_j^{(h)}) = \frac{|\theta_{a_i}^{(k)} - \theta_{b_j}^{(h)}|}{\theta_{a_i}^{(k)} + \theta_{b_j}^{(h)}} \left| \frac{l_{a_i}^{(k)}}{L_A^{(k)}} - \frac{l_{b_j}^{(h)}}{L_B^{(h)}} \right|, \tag{4}$$

where $\theta_{a_i}^{(k)}$ and $\theta_{b_j}^{(h)}$ denote rotation angles of tangent vectors along the contours, $l_{a_i}^{(k)}$ and $l_{b_j}^{(h)}$ denote length of the contours, $L_A^{(k)}$ and $L_B^{(h)}$ denote total segment length of the sequences $A$ and $B$ at scales $\sigma^{(k)}$ and $\sigma^{(h)}$. According to the above definition, large differences can be assigned when difference of rotation angle or relative length is large. Continuous $2n - 1$ segments can be integrated into one segment at higher scale. Difference between the replaced segments and another segment can be defined analogously, with additive replacement cost that suppresses excessive replacement.

Their measure would be powerful in recognizing correspondence between largely distorted planar curves because it provides constant value for curves with affine transformation. However, this measure cannot directly be applied to temporal data because a data value itself has far important meaning than that in the planar curves. Two important issues associated with this property are summarized below.

1. Rotation of a planar curve corresponds to shift of phase in a temporal sequence. Although the above dissimilarity measure can be used to absorb shift of time and difference of sampling duration, we should suppress excessive back-shift of sequences in order to correctly distinguish the early-phase events from late-phase events.

2. It prevents us from evaluating difference of trends. Since rotation angle of a segment is defined as an accumulated change of angle of the tangent vector along the segment, it produces zero dissimilarity for vertically mirrored sequences that have inverse characteristics on their trends. This means that by this dissimilarity measure we cannot distinguish an increasing trend from a decreasing trend. Figure 2 shows an example of this second problem. A black point shows place of an inflection point. Each of the subsequences between adjacent inflection points, $a, \ldots, d, a', \ldots, d'$ represents a segment. All of the segments in this example are generated by inverting or vertically mirroring one basic segment $a$. Although polarities of the segments are not the same for convex and concave segments, all of their rotation angles, lengths, and phases are the same. For sequences $A$ and $B$, the zero dissimilarity, which represents the best match, would be obtained when one makes successive match of the segments, e.g., $a$-$a'$, $b$-$b'$, from head to tail. However, this is not appropriate from the viewpoint of human perception because they have obvious difference in their long-term trends; sequence $A$ has increasing trend and sequence $B$ has decreasing trend. This problem arises from the fact that, for the purpose of comparing similarity of the convex and concave structure of the planar curves, the dissimilarity measure in Equation (4) evaluates divergence of the data value not from the vertical origin but from the line that bridges inflection points.

**Fig. 2.** An example of sequences that have different trends but produce the same dissimilarity.

In order to elude these problems, we have proposed the following new dissimilarity measure for multiscale comparison of temporal sequences that employs difference on phase and gradient in addition to these two factors.

$$d(a_i^{(k)}, b_j^{(h)}) = \max(\theta, l, \phi, g), \tag{5}$$

where $\theta$ and $l$ correspond to the first and second product terms in Equation (4) respectively, and $\phi$ and $g$ denote segment difference on phase and gradient defined below.

$$\phi(a_i^{(k)}, b_j^{(h)}) = \left| \frac{\phi_{a_i}^{(k)}}{\Phi_A^{(k)}} - \frac{\phi_{b_j}^{(h)}}{\Phi_B^{(h)}} \right|, \tag{6}$$

$$g(a_i^{(k)}, b_j^{(h)}) = \begin{cases} 1, & \text{if } g_{a_i}^{(k)} \times g_{b_j}^{(h)} < 0 \\ \left| g_{a_i}^{(k)} - g_{b_j}^{(h)} \right|, & \text{otherwise.} \end{cases} \tag{7}$$

where $\phi_{a_i}^{(k)}$ denotes temporal delay from the first time of data acquisition, $\Phi_A^{(k)}$ denotes durations of data acquisition of sequence $A$, $g_{a_i}^{(k)}$ denotes difference of data values at both ends of segment $a_i^{(k)}$, and $\sigma$ denotes standard deviation of the data values. The third term $\phi$ defined in Equation (6) emphasizes difference on phase. Phase $\phi_{a_i}^{(k)}$ is defined as an acquisition time $t$ of the head point of segment $a_i^{(k)}$. It will be normalized by the acquisition durations $\Phi_A^{(k)}$ before taking subtraction to $\phi_{b_j}^{(h)}/\Phi_B^{(h)}$. The last term $g$ defined in Equation (7) emphasizes difference on gradient normalized by the standard deviation of the corresponding attribute value. Figure 2 illustrates meaning of these terms. By this extension, we simultaneously evaluate dissimilarity of two events from the following aspects: (1) intenseness of increase/decrease of data values, (2) length of the events (3) dates of the events (4) global trends of the events. Besides, by taking maximum of these four factors, we improve discrepancy between sequences.

There is a strict restriction for selection of segment pairs. The resultant set of segment pairs must not be redundant or insufficient to represent the original sequences. Namely, by concatenating all subsequences in the set, the original sequence must be completely reconstructed without any partial intervals or overlaps. Therefore, a pair of segments that locally takes very low dissimilarity may not be included in the final set if selecting the pair distorts completeness of the

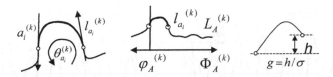

**Fig. 3.** Components of the dissimilarity measure.

sequence. This makes it difficult for us to recognize which term in the dissimilarity measure actually contributes to determination of total dissimilarity and how a small change of local dissimilarity affects the results.

## 3    Experimental Results

For the purpose of recognizing fundamental characteristics of the dissimilarity measure presented in the previous section, we applied multiscale matching to some basic sequences and compared the produced dissimilarities with those produced by dynamic time warping (DTW) [5]. The sequences used were listed below.

$$w_1 : \quad y(t) = \sin(2.5t)$$
$$w_2 : \quad y(t) = 2\sin(2.5t)$$
$$w_3 : \quad y(t) = 0.5\sin(2.5t)$$
$$w_4 : \quad y(t) = \sin(2.5t + 0.5\pi)$$

$$w_5 : \quad y(t) = \sin(2.5t) + 0.2(t - 9.0)$$
$$w_6 : \quad y(t) = \sin(2.5t) - 0.2(t - 9.0)$$
$$w_7 : \quad y(t) = 0.5e^{0.1t}\sin(2.5t)$$
$$w_8 : \quad y(t) = 0.5e^{-0.1t+0.6\pi}\sin(2.5t)$$
$$w_9 : \quad y(t) = 2 \times \sin(2 * 2.5t)$$

The range of $t(= \Phi)$ was set to $0 \leq t < 6\pi$. The sampling interval was $1/500\Phi$. Thus each data consisted of 500 points. The scale $\sigma$ was changed for 30 levels, starting from 1.0 to 30.0 with the interval of 1.0. Note that theoretically replacement of segments would never occur because all of the eight sequences were generated from single sine wave. Practically, some minor replacement occurred because implementation of the algorithm required exceptional treatment at the both ends of the sequences. However, since they affected all the sequences commonly, we simply ignored the influence.

Sequence $w_1$ was a simple sine wave and was the basic wave for generating other seven waves. Sequences $w_2$ and $w_3$ were generated by changing amplitude of $w_1$ to twice and half respectively. These two sequences and $w_1$ had inflection points at the same places and their corresponding subsequences had the same lengths, phases, and gradients. Thus we used these sequences for evaluation of contribution of rotation angles to representing difference on amplitude. Sequence $w_4$ was generated by adding $-0.5\pi$ delay to $w_1$ and used for evaluation of contribution of the phase term. Sequence $w_5$ and $w_6$ were generated by adding long-term increasing and decreasing trends to $w_1$ and thus were used for evaluating the contribution of the gradient term. Finally, sequences $w_7$ and $w_8$ were generated by exponentially changing amplitude of $w_1$. They were used for testing

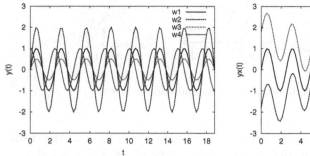

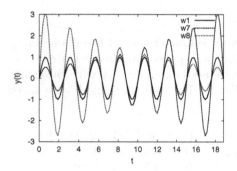

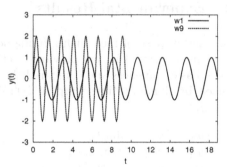

**Fig. 4.** Test sequences $w_1$–$w_4$.          **Fig. 5.** Test sequences $w_5$ and $w_6$.

**Fig. 6.** Test sequences $w_7$ and $w_8$.          **Fig. 7.** Test sequence $w_9$.

how the dissimilarity behaves for nonlinear change of amplitude. Sequence $w_9$ was generated by changing frequency and amplitude of $w_1$ to twice. It was used to test sensitivity to compression in time domain. Note that we did not directly evaluated the length term because it was hard to create a wave such that only length of a subsequence changes while preserving other factors. Figures 3-5 show each of the sequences from $w_1$ to $w_8$.

Tables 1 and 2 provide the dissimilarity matrices obtained by applying multiscale matching and DTW to each pairs of the nine sequences, respectively. In order to evaluate basic topological property of the dissimilarity, we here listed all elements in the matrix. From Table 1, it can be confirmed that the dissimilarity is non-negative ($d(w_i, w_j) \geq 0$), and satisfies both of reflectivity ($d(w_i, w_i) = 0$) and symmetry ($d(w_i, w_j) = d(w_j, w_i)$). These three properties are empirically known to be preserved for other types of data including real-life ones. However, triangular inequality is known to be violated in some cases, for example, when length of sequences are substantially different. Simply, two sine waves containing $n$ periods and $n + 1$ periods never matches. Therefore, if there is one sequence partly containing their harmonics and matches to each of them at higher scales, the triangular inequality will not be satisfied.

**Table 1.** Dissimilarity matrix produced by multiscale matching (normalized by the maximum value).

|       | $w_1$ | $w_2$ | $w_3$ | $w_4$ | $w_5$ | $w_6$ | $w_7$ | $w_8$ | $w_9$ |
|-------|-------|-------|-------|-------|-------|-------|-------|-------|-------|
| $w_1$ | 0.000 | 0.574 | 0.455 | 0.644 | 0.541 | 0.611 | 0.591 | 0.662 | 0.782 |
| $w_2$ | 0.574 | 0.000 | 0.774 | 0.749 | 0.736 | 0.675 | 0.641 | 0.575 | 0.451 |
| $w_3$ | 0.455 | 0.774 | 0.000 | 0.834 | 0.720 | 0.666 | 0.586 | 0.736 | 0.950 |
| $w_4$ | 0.644 | 0.749 | 0.834 | 0.000 | 0.816 | 0.698 | 0.799 | 0.635 | 0.745 |
| $w_5$ | 0.541 | 0.736 | 0.720 | 0.816 | 0.000 | 0.917 | 0.723 | 0.624 | 0.843 |
| $w_6$ | 0.611 | 0.675 | 0.666 | 0.698 | 0.917 | 0.000 | 0.624 | 0.726 | 0.806 |
| $w_7$ | 0.591 | 0.641 | 0.586 | 0.799 | 0.723 | 0.624 | 0.000 | 1.000 | 0.765 |
| $w_8$ | 0.662 | 0.575 | 0.736 | 0.635 | 0.624 | 0.726 | 1.000 | 0.000 | 0.683 |
| $w_9$ | 0.782 | 0.451 | 0.950 | 0.745 | 0.843 | 0.806 | 0.765 | 0.683 | 0.000 |

**Table 2.** Dissimilarity matrix produced by DTW (normalized by the maximum value).

|       | $w_1$ | $w_2$ | $w_3$ | $w_4$ | $w_5$ | $w_6$ | $w_7$ | $w_8$ | $w_9$ |
|-------|-------|-------|-------|-------|-------|-------|-------|-------|-------|
| $w_1$ | 0.000 | 0.268 | 0.134 | 0.030 | 0.399 | 0.400 | 0.187 | 0.187 | 0.164 |
| $w_2$ | 0.268 | 0.000 | 0.480 | 0.283 | 0.447 | 0.445 | 0.224 | 0.224 | 0.033 |
| $w_3$ | 0.134 | 0.480 | 0.000 | 0.146 | 0.470 | 0.472 | 0.307 | 0.307 | 0.268 |
| $w_4$ | 0.030 | 0.283 | 0.146 | 0.000 | 0.407 | 0.379 | 0.199 | 0.201 | 0.184 |
| $w_5$ | 0.399 | 0.447 | 0.470 | 0.407 | 0.000 | 1.000 | 0.384 | 0.477 | 0.264 |
| $w_6$ | 0.400 | 0.445 | 0.472 | 0.379 | 1.000 | 0.000 | 0.450 | 0.411 | 0.262 |
| $w_7$ | 0.187 | 0.224 | 0.307 | 0.199 | 0.384 | 0.450 | 0.000 | 0.372 | 0.151 |
| $w_8$ | 0.187 | 0.224 | 0.307 | 0.201 | 0.477 | 0.411 | 0.372 | 0.000 | 0.151 |
| $w_9$ | 0.164 | 0.033 | 0.268 | 0.184 | 0.264 | 0.262 | 0.151 | 0.151 | 0.000 |

Comparison of $w_2$ and $w_3$ with $w_1$ yielded $d(w_2, w_3) > d(w_1, w_2) > d(w_1, w_3)$, meaning that the large amplitude induced large dissimilarity. The order was the same as that of DTW. As mentioned above, these three sequences had completely the same factors except for rotation angle. Thus rotation angle successfully captured difference of amplitudes as that difference of shapes. Comparison of $w_4$ with $w_1$ showed that difference of phase was successfully translated to the dissimilarity. Taking $w_2$ and $w_3$ into account, one may argue that the order of dissimilarities does not follow the order of dissimilarities produced by DTW. We consider that this occurred because, due to phase shift, the shape of $w_4$ at the edge became different from those of $w_1$, $w_2$ and $w_3$. Therefore matching was performed accompanying replacement of segments at higher scale and thus cost for segment replacement might be added to the dissimilarity.

Comparison of $w_5$ and $w_6$ with $w_1$ yielded $d(w_5, w_6) >> d(w_1, w_6) > d(w_1, w_5)$. This represents that dissimilarity between $w_5$ and $w_6$ that have completely different trends was far larger than the dissimilarity to $w_1$ that has flat trend. Dissimilarities $d(w_1, w_5)$ and $d(w_1, w_6)$ were not the same due to the characteristics of the test sequences; since $w_5$ had increasing trends and first diverged towards the vertical origin, it reached to the first inflection points in shorter route than that in $w_6$. The order of dissimilarities was the same as that of DTW. Comparison of $w_7$ and $w_8$ with $w_1$ yielded $d(w_7, w_8) >> d(w_1, w_7) > d(w_1, w_8)$, meaning that difference on amplitude was accumulated and far larger dissimilarity was assigned to $d(w_7, w_8)$ than $d(w_1, w_7)$ or $d(w_1, w_8)$. Finally, comparison of $w_9$ with $w_1$ and $w_2$ yielded $d(w_1, w_9) >> d(w_1, w_2)$. This represents that the change of sharpness was captured as rotation angle. DTW produced quite small dissimilarities between $w_1$ and $w_9$ because of its one-to-many matching property.

## 4   Conclusions

In this paper we have reported the basic characteristics of the dissimilarity measure for multiscale matching that were empirically observed on the simple sine wave and its variants. Although experiments were performed under the very simplified condition, we could confirm that difference of amplitude of temporal sequences were successfully captured using rotation term, and that differences on phases and trends were also successfully reflected in the dissimilarity. However, it also revealed that their changes lack linearly compared with DTW. In the future we will make further optimization of the dissimilarity measure so that it naturally follows human perception.

**Acknowledgments.** This work was supported in part by the Grant-in-Aid for Scientific Research on Priority Area (B)(No.759) "Implementation of Active Mining in the Era of Information Flood" by the Ministry of Education, Culture, Science and Technology of Japan.

## References

1. E. Keogh (2001): Mining and Indexing Time Series Data. Tutorial at the 2001 IEEE International Conference on Data Mining.
2. S. Hirano and S. Tsumoto (2002): Mining Similar Temporal Patterns in Long Time-series Data and Its Application to Medicine. Proceedings of the IEEE 2002 International Conference on Data Mining: pp. 219–226.
3. F. Mokhtarian and A. K. Mackworth (1986): Scale-based Description and Recognition of planar Curves and Two Dimensional Shapes. IEEE Transactions on Pattern Analysis and Machine Intelligence, PAMI-8(1): 24-43
4. N. Ueda and S. Suzuki (1990): A Matching Algorithm of Deformed Planar Curves Using Multiscale Convex/Concave Structures. IEICE Transactions on Information and Systems, J73-D-II(7): 992–1000.
5. D. J. Berndt and J. Clifford (1994): Using dynamic time warping to find patterns in time series. Proceedings of AAAI Workshop on Knowledge Discovery in Databases: 359-370.

# First-Order Rules Mining Guided by Information Gain[*]

Xinwu Yang[1], Chunnian Liu[1], and Ning Zhong[2]

[1] Beijing Municipal Key Lab. of Multimedia and Intelligent Software Tech.
School of Computer Science, Beijing University of Technology, China
yang_xinwu@yahoo.com,
[2] Dept. of Information Eng., Maebashi Institute of Technology, Japan

**Abstract.** The key of using genetic algorithm to mine first-order rules is how to precisely evaluate the quality of first-order rules. By adopting the concept of binding and information theory, a new fitness function based on information gain is proposed. The new fitness function not only measures the quality of first-order rules precisely but also solves the equivalence class problem, which exists in the common evaluation criteria based on the number of examples covered by rules.

## 1 Introduction

The data mining methods based on first-order logic have gained more attention recently[1]. The task of mining first-order rules is essentially a combination optimization problem of condition atoms constructed by target predicate and background knowledge predicates. Genetic algorithm possesses global search ability and does not demand much future knowledge about the mined rules. Thus, using genetic algorithm as search strategy, the robustness and adaptability of the first-order rule mining algorithm will be enhanced. There are some initial exploring researches in this field[2,3].We have put forward GILP algorithm[4].

But the common evaluation criterion is based on the number of examples covered by rules[2,3], which does not distinguish the quality of equivalence rules. The equivalence class problem will badly reduce the search efficiency of algorithm and the readability of rules. Based on the concept of binding[5], a new fitness function based on information gain is proposed. By adequately utilizing the information hidden in examples and background knowledge, the new fitness function can distinguish the exact influence of the condition atoms of rules on the description of data feature and discriminate the quality of equivalence rules. An analysis and contrastive experiment demonstrate that the new fitness function can more effectively guide the search direction of algorithm and enhance search efficiency of algorithm and the readability of rules.

---

[*] This project is supported by the National Natural Science Foundation of China (60173014), and by the Municipal Natural Science Foundation of Beijing, China (4022003)

N. Zhong et al. (Eds.): ISMIS 2003, LNAI 2871, pp. 463–467, 2003.

# 2   Fitness Function Based on Information Gain

## 2.1   Information Gain

Before introducing the Information gain, we firstly induce the concept of binding[5]. A substitution $\theta=\{X_{p1}/t_{p1}, \ldots, X_{pn}/t_{pn}, X_{q1}/t_{q1} \ldots, X_{qm}/t_{qm}, X_{r1}/t_{r1}, \ldots, X_{ri}/t_{ri}\}$ maps all variables of rule R=$p(X_{p1},\ldots,X_{pn})$ :- $q(X_{q1},\ldots,X_{qm})$, ,.... $r(X_{r1},\ldots,X_{ri})$. into the constants in data.

**Definition 1** *If the condition of rule R is true under a substitution $\theta$, then the substitution $\theta$ is called as a binding of rule R. And if under the substitution $\theta$, the conclusion of rule R is true, i.e., there is corresponding positive examples in data, then the substitution $\theta$ is called as a positive binding of rule R, otherwise, it is called as a negative binding of rule R.*

The concept of binding considers various cases that the condition of rules is true, and can utilize thoroughly the information hidden in examples and background knowledge to quantify the influence of the condition atoms on description accuracy of data feature.

**Definition 2** *If all bindings of a rule are positive bindings, then the rule is a complete rule.*

A complete rule covers a subset of positive examples and rejects all negative examples. The purpose of mining first-order rules is to find out a set of complete rules, which together cover all positive examples and reject all negative examples.

But GILP adopts genetic algorithm not hill-climbing as its search strategy. The parent rules of sub-generation are not identity and the parent rules are not sole in crossover operation, so the evaluation criterion used by FOIL[5] is not applicable in GILP. GILP selects parent rules operated by crossover or mutation operator is according to the fitness of parent rules, which should only depend on the structures of parent rules, and since the heads of rules are identity, which should only depend on the structures of their conditions. Each of rules can be viewed as a rule obtained by adding the corresponding condition to the rule without condition. Thus, we can quantify the quality of rules according to the information gain of these rules over the rule without condition.

The condition part of the rule without condition is identically-true, its binding set is the set of examples. We use $T_0$ to represent the set of examples, and $T_0$ includes $T_0^+$ positive examples and $T_0^-$ negative examples. Similarly, $T_1$ represents the binding set of any rule $R_1$ with condition, and $T_1$ includes $T_1^+$ positive bindings and $T_1^-$ negative bindings . A positive binding of $T_1$ is corresponding to a positive example of $T_0$. For each example covered by rule $R_1$, rule $R_1$ has got the same amount of information gain. Thus, The total information gain of rule $R_1$ is: the number $T_0^s$ of positive examples covered by rule $R_1$ is multiplied by the information gain of rule $R_1$ over a single positive example.

$$Gain(R_1) = T_0^s \times (\log_2(T_1^+/(T_1^+ + T_1^-)) - \log_2(T_0^+/(T_0^+ + T_0^-))) . \quad (1)$$

GILP uses information gain shown in equation (1) as its fitness function.

## 2.2   The Information Gain of Equivalence Rules

Rule $R_r$ and rule R represent two equivalence rules in current rule population. Rule R is longer than rule $R_r$, i.e., rule R has more condition atoms. The number of the positive bindings and negative bindings of rule $R_r$ are represented with $P_1$ and $N_1$ respectively. Similarly, the ones of rule R are represented with $P_2$ and $N_2$. Rule R can be viewed as adding new condition atoms to rule $R_r$. New condition atoms induce more new variables, which will change the binding number of rule $R_r$. The variation ratios of positive and negative binding are respectively represented with $\delta$ and $\varepsilon$, i.e., $P_2 = P_1(1+\delta)$ and $N_2 = N_1(1+\varepsilon)$. For the equivalence rules in a same equivalence class, their $T_0^s$ are equal. According to the definition of information gain, the proportion variation of the positive bindings of equivalence rules can directly indicates the difference of their quality. The proportions of the positive bindings of rule $R_r$ and rule R are respectively:

$$\frac{P_1}{P_1+N_1} \quad , \qquad \frac{P_2}{N_2+P_2} = \frac{P_1(1+\delta)}{P_1(1+\delta)+N_1(1+\varepsilon)} \qquad (2)$$

The result of the former divided by the latter is

$$\frac{P_1(1+\delta)+N_1(1+\varepsilon)}{(1+\delta)(P_1+N_1)} \qquad (3)$$

After the numerator of the above formula plus and minus term $P_1 \cdot \varepsilon$ , and then eliminating the common factor $(P_1+N_1)$, the result is

$$\frac{1+\frac{P_1}{P_1+N_1} \cdot (\delta-\varepsilon)+\varepsilon}{1+\delta} \qquad (4)$$

The formula can be classified into three classes in terms of the relation of $\delta$ and $\varepsilon$:

(1) $\delta > \varepsilon$, that is the increase of the number of the positive bindings of rule R is more than the increase of its negative bindings,

$$\frac{1+\frac{P_1}{P_1+N_1} \cdot (\delta-\varepsilon)+\varepsilon}{1+\delta} < 1 \qquad (5)$$

In this case, the additional condition atoms of t rule R enhances its description accuracy. The information gain of rule R is greater than rule $R_r$.

(2) $\delta=\varepsilon$, that is the increase of the number of the positive bindings of rule R is equal to the increase of the number of its negative bindings,

$$\frac{1+\frac{P_1}{P_1+N_1} \cdot (\delta-\varepsilon)+\varepsilon}{1+\delta} = 1 \qquad (6)$$

In this case, the additional condition atoms of rule R does not change its description accuracy.The information gain of rule R is the same as rule $R_r$.

(3) $\delta < \varepsilon$, that is the increase of the number of positive bindings of rule R is fewer than the increase of its negative bindings,

$$\frac{1 + \frac{P_1}{P_1+N_1} \cdot (\delta - \varepsilon) + \varepsilon}{1 + \delta} > 1 \tag{7}$$

In this case, the additional condition atoms of rule R reduces its description accuracy. The information gain of rule R is lower than rule $R_r$.

Adding condition atoms to a rule has two purposes: a purpose is to increase the proportion of positive bindings to make the rule be close to the complete rule; another purpose is to induce the new variables needed in the complete rule. In the case shown in (1), additional condition atoms of rule R increase the proportion of its positive bindings, and make rule R be more close to the final complete rule. That meets the first purpose, and rule R should have higher fitness. In the case shown in (3), additional condition atoms of rule R reduce the proportion of its positive bindings and make rule R deviate from the final complete rule, so rule R should have lower fitness. In the case shown in (2), although the additional condition atoms of rule R don't increase the proportion of its positive bindings, they don't reduce the proportion. And they may induce the new variables needed in the final complete rule, so we should keep its fitness the same as the fitness of rule $R_r$, and make rule R compete with rule $R_r$ to ensure the necessity of the new variables.

## 3    A Simulation Experiment

The details of the coding, crossover and mutation operator of GILP algorithm are given in the reference[4]. Over the task of directional network[5],we test the fitness functions respectively based on the proportion of positive examples covered by rules and information gain of rules. The variation of the average length and the average fitness of population along to the evolution generation are respectively shown in Fig. 1 and Fig. 2. The two curves shown in Fig.1 represent respectively the variation of the average length along to the evolution generation under the above two fitness functions. The two curves shown in Fig.2 represent respectively the variation of the average fitness of population along to the evolution generation under the above two fitness functions.To compare, the fitness value of information gain is multiplied by a factor 0.1.

As shown in the figures, although the variation tendency of the average fitness of population are same under the two fitness function, the average length of population under information gain is lower than the one under the proportion of covered positive examples. The reason is that, under information gain, the effect of condition atoms of a rule is quantified precisely, which reduces the risk of the inherent tendency to longer equivalence rule of GILP algorithm. As using first logic as description language, when GILP compute the fitness of a rule, it will consider various combinations of rule variables taking data constants. The longer the average length of population is and the more combinations are. That increases the computing expense, and the expense will be multiplied by population size, which will reduce the search performance remarkably. Furthermore, the increase of rule length also increase the complexity of rule structure and

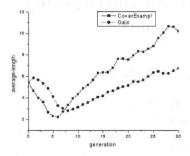

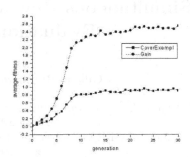

**Fig. 1.** The variety of individual average length

**Fig. 2.** The variety of individual average fitness

reduce the readability of rule. Thus, using information gain as fitness function will enhance the search performance of algorithm and the readability of rules.

## 4   Conclusions

A new fitness function based on information gain is proposed. By adequately utilizing the information hidden in examples and background knowledge, the new fitness function not only measures the quality of first-order rules precisely, but also it can discriminate the quality of equivalence rules. The analysis and a contrastive experiment demonstrate that the new fitness function can more effectively guide the search direction of algorithm and enhance search efficiency of algorithm and the readability of rules.

## References

1. Dzeroski S., LaVrac N.: Relation Data Mining, Springer-Verlag, Berlin Heidelberg New York (2001)
2. Po Shun Ngan, Man leung Wong, Kwong Sak Leung, Jack C. Y. Cheng: Using grammar based genetic programming for data mining of medical knowledge. In: Proc. of the Third Annual Genetic Programming Conference. (1998), 254-259.
3. Kkai, G.: GeLog - A System Combining Genetic Algorithm with Inductive Logic Programming. In Proc. of the International Conference on Computational Intelligence, LNCS 22062, (2001), 326-345
4. Yang Xinwu, Liu Chunnian: Bits string representation of rules in Design of inducing logic programs by genetic algorithm. Journal of Beijing Polytechnic university, Vol.27, No.3, (2001), 297-302
5. Quinlan, J. R. Learning logical definitions from relations. Machine Learning, Vol.5, (1990), 239-266

# Simultaneous Row and Column Partitioning: Evaluation of a Heuristic

Gilbert Ritschard[1] and Djamel A. Zighed[2]

[1] Dept of Econometrics, University of Geneva, CH-1211 Geneva 4, Switzerland
`ritschard@themes.unige.ch`
[2] Laboratoire ERIC, University of Lyon 2, C.P.11 F-69676 Bron Cedex, France
`zighed@univ-lyon2.fr`

**Abstract.** This paper is concerned with the determination, in a cross table, of the simultaneous merging of rows and columns that maximizes the association between the row and column variables. We present a heuristic, first introduced in [2], and discuss its reliability. The heuristic reduces drastically the complexity of the exhaustive scanning of all possible groupings. Reliability is assessed by means of a series of simulation runs. The outcomes reported show that though the quasi optima may often miss the true global optima, they provide very close solutions.

## 1 Introduction

When investigating the relationship between the row and column variables in a cross table, too much empty cells or cells with small frequencies may lead to unreliable results. The usual remedy consists in aggregating categories. This should be done carefully, however, since the merging of categories may affect the strength of the association. It is well known for instance that while merging identically distributed rows or columns does not affect the Pearson or Likelihood ratio Chi-squares, it increases generally the value of association measures as illustrated for instance by the simulations reported in [1].

In many settings, the objective is the maximization of the association. For example, in supervised learning we are interested in the best way of using the predictors to discriminate between the values of the response variable. Considering the table that crosses the response variable with the composite variable obtained by crossing all predictors, the problem may be expressed as the search of the simultaneous partitions of the rows and columns that maximize the association between the (row) response variable and the (column) composite predictor. Another example is social sciences, where researchers look for the grouping of the items of surveys that best demonstrates their hypotheses on the role of explanatory factors, the role of social origin on the type of family organization for instance. This paper focuses on this maximization of the association.

Grouping values of variables has to do with categorization and discretization. In this framework, the univariate approach that handles each variable independently has been abundantly studied. The main distinction is here between contextual and non contextual approaches. The former seeks the partitioning that

N. Zhong et al. (Eds.): ISMIS 2003, LNAI 2871, pp. 468–472, 2003.

maximizes a contextual criteria like the predictive power of a classifier. See for instance [4] for a survey.

The effect of the groupings on one variable upon the association with a second variable depends obviously on those made on the latter. It is then natural to consider a multidimensional approach that proceeds simultaneously to the aggregation of both variables. The literature about this multidimensional case is less rich.

Clearly, the exhaustive scanning of all combinations of partitions of each of the two variables is not practicable for large tables. We have thus proposed a heuristic algorithm in [2] that successively looks for the optimal grouping of two row or column categories. The effect of the merging of two categories on the most popular association measures has been examined analytically in [3]. The purpose of this paper is to empirically investigate the efficacy of the algorithm.

The formal framework and the heuristic are defined in Section2. Section 3 exhibits the outcomes of a series of simulation studies carried out to assess the reliability of the heuristic. Finally, Section 4 proposes some concluding remarks.

## 2    Formal Framework

Let $x$ and $y$ be two variables with respectively $r$ and $c$ different states. Crossing variable $x$ with $y$ generates a contingency table $\mathbf{T}_{r \times c}$ with $r$ rows and $c$ columns.

Let $\theta_{xy} = \theta(\mathbf{T}_{r \times c})$ denote a generic association criterion for table $\mathbf{T}_{r \times c}$. This criterion $\theta_{xy}$ may thus be the Cramer $v$ or Kendall $\tau_b$ for table $\mathbf{T}_{r \times c}$.

Let $P_x$ be a partition of the values of the row variable $x$, and $P_y$ a partition of the states of $y$. Each couple $(P_x, P_y)$ defines then a contingency table $\mathbf{T}(P_x, P_y)$. The optimization problem considered is then to find the couple $(P_x, P_y)$ of partitions that maximizes the association $\theta_{xy}$, i.e.

$$\arg \max_{P_x, P_y} \theta\big(\mathbf{T}(P_x, P_y)\big) \ . \tag{1}$$

For ordinal variables, hence for interval or ratio variables, only partitions obtained by merging adjacent categories make sense. The above program must then be restricted with the constraints $P_x \in \mathcal{A}_x$ and $P_y \in \mathcal{A}_y$ where $\mathcal{A}_x$ and $\mathcal{A}_y$ stand for the sets of partitions obtained by grouping adjacent values of $x$ and $y$. Finally, note that ordinal association measures may take negative values. Then, for maximizing the strength of the association, the objective function $\theta\big(\mathbf{T}(P_x, P_y)\big)$ should be the absolute value of the ordinal association measure.

**The Heuristic.** The heuristic, first introduced in [2], is an iterative process that successively merges the two rows or columns that most improve the association criteria $\theta(\mathbf{T})$. Formally, the configuration $(P_x^k, P_y^k)$ obtained at step $k$ is the solution of

$$
\begin{cases}
\arg\max_{P_x, P_y} \ \theta\big(\mathbf{T}(P_x, P_y)\big) \\[4pt]
\text{s.t. } P_x = P_x^{(k-1)} \text{ and } P_y \in \mathcal{P}_y^{(k-1)} \\[4pt]
\text{or} \\[4pt]
\quad\ P_x \in \mathcal{P}_x^{(k-1)} \text{ and } P_y = P_y^{(k-1)}
\end{cases}
\tag{2}
$$

where $\mathcal{P}_x^{(k-1)}$ stands for the set of partitions on $x$ resulting from the grouping of two classes of the partition $P_x^{(k-1)}$.

For ordinal variables, $\mathcal{P}_x^{(k-1)}$ and $\mathcal{P}_y^{(k-1)}$ should be replaced by the sets $\mathcal{A}_x^{(k-1)}$ and $\mathcal{A}_y^{(k-1)}$ of partitions resulting from the aggregation of two adjacent elements.

Starting with $\mathbf{T}^0 = \mathbf{T}_{r\times c}$ the table associated to the finest categories of variables $x$ and $y$, the algorithm successively determines the tables $\mathbf{T}^k, k = 1, 2, \ldots$ corresponding to the partitions solution of (2). The process continues while $\theta(\mathbf{T}^k) \geq \theta(\mathbf{T}^{(k-1)})$ and is stopped when the best grouping of two categories leads to a reduction of the criteria.

The *quasi-optimal grouping* is the couple $(P_x^k, P_y^k)$ solution of (2) at the step $k$ where $\theta\big(\mathbf{T}^{(k+1)}\big) - \theta\big(\mathbf{T}^k\big) < 0$   and   $\theta\big(\mathbf{T}^k\big) - \theta\big(\mathbf{T}^{(k-1)}\big) \geq 0$ . By convention, we set the value of the association criteria $\theta(\mathbf{T})$ to zero for any table with a single row or column. The algorithm then ends up with such a single value table, if and only if all rows (columns), are equivalently distributed.

The actual number of couples $(P_x, P_y)$ explored by the heuristic depends on when the stopping criterion is reached. Assuming $c \leq r$, the upper bound is in the nominal case, ,

$$
\sum_{i=2}^{c}\left[\binom{i}{2}+\binom{r}{2}\right] + \sum_{j=2}^{r}\binom{j}{2}+1 = \frac{r(r^2-1)+c(c^2-1)}{6} + \frac{(c-1)r(r-1)}{2}+1
$$

and reads for the ordinal case

$$
\frac{(r+c-1)(r+c-2)}{2}+1 \ .
$$

For $c = r = 10$, these bounds are respectively 736 and 172. These figures are dramatically less than the total number of partitions scanned by the exhaustive search which exceeds $1.3 \cdot 10^{10}$ in the nominal case and is 262144 for ordinal variables.

## 3   Reliability of the Heuristic

To assess the reliability of the results provided by the heuristic, we have run a series of simulation studies to investigate: i) the number of global optima missed by the heuristic and ii) how far the quasi-optimum provided by the heuristic is from the global one.

Several association measures have been examined. Due to space constraints, we report here only outcomes for the $t$ of Tschuprow. Among the measures

**Table 1.** Simulations: $t$ of Tschuprow

| Tschuprow | nominal | | | ordinal | | |
|---|---|---|---|---|---|---|
| Size | $4 \times 4$ | $5 \times 5$ | $6 \times 6$ | $4 \times 4$ | $5 \times 5$ | $6 \times 6$ |
| Non zero deviations | 39.5% | 62.5% | 74.5% | 23.5% | 36% | 46.5% |
| maximum | 0.073 | 0.074 | 0.077 | 0.077 | 0.063 | 0.108 |
| mean | 0.025 | 0.023 | 0.028 | 0.019 | 0.019 | 0.012 |
| standard deviation | 0.015 | 0.014 | 0.016 | 0.014 | 0.016 | 0.015 |
| skewness | 0.986 | 0.979 | 0.598 | 1.674 | 0.972 | 3.394 |
| With zero deviations | | | | | | |
| mean | 0.010 | 0.015 | 0.021 | 0.005 | 0.007 | 0.006 |
| standard deviation | 0.016 | 0.016 | 0.018 | 0.011 | 0.013 | 0.012 |
| skewness | 1.677 | 1.062 | 0.615 | 3.168 | 2.211 | 4.457 |
| Relative deviations | | | | | | |
| maximum | 0.168 | 0.198 | 0.221 | 0.179 | 0.194 | 0.307 |
| mean | 0.079 | 0.077 | 0.093 | 0.063 | 0.066 | 0.046 |
| Mean initial association | 0.260 | 0.240 | 0.226 | 0.263 | 0.244 | 0.228 |
| Mean global optimum | 0.340 | 0.316 | 0.303 | 0.301 | 0.275 | 0.250 |

considered the $t$ of Tschuprow provides the worse scores for both the number of missed optima and the deviations from the global optima.

The comparison between quasi and global optima is done for square tables of size 4, 5 and 6. Above 6, the global optimum can no longer be obtained in a reasonable time. We report in Table 1 results for the nominal case as well as for the ordinal case.

For each size and variable type, 200 contingency tables have been randomly generated. Each table was obtained by distributing 10000 cases among its $r \times c$ cells with a random uniform process. This differs from the solution used to generate the results given in [3], which were obtained by distributing the cases with nested conditional uniform distributions: first a random percentage of the cases is attributed to the first row, then a random percentage of the remaining cases is affected to the second row and so on until the last row; the total of each row is then likewise distributed among the columns. The solution retained here generates indeed tables that are closer to the uniform distribution and should therefore exhibit lower association. As will be shown, low association are the less favorable situations for the heuristic. Thus, we can expect the results obtained with this random uniform generating process to provide some upper bounds for the deviations from the global optima.

Table 1 exhibits, for each series of tables generated, the proportion of optima missed and characteristic values (maximum, mean value, standard deviation, skewness) of the distribution of the deviations between global and quasi optima. Relative deviations, of which the maximum and the mean value are reported, are the ratios between deviations and global optima. The last two rows give respectively the average of the initial values of the criterion and the mean value of the global optima.

Looking at Table 1, we see that the proportion of optima missed by the heuristic is relatively important and tends to increase with the size of the table. This high percentage of missed optima is luckily balanced by the small deviation between the quasi and global optima. The mean value of the non zero deviations is roughly less than half the difference between the initial value of the criterion and the global optimum. In the case of stronger initial associations than those generated here with a uniform random distribution, this ratio becomes largely more favorable, i.e. smaller. The level and dispersion of the non zero deviations seems to remain stable when the size of the table increases. These deviations tend naturally to be larger when the association measures provides larger values. Inversely, the relative deviations take larger values when the association measure tends to zero.

Globally, the outcomes of these simulation studies show that the cost in terms of reliability of the heuristic remains moderate when compared with the dramatic increase of performance.

## 4    Further Developments

The issue considered is the finding of the optimal way to merge row and column categories in a crosstable. We focused on the maximization of the association. Other criteria may obviously be considered and should be investigated. For instance, when the data collected in the table are a sample of a larger population, the association computed is an estimate and one should then also care about its standard error. Beside this aspect we are presently working on a strategy to find an optimal aggregation under some constraints. Indeed, following our introductory argument, the primary objective of the reduction of the size of the table is to avoid cells with low frequencies. Therefore, it is worth to be able to maximize for instance the association under a constraint on the minimal cell frequency. On the algorithmic side, we are working on a top-down divisive approach in which, starting from the completely aggregated table we would iteratively split rows or columns.

## References

1. Olszak, M., Ritschard, G.: The behaviour of nominal and ordinal partial association measures. *The Statistician* **44** (1995) 195–212
2. Ritschard, G., Nicoloyannis, N.: Aggregation and association in cross tables. In Zighed, Komorowski, Zytkow, eds.: *Principles of Data Mining and Knowledge Discovery.* Springer-Verlag, Berlin (2000) 593–598
3. Ritschard, G., Zighed, D.A., Nicoloyannis, N.: Maximisation de l'association par regroupement de lignes ou colonnes d'un tableau croisé. *Revue Mathématiques Sciences Humaines* **39** (2001) 81–97
4. Zighed, D.A., Rabaseda, S., Rakotomalala, R., Feschet, F.: Discretization methods in supervised learning. *Encyclopedia of Computer Science and Technology* **40** (1999) 35–50

# Partial Prefix Sum Method for Large Data Warehouses

Seok-Ju Chun

Department of Internet Information, Ansan College
752, Il-Dong, Sangrok-Ku, Ansan, Korea
chunsj@ansan.ac.kr

**Abstract.** A range-sum query computes aggregate information over a data cube in the query range specified by a user. Existing methods based on the prefix-sum approach use an additional cube called the prefix-sum cube (PC), to store the cumulative sums of data, causing a high space overhead. This space overhead not only leads to extra costs for storage devices, but also causes additional propagations of updates and longer access time on physical devices. In this paper, we propose a new cube called Partial Prefix-sum Cube (PPC) that drastically reduces the space of the PC in a large data warehouse. The PPC decreases the update propagation caused by the dependency between values in cells of the PC. We perform an extensive experiment with respect to various dimensions of the data cube and query sizes, and examine the effectiveness and performance of our proposed method. Experimental results show that the PPC drastically reduces the space requirements, while having reasonable query performances.

**Keywords:** Data cube, Data warehouses, OLAP, Range-sum query

## 1 Introduction

Data cubes are powerful tools to support the analysis the contents of data warehouses and databases. A data cube is constructed from a subset of attributes in the database. To build a data cube for a data warehouse, certain attributes are chosen to be measure attributes, i.e., the attributes whose values are of interest to an analyst. Other attributes are selected as dimensions or functional attributes. The measure attributes are aggregated according to the dimensions. The data cube is a data structure that enables a range-sum query that applies an aggregate operation to the measure attribute within the range of the query. Ho, et el. [4] have presented an elegant algorithm for computing range-sum queries in data cubes which we call the *prefix sum* (PS) method. In the PS method, a prefix-sum cube (PC) stores various precomputed prefix-sums of the data cube. Each cell of PC contains the sum of all cells up to and including itself in the data cube.

The PS method turned out to be very powerful. Range-sum queries were processed in constant time regardless of the size of the data cube. But, it is very expensive to maintain the PC when data elements in the cube are frequently changed. In worst case of the value of the first cell C[0,...,0] be changed, the total cells of the PC should be changed. In typical OLAP applications, the data are massive and commonly sparse,

N. Zhong et al. (Eds.): ISMIS 2003, LNAI 2871, pp. 473–477, 2003.

that is, number of nonzero cells in the data cube is much smaller than the total number of cells.

However, the PC is always dense since it stores the cumulative sums of data cube cells even though the data cube is sparse.

The PS method causes a severe storage overhead and also incurs an update propagation problem caused by the dependency between values in cells of the PC. Furthermore, the update propagation problem is amplified as the size of the data cube increases. In this paper, we present a new cube called *partial prefix-sum cube* (PPC) that stores large prefix-sums in a space-efficient manner. Based on dense intervals, we identify a set of dense sub-cubes with respect to a given density threshold. We build multiple PPCs, one for each sub-cube in the set. The PPC reduces drastically the space requirement.

# 2   Partial Prefix Sum (PPS) Method

## 2.1   Finding Dense Sub-cubes

Various clustering methods, such as [1,2,5,6,7], have been studied in database communities. However, finding dense sub-cubes should be handled in a way different from the existing clustering methods in the sense that the shapes of sub-cubes are confined to hyper-rectangles. Let $D = \{1, 2, \ldots, d\}$ denote the set of dimensions and $n_i$ denote the cardinality of dimension $i$. Then, we represent a $d$-dimensional data cube by $C[0{:}n_1{-}1, \ldots, 0{:}n_d{-}1]$. The sparse cube may have a number of dense regions and thus be represented by sub-cubes $SC[l_1{:}h_1,\ldots,l_d{:}h_d]$ where $l_i$ and $h_i$ are lower bound and upper bound, respectively, such that $0 \le l_i \le h_i \le n_i{-}1$. Then, the problem of finding sub-cubes is formalized as follows:

*Given:* A $d$-dimensional data cube C, the minimum number of cells *minCells* in a sub-cube, and the density thresholds $\delta_1$, $\delta_2$
*Target:* To find a set of dense sub-cubes that satisfies the predefined conditions

An input parameter $\delta_1$ is needed to determine the dense intervals in each dimension, while $\delta_2$ is used to control the merging and shrinking of produced sub-cubes. An input parameter *minCells* is needed to determine outliers. If a sub-cube has cells less than this value, the populated (non-empty) cells in the sub-cube are regarded as outliers. This value is of course heuristically determined depending on applications. A too small value of *minCells* makes unimportant sub-cubes be identified, degrading the memory utilization, while a too large value makes meaningful sub-cubes be missed.

The procedure for finding dense sub-cubes from a given data cube is as follows:

**Step 1.** In the first step, we mark populated cells in the data cube.
**Step 2.** Nextly, dense intervals in each dimension are identified by the projection of marked cells to a *one*-dimensional array of each dimension and the computation of the density. Based on the dense intervals, we build the initial sub-cubes. For each sub-cube built, dense intervals are identified and sub-cubes

are built again based on new dense intervals. This process is applied repeatedly until a sub-cube is dense enough.

**Step 3.** In the third step, candidate sub-cubes produced in the step 2 are refined with respect to the given density threshold. The sub-cubes that are closely placed may be merged together in the growing phase, while sparse surfaces of candidate sub-cubes are pruned from the cubes in the shrinking phase.

**Step 4.** We get a set of sound sub-cubes as a result of Step 3.

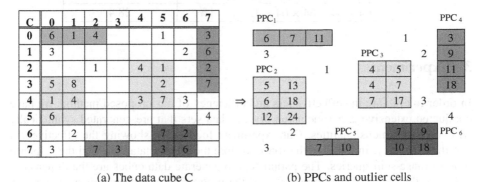

(a) The data cube C                (b) PPCs and outlier cells

**Fig. 1.** The basic concepts of the PPC

## 2.2  Constructing PPC from Dense Sub-cubes

In this section, we discuss the algorithm that builds PPCs from dense sub-cubes. The problem of computing a range-sum query in a $d$-dimensional data cube can be formulated as follows:

$$sum(l_1{:}h_1, l_2{:}h_2, \dots, l_d{:}h_d) = \sum_{i_1=l_1}^{h_1} \dots \sum_{i_d=l_d}^{h_d} C\,[i_1, \cdots, i_d]. \tag{1}$$

The range parameters $l_j$, $h_j$ for all $j \in D$ is specified by a user and typically not known in advance. We construct PPCs from dense sub-cubes found in Section 2.1.

We represent a $d$-dimensional PPC built from a sub-cube $SC[l_1{:}h_1, \dots, l_d{:}h_d]$ by $PPC[l_1{:}h_1, \dots, l_d{:}h_d]$. PPC will be used to store precomputed prefix-sums of a sub-cube. We will precompute, for all $0 \le l_j \le x_j \le h_j < n_j$ and $j \in D$,

$$PPC[x_1, x_2, \dots, x_d] = sum(l_1{:}x_1, l_2{:}x_2, \dots, l_d{:}x_d) = \sum_{i_1=l_1}^{x_1} \sum_{i_2=l_2}^{x_2} \dots \sum_{i_d=l_d}^{x_d} SC\,[i_1, \cdots, i_d]. \tag{2}$$

For example, we consider the sparse data cube shown in Fig. 1(a). Let six dense sub-cubes be identified in the process of finding dense sub-cubes. We can build six PPCs from six dense sub-cubes using Equation 1. Fig. 1(b) shows them ($PPC_1 \sim PPC_6$). Many outlier cells may remain in a data cube after having constructed PPCs. Outlier cells can be considered as multi-dimensional data. A traditional method to store multi-dimensional data is to use multi-dimensional arrays. Multi-dimensional arrays also are stored as chunks. A chunk is a block of data from the multi-dimensional array that contains data in all dimensions. Thus it is needed to store only the sparse portions of outlier cells. The simplest scheme to store sparse data is the index of a position in a multi-dimensional array together with data. We also use *index-value pairs* scheme in order to outlier cells. For more details on storing sparse data, refer to [3].

**Table 1.** Parameters used to generate sparse data cubes

| $d$ | $s$ | $p$ | avg. #sub-cubes |
|---|---|---|---|
| 3 | $512 \times 512 \times 512$ | 10% | 10.3 |
| 4 | $128 \times 128 \times 128 \times 128$ | 5% | 16.7 |
| 5 | $64 \times 64 \times 64 \times 64 \times 32$ | 1% | 28.4 |

## 3 Experiments

In order to evaluate the effectiveness and efficiency of our proposed method, we have conducted extensive experiments on diverse data sets that are generated synthetically with various dimensionalities. Our experiment focuses on showing the effectiveness and the efficiency, in terms of the space to store the sparse data cube and the response time to range-sum queries. The parameters to generate data cubes are the dimensionality ($d$), the size of a data cube ($s$), and the proportion of the number of non-empty cells to s ($p$). Table 1 shows parameters that are used to generate data cubes. The experiment was conducted for three dimensions ($d = 3,4,5$) for convenience, but our method does not restrict the dimensionality of data sets. For each dimension, we generated 10 data cubes, resulting in 30 data cubes. The average number of sub-cubes generated for each dimension is showed in Table 1.

For the evaluation of the query performance, we have used various queries with different sizes. The edge lengths of query rectangles are selected as 50%, 40%, 30%, 20%, and 10% of the corresponding dimension length of the data cube. We have generated 20 range queries for each size and for each data cube. The primary advantage of the proposed method is that it greatly reduces the storage to store the cubes. The total volume of sub-cubes produced by our method is generally much smaller than that of the PC, causing a remarkable storage reduction. Fig. 2 shows that the storage requirement for the PSS Method increases slowly as the dimensionality increases, while the PS Method increases with a steep slope. It means that the PPS method achieves a better performance for high dimensional data cube.

The query performance was measured by the number of the page I/Os accessed during the query processing in both the PS and PPS methods. We have executed 10 queries for each query size, each dimension, and each data cube and have taken the average of the query results. We examined the query performance of range-sum queries in the dimensionality of 3, 4, and 5 for various query sizes. The result showed that the PPS Method drastically reduces the space requirements, while having reasonable query performances.

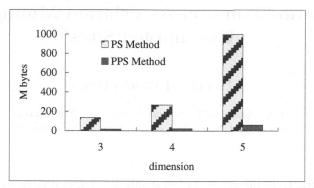

**Fig. 2.** Comparison of storage requirements between PS and PPS Method

# 4 Conclusion

In a real OLAP environment, analysts may want to explore the relationship among diverse attributes to find business trends and opportunities. A data cube for such analyses generally has a high dimensionality causing the data cube to be very sparse. This is the motivation that we proposed a new cube called *'Partial Prefix-sum Cube'* that drastically reduces the space of the PC in a large data warehouse. The PPC drasti cally reduces the space requirement for large data warehouses. We demonstrated the effect of the storage reduction for various sizes of the data cube and query sizes. Experimental results show that our method reduces almost 82 – 93% of the space of the PC while having a reasonable query performance.

# References

1. R. Agrawal, J. Gehrke, D. Gunopulos, and P. Raghavan: Automatic subspace clustering of high dimensional data for data mining applications. Proc. of ACM SIGMOD Conference (1998) 94–105
2. M. Ester, H. P. Kriegel, J. Sander, and X. Xu: A density-based algorithm for discovering clusters in large spatial databases with noise. Proc. of ACM SIGKDD Conference (1996) 226–231
3. S. Goil and A. Choudhary. BESS: Sparse data storage of multi-dimensional data for OLAP and data mining. Technical report, Northwestern University (1997)
4. C. Ho, R. Agrawal, N. Megido, R. Srikant: Range queries in OLAP Data Cubes. Proc. of ACM SIGMOD Conference (1997) 73–88
5. R. T. Ng and J. Han: Efficient and effective clustering methods for spatial data mining. Proc. of ACM VLDB Conference (1996) 144–155
6. S. Guha, R. Rastogi, and K. Shim, CURE: An efficient clustering algorithm for large databases. Proc. of ACM SIGMOD Conference (1998) 73–84
7. T. Zhang, R. Ramakrishnan, and M. Livny, BIRCH: An efficient data clustering method for very large databases. Proc. of ACM SIGMOD Conference (1996) 103–114 Appendix: Springer-Author Discount

# Spatio-Temporal Association Mining for Un-sampled Sites*

Dan Li and Jitender Deogun

Department of Computer Science and Engineering
University of Nebraska-Lincoln, Lincoln NE 68588-0115

**Abstract.** In this paper, we investigate interpolation methods that are suitable for discovering spatio-temporal association rules for unsampled points with an initial focus on drought risk management. For drought risk management, raw weather data is collected, converted to various indices, and then mined for association rules. To generate association rules for unsampled sites, interpolation methods can be applied at any stage of this data mining process. We develop and integrate three interpolation models into our association rule mining algorithm. The performance of these three models is experimentally evaluated comparing interpolated association rules with rules discovered from actual raw data.

## 1 Introduction

Nationally, drought events are the dominant cause of crop loss. We are in the process of developing a Geo-spatial Decision Support System (GDSS) that provides farmers and government agencies with critical ongoing information for drought risk management [1]. One of our project objectives is to discover interpretable patterns and rules associated with ocean parameters, atmospheric indices and climatic data. These rules capture the influence of ocean parameters (e.g, Multivariate ENSO Index (MEI)) upon climatic and drought indices (e.g, Standardized Precipitation Index (SPI), Palmer Drought Severity Index (PDSI)). Association rule mining, one of the most important Knowledge Discovery in Databases (KDD) techniques in data mining, is applied to meet our goal.

We collect raw weather data and oceanic indices from a variety of sources, e.g, precipitation and temperature data from High Plains Regional Climate Center (HPRCC), and the MEI from Climate Prediction Center. However, cost and technical considerations do not allow data to be sampled at all points in a region, therefore, spatial interpolation has been widely used in geographical information systems (GIS). It has the potential to find the functions that best represent the entire area. Such functions predict data values at unsampled points given a set of spatial data at sample points.

* This research was supported in part by NSF Digital Government Grant No. EIA-0091530, USDA RMA Grant NO. 02IE08310228, and NSF EPSCOR, Grant No. EPS-0091900.

N. Zhong et al. (Eds.): ISMIS 2003, LNAI 2871, pp. 478–485, 2003.

We develop three interpolation models to discover association rules for un-sampled sites. We apply Leave-One-Out (LOO) cross-validation to estimate errors generated by the interpolation models. The analysis and evaluation of the three proposed models is based on two quality metrics, *precision* and *recall*, and on the comparison of the interpolated rules with the rules discovered from actual data.

## 2  Spatio-Temporal Data Mining and Interpolation Concepts

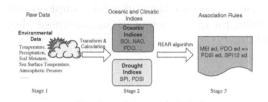

**Fig. 1.** A conceptual model of mining process.

A typical association rule has the form of $X \Rightarrow Y$, where $X$ is antecedent episode, $Y$ is the consequent episode, and $X \cap Y = \emptyset$. Here, an *episode* is a collection of events occurring close enough in time. In an earlier paper, we present *REAR* algorithm [1] which allows the user to efficiently discover user specified target episodes. Rules generated by the REAR demonstrate the importance and potential use of the spatio-temporal data mining algorithms in monitoring drought using the oceanic and atmospheric indices.

A conceptual model of the three-step data mining process is given in Figure 1. We use historical and current climatology data, including precipitation data, atmospheric pressure data, and sea surface temperatures collected at various weather stations around the world. Drought indices, e.g. SPI and PDSI, are calculated based on these raw datasets. The REAR algorithm is used to find relationships between the oceanic indices and the drought indices. These rules provide useful information for drought risk management and decision making.

To discover association rule for unsampled sites, we use two basic interpolation methods, IDW [3] and Kriging [4]. The IDW interpolation assumes that each input point has a local influence that diminishes with distance. In IDW the points closer to the unsampled point are assigned greater weight than those that are further away. The simplest form of IDW interpolation is defined as $F(x,y) = \sum_{i=1}^{n} w_i f_i(x_i, y_i)$, where $n$ is the number of sampled points in the data set, $w_i$ are weight functions assigned to each sample point, and $f_i(x_i, y_i)$ are the data values at each sample point with coordinate $(x_i, y_i)$. $(x,y)$ denote the coordinates of the interpolated (unsampled) points. The weight function is calculated as $w_i = h_i^{-p} / \sum_{j=1}^{n} h_j^{-p}$, where $p$ is the *power* parameter, and $h_i$ is the Euclidean distance from the sample point to the interpolated point. It may be noted that $p$ controls the significance of the surrounding points upon the interpolated value. Weight functions are normalized so that the sum of weights of all sample points equals 1, and the closer a sample points is to the interpolated point, the greater the weight is. In comparison to IDW, Kriging interpolation uses different kind of weight function that does not only depend on the distance but also on the geographic orientation of the sample point with respect to the interpolated node [4].

# 3   Interpolation Models for Un-sampled Sites

The interpolation can be applied to any one of the three stages in the spatio-temporal data mining process, as shown in Figure 1: (1) *Interpolate raw data.* The interpolated datasets become the "raw" datasets for unsampled sites. (2) *Interpolate climatic indices.* Raw data is processed into indices, and then the indices are interpolated to obtain the indices for unsampled points. (3) *Interpolate association rules.* We first discover association rules for sample points, then interpolate rules to discover rules for query points. Based on these ideas, we develop three interpolation models.

## 3.1   Pre-order Interpolation

The basic steps in the pre-order interpolation model are as: (1) *interpolate raw data*; (2) *calculate drought indices*; and (3) *mine data*. In the raw data interpolation process, we first apply basic IDW and Kriging interpolation methods to obtain the interpolated "raw" data sets for unsampled sites. In the basic IDW method, the weight functions merely depend on the distances between the interpolation point and a collection of sample points. In a geo-spatial system, however, we need to consider geographic or other properties that may influence the interpolated data value. For instance, in our GDSS project, we need to take climatic region information into consideration when we interpolate weather related datasets, because it is most likely that sites within the same climatic region share the similar climatic pattern [1]. To integrate such information into interpolation algorithms, we propose a new version of IDW method by modifying the weight functions. Higher weights are assigned to the sample points that are in the same climatic region as the interpolation point and lower weights to other points. We propose to change the distance functions as

$$h_i = \begin{cases} k \times h_i, & \text{if in the same climatic region;} \\ h_i, & \text{otherwise.} \end{cases} \qquad (1)$$

where $k$ $(0 < k \leq 1)$ is a constant that can be determined empirically.

After data is generated for unsampled sites by the pre-order interpolation model, we calculate climatic indices, e.g. 3-month SPI (SPI3) and PDSI, based on the specific time scale. After processing indices, the data is ready for knowledge discovery. In this paper, REAR association rule mining algorithm is applied to discover relationships between environmental and climatic parameters.

## 3.2   In-Order Interpolation

The difference between pre-order and in-order interpolation models is that we apply the interpolation to indices rather than raw data. That means the raw weather data for sampled sites is processed into climatic indices, and then these indices are taken as the input of the interpolation algorithms to get the indices for unsampled sites. For the interpolation of indices, we apply the same spatial interpolation methods, i.e. the basic IDW, the modified IDW and the Kriging.

---

*Input:* Two association rules $r1 : A1 \Rightarrow C1$ $(conf1)$, $r2 : A2 \Rightarrow C2$ $(conf2)$.
*Output:* An interpolated rule $r : A \Rightarrow C$ $(conf)$.
**Case 1:** $A1 = A2 = A$, $C1 \cap C2 = C \neq \emptyset$, then output $A \Rightarrow C$, $conf = IDW(conf1, conf2)$;
**Case 2:** $A1 = A2 = A$, $C1 \cap C2 = \emptyset$, but $clustering(C1) \cap clustering(C2) = C_G \neq \emptyset$, then let $C1'$ and $C2'$ be the subset of $C1$ and $C2$ such that $clustering(C1') = clustering(C2') = C_G$. Let $C = ROUND(IDW(C1', C2'))$, output $A \Rightarrow C$, $conf = IDW(conf1, conf2)$;
**Case 3:** $A1 \neq A2$, but $|A1| = |A2|$, $clustering(A1) = clustering(A2)$, and $C1 \cap C2 = C \neq \emptyset$, then let $A = ROUND(IDW(A1, A2))$, output $A \Rightarrow C$, $conf = IDW(conf1, conf2)$;
**Case 4:** $A1 \neq A2$, but $|A1| = |A2|$, $clustering(A1) = clustering(A2)$, and $C1 \cap C2 = \emptyset$, but $clustering(C1) \cap clustering(C2) = C_G \neq \emptyset$, then let $A = ROUND(IDW(A1, A2))$, let $C1'$ and $C2'$ be the subset of $C1$ and $C2$ such that $clustering(C1') = clustering(C2') = C_G$. Let $C = ROUND(IDW(C1', C2'))$. Output $A \Rightarrow C$, $conf = IDW(conf1, conf2)$;
**Case 5:** Otherwise, do nothing.

---

**Fig. 2.** Rule interpolation algorithm.

## 3.3 Post-order Interpolation

The guiding principle for the post-order interpolation is that the relationships between environmental and climatic indices for sites that are spatially close may be similar. We develop rule interpolation algorithms to interpolate rules from sampled sites to obtain association rules for unsampled sites.

Rule *clustering* is an important operation in rule interpolation. Suppose a rule or several similar rules occur at the surrounding sites, with high possibility, then this or a similar rule may occur at the interpolated site. We say rules are *similar* if they indicate the associations between the same indices. In a geo-spatial decision support system, it is reasonable to make such assumption because the effect of some indices on other indices can be similar within a certain geographical area. Thus, the purpose of clustering is to include the rules — which occur in two or more sample sites and reflect the relationships between the same indices, but may be in different drought-intensity categories, in the interpolated rule set.

The rule interpolation algorithm, shown in Figure 2, is divided into five cases. This algorithm shows how to interpolate two association rules which occur in two different sample sites. The five cases deal with different conditions of antecedent or consequent episodes in two rules. For example, in cases 2, 3, and 4, either we do not have exactly the same sets of antecedent episodes, or we have, but no common event in the consequent sets. In such cases, the clustering operation is needed to find out whether two rules have the same drought indices in the antecedent and consequent sets respectively. If so, that means the two rules reflect the relationships among some common indices, therefore, can be interpolated.

## 4    Quality Metrics

Cross-validation (CV) is a resampling method for evaluating the performance of data models [2]. In $k$-fold cross validation, the data set is divided into k subsets of (approximately) equal size. Leave-one-out (LOO) cross-validation is $k$-fold cross-validation taken to its logical extreme, with $k$ equal to $n$, the number of data points in the set. That means that $n$ separate times, the function approximator is trained on all the data except for one point and a prediction is made for that point. Since LOO cross-validation often works well for estimating errors for continuous error functions [6], in this paper, we use the Root Mean Squared Error (RMSE) to evaluate the overall performance of interpolation models. RMSE error analysis metric is defined as $RMSE = \sqrt{\sum_{i=1}^{n} |F_i - f_i|^2 / n}$, where $n$ is the total number of test points, $F_i$ are the interpolated data values, and $f_i$ are the actual data values.

Our objective is to investigate interpolation models that can discover as many association rules as possible, and as few non-actual rules as possible. We use two quality metrics, precision and recall [5]. *Precision* is defined as the percentage of actual rules correctly discovered among all discovered rules by an interpolation model. *Recall* is defined as the percentage of actual rules discovered by an interpolation model to the number of actual rules discovered with sample raw data sets. *Exact match* and *fuzzy match* are defined when we compare new rule sets with actual rule sets. Two rules are exact match if they have the same antecedent and consequent episodes. Two rules are fuzzy match if they are exact match after *clustering* operation. The consideration of fuzzy match gives the ability to discover more similarity between generated rules and actual rules at the cost of accuracy.

## 5    Experimental Results

To test our interpolation models, we conducted experiments on the weather datasets available for Nebraska, USA, from 1951 to 2000. We choose 98 weather stations as our training and testing data sources.

**Pre-order Interpolator.** For pre-order interpolator, the interpolation is conducted on raw precipitation data. Figure 3 shows the performance of this interpolator. In figure (a)-(d), the vertical or horizontal distance of each point from the 45-degree line provides the estimation error for the testing site at Omaha, NE from 1997 to 2000. Figure 3 (a) shows the effect of the power parameter; (b) shows the effect of the number of nearest neighbors; (c) shows the effect of the constant factor we added to the distance function; and (d) provides the comparison of three interpolation methods, i.e. basic IDW, modified IDW and-Kriging, in the pre-order interpolation model[1]. The figure leads to the following conclusions: (1) when $p = 3$ (from (a)) and $NeighborNumber = 10$ (from (b)), the IDW methods yield the best data values. (2) For the modified IDW method, when $k = 1/2$ (from (c)), the interpolation model shows the best interpolation

---

[1] The experiments are based on the following input parameters: for IDW method, we select 4 nearest neighbors for each interpolation point, power = 2; for modified IDW, k = 1/2; for Kriging, sill = 0.953, nugget = 0.049, and we choose general exponential variogram model and ordinary Kriging method.

results. (3) The modified IDW method improves the basic IDW method slightly, and the Kriging method outperforms the two IDW methods obviously (from (d)).

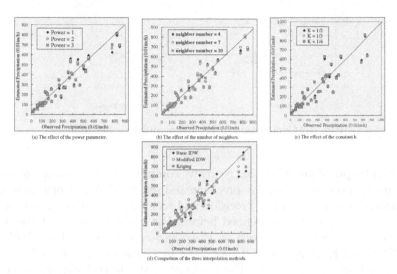

(a) The effect of the power parameter.    (b) The effect of the number of neighbors.    (c) The effect of the constant k.

(d) Comparison of the three interpolation methods.

**Fig. 3.** Pre-order Interpolation.

Table 1 presents the overall statistical analysis of the performance of the three basic methods in the pre-order model. The experiment is based on the average RMSE values over all 98 testing stations for all available datasets. We can see that the Kriging method outperforms the other two methods, and the input parameters for IDWs affect the performance of data models slightly different as we previously described.

**Table 1.** RMSE in Pre-order Interpolation.

| Basic IDW | | | | Modified IDW | | Kriging |
|---|---|---|---|---|---|---|
| $n = 4$ | | $p = 2$ | | $p = 2$, $n = 4$ | | |
| $p = 1$ | 0.96 | $n = 4$ | 0.92 | $k = 1/2$ | 0.92 | 0.58 |
| $p = 2$ | 0.92 | $n = 7$ | 0.92 | $k = 1/3$ | 0.94 | |
| $p = 3$ | 0.90 | $n = 10$ | 0.91 | $k = 1/4$ | 0.95 | |

**Pre-order vs. In-Order Interpolators.** Although the pre-order and the in-order interpolation models work on different input data sets, they can be compared by transforming the interpolated data sets produced by the pre-order model into drought related indices. Figure 4 shows the RMSE of two year's monthly SPI3 produced by these two models with basic IDW and Kriging methods for all testing stations. From the Figure, the Kriging method in pre-order interpolation model presents better quality than the basic IDW approach.

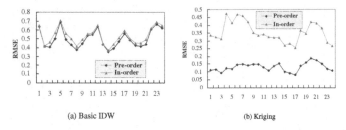

(a) Basic IDW                    (b) Kriging

**Fig. 4.** Comparison of pre-order and in-order models.

**Three Interpolation Models.** Next, we compare all three interpolation models by using two quality metrics, precision and recall. REAR algorithm is applied to generate association rules. Precision and recall are calculated based on exact match and fuzzy match as defined before. For the pre-order and the in-order interpolation approaches, we test on three basic methods, i.e. basic IDW, modified IDW and Kriging. Table 2 shows the precision and recall with respect to exact match and fuzzy match. The modified IDW method slightly outperforms the basic IDW method no matter which interpolation model is considered, and the pre-order model presents better performance than the in-order model considering both IDWs and Kriging methods. Overall, the Kriging method in the pre-order model provides the highest recall, while the post-order interpolation model provides the highest precision. The performance of the post-order interpolator is weakened due to the intersection operation in the rule interpolate algorithm.

**Table 2.** Comparison of the three interpolation models.

|  | Exact Match | | Fuzzy Match | | Comments |
|---|---|---|---|---|---|
|  | precision | recall | precision | recall |  |
| Pre-IDW | 0.48 | 0.48 | 0.62 | 0.62 |  |
| Pre-Mod-IDW | 0.48 | 0.51 | 0.62 | 0.64 |  |
| Pre-Krig | 0.43 | 0.62 | 0.53 | 0.8 | highest recall |
| In-IDW | 0.23 | 0.3 | 0.39 | 0.59 |  |
| In-Mod-IDW | 0.28 | 0.31 | 0.39 | 0.6 |  |
| In-Krig | 0.36 | 0.47 | 0.47 | 0.71 |  |
| Post | 0.53 | 0.27 | 0.69 | 0.35 | highest precision |

# 6    Conclusion

In this paper, we focus on enhancing data mining techniques in the context of Geo-spatial Decision Support System (GDSS) [1] by integrating spatial interpolation techniques into the KDD process. For spatio-temporal data mining in our GDSS, datasets are collected from a variety of sources. However, it is not feasible to collect data for all sites that users are interested in. To find association rules for unsampled sites, we integrate three interpolation models into data mining algorithms. IDW and Kriging methods are applied to interpolate observed datasets. To obtain more accuracy, we modify the weight function in basic IDW to accommodate some geographic features. We compare the pre-order interpolation method with the in-order interpolation method through error analysis based on Leave-one-out cross-validation. Precision and recall are considered as two quality metrics to test accuracy of the generated rules. Based on our experiments, we discovered that the Kriging method outperforms the IDW method in both pre-order and in-order models, and the modified IDW performs slightly better than the the basic IDW in these two models. Overall, the post-order interpolation model provides the highest precision among the three models, and the Kriging method in the pre-order interpolation model presents the highest recall.

# References

1. S. Harms, D. Li, J. Deogun, and T. Tadesse. Efficient rule discovery in a geo-spatial desicion support system. In *Proceedings of the 2002 National Conference on Digital Government Research*, pages 235–241, Los Angeles, California, USA, May 2002.
2. Ron Kohavi. A study of cross-validation and bootstrap for accuracy estimation and model selection. In *IJCAI*, pages 1137–1145, 1995.
3. N. Lam. Spatial interpolation methods: A review. *The American Cartographer*, 10(2):129–149, October 1983.
4. M. Oliver and R. Webster. Kriging: a method of interpolation for geographical information system. *INT. J. Geographical Information Systems*, 4(3):313–332, 1990.
5. V.V. Raghavan, G.S. Jung, and P. Bollman. A critical investigation of recall and precision as measures of retrieval system performance. *ACM Transactions on Information Systems*, 7(3):205–229, July 1989.
6. J. Shao. Linear model selection by cross-validation. *Journal of the American Statistical Association*, 88(422):486–494, 1993.

# Development of Generic Search Method Based on Transformation Invariance

Fuminori Adachi[1], Takashi Washio[1], Hiroshi Motoda[1], Atsushi Fujimoto[1], and
Hidemitsu Hanafusa[2]

[1] ISIR, Osaka University,
{adachi, wasahio, motoda, fujimoto}@ar.sanken.osaka-u.ac.jp
[2] INSS Inc., hanafusa@inss.co.jp

**Abstract.** The needs of efficient and flexible information retrieval on
multi-structural data stored in database and network are significantly
growing. Most of the existing approaches is designed for a particular
content and data structure, e.g., natural text and relational database.
We propose a generic information retrieval method directly applicable
to various types of contents and data structures. The power of this approach comes from the use of a generic and invariant feature information obtained from byte patterns in the files through some mathematical
transformation. The experimental evaluation of the proposed approach
for both artificial and real data indicates its high feasibility.

## 1 Introduction

The recent progress of information technology increases the mutiformity of the
data structure in addition to their amount of quantity accumulated in the
database and the network. The flexible information retrieval on multi-structured
data is crucial to acquire relevant information for users. However, the state of
the art remains within the retrieval for each specific data structure, e.g., natural text, relational data and sequential data [1,2,3]. Accordingly, the retrieval
on mixed structured data such as multimedia data containing documents, pictures and sounds requires the combined use of the retrieval mechanisms [4,5].
Because of this nature, the current approach necessarily increases the developmental and maintenance cost of the retrieval system. To alleviate this difficulty,
we propose a novel retrieval approach that uses the most basic nature of the
data representation. All real world data are represented by the sequence of bits
or bytes. Accordingly, a generic retrieval method is established if a set of data
which is similar on this basic representation can be appropriately searched. The
main issue is the definition of the similarity in the low level representation which
appropriately reflects the similarity at the content level. Though the perfect
correspondence is hard to attain, the followings operation and assumption are
thought reasonable to enhance the feasibility.

1) Search is made for commonly seen byte sequences in approximately similar
   order and length.

N. Zhong et al. (Eds.): ISMIS 2003, LNAI 2871, pp. 486–495, 2003.
© Springer-Verlag Berlin Heidelberg 2003

2) Similarity is not significantly affected by the location of the patterns in the byte sequences.
3) Similarity is not significantly affected by the noise and the slight difference in the byte sequences.
4) Similarity of the entire files is evaluated by the frequency of the similar byte sequences shared among the files.
5) Similar byte sequences shared by most of the files can be removed as they do not characterize the specific similarity.

The last point has also been addressed by the idea of TFIDF (Term Frequency Inversed Document Frequency) [6] and the idea of "Stop List" [7]. In this work, a generic method to retrieve similar files in terms of the byte sequences is studied. A certain mathematical transformation on the byte sequences is used by treating each byte as a numeral. This can extract invariant properties of the sequences from which the relevant files can be retrieved. The basic performance of the proposed approach is evaluated through numerical experiments and a realistic application to the retrieval of raw binary format data of a word processor.

## 2 Principle of Similarity Judgment and Its Preliminary Study

The aforementioned point (1) is easily achieved by the direct comparison among byte sequences. However, the point (2) requires a type of comparison among sequences that is invariant against the shit of the sequences. If the direct pair wise comparison between all subsequences is applied, the computational complexity is $O(n_1^2 n_2^2)$ where $n_1$ and $n_2$ are the numbers of bytes in the two sequences. To avoid this high complexity, our approach applies a mathematical transformation to the byte sequence in each file. The transformation has the property of "shift invariance". To address the point (3), the result of the transformation should be quite robust against the noise and slight difference in the sequence. One of the representative mathematical transformation to suffice these requirements is the Fast Fourier Transform (FFT) [8]. It requires only computation time of $O(n \log n)$ in theory when the length of the byte sequence is $n$, and a number of methods for practical implementation are available. In addition, the resultant coefficients can be compressed into half of the original if only their absolute values are retained. However, when the transformation is applied to very long sequences or sub-sequences contained in a large file where each part of the file indicates a specific meaning, the characteristics of the local byte sequence reflecting the meaning in the contents level will be mixed with the characteristics of the other local part. Accordingly, we partition the byte sequence in a file into an appropriate length, and apply the FFT to each part to derive a feature vector consisting the absolute values of the Fourier coefficients.

The feasibility and the characteristics of the proposed method have been assessed though some numerical experiments on some pieces of byte sequences. In the experiment, the length of each byte sequence is chosen to be 8 bytes because it is the length of byte sequences to represent a word in various languages. A number 128 is subtracted from the value of each byte to eliminate the bias of the FTT coefficient of order 0, while each byte takes an integer value in the range of [0, 255]. First, we shift the byte sequences to the left randomly, and the bytes out of the edge are pushed back in the right in the same order. Thus, the byte sequences are shifted in circular manners. Because of the mathematical nature of FFT, i.e., shift invariance, we observed that this did not cause any change on the absolute value of the transformed coefficients. Next, the effect of the random replacement of some bytes is evaluated. Table 1 exemplifies the effects of the replacement in a basic sequence "26dy10mo" on the absolute coefficients. The distance in the table represents the Hamming distance, i.e., the number of the different bytes from the original. The absolute coefficients from f5 to f8 are omitted due to the symmetry of Fourier Transform. In general, only $n/2 + 1$ coefficients for an even number $n$ and $(n+1)/2$ for an odd number $n$ are retained. The numbers of the absolute coefficients are quite similar within the Hamming distance 2 in many cases. However, they can be different to some extent even in the case of distance 2 such as "(LF)5dy10mo" where the value of "(LF)" is quite different from that of "2". Accordingly, some counter measure to absorb this type of change or noise in the similarity judgment must be introduced.

If the absolute coefficients are discretized in an appropriate manner, the slight differences of the coefficient vales do not affect the similarity judgment of the byte sequence. An important issue is the criterion to define the

**Table 1.** Effect of byte replacements on FFT coefficients

| Sequences | f0 | f1 | f2 | f3 | f4 | Distance |
|-----------|----|----|----|----|----|----------|
| 26dy10mo | 144 | 112.9 | 345.6 | 103.8 | 108 | 0 |
| 20dy10mo | 150 | 112.4 | 350.7 | 103.9 | 102 | 1 |
| 19dy10mo | 142 | 113.8 | 343.6 | 103.1 | 112 | 2 |
| (LF)5dy10mo | 174 | 89.9 | 361.2 | 136.2 | 156 | 2 |
| (LF)5dy11mo | 178 | 86.6 | 364.4 | 137.3 | 152 | 3 |
| (LF)5dy09mo | 180 | 88.6 | 365.8 | 136.8 | 152 | 4 |

threshold values for the discretization. A reasonable and efficient way to define the thresholds of the absolute coefficients for arbitrary sequences is that the absolute coefficient obtained from a randomly chosen sequence falls into an interval under an identical probability. To define the thresholds of the absolute coefficient in every order for a certain length of byte sequences, i.e., the length $n$, we calculated the absolute coefficient value distribution for all $2^{8n}$ byte sequences for every order. This computation is not tractable. However in practice, this is quite easily achieved by using the symmetric and invariant characteristics of the absolute values of the FFT coefficients on various sequence patterns. Using these characteristics of the absolute FFT coefficients, the space of the sequences consisting of 8 bytes to be assessed for the derivation of the exact absolute coefficient value distributions is significantly reduced, and the distributions are obtained in a few hours computation. Upon the obtained absolute coefficient distribution for every order, $(m-1)$ threshold values are defined for every order where every interval covers the identical probability $1/m$ in the appearance of a coefficient. We tested various number $m$, and chose the value $m = 16$ empirically which is sufficient to characterize the similarity of the byte sequence in generic means. Through this process, the information of a FFT coefficient for every order is compressed into 16 labels. In summary, a feature vector consisting of $n/2 + 1$ or $(n + 1)/2$ elements for an even or odd number $n$ is derived where each element is one of the 16 labels.

Moreover, the moving window of a fixed length byte sequence is applied to generate a set of feature vectors for a file as depicted in Fig. 1. First, a feature vector of the byte sequence of a length $n(=8)$ at the beginning of the file is calculated. Then another feature vector of the sequence having the same length $n$ but shifted with one byte toward the end of the file is calculated. This procedure is repeated until the feature vector of the last sequence at the end of the file is obtained. This approach also enhances the robustness of the similarity judgment among files. For example, the feature vectors of the first 8 bytes windows of "26dy10mo02yr" and "(LF)5dy10mo02yr" are quite different as shown in Table 1. However, the feature vectors for the 8 bytes windows shifted by one byte, i.e., "6dy10mn0" and "5dy10mn0", are very similar. Furthermore, the vectors for the windows shifted by two bytes become identical because both byte sequences are "dy10mo02". This moving window approach enhances the performance of the frequency counting of the parts having similar patterns among files. Thus, the point (4) mentioned in the first section is addressed where the similarity of the entire files is evaluated by the frequency of the similar byte sequences shared among the files. To address the point (5), the feature vectors obtained from a given set of files more than a certain frequency threshold are registered as "Unusable Vectors", and such unusable vectors are not used in the stage of the file retrieval.

## 3   Fast Algorithm of Retrieval

The data structure to store the feature vectors for given vast number of files must be well organized to perform an efficient file retrieval based on the similarity of the byte sequences. The approach taken in this work is the "inversed file indexing" method which is popular and known to be the most efficient in terms of retrieval time [3,9]. Through the procedure described in the former section, the corre-

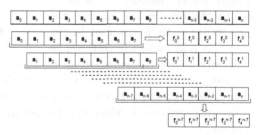

**Fig. 1.** FFT on moving windows

spondence from each file to a set of feature vectors derived from the file is obtained. Based on this information, the inversed indexing from each feature vector to a set of files which produced the vector is derived. The data containing this inversed indexing information is called "inversed indexing data". By using the inversed correspondence in this data, all files containing patterns which are similar with a given feature vector are enumerated efficiently.

Figure 2 outlines our retrieval approach. The path represented by solid arrows is the aforementioned preprocessing. The "Data Extraction" part applies the moving window extraction of byte sequences to each file in a given set of data files. The extracted byte sequences are transformed by FFT in the "Mathematical Transformation" part. The "Vector Discretization" part discretizes the resulted coefficients by the given thresholds, and the feature vectors are generated. The "Vector Summarization" part produces the correspondence data from each file to feature vectors while removing the redundant feature vectors among the vectors derived from each file. Finally, the "Inversed Indexing" part derives the inverse correspondence data from each feature vector to files together with the "Unusable Vectors List".

The file retrieval is conducted along the path represented by the dashed arrows. A key file for the retrieval is given to the "Data Extraction" part, and the identical information processing from "Data Extraction" to "Vector Summarization" derives the set of the feature vectors of the key file. Subsequently, the unusable vectors are removed from the set in the "Unusable Vectors Removal" part. Finally, the files corresponding to the feature vectors in the set are enumerated based on the inverse correspondence data in the "Vector Matching" part. First, the "frequency" of the complete match of every feature vector in the set to the one in the inverse corresponding data is counted in this part. Then to focus the retrieval result only on files having strong relevance with the key file, the total sum of the frequencies of all feature vectors in the set are calculated. If the total frequency is less than a given "frequency threshold value", the file is not retained in the retrieval result. Moreover, the result is sorted in the order of the matching frequency.

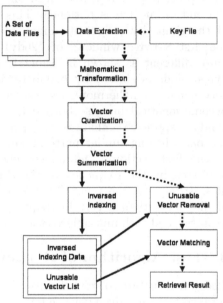

**Fig. 2.** Outline of retrieval system

## 4    Basic Performance Evaluation

A program based on the proposed method has been implemented, and its basic performance was evaluated by using artificial data sets. The specification of the computer used in this experiment is CPU: AMD Athlon 1400MHz, RAM: PC2100 DDRSDRAM 348MB, HDD: Seagate ST340824A and OS: LASER5 Linux 7.1. 500 files having the normal distribution in their sizes were generated.

Their average size is 30KB and the standard deviation 10KB. Once the size of a file is determined, the byte data in the file were generated by using the uniform random distribution. In the next stage, 5 specific sequences in the length of 16 bytes, which were labeled as No.1 to No.5, were embedded in each file. They were embedded not to overlap, and moreover it is verified that there is no sequences that are same with these 5 sequences in the random generation of the byte data. The moving window size of 8 bytes, the 16 level of discretization of the FFT coefficients for each order and 70% for the threshold frequency to determine the unusable vector are set for the generation of the feature vectors.

The performance indices used in the experiment is the precision and the recall. In ideal situation, both values are close to 1. However, they have a trade off relation in general. Table 2 shows the performance of the retrieval by the key file consisting of the sequence No.1. The thresholds in the table are the frequency threshold values to evaluate the similarity of the files in the "Vector Matching" part in Fig.2.

**Table 2.** Retrieval by key file No.1

| Seq. No. | Thres. | Retrieved Files | Correct Files | Precision | Recall | Comp. Time |
|---|---|---|---|---|---|---|
| 1 | 1.0 | 250 | 250 | 1.00 | 1.00 | 1.6 |
| | 0.25 | 261 | 250 | 0.96 | 1.00 | |
| | 0.125 | 344 | 250 | 0.73 | 1.00 | |

When threshold values are high, only highly similar files are retained. The sequence No.1 is embedded in the 250 files in the 500 test files. This is reflected in the result of the threshold equal to 1.0, i.e., the key file consisting of the sequence No.1 is certainly included in these files as a subsequence. For lower values of the threshold, some files containing subsequence that are similar to the sequence No.1 are also retrieved. Thus, the precision decreases. In this regard, our proposing approach has a characteristic to retrieve a specified key pattern similarly to the conventional keyword retrieval when the threshold is high.

**Table 3.** Retrieval by shifted key file No.1

(a) Result by proposed method using FFT

| Seq. No. | Thres. | Retrieved Files | Correct Files | Precision | Recall | Comp. Time |
|---|---|---|---|---|---|---|
| 1 | 0.66 | 2 | 2 | 1.00 | 0.01 | 0.7 |
| | 0.55 | 37 | 37 | 1.00 | 0.15 | |
| | 0.44 | 250 | 250 | 1.00 | 1.00 | |
| | 0.33 | 252 | 250 | 0.99 | 1.00 | |
| | 0.22 | 266 | 250 | 0.94 | 1.00 | |
| | 0.11 | 326 | 250 | 0.77 | 1.00 | |

(b) Result by conventional keyword matching

| Seq. No. | Thres. | Retrieved Files | Correct Files | Precision | Recall | Comp. Time |
|---|---|---|---|---|---|---|
| 1 | - | 0 | 0 | 0.00 | 0.00 | 0.5 |

Table 3 (a) shows the result of the retrieval where the key sequence No.1 is shifted randomly in circular manner. Because the lengths of the embedded sequences and the key sequence are 16 bytes, but that of the moving window for FFT is only 8 bytes, the FFT coefficients do not remain identical even under its shift invariance characteristics. Accordingly, the feature vectors of the key sequence do not completely match with those of the embedded sequences. However, the coefficients of FFT reflects their partial similarity to some extent, and thus the excellent combination of the values of the precision and the recall is obtained under the frequency threshold values around [0.2, 0.4]. Similar results were obtained in case of the other key sequences. In contrast, when we applied the conventional retrieval approach based on the direct matching without using the FFT to derive the feature vectors, very low values of the precision and the recall were obtained as shown in Table 3 (b). Table 4 represents the results for noisy data. 2 bytes are randomly chosen in each original 16 bytes sequence, and they are replaced by random numbers. Similarly to the former experiment, the excellent combination of the precision and the recall was obtained for most of the key sequences under the threshold value of [0.3, 0.5]. If the distortion on the embedded sequences by the replacement becomes larger, i.e., the increase of the number of bytes to be replaced, the values of precision and the recall decreases.

But, the sufficient robustness of the proposed retrieval approach under the random replacement of 3 or 4 bytes in the 16 bytes sequence has been confirmed through the experiments.

The computation time to finish a retrieval for a given key file is around 1 second due to the efficient inverse indexing approach. Thus, the proposed method is thought to be practical enough for this scale of problems. In short summary, the basic function of our approach subsumes the function of the conventional retrieval approach, because the retrieval equivalent to the conventional retrieval is performed by setting the frequency threshold value at a high value as shown in Table 2. Moreover, this approach can retrieve files having some generic similarity.

**Table 4.** Retrieval on Noisy Data

| Seq. No. | Thres. | Retrieved Files | Correct Files | Precision | Recall | Comp. Time |
|------|--------|-----------------|---------------|-----------|--------|------------|
| 1 | 0.33 | 3 | 2 | 0.67 | 0.01 | 0.9 |
|   | 0.22 | 27 | 18 | 0.67 | 0.07 |   |
|   | 0.11 | 159 | 92 | 0.59 | 0.37 |   |
| 2 | 0.77 | 1 | 1 | 1.00 | 0.01 | 1.2 |
|   | 0.66 | 15 | 15 | 1.00 | 0.04 |   |
|   | 0.55 | 125 | 125 | 1.00 | 1.00 |   |
|   | 0.22 | 140 | 125 | 0.89 | 1.00 |   |
|   | 0.11 | 203 | 125 | 0.62 | 1.00 |   |
| 3 | 0.625 | 1 | 1 | 1.00 | 0.01 | 1.0 |
|   | 0.500 | 3 | 3 | 1.00 | 0.03 |   |
|   | 0.375 | 631 | 28 | 0.90 | 0.28 |   |
|   | 0.250 | 120 | 100 | 0.83 | 1.00 |   |
|   | 0.125 | 229 | 100 | 0.44 | 1.00 |   |
| 4 | 0.375 | 1 | 1 | 1.00 | 0.02 | 1.1 |
|   | 0.250 | 38 | 14 | 0.37 | 0.28 |   |
|   | 0.125 | 178 | 50 | 0.28 | 1.00 |   |
| 5 | 0.66 | 3 | 3 | 1.00 | 0.12 | 1.2 |
|   | 0.55 | 25 | 25 | 1.00 | 1.00 |   |
|   | 0.22 | 34 | 25 | 0.74 | 1.00 |   |
|   | 0.11 | 127 | 25 | 0.20 | 1.00 |   |

## 5    Evaluation on Semi-real-World Word Processor Files

The practical performance of our proposed method is evaluated by using real world data. The data is a set of 2253 word processor files having Microsoft Word doc format. The average size of a file is around 20KB. Each contains a text document consisting of 600 characters coded in a specific binary format. Accordingly, the conventional text keyword retrieval is not applicable to this retrieval problem. To evaluate the ability to retrieve similar content files within our proposing approach, the raw Microsoft Word data are numbered from No.1 to No. 2253, and they are processed to have stronger similarity in terms of contents when the number labels of the files are closer. Initially, a seed file is selected from the original set of word processor files and numbered as No.1. Then, another file $X$ is randomly chosen from the raw file set, and a sequence consisting 16 characters is selected from the file. Then, a randomly chosen part consisting of 16 characters sequence in the original file No.1 is overwritten by the sequence selected from the file $X$, and the new file is numbered as No.2. Starting from this stage, a part of 16 characters randomly chosen in the file No. $n$ is overwritten by the sequence of 16 characters selected from another randomly chosen file $X$, and the new file is numbered as No. $n+1$. This process is repeated 2253 times to gradually and randomly change the original seed file and newly generate similar files. As a result, 2253 files in total are generated where the files having close number labels have some similarity.

Based on this semi-real world data, the inversed indexing data and unusable vector list are generated in the preprocessing stage of our approach. Subsequently, 5 key files arbitrary chosen from the semi-real world files are used to retrieve their similar files. Each key file is given to the retrieval system and processed along the dashed line in Fig. 2. Table 5 show the result of the top 10 retrieved files in the order of the similarity in the feature vector matching for the 5 key files. The result clearly shows that the files having close number to the key file are retrieved. Some files are missed to be retrieved even when their numbers are close to the number of the given key file. This is because the character sequence for the replacement can be quite different from the original overwritten sequence as numerical series data, and this replacement significantly affects the coefficients of FFT in the feature vectors. This effect has been already discussed in the example of the feature vectors of "26dy10mo02yr" and "(LF)5dy10mo02yr" in Table 1. Though the moving window approach alleviates this type of distortion in the judgment of similarity, the judgment is infected to some extent even under this approach when the character sequence for the replacement is much different from the overwritten sequence. The third row from the bottom in the table indicates the standard deviation of the number labels of the top 50 retrieved files, and the second row from the bottom shows the chi-squared value on the difference of the distribution from the expected distribution of the number labels of randomly sampled 50 files. The numbers from 1 to 2253 are divided into the 50 sections, then the expected number of files in each section is 1 when 50 files are sampled randomly. At this time, the chi-squared value follows chi-squared distribution which flexibility is 49. If the chi-squared value is more than 94.6, the probability that the files retrieved are randomly sampled is less than 0.0001. Therefore, the distributions of the retrieval results are sufficiently skewed around the key files in the sense of the similarity. The bottom row represents the computation time to retrieve the 50 files for each key files. The 50 similar files are retrieved within a second among the 2253 doc files for each key file. The difference of the time for retrieval is due to the difference of the number of the feature vectors which is not unusable for each key file. For example, the number of the usable feature vector of the key file No.1500 is 1474 while it is only 593 for the key file No. 2000. This difference is reflected on the retrieval time. The retrieval time is almost linear with the number of the effective feature vectors of each key file.

## 6   Discussion and Related Work

The signature files method to use moving windows of byte sequences having a fixed length in the files has been proposed for file retrieval [2]. This method compresses each byte sequence in incomplete and irreversible fashion by introducing hash functions, and efficiently focuses on similar key sequence patterns on the reduced size of binary signature data. However, the direct matching of

**Table 5.** Retrieval on semi-real world data

| Key File No.100 | Key File No.500 | Key File No.1000 | Key File No.1500 | Key File No.2000 |
|---|---|---|---|---|
| 100 | 500 | 1000 | 1500 | 2000 |
| 102 | 676 | 789 | 1499 | 2001 |
| 99 | 664 | 979 | 1494 | 1999 |
| 104 | 508 | 648 | 1498 | 1995 |
| 96 | 554 | 999 | 1502 | 2158 |
| 97 | 508 | 967 | 1497 | 2258 |
| 105 | 579 | 997 | 1496 | 1868 |
| 106 | 561 | 856 | 1503 | 2019 |
| 103 | 543 | 852 | 1504 | 1989 |
| 98 | 485 | 543 | 1506 | 1877 |
| Std. 17.0 | Std. 142.4 | Std. 176.4 | Std. 190.0 | Std. 108.2 |
| $\chi^2=$ 1352 | $\chi^2=$ 316 | $\chi^2=$ 256 | $\chi^2=$ 1765 | $\chi^2=$ 385 |
| 0.642 sec. | 0.466 sec. | 0.422 sec. | 0.844 sec. | 0.370 sec. |

key sequence is required at the final stage of the retrieval to achieve the complete retrieval because of the incompleteness of the signature matching. On the other hand, the inversed indexing approach where the files containing each key are listed in advance are often used for the practically fast retrieval [3]. One of the representative system is Namazu for Japanese documents [9]. Though this approach needs considerably large space for the indexing data storage, the recent increase in the capacity of the storage devices is alleviating this difficulty. However, this approach is for the complete keyword matching in the files such as text documents.

In contrast, our proposing method applies a mathematical transformation having some invariance and compression properties to retain the information of certain similarities among files rather than the ordinary hash compression function. Because of the nature of the mathematical transformation, the complete matching is easily achieved in our framework if the threshold value for feature vector matching is taken at a high frequency. Moreover, the incomplete matching to retrieve files containing similar patterns in terms of the invariance and robustness of the transformation is also achieved by applying the lower threshold value. The efficiency of the retrieval is comparable with the ordinary inversed indexing approach because our approach also uses the inversed indexing on the representation of feature vectors.

## 7    Conclusion

In this work, a generic retrieval approach for the data was proposed where one dimensional byte sequences reflect the contents of the data. The proposed approach covers most of the advantage of the conventional approaches. Moreover the generic applicability of this method is superior to the conventional ones.

Currently, a study to extend this approach to image which has two dimentional bytes sequences is in progress. However, some issues remain. First a problem is the amount of disk used by inversed indexing data. In case described in this paper, the substaintial size of inversed indexing data which is 265 Mega Bytes required, while the original data for retrieval is only 60 Mega Bytes.The problem should be adressed in the future work. One measure will be to introduce some data compression technique. Futhermore our approach cannot retrieve files having different format such as mixture of MS Word format and plain text. This is because the sequence changes according to the formats, even if the sequences express the same matter. For example, MS Word adopts unicode as the format records text data, while plain text adopts ascii code. This matter must be also adressed in future.

## References

1. Baeza-Yates, R.A.: String Searching Algorithms, Information Retrieval, Data Structures & Algorithms, Chapter 10, ed. Baeza-Yates, R.A., New Jersey: Prentice Hall, pp. 219–240 (1992).
2. Faloutsos, C: Signature Files, Information Retrieval, Data Structures & Algorithms, Chapter 4, ed. Baeza-Yates, R.A., New Jersey: Prentice Hall, pp. 44–65 (1992).
3. Harman, D., Fox, E. and Baeza-Yates, R.A.: Inverted Files, Information Retrieval, Data Structures & Algorithms, Chapter 3, ed. Baeza-Yates, R.A., New Jersey: Prentice Hall, pp. 28–43 (1992).
4. Ogle, V.E., Stonebraker, M: Chabot: Retrieval from a Relational Database of Images, IEEE Computer, Vol. 28, No. 9, pp. 1–18 (1995).
5. Faloutsos, C., Equitz, W., Flickner, M., Niblack, W., Petkovic, D., Barber, R.: Efficient and Effective Querying by Image Content, Journal of Intelligence Information Systems, 3, 3/4, pp. 231–262 (1994).
6. Salton, G. and McGill, M.J.: Introduction to Modern Information Retrieval, McGraw-Hill Book Company (1983).
7. Fox, C: Lexical Analysis and Stoplists, Information Retrieval, Data Structures & Algorithms, Chapter 7, ed. Baeza-Yates, R.A., New Jersey: Prentice Hall, pp. 102–130 (1992).
8. Digital Signal Processing, The Institute of Electronics, Information and Communication Engineers (IEICE) 10th Ed., Gihoudou, pp. 49–61 (1983) (in Japanese).
9. http://www.namazu.org/

# Hierarchical Ordering for Approximate Similarity Ranking

Joselíto J. Chua and Peter E. Tischer

School of Computer Science and Software Engineering
Monash University, Victoria 3800, Australia
jjchua@mail.csse.monash.edu.au

**Abstract.** We propose a partial ordering that approximates a ranking of
the items in a database according to their similarity to a query item. The
partial ordering uses a single-link hierarchical clustering of the data items
to rank them with respect to the query's closest match. The technique
avoids the $O(kn)$ cost of calculating the similarity measure between the
query and every item in the database. It requires only $O(n)$ space for
pre-computed information. The technique can also provide a criterion
for determining which items may not need to be included in the ranking.
The results of our experiments suggest that the partial ordering provides
a good approximation to the similarity ranking.

## 1  Introduction

We consider the information retrieval problem of ranking the items in a database
according to their similarity to a query item. A large part of the cost is due to the
calculation of the similarity measure. In order to rank the data items according
to their similarity to the query, the similarity measure needs to be calculated
between the query and every item in the database. For example, if the data items
are $k$-dimensional vectors, and similarity is measured by the Euclidean distance,
then ranking the items in a database of size $n$ will cost $O(kn)$ computations.
A large portion of those calculations can be avoided if we can determine which
items are so far away from the query, that they need not be included in the
ranking, without having to compute the similarity measure between them and
the query.

One solution is to avoid the calculation of the similarity measure between the
query and every item in the database by ranking the items according to their
similarity to the query item's *closest match* instead. The idea is that items which
are similar to the closest match are also likely to be similar to the query item.
There are a number of fast nearest-neighbour (NN) search techniques that can
be used for finding a query item's closest match in the database [1]. An $O(n^2)$
*proximity table* that lists the value of the similarity measure between data items
can be pre-computed. The data items can be ranked with respect to the closest
matching item by looking up the table, and sorting the data items according to
their similarities to the closest match. The problem with this approach is that the

N. Zhong et al. (Eds.): ISMIS 2003, LNAI 2871, pp. 496–500, 2003.

$O(n^2)$ space required by the proximity table can be prohibitive in applications involving large databases.

The solution we propose in this paper is to cluster the data items hierarchically using a *minimal cost spanning tree (MCST)*, and to use the resulting partial ordering to rank the data items relative to the closest match. The MCST represents a *single-link hierarchical clustering* of the data [2], [3]. The clustering is also invariant under monotonic transformations of the distance function. If the similarity measure is a metric, then the triangle inequality provides a criterion for determining sections of the MCST which contain items that may be considered too far away to be included in the ranking. We shall outline our technique and its performance in this paper. A more detailed discussion of the technique, an illustrated example, and results of further experiments are provided in [4].

## 2   Hierarchical Ordering

Consider an MCST where each vertex is a data item, and the weight of an edge between two vertices is the value of the (dis)similarity measure between the data items connected by that edge. An MCST can be stored in $O(n)$ space. An important well-known property of an MCST is as follows:

*Property 1.* Every edge in an MCST partitions the vertices into two clusters, such that no other pair of vertices between those clusters are closer to each other than the two vertices connected by the partitioning edge.

Suppose the database consists of items $y_1, y_2, \ldots, y_n$, and $x$ is the query item. Property 1 implies that every $y_i$ is connected to the MCST through one of its closest matching items. That is, $y_i$ is connected to one of its nearest neighbours, which in turn is connected to one of its own nearest neighbours, and so on. This creates a "chain" of nearest-neighbouring items in the MCST. Each chain terminates at an edge that connects two mutual nearest neighbours. Disjoint chains are connected in the MCST by the shortest path from one of the vertices in one chain to a vertex in another chain. We obtain a partial ordering of the data items by following the nearest-neighbour chains, starting from the query's closest match.

The partial ordering is based on the single-link hierarchical clustering represented in the MCST. We use the single-link clustering algorithm proposed by Gower and Ross [2], where the sorted weights of all the edges in the MCST determine the thresholds. The resulting clustering information is represented by a *dendogram.*

We implement the dendogram as a binary tree where each child node has a pointer to its parent node. Each non-leaf node represents the MCST edge connecting two mutually exclusive subtrees of the MCST. Each subtree represents a cluster, and the leaves are the items in the cluster represented by that subtree. The partial ordering is obtained by traversing the dendogram recursively according to the links provided by the nodes. The resulting ordering is *hierarchical* in the sense that the clusters are traversed recursively from the lowest to the highest level of the hierarchy. Clusters closest to the smallest cluster containing the starting leaf are traversed first. The dendogram makes it easy to find another NN chain that can link to the current NN chain, because the link is given by the node with which the current cluster is connected to the rest of the dendogram. We obtain an approximate similarity ranking of the items by traversing the dendogram from the leaf that corresponds to the query's closest match.

## 3   Terminating Criterion

If the similarity measure, $d(\cdot, \cdot)$, is a metric, then the triangle inequality provides a *criterion* for pruning the ranked list of items. The triangle inequality guarantees that if $h = d(\mathbf{x}, \mathbf{y}_{\mathrm{curr}})$ and $d(\mathbf{y}_i, \mathbf{y}_{\mathrm{curr}}) > 2h$, then $d(\mathbf{x}, \mathbf{y}_i) > h$ [5]. Suppose item $\mathbf{y}_j$ is followed immediately by item $\mathbf{y}_i$ in an hierarchical ordering which starts from $\mathbf{y}_{\mathrm{curr}}$. Property 1 and the triangle inequality imply that if $d(\mathbf{y}_j, \mathbf{y}_i) > 2h$, then $\mathbf{y}_i$, as well as all the items that follow it in the ordering, cannot be closer than $\mathbf{y}_{\mathrm{curr}}$ to $\mathbf{x}$ [6]. Thus, we can terminate the partial ordering with respect to $\mathbf{y}_{\mathrm{curr}}$ as soon as we find two consecutive items which are connected by an edge of weight greater than $2h$.

Furthermore, the triangle inequality ensures that all the closest matches of $\mathbf{x}$ are included in the pruned list at that stage of the partial ordering [6]. This can be useful in applications where a good match, though not necessarily the closest, can be obtained inexpensively. For example, our experiments in [1] suggest that a variation of the $k$-d tree proposed in [7] can yield good approximate matches at $O(\log n)$ scalar decisions. The hierarchical ordering can start at the approximate match, and terminate as soon as the terminating criterion is satisfied. All the closest matches of $\mathbf{x}$ are contained in the pruned list.

## 4   Results of Experiments

We demonstrate the technique proposed in this paper using data sets from vector quantisation (VQ) coding of images. Each data item is an image block from an 8-bit grayscale image. The database is a VQ codebook trained over an image using the LBG algorithm [8]. We use various image block and codebook sizes in our experiments. We present the results for the image len ("Lenna"), which is a $512 \times 512$ image of a woman. The results of other experiments are discussed in [4]. The Euclidean distance function is used as the similarity measure. Table 1 shows the average results over the total number of queries, QTotal. The query set is the same as the training set used to generate the VQ codebook.

Column NNCost shows the average cost of finding the query's closest match. We used the fast NN search algorithm proposed in [1]. The algorithm uses $O(n)$ pre-computed information. The algorithm also uses the MCST to speed up the search. The cost of the search is expressed in the tables as the equivalent number of $O(k)$ distance function evaluations. Compared to the $O(kn)$ arithmetic cost of an actual similarity ranking, the cost of finding a closest match is considerably smaller.

**Table 1.** Results for query sets which are the same as the VQ codebook's training data.

| Image | Block size | Codebk size ($n$) | Performance: | | | | |
|---|---|---|---|---|---|---|---|
| | | | QTotal | NNCost | ShiftsF | RSize | ShiftsR |
| len 512 × 512 | 2 × 2 ($k=4$) | 1024 | 65536 | 11.552 | 0.380 | 2.418 | 0.049 |
| | | 256 | 65536 | 5.898 | 0.362 | 2.419 | 0.050 |
| | 4 × 4 ($k=16$) | 1024 | 16384 | 28.082 | 0.361 | 7.575 | 0.094 |
| | | 256 | 16384 | 8.793 | 0.353 | 4.139 | 0.056 |
| | 8 × 8 ($k=64$) | 256 | 4096 | 13.748 | 0.337 | 7.780 | 0.075 |
| | | 128 | 4096 | 7.879 | 0.330 | 4.223 | 0.047 |
| | 16 × 16 ($k=256$) | 128 | 1024 | 10.845 | 0.306 | 7.111 | 0.082 |
| | | 64 | 1024 | 7.457 | 0.309 | 5.066 | 0.054 |

We evaluate the approximate similarity ranking from the hierarchical ordering according to the "sortedness" of the resulting list. We measure this in terms of the amount of work that a sorting algorithm would require to re-arrange the items in the order that an actual similarity ranking would list them. We count the number of *element shifts* that the insertion sort algorithm has to perform to re-arrange the items so that their distances to the query are in increasing order. We chose the insertion sort algorithm because it returns the best result if the distances were already in sorted order, so that no element in the list needs to be shifted. The worst case result occurs when the distances are in reversed (decreasing) order, resulting in $\frac{N(N-1)}{2}$ shifts (where $N$ is the number of items in the list). We scale the results by taking the *ratio* between the actual number of element shifts over the number of shifts in the worst case. The performance value ranges from 0 (best) to 1 (worst).

Column ShiftsF shows the performance when all the items are ordered hierarchically. Further experiments in [4] suggest that the performance may be dependent on the relative distances between the items in the database. Because hierarchical ordering is based on a single-link hierarchical clustering of the data items, the technique is likely to perform better in cases where the items tend to form small dense clusters which are distant from each other.

Column RSize shows the average size of the pruned list when the criterion based on the triangle inequality is used to terminate the partial ordering. The comparatively small size of the pruned list indicates that a large part of the result in Column ShiftsF is probably due to data items that may not need to be included in the ranking because they are relatively far away from the query. Column ShiftsR indicates the "sortedness" of the items in the pruned list. The comparatively small element shift ratios suggest that the items in the pruned list are often already arranged in nearly the same order in which an actual similarity ranking would list them.

# 5   Conclusion

The results of our experiments suggest that hierarchical ordering is able to provide a good approximate similarity ranking at a fraction of the cost of an actual similarity ranking. The technique is efficient in terms of both arithmetic cost and storage space requirements. The cost of finding the closest match for the hierarchical ordering is only a fraction of the $O(kn)$ cost of an actual similarity ranking. Hierarchical ordering itself requires only scalar decisions to traverse the dendogram. It also requires only $O(n)$ space for the dendogram, compared to the $O(n^2)$ space required by the proximity table. If the similarity measure is a metric, then the triangle inequality provides a criterion for determining a partial list of ranked items.

The efficiency and performance of hierarchical ordering can allow researchers to consider sophisticated similarity measures despite the arithmetic complexity of those measures [9]. Of interest to the authors are data mining and case-based reasoning applications, where large databases have been accumulated over the years in an *ad hoc* manner. Given an appropriate similarity measure, a single-link hierarchical clustering can provide the needed structure for such databases.

# References

1. Joselíto J. Chua. Fast full-search equivalent nearest-neighbour search algorithms. Master of Computing, School of Computer Science and Software Engineering, Faculty of Information Technology, Monash University, 1999.
2. J. C. Gower and G. J. S. Ross. Minimum spanning trees and single linkage cluster analysis. *Applied Statistics*, 10:54–64, 1969.
3. F. James Rohlf. Single-link clustering algorithms. In P.R. Krishnaiah and L.N. Kanal, editors, *Handbook of Statistics, vol. 2*, pages 267–284. Elsevier Science Publishers, Amsterdam, The Netherlands, 1982.
4. Joselíto J. Chua and Peter E. Tischer. Hierarchical ordering for approximate similarity ranking. Technical Report 2003/141, School of Computer Science and Software Engineering, Monash University, Victoria 3800, Australia, 2003.
5. C.-M. Huang, Q. Bi, G. S. Stiles, and R. W. Harris. Fast full search equivalent encoding algorithms for image compression using vector quantization. *IEEE Transactions on Image Processing*, 1(3):413–416, July 1992.
6. Joselíto Chua and Peter Tischer. Minimal cost spanning trees for nearest-neighbour matching. In Masoud Mohammadian, editor, *Computational Intelligence for Modelling, Control and Automation: Intelligent Image Processing, Data Analysis and Information Retrieval*, pages 7–12. IOS Press, 1999.
7. Jerome H. Friedman, Jon Louis Bentley, and Raphael Ari Finkel. An algorithm for finding best matches in logarithmic expected time. *ACM Transactions on Mathematical Software*, 3(2):209–226, June 1977.
8. Yoseph Linde, Andrés Buzo, and Robert M. Gray. An algorithm for vector quantizer design. *IEEE Transactions on Communications*, COM-28(1):84–95, January 1980.
9. Nicu Sebe, Michael S. Lew, and Dionysius P. Huijsmans. Toward improved ranking metrics. *IEEE Transactions on Pattern Analysis and Machine Intelligence*, 22(10):1132–1143, October 2000.

# Space Transformation Based Approach for Effective Content-Based Image Retrieval

Biren Shah and Vijay Raghavan

University of Louisiana at Lafayette, CACS, P.O.Box 44330, Lafayette, LA 70503, USA
{bshah, raghavan}@cacs.louisiana.edu

**Abstract.** In this paper, we extend the work done by Choubey and Raghavan, which proposed an approach to content-based image retrieval that uses the space transformation methods proposed by Goldfarb to transform the original low-level image space into a feature space, where images are represented as vectors of high-level features that enable efficient query processing. The resulting retrieval system consists of three phases: database population, online addition and image retrieval. In the current work, we investigate issues relating to online addition of new images, during database population phase, in incremental stages. The results show that our approach is effective in retrieving images even when the image database is dynamic.

## 1  Introduction

Interest in applications involving the search and management of digital images has increased tremendously over the last few years. Image databases can be huge, containing hundreds of thousands of images. However, it is not possible to access or make use of this information unless it is organized to allow for efficient browsing and retrieval. Content-Based Image Retrieval (CBIR) systems are required to effectively and efficiently access images using information contained in image databases. A CBIR system uses information from the content of images for retrieval and helps the user retrieve database images relevant to the contents of a query image [2].

The selection of an approach to CBIR is influenced by the type of image features to be extracted, the level of abstraction to be revealed in the features and the extent of desired domain independence. The use of low-level (or measurable, automatically extractable) features, for example, color, texture or shape, in image retrieval makes the approach automatic but not necessarily efficient. Inter-image distances computed using the low-level features are called *real* (or actual) inter-image distances. Inter-image distances computed using the high-level features obtained, following space transformation, are called *estimated* inter-image distances. There is an urgent need for an efficient and effective CBIR system. Our goal is to develop such an automatic system that supports incremental addition of new images into the image database.

## 2  Related Work and Motivation

A review of the literature [1, 3] shows that the use of real distances in image retrieval during query processing is computationally expensive.

N. Zhong et al. (Eds.): ISMIS 2003, LNAI 2871, pp. 501–505, 2003.

CBIR is a type of a pattern recognition problem. Goldfarb [4] proposed some ideas that use space transformation to efficiently solve pattern recognition problems. Space transformation methods provide a way of mapping original samples into a low-dimensional vector space, preserving discriminatory information contained in original sample representation. These methods allow the utilization of the analytical tools available in a vector space. Goldfarb [4] proposed the *First* and the *Main* Embedding space transformation methods to represent the original visual content in a completely new multi-dimensional space. According to Goldfarb's results, the distance preservation is guaranteed, as long as the real distance function is pseudo-metric.

Choubey and Raghavan [2] used the space transformation ideas proposed by Goldfarb to develop a generic and fully automatic CBIR architecture. A step in their CBIR approach requires the selection of a subset of database images, called the *initial* (or representative) set. Their experiments, for reasons of simplicity, were done under the assumption that the whole database corresponded to the initial set. Not all aspects of his approach were investigated.

Our approach, to solving the image retrieval problem, extends the work done by Choubey and Raghavan [2]. It involves using the First Embedding space transformation method proposed by Goldfarb [4]. Other alternative embedding methods are not considered, since they are not suitable for situations requiring online addition [4]. Inter-image comparisons are made using the high-level feature vectors of the transformed space. Our estimated distance is more accurate compared to the estimated distance used by Faloutsos [3]. Our approach supports adding new images online into the image database. Our approach is applicable to the following two cases:

1.  Original feature space represents images as feature vectors.
2.  Only proximity data (e.g., inter-object distance data) is given.

## 3   CBIR System Architecture

Our focus is on the First Embedding space transformation method proposed by Goldfarb [4] to transform the original space into an efficient and effective domain independent vector space, since the Main Embedding method does not support online addition of new images. Our approach supports the online addition of new images into the image database. A high-level feature vector finally represents each image. Inter-image comparisons are made using the high-level feature vectors of the transformed space. The pseudo-Euclidean distance function, which is computationally faster than the original real distance function, is used to calculate the estimated inter-image distance. If $i$ and $j$ represent the high-level feature vectors of any two images and $(m,n)$ is the vector signature, then the pseudo-Euclidean distance function $D(i,j)$ used to compute the estimated distance, is as follows:

$$D(i, j) = \left[ (i_1 - j_1)^2 + \ldots + (i_m - j_m)^2 - (i_{m+1} - j_{m+1})^2 - \ldots - (i_{m+n} - j_{m+n})^2 \right]^{\frac{1}{2}} \qquad (1)$$

The image database to be populated is divided into an initial set and an incremental set using the Maxmin [7] clustering algorithm. The initial set should represent images from all possible classes. We, therefore, cluster all images and make up the initial set by selecting the centroid (or representative) image from each cluster. The incremental set denotes the set of images that can be added online without affecting the structure of the representation space of the existing image database. The CBIR system using the First Embedding method involves the following three phases:

1.    Database Population: The Database Population phase uses low-level image properties, such as color, for computing the real inter-image distances to the images in the initial set. The size of the initial set is much smaller than that of the eventual whole image database. Starting from the real inter-image distances, the high-level image feature vectors for these images are computed using the First Embedding algorithm. At the same time, the training set is also generated. The training set is comprised of feature vectors corresponding to the images of the initial set. These feature vectors can have significantly fewer features, compared to the representation of images based on low-level image properties. Components of derived feature vectors that have a negligible effect (close to zero) on the overall representation of the vectors can be discarded to further reduce the dimension of the feature space and hence the complexity of the process of distance computation during retrieval.

2.    Online Addition: The Online Addition phase allows addition of a new image into the image database. The idea here is to project the new image onto the existing vector space in such a manner that the feature vector corresponding to the new image preserves certain properties relative to the objects in the existing transformed space [4]. First, the low level representation of a new image is obtained. The low-level features are used to compute inter-image distances of the images in the initial set. Finally, the high-level feature vector for the incoming image is computed.

3.    Image Retrieval: In the Image Retrieval phase, relevant images that are close to the query image are retrieved from the image database. The main advantage of online addition is that, for a query image, the system has to compute the real distance to only the images in the initial set, as opposed to all the images in the database. This makes the query processing a lot more efficient when compared to the conventional approach. After the high-level feature vector is computed for the query image, online retrieval is performed by computing the estimated distance of the query image feature vector to the feature vector of each of the other database images (i.e. images not in the initial set) as estimates of the corresponding real distances. The estimated distances correspond to distances in the resulting pseudo-Euclidean space.

## 4    Experimental Setup and Results

A detailed set of experiments were carried out in order to achieve the following goals:
1.    To measure the degree of order and distance preservation of images that were added online using the First Embedding method.
2.    To determine the effect of using threshold value.

To achieve the above goals, two sets of experiments were conducted, using images from the Department of Water Resources (DWR) repository maintained at University of California, Berkeley. Experiments were performed with two image data sets: one with 32 images (DWR32) and other with 75 images (DWR75). The images used in the experiments can be downloaded from [8]. We have used color as the low-level feature to illustrate the principles behind the proposed scheme. For the experiments, we used the RGB color space and the images were all quantized to 64 color bins using the median cut [5] quantization algorithm for extracting the low-level feature vectors.

**Table 1.** Kendall's Tau values. Order preservation results of experiment I

| # Of Images (Initial Set) | # Of Images (Online Added) | DWR32 | | | # Of Images (Initial Set) | # Of Images (Online Added) | DWR75 | |
|---|---|---|---|---|---|---|---|---|
| | | No Thresh old | T1 | T2 | | | No Thresh old | T1 |
| 8 | 20 | 0.5782 | 0.5017 | -0.5664 | 20 | 48 | 0.9271 | -0.2814 |
| 14 | 14 | 0.8471 | 0.4811 | -0.3165 | 34 | 34 | 0.8918 | -0.7214 |
| 19 | 9 | 0.9677 | 0.6337 | 0.1060 | 42 | 26 | 0.7575 | 0.2460 |

The real inter-image function $d_{ij}$ between two images $O_i = (x_{i1}, x_{i2}, ..., x_{il})$ and $O_j = (x_{j1}, x_{j2}, ..., x_{jl})$, can be computed as follows:

$$d_{ij} = (O_i - O_j)A(O_i - O_j)^T$$  (2)

where $A$ is the color-color similarity matrix.

Images used in the experiments were classified into two distinct sets: the initial set and the online added set. Database population was performed using the images from the set labeled as "Initial Set". Online addition was performed using the images from the set labeled as "Online Added Set".

Each set of experiments was carried out with different threshold values that we use to determine the number of high-level image features to be retained. T1 and T2 in DWR32 indicate that one and three components (the worst), respectively, of the feature vector were discarded. T1 in DWR75 indicates that two least influential components of the feature vector were discarded.

## 4.1 Experiment I (Order Preservation When Using Online Addition)

This experiment was performed to check the order preservation property of images that were added online using the First Embedding method. Kendall's Tau [6] was used to measure the order preservation by comparing the order of the real inter-image distance and the estimated inter-image distance of all online added images with that of the images in the initial set. A value of 1 implies that the degree of association between the two orderings is at its positive extreme and a value of –1 implies that the strength of association is the worst possible.

The order preservation results are summarized in Table 1. The results show that the Kendall's Tau value is greater that 0.84 for more than 65% of the cases when no feature component in the transformed space is discarded, which implies that the order preservation is good. With threshold values T1 and T2, the maximum Kendall's Tau value is 0.6337, which implies that the order preservation is poor.

## 4.2 Experiment II (Distance Preservation When Using Online Addition)

This experiment was performed to check the distance preservation property of images that were added online using the First Embedding method. $L_2$-Norm was used to measure the distance preservation by comparing the real inter-image distance and the estimated inter-image distance of all online added images with that of the images in the initial set. A value of 0 implies 100% inter-image distance preservation. As the corresponding values increases, distance preservation gets poorer and poorer.

**Table 2.** $L_2$-Norm values. Distance preservation results of experiment II

| # Of Images (Initial Set) | # Of Images (Online Added) | DWR32 | | | # Of Images (Initial Set) | # Of Images (Online Added) | DWR75 | |
|---|---|---|---|---|---|---|---|---|
| | | No Thresh old $(x\ 10^7)$ | T1 $(x\ 10^8)$ | T2 $(x\ 10^8)$ | | | No Thresh old $(x\ 10^7)$ | T1 $(x\ 10^8)$ |
| 8 | 20 | 4.0479 | 4.1438 | 35.6269 | 20 | 48 | 1.6574 | 275.363 |
| 14 | 14 | 1.1576 | 4.6016 | 21.9579 | 34 | 34 | 1.5845 | 69.3540 |
| 19 | 9 | 0.6525 | 2.7901 | 17.6205 | 42 | 26 | 6.0523 | 21.3853 |

The distance preservation results are summarized in Table 2. The results show that the distance preservation is high when no threshold value is used and low with threshold values T1 and T2, i.e., average $L_2$-Norm value for a pair is in the order of $10^7/^{32}C_2 \approx 2.01E4$ for DWR32 and $10^7/^{75}C_2 \approx 3.6E3$ for DWR75, which is small when compared with the actual real distance value.

# 5  Conclusion and Future Work

We have extended and developed an effective and fully automated CBIR system that supports online addition of new images into the image database. Our experiments show that the First Embedding space transformation method that we investigated preserves the distances and the order of the distances in the transformed space. To perform effective image retrieval, it is not recommended to reduce the dimension of the feature vector space. As a part of our future work, we plan to measure the retrieval efficiency and also test the scalability of our approach.

# References

1.  S. Chang, A. Eleftheriadis, D. Anastassiou, "Development of Columbia's Video on demand Testbed," *Intl. Journal of Image Comm.-Signal Processing, 8*(1996), pp. 191–207.
2.  S. Choubey, V. Raghavan, "Generic and Fully Automatic Content-Based Image Retrieval Using Color," *Pattern Recognition Letters, 18*(1997), pp. 1233–1240.
3.  C. Faloutsos, "Efficient and Effective Querying by Image Content," *Journal of Intelligent Information Systems, 3*(1994), pp. 231–262.
4.  L. Goldfarb, "A Unified Approach to Pattern Recognition," In *Pattern Recognition, 17*(1985), pp. 575–582.
5.  P. Heckbert, "Color Image Quantization for Frame-Buffer Display," *Computer Graphics, 16* (1980), pp. 297–307.
6.  W. Hays, P. Winkler, "Nonparametric Methods," In *Statistics: Probability, Inference, and Decision* (New York, NY: Holt, Rinehart and Winston, Inc., 1970), vol. II, pp. 182–264.
7.  J.Tou, R.Gonzalez, *Pattern Recognition Principles* (Boston, MA: Addison-Wesley, 1972).
8.  http://www.cacs.louisiana.edu/~bns0742/CBIR/Images/DWR/DWR.html, Date: 16th June 2003, Time: 5:43 p.m.

# Collaborative Filtering – Safe and Sound?

Michael P. O'Mahony, Neil J. Hurley, and Guénolé C.M. Silvestre

Department of Computer Science, University College Dublin,
Belfield, Dublin 4, Ireland
{michael.p.omahony, neil.hurley,guenole.silvestre}@ucd.ie

**Abstract.** Recommender systems are now widely used to overcome the information overload problem. Security is an ever-present concern, and since many of these systems operate in an on-line environment, it is necessary to understand and remove any security issues that may exist. In earlier work, we have demonstrated that collaborative recommender systems are indeed vulnerable to biased noise attacks. In this paper, we expand on our previous work by adapting techniques from the field of Reputation Reporting Systems that substantially improve the robustness of recommender systems.

## 1   Introduction

Recommender systems are now an established component of many e-commerce applications and assist customers to find relevant products from the many items that are frequently on offer. The *collaborative filtering* approach [7,9,1] is frequently used in the implementation of many of these systems.

While the performance of recommender systems from the accuracy, coverage and efficiency perspectives has been extensively researched in the literature [1, 3,8], in previous work [5,6] we have outlined the need for a further performance measure – that is the *robustness* of the system. Robustness measures the power of an algorithm to make consistent predictions in the presence of biased or unbiased noise. In [5,6] we have shown that collaborative filtering systems are vulnerable to a biased noise attack, and that a small amount of data, relative to the overall database size, can dramatically change a system's output.

In this paper, we focus on improving the robustness of collaborative filtering algorithms by introducing an approach from the field of Reputation Reporting Systems [2]. We demonstrate that, by modifying and extending this approach to suit the requirements of collaborative filtering, a substantial improvement in the robustness of recommender systems can be achieved.

## 2   Collaborative Filtering

One of the most commonly-used collaborative filtering algorithms is described in [7], in which a prediction for a user $a$ (termed the active user) for an item $j$ is calculated as follows:

N. Zhong et al. (Eds.): ISMIS 2003, LNAI 2871, pp. 506–510, 2003.

$$p_{a,j} = \bar{v}_a + \kappa \sum_{i=1}^{n} w(a,i)(v_{i,j} - \bar{v}_i) \tag{1}$$

where $p_{a,j}$ is the predicted rating for item $j$, $\bar{v}_a$ is the mean rating for user $a$, $v_{i,j}$ is the rating of neighbour $i$ for item $j$, and $\kappa$ is a normalising factor. The number of neighbours considered in the calculation of the predicted rating is given by $n$. Various similarity measures have been proposed to calculate the weights, $w(a,i)$. Here, we consider three of the most widely used measures, cosine (or vector) similarity [1], Pearson correlation [7] and Spearman rank correlation [3].

## 2.1 Robustness of Collaborative Filtering Systems

In the context of collaborative filtering, we define robustness as a measure of a system's ability to deliver stable or consistent predictions in the presence of noisy data. To evaluate robustness, we define *mean absolute prediction error* (MAPE) as the average difference in pre- and post-attack predictions. Note that this metric is independent of any accuracy measurement. The MAPE metric enables us to determine exactly the effect of any noise (biased or unbiased) on a system's output.

We restrict our discussion to one particular class of attacks – *product nuke* attacks. The objective of these attacks is to force a recommender system to output low ratings for targeted items. (A similar analysis to that below applies to product push attacks, in which the goal is to promote targeted item ratings). In all cases, attacks are implemented by creating false user profiles and inserting them through the normal user interface – i.e. no further access to a system's database is assumed for attackers.

Furthermore, with respect to (1), we focus on the nearest-neighbour neighbourhood formation scheme since this approach is known to provide reasonable accuracy while maintaining a high degree of coverage [3]. For a successful attack on a system, the neighbourhood will need to be at least partially formed by the false profiles inserted by the attacker. In the next section, we discuss our scheme that aims to filter any false neighbours that may be present in a neighbourhood.

## 3 Neighbourhood Filtering

We propose the following neighbourhood filtering scheme that is adopted from the field of Reputation Reporting Systems. The reputation system described in [2] is as follows. The goal of the system is to enable a buyer $b$ to obtain a reputation estimate for a particular seller $s$, based on the previous ratings given by other buyers for $s$. (In this way, the reputation system is directly analogous to our work, with buyers taking on the role of users and sellers taking the role of items). The first step in the calculation of a reputation estimate is to form a neighbourhood of the most similar buyers to $b$ that have given a rating for $s$. The next step is to *filter* the neighbourhood and remove any possible malicious ratings (here, only unfairly high ratings are assumed to be present - see [2] for details). Filtering takes place by clustering the ratings for $s$ into two groups, and by assuming that the group with the highest mean contains the malicious ratings. Note that filtering is performed in all cases – no attempt is made to determine whether any malicious ratings are actually present in the neighbourhood. In the final step, a reputation estimate based on those ratings for $s$ contained in the genuine group only is calculated.

With regard to robustness of collaborative filtering systems, we now adopt the above approach with the following modifications. In the first instance, we do not assume that an attack has taken place in all cases, rather we analyse the difference in the cluster means to determine if a significant difference exists from that of an un-attacked system (of course, this requires *a priori* knowledge of the distribution of the difference in cluster means in an un-attacked system). If we deem an attack has occurred, we further need to determine the attack cluster. To this end, the cluster containing the false profiles is assumed to be the one with the lowest standard deviation in the item ratings for which a prediction is being sought. The motivation is that, for example, in a product nuke attack, false ratings are likely to be consistently low.

## 3.1   Attack Strategy

To illustrate our neighbourhood filtering scheme, we consider product nuke attacks in which the goal is to reduce predicted values of targeted items. In general, if these attacks are to be successful (from the attacker's perspective), the attacker needs to ensure that the false profiles correlate in the same direction with genuine users in the database. Thus, along with the item to be nuked, the false profiles consists of items from two "groups". The first group consists of items that are generally rated higher than average in the database (i.e. *liked* items), and the second group consists of items that are generally rated lower than average (*disliked* items). By assigning a high rating to the liked items and a lower rating to the disliked items, we can be confident that these false profiles will correlate in the same direction with the majority of the genuine users in the database. In addition, if the groups are formed by selecting relatively popular items (i.e. those that have been rated by many users), the probability of achieving higher similarities between genuine and false users in increased.

While this strategy requires a certain knowledge of the data contained in databases, it is not unreasonable to assume that such knowledge is possible to estimate (e.g. in movie domains) or to mine (e.g. on Amazon.com, using feedback provided by users on items offered for sale).

## 4   Results

To evaluate our filtering scheme, we used the MovieLens [4] dataset which consists of 943 users and 1,682 movies, and contains 100,000 ratings on a scale of 1 to 5. In addition, we evaluated our scheme on the EachMovie database ( provided by Compaq Equipment Corporation) but, due to limitations of space, we omit these results. Note, however, that the trends observed for EachMovie were similar to MovieLens.

The experimental protocol adopted is to form the test set by removing a single user-item pair from the database and then making a prediction for this pair using all the remaining data. The MAPE over each item is calculated by removing each of the associated user-item pairs in turn and computing the average (absolute) difference between pre- and post-attack predictions. The performance over the entire database is then evaluated by taking an average of the MAPE's calculated for each item.

With respect to (1), the contribution of any potential neighbour to a particular prediction depends on the magnitude or the difference term $(v_{i,j} - \bar{v}_i)$. For attack profiles, the obvious strategy is to choose ratings for the item groups that will maximise this term. Thus the maximum rating, $R_{max}$, is assigned to the liked items and a rating of $R_{max} - 1$ to the disliked items. In the first attack, the lowest rating is assigned to the item being nuked, thereby maximising the difference term for the false profiles. The number of items in each false profile is approximately 50.

**Table 1.** Robustness of collaborative filtering with and without neighbourhood filtering for various similarity measures

|  | Cosine | | Pearson | | Spearman | |
|---|---|---|---|---|---|---|
|  | % unchanged | MAPE | % unchanged | MAPE | % unchanged | MAPE |
| pn1 | 0.30 | 1.63 | 0.18 | 2.82 | 0.17 | 2.79 |
| pn1+ | 0.45 | 0.76 | 0.28 | 0.74 | 0.27 | 0.74 |
| pn2 | 0.30 | 1.42 | 0.18 | 2.36 | 0.17 | 2.34 |
| pn2+ | 0.32 | 0.98 | 0.18 | 1.47 | 0.18 | 1.45 |

Results are presented in Table 1 (labelled **pn1**) for an attack strength of 50 false profiles. Without any filtering of the neighbourhoods taking place and when Pearson correlation is used, an average of only 18% of predictions remained unchained after the attack. For those that were changed, the MAPE was 2.82, of which 98% were negative (i.e. shifted towards the minimum rating). At this attack strength, the average percentage of false profiles in the neighbourhoods was 84%. These results indicate a successful attack, given that a shift of 2.82 is sufficient to change a prediction from "like" to "dislike". When neighbourhood filtering is used (**pn1+**), the improvement in robustness achieved was significant with 28% of predictions remaining unchanged, and for the remainder, the MAPE was reduced to 0.74 (Pearson correlation).

In our next attack, we attempt to defeat the filtering scheme by causing it to mis-identify the attack cluster. Since the attack cluster is assumed to be the one with the lowest variation in the item ratings for which a prediction is being sought, we increased the variation of the ratings for the nuked item in the attack profiles. Results are shown in Table 1 with and without neighbourhood filtering (**pn2** and **pn2+** respectively). In this case, for all similarity measures, neighbourhood filtering was less successful, with an MAPE of 1.47 achieved for 82% of all predicted values using Pearson correlation. Nevertheless, it is apparent that a substantial improvement in robustness over an unfiltered system remains.

Finally, we should note that the filtering scheme does not significantly affect accuracy or coverage when no attack is present. For example, in the first attack, accuracy calculated according to mean absolute error [1] changed from 0.80 to 0.88 after filtering, while coverage remained the same at 92%.

## 5   Conclusion

In this paper, we have described a neighbourhood filtering scheme that improves the robustness of collaborative recommender systems. The scheme performs reasonably well but it vulnerable to more sophisticated attack strategies. In future work, we will continue to expand on this approach and examine ways to improve its performance against various attack types.

## References

1. J. S. Breese, D. Heckerman, and C. Kadie. Empirical analysis of predictive algorithms for collaborative filtering. In *Proceedings of the Fourteenth Annual Conference on Uncertainty in Artificial Intelligence*, pages 43–52, July 1998.
2. C. Dellarocas. Immunizing online reputation reporting Systems against unfair ratings and discriminatory behavior. In *Proceedings of the 2nd ACM Conference on Electronic Commerce, Minneapolis, MN*, 2000.
3. J. Herlocker, J. Konstan, A. Borchers, and J. Riedl. An algorithmic framework for performing collaborative filtering. In *Proceedings of the SIGIR*. ACM, August 1999.
4. http://movielens.umn.edu/.
5. M. P. O'Mahony, N. J. Hurley, N. Kushmerick, and G. C. M. Silvestre. Collaborative recommendation: A robustness analysis. In *ACM Transactions on Internet Technology (to appear)*, 2003.
6. M. P. O'Mahony, N. J. Hurley, and G. C. M. Silvestre. Towards robust collaborative filtering. In *Proceedings of the 19th Irish International Conference, AICS 2002, Limerick*, Ireland, pages 87–94, 2002.
7. P. Resnick, N. Iacovou, M. Suchak, P. Bergstrom, and J.Riedl. Grouplens: An Open architecture for collaborative filtering of netnews. In *Proceedings of the ACM Conference on Computer Supported Cooperative Work*. ACM, 1994.
8. B. M. Sarwar, G. Karypis, J. A. Konstan, and J. Riedl. Analysis of recommendation algorithms for e-commerce. In *ACM Conference on Electronic Commerce*, pages 158–167, 2000.
9. U. Shardanand and P. Maes. Social information filtering: Algorithms for automating word of mouth. In *Proceedings of ACM CHI'95 Conference on Human Factors in Computing Systems*, pages 210–217, 1995.

# RNA Structure as Permutation: A GA Approach Comparing Different Genetic Sequencing Operators

Kay C. Wiese and Edward Glen

Simon Fraser University, Information Technology
2400 Central City, 10153 King George Highway
Surrey, BC V3T 2W1, CANADA
Phone: (604) 268.7436, Fax: (604) 268.7488
{wiese,eglen}@sfu.ca

**Abstract.** This paper presents a genetic algorithm (GA) to predict the secondary structure of RNA molecules, where the secondary structure is encoded as a permutation. More specifically the proposed algorithm predicts which specific canonical base pairs will form hydrogen bonds and build helices, also known as stem loops. Since RNA is involved in both transcription and translation and also has catalytic and structural roles in the cell, knowing its structure is of fundamental importance since it will determine the function of the RNA molecule. We discuss results on RNA sequences of lengths 76, 681, and 785 nucleotides and present several improvements to our algorithm. We show that the Keep-Best Reproduction operator has similar benefits as in the TSP domain. In addition, a comparison of several crossover operators is provided, demonstrating that CX, an operator that is marginal in the TSP domain, performs very well in the RNA folding domain.

**Keywords:** Evolutionary Computation, Soft Computing, Bioinformatics

## 1 Introduction

Ribonucleic Acid (RNA) is essential for the functioning of a cell and is the product of gene transcription. In a process known as translation, the RNA is involved in the building of proteins. While Deoxyribonucleic Acid (DNA) consists of a sequence of molecules made from the 4 nucleotides Adenine (A), Cytosine(C), Guanine (G), and Thymine (T), RNA consists of A, C, G, and Uracil (U), which replaces Thymine. In the translation process, a ribosome uses the additional tRNA available in the cell to produce a protein where 3 RNA nucleotides form a codon which encodes for one of the 20+ amino acids. The structure of the RNA molecule is important as it largely determines its function. This can be exploited for understanding RNA-Protein interactions which are relevant in pharmacology as well as the understanding and cure of genetic diseases. We can adequately describe the secondary structure of an RNA molecule as a set of stem loops consisting of a set of consecutive base pairs connected through hydrogen bonds (see Sect. 2 for more details and examples).

VanBatenburg et. al. [11] have demonstrated that a genetic algorithm (GA) can be used to closely predict the secondary structure of RNA and also to approximate the folding pathway that the RNA molecule may take during the folding process by add-

N. Zhong et al. (Eds.): ISMIS 2003, LNAI 2871, pp. 511–520, 2003.

ing and deleting stem loops. Their implementation used a binary representation for the solutions and they made several additions to the GA such as elitism that improved the results. Their initial algorithm had very poor performance and did not converge at all due to the inherent incompatibilities of stem loops in the binary representation of the solutions. Subsequently, the authors suggest ways of "repairing" the solutions to yield feasible ones. A massively parallel GA for the RNA folding problem is discussed in [10] and an improved mutation operator is discussed in a subsequent paper [9]. In the latter paper, the authors demonstrate that the improved GA predicts more correct (true-positive) stem loops and more correct base pairs than what could be predicted with a dynamic programming algorithm (DPA). While DPAs can accurately compute the minimum energy within a given thermodynamic model, the natural fold of RNA is often in a sub-optimal energy state. It can be argued that the natural folding process of RNA and the simulated folding of RNA using a GA (which includes intermediate folds) have many similarities, especially with regards to stem loop additions and deletions [11]. We propose to use a permutation based genetic algorithm to predict which helices (see exact definition in the next section) will form in the final secondary structure of the molecule. The objectives of this paper are as follows:

1. To introduce an alternative representation for RNA secondary structure that allows the use of a permutation based GA for the RNA folding problem
2. To present an evaluation of the GA, including convergence behavior, efficiency, and effectiveness
3. To study the effects of different selection strategies on the GA
4. To investigate whether KBR [13], a selection strategy that combines both fitness proportional selection and rank based selection, has similar benefits as in the traveling salesman problem (TSP)
5. To examine the effect of different crossover operators on solution quality and convergence behavior

We presented initial results of our algorithm in [15]. The work presented here discusses the above objectives in the context of differing crossover operators. In Section 2, we give an introduction to RNA structural elements. We describe how the problem can be decomposed into a combinatorial problem of finding the sub-set of helices from a set of feasible helices leading to a near minimum energy in the molecule. We describe the permutation based GA that we use to solve the RNA folding problem in Section 3. Section 4 contains our empirical results. A discussion and conclusions are outlined in Section 5 and Section 6, respectively.

## 2   RNA Secondary Structure

The formation of RNA secondary structure is the result of a natural folding process in which chemical bonds (hydrogen bonds) form between canonical base pairs. It is important to note that the hydrogen bonds are not the cause of the folding, but rather the result. These hydrogen bonds can only form between certain pairs of nucleotides, i.e. GC, AU, GU, and their mirrors, CG, UA, UG, hence the name canonical base pair. Searching a nucleotide sequence for all possible base pairs is a fast and simple procedure. The difficulty comes in predicting which ones, out of all the possibilities, will form bonds.

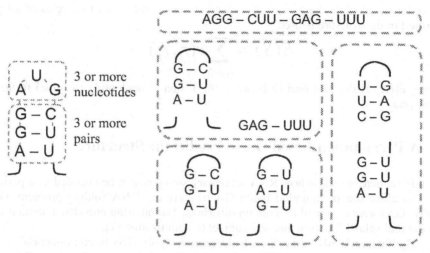

**Fig. 1.** Rules for stem loop formation

**Fig. 2.** Sample sequence fragment (top) and examples of possible helices that could form.

Stacked pairs, which form helices, provide stability in the secondary structure. A set of stacked pairs is formed by two or more base pairs (i, j), ..., (i+n, j-n) 1<=n<=m such that the ends of the pairs are adjacent, forming a ladder type structure.

Finding all possible helices made from these stacked pairs assists in determining the secondary structure. There are certain requirements that must be met in order for a helix to form, as illustrated in Fig. 1. We consider a helix to consist of at least three consecutive canonical base pairs forming a stack, and the loop connecting the two strands must be at least 3 nucleotides in length. These are chemical requirements for the stable formation of stem loops. Considering these constraints for the formation of helices, it is now possible to compute the set $H$ of all helices that could potentially form. This can be accomplished by a simple nested for-loop that scans through the whole sequence, identifies adjacent base pairs and ensures that the strand connecting them is at least 3 nucleotides long. The solution to the secondary structure prediction problem is a subset $S$ of $H$, which contains the helices that make up the final structure. Of course, care must be taken to only include helices in $S$ that are mutually exclusive, i.e., do not share one or more nucleotides (again, chemically such structures are infeasible). Since there are $2^{|H|}$ subsets of $|H|$, the problem is highly combinatorial. As Fig. 2 demonstrates, there are many possible helices from even a short sequence.

The technique employed to direct the GA through this large search space is energy minimization. As an RNA molecule will fold into a structure with near minimal energy, the GA attempts to find the combination of helices that result in the lowest energy possible. The energy function used in this paper takes into account the bonding energies of the helices. A change in free energy ($\Delta G$) is associated with each canonical base pair:

$$\Delta G(GC) = \Delta G(CG) = -3 \text{ kcal/mol}$$
$$\Delta G(AU) = \Delta G(UA) = -2 \text{ kcal/mol} \quad \text{(all at 37°C).}$$
$$\Delta G(GU) = \Delta G(UG) = -1 \text{ kcal/mol}$$

In order to calculate the energy of a given structure, the sum of energies of all pairs formed in the structure is used:

$$E(S) = \sum_{i,j \in S} e(r_i, r_j).$$

Here, $e(r_i, r_j)$ is the free energy between the $i^{th}$ and $j^{th}$ nucleotide (residue) forming a base pair.

## 3   A Permutation Based GA to Predict the Structure

In this section, we show how RNA secondary structure can be encoded as a permutation to allow our permutation based GA to solve the RNA folding problem. Originally, GAs were designed to work on bitstrings. The bitstring encoded a domain value of the real valued function that was subject to optimization [7].

By the mid 1980s, researchers had started to apply GAs to combinatorial optimization problems such as the TSP and the Job Shop Scheduling Problem (JSSP). For the TSP, a solution (a tour visiting each city exactly once and returning to the start city) can be encoded as a permutation of the individual city numbers. For example, a permutation (3 4 2 1 5 6) means start at city 3, then go to city 4, then to city 2, and so on. Such a representation, however, is not suitable for standard "cut and paste" binary crossover operators since such operators would create offspring that are not permutations anymore due to duplications and omissions of cities. The literature contains operators that are suitable for permutations, i.e., will always create a permutation again. Also, these operators try to preserve and promote either absolute position of cities, partial order between cities, or adjacency between cities. Some of the operators discussed in the literature for direct representation include *partially mapped crossover* (PMX) [2], *order crossover* (OX) [1], and *cycle crossover* (CX) [6]. Similarly, for other ordering problems such as the JSSP a solution can be encoded as a permutation of orders for the varying machines on the shop floor.

As outlined in Section 2, the problem of predicting the secondary structure of RNA can be decomposed to become a problem of picking the sub-set $S$ of helices from the set of all helices $H$, such that $E(S)$ is minimized and that no helices in $S$ share one or more base pairs. In order to use a GA to solve this problem we need to decide on a representation and operators. We propose the following: If the set of all helices $H$ contains $n$ helices then use a permutation of length $n$ to represent a candidate solution. The order in which a helix appears in the permutation is the order in which it is picked by the decoder to be inserted into the final structure. Helices that are incompatible with any previously selected helices are rejected.

This decoding algorithm will ensure that only valid secondary structures are produced by the GA. We can now run a GA using permutation based crossovers such as CX [6], PMX [2], and OX [1] on the permutations which encode for secondary RNA structures.

Another operator that is critical for the performance of a GA is the selection operator. In our study we use both standard roulette wheel selection (STDS) and a strategy called Keep-Best Reproduction (KBR) introduced in [13] where parents are chosen by Roulette Wheel selection, then crossover and mutation are performed and the set of parents and offspring undergo an additional selection step where the fittest parent and the fittest offspring survive and are inserted into the next generation. We have shown that the KBR operator increases both the efficiency and the effectiveness of the GA in the TSP domain and we also demonstrated that it is more robust with regard to algorithm parameter settings [13]. Here we demonstrate that KBR has similar benefits in the RNA prediction domain as in the TSP domain and hence the benefits of KBR can be observed in independent domains.

# 4 Results

In this section we discuss our results related to the algorithm's performance. We have tested three sequences of length 76nt, 681nt and 785nt. Our discussion will focus on an in-depth analysis of the results of the 785nt sequence. Results with the 681nt sequence are similar and are not included here due to space limitations. After discussing our initial results, we introduce several improvements to the algorithm, which include the use of 1-elitism and the use of an improved selection strategy, namely, Keep-Best Reproduction [13] (see the previous section for a brief explanation of this operator).

Three parameters control the workings of our GA: population size, crossover probability $P_c$ and mutation probability $P_m$. We tested a large number of different combinations of $P_c$ and $P_m$ in this domain and an even larger number of combinations were tested in [13] ranging from 0.0 to 1.0 in increments of 0.01 and 0.1 to cover a wide range of possibilities. We used this data to determine the best ranges of settings for our algorithm and the results reported here are the best results and the respective parameter settings.

## 4.1 Initial Evaluation

During preliminary testing, a short 76 nucleotide tRNA sequence (Saccharomyces cerevisiae tRNA-Phe gene, GI:176479) resulting in 90 possible helices, was used. The structure with minimal energy found at the end of the run was only marginally better (–93 kcal/mol) than the structure with minimal energy of the initial random population (–86 kcal/mol). Additional tests yielded a best solution of –97 kcal/mol. In light of the initial findings with the small tRNA sequence, we decided to study longer sequences as well as increase the size of the population and number of generations.

The parameters used for this run were largely the same as those used for the smaller sequence with the exceptions being a longer RNA sequence consisting of 785 nucleotides (homo sapiens mRNA containing U19H snoRNA, GI:2853215), a population size of 700, and a run length of 400 generations. Fig. 3 shows the behavior of the algorithm using CX. The outer envelope of the plot shows the extremities of each generation (maximum and minimum energies present), while the darker, inner, envelope shows the mean free energy of the population with standard deviation. As the mean clearly shows, there is a steady trend of the population towards structures with lower free energy. As well, the population remains quite diverse during the run.

While there is progress towards a low free energy solution, the convergence is very slow, requiring many generations. Noteworthy is also that the best structure at generation 400 has a higher energy than some of the best structures found in previous

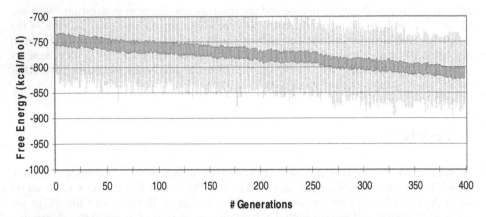

**Fig. 3.** 10480 Possible Helices, $P_m$=5%, $P_c$=70%, pop_size = 700, CX, STDS, no elitism

generations. For example, a structure with G = –896 kcal/mol was found at generation 388, but was subsequently lost.

In order to preserve the best result from each generation, elitism was used to replace the structure with the highest free energy in generation $i$ with the structure with lowest free energy from generation $i$-1. Results are displayed in Fig. 4. Due to the 1-elitism, the lower extremity of the graph is not as ragged as in Fig. 3 and an improved solution with a free energy of –916 kcal/mol is found. This is an improvement of 13.2% over the best structure found in the initial random population. Overall, the convergence speed of the algorithm using standard selection is very slow and the improvement over 400 generations is moderate.

## 4.2 Selection Strategies

The next step in testing was to use Keep Best Reproduction (KBR) [13] to increase selection pressure. This increased selection pressure requires that the mutation probability be dramatically increased in order to help maintain diversity in the population.

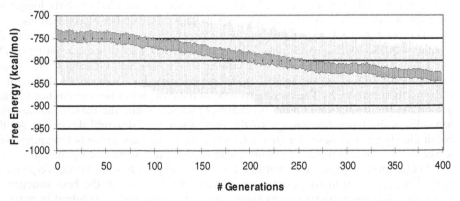

**Fig. 4.** 10480 Possible Helices, $P_m$=5%, $P_c$=70%, pop_size = 700, CX, STDS, 1-elitism

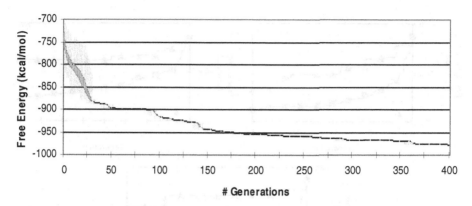

**Fig. 5.** 10480 Possible Helices, $P_m$=80%, $P_c$=70%, pop_size = 700, CX, KBR, 1-elitism

As a result, the parameters different from the previous example are the mutation probability and the selection operator. $P_m$ is now 80% rather than 5% and KBR is used instead of STDS.

As is evident in Fig. 5, convergence is much faster with the KBR selection operator, arriving at better solutions sooner than with STDS. As a result of this rapid convergence, the diversity of the population is swiftly decreased and most benefits past 100 generations are the result of the extremely high mutation rate. However, this does not pose a problem for the algorithm. For example, in the experiment graphed in Fig. 5, after 50 generations KBR has a peak result of –899 kcal/mol whereas STDS has a peak result of –853 kcal/mol. After 100 generations, KBR has found a solution of – 923 kcal/mol, while STDS has found a result of –866 kcal/mol. At the end of 400 generations, the KBR technique resulted in a solution of –980 kcal/mol, a ~21% decrease in free energy compared to the STDS decrease of ~13% at –916 kcal/mol.

### 4.3 Crossover Operators

Fig. 6 depicts the results for the 785 nt sequence. As we can see from Fig. 6 the convergence speed and quality of the solution is much better for the KBR selection operator than for the standard selection operator, regardless of crossover operator used. Specifically, the overall improvement of KBR vs. STDS as measured in total energy reduction over the initial energy is: 38.2% for CX, 151.0% for OX, and 144.6% for PMX. The best structure in the initial population had energy –825 kcal/mol. After 400 generations, CX found a structure with –935 kcal/mol using STDS and –977 kcal/mol using KBR. OX managed to find a structure with –876 kcal/mol for STDS and –953 kcal/mol for KBR. PMX found a structure with free energy –881 kcal/mol for STDS and –962 kcal/mol for KBR. We know that CX found the best structures overall and, especially under STDS is able to make progress where PMX and OX get stuck in a local optimum.

In [14] CX performed rather poorly and was outperformed by a wide margin by OX in the traveling salesman domain. CX preserves absolute position, which is not very useful in the TSP domain, but is important in the RNA folding domain as the absolute position of a helix contributes to the probability of it being picked for the sec

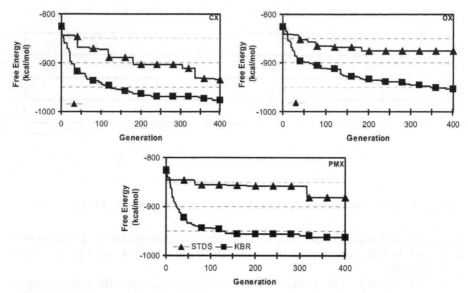

**Fig. 6.** 785nt sequence STDS vs. KBR for CX (upper left), OX (upper right), PMX (bottom

ondary structure. This difference may explain why CX performs so poorly in the TSP domain and so well in the RNA folding domain. On the other hand, OX, which performed extremely well in the TSP domain, especially on asymmetric TSPs [14], performs mediocre in the RNA domain.

Fig. 7 illustrates the different convergence speeds of KBR vs. STDS and also compares the relative performance of the crossover operators CX, OX, and PMX. As the left graph illustrates, PMX and CX both perform similarly well at the early stages of the algorithm up to about 160 generations. After that, CX is able to make more progress than PMX. Contrary to that, OX clearly has the worst performance. With STDS (right graph in Fig. 7) PMX and OX show a similar mediocre performance while CX clearly makes better progress towards structures with lower free energy. Runs with another medium length sequence (681 nt Hs_U19H2) have given similar results but are not included here due to space limitations.

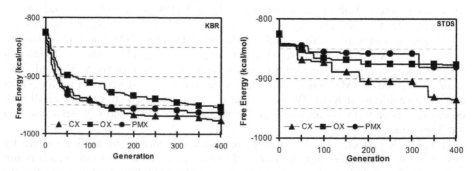

**Fig. 7.** A comparison of crossover operators CX, OX, and PMX.

## 5 Discussion

Our findings clearly indicate that our proposal to use a permutation to represent RNA secondary structure is valid in the context of a GA. While the convergence speed and solution quality with a standard selection operator are modest, the algorithm's behavior improves substantially with the use of keep-best reproduction. Also, our findings indicate that cycle crossover is a very good crossover operator for this domain and outperforms PMX and OX.

Also, the study of additional crossover operators and the study of larger sequences will reveal further insight into how well a permutation based encoding is suited for the RNA structure prediction domain. Predicted structures of low energy should be compared to the structures predicted by dynamic programming approaches and to known structures.

## 6 Conclusions

We have proposed a novel permutation based genetic algorithm to predict the secondary structure of RNA molecules using a simplistic energy function that accounts for the energy contribution of individual hydrogen bonds. The results on a sequence of 681 and a sequence of 785 nucleotides demonstrate a good convergence behavior of the algorithm and the GA is able to improve the initial random solutions substantially.

With regards to selection strategies, 1-elitism has proven useful for both STDS and KBR, where clearly, STDS benefits more from elitism than KBR. The best results overall were achieved with the KBR selection operator (both with and without elitism). With KBR, both the efficiency and the effectiveness of the algorithm increase substantially. This gives further evidence to our claim in [13] that KBR is a superior selection operator regardless of problem domain.

While CX performs rather poorly on TSPs [14], it outperformed OX and PMX in the RNA folding domain in this study. We attribute this to the fact that CX preserves absolute position, which in the TSP domain is not important, but is of importance when the permutation codes RNA structure. Overall, we conclude that using a permutation based GA is a promising approach to predict RNA secondary structure, especially when combined with KBR and CX.

**Acknowledgements.** The first author would like to acknowledge the support of the National Science and Engineering Research Council (NSERC), Canada, for the support of this research under Research Grant number RG-PIN 238298 and Equipment Grant number EQPEQ 240868. He would also like to acknowledge the support of the InfoNet Media Center funded by the Canada Foundation for Innovation (CFI) under grant number CFI-3648.

# References

[1]     Davis, L. (1985), "Job Shop Scheduling with Genetic Algorithms", *Proceedings of the 1ˢᵗ International Conf. on Genetic Algorithms,* ICGA-85, pp. 136–140

[2]     Chen, J.H., Shi-Yun, L. and Jacob V. Maizel (2000), "Prediction of common secondary structures of RNAs: A genetic Algorithm Approach", *Nucleic Acids Research,* Vol. 28 (4), Oxford University Press, pp. 991–999

[3]     Currey, K.M. and  Shapiro, B.A.(1997), "Secondary structure computer prediction of the poliovirus 5' non-coding region is improved by a genetic algorithm", *Computer Applications in the Biosciences,* Vol. 13 (1), pp. 1–12

[4]     Goldberg D.E., Lingle R. Jr. (1985), "Alleles, Loci, and the Traveling Salesman Problem", Proceedings of the 1ˢᵗ *International Conference on Genetic Algorithms ICGA-85,* pp. 154–159

[5]     Gultyaev, A.P., VanBatenburg, F.H.D., and Pleij, C.W.A. (1998), "RNA folding dynamics: Computer simulations by a genetic algorithm", *Molecular Modeling of Nucleic Acids, ACS Symposium Series,* 682, pp. 229–245

[6]     Higgs, P.G.(2000), "RNA secondary structure: Physical and computational aspects", *Quarterly Reviews for Biophysics,* Vol. 33 (3), Cambridge University Press, pp. 199–253

[7]     Holland, J.H. (1975), *Adaptation in Natural and Artificial Systems,* Ann Arbor, MI, Michigan University Press

[8]     Shapiro, B.A., Wu, J.C., Bengali, D., and Potts M.J. (2001), "The massively parallel genetic algorithm for RNA folding: MIMD implementation and population variation", *Bioinformatics,* 17(2), pp. 137–148

[9]     Shapiro, B. A. and Wu, J. C. (1996), "An annealing mutation operator in the genetic algorithms for RNA folding". *Comput. Appl. Biosci.* 12(3): 171–180

[10]    Shapiro, B. A. and Navetta, J. (1994), "A massively parallel genetic algorithm for RNA secondary structure prediction", *Journal of Supercomputing,* 8(3), pp. 195–207

[11]    VanBatenburg, F.H.D., Gultyaev, A.P., and Pleij, C.W.A. (1995), "An APL-programmed Genetic Algorithm for the Prediction of RNA Secondary Structure", *Journal of theoretical Biology,* 174(3), pp. 269–280

[12]    Oliver, I.M., Smith, D.J., and Holland, J.R.C. (1987), "A Study on Permutation Crossover Operators on the Traveling Salesman Problem", Proceedings of the 2ⁿᵈ *International Conf. on Genetic Algorithms ICGA-8,* pp. 224–230

[13]    Wiese, K.C. and Goodwin, S.D. (2001), "Keep-Best Reproduction: A Local Family Competition Selection Strategy and the Environment it Flourishes in", *Constraints,* Vol. 6, Kluwer Academic Publishers, pp. 399–422

[14]    Wiese, K.C., Goodwin, S.D., and Nagarajan, S. (2000), "ASERC – A Genetic Sequencing Operator for Asymmetric Permutation Problems", *Lecture Notes in Artificial Intelligence,* Vol. 1822, Springer, pp. 201–213

[15]    Wiese, K.C. and Glen, E. (2002), "A Permutation Based Genetic Algorithm for RNA Secondary Structure Prediction", *Frontiers in Artificial Intelligence and Applications,* Vol. 87, Abraham, A., Ruiz-del-Solar, J., Köppen, M., (eds.), IOS Press, 173–182

# Evolutionary Computation for Optimal Ensemble Classifier in Lymphoma Cancer Classification*

Chanho Park and Sung-Bae Cho

Dept. of Computer Science, Yonsei University
134 Shinchon-dong, Sudaemoon-ku, Seoul 120-749, Korea
cpark@candy.yonsei.ac.kr, sbcho@csai.yonsei.ac.kr

**Abstract.** Owing to the development of DNA microarray technologies, it is possible to get thousands of expression levels of genes at once. If we make the effective classification system with such acquired data, we can predict the class of new sample, whether it is normal or patient. For the classification system, we can use many feature selection methods and classifiers, but a method cannot be superior to the others absolutely for feature selection or classification. Ensemble classifier has been using to yield improved performance in this situation, but it is almost impossible to get all ensemble results, if there are many feature selection methods and classifiers to be used for ensemble. In this paper, we propose GA based method for searching optimal ensemble of feature-classifier pairs on Lymphoma cancer dataset. We have used two ensemble methods, and GA finds optimal ensemble very efficiently.

## 1 Introduction

Although early detection and correct class prediction of cancer have been seriously studied over the past years, there has been no exceptional way to work out this problem. It is because there can be so many pathways causing cancer, there exist tremendous number of varieties, and there are relatively small amount of experimental data. Recently, array technologies are developed enough to acquire thousands of gene expression levels at once. These gene expression profiles, however, are just simple sequence of numbers, so effective analysis tools are needed to find meaningful information in the numbers. Relating to this, many studies have been going on and published [1].

In general, the data from microarray is first normalized because raw data can be hardly used directly [2]. Then, we select informative genes by feature selection method, because the number of genes is much greater than that of samples, moreover many of them do not give help classification [3]. After feature selection, classifier operates with selected genes. Various feature selection methods and classifiers exist,

---

* This paper was supported in part by Biometrics Engineering Research Center, KOSEF, and Brain Science and Engineering Research Program sponsored by Korean Ministry of Science and Technology in Korea.

N. Zhong et al. (Eds.): ISMIS 2003, LNAI 2871, pp. 521–530, 2003.

and they produce many feature-classifiers (combination of feature selection method and classifier). In this paper, we have used seven feature selection methods and six classifiers, leading to 42 different feature-classifiers. On the other hand, it is hard to find a feature-classifier that always shows better performance than any other ones. In this situation, we can expect to get wide and improved result through the ensemble classifier [4]. Ensemble is behaved with element feature-classifiers, and $2^{42}$ ensembles are available in our case. It is practically impossible to calculate all ensemble results, and if feature-classifiers are added, then the time increases exponentially.

To remedy these drawbacks, we propose a method based on the genetic algorithm for finding optimal ensemble of feature-classifier pairs efficiently. We have tried to test the proposed method on Lymphoma cancer dataset which is well known as benchmark data, and systematically analyze its usefulness.

The rest of the paper is organized as follows. In section 2, the backgrounds for this paper, such as DNA microarray and genetic algorithm, are illustrated. In section 3, the whole system for classifying gene expression profile is explained, such as feature selection methods, classifiers, ensemble classifier, and searching process by genetic algorithm. Section 4 presents the experiments and its results. Section 5 is the concluding remarks.

## 2 Background

### 2.1 DNA Microarray

DNA microarray consists of a large number of DNA molecules spotted in a systemic order on a solid substrate. Two DNA microarray types currently in wide use are cDNA array type and high density synthetic oligonucleotide array type. Here we only focus on oligonucleotide arrays. Oligonucleotide expression arrays include both short oligo (20-25mers) arrays and long oligo (50-70 mers) arrays [5].

DNA microarrays are composed of thousands of individual DNA sequences printed in a high density array on a glass microscope slide using a robotic arrayer. The relative abundance of these spotted DNA sequences in two DNA or RNA samples may be assessed by monitoring the differential hybridization of the two samples to the sequences on the array. For mRNA samples, the two samples are reverse-transcribed into cDNA, labeled using different fluorescent dyes mixed (red-fluorescent dye Cy5 and green-fluorescent dye Cy3). After the hybridization of these samples with the arrayed DNA probes, the slides are imaged using scanner that makes fluorescence measurements for each dye. The log ratio between the two intensities of each dye is used as the gene expression data.

Hybridization of fluorescently labeled RNA and DNA-derived samples to DNA microarrays allows the monitoring of gene expression or occurrence of polymorphisms in genomic DNA.

$$gene \_ expression = \log_2 \frac{\text{Int(Cy5)}}{\text{Int(Cy3)}} \tag{1}$$

## 2.2  Genetic Algorithm

Genetic algorithms are stochastic search methods that have been successfully applied in many search, optimization, and machine learning problems [6]. Unlike most other optimization techniques, GAs maintain a population of encoded tentative solutions that are competitively manipulated by applying some variation operators to find a global optimum. A population consists of many chromosomes that can be a candidate solution. A chromosome is composed of bit strings that express a specific status or value.

A sequential GA proceeds in an iterative manner by generating new populations of strings from the old ones. Every string is the encoded (binary, real, ...) version of a candidate solution. An evaluation function associates a fitness measure to every string indicating its fitness to the problem. The standard GA applies genetic operators such as selection, crossover, and mutation on an initially random population in order to compute a whole generation of new strings.

# 3  Cancer Prediction System

The classification architecture for DNA microarray is composed of a series of processes to classify samples. The architecture contains feature selection, classifier, and finding optimal ensemble using GA. The system is as shown in Fig. 1.

## 3.1  Gene Selection Methods

We use seven feature selection methods to select informative genes. They are based on representative three fields of feature selection, such as statistical correlation, measurement of distance, and information theory.

**Statistical approach.** Using the statistical correlation analysis, we can see the linear relationship and the direction of relation between two variables. Correlation coefficient $r$ varies from $-1$ to $+1$, so that the data distributed near the line biased to $(+)$ direction will have positive coefficients, and the data near the line biased to $(-)$ direction will have negative coefficients.

Suppose that we have a gene expression pattern $g_i$ ($i = 1 \sim m$, where $m$ is the number of genes). Each $g_i$ is a vector of gene expression levels from $n$ samples, $g_i = (e_1, e_2, ..., e_n)$. Some elements are examples of class 1, and the others are those from class 0. An ideal gene pattern that belongs to class 1 is defined by $g_{ideal\_c1} = (1, ..., 1, 0, ..., 0)$, so that all the elements from class 1's samples are 1 and the others are 0.

In this paper, we have calculated the correlation coefficients between this $g_{ideal}$ and the expression pattern of each gene. When we have two vectors $X$ and $Y$ that contain - $N$ elements, $r_{Pearson}$ (PC) and $r_{Spearman}$ (SC) are calculated as follows:

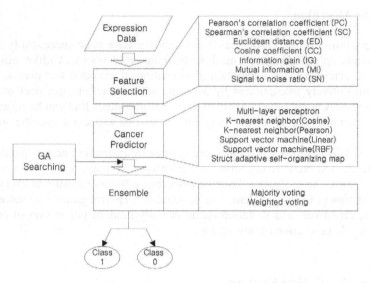

**Fig. 1.** The Cancer Prediction System

$$r_{Pearson} = \frac{\sum XY - \frac{\sum X \sum Y}{N}}{\sqrt{\left(\sum X^2 - \frac{(\sum X)^2}{N}\right)\left(\sum Y^2 - \frac{(\sum Y)^2}{N}\right)}} \qquad (2)$$

$$r_{Spearman} = 1 - \frac{6\sum (D_x - D_y)^2}{N(N^2 - 1)} \qquad (3)$$

where $D_x$ and $D_y$ are the rank matrices of $X$ and $Y$, respectively.

**Distance measure approach.** The similarity between two input vectors $X$ and $Y$ can be thought of as distance. Distance is a measure on how far the two vectors are located, and the distance between $g_{ideal\_c1}$ and $g_i$ tells us how much the $g_i$ is likely to the class 1. Calculating the distance between them, if it is bigger than certain threshold, the gene $g_i$ would belong to class 1, otherwise $g_i$ belongs to class 0. In this paper, we have adopted Euclidean distance ($r_{Eclidean}$, ED) and cosine coefficient ($r_{Cosine}$, CC) represented by the following equations:

$$r_{Eclidean} = \sqrt{\sum (X - Y)^2} \qquad (4)$$

$$r_{Cosine} = \frac{\sum XY}{\sqrt{\sum X^2 \sum Y^2}} \qquad (5)$$

**Information-theoretic approach.** We have utilized the information gain and mutual information that are widely used in many fields such as text categorization and data mining. If we count the number of genes excited ($P(g_i)$) or not excited ($P(g_i)$) in category $c_j$ $(P(c_j))$, the coefficients of the information gain (IG) and mutual information (MI) become as follows:

$$IG(g_i, c_j) = P(g_i \mid c_j) \log \frac{P(g_i \mid c_j)}{P(c_j) \cdot P(g_i)} + P(\bar{g}_i \mid c_i) \log \frac{P(\bar{g}_i \mid c_j)}{P(c_j) \cdot P(\bar{g}_i)} \qquad (6)$$

$$MI(g_i, c_j) = \log \frac{P(g_i, c_j)}{P(c_j) \cdot P(g_i)} \qquad (7)$$

Mutual information tells us the dependency relationship between two probabilistic variables of events. If two events are completely independent, the mutual information is 0. The more they are related, the higher the mutual information gets. Information gain is used when the features of samples are extracted by inducing the relationship between gene and class by the presence frequency of the gene in the sample. Information gain measures the goodness of gene using the presence and absence within the corresponding class.

For each gene $g_i$, some are from class 1, and some are from class 0. If we calculate the mean $\mu$ and standard deviation $\sigma$ from the distribution of gene expressions within their classes, the signal to noise ratio of gene $g_i$, $SN(g_i)$, is defined by:

$$SN(g_i) = \frac{\mu_{c1}(g_i) - \mu_{c0}(g_i)}{\sigma_{c1}(g_i) + \sigma_{c0}(g_i)} \qquad (8)$$

## 3.2 Classifiers

**Multilayer perceptron.** Error backpropagation neural network is a feed-forward multilayer perceptron (MLP) that is applied in many fields due to its powerful and stable learning algorithm [7]. The neural network learns the training examples by adjusting the synaptic weight of neurons according to the error occurred on the output layer. The power of the backpropagation algorithm lies in two main aspects: local for updating the synaptic weights and biases, and efficient for computing all the partial derivatives of the cost function with respect to these free parameters.

**K-nearest neighbor.** $K$-nearest neighbor (KNN) is one of the most common methods for memory based induction. Given an input vector, KNN extracts $k$ closest vectors in the reference set based on similarity measures, and makes decision for the label of input vector using the labels of the $k$ nearest neighbors [8]. Pearson's correlation and cosine coefficient have been used as the similarity measure.

**Support vector machine.** Support vector machine (SVM) estimates the function classifying the data into two classes [9]. SVM builds up a hyperplane as the decision surface in such a way to maximize the margin of separation between positive and negative examples. SVM achieves this by the structural risk minimization principle that the error rate of a learning machine on the test data is bounded by the sum of the training-error rate and a term that depends on the Vapnik-Chervonenkis (VC) dimension. We have used linear kernel and RBF kernel in SVM[light] module. (available at: http://svmlight.joachims.org/)

**Structure adaptive SOM.** Even though SOM is well known for its good performance of topology preserving, it is difficult to apply it to practical classification since the topology should be fixed before training. A structure adaptive self-organizing map (SASOM) was proposed to overcome this shortcoming [10]. SASOM starts with 4×4 map, and dynamically splits the output nodes of the map, where the data from different classes are mixed, trained with the LVQ learning algorithm.

## 3.3 Ensemble Classifier

Though there are various feature selection methods and classifiers, it is hard to find the perfect method for classification. Besides it is difficult to decide the number of informative genes, and setting of parameters. In a situation like these, we cannot expect that one feature-classifier always produces good performance. At this time, ensemble classifier can be used usefully through the combination of feature-classifier pairs. Researchers are used as ensemble methods such as majority voting, Bayesian average, neural network, and so on [11].

If we just use a feature-classifier pair, we get only 42 results of classification because we have used seven feature selection methods and six classifiers. However, we can get about 4-tera results by ensemble classifier. It means that we can search much wider solution space. We have applied this idea to the classification framework as shown in Fig. 1. We have chosen majority voting and weighted voting as ensemble methods, they are shown in the Table 1.

**Table 1.** Ensemble methods (when $x$ is input, $c_{1i}(x) = 1$, if $e_i(x) = 1$, otherwise $c_{1i}(x) = 0$, $c_{0i}(x) = 1$, if $e_i(x) = 0$, otherwise $c_{0i}(x) = 0$, $w_i$ is accuracy of $e_i(x)$, and $e_i(x)$ is element feature-classifier)

| Ensemble method | Output | Condition |
|---|---|---|
| Majority voting | 1 | $\sum_i (c_{1i}(x)) > \sum_i (c_{0i}(x))$ |
|  | 0 | otherwise |
| Weighted voting | 1 | $\sum_i (c_{1i}(x)w_i) > \sum_i (c_{0i}(x)w_i)$ |
|  | 0 | otherwise |

## 3.4 Searching Optimal Ensemble Using GA

It takes so long time to calculate all possible ensembles. Moreover, if we added one feature-classifier pair, it would increase spending time exponentially. Therefore efficient method for finding optimal ensemble is needed, so that we have proposed the method with GA. The structure of chromosome is as shown in Fig. 2.

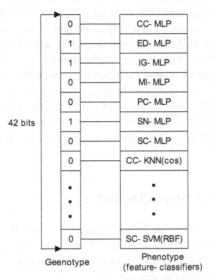

**Fig. 2.** The Design of Chromosome

Each chromosome is composed of 42 bits, and each bit means that the corresponding feature-classifier is included or not. Each bit corresponding specific feature-classifier like Fig. 2. Fig. 2 means the ensemble of second, third, and sixth feature-classifier pairs because those bits are 1. After initial population is created, fitness is evaluated with ensemble result.

## 4 Experiments

### 4.1 Experimental Dataset

B cell diffuse large cell lymphoma(B-DLCL) is a heterogeneous group of tumors, based on significant variations in morphology, clinical presentation, and response to treatment. Gene expression profiling has revealed two distinct tumor subtypes of B-DLCL: germinal center B cell-like DLCL and activated B cell-like DLCL [12]. Lymphoma dataset consists of 24 samples of GC B-like and 23 samples of activated B-like. 22 out of 47 samples were used as training data and the remaining were used as test data in this paper. (Available at: http://genome-www.stanford.edu/lymphoma)

### 4.2 Experimental Environment

The experimental process is composed of gene selection, classification, and searching optimal ensemble using GA. For gene selection, we rank the genes according to its feature score, and select 25 highly scored genes. For classifier, we have used MLP with 8 hidden nodes, 2 output nodes, 0.01~0.50 of learning rate, 0.9 of momentum, 500 of maximum iterations, and 98% of goal accuracy. In $k$NN, we have set $k$ from 1 to 8, and used Pearson correlation coefficient and cosine coefficient as similarity measures. We have used SVM with linear and RBF kernel function. In SASOM, we have used initial $4\times4$ map which has rectangle shape.

Preliminary experiments for searching optimal ensemble using GA show converge to local minimum when we use only tens of chromosomes. So we set the sizes of population to 100, 200, 500, 1000, 1500, and 2000. Many crossover rates and mutation rates are applied to various size of population. We use roulette wheel rule as a selection method, and give higher fitness to chromosome that have small number of feature-classifier pairs.

### 4.3  Results of Element Feature-Classifier

There are results for all element feature-classifier pairs in Table 2. $K$NN(Cosine) classifier records good accuracy and IG shows outstanding performance for all classifiers. Feature selection methods based on information-theoretic approach show better performance than others in this dataset.

**Table 2.** Recognition rate with features and classifiers (%) in Lymphoma dataset

|      | MLP  | SASOM | SVM |      | KNN |      |
|------|------|-------|--------|------|--------|---------|
|      |      |       | Linear | RBF  | Cosine | Pearson |
| PC   | 64.0 | 48.0  | 56.0   | 60.0 | 76.0   | 60.0    |
| SC   | 60.0 | 68.0  | 44.0   | 44.0 | 60.0   | 60.0    |
| ED   | 56.0 | 52.0  | 56.0   | 56.0 | 68.0   | 56.0    |
| CC   | 68.0 | 52.0  | 56.0   | 56.0 | 72.0   | 60.0    |
| IG   | 92.0 | 84.0  | 92.0   | 92.0 | 92.0   | 92.0    |
| MI   | 72.0 | 64.0  | 64.0   | 64.0 | 64.0   | 80.0    |
| SN   | 76.0 | 76.0  | 72.0   | 76.0 | 80.0   | 76.0    |
| Avg. | 69.7 | 63.4  | 62.9   | 63.4 | 73.1   | 69.1    |

### 4.4  Results of Optimal Ensemble with GA

Before finding optimal ensemble, we investigate the change of average fitness to see if GA evolves. It is because optimal ensemble can be found accidentally. Fig. 3 shows the change of average fitness. We can see that average fitness increases by iteration and it converge after about 100 iterations. Fig. 4 is a plot for relation of population size and generation that find optimal ensemble. It shows that population size is inverse proportion to the finding generation.

We could not get good performances by element feature-classifier pairs. It means that there exists high possibility of improving performance, and GA practically finds ensembles that record improved performance than any other element feature-classifier pairs. The accuracy of element feature-classifier pair is 44~92%, and average is 67%.

Nevertheless, GA finds the ensemble of 100% that is composed of supplemented pairs of feature-classifier. Ensembles searched by GA have ranged 92~100% accuracy, and recorded 96.67% on average. Some optimal ensembles are in Table 3.

The real usefulness of GA lies in its time-efficiency. We have experimented with all the ensembles that are composed of 3, 5 and 7 feature-classifier pairs without using GA, and it takes about 20 minutes. Therefore, it is almost impossible to test all the ensembles. However, it takes only 60 seconds averagely with GA of 2000 population size when finding optimal ensemble.

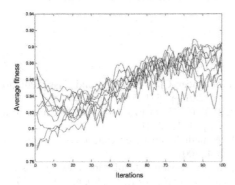
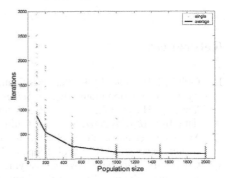

**Fig. 3.** The Change of Average Fitness

**Fig. 4.** The Population Size and Generation that finds Optimal Ensemble

**Table 3.** Optimal ensembles of Lymphoma dataset

| Methods | Feature-classifier pairs |
|---|---|
| Majority voting | CC-KNN(P), MI-KNN(C), SN-KNN(C), SS-SASOM, IG-SVM(L) |
| | IG-KNN(C), MI-KNN(C), PC-KNN(C), SN-KNN(P), SN-SASOM |
| Weighted voting | IG-KNN(C), IG-KNN(P), PC-KNN(P), SN-KNN(P), CC-SASOM |
| | IG-KNN(C), MI-KNN(C), SN-KNN(C), SN-KNN(P), CC-SASOM, IG-SASOM, PC-SVM(R) |

## 5   Concluding Remarks

This paper uses GA for efficiently analyzing gene expression profiles. Experimental results show that GA finds ensembles that produce higher performance than any individual feature-classifier pairs. Though we can find optimal ensemble without using GA, it is so time-consuming work for evaluating all ensembles. GA finds optimal solution quickly, and it is more useful when feature selection method or classifier is added to the system. In addition, we can see that GA finds optimal solution through the increasing average fitness. This means that chromosomes evolve to right way.

On the other hand, though we have just used simple GA and ensemble methods, we will investigate more methods and conditions. Moreover, we are going to experiment on the other datasets to establish our proposed method. Though we cannot know the meaning of genes that related optimal ensembles found by GA, but there exists biological worth, and these studies will be good for interdisciplinary work.

# References

1.  Golub, T. R., et al.: Molecular classification of cancer: Class discovery and class prediction by gene expression monitoring. In *Science*, vol. 286, pp. 531–537, 1999.
2.  Yang, Y. H., Dudoit, S., Luu, P. and Speed, T. P.: Normalization for cDNA microarray data. In *SPIE Bios 2001*, San Jose, California, pp. 1–12, 2001.
3.  Model, F., et al.: Feature selection for DNA methylation based cancer classification. In *Bioinformatics*, vol. 17 Suppl. 1, pp. s157–s164, 2001.
4.  Cho, S.-B. and Ryu, J.-W.: Classifying gene expression data of cancer using classifier ensemble with mutually exclusive features. In *Proc. of the IEEE*, vol. 90, no. 11, pp. 1744–1753, 2002.
5.  Li, F. and Stormo, G. D.: Selection of optimal DNA oligos for gene expression arrays. In *Bioinformatics*. vol. 17, no. 11, pp. 1067–1076, 2001.
6.  Mitchell, T. M.: *Machine Learning*, Carnegie Mellon University, 1997.
7.  Khan, J., et al.: Classification and diagnostic prediction of cancers using gene expression profiling and artificial neural networks. In *Nature*, vol. 7, no. 6, pp. 673–679, 2001.
8.  Duda, R. O., Hart, P. E., and Stork, D. G.: *Pattern Classification, 2nd Ed.* Wiley Interscience, 2001.
9.  Furey, T. S., et al.: Support vector machine classification and validation of cancer tissue samples using microarray expression data. In *Bioinformatics*, vol. 16, no. 10, pp. 906–914, 2000.
10. Kim, H. D. and Cho, S.-B.: Genetic optimization of structure-adaptive self-organizing map for efficient classification. In *Proc. of International Conference on Soft Computing*, pp. 34–39, 2000.
11. Ben-Dor, A., et al.: Tissue classification with gene expression profiles. In *Journal of Computational Biology*, vol. 7. pp. 559–584, 2000.
12. Alizadeh, A. A., et al.: Distinct types of diffuse large B-cell lymphoma identified by gene expression profiling. In *Nature*, vol. 403, pp. 503–511, 2000.

# Floorplan Design Using Improved Genetic Algorithm

Kenichi Ida and Yosuke Kimura

Department of Systems and Information Engineering,
Maebashi Institute of Technology,
Maebashi, 371-0816 Japan
ida@maebashi-it.ac.jp

**Abstract.** Genetic Algorithm (GA) which is a part of soft computing is attracting attention as an approximation method to combinatorial optimization problems. The floorplan design problem (FDP) belongs to the category of these kinds of problems; it is difficult to find a true optimal solution in real time. A floorplan design problem is classified into the slicing structure and the non-slicing structure, from the arrangement structure. Recently, we proposed the new immune algorithm for the floorplan design with slicing structure, which was an application of GA. In this paper, we propose an improved genetic algorithm (pIGA) combining the advantage of our proposed immune algorithm to the floorplan design with non-slicing structure. pIGA is improved aiming at the further improvement in the convergence speed and the accuracy of a solution. Moreover, we apply pIGA to the MCNC benchmark problem. The experimental results show that the proposed pIGA has better performance than the existing methods.

## 1 Introduction

Soft computing is attracting attention as an efficient technique to complicated problems. It includes fuzzy logic (FL), neural network (NN) and genetic algorithm (GA). And immunity algorithm (IA) developed from GA.

As an example of application, it is known that GA is effective in a floorplan design problem. A floorplan design is a kind of combinatorial optimization problem. The object of the problem is to obtain arrangement of which area is the minimum. But when many restricted conditions about blocks were given, this kind of combinatorial optimization problem makes it difficult to obtain a strict solution within a practical limited time.

As concrete application to a floorplan design, there are the method of Cohoon et al.[2], Someya's method[3], Shigehiro's method[4], Nakaya's method[5] about GA, and Tazawa's methods[6,7] about IA. Cohoon et al., Someya, and Tazawa treated the floorplan design of slicing structure. On the other hand, Shigehiro and Nakaya treated non-slicing structure. The slicing structure regards layout as a repetition of dividing such as horizontal and vertical slicing. It can be

N. Zhong et al. (Eds.): ISMIS 2003, LNAI 2871, pp. 531–538, 2003.

represented by tree structure. When using genetic algorithm, this tree structure is often expressed by reverse polish notation.

Recently, we proposed new algorithm[8] that treats the slicing floorplan. It was improved at a convergence speed and the processing speed which had been the fault of IA. Moreover, It aimed at conquest of the complexity of a parameter setup, and improvement in solution accuracy. We compared this technique with the Someya's method[3], Tazawa's method[7], etc.

On the other hand, because non-slicing floorplan cannot be expressed by reverse polish notation, sequence-pair is proposed. Since sequence-pair can express all the floorplans that are the candidate of the optimal solution, it was adopted in the Shigehiro's method[4], the Nakaya's method[5], etc., and has obtained the outstanding result.

In this paper, we propose improved GA which aimed at the further improvement in a convergence speed of solution candidates and the accuracy of a solution, applying the advantage of our improved IA[8] to this non-slicing floorplan. These improvements are maintenance of the diversity by double populations, application of Hayashi's quantification method type four[9] for acquisition of outstanding initial individual, the simplification of parameter setup, use of local search, etc. Furthermore, using a benchmark problem, our algorithm was compared with the existing methods.

## 2     Floorplan Design Problem

In this paper, a set $r_i(1 \leq i \leq n)$ of rectangular blocks lie parallel to the coordinate axes. Each rectangular block $r_i$ is defined by a elements $(h_i, w_i)$, where $h_i$ and $w_i$ are the height and the width of the block $r_i$, respectively. A placement $(x_i, y_i)$ is an assignment of coordinates to center the rectangular blocks such that there is no two rectangular blocks overlapping. That is, the restrictions to $x_i, y_i (1 \leq i \leq n)$ are such that the following equation is consistent to any $i, j (1 \leq i \leq n, 1 \leq i \leq n, i \neq j)$.

$$|x_i - x_j| \geq \frac{(w_i + w_j)}{2} \tag{1}$$

$$|y_i - y_j| \geq \frac{(h_i + h_j)}{2} \tag{2}$$

The cost function we use for a placement consists of two parts. One is the area of the smallest rectangle that encloses the placement. This is expressed with the following equations.

$$s = \{\max_i(x_i + \frac{w_i}{2}) - \min_i(x_i - \frac{w_i}{2})\}$$
$$\times \{\max_i(y_i + \frac{h_i}{2}) - \min_i(y_i - \frac{h_i}{2})\} \tag{3}$$

Another is the interconnection cost between rectangular blocks. In this case, we use the Manhattan distance between the central coordinates of each rectangle block as an approximation. The interconnection cost between rectangular blocks $r_i$ and $r_j$ is expressed as $m_{ij}$. Thus, another part of the cost function is represented with the following equations.

$$l = \sum_{i=1}^{n}\sum_{j=1}^{n}\{(|x_i - x_j| + |y_i - y_j|) \times m_{ij}\} \qquad (4)$$

Finally, $e = s + \lambda l$ becomes a objective function. This problem aims at minimizing this function. Here, $\lambda$ is the weight of the interconnection cost in this function.

# 3 Proposed Method

## 3.1 Improved Points

1. This technique has adapted the thinking of a hash method. It makes a different gene exist in population, using a function that accepts a hash key, and returns a hash result with uniform distribution. When a collision happens, the fitness of the individual that was stored there and the individual that was newly produced are compared. The one with the higher fitness remains. This maintains diversity.

2. Genetic operations (for example, crossover, mutation) have been performed based on the genotype on the floorplan design problem as a general method. This method operates these modules using coordinates that are equivalent to the phenotype. Thus, similar solutions are generated easily, and a local search is performed.

3. The proposed technique uses units (this unit is called meme after this) that have information which population will be operated by which genetic operation. This is prepared beforehand. The effective meme is bred, and the low meme of an effect is extinguished, like an individual.

4. This method prepares two kinds of populations. Each population shares search as before and maintenance of diversity. The individual that maintains diversity is called a heroic individual in this paper. Almost all individuals are a copy of one of the heroic individuals. The outstanding individual created as a result of the search can replace only the heroic individual that became an ancestor. We will call the information in which a heroic individual is an ancestor, blood after this.

5. The outstanding initial individual is obtained using Hayashi's quantification method type four[9].

6. We applied two kinds of Hill Climbing local searches. These use almost all mutations. Two kinds of searches are performed by two kinds of fitness functions. One function simply uses an evaluation function to provide fitness, and the other distributes the solutions in landscapes like a Sharing. The Hill Climbing local search was usually repeated until processing of the target individual was completed. However, since search stops after a defined number of evaluating, the amount of calculation in this method is adjusted.

## 3.2 Algorithm

**Step 1.** Recognition of restriction conditions
Input the objective function and restriction conditions into the system. If there are parameters, which control them, input these also.

**Step 2.** Determination of the genotype
Express genes as sign sequences. Here, we use the already proposed sequence-pair.

**Step 3.** Creation of the initial population
Copy outstanding heroic individuals generated in the past. If a heroic individual did not exist, generate these one at random. Give peculiar blood to each hero individual. Generate an individual group, choosing method by equal probability between randomness and using the Hayashi's Quantification Third Method.

**Step 4.** Creation of meme
Generate a fixed number of memes that have information on which individuals will be operated by which genetic operations.

**Step 5.** Shift from heroic individuals to individuals
Choose a heroic individual. It can choose by equal probability whether to leave it as it is or to change it for an individual with the lowest fitness.

**Step 6.** Creation of individuals
Generate offspring by crossover and mutation. Each individual are given the parents' blood. Store the generated individuals by hashing, and breed effective memes.

**Step 7.** Hill Climbing local search that maintains diversity
Perform the Hill Climbing local search which distributes individuals into the landscapes in the first stage of search.

**Step 8.** The straightforward Hill Climbing local search
Perform the straightforward Hill Climbing local search at the end of the search.

**Step 9.** Shift from individuals to heroic individuals Choose whether to leave it in a population, or shift from heroic individuals about each blood which exists in a population

Repeat Step5 to Step9 until a predefined number of generations is achieved.

## 4 Numerical Experiment

The purpose of the numerical experiment is to ensure that the proposed improved Genetic Algorithm (pIGA) is better than the existing methods. We compared pIGA with Shigehiro's method (GA)[4] and Nakaya's method (EAGA)[5]. Moreover, since Nakaya compared his method with Someya's method (GSA)[3], that we also consider the performance of Someya's method. These methods were applied to two MCNC examples: ami33 and ami49. It is used when consider about application to VLSI layouts. The terminal with three or more Net Degree was divided into the terminal with two Net Degree. All the aspect ratios were fixed to 1. We calculated for 30 minutes. And we ran experiment 10 times on ami33, 30 times on ami49.

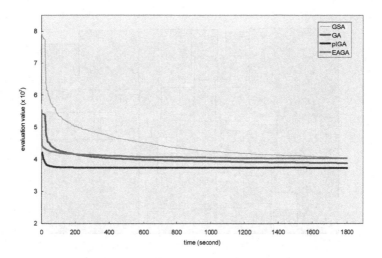

**Fig. 1.** Convergence process

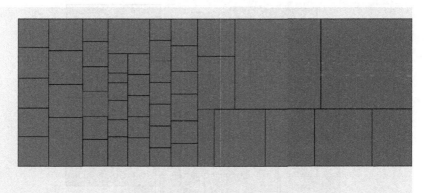

**Fig. 2.** Result of GSA (ami49)

**Table 1.** Experimental result by each method

| Problem | Solution | Algorithm | | | |
|---|---|---|---|---|---|
| | | pIGA | GA | EAGA | GSA |
| ami49 (x $10^7$) | Best | 3.6691 | 3.7431 | 3.8479 | 3.8715 |
| | Worst | 3.7964 | 3.9733 | 4.2398 | 4.4116 |
| | Average | 3.7181 | 3.8685 | 4.0268 | 4.0342 |
| ami33 (x $10^6$) | Best | 1.5551 | 1.6067 | 1.9875 | 1.6277 |
| | Worst | 1.6141 | 1.6845 | 2.0902 | 1.6939 |
| | Average | 1.5908 | 1.6402 | 2.0283 | 1.6456 |

Average convergence process to ami49 is shown in Figure 1. Each example of result of these methods is shown in Figure 2, 3, 4, and 5.

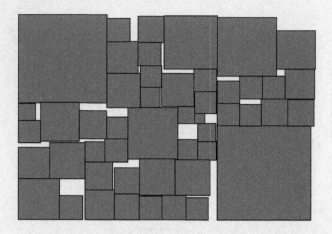

**Fig. 3.** Result of GA (ami49)

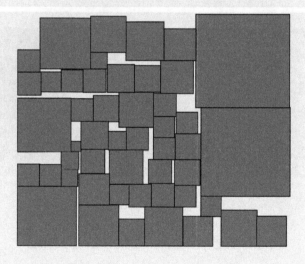

**Fig. 4.** Result of EAGA (ami49)

Best, worst and average costs of each method are shown in Table 1 and Figure 6. In Figure 6, minimum values of two results of problems are made 0 and standard deviation of two results of problems are made 100 in order to make the figure clear.

Acculate and efficient convergence of the pIGA is shown in Figure 1. From this figure, we can conjecture that GSA can still improve solution. But it takes long time to improve the solution by GSA. It is supposed that GA and EAGA will not obtain a better solution than pIGA. Figure 2, 3, 4, and 5 show that pIGA has the minimum deadspace. Tabele 1 and Figure 6 shows that pIGA gets the minimum cost in arbitrary items.

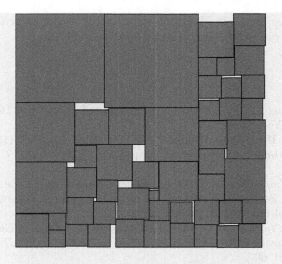

**Fig. 5.** Result of pIGA (ami49)

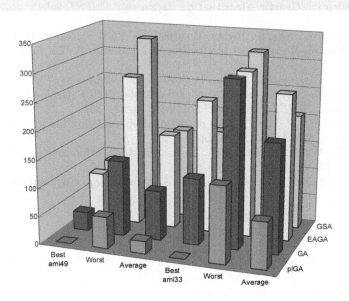

**Fig. 6.** Experimental result by each method

## 5   Conclusions

In this paper, we proposed new GA for floorplan design, which aimed at "the convergence speed of the solution candidate", "improvement in the accuracy of a solution by maintenance of diversity" and "simplification of a parameter setup". The algorithm can't always calculate the strict optimal solution. But the experimental results showed that the proposed method performed better than the existing methods. And it is supposed that the algorithm is practical, because it does not need a complicated parameter setup.

# References

1. Gen, M., Cheng, R. (1997), *Genetic Algorithms and Engineering Design*, John Wiley & Sons, New York.
2. Cohoon, J.P., Hedge, S.U., Martin, W.N. and Richards, D.S. (1991), Distributed genetic algorithms for floorplan design problem, *IEEE Trans. CAD*, vol.10, no.4, pp.483–492.
3. Someya, H., Yamamura, M. (1999), A Genetic Algorithms for the Floorplan Design Problem with Search Area Adaptation along with Search Stage (in Japanese), *T. IEE Japan*, vol.119-C, no.3, pp.393–403.
4. Shigehiro, Y., Yamaguchi, S., Inoue, M., Masuda, T. (2001), A Genetic Algorithms Based on Sequence-Pair for Floorplan Design (in Japanese), *T. IEE Japan*, vol.121-C, no.3, pp.601–607.
5. Nakaya, S., Koide, T., Wakabayashi, S. (2002), A VLSI Floorplanning Method Based on an Adaptive Genetic Algorithm (in Japanese), *J. IPSJ*, vol.43, no.5, pp.1361–1371.
6. Tazawa, I., Koakutsu, S., Hirata, H. (1995), A VLSI Floorplan Design Based on Genetic Immune Recruitment Mechanism (in Japanese), *T. IEE Japan*, vol.31, no.5, pp.615–621.
7. Tazawa, I., Koakutsu, S., Hirata, H. (1997), An Evolutionary Optimization based on the Immune System and its Application to the VLSI Floorplan Design Problem (in Japanese), *T. IEE Japan*, vol.117-C no.7, pp.821–827.
8. Ida, K., Kimura, Y. (2002), Layout Design Problem Using Immune Algorithm (in Japanese), *J. SPEJ* vol.14, no.3, pp.207–213.
9. Tanaka, Y., Wakimoto, K. (1998), *Methods of Multivariate Statistical Analysis* (in Japanese), Gendaisuugakusha, pp.161–171.
10. Kitano, H. (1995), *Genetic Algorithms 2* (in Japanese), Sangyoutosho, pp.37–38.

# Some Enhancements in Genetic Learning:
# A Case Study on Initial Population

Ivan Bruha

McMaster University, Dept. Computing & Software
Hamilton, Ont., Canada, L8S4L7
bruha@mcmaster.ca

**Abstract**. In our project, we have selected the paradigm of genetic algorithms (GAs) for search through a space of all possible concept descriptions. We designed and implemented a system that integrates a domain-independent GA into the covering learning algorithm CN4, a large extension of the well-known CN2; we call it GA-CN4.
This paper focuses on some enhancements of the above learning algorithm. Particularly, (a) discretization and fuzzification of numerical attributes for GAs (their genuine form is not able to process these attributes), (b) representation of chromosomes (objects, individuals) in GAs, and (c) the ways of initialization of a population for a GA.

## 1  Introduction:  Genetic Algorithm as a Learner

*Genetic algorithms* (GAs) seem to be a relativelynew efficient paradigm for inducing new concepts. They emulate biological evolution and are utilized in optimization processes, similarly to simulated annealing, rough sets, and neural nets. The optimization is performed by processing a population of individuals (objects, chromosomes). A designer of a GA has to provide an evaluation function, called *fitness*, that evaluates any individual (chromosome). The fitter individual has the greater chance in forming a new population. Given an initial population of individuals, a genetic algorithm proceeds by choosing individuals to become parents and then replacing members of the current population by the new individuals (offsprings) that are modified copies of their parents. The designer must also select types of *genetic operators*, namely *selection, crossover*, and *mutation*.

GA's have become an attractive alternative to classical search algorithms for exploring large spaces of concept descriptions. They are two important characteristics of the search performed by a GA: the search is usually global and is parallel in nature since a GA processes not just a single individual (chromosome) but a large set (population) of individuals.

As we have already stated, GAs exhibit various parameters that must be selected by a designer; there are, however, two important parameters whose selection and/or definition is the most important, namely the initialization of the population of individuals and their representation. Besides, the genuine GAs can process individuals represented by discrete attributes only. Therefore, the other important issue is the discretization of numerical attributes.

## 2  GA-CN4:  Genetic-Based Learner

A GA starts with an initial population of chromosomes and lets them evolve by combining them by means of genetic operators. Its behaviour generally depends on the types of genetic operators, the shape of the fitness function, and the initial population's initialization procedure. We designed the rule-inducing CN4 learning algorithm [3], a large extension of the well-known algorithm CN2 [6] by many efficient routines. In our new genetic learner GA-CN4, we have replaced the original search strategy by a domain-independent GA.

N. Zhong et al. (Eds.): ISMIS 2003, LNAI 2871, pp. 539–543, 2003.

A single rule is treated as an individual (chromosome). After a stopping condition is satisfied, the best individual (decision rule) is selected. GA-CN4 generates decision rules from a set of $K$ training examples, each accompanied by its *desired class* $C_r$, $r = 1,...,R$. Examples are represented by $N$ discrete (symbolic) *attributes*. An attribute $A_n$, n=1,...,N, comprises $J(n)$ distinct values $V_1,...,V_{J(n)}$. The algorithm yields an *ordered* list of decision rules of the form

$$\text{Rule: if } Cond \text{ then class is } C_r \qquad (1)$$

The condition *Cond* is represented by a conjunction of selectors (attribute-value pairs).

Our domain-independent GA(*T*) processes the fixed-length chromosomes:

**procedure** GA(*T*)                                                                                          // *T* is a training set
1.    Initialize a new population
2.    **Until** stopping condition is satisfied **do**
      2.1    Select individuals by the tournament selection operator
      2.2    Generate offsprings by the two-point crossover operator
      2.3    Perform the bit mutation
      2.4    Execute the hill-climbing local-optimization
      2.5    Check whether each new individual has the correct attribute and class values (within their
           ranges); if not the individual's fitness is set to 0 (the worst value)
    **enddo**
3.    Select the fittest individual (i.e. a decision rule)
4.    **If** this object is statistically significant **then** return this object
    **else** return nil

Details of our genetic learner can be found in [4]. The fitness function is calculated by the Laplacian criterion for expected accuracy (for the class $C_r$)

$$Lapl(C_r, Cond) = \frac{K_r(Cond)+1}{K(Cond)+R} \qquad (2)$$

where $K_r(Cond)$ is the number of training examples of the class $C_r$ covered by the condition *Cond*, $K(Cond)$ the number of examples covered by the condition, $R$ the number of classes.

# 3    Some Enhancements

## 3.1  Discretization/Fuzzification of Numerical Attributes

The genuine GAs are not able to process numerical (continuous) attributes; some discretization/fuzzification procedure has to be performed. In our genetic learner, we discretize numerical attributes by invoking the discretization off-line preprocessor of the learning algorithm KEX [1], [2], [4] before a generic algorithm is called. The rudimentary idea is to create intervals for which the *aposteriori* class distribution $P(C_r|interval)$ significantly differs from the *apriori* one $P(C_r)$, r=1,...,R, in the entire training set. Thus, the performance of this procedure leads to a rule of the form (1) where one of the selectors of the condition is $A_n$ 0 *interval*.

Discretization of numerical attributes into crisp intervals (sharp bounds between intervals) does not correspond to real situations in many application areas. Therefore, KEX also generates fuzzy intervals in order to eliminate such an impurity around the interval borders.

## 3.2  Representation of Rules

As we have already stated, each decision rule generated by the genetic learner are portrayed by a chromosome (individual). Since the number $N$ of attributes for a task (problem) is given, each chromosome (decision rule) is represented by a fixed-length string of the length of $N$ fields.

There exist various ways of actual depiction of these fields that form the entire string (i.e., chromosome's representation). We now survey the most interesting ones [7].

(a) In *Byte Representation*, each attribute field is placed in one byte (8 bits); i.e., maximum range of values of any attribute is from 0 to 255. – Let us illustrate this representation on the well-known 'weather' problem [8] with these attributes:

```
windy:              false, true
humidity:           normal, high
temperature:        cool, mild, hot
outlook:            rain, overcast, sunny
```

Each rule is represented by a string of 4 bytes, each attribute value by an integer from the range 0 to $J(n)$. If a byte is within this range, then it is interpreted as the corresponding attribute value; otherwise, the given selector is excluded from the rule. For instance, the string

```
00000001 10111101 01011111 11001011
```

corresponds to values 1, 189, 95, 203; since only the 1st value is permissible, i.e. it represents

```
if windy=true then class is C
```

where $C$ is the majority class of the training examples covered by this rule.

Evidently, this representation requires *Lchrom* = 8 * $N$ bits. The probability of inserting a selector $A_n$ into a rule is thus

$$Pins(A_n) = \frac{J(n)}{256}$$

i.e. usually very small. In our example, the probability $Pins(\texttt{windy}) = 0.0078$ (0.78%).

However, this representation allows to easily introduce a negation of a selector. The left-most bit in any byte can serve as a flag for negation (equal 1 if the selector is to be negated). The maximum range of attribute values is consequently half, i.e. from 0 to 127.

(b) In *Reduced Mask Representation* each attribute $A_n$ in a chromosome representation is depicted by *Lmask*(n) bits which is the minimum integer greater than or equal to $J(n)$. The probability of inserting a selector $A_n$ into a rule looks thus better:

$$Pins(A_n) = \frac{J(n)}{Lmask(n)+1}$$

In our example, $Pins(\texttt{windy}) = 0.75$. – Also, by adding an extra bit for each rule allows to introduce a negation of the corresponding selector.

(c) In *Bit representation* each attribute $A_n$ is represented by $J(n)+1$ bits. Each attribute field begins with one bit (toggle) for negation. Each remaining bit exhibits one value of this attribute; it is set up to 1 if the corresponding value is present in the selector. E.g., the string

```
0 01 1 00 1 101 1 001
```

in our task represents this rule:

```
if windy=true && temperature\=[cool or hot] && outlook\=sunny
    then class is C
```

Hence, this representation allows negation, internal disjunction, and negation of the internal disjunction. The length of a chromosome is

$$Lchrom = N + \int_{n=1}^{N} J(n)$$

and the probability of inserting a selector $A_n$ into a rule is always 0.5.

(d) *Representation of a numerical attribute* $A_n$ is done by two real numbers; the lower bound $Lbound_n$ of an interval and its upper bound $Ubound_n$, i.e. this field depicts the interval

$$Lbound_n < A_n \text{ \# } Ubound_n \tag{3}$$

If a bound does not fit to the entire range of the numerical attribute, then it is eliminated from (3); if both bounds do not fit, or if the lower bound is greater than the upper one, then the entire selector is eliminated from the corresponding rule.

### 3.3 Initialization of a Population

Another important issue of defining or selecting parameters for a genetic algorithm is the initialization of the initial population.

First, the initialization of a population could be done either
*(1)*   randomly (using a pseudo-random number generator), or
*(2)*   by utilizing an initial domain-specific ('external') knowledge base (KB).

In the latter case, KB is available from an 'external' agent; consequently, our genetic learner then serves as a refinement agent. The initial population is in this case formed by chromosomes that correspond to the conditions of 'external' rules and their subsets until the entire size of the population is generated [5]:

**procedure** Initialize
1.    Convert all the external rules to chromosomes of the initial population
2.    **Until** the required number of initial chromosomes (size of population) is generated **do**
      2.1    **If** there is no external (generalized) rule left **then**
                    generate randomly the rest of initial chromosomes and **exit**
      2.3    Generalize the external rules by removing last selector from their conditions
      2.4    Convert all these new rules to initial chromosomes
    **enddo**

Next, we have to realize that a population is initialized before a new rule is generated (step 1 of the procedure GA above). There exist two possibilities: either
*(A)*   to initialize a new population for each new rule, or
*(B)*   to initialize a new population for the first rule only, thus using the final population from the last call (loop) as the new one for the current call of the procedure GA.

In our genetic learner, we thus provide four possible routines of initialization: *(A1)*, *(A2)*, *(B1)*, and *(B2)*.

## 4    Experiments

To compare and analyze the efficiency and power of three important routines/parameters (discretization, chromosome representation, and population initialization) in our genetic learner GA-CN4, we run various tests above several datasets from the Machine Learning Repository and other sources. – Each of the databases was randomly separated to two subsets (70% learning, 30% testing) and this 'splitting' has been executed 15 times. Comparison of the various routines was done as been by the paired t-test at the significant level 2.5%.

Since the lack of space, we do not exhibit the results of tests for the discretization/fuzzification of numerical attributes. – The experiments carried out for various representations of rules, however, did have not bring any significant difference in the classification accuracy. – Performance of various routines for population initializations is in Table 1. The C4.5 served as the external domain-specific agent that formed the initial population for the case *(2)*. Its pruning factor was 50% so rather inconsistent knowledge bases were generated; consequently, our genetic learner with a population initialized by this external knowledge base (KB) had enough 'space' to show its power by modifying this initial population.

## 5    Analysis and Future Research

We introduced some enhancements of our genetic algorithm GA-CN4, namely (a) discretization and fuzzification of numerical attributes, (b) representation of chromosomes in the genetic algorithm, (c) the ways of initialization of a population for the genetic algorithm.

**Table 1.** Classification accuracy for various initializations of populations for GA-CN4. Here *(A)*: initialize a new population for each new rule, *(B)*: initialize a new population by using the final population from the last call

| database | *(1)* randomly (A) | *(2)* external KB (A) | *(1)* randomly (B) | *(2)* external KB (B) |
|---|---|---|---|---|
| *Japanese Credit* | 97 | 98 | 97 | 98 |
| *Iris* | 98 | 98 | 98 | 97 |
| *Pima Indian Diabetes* | 86 | 89 | 87 | 89 |
| *Australian Credit* | 92 | 94 | 93 | 94 |
| *Thyreosis21* | 97 | 98 | 96 | 98 |
| *Onco7* | 77 | 79 | 77 | 80 |
| *Onco8* | 66 | 69 | 67 | 68 |

As for the discretization/fuzzification, our analysis came to the following:

- When applying the preprocessors, we lost up to 4% of the maximum possible accuracy. The algorithms with their internal discretization procedures behave significantly better.
- We intuitively anticipated that the fuzzification would yield significantly better performance than the discretization. The results, however, did not reveal that.

The experiments with various chromosome representation did not bring anything substantial as for the classification accuracy; the t-test exhibited no significant difference.

Next, the tests performed for various initialization procedures revealed the following:

- there is no significant difference between the cases *(A)* and *(B)*;
- initialization by an external KB became significantly better than the random one.

Generally, we found out that the genetic learner has better classification performance than the traditional learning algorithms. We explain this better behaviour by the fact that the traditional algorithms explore a small number of hypotheses at a time, whereas the genetic algorithm carries out a search within a robust population, in parallel in nature. The only disadvantage of GA is time consumption.

By analyzing the results achieved we plan to add and explore the following directions:

- to build in an internal discretizing routine in our GA to improve its performance;
- to exploit and test various rule representations in GA from the viewpoint of the complexity and comprehensibility of the knowledge base (KB) induced;
- to incorporate the genuine global search into the genetic learner by considering the entire set of decision rules as a single chromosome in a population.

# References

1. P. Berka, I. Bruha: Various discretizing procedures of numerical attributes: Empirical comparisons. 8th European Conference Machine Learning, Workshop Statistics, Machine Learning, and Knowledge Discovery in Databases, Heraklion, Crete (1995), 136–141
2. I. Bruha, P. Berka: Numerical attributes in symbolic learning algorithms: Discretization and fuzzification. 2nd International Conf. Neural Networks & Expert Systems in Medicine, Plymouth, UK (1996), 131–138
3. I. Bruha, S. Kockova: A support for decision making: Cost-sensitive learning system. Artificial Intelligence in Medicine, 6 (1994), 67–82
4. I. Bruha, P. Kralik, P. Berka: Genetic learner: Discretization and fuzzification of numerical attributes. Intelligent Data Analysis J., 4 (2000), 445–460
5. I. Bruha, P. Kralik: Genetic learner GA-CN4: The ways of initializations of new populations. Dept Computing & Software, McMaster Univ, Techn. Rept. (2002)
6. P. Clark, R. Boswell: Rule induction with CN2: Some recent improvements. EWSL-91, Porto, Springer-Verlag (1991), 151–163
7. P. Kralik: Application of genetic algorithms in machine learning. PhD thesis, Czech Techn. Univ., Brno, 2001
8. J.R. Quinlan: Induction of decision trees. Machine Learning, 1 (1986), 81–106

# Comparing Hierarchical Markov Networks and Multiply Sectioned Bayesian Networks

C.J. Butz and H. Geng

Department of Computer Science, University of Regina
Regina, Saskatchewan, Canada S4S 0A2
{butz,gengho}@cs.uregina.ca

**Abstract.** *Multiply sectioned Bayesian networks* (MSBNs) were originally proposed as a modular representation of uncertain knowledge by sectioning a large *Bayesian network* (BN) into smaller units. More recently, *hierarchical Markov networks* (HMNs) were developed in part as an hierarchical representation of the flat BN.

In this paper, we compare the MSBN and HMN representations. The MSBN representation does not specify how to section a BN, nor is it a faithful representation of BNs. On the contrary, a given BN has a *unique* HMN representation, which encodes *precisely* those independencies encoded in the BN. More importantly, we show that failure to encode known independencies can lead to unnecessary computation in the MSBN representation. These results, in particular, suggest that HMNs may be a more natural representation of BNs than MSBNs.

## 1 Introduction

Probabilistic reasoning with *Bayesian networks* (BNs) [5] has been an active field of research over the past two decades. To facilitate the inference process, a BN is represented as a secondary network, usually a (decomposable) *Markov network* (MN) [5]. Several researchers, however, have suggested alternative representations of BNs, including *hierarchical Markov networks* (HMNs) [10], *multiply sectioned Bayesian networks* (MSBNs) [12], *multiple undirected graphs* [6], *nested jointrees* [2], and *maximal prime decompositions* [4]. Our discussion here focuses on the HMN and MSBN representations.

As the name suggests, the *hierarchical Markov network* (HMN) framework represents a BN as a hierarchy of MNs. It was also shown in [10] that HMNs have several advantages over the MN, multiple undirected graphs, and nested jointree representations. Very recently, it was shown in [1] that the HMN representation has the same advantages over the *maximal prime decomposition* [4] representation. Hence, the HMN representation seems to be a favorable framework for representing uncertain knowledge.

On the other hand, MSBNs were originally proposed as a modular representation of a large and sparse BN. By sectioning one BN into several smaller units, inference computation can be performed on one local network in a more efficient manner than on one conventional MN. Xiang [11] showed that Srinivas's

N. Zhong et al. (Eds.): ISMIS 2003, LNAI 2871, pp. 544–553, 2003.

work in [7] was actually an application of a special case of MSBN to hierarchical model-based diagnosis. The MSBN representation supports object-oriented inference, as emphasized by Koller and Pfeffer [3]. As MSBNs seem to be another desirable representation of uncertainty, it is natural to compare the HMN and MSBN representations.

Despite its name, we first show in this paper that a MSBN is in fact a two-level hierarchy of MNs. Although the HMN representation is guaranteed to encode precisely those independencies in a BN [10], we next show that a MSBN does not. This is a crucial difference as efficient probabilistic inference is based on utilizing independencies. We explicitly demonstrate in Ex. 7 that failure to represent known independencies leads to unnecessary computation. Moreover, Xiang et al.[13] point out some limitations of sectioning a BN as a MSBN. The MSBN technique makes the natural localization assumption. Hence, localization does not dictate exactly what should be the boundary conditions between different subnets [13]. In order to provide a coherent framework for probabilistic inference, technical constraints are imposed. Xiang, Olesen and Jensen [15] recently acknowledged that how to satisfy these technical constraints may not be obvious to a practitioner. This means that the MSBN representation itself does not indicate how the BN is to be sectioned, while the knowledge engineer may not know how to satisfy the technical constraints required to make a workable MSBN. On the other hand, our constructed HMN representation is *unique* for a given BN [10]. This sectioning is defined solely by the structure of the BN. It does not involve any technical constraints, nor does it require any type of practitioner input. Our analysis then suggests that it is perhaps more useful to represent a given BN as a HMN rather than as a MSBN.

This paper is organized as follows. In Section 2, we review BNs and MNs. We outline the MSBN and HMN representations in Section 3. In Section 4, we compare these two representations. The conclusion is given in Section 5.

## 2    Background Knowledge

Let $U$ be a finite set of discrete random variables, each with a finite set of mutually exclusive states. Obviously, it may be impractical to define a joint distribution on $U$ directly: for example, one would have to specify $2^n$ entries for a distribution over $n$ binary variables. BNs utilize *conditional independencies* [9] to facilitate the acquisition of probabilistic knowledge.

Let $X, Y$ and $Z$ be disjoint subsets of variables in $R$. Let $x$, $y$, and $z$ denote arbitrary values of $X, Y$ and $Z$, respectively. We say $Y$ and $Z$ are *conditionally independent* given $X$ under the joint probability distribution $p$, denoted $I(Y, X, Z)$, if

$$p(y \mid x, z) = p(y \mid x), \tag{1}$$

whenever $p(x, z) > 0$. $I(Y, X, Z)$ can be equivalently written as

$$p(y, x, z) = \frac{p(y, x) \cdot p(x, z)}{p(x)}. \tag{2}$$

A *Bayesian network* (BN) [5] is a pair $\mathcal{B} = (D, C)$. In this pair, $D$ is a *directed acyclic graph* (DAG) on a set $U$ of variables, and $C = \{p(a_i|P_i) \mid a_i \in D\}$ is the corresponding set of *conditional probability tables* (CPTs), where $P_i$ denotes the *parent set* of variable $a_i$ in the DAG $D$. The *family set* of a variable $a_i \in D$, denoted $F_i$, is defined as $F_i = \{a_i\} \cup P_i$. The *d-separation* method [5] can be used to read independencies from a DAG. For instance, $I(d, b, e)$, $I(c, \emptyset, f)$, $I(h, g, i)$ and $I(defh, b, g)$ all hold by d-separation in the DAG $D$ in Fig. 1.

*Example 1.* Consider the BN $\mathcal{B} = (D, C)$, where $D$ is the DAG in Fig. 1 on $U = \{a, b, c, d, e, f, g, h, i, j, k\} = abcdefghijk$, and $C$ is the corresponding set of CPTs. The conditional independencies encoded in the DAG $D$ indicate that the product of the CPTs in $C$ defines a *unique* joint probability distribution $p(U)$:

$$p(U) = p(a) \cdot p(b) \cdot p(c|a) \cdot p(d|b) \cdot p(e|b) \cdot p(f|d, e) \cdot p(g|b) \cdot p(h|c, f) \cdot p(i|g)$$
$$\cdot p(j|g, h, i) \cdot p(k|h). \tag{3}$$

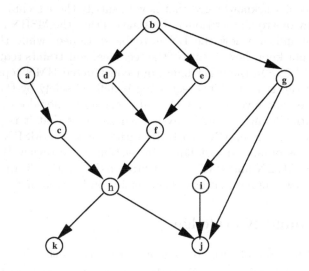

**Fig. 1.** A Bayesian network on variables $U = \{a, b, c, d, e, f, g, h, i, j, k\}$.

To facilitate probabilistic inference, a BN is usually transformed into a *Markov network* (MN), which Pearl [5] calls a *decomposable* MN. A MN consists of a *triangulated* (*chordal*) graph together with a potential defined over each maximal clique of $D^t$ (defined below). Given a DAG $D$, the *moralization* $D^m$ of $D$ is the undirected graph defined as

$$D^m = \{(a, b) \mid a, b \in F_i \text{ for the family set } F_i \text{ of each variable } a_i \in D\}. \tag{4}$$

If necessary, edges are added to $D^m$ to obtain a *triangulated* graph $D^t$. The *maximal cliques* (maximal complete subgraphs) of $D^t$ are organized as *jointree* $J$. Finally, the CPTs of the BN are assigned to nodes of $J$.

*Example 2.* Consider the BN $\mathcal{D} = (D, C)$ above. The *moralization* $D^m$ of $D$ is shown in Fig. 2. A minimum *triangulation* $D^t$ can be obtained by adding the two edges $(b, f)$ and $(f, g)$ to $D^m$. The maximal cliques of the triangulated graph $D^t$ are $bdef$, $bfg$, $fgh$, $cfh$, $ac$, $hk$, and $ghij$. These cliques are organized as a *jointree J*, as shown in Fig. 3.

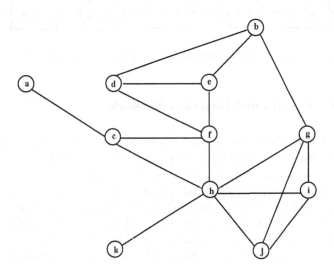

**Fig. 2.** The *moralization* $D^m$ of the DAG $D$ in Fig. 1.

*Example 3.* Given the BN in Fig. 1, one possible MN is illustrated in Fig. 3. This MN expresses the joint distribution in Ex. 1 as

$$p(U) = \frac{p(bdef) \cdot p(bfg) \cdot p(fgh) \cdot p(ghij) \cdot p(cfh) \cdot p(ac) \cdot p(hk)}{p(bf) \cdot p(fg) \cdot p(gh) \cdot p(fh) \cdot p(c) \cdot p(h)}. \tag{5}$$

Although the MN representation facilitates the probabilistic inference process, it may not represent all of the independencies in a BN. For instance, while the BN in Ex. 1 encodes $I(h, g, i)$, this conditional independence of $h$ and $i$ given $g$ is not encoded in the MN in Ex. 3. This undesirable characteristic has lead to the proposal of other representations of BNs [2,4,10], including the hierarchical Markov network representation discussed in the next section.

## 3    The MSBN and HMN Representations

Here we review two favorable representations of probabilistic knowledge, namely, multiply sectioned Bayesian networks and hierarchical Markov networks.

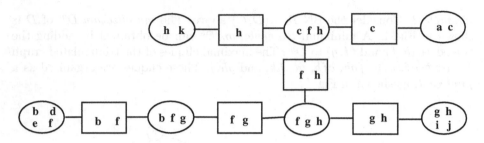

**Fig. 3.** One possible *Markov network* (MN) of the BN in Fig. 1.

### 3.1   Multiply Sectioned Bayesian Networks

*Multiply sectioned Bayesian networks* (MSBNs) [12,13,15] were originally proposed as a modular representation of a large and sparse BN.

Despite its name, a MSBN is a two-level hierarchy of MNs. There are only two differences between a MSBN and a traditional MN. First, the root level MN in a MSBN is not necessarily obtained via the moralization and triangulation procedures. Second, each node in the root level MN has a local MN nested in it. One technical constraint imposed on the root level MN is that, for any variable appearing in more than one node, there exists a node containing its parent set.

*Example 4.* The BN in Fig. 1 can be represented by the MSBN in Fig. 4. (The root level MN satisfies the MSBN restriction, since the parent set $\{a\}$ of $c$ is contained in the node $\{a,c\}$, the parent set $\{b\}$ of $g$ is contained in the node $\{b,c,d,e,f,g,h\}$, and the parent set $\{c,f\}$ of $h$ is contained in the node $\{b,c,d,e,f,g,h\}$.) This MSBN encodes the following independency information:

$$p(U) = \frac{p(ac) \cdot p(bcdefgh) \cdot p(ghij) \cdot p(hk)}{p(c) \cdot p(gh) \cdot p(h)}, \qquad (6)$$

$$p(bcdefgh) = \frac{p(cfh) \cdot p(def) \cdot p(bde) \cdot p(bg)}{p(f) \cdot p(de) \cdot p(b)}. \qquad (7)$$

It is perhaps worthwhile here to elaborate on the MSBN construction process. Given the root MN $J$ for a MSBN representation, an embedded MN $J_X$ is constructed for each node $X$ of $J$ by the following four steps:

(i)     compute the *subDAG* $D_X$ of DAG $D$ onto the subset $X$ of variables,
(ii)    apply the *MSBN moralization* to $D_X$ giving the undirected graph $D_X^{m'}$,
(iii)   triangulate $D_X^{m'}$ if necessary,
(iv)    construct a jointree $J_X$ for the triangulated graph in (iii).

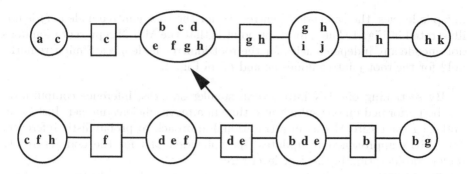

**Fig. 4.** One possible *multiply sectioned Bayesian network* (MSBN) of the BN in Fig. 1.

The new notions of subDAG and MSBN moralization are now defined. Given a BN $D$ on $U$, the subDAG $D_X$ of $D$ onto the subset $X$ of $U$ is defined as:

$$D_X = \{ \ (a,b) \mid (a,b) \in D \text{ and } a,b \in X \ \}.$$

Since the parent set of a node might not be contained in the same subDAG as the node itself, the moralization procedure is modified as follows. The *MSBN moralization* $D_X^{m'}$ of a subDAG $D_X$ means the moralization in Eq. (4) except that the family set $F_i$ of variable $u_i$ is defined with respect to $D_X$.

*Example 5.* Consider the node $X = bcdefgh$ in the MSBN root MN in Fig. 4. By definition, the subDAG $D_X$ is:

$$D_X = \{ \ (b,d), (b,e), (b,g), (c,h), (d,f), (e,f), (f,h) \ \}.$$

The MSBN moralization $D_X^{m'}$ is then:

$$D_X^{m'} = \{ \ (b,d), \ (b,e), \ (b,g), \ (c,f), \ (d,e), \ (d,f), \ (e,f) \ \}.$$

No additional edges have to be added to $D_X^{m'}$, as it is already a triangulated graph. The maximal cliques of $D_X^{m'}$ are $cfh$, $def$, $bde$, $bg$. There is only one jointree $J_X$ for these four cliques, namely, the one shown in Fig. 4.

On the other hand, consider the root jointree node $ghij$ in Fig. 4. The sub-DAG $D_{ghij}$ is

$$D_{ghij} = \{ \ (g,i), (g,j), (h,j), (i,j) \ \},$$

and the MSBN moralization $D_{ghij}^{m'}$ is

$$D_{ghij}^{m'} = \{ \ (g,h), (g,i), (g,j), (h,i), (h,j), (i,j) \ \}.$$

Not only is $D_{ghij}^{m'}$ a triangulated graph, but it is in fact a *complete* graph, i.e., $D_{ghij}^{m'}$ has only one maximal clique. By definition, the jointree $J_X$ for $D_{ghij}^{m'}$ has only one node. Since any jointree defined by a single node does *not* encode any independencies, the embedded jointree $J_X$ for the root jointree node $ghij$ is not illustrated in Fig. 4. The important point is that the MSBN representation does not encode any independencies for the root jointree node $ghij$. Similar remarks hold for the root jointree nodes $ac$ and $hk$ in Fig. 4.

By sectioning one BN into several smaller subnets, inference computation can be performed on one subnet at a time in a more efficient manner. Instead of updating the entire MN as in a traditional approach to probabilistic inference, the MSBN approach only updates the embedded MN for the node currently under consideration in the root level MN.

The MSBN representation is quite robust as it can be applied to large diagnostic systems [15], in either a single agent or a multi-agent paradigm [12], and supports object-oriented inference as emphasized in [3].

## 3.2   Hierarchical Markov Networks

In [10], Wong et al. suggested that a BN be transformed into a *hierarchical Markov network* (HMN). An HMN is a hierarchy of MNs (jointrees).

Due to space limitations, we use an example to illustrate HMNs, and refer readers to [10] for a thorough discussion on the automated procedure for constructing the unique HMN representation of a given BN.

*Example 6.* The BN in Fig. 1 can be represented by the unique HMN in Fig. 5. This HMN encodes the following independency information:

$$p(U) = \frac{p(ac) \cdot p(cfh) \cdot p(hk) \cdot p(bdefgh) \cdot p(ghij)}{p(c) \cdot p(h) \cdot p(fh) \cdot p(gh)}, \tag{8}$$

$$p(cf) = p(c) \cdot p(f), \tag{9}$$

$$p(bdefgh) = \frac{p(fh) \cdot p(def) \cdot p(bde) \cdot p(bg)}{p(f) \cdot p(de) \cdot p(b)}, \tag{10}$$

$$p(bde) = \frac{p(bd) \cdot p(be)}{p(b)}, \tag{11}$$

$$p(ghi) = \frac{p(gh) \cdot p(gi)}{p(g)}. \tag{12}$$

In [10], it was shown that HMNs have several advantages over the MN, multiple undirected graphs, and nested jointree representations. In particular, the HMN can optimize queries using independencies that would go unnoticed in other representations [10]. More recently, it was explicitly demonstrated in [1] that HMNs possess several important characteristics, which the maximal prime decomposition representation does not. In the next section, we bring the elegance of the HMN representation down to bear on the MSBN representation.

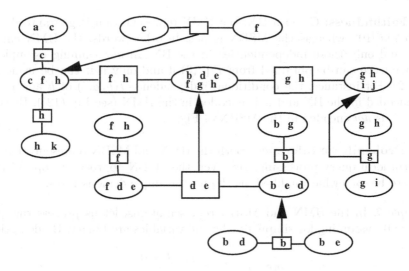

**Fig. 5.** The *hierarchical Markov network* (HMN) for the DAG $D$ in Fig. 1.

## 4  Comparing the MSBN and HMN Representations

In this section, we present a comprehensive comparison of the HMN and MSBN representations based on seven relevant factors.

**(i) Assumptions:** The MSBN representation makes the natural localization assumption. Hence, *localization does not dictate exactly what should be the boundary conditions between different subnets* [13]. The HMN representation does not require any assumptions when sectioning a BN.

**(ii) Technical constraints:** In order to make a workable MSBN, technical constraints such as the *d-sepset* condition need to be imposed [13]. The HMN representation does not impose any technical constraints.

**(iii) Practitioner input:** The sectioning of a BN into a MSBN is performed by a knowledge engineer. Xiang et al. [15] recently acknowledged that how to satisfy these technical constraints may not be obvious to a practitioner. Constructing a HMN from a BN is an *automated* procedure; it does not require any human input.

**(iv) Restriction on the number of levels:** By definition, the MSBN representation always has precisely two levels. The number of levels in a HMN is determined solely by the structure of a BN, and is not confined to two levels. For instance, the HMN in Fig. 5 has three levels.

**(v) Uniqueness:** While there may be multiple MSBN representations for a given BN, the constructed HMN representation is always *unique* [10].

**(vi) Faithfulness:** Given a BN, the HMN representation is guaranteed to be *equivalent* [10], whereas the MSBN is not. In other words, the HMN encodes those and only those independencies in the BN. In our running example, an independence can be obtained from Eq. (3) if and only if it can be using Eqs. (8)-(12). For instance, the conditional independence $I(h, g, i)$ of $h$ and $i$ given $g$ is encoded in the BN and it is encoded in the HMN (see Eq. (12)). However, $I(h, g, i)$ is *not* encoded in the MSBN of Fig. 4.

**(vii) Probabilistic Inference:** Both the HMN and MSBN representations can perform local query processing. However, the MSBN approach to optimization needs to be somewhat qualified, as the next example demonstrates.

*Example 7.* In the HMN and MSBN representations, let us process the query $p(c|f = 0)$, assuming for simplicity that all variables are binary. By definition,

$$p(c \mid f = 0) = \frac{p(c, f = 0)}{p(f = 0)}. \tag{13}$$

The MSBN can use its only embedded jointree as follows. Two additions are required to compute $p(c, f = 0)$ from the stored distribution $p(c, f, h)$. One more addition is required to derive $p(f = 0)$ from $p(c, f = 0)$. Two divisions are needed to compute the desired result $p(c|f = 0)$ using $p(c, f = 0)$ and $p(f = 0)$. Thus, the MSBN approach requires three additions and two divisions to compute $p(c|f = 0)$. On the contrary, the HMN approach requires zero additions and zero divisions to compute $p(c|f = 0)$. The reason is that the HMN encodes $I(c, \emptyset, f)$ meaning that Eq. (13) can be rewritten as:

$$p(c \mid f = 0) = \frac{p(c, f = 0)}{p(f = 0)} = \frac{p(c) \cdot p(f = 0)}{p(f = 0)} = p(c). \tag{14}$$

The marginal $p(c)$ is already stored in the HMN representation.

Query optimization means taking advantage of independencies during processing. Our HMN encodes $I(c, \emptyset, f)$, which is given in the BN. Since $c$ and $f$ are unconditionally independent, $p(c|f = 0) = p(c)$ as shown in Eq. (14). Since $p(c)$ is a marginal already stored in the HMN, the query $p(c|f = 0)$ can be answered without any additional computation. On the contrary, the MSBN sacrifices $I(c, \emptyset, f)$. Failure to represent $I(c, \emptyset, f)$ leads to unnecessary work in the MSBN computation of $p(c|f = 0)$, as Ex. 7 demonstrates.

## 5   Conclusion

In this paper, we exposed the MSBN representation as a very limited hierarchical representation; one that always consists of precisely two levels. More importantly, we explicitly demonstrated that the MSBN may not represent all the independencies encoded in a BN. This has important practical ramifications. As Ex. 7

explicitly shows, failure to represent known independencies results in unnecessary computation in the MSBN representation. Moreover, the MSBN approach is not unique, makes assumptions, and imposes technical constraints. Xiang et al. [15] recently acknowledged that how to satisfy these technical constraints may not be obvious to a practitioner. On the contrary, the HMN is a unique and equivalent representation of BNs, which does not require assumptions, technical constraints, and practitioner input. Our analysis then suggests that HMNs may be a better representation of BNs than MSBNs.

# References

1. C.J. Butz, Q. Hu and X.D. Yang: Critical remarks on the maximal prime decomposition of Bayesian networks. To appear in *Proc. 9th International Conf. on Rough Sets, Fuzzy Sets, Data Mining and Granular Computing* 2003.
2. U. Kjaerulff: Nested junction trees. In *Proc. 13th Conf. on Uncertainty in Artificial Intelligence*, 302–313, 1997.
3. D. Koller and A. Pfeffer: Object-oriented Bayesian networks. In *Thirteenth Conference on Uncertainty in Artificial Intelligence*, 302–313, 1997.
4. K.G. Olesen and A.L. Madsen: Maximal prime subgraph decomposition of Bayesian networks. *IEEE Transactions on Systems, Man, and Cybernetics*, B, 32(1):21–31, 2002.
5. J. Pearl: *Probabilistic Reasoning in Intelligent Systems: Networks of Plausible Inference*, Morgan Kaufmann, San Francisco, California, 1988.
6. R.D. Shachter: A graph-based inference method for conditional independence. *Proc. 7th Conf. on Uncertainty in Artificial Intelligence*, 353–360, 1991.
7. S. Srinivas: A probabilistic approach to hierarchical model-based diagnosis. *Proc. 10th Conf. on Uncertainty in Artificial Intelligence*, 538–545, 1994.
8. S.K.M. Wong and C.J. Butz: Constructing the dependency structure of a multi-agent probabilistic network. *IEEE Trans. Knowl. Data Eng.*, 13(3):395–415, 2001.
9. S.K.M. Wong, C.J. Butz, and D. Wu: On the implication problem for probabilistic conditional independency. *IEEE Transactions on Systems, Man, and Cybernetics*, A, 30(6): 785–805, 2000.
10. S.K.M. Wong, C.J. Butz, and D. Wu: On undirected representations of Bayesian networks. *ACM SIGIR Workshop on Mathematical/Formal Models in Information Retrieval*, 52–59, 2001.
11. Y. Xiang: Optimization of inter-subnet belief updating in multiply sectioned Bayesian networks. *Proc. 11th Conf. on Uncertainty in Artificial Intelligence*, 565–573, 1995.
12. Y. Xiang: *Probabilistic Reasoning in Multi-Agent Systems: A Graphical Models Approach*. Cambridge Publishers, 2002.
13. Y. Xiang, D. Poole, and M. Beddoes: Exploring localization in Bayesian networks for large expert systems. *Proc. 8th Conf. on Uncertainty in Artificial Intelligence*, 344–351, 1992.
14. Y. Xiang, D. Poole, and M. Beddoes: Multiply sectioned Bayesian networks and junction forests for large knowledge based systems. *Computational Intelligence*, 9(2):171–220, 1993.
15. Y. Xiang, K.G. Olesen, and F.V. Jensen. Practical issues in modeling large diagnostic systems with multiply sectioned Bayesian networks. *International Journal of Pattern Recognition and Artificial Intelligence*, 14(1):59–71, 2000.

# Constraint Propagation to Semantic Web Services Discovery

Salima Benbernou[1], Etienne Canaud[1], Mohand-Said Hacid[1], and
Farouk Toumani[2]

[1] LIRIS – Université Claude Bernard Lyon 1, 43, boulevard du 11 novembre 1918
69622 Villeurbanne, France
{sbenbern, ecanaud, mshacid}@liris.univ-lyon1.fr
[2] Laboratoire LIMOS, ISIMA – Campus des Cezeaux – B.P. 125
63173 AUBIERE Cedex, France
ftoumani@isima.fr

**Abstract.** This paper proposes a framework for semantic web services
discovery. Services are described by means of terminological axioms. We
propose a method for services discovery based on constraint propagation. We apply specific propagation rules to make explicit a part of the
knowledge about services which is implicitly available in the query.

## 1 Introduction

There are several research works (see, among others, [1,2,3,4,5,6]) that propose
to apply the semantic web technology to web services. These works address some
challenging issues related to the problem of describing service capabilities in a
machine understandable form as well as the development of reasoning mechanisms that support automation of web services.

Examples of such efforts include the DAML-S [7] initiative and the WSMF-
Web Services Modeling Framework [3].

Until now, most of the efforts have been achieved on low-level composition
of already discovered services [8]. This paper concentrates on the reasoning
issue to automate the discovery of e-services. Given a query Q and a set of
services descriptions S, we are interested in computing the set of services answers to the query. This process is seen as a rewriting by constraint propagation.

Although, in the basic form that we give here, the languages do not account
for all aspects of web services, they constitute kernels to be extended. Showing
how we can reason about web services is useful and significant.

The rest of the paper is organized as follows: Section 2 gives an introductory
example. Section 3 discusses related work. Section 4 gives the syntax and semantics of the languages for describing and querying services. Section 5 provides a
calculus for services discovery. We conclude in Section 6.

N. Zhong et al. (Eds.): ISMIS 2003, LNAI 2871, pp. 554–561, 2003.

## 2  An Introductory Example

Our work focuses on automatic discovery of services. In general, a service can be described by input and output attributes. The input attributes specify the information that the service requires to be executed. The output attributes describe the result of the operation of the service.

A query is a declarative specification involving constraints that have to match some inputs of candidate services (see figure 1).

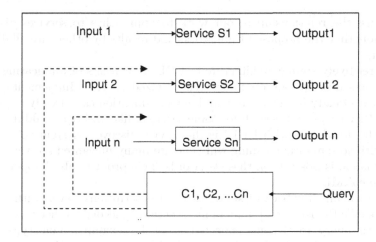

**Fig. 1.** Web Service Discovery

To illustrate our approach, let us consider the following services:

- *Transport* service gives a list of trips (by plane, by train, by boat, ...) given a departure place, an arrival place, a departure date, a departure time and a price, which are the inputs allowing the service to be executed.
- *Lodging* service gives a list of lodging (Hotel, Camping, House, ..) where inputs are destination place and rate.

Let us consider the following query "I want to go from Lyon to Tokyo next week end with price P and I would like to stay 2 days there".
Formally, the e-services *Transport* and *Lodging* can be specified as a *structural description* in some language. The query is expressed as a *relational description* with constraints.

The query involves a first constraint, namely, *departure place*. Starting with that constraint, one has to scan the services looking for those displaying an input that entails the constraint. If such a service is found (in our case the transport service), then all its inputs are returned as requirements for the service to be executed. The inputs and the remaining constraints in the query are checked for satisfiability.

The mechanism of constraint-driven search for services is repeated for each constraint in the query. At the end, a combination of services is obtained. That combination satisfies as much as possible the outputs of the query and requires as less as possible of inputs that are provided in the query.

## 3  Related Work

We discuss the relationship of our work to approaches to services discovery. Please note that the proposed frameworks and results by others are all different from ours.

The relatively simple architecture of UDDI[9] consists of duplicating all the web services descriptions on many synchronized servers. Implementations of UDDI have already been achieved, and any organization can already register the services they propose or search for some services, like on http://uddi.us.com/ . One of the drawbacks with UDDI is the service discovery system : simple keywords with no semantic meaning will generate many unwanted answers, and no approximation is possible on these keywords. This problem also happens in systems like ebXML.

This is the main drawback of keyword-based descriptions : even with powerful API to handle Registries[10], human intervention is needed to check whether answers to the query are the ones expected or not. For example, if one types "white house" as key words, one doesn't know whether the answer will refer to the US white house or to a house which color is white. The lack of semantic often leads to ambiguity, thus making an automated handling of answers or composition of services impossible, unlike in semantic web services. [1,4].

## 4  Describing Services

Here we specify syntax and semantics of the Services Description Language ($\mathcal{SDL}$).

The elementary building blocks are primitive concepts (ranged over by the letter $A$) and primitive roles (ranged over by $P$). Intuitively, concepts describe sets and thus correspond to unary predicates while attributes describe relations and thus correspond to binary predicates.

In the *Services Description Language $\mathcal{SDL}$*, concepts (ranged over by C, D) are formed according to the following syntax rule:

$$C, D \rightarrow \quad A \mid$$
$$\forall P.A$$
$$(\geq nP)$$
$$(\leq nP)$$

Axioms come in the two forms:

$$A \sqsubseteq C, \; P \sqsubseteq A_1 \times A_2$$

where $A, A_1, A_2$ are primitive concepts, $C$ is an arbitrary $\mathcal{SDL}$ concept, and $P$ a primitive role. The first axiom states that all instances of $A$ are instances of $C$. So $C$ gives necessary conditions for membership in $A$. The second axiom states that the role $P$ has domain $A_1$ and range $A_2$. A $\mathcal{SDL}$ description $\Sigma$ consists of a set of axioms.

Given a fixed interpretation, each formula denotes a binary or unary relation over the domain. Thus we can immediately formulate the semantics of attributes and concepts in terms of relations and sets without the detour through predicate logic notation. An interpretation $\mathcal{I} = (\Delta^{\mathcal{I}}, \cdot^{\mathcal{I}})$ consists of a set $\Delta^{\mathcal{I}}$ (the domain of $\mathcal{I}$) and a function $\cdot^{\mathcal{I}}$ (the extension function of $\mathcal{I}$) that maps every concept to a subset of $\Delta^{\mathcal{I}}$, every constant to an element of $\Delta^{\mathcal{I}}$ and every role to a subset of $\Delta^{\mathcal{I}} \times \Delta^{\mathcal{I}}$. Moreover, we assume that distinct constants have distinct images (Unique Name Assumption). The interpretation function can then be extended to arbitrary concepts as follows: ($\#S$ denotes the cardinality of the set $S$)

| Construct | Set Semantics |
|---|---|
| $\forall P.A$ | $\{d_1 \in \Delta^{\mathcal{I}} \mid \forall d_2.(d_1, d_2) \in P^{\mathcal{I}} \Rightarrow d_2 \in A^{\mathcal{I}}\}$ |
| $(\geq nP)$ | $\{d_1 \in \Delta^{\mathcal{I}} \mid \#\{d_2 \mid (d_1, d_2) \in P^{\mathcal{I}} \wedge d_2 \in A^{\mathcal{I}}\} \geq n\}$ |
| $(\leq nP)$ | $\{d_1 \in \Delta^{\mathcal{I}} \mid \#\{d_2 \mid (d_1, d_2) \in P^{\mathcal{I}} \wedge d_2 \in A^{\mathcal{I}}\} \leq n\}$ |

We say that two concepts $C, D$ are equivalent if $C^{\mathcal{I}} = D^{\mathcal{I}}$ for every interpretation $\mathcal{I}$, i.e., equivalent concepts always describe the same sets.

We say that an interpretation $\mathcal{I}$ satisfies the axiom $A \sqsubseteq C$ if $A^{\mathcal{I}} \subseteq C^{\mathcal{I}}$ and the axiom $P \sqsubseteq A_1 \times A_2$ if $P^{\mathcal{I}} \subseteq A_1^{\mathcal{I}} \times A_2^{\mathcal{I}}$. If $\Sigma$ is a set of axioms, an interpretation $\mathcal{I}$ that satisfies all axioms in $\Sigma$ is called a $\Sigma$-interpretation. A concept $C$ is $\Sigma$-satisfiable if there is a $\Sigma$-interpretation $\mathcal{I}$ such that $C^{\mathcal{I}} \neq \emptyset$. We say that $C$ is $\Sigma$-subsumed by $D$ (written $C \sqsubseteq_\Sigma D$) if $C^{\mathcal{I}} \subseteq D^{\mathcal{I}}$ for every $\Sigma$-interpretation $\mathcal{I}$.

## 5  A Calculus for Services Discovery

To formulate the calculus we augment our syntax by variables (ranged over by $x, y$). We will refer to constants and variables alike as individuals (denoted by the letters $s, t$). Our calculus works on syntactic entities called constraints that have one of the forms:

$$s : C, sPt, s \not\equiv t$$

where $C$ is a concept, $P$ is an attribute, and $s, t$ are individuals. The first constraint says that $s$ is an instance of $C$, and the second that $t$ is a $P$-filler of $s$. A constraint system is a set of constraints.

We also extend the semantics. An interpretation $\mathcal{I}$ maps a variable $x$ to an element $x^{\mathcal{I}}$ of its domain. It *satisfies* a constraint $s : C$ if $s^{\mathcal{I}} \in C^{\mathcal{I}}$, a constraint $sPt$ if $(s^{\mathcal{I}}, t^{\mathcal{I}}) \in P^{\mathcal{I}}$, and a constraint $s \neq t$ if $s^{\mathcal{I}} \neq t^{\mathcal{I}}$. We say that a $\Sigma$-interpretation $\mathcal{I}$ is a $\Sigma$-model of a constraint $c$ if it satisfies $c$. A constraint is $\Sigma$-*satisfiable* if it has a $\Sigma$-model. The notions of satisfaction, model, and satisfiability are extended to constraint systems as one would expect.

## 5.1   Query Answering

In the following we refer to a description of services $\Sigma$ and to a query $Q = q_1, \ldots, q_n \& \beta_1, \ldots, \beta_m$ posed to $\Sigma$.

The calculus makes use of 5 propagation rules (see figure 2). The rules work on a constraint system $\mathcal{F}$. In order to compute the services which are the answer to the query, we start with the constraint system $\{q_1, \ldots, q_n\}$. The rules will add more facts until no more rule is applicable.

We say that $s$ and $t$ are separated in a constraint system if the constraint $s \neq t$ is in the constraint system.

Given a constraint system $\mathcal{F}$ and an individual $s$, we define the function $\sigma(., .)$ as follows: $\sigma(\mathcal{F}, s) := \{C \mid s : C \in \mathcal{F}\}$. We say that two variables $x$ and $y$ are $\mathcal{F}$-equivalent, written $x \equiv_{\mathcal{F}} y$, if $\sigma(\mathcal{F}, x) = \sigma(\mathcal{F}, y)$. Intuitively, two $\mathcal{F}$-equivalent variables can represent the same element in the potential interpretation built by the rules, unless they are separated.

$r_1:$    $\mathcal{F} \to \mathcal{F} \cup \{s : C\}$
     if $s : A$ is in $\mathcal{F}$, $A \sqsubseteq C$ is in $\Sigma$ ($C$ is an arbitrary concept) and $s : C$ is not in $\mathcal{F}$

$r_2:$    $\mathcal{F} \to \mathcal{F} \cup \{s : A_1, t : A_2\}$
     if $(s, t) : P$ is in $\mathcal{F}$, $P \sqsubseteq A_1 \times A_2$ is in $\Sigma$ and $s : A_1$ or $t : A_2$ is not in $\mathcal{F}$

$r_3:$    $\mathcal{F} \to \mathcal{F} \cup \{t : A'\}$
     if $s : A$ is in $\mathcal{F}$, $(s, t) : P$ is in $\mathcal{F}$, $A \sqsubseteq \forall P.A'$ is in $\Sigma$ and $t : A'$ is not in $\mathcal{F}$

$r_4:$    $\mathcal{F} \to \mathcal{F} \cup \{sPy_1, \ldots sPy_n\} \cup \{y_i \neq y_j | i, j \in 1..n, i \neq j\}$
     if $s : (\geq nP)$ is in $\mathcal{F}$
     $y_1, \ldots y_n$ are new variables
     there do not exist $n$ pairwise separated $P$-successors of $s$ in $\mathcal{F}$

$r_5:$    $\mathcal{F} \to \mathcal{F}[y/t]$
     if $s : (\leq nP)$ is in $\mathcal{F}$
     $s$ has more than $n$ $P$-successors in $\mathcal{F}$
     $y, t$ are two $P$-successors of $s$ which are not separated.

**Fig. 2.** Propagation rules

**Proposition 1. (Invariance)** *Suppose $\mathcal{F}'$ has been derived from $\mathcal{F}$ by applying a rule. Then every $\Sigma$-model $\mathcal{I}$ of $\mathcal{F}$ can be turned into a $\Sigma$-model $\mathcal{I}'$ of $\mathcal{F}'$.*

## 5.2   Example

As an example, we use the calculus to rewrite the query given in section 2:

$$departurePlace(F, A), arrivalPlace(F, B), price(F, P),$$
$$Accommodation(C), rate(C, R)\&P \leq 2000, R \leq 60, A = Lyon, B = Tokyo$$

Figure 3 gives an ontology associated with the services *Transport* and *Lodging*. Flights are grouped in companies which are structured in a subsumption hierarchy given figure 4.

$Accommodation \sqsubseteq \forall location.City$
$Accommodation \sqsubseteq \forall category.Category$
$Accommodation \sqsubseteq \forall rate.Number$
$Hotel \sqsubseteq Accommodation$
$Hotel \sqsubseteq \forall chain.Chain$
$House \sqsubseteq Accommodation$
$Flat \sqsubseteq Accommodation$
$Restaurant \sqsubseteq \forall address.City$
$Restaurant \sqsubseteq \forall minimumprice.Number$
$Restaurant \sqsubseteq \forall speciality.Speciality$
$Flight \sqsubseteq TransportationMean$
$Flight \sqsubseteq \forall company.FlightCompany$
$Flight \sqsubseteq \forall price.Number$
$Flight \sqsubseteq \forall departureDate.Date$
$Flight \sqsubseteq \forall arrivalDate.Date$
$Flight \sqsubseteq \forall departurePlace.Airport$
$Flight \sqsubseteq \forall arrivalPlace.Airport$
$Flight \sqsubseteq \forall departureTime.Time$
$Flight \sqsubseteq \forall arrivalTime.Time$

$location \sqsubseteq Accommodation \times City$
$categoty \sqsubseteq Accommodation \times Category$
$rate \sqsubseteq Accommodation \times Number$
$chain \sqsubseteq Hotel \times Chain$
$address \sqsubseteq Restaurant \times City$
$minimumprice \sqsubseteq Restaurant \times Number$
$speciality \sqsubseteq Restaurant \times Speciality$
$company \sqsubseteq Flight \times Company$
$price \sqsubseteq Flight \times Number$
$departureDate \sqsubseteq Flight \times Date$
$arrivalDate \sqsubseteq Flight \times Date$
$departurePlace \sqsubseteq Flight \times Airport$
$arrivalPlace \sqsubseteq Flight \times Airport$
$departureTime \sqsubseteq Flight \times Time$
$arrivalTime \sqsubseteq Flight \times Time$

**Fig. 3.** A part of a tourism ontology

The first part of the query can be rewritten as follows:

$departurePlace(F, A)$ as $(F, A) : departurePlace$
$arrivalPlace(F, B)$ as $(F, B) : arrivalPlace$
$price(F, P)$ as $(F, P) : price$
$Accommodation(C)$ as $C : Accommodation$
$rate(C, R)$ as $(C, R) : rate$

We start with the constraint system :

$$\mathcal{F}_0 = \{(F, A) : departurePlace, (F, B) : arrivalPlace, (F, P) : price,$$
$$C : Accommodation, (C, R) : rate\}$$

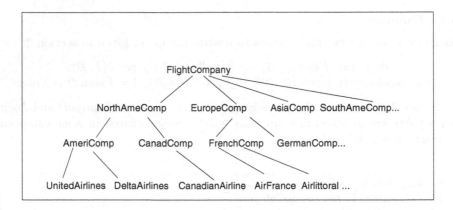

**Fig. 4.** A hierarchical structure of flight Company

Figure 5 shows the sequence of rule applications. The constraint $(F, A)$ : *departurePlace*, combined with the axiom *departurePlace* $\sqsubseteq$ *Flight* $\times$ *Airport* by using the rule $r_2$ produces the two constraints $F$ : *Flight* and $A$ : *Airport*. Similar reasoning is applied to all the constraints until no propagation rule applies. From the query, $P, R, A$ and $B$ are bound variables, whereas $F$ and $C$ are not. From $\mathcal{F}_5$ (see figure 5) the services *Flight* and *Accommodation* are possible solutions to the query.

$$
\begin{aligned}
\mathcal{F}_1 &= \mathcal{F}_0 \cup \{F : Flight, A : Airport\} \quad r_2 \\
\mathcal{F}_2 &= \mathcal{F}_1 \cup \{B : Airport\} \quad\quad\quad\quad r_2 \\
\mathcal{F}_3 &= \mathcal{F}_2 \cup \{P : Number\} \quad\quad\quad\; r_2 \\
\mathcal{F}_4 &= \mathcal{F}_3 \cup \{C : Accommodation\} \quad\; r_1 \\
\mathcal{F}_5 &= \mathcal{F}_4 \cup \{R : Number\} \quad\quad\quad\; r_3
\end{aligned}
$$

**Fig. 5.** A sequence of rule applications

# 6   Conclusion

Existing solutions that achieve discovery of e-services rely on simple query mechanisms to provide *individual* services that exactly match the query. Clearly, a semantic match like the one proposed in this paper is beyond the representation capabilities of the emerging XML based standards and current e-services platforms.

We have investigated the problem of e-services discovery by constraint propagation in a restricted framework of description logics. However, the languages that are recommended to realize the semantic web vision tend to be more expressive. That's why our future work will be devoted to the extension of the proposed framework to hold the use of constraint propagation for more expressive description logics and full rule constraint query languages.

# References

1. S. McIlraith, T. C. Son, and H. Zeng. Semantic Web Services. *IEEE Intelligent Systems. Special Issue on Semantic Web*, 16(2):46–53, March/April 2001.
2. D. Chakraborty, F. Perich, S. Avancha, and A. Joshi. DReggie: Semantic Service Discovery for M-Commerce Applications. In *Workshop on Reliable and Secure Applications in Mobile Environment, 20th Symposium on Reliable Distributed Systems*, pages 28–31, June 2001.
3. D. Fensel, C. Bussler, and A. Maedche. Semantic Web Enabled Web Services. In *Proceedings of the International Semantic Web Conference*, pages 1–2, Sardinia, Italy, June 2002.
4. D. Fensel and C. Bussler. The Web Service Modeling Framework WSMF. http://www.cs.vu.nl/˜dieter/wese/publications.html.
5. The DAML Services Coalition. DAML-S: Web Service Description for the Semantic Web. In *The First International Semantic Web Conference (ISWC)*, pages 348–363, June 2002.
6. A. Bernstein and M. Klein. Discovering Services: Towards High Precision Service Retrieval. In *CaiSE Workshop on Web Services, e-Business, and the Semantic Web: Foundations, Models, Architecture, Engineering and Applications*, Toronto, May 2002.
7. http://www.daml.org/services.
8. S. Narayanan and S. McIlraith. Simulation, verification and automated composition of web services. In *Eleventh International World Wide Web Conference*, Honolulu, HAWAII, USA, May 2002.
9. UDDI Home Page. http://www.uddi.org/, 2003.
10. ebXML Home Page. http://www.ebxml.org/, 2003.

# Reasoning in Data Integration Systems: Why LAV and GAV Are Siblings

Andrea Calì

Dipartimento di Informatica e Sistemistica
Università di Roma "La Sapienza"
Via Salaria 113, I-00198 Roma, Italy
cali@dis.uniroma1.it

**Abstract.** Data integration consists in providing a uniform access to a set of data sources, through a unified representation of the data called *global schema*; a *mapping* specifies the relationship between the global schema and the sources. Integrity constraints (ICs) are expressed on the global schema to better represent the domain of interest; in general, ICs are not satisfied by the data at the sources. In this paper we address the problem of query answering in GLAV data integration systems, where tuple-generating dependencies are expressed on the global schema. We solve the problem in an intensional fashion, by presenting a rewriting technique that, taking into account both the ICs and the mapping, allows us to compute the answers to a query, expressed over the global schema, by evaluating the rewritten query directly over the sources. Since the GLAV approach is a generalisation of the basic approaches LAV and GAV, we show that query answering under ICs can be done in the same way in LAV and GAV systems, thus proving that LAV and GAV are siblings, and not opposites.

## 1 Introduction

The task of a data integration system is to provide the user with a unified view, called *global schema*, of a set of heterogeneous data sources. Once the user issues a query over the global schema, the system carries out the task of suitably accessing the different sources and assemble the retrieved data into the final answer to the query. In this context, a crucial issue is the specification of the relationship between the global schema and the sources, which is called *mapping* [15]. There are two basic approaches for specifying a mapping in a data integration system [12,15]. The first one, called *global-as-view (GAV)*, requires that to each element of the global schema a view over the sources is associated. The second approach, called *local-as-view (LAV)*, requires that to each source a view over the global schema is associated. Besides GAV and LAV, a mixed approach, called GLAV [9,8], consists in associating views over the global schema to views over the sources.

Since the global schema is a representation of the domain of interest of the system, it needs to be represented by means of a flexible an expressive formalism: to this aim, *integrity constraints* are expressed on it. The data at the sources may not satisfy the constraints on the global schema; in this case a common assumption (which is the one

N. Zhong et al. (Eds.): ISMIS 2003, LNAI 2871, pp. 562–571, 2003.

adopted in this paper) is to to consider the sources as *sound*, i.e., they provide a *subset* of the data that satisfy the global schema.

In this paper we address the problem of data integration in the relational context, where the mapping is GLAV, and in the presence of *tuple-generating dependencies (TGDs)* on the global schema; TGDs are an extension of *inclusion dependencies*, which are an important class of dependencies in database schemata [1,13].

First, we generalise the notion of *retrieved global database (RGD)* [4] to GLAV systems, showing that in our case the treatment of integrity constraints is based on a *repairing* of the RGD, performed with a procedure called *chase* [13]. The correct answers to a query are obtained by evaluating the query over the repaired retrieved global database; from this perspective, LAV and GAV (and GLAV) systems are analogous with respect to the treatment of integrity constraints. Then, we present a technique for rewriting a query in such a way that the knowledge about integrity constraints is encoded in the rewritten query; in particular, the evaluation of the rewritten query over the retrieved global database returns the same answers as the evaluation of the original query over the repaired RGD: this allows us to avoid the repairing of the RGD. Since in the case of arbitrary TGDs the problem of query answering is undecidable [14], the technique applies to a restricted class of TGDs for which the problem is decidable. Finally, we present a query rewriting technique that takes the mapping into account: the GLAV data integration system is first compiled into an equivalent GAV one. At this point, once we have taken into account the integrity constraints in the previous rewriting step, we can proceed with the traditional rewriting technique for query processing in GAV, i.e., *unfolding*. In this way, we are able to avoid the construction of the RGD.

In conclusion, we are able to take into account the integrity constraints on the global schema and the mapping in two distinct rewriting steps, in a purely intensional fashion. The rewritten query can be thus evaluated on the data sources, providing the correct answers to the query.

## 2   Framework

In this section we define a logical framework for data integration, based on the relational model with integrity constraints.

**Syntax.** We consider to have an infinite, fixed alphabet $\Gamma$ of constants representing real world objects, and will take into account only databases having $\Gamma$ as domain. Formally, a data integration system $\mathcal{I}$ is a triple $\langle \mathcal{G}, \mathcal{S}, \mathcal{M} \rangle$, where:

1. $\mathcal{G}$ is the *global schema* expressed in the relational model with integrity constraints. In particular, $\mathcal{G} = \langle \Psi, \Sigma_T \rangle$, where: *(i)* $\Psi$ is a set of relations, each with an associated arity that indicates the number of its attributes. A relation $R$ of arity $n$ is denoted by $R/n$. *(ii)* $\Sigma_T$ is a set of *tuple-generating dependencies (TGDs)*. A TGD [1,8] is a first-order formula of the form

$$\forall \boldsymbol{X}(\exists \boldsymbol{Y}\, \chi(\boldsymbol{X}, \boldsymbol{Y}) \;\rightarrow\; \exists \boldsymbol{Z}\, \psi(\boldsymbol{X}, \boldsymbol{Z}))$$

where $\boldsymbol{X}, \boldsymbol{Y}, \boldsymbol{Z}$ are sets of variables, and $\chi$ and $\psi$ are conjunctions of atoms whose predicate symbols are in $\Psi$. Henceforth, for the sake of conciseness, we will omit the quantifiers in TGDs.

2. $\mathcal{S}$ is the *source schema*, constituted by the schemata of the different sources. We assume that the sources are relational, and in particular each source is represented by a relation; furthermore, we assume that no integrity constraint is expressed on the source schema. Considering relational sources is not a restriction, since we may assume that sources that are not relational are suitably presented in relational form by software modules called *wrappers*.

3. $\mathcal{M}$ is the *mapping* between $\mathcal{G}$ and $\mathcal{S}$, specifying the relationship between the global schema and the source schema. The mapping $\mathcal{M}$ is a set of first-order formulae of the form

$$\forall \boldsymbol{X}(\exists \boldsymbol{Y} \varphi_{\mathcal{S}}(\boldsymbol{X}, \boldsymbol{Y}) \ \rightarrow \ \exists \boldsymbol{Z} \varphi_{\mathcal{G}}(\boldsymbol{X}, \boldsymbol{Z}))$$

where $\boldsymbol{X}, \boldsymbol{Y}, \boldsymbol{Z}$ are sets of variables or constants, and $\varphi_{\mathcal{S}}$ and $\varphi_{\mathcal{G}}$ are conjunctions of atoms whose predicate symbols are in $\mathcal{S}$ and $\Psi$ respectively. Henceforth, we will omit quantifiers in mapping formulae. Note that this kind of mapping assertions is a generalisation of both LAV and GAV assertions; in particular, in a LAV assertion a view (conjunction of atoms) over the global schema is associated to a source relation, while in a GAV assertion a view over the source schema is associated to a relation symbol in $\Psi$. Henceforth, consistently with [9], we will call *GLAV (global-local-as-view)* this approach.

Now we come to queries expressed over the global schema; a $n$-ary *relational query* (relational query of arity $n$) is a formula that is intended to specify a set of $n$-tuples of constants in $\Gamma$, that constitute the *answer* to the query. In our setting, we assume that queries over the global schema are expressed in the language of *union of conjunctive queries (UCQs)*. A conjunctive query (CQ) of arity $n$ is a formula of the form $q(\boldsymbol{X}) \leftarrow \omega(\boldsymbol{X}, \boldsymbol{Y})$ where $\boldsymbol{X}$ is a set of variables called *distinguished variables*, $\boldsymbol{Y}$ is a set of symbols that are either variables (called *non-distinguished*) or constants, $q$ is a predicate symbol not appearing in $\Psi$ or $\mathcal{S}$, and $\omega$ is a conjunction of atoms whose predicate symbols are in $\Psi$. The atom $q(\boldsymbol{X})$ is called *head* of the query (denoted $head(q)$), while $\omega(\boldsymbol{X}, \boldsymbol{Y})$ is called *body* (denoted $body(q)$). A UCQ of arity $n$ is a set of conjunctive queries $Q$ such that each $q \in Q$ has the same arity $n$ and uses the same predicate symbol in the head.

**Semantics.** A *database instance* (or simply *database*) $\mathcal{C}$ for a relational schema $\mathcal{R}$ is a set of facts of the form $R(t)$ where $R$ is a relation of arity $n$ in $\mathcal{R}$ and $t$ is an $n$-tuple of constants of the alphabet $\Gamma$. We denote as $R^{\mathcal{C}}$ the set of tuples of the form $\{t \mid R(t) \in \mathcal{C}\}$.

In the following, we shall often make use of the notion of substitution. A *substitution* of variables $\sigma$ is a partial function that associates to a variable either a constant or a variable, and to each constant the constant itself. Given a formula $F$ and a substitution $\sigma$, we denote with $\sigma(F)$ the formula obtained by replacing each variable (or constant) $X$ appearing in $F$ with $\sigma(X)$. Given two substitutions $\sigma_1$ and $\sigma_2$ we use $\sigma_1\sigma_2(F)$ as a shortcut for $\sigma_1(\sigma_2(F))$.

Given a CQ $q$ of arity $n$ and a database instance $\mathcal{C}$, we denote as $q^{\mathcal{C}}$ the evaluation of $q$ over $\mathcal{C}$, i.e., the set of $n$-tuples $\bar{t}$ of constants of $\Gamma$ such that there exists a substitution that sends the atoms of $q$ to facts of $\mathcal{C}$ and the head to $q(\bar{t})$. Moreover, given a UCQ $Q$, we define the evaluation of $Q$ over $\mathcal{C}$ as $Q^{\mathcal{C}} = \bigcup_{q \in Q} q^{\mathcal{C}}$

*Example 1.* Consider a data integration system $\mathcal{I} = \langle \mathcal{G}, \mathcal{S}, \mathcal{M} \rangle$, with $\mathcal{G} = \langle \Psi, \Sigma_T \rangle$. The schema $\Psi$ is constituted by the relations $R_1/2$ and $R_2/2$, the source schema by relations $S_1/2, S_2/1$. The set of TGDs $\Sigma_T$ contains the single TGD $\theta : R_1(X, Y) \rightarrow R_1(Y, W), R_2(Y, X)$. The mapping $\mathcal{M}$ consists of the assertions $S_1(X, c) \rightarrow R_1(X, Y), R_2(Y, Z)$ and $S_2(X) \rightarrow R_2(X, Y)$. ∎

Now we come to the semantics of a data integration system $\mathcal{I} = \langle \mathcal{G}, \mathcal{S}, \mathcal{M} \rangle$. Such a semantics is defined by first considering a *source database* for $\mathcal{I}$, i.e., a database $\mathcal{D}$ for the source schema $\mathcal{S}$. We call *global database* for $\mathcal{I}$ any database for $\mathcal{G}$. Given a source database $\mathcal{D}$ for $\mathcal{I} = \langle \mathcal{G}, \mathcal{S}, \mathcal{M} \rangle$, the semantics $sem(\mathcal{I}, \mathcal{D})$ of $\mathcal{I}$ w.r.t. $\mathcal{D}$ is the set of global databases $\mathcal{B}$ for $\mathcal{I}$ such that:

1. $\mathcal{B}$ satisfies the set $\Sigma_T$ of TGDs in $\mathcal{G}$; in particular, $\mathcal{B}$ satisfies a TGD $\chi(\boldsymbol{X}, \boldsymbol{Y}) \rightarrow \psi(\boldsymbol{X}, \boldsymbol{Z})$ when, if there exists a substitution $\sigma$ that sends $\chi(\boldsymbol{X}, \boldsymbol{Y})$ to a set of facts of $\mathcal{B}$, then there exists another substitution $\sigma'$ that sends $\psi(\boldsymbol{X}, \boldsymbol{Z})$ to $\sigma(\chi(\boldsymbol{X}, \boldsymbol{Y}))$ and those of $\chi(\boldsymbol{X}, \boldsymbol{Y})$ to sets of facts of $\mathcal{B}$. In other words, $\sigma'$ is a generalisation of $\sigma$ that sends the atoms of $\psi(\boldsymbol{X}, \boldsymbol{Z})$ to sets of facts of $\mathcal{B}$.

2. $\mathcal{B}$ satisfies $\mathcal{M}$ w.r.t. $\mathcal{D}$. In particular, $\mathcal{B}$ satisfies a GLAV mapping $\mathcal{M}$ w.r.t. $\mathcal{D}$ if for each mapping formula $\varphi_{\mathcal{S}}(\boldsymbol{X}, \boldsymbol{Y}) \rightarrow \varphi_{\mathcal{G}}(\boldsymbol{X}, \boldsymbol{Z})$ we have that, if there exists a substitution $\sigma$ that sends $\varphi_{\mathcal{S}}(\boldsymbol{X}, \boldsymbol{Y})$ to a set of facts of $\mathcal{D}$, then there exists a generalisation $\sigma'$ of $\sigma$ that sends $\varphi_{\mathcal{G}}(\boldsymbol{X}, \boldsymbol{Z})$ to a set of facts of $\mathcal{B}$. Note that the above definition amounts to consider the mapping as *sound* but not necessarily complete; intuitively, for each mapping formula, the data retrievable at the sources are a *subset* of the data that satisfy the corresponding fragment of global schema.

We now give the semantics of queries. Formally, given a source database $\mathcal{D}$ for $\mathcal{I}$ we call *certain answers* to a query $q$ of arity $n$ w.r.t. $\mathcal{I}$ and $\mathcal{D}$, the set $cert(Q, \mathcal{I}, \mathcal{D}) = \{\bar{t} \mid \bar{t} \in Q^{\mathcal{B}}$ for each $\mathcal{B} \in sem(\mathcal{I}, \mathcal{D})\}$, or equivalently $cert(Q, \mathcal{I}, \mathcal{D}) = \bigcap_{\mathcal{B} \in sem(\mathcal{I}, \mathcal{D})} Q^{\mathcal{B}}$.

## 3  Query Answering in GLAV Systems

In this section we present a framework for query answering in the GLAV approach.

**Definition 1.** *Let* $\mathcal{I} = \langle \mathcal{G}, \mathcal{S}, \mathcal{M} \rangle$ *be a GLAV data integration system, and $\mathcal{D}$ a source database for $\mathcal{I}$. The retrieved global database $ret(\mathcal{I}, \mathcal{D})$ is defined constructively as follows. Consider a mapping assertion $\varphi_{\mathcal{S}}(\boldsymbol{X}, \boldsymbol{Y}) \rightarrow \varphi_{\mathcal{G}}(\boldsymbol{X}, \boldsymbol{Z})$. For each set $H$ of facts of $\mathcal{D}$ such that there exists a substitution $\sigma$ that sends the atoms of $\varphi_{\mathcal{S}}(\boldsymbol{X}, \boldsymbol{Y})$ to $H$: (i) we first define a substitution $\sigma'$ such that $\sigma'(X_i) = \sigma(X_i)$ for each $X_i$ in $\boldsymbol{X}$, and $\sigma'(Z_j) = z_j$ for each $Z_j$ in $\boldsymbol{Z}$, where $z_j$ is a fresh constant, not introduced before and not appearing in $\mathcal{D}$; (ii) we add to $ret(\mathcal{I}, \mathcal{D})$ the set of facts that are in $\sigma'(\varphi_{\mathcal{G}}(\boldsymbol{X}, \boldsymbol{Z}))$.*

Now we come to the role of integrity constraints. Here, we will consider a restricted class of TGDs, called *weakly-full TGDs*, for which query answering is decidable. In fact, it is known that query answering under general TGDs is undecidable [14].

**Definition 2.** *A TGD of the form* $\chi(\boldsymbol{X}, \boldsymbol{Y}) \rightarrow \psi(\boldsymbol{X}, \boldsymbol{Z})$ *is a weakly-full* TGD[1]*(WFTGD) if each* $Y_i \in \boldsymbol{Y}$ *appears at most once in* $\chi(\boldsymbol{X}, \boldsymbol{Y})$.

Given a retrieved global database $ret(\mathcal{I}, \mathcal{D})$, in general it does not satisfy the integrity constraints on the global schema, expressed in terms of WFTGDs. Due to the assumption of soundness of views, we are allowed to repair such constraints by suitably adding tuples to the RGD. In general, this can be done in several ways, therefore $sem(\mathcal{I}, \mathcal{D})$ consists of several databases. In the case of WFTGDs, as in other classes of dependencies treated in the literature [4,8], there exists a database that is a representative of all databases in $sem(\mathcal{I}, \mathcal{D})$. Such a database, called *chase*, is constructed by repairing the violations of a set of WFTGDs $\Sigma_T$ defined on a schema $\Psi$, by repeatedly applying, as long it is applicable, the *TGD chase rule*; it is denoted by $chase(\Psi, \Sigma_T, \mathcal{B})$.

> TGD CHASE RULE. Consider a database $\mathcal{B}$ for a schema $\Psi$, and a TGD $\theta$ of the form $\chi(\boldsymbol{X}, \boldsymbol{Y}) \rightarrow \psi(\boldsymbol{X}, \boldsymbol{Z})$. The TGD $\theta$ is *applicable* to $\mathcal{B}$ if there is a substitution $\sigma$ that sends the atoms of $\chi(\boldsymbol{X}, \boldsymbol{Y})$ to tuples of $\mathcal{B}$, and there is no generalisation of $\sigma$ that sends the atoms of $\psi(\boldsymbol{X}, \boldsymbol{Z})$ to tuples of $\mathcal{B}$. In this case: *(i)* we define a substitution $\sigma'$ such that $\sigma'(X_i) = \sigma(X_i)$ for each $X_i$ in $\boldsymbol{X}$, and $\sigma'(Z_j) = z_j$ for each $Z_j$ in $\boldsymbol{Z}$, where $z_j$ is a fresh constant of $\Gamma$, not already introduced in the construction and not appearing in $\mathcal{B}$; *(ii)* we add to $\mathcal{B}$ the facts of $\sigma'(\varphi_{\mathcal{G}}(\boldsymbol{X}, \boldsymbol{Z}))$ that are not already in $\mathcal{B}$.

Note that in the case of WFTGDs, the chase may be infinite.

*Example 2.* Consider Example 1, and let $\mathcal{B}$ be a RGD constituted by a single fact $R_1(a, b)$. Let us construct $chase(\Psi, \Sigma_T, \mathcal{B})$: at the first step we add the facts $R_1(b, z_1), R_2(b, a)$; at the second step the facts $R_1(z_1, z_2), R_2(z_1, b)$; note that the construction process is infinite. ∎

Finally, we prove that the chase of the RGD, constructed according to the set of WFTGDs $\Sigma_T$, is a representative of all databases of $sem(\mathcal{I}, \mathcal{D})$.

**Theorem 1.** *Consider a data integration system* $\mathcal{I} = \langle \mathcal{G}, \mathcal{S}, \mathcal{M} \rangle$, *with* $\mathcal{G} = \Psi$, *where* $\Sigma_T$ *is a set of WFTGDs. Let* $\mathcal{D}$ *be a source database for* $\mathcal{I}$, *and let* $Q$ *be a UCQ expressed over the global schema. We have that* $cert(Q, \mathcal{I}, \mathcal{D}) = Q^{chase(\Psi, \Sigma_T, ret(\mathcal{I}, \mathcal{D}))}$.

## 4   Query Rewriting for Tuple-Generating Dependencies

In this section we present a rewriting technique that takes into account the WFTGDs expressed on the global schema. Such a technique is an extension of that presented in [6], which works in the case of inclusion dependencies.

---

[1] We recall that a TGD is *full* if its right-hand side has no existentially quantified variables, i.e., all variables appearing in the conjunction $\psi$ appear also in $\chi$ [1].

**Algorithm** reduce($q, g_1, g_2$)
**Input:** conjunctive query $q$,
    atoms $g_1, g_2 \in body(q)$
    such that $g_1$ and $g_2$ unify
**Output:** reduced CQ $q'$
$q' = q$;
$\sigma := \text{mgu}(g_1, g_2)$;
$body(q') := body(q') - \{g_2\}$;
$q' := \sigma(q')$;
$q' := \tau(q')$;
**return** $q'$

**Algorithm** rewrite($q, G, \theta$)
**Input:** conjunctive query $q$,
    set of atoms $G \subseteq body(q)$,
    WFTGD $\theta$ such that
    $\theta$ is applicable to $G$
**Output:** rewritten CQ $q'$
$q' := q$;
$body(q') := body(q') - G$;
$q' := \sigma_{G,\theta}(q')$;
$body(q') := body(q') \cup rew(G, \theta)$;
**return** $q'$

**Fig. 1.** The auxiliary algorithms reduce and rewrite

## 4.1 Preliminaries

Given a conjunctive query $q$, we say that a variable $X$ is *unbound* in $q$ if it occurs only once in $q$, otherwise we say that $X$ is *bound* in $q$. Notice that variables occurring in the head of the query are necessarily bound, since each one of them must also occur in the query body. A *bound term* is either a bound variable or a constant. Analogously to the standard notation used in deductive databases, we adopt the special symbol "$\star$" for all unbound variables in the query $q$ (deductive database systems use the symbol "_").

**Definition 3.** *Given an atom $g_1 = r(X_1, \ldots, X_n)$ and an atom $g_2 = r(Y_1, \ldots, Y_n)$, we say that $g_1$ and $g_2$* unify *if there exists a variable substitution $\sigma$ such that $\sigma(g_1) = \sigma(g_2)$. Each such a $\sigma$ is called* unifier. *Moreover, if $g_1$ and $g_2$ unify, we denote as $\text{mgu}(g_1, g_2)$ a most general unifier (mgu) of $g_1$ and $g_2$ (we recall that $\sigma$ is a mgu if for every unifier $\sigma'$ of $g_1$ and $g_2$ there exists a substitution $\gamma$ such that $\sigma' = \gamma\sigma$).*

**Definition 4.** *Given a set of atoms $G = \{g_1, \ldots, g_k\}$ and a WFTGD $\theta : \chi(\boldsymbol{X}, \boldsymbol{Y}) \rightarrow \psi(\boldsymbol{X}, \boldsymbol{Z})$, we say that $\theta$ is* applicable *to $G$ if there exists a substitution $\sigma$ such that: (i) $\sigma$ sends the atoms of $\psi(\boldsymbol{X}, \boldsymbol{Z})$ to $g_1, \ldots, g_k$; (ii) for any variable or constant $W \neq \star$ in $G$ (i.e., for any bound term $W$ in $G$), there is at least one variable $X$ in $\boldsymbol{X}$ such that $\sigma(X) = W$. If such a $\sigma$ exists, we denote with $\sigma_{G,\theta}$ the most general substitution that verifies the above conditions. Moreover, we denote with $rew(G, \theta)$ the conjunction of atoms $\sigma_{G,\theta}(\chi(\boldsymbol{X}, \boldsymbol{Y}))$.*

## 4.2 The Algorithm TGDrewrite

In Figure 2 we define the algorithm TGDrewrite that computes the rewriting of a UCQ $Q$ expressed over the global schema. We will show that such a rewriting, when evaluated on the RGD, returns the result of the evaluation of $Q$ over the chase of the RGD, i.e., the certain answers to $Q$. In the algorithm, it is assumed that unbound variables in the input query $Q$ are represented by the symbol $\star$.

**Algorithm** TGDrewrite($\Psi, \Sigma_I, Q$)
**Input:** relational schema $\Psi$,
      set of WFTGDs $\Sigma_T$, UCQ $Q$
**Output:** rewritten query $Q'$
$Q' := Q$;
**repeat**
   $Q_{aux} := Q'$;
   **for each** $q \in Q_{aux}$ **do**
   (a) **for each** $g_1, g_2 \in body(q)$ **do**
      **if** $g_1$ and $g_2$ unify
         **then** $Q' := Q' \cup \{\text{reduce}(q, g_1, g_2)\}$;
   (b) **for each** $G \subseteq body(q)$ **do**
      **for each** $\theta \in \Sigma_T$ **do**
         **if** $\theta$ is applicable to $G$
            **then** $Q' := Q' \cup \{\text{rewrite}(q, g, I)\}$
**until** $Q_{aux} = Q'$;
**return** $Q'$

**Fig. 2.** The algorithm TGDrewrite

More specifically, the algorithm TGDrewrite makes use of the auxiliary algorithms reduce and rewrite; it generates a set of conjunctive queries, whose union is the rewritten query, according to the following rules, applied to $Q$ until the fixpoint is reached. (1) For each pair of atoms $g_1$ and $g_2$ that unify in the body of a CQ $q \in Q$, then the algorithm adds to $Q$ the conjunctive query reduce$(q, g_1, g_2)$. Note that the most general unifier mgu$(g_1, g_2)$ is applied to the whole CQ $q$. Finally, a function $\tau$ replaces with $\star$ each unbound variable symbol; this is necessary in order to guarantee that the generated query has the required form. (2) If there exists a WFTGD $\theta$ and a conjunctive query $q \in Q$ such that $\theta$ is applicable to a set of atoms $G \subseteq body(q)$, then the algorithm adds to $Q$ the query obtained from $q$ by replacing $G$ with $rew(G, \theta)$ and by applying the substitution $\sigma_{G,\theta}$ to $q$. This step adds new CQs obtained by applying WFTGDs as rewriting rules (applied from right to left). The above two rules correspond to steps (a) and (b) of the algorithm, which make use of the algorithms reduce and rewrite respectively. Termination is guaranteed by the fact that no new symbols are introduced in the rewriting process, and the number of atoms that can be written with a finite set of relation symbols in $\Psi$, variables (including the special symbol $\star$) and constants is finite.

*Example 3.* Consider Example 1 and a CQ $q(X_1) \leftarrow R_1(X_1, X_2), R_2(X_1, X_3)$, represented as $q(X_1) \leftarrow R_1(X_1, \star), R_2(X_1, \star)$. The WFTGD $\theta$ is applicable to $G = \{R_1(X_1, \star), R_2(X_1, \star)\}$, and the application of rewrite yields the CQ $q(X_1) \leftarrow R_1(X_3, X_1)$, being $\sigma_{G,\theta} = \{X \rightarrow X_3, Y \rightarrow X_1, W \rightarrow X_2\}$. The rewritten CQ is represented as $q(X_1) \leftarrow R_1(\star, X_1)$, after the application of $\tau$. ∎

We can now give the main result about the algorithm TGDrewrite.

**Theorem 2.** *Consider a data integration system* $\mathcal{I} = \langle \mathcal{G}, \mathcal{S}, \mathcal{M} \rangle$, *with* $\mathcal{G} = \langle \Psi, \Sigma_T \rangle$, *a source database* $\mathcal{D}$ *for* $\mathcal{I}$, *and a UCQ* $Q$ *expressed over* $\mathcal{G}$. *We have that* TGDrewrite$(Q)^{ret(\mathcal{I},\mathcal{D})} = Q^{chase(\Psi, \Sigma_T, ret(\mathcal{I},\mathcal{D}))}$.

## 5   Query Rewriting for the Mapping

In the previous section we have shown a technique that allows us to obtain the certain answers by evaluating a rewriting of the query $Q$ over the RGD, thus avoiding the construction of the (possibly infinite) chase. In this section we will present a rewriting technique that allows us to avoid even the construction of the RGD. The technique is based on a transformation of the given GLAV system into an equivalent GAV one, and then on the application of a variant of the known techniques for GAV [15], namely, the *unfolding*.

## 5.1 From GLAV to GAV

Here we present a technique for compiling a GLAV system into an equivalent GAV one. The notion of equivalence is given in terms of queries, and it is the same as in [3]. In particular, given two integration systems $\mathcal{I} = \langle \mathcal{G}, \mathcal{S}, \mathcal{M} \rangle$ and $\mathcal{I}' = \langle \mathcal{G}', \mathcal{S}, \mathcal{M}' \rangle$ over the same source schema $\mathcal{S}$ and such that all relations of $\mathcal{G}$ are also relations of $\mathcal{G}'$, we say that $\mathcal{I}'$ is *query-preserving* with respect to $\mathcal{I}$, if for every query $q$ over $\mathcal{I}$ and for every source database $\mathcal{D}$ for $\mathcal{S}$, we have that $cert(q, \mathcal{I}, \mathcal{D}) = cert(q, \mathcal{I}', \mathcal{D})$. The transformation of a GLAV system into a GAV one is an extension of the one presented in [3], which transforms LAV systems without integrity constraints into GAV ones; we improve the technique as follows: *(i)* we transform GLAV systems instead of LAV ones; as already observed in Section 2, the class of GLAV systems is a generalisation of both GAV and LAV; *(ii)* we allow the presence of dependencies belonging to the class of WFTGDs in the original GLAV system.

Let $\mathcal{I} = \langle \mathcal{G}, \mathcal{S}, \mathcal{M} \rangle$ be the initial GLAV system, with $\mathcal{G} = \langle \Psi, \Sigma_T \rangle$ and $\mathcal{I}' = \langle \mathcal{G}', \mathcal{S}, \mathcal{M}' \rangle$, with $\mathcal{G}' = \langle \Psi', \Sigma'_T \rangle$ be the transformed GAV one. The transformation is performed as follows. (1) The set of sources $\mathcal{S}$ remains unchanged. (2) The global schema $\mathcal{G}'$ is obtained from $\mathcal{G}$ by introducing: *(i)* a new relation $R/n_d$ for each mapping formula $\varphi_{\mathcal{S}}(\boldsymbol{X}, \boldsymbol{Y}) \to \varphi_{\mathcal{G}}(\boldsymbol{X}, \boldsymbol{Z})$, where $n_d$ is the number of symbols in $\boldsymbol{X} = X_1, \ldots, X_{n_d}$; *(ii)* a new relation $R_{\exp}/(n_d + n_n)$ for each relation $R$ introduced in the previous step, where $n_n$ is the number of symbols in $\boldsymbol{Z} = Z_1, \ldots, Z_{n_n}$ (3) The GAV mapping $\mathcal{M}'$ associates to each global relation $R$ the query $R(X_1, \ldots, X_{n_d}) \leftarrow \varphi_{\mathcal{S}}(\boldsymbol{X}, \boldsymbol{Y})$. We do not associate any query to the remaining global relations. (4) For each mapping assertion $\varphi_{\mathcal{S}}(\boldsymbol{X}, \boldsymbol{Y}) \to \varphi_{\mathcal{G}}(\boldsymbol{X}, \boldsymbol{Z})$ and its corresponding introduced relation symbol $R_{\exp}$: *(i)* we add the WFTGD $R(X_1, \ldots, X_{n_d}) \to R_{\exp}(X_1, \ldots, X_{n_d}, Z_1, \ldots, Z_{n_n})$; *(ii)* we add the full TGD $R_{\exp}(X_1, \ldots, X_{n_d}, Z_1, \ldots, Z_{n_n}) \to \varphi_{\mathcal{G}}(\boldsymbol{X}, \boldsymbol{Z})$.

It is immediate to verify that, given a GLAV integration system $\mathcal{I}$, the corresponding GAV integration system $\mathcal{I}'$ defined as above can be constructed in time that is linear in the size of $\mathcal{I}$. We now show that the above transformation is query-preserving.

**Theorem 3.** *Let $\mathcal{I} = \langle \mathcal{G}, \mathcal{S}, \mathcal{M} \rangle$ be a GLAV integration system, with $\mathcal{G} = \langle \Psi, \Sigma_T \rangle$ and let $\mathcal{I}' = \langle \mathcal{G}', \mathcal{S}, \mathcal{M}' \rangle$, with $\mathcal{G} = \langle \Psi', \Sigma'_T \rangle$, be the corresponding GAV integration system defined as above. Then $\mathcal{I}'$ is query-preserving with respect to $\mathcal{I}$.*

## 5.2 Unfolding

We now go back to query rewriting. The algorithm IDrewrite provides a rewriting of a UCQ $Q$ that returns the certain answers to $Q$ when evaluated over the RGD; however, we are interested in expressing the query in terms of the source relations is $\mathcal{S}$. In order to do this, we define a transformation *unfold* that "unfolds" the rewritten query by using the GAV mapping $\mathcal{M}$. The following definition formally extends the well-known concept of query unfolding.

**Definition 5.** *Given a conjunctive query $q$ of the form $q(\boldsymbol{X}) \leftarrow g_1, \ldots, g_k$ over $\mathcal{G}$, and a GAV mapping $\mathcal{M}$, we say that an atom $g_i$ is unfoldable in $\mathcal{M}$ if and only if there exists a mapping assertion in $\mathcal{M}$ whose head unifies with $g_i$. Moreover, we say that $q$ is unfoldable in $\mathcal{M}$ if, for each $j$ such that $1 \leq j \leq k$, $\sigma_{j-1} \ldots \sigma_1(g_j)$ is unfoldable in $\mathcal{M}$*

*with most general unifier $\sigma_j$. If q is unfoldable in $\mathcal{M}$, we denote as $unfold(q, \mathcal{M})$ the CQ*

$$\sigma_k \ldots \sigma_1(q(\boldsymbol{X})) \leftarrow unfold(g_1, \mathcal{M}), unfold(\sigma_1(g_2), \mathcal{M}), \ldots, unfold(\sigma_{k-1} \ldots \sigma_1(g_k), \mathcal{M})$$

*otherwise, $unfold(q, \mathcal{M}) = \emptyset$. Finally, given a UCQ Q, we define $unfold(Q, \mathcal{M}) = \{unfold(q, \mathcal{M}) \mid q \in Q\}$*

**Theorem 4.** *Let $\mathcal{I} = \langle \mathcal{G}, \mathcal{S}, \mathcal{M} \rangle$ be an integration system with $\mathcal{G} = \langle \Psi, \Sigma_T \rangle$; let $\mathcal{D}$ be a source database for $\mathcal{I}$, and Q be a UCQ over $\mathcal{G}$. Then, $unfold(\mathsf{TGDrewrite}(\Psi, \Sigma_T, Q), \mathcal{M})^{\mathcal{D}} = cert(Q, \mathcal{I}, \mathcal{D})$.*

# 6   Discussion

In this paper we have addressed the problem of query answering in GLAV data integration systems, in the presence of WFTGDs, a restricted class of tuple-generating dependencies for which query answering is decidable.

Several works in the literature address the problem of query answering under integrity constraints, both in a single database context [5,2,10] and in data integration [7, 8,6,14,4,11,16]. In particular, [14] presents a technique for query rewriting under *conjunctive inclusion dependencies (CIDs)*, that are analogous to TGDs; however, this work considers *acyclic* CIDs, so that the problem of having an infinite chase is not addressed. Also, the excellent work of Fagin et al. [8], in the context of *data exchange*, deals with a class of ICs that is incomparable to the one treated in this paper; this work considers a class of TGDs (the *weakly-acyclic* TGDs) together with *equality-generating dependencies*; also in this case, due to the fact that in data exchange the chase is to be materialised, the chase turns out to be finite.

First, we have presented a framework for dealing with integrity constraints in the GLAV approach, based on the notions of retrieved global database [15] and chase [13]; since GLAV is a generalisation of both LAV and GAV, we have thus shown that LAV and GAV are siblings and not opposites, as often stated in the literature. Then, we have presented a further rewriting technique that allows us to take into account the mapping, once it is "compiled" into an equivalent GAV one.

The tractability of our techniques is easily proved, since the evaluation of a UCQ over a database can be done in PTIME in data complexity, i.e., w.r.t. the size of the data; we recall that data complexity is the one that is usually considered in a database context, since the size of the queries is assumed to be much smaller than the size of the data. Due to space limitations, we are not able to give a detailed analysis of the computational complexity of query rewriting in our case.

**Acknowledgements.** This work was supported by the following projects: INFOMIX (IST-2001-33570), funded by the EU; FIRB-MAIS and "Società dell'Informazione", both funded by MIUR. The author wishes to thank Maurizio Lenzerini, Riccardo Rosati and Domenico Lembo for their insightful comments about this material.

# References

1. Serge Abiteboul, Richard Hull, and Victor Vianu. *Foundations of Databases*. Addison Wesley Publ. Co., Reading, Massachussetts, 1995.
2. Marcelo Arenas, Leopoldo E. Bertossi, and Jan Chomicki. Consistent query answers in inconsistent databases. In *Proc. of PODS'99*, pages 68–79.
3. Andrea Calì, Diego Calvanese, Giuseppe De Giacomo, and Maurizio Lenzerini. On the expressive power of data integration systems. In *Proc. of ER 2002*.
4. Andrea Calì, Diego Calvanese, Giuseppe De Giacomo, and Maurizio Lenzerini. Data integration under integrity constraints. *Information Systems*, 2003. To appear.
5. Andrea Calì, Domenico Lembo, and Riccardo Rosati. On the decidability and complexity of query answering over inconsistent and incomplete databases. In *Proc. of PODS 2003*.
6. Andrea Calì, Domenico Lembo, and Riccardo Rosati. Query rewriting and answering under constraints in data integration systems. In *Proc. of IJCAI 2003*. To appear.
7. Oliver M. Duschka and Michael R. Genesereth. Answering recursive queries using views. In *Proc. of PODS'97*, pages 109–116.
8. Ronald Fagin, Phokion Kolaitis, Renee J. Miller, and Lucian Popa. Data exchange: Semantics and query answering. In *Proc. of ICDT 2003*, pages 207–224.
9. Marc Friedman, Alon Levy, and Todd Millstein. Navigational plans for data integration. In *Proc. of AAAI'99*, pages 67–73, 1999.
10. Gianluigi Greco, Sergio Greco, and Ester Zumpano. A logic programming approach to the integration, repairing and querying of inconsistent databases. In *Proc. of ICLP'01*, volume 2237 of *LNAI*, pages 348–364. Springer.
11. Jarek Gryz. Query rewriting using views in the presence of functional and inclusion dependencies. *Information Systems*, 24(7):597–612, 1999.
12. Alon Y. Halevy. Answering queries using views: A survey. *VLDB Journal*, 10(4):270–294, 2001.
13. David S. Johnson and Anthony C. Klug. Testing containment of conjunctive queries under functional and inclusion dependencies. *J. of Computer and System Sciences*, 28(1):167–189, 1984.
14. Christoph Koch. Query rewriting with symmetric constraints. In *Proc. of FoIKS'02*, pages 130–147.
15. Maurizio Lenzerini. Data integration: a theoretical perspective. In *Proc. of PODS 2002*.
16. Jinxin Lin and Alberto O. Mendelzon. Merging databases under constraints. *Int. J. of Cooperative Information Systems*, 7(1):55–76, 1998.

# Design of an Adaptive Web Merchandising System Using Data Mining

Sung Ho Ha

School of Business Administration,
College of Economics & Commerce,
Kyungpook National University,
702-701, Sangyeok-dong, Buk-gu, Daegu, Korea
hsh@bh.knu.ac.kr

**Abstract.** In this paper, an intelligent system for making Web merchandising plans and improving Web merchandising effectiveness is proposed for online retailers to succeed in gaining competitive advantage in highly competitive environment. The system utilizes data mining techniques and focuses on generating Web merchandising rules that are used to estimate customer's demand and to plan merchandise for it. Additionally it concentrates on monitoring effectiveness of the merchandising rules over time, and refining the static merchandising rules or generating new rules for products.

## 1 Introduction

In general, the Web sites' effectiveness can be evaluated from merchandising perspectives. However useful metrics and analysis tools for Web merchandising still lag behind. The rise of Web merchandising analysis in business-to-consumer electronic commerce is mainly attributed to this reason.

Web merchandising helps online retailers to choose the right products appeal to the customers, and to present them to motivate purchase via cross-sells, up-sells, promotions, and recommendations. It also helps provide shoppers with a means to quickly find interesting products, and make adjustments to the Web site content suitable for customer purchase behaviors to build loyalty among those customers considered most profitable and to sustain competitive advantage [1]. In general, Web merchandising analysis consists of four areas: product assortment, merchandising cues, shopping metaphor, and Web design features [4]. The essential components for successful building of Web merchandising system comprise accurate demand forecasting [3, 6], appropriate supplier selection and purchase negotiation [5], and desirable merchandise selection and evaluation [2].

This paper focuses on designing a Web merchandising system utilizing data mining techniques, such as clustering, sequential patterns generation, and association rules mining. It generates merchandising rules used for estimating customer's demand, selects and plans desirable merchandise. Additionally it concentrates on monitoring

N. Zhong et al. (Eds.): ISMIS 2003, LNAI 2871, pp. 572–576, 2003.

effectiveness of the merchandising rules over time, and refining the static merchandising rules (merchandising plans) or generating new rules for products.

## 2 Static Web Merchandising System

The essential components of a static Web merchandising system consist of such functionalities as *Customer segmentation, Product classification, Sequential pattern mining,* and *Association mining*, as shown in Figure 1.

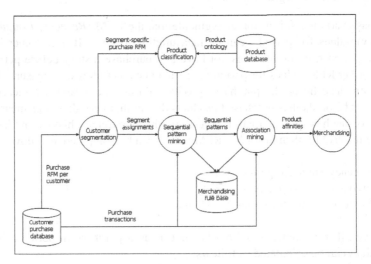

**Fig. 1.** The static Web merchandising system for a specific time period

## 3 Adaptive Web Merchandising System

After a merchandising system observes merchandising effectiveness over time, it generates new merchandising rules or updates the static ones for each product. The following sections describe an adaptive Web merchandising system.

### 3.1 Goodness-of-Fit of the Previous Merchandising Rules

An adaptive merchandising system sees whether merchandising rules derived at the previous period $t-1$ can be applied to the planning for the current period $t$. So-called goodness-of-fit test of the previous merchandising rules is based on the following procedure: 1) Identify a list of products that customers – who belong to the same customer segment – purchase; 2) To evaluate the merchandising plans for each product in the list, the actual sales amount of each product is compared with the plan via the Student's t-test between the two means; 3) If the difference is not statistically significant, the merchandising rules for period *t-1* still remain valid for the next period, *t*. Thus each product's merchandising plan for period *t* is based on its previous period's rules which are stored within the merchandising rule base. On the other hand, if the difference is statistically significant, the merchandising rules for period *t-1* can not be used again for period *t*. This is because the characteristics of each customer segment have been significantly changed since the last segmentation. In this case, new customer segmentation reflecting the changes in customers is needed for an adaptive merchandising planning.

## 3.2  New Customer Segmentation

As the base variables for customer segmentation, the RFM (*Recency, Frequency, and Monetary*) values for period *t* can be measured as follows: If a customer is a newcomer in period *t*, he or she does not have any purchase history before period *t*, and thus his or her RFM values for period *t* are calculated as follows; $r_t$ measures how long it has been since he or she purchases products during the period *t*; $f_t$ measures how many times he or she has purchased products during that period; and $m_t$ measures how much he or she has spent in total. If a customer had a purchase history and has made a purchase in period *t*, then his or her RFM values can be computed as follows:

- Recency value for period $t = r_t$
- Frequency value for period $t = F_{t-1} + f_t$
- Monetary value for period $t = M_{t-1} + m_t$

However, if a customer is old but has not made a purchase in period *t*, his or her RFM values can be calculated as follows:

- Recency value for period $t = R_{t-1}$ + an observation period
- Frequency value for period $t = F_{t-1}$
- Monetary value for period $t = M_{t-1}$

Notice that $R_{t-1}$, $F_{t-1}$, and $M_{t-1}$ stand for cumulative recency, frequency, and monetary values to period *t-1*. These RFM data at period *t* are used as a training data set for the new segmentation. Purchase RFM values of 2,036 customers are gathered, and the observation period falls three months.

## 3.3  Goodness-of-Fit of Customer Segmentation and Refinement of Rules

Table 1 presents the number of customers before segment shifts and after segment shifts. Using this table, it is possible to track the segment shifts of individual members of each segment after the new segmentation at period *t*. The *rows* in this table show the retention of customers on one segment and the *outflow* of customers to another segment; the *columns* represent the retention of customers on one segment and the *inflow* of customers from the other segments.

**Table 1.** Segment shifts of customers among the customer segments

| Segment | Customers before shifts | Segment shifts (To) | | | | Customers after shifts |
|---|---|---|---|---|---|---|
| | | **A** | **B** | **C** | **D** | |
| **A** | 627 | 527 (84.1%) | 86 (13.7%) | 0 | 14 (2.2%) | 641 |
| **B** | 140 | 11 (7.9%) | 113 (80.7%) | 14 (10%) | 2 (1.4%) | 199 |
| **C** | 416 | 26 (6.3%) | 0 | 352 (84.6%) | 38 (9.1%) | 884 |
| **D** | 853 | 77 (9.0%) | 0 | 518 (60.7%) | 258 (30.3%) | 312 |

After acquiring the segment shift information, the merchandising system observes the retention of customers on segments. Larger retention rates mean that the previous and new segments are much the same. A merchandiser can choose the threshold (e.g., 80% of the retention rate) as a criterion of similarity. If the previous and new segments are different, the merchandising system proceeds to make new Web merchandising rules for period $t$. If the segments for period $t-1$ are similar to new ones for period $t$, the previous merchandising rules could be reused for period $t$ after appropriate refinement of the rules. This increases the degree of reusability of merchandising rules.

The refining procedure for tailoring the previous rules to the new customer segments is summarized as follows: 1) Identify the retention of customers on segments, the inflow of customers from other segments, and the outflow of customers to other segments; 2) For each sequential pattern for previous period, make sure that the same patterns can be extracted from purchase history of the incoming or outgoing customers. If so, customer inflow increases correlation scores of sequential patterns but customer outflow decreases them (A correlation score measures the strength of a sequential pattern); 3) Refine the association rules as the same way as sequential patterns: customer inflow entails the increase in confidence of the association rule but customer outflow entails the decrease.

To illustrate how to refine the sequential patterns, consider a specific segment $A$ in Table 1. 527 customers remain on the same segment. 17 customers out of the incomers to that segment buy "Game driver," followed by "CD title" within average 52 working days. 6 customers left that segment buy "Game driver," followed by "CD title" within average 48 working days. Thus refining the sequential pattern brings about the following results:

- *The old pattern in the Web merchandising rule base*: "27% of customers who belong to the customer segment $A$ and buy "Game driver", also buy "CD title" within average 35 working days";
- *The refined pattern*: "**28%** of customers who belong to the customer segment $A$ and buy "Game driver," also buy "CD title" within average **36** working days."

The new correlation score of the refined pattern is computed by the expression (1):

$$[(627 \times 0.27) + 11]/641 \cong 0.28 \tag{1}$$

where $(627 \times 0.27)$ indicates the number of customers who show the pattern before shift, 11 shows a net increase in the number of customers after shift, and 641 shows the total number of customers in the segment $A$ after shift.

The new average period is calculated by the expression (2):

$$[(627 \times 0.27) \times 35 + 17 \times 52 - 6 \times 48]/[(627 \times 0.27) + 17 - 6] \cong 36 \tag{2}$$

where the denominator shows the number of customers who have the pattern in the segment $A$ after shift, and the numerator shows the average period of these customers.

## 4   Conclusion

This paper presented online merchandising strategies to increase the sales amount of the target online store as well as to improve customer satisfaction. It also presented the details of deriving merchandising rules (merchandising plans) by using data mining techniques. The effective Web merchandising rules generated by this system made it possible to satisfy the customers through acquiring particular products needed by the customers and making them available to the customers. Through the empirical data, this paper demonstrated how the proposed methods could be used to understand the customers' shopping behavior in an online store and to derive the merchandising plans. The merchandising system presented in this paper is currently being implemented as a part of a business intelligence system that manages and integrates multiple sources of data from the e-commerce site, and provides intelligent capabilities for examining and analyzing the business data.

## References

1.  B. Berman, and J.R. Evans, *Retail Management: A Strategic Approach, 8<sup>th</sup> Ed.* Prentice-Hall, Inc., Englewood Cliffs, NJ, 2000.
2.  R.P. Cash, J.W. Wingate, and J.S. Freidlander, *Management of Retail Buying*, Wiley, New York, 1995.
3.  J. Korpela, and M. Tuominen, Inventory forecasting with a multiple criteria decision tool. *International Journal of Production Economics*, 45, 1996, pp. 159–168.
4.  J. Lee, M. Podlaseck, E. Schonberg, and R. Hoch, Visualization and Analysis of Clickstream Data of Online Stores for Understanding Web Merchandising. In: *Applications of Data Mining to Electronic Commerce*, R. Kohavi, and F. Provost, F (eds), Kluwer Academic Publishers, Boston, 2001, pp. 59–84.
5.  R.T., McIvor, M.D. Mulvenna, and P.K. Humphreys, A hybrid knowledge-based system for strategic purchasing. *Expert Systems with Applications*, 12, 1997, pp. 497–512.
6.  J.R. Stock, and D.M. Lambert, *Strategic Logistics Management*. Irwin, Homewood, IL, 1987.

# Minutiae Extraction from Fingerprint Images Using Run-Length Code

Jung-Hwan Shin, Hui-Yeoun Hwang, and Sung-Il Chien

School of Electronic and Electrical Engineering, Kyungpook National University,
Daegu, 702-701, Korea
{jhshin, huiyeoun}@palgong.knu.ac.kr
sichien@ee.knu.ac.kr
http://hci.knu.ac.kr/

**Abstract.** Minutiae extraction is often carried out on thinned images. Thinning is a time-consuming process and causes undesired spikes and breaks. In this paper, a minutiae-extracting method is presented by encoding run-length code from binary images without a thinning process. Ridges in fingerprint images are represented as a cascade of runs, and minutiae detection has been accomplished by searching for starting or ending runs and merging or splitting runs. Experimental results show that the proposed method is fairly reliable and fast, when compared to a thinning-based method.

## 1 Introduction

Among human biometric features to confirm the identity, fingerprint matching is the most popular and reliable technique for automatic personal identification. This popularity can be attributed to many reasons [1]. First, it is a relatively non-invasive technology which less irritates people in fingerprint acquisition. Second, many inexpensive high quality devices for fingerprint scanning are now available on the market. Third, fingerprints have uniqueness and immutability properties. The uniqueness of an individual fingerprint is exclusively determined by minutiae. There are various types of minutiae in a fingerprint, but widely used fingerprint features are restricted to a ridge ending and a ridge bifurcation [2]. The performance of automatic fingerprint identification systems heavily relies on how well these minutiae are extracted.

In this paper, a novel method is proposed for fast extraction of fingerprint minutiae that are based on run-length encoding from binary images without a time-consuming thinning process. Ridges in fingerprint images can be represented by a cascade of runs via run-length encoding. Ridge endings and ridge bifurcations in fingerprint images are defined as starting or ending runs and merging or splitting runs, which are defined as characteristic runs in this research, respectively. Characteristic runs are detected by considering the geometrical relationship of runs. Sets of geometric constraints are also introduced in order to reject false minutiae from the characteristic runs.

N. Zhong et al. (Eds.): ISMIS 2003, LNAI 2871, pp. 577–584, 2003.

## 2   Preprocessing

The quality of fingerprint images is often to be poor due to many factors, such as variations in impression conditions, skin conditions, acquisition devices, etc. In order to improve the clarity of the ridge structure and to accurately extract the minutiae of a fingerprint, two steps of the preprocessing are applied.

*Step 1: Segmentation.* The goal of segmentation is to reduce the size of the input data, eliminating undesired background or poor-quality areas. Poor-quality areas give rise to a serious problem of generation of spurious minutiae. Consequently, the proper segmentation is needed to remove false minutiae for better identification by retaining as many details of ridge structure as possible. In this paper, segmentation is performed using the difference between minimum and maximum values of directional slit sums [3]. Figure 1(b) shows a result of segmentation.

*Step 2: Binarization.* In a local subblock, the flow of ridge or valley varies slowly. Therefore, Gabor filter can be efficiently used in the process of removing undesired noise because of its frequency- and orientation-selective properties. The even-symmetric Gabor filter in the spatial domain is tuned by the estimated orientation and frequency of the local ridge through the least mean-square orientation estimation algorithm [4] and the local frequency estimation method in [5]. In the experiments, the filter with a mask size of 13 by 13 and 16 orientations are used. The Gabor-filtered image is binarized using the well-known method suggested by Otsu. Example of the binarized fingerprint image after the Gabor filtering is shown in Fig. 1(c). As shown in this figure, the clarity of the ridge and valley structures is improved.

## 3   Run-Length Code-Based Minutiae Extraction

A binary image is completely specified by a linked list of its run [6]. In this paper, a binarized fingerprint image is also represented by a linked list of its run. In a fingerprint image, the ridge ending is the starting or ending point of a ridge flow and the ridge bifurcation is the merging or splitting point of two ridges. The underlying idea of the proposed method is detecting these points by tracking ridge flows connected to them not in a binary image but in a run-length code. The following steps are performed in the method.

### 3.1   Run-Length Encoding

A run-length encoding is an efficient coding scheme for binary or labeled images because it can not only reduce memory space but also speed up image processing time [7]. In a binary image, successive black pixels along the scan line are defined as a run. Generally, a run-length encoding of a binary image is a list of contiguous runs of black-pixels. For each run, locations of the starting and the ending pixel of a run (or the length of a run) are recorded in the run-length code. Figure 2 shows

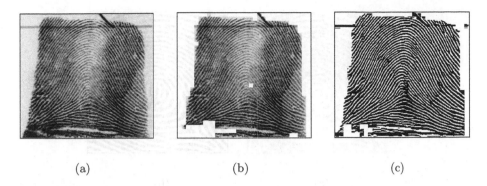

(a)                          (b)                          (c)

**Fig. 1.** Result fingerprint images after preprocessing. (a) Original gray-level fingerprint image. (b) Segmented fingerprint image. (c) Enhanced binarized fingerprint image after Otsu thresholding and Gabor filtering

how to express the minutiae in the run representation. As shown in Figs. 2(c) and (d), the endmost run stands for the ridge ending. A merging or splitting run in Figs. 2(e) and (f) signifies the ridge bifurcation. For reliable detection of these runs, two different scans with orthogonal directions, top-to-bottom and left-to-right, must be carried out. The major reason of using both horizontal and vertical scans is that a minutia, in which a ridge flows along to the direction of scan, cannot be detected properly as shown in Fig. 3. Figures 3(a) and (b) show a binarized fingerprint image and a ridge ending on it, respectively. Figures 3(c) and (d) show ridges represented by vertical and horizontal runs, respectively. In case of a slanted ridge, as horizontal and vertical runs have little difference in width, both will be represented well as minutiae. In a horizontal scan, a horizontal run is specified by three parameters: the order of a row and two positions of a starting and an ending column of the run. Similarly, in a vertical scan, a vertical run is specified by the order of a column and two positions of a starting and an ending row of the run.

### 3.2   Adjacency-Checking Rules

Every run is checked against runs on the previous and the next scan line for their adjacency. Before checking adjacency, we need to elaborate several definitions originally offered in [6].

*Definition 1.* Two runs are said to be *adjacent* if they lie in adjacent scan lines and touch one another in an 8-neighbor sense.

*Definition 2.* A ridge is composed of a sequence of runs.
    $ridge = \{P_1, P_2, P_3, \cdots, P_n,$ where $P_{i+1}$ is adjacent to $P_i$, $1 \leq i \leq n-1\}$.
If a set $S$ is a ridge in binarized fingerprint image, and $P_1$ and $P_n$ are any pair of runs in the $S$, then we say that $P_1$ and $P_n$ are connected in the ridge $S$ and a sequence from $P_1$ and $P_n$ is a *path*.

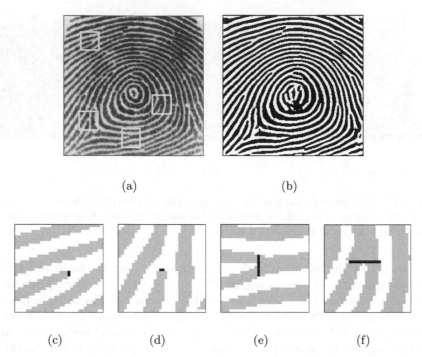

(a)                              (b)

(c)          (d)          (e)          (f)

**Fig. 2.** Minutiae in run representation. (a) Original gray-level fingerprint image. (b) Enhanced binarized fingerprint image. Ridge ending (c) in vertical and (d) horizontal run. Ridge bifurcation (e) in vertical and (f) horizontal run

*Definition 3.* A run is *regular* if it has one previous adjacent run and one next adjacent run. If a run is not regular, it is *singular*.

*Definition 4.* A starting run is a run with no previous adjacent run. An ending run is a run with no next adjacent run. A merging run is a run that has two previous adjacent runs and one next adjacent run. A splitting run is a run that has one previous adjacent run and two next adjacent runs.

During the adjacency checking, the following five cases occur:
*Case 1.* No adjacent run in both the previous and the next scan line
*Case 2.* One adjacent run in both the previous and the next scan line
*Case 3.* One adjacent run in either the previous or the next scan line
*Case 4.* Two adjacent runs in either the previous or the next scan line
*Case 5.* More than two adjacent runs in either the previous or the next scan line

*Case 1* means the run is one pixel spot or an isolated line with more than one pixel width. *Case 2* means the run is part of a ridge flow. *Case 3* means the run is either the starting or the ending point of ridge flow. *Case 4* means two runs on the previous scan line are merging or one run is splitting into two runs on the next scan line. Finally, *Case 5* has not been considered in the current experiment

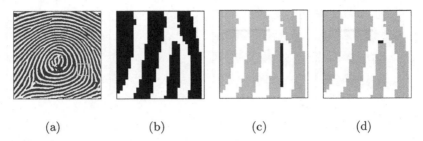

**Fig. 3.** Ridge is represented by two directional scans. (a) Enhanced binarized fingerprint image. (b) Ridge ending in binary image. (c) Ridge ending was not properly detected in vertical run. (d) Ridge ending was detected in horizontal run

because a confluence point, which is composed of more than two ridge flows, is not a minutia in most AFIS. The runs in both *Cases 3* and *4* are singular runs and are especially called characteristic runs in this study, whereas the runs in *Case 2* are called regular runs. Characteristic runs of *Case 3* correspond to ridge endings and those of *Case 4* stand for ridge bifurcations in a fingerprint image.

### 3.3 Validity of Characteristic Run for Minutiae

Although the characteristic runs are extracted from the run-length codes, validity-checking process for true minutiae is needed. For example, very short ridges generated by the noise in an input image or small protrusions on the contours of the ridge tend to result in false characteristic runs. In this research, three properties are used to eliminate false characteristic runs. The first one is a length of each run. If the length of a characteristic run is longer than $2\lambda$, where $\lambda$ is a local ridge width estimated in preprocessing, the run is determined as false minutiae and removed from the characteristic run list. The second one is the gap between two previous adjacent runs or two next adjacent runs of a characteristic run. If the gap is larger than $3\lambda$, the run is considered as a curved ridge with small curvature and is then removed. The third one is the path length measured by tracking along the adjacent runs from a characteristic run. If the tracked distance from the characteristic run in the current scan line to another one is smaller than $2\lambda$, it is also removed. Some typical structures of characteristic runs, which will be turned out to be false minutiae, are shown in Fig. 4.

## 4   Experimental Results

The minutiae extraction algorithm described in this paper has been implemented and tested on the two sets of databases. The first database (*Database1*) is composed of 120 fingerprint images through an optical sensor. Each gray-level fingerprint image has 256×256 pixels with the resolution of 500 dpi. The second database (*Database2*) is 21 fingerprints from the NIST Special Database 4 containing gray-level images. Each image has 512×512 pixels with 32 rows of white

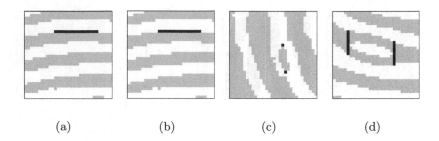

(a)          (b)          (c)          (d)

**Fig. 4.** Examples of structures of characteristic runs that turn to be false minutiae.

space at the bottom of the image. The performance of different methods has been reliably evaluated by comparing the detected minutiae with the set of minutiae obtained from the same image by a human expert. A thinning process has been carried out by the algorithm presented in [8] and the postprocessing method in [9], which is recently published and is carefully implemented for fair comparison, is used. Examples of extracted minutiae by two methods are shown in Fig. 5. Extracted minutiae are marked on the gray-level images for comparison. Figures 5(a) and (b) are the result images that were tested on *Database1* and Figs. 5(c) and (d) are the results tested on *Database2*. The entire minutiae extraction procedures are executed on a Pentium III-500Mhz.

Although the process of eliminating false minutiae is adopted for both methods, some false minutiae are observable in both methods. The false minutiae are generated by preprocessing and noise in the input image. The proposed method sometimes could not remove broken structures but it is robust in island structures. The following definitions are needed to compare the experimental results.

- *True minutiae*: Minutiae detected by an expert are said to be true minutiae.
- *Paired minutiae*: If the minutiae extracted by an algorithm coincide with true minutiae, they are said to be paired minutiae.
- *False minutiae*: If the minutiae extracted by an algorithm do not coincide with true minutiae, they are said to be false minutiae.
- *Dropped minutiae*: If the true minutiae are not detected by an algorithm, they are said to be dropped minutiae.
- *Exchanged minutiae*: Minutiae with different (exchanged) type are said to be exchanged minutiae, although the minutiae extracted by an algorithm coincide with true minutiae.

True minutiae ratio (TMR) is the ratio of paired minutiae to true ones. A large value of TMR implies good performance of the algorithm for a fingerprint image. False minutiae ratio (FMR) is the ratio of false minutiae to true ones. The purpose of the postprocessing is the reduction of FMR while preserving or increasing TMR. Dropped minutiae ratio (DMR) is the ratio of dropped minutiae to true ones and exchanged minutiae ratio (EMR) is the ratio of exchanged minutiae to true ones. The sum of TMR, DMR, and EMR is 100%. Table 1 shows the performance and computational time of the minutiae extraction algorithms. In

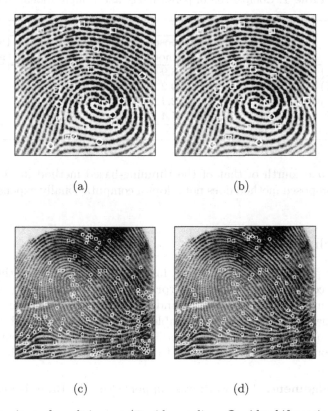

(a)                    (b)

(c)                    (d)

**Fig. 5.** Comparison of result images (□: ridge ending, ○: ridge bifurcation). Result of (a) thinning-based and (b) proposed method from *Database1*. Result of (c) thinning-based and (d) proposed method from *Database2*

case of *Database1*, two methods show similar ratio in four factors. That means the performance of the proposed method is comparable to that of the thinning-based method. Most of the errors of two methods except FMR are minutiae exchanges. EMR is mainly due to the conversion process of a gray image into a binary one. In case of *Database2*, overall errors of the proposed method are a little lower than the thinning-based method. Two methods have high FMR, but these could be decreased by more sophisticated postprocessing. It was pointed out from the visual consideration that the thinning-based method generated more false ridge bifurcations in the island structure (closely located ridge bifurcations) than the proposed method. Therefore, the FMR of the proposed method is about 2.9% lower than the thinning-based method. However, the TMR of the proposed method is about 3.9% higher than that of the thinning-based method. The DMR of the proposed method is about 3.2% lower than the thinning-based method. In terms of computational complexity, the proposed method is much faster than the thinning-based method. The average computational time of the proposed method is about one third of that of the thinning-based method in *Database1*

**Table 1.** Comparison of performance and computational time

|  | Database1 | | Database2 | |
|---|---|---|---|---|
|  | Thinning-based method | Proposed method | Thinning-based method | Proposed method |
| FMR (%) | 18.5 | 18.9 | 46.1 | 43.2 |
| TMR (%) | 69.9 | 70.2 | 64.6 | 68.5 |
| DMR (%) | 12.9 | 12.4 | 12.4 | 9.2 |
| EMR (%) | 17.2 | 17.4 | 23.0 | 22.3 |
| Time (ms) | 117 | 35 | 570 | 140 |

and about one fourth of that of the thinning-based method in *Database2*, because the proposed method does not adopt a computationally expensive thinning process.

## 5    Conclusions

This paper proposes the reliable and fast feature extraction method based on run-length code from binarized fingerprint images. By detecting characteristic runs as feature from run-length code and effectively removing false minutiae, the proposed method has performed reliable minutiae extraction. Moreover, when compared to a thinning-based method, the proposed method shows much reduced computational time and seems to be more suitable for on-line AFIS.

**Acknowledgement.** This work was supported by the Brain Korea 21 Project in 2003.

## References

1. Dale, L.: Schools Learn about the Benefits of Biometrics. Biometric Technology Today. **9(6)** Elsevier Science. (2001) 7–8
2. Lee, H.C., Gaensslen, R.E.: Adavances in Fingerprint Technology. 2nd edn. CRC Press, Boca Raton London New York Washington D.C. (2001)
3. Wilson, C.L., Candela, G.T., Watson, C.I.: Neural-Network Fingerprint Classification. J. Artif. Neur. Net. **1(2)** (1994) 203–228
4. Ratha, N.K., Chen, S., Jain, A.K.: Adaptive Flow Orientation-based Feature Extraction in Fingerprint Images. Pattern Recog. **28(11)** (1995) 1657–1672
5. Hong, L., Wan, Y., Jain, A.K.: Fingerprint Image Enhancement: Algorithm and Performance Evaluation. IEEE Trans. Patt. Anal. Mach. Intell. **18(1)** (1996) 83–89
6. Zenzo, S.D., Cinque, L., Levialdi, S.: Run-based Algorithms for Binary Image Analysis and Processing. IEEE Tran. Patt. Anal. Mach. Intell. **18(1)** (1996) 83–88
7. Shapiro, L.G., Stockman, G.C.: Computer Vision. Prentice Hall. (2001)
8. Chen, Y.S., Hsu, W.H.: A Modified Fast Parallel Algorithm for Thinning Digital Patterns. Pattern Recog. Lett. **7** (1988) 99–106
9. Kim, S.J., Lee, D.J., Kim, J.H.: Algorithm for Detection and Elimination of False Minutiae in Fingerprint Images. Lecture Notes in Computer Science, Vol. 2091. Springer-Verlag, Berlin Heidelberg New York (2001) 235–240

# Endpoint Detection of Isolated Korean Utterances for Bimodal Speech Recognition in Acoustic Noisy Environments

Hyun-Hwa Oh, Hong-Seok Kwon, Jong-Mok Son, Keun-Sung Bae, and
Sung-Il Chien

School of Electronic and Electrical Engineering, Kyungpook National University,
Daegu, 702-701, Korea
ohh@palgong.knu.ac.kr, {hskwon, sjm}@mir.knu.ac.kr
{ksbae, sichien}@ee.knu.ac.kr
http://hci.knu.ac.kr/main/main.htm

**Abstract.** This paper proposes a reliable endpoint detection method
for a bimodal system in an acoustically noisy environment. Endpoints
are detected in the audio and video signals, and then suitable ones are
selected depending on the signal-to-noise ratio (SNR) estimated in the
input audio signal. Experimental results show that the proposed method
can significantly reduce a detection error rate and produce acceptable
recognition accuracy in a bimodal system, even with a very low SNR.

## 1 Introduction

Bimodal systems [1][2][3] have been introduced as a means of constructing a
noise-tolerant speech recognition system based on utilizing the visual information related to speech, often referred to as lipreading [4][5]. Endpoint detection
is crucial for a good recognition performance in a bimodal system as well as in
an automatic speech recognition (ASR) system that only uses acoustic information, because endpoint detection error cannot be recovered in the later stage of
recognition. Although various studies have already reported on endpoint detection for an ASR system, few studies have focused on endpoint detection for a
bimodal system. Existing approaches in the ASR system include those based on
an energy and zero-crossing rate [6], level equalizer [7], Teager energy [8], spectrum analysis, cepstral analysis [9], and fusion [10], and many other methods.
However, these methods often fail to reliably determine endpoints under noisy
circumstances, thereby dramatically degrading the recognition accuracy of the
ASR. The application of conventional endpoint detectors used for audio signals
to a bimodal system in an adverse acoustic environment needs more elaboration. Generally, it is well-known that a video signal is immune to acoustic noise.
Accordingly, this paper proposes the use of an endpoint detector from the video
signal of which accuracy is slightly inferior to that from an audio signal with a
high SNR. Thereafter, an endpoint selection method is proposed that chooses
either the endpoints detected from the audio signal or the ones detected from
the video signal, according to the SNR estimated in the input audio signal.

N. Zhong et al. (Eds.): ISMIS 2003, LNAI 2871, pp. 585–592, 2003.

## 2  Endpoint Detection for Bimodal System

### 2.1  Bimodal System under Study

For the current study, a typical bimodal system was implemented as shown in Fig. 1. This system receives two input signals for isolated Korean word utterances: a 4-channel audio signal sampled at 100kHz with a 16-bit quantization level and a video signal acquired at 30frames/sec. The resolution of the lip images is 320×240 pixels with an 8-bit gray level. First, a speech enhancement technique using a 4-channel microphone array [11] is used to reduce the effect of acoustic noise causing inaccurate endpoints. The enhanced speech signal is then pre-emphasized based on a factor of 0.95 and analyzed with a hamming window. The analysis frame size of audio signal is set to 25.6ms with 11.1ms overlap between two audio frames. The acoustic and visual features are extracted from the respective signals within the speech region, which is bounded by beginning and ending points. The acoustic features consist of 13th order mel-frequency cepstral coefficients (MFCC), the single energy, and their delta values calculated over seven audio frames. The visual features consist of 64th order mesh features extracted from the region of interest (ROI), including the lips, from each video frame in the image sequence [4]. The visual and acoustic classifiers are both based on a continuous hidden Markov model (HMM) with the same structure. Finally, a late-integration technique is used to combine the two classifiers by typically weighting their respective log-likelihoods, $\log P(w_i|V)$ and $\log P(w_i|A)$ [1]. In other words, the recognized word $w^*$ is determined by

$$w^* = \arg \max_{i=1,2,\ldots,N} \{\alpha \log P(w_i \mid V) + (1-\alpha) \log P(w_i \mid A)\}$$

where $\alpha$ is a video weighting factor which is dependent on the quality of the acoustic signal.

### 2.2  Endpoint Detection in Audio and Video Signals

Energy-based endpoint detection is widely used for determining endpoints in an audio signal. While the conventional root mean square energy only reflects the

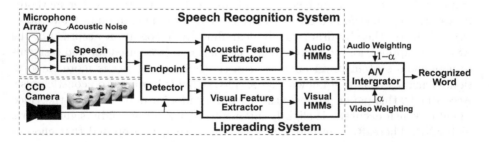

**Fig. 1.** Overall block diagram of bimodal speech recognition system

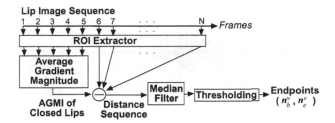

**Fig. 2.** Schematic diagram of endpoint detection in video signal

square of the amplitude, the Teager energy is proportional to the square of the frequency as well as the amplitude of the audio signal. This property creates a high energy level in both unvoiced and voiced sounds with only a slight computational load. Therefore, in this paper, the frame-based Teager energy [8], defined as the total Teager energy measured in a frame, is used for endpoint detection in the audio signal. The average frame-based Teager energy is calculated from the first six audio frames based on assuming that the beginning part of utterance can be regarded as a silence region. Then, the threshold for endpoint detection is determined empirically. Finally, the endpoints ($n_b^a$ and $n_e^a$) are detected by comparing the threshold with the frame-based Teager energy of successive audio frames.

Until now, there have been few studies on endpoint detection in a video signal. Therefore, the current paper introduces simple endpoint detection in an image sequence, as shown in Fig. 2. When the audio/visual data for an isolated word utterance was recorded for our experiments, each speaker was instructed to start and end each word utterance with their lips in the closed position. As such, since it can be assumed that the speaker's lips are closed in at least the first five frames of every image sequence, the gradient magnitudes of the ROIs extracted from these first five video frames can be averaged and defined as the average gradient magnitude image (AGMI) of closed lips. Thereafter, the Euclidean distance between the AGMI of closed lips and the gradient magnitudes of the ROIs extracted from the consecutive frames after the sixth video frame is simply calculated. From that, a one-dimensional distance sequence is obtained. As a result, after applying a median filter and thresholding to the distance sequence, the endpoints ($n_b^v$ and $n_e^v$) of the speech region are determined.

Figure 3 shows the enhanced speech waveform of an isolated Korean word 'Dongdaegu [dôŋdægu]' and the detected endpoints. Here, $n_b^m$ and $n_e^m$ represent the manually detected beginning and ending points, respectively, which are considered as true ones. As seen in Fig. 3, with a high SNR of 0dB, when the only audio or video signal is used for endpoint detection, the beginning point is usually located earlier than the true beginning point, while the ending point is usually located later than the true ending point. In addition, it is observed that both the beginning and ending points detected in the audio signal are more accurate than those detected in the video signal. However, with a lower SNR,

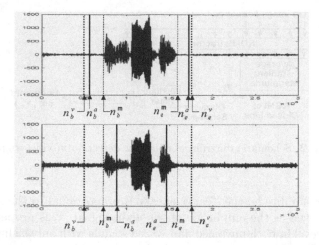

**Fig. 3.** Enhanced speech waveform of 'Dongdaegu [dôŋdæɡu] and endpoints detected manually, $(n_b^m, n_e^m)$ and detected automatically in audio signal ( $n_b^a, n_e^a$ ) and in video signal ( $n_b^v, n_e^v$ ) with SNRs of 0dB (*top*) and -15dB (*bottom*)

like -15dB, the endpoint detector using the audio signal exhibited a tendency to erroneously detect the beginning and ending points inside the actual speech region bounded by the manually detected points.

## 2.3   Proposed Method

As shown by the schematic diagram in Fig. 4, an endpoint selection method is proposed that chooses one set from the two sets of endpoints obtained from audio and video channels, depending on the SNR estimated in the input audio signal. First, the noisy audio signal of the first channel is downsampled at 10kHz. For an isolated word utterance, since the lip movements start earlier and stop later than the corresponding acoustic case [2], the first five frames of the input audio signal are assumed to be a silence region, i.e., noise-only period. Moreover, it can also be assumed that both acoustic speech and noise exist within the speech region determined by the input video signal. Accordingly, the SNR $\hat{\gamma}$ can be obtained from the noisy audio signal $x(n)$ by Eq. (2).

$$\hat{\gamma}[dB] = 10 \log_{10} \left( \frac{\frac{1}{n_e^v - n_b^v + 1} \sum\limits_{n=n_b^v}^{n_e^v} |x(n)|^2}{\frac{1}{5N} \sum\limits_{n=0}^{5N-1} |x(n)|^2} - 1 \right) \tag{1}$$

where $N$ is the audio frame length. If the estimated input SNR is greater than the predefined threshold $\gamma_{th}$, the endpoints detected in the audio signal are selected as the final ones. Otherwise, the endpoints detected in the video signal are selected. Here, the threshold $\gamma_{th}$ was empirically predetermined from the 10kHz downsampled audio signal.

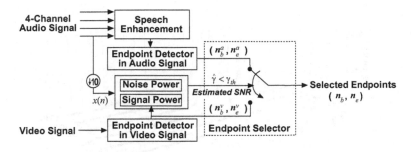

**Fig. 4.** Schematic diagram of proposed endpoint selection method

# 3   Experimental Results and Discussion

There are two possible ways to evaluate the performance of endpoint detection method: one is to compare the detection error via visual inspection [7][8], and the other is to examine the recognition rate of bimodal recognition system by passing the bounded word into the recognizer [12]. In the following, both of two manners are used to test the performance of endpoint detectors and the evaluation results are discussed.

## 3.1   Evaluation on Endpoint Detection Methods

The endpoint detection for the bimodal system has been tested using 4000 audio/visual data. The database consisted of the utterances of 20 speakers (11 males and 9 females) repeating 20 isolated Korean words composed of two or three syllables (names of railroad stations) 10 times. To evaluate the performance of the endpoint detector in an acoustically noisy situation, white Gaussian random noise was artificially added to the 100kHz input audio signals with different SNRs, including 0dB, -5dB, -10dB, and -15dB.

Before the experiments, endpoints were manually located for every utterance and then used as references for comparing the automatically detected endpoints, $n_b^a$ and $n_e^a$. Here, the differences between automatically detected beginning or ending points and their respective reference points, were defined by $d_b = n_b^a - n_b^m$ and $d_e = n_e^a - n_e^m$, respectively.

The histograms of the differences are shown in Fig. 5. The positive difference in the beginning point (*top*) and the negative difference in the ending point (*bottom*) are represented by dark-gray color. In the case of the beginning point, a positive difference value means that the beginning point is located erroneously within the true speech region, as seen in Fig. 3 (*bottom*). As for the ending point, a negative difference value means that the ending point is located erroneously within the true speech region. In isolated word recognition, such an error causes the loss of meaningful speech region, which cannot be recovered in the subsequent steps of recognition. As a result, the recognition accuracy of recognizer can be severely degraded. In the case of the audio signal with a SNR of -10dB or -15dB, the occurrence frequency of dark-gray part was increased dramatically and was

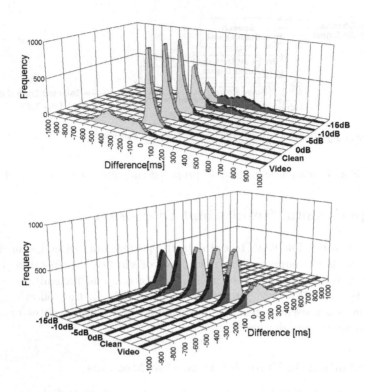

**Fig. 5.** (*Top*) Histogram of differences between beginning points detected manually and ones detected automatically in audio or video signal, in which dark-gray and bright-gray represent positive and negative difference, respectively. (*Bottom*) Histogram of differences between ending points, in which dark-gray and bright-gray represent negative and positive difference, respectively

observed through wide range of difference in both cases of the beginning and the ending points in Fig. 5.

The bright-gray part in Fig. 5 means that non-speech region is included erroneously in the speech-region. In many isolated word utterances,the lips begin to move before the actual speech utterance and sometimes remain opened for a while after termination of speech utterance. Therefore,the non-speech regions tend to be included in speech region determined by the video signal. Commonly, it is expected that lots of non-speech regions affect negatively and severely to recognition accuracy. However, the recognition rate of the bimodal system with endpoint detector using the video signal was found to be relatively good compared to that using the audio signal with very low SNR, because the inclusion of a non-speech region could be modeled by a state for non-speech regions in the HMM-based classifier.

## 3.2  Recognition Results of Bimodal System

Now, the recognition rate of the current bimodal system was evaluated according to each endpoint detection method. Among the 4000 utterances, 2800 were used as an audio/visual database for training and the remaining 1200 used for testing. In addition, acoustic and visual features were extracted from the manually determined speech regions and used to train the respective HMM classifiers in the bimodal system. In the late-integration procedure, the video weighting factor ranged from 0.1 to 0.9 depending on the SNR.

The recognition results of the bimodal system with respect to the SNR and endpoint detectors are depicted in Table 1. When the endpoints were detected automatically in the audio signal, the recognition rate of the bimodal system decreased sharply with SNRs of -10dB and -15dB, because of a soaring detection error corresponding to the dark-gray part in Fig. 5. Conversely, a video signal is insensitive to acoustic noise. Accordingly, when the endpoints were detected in video signal, the bimodal system achieved more than 90% recognition rate with an SNR of -10dB or below, whereas the recognition rate tended to be lower than that in the audio signal with an SNR of -5dB or above. In the case of the bimodal system with the proposed endpoint detector, satisfactory recognition rates were attained with all the SNR levels, ranging from 91.3% (-10dB) to 98.9% (clean). Consequently, the bimodal system with the proposed endpoint detector achieved good recognition accuracy due to reliable endpoints for all noisy audio signals, compared to that with the other two methods.

**Table 1.** Video weighting factor for late-integration and recognition rates of bimodal system with respect to SNRs of audio signals and endpoint detection methods

| SNR of 100kHz input audio signal | | Clean | 0dB | -5dB | -10dB | -15dB |
|---|---|---|---|---|---|---|
| Video weighting ($\alpha$) | | 0.1 | 0.3 | 0.5 | 0.7 | 0.9 |
| Endpoint detection | In audio signal (manually) | 100% | 99.8% | 98.2% | 96.7% | 96.8% |
| | In audio signal (automatically) | 99.2% | 98.7% | 96.3% | 87.3% | 68.9% |
| | In video signal (automatically) | 99.2% | 97.8% | 93.9% | 91.5% | 91.6% |
| | Proposed method | 98.9% | 98.4% | 94.6% | 91.3% | 91.6% |

## 4  Conclusions

This paper proposed a reliable endpoint detection method for a bimodal system with various levels of acoustic noise. The endpoints detected in the audio signal showed higher detection error as acoustic noise increased, therefore, the recognition rate of the bimodal system remarkably declined with a very low SNR. Meanwhile, the recognition rate of the bimodal system with endpoint detector in the video signal outperformed that in the audio signal with a very low SNR, although part of the non-speech region was included in the speech region. The proposed method detected endpoints in the audio signal when the estimated input SNR was high, and detected endpoints in the video signal when the estimated SNR was low. Consequently, with the proposed endpoint selection method, reliable endpoints could be determined for the bimodal system with various noise levels, thereby achieving satisfactory recognition rates irrespective of acoustic noise, even in acoustically very low SNR situations.

**Acknowledgement.** This work was supported by grant No. (R01-1999-000-00233-0) from the Basic Research Program of the Korea Science & Engineering Foundation.

# References

1. Teissier, P., Ribes, J.R., Schwartz, J.-L., Dugue, A.G.: Comparing Models for Audiovisual Fusion in a Noisy-Vowel Recognition Task. IEEE Trans. Speech Audio Processing **7(6)** (1999) 629–642
2. Bregler, C., Konig, Y.: Eigenlips for Robust Speech Recognition. Proc. IEEE ICASSP-94(2) (1994) 669–672
3. Chen, T.: Audiovisual Speech Processing: Lip Reading and Lip Synchronization. IEEE Signal Processing Mag. **18(1)** (2001) 9–21
4. Oh, H.-H., Jeoun, Y.-M., Chien, S.-I.: A Set of Mesh Features for Automatic Visual Speech Recognition. Proc. IARP MVA2002 (2002) 488–491
5. Matthews, I., Cootes, T.F., Bangham, J.A., Cox, S., Harvey, R.: Extraction of Visual Features for Lipreadig. IEEE Trans. Pattern Anal. Machine Intell. **24(2)** (2002) 198–213
6. Rabiner, L.R. Sambur, M.R.: An Algorithm for Determining the Endpoints of Isolated Uttrances. Bell Syst. Tech. J. **54(2)** (1975) 297–315
7. Lamel, L.F., Rabiner, L.R., Rosenberg, A.E., Wilpon, J.G.: An Improved Endpoint Detector for Isolated Word Recognition. IEEE Trans. Acoust., Speech, Signal Processing ASSP-29(4) (1981) 777–785
8. Ying, G.S., Mitchell, C.D., Jamieson, L.H.: Endpoint Detection of Isolated Utterances Based on a Modified Teager Energy Measurement. Proc. IEEE ICASSP-93 (1993) 732–735
9. Haigh, J.A., Mason, J.S.: Robust Voice Activity Detection Using Cepstral Features. Proc. IEEE TENCON-99 (1999) 321–324
10. Tanyer, S.G., Özer, H.: Voice Activity Detection in Nonstationary Noise. IEEE Trans. Speech Audio Processing **8** (2000) 478–482
11. Kwon, H.-S., Son, J.-M., Jung, S.-Y., Bae, K.-S.: Speech Enhancement Using Microphone Array with MMSE-STSA Based Post-Processing. Proc. ICEIC2002 (2002) 186–189
12. Bou-Ghazale, S., Assaleh, K.: A Robust Endpoint Detection of Speech for Noisy Environments with Application to Automatic Speech Recognition. Proc. IEEE ICASSP-02 (2002) IV-3808–IV-3811

# Enhanced Active Shape Models with Global Texture Constraints for Image Analysis

Shiguang Shan, Wen Gao, Wei Wang, Debin Zhao, and Baocai Yin

Institute of Computing Technology, Chinese Academy of Sciences, Beijing, China, 100080
College of computer science, Beijing polytechnic university, Beijing, China, 100022
{sgshan, wgao, wwang, dbzhao}@jdl.ac.cn, ybc@bjpu.edu.cn

**Abstract.** Active Shape Model (ASM) has been widely recognized as one of the best methods for image understanding. In this paper, we propose to enhance ASMs by introducing global texture constraints expressed by its reconstruction residual in the texture subspace. In the proposed method, each landmark is firstly matched by its local profile in its current neighborhood, and the overall configure of all the landmarks is re-shaped by the statistical shape constraint as in the ASMs. Then, the global texture is warped out from the original image according to the current shape model, and its reconstruction residual from the pre-trained texture subspace is further exploited to evaluate the fitting degree of the current shape model to the novel image. Also, the texture is exploited to predict and update the shape model parameters before we turn to the next iterative local matching for each landmark. Our experiments on the facial feature analysis have shown the effectiveness of the proposed method.

**Keywords:** Active Shape Models (ASMs), Active Appearance Models (AAMs), Enhanced Active Shape Models (EASMs), Global Texture Constraints (GTC)

## 1 Introduction

In most pattern recognition and computer vision tasks, the localization and alignment of target object from an image is a task of great importance. To deal with the problem, many methods have been presented in recent years including active contour models (snake)[1], deformable template [2], elastic bunch graph matching [3], Gabor wavelet networks [4], Active Shape Models (ASMs) [5] and Active Appearance Models (AAMs)[6] etc. Among them, ASMs and AAMs are both based on statistical models, which are demonstrated to be efficient and effective for image interpretation. This paper presents an Enhanced ASM (EASM) by combining global texture constraints into ASM, which is essentially a strategy by combining ASM's local profile matching with AAM's global texture models. To integrate the local profile matching, the overall shape constraints, and the global texture constraints, the reconstruction residual of the global texture in its subspace is exploited to evaluate the fitting degree of the current model for the novel image. In addition, the global texture is also exploited to predict and update the shape model parameters. Therefore, with such an interleaving iteration of local profile matching, overall shape constraints, and global

N. Zhong et al. (Eds.): ISMIS 2003, LNAI 2871, pp. 593–597, 2003.

texture constraints, our method takes advantages of both ASMs and AAMs, meanwhile avoids their deficiencies.

## 2   EASMs with Global Texture Constraints

### 2.1   Fitting Degree Measurement in EASM

As is well known, the goal of the analysis-by-synthesis is to optimize the parameters of the model in order that the synthesized model matches the novel image to the utmost. Therefore, it is one of the most important tasks to define the objective function measuring the fitting degree between the novel image and the model, which should be minimized during the optimization.

As illustrated in Fig.1, mis-matched shape implies distorted texture. Therefore, the mis-fitting degree is equivalent to the distortion degree in some sense. In this paper, the reconstruction residual of the current texture in the texture subspace is exploited as the fitting degree to be minimized.

**Fig. 1.** Mis-matched shape model and corresponding distorted texture

As in AAM, statistical texture model is pre-learned from a number of manually annotated images by applying PCA. The texture, $g$, warped from an image, can then be reconstructed as $g' = \overline{g} + P_g b_g$, where texture parameters, $b_g = P_g^T (g - \overline{g})$. So, the reconstruction residual can then be computed by:

$$\varepsilon = \left| g - g' \right| \tag{1}$$

If the model shape is well matched to the target object image, the texture is expected to be a normal patch without background and distortion. Therefore, according to the theory of the Eigen-analysis, the texture should be reconstructed "perfectly", that is, the reconstruction residual should be relatively small. Otherwise, the residual would be very large. To demonstrate this point, we systematically perturb the ground truth shape in scale (from 0.75 to 1.25), rotation (from −25° to +25°), and translation (from −15 pixels to 15 pixels along the X and Y axis respectively). Figure 1 illustrates the corresponding relationship between the reconstruction residual and the parameters displacements in our experiment. Each curve represents a series of parameter variations for one image. From these figures, approximate monotony relationship between the reconstruction residual and the shape parameters displacement can be observed in a certain range. Especially, when the displacement ranges within a certain limit, the monotony attribute is quite ideal. So, it is reasonable to use the reconstruction residual as the fitting degree measurement, i.e. the objective function, to be minimized.

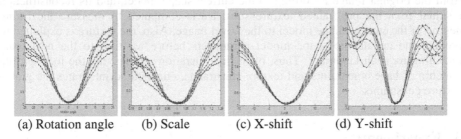

| (a) Rotation angle | (b) Scale | (c) X-shift | (d) Y-shift |

**Fig. 2.** Relationship between the shape parameters variations and the reconstruction residual

## 2.2 Updating Shape Model According to the Global Texture

Similar to AAMs, we also make use of the approximate linear relationship assumption between the texture displacement, $\delta g$, i.e. the shifting from the pre-trained mean texture, and the displacement of the shape parameter $\delta b$ (However, we do not go all the way as AAMs, where appearance parameter is used.) [6]. That is, $\delta b$ can be predicted by linear regression: $\delta b = R_b \delta g$, $\delta t = R_t \delta g$, where $\delta b$ and $\delta t$ are the shape parameter displacement and the affine transformation parameters respectively. The linear regression mapping $R_b$ and $R_t$ is computed in the same way as AAMs.

## 2.3 EASM with Global Texture Constraints for Image Feature Analysis

To sum up, the enhanced ASM with global texture constraints are outlined as follows:

1. *Initialize the mean shape in the novel image;*
2. *Move each landmark locally to its "best position" by profile matching as in ASMs;*
3. *Adjust the 2D affine parameters, and update the shape parameters under the statistical shape models constraints as in ASMs;*
4. *Warp the novel image to the mean shape according to the new shape to obtain the global texture g, and compute the fitting degree measurement, i.e. the reconstruction residual ε in the pre-learned texture subspace;*
5. *If ε is small enough, convergence is declared;*
   *else {if ε is smaller than its previous value, go to step 2;*
       *else, go to the next step;}*
6. *Predict and update the shape parameters according to g;*
7. *Perform the same operation as Step 4;*
8. *If ε is smaller than its previous value, go to step 6 again; otherwise go to step 2;*
9. *The above iteration is continued until no further improvement is observed.*

In the above iteration, each landmark is firstly matched by its local profile in its neighborhood, and the overall configure of all the landmarks is re-shaped by the statistical shape constraint as in the ASMs. Then, the global texture is warped out from the original image according to the current shape model, and its reconstruction residual from the pre-trained texture subspace is computed to measure the fitting degree of the current shape model to the novel image. Also, the texture is exploited to predict and update the shape model parameters before we turn to the next local matching for each landmark. Thus, by such an iteration interleaving the local profile matching, shape constraints and texture constraints, our method integrates the global texture constraints.

## 3   Experiments

By taking face image analysis for example, we conducted experiments to demonstrate the effectiveness of the proposed EASMs. A face database containing 500 face images manually labeled is exploited, in which all the faces possess different expressions including laugh, surprise and angry and all the faces are near frontal with slight illumination variation. To analyze the face image, we defined 103 landmarks on the face, whose coordinates form the face shape in our experiments.

In our experiments, the performance is evaluated by calculating the mean point distance between the resulting shapes and the labeled ones (ground-truth). The distance can be denoted as:

$$d = \frac{1}{N}\sum_{i=1}^{N}\left(\frac{1}{n}\sum_{j=1}^{n} dist(P_{ij}, P_{ij}')\right) \tag{2}$$

where $N$ is the total number of the test images, $n$ is the number of the landmark points in the shape (for our face case, $n=103$), $P_{ij}$ and $P_{ij}'$ are respectively the labeled

**Table 1.** Performance comparison of different methods

| Method | $d$ (pixel) | Variance of $d$ (pixel) |
|--------|-------------|-------------------------|
| ASMs   | 3.05        | 3.23                    |
| EASMs  | 2.59        | 2.71                    |

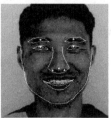
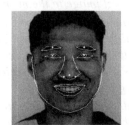

Results of ASM                    Results of our EASM

**Fig. 3.** Comparison between our method and ASM

coordinate and the resulting coordinate for the $j$-th landmark of the $i$-th test image. The function $dist(p_{ij}, p'_{ij})$ is the Euclidean distance between the two points.

In the experiment, 350 images are randomly selected from the 500 images as the training set to build both the statistical texture model and the statistical shape model. The remaining 150 images are used for testing. Similar experiments are conducted 10 times for statistics. Table 1 shows the average experimental results of both ASMs and the proposed EASMs, from which some improvement of our method over ASMs can be observed. Figure 3 shows some example results of both ASM and EASM. As illustrated in this figure, the matching result of the mouth for ASM is not ideal due to the variation of expression, but the EASM works better.

# 4  Conclusion

In this paper, we propose the Enhanced ASMs by introducing global texture constraints expressed by its reconstruction residual in the texture subspace. The global texture is also exploited to predict and update the shape models. The method is essentially a combination of the ASM and AAM. Experiments have shown that our proposed method performs better than standard ASM.

**Acknowledgement.** This research is partly sponsored by National Hi-Tech Program of China (No.2001AA114190 and No. 2002AA118010), and IS' VISION Corp.

# References

[1]    M.Kass, A.Witkin,and D.Terzopoulos. Snakes: Active contour models. Int. Journal of Computer Vision, pp.321–331, 1988.

[2]    A.L.Yuille, Deformable templates for face detection, J. Cogn. neurosci. 3, 59–70, 1991.

[3]    L. Wiskott, J.M. Fellous, N. Kruger, C.v.d.Malsburg, Face Recogniton by Elastic Bunch Graph Matching, IEEE Trans. On PAMI, Vol.19, No. 7, pp775–779, 1997

[4]    V. Krüger and G. Sommer. Gabor wavelet networks for object representation. Technical Report 2002, Institute of Computer Science, University of Kiel, 2000.

[5]    T.F.Cootes, C.J.Taylor, D.Cooper, and J. Graham. Active shape models--their training and application. Computer vision and image understanding, 61(1): pp38–59, 1995.

[6]    T.F.Cootes, C.J.Taylor. "Statistical models of appearance for computer vision", http://www.isbe.man.ac.uk/~bin/refs.html, 2001

# Discovering Structures in Video Databases

Hicham Hajji[1], Mohand-Said Hacid[1], and Farouk Toumani[2]

[1] LIRIS - Université Claude Bernard Lyon 1
43, boulevard du 11 novembre 1918
69622 Villeurbanne - France
{hhajji, mshacid}@liris.univ-lyon1.fr
[2] Laboratoire LIMOS
ISIMA - Campus des Cezeaux - B.P. 125
63173 AUBIERE Cedex - France
ftoumani@isima.fr

**Abstract.** This paper presents an automated technique that combines manual annotations and knowledge produced by an automatic content characterization technique[1] to build higher level abstraction of video content. We develop a method based on concept languages for automatically discovering structural associations within video sequences. The obtained abstraction of the contents of video sequences can be used, by navigating the tree structure.

**Keywords:** Mining Multimedia Data, Concepts Classification, Reasoning.

## 1 Introduction

Content-based video browsing and retrieval are becoming important research topics in recent years. Research interest in this field has escalated because of the proliferation of video data in digital form. For databases with large numbers of video sequences, it is not feasible to browse linearly through the videos in the database. A desirable characteristic of a browsing system is to let the user navigate through the database in a structured manner.

We develop an approach to automatically create a hierarchical clustering of the videos in the database and use the resulting tree structure to navigate through the videos. To represent the various aspects of a video object's characteristics, we propose a model which consists of two layers: (1) Feature & Content Layer, intended to contain video visual features such as color, texture, shape; (2) Semantic Layer, which provides the (conceptual) content dimension of video data. Objects of the Semantic Layer make reference to objects of the Feature & Content Layer through a particular attribute called *sequence*. On top of these two layers, we propose to automatically build a *Schema Layer*, which will contain the structured abstractions of video sequences, i.e., a general schema about the

---

[1] i.e., Clustering algorithms.

N. Zhong et al. (Eds.): ISMIS 2003, LNAI 2871, pp. 598–602, 2003.

classes of objects represented in the previous layers. This process is shown in figure 1. To do that, we assume video sequences in the Feature & Content Layer are clustered according to some algorithms. Video sequences are grouped by similarity. Each cluster is seen as a class. Given those clusters and data of the Semantic Layer[2], we proceed in two steps for building the *Schema Layer*: (1) computing the most specific abstraction of each object in the Semantic Layer; (2) a minimal representation of the (partial) structure of the Semantic Layer is then derived by computing *least common subsumers* of appropriate concepts generated in the first step.

To our knowledge, this is the first proposal for automatically building an abstract layer, in the form of structural associations, on top of a video database.

**Paper outline:** In Section 2 we provide the syntax and semantics of the concept language we use for describing the extracted structural abstractions. Section 3 develops our algorithms for discovering structural associations from video content descriptions. We conclude in Section 4.

## 2    Representing Structural Associations

In the following, we introduce the description logic which will be used to represent the extracted structural associations. The set of constructors allowed by the language are given below.

**Definition 1. (Syntax)** *Let $C$ and $\mathcal{R}$ be two pairwise disjoint sets of concept names and role names respectively. Let $A \in C$ be a concept name and $R \in \mathcal{R}$ be a role name. Concepts $C$, $D$ are defined inductively by the following rules:*

$$C, D \longrightarrow \top \mid \bot \mid A \mid C \sqcap D \mid \exists R.C$$

Here, the concept $\top$ (top) denotes the entire domain of an interpretation, while the concept $\bot$ (bottom) denotes the empty set of objects. In the following, we call this language $\mathcal{LSA}$[3].

**Definition 2. (Semantics)** *The semantics is given by an interpretation $\mathcal{J} = (\Delta^{\mathcal{J}}, \cdot^{\mathcal{J}})$, which consists of an (abstract) interpretation domain $\Delta^{\mathcal{J}}$, and an interpretation function $\cdot^{\mathcal{J}}$, which associates each concept $C$ with a subset $C^{\mathcal{J}}$ of $\Delta^{\mathcal{J}}$ and each role $R$ with a binary relation $R^{\mathcal{J}}$ on $\Delta^{\mathcal{J}}$. Additionally, $\mathcal{J}$ has to satisfy the following equations:*

$$\top^{\mathcal{J}} = \Delta^{\mathcal{J}}$$
$$\bot^{\mathcal{J}} = \emptyset$$
$$(C \sqcap D)^{\mathcal{J}} = C^{\mathcal{J}} \cap D^{\mathcal{J}}$$
$$(\exists R.C)^{\mathcal{J}} = \{d_1 \in \Delta^{\mathcal{J}} \mid$$
$$\exists d_2 : (d_1, d_2) \in R^{\mathcal{J}} \wedge d_2 \in C^{\mathcal{J}}\}$$

---

[2] Data in this layer is expressed in a semistructured data model proposed in [4].
[3] Language for Structural Associations.

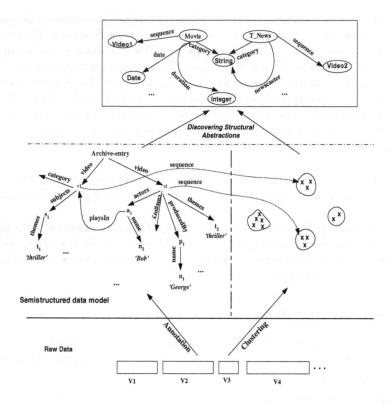

**Fig. 1.** Framework for discovering structural associations

**Definition 3. (Least Common Subsumer** [2]) *Let* $C_1, \ldots, C_n$ *and* $E$ *be concept descriptions in* $\mathcal{LSA}$. *The concept description* $E$ *is a least common subsumer of* $C_1, \ldots, C_n$ *(noted* $E = lcs(C_1, \ldots, C_n)$*) iff*

- $C_i \sqsubseteq E \; \forall i \in [1, n]$, *and*
- $E$ *is the least concept description with this property, i.e., if* $E'$ *is a concept description satisfying* $C_i \sqsubseteq E' \; \forall i \in [1, n]$, *then* $E \sqsubseteq E'$

The msc is a process that abstracts an object $o$ by constructing a very specific description $msc(o)$ that characterizes $o$.

**Definition 4. (Most Specific Concept)** *Let* $A$ *be an ABox,* $o$ *be an object in* $A$, *and* $C$ *be a concept description.* $C$ *is the* most specific concept *for* $o$ *in* $A$, *noted* $C = msc(o)$, *iff* $o \in C^{\mathcal{J}}$ *and if* $C'$ *is a concept description satisfying* $o \in C'^{\mathcal{J}}$, *then* $C \sqsubseteq C'$.

Techniques for computing least common subsumers and most specific concepts are described in [3,1]. Subsumption in $\mathcal{LSA}$ can be decided in polynomial time. Computing the *lcs* of two $\mathcal{LSA}$-descriptions $C, D$ can be done in polynomial time and the size of the *lcs* is polynomial in the size of $C$ and $D$ [2].

# 3   Discovering Structural Associations

**Extracting the Most Specific Schema.** We propose an algorithm, called
Gen$\mathcal{K}$, that allows to *abstract* objects of a data graph. Recall that data in the
Semantic Layer is expressed in the form of semistructured data model denoting
graphs. It consists in retrieving all the assertions characterizing a given object
$o$ and collecting them into a single concept. Such a concept has the property of
being the most specific concept expressible in $\mathcal{LSA}$ of which the object $o$ is an
instance.

---

**Algorithm 1 (Gen$\mathcal{K}$)**

---

**Require:** a data graph $DB = (V_a \cup V_c, E, L, v, r)$
**Ensure:** a knowledge base $\mathcal{K} = (\mathcal{T_S}, \mathcal{A})$.
    {Step 1 : Generating $\mathcal{A}$}
 1: **for** each $(o_i, l, o_j) \in E$ **do**
 2:    $\mathcal{A} \leftarrow \mathcal{A} \cup \{l(o_i, o_j)\}$
 3: **end for**
    {Step 2 : Generating $\mathcal{T_S}$}
    {Initialization of specific descriptions and atomic types}
 4: **for** each $o_i$ in $V_a$ **do**
 5:    {If an object $o_j$ is atomic we denotes by $type(o_j)$ its atomic type}
 6:    $N_{o_j} \leftarrow type(o_j)$
 7: **end for**
 8: **for** each $o_i$ in $V_c$ **do**
 9:    $\delta_{o_i} \leftarrow \emptyset$
10: **end for**
    {Computation of the exact structure for each object}
11: **for** each $l(o_i, o_j) \in \mathcal{A}$ **do**
12:    $\delta_{o_i} \leftarrow \delta_{o_i} \sqcap \exists l.N_{o_j}$
13: **end for**
14: **for** each generated $\delta_{o_i}$ **do**
15:    $\mathcal{T_S} \leftarrow \mathcal{T_S} \cup \{N_{o_i} = \delta_{o_i}\}$
16: **end for**
    {Step 3 : Merging equivalent concepts}
17: Merge together equivalent concepts in $\mathcal{T_S}$
18: **return** $\mathcal{K} = (\mathcal{T_S}, \mathcal{A})$

---

## 3.1   Approximate Typing

In the previous section we provided an algorithm for extracting the most specific
schema abstracting a data graph. In general, we do not expect to find strict
regular structures in video data. Indeed, in a data graph many of the most
interesting structures show up in a slightly different forms. So, we can be often
satisfied by a compact graph schema which roughly describes the input data
graph.

In the following, we propose an approach for reducing the size of the most specific schema by grouping together the concepts that have similar structures. To do that, we replace sets of concept descriptions by their least common subsumer.

---

**Algorithm 2 (Comp$\mathcal{T}$)**

---

**Require:** a data graph $DB$, a threshold $k$
**Ensure:** a knowledge base $\mathcal{K} = (\mathcal{T}, \mathcal{A})$
 1: Gen$\mathcal{K}$'($DB$)
 2: Let $\mathcal{K} = (\mathcal{T}_S, \mathcal{A})$ be the knowledge base generated by Gen$\mathcal{K}$'.
 3: Compute $Candidate_k(C_{T_S})$
 4: **for all** $C \in Candidate_k(C_{T_S})$ **do**
 5:     Compute $lcs[C]$
 6:     **if** $lcs[C] \not\equiv \top$ **then**
 7:         $\mathcal{T} \leftarrow \mathcal{T} \cup \{N_C = lcs[C]\}$
 8:     **end if**
 9: **end for**
10: Merge equivalent concepts in $\mathcal{T}$
11: Cleaning($\mathcal{T}$)
12: **return** $\mathcal{K} = (\mathcal{T}, \mathcal{A})$

---

## 4    Conclusion

We presented a knowledge-based approach for structural associations discovery in video databases. We considered first the extraction of the schema that best describes the data of the Semantic Layer. The result of this step is a most specific schema abstracting the Semantic Layer content. Second, due to the irregularity of structures in video databases, perfect typing may lead to large sets of descriptions. We have shown that it is possible to identify similar, and not only identical, objects, and providing an approximate typing.

## References

1. F. Baader and R. Küsters. Computing the Least Common Subsumer and the Most Specific Concept in the Presence of Cyclic $\mathcal{ALN}$-Concept Descriptions. In *Proceedings of KI-98*, volume 1504 of *LNCS*, pages 129–140. Springer–Verlag, 1998.
2. F. Baader, R. Küsters, and R. Molitor. Computing Least Common Subsumer in Description Logics with Existential Restrictions. In T. Dean, editor, *Proceedings of IJCAI'99*, pages 96–101, 1999.
3. F. Donini and A. Era. Most Specific Concepts Technique for Knowledge Bases with Incomplete Information. In *Proceedings of the 1992 International Conference on Information and Knowledge Management (CIKM), Baltimore, Maryland*, pages 545–551. Springer Verlag, Aug. 1992.
4. M.-S. Hacid, C. Decleir, and J. Kouloumdjian. A Database Approach for Modeling and Querying Video Data. *IEEE Transactions on Knowledge and Data Engineering (IEEE TKDE)*, 12(5):729–750, 2000.

# Theoretical Evaluation of Ring-Based Architectural Model for Middle Agents in Agent-Based System

Chunsheng Li, Chengqi Zhang, and Longbing Cao

Faculty of Information Technology, University of Technology, Sydney
PO Box 123, BROADWAY, NSW 2007, AUSTRALIA
{csli, chengqi, lbcao}@it.uts.edu.au

**Abstract.** Ring-based architectural model is usually employed to promote the scalability and robustness of agent-based systems. However there are no criteria for evaluating the performance of ring-based architectural model. In this paper, we introduce an evaluation approach to comparing the performance of ring-based architectural model with other ones. In order to evaluate ring-based architectural model, we proposed an application-based information-gathering system with middle agents, which are organized with ring-based architectural model and solve the matching problem between service provider agents and requester agents. We evaluate the ring-based architectural model with performance predictability, adaptability, and availability. We demonstrate the potentials of ring-based architectural model by the results of evaluation.

## 1 Introduction

The organizational structure and coordination mechanism of an agent-based system determine the interaction performance among agents. Organizational structure presents the interrelationship among agents in a system. The organizational structures have been modeled into four types, namely, Peer-to-Peer (P), Tree (T), Grouping with facilitator (F), and Ring (R) in practical agent-based systems [3]. Coordination mechanism is the protocols to manage inter-dependencies between the activities of agents. Coordination mechanisms have been classified into five patterns, namely, Direct search (D), Matchmaker (M), Broker (B), Contract-net (C), and Token Ring (TR) [3]. Twelve architectural models for agent-based systems have been proposed by combination of the organizational structures (OS) and coordination mechanisms as shown in Table 1.

**Table 1.** Practical architectural models

| OS | D | M | B | C | TR |
|----|-----|-----|-----|-----|------|
| P | P-D | - | - | P-C | P-TR |
| F | - | F-M | F-B | F-C | - |
| T | - | - | T-B | T-C | - |
| R | - | R-M | R-B | R-C | R-TR |

N. Zhong et al. (Eds.): ISMIS 2003, LNAI 2871, pp. 603–607, 2003.

A key issue concerning agent-based systems with middle agents is how to organize requester agents, middle agents, and service provider agents so that the requester agents can receive appropriate services quickly and efficiently. The combination of R-M and R-TR architectural models can solve the problem because they concentrate on the features of middle agents [3]. However there are no criteria for evaluating the performance of ring-based architectural model. In this paper, we introduce an evaluation approach to comparing the performance of ring-based architectural model with other ones. In order to evaluate ring-based architectural model, an application-based information-gathering system from websites is designed. We evaluate the practical architectural models with performance predictability, adaptability, and availability. We demonstrate the potentials of ring-based architectural model by the result of evaluation.

The remaining sections of this paper are organized as follows: Section 2 chiefly presents the related work about this research. Section 3 introduces the evaluation approach. Section 4 concludes the paper.

## 2   Review of Related Work

The evaluation paradigms of agent-oriented technology might be categorized into three levels: agent coordination level, individual agent behavior level, and agent-oriented methodology level. Bourne et al. proposed a formal framework within which autonomous agents could dynamically select and apply different mechanisms to coordinate their interactions with one another [1]. Agents used the task attributes and environmental conditions to evaluate which mechanism maximized their expected utility. Mali et al. defined power, usefulness, flexibility, modularity, and reliability to evaluate properties of agent behavior sets [4]. Cernuzzi et al. proposed a framework for evaluating methodologies, so that agent-based system designers and authors of agent-oriented methodologies might carry out the evaluation and accumulation of experience [2]. However the framework lacks enough accurate methods to evaluate every attribute. Our research promotes the interaction attribute of the attribute tree of the framework.

## 3   Evaluation of Ring-Based Architecture

We evaluate the ring-based architectural model with performance predictability, adaptability, and availability. The performance predictability can be measured by complexity and efficiency of the system. Adaptability is measured by extendibility of the system. (Note that all following comparisons are based on Lee and Kim's research at Korea University).

### 3.1   Complexity

Complexity measures the number of links among agents or middle agents in organizational structure. The more the number of interactions between agents is, the more complex agent-based system is. If agent-based system is designed by using the peer-to-peer structure, the complexity of the system will be highest because agents in peer-to-peer structure are fully connected. Complexity (C) is defined as following.

C = *Number of links among agents*

For each organizational structure, the detail formula for the complexity is different. The formulae for each structure are defined as following ($C_p$ means the complexity of peer-to-peer structure; $C_f$ means the complexity of grouping with facilitator structure; $C_t$ means the complexity of tree structure; $C_r$ means the complexity of ring structure).

$C_p = n(n-1)/2$

where n is the number of agents.

$C_f = f(f-1)/2 + \sum(n_i(n_i+1)/2)$

where f is the number of middle agents; $n_i$ is the number of agents under the $_i$th middle agent.

$C_t = \text{sum(in-degree}(f_i), \text{out-degree}(f_i))$

where $f_i$ means $_i$th middle agent (i = 1,2...n); n is the number of middle agents in the tree structure.

$C_r = N_f + N_s + 2m + mN_s + \sum(n_i(n_i-1)/2)$

where $N_f$ means the number of middle agents; $N_s$ means the number of service provider agents; $n_i$ means the number of requester agents in Group$_i$ (i = 1,2...m; m is the number of groups).

According to the case study (the system includes 9 agents and 4 middle agents) in our research, the Cr is 26, which is worse than Tree (less than 20) but better than Peer-to-Peer and Grouping with facilitator (between 30 to 70).

## 3.2 Efficiency

Efficiency measures the number of links from service request to completion of the service. Efficiency (E) is defined as following.

E = *Number of interactions until completion after receiving request*

The formulae for each structure are defined as following ($E_p$ means the efficiency of peer-to-peer with contract-net coordination mechanism; $E_f$ means the efficiency of grouping with facilitator; $E_t$ means the efficiency of tree structure with broker coordination mechanism; $E_r$ means the efficiency of ring structure).

$E_p = (n-1)*3+1$

where n is the number of agents.

$E_f = N_l + N_f + N_r$

where $N_l$ is the number of interactions among agents under a local middle agent; $N_f$ is the number of interactions among local middle agents; $N_r$ is the number of interactions among agents under the remote middle agent.

$E_t = N_l + N_f + N_r$

where $N_l$ is the number of interactions between agents and local middle agent; $N_f$ is the number of interactions between local middle agent and global agent; $N_r$ is the number of interactions between remote middle agent and agents under it.

$E_r = N_l + N_f + N_r + N_s$

where $N_l$ is the number of interactions among agents under a group; $N_f$ is the number of interactions between agent and its middle agent; $N_r$ is the number of interactions among middle agents; $N_s$ is the number of interactions between requester agent and service provider agent.

According to the case study, the $E_r$ is 20, which is better than Tree, Peer-to-Peer and Grouping with facilitator (Between 30 to 50).

## 3.3 Extendibility

Extendibility is to evaluate the adaptability of agent-based system. When a new type of service request is introduced into the system, it is necessary to reconfigure the existing system. Reconfiguration includes change, replacement, deletion and addition of agent or middle agent. Extendibility (EL) measures the resources that need to add an agent or middle agent to the existing system. It is defined as following.

$EL$ = *Number of links that need to add agent or middle agent*

The formulae for each structure are defined as following ($EL_p$ means the extendibility of peer-to-peer structure; $EL_f$ means the extendibility of grouping with facilitator structure; $EL_t$ means the extendibility of tree structure; $EL_r$ means the extendibility of ring structure).

$EL_p = n$

where n is the number of agents.

$EL_f = n+1$ (if an agent is added) or

$EL_f = 2$ (if a middle agent is added)

where n is the number of agents under the middle agent.

$EL_t = 1$

$EL_r = n$ (if a requester agent is added) or

$EL_r = 4$ (if a pair of middle agents are added) or

$EL_r = 1$ (if a service provider agent is added)

where n means the number of requester agents in the group.

According to the case study, the most $EL_r$ is 4, which is worse than Tree (1) but better than Peer-to-Peer and Grouping with facilitator (7, 12 respectively). From this measure, we can reason whether an organizational structure can be easily extend. Ring structure is more scalable than peer-to-peer and grouping with facilitator.

## 3.4 Availability

When agent or middle agent is abnormal, agent-based system may occur erroneous behaviors. The abnormal situations can be occurred by fault or malicious action. If local middle agent in tree structure is abnormal, agents under the middle agent cannot act and consequently the availability of system decreases. Availability (A) is defined as following.

$A = (C-F)/C$

where: *C means Complexity;*

$F$ = *Number of links connected to abnormal agent or middle agent.*

The formulae for each structure are defined as following ($A_p$ means the availability of peer-to-peer structure; $A_f$ means the availability of grouping with facilitator; $A_t$ means the availability of tree structure; $A_r$ means the availability of ring structure).

$A_p = (C_p - F_p)/C_p$

$F_p = n-1$

where n is the number of agents.

$A_f = (C_f - F_f)/C_f$

$F_f$ = sum(the number of peer middle agents, the number of agents connected to the fault middle agent)

$A_t = (C_t - F_t)/C_t$

$F_t = 1$ (If an agent is abnormal) or

$F_t$ = sum(in-degree($f_i$), out-degree($f_i$)) (If a local middle agent is abnormal) or

$F_t = C_t$ (If global middle agent is abnormal)

where $f_i$ means ith middle agent ($_i$ = 1,2...n); n is the number of middle agents in the tree structure; out-degree($f_i$) includes all offspring links of $f_i$.

$A_r = (C_r - F_r)/C_r$

$F_r = n_i$ (If a requester agent is abnormal) or

$F_r = 4$ (If a middle agent is abnormal) or

$F_r = 1$ (If service provider is abnormal)

where $n_i$ means the number of requester agents in Group$_i$ (i = 1,2...m; m is the number of groups).

According to the case study, the least $A_r$ is 0.85, which is similar with Tree, Peer-to-Peer and Grouping with facilitator (Between 0.8 to 0.9). If the coordinator in ring structure is abnormal, $A_r$ will decrease to a lower point (about 0.65). However, the coordinator can be automatically regenerated if it is abnormal.


# 4  Conclusion

Although the extendibility and availability are not better than tree structure, these factors can be improved by organizing the agents in a group (application) when the application is designed. The result of this research shows that the ring-based middle agent architectural model can be used as a basis for the agent-based systems that need to use middle agents.


# References

1. Bourne, R.A., Shoop, K. and Jennings, N.R., Dynamic evaluation of coordination mechanisms for autonomous agents, in proceedings of 10th Portuguese Conference on Artificial Intelligence, LNAI 2258, 2001, Springer, 155–168.
2. Cernuzzi, L. and Rossi, G., On the evaluation of agent oriented methodologies, In Proceedings of the OOPSLA 2002 Workshop on Agent-Oriented Methodologies (Seattle, USA, November, 2002), 21–30.
3. Li, C., Zhang, C., Chen, Q. and Zhang, Z., A scalable and robust framework for agent-based heterogeneous database operation, in Proceedings of the 2003 International Conference on Intelligent Agents, Web Technologies and Internet Commerce (Vienna, Austria, February, 2003), 260–271.
4. Mali, A.D., On the evaluation of agent behaviors, Artificial Intelligence, 143, 2003, 1–17.

# Multi-attributes-Based Negotiation Agent and E-marketplace in Customer-to-Customer Electronic Commerce

Wooju Kim[1], June S. Hong[2], and Yong U. Song[3]

[1] Department of Industrial System Engineering, Chonbuk National University, Korea
wjkim@chonbuk.ac.kr
[2] Department of Management Information Systems, Kyonggi University, Korea
junehong@kyonggi.ac.kr
[3] Department of Management Information Systems, Yonsei University, Korea
yusong@dragon.yonsei.ac.kr

**Abstract.** Since people have come to access more and more information about products with the proliferation of the Internet, more and more customer-to-customer e-marketplaces are being introduced with rapidly increasing transaction volumes. Much research has delved into developing intelligent agent systems to efficiently support customer-to-customer EC. However, most of this research has focused only on supporting simple negotiation for the price of common goods. To expand the negotiation object to the differentiated goods, the customer must be allowed to negotiate over multi-attributes of the product besides the price. To satisfy this requirement, we propose an agent marketplace for differentiated goods where the agent of a customer can negotiate not only the price but also the various attributes of the product and the transaction. The formal protocol and the architecture issues to support the proposed e-marketplace and agents are also addressed.

## 1 Introduction

Since EC has become popular with the proliferation of the Internet, the volume of the exchange of property or merchandise between consumers has rapidly grown. Many types of systems have been developed to support customer-to-customer exchange. One of the most popular and powerful among them is an agent-based system. From the survey of related research, most approaches do not support the function of multiple-attribute negotiation between consumers. If there exists an exchange market that allows consumers to negotiate multiple attributes of the product and the transaction activity, additional benefits may be automatically expected.

First, if a party who wishes to sell can provide modifications on the configuration of a product, he may negotiate with a broader range of consumers, which may eventually be of further benefit to both buyer and seller. Second, negotiation over multiple attributes generally results in better satisfaction for both sides than simple negotiation over only one attribute, such as price. Lastly, there is no available system to support this kind of negotiation process for the customer-to-customer exchange

N. Zhong et al. (Eds.): ISMIS 2003, LNAI 2871, pp. 608–612, 2003.
© Springer-Verlag Berlin Heidelberg 2003

market in the electronic commerce environment. Therefore, such an e-marketplace will create new markets in the e-commerce economy while helping to increase efficiency.

## 2 Related Work

Since the advent of the EC, numerous agent-based consumer support systems have been introduced. In a real sense, Kasbah [1] is the first negotiation agent supporting competitive negotiation. To match a buying agent and a selling agent, Kasbah uses a negotiation process that continuously adjusts the price along the time span. Multiple transaction attributes are taken into account in Tête-à-Tête [2], which allows the consumer to present his preferences on the multiple attributes and searches for the most appropriate product and its seller. Recently, the MARI project [3] began development to establish a generalized platform for the brokering of heterogeneous goods and services. MARI finds the best-matched partner to a participant using relative preferences and permissible trade-off ranges for multiple attributes.

As discussed in this section, previous research has not paid enough attention to the negotiation over multiple transaction attributes in the context of the customer-to-customer differentiated goods exchange market. Our methodology complements the above approaches.

## 3 An Approach to E-marketplace for Differentiated Goods

To establish a customer-to-customer e-marketplace for the differentiated goods, appropriate schemes for two well-known prerequisites should be prepared. The first prerequisite is a mechanism for considering trade-offs between the multiple transaction attributes in a unified evaluating framework. Secondly, an agent's negotiation strategy should not be disclosed to other agents before a negotiation action is taken to avoid loss to the side whose strategy was disclosed.

### 3.1 Measuring Utility with Monetary Scale

To obtain a unified utility evaluating mechanism across transaction attributes, most of the previous research forced buyers and sellers to choose a set of predefined utility functions for transaction attributes to be considered. However, selecting the most appropriate utility function out of various functions is an obscure task for users and it can be difficult for them to appreciate how their choices eventually affect the resulting transaction and the trade-offs between transaction attributes. To reduce this kind of difficulty in describing the user utilities, we propose a utility representation mechanism based on a monetary scale.

Our major plan here is that once the buyer (or the seller) quotes the bid (or ask) price for the initial configuration of the product to buy (or sell), a large portion of the buyer's (or the seller's) utility is automatically reflected into that price in terms of a monetary scale. The only additional information that is needed is about his marginal willingness to pay (or be compensated) for any potential changes in the initial transaction attributes. The buyer (or the seller) can represent his marginal willingness in terms of a monetary scale easily and accurately for each transaction attribute.

### 3.2 Two Stages of the Negotiation Process

To satisfy the prerequisite that one agent's negotiation strategy should not be disclosed to other agents prior to an action on the negotiation, the negotiation process is split into two stages: transaction attributes negotiation and price negotiation. In the transaction attributes negotiation stage, both the buyer agent and the seller agent negotiate over all transaction attributes except the price. Therefore, each agent can sense only the other's preference on the transaction attributes without obtaining any information about the partner's utility. Agents from both sides negotiate over the price with each other in the price negotiation stage. To prevent an unfair situation the simultaneous exchange of information about the bid and the ask prices is mandatory in this stage. The agents of the buyers and sellers keep the iteration of these two stages till a matched partner in terms of both the configuration and the price is found or till the negotiation completion time initially set by the owner of the agent is past.

## 4 Automated Negotiation Protocol

To enable the e-marketplace to operate practically and allow its agents to perform their respective roles harmoniously, a formally defined negotiation process and message protocol for communication between the agents must be established in advance. When the negotiation process begins, the buyer (or seller) agent passes through our proposed negotiation process steps consecutively to eventually find the best matching partner who will provide the best configuration including the price.

**Step 1. Negotiation Triggering.** The registered buyer (or seller) agent can initiate a negotiation process by sending the message "request for transaction" to the e-marketplace agent. When the e-marketplace agent receives third message "negotiable range" from the buyer (or seller) agent, it sends the message which is comprised of a list of potential partners and intersection ranges of each attribute.

**Step 2. Configuration Consenting.** In this step, any participant can submit an initial proposal containing information about the desired configuration, except the price. After the initial proposal is initiated, both sides of the transaction may be repeated until one side accepts the other side's proposal by submitting the message "acceptance", or until no more configuration proposals are available from either sides.

**Step 3. Price Comparing.** The price comparing step begins whenever a participant submits his "bid price" (or "ask price") to the price negotiation agent. To preserve a simultaneous exchange of price information, the e-marketplace agent does not release any information that arrives until both "ask price" and "bid price" proposals for a transaction are received. When the e-marketplace agent obtains both bid and ask prices, it relays the price comparing results to the corresponding agents.

**Step 4. Negotiation Settling.** This step completes the whole negotiation process whenever anyone who has received the successful "comparison result" message, requests the settlement of the negotiation and the other party agrees to this request by responding with the message "settlement response."

# 5  Customer Agents in NegoPlace

A participating agent in the e-marketplace represents its owner (buyer or seller) and is supposed to find the optimal deal and a corresponding partner while complying with the protocol and procedures of the marketplace. For an agent to perform this role, it requires an ability to generate a feasible and best offer and evaluate an offer from the partner in terms of customer's utility.

## 5.1  Searching Optimal Offer

We adopt a kind of bounded and incremental search approach for an optimal offer by estimating the other agent's valuation mechanism. The only thing for agent to do in initial stage is to maximize the potential value of the offer. But once it has accumulated information about the partner, it tries to ensure available gains as much as possible. The more the partner's preferences are revealed the more consideration is moved from the potential gain to the obtainable gain.

The agent uses initial attribute value combination as an initial offer. As an agent becomes to know about a partner's preferences on attributes partially or fully, the agent can compute the obtainable gains for an offer based on the acquired information so far. The offer by investigating a offer space to find a best offer that provides the maximum gain in the region is used to generate the next counter proposal to the partner. If this optimal offer searching process is ended for a given partner, then the found optimal offer needs to be compared to optimal offers from other partners.

## 5.2  Customer Agent's Architecture and a Formal Negotiation Process

A customer agent consists of two types of subagents, partner negotiation agent and meta-negotiation agent according to their purposes. A formal negotiation process of the partner negotiation agent consists of six consecutive steps as follows. First, an agent submits an initial offer to the partner by using the initial attribute value combination. In second step, the agent receives and evaluates the partner's offer by comparing the obtainable gain with gains of registered offers. Third, the agent generates a new offer by using the optimal offer searching approach. Fourth, it waits for the configuration consenting acceptance message from the partner for the proposed offer. Fifth, the agent exchanges its ask (bid) price for an agreed offer with the partner agent simultaneously through the e-marketplace agent. Sixth, the agent computes the obtainable gain from the offer that was successful in previous step and examine whether or not the computed gain exceeds the minimum required gain.

An equal number of partner negotiation agents to the number of partners to negotiate with are generated in the meta-negotiation agent that can control these multiple and simultaneous negotiation processes. Whenever a partner agent returns with a satisfactory offer in terms of minimum required gain, it sends the transaction settlement request message to that partner and waits for the transaction settlement acceptance message from the selected partner. When this message arrives, the overall negotiation process ends while canceling all ongoing negotiations. But if the partner negotiation agent returns with an unsatisfactory offer, then it holds the offer until every other partner negotiation agent finishes his negotiations.

## 6 Conclusions

We have proposed an agent-based approach in order to take into account not only the price but also transaction attributes when the buyer and the seller agents negotiate over the differentiated goods in the customer-to-customer e-marketplace environment. A brief summary of our contributions is as follows. First, we propose an efficient and accurate utility representation and acquisition mechanism based on a monetary scale while minimizing the user interactions with the agent. Second, we allow both the buyer and the seller to negotiate over not only the price but also various transaction attributes in the customer-to-customer e-marketplace by providing a multi-attribute negotiation framework based on the attribute utility evaluation mechanism. Third, we have designed the architecture of the e-marketplace agent and agents for customers to support the framework and mechanisms proposed above. The formal protocol has also been developed to create and to control the required messages for the negotiation.

## References

[1] Chavez, A. and P. Maes, "Kasbah: An Agent Marketplace for Buying and Selling Goods," Proceedings of the First International Conference on the Practical Application of Intelligent Agents and Multi-Agent Technology(PAAM'96), London, UK, Apr. 1996.
[2] Maes, P., Guttman, R. and A. Moukas, "Agents that Buy and Sell: Transforming Commerce as We Know It", Communications of the ACM, Mar. 1999.
[3] Tewari, G., Berkovich, A., Gavovich, V., Liang, S., Ramakrishnan, A. and P. Maes, "Sustaining Individual Incentives While Maximizing Aggregate Social Welfare: A Mediated Brokering Technique for Trading Agents in Next-Generation Electronic Markets," Proceedings of the International Conference on Internet Computing (IC'2001), LasVegas, Nevada, USA, Jun., 2001.

# A Feature Analysis Framework for Evaluating Multi-agent System Development Methodologies

Quynh-Nhu Numi Tran[1], Graham Low[1], and Mary-Anne Williams[2]

[1] School of Information Systems, Technology and Management
The University of New South Wales
New South Wales, Australia
{numitran, g.low}@unsw.edu.au
[2] Innovation and Technology Research Laboratory
Faculty of Information Technology, University of Technology Sydney
New South Wales, Australia
Mary-Anne@it.uts.edu.au

**Abstract.** This paper proposes a comprehensive and multi-dimensional feature analysis framework for evaluating and comparing methodologies for developing multi-agent systems (MAS). Developed from a synthesis of various existing evaluation frameworks, the novelty of our framework lies in the high degree of its completeness and the relevance of its evaluation criteria. The paper also presents a pioneering effort in identifying the standard steps and concepts to be supported by a MAS-development process and models.

## 1 Introduction

Today, with the availability of numerous methodologies for analyzing and designing multi-agent systems (MAS), MAS-developers have to deal with a difficulty that has plagued object-oriented (OO) developers, i.e. comparing the available MAS-development methodologies, thereafter deciding on the most appropriate methodology to use in a specific application. Unfortunately, the numerous feature analysis frameworks for evaluating conventional system development methodologies do not assess the agent-oriented aspects of MAS development. On the other hand, due to the recent emergence of MAS and their inherent complexity, few frameworks exist for evaluating MAS-development methodologies ([5], [6], [7], [8]). These frameworks mainly examine MAS-specific characteristics without adequately considering the system engineering dimensions. We fill the current void by proposing a comprehensive, multi-dimensional framework that evaluates a MAS-development methodology from both the dimensions of system engineering and those specific to MAS engineering.

Instead of developing the framework from scratch, we built on the established work in the literature by, firstly, selecting the relevant evaluation criteria from the various existing feature analysis frameworks, thereafter synthesizing these criteria into a new comprehensive framework. Our pool of resources consists of a) the most outstanding and well-documented evaluation frameworks for conventional system development methodologies including OO methodologies – namely [1], [2], [3] and [4], and b) all the identified frameworks for MAS-methodology evaluation – namely [5],

N. Zhong et al. (Eds.): ISMIS 2003, LNAI 2871, pp. 613–617, 2003.

[6], [7] and [8]. The former provides a well-established account of the generic system engineering features to be subject to methodological evaluation, while the latter presents various agent-oriented and MAS-specific aspects for assessment.

To promote the relevance of our framework, we adopted the evaluation criteria that are representative, case-generic, and centered on the capabilities and usefulness of a methodology. We also added several evaluation criteria that are not yet accounted for in the existing evaluation frameworks, e.g. a methodology's approach towards MAS development, support for mobile agents, and support for ontology.

## 2  Specification of the New Feature Analysis Framework

Our evaluation framework is comprised of four components (Table 1):
- *Process Related Criteria*: evaluating a methodology's support for the MAS-development process
- *Technique Related Criteria:* assessing the methodology's techniques to develop MAS
- *Model Related Criteria*: examining the capabilities of the methodology's models
- *Supportive Feature Criteria*: evaluating a variety of high-level methodological capabilities

This structure highlights the completeness of our framework, as it targets at all three major components of a system development methodology – process, models, and techniques – as defined by OPEN [9]. Full details of how the framework was specified are not presented due to space constraints.

**Table 1.** Feature analysis framework for evaluating MAS-development methodologies

| Process Related Criteria |
| --- |
| 1. **Development lifecycle:** What development lifecycle best describes the methodology (e.g. waterfall)? |
| 2. **Coverage of the lifecycle:** What phases of the lifecycle are covered by the methodology (e.g. analysis, design, and implementation)? |
| 3. **Development approach:** What development approach is supported (i.e. top-down or bottom-up)? |
| 4. **Application domain:** Is the methodology applicable to a specific or multiple application domains? |
| 5. **Scope of effort:** What size of MAS is the methodology suited for (i.e. small, medium, or large)? |
| 6. **Agent nature:** Does the methodology support only homogeneous agents, or heterogeneous agents? |
| 7. **Support for verification and validation:** Does the methodology contain rules to allow for the verification and validation of correctness of developed models and specifications? |
| 8. **Steps in the development process:** What development steps are supported by the methodology? |
| 9. **Notational components:** What models and diagrams are generated from each process step? |
| 10. **Comments on the overall strengths/weaknesses of each step:** This criterion allows the evaluator to record any comments on a process step that cannot be recorded anywhere else. |
| 11. **Ease of understanding of the process steps:** Are the process steps easy to understand? |
| 12. **Usability of the methodology:** Are the process steps easy to follow? |
| 13. **Definition of inputs and outputs:** Are inputs and outputs to each process step defined, with possible examples? |
| 14. **Refinability:** Do the process steps provide a clear path for refining the methodology's models through gradual stages to reach an implementation, or at least for clearly connecting the implementation level to the design specification? |
| 15. **Approach towards MAS development:** Is the methodology<br>  a.   OO-based or knowledge-engineering based?<br>  b.   Role-oriented or non-role-oriented regarding its approach towards agent identification? |

   c. Goal-oriented, behavior-oriented, or organization-oriented in the identification of roles (if a role-oriented approach in b. applies)?

   d. Architecture-independent or architecture-dependent?

## Technique Related Criteria

1. **Availability of techniques and heuristics:**
   a. What are the techniques to perform each process step?
   b. What are the techniques to produce each notational component (i.e. modeling techniques)?
2. **Comments on the strengths/weaknesses of the techniques:** This criterion allows the evaluator to record any comments on the techniques to perform each step or to produce each model.
3. **Ease of understanding of techniques:** Are the techniques easy to understand?
4. **Usability of techniques:** Are the techniques easy to follow?
5. **Provision of examples and heuristics:** Are examples and heuristics of the techniques provided?

## Model Related Criteria

1. **Concepts:** What concepts are the methodology's models capable of expressing?
2. **Expressiveness:** How well can the models express these concepts and relationships between concepts? (e.g. are the models capable of capturing each concept at a great level of detail, or from different angles?)
3. **Completeness:** Are all necessary agent-oriented concepts that describe the target MAS captured?
4. **Formalization/Preciseness of models:**
   a. Are notation (syntax) and semantics of the models clearly defined?
   b. Are examples of the models presented?
5. **Model derivation:** Does there exist explicit process/logic and guidelines for transforming models into other models, or partially creating a model from information present in another?
6. **Consistency:**
   a. Are there rules and guidelines to ensure consistency between levels of abstractions within each model (i.e. internal consistency), and between different models?
   b. Are representations expressed in a manner that allows for consistency checking between them?
7. **Complexity:**
   a. Is there a manageable number of concepts expressed in a single model/diagram?
   b. Is notation semantically and syntactically simple across models?
8. **Ease of understanding of models:** Are the models easy to understand?
9. **Modularity:** Does the methodology and its models provide support for modularity of agents?
10. **Abstraction:** Does the methodology allow for producing models at various levels of detail and abstraction?
11. **Autonomy:** Can the models support and represent the autonomous feature of agents?
12. **Adaptability:** Can the models support and represent the adaptability feature of agents (i.e. the ability to learn and improve with experience)?
13. **Cooperative behavior:** Can the models support and represent the cooperative behavior of agents (i.e. the ability to work together with other agents to achieve a common goal)?
14. **Inferential capability:** Can the models support and represent the inferential capability feature of agents (i.e. the ability to act on abstract task specifications)?
15. **Communication ability:** Can the models support and represent "knowledge-level" communication ability (i.e. the ability to communicate with other agents using language resembling human-like speech acts)?
16. **Personality:** Can the models support and represent the personality of agents (i.e. the ability to manifest attributes of a "believable" human character)?
17. **Reactivity:** Can the models support and represent reactivity of agents (i.e. the ability to selectively sense and act)?
18. **Temporal continuity:** Can the models support and represent temporal continuity of agents (i.e. persistence of identity and state over long periods of time)?
19. **Deliberative behavior:** Can the models support and represent deliberative behavior of agents (i.e. the ability to decide in a deliberation, or proactiveness)?
20. **Concurrency:** Does the methodology allow for producing models to capture concurrency (e.g. representation of concurrent processes and synchronization of concurrent processes)?
21. **Human Computer Interaction:** Does the methodology allow for producing models to represent user interface and system-user interaction?

| |
|---|
| **22. Sub-system interaction:** Does the methodology allow for producing models to capture interaction/relationships between subsystems in MAS? |
| **23. Models Reuse:** Does the methodology provide, or make it possible to use, a library of reusable models? |

**Supportive Feature Criteria**

1. **Software and methodological support:** Is the methodology supported by tools and libraries (e.g. libraries of agents, agent components, organizations, architectures and technical support)?
2. **Open systems and scalability:** Does the methodology provide support for open systems and scalability (e.g. the methodology allows for dynamic integration/removal of new agents/resources)?
3. **Dynamic structure:** Does the methodology provide support for dynamic structure (e.g. the methodology allows for dynamic system reconfiguration when agents are created/destroyed during execution)?
4. **Agility and robustness:** Does the methodology provide support for agility and robustness (e.g. the methodology captures normal processing and exception processing, provides techniques to analyze system performance for all configurations, or provides techniques to detect/recover from failures)?
5. **Support for conventional objects:** Does the methodology support the use/integration of ordinary objects in MAS (e.g. the methodology models the agents' interfaces with objects)?
6. **Support for mobile agents:** Does the methodology cater for the use/integration of mobile agents in MAS (e.g. the methodology models which/when/how agent should be mobile)?
7. **Support for self-interested agents:** Does the methodology provide support for MAS with self-interest agents (whose goals may be independent or enter in conflict with other agents' goals)?
8. **Support for ontology:** Does the methodology cater for the use/integration of ontology in MAS (i.e. ontology-driven agent systems)?

To evaluate the criteria "*Steps in the development process*" and "*Concepts*", it is helpful to have a list of "standard" process steps and concepts to serve as an assessment checklist. To date, no study has been found that identifies the representative steps and concepts to be supported by a typical MAS-development process and models. We therefore provide a pioneering effort in this area. The following list of standard steps and concepts (Fig. 1) were determined from our investigation of the existing MAS-development methodologies (references [10] to [15][1]). Full details on the specification of these standard steps and concepts will be presented in a separate paper.

**Steps**

Identify system goals
Identify system roles
Develop system use cases/scenarios
Identify system functionality
Identify design requirements
Identify agent classes
Specify agent interaction pathways
Define exchanged messages
Specify interaction protocols
Specify contracts/commitments
Specify ACL

Specify conflict resolution mechanisms
Define agent architecture
Define agents' mental attitudes (goals, plans, beliefs...)
Define agents' interface (capabilities, services...)
Fulfill agent architecture
Define system architecture
Specify organizational structure
Specify group behavior

Specify agent relationships (inheritance, aggregation & association)
Specify co-existing entities
Specify environment facilities
Specify agent-environment interaction
Instantiate agent classes
Specify agent instances location

**Concepts**

System goals
System roles
System functionality
Task responsibilities/procedures
Design requirements
Use case/scenarios
Agent classes
Agent instances
Agent's knowledge/beliefs
Agent's plans
Agent's goals
Agent's roles

Agent's functionality
Percepts/Events
Agent mobility
Interaction pathways
Exchanged messages
Interaction protocols
Interaction constraints
Conflict resolution mechanisms
Contracts/commitments
ACL
Ontology
Agent inheritance

Agent aggregation
Agent association
Co-existing entities
Environment facilities
Organizational structure
Group behavior
Agent-environment interaction
Environment characteristics
Agent architecture
System architecture
Location of agent instances
Sources of agent instances

**Fig. 1.** List of standard steps and concepts to be supported by a MAS-development process and models

[1] Due to space constraints, only some of the investigated methodologies are listed here.

# 3 Conclusion

The completeness and relevance of our evaluation framework for MAS-development methodologies are reflected via its attention to both system engineering dimensions and agent-specific aspects, its focus on all three major components of the methodology (i.e. process, techniques and models), and its representative, case-generic evaluation criteria which center on the capabilities and usefulness of the methodology. We also proposed a list of standard steps and concepts to be supported by a MAS development process and models. Future work includes applying the framework to a comparative analysis of existing MAS-development methodologies, validating the proposed list of standard steps and concepts, and using the framework and the list to develop a new, unified MAS-development methodology.

# References

1.  Wood, B., Pethia, R., Gold, L.R., Firth, R.: A Guide to the Assessment of Software Development Methods. Technical Report CMUSEI-88-TR-8, SEI, Software Engineering Institute, Carnegie Mellon University (1988)
2.  Jayaratna, N.: Understanding and Evaluating Methodologies - NIMSAD A Systematic Framework. McGraw-Hill, England (1994)
3.  Olle, T.W., Sol, H.G., Tully, C.J. (eds.): Information Systems Design Methodologies - A Feature Analysis. Elsevier Science Publishers, Amsterdam (1983)
4.  The Object Agency Inc.: A Comparison of Object-Oriented Development methodologies. http://www.toa.com/smnn?mcr.html (1995)
5.  Shehory, O., Sturm, A.: Evaluation of modeling techniques for agent-based systems. Proc. of the 5th Int. Conf. on Autonomous agents (2001) 624-631.
6.  O'Malley, S.A., DeLoach, S.A.: Determining When to Use an Agent-Oriented Software Engineering Paradigm. Proc. of the 2nd Int. Workshop on Agent-Oriented Software Engineering (AOSE) (2001).
7.  Cernuzzi, L., Rossi, G.: On the Evaluation of Agent-Oriented Modelling Methods. Proc. of the OOPSLA Workshop on Agent-Oriented Methodologies (2002)
8.  Sabas, A., Badri, M., Delisle, S.: A Multidimentional Framework for the Evaluation of Multiagent System Methodologies. Proc. of the 6th World Multiconference on Systemics, Cybernetics and Informatics (SCI-2002), 211-216.
9.  Henderson-Sellers, B., Simons, A., Younessi, H.: The OPEN Toolbox of Techniques. Addison Wesley Longman Ltd., England (1998)
10. Wood, M.: Multiagent Systems Engineering: A Methodology for Analysis and Design of Multiagent Systems. MS Thesis, Air Force Institute of Technology, Ohio (2000)
11. Lind, J.: MASSIVE: Software Engineering for Multiagent Systems. PhD Thesis, University of Saarland, Saarbrucken (1999)
12. Wooldridge, M., Jennings, N.R., Kinny, D.: The Gaia Methodology for Agent-Oriented Analysis and Design. Autonomous Agents and Multi-Agent Systems 3(3) (2000) 285-312
13. Eurescom: MESSAGE - Methodology for Engineering Systems of Software Agents. http://www.eurescom.de/public/projectresults/P900-series/907ti1.asp (2001)
14. Padgham, L., Winikoff, M.: Prometheus: A Methodology for Developing Intelligent Agents. Proc. of the 3rd Int. Workshop on Agent-Oriented Software Engineering (AOSE) (2002)
15. Glaser, N.: Contribution to Knowledge Acquisition and Modelling in a Multi-Agent Framework (the CoMoMAS Approach). PhD Thesis, University of Nancy 1, France (1996)

# Decentralized Control
## Obligations and Permissions in Virtual Communities of Agents

Guido Boella[1] and Leendert van der Torre[2]

[1] Dipartimento di Informatica, Università di Torino, Italy
guido@di.unito.it
[2] CWI, Amsterdam, The Netherlands
torre@cwi.nl

**Abstract.** In this paper we introduce a model of local and global control policies regulating decentralized virtual communities of heterogeneous agents. We illustrate how the model can be formalized if agents attribute mental attitudes to normative systems.

## 1 Introduction

In highly decentralized structures such as peer-to-peer systems and grid architectures, there is neither a central design nor a central administrator, agents play both the role of resource consumers and providers, and they have the power to control their resources by expressing their own *local access policies*. But to form a *virtual community* local access policies should be organized according to global policies that define resource sharing among the members of the community. According to Pearlman *et al.* [10], "a key problem associated with the formation and operation of distributed virtual communities is that of how to specify and enforce community policies." Since there is no plausible way to enforce the respect of global policies by constraining the architecture, it is necessary to have a *normative system* able to specify global policies about local policies.

In [2] we argue that the interaction between an agent and its normative system can be modelled as a game between them when the agent attributes mental attitudes to the normative system, and in [3] we extended this argument to norm creation. In this paper we address the following two questions:

1. How to model decentralized control in virtual communities using a normative system with local and global control policies?
2. How can the attribution of mental attitudes to normative systems be used to reason about obligations and permissions regulating virtual communities of heterogeneous agents?

This paper is organized as follows. In Section 2 we discuss the first question of modelling decentralized control, in Section 3 we discuss the second question on the attribution of mental attitudes to normative systems, and in Section 4 we discuss how our model of decentralized control could be formalized.

N. Zhong et al. (Eds.): ISMIS 2003, LNAI 2871, pp. 618–622, 2003.

# 2    How to Model Decentralized Control?

A normative system which specifies what is obliged or permitted is not sufficient to regulate a virtual community, because the "exercise of rights is effective only if the resource provider has granted those rights to the community" [10]. Moreover, the global authority must be able to *motivate* local authorities such as these resource providers to issue policies which respect the global ones, besides motivating resource consumers to respect the norms. However, Firozabadi and Sergot [9] argue that in a virtual community of heterogeneous agents, a local authority can deliberately fail to comply with global policies: "Upon an access request from $a_1$, $a_2$ has to decide whether to grant the access to $a_1$ or not. There are several possible cases:

1. $a_1$ is permitted to access the resource, but there is no obligation on $a_2$ to grant that access. $a_2$ will not violate any policy regardless of whether it grants or denies the access.
2. $a_1$ is not only permitted to access the resource, but is also *entitled* to it. This means that $a_2$ has an obligation to grant the access whenever $a_1$ requests it. A typical scenario is when $a_1$ is the owner of $d$ and $a_2$ is the storage service provider for $d$.
3. $a_1$ has no permission to access d, and so $a_2$ is forbidden to grant the access. Note that $a_2$ may have the practical possibility to give access to $a_1$ even if it is not permitted to do so."

Consequently, a model of community policies and decentralized control should be able to deal with the following two issues. First, it should model local authorities that can deliberately fail to comply with global policies, and it should model how the global authority motivates and sanctions local authorities. In [2] we argue that a model of norm-evading agents can be based on interpreting normative systems as agents, for example by attributing mental attitudes to them. This attribution of mental attitudes is also the basis of the model in this paper.

Second, it should model various distinctions. E.g., Firozabadi and Sergot observe that in the literature on computer security, the terms *right, permission* and *privilege* often have the same meaning, whereas the term *entitlement* emphasizes a concept which is stronger than mere permission. In this paper, notions like entitlement are expressed as the obligations and permissions posed by a global authority on access permissions of the resource consumers. Entitlement is an obligation of the global authority to make a behavior permitted. Moreover, since something is obliged if its absence counts as a violation, it is defined as the obligation that the local authority does not count this behavior as a violation (2. above). The local authority, however, can still violate this global policy and forbid access to users if it prefers to face the sanction. Similarly, the obligation to forbid access can be modelled as a global obligation that local authorities count access as a violation (3. above). The permission to forbid access never leads to a violation of the local authority, regardless of whether it counts access as a violation. Analogously, the permission to permit access does not lead to a violation if the local authority does not count access as a violation (1. above).

# 3    Our Approach: Normative Systems as Agents!

Normative systems that control and regulate behavior like legal, moral or security systems are autonomous, they react to changes in their environment, and they are pro-active. For example, the process of deciding whether behavior counts as a violation is an autonomous activity. Since these properties have been identified as the properties of autonomous or intelligent agents by [11], normative systems may be called *normative agents*. This goes beyond the observation that a normative system may contain agents, like a legal system contains legislators, judges and policemen, because *a normative system itself is called an agent*.

The first advantage of the normative systems as agents perspective is that the interaction between an agent and the normative system which creates and controls its obligations can be modelled as a game between two agents. Consequently, methods and tools used in game theory such as equilibrium analysis can be applied to normative reasoning. For example, the game theories in [1,2] are based on *recursive modelling* of the normative system by the bearer of the obligation. The agent bases its decision on the consequences of the normative system's anticipated reaction, in particular, whether the system considers the agent a violator and thus sanctions it. Analogously, the normative system can base its decision regarding which norm to create on the consequences of the agent's anticipated reaction [3].

The second advantage of the normative systems as agents perspective is that, since mental attitudes can be attributed to agents, we can attribute mental attitudes to normative systems. A consequence of the second advantage is that obligations can be defined in the standard BDI framework. In particular, Boella and Lesmo [1] suggest that we can attribute mental attitudes to normative systems, such that obligations of an agent can be interpreted as the wishes, desires or goals of the normative system. The motivation of their interpretation is the study of reasons why agents fulfil or violate sanction-based obligations.

In this paper, normative systems do not contain one authority only but they are composed of a set of authorities which are in control of their own resources. A distinguished authority (usually called *community authorization service*) plays the role of a global authority which, even if it is not in control of the local resources, issues the norms representing local policies and negotiates the conditions for the participation of agents to the virtual community. We model global policies which forbid or permit local policies to constrain the behavior of users by norms concerning other norms.

The global authority creates obligations about which behaviors the local authorities should count as violations and thus sanction. This is its way to motivate local authorities. There are two ways to formalize the relation between global and local authorities when obligations are interpreted as the goals of the authority: either the global authority has the goal that the local authority has the goal to grant access, or the global authority has the goal that the local authority grants access, but it not necessarily has the goal that the local authority has this goal. In this paper we choose the second solution, since the local authorities cannot be assumed to have the same goal as the global one.

# 4    Toward Formalization

The agents' abilities, their beliefs and their motivations (goals and desires) must be distinguished. For example, these mental attitudes can be modelled as conditional rules in a qualitative decision theory inspired by the BOID architecture [7]. Belief rules can be used to infer the beliefs of agents using a priority relation to resolve conflicts. Goal and desire rules can be used to value a decision according to which motivations remain unsatisfied. Moreover, it must be formalized when behavior counts as a violation. There are two distinctions with the formalization sketched in [2,3].

- In [2,3] an obligation for $x$ is defined as the belief that absence of $a$ counts as a violation of some norm $n$. In this paper, we do not explicitly formalize the norm $n$. Instead, we write $V(\neg x)$ for 'the absence of $x$ counts as a violation', see [6] for further details on this approach.
- In contrast to [2,3] the counts-as-a-violation operator is indexed by an agent, we write $V_A(\neg x)$ for 'the absence of $x$ counts as a violation by agent A'. Moreover, we also consider nested counts-as-a-violations. For example, we write $V_B(\neg V_A(\neg x))$ for 'the absence of counting $x$ as a violation by agent A counts as a violation by agent B'.

Let agent A be a resource consumer agent B a resource provider, and consider the perspective of agent A. If agent A is obliged to $x$ in context $q$, then agent B may decide that the absence of $x$ counts as a violation and that agent A must be sanctioned with $s$, written as $O_{A,B}(x, s \mid q)$, if and only if:

1. Agent A believes that agent B desires that agent A does $x$ if $q$.
2. Agent A believes that agent B desires $\neg V_A(\neg x)$, that there is no violation by agent A, but if agent B believes $\neg x \wedge q$ then it has the goal $V_A(\neg x)$, $\neg x$ counts as a violation by agent $A$.
3. Agent A believes that agent B desires $\neg s$, not to sanction, but if agent B decides that $x$ is a violation by agent A, $V_A(\neg x)$, then it has as a goal that it sanctions agent A by doing $s$. Agent B only sanctions in case of violation. Moreover, agent A believes that agent B has a way to apply the sanction.
4. Agent A desires $\neg s$: it does not like the sanction.

Symmetrically, permission can be modelled as an exceptional situation which does not count as a violation. A permission to do $\neg x$ in context $q$, $P_{A,B}(\neg x \mid q)$ is an exception to an obligation to do $x$ if in context $q$, if and only if agent B has the goal that $\neg x$ does not count as a violation if $q$.

Finally, entitlement and other nested concepts are defined as follows, where agent C is a global authority:

- Agent B believes that it is *obliged* by agent C to oblige agent A to do $x$ with sanction $s$ in context $q$ iff $O_{B,C}(V_A(\neg x), s \mid q \wedge \neg x)$;
- Agent B believes that it is *obliged* by agent C to permit agent A not to do $x$ with sanction $s$ in context $q$ iff $O_{B,C}(\neg V_A(\neg x), s' \mid q \wedge \neg x)$;
- Agent B believes that it is *permitted* by agent C to permit agent A not to do $x$ in context $q$ iff $P_{B,C}(\neg V_A(\neg x) \mid q \wedge \neg x)$.

# 5  Concluding Remarks

A consequence of the attribution of mental attitudes to normative systems [2, 3] is that the multi agent system and the normative system are unified into a single system. In this paper we show that this unification is useful to model decentralized control, because also in virtual communities the distinction between multi agent system and normative system is disappearing.

In related research we further detail our model of decentralized control in virtual communities by introducing the defender role in obligations [4] and studying decisions of agents reasoning about local and global policies [5]. Further issues of research are the distinction of the roles of legislative authorities (creating norms), judicial (deciding if behavior counts as a violation) and executive ones (applying sanctions), where the former can be based on the creation of norms developed in [3]. Another issue for further research is the distinction between enacting a permission and granting an authorization [8].

# References

1. G. Boella and L. Lesmo. A game theoretic approach to norms. *Cognitive Science Quarterly*, 2(3-4):492–512, 2002.
2. G. Boella and L. van der Torre. Attributing mental attitudes to normative systems. In *Proceedings of the Second International Joint Conference on Autonomous Agents and Multi Agent Systems (AAMAS'03)*, 2003.
3. G. Boella and L. van der Torre. Rational norm creation: Attributing mental states to normative systems, part 2. In *Proceedings of the Eighth International Conference on Artificial Intelligence and Law (ICAIL'03)*. ACM, 2003.
4. G. Boella and L. van der Torre. Norm governed multiagent systems: The delegation of control to autonomous agents. In *Proceedings of the 2003 IEEE/WIC International Conference on Intelligent Agent Technology (IAT'03)*. IEEE, 2003.
5. G. Boella and L. van der Torre. Local policies for the control of virtual communities. In *Proceedings of the 2003 IEEE/WIC International Conference on Web Intelligence (WI'03)*. IEEE, 2003.
6. G. Boella and L. van der Torre. Obligations as social constructs. In *Proceedings of the Italian Conference on Artificial Intelligence (AI*IA'03)*, LNAI. Springer, 2003.
7. J. Broersen, M. Dastani, J. Hulstijn, and L. van der Torre. Goal generation in the BOID architecture. *Cognitive Science Quarterly*, 2(3-4):428–447, 2002.
8. E. Bulygin. Permissive norms and normative systems. In A. Martino and F. S. Natali, editors, *Automated Analysis of Legal Texts*, pages 211–218. Publishing Company, Amsterdam, 1986.
9. B. S. Firozabadi and M. Sergot. Contractual access control. In *Proceedings of the Tenth International Workshop of Security Protocols*, Cambridge (UK), 2002.
10. L. Pearlman, V. Welch, I. Foster, C. Kesselman, and S. Tuecke. A community authorization service for group collaboration. In *Proceedings of the Third International Workshop on Policies for Distributed Systems and Networks*, pages 50–59. IEEE, 2002.
11. M. J. Wooldridge and N. R. Jennings. Intelligent agents: Theory and practice. *Knowledge Engineering Review*, 10(2):115–152, 1995.

# An Intelligent Agent for Automatic Course Adaptation

Mohammed Abdel Razek, Claude Frasson, and Marc Kaltenbach

Computer Science Department and Operational Research University of Montreal,
C.P. 6128, Succ. Centre-ville Montreal,
Québec H3C 3J7 Canada
{abdelram, frasson, kaltenba }@iro.umontreal.ca

**Abstract.** In this paper, we propose our proposed technique for building an automatically adaptive course presentation on the Web. Our method uses an intelligent agent approach in order to keep track the learner's behavior during a learning session and then not only adapts the next presentation but also updates the domain model accordingly. We use Java-Servlets to build the confidence agent, XML to represent the database of course contents, and JSP to achieve a dynamic course presentation

## 1 Introduction

Generally, a course includes resources such as text, images, and multimedia. Learners use these resources to participate in various activities. Some learners (inductive types) prefer to start with examples, moving to explanations, in contrast, others (deductive types) prefer to start with explanations, moving to examples. Though, most of those learners prefer inductive rather than deductive learning, it is very difficult for tutors to monitor and analyze all the activities. Therefore, we desperately need an automatic way to track a learner's learning style and browsing behavior, and adapt the course presentation accordingly.

To fulfill this goal, we build an agent called confidence agent. This agent works on the server side. Based on the domain model (the granularity level of materials) and the user model (i.e. learning style, goals, etc.) of the Confidence Intelligent Tutoring System (CITS) [2], the agent can observe the learners' behaviors, allow them to insert and remove parts, and update the course materials. The next section illustrates the role of this confidence agent.

## 2 Confidence Agent

According to [1,5], the architecture of the Adaptive Hypermedia Application Model (AHAM) relies on three factors: a domain model, a user model, and an adaptation model. The confidence agent takes into consideration the following conditions to present the mate-rials that best meet the learner's needs; i)The user model: learner's goals, learning style, behaviors, and preferences, ii)The domain model: a granularity level of the course materials.

N. Zhong et al. (Eds.): ISMIS 2003, LNAI 2871, pp. 623–627, 2003.

In the confidence agent, the user model represents the relationship between the user and the domain model. The domain model is represented as a hierarchy of concepts. There are some dominant meanings to define each concept [2]. These dominant meanings consist of a set of keywords that best fit a concept or that reflect the particular view of specific learners on the concept [3]. In our domain model graph, the concept consists of 5 fragments: back-ground, definition, problems, examples, and exercises. For each fragment, there are links to three chunks that define it. Each chunk consists of atomic units, such as text, images, audio, and video.

The adaptive course presentation is implemented through a 2-Tier architecture, as shown in Fig. 1. The first tier is implemented through the browser on the client side. In this tier, JSP and HTML techniques are employed to present the course. The second tier is implemented on the server side. This tier executes the roles of the confidence agent based on the learner's learning style, XML-based course materials, and adaptive pattern modules.

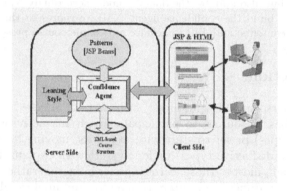

**Fig. 1.** Confidence Agent Architecture

Our approach keeps track of learners' evolving characteristics of the learner, such as chunks read, added and erased. These values are recorded in the user model and are used to be one item for determining the granularity level of each chunk. The second item is to determine the dominant meaning probability between a chunk and the concept, which is taught [2]. The adaptation algorithm [3] sorts the chunks in decreasing order and then returns the first three chunks to be presented with the current fragment. The next section explains how we can represent course materials using XML [6].

## 3  Models Representation Using XML

Using XML and JavaServer Pages (JSP), we can create an Adaptive Presentation Pattern (APP). APP adapts course presentation by applying conditions. In this paper, the conditions are the granularity level of the chunk, the course requirements, and the learner's goals and learning style. In order to effectively control the domain model, we use XML [6] to define the fixed structure of the user and the domain model.

## 3.1    User Model Meta-data

In our system, each learner has a personal XML file described using DTD. The learner models are automatically created and managed by the confidence agent. The XML file contains information about the user that will assist in the adaptation process, such as setting learner's goals, learning style, browsing behavior, and preferences. The following example shows a simplified version of an XML file representing knowledge about a specific learner.

```
<Model description="user model">
<Name>A<Name>
<Learner-style> Visual </ Learner-style>
<Visit>
<Concept> C1 </Concept>
<Chunks-Recommended> C11, C12 </Chunks-Recommended>
<Chunks-Erased>C21 </Chunks-Erased>
</Visit> < /Model>
```

## 3.2    Domain Model Meta-data

The domain model, the dominant meanings, and the chunks are described textually in the XML documents. The following example shows the background fragment for the concept of a "heap" in a course on data structures.

```
<Fragment description="Fragment" >
<Concept>Heap<Concept>
<ID> 1 </ID>
<Prerequisites> <ID ref="0" > </Prerequisites>
<Name> Background </Name>
<Chunk1>C11</Chunk1>
<Chunk2>C21</Chunk2>
<Chunk3>C31</Chunk3>
</Fragment>
```

The background fragment consists of three chunks: C11, C21, and C31. The following example illustrates the creation of an instance of the chunk C11:

```
< Chunk description=" Chunk "Visible-Image="yes"
Visible-Audio="yes" Visible-Applets="yes" Granularity-Value="yes">
<Concept>Heap<Concept>
<ID> C11 </ID>
<Type> Background </Type>
<Granularity> 0.97 </Granularity>
<Dominant-Meaning>
<D1> Binary tree </D1> <D2> Complete tree </D2>
</Dominant-Meaning>
<Text>
Heaps are based on the notion of a complete tree, for which we
gave an informal definition earlier. Formally: A binary tree is
completely full if it is of height, h, and has 2^{h+1-1} nodes
</Text>
<Media>
<Condition Learner-style ="Visual" Images="heap1.jpg">
</Condition>
<Condition Learner-style ="Auditory " Images="heap1.wav">
</Condition>
<Condition Learner-style ="Kinaesthetic" mages="Animation1.jpg">
</Condition>
</Media>
</Chunk>
```

The element with the attribute "Visible-Image" indicates that when the chunk element is presented, the image will be displayed if the value is equal to "yes" and hidden otherwise. The domain model in our confidence agent supports the definition of adaptive elements in the model itself by introducing conditions on any part of the structure. For example, on lines 16 to 21, the presented elements were adapted to the student's learning style. If the learner's learning style is visual, auditory, or kinaesthetic, the system selects the image file "heap1.jpg", the audio files "heap1.wav", or the animation file (applet file) respectively.

In this sense, we can build an adaptive model that depends on the user model. Using JSP, we apply further adaptation conditions to complete the modification of the course structure.

### 3.3   Automatics Adaptive Representation Course

To create an adaptive page, we use JSP in addition to HTML. JSP allows developers to design patterns with control statements by adding Java expressions < %=and %> to the HTML code. The following example illustrates the pattern with a background fragment for the concept of a heap mentioned previously: Fig. 2 shows the resulting page for the previous example.

```
<h2> <center> < %= Fragment.Concept % > </h2> </center>
<P> < %= Fragment.Name % > </P >
<BR> < %= Fragment.Chunk.Chunk1 % >
```

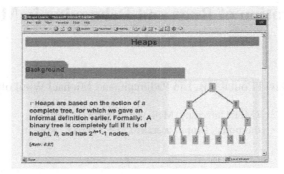

**Fig. 2.** Web page of the chunk Background at the concept Heaps.

## 4 Conclusions

We introduced in this paper our confidence agent, which is designed to maintain course materials and adapt a course presentation. Based on XML, we proposed a representation for the domain model that allows the confidence agent to insert, remove and exchange course materials easily. The agent was implemented using Java-Servlets, the database of course contents uses XML, and dynamic course presentation uses JSP. Apache Tomcat 3.2.1 launches the CITS system (including the confidence agent) and provides it with an environment to activate the JSP file.

## References

1. De Bra, P., Houben, G.J., Wu, H: AHAM: A Dexter-based Reference Model for Adaptive Hypermedia. Proceedings of the ACM Conference on Hypertext and Hypermedia, pp. 147–156, Darmstadt, Germany, 1999.
2. Abdel Razek M., Frasson, C., Kaltenbach M.: Context-Based Information Agent for Supporting Intelligent Distance Learning Environment. The Twelfth International World Wide Web Conference , WWW03, 20–24 May, Budapest, Hungary, 2003.
3. Abdel Razek M., Frasson, C., Kaltenbach M.: Using Adaptability to Create an automatically Adaptive Course Presentation on the Web. IEEE International Conference on Advanced Learning Technologies (ICALT2003). July 9–11, Athens, Greece, 2003.
4. Abdel Razek M., Frasson, C., Kaltenbach M.: Web Course Self-Adaptation. The 2003 IEEE/WIC International Conference on Intelligent Agent Technology (IAT 2003) October 13–17, Halifax, Canada,2003.
5. Wu, H., De Kort, E., De Bra, P.: Design Issues for General-Purpose Adaptive Hypermedia Systems. Proceedings of the ACM Conference on Hypertext and Hypermedia, pp. 141–150, Aarhus, Denmark, August 2001.
6. W3 Recommendation: Extensible Markup Language (XML). http://www.w3.org/, 1999.

# An Exploration of Bugs and Debugging in Multi-agent Systems

David Poutakidis, Lin Padgham, and Michael Winikoff

RMIT University, Melbourne, Victoria, Australia,
{davpout,linpa,winikoff}@cs.rmit.edu.au

**Abstract.** Debugging multi-agent systems, which are concurrent, distributed, and consist of complex components, is difficult, yet crucial. In earlier work we have proposed mechanisms whereby protocol specifications available from the design process can be used for monitoring the execution of the multi-agent system they describe. Protocol specifications can be used at run-time for reporting any discrepancies in interactions compared to that which was specified. In this paper we describe and categorise a range of bugs found in actual multi-agent systems developed by students in an Agent Oriented Programming and Design class. We then indicate how these bugs manifest to the debugging agent and what information it is able to provide to the user to assist in locating and diagnosing the problem.

## 1 Introduction

Based on foundational work in AI and Philosophy, *agent technology* has significant applications in a wide range of domains [5]. Agent based software engineering methodologies [1] have emerged to facilitate the development of agent based applications. These applications are often developed as multi-agent systems and are notoriously difficult to debug since they are distributed, concurrent, and complex. Under these circumstances good debugging tools are essential.

Despite this, little work has focused on debugging multi-agent systems. Most of the existing prototype or research tools rely on visualisation of the messages passing between agents, possibly with some filtering applied to these [4]. However these are often not useful as there is too much information for the developer to be able to detect that there may be a problem.

Exception detection and resolution and domain independent exception handling services [6] is a similar domain to debugging. However the techniques are not appropriate for multi-agent systems that are not the traditional problem solving or workflow systems seen in [6]. Many agent system do not have a concrete representation of tasks, resources and other properties required to make use of these exception handling services.

In an earlier paper [2] we proposed that protocol specifications, produced during the design stages of system development, could be used during debugging to monitor what message exchanges are expected and to locate bugs by detecting unexpected patterns of message exchange. We proposed a mechanism for taking protocol diagrams developed in Agent UML (AUML) [3], converting them to equivalent Petri nets, and then using them to monitor execution and detect problems. The protocol diagrams being used were

N. Zhong et al. (Eds.): ISMIS 2003, LNAI 2871, pp. 628–632, 2003.

typical of those produced during the architectural design phase of the Prometheus design methodology for agent systems [1]. The key point is that instead of presenting messages to the programmer and relying on him or her to detect problems, the debugging agent proposed in [2] monitors conversations and detects problems by identifying messages that are not permissible in the conversation defined by the protocols.

In this paper we describe the results of applying the debugging agent from [2] to actual agent applications. Our aims are to:

- Determine what types of bugs occur in practice.
- Determine to what extent the debugging agent is able to assist with detecting these bugs.
- Apply these results to determine the usefulness of applying design documents in debugging multi-agent systems.

## 2  A Description of the Debugging Agent

In Poutakidis et. al. [2] we proposed that the design documents (specifically interaction protocols) produced in pre-implementation could be used by a debugging system to provide run-time error detection and debugging support. It was suggested that the design documents could be converted into an internal representation that the debugging agent could use to compare against run-time execution. Execution that differed from what was defined by the design documents is reported to the developer.

Petri nets were used as an internal representation for protocols since they are a formal graphical modelling notation that can easily be interpreted by both the human user and a program. Importantly, Petri nets are also able to capture concurrency. We discussed a process for converting AUML interaction protocols to an internal Petri net form in [2].

The debugging agent takes as input a set of these Petri net protocols, one for each AUML interaction protocol. These Petri net protocols are used by the debugging agent to both monitor interactions for errors and to reason about how the errors may have occurred. This process is discussed in detail in [2].

Whenever a message is received the debugging agent needs to determine which protocol the message belongs to. The decision is facilitated by the parameters that agents are required to include with their messages. Messages that the debugging agent receives must include a *sender, receiver, message type,* and *conversation id.*

Briefly, for each incoming message the debugging agent determines which conversation the message belongs to and a token is then placed on the appropriate *message place.* The Petri Net is then fired to determine the next state of the conversation. If any message places have tokens after firing then that message was not expected and a bug is reported.

## 3  Debugging with the Debugging Agent

As part of our investigation into the types of bugs that occur in multi-agent systems and the methods that can be used to detect them we examined 15 multi-agent applications and their associated bug logs. The bugs encontered in the application and the bug logs are presented. For each type of bug we explain what the bug is, what typical errors that programmers make lead to the bugs, any variations of the bug (where relevant), how we tested these bugs, and the results from the tests.

The following is a brief description of the types of bugs we found while inspecting a set of agent programs developed by third year software engineering students. After identifying the bugs we then introduced each of them into a single application. This application simulates an ambulance response service where patients are generated and ambulances are called on to handle requests by picking up patients and taking them to a hospital. The application consists of three agent types: one Controller agent named Controller, ten Ambulance agents named Unit-X, where X is a number between one and ten and an ExternalSimulator agent that is not discussed further in this paper.

**Failure to send a message:** An example of a failure to send a message that occurred in the test application involved the top level *Dispatcher* plan. This plan is responsible for assigning Ambulance agents to patients and then instructing the Ambulance agents, via a "PickUpPatient" message, to collect the patient and deliver them to a hospital.

There is a logic error that causes the plan to fail, the result is that no message is sent and the Dispatcher stops responding. This is a breach of the protocol however in this instance the debugging agent did not alert us to an error. This is however to be expected given the design of the debugging agent. The debugging agent focuses on debugging interaction and since the debugging agent did not receive any messages it can not know that the agent was supposed to begin a conversation. Therefore, a limitation of our debugging agent is that it is unable to detect a failure to send a message if the message is the first in the protocol.

The first message in a protocol is a special case and although we would like to be able to detect failure when it occurs in this situation, at present we cannot. However the debugging agent is capable of detecting an error if the failure is from any message other than the first message. To test this we modified the test application so that the failure would occur after the conversation had begun. In this example the debugging agent indicated that there was a warning, not an error. Since the lack of a message is detected using a timeout it is not possible to guarantee that the message will not arrive at some point in the future.

**Uninitialised agents:** When an agent sends a message to another agent that agent must be in the position to receive the message. If the intended recipient has not yet been initialised it will not receive the message and the protocol will not be able to complete.

In our test application when we introduced an error that resulted in one of the agents sending a message to another that had not yet had time to initialise an error message was generated. It is interesting to note that the error message is the same type of error as *failure to send a message*. Although the cause of the bugs are different, the debugging agent cannot tell the difference between the two. The debugging agent is able to determine that an error has occurred but can offer little more advice. This is due to the fact that by sending a message to an uninitialised agent you are guaranteeing that a response will not be returned, hence the bug is presented in the same way.

**Sending a message to the wrong recipient:** We have seen how the debugging agent deals with the sending of a message to agents that don't yet exist, or will never exist. We now present the results of sending a message to the wrong recipient where the recipient actually exists but was not the intended recipient.

A message is addressed to the wrong agent, it should be addressed to the Controller agent but is instead addressed to Unit-4 who is a valid agent but the debugging agent does not have it as one of the agents in the role map. Only Unit-1 and the Controller agent are valid agents in this conversation. The token is rejected from the message place and an error message indicating that the agent is not the intended recipient is generated. We are given specific information as to which protocol was being followed and which agent was supposed to receive the message.

**Sending the wrong message:** In the case that the message does not exist in the protocol and the case that the message is valid in the protocol but not at the time it was sent the debugging agent is able to determine that an error occurred. The test application was modified so that after Unit-1 received a "PickUpPatient" request it would send the wrong message in reply. The debugging agent receives a copy of the wrong message, places it in the associated message place and then fires the net. After the net is fired a token remains in the message place indicating that an error has occurred. The debugging agent informs us that the wrong message was sent and details of the status of the conversation are presented.

**Sending the same message multiple times:** This can result in unintended consequences and unless the design of the protocol allows for it it should be considered an error. We instructed our agents to send the same message twice in immediate succession. The debugging agent is able to determine that an error has occurred but it does not specify that the error was that the same message was received twice. It is obvious how to extend the debugging agent to handle this as the necessary information is available. The sequence of messages that have been received is known and the debugging agent could check to see if the last two messages are the same.

# 4   Conclusion

We identified a range of bugs and demonstrated how the debugging agent was able to assist in detecting them. Figure 1 summarises the different bug types that we found, and how well the debugging agent is able to assist in detecting them. As can be seen, the debugging agent is able to detect most of the bugs that we found and in many cases gives precise feedback that assists in localising the cause of the bug.

We then summarised the design of a debugging agent (presented in [2]). Having identified a range of bugs, and described a debugging agent, we then selected a particular application and showed how the debugging agent was able to assist in detecting a range of bugs, both actual, and seeded (based on bugs that were found in other applications). Figure 1 summarises the different bug types that we found, and how well the debugging agent is able to assist in detecting them and in localising their cause. As can be seen, the debugging agent is able to detect most of the bugs that we found and in many cases gives precise feedback that assists in localising the cause of the bug.

| Bug Type | Debugging Agent |
|---|:---:|
| **Uninitialised Agent:** | ★ |
| **Failure to send:** | |
| first message in conversation | ✗ |
| not first message | ✔ |
| **Wrong recipient:** | |
| recipient non-existent | ★ |
| recipient exists and first message | ★ |
| recipient exists and not first message | ✔ |
| **Message sent multiple times:** | ✔ |
| **Wrong message sent:** | ✔ |

**Fig. 1.** Bug types and how well the debugging agent handled them. A "✔" or "★" indicates that the debugging agent can handle the bug. A "✔" means that the agent also gave a precise error message, a "★" means that the error message was not precise, but still useful. A "✗" indicates that the bug is not handled.

The debugging agent is an improvement over existing debuggers in that it doesn't rely on the programmer to interpret information and detect bugs. Rather, it diagnoses bugs itself based on design information. *Our results show that design documents and system models, specifically in this case interaction protocols, can be successfully and usefully applied to debugging agent systems.* Future work includes extending to design models other than interaction protocols and extending the debugger to look at events posted *within* agents, in addition to messages *between* agents.

# References

1. L. Padgham and M. Winikoff. Prometheus: A Methodology for Developing Intelligent Agents. Proceedings of the Third International Workshop on Agent-Oriented Software Engineering (AOSE), 2002.
2. D. Poutakidis and L. Padgham and M. Winikoff. Debugging Multi-Agent Systems using Design Artifacts: The case of Interaction Protocols. First International Joint Conference on Autonomous Agents and Multi-Agent Systems (AAMAS), 2002.
3. Foundation for Intelligent Physical Agents (FIPA). FIPA Interaction Protocol Library Specification. Document number XC00025D, version 2001/01/29, www.fipa.org
4. M. Liedekerke and N. Avouris. Debugging multi-agent systems. Information and Software Technology, 37(2), pg 102–112.
5. N.R. Jennings and M.J. Wooldridge. Agent Technology: Foundations, Applications, and Markets. Chapter 1 pages 3–28, 1998.
6. Mark Klein and Chrysanthos Dellarocas  Exception Handling in Agent Systems. Third International Conference on Autonomous Agents, 1999.

# A Framework for Building Competency-Based Systems Dedicated to Human Resource Management

Francky Trichet and Michel Leclère

IRIN - Computer Science Research Institute
University of Nantes
2 rue de la Houssinière - BP 92208
44322 Nantes Cedex 3, France
{trichet,leclere}@irin.univ-nantes.fr

**Abstract.** CommOn is a framework which aims at developing operational systems dedicated to the management of competencies. Such a Competency-Based System can be used for different purposes such as staff development and deployment, job analysis or economic evaluation. CommOn is based on two models (implemented with specific tools) which guide (i) the building of competency reference systems related to particular domains such as Healthcare or Information and Telecommunication, (ii) the identification and the formal representation of competency profiles and (iii) the matching of competency profiles. Developed in the context of Semantic Web Technology, the CommOn framework allows one to build shareable ontologies and knowledge bases represented with Semantic Web Languages and to develop Competency-Based Web Services dedicated to Human Resource Management. The use of CommOn is illustrated in the context of a project related to e-recruitment (http://www.sciences.univ-nantes.fr/irin/commoncv/).

## 1 Introduction

Knowledge Management Systems (KMS) have been defined as an emerging line of systems which target professional and managerial activities by focusing on creating, gathering, organizing and disseminating an organization's knowledge as opposed to information or data [1]. People-Finder KMS (also known as yellow pages) are repositories that allow managing knowledge by holding pointers to experts who possess specific knowledge within an organization.

CommOn (*Competency Management through Ontologies*) is a generic framework dedicated to the development of Competency-Based Systems, i.e. specific People-Finder KMS. This framework is based on the following definition: " a *Competency*[1] is the effect of combining and implementing *Resources* in a specific *Context* (including physical, social, organizational, cultural and/or economical aspects) for reaching an *Objective* (or fulfilling a mission)". Three types

---

[1] We voluntarily use the expression *competency* (or *competence*) in order to avoid confusion with skill, ability or know-how.

N. Zhong et al. (Eds.): ISMIS 2003, LNAI 2871, pp. 633–639, 2003.

of resources are distinguished: *Knowledge* which includes theoretical knowledge (e.g. knowing the second law of thermodynamics) and procedural knowledge (e.g. knowing the procedure for assembling a particular electronic card), *Skills* which include formalized know-how (e.g. the application of working procedures) and empirical know-how (e.g. tricks, abilities or talents) and *Behavioural aptitudes* which refer to the potential for performing an activity and correspond to the characteristics which underlie an individual's behaviour at work. This definition, which highlights the singular dimension of a competency, integrates the traditional view of KSA (Knowledge, Skills and Aptitudes). Indeed, in our approach, KSA are not competencies but only resources of competencies. Note that although "competency logic" is not a new approach in Human Resource Management, it has not been implemented yet in KMS in the sense that no operational competency-based systems are currently used in organizations.

Practically, CommOn is composed of three complementary tools. These tools, which are based on models defined through our conception of competency, allow one (i) to build "competency reference systems" related to particular domains, (ii) to identify the competencies and the behavioural aptitudes a person has or a task (a job-position) requires and (iii) to compare competency profiles. Following the work of the HR-XML Consortium (`http://www.hr-xml.org`), these tools are defined within the Semantic Web context. Thus, the CommOn models are represented as RDFS ontologies (`http://www.w3.org/TR/2000/rdf-schema`), the knowledge bases constructed from the models are represented as RDF assertions, and the proposed tools are seen as Web Services.

CommOn is currently being experimented in the context of the CommOnCV project[2] (*competency@ontology.cv*) which aims at dealing with e−recruitment by considering a new approach based on competency management. The principle underlying CommOnCV consists in considering a Curriculum Vitae (respectively a job offer) as a synthetic view (expressed, in natural language, in terms of qualifications, work experiences and extracurricular activities) of a richer network of competencies. According to this principle, the first goal of the project is to allow the end-user (i.e. a job seeker or a recruiter) to make all the competencies underlying her/his resources (i.e. a CV or a job offer) explicit. The second goal is to formally represent these competencies in order to provide more powerful e−recruitment services since the content (expressed in terms of competencies) of CVs and job offers must be manageable by computers in order to carry out automatic matching processes.

Section 2 presents the model of a competency reference system we advocate and the tool we have developed for building the reference systems of particular domains. Section 3 presents the competency model and the tools we propose for identifying competencies and behavioural aptitudes.

---

[2] This multidisciplinary project (`http://www.sciences.univ-nantes.fr/irin/commoncv/`), which involves researchers from Communication Science, Computer Science and Industrial Engineering, is funded by the research foundation of VediorBis, a firm specialized in temporary employment (`http://www.vediorbis.com`).

## 2 Building Competency Reference Systems

### 2.1 The Model

The model we advocate provides all the concepts (structured according to the *Specialisation/Generalisation* relationship) and the relations which must be identified when defining a competency reference system for a specific domain such as Healthcare or Banking and Finance. As shown in figure 1, this model specifies that a competency reference system is defined by a set of tasks (a Task can be an Elementary Task or a Composite Task) which are respectively based on Resources (Knowledge, Skill or Aptitude) also structured hierarchically.

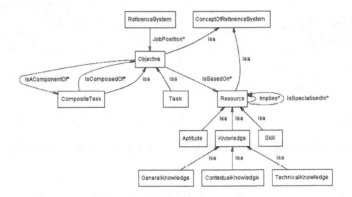

**Fig. 1.** The model of a competency reference system

### 2.2 The CommonReference Tool

CommonReference is the tool which implements the model presented above; it allows one to build a knowledge base characterising a specific competency reference system. Such a knowledge base includes a fine-grained description of all KSA required for the job-position (and their associated tasks) of the considered domain. For instance, in the context of the Information and Telecommunication domain, this knowledge base includes a description of all the KSA and tasks required for performing job-positions such as Database Administrator, Desktop Technician or System Analyst. From a technical point of view, a prototype of CommonReference has been developed from Protégé-2000 [4] (http://protege.stanford.edu).

The use of CommonReference is illustrated in figure 2 in the context of a competency reference system which has been developed for the CommOnCV project. This reference system is related to the domain of Information and Telecommunication Technology (ITT). It has been built from a report provided by the Cigref (http://www.cigref.fr), an independent/non-profit organisation which includes the major ITT French corporations such as Air France or France Télécom.

The extract of the knowledge base presented in figure 2 shows that the composite task Network & Telecommunications Technician (considered as

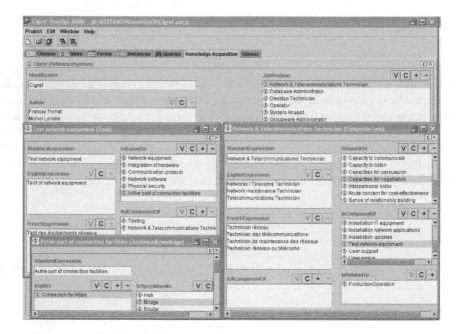

**Fig. 2.** Extract of the knowledge base corresponding to the Cigref

a JobPosition of the Cigref) is composed of several elementary tasks such as Test network equipment or User support. Synonyms of this job-position are Telecommunications Technician or Network/Telecoms Technician. Performing this job-position requires behavioural aptitudes such as Capacities for negotiation or Sense of relationship building. The elementary task Test network equipment is based both on general knowledge such as Physical security and on technical knowledge such as Communication protocol or Active part of connection facilities. The latter necessarily implies knowledge of Connection facilities; it can be specialised in knowledge of Hub, Bridge or Router.

## 3   Building Competency Profiles

### 3.1   The Model

In our work (cf. the definition proposed in introduction), a competency $C_i$ is defined by the quintuplet $(K, B, C, A, o)$ (this quintuplet is justified in [2]) where:

- $K$ is a set of Knowledge necessary for $C_i$, $B$ a set of Behavioural Aptitudes necessary for $C_i$ and $C$ is a set of more basic Competencies necessary for $C_i$ (in its more atomic form, an element of this latter set corresponds to a formalized or empirical skill). (K,B,C) corresponds to the resources of $C_i$;

 – $A$ is a set of aspects which define the context of $C_i$ such as social, organizational, economical, physical or informational aspects;
 – $o$ is an objective which can correspond to a job-position, a mission to carry out or a task to achieve.

### 3.2  Identifying Behavioural Aptitudes with CommonAptitude

CommonAptitude is a tool which allows the end-user of a CBS to identify its personality traits and then to automatically match these traits with behavioural aptitudes. CommonAptitude reuses a predefined tool called Performanse-Echo which allows the user to identify human traits; Performanse-Echo has been developed by Performanse (http://www.performanse.com), a French firm specialized in the development of software dedicated to the analysis of individual behaviour.

The approach we advocate for evaluating behavioural aptitudes is based on a two-step process: (1) evaluation of human traits from answers to questions and (2) identification of behavioural aptitudes from evaluated human traits.

The *questionnaire* used to perform the first step is composed of 75 closed questions such as "I think that any experience, pleasant or not, is an occasion (1) to discover something or (2) to verify something" or "To get interesting results, I prefer (1) to control my actions or (2) to adapt my actions". This questionnaire has been put together by the psychologist from Performanse. Its objective is to evaluate twenty human traits such as Self-assertion/Self-questioning, Extroversion/Introversion or Anxiety/Relaxation. These traits are related to a model corresponding to a refinement of the five-factor model (Openness to experience, Conscientiousness, Extroversion, Agreeableness and Neuroticism), more well-known as the Big Five dimensions of personality. Each question is dedicated to the evaluation of one of several human traits. A human trait can be evaluated from several questions; some questions can increase the weight of a trait whereas others can decrease this weight. Thus, answering the 75 questions leads to an individual assessment composed of the twenty human traits respectively characterised by a weight (expressed as a percentage). An extract of such an assessment can be expressed as follows: *Self-assertion: 23%, Extroversion: 88%, Anxiety:54%, ...*

The *expertise* used to perform the second step is composed of inference rules. These rules have been defined in collaboration with the psychologist from Performanse. Each rule defines a way to attest a behavioural aptitude from a combination of human traits. Thus, the hypothesis of a rule is composed of a conjunction of human traits characterised by an interval and the conclusion of a rule is a linguistic expression characterising a behavioural aptitude. An example of such a rule related to the aptitude called "Negotiation and Persuasion" is expressed as follows: *(Self-assertion $\in$ [60..70])* and *(Anxiety $\in$ [40..60])* and *(Combativeness $\geq$ 60)* and *(Extroversion $\in$ [33..50]) $\rightarrow$ Negotiation and Persuasion.*

### 3.3  Identifying Competencies with CommonCompetency

Based on the use of the knowledge bases constructed with CommonReference and on the integration of the results produced by CommonAptitude, the first functionality of CommonCompetency is to facilitate the identification of competencies expressed in terms of *Resources* mobilized, combined and implemented in a *Context* for reaching an *Objective*. In the context of one competency, this task which is performed by the end-user (for instance a job seeker who wants to annotate its CV) consists in first searching through all the tasks described in the given competency reference system for the task which best characterises the intended *Objective* and then focusing on the *Resources* needed to reach this objective. For resources related to Aptitudes, the results provided by CommonAptitude can be used directly. For resources related to Knowledge or Skills, the end-user can attest or refute the ones proposed by the system (because in the knowledge base they are associated with the selected task) and/or define new ones. For describing the *Context*, we plan to use existing domain ontology dedicated to the modeling of organisations such as Enterprise ontology [3]; this work has not yet been studied.

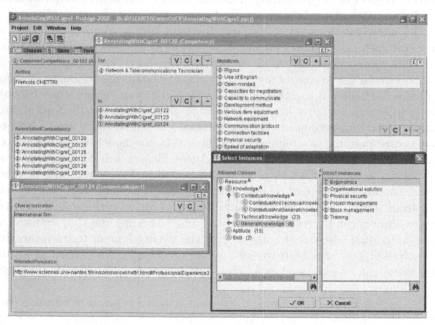

**Fig. 3.** Annotating electronic documents with CommonCompetency

Figure 3 shows an extract of a prototype used to put our approach into practice. Annotating an electronic resource from a competency point of view (for instance the second professional experience of Mr Chettri identified by the URI http://www.sciences...chettri.html#ProfessionalExperience2) consists in attesting a set of competency instances (e.g. AnnotatingWithCigref_00120 ... AnnotatingWithCigref_00129) where each instance is described by using the three relations involve in our definition: Mobilizes(Competency,Resource), For(Competency,Objective), In(Competency,Context). Each instance of the In relation is related to an economical, social or technical aspect; this allows the user to describe a competency context including several dimensions. As specified by the signature of the For relation, the objective of a competency can only be a job-position (considered as a Composite Task in our model) or a task of a job-position described in the considered reference system. This approach seems to be relevant in a context of e-recruitment because when an applicant wants to describe an experience, he always think about the job or the tasks he has performed. For the relation Mobilizes, the end-user can attest all (or only a part of) the resources automatically proposed by the system because they are connected (by the relation IsBasedOn) to the selected Objective in the considered reference system. He can also add new resources. This process leads to a set of RDF statements which verify a specific RDFS file corresponding to our competency model (cf. the CommOnCV website for examples of RDF files).

## 4 Conclusion

CommOn is a generic framework which aims at developing operational Competency-Based Systems. Based on a fine-grained description of the competency concept and on a semantic web approach, this framework facilitates the construction of competency reference systems for particular domains and the exploitation of such reference systems for identifying and matching competency profiles. Moreover, the integration of a tool especially dedicated to an automatic identification of behavioural aptitudes allows us to consider CommOn as a complete and innovative framework. This work is currently in progress towards the definition of more powerful operators dedicated to matching *required competency profiles* and *acquired competency profiles*. These operators will be based on the reasoning mechanisms provided by the semantic web languages.

**Acknowledgements.** For their valuable contributions for this work, we are grateful to Michel BOURSE (South East European University, Republic of Macedonia), Mounira HARZALLAH (University of Nantes) and Serge BAQUEDANO (the psychologist from Performanse).

## References

1. M. Alavi and D. Leidner. Knowledge management systems: issues, challenges and benefits. In *Communications of the Association for Information Systems*, volume 1(7), 1999.
2. M. Bourse, M. Harzallah, M. Leclère, and F. Trichet. Commoncv: modelling the competencies underlying a curriculum vitae. In *Proceedings of the 14th international conference on Software Engineering and Knowledge Engineering (SEKE'2002)*, pages 65–73. ACM Press, 2002.
3. M. Fox and M. Gruninger. Enterprise modeling. *AI Magazine*, 19(3):109–121, 1999.
4. N. F. Noy, M. Sintek, S. Decker, M. Crubezy, W. Fergerson, and M. A. Musen. Creating semantic web contents with protege-2000. In *IEEE Intelligent Systems*, volume 16(2), pages 60–71, 2001.

# Extracting the Most Discriminant Subset from a Pool of Candidates to Optimize Discriminant Classifier Training*

Carlos E. Vivaracho[1], Javier Ortega-Garcia[2], Luis Alonso[3], and Q. Isaac Moro[1]

[1] Dep. Informática, U. de Valladolid, {cevp,isaac}@infor.uva.es
[2] Biometric Research Lab, U. Politécnica de Madrid, jortega@diac.upm.es
[3] Dep. Automática e Informática, U. de Salamanca, lalonso@usal.es

**Abstract.** Our work is concerned with the problem of classifying a sample as belonging or not to a *Target Class* (TC) by means of a discriminant classifier. To yield this goal, the classifier must be trained with samples of the TC and *Non-Target Class* (NTC). The problem arises when, as in many real applications, the number of the NTC examples is much higher than that of the TC, leading the classifier, if all the examples are used in training, to overlearn the NTC. This paper is focused in the task of extracting, from the pool of NTC representatives, the most discriminant training subset with regard to the TC, and with the optimum size: too few NTC examples would be non-representative and the classifier tends to missaccept, and with too many the classifier tends to misreject. A new heuristic search method is presented that improves the performance of the traditional problem solution, the random selection, eliminating the random behavior of the system. To prove this advantages the new technique will be applied to speaker verification task by means of neural networks, achieving in this way a more competitive system.

## 1 Introduction

To train a two class discriminant classifier, samples of both classes to discriminate must be used. In many real applications, as for example biometric authentication of persons, one of the classes is clearly defined, the called *Target Class* (TC), and the goal is to classify the input sample as belonging or not to this class. The problem arises when the *Non-Target Class* (NTC) training samples must be chosen, since normally this class is not so clearly defined, as happens in the biometric authentication example, where this class is the "rest of the people". Then, a representative subset of the NTC must be used.

The main problems in the NTC representative subset selection are: i) the size of the subset: too few examples would be non-representative and the classifier would tend to missaccept, and with too many the classifier tends to misreject, and ii) the representativeness of the subset: given a TC the most discriminant subset with regard to this particular class should be chosen.

---

* This work has been supported by Ministerio de Ciencia y Tecnología, Spain, under Project TIC2000-1669-C03

N. Zhong et al. (Eds.): ISMIS 2003, LNAI 2871, pp. 640–645, 2003.

The lack of research into this subject, and its importance in order to adjust the system performance, have led us to focus on it. The traditional solution has been the random selection, that means a system unpredictable behavior, doing impossible to find an optimum solution to previous problems.

In the section 3, a new heuristic search method of the NTC training samples is presented, allowing an optimum extraction of these samples from the pool of candidates. This method will be called *Non-Target Incremental Learning (NTIL)*.

Next, an example of application of the NTIL method will be seen. Our work is mainly concerned with the Speaker Verification (SV) by means of discriminant Neural Networks [4], that was a very popular approach at the beginning of the 90s, but with few attention currently, where systems based in Gaussian Mixture Models (GMMs) are the most used. It will be shown that the use of NTIL, besides solving the previous problems in NTC training samples selection, allows to achieve improvements of over 20% with regard to the best performance of the system with random selection. The achieved performance can be considered competitive with respect to another systems as this paper shows.

## 2    The Selection Problem

To reduce notation the NTC samples used in the classifier learning will be called *Impostors for Training* (IT), and the pool of NTC examples, those from the IT are extracted, will be called the *Development Set* (DS).

To show the IT selection problem better, a 2-dimension linear separable example will be used; although simple, it will show clearly the IT size and composition importance. Let us suppose that the distribution of the characteristic vectors extracted from the training samples is that shown in Fig. 1(left), where $t_i$ are the vectors extracted from the TC training sample/s $i$, and $i_j$ are those extracted from the DS samples. If, without loss of generalization in the reasoning, linear discriminant functions are used, the best selection to train, e.g., the TC 2 classifier are the samples of the NTCs 2, 4 and 7, whose characteristic vectors are the nearest to TC 2 ones. An example of the linear discriminant frontiers achieved are shown in Fig. 1(middle). In this figure can be seen that the use of another DS samples do not add any information to the classification, and can make worse the system performance. If random selection was used, the IT could be, for example, the samples of NTCs 2, 5 and 8, and then, the probability of missaccept NTC samples would be very high, as can be seen in Fig. 1(right).

## 3    Non-target Incremental Learning

A first heuristic search was tested, based on modelling, by means of a Auto-Associative Neural Network (AANN), the distribution of the characteristic vectors extracted from the TC training sample/s, and calculating the distance between this model and each sample in the DS. The $M$ samples with the smallest distances, i.e., the "$M$ nearest neighbours to the TC training sample/s" are chosen as IT. The AANN was used due to its ability to model the probability

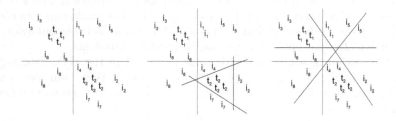

**Fig. 1.** Example of characteristic vectors distribution (left). Example of good (middle) and bad (right) IT selection to classify TC 2, by means of linear discriminant functions.

distribution of the training data [5], without previous assumptions about the shape of that distribution, as in parametric models. Several tests were carried out, achieving a system performance similar to the mean with random selection. Although it is not a bad performance, other methods to model the vectors distribution, e.g. GMMs or VQ, were not tested due to the NTIL advantages.

The main problem regarding the previous approach, and similar ones, is that the classifier and the system used to select the IT are not the same, and, then, the IT selected cannot ensure to be the most discriminant with respect to the classifier training. Another problem is the impossibility to correctly model the training vectors distribution. The proposed search method avoids these problems because is the classifier itself during the learning stage, who selects the most discriminant subset of IT, without the need of modelling the training vector distribution. The NTIL methodology is an iterative proposal, based on *Incremental Learning* idea, that searches "not learned" NTC examples in each iteration, in order to increase with them the IT set. The proposed technique can be formulated as follows:

a) The size of the IT, *MaxIT*, and the ending criteria of the classifier training, *EndCri*, are selected, using, for example, a validation set.
b) The classifier is trained using the target training sample/s and one of those in the DS, until *EndCri* is reached.
c) The score of the classifier $S(X)$ is obtained for each of the remaining samples of the DS, and the $P$ samples with the highest values[1] are chosen as the most similar (nearest) to the TC. If the classifier was used for classification, these $P$ samples would be those with the highest probability of producing false acceptances; though, due to their discriminant capability, these are selected to train the classifier in the next phase.
d) The $P$ samples chosen in step c) are included into the IT set and the classifier is trained once again.
e) Steps c) and d) are repeated until *MaxIT* is reached.

In order to avoid random initialization of IT, even the first of the IT (step b) is also heuristically selected, using the methodology shown at the beginning.

---

[1] We are assuming that the classifier is trained to get TC samples scores higher than those for the NTC ones. If not, the modification in the reasoning is immediate.

## 4    Example of Application: Speaker Verification

In SV the goal is to accept or to reject the claimed identity of the user (target class) by means of his/her voice.

### 4.1    System Description

Standard feature extraction is accomplished from each speech sample, through 14 mel-frequency cepstral coefficients (MFCC) plus 14 $\Delta$MFCC vectors; these are extracted from 32 ms frames, taken every 16 ms with Hamming windowing. Cepstral Mean Normalization is applied as channel compensation scheme.

The classification stage is based on Artificial Neural Networks (ANNs) [4]. A Multilayer Perceptron (MLP) per speaker is trained, with 28-32-1 neurons in the input-hidden-output layer. The desired output was 1.0 for TC vectors and 0.0 for IT ones. Then, the MLP output for input vector $x_i$ can be seen as the $P(\lambda_c/x_i)$, being $\lambda_c$ the client $c$ MLP. A modification with regard to [4] is introduced, as not all of the $N$ vectors of the input sample $X$, $X = \{x_1, x_2, ..., x_N\}$, are used to calculate the final system score $S(X)$, being this calculation as follows:

$$S(X) = \frac{1}{N_R} \sum_{i=1}^{N_R} \log(P(\lambda_c/x_i)) \ \forall x_i/P(\lambda_c/x_i) \notin (0.2, 0.8) \tag{1}$$

Where $N_R$ is the number of vectors $x_i$ that verify the rule in (1). The use of this rule, called R262, has shown some improvements in system performance [6].

System performance is measured by means of the Equal Error Rate (EER), that is the error of the system when the decision threshold is such that the False Match Rate equals the False Non Match Rate. The EER is calculated using a common threshold for all the target speakers, using Z-Norm [1] in order to normalize the score distributions of the different classifiers.

The experiments have been performed using the subset of AHUMADA corpus [3] included in the NIST (National Institute of Standards and Technology, USA) 00 and 01 evaluations [2]. It is a telephonic subcorpus in Spanish, only with male speakers and channel mismatch between training (a speech recording of about 60s.) and testing (two different speech recordings of about 60s.) samples.

### 4.2    NTIL Effectiveness and Robustness Test

The experiments carried out analyze the behavior of the system with respect to the IT set size, the training epochs and the $P$ value in the NTIL technique, testing $P=1$ and $P>1$ values to compare results when the IT set is increased in one or in various at a time. In order to demonstrate the robustness of the NTIL procedure with respect to the DS, experiments with two different DS have been performed, using: i) the DS supplied with NIST-AHUMADA subcorpus (AhumadaDev), that consists of 122 male spanish speakers, each of them with speech samples of about 30 s. of duration, ii) the created using the CSLU database (CsluDev), with 122 American speakers samples, and an average speech duration of 12 s. To compare NTIL effectiveness 5 experiments were carried out with different random choices of the IT using AhumadaDev and 6 using CsluDev. Analyzing the system performance evolution, training the network for 150 epochs is chosen as the ending criteria (*EndCri* in NTIL) for the learning stage. In table 1 can be seen a summary of the most relevant results, showing the improvements achieved with the use of NTIL. For *P>1* is improved not only the average performance but also that of the best random case. Besides this advantage, the computational load of the training process is smaller than for *P=1*.

**Table 1.** System EER (in %). The **IT Size** column shows the number of samples from the DS in the IT set. The **Al**$_{best}$ and **Al**$_{med}$ columns show the best and average results with random selection, respectively. With NTIL selection the values of P, when *P>1*, are chosen to get a similar IT set increase, increase measured in number of vectors, for AHUMADA and CSLU DSs. The best results are emphasized with bold face.

| AhumadaDev | | | | | CsluDev | | | | |
|---|---|---|---|---|---|---|---|---|---|
| | Random | | NTIL | | | Random | | NTIL | |
| IT Size | Al$_{best}$ | Al$_{med}$ | P=1 | P=5 | IT Size | Al$_{best}$ | Al$_{med}$ | P=1 | P=10 |
| 11 | 16.0 | 16.0 | 17.0 | 16.0 | 21 | 15.0 | 17.0 | 16.0 | 15.2 |
| 16 | 16.7 | 17.0 | 16.6 | **14.0** | 31 | 15.0 | 16.9 | 14.5 | 17.0 |
| 21 | 16.0 | 17.0 | 16.2 | **15.0** | 41 | 15.2 | 17.0 | 17.0 | **13.0** |
| 26 | 17.0 | 17.5 | 16.6 | 15.8 | 51 | 18.7 | 18.5 | - | **13.3** |

### 4.3  IT Size Optimization

Having improved performance, there is still to be solved the problem of IT set size optimization, as NTIL allows this parameter to be defined. In Fig. 2 can be seen the system performance evolution using NTIL selection (P=5 for AhumadaDev and P=10 for CsluDev) with respect to the ratio between the number of the TC and the IT training vectors. The figure shows a similar evolution for both DS, in spite of the great differences between them; and this reinforces the robustness of the NTIL selection. The best results are obtained with 7-9 vectors of the IT for each TC training vector, with an improvement of over 20% with respect to the best mean EER with random selection. It can also be derived from Fig. 2, that even for non-optimum IT sizes, the system performance is almost always better (and, in the worst case, similar to) to the performance with random selection.

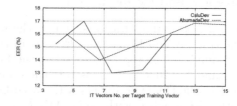

**Fig. 2.** System performance evolution with IT size.

## 4.4    About Discriminant MLP Competitiveness in SV

As the NIST evaluation results are not public, the comparison with other systems with the same data is impossible, then the results shown in [5] (table 2) will be used as reference, as these were obtained under the same experimental conditions than ours. Our system final result is the average of those achieved in the optimum IT size, once shown this parameter can be defined. Using MLP the number of model parameters is as few as 961 (weights+bias), as opposed to 1847 used by AANN-based system and 9728 used by GMM-based system.

**Table 2.** Results of MLP-based SV system compared with those achieved with GMM-based (state of the art) and AANN-based (an alternative to GMMs) systems applied on NIST99-00 databases, under training and testing channel mismatched conditions.

| GMM | | AANN | | MLP |
| --- | --- | --- | --- | --- |
| NIST'99 | NIST'00 | NIST'99 | NIST'00 | NIST-AHUMADA |
| 10.0% | 11.0% | 14.4% | 14.8% | 13.5% |

## 5    Conclusions

To reach a competitive system, unpredictable behavior must be eliminated. With discriminant classifiers, one of the main causes of unpredictability is random selection of the IT. Applying the new search technique NTIL not only the system performance is improved, but it also allows a parameter optimization, independently of the DS used. These advantages have been shown in SV with discriminant MLP, where the use of NTIL has allowed to improve the performance of the system, achieving competitive results.

**Acknowledgment.** We wish to acknowledge the CSLU (Oregon Graduate Institute) for providing us the Speaker Recognition V1.1 Database.

## References

1. Auckenthaler, R., Carey, M., Harvey, Ll.: Score Normalization for Text-Independent Speaker Verification Systems. Digital Signal Processing, Vol. 10 (2000) 42–54
2. Martin, A., Przyboki, M.: The NIST Speaker Recognition Evaluations: 1996-2001. Proc. of the 2001: The Speaker Odyssey, The Speaker Recognition Workshop (2001)
3. Ortega-Garcia, J., Gonzalez-Rodriguez, J., Marrero-Aguiar, V.: An Approach to Forensic Speaker Verification Using AHUMADA Large Speech Corpus in Spanish. Speech Communication, Vol. 31 (2000) 255–264
4. Vivaracho, C., Ortega-Garcia, J., Alonso, L., Moro, Q.: A Comparative Study of MLP-based Artificial Neural Networks in Text-Independent Speaker Verification against GMM-based Systems. Proc. of Eurospeech01, Vol. 3 (2001) 1753–1756
5. Yegnanarayana, B., Kishore, S.: AANN: an Alternative to GMM for Pattern Recognition. Neural Networks, Vol. 15, No. 3 (2002) 459–469
6. Vivaracho, C., Ortega-Garcia, J., Alonso, L., Moro, Q.: Improving the Competitiveness of Discriminant Neural Networks in Speaker Verification. Proc. Eurospeech 03 (to appear) (2003)

# Knowledge Engineering of Intelligent Sales-Recruitment System Using Multi-layered Agent Methodology

R. Khosla[1], T. Goonesekera[1], and Y. Mitsukura[2]

[1]School of Business
La Trobe University
Melbourne, Victoria – 3086, Australia
Fax: (613) 94795971, Tel: (613) 94793064
R.Khosla@latrobe.edu.au

[2]Dept. of Information Science & Intelligent Systems .
University of Tokushima
2- 1, Minami-Josanjima
Tokushima, Japan

**Abstract.** In this paper we outline a multi-layered multi-agent distributed soft computing architecture for providing support to practitioners and problem solvers at four levels, namely, distributed processing, technology, optimization and problem solving level respectively. The architecture has been applied in complex problems like image recognition, web mining, alarm processing, and medical diagnosis. We illustrate some aspects of the architecture with help of e-Sales recruitment (e-SRS) application. An earlier version of e-SRS (expert system ) is also in commercial use.

## 1 Introduction

Intelligent agents today are being applied in a range of areas including image processing, engineering, process control and others. In the process of applying intelligent and soft computing agents to complex real world problems three phenomena have emerged. Firstly, the application of soft computing agents in distributed environments has resulted in merger of techniques from soft computing area with those in distributed artificial intelligence. Secondly, in an effort to improve the quality of soft computing solution (or optimizing) researchers have been combining and fusing technologies. This has resulted in hybrid configurations of soft computing technologies. Finally, from a practitioners perspective, as the soft computing technologies have moved out of laboratories into the real world the need for knowledge or problem solving level practitioner-centered technology independent constructs for modeling complex problems has emerged. In this paper we outline a multi-layered multi-agent architecture for designing soft computing agents which models these three phenomena. We also illustrate some aspects of the architecture with the help of intelligent e-sales recruitment application

The paper is organised as follows. Section 2 outlines the distributed multi-layered multi-agent soft computing architecture. Section 3 describes the application of the architecture in e-sales recruitment domain. Section 4 concludes the paper.

N. Zhong et al. (Eds.): ISMIS 2003, LNAI 2871, pp. 646–651, 2003.

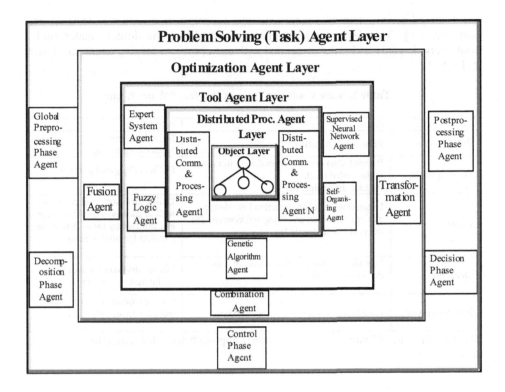

**Fig. 1.** Distributed Multi-Agent Soft Computing Architecture

## 2 Distributed Multi-agent Architecture

The layered multi-agent architecture is shown in Figure 1. It is derived from integration of intelligent technologies like expert systems, fuzzy logic, neural network and genetic algorithms and their hybrid configurations (fusion, combination, transformation and association [3]), agent and object models, operating system process model and problem solving ontology model [3]. The layered architecture in Figure 1 consists of five layers, the object layer, which defines the data architecture or structural content of an application. The distributed processing agent layer helps to define the distributed processing and communication constructs used for receiving, depositing and processing data in a distributed environment. The tool or technology agent layer defines the constructs for various intelligent and soft computing tools. The optimization agent layer defines constructs for fusion, combination and transformation technologies which are used for optimizing the quality of solution (e.g., accuracy). Finally, the problem solving ontology (task) agent layer defines the constructs related to the problem solving agents or adapters[1] namely, preprocessing, decomposition, control, decision and postprocessing. This layer models practitioners tasks in the domain under study. Some generic goals and tasks associated with each problem solving agent are shown in Table 1.

**Table 1.** Some Goals and Tasks of Problem Solving Agents

| Phase | Goal | Some Tasks |
|---|---|---|
| Preprocessing | Improve data quality | Noise Filtering<br>Input Conditioning |
| Decomposition | Restrict data context from the environment at the global level.<br>Reduce the complexity | Define orthogonal concepts |
| Control | Determine decision selection knowledge constructs within an orthogonal concept for the problem under study . | Define decision level concepts with in each orthogonal concept as identified by users Determine Conflict Resolution rules |
| Decision | Provide decision instance results in a user defined decision concept. | Define decision instance of interest to the user |
| Post-processing | Establish outcomes as desired outcomes | Concept validation. Decision instance result validation |

The five layers facilitate a component based approach for soft computing software design.

# 3   Application in E-sales Recruitment

In this section we illustrate the application of the task, optimization and technology ( tool) layers of the architecture. in an e-sales recruitment application. It may be noted that we have applied the architecture on very complex problems like alarm processing (in a power system control centre), image processing and image retrieval. Further, the application represents a novel integration of psychology based selling behaviour model with AI and soft computing agents like expert systems and fuzzy-k-means[1] for on-line prediction of selling behaviour profile of a sales candidate.

Most organizations rely on interview as the main strategy for recruiting salespersons. Some of the limitations of interview procedure are a) In the limited interview time, it is difficult to realistically assess all the factors which affect the selling behavior of a salesperson, and b) The sales manager and the top management view the selling behavior of the salesperson based on their traits, whims/mood and experience which introduces inconsistency & subjectivity in the whole process. We next describe some aspects of selling behaviour analysis to develop an e-sales recruitment system which can be used consistently & objectively.

---

[1] Problem solving adapter is a generic problem solving primitive used for modeling a subset of a problem under study. The term "adapter" has its underpinnings in design patterns in software engineering. Problem solving adapter are more complex than design patterns.

## 3.1  Selling Behaviour Analysis

The selling behavioral analysis is based on the selling behavior model [2] shown in Figure 2. It is used to derive four behavioral categories; namely, dominant hostile, submissive warm, dominant warm, and submissive hostile. These four categories are based on two dimensions, namely,  "Submissive------Dominant, and Warm-----Hostile" as shown in Figure 2. In order to analyze the behavior of a sales candidate sixteen areas have been identified.   These include selling (as a profession), decisiveness, assertiveness, competition,  customer, job satisfaction, and others.  In order to quantify the varying degree of importance attached to the different areas of selling and buying behavior by the domain experts, weights have been assigned to them on a scale of 1 to 10. After determining the different areas and their weights, attributes in the form of questions  related to each of these areas with respect to different behavioral categories have been determined. The questions are used to take feedback from the salesperson. Heuristics and  the behavioral model are used to compute the category scores of the sales candidate.

**Fig. 2.** Selling Behavior Model

## 3.2  E-sales Recruitment System (E-SRS) Modelling

Figure 3 shows an overview of problem solving level modelling of e-SRS . In order to facilitate decision making  two models of selling behavior categorization have been developed. These are the Expert System (ES) Model (ES selling behavior categorization and profiling agent) and  Behavioral Clustering Model (Behavior clustering agent).  The user (sales manger or a recruitment manager)  employs both the models to  accept or reject the behavioral categorization providing by them.  For purpose of optimization, we use the accept and reject cases as  positive and negative examples for training a Neural Network (NN) agent. The NN agent is employed  in combination configuration with existing ES and clustering (Fuzzy K-means) agents. The trained NN agent is used to predict  whether the behavior  categorization made by the  two (ES and Clustering) agents is likely to be accepted or rejected by the user based on past experience (incorporated during training of the neural network). In the technology layer  we  also use a fuzzy k-means agent[1] to introduce further granularity in the behaviour categories. That is, the four categories SH, SW, DH, and DW are refined using linguistic variable like high, medium and low.   So, we have twelve clusters  (SH (high, medium and low), and three each for the other three categories) instead of the original four   shown in Figure 2. Qualitatively, the linguistic variables provide information on the intensity (or extent to which a candidate's behaviour belongs to a category) of each category . Qualitative interpretation of behaviour  categorization results is shown in Figure 4.

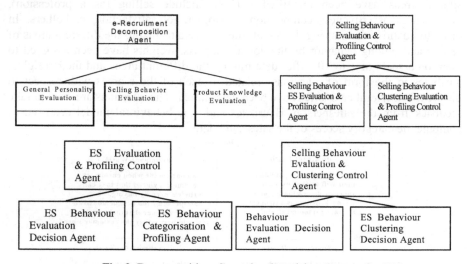

**Fig. 3.** Decomposition, Control and Decision Agents of e-SRS

## 4   Conclusion

We have outlined a multi-layered multi-agent soft computing architecture which provides support to users to model complex problems like e-sales recruitment at problem solving, optimization, technology and distributed processing levels

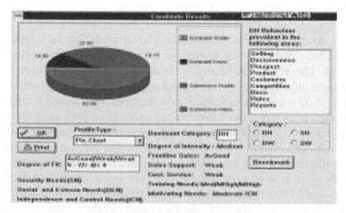

**Fig. 4.** Candidate Result Screen

# References

[1] Bezdek, J.C. "Pattern Recognition with Fuzzy Objective Function Algorithms,' Advanced Applications in Pattern Recognition," Plenum Press 1981, USA

[2] Buzzotte, V. R., et. al., Effective Selling through Psychology, Psychological Associates, New York, 1981.

[3] Khosla, R. Damiani, E., and Grosky, W. Human-Centered E-Business, Kluwer Academic Publishers, MA, USA, 2003

# The KAMET II[1] Methodology: A Modern Approach for Building Diagnosis-Specialized Knowledge-Based Systems

Osvaldo Cairó and Julio César Alvarez

Instituto Tecnológico Autónomo de México (ITAM)
Department of Computer Science
Río Hondo 1, Mexico City, Mexico
cairo@itam.mx, calvarez@alumnos.itam.mx

**Abstract.** Knowledge engineering (KE) is not "mining from the expert's head" as it was in the first generation of knowledge-based systems (KBS). Modern KE is considered more a modeling activity. Models are useful due to the incomplete accessibility that knowledge engineer has to the experts knowledge and because not all the knowledge is completely necessary to reach the majority of projects goals. KAMET II[2], the evolution of KAMET (Knowledge-Acquisition Methodology), is a modern approach for building diagnosis-specialized knowledge models. This new diagnosis methodology pursues the objective of being a complete robust methodology to lead knowledge engineers and project managers (PM) to build powerful KBS by giving the appropriate modeling tools and by reducing KE-specific risks. Not only KAMET II encompasses the conceptual modeling tools, but it presents the adaptation to the implementation tool Protégé 2000 [6] for visual modeling and knowledge-base-editing as well. However, only the methodological part is presented in this paper.

## 1 Introduction

Knowledge acquisition (KA) has been recognized as the critical phase and bottleneck for the KBS construction. The KAMET [1][2] methodology was born during the last third of the nineties. The life-cycle of KAMET's first version was constituted mainly by two phases. The first one, analyzes and acquires the knowledge of different sources involved in the system. The second one, models and processes this knowledge. KAMET was inspired by two basic ideas: the spiral model proposed by Boehm and the essence of cooperative processes. Both ideas are closely related to the concept

---

[1] This project has been founded by CONACyT, as project number 33038-A, and Asociación Mexicana de Cultura, A.C.

[2] KAMET II is a project that is being carried out in collaboration with the SWI Group at Amsterdam University and Universidad Politécnica de Madrid.

N. Zhong et al. (Eds.): ISMIS 2003, LNAI 2871, pp. 652–656, 2003.

of risk reduction. This has led KAMET to successful applications in the medicine, telecommunications and human resources areas. The integration of the ideas of diagnosis specialization and the KAMET methodology converges in the KAMET II methodology which comes up to be a specialized, complete and robust methodology in the diagnosis area by focusing on KA from multiple sources. The objective of KAMET II, which is the new version of KAMET, is, in a certain sense, to specialize the phases of this methodology in knowledge acquisition and knowledge modeling. KAMET II provides a precise description of a methodology. We assume a methodology as a software engineering technology where each layer can be seen like a construction block used by the superior layers. Fig. 1 shows KAMET-II's methodological pyramid.

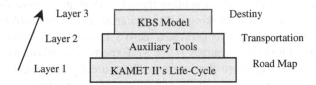

**Fig. 1.** KAMET II's Methodological Pyramid

Fig. 1 shows the Methodological Pyramid of KAMET II. KAMET-II's life cycle: it represents the methodology itself; it is the beginning to reach the goal. Auxiliary tools provide an automated or semi-automated support for the process and the methods. A KBS Model represents a KBS detailed description, in form of models. This has led KAMET to successful applications in the medicine, telecommunications and human resources areas. The integration of diagnosis specialization and the KAMET methodology ideas converges in the KAMET II methodology which is a specialized methodology in the diagnosis area by focusing on KA from multiple sources. Although KAMET provides a framework for managing the phase of knowledge modeling process in a systematic and disciplined way, the manner to obtain additional organizational objectives like predictability, consistency and improvement in quality and productivity is still not well defined within the KAMET Life-Cycle Model (LCM). Fig. 2 shows a schema of the environment used by KAMET II.

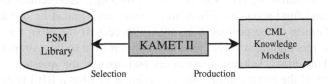

**Fig. 2.** KAMET II's Environment

# 2 The KAMET II Life-Cycle

The KAMET II life-cycle model (LCM) provides a framework for managing both the phase of KA from multiple knowledge sources and the knowledge modeling process. The approaches also helps set up and facilitate ways to characterize and organize the knowledge acquired from multiple knowledge sources, implement the required actions, review the project situation, identify risks of not reaching objectives, monitor project progress, and check the control quality project. In KAMET, it has been considered appropriate to distinguish among different kinds of knowledge sources. We therefore distinguish between active knowledge sources (AKS) and passive knowledge sources (PKS). Human Experts (HE) represent AKS. These experts deal with private type of knowledge, knowledge that manifests itself through experience and abilities acquired over time, thus enabling them to establish a diagnosis with acceptable plausibility, even when working with inaccurate and/or incomplete information. Within AKS, we also perceive dedicated active knowledge sources (DAKS) and consulting active knowledge sources (CAKS). Experts with whom knowledge engineers interact largely represent the formers. These are the HE directly linked to the project. The latter are represented by specialists who contribute to the project by providing ideas, experiences and suggesting alternatives, without being totally devoted to the project. KAMET provides a strong mechanism with which to achieve KA from multiple knowledge sources in an incremental fashion, and in a cooperative environment. The number and type of stages, the input and output for each one of them, the steps that constitute the stages, as well as the activities related to each one of the steps, is the result of a careful research process and later testing. It must also be remembered that stages, steps and activities were defined only as guidance for the PM. KAMET consists of four stages: the strategic planning of the project, construction of the initial model, construction of the feedback model, and construction of the final model.

## 2.1 The Strategic Planning

The first stage, the strategic planning of the project, is essential for the development of the project. The PM and the four groups involved in the project (KE responsible for KBS implementation, HE who provide knowledge, representatives of potential users (PU), and fund sponsors (FS) who provide funds) must be in total agreement with the definition of the project to assure its success. If the groups are experienced in projects of this nature, strategic planning may turn out to be a simple task. Participants contribute ideas, suggest alternatives and answer the questions asked by the PM. However, if the groups have only vague ideas of what a KBS is and what it can achieve, defining the project may prove to be a complex task. In these instances, it might be convenient for the PM to initially explain the following questions to the participants in a precise way: What is a KBS? How does it work? What does KA consist of? and what are the roles played by the group members in the project?

## 2.2 The Initial Model

In the second stage, KE elicit knowledge from PKS and DAKS and proceed to construct the initial model. An initial model is constituted by one o more models -it will be explained in section five-. This stage involves the largest number of risks, which mainly arise because interviews involve introspection and verbal expression of knowledge, resulting in a difficult task for humans, and especially for experts. On the other hand, if the communication language among PM, knowledge engineers and human experts is not clear, this may also cause conflicts. The knowledge elicitation in these instances may be monotonous and ineffective. These problems lead to consider a certain degree of inaccuracy in the formulation of the initial model. Because of this, it is advised to walk through the following two stages.

## 2.3 The Feedback Model

The opinion of consulting active knowledge sources is obtained in the third stage. The KE distributes the initial model among the CAKS for its analysis, and ideas, experiences or perspectives are exchanged about it. Finally, the PM, KE, jointly with the DAKS, reviews and analyzes the changes introduced to the initial model and constructs the feedback model. The inaccuracy of the model at the end of the stage must be less, since the model now expresses the knowledge of several specialists in the knowledge domain of the application. It must be remembered that the feedback model is only a refined and better initial model.

## 2.4 The Final Model

In the last stage, active knowledge sources participate in a series of interviews, under the coordination of the PM, to develop the final model. The stage is considered to be over when the model satisfies the proposed objectives with a high degree of plausibility and/or there are no AKS capable of further transforming it. Inaccuracy at the end of the stage must be minimal, since the model now expresses the knowledge acquired
from multiple knowledge sources, and of course from multiple human experts who collaborated in different degrees and ways to solve the problem. Remember that the final model is only an improve version of the feedback model. Detailed information about these stages can be found in [2].

## 2.5 The Project Management Dimension

Although KAMET provides a framework for managing both the phase of knowledge modeling process in a systematic and disciplined way, the manner to catch up with some additional organizational objectives like predictability, consistency and improvement in quality and productivity is still unclear and that is why KAMET II,

KAMET's new version, supports most aspects of a KBS development project, including organizational analysis, KA from multiple sources, conceptual modeling and user interaction. A software project has two main activity dimensions: engineering and project management. The second dimension deals with properly planning and controlling of the engineering activities to meet the project goals for cost, schedule and quality. Project Management is a process that involves several things including planning, putting the project plan into action, and measuring progress and performance. Project management processes organize and describe the work of the project.

## 3 Conclusions

In this paper we presented the diagnosis -specialized methodology KAMET II, which is the new version of KAMET. There were presented all the roles involved within the process of construction of KBS. We presented the project management dimension which tackles KE-specific risks. KAMET II is a complete methodology with KE representation adapted to metaclass models like Protégé's. This is explained in detail [5].

## References

1.   Cairó, O.: A Comprehensive Methodology for Knowledge Acquisition from Multiple Knowledge Sources. Expert Systems with Applications (1998) 1–16
2.   Cairó, O.: The KAMET Methodology: Content, Usage and Knowledge Modeling. In: Gaines, B. and Musen, M., (eds.): Proceedings of the 11th Banff Knowledge Acquisition for Knowledge-Based Systems Workshop. SRGD Publications (1998) 1–20
3.   Cairó, O., Barreiro, J., Solsona, F.: Software Methodologies at Risk. In: Fensel, D. and Studer, R., (eds.): 11th European Workshop on Knowledge Acquisition, Modeling and Management. Lecture Notes in Artificial Intelligence, Vol. 1621. Springer-Verlag (1999) 319–324
4.   Cairó, O., Barreiro, J., Solsona, F.: Risks Inside-out. In: Cairó, O., Sucar, L. and Cantu, F., (eds.): MICAI 2000: Advances in Artificial Intelligence. Lecture Notes in Artificial Intelligence, Vol. 1793. Springer-Verlag (2000) 426–435
5.   Cairó, O., Alvarez, J.:KAMET II: An Extended Knowledge=Acquisition Methodology. KES 2003: Advances in Artificial Intelligence. Lecture Notes in Artificial Intelligence. Oxford, England. Springer-Verlag (2003).
6.   Fridman, N., Fergerson, R., Musen, M.: The Knowledge Model of Protégé-2000: Combining Interoperability and Flexibility. In: Dieng, R. and Corby, O., (eds.): 12th International Conference, EKAW 2000. Lecture Notes in Artificial Intelligence, Vol. 1937. Springer-Verlag (2000) 17–32 Juan-les-Pins, France.
7.   Schreiber, G., Crubézy, M., Musen, M.: A Case Study in Using Protégé-2000 as a Tool for CommonKADS. In: Dieng, R. and Corby, O., (eds.): 12th International Conference, EKAW 2000. Lecture Notes in Artificial Intelligence, Vol. 1937. Sp ringer-Verlag (2000) 33–48

# A Formal Approach to Describing Action Concepts in Taxonomical Knowledge Bases

Christel Kemke

Department of Computer Science
562 Machray Hall
University of Manitoba
Winnipeg, Manitoba, R3T 2N2, Canada
ckemke@cs.umanitoba.ca

**Abstract.** This paper outlines a formal theory for defining action concepts in taxonomical knowledge representation languages, in a form closely related to description logics. The central problems of defining an extensional semantics, and, based on this, a subsumption/specialization relation as well as the inheritance of descriptions for action concepts is addressed, as an extension to the respective notions for static object concepts. The suggested approach is based on the view of actions as transformers between world states, where a world state corresponds to an instantiation of object concepts coherent with the knowledge base. A model-theoretic, extensional semantics for action concepts is defined - in accordance with the semantics for object concepts - as the set of world states which are in the domain/range of the transformation function associated with the action concept, as specified through the precondition and effect formulae stated in the action description. The specialization/subsumption relation for action concepts is defined based on the set inclusion of the sets of world states which fulfill the precondition (effect) formula.

## 1 Introduction

Taxonomical or terminological knowledge representation languages present a formal notion of inheritance hierarchies, and are in the focus of attention at least since the early eighties, with the rise of KL-ONE [7] and related languages. KL-ONE was mainly concerned with modeling and representing object-concepts which could be described as static entities through attributes and relations to other concepts. In the mid 90ies it became obvious that dynamic entities, in particular action concepts, have to be integrated into these knowledge representation formalisms. Several groups of researchers have dealt with the integration of action concepts into terminological knowledge representation languages [1-6][8-9][16-18]. Most of these approaches, however, developed into sophisticated, complex language systems featuring the representation of time [1-6] or planning and plan recognition methods [17-18], or are more practically oriented and deal with the implementation of action representations in terminological languages [16].

In this paper, we propose a formal semantics of action concepts with a definition of the subsumption/specialization relation. The formal framework bases the definition of action concepts on a functional view of actions as transformers between world states, where these world states comprise of instantiations of object concepts including their attributes and roles/relations to other object concepts, as described in the knowledge base. In addition, precondition and effect formulae are part of the action description and they specify further constraints on the world states involved in the transformation. This approach provides a grounding of action concepts and their descriptions in the static, object part of the

N. Zhong et al. (Eds.): ISMIS 2003, LNAI 2871, pp. 657–662, 2003.

taxonomy, and thus allows the definition of an extensional semantics for action concepts. The extensional semantics provides a basis for defining the subsumption/specialization relation for action concepts, and the inheritance for action concepts, including their preconditions and effects described as formulae-valued attributes of action concepts.

## 2     The General Concept Terminology Language

*Concepts* are assumed to correspond to unary predicates, i.e. they consist of simple sets of elements which are also called *instances*. *Attributes* or *features* correspond to functions or functional relations, with object concepts specifying the domain and range. *Roles* correspond to binary predicates or relations. The concepts defined within a taxonomical knowledge base are divided into *object concepts* which describe structural, static entities and *action concepts*, which describe temporal, dynamic entities.

Furthermore, we assume a distinction of characteristics of concepts (roles and features, and their values) into those which are definitional and cannot be changed, and those which are accidental or temporary and changeable. The second class compares to the general concept of *Fluents*.

### 2.1     The Object Concept Taxonomy

Object concepts are in general described by a set of roles and features. Roles and features are inherited from the subsuming concept(s) and additional ones can be specified for the specialized concept. The extension of a concept is defined as the set of all instances which fulfill all the definitional constraints specified in the description of the concept. Each instance is vice versa associated with a concept.

The subsumption relation for object concepts is defined as:

$$C \text{ } subsumes \text{ } C' \text{ } (C' \text{ } specializes \text{ } C) :\Leftrightarrow \forall x: (x \in C' \Rightarrow x \in C)$$

This is equivalent to the Predicate Logic expression:

$$\forall x: C'(x) \Rightarrow C(x)$$

## 3     Action Concepts – Description, Semantics, and Inheritance

### 3.1     Describing Action Concepts

*Action concepts* are described by a set of *parameters* or *object variables*[1], which refer to concepts in the object taxonomy, and a precondition as well as an effect formula, which are stored as features of the action concept.

The parameters of an action concept specify the object concept, including features or roles, which are affected by the action. These parameters are also used in the precondition and effect formulae of the action, as predicates, functions, or constants.

Precondition and effect formulae are simple First-Order Predicate Logic formulae:
- simple or negated atomic formulae, like $P(x)$, $P(c)$, $\neg P(x)$;
- quantified atomic formulae, like $\forall x: P(x)$, $\exists x: P(x)$;
- conjuncts and disjuncts of the above, like $P(x) \wedge Q(x)$ or $P(x) \vee Q(x)$.

---

[1] It should be mentioned here that the idea to describe action concepts by including parameter objects has been described by the author already in [10-11], prior to [9].

In these formulae, the free variables refer to the parameters of the action; they are supposed to be instantiated (bound to object constants) when a respective concrete action occurs. These parameters define constraints on the set of possible worlds (interpretations) which satisfy the precondition and effect formulae. Variables bound by a quantifier are supposed to be evaluated for the current knowledge base, i.e. the current set of object instances, when a concrete action occurs, i.e. an action concept is instantiated. This approach assumes a kind of "temporary closed world" in which object instances are stable and known at each time instance but the set of objects can change over the time. This is consistent with the general STRIPS methodology but it provides a neat extension for standard STRIPS based planning algorithms which deal only with atomic formulae.

## 3.2 World States and the Subsumption Relation for Actions

We regard action concepts in a traditional way as generic transformers between world states, similar to functions, where the domain of the transformation function is the set of worlds fulfilling the precondition of an action, and the range is specified by the effect formula of the action concept.

In taxonomical knowledge bases or terminologies, a possible world state refers to a set of object instances which adheres to the concept definitions specified in the terminology. A terminological knowledge base then specifies a set of such world states. On the extensional, interpretation level a single world state is specified by an interpretation of the conceptual objects, i.e. the object instances which constitute the knowledge base, or A-Box.

We define the subsumption relation for actions based on the set inclusion of the extension of the concept, which is in the case of action concepts defined via the sets of worlds which are specified through the precondition / effect formulae of the action concept, and which correspond to the domain / range of the transformation function when we regard the action as a transformer between world states – always based on the object terminology.

## 3.3 Example of an Action Concept with Semantics

We consider as a general example the generic action 'change-feature-value':

```
CHANGE-FEATURE-VALUE-ACTION
is-a           a    action
parameter1     c    object-concept        C
parameter2     d    value-concept         D
parameter3     f    feature               f:C→D
precondition   ∃x:  D(x) ∧ c.f = x        α_pre
effect         c.f = d                    α_post
```

Fig. 1. Example of a generic action concept for changing a feature value.

This action has three parameters or variables, which are described by their types or object concepts, for example C, and an associated constant or individual which refers to the value of that parameter for an instantiation of that action, e.g. the new feature-value $d \in D$.

This action concept specifies a set of worlds W1 in which the precondition states that the respective object has to have the relevant feature. This is more a terminological constraint than a constraint related to concrete world states as used in STRIPS-like action specifications. Thus, the action is applicable to all objects of a concept category which have the respective feature, filled by an arbitrary value x, and this is so far the only constraint on worlds in W1.

The generic effect formula of the action describes also a type constraint which states that the concept category of the feature value is of the type specified in parameter2, i.e. the feature-value-concept. Altogether, this means that W1 is constrained by the typing of parameter1 including the existence of an appropriate feature at the object-concept of parameter1, and that W2 is constrained through a typing of the respective feature-values of the object-concept as specified by parameter2. Thus, on the terminological level, the set of worlds (or taxonomies) is with respect to the action definition and the parameter objects involved, restricted through these typing constraints.

### 3.4     Formalizing the Subsumption Relation for Action Concepts

We now define the subsumption relation for action concepts $a$, $a'$ via a subsumption relation between the corresponding world sets described by precondition and effect formulae

$$a' \text{ specializes } a \ (a \text{ subsumes } a') :\Leftrightarrow W_{a',pre} \subseteq W_{a,pre} \text{ or } W_{a',post} \subseteq W_{a,post}$$

where $W_{a,pre}$ denotes the set of worlds specified through the precondition formula of $a$ and $W_{a,post}$ denotes the set of worlds specified by the effect formula of action $a$ (equivalent for $a'$).

Since the notion and interpretation of world states used above is equivalent to the notion of interpretation of the corresponding First-Order Predicate Logic (FOPL) formulae, we can formulate a definition of the subsumption relation for world states described by formulae as above, and subsequently define the subsumption relation for action concepts, based on the well-known equivalence of logical consequence and formal inference of formulae in FOPL. In order to achieve this correspondence, we relate the FOPL formulae to the terminology or taxonomical knowledge base under consideration, by constraining the set of predicate symbols to roles and the set of function symbols to features described in the knowledge base, and demand that these constructs are used in coherence with the terminology.

Let $\alpha$, $\alpha'$ be FOPL formulae adhering to a given taxonomical knowledge base, and let $\alpha$, $\alpha'$ describe preconditions (or effects) of action concepts a and a', respectively. $W_\alpha$, $W_{\alpha'}$ is the set of possible interpretations of $\alpha$, $\alpha'$ based on the terminology. We define the specialization/subsumption relation for action concepts:

$$\alpha' \text{ specializes } \alpha \ (\alpha \text{ subsumes } \alpha') :\Leftrightarrow W_{\alpha'} \subseteq W_\alpha$$

This is equivalent to

$$\alpha' \text{ specializes } \alpha \ (\alpha \text{ subsumes } \alpha') \Leftrightarrow \Phi_{KB} \cup \alpha' \models \Phi_{KB} \cup \alpha$$

where $\Phi_{KB}$ is the set of formulae describing the object-part of the knowledge base KB, since the worlds $W_\alpha$ and $W_{\alpha'}$ are defined as possible interpretations of the formulae $\alpha$ and $\alpha'$, given the taxonomical knowledge base KB.

Using the correspondence of logical consequence and formal inference

$$\alpha' \models \alpha \Leftrightarrow \alpha' \vdash \alpha$$

we derive the following equivalences, relating the subsumption relation for action concepts $a$ and $a'$ to the notions of logical consequence and formal inference between the two formulae $\alpha$ and $\alpha'$:

$$a' \text{ specializes } a \quad (a \text{ subsumes } a')$$

$$\Leftrightarrow [\Phi_{KB} \cup a' \models \Phi_{KB} \cup a]$$

$$\Leftrightarrow [\Phi_{KB} \cup a' \vdash \Phi_{KB} \cup a]$$

This leads to a general notion of the specialization of FOPL formulae, which are grounded in a terminological, taxonomic knowledge base. For object concept definitions and their extensional semantics, this does not yield anything new and is consistent with the standard definition of subsumption. For action concepts, this yields a new way of dealing with the subsumption/ specialization relation, based on the definition of an extensional semantics of action concepts as the set of world states specified through precondition and effect formulae, in accordance with the object-concept taxonomy.

### 3.5    Example of Specializing and Instantiating an Action Concept

We can now define and interpret specializations of action concepts. As an example, we modify the general action for changing the value of a feature as shown in figure 1 above. We can specialize this general action, for example by specifying the feature to be 'colour'. Since the colour-feature function maps 'coloured-things' to 'colour-concept', the sets of possible fillers for parameter1 and parameter2 are constrained to sub-concepts of object-concept and value-concept, respectively :

```
CHANGE-COLOUR
is-a            action
parameter1      c    coloured-thing
parameter2      d    colour-concept
parameter3      f    colour
precondition    ∃x: colour-concept(x) ∧ c.colour = x
effect          c.colour = d
```

Fig. 2. Action concept 'change-colour' derived from 'change-feature-value'

An instantiation of the generic action 'change-colour' is shown in figure 3.

```
CHANGE-COLOUR#1
instance-of    change-colour
parameter1     wall#1    instance-name
parameter2     pink      new value
parameter3     colour    as inherited
precondition   True      based on evaluation of inherited formula
effect         wall#1.colour = pink    substituting parameters with
                                       concrete instances and values
```

Fig. 3. Concrete action as instance of the generic action 'change-colour'

With this action, we have coloured wall#1 in pink, i.e. the new state of the world will contain the instance wall#1 of 'wall' with the value 'pink' of its colour-feature.

## 4    Resumee and Outlook

We presented a framework for describing action concepts in taxonomical knowledge bases with a focus on defining the semantics and a subsumption relation in parallel to the respective notions for object concepts. The basis of this approach is the view of actions as defining transformations of world states, and an anchoring of action descriptions in the object concept part of the taxonomical knowledge base.

The formal framework outlined here is currently implemented as a knowledge representation and knowledge base design system for object and action definitions. In the near future, the system will be integrated with a planning system.

# References

1.  Artale A. and E. Franconi, A Temporal Description Logic for Reasoning about Actions and Plans, *Journal of Artificial Intelligence Research,* 9,pp. 463–506, 1998
2.  Artale A. and E. Franconi, A Computational Account for a Description Logic of Time and Action, *Proceedings of the Fourth International Conference on Principles of Knowledge Representation and Reasoning,* pp. 3–14, Bonn, Germany, 1994
3.  Artale A. and E. Franconi, Time, Actions, and Plans Representation in a Description Logic, *International Journal of Intelligent Systems,* 1995
4.  Artale A. and E. Franconi, Hierarchical Plans in a Description Logic of Time and Action,
5.  Bettini, C. A Formalization of Interval-Based temporal Subsumption in First-Order Logic, In: *Lecture Notes in Artificial Intelligence,* LNAI-810, Springer, 1994
6.  Bettini, C. Time Dependent Concepts: Representation and Reasoning Using Temporal Description Logics, *Data and Knowledge Engineering,* 22(1), pp.1–38, 1997
7.  Brachman, R.J. and J.G. Schmolze, An Overview of the KL-ONE Knowledge Representation System. *Cognitive Science* 9(2):171–216, 1985. Also *Fairchild Technical Report No 655,* 1984
8.  Devanbu, P. T. and D. J. Litman, Taxonomic Plan Reasoning, *Artificial Intelligence,* 84, pp. 1–35, 1996
9.  Heinsohn, J., D. Kudenko, B. Nebel, and H.-J. Profitlich, *RAT: Representation of Actions Using Terminological Logics,* DFKI Technical Report, 1992
10. Kemke, C. Die Darstellung von Aktionen in Vererbungshierarchien (The Representation of Actions in Inheritance Hierarchies). In: Hoeppner (ed.), *GWAI-88, Proceedings of the German Workshop on Artificial Intelligence,* Springer, 1988
11. Kemke, C. Representation of Domain Knowledge in an Intelligent Help System. In *Proceedings of the Second IFP Conference on Human-Computer Interaction INTER-ACT'87,* pp. 215–200, Stuttgart, FRG, 1987
12. Kemke, C. What Do You Know about Mail? Knowledge Representation in the SINIX Consultant. *Artificial Intelligence Review,* **14**: 253–275, Kluwer Academic Publishers, 2000. Reprinted in Stephen J. Hegner, Paul McKevitt, Peter Norvig, Robert Wilensky (eds.): *Intelligent Help Systems for UNIX.* Kluwer Academic Publishers, Boston, USA & Dordrecht, The Netherlands, 2000
13. Kemke, C. *About the Ontology of Actions.* Technical Report MCCS-01-328, Computing Research Laboratory, New Mexico State University, 2001
14. Lifschitz, V. On the Semantics of STRIPS, In: *The 1986 Workshop on Reasoning about Actions and Plans,* pp.1–10, Morgan Kaufmann, 1987
15. Patel-Schneider, P. F., B. Owsnicki-Klewe, A. Kobsa, N. Guarino, R. MacGregor, W. S. Mark, D. L. McGuiness, B. Nebel, A. Schmiedel, and J. Yen, Term Subsumption Languages in Knowledge Representation, *AI Magazine,* 11(2): 16–23, 1990
16. Liebig, T. and D. Roesner, Action Hierarchies in Description Logics, Workshop on Description Logics, 1995.
17. Weida R. and D, Litman, Terminological Reasoning with Constraint Networks and an Application to Plan Recognition, *Proceedings of the Third International Conference on Principles of Knowledge Representation and Reasoning,* pp. 282–293, Cambridge, MA, 1992
18. Weida R. and D, Litman, Subsumption and Recognition of Heterogeneous Constraint Networks, *Proceedings of CAIA-94,* 1994

# An Efficient Algorithm for Computing Core Attributes in Database Systems

Jianchao Han[1], Xiaohua Hu[2], and T.Y. Lin[3]

[1] Dept. of Computer Science, California State University Dominguez Hills
1000 E. Victoria St., Carson, CA 90747, USA    jhan@csudh.edu
[2] College of Information Science and Technology, Drexel University
3141 Chestnut St., Philadelphia, PA 19104, USA    thu@cis.drexell.edu
[3] Dept. of Computer Science, San Jose State University
One Washington Square, San Jose, CA 94403, USA    tylin@cs.sjsu.edu

**Abstract.** A new approach to computing core attributes in rough set theory is proposed based on relational database systems. Especially, the fundamental operators of relational algebra are used to define the necessary and sufficient conditions that an attribute is a core attribute under the condition of the data table being consistent. Furthermore, inconsistent data table can be easily checked out and noise data can be efficiently eliminated. With this approach, we present an efficient and scalable algorithm for computing core attributes.

## 1 Introduction

Rough sets theory has been widely applied in different real applications such as machine learning, data mining and knowledge discovery, expert systems, etc. [4,5]. It provides a powerful tool for data analysis and data exploration from imprecise and ambiguous data. Many rough sets models have been developed in the rough set community. Some of them have been applied in the industrial data mining projects such as stock market prediction, patient symptom diagnosis, telecommunication churner prediction, and financial bank customer attrition analysis to solve challenging business problems. These rough set models focus on extending the original model proposed by Pawlak [6] and attempt to deal with its limitations, but haven't paid much attention on the efficiency of the model implementation, like the core and reduct generation.

Based on our own experience of applying rough set models in data mining applications, we found that one of the strong drawbacks of existing rough set models is the inefficiency and unscalability of their implementations to compute the core and reduct and identify the dispensable attributes, which limits their suitability in data mining applications with large data sets. Most existing rough set methods do not integrate with the efficient and high performance relational database set operations, while some authors have proposed ideas to do data reduction using relational database system techniques [2,3]. In this paper, we propose a new approach to efficiently find the core attributes by means of relational database set-oriented operations. We prove that our approach is equivalent to the traditional rough set model, but much more efficient and scalable.

N. Zhong et al. (Eds.): ISMIS 2003, LNAI 2871, pp. 663–667, 2003.
© Springer-Verlag Berlin Heidelberg 2003

## 2   Preliminary

An *information system IS* is usually defined as $IS = < U, C, D, \{V_a\}_{a \in C \cup D}, f >$, where $U = \{u_1, u_2, ...u_n\}$ is a non-empty set of tuples, called data set or data table, $C$ is a non-empty set of condition attributes, and $D$ is a non-empty set of decision attributes and $C \cap D = \emptyset$. $V_a$ is the domain of attribute "$a$" with at least two elements. $f$ is a function: $U \times (C \cup D) \to V = \bigcup_{a \in C \cup D} V_a$, which maps each pair of tuple and attribute to an attribute value.

Two examples with the same attribute values are indiscernible. The *indiscernibility relation*, denoted $IND$, is an equivalent relation on $U$. The ordered pair $< U, IND >$ is called an *approximation space*. It partitions $U$ into *equivalent classes*, each of which is labelled by a *description*, and called an *elementary set*. Any finite union of elementary set is called a *definable* set in $< U, IND >$.

Let $[D] = \{D_1, D_2, \ldots, D_k\}$ be the set of elementary sets based on the decision attributes set $D$. Assume $A$ is a subset of condition attributes, $A \subseteq C$, and $[A] = \{A_1, A_2, \ldots, A_h\}$ is the set of elementary sets based on $A$.

**Definition 1.** $\forall D_j \in [D], 1 \leq j \leq k$, the lower approximation of $D_j$ based on $A$, denoted $Lower_A(D_j)$, is defined as $Lower_A(D_j) = \bigcup\{A_i | A_i \subseteq D_j, i = 1, 2, \ldots, h\}$. All tuples in $Lower_A(D_j)$ can be certainly classified to $D_j$. The lower approximation of $[D]$, denoted $Lower_A([D])$, is defined as $Lower_A([D]) = \bigcup_{j=1}^{k} Lower_A(D_j)$. All tuples in $Lower_A([D])$ can be certainly classified.

Similarly, $\forall D_j \in [D], 1 \leq j \leq k$, the upper approximation of $D_j$ based on $A$, denoted $Upper_A(D_j)$, is defined as $Upper_A(D_j) = \bigcup\{A_i | A_i \cap D_j \neq \emptyset, i = 1, 2, \ldots, h\}$. All tuples in $Upper_A(D_j)$ can be probably classified to $D_j$. The upper approximation of $[D]$, denoted $Upper_A([D])$, is defined as $Upper_A([D]) = \bigcup_{j=1}^{k} Upper_A(D_j)$. All tuples in $Upper_A([D])$ can be probably classified.

The boundary of $[D]$ based on $A$, denoted $Boundary_A([D])$, is defined as $Boundary_A([D]) = Upper_A([D]) - Lower_A([D])$. All tuples in $Boundary_A([D])$ can not be classified in terms of $A$ and $D$. □

Rough sets theory can tell us whether the information for classification of tuples is consistent based on the data table itself. If the data is inconsistent, it suggests more information about the tuples need to be collected in order to build a good classification model for all tuples. If there exist a pair of tuples in $U$ such that they have the same condition attributes values but different decision attributes values, $U$ is said to contain *contradictory* tuples.

**Definition 2.** $U$ is consistent if no contradictory pair of tuples exist in $U$, that is, $\forall t_1, t_2 \in U$, if $t_1[D] \neq t_2[D]$, then $t_1[C] \neq t_2[C]$. □

Usually, the existence of contradictory tuples indicates that the information contained in $U$ is not enough to classify all tuples, and there must be some contradictory tuples contained in the boundary area. On the other hand, if the data is consistent, rough sets theory can also determine whether there are more than sufficient or redundant information in the data set and provide approaches to finding the minimum data needed for classification model. This property of rough sets theory is very important for applications where domain knowledge is limited or data collection is expensive/laborious, because it ensures that the data collected is right (not more or less) to build a good classification model without sacrificing the accuracy of the classification model or wasting time and effort to gather extra information. Furthermore, rough sets theory classifies all the attributes into three categories: core attributes, reduct attributes, and dispensable attributes. Core attributes have the essential information to make correct classification for the data set and should be retained in the data set; dispensable attributes are the redundant ones in the data set and should be eliminated without loss of any useful information; while reduct attributes are in the middle between. A reduct attribute may or may not be essential.

**Definition 3.** *A condition attribute $a \in C$ is a dispensable attribute w.r.t $D$ if $Lower_C([D]) = Lower_{C-\{a\}}([D])$. Otherwise, $a \in C$ is called a core attribute w.r.t $D$.*  □

## 3   Computing Core Attributes Using Relational Algebra

One of limitations that the rough sets theory bears is the inefficiency in computation of core attributes and reducts, which limits its suitability for large data sets. In order to find core attributes, dispensable attributes, or reducts, rough set model needs to construct all the equivalent classes based on the values of condition and decision attributes of all tuples in the data set. It is very time-consuming and infeasible, since most data mining applications require efficient algorithms to deal with scalable data sets.

We propose a computation approach based on the relational algebra to find the core attributes of the given attribute sets in this section and present its implementation in relational database systems. For the definitions of set-oriented operations like Count (Card), Selection ($\sigma$) Projection ($\Pi$), Rename ($\rho$) and $\Theta$-Join ($\Theta$) utilized in relational database systems, one can refer [1]. Our approach is based on the following facts:

**Fact 1:** The data table $U$ is consistent if and only if $U = Lower_C([D]) = Upper_C([D])$ and $Boundary_C([D]) = \emptyset$.  □

**Fact 2:** Let $A \subset B \subseteq C$. Assume $[A] = \{A_1, A_2, \ldots, A_m\}$ and $[B] = \{B_1, B_2, \ldots, B_n\}$ are the set of equivalent classes induced by $A$ and $B$, respectively, then $\forall\ B_i \in [B], i = 1, 2, \ldots, n$, and $A_j \in [A], j = 1, 2, \ldots, m$, either $B_i \cap A_j = \emptyset$ or $B_i \subseteq A_j$. $[B]$ is said a refinement of $[A]$.  □

With these facts, one can easily verify the following two propositions, which together lead to Theorem 1.

**Proposition 1.** *(1.) $\forall\ a \in C$, if $Lower_C([D]) \neq Lower_{C-\{a\}}([D])$, then $Card(\Pi_{C-\{a\}}(U)) < Card(\Pi_{C-\{a\}+D}(U))$.*  □

**Proposition 2.** *(2.) $\forall\ a \in C$, if $Card(\Pi_{C-\{a\}}(U)) < Card(\Pi_{C-\{a\}+D}(U))$ and $U$ is consistent, then $Lower_C([D]) \neq Lower_{C-\{a\}}([D])$.*  □

**Theorem 1.** *(1.) If the data table $U$ is consistent, then $a$ is a core attribute in $C$ w.r.t $D$ if and only if $Card(\Pi_{C-\{a\}}(U)) < Card(\Pi_{C-\{a\}+D}(U))$.*

*If the data table $U$ is consistent, then $a$ is a dispensable attribute in $C$ w.r.t $D$ if and only if $Card(\Pi_{C-\{a\}+D}(U)) = Card(\Pi_{C-\{a\}}(U))$.*    □

Thus, to check whether an attribute $a \in C$ is a core attribute, we only need to take two projections of the table: one on the attribute set $C - \{a\} + D$, and the other on $C - \{a\}$, and then count the distinct number of tuples in these projections. If the two projection tables have the same cardinality, then no information is lost in removing the dispensable attribute $a$. Otherwise, $a$ is a core attribute.

Theorem 1 proposes the necessary and sufficient condition of a condition attribute being a core attribute if the data table is consistent. In real applications, however, the data table may not be consistent. If this is the case, either more information needs to be collected or contradictory tuples should be eliminated. Therefore, before the data table is actually used, the consistency of the data table should be investigated. In terms of relational databases operations, we have the following theorems.

**Theorem 2.** *(2.) If $Card(\Pi_C(U)) < Card(\Pi_{C+D}(U))$, then $U$ is inconsistent.*    □

**Theorem 3.** *(3.) $\Pi_{C+D}(U\Theta_{U.C=V.C \wedge U.D \neq V.D}(\rho_U(V))) = Boundary_C([D])$.*    □

Theorem 2 suggests a simple method to check whether a data table is consistent, while Theorem 3 suggests an approach to eliminating contradictory tuples from the data table.

## 4    An Efficient Algorithm for Computing Core Attributes

We propose a new algorithm based on the theorems in the previous section to find all core attributes of a data table. The data table, however, may contain contradictory tuples which can not be classified. Thus, the contradictory tuples should be first eliminated from the table. Here we assume the contradictory tuples are noisy data, otherwise more attributes and values for tuples should be collected further to ensure the data table is consistent.

**Algorithm** *FindCore*: Find the set of core attributes of a decision table
**Input**: A decision table $T(C, D)$
**Output**: $Core$ – the set of core attributes of $T$
    1.     **If** $Card(\Pi_C(U)) < Card(\Pi_{C+D}(U))$
    2.       **Then** $U \leftarrow U - \Pi_{C+D}(U\Theta_{U.C=V.C \wedge U.D \neq V.D}(\rho_V(U)))$
    3.     Set $Core \Leftarrow \emptyset$
    4.     **For** each attribute $a \in C$
    5.       **If** $Card(\Pi_{C-\{a\}}(U)) < Card(\Pi_{C-\{a\}+D}(U))$
    6.         **Then** $Core \Leftarrow Core \cup \{a\}$
    7.     Return $Core$

Theorems 2 and 3 ensure that all contradictory tuples and only those tuples are eliminated in Lines 1 and 2. Lines 4 through 6 check all condition attributes one by one to see if they are core attributes, and keep core attributes in *Core*. Theorem 1 ensures that the output of the algorithm *FindCore* contains all core attributes and only those attributes. Thus, we have the following theorems.

**Theorem 4.** *(4.) The output of FindCore contains and only contains all core attributes of the given condition attributes w.r.t. the decision attributes.*     □

**Theorem 5.** *(5.) If the database system implements the $\Theta$-Join using Hash table, then the algorithm FindCore can be implemented in $O(mn)$ time, where m is the number of condition attributes and n is the number of tuples (rows).*  □

## 5   Concluding Remarks

Most existing rough set models do not integrate with database systems to generate core, reduct, and rule induction, which limits their applicability for large data set in data mining applications.

In order to take advantage of efficient data structures and algorithms developed and implemented in relational database systems, we propose a new approach for rough set theory using relational algebra operations in this paper. With this approach, we present an algorithm to eliminating contradictory tuples, if any, and computing core attributes. Since these relational algebra operations have been efficiently implemented in most widely-used relational database systems, the algorithm presented can be extensively applied to relational database systems and adapted to a wide range of real-life applications. Another pros of this algorithm is its scalability, because existing relational database systems have demonstrated that their implementations of relational algebra operations are suitable to process very large data sets.

Our future work will focus on the applications of this approach to reduct generation, features selection, and rule induction for knowledge discovery in very large data sets.

## References

1. Garcia-Molina, H., Ullman, J. D., Widom, J., Database System Implementation, Prentice Hall, 2000.
2. Hu, X., Lin, T. Y., Han, J., A New Rough Sets Model Based on Database Systems, RSFDGrC 2003, 114–121.
3. Kumar, A., A New Technique for Data Reduction in A Database System for Knowledge Discovery Applications, J. of Intelligent Systems, 10(3), 2002.
4. Lin, T.Y and Cercone, N., Applications of Rough Sets Theory and Data Mining, Kluwer Academic Publishers, 1997.
5. Lin, T. Y., Yao, Y. Y., and Zadeh, L. A., Data Mining, Rough Sets and Granular Computing, Physical-Verlag, 2002.
6. Pawlak, Z., Rough Sets, International Journal of Information and Computer Science, 11(5), 1982.

# Similarity Graphs

Rasmus Knappe, Henrik Bulskov, and Troels Andreasen

Department of Computer Science,
Roskilde University,
P.O. Box 260, DK-4000 Roskilde, Denmark
{knappe,bulskov,troels}@ruc.dk

**Abstract.** The focus of this paper is approaches to measuring similarity for application in content-based query evaluation. Rather than only comparing at the level of words, the issue here is conceptual resemblance. The basis is a knowledge base defining major concepts of the domain and may include taxonomic and ontological domain knowledge. The challenge for support of queries in this context is an evaluation principle that on the one hand respects the formation rules for concepts in the concept language and on the other is sufficiently efficient to candidate as a realistic principle for query evaluation. We present and discuss principles where efficiency is obtained by reducing the matching problem - which basically is a matter of conceptual reasoning - to numerical similarity computation.

## 1 Introduction

The objective of this paper is to devise a similarity measure that utilizes knowledge from a domain-specific ontology to obtain better answers on a semantical level, thus comparing concepts rather than terms. Better answers are primarily better ranked information base objects which in turn is a matter of better means for computing the similarity between a query and an object from the information base. The basis is an ontology that defines and relates concepts and a concept language ONTOLOG [6] for expressing the semantics of queries and objects in the information base.

The approach presented in the paper is a refinement of [5] on similarity measures based on the notion of shared nodes. We aim to devise a similarity measure that can capture the aspect exemplified by the intuition that for example the similarity between concepts "*grey cat*" and "*grey dog*" is intuitively higher than the similarity between "*grey cat*" and "*yellow bird*", because the former share the same color.

This is sought done by introducing the notion of similarity graphs, as the subset of the ontology covering the concepts being compared, thereby capturing semantics without the loss of scalability.

N. Zhong et al. (Eds.): ISMIS 2003, LNAI 2871, pp. 668–672, 2003.

## 2    Similarity Graphs

The basis for the ontology is a simple taxonomic concept inclusion relation $\text{ISA}_{\text{KB}}$ which is considered as domain or world knowledge and may for instance express the view of a domain expert. The concepts in the ontology can be divided into two sets; atomic and compound concepts. The latter are formed by attribution of atomic concepts with a relation to form a compound concept. Take as an example the compound concept "black cat", denoted $cat[\text{CHR}: black]$ in the concept language ONTOLOG.

The general idea now is a similarity measure between concepts $c_1$ and $c_2$ based upon the set of all nodes reachable from both concepts in the similarity graph, representing the part of the ontology covering $c_1$ and $c_2$. These shared nodes reflect the similarity between concepts, both in terms of subsuming concepts and similar attribution.

Consider Figure 1. The solid edges are $\text{ISA}_{\text{KB}}$ references and the broken are references by other semantic relations - in this example only CHR. Each compound concept has broken edges to its attributed concepts.

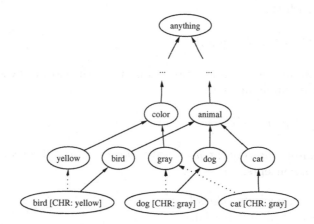

**Fig. 1.** An ontology covering colored pets.

If we consider only the $\text{ISA}_{\text{KB}}$-edges then there is no difference in similarity between any pair of $dog[\text{CHR}: grey]$, $cat[\text{CHR}: grey]$ and $bird[\text{CHR}: yellow]$ due to the fact that they are all specializations (sub-classes) of pet.

If we on the other hand also consider broken edges, then we can add the aspect of shared attribution to the computation of similarity. In the case of Figure 1 we can, by including the broken edges, capture the intuitive difference in similarity between two grey pets compared to the similarity between a grey and a yellow pet. This difference is visualized by the existence of a path, that includes the shared concept, between the two concepts sharing attribution.

One possible way to include the attributes of compound concepts in the basis for a similarity graph is to perform a term-decomposition of the concepts. To further include the semantics, given by the inclusion relation of the ontology we can expand every atomic concept in the decomposition with all nodes upwards reachable in the ontology.

The term-decomposition is defined as the set of all terms appearing in $c$. The present term-decomposition differs from earlier definitions [5] in that it does not generate all generative subsuming concepts. We only need to maintain the compound nestings and the atomic concepts of a given concept when decomposing. For instance, we do not need to include $noise[\text{CBY}: dog]$ in the decomposition of $noise[\text{CBY}: dog[\text{CHR}: black]]$, because this concept will the included in any specialization of $noise[\text{CBY}: dog]$.

If we for a concept $c = c_0[r_1 : c_1, \dots, r_n : c_n]$, where $c_0$ is the atomic concept attributed in $c$ and $c_1, \dots, c_n$ are the attributes (which are atomic concepts or further compound concepts), define:

$$subterm(c) = \{c_0, c_1, \dots, c_n\}$$

and straightforwardly extend $subterm$ to be defined on a set of concepts $C = \{c_1, \dots, c_n\}$, such that

$$subterm(C) = \cup_i subterm(c_i)$$

then we can obtain the term-decomposition of $c$ as the closure by subterm, that is, by repeatedly applying $subterm$:

$$\tau(c) = \{c\} \cup \{x | x \in subterm^k(c) \text{ for some k}\}$$

As an example the concept $noise[\text{CBY}: dog[\text{CHR}: black]]$ decomposes to the following set of concepts:

$$\tau(noise[\text{CBY}: dog[\text{CHR}: black]]) =$$
$$\{noise[\text{CBY}: dog[\text{CHR}: black]],$$
$$noise, dog[\text{CHR}: black], dog, black\}$$

The upwards expansion, i.e. nodes upwards reachable in the ontology, $\omega(C)$ of a set of concepts $C$ is then the transitive closure of $C$ with respect to $\text{ISA}_{\text{KB}}$.

$$\omega(C) = \{x | x \in C \vee y \in C, y \text{ ISA } x\}$$

where ISA is the transitive closure of $\text{ISA}_{\text{KB}}$. This expansion thus only adds atoms to C.

Now a similarity graph $\gamma(C)$ is defined for a set of concepts $C = \{c_1, \dots, c_n\}$ as the graph that appears when decomposing $C$ and connecting the resulting set of terms with edges corresponding to the $\text{ISA}_{\text{KB}}$ relation and to the semantic relations used in attribution of elements in C. We define the triple $(x, y, r)$ as the edge of type $r$ from concept $x$ to concept $y$.

$$\gamma(C) = \cup \begin{array}{l} \{(x, y, \text{ISA}) | x, y \in \omega(\tau(C)), x \text{ ISA}_{\text{KB}} \ y\} \\ \{(x, y, r) | x, y \in \omega(\tau(C)), r \in \mathbf{R}, x[r : y] \in \tau(C)\} \end{array}$$

Fig. 2 shows an example of a similarity graph covering two terms $cat[\text{CHR}: black]$ and $poodle[\text{CHR}: black]$, capturing similar attributes and subsuming concepts.

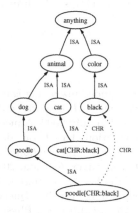

**Fig. 2.** An example of a similarity graph for the concepts *cat*[chr: *black*] and *poodle*[chr: *black*].

A similarity graph expresses the similarity between two concepts $c_1$ and $c_2$. We can therefore, by generalizing to every pair of concepts in an ontology, identify similar concepts $\{c_1, \dots, c_n\}$ to a given concept $c$. This set can be expressed as a fuzzy set where the membership grade for a given element $w_i/c_i$ is the similarity between $c$ and $c_i$.

## 3   Conclusion

The notion of measuring similarity based on the notion of similarity graphs, seems to indicate a usable theoretical foundation for design of similarity measures. The inclusion of the attribution of concepts, by means of shared nodes, in the calculation of similarity, gives a possible approach for a measure that captures more details and at the same time scale to large systems.

The purpose of similarity measures in connection with querying is of course to look for similar rather than for exactly matching values, that is, to introduce soft rather than crisp evaluation. As indicated through examples above one approach to introduce similar values is to expand crisp values into fuzzy sets including also similar values. Query evaluation in such an environment raises the need for aggregation principles that supports nested aggregation over fuzzy sets [7] as described in [1].

Expansion of this kind, applying similarity based on knowledge in the knowledge base, is a simplification replacing direct reasoning over the knowledge base during query evaluation. The graded similarity is the obvious means to make expansion a useful - by using simple threshold values for similarity the size of the answer can be fully controlled.

**Acknowledgments.** The work described in this paper is part of the Onto-Query[1][4] project supported by the Danish Technical Research Council and the Danish IT University.

## References

[1] Andreasen, T.: On knowledge-guided fuzzy aggregation. In *IPMU'2002, 9th International Conference on Information Processing and Management of Uncertainty in Knowledge-Based Systems*, 1–5 July 2002, Annecy, France

[2] Andreasen, T.: Query evaluation based on domain-specific ontologies. In *NAFIPS'2001, 20th IFSA / NAFIPS International Conference Fuzziness and Soft Computing*, pp. 1844–1849, Vancouver, Canada, 2001.

[3] Andreasen, T., Nilsson, J. Fischer & Thomsen, H. Erdman: Ontology-based Querying, in Larsen, H.L. *et al.* (eds.) Flexible Query Answering Systems, *Flexible Query Answering Systems, Recent Advances*, Physica-Verlag, Springer, 2000. pp. 15–26.

[4] Andreasen, T., Jensen, P. Anker, Nilsson, J. Fischer, Paggio, P., Pedersen, B. Sandford & Thomsen, H. Erdman: Ontological Extraction of Content for Text Querying, to appear in NLDB 2002, Stockholm, Sweden, 2002.

[5] Knappe, R., Bulskov, H. and Andreasen, T.: On Similarity Measures for Content-based Querying, LNAI, to appear in International Fuzzy Sysytems Association, World Congress, June 29-July 2, Istanbul, Turkey, 2003, Proceedings

[6] Nilsson, J. Fischer: A Logico-algebraic Framework for Ontologies ONTOLOG, in Jensen, P. Anker & Skadhauge, P. (eds.): Proceedings of the First International OntoQuery Workshop *Ontology-based interpretation of NP's*. Department of Business Communication and Information Science, University of Southern Denmark, Kolding, 2001.

[7] Yager, R.R.: A hierarchical document retrieval language, in Information Retrieval vol 3, Issue 4, Kluwer Academic Publishers pp. 357–377, 2000.

---

[1] The project has the following participating institutions: Centre for Language Technology, The Technical University of Denmark, Copenhagen Business School, Roskilde University, and the University of Southern Denmark.

# Image-Based Flame Control of a Premixed Gas Burner Using Fuzzy Logics

Apichart Tuntrakoon and Suwat Kuntanapreeda

Research and Development Center for Intelligent Systems
Faculty of Engineering
King Mongkut's Institute of Technology North Bangkok
1518 Pibulsongkram Rd., Bangkok, THAILAND 10800
suwat@kmitnb.ac.th

**Abstract.** This paper presents an application of fuzzy logics for controlling the combustion flame of a premixed gas burner. The control objective is to achieve a good characteristic of combustion flame by visualizing the colors of the flame while maintaining its size as desired. The fuzzy logic controller adjusts the flow rates of gas and air independently through two stepper-driven needle valves. A CCD camera with an image-processing/frame-grabber card is utilized as a sensor unit. The image captured by the CCD camera is processed in real time to extract the color and size information of the flame. This information is then used as a feedback signal for the controller. The study results show that the fuzzy logic controller is able to automatically regulate the flame to achieve the objective as desired.

## 1 Introduction

In recent year, there has been a growing interest in image-based analysis and feedback control applied to engineering problems. Visual servo control of robotic manipulators is a well-known example. There is also a number of research publications indicating good potential applications of this image-based analysis and control in combustion processes. The references [1, 2] provide excellent overviews of this subject. Iion et al. [3] conducted experiments using image processing techniques to study dynamics behavior of flames and timewise variation of high-luminous region in flames. One of their results indicated that the apparent flow velocity of the high-luminous region is approximately constant and is independent of the fuel velocity. Tao and Burkhardt [4] and Oest and Burkhardt [5] presented implementations of a vision-guided flame control system using a fuzzy logic plus neural network technique and an iterative minimization method, respectively. The experimental results of both works showed that the designed controllers performed satisfactorily.

This paper presents an experimental study of utilizing fuzzy logics as an image feedback controller for regulating the combustion flame of a premixed gas burner. The control objective is to achieve a good characteristic of combustion flame by visualizing the colors of the flame while maintaining its size as desired.

N. Zhong et al. (Eds.): ISMIS 2003, LNAI 2871, pp. 673–677, 2003.
© Springer-Verlag Berlin Heidelberg 2003

## 2 Experimental System

As shown in Fig. 1, the experimental system employed in this work comprises (1) a premixed gas burner (2) a pc-computer with an image-processing/frame grabber card, (3) a camera, and (4) two stepper-driven needle valves for adjusting the flow rates of gas and air. The burner used here is known as a Meker burner, which is very similar to the well-known Bunsen burner. In operating the burner is installed in a chamber as shown in Fig. 2. The main processor of the image-processing/frame grabber card is TMS320C81-MVP (Multimedia Video Processor) which consists of four DSPs (Digital Signal Processors) running in parallel. The camera is a CCD (Charge Coupled Device) mono camera. The gas used as the fuel is liquid petroleum gas (LPG). The air comes directly from an air compressor.

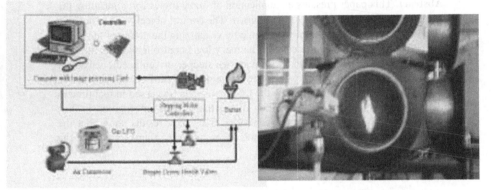

**Fig. 1.** Experimental System          **Fig. 2.** Burner in operating

## 3 Flame Analysis

In this paper we assume that the structure of the combustion flame consisting of two portions: blue and orange portions (see Fig. 3). Moreover, flame analysis is based only on the colors of the flame. Three main color components detected by the camera are black, orange, and blue. The black color is the color of the background while the orange and blue colors are of the flame. These two last colors that we are interested are related to the performance of the combustion process. In general a good combustion flame should have solely the blue. The orange dues to soot and indicates that the combustion process is lacking of air.

In this paper the images captured by the CCD camera is gray. Each pixel of the images then can be represented by an 8-bit word that has the value between 0 and 255. Here, we process the image to extract the amount of the blue and orange by two threshold processes and one XOR operation. An example of the processed results is shown in Fig. 4. Note that the numbers of white pixel of the bottom left and right pictures, which are 27.5 and 9.5, indicated the size of the orange and blue portions, respectively. These numbers are not the actual numbers of the white pixels, but they are some kind of the index that is equivalent to the size.

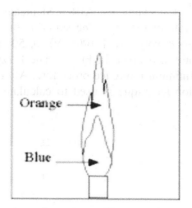
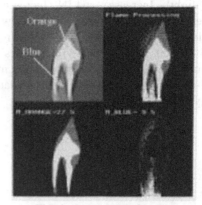

Fig. 3. Combustion flame structure        **Fig. 4.** Processed Images

## 4 Fuzzy Logic Controller

In this paper the control system consists of two fuzzy logics acting as a nonlinear controller. As shown in Fig. 5, the first fuzzy logic controls the flow rate of the air while the other controls the flow rate of the gas. The two inputs for both fuzzy logics are identical which are the size errors of the orange and the blue portions of the flame. Note that the sizes are obtained in real time from the image processing processes as mentioned before. Here, the desired size of the orange is set to zero since we want to minimize this portion.

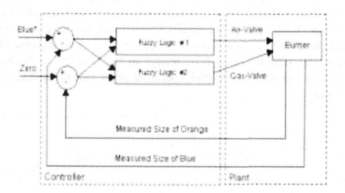

**Fig. 5.** Control block diagram

The membership functions of the fuzzy sets for the inputs are triangular functions with the finite supports as shown in Fig. 6. Their linguistic variables are defined as NL (Negative Large), NS (Negative Small), ZE (Zero), PS (Positive Small), and PL (Positive Large). Here, for example, BLUE = NL means the size of the blue portion of the flame is very small compared to the desired size. The outputs are fuzzy singletons with the variables DE (Decrease), SD (Slightly Decrease), ZE (Zero),

SI (Slightly Increase), and IN (Increase). For examples, AIR = SI means the controller should slightly increase the flow rate of the air. The supports of the fuzzy singleton for the air- and gas-valves, respectively, are {-100, -50, 0, 50, 100} and {-75, -40, 0, 40, 75}. The fuzzy rules are also given in Fig. 6. The fuzzy control commands are determined through the minimum inference procedure. After that, the well-known center average defuzzyfication technique is used to calculate the non-fuzzy control commands.

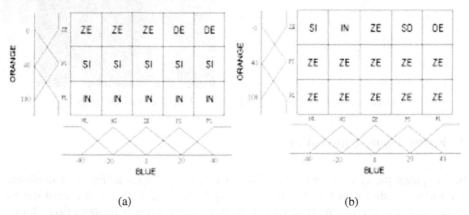

(a)                                             (b)

**Fig. 6.** Fuzzy input functions and rules: (a) for the air-valve (b) for the gas-valve

## 5   Results

Fig. 7 and 8 show examples of the control results. In Fig. 7 the flame initially started with very small size of both the blue and orange flames. The desired blue is set at the value of 25 (i.e., Blue* = 25). The results showed that the designed fuzzy logic controller is able to adjust the flow rates of the gas and the air to increase the size of the blue while maintaining the size of the orange to be minimum as desired. The time-history graph shows that the desired operating point can be automatically achieve within 13 seconds.

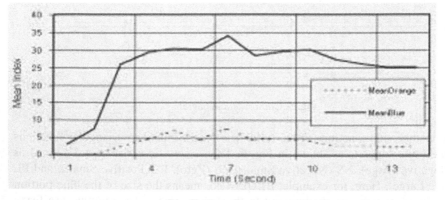

**Fig. 7.** Control responses: Case1

Fig. 8 presents the control results of the second case when the initial size of the blue flame was larger than the desired size which is set to equal 10. Similar to the first case, the designed controller was able to adjust the flow rate of the gas and the air to decrease the size of the blue portion correctly and to reduce the orange to the minimum value in the same time.

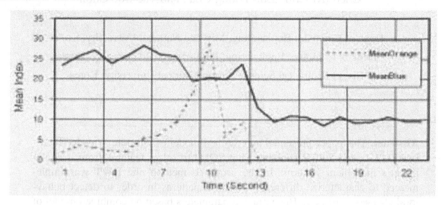

**Fig. 8.** Control responses: Case2

# 6 Conclusions

An experimental study of fuzzy logic control for a Meker burner has been presented in this paper. The control system consists of two fuzzy logics. The objective of the control is to achieve a good characteristic of combustion flame by visualizing the flame colors. The image of the flame captured by a CCD camera is processed in real time to extract the equivalent sizes of the blue and orange portions of the flame. These sizes are used to feedback to the designed fuzzy controller. The control results, in general, are satisfactory. The controller can regulate the flame to have the size of the blue portion of the flame as desired while minimizes the orange portion.

# References

1. H. Burkhardt, "Image Analysis and Control of Combusion Processes" The International Seminar on Imaging in Transport Processes, Athen, May 1992
2. N. Decquier and S. Candel, "Combustion Control and Sensors: a review", Progress in Energy and Combustion Science, 28, 2002
3. N. Iino, F. Tsuchino, S. Torii, and T. Yano, "Timewise Variation of Turbulent Jet Diffusion Flame Shape by Means of Image Processing" J. Flow Visualization and Image Processing, Vol. 5, 1998
4. W. Tao and H. Burkhardt, "Vision-Guided Flame Control using Fuzzy Logic and Neural Networks" The Third Meeting of European Concerted Action on Process Tomography (ECAPT), Oporto, Portugal, March 1994
5. L. Oest and and H. Burkhardt, "Application of a New Iterative Minimization Method to Vision-Guided Flame Control" The Fourth Meeting of European Concerted Action on Process Tomography (ECAPT), Bergen, Norway, April 1995

# Intelligent Pattern Recognition by Feature Selection through Combined Model of *DWT* and *ANN*

Cheol-Ki Kim[1], Eui-Young Cha[2], and Tae-Soo Chon[3]

[1]Dept. of Computer Engineering, Miryang National University, Korea
[2]Dept. of Computer Engineering, Pusan National University, Korea
[3]Div. of Biological Science, Pusan National University, Korea

**Abstract.** This paper presented a combined model of Discrete Wavelet Transform(DWT) and Self-Organizing Map(SOM) to select features from irregular insect's movement patterns. In the proposed method, the DWT was implemented to characterize different movement patterns in order to detect behavioral changes of insects. The extracted parameters based on combined model of DWT and SOM were subsequently provided to artificial neural networks to be trained to represent different patterns of the movement tracks before and after treatments of the insecticide. Finally, the proposed combined model of DWT and SOM was able to point out the occurrence of characteristic movement patterns, and could be a method for automatically detecting irregular patterns for nonlinear movements.

## 1 Introduction

In biological-related fields, ANNs have been implemented in data organization and classification of groups[1], patterning complex relationships between variables[2][3], and predicting population development[4]. Behavioral responses have been reported to be sensitive to sub-lethal exposures to various chemical pollutants[5]. [5] indicated that a behavioral bioassay could be more sensitive than other types of testing. In recent years, researches on the effects of sub-lethal levels of toxic substances have been rapidly accumulating for various taxa including crustacean's fish and insects. However, these studies are mostly based on observation of single or combinations of single behaviors with qualitative descriptions. Not many quantitative researches have been conducted on behavioral changes in spatial and temporal domain in response to treatments of toxic chemicals. The continuous observations of the movement tracks of small size insects have been separately initiated in the field of search behavior in chemical ecology[6]. In this paper, we utilize the feasibility of combined model of *DWT* and *ANN*s in classification of the movement data and attempted to elucidate spatial and temporal patterning of the movement tracks with less contraction of information in feature extraction.

N. Zhong et al. (Eds.): ISMIS 2003, LNAI 2871, pp. 678–683, 2003.

## 2  Proposed Methods

The specimens of Chironomus flaviplumus were collected from an urbanized stream. The stock populations were maintained in a plastic container under the light regime of Light Condition-10hours and Dark Condition. Cabofuran was applied at the concentration of 0.1 mg/l directly into an aquarium in insect resided.

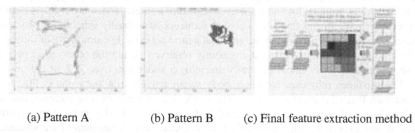

(a) Pattern A                (b) Pattern B        (c) Final feature extraction method

**Fig. 1.** Example of the movement tracks of *Chironomus flaviplumus* and feature extraction

During the observational period, individual insect's vertical position was observed at 0.25 second intervals using a CCD for four days (2 days before the treatment and 2 days after the treatment). Then, center of partial body movement was detected by difference image method and its two-dimensional location of was automatically recorded.

The back-propagation algorithm(BP) was used for training input and output pair in a supervised manner. Training proceeds on an iterative gradient algorithm designed to minimize the mean square error between the actual output and the desired output or the target value. After parameters charactering the movement track were selected through wavelet transform, they were trained by artificial neural networks. The value of activation function coefficients, $\lambda$, used in this study was 1.0, and the learning coefficient, which updates the weights in iterative calculation, was set to 0.01. The level of error tolerance was 1.0, and the threshold for determining the binary level for the activation function was 0.5. Network pruning was not required during the training process in this study. The movement tracks were investigated during 60-seconds in this study. For simplicity of training, we selected two most frequently observed patterns. Pattern A generally represented the active movement spanning a wider area of the observation cage. The specimen fully used its whole body, and swam actively in a linear phase, while briefly twitching to propel its advancement. In contrast, pattern B showed a higher degree of shaking with curve-linear movements. In the preparatory experiments, pattern A was observed with a relatively low frequency after the treatments, while pattern B increased after the treatments. Based on experience on behavior of Chironomus flaviplumus and suggestions in previous studies on the movement tracks[6], the following parameters were selected in 60 seconds duration as input for the wavelet analysis: number of backward movements, stop duration (total time of stops; sec), meander (total abstract angle changes divided by the total path length; radian/mm), angle acceleration (radian/sec$^2$) and maximum distance along short term segment (mm). The maximum distance was calculated as the maximum distance of five segments per window. In total 10 specimens were observed. Considering individual variations in the movement patterns, we selected 7 individuals with similar movement patterns. Four specimens were chosen for training, while the data sets for the rest three specimens were used for evaluation. Twenty-one observations in one-minute duration were selected for each pattern A and B, and the five parameters mentioned above were measured separately for input data to the network (5 nodes in the input layer), while binary information either for pattern A or pattern B, was used for the matching output (1 node in the output layer). For training, four nodes were assigned to a single hidden layer. It has been shown in preparatory experiments that sixty seconds sequence was usually suitable for characterizing the track's pattern for training with the artificial neural network. For simplicity of the modeling, we selected two typical pattern most frequently observed during the observation period. Fig. 1(a) shows an active movement generally spanning a wider area over 50% of the observation cage. The specimen fully used its whole body swam actively in a linear phase. Fig. 1(b) is in contrast with Pattern A in many aspects. The movements were in circular patterns, and showed a higher degree of shaking with the partial body movement. In the preparatory experiments, pattern A was observed with a relatively low frequency after treatments of carbofuran, while the frequency of pattern B increased.

In above paragraph, we referred five used feature parameters for training. In this section, we present a method to extract these five feature parameters. For these procedure, we used twelve feature parameter(4-directional movement, speed, acceleration, angle acceleration, number of backward movement, stop duration, stop number, maximum length, locomotory rate, turning rate, meander, maximum distance along short term segment).

To extract final feature parameters, we used a combined model of *DWT* and *SOFM*. Using *DWT* coefficients of twelve feature parameter, the transformed coefficients are clustered by *SOFM*. In the similar clusters, we finally select parameters corresponding to high energy distribution. Fig 1(c) shows the procedure of extracting feature parameters. Fig 2 shows flow-charts for implementing wavelets and artificial neural networks for pattern recognition of the movement tracks. From training (or evaluation) data, parameters mentioned above were obtained, and were subsequently given to *DWT* with basic function of Daubechies'4. The Approximation coefficients at level 3 are extracted, and feature coefficients are selected to the provided as input to *ANN*s. The *BP* was used in this paper. While the approximation coefficients are given as input to the network, the corresponding patterns are given as output in a binary format. Evaluation data are newly selected, and feature coefficients of the parameters are similarly obtained through *DWT*. The newly obtained coefficients are in turn recognized by *ANN*.

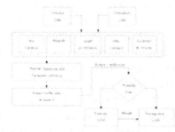

**Fig. 2.** Overall system flow-chart using wavelet transform and artificial neural network..

## 3  Results

The input data were effectively trained and the training rates appeared to be over 98%. New evaluation data sets for three specimens were sequentially given to the trained network as mentioned previously, and the network was capable of recognizing patterns A and B effectively. Fig. 4 shows the changes in representative behavioral patterns after the treatments of an insecticide.

Table 1 show results of average detection rates (percents) before and after the treatments of insecticides. The values shown in the table were obtained as follows : The number of detecting pattern A or pattern B in each one-minute data segment was counted through a period of 6060 seconds (approximately 100 minutes), and the total count was expressed in percents relative to the total number of one minute observations in the period of 6060 seconds.

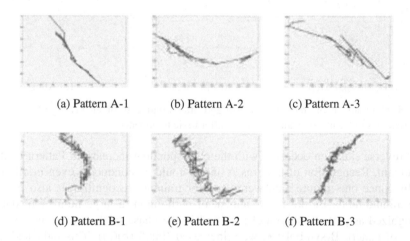

(a) Pattern A-1          (b) Pattern A-2          (c) Pattern A-3

(d) Pattern B-1          (e) Pattern B-2          (f) Pattern B-3

**Fig. 4.** Changes in representative behavioral patterns before and after toxic treatments.

**Table 1.** Comparison of recognition rates (percents) by the trained artificial neural networks for Pattern A and B in the movement tracks of *chironomids* treated with carbofuran.

|  | Specimens | Specimen 1 |  | Specimen 2 |  | Specimen 3 |  |
|---|---|---|---|---|---|---|---|
|  | Patterns | A | B | A | B | A | B |
| Before Treatment | Mean | 74.50 | 10.59 | 70.71 | 11.09 | 74.44 | 12.11 |
| | SD | 8.08 | 6.67 | 10.63 | 9.25 | 14.54 | 9.31 |
| After Treatment | Mean | 55.67 | 31.01 | 64.20 | 22.20 | 68.83 | 22.83 |
| | SD | 5.52 | 8.34 | 12.60 | 13.40 | 10.53 | 7.47 |

The overlapping of one-minute window was 30 seconds. The recognition rate for the pattern ranged 70.7~74.5% before the treatment, and corresponding by decreased to 55.7~68.8% after the treatment for all the observed specimens. In contrast, the recognition rate of pattern B was low in 11.0~12.1% before the treatments; however increased consistently and distinctively to 22.2~31.0% for all the specimens after the treatment. As mentioned before, patterns A and B were both detected in the movement tracks before and after the treatments of insecticides. This is understandable that, by considering the treatment dose is in the sub-lethal range, pattern A may also occur after the treatment if the treated specimens recover to pattern A state briefly. Appearance of the two patterns, however, changed greatly after the carbofuran treatment. Pattern A decreased significantly while pattern B correspondingly increased in a great degree after the treatment of the insecticide. Fig 5(a) shows an example of detecting changes in movement patterns in 100 minute units during the whole observation period. Initially Pattern A was abundant, however, the pattern distinctively decreased after treatments of carbofuran (Fig. 5(a)).

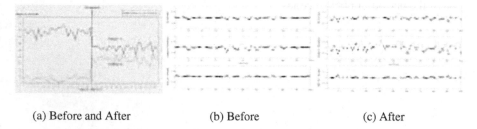

(a) Before and After              (b) Before              (c) After

**Fig. 5.** Comparison of frequency before and after treatments of an insecticide, and wavelet coefficient's recognition result before and after toxic treatments.

The reverse situation occurred with the corresponding increase in Pattern B after the treatment. Recognition of patterns A and B could be conducted even in a fine timescale. Since one-minute data were used for training, recognition is also possible in one-minute units. Before the treatment of carbofuran, a large number of data were recognized as pattern A(symbol : ×), and in the phase of the treatment, recognition rates of pattern B(symbol : •) were increased (Fig.5 (b)(c)). This indicated that the network and wavelet transform could be useful for detecting the response behavior on the real time basis.

## 4  Conclusion

This paper demonstrated that biological behavior's differences of animals in response to an insecticide could be successfully detected by the trained *ANN*. For each individual every one-minute segment was observed continuously for four days. Besides time consumption of classification, objectivity in judgments for classification was another problem. In this regard the pattern recognition by *ANN* could be an alternative for detection the movement tracks of animals exposed to toxic chemicals in environment. The carbofuran showed a high toxicity to organisms, especially *Chironomus flaviplumus* and aquatic invertebrates although it had relatively low toxic effects on mammals and humans. Pattern A and B were observed at the same time before and after the treatment as table 1, and this suggested that behaviors resulting from the sub-lethal treatments are not deterministic. The occurrence of behaviors appeared to be probabilistic depending upon the specimen's internal and external conditions. These stochastic occurrences of patterns were effectively revealed by continuous recognition by the trained artificial neural network. However, the occurrence of Pattern A and B in the same period might also suggest that the parameters may not be effectively selected to specifically separate Pattern A or B before and after the treatments of carbofuran. The trained *ANN* could be useful for detecting presence of toxic chemicals in environment as for an *in-situ* behavioral monitoring tool and Wavelet transform is shown that it had good time analysis ability. Further study on improving feature extraction of the movement data are needed in the future.

**Acknowledgement.** This paper was supported by the Korea Science and Engineering Foundation (KOSEF; Project Number 98-0401-02-01-3)

# References

1. Chon, T.-S., Park, Y.S., Moon, K.H., Cha, E.Y., Patternizing communities by using an artificial neural network. *Journal of Ecological Modeling,* vol. 90, pp.69–78,1996.
2. Lek, S., Delacoste, M., Baran, P., Dimopoulos, I., Lauga, J., Aulagnier, S., Application of Neural Networks to Modelling Nonlinear Relationships in Ecology. *Journal of Ecological Modelling*, vol. 90, pp.39–52,1996
3. Huntingford, C., Cox, P.M., Use of statistical and neural network techniques to detect how stomatal conductance responds to changes in the local environment. *Journal of Ecological Modelling*, vol. 97, pp.217–246,1996.
4. Elizondo, D.A., McClendon, R.W., Hoongenboom, G., Neural network models for predicting flowering and physiological maturity of soybean. *Transactions of the ASAE* 37(3), pp.981–988,1994
5. Dutta, H., Marcelino, J., Richmonds, Ch., Brain acetylcholinesterase activity and optomotor behavior in bluegills, Lepomis macrochirus exposed to different concentrations of carbofuran. Arch. Intern. Physiol. Biochim. Biophys. 100(5), pp.331–334, 1992.
6. Collins, R.D., Gargesh, R.N., Maltby, A.D., Roggero, R.J., Tourtellot, M.K., Bell, W.J., Innate control of local search behaviour in the house fly, Musca domestica. Physiological Entomology 19, pp.165–172, 1994.

# Applying Neural Networks to Study the Mesoscale Variability of Oceanic Boundary Currents

Silvia S.C. Botelho, Mauricio M. Mata, Rodrigo de Bem, and Igor Almeida

Dep. Fisica - Fundação Universidade Federal do Rio Grande, FURG,
Av. Itália Km 8, Rio Grande, RS, Brazil,
{silviacb,dfsmata,debem,igor}@ee.furg.br
http://www.ee.furg.br/pavao/pavao.html

**Abstract.** In this paper we apply a Neural Network (NN) to distill massive oceanographic datasets down to a new space of smaller dimension, thus characterizing the essential information contained in the data. Due to the natural nonlinearity of those data, traditional multivariate analysis may not represent reality. This work presents the methodology associated with the use of a multi-layer NN with a bottleneck to extract nonlinear information of the data.

## 1 Introduction

A typical problem faced in oceanography is to reduce the dimensions of large datasets in order to make sense of the bulk information contained in them. This reduction is relevant when one is focusing in describing the variability associated with ocean currents, fronts, and other dynamic marine systems.

A classical approach to go about this problem is to use linear solvers based in multivariate statistics like the Principal Component Analysis (PCA) [1]. The PCA finds the eigenmodes of the data covariance matrix and, with this result, one is able to reduce dimensionality and analyze the main patterns of variability present in the dataset. The fact that PCA solves the eigenmode problem using a linear approach may lead the result to be an oversimplification of the variability contained in the dataset, especially if the processes ruling this variability have a non-linear nature, like oceanic mesoscale variability.

The artificial Neural Network (NN) approach has been proposed by several authors as a tool to try to overcome the limitations imposed by linear PCA in oceanography and marine ecology problems [2,3,4]. The main advantage besides being able to take nonlinearity into account is that the computational process can occur unbiased by our knowledge about the samples and about the physical aspects that ultimately control the study area. Hence, this work aims to evaluate the potential of a NN approach to investigate the variability in an ocean area dominated by strong mesoscale dynamics, using a time-series of sea surface temperature satellite images of the southwestern Pacific Ocean as example.

N. Zhong et al. (Eds.): ISMIS 2003, LNAI 2871, pp. 684–688, 2003.

## 2    The Theory of NLPCA

In order to analyze large fields of satellite oceanographic data $\mathbf{x}$, one works finding the principal modes of variability, thus reducing dimensionality and allowing feature extraction of $\mathbf{x}$.

A satellite image can be viewed as a vector. If the images width and height are $w$ and $h$ pixels respectively, the number of components of this vector will be $w*h$. Each pixel is coded by one vector component. The construction of this vector, called *image vector*, from an image is performed by a simple concatenation - the rows of the image are placed beside each other [5]. The *image vector* belongs to a space called *image space*, which is the space of all images whose dimension is $w*h$ pixels. Typically our satellite images can be divided into several physical features which are very similar from image to image (i.e. land masses, clouds, equal temperature zones, etc). Thus, when plotting the *image vectors* they tend to group together to form a narrow cluster in the common image space. The goal of the PCA is to reduce the dimension of the original set or space so that the new basis better describes the typical "models" of the set.

**Theory of PCA.** Let $x(t) = [x_1, ..., x_p]$ be a set of sea surface satellite data, where each variable $x_i, (i = 1, ..., p)$ is a time series containing $n$ observations. PCA transformation is given by a linear combination of the $x_i$, time function $u$, and an associated vector $\mathbf{a}$: $u(t) = \mathbf{a} * \mathbf{x}(t)$, so that $\ll \|\mathbf{x}(t) - \mathbf{a}u(t)\|^2 \gg$, is minimized ($\ll ... \gg$ denotes a sample or time mean). Here $u$, called the first principal component (PC) is a time series, while $\mathbf{a}$, the first eigenvector of the data covariance matrix, often describes a spatial pattern. From the residual, $\mathbf{x} - \mathbf{a}u$, the second PCA mode can be obtained, and so on for higher modes.

PCA only allows a linear mapping from $\mathbf{x}$ to $\mathbf{u}$. On the other hand, NLPC is obtained using a multi layer Neural Network (NN), see figure 1 [6]. To perform NLPCA, the NN contains 3 hidden layers of neurons between the input and output layers. Hidden layers have nonlinear activation functions between the input and bottleneck layers and between the bottleneck and output layers. Hence, the network models a composition of functions. The five-layer NLPCA network has $p$ nodes in the input layer, $r$ nodes in the third (bottleneck) layer, and $p$ in the output layer. The nodes in layer 2 and 4 must have nonlinear activation functions so that layers 1,2 and 3 and 3,4, and 5 can represent arbitrary smooth functions. NLPCA network allows data compression because the $p$-dimensional inputs must pass through the $r$-dimensional bottleneck layer before reproducing the inputs. Once the network has been trained, the bottleneck node activation values give the scores.

Let $\mathbf{f} : \Re^p \rightarrow \Re^r$ denotes the function modeled by layers 1, 2 and 3, and let $\mathbf{s} : \Re^r \rightarrow \Re^p$ denotes the function modeled by layers 3, 4 and 5. Using this notation, the weights in the NLPCA network (associated with $n$ sets of input data $x$) are determined under the following objective function:

$$\min \sum_{l=1}^{n} \|x_l - x_l'\| \tag{1}$$

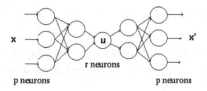

**Fig. 1.** Neural Network to map Nonlinear Components.

where $\mathbf{x}'$ is the output of the network. The PCA relation $u$ is now generalized to $u = \mathbf{f}(\mathbf{x})$, where $\mathbf{f}$ can be any nonlinear function explained by a feed-forward NN mapping from input layer to the bottleneck layer, $\|x_l - x_l'\|$ is minimized by nonlinear mapping functions, $\mathbf{x}' = \mathbf{s}(u)$. The residual $\|x_l - x_l'\|$, can be input into the same network to extract the second NLPCA mode, and so on for the higher modes [4].

## 3    Implementation of NLPCA

The hidden neurons have hyperbolic tangent function as nonlinear transfer function. For the other neurons, NLPCA was implemented using an identity function. The choice of $m$, the number of hidden neurons in both hidden layers, follows a general principle of parsimony. A larger $m$ increases the nonlinear modeling capability of the network, but could also lead to overfitted solutions (i.e irregular solutions which fit to the noise in the data). A set of 30 NNs with initial weights was run and the NN sensivity tests were followed to avoid local minima problems (see [3] for details).

The data used is a series of 128 Sea Surface Temperature (SST) satellite images (from 1991 to 1994) of 60 x 60 pixels, covering the area from $31^o$ do $36^oS$ and $150.5^o$ and $155.5^oE$ (Figure 2.a) The region was chosen for the pilot study since it is one of the most energetic in the world ocean with a clear and distinct mesoscale signal [7]. Due to the wide range of the magnitude of the input data, an appropriated normalization algorithm is used (subtraction of the mean and division by the standard deviation).

## 4    Results and Discussion

The data present 3600 spatial variables and 128 time points. Thus, there are too many spatial variables for this dataset to be directly analyzed by the NLPCA (see [3] for more details). To reduce the number of input variables, pre-filtering the SST data using PCA is one possible solution. That is a reasonable approach because one can expect that the first 2 or 3 PCs would be able to explain almost the totality of the data variance. Indeed, that is confirmed by computing the PCA modes from the dataset, which revealed that the eigenvalues associated to spatial modes 1, 2 and 3 accounted for 89.65%, 1.86% and 1.46% of the total variance, respectively (the 3 modes combined explain $\sim 93\%$ of the total

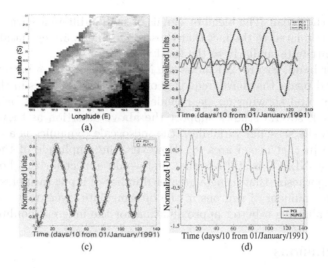

**Fig. 2.** Study area and results.

variance).Thus PC1, PC2 and PC3 are used as the input **x** for the NLPCA network.

The first 3 PCs (time series) computed from the dataset are shown in Figure 2.b. Looking at this figure, one can perceive the ample dominance of the first mode variability over the higher ones. Having a frequency of about 1 year, it is related to the seasonal heating and cooling of sea surface waters following the annual cycle of solar radiation. The second and third modes seem to be dominated by a higher than seasonal frequency, however, this signal seems also contaminated by a long term component. This is a clear sign of the inability of the PCA to separate in different modes signals that either are typically nonlinear, not dominant in the series or have similar energy levels (contribute equally to the total variance).

As the solution of the first PCA mode is linear, and it dominates unquestionably the dataset variability, one would expect that the NLPC1 would have quite a similar pattern. Indeed, that is confirmed in Figure 2.c, where it is clear the excellent agreement between the PC1 and NLPC1 functions while, at the same time, the higher PCs describe a completely different pattern (note that the amplitudes of the PC2 and PC3 functions have been exaggerated for clarity). Conversely, one can expect different pattern when comparing the PCA solution for the higher modes (mode 2 for example) with the correspondent NLPCs. After computing NLPC2, it is plotted together with PC2 in Figure 2.d. One can see how different they look and, taking advantage of the use of normalized units, it is clearly notable that PC2 contains a combination of a higher frequency phenomenon (about 70 days) with a lower frequency one (about 3 years). The 70 days signal should be basically composed by marine mesoscale phenomena while the 3 years one should be related to a residual of the interannual signal in the sea surface temperatures such as "El Ninõ" events, which can be quite intense in this part of the ocean. The blend of signals of such a different nature in only one PCA mode is related to the fact that those phenomena are essentially nonlinear and also contribute similarly to the total variance.

On other hand, Figure 2.d shows the NLPC2 describing a pattern with only some isolated peaks that have frequency of about 120-180 days in the beginning of the series, and showing no clear evidence of another signal being superimposed. Indeed, several studies support the above assertion as they have found that besides the seasonal variability, the mesoscale dynamics is a quite important feature in that ocean area [8]. However, the amplitude of the variability illustrated by NLPC2 is still less that one would expect for this boundary current. We hypothesize that using a greater number of input variables (more PCs) and a greater number of neurons in the intermediate layers may overcome this problem by allowing a better approximation for the inherent nonlinearity [3].

## 5   Conclusions

In the present study, we investigate the NN approach proposed by [3] specifically to study the mesoscale variability of an oceanic boundary current. We have shown in section 3 that the aforementioned multivariate statistics, like the PCA, leads to good approximation of the variability only to the first and most dominant mode. The higher modes, however, have a nonlinear nature and are not prominent when considering the total variance of the dataset. As a result, the PCA can not fully isolate those modes from each other and the computation leads to time series containing more that one signal associated with distinct physical processes. On the other hand, the NLPCA network has demonstrated the capability of isolating the second mode of variability which seems to be related with the mesoscale variability for the southwestern in Pacific Ocean.

## References

1. Preisendorfer, R.W.: PCA in Metereology and Oceanography. Developments in Atmospherics Science. Volume 17. Elsevier (1988)
2. Lek, S., Guegan, J.: Artificial neural networks as a tool in ecological modelling an introduction. Ecological Modelling **120** (1999) 65–73
3. Hsieh, W.: Nonlinear canonical correlation analysis by neural networks. Neural Networks **13** (2000) 1095–1105
4. Monahan, A.: Nonlinear principal component analysis of climate data. PhD thesis, University of British Columbia (2000)
5. Romdhani, S., Psarrou, A., Gong, S.: Multi-view nonlinear active shape model using kernel pca. In: Tenth British Machine Vision Conference. (1999)
6. Kirby, M., Sirovich, L.: Application of karhunen-loeve procedure for the caracterization of human faces. IEEE On pattern analysis and machine intelligence (1990)
7. Walker, A.E., Wilkin, J.L.: Optimal averaging of noaa/nasa pathfinder satellite sea surface temperature data. Geophys. Res. **102** (1997) 22921–22936
8. Mata, M., Tomczak, M., Wijffels, S., Church, J.: East australian current volume transport at 30°s: Estimates from the woce hydrographic sections pr11//p6 and pcm3 current meter array. J. Geophys. Res. **105** (2000) 28509–28526

# Dialog Planning and Domain Knowledge Modeled in Terms of Tasks and Methods: A Flexible Framework for Dialog Managing

Fabien Delorme[1] and Jérôme Lehuen[2]

[1] PSI, Université de Rouen, 76821 Mont-Saint-Aignan Cedex, FRANCE
fdelorme@insa-rouen.fr
[2] LIUM, Université du Maine, 72085 Le Mans Cedex 09, FRANCE
Jerome.Lehuen@lium.univ-lemans.fr

**Abstract.** This paper describes a work in progress about dialog managing in the context of a Computer Assisted Language Learning (CALL) research. In this paper, we choose to focus on the dialog management which is modeled in terms of tasks and methods. This approach is coming from research on generic mechanisms for problem-solving. First, we describe the context of this work. The following sections describe respectively the dialog and the domain levels.

## 1 Context of This Work

This paper takes place in a specific context of dialogue management that concerns the conception of a CALL environment called Sampras [1] [2]. In this environment, the learner is implicated in a task that (s)he has to complete by interacting with a virtual partner using his/her language competencies. The underlying pedagogical approaches are the "communicative" and the "actional" ones. Related works exist and so we can mention [3] [4] and [5]. The learner acts within a 2D virtual world. Two ways of acting in the world exist: verbal and non-verbal actions. The user dialogues with his/her partner via a dialog panel and can directly manipulate objects on the GUI, and so does the partner. An activity is based on a Problem Situation ("how to make a chocolate cake") and one Interaction Type (Fig. 1).

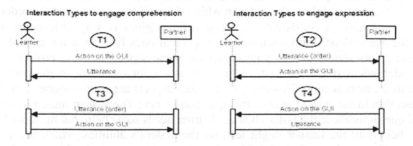

**Fig. 1.** Four Interaction Types

In the following sections, we respectively describe the dialog and the domain levels. They are both modeled into the Task-Method (TM) framework [6] [7].

N. Zhong et al. (Eds.): ISMIS 2003, LNAI 2871, pp. 689–693, 2003.
© Springer-Verlag Berlin Heidelberg 2003

## 2 The Dialogue Level

### 2.1 Implementation Formalism

Our TM engine is based on the CLIPS[1] production system. We have defined a "language" to write tasks and methods (Fig. 2). We saw in §1 that different activities might take place in our environment and each activity corresponds to a specific interaction type; it is also important to specify a social context in which the dialog takes place for each interaction type in order to make it more realistic. In the case of the "T2" interaction type (the learner wants the system to perform a given task and he has to give him orders in French), the social context can be: You (the learner) are having a cooking exam. You are given a recipe, and are supposed to make your teacher (the partner) prepare the meal, by the way of orders.

```
(task (name    T-structure-dialog)
      (methods M-structure-dialog))

(method-decomp (name  M-structure-dialog)
               (tasks T-open-dialog T-dialog T-close-dialog))

(task (name    T-open-dialog)
      (methods M-open-dialog))

(method-exec (name    M-open-dialog)
             (function F-open-dialog))

(deffunction MAIN::F-open-dialog ()
   (printout t "Hello, can you explain to me how to make a
                chocolate cake?"))
```

**Fig. 2.** Some tasks and methods to engage a dialog

### 2.2 Study around "T2" Interaction Type

A wizard of Oz-like study was set up so as to have an idea of how such an activity could take place. The results of this experience have shown us the following points: (1) The learner asks questions when he is in trouble, like "How can we do this?" (2) He doesn't necessary follow the order in which the recipe is written and the order he chooses is not always consistent. (3) He sometimes gives very specific orders like "open the fridge door" but sometimes gives general ones like "melt the chocolate". All these points should be taken into account. Some aspects of these problems are domain-dependent (the answers to a given question for example) so they will be treated in the next section. However, some other aspects are context-dependent. For example, should the system answer this question or not? The system must be able to answer questions about the task, when the learner needs some help, but he should not always help him: the learner might lean on the system's abilities, which is not the objective. This is why we have introduced a cooperation rate mechanism: the highest the rate is, the more cooperative the system is. This way, the system will not answer questions every time. From this study, we can build a decision tree (Fig. 3) which is implemented as a set of tasks and methods (Fig. 4).

---

[1] CLIPS web site: http://www.ghg.net/clips/CLIPS.html

| | |
|---|---|
| If the sentence can't be understood → **Say it** | M-respond-case-0 |
| If the sentence read from the learner is an order → | |
|    If the order is a precise one → **Perform it** | M-respond-case-1 |
|    If the order is a general one → | |
|       If the cooperation rate is high → **Perform it** | M-respond-case-2 |
|       Else → **Don't perform it** | M-respond-case-3 |
| Etc. | |

**Fig. 3.** Part of the decision tree for the "T2" interaction type

```
(task (name    T-respond)
       (methods M-respond-case-0 M-respond-case-1 ... ))

(method-exec (name      M-respond-case-0)
              (precond  "(not (analyzed))")
              (function F-respond-case-0))

(deffunction MAIN::F-respond-case-0 ()
  (printout t "Sorry but I don't understand your sentence."))
```

**Fig. 4.** Method which implement the case 0 of the decision tree

# 3   The Domain Level

The domain level contains the useful knowledge to describe and perform a complex task as cooking a recipe. This section deals with the way a task is described and can be performed.

## 3.1   How to Make a Recipe

When you read a recipe, you can see a list of instructions to be performed, not necessarily in the order they are written. However, you cannot perform the instructions in any order: thus, actions can be associated to a set of preconditions to be checked before they can be accomplished (Fig. 5). Besides, they are associated with effects which happen once the action is performed: if you open the fridge, you can take eggs from it. The precondition "eggs available" is then checked.

```
(task (name        T-take-eggs)
      (post-cond "(eggs available)")
      (methods    M-take-eggs-from-opened-fridge
                  M-take-eggs-from-closed-fridge))

(method-decomp (name     M-take-eggs-from-opened-fridge)
               (context "(not (eggs available))"
                        "(fridge opened)"
                        "(fridge contains eggs)")
               (tasks    T-take-eggs-from-fridge))

(method-decomp (name     M-take-eggs-from-closed-fridge)
               (context "(not (eggs available))"
                        "(fridge closed)"
                        "(fridge contains eggs)")
               (tasks    T-open-fridge T-take-eggs-from-fridge))
```

**Fig. 5.** Task "To take eggs"

## 3.2   High-Level and Low-Level Tasks

When you ask somebody to make a recipe, you can give him low-level orders, or more general orders you know (s)he will understand (Fig. 5). Consider the activity to be performed as a tree of tasks, the top-level one being "make a chocolate cake", and low-level ones corresponding to actions on the GUI (taking an object, etc.).

## 3.3   Performing Orders and Answering Questions

The model we have just described has an intrinsic ability of dealing with questions, high-level orders and non-executable orders. When the system is asked to perform a low-level task for which preconditions are checked, it just has to perform the underlying action on the GUI and to add the effects to the facts list. When the system is asked to perform a high-level task, it has to perform all the underlying actions. If the learner gives an order for an action whose preconditions are not checked, the system is able to perform it, by finding and performing an action making these preconditions become true. If this action is not executable either, it runs this process once more, and so on: to mix the eggs, you need a whip and the eggs need to be in a bowl; to make the eggs be in the bowl, you can perform the action "put the eggs in the bowl". Sometimes, the learner wants to perform an action, but some constraints are not checked. He asks the system how to do. The system thus indicates actions that will allow, once performed, the checking of missing preconditions. Let's consider the learner wants to know how to get the eggs. Since the fact "eggs available" is the effect of the action "take the eggs from the fridge", the system will answer "take them from the fridge".

# 4   Links between the Dialogue and the Domain Levels

According to the definition we gave for the interaction types and the problem situation, we assume that any problem situation can be applied to any task. Thus, an activity can be thought of as the aggregation of a problem situation and an interaction. However these two levels aren't completely independent since the dialog takes place around the activity. Some preconditions of the dialog level are about some domain level elements and the domain level is controlled by some tasks of the dialog level.

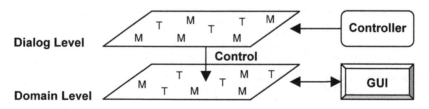

**Fig. 6.** Dialog and Domain Levels

According to [7], a TM model can be decomposed into four layers, each layer manipulating data from the lower one. The highest one, named control, deals with the way the task is performed (a simple algorithm, a classical expert system, or a higher-level TM engine). In our case, the control of the dialog level is performed by an simple algorithm, whereas the control of the domain level is performed by specific methods of the dialog level.

## 5    Conclusion

In this article, we have proposed a generic framework based on the TM paradigm to build dialog systems. This framework is applied to the design of a CALL environment, but we assume that our architecture can be reused in other dialog contexts. The generic aspects of this work come from the high abstraction of the concepts we implemented, particularly from the TM approach which fits into the scheme of the Knowledge Level framework [6]. We don't have any evaluation of this work in progress yet, but we are trying to take advantage of a quite good experience on designing dialog systems.

## References

[1]    Lehuen, J. (2000), "A Dialogue-Based Architecture for Computer Aided Language Learning", In: *Proceedings of AAAI Fall Symposium on Building Dialogue Systems for Tutorial Applications*, Cape-Cod (USA), 3-5 november 2000, (20–27).

[2]    Michel, J. and Lehuen, J. (2002), "Conception of a Language Learning Environment based on the Communicative and Actional Approaches", In: Cerri, S., Gouardères, G. and Paraguaçu, F. (ed.), *Notes in Computer Science (Intelligent Tutoring Systems)*, Springer-Verlag, Proceedings of ITS'2002, Biarritz (France), 5-8 juin 2002, (651–660).

[3]    Hamburger, H. (1994), "Foreign language immersion: Science, practice, and a System", In: *JAIED Special Issue on Language Learning*, vol. 5(4) (429–453).

[4]    Boylan, P. and Micarelli, A. (1998), "Learning languages as "culture" with CALL", In Calvi, L. and Geerts, W. (ed.), *CALL, Culture and the language curriculum*, Springer-Verlag, (60–72).

[5]    Reeder, F. (2000), "Could you repeat the question?" In: *Proceedings of AAAI Fall Symposium on Building Dialogue Systems for Tutorial Applications*, Cape-Cod (USA), 3–5 november 2000, (144–147).

[6]    Newell, A. (1982), "The Knowledge Level", In: *Artificial Intelligence*, vol. 18 (87–127).

[7]    Trichet, F. and Tchounikine, P. (1999), "DSTM: a Framework to operationalise and Refine a Problem-Solving Method modeled in terms of Tasks and Methods", In: *International Journal of Expert Systems with Applications*, vol. 16 (105–120).

# Author Index

Abdel Razek, Mohammed  623
Abou-Assaleh, Tony  397
Adachi, Fuminori  486
Aida, Takumi  242
Almeida, Igor  684
Alonso, Luis  640
Alvarez, Julio César  652
Andreasen, Troels  668
Angelopoulos, Nicos  365
Appice, Annalisa  49
Arara, Ahmed  339

Bae, Keun-Sung  585
Bai, Yun  292, 349
Basile, T.M.A.  384
Bazan, Jan  160
Bem, Rodrigo de  684
Benbernou, Salima  554
Benoit, Eric  88
Benslimane, Djamal  339
Bertino, Elisa  65
Boella, Guido  618
Botelho, Silvia S.C.  684
Brand, Peter van den  226
Bruha, Ivan  539
Bruza, Peter  297
Buche, Patrice  98
Bulskov, Henrik  668
Butz, C.J.  544

Cairó, Osvaldo  652
Calì, Andrea  562
Canaud, Etienne  554
Cao, Longbing  603
Ceci, Michelangelo  49
Cercone, Nick  397
Cha, Eui-Young  678
Chan, Kevin  197
Chang, Jae-young  326
Chang, Matthew  344
Chang, Tseng-Chung  285
Chen, Xiang  108
Chen, Yiqiang  108
Chien, Sung-Il  577, 585
Cho, Sung-Bae  521

Choi, Joongmin  179
Chon, Tae-Soo  678
Choo, Kyonam  433
Chu, Shu-Chuan  279
Chua, Joselíto J.  496
Chun, Seok-Ju  473
Chung, Ken C.K.  124
Corbett, Dan  75

Dapoigny, Richard  88
Delorme, Fabien  689
Deogun, Jitender  402, 478
Duan, Lijuan  108

Elomaa, Tapio  445
Esposito, F.  384

Ferilli, S.  384
Flouret, Marianne  221
Foulloy, Laurent  88
Fournier, Dominique  221
Frasson, Claude  623
Fujimoto, Atsushi  486

Gao, Wen  108, 593
Geng, H.  544
Glen, Edward  511
Goonesekera, T.  646
Goschnick, Steve  187
Gouaich, Abdelkader  211, 216
Guiraud, Yves  216

Ha, Sung Ho  572
Hacid, Mohand-Said  554, 598
Haemmerlé, Ollivier  98
Hajji, Hicham  598
Han, Jianchao  663
Han, Kwang-Rok  320
Hanafusa, Hidemitsu  486
Hirano, Shoji  454
Hogo, Mofreh  169
Hong, June S.  608
Hu, Xiaohua  663
Huang, Shang-Ming  252
Huang, Zi  297
Hurley, Neil J.  506

Hwang, Chang Ha    440
Hwang, Hui-Yeoun    577

Ida, Kenichi    531
Intan, Rolly    174, 427

Jeansoulin, R.    83
Jia, Dong    357
Jiang, Liying    402

Kaltenbach, Marc    623
Kang, Dae-Ki    179
Kang, Seokhoon    433
Kemke, Christel    657
Kešelj, Vlado    397
Khosla, R.    646
Kim, Byung Joo    440
Kim, Cheol-Ki    678
Kim, Dae-Won    422
Kim, Han-joon    326
Kim, Il Kon    440
Kim, Wooju    608
Kimura, Yosuke    531
Knappe, Rasmus    668
Koo, Sang Ok    93
Kuntanapreeda, Suwat    673
Kurihara, Masahito    374
Kwan, Alvin C.M.    124
Kwon, Hong-Seok    585

Lau, Raymond Y.K.    226, 297
Lavi, Inbal    24
Leclère, Michel    633
Lee, Chung-Hong    307, 334
Lee, Kwang H.    422
Lee, Sang Jo    93
Lehuen, Jérôme    689
Leonard, Bill    169
Li, Chunsheng    603
Li, Dan    478
Li, Zhanhuai    315
Liau, Churn-Jung    152
Lim, Soo Yeon    93
Lin, T.Y.    663
Ling, Charles X.    108
Lingras, Pawan    169
Liu, Chao-Lin    252, 285
Liu, Chunnian    357, 463
Liu, Jiming    1
Liu, Kun-Hao    252

Low, Graham    613

Maimon, Oded    24
Malerba, Donato    49
Malinen, Tuomo    445
Maluf, David A.    231
Mata, Mauricio M.    684
Mathieu, Philippe    206
Mauro, N. Di    384
Mermet, Bruno    221
Mileo, Alessandra    65
Min, Hongki    433
Mitsukura, Y.    646
Miyamoto, Sadaaki    417
Mizutani, Kiyotaka    417
Moro, Q. Isaac    640
Motoda, Hiroshi    486
Mukaidono, Masao    174, 427

Nakashima, Hideyuki    7
Numazawa, Masanobu    374

O'Mahony, Michael P.    506
Ogiela, Marek R.    116
Oh, Hyun-Hwa    585
Ohsuga, Setsuo    242
Ortega-Garcia, Javier    640

Padgham, Lin    628
Pan, Jeng-Shyang    279
Park, Chanho    521
Park, Hyunjae    433
Peters, James F.    262
Pham, T.T.    83
Phan-Luong, V.    83
Poon, Chung Keung    344
Poutakidis, David    628
Provetti, Alessandro    65

Raś, Zbigniew W.    135
Raghavan, Vijay    402, 501
Ramakrishnan, Raghu    12
Rim, Kee-Wook    320
Ritschard, Gilbert    57, 468
Roddick, John F.    279
Rokach, Lior    24
Roussey, Catherine    339
Routier, Jean-Christophe    206
Ruan, Chun    392
Ryu, Je    320

Sakai, Hiroshi   143
Secq, Yann   206
Shah, Biren   501
Shan, Shiguang   593
Shim, Joo Yong   440
Shin, Jung-Hwan   577
Silvestre, Guénolé C.M.   506
Simon, Gaële   221
Skowron, Andrzej   160
Ślęzak, Dominik   160, 408
Snorek, Miroslav   169
Son, Jong-Mok   585
Song, Dawei   297
Song, Joon Hyun   440
Song, Yong U.   608
Sterling, Leon   197
Struzik, Zbigniew R.   32
Su, Che-Jen   279
Synak, Piotr   270
Szczuka, Marcin   408

Tadeusiewicz, Ryszard   116
Talia, Domenico   14
Tam, Vincent   124
Thomopoulos, Rallou   98
Tischer, Peter E.   496
Torre, Leendert van der   618
Toumani, Farouk   554, 598
Tran, Peter B.   231
Tran, Quynh-Nhu Numi   613
Trichet, Francky   633
Tsay, Li-Shiang   135
Tsumoto, Shusaku   40, 454

Tuntrakoon, Apichart   673

Vangenot, Christelle   339
Varadharajan, Vijay   392
Vivaracho, Carlos E.   640

Wang, Wei   593
Washio, Takashi   486
Wieczorkowska, Alicja A.   135
Wiese, Kay C.   511
Williams, Mary-Anne   613
Winikoff, Michael   628
Woo, Yoseop   433
Wróblewski, Jakub   160, 408

Xie, Ying   402

Yan, Jianfeng   315
Yang, Hsin-Chang   307, 334
Yang, Hsiu-Ming   252
Yang, Xinwu   463
Yao, Yiyu   152
Yin, Baocai   593
Yip, Kammy K.K.   124

Zhang, Chengqi   603
Zhang, Lijun   315
Zhang, Yan   292, 349
Zhang, Yang   315
Zhao, Debin   593
Zheng, Lei   357
Zhong, Ning   152, 357, 463
Zighed, Djamel A.   57, 468